T0180715

# IFIP Advances in Information and Communication Technology 629

## Editor-in-Chief

## IFIP – The International Federation for Information Processing

IFIP was founded in 1960 under the auspices of UNESCO, following the first World Computer Congress held in Paris the previous year. A federation for societies working in information processing, IFIP's aim is two-fold: to support information processing in the countries of its members and to encourage technology transfer to developing nations. As its mission statement clearly states:

> *IFIP is the global non-profit federation of societies of ICT professionals that aims at achieving a worldwide professional and socially responsible development and application of information and communication technologies.*

IFIP is a non-profit-making organization, run almost solely by 2500 volunteers. It operates through a number of technical committees and working groups, which organize events and publications. IFIP's events range from large international open conferences to working conferences and local seminars.

The flagship event is the IFIP World Computer Congress, at which both invited and contributed papers are presented. Contributed papers are rigorously refereed and the rejection rate is high.

As with the Congress, participation in the open conferences is open to all and papers may be invited or submitted. Again, submitted papers are stringently refereed.

The working conferences are structured differently. They are usually run by a working group and attendance is generally smaller and occasionally by invitation only. Their purpose is to create an atmosphere conducive to innovation and development. Refereeing is also rigorous and papers are subjected to extensive group discussion.

Publications arising from IFIP events vary. The papers presented at the IFIP World Computer Congress and at open conferences are published as conference proceedings, while the results of the working conferences are often published as collections of selected and edited papers.

IFIP distinguishes three types of institutional membership: Country Representative Members, Members at Large, and Associate Members. The type of organization that can apply for membership is a wide variety and includes national or international societies of individual computer scientists/ICT professionals, associations or federations of such societies, government institutions/government related organizations, national or international research institutes or consortia, universities, academies of sciences, companies, national or international associations or federations of companies.

More information about this series at http://www.springer.com/series/6102

Luis M. Camarinha-Matos ·
Xavier Boucher · Hamideh Afsarmanesh (Eds.)

# Smart and Sustainable Collaborative Networks 4.0

## 22nd IFIP WG 5.5 Working Conference on Virtual Enterprises, PRO-VE 2021 Saint-Étienne, France, November 22–24, 2021 Proceedings

*Editors*
Luis M. Camarinha-Matos
NOVA University of Lisbon
Caparica, Portugal

Hamideh Afsarmanesh
University of Amsterdam
Amsterdam, The Netherlands

Xavier Boucher
Mines Saint-Étienne
Saint-Étienne, France

Clermont Auvergne University
Clermont-Ferrand, France

ISSN 1868-4238 ISSN 1868-422X (electronic)
IFIP Advances in Information and Communication Technology
ISBN 978-3-030-85971-8 ISBN 978-3-030-85969-5 (eBook)
https://doi.org/10.1007/978-3-030-85969-5



This Springer imprint is published by the registered company Springer Nature Switzerland AG
The registered company address is: Gewerbestrasse 11, 6330 Cham, Switzerland

# Preface

Widespread digital transformation in industry and services is strongly enabled by the results achieved through more than two decades of research and development in the inter-disciplinary Collaborative Networks (CNs) paradigm. The PRO-VE series of conferences, now in its 22nd edition, has been a successful vessel for presenting innovative concepts and tools as well as providing a proper sand box to investigate and intersect new models and approaches that address the challenges raised. As such, this annual conference gives a bird's-eye view of the CN area and its achieved milestones, identifies forthcoming open challenges, and proposes research directions that require developing novel and/or disruptive solutions.

In the very last edition of the PRO-VE conference series, in 2020, the highlights of the past achievements in Collaborative Networks were structured as CN 1.0, CN 2.0, and CN 3.0. It further addressed the new emerging challenges in this area, e.g., the exponential increase in the availability of both data and intelligence, the vast progress in digitalization, and the proper positioning of humans in highly collaborative, dynamic, and resilient networks. The academic world was then invited to focus on addressing its newly introduced notion of Collaborative Networks 4.0, as the next generation of collaborative networks, in the era of applied artificial intelligence and digital transformation. By then, the following items were identified as the main challenges on which to focus: hybridization in CN structure, where network entities constitute organizations, people, intelligent systems, and machines; formation of distributed cognitive systems; collaborative decision making among humans and intelligent autonomous systems; managing big data; mass collaboration and collaborative creativity; and modeling and formalizing rights and liabilities, monetization, accountability, ethics, trust, and risk/disruption management. With this, the conference directed the community to focus on understanding and creating new collaboration culture and business models, with the purpose of addressing sustainable collaborative value creation.

Meanwhile, since last year, the world has encountered major health and economic crises caused by the COVID-19 pandemic, which emphasized that disruptive situations, at different scales, tend to be increasingly frequent and have strong impacts on society. As predicted by PRO-VE, smart and digital technologies supporting agility, scalability, resilience, and adaptability, which characterize CN 4.0, have nowadays become the critical features for most sectors of our modern societies, including the manufacturing industry and services sectors. Many properties of CN 4.0 can contribute to building a more resilient and sustainable world, providing that the socio-economic actors can implement efficient learning mechanisms, applying the lessons learned from recent crises. The crucial importance of Collaborative Networks in the current situation has led us to highlight the theme of the 2021 conference, targeting "Smart and Sustainable Collaborative Networks 4.0". Agile and sustainable systems and business models, based on open collaborative processes, are not only the answer to the increasing need for customization but also provide higher resilience, i.e., through joint reconfiguration of market-offers, production processes, and consumption patterns, among others. Digitalization of both products and services enable a transition towards a larger vision of value creation. Furthermore, digitalization strengthens research trends on societal impacts, and makes it possible to focus progressively on the more ecological value chains, based on circular and collaborative economy.

Combined with the current boom of applied artificial intelligence including machine learning, the Collaborative Networks facilitate high potentials to boost Industry 4.0. The PRO-VE Working Conference sheds light on many applications within the industrial economy, at different levels of organization, spanning from human/robot collaboration at the detail process level to the high-level management of a manufacturing system's lifecycle, design and management of supply/value networks, and running the business ecosystems. However, the digital transition similarly affects all sectors of the economy, as strongly as each industry itself. Many other activity sectors are also concerned, where agility, resilience, and sustainability are the key challenges, e.g., Health 4.0, Agriculture 4.0, Cities 4.0, Transportation 4.0, Logistics 4.0, Education 4.0, and even Tourism 4.0. With an eye on these diverse application fields, PRO-VE 2021 provided a forum for sharing experiences, discussing trends, and identifying new opportunities, thus introducing innovative solutions for the new generation of Smart and Sustainable Collaborative Networks 4.0. Today more than ever, everyone realizes the need to network and boost collaboration at all levels of our modern societies, and to interlink different types of organizations, including private companies, public institutions, business, and non-profit organizations, down to the level of their industrial- and service-oriented processes. Therefore, the resilience and efficiency of our modern societies as a whole appear to be based on collaborative networking.

To better tackle the multidimensional complexity of Collaborative Networks, PRO-VE 2021 aimed to put forth a multidisciplinary forum, with conference contributions coming from both the engineering/computer science and the managerial/socio-human communities, including industrial and electrical engineering, computer science, manufacturing, organization science, logistics, managerial, and social sciences. These multiple points of view fuel both the interdisciplinary nature of the research and development on Collaborative Networks, as well as the multidisciplinary networking spirit of the PRO-VE Working Conferences.

PRO-VE 2021 was the 22nd event in a series of successful conferences, which included PRO-VE 1999 (Porto, Portugal), PRO-VE 2000 (Florianopolis, Brazil), PRO-VE 2002 (Sesimbra, Portugal), PRO-VE 2003 (Lugano, Switzerland), PRO-VE 2004 (Toulouse, France), PRO-VE 2005 (Valencia, Spain), PRO-VE 2006 (Helsinki, Finland), PRO-VE 2007 (Guimarães, Portugal), PRO-VE 2008 (Poznan, Poland), PRO-VE 2009 (Thessaloniki, Greece), PRO-VE 2010 (St. Etienne, France), PRO-VE 2011 (São Paulo, Brazil), PRO-VE 2012 (Bournemouth, UK), PRO-VE 2013 (Dresden, Germany) , PROVE 2014 (Amsterdam, The Netherlands), PRO-VE 2015 (Albi, France), PRO-VE 2016 (Porto, Portugal), PRO-VE 2017 (Vicenza, Italy), PRO-VE 2018 (Cardiff, UK), PRO-VE 2019 (Torino, Italy), and PRO-VE 2020 (Valencia, Spain).

This proceedings includes selected papers from the PRO-VE 2021 conference submissions. It provides a comprehensive overview of major challenges that are being currently addressed related to sustainability and resilience and, specifically, recent advances in various domains related to Collaborative Networks and their applications. In this direction, the following five key areas are highlighted in these proceedings:

- Resilience and sustainability of Collaborative Networks and their ecosystems
- Collaboration management, spanning from operational life-cycle management to value creation boosting
- Digitalization of Collaborative Networks, embracing the definition of digital strategies and the multiple applications of ontologies, IoT, and CPS
- Multiple dimensions of the Factory of the Future
- Advanced collaborative learning environments, contributing to the deployment of an eco-systemic culture on CN 4.0

At a more detailed level, the 2021 conference papers are organized around the following subject headings:

- Sustainable Collaborative Networks
- Sustainability via Digitalization
- Analysis and Assessment of Business Ecosystems
- Human Factors in Collaboration 4.0
- Maintenance and Life-Cycle Management
- Policies and New Digital Services
- Safety and Collaboration Management
- Simulation and Optimization
- Complex Collaborative Systems and Ontologies
- Value Co-creation in Digitally Enabled Ecosystems
- Digitalization Strategy in Collaborative Enterprises' Networks
- Pathways and Tools for Digital Innovation Hubs
- Socio-technical Perspectives on Smart Product-Service Systems
- Knowledge Transfer and Accelerated Innovation in Factories of the Future
- Interoperability of IoT and CPS for Industrial CNs
- Sentient Immersive Response Network
- Digital Tools and Applications for Collaborative Healthcare
- Collaborative Networks and Open Innovation in Education 4.0
- Collaborative Learning Networks with Industry and Academia
- Industrial Workshop

We would like to express our thanks to all the authors from academia, research, and industry for their contributions. Continuing with the tradition of the PRO-VE conferences, we hope this collection of papers represents both a valuable tool for those interested in research advances and emerging applications in Collaborative Networks, and in identifying future open challenges for research and development in this area. We also very much appreciate the dedicated time and effort spent by the members of the PRO-VE International Program Committee, who supported us with the selection of articles for the conference and provided valuable and constructive comments to help authors with improving the quality of their papers.

November 2021

Luis M. Camarinha-Matos
Xavier Boucher
Hamideh Afsarmanesh

# Organization

**PRO-VE 2021 – 22nd IFIP Working Conference on VIRTUAL ENTERPRISES**

Saint-Étienne, France, November 22–24, 2021

## Conference Chair

| | |
|---|---|
| Xavier Boucher | Ecole des Mines de Saint-Etienne, France |

## Program Committee Chair

| | |
|---|---|
| Luis M. Camarinha-Matos | NOVA University of Lisbon, Portugal |

## Program Committee Co-chair

| | |
|---|---|
| Hamideh Afsarmanesh | University of Amsterdam, The Netherlands |

## International Program Committee

| | |
|---|---|
| Antonio Abreu | Polytechnic Institute of Lisbon, Portugal |
| Hamideh Afsarmanesh | University of Amsterdam, The Netherlands |
| Thecle Alix | Institut de Mécanique et d'Ingénierie de Bordeaux, France |
| Dario Antonelli | Politecnico di Torino, Italy |
| Vincent Augusto | Ecole des Mines de Saint-Etienne, France |
| Américo Azevedo | University of Porto, Portugal |
| Thomas Beach | Cardiff University, UK |
| Frédérick Bénaben | Ecole des Mines d'Albi-Carmaux, France |
| Peter Bernus | Griffith University, Australia |
| Valérie Botta-Genoulaz | INSA-Lyon, France |
| Xavier Boucher | Ecole des Mines de Saint-Etienne, France |
| Jeremy Bryans | Coventry University, UK |
| Luis M. Camarinha-Matos | NOVA University of Lisbon, Portugal |
| Wojciech Cellary | Poznan University of Economics and Business, Poland |
| Audrey Cerqueus | Ecole des Mines de Saint-Etienne, France |
| Nicolas Daclin | Ecole des Mines d'Alès, France |
| Rob Dekkers | University of Glasgow, UK |
| Xavier Delorme | Ecole des Mines de Saint-Etienne, France |

| | |
|---|---|
| Filipa Ferrada | NOVA University of Lisbon, Portugal |
| Hans-Georg Fill | University of Fribourg, Switzerland |
| Adriano Fiorese | University of the State of Santa Catarina, Brazil |
| Adrian Florea | 'Lucian Blaga' University of Sibiu, Romania |
| Rosanna Fornasiero | ITIA-CNR, Italy |
| Gary Fragidis | International Hellenic University, Greece |
| Cesar Garita | ITCR, Costa Rica |
| Ted Goranson | Sirius-Beta, USA |
| Juanqiong Gou | Beijing Jiaotong University, China |
| Paul Grefen | Eindhoven University of Technology, The Netherlands |
| Didier Gourc | Ecole des Mines d'Albi-Carmaux, France |
| Lilia Gzara | INSA Lyon, France |
| Hichem Haddou | IMT Atlantique, France |
| Dmitri Ivanov | Berlin School of Economics and Law, Germany |
| Tomasz Janowski | Gdańsk University of Technology, Poland |
| Eleni Kaldoudi | Democritus University of Thrace, Greece |
| Dimitris Karagiannis | University of Vienna, Austria |
| Adamantios Koumpis | Berner Fachhochschule, Germany |
| Matthieu Lauras | École des Mines d'Albi-Carmaux, France |
| Mario Lezoche | University of Lorraine, France |
| Leandro Loss | UFSC, Brazil |
| António Lucas Soares | University of Porto, Portugal |
| Laura Macchion | University of Padova, Italy |
| Patricia Macedo | Polytechnic Institute of Setubal, Portugal |
| Khaled Medini | Ecole des Mines de Saint-Etienne, France |
| Kyrill Meyer | Institut für Digitale Technologien, Germany |
| Istvan Mezgar | Hungarian Academy of Sciences, Hungary |
| Paulo Miyagi | University of S Paulo, Brazil |
| Nejib Moalla | Université Lumière Lyon 2, France |
| Arturo Molina | Tecnológico de Monterrey, Mexico |
| Ovidiu Noran | Griffith University, Australia |
| Paulo Novais | University of Minho, Portugal |
| Adegboyega Ojo | Maynooth University, Ireland |
| Ana Inês Oliveira | NOVA University of Lisbon, Portugal |
| Martin Ollus | VTT (retired), Finland |
| Angel Ortiz | Universitat Politècnica de València, Spain |
| A. Luis Osório | Polytechnic Institute of Lisbon, Portugal |
| Yacine Ouzrout | Université Lumiere Lyon 2, France |
| Hervé Panetto | University of Lorraine, France |
| Iraklis Paraskakis | South East European Research Centre, Greece |
| Adam Pawlak | Silesian University of Technology, Poland |
| Jorge Pinho Sousa | University of Porto, Portugal |
| Raul Poler | Universitat Politècnica de València, Spain |
| Ricardo Rabelo | Federal University of Santa Catarina, Brazil |
| David Romero | Tecnológico de Monterrey, Mexico |
| João Rosas | NOVA University of Lisbon, Portugal |

| | |
|---|---|
| Hans Schaffers | Technology and Societal Change, The Netherlands |
| Jens Schütze | Chemnitz University of Technology, Germany |
| Volker Stich | RWTH Aachen University, Germany |
| Chrysostomos Stylios | University of Ioannina, Greece |
| Thomas Suesse | Bielefeld University of Applied Science, Germany |
| Klaus-Dieter Thoben | University of Bremen, Germany |
| Lorna Uden | Staffordshire University, UK |
| Paula Urze | NOVA University of Lisbon, Portugal |
| Katri Valkokari | VTT, Finland |
| Rolando Vallejos | SENAI, Brazil |
| Elise Vareilles | ISAE-SUPAERO Toulouse, France |
| Agostino Villa | Politecnico di Torino, Italy |
| Antonio Volpentesta | University of Calabria, Italy |
| Shaun West | Lucerne University of Applied Sciences and Art, Switzerland |
| Stefan Wiesner | Bremer Institut für Produktion und Logistik, Germany |
| Lai Xu | Bournemouth University, UK |
| Claude Yugma | Ecole des Mines de Saint-Etienne, France |
| Peter Weiß | Pforzheim University, Germany |
| Greg Zacharewicz | Ecole des Mines d'Alès, France |

## Special Session Organizers

### Special Session on Complex Collaborative Systems and Ontologies

Claude Yugma, France
Lars Moench, Germany
Abdelhak Khemiri, France

### Special Session on Value Co-creation in Digitally Enabled Ecosystems

Shaun West, Switzerland
Tobias Larsson, Sweden

### Special Session on Digitalization Strategy in Collaborative Enterprises' Networks

Lilia Gzara, France
Alejandro G. Frank, Brazil

### Special Session on Pathways and Tools for DIHs

Gustavo Dalmarco, Portugal
Ana Cristina Barros, Portugal
António Lucas Soares, Portugal
Sergio Gusmeroli, Italy
Vasco Bernardo Teles, Portugal

**Special Session on Socio-technical Perspectives on Smart Product-Service Systems**

António Lucas Soares, Portugal
Henrique Silva, Portugal

**Special Session on Knowledge Transfer and Accelerated Innovation in FoF**

Adrian Florea, Romania
Luis M. Camarinha-Matos, Portugal
Fabiana Pirola, Italy
Arkadiusz Jurczuk, Poland

**Special Session on Interoperability of IoT and CPS for Industrial CNs**

Yacine Ouzrout, France
Keshav Dahal, UK
Nejib Moalla, France

**Special Session on Sentient Immersive Response Network**

Frederick Benaben, France
Benoit Montreuil, USA
Matthieu Lauras, France

**Special Session on Digital Tools and Applications for Collaborative Healthcare**

Daniele Spoladore, Italy
Elena Pessot, Italy

**Special Session on Collaborative Networks and Open Innovation in Education 4.0**

Arturo Molina, Mexico
María Soledad Ramírez-Montoya, Mexico
Jhonattan Miranda, Mexico

**Special Session on Collaborative Learning Networks with Industry and Academia**

Ana Correia Simões, Portugal
António Almeida, Portugal
Américo Lopes Azevedo, Portugal

**Industrial Workshop**

Carlo Leardi, Italy
Xavier Delorme, France
Vincent Chapurlat, France

## Technical Sponsors

IFIP WG 5.5 COVE
Cooperation Infrastructure for Virtual Enterprises and Electronic Business

Society of Collaborative Networks

Project

## Organizational Cosponsors

# Contents

## Human Factors in Collaboration 4.0



## Maintenance and Life-Cycle Management



## Policies and New Digital Services

## Safety and Collaboration Management



## Simulation and Optimization



## Complex Collaborative Systems and Ontologies

## Value Co-creation in Digitally Enabled Ecosystems



## Digitalization Strategy in Collaborative Enterprises Networks

**Pathways and Tools for Digital Innovation Hubs**



**Socio-Technical Perspectives on Smart Product-Service Systems**



**Knowledge Transfer and Accelerated Innovation in FoF**

**Interoperability of IoT and CPS for Industrial CNs**



**Sentient Immersive Response Network**

## Digital Tools and Applications for Collaborative Healthcare



## Collaborative Networks and Open Innovation in Education 4.0

# Sustainable Collaborative Networks

# Brief Overview of Collaborative Approaches in Sustainable Manufacturing

Luis M. Camarinha-Matos[1], Andre Dionisio Rocha[1(✉)], and Paula Graça[1,2]

[1] School of Science and Technology and Uninova-CTS, NOVA University of Lisbon, Campus de Caparica, 2829-516 Caparica, Portugal
{cam,andre.rocha}@uninova.pt, paula.graca@isel.pt

[2] Instituto Superior de Engenharia de Lisboa, Instituto Politécnico de Lisboa, Rua Conselheiro Emídio Navarro 1, 1959-007 Lisbon, Portugal

**Abstract.** The manufacturing sector is experiencing a profound transformation as reflected in the Industry 4.0 movement, combined with the growing societal concerns for sustainability. This trend has led to the notion of sustainable manufacturing. On the other hand, the increasing interconnectivity among organisations, people, and physical systems, supported by recent developments in communication technologies, points to the important role that collaborative networks have in the ongoing digital transformation processes. As such, this paper analyses the synergies between sustainable manufacturing and collaborative networks. More specifically, the goal is to analyse how the responsibility for the various facets of sustainability can be distributed among the multiple entities involved in manufacturing. This study is based on both literature survey and our experience in various research projects in the area and is organised according to the typical six dimensions of Industry 4.0. The work is complemented with a brief summary of proposed indicators to measure sustainability under this networked manufacturing perspective.

**Keywords:** Collaborative networks · Sustainability · Sustainable manufacturing · Industry 4.0 · Digital transformation · Sustainability indicators

## 1 Introduction

The manufacturing sector has experienced considerable evolution in the last decade as reflected in the Industry 4.0 and digital transformation "movement". The convergence of multiple new technologies and the political support to this "industrial revolution" led to the emergence of new organisational and managerial forms, new processes, extended notion of product-service, and new business models.

In parallel, the manufacturing world also faces the challenge of coping with a growing societal claim for sustainability. This is reflected, for instance, in the UN Agenda 2030 [1], which establishes 17 goals for sustainable development. Manufacturing has a crucial role in this context, as addressed in the various sub-items of Goal 9, "Build resilient


Published by Springer Nature Switzerland AG 2021
L. M. Camarinha-Matos et al. (Eds.): PRO-VE 2021, IFIP AICT 629, pp. 3–18, 2021.
https://doi.org/10.1007/978-3-030-85969-5_1

infrastructure, promote inclusive and sustainable industrialisation and foster innovation". But other (indirect) links to manufacturing can also be found in other goals of the Agenda, e.g., "double the global rate of improvement in energy efficiency", "achieve higher levels of economic productivity through diversification, technological upgrading and innovation", "promote development-oriented policies that support productive activities, decent job creation, entrepreneurship, creativity and innovation, and encourage the formalisation and growth of micro-, small- and medium-sized enterprises", etc. As such, in recent years the term "sustainable manufacturing" [2] is becoming more relevant.

As identified in [3], there is a great potential for mutual beneficial synergies between the fields of collaborative networks and sustainability science. This was one of the earliest works arguing that sustainability requires a wide collaboration among multiple stakeholders, not being possible to achieve by individual entities. On the other hand, collaborative networks have also been pointed out as a core enabler for Industry 4.0 and digital transformation [4, 5]. Given this context, this work is guided by the following general research question: *What is the role of collaborative networks in sustainable manufacturing?* More specifically, we are interested in analysing how the responsibility for the various facets of sustainability can be distributed among the multiple entities involved in networked manufacturing systems.

As this research is ongoing work, this paper mainly tries to identify and categorise relevant examples and trends to help understand the synergies among these three areas: collaborative networks, manufacturing, and sustainability.

## 2 Base Concepts and Research Method

In this section, some base concepts are briefly revisited in order to provide a context for the following discussion.

The notion of sustainability is typically analysed under three perspectives: environmental, economic, and social [3]. Such a notion involves considerable complexity, not only because of this multi-dimensional nature, but also because it calls for a difficult balance among objectives that are often conflicting and involving multiple stakeholders. When it comes to manufacturing, various related terms are often used, including sustainable manufacturing, industrial symbiosis, and circular economy.

**Sustainable manufacturing** has emerged in recent years as the "*integration of processes and systems capable to produce high quality products and services using less and more sustainable resources (energy and materials), being safer for employees, customers and communities surrounding, and being able to mitigate environmental and social impacts throughout its whole life cycle*" [6]. A similar definition is provided in [i], which further refers the need to be "economically sound".

**Industrial symbiosis** can be seen as one specific implementation of sustainable manufacturing representing a "*process by which the wastes or by-products of an industry or industrial process become the raw materials for another*" [7]. This notion implies a collective endeavour through which a group of separate industries form a kind of collaborative business ecosystem to exchange materials, energy, water and by-products [8]. It implies moving from a linear model of "take-make-dispose" to a circular model in which waste is valorised as a resource.

**Circular economy** is a more general concept, which focuses on "*higher resource utilisation by recollecting and reusing components of products after their use is over*" [9]. In other words, it "*enables the reintegration of materials into production processes through their reuse, recycling, and recovery*" [10]. From a traditional point of view, while circular economy focuses on the entire economy, sustainable manufacturing appears focused solely on the manufacturing phase [11]. However, when we take the Industry 4.0 view, and the notion of extended smart product and the need of considering the whole life cycle of the product, the notions of sustainable manufacturing and circular economy get a bigger overlapping.

The effective materialisation of all the above notions implies some form of collaboration among multiple stakeholders, and thus, the role of collaborative networks in support of sustainable manufacturing deserves attention. In fact, the common notion of **collaborative network** as "*composed of a variety of entities – organisations people* and even smart machines – *which are largely autonomous, geographically distributed, and heterogeneous in terms of their operating environment, culture, social capital and goals... that collaborate to (better) achieve common or compatible goals*" [12] provides a comprehensive view of the interactions and inter-dependencies among the multiple entities involved in a manufacturing system. The notion of community or business ecosystem, as implicit in Virtual organisation Breeding Environments, helps to build a better perception of co-responsibility of all involved actors regarding the sustainability challenges [3].

In this work, as a preliminary stage to understand the synergies among sustainability, manufacturing, and collaborative networks, we adopted a mixed method, combining a systematic mapping study based on literature with case studies/acquired experiences from various research projects. On the other hand, the study of such synergies is also expected to contribute to a better understanding of the next generation of collaborative networks. In fact, a business ecosystem or any other form of a collaborative network not only involves collaboration but rather a complex and dynamic mix of collaboration and competition. In such business communities, there is some form of "survival instinct" and shared vision that can lead members to align their commitments and to find mutually supportive roles. By further expanding these ideas, we hope to acquire new insights on better organisational and governance principles that will likely contribute to more sustainable business ecosystems.

## 3 A Collaborative Networks View of Manufacturing Systems

Various recent works have presented collaborative networks as one of the core enablers for Industry 4.0 and the ongoing digital transformation process [4, 5, 13, 14]. In fact, considering the typical dimensions of the current industrial revolution, including both the manufacturing system and product/service perspectives, it becomes clear that we need to deal with, at all levels, networks involving multiple actors, being them organisations, people, smart machines, and smart systems, with varying degrees of autonomy and heterogeneity. The highlights of such a trend are illustrated in Fig. 1, which go far beyond the traditional view of networks applied to value chains and rather influence all dimensions of Industry 4.0.

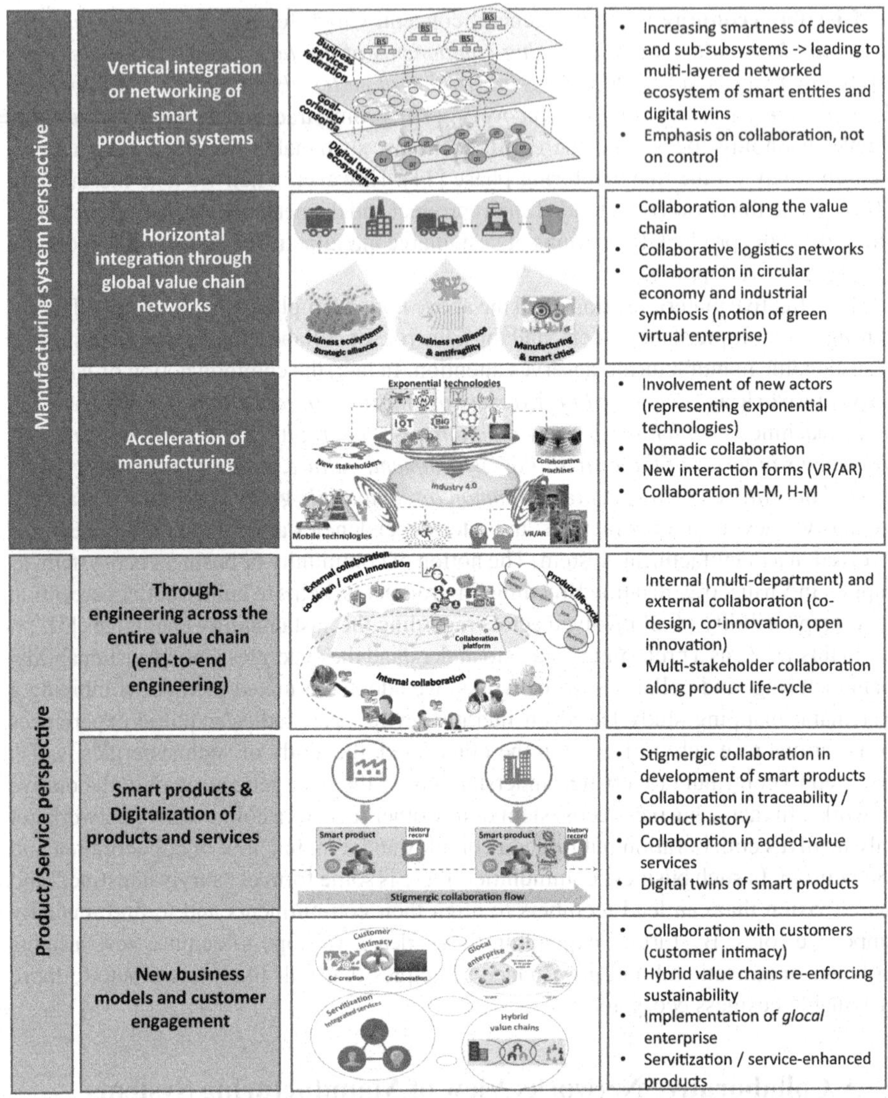

Manufacturing system perspective
Vertical integration or networking of smart production systems
Business services federation
Goal-oriented consortia
Digital twins ecosystem
Increasing smartness of devices and sub-subsystems -> leading to multi-layered networked ecosystem of smart entities and digital twins
Emphasis on collaboration, not on control
Horizontal integration through global value chain networks
Business ecosystems Strategic alliances
Business resilience & antifragility
Manufacturing & smart cities
Collaboration along the value chain
Collaborative logistics networks
Collaboration in circular economy and industrial symbiosis (notion of green virtual enterprise)
Acceleration of manufacturing
Exponential technologies
New stakeholders
Collaborative machines
Industry 4.0
Mobile technologies
VR/AR
Involvement of new actors (representing exponential technologies)
Nomadic collaboration
New interaction forms (VR/AR)
Collaboration M-M, H-M
Product/Service perspective
Through-engineering across the entire value chain (end-to-end engineering)
External collaboration co-design / open innovation
Product life-cycle
Collaboration platform
Internal collaboration
Internal (multi-department) and external collaboration (co-design, co-innovation, open innovation)
Multi-stakeholder collaboration along product life-cycle
Smart products & Digitalization of products and services
Smart product
history record
Stigmergic collaboration flow
Stigmergic collaboration in development of smart products
Collaboration in traceability / product history
Collaboration in added-value services
Digital twins of smart products
New business models and customer engagement
Customer intimacy
Co-creation
Co-innovation
Glocal enterprise
Servitization
Integrated services
Hybrid value chains
Collaboration with customers (customer intimacy)
Hybrid value chains re-enforcing sustainability
Implementation of glocal enterprise
Servitization / service-enhanced products


**Fig. 1.** Dimensions of Industry 4.0 and role of collaborative networks

This view of a manufacturing system as composed of multiple networks of autonomous or partially autonomous entities implies a distribution of responsibilities among these entities. As such, also the issue of sustainability needs to be analysed under a collaborative networks perspective in the sense that multiple entities/sub-systems are co-responsible for the sustainability level of the manufacturing system.

The role of CNs in sustainability has been addressed in relation to the horizontal integration dimension, namely in terms of circular economy and industrial symbiosis, or in relation to new business models, such as some cases of hybrid value chains

[8, 10]. However, the issue has been less studied in the case of the other dimensions, which justifies an effort to analyse existing trends and relevant examples in order to characterise research gaps.

## 4 Trends and Examples

The latest developments associated with Industry 4.0 have focused on developing solutions aimed at introducing more sustainable manufacturing practices, not only from the point of view of costs and profit but also considering the other two pillars of sustainability, related to social and environmental aspects. Although this trend towards more sustainable ecosystems can be noticed, an assessment is not usually made of how the collaboration aspects are directly or indirectly related to improving these complex ecosystems. These distributed and complex systems imply constant communication between the players to optimise the systems, whether from an economic, social and/or environmental points of view.

The association of the collaborative perspective with these systems is usually not much explicit in the manufacturing literature, besides the obvious case of the horizontal dimension. However, in many studies, it is possible to identify that collaboration is an essential aspect in the design and operation of these complex environments. For example, it is possible to find shopfloors' implementation where machines collaborate with each other and/or with the operators. Another case widely observed in the literature is the optimisation of distributed manufacturing systems where different factories, suppliers, and transportation systems work together to optimise themselves as a whole. Products are also beginning to emerge with new features such as connectivity to the cloud that allows data extraction from products and changing their functionality remotely by manufacturers. This aspect also contributes to the product design being done collaboratively between the company's different departments, including the customer and the product itself in this process. This new reality is becoming clear with the introduction of new emerging technologies such as Additive Manufacturing, Artificial Intelligence or Cyber-Physical Systems that will force companies to apply new business models.

A summary of studies focusing on developing sustainable manufacturing systems in which collaborative aspects are presented is shown in Table 1. This table covers the infrastructure perspective and presents examples aiming to increase the sustainability of manufacturing systems through collaboration.

Similar to Table 1, Table 2 presents the elements of collaboration and added value regarding sustainability that are found in studies related to the dimensions of End-to-End Engineering, Smart Products, and the creation of new business models.

It is possible to verify by the results summarised in Table 1 and Table 2 that some work has already been done in order to develop more sustainable systems using as a base the combination of practices of Industry 4.0 and collaborative networks. In most of the studied works, the collaboration aspects are not usually highlighted; nevertheless, the synergy between sustainable manufacturing and collaborative networks can be inferred. For instance, a research project in sustainable manufacturing in which our research centre participated is illustrated in Fig. 2, where it is possible to identify the role of collaborative aspects at different levels.

**Table 1.** Examples of sustainability aspects in the manufacturing infrastructure dimensions.

| | Economic | Social | Environmental |
|---|---|---|---|
| Vertical integration | • Collaboration between machines to reduce costs and increase productivity. [15, 16]<br>• Increase productivity using human-robot collaboration [17, 18]<br>• Share factories to increase efficiency [19] | • Human-robot collaboration (Improve working conditions, reduce health problems) [17, 18, 20–22] | • Implementation of shared factories to reduce energy and natural resources consumption [19]<br>• Human robot collaboration in order to improve recycling process, reducing waste [21, 22] |
| Horizontal integration | • Collaborative resource allocation. [16, 23]<br>• Increase efficiency sharing spaces and machines [24]<br>• Shared logistics for cost reduction [25]<br>• Collaborative strategies for pickup and delivery network of eco-packages through resource sharing [26]<br>• Contributions of environmental collaboration to firm performance [27] | • Auction-based logistics for social welfare [25]<br>• Collaborative platforms to ensure human rights protection, patient confidentially and welfare. [23]<br>• Role of green supply chain to improve brands and customer value [28]<br>• Sustainable collaborative governance of supply chains [29] | • Reduce resources' waste sharing spaces and machines [24]<br>• Reduce carbon footprint and energy consumption through trustable collaborative supply chain [23, 30, 31]<br>• Various methods to select suppliers for sustainable supply chains using the 3 dimensions of sustainability [32–34] |
| Acceleration of manufacturing | • CPS systems for allowing interoperability among factory resources [15]<br>• Digital Twins to design products by different teams and in different stages [35]<br>• Digital Twins to optimise shared resources' allocation [24]<br>• Self-organised approaches to optimise network of resources [19]<br>• Blockchain to increase trustability among suppliers [23] | • Additive manufacturing and 3D printing as part of circular production and consumption. [36, 37]<br>• Digital Twins to increase the collaboration between human and robots [17]<br>• Blockchain to ensure social aspects in a collaborative distributed ecosystem [23] | • Distributed manufacturing of 3D printed products to reduce energy and material consumption [38]<br>• Overall reduction of energy and material consumption using Digital Twins [24, 30]<br>• Blockchain technology to allow a trustable waste and resources consumption reduction in collaborative supply chains [23] |

**Table 2.** Examples of sustainability aspects in the product/service dimensions.

| | Economic | Social | Environmental |
|---|---|---|---|
| End-to-end engineering | • Co-creation and user innovation [37, 39, 40]<br>• Shorten design cycles and reduce costs using the data collected from products and customers. [35, 41] | • (Re)design products according to customer needs and desires based on product data [39]<br>• Guarantee product quality through remote product analysis during execution [42]<br>• Value co-creation network [40] | • Utilisation of the collected data from the product to design more ecofriendly transport conditions [43] |
| Smart products/digitalisation | • Product data extraction to (re)design better products [39]<br>• Extract and analyse products' data along the supply chain to reduce costs [39]<br>• Symbiosis network [40] | • Extract data to assess product quality and execution [42]<br>• Extract and analyse data from the product to reduce delivering time [39] | • Constant assessment of products' conditions during transportation [43]<br>• Extract and analyse products' data along the supply chain to reduce environmental impact [39]<br>• Smart products contribution to circular economy [44] |
| New business models | • Sharing economy to increase competitiveness [19, 24]<br>• Application of industrial symbiosis [31, 45] | • Increase customer involvement [36, 37]<br>• Stigmergic Mass customization, co-creation, co-design [46]<br>• Hybrid value chains and social innovation [47, 48] | • Circular economy-based model [21, 36]<br>• Distributed manufacturing model [38, 49]<br>• Sharing economy to reduce wastes and consumptions [19, 24]<br>• Application of industrial symbiosis [31, 45]<br>• Global business sustainability [50] |

From the analysed examples, as summarised in the tables above, it is possible to verify that the collaborative aspects are already present in various cases of applying the Industry 4.0 concepts to achieve sustainability. It can also be noticed that these aspects appear more frequently in terms of the vertical and horizontal integration dimensions. Another interesting point is that emerging technologies, included under the acceleration of manufacturing, are particularly relevant in the efficient application of the collaborative aspects. However, it is important to underline that the combination of manufacturing, sustainability and collaborative networks are not always explicitly presented in the studied literature, but it is possible to infer their importance, as summarised in Table 1 and Table 2.

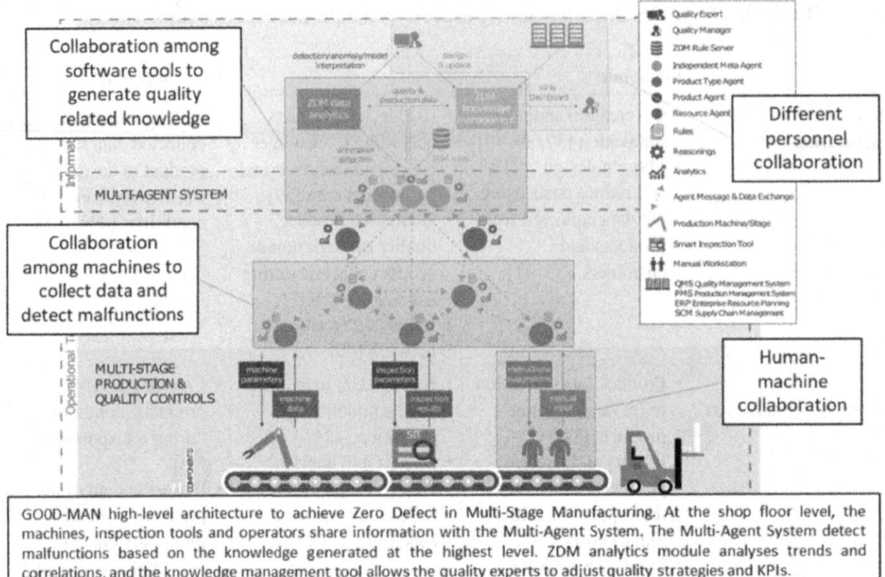
Collaboration among software tools to generate quality related knowledge
Different personnel collaboration
Collaboration among machines to collect data and detect malfunctions
Human-machine collaboration
MULTI-AGENT SYSTEM
MULTI-STAGE PRODUCTION & QUALITY CONTROLS
GOOD-MAN high-level architecture to achieve Zero Defect in Multi-Stage Manufacturing. At the shop floor level, the machines, inspection tools and operators share information with the Multi-Agent System. The Multi-Agent System detect malfunctions based on the knowledge generated at the highest level. ZDM analytics module analyses trends and correlations, and the knowledge management tool allows the quality experts to adjust quality strategies and KPIs.

**Fig. 2.** GOODMAN High-Level Architecture and Collaborative Aspects (adapted from [51])

## 5 Measuring Sustainability

Although it is widely agreed that sustainability is one of the main concerns for manufacturing, to be more effective, sustainability must be measured and proper sustainability-related performance indicators established. As summarised in Table 3 and Table 4, some examples of efforts on measuring sustainability under a collaborative perspective and addressing the economic, social, and environmental concerns can already be found in the literature.

The examples in Table 3, addressing the manufacturing infrastructure perspective, propose mainly metrics and indicators to evaluate sustainability performance, borrowed from traditional manufacturing and supply chains. Concerning the collaboration perspective, some attempts can be found, underlining the importance of collaboration between the various players towards better sustainability.

**Table 3.** Examples of sustainability metrics/indicators in the manufacturing infrastructure dimensions.

| | Economic | Social | Environmental |
|---|---|---|---|
| Vertical integration | • Metrics for evaluation of manufacturing sustainability performance at the production line level [52]<br>• Framework to map and analyse the interconnections between technical and economic performance metrics at the operation [53] | • Metrics for evaluation of manufacturing sustainability performance at the production line/plant level [52]<br>• Framework to map and analyse the interconnections between technical and social performance metrics at the operation [53] | • Metrics for evaluation of manufacturing sustainability performance at the production line/plant level [52]<br>• Framework to map and analyse the interconnections between technical and environmental performance metrics at the operation [53] |
| Horizontal integration | • Dashboard of KPIs of a Virtual Factory processes [54]<br>• Framework to develop metrics for evaluating system effectiveness to improve sustainability [55]<br>• Proposal for a sustainability index to show performance at manufacturer and supply chain level [56]<br>• Measurement of sustainability performance in products and processes for manufacturing companies [57] | • Framework to develop metrics for evaluating system effectiveness to improve sustainability [55]<br>• Proposal for a sustainability index to show performance at manufacturer and supply chain level [56]<br>• Social responsibility metrics to evaluate and select sustainable suppliers [32]<br>• Measurement of sustainability performance in products and processes for manufacturing companies [57]<br>• Sustainability performance indicators for an Industry 4.0 virtual learning environment [58] | • Dashboard of KPIs of a Virtual Factory processes [54]<br>• Framework to develop metrics for evaluating system effectiveness to improve sustainability [55]<br>• Proposal for a sustainability index to show performance at manufacturer and supply chain level [56]<br>• Environmental metrics to evaluate & select sustainable suppliers [32]<br>• Measurement of sustainability performance in products and processes for manufacturing companies [57]<br>• Sustainability performance indicators for an Industry 4.0 virtual learning environment [58]<br>• Model for the assessment of the performance of a supply chain, based the perspectives used in the balanced scorecard e[59] |

*(continued)*

**Table 3.** (*continued*)

| | Economic | Social | Environmental |
|---|---|---|---|
| Acceleration of manufacturing | • Indicators/practices to optimise economic returns [60]<br>• Metrics to evaluate the influence of Industry 4.0 on sustainable manufacturing [11]<br>• Study to integrate the sustainable smart manufacturing performance by incorporating sustainable manufacturing measures [61]<br>• Metrics framework for assessing sustainability benefits in cyber manufacturing systems [62] | • Indicators/practices to optimise social returns [60]<br>• Measures for talent attractiveness in SMEs to achieve social sustainability in the cities of the future [63]<br>• Metrics to evaluate the influence of Industry 4.0 on sustainable manufacturing [11]<br>• Study to integrate the sustainable smart manufacturing performance by incorporating sustainable manufacturing measures [61]<br>• Metrics framework for assessing sustainability benefits in cyber manufacturing systems [62] | • Indicators/practices to optimise environmental returns [60]<br>• Metrics to evaluate the influence of Industry 4.0 on sustainable manufacturing [11]<br>• Study to integrate the sustainable smart manufacturing performance by incorporating sustainable manufacturing measures [61]<br>• Metrics framework for assessing sustainability benefits in cyber manufacturing systems [62] |

Table 4 presents examples related to sustainability metrics and indicators focused on smart products, digitalisation and new business models. Under this perspective, the identified attempts are preliminary approaches to measurement models, identification of benefits, and insights on the influence of these products and services on sustainable performance. At this level, the collaboration that is more worth highlighting is between human-machine.

This study only presents some examples and not an exhaustive list of cases. Nevertheless, and despite some valuable attempts, there is still a lack of concrete performance indicators to assess the benefits of collaboration towards a better manufacturing sustainability performance.

**Table 4.** Examples of sustainability metrics/indicators in the product/service dimensions.

| | Economic | Social | Environmental |
|---|---|---|---|
| End-to-end engineering | • Preliminary approach towards a measurement model for value co-creation in service design [64] | • Identification of benefits for customers from co-creation [65] | |
| Smart products/digitalisation | • Smart targets to smart energy systems transition with economic impact [66] | • Smart targets to smart energy systems transition with social impact [66] | • Smart targets to smart energy systems transition with environmental impact [66] |
| New business models | • Insights that servitisation and lean bundles have complementarity effects on sustainable performance [67]<br>• Index to assess the sustainability and the circularity of manufacturing companies [10]<br>• Framework based on concepts of circular economy to assess sustainability performance of manufacturing companies [60]<br>• Quantitative framework for Industry 4.0 enabled circular economy [68] | • Index to assess the sustainability and the circularity of manufacturing companies [10]<br>• Framework based on concepts of circular economy to assess sustainability performance of manufacturing companies [60] | • Insights that servitisation and lean bundles have complementarity effects on sustainable performance [67]<br>• Index to assess the sustainability and the circularity of manufacturing companies [10]<br>• Framework based on concepts of circular economy to assess the sustainability performance of manufacturing companies [60]<br>• Quantitative framework for Industry 4.0 enabled circular economy [68] |

## 6 Conclusions

Sustainability is a major challenge for modern manufacturing systems. Although the manufacturing sector has received a renewed attention in the last years, as reflected in the multiplication of initiatives around Industry 4.0 and digital transformation, making such systems more sustainable remains a crucial challenge.

On the other hand, as manufacturing systems become increasingly smart, autonomous, and interconnected, reflecting a kind of distributed intelligence, the issues of sustainability need to be analysed under a distributed and collaborative perspective. To this aim, the synergies between collaborative networks and sustainable manufacturing need to be further explored.

This study reveals a good number of steps in this direction, both at the manufacturing infrastructure level and at the product/service/business model level. However, the collaboration aspects among all the entities present in these ecosystems are still not usually considered and analysed. But it is clear that despite the identified positive examples, there is a need to substantially pursue the exploitation of synergies among the areas of sustainability, manufacturing, and collaborative networks and develop corresponding assessment methodologies and indicators.

**Acknowledgments.** This work was funded in part by Fundação para a Ciência e Tecnologia through the program UIDB/00066/2020 and Center of Technology and Systems (CTS).

## References

1. United Nations. Transforming our world: the 2030 agenda for sustainable development department of economic and social affairs (2015). https://sdgs.un.org/2030agenda. Accessed 6 Apr 2021
2. OCDE: The OECD sustainable manufacturing toolkit (2021). https://www.oecd.org/innovation/green/toolkit/48704993.pdf. Accessed 6 Apr 2021
3. Camarinha-Matos, L.M., Afsarmanesh, H., Boucher, X.: The role of collaborative networks in sustainability. In: Camarinha-Matos, L.M., Boucher, X., Afsarmanesh, H. (eds.) PRO-VE 2010. IAICT, vol. 336, pp. 1–16. Springer, Heidelberg (2010). https://doi.org/10.1007/978-3-642-15961-9_1
4. Camarinha-Matos, L.M., Fornasiero, R., Afsarmanesh, H.: Collaborative networks as a core enabler of Industry 4.0. In: Camarinha-Matos, L.M., Afsarmanesh, H., Fornasiero, R. (eds.) PRO-VE 2017. IAICT, vol. 506, pp. 3–17. Springer, Cham (2017). https://doi.org/10.1007/978-3-319-65151-4_1
5. Camarinha-Matos, L.M., Fornasiero, R., Ramezani, J., Ferrada, F.: Collaborative networks: a pillar of digital transformation. Appl. Sci. **9**(24), 5431 (2019). https://doi.org/10.3390/app9245431
6. Gonçalves Machado, C., Winroth, M.P., Hans Dener Ribeiro da Silva, E.: Sustainable manufacturing in Industry 4.0: an emerging research agenda. Int. J. Prod. Res. 58(5), 1462–1484 (2020)https://doi.org/10.1080/00207543.2019.1652777
7. EGC (2018). https://ec.europa.eu/environment/europeangreencapital/wp-content/uploads/2018/05/Industrial_Symbiosis.pdf. Accessed 2 Apr 2021
8. Baldassarre, B., Schepers, M., Bocken, N., Cuppen, E., Korevaar, G., Calabretta, G.: Industrial symbiosis: towards a design process for eco-industrial clusters by integrating circular economy and industrial ecology perspectives. J. Clean. Prod. **216**, 446–460 (2019). https://doi.org/10.1016/j.jclepro.2019.01.091
9. Pomponi, F., Moncaster, A.: Circular economy for the built environment: a research framework. J. Clean. Prod. **143**, 710–718 (2017). https://doi.org/10.1016/j.jclepro.2016.12.055
10. Azevedo, S., Godina, R., Matias, J.: Proposal of a sustainable circular index for manufacturing companies. Resources **6**(4), 63 (2017). https://doi.org/10.3390/resources6040063
11. Enyoghasi, C., Badurdeen, F.: Industry 4.0 for sustainable manufacturing: opportunities at the product, process, and system levels. Resour. Conserv. Recycl. **166**, 105362 (2021). https://doi.org/10.1016/j.resconrec.2020.105362
12. Camarinha-Matos, L.M., Afsarmanesh, H., Galeano, N., Molina, A.: Collaborative networked organisations - concepts and practice in manufacturing enterprises. Comput. Ind. Eng. **57**(1), 46–60 (2009). https://doi.org/10.1016/j.cie.2008.11.024
13. Santos, L.M.A.L.D., et al.: Industry 4.0 collaborative networks for industrial performance. J. Manuf. Technol. Manage. **32**(2), 245–265 (2020). https://doi.org/10.1108/JMTM-04-2020-0156

14. Torn, I.A.R., Vaneker, T.H.J.: Mass personalization with Industry 4.0 by SMEs: a concept for collaborative networks. Procedia Manuf. **28**, 135–141 (2019). https://doi.org/10.1016/j.promfg.2018.12.022
15. Adamson, G., Wang, L., Moore, P.: Feature-based control and information framework for adaptive and distributed manufacturing in cyber physical systems. J. Manuf. Syst. **43**, 305–315 (Apr 2017). https://doi.org/10.1016/j.jmsy.2016.12.003
16. Li, K., Zhou, T., Liu, B.-H., Li, H.: A multi-agent system for sharing distributed manufacturing resources. Expert Syst. Appl. **99**, 32–43 (2018). https://doi.org/10.1016/j.eswa.2018.01.027
17. Lv, Q., Zhang, R., Sun, X., Yuqian, L., Bao, J.: A digital twin-driven human-robot collaborative assembly approach in the wake of covid-19. J. Manuf. Syst. (Feb 2021). https://doi.org/10.1016/j.jmsy.2021.02.011
18. Gualtieri, L., Palomba, I., Merati, F.A., Rauch, E., Vidoni, R.: Design of Human-centered collaborative assembly workstations for the improvement of operators' physical ergonomics and production efficiency: a case study. Sustainability **12**(9), 3606 (2020)
19. Li, P., Jiang, P.: Enhanced agents in shared factory: enabling high-efficiency self-organisation and sustainability of the shared manufacturing resources. J. Clean. Prod. **292**, 126020 (2021). https://doi.org/10.1016/j.jclepro.2021.126020
20. Ansari, F., Hold, P., Khobreh, M.: A knowledge-based approach for representing jobholder profile toward optimal human–machine collaboration in cyber physical production systems. CIRP J. Manuf. Sci. Technol. **28**, 87–106 (2020). https://doi.org/10.1016/j.cirpj.2019.11.005
21. Renteria, A., Alvarez-de-los-Mozos, E.: Human-robot collaboration as a new paradigm in circular economy for WEEE management. Procedia Manuf. **38**, 375–382 (2019). https://doi.org/10.1016/j.promfg.2020.01.048
22. Poschmann, H., Brüggemann, H., Goldmann, D.: Fostering end-of-life utilization by information-driven robotic disassembly. Procedia CIRP **98**, 282–287 (2021). https://doi.org/10.1016/j.procir.2021.01.104
23. Upadhyay, A., Mukhuty, S., Kumar, V., Kazancoglu, Y.: Blockchain technology and the circular economy: Implications for sustainability and social responsibility. J. Clean. Prod. **293**, 126130 (2021)
24. Wang, G., Zhang, G., Guo, X., Zhang, Y.: Digital twin-driven service model and optimal allocation of manufacturing resources in shared manufacturing. J. Manuf. Syst. **59**, 165–179 (2021). https://doi.org/10.1016/j.jmsy.2021.02.008
25. Kang, K., Zhong, R.Y., Su Xiu, X., Tan, B.Q., Wang, L., Peng, T.: Auction-based cloud service allocation and sharing for logistics product service system. J. Clean. Prod. **278**, 123881 (2021). https://doi.org/10.1016/j.jclepro.2020.123881
26. Wang, Y., et al.: Collaborative logistics pickup and delivery problem with eco-packages based on time–space network. Expert Syst. Appl. **170**, 114561 (2021). https://doi.org/10.1016/j.eswa.2021.114561
27. Grekova, K., Calantone, R.J., Bremmers, H.J., Trienekens, J.H., Omta, S.W.F.: How environmental collaboration with suppliers and customers influences firm performance: evidence from dutch food and beverage processors. J. Clean. Prod. **112**, 1861–1871 (2016). https://doi.org/10.1016/j.jclepro.2015.03.022
28. Lintukangas, K., Kähkönen, A.-K., Ritala, P.: Supply risks as drivers of green supply management adoption. J. Clean. Prod. **112**, 1901–1909 (2016). https://doi.org/10.1016/j.jclepro.2014.10.089
29. Wang, J., Ran, B.: Sustainable collaborative governance in supply chain. Sustainability **10**(2), 171 (2018). https://doi.org/10.3390/su10010171
30. Glatt, M., Kölsch, P., Siedler, C., Langlotz, P., Ehmsen, S., Aurich, J.C.: Edge-based digital twin to trace and ensure sustainability in cross-company production networks. Procedia CIRP **98**, 276–281 (2021). https://doi.org/10.1016/j.procir.2021.01.103

31. Chen, P.-C., Liu, K.-H.: Development of an interactive industrial symbiosis query system with structured industrial waste database in taiwan. J. Clean. Prod. **297**, 126673 (2021). https://doi.org/10.1016/j.jclepro.2021.126673
32. Sarkis, J., Dhavale, D.G.: Supplier selection for sustainable operations: a triple-bottom-line approach using a bayesian framework. Int. J. Prod. Econ. **166**, 177–191 (2015). https://doi.org/10.1016/j.ijpe.2014.11.007
33. Trapp, A.C., Sarkis, J.: Identifying robust portfolios of suppliers: a sustainability selection and development perspective. J. Clean. Prod. **112**, 2088–2100 (2016). https://doi.org/10.1016/j.jclepro.2014.09.062
34. Chong, W., Barnes, D.: An integrated model for green partner selection and supply chain construction. J. Clean. Prod. **112**, 2114–2132 (2016). https://doi.org/10.1016/j.jclepro.2015.02.023
35. Tao, F., et al.: Digital twin-driven product design framework. Int. J. Prod. Res. **57**(12), 3935–3953 (2019). https://doi.org/10.1080/00207543.2018.1443229
36. Turner, C., et al.: Sustainable production in a circular economy: A business model for re-distributed manufacturing. Sustainability **11**(16), 4291 (2019). https://doi.org/10.3390/su11164291
37. Rayna, T., Striukova, L., Darlington, J.: Co-creation and user innovation: the role of online 3D printing platforms. J. Eng. Tech. Manage. **37**, 90–102 (2015). https://doi.org/10.1016/j.jengtecman.2015.07.002
38. Cerdas, F., Juraschek, M., Thiede, S., Herrmann, C.: Life cycle assessment of 3D printed products in a distributed manufacturing system. J. Ind. Ecol. **21**(S1), S80–S93 (2017). https://doi.org/10.1111/jiec.12618
39. Zheng, P., Lin, T.-J., Chen, C.-H., Xun, X.: A systematic design approach for service innovation of smart product-service systems. J. Clean. Prod. **201**, 657–667 (Nov 2018). https://doi.org/10.1016/j.jclepro.2018.08.101
40. Yin, D., Ming, X., Zhang, X.: Sustainable and smart product innovation ecosystem: an integrative status review and future perspectives. J. Clean. Prod. **274**, 123005 (2020). https://doi.org/10.1016/j.jclepro.2020.123005
41. Verhagen, W.J.C., de Vrught, B., Schut, J., Curran, R.: A method for identification of automation potential through modelling of engineering processes and quantification of information waste. Adv. Eng. Inform. **29**(3), 307–321 (2015). https://doi.org/10.1016/j.aei.2015.03.003
42. Maleki, E., et al.: Ontology-based framework enabling smart product-service systems: application of sensing systems for machine health monitoring. IEEE Internet Things J. **5**(6), 4496–4505 (2018). https://doi.org/10.1109/JIOT.2018.2831279
43. Inés Cabot, M., Luque, A., De Las Heras, A., Aguayo,F.: Aspects of sustainability and design engineering for the production of interconnected smart food packaging. PloS ONE **14**(5), e0216555 (2019)https://doi.org/10.1371/journal.pone.0216555
44. Alcayaga, A., Hansen, E.G.: Smart products as enabler for circular business models: the case of B2B textile washing services. In: 3rd PLATE 2019 Conference, Berlin, Germany, pp. 18–20 (2019)
45. Gao, N., Li, Y., Mai, Y., Xu, H.: Optimisation of multiple products transportation under the background of industrial symbiosis network. In: 2020 IEEE International Conference on Industrial Engineering and Engineering Management (IEEM), pp. 1281–1285 (2020). https://doi.org/10.1109/IEEM45057.2020.9309810
46. Ogunsakin, R., Marin, C.A., Mehandjiev, N.: Towards engineering manufacturing systems for mass personalisation: a stigmergic approach. Int. J. Comput. Integr. Manuf. **34**(4), 341–369 (2021). https://doi.org/10.1080/0951192X.2020.1858508
47. Budinich, V., Manno Reott, K., Schmidt, S.: Hybrid value chains: social innovations and the development of the small farmer irrigation market in Mexico. SSRN 981223 (2007)

48. Doherty, B., Kittipanya-Ngam, P.: The role of social enterprise hybrid business models in inclusive value chain development. Sustainability **13**(2), 499 (2021)
49. Gupta, H., Lawal, J.N., Orji, I.J., Kusi-Sarpong, S.: Closing the gap: the role of distributed manufacturing systems for overcoming the barriers to manufacturing sustainability. IEEE Trans. Eng. Manage. 1–20 (2021) https://doi.org/10.1109/TEM.2021.3059231
50. Svensson, G., Padin, C., Eriksson, D.: Glocal business sustainability - performance beyond zero! Int. J. Procurement Manage. **9**(1), 15–26 (Jan 2016). https://doi.org/10.1504/IJPM.2016.073385
51. Angione, G., Cristalli, C., Barbosa, J., Leitão, P.: Integration challenges for the deployment of a multi-stage zero-defect manufacturing architecture. In: 2019 IEEE 17th International Conference on Industrial Informatics (INDIN), vol. 1, pp. 1615–1620 (2019). https://doi.org/10.1109/INDIN41052.2019.8972259
52. Huang, A., Badurdeen, F.: Metrics-based approach to evaluate sustainable manufacturing performance at the production line and plant levels. J. Clean. Prod. **192**, 462–476 (Aug 2018). https://doi.org/10.1016/j.jclepro.2018.04.234
53. Zhang, H., Veltri, A., Calvo-Amodio, J., Haapala, K.R.: Making the business case for sustainable manufacturing in small and medium-sized manufacturing enterprises: a systems decision making approach. J. Clean. Prod. **287**, 125038 (2021). https://doi.org/10.1016/j.jclepro.2020.125038
54. Hao, Y., Helo, P., Shamsuzzoha, A.: Virtual factory system design and implementation: integrated sustainable manufacturing. Int. J. Syst. Sci. Oper. Logistics **5**(2), 116–132 (2018). https://doi.org/10.1080/23302674.2016.1242819
55. Koren, Y., Gu, X., Badurdeen, F., Jawahir, I.S.: Sustainable living factories for next generation manufacturing. Procedia Manuf. **21**, 26–36 (2018)https://doi.org/10.1016/j.promfg.2018.02.091
56. Salvado, M., Azevedo, S., Matias, J., Ferreira, L.: Proposal of a sustainability index for the automotive industry. Sustainability **7**(2), 2113–2144 (2015). https://doi.org/10.3390/su7022113
57. Feng, S.C., Joung, C.-B., Li, G.: Development overview of sustainable manufacturing metrics. In: Proceedings of the 17th CIRP International Conference on Life Cycle Engineering, vol. 6, p. 12. Citeseer (2010)
58. Chaim, O., Muschard, B., Cazarini, E., Rozenfeld, H.: Insertion of sustainability performance indicators in an Industry 4.0 virtual learning environment. Procedia Manuf. **21**, 446–453 (2018). https://doi.org/10.1016/j.promfg.2018.02.143
59. Luís, M.D., Ferreira, F., Silva, C., Azevedo, S.G.: An environmental balanced scorecard for supply chain performance measurement (env_bsc_4_scpm). Benchmarking Int. J. **23**(6), 1398–1422 (2016). https://doi.org/10.1108/BIJ-08-2013-0087
60. Gupta, H., Kumar, A., Wasan, P.: Industry 4.0, cleaner production and circular economy: an integrative framework for evaluating ethical and sustainable business performance of manufacturing organizations. J. Cleaner Prod. **295**, 126253 (2021). https://doi.org/10.1016/j.jclepro.2021.126253
61. Abubakr, M., Abbas, A.T., Tomaz, I., Soliman, M.S., Luqman, M., Hegab, H.: Sustainable and smart manufacturing: an integrated approach. Sustainability **12**(6), 2280 (2020). https://doi.org/10.3390/su12062280
62. Song, Z., Moon, Y.: Assessing sustainability benefits of cybermanufacturing systems. Int. J. Adv. Manuf. Technol. **90**(5–8), 1365–1382 (2016). https://doi.org/10.1007/s00170-016-9428-0
63. Matt, D.T., Orzes, G., Rauch, E., Dallasega, P.: Urban production – a socially sustainable factory concept to overcome shortcomings of qualified workers in smart smes. Comput. Ind. Eng. **139**, 105384 (2020). https://doi.org/10.1016/j.cie.2018.08.035

64. Botti, A., Grimaldi, M., Vesci, M.: Customer value co-creation in a service-dominant logic perspective: some steps toward the development of a measurement scale. In: Barile, S., Pellicano, M., Polese, F. (eds.) Social Dynamics in a Systems Perspective. NEW, pp. 137–157. Springer, Cham (2018). https://doi.org/10.1007/978-3-319-61967-5_8
65. Lee, A.R., Kim, K.K.: Customer benefits and value co-creation activities in corporate social networking services. Behav. Inf. Technol. **37**(7), 675–692 (2018). https://doi.org/10.1080/0144929X.2018.1474252
66. Dincer, I., Acar, C.: Smart energy systems for a sustainable future. Appl. Energy **194**, 225–235 (May 2017). https://doi.org/10.1016/j.apenergy.2016.12.058
67. Hao, Z., Liu, C., Goh, M.: Determining the effects of lean production and servitisation of manufacturing on sustainable performance. Sustain. Prod. Consump. **25**, 374–389 (2021). https://doi.org/10.1016/j.spc.2020.11.018
68. Spaltini, M., Poletti, A., Acerbi, F., Taisch, M.: A quantitative framework for industry 4.0 enabled circular economy. Procedia CIRP **98**, 115–120 (2021). https://doi.org/10.1016/j.procir.2021.01.015

# A Systematic Review of Sustainable Supply Chain Management Practices in Food Industry

Federica Minardi[1], Valérie Botta-Genoulaz[1(✉)], and Giulio Mangano[2]

[1] Univ Lyon, INSA Lyon, Université Claude Bernard Lyon 1, Univ Lumière Lyon 2, DISP, EA4570, 69621 Villeurbanne, France
{federica.minardi,valerie.botta}@insa-lyon.fr

[2] Department of Management and Production Engineering, Politecnico di Torino, 10129 Turin, Italy
giulio.mangano@polito.it

**Abstract.** The food industry is central to human beings and heavily impacts the lives of the entire society. Nowadays, the sustainable development goal and the introduction of new information and communication technologies has led food companies to deal with this new paradigm. They require sustainable practices that have the dual objective of improving the overall performance of the company itself and fulfilling the sustainability requirement. Research works on sustainable supply chain management practices in the food industry is quite fragmented, as it often considers just a part of the chain. Therefore, through a systematic literature review, this paper aims to provide an up-to-date analysis of supply chain management practices within the scope of sustainability, studying the findings of 224 reviewed papers. The implications of this work are relevant for academic research as they enlarge the body of knowledge and highlight key points where there is the need to investigate further. From a practical point of view this study proposes an overview of the most common and adopted practices that can be implemented in order to achieve sustainable development in the food industry.

**Keywords:** Systematic literature review · Supply chain management · Sustainable development · Food industry

## 1 Introduction

Food Supply Chain (FSC) refers to the set of processes that describe how food from a farm ends up on the table. Several dimensions are particularly critical in a FSC namely quality, safety, sustainability, and logistic efficiency [1, 2]. Moreover, "*internationalization, along with the need to keep up with sustainable development goals, has increased the level of global competition among companies, with conventional business models struggling to find adequate solutions*" [3]. In order to achieve a competitive advantage in the market, firms are called to integrate the concept of sustainability in their supply chain operations [4]. Sustainability or Sustainable Development (SD) is defined as "*the development that meets the needs of the present without compromising the ability of future*


Published by Springer Nature Switzerland AG 2021
L. M. Camarinha-Matos et al. (Eds.): PRO-VE 2021, IFIP AICT 629, pp. 19–30, 2021.
https://doi.org/10.1007/978-3-030-85969-5_2

*generations to meet their own needs*" [5]. SD concept applied to operations is introduced by Elkington [6], whilst also conceptualized the Triple-Bottom Line (TBL) approach i.e., the Economic-Social-Environmental impacts that businesses should be accountable for [7]. In addition, for facing unsustainable trajectories of the existing business model, the Circular Economy principle is widely considered as a paradigm to achieve SD [3]. The Circular Economy concept underlines the issue of transforming products by applying the 4R principles: reduce, recycle, reuse and recover at the individual company, industrial park and regional level, thus reducing the need for new inputs into production system [8, 9]. As a matter of fact, Circular Economy is "*expected to promote economic growth by creating new businesses and job opportunities, saving materials' cost, dampening price volatility, improving security of supply while at the same time reducing environmental pressures and social impacts*" [10] thereby addressing all the three dimensions of the TBL.

In general terms, a supply chain (SC) is designed to meet consumers' demands as efficiently and profitability as possible. The efficiency of planning, manufacturing and distributing a product in a network determines the success of a company [11]. Aiming at achieving the sustainability goal, different terms used to describe several types of SC can be identified: sustainable, closed-loop, lean [12] and short SC. The alignment of supply chain management (SCM) to the three issues of the TBL makes up the core concepts of Sustainable Supply Chain Management (SSCM) [12]. A Closed-Loop SC describes both forward distribution operations and reverse flows. The forward SC includes the activities of procurement, design, manufacturing and distribution to consumer. On the contrary, reverse SC is related to the handling, storage, and transport of reusable products, components, waste or packaging [2]. Therefore, a Closed-Loop SC is referred to as 'product-recovery management' [13] or 'reverse SCM' [8], a concept closed to circular industry. Besides, adopting Lean paradigm in SCM helps to focus on waste reduction that are processes or resources that have no value added for the end consumers, enhancing the importance of the workforce commitment [14]. Nowadays, a continuous increase of consumers' demand on safety, product diversity, local, organic and seasonal food, higher packaging and quality of services determines the adoption of shortest ways of delivering food, directly from producers to final consumers [15]. A Short FSC is defined as "a limited number of economic operators, committed to co-operation, local economic development, and close geographical and social relations between producers, processors and consumers" [16]. Short Food Supply chains are identified as an economic opportunity for agriculture, as well as a driver for a more sustainable farming system [17].

The increasing attention paid to SD and SSCM concepts and the most recent scientific papers allow to figure out the well-known or best practices that companies should pursue to "green" their operations. However, studies across these topics frequently fail in taking into consideration the whole FSC. A best practice is defined as: "*Any practice or experience which has proved its value or which is used in an efficient way in an organization, and can be applied in other organizations*"[1]. A best practice has three characteristics: it is formalized, reusable and effective [12]. The third criteria include the relevance, coherence, effectiveness, efficiency, robustness and sustainability of the value created by the implementation of a practice.

[1] American Productivity and Quality Council (APQC). Available on http://www.apqc.org.

This literature review allows to identify current trends and recent developments in this specific research direction. After a description of the research methodology, in Sect. 2, the analysis of the literature review is presented in Sect. 3. Section 4 provides the major SSCM practices. Finally, conclusions and future research directions are proposed in Sect. 5.

## 2 Research Methodology

The systematic literature review methodology is adopted as it is an approach of making sense of large bodies of information in a systematic way in order to provide coherent and robust evidence to address some compelling issues [18]. In this research, the main objective is to identify the present status of the literature in the area of SSCM in the food industry, in order to assess which are the practices that a company should implement in order to achieve the SD goal. To this end, the terms "Sustainable AND Supply AND Chain AND Management" and "Food AND Supply AND Chain" are applied to the titles, abstracts and keywords of research journal articles or review articles to sample the open access documents published in Scopus and ScienceDirect databases as they are internationally recognized and relevant scientific databases. Some filters are adopted by considering the subject are of the documents, such as "chemical engineering", "immunology", "biology", "veterinary", "neuroscience", "nursing". This allows to exclude not relevant contributions. Finally, a total of 324 relevant articles are identified (11 are found in the two databases at issue). Abstracts and conclusions of the selected papers are then read and analyzed. The documents dealing with Food-Energy-Water nexus, food rescue, Hotel, Restaurant and Catering SC are out of the boundaries of SSCM practices field and so not examined further. For the same reasons, some papers are excluded after the analysis of the full text. In the end, the selected articles cover two main topics: sustainable food SCM and the role of Information and Communication Technology in the food industry. This made up the initial corpus of papers. Furthermore, a forward and backward snowballing procedure have been carried out to ensure that all valuable knowledge has been identified [19] also from the studies not identified through the initial search process [20]. In the end, 224 articles are considered relevant for the further analysis.

## 3 Results and Discussion

By considering the year-wise distribution of the papers, this topic appears to be little discussed in the literature from 2008 (first year found through the query) to 2010 (2 out of 224). Then, the papers fluctuate slightly from 2012 to 2014 (22 out of 224). Another change of emphasis in research can be observed from 2015 to 2017 (62 out of 224). More recently, there is a considerable increase of research related to this topic (138 papers published between 2018 and 2020). This points out that the sustainability in the food industry is a recent field of study and that the general interests on this subject might be expected to increase in the future. Moreover, it is worth noticing that papers included after the forward analysis are twice with respect to the backward one. One of the most influential factors requiring food industries to move towards a more sustainable future is represented by the "2030 Agenda" dealing with the Sustainable Development Goals, agreed in 2015 by the United Nations General Assembly.

Most of the reviewed papers are coming from leading international journals such as Sustainability, Journal of Cleaner Production and International Journal of Production Economics. The contribution of these three ones represents exactly 50% of the documents set, the remaining 50% is made up by 79 different journals with a frequency of less than 5 articles per journal. Therefore, sustainability in the food industry is a granular and horizontal topic, discussed from the point of view of different journals.

The articles are classified in case-studies (43%), empirical research (39%) and literature reviews (18%). Case-studies answer to both "why" and "how" questions in relation to a dynamic presented within the situation analyzed. Empirical research aims at answering empirical question through observation and documentation. Literature reviews are intended to evaluate and interpret the results obtained from previous academic findings. Six research methodologies are differentiated based on the way in which data are analyzed (cf. Fig. 1).

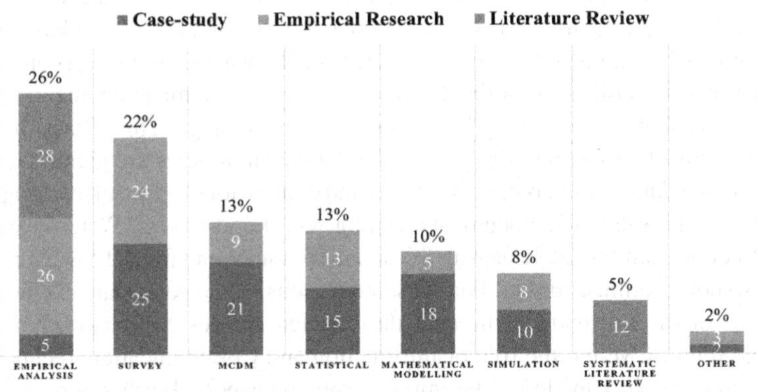


**Fig. 1.** Classification based on paper type and methodology.

Most of the works are developed by analyzing a set of both primary and/or secondary data that according to [21] are information that are collected for the specific research problem. These studies are grouped under the Empirical Analysis label. Surveys (semi-structured interviews, direct or online interviews, field observation, workshops or surveys itself) are mostly carried out to evaluate the level of satisfaction of several individuals (Ex-post survey). In fact, only the 14% of these are intended to appraise the potential interest concerning the selected topic (Ex-ante survey). Statistical analyses are generally conducted to test hypotheses and uncover trends. Conversely, simulations are performed to optimize a given situation. With the intent to assess and predict possible outcomes, these are mostly adopted in Ex-ante evaluation. Multicriteria decision making analysis is a widespread methodology that deals with the economic, environmental and social impacts i.e., the three recognized dimensions of sustainability, that are perceived in the food chain. The multicriteria decision making methodologies used are for example the life cycle thinking approach or the Analytical Hierarchy Problem technique. These ones are intended to capture the real time situation and support decision makers by providing alternative strategies. Even if the life cycle thinking seems to be widely applied, the adoption of this approach to deal with sustainability issue is critically questioned in the literature. In the end, mathematical modelling includes Multi Integer Linear Programming or Multi Objectives Linear Programming problems, Inventory Routing Problems or it simply refers to mathematical models. When it comes to delivering general judgements on sustainability, models that rely only on quantitative data struggle with the quantification of intangible benefits that mostly compose the social aspect. Thus, some authors perform both qualitative and quantitative analysis. In fact, the approach of the reviewed studies is mainly qualitative (56%) rather than quantitative (34%) or both (10%).

Since this literature review is intended to look at the SC operations, it is worth noticing in which part of the network the reviewed studies are focused on. The framework selected is the generic FSC model proposed by Gustavsson et al. [22]. Moreover, the End-of-life stage is added to this model in order to count for papers that deal with the recycling, reuse, recovery and disposal of materials. With reference to the obtained results (cf. Fig. 2), papers generally consider more than one stage. It is worth noticing that 57 over 224 studies are not focused specifically on one or more stages of the SC. Agricultural production, that includes also breeding and fisheries activities, processing and distribution stages are equally addressed. So that, dealing with sustainability in the food industry, primary production activities have to be analyzed with the same importance as all the other more industry-related steps. Surprisingly, the end-of-life stage appears to be less addressed in the scholarly papers despite the importance of Circular Economy paradigm and the creation of Closed-Loop SC for achieving SD.

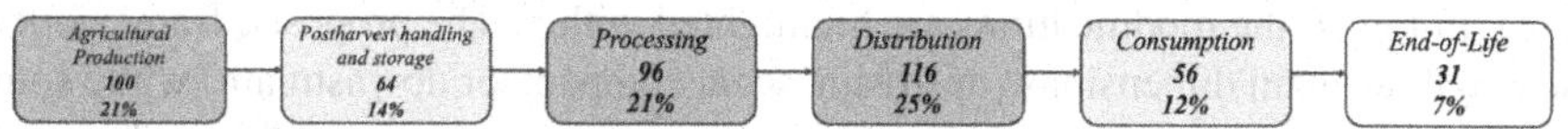


**Fig. 2.** Generic FSC model.

This shows that even if the sustainability challenge of the food sector is increasingly studied, the research papers are mostly conducted for quantifying the impacts instead for finding solutions. In line with this, Ex-post works i.e., the analysis is performed by looking at the result of an event, account for 73% of the total while Ex-ante studies account for 27% of the total.

Articles vary in terms of geographical positioning: most of the articles are focused on European countries or developed nations in general. This is in line with the conclusions traced by Rehman Khan et al. [4] that emphasize the strong acceptability of sustainability ideas in developed nations, while developing countries are beginning to realize the importance and benefits of sustainable practices. The six leading European countries in terms of both number of authors and number of studies are the UK, Italy, Spain, France, The Netherlands and Germany. The same countries are the largest EU food and drink producers by turnover with reference to the 2020 report provided by the FoodDrink Europe organization [23]. Papers are focused more on unprocessed or minimally processed foodstuffs (78%), rather than processed products (17%) or culinary ingredients (5%) according to the classification provided by Monteiro [24].

Finally, the integration of TBL axes is considered (cf. Fig. 3). As a result, while the economic and environmental aspects are generally included in the studies, the social aspect remains slightly less analyzed. Economically, cost remains the key factor. By considering the environmental dimension, the focus is on lowering the environmental burden that derives from human production and consumption. The social aspect refers to the development of the community and the image of the firm and their goods from the point of view of various stakeholders.

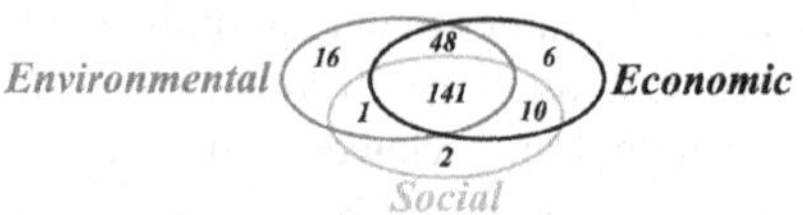


**Fig. 3.** TBL papers distribution.

## 4 Overview of SSCM Practices

This section investigates the way a food company accomplishes the need to achieve SD i.e., the most common practices that can be implemented to reach this goal. A proper balancing between social responsibility, environmental preservation, economic prosperity and technological revolution plays the most prominent role [9, 13]. The model proposed by Zimon et al. [25] is used as a starting point to classify sustainable practices and it has been enlarged according to the findings of the literature review performed (cf. Fig. 4). In Fig. 4, the modifications are highlighted with *. The proposed framework is based on three main dimensions (upstream, focal company or downstream) while some other practices overlap with multiple dimensions (transverse). In addition, the waste management issue, introduced by Papargyropoulou et al. [26] is considered. Prevention (10.4%) and disposal (1.0%) practices are investigated together with material and *product recycling* (P4) and *product recovery and remanufacturing* (P9). Prevention is the most desirable form of practices. On the contrary, disposal practices are the last ones that should be addressed. Percentages in brackets (cf. Fig. 4) refer to the relative attention the literature gives to each practice, by considering 1360 practices for a total of 224 papers. Differences from the original model are highlighted.

### 4.1 Sustainable Supplier Management (Upstream)

Sustainable Supplier Management, upstream the focal firm, includes sustainable sourcing and green purchasing. The former refers to *suppliers' assessment* (P1) and *collaboration with suppliers* (P2) [27], while *green purchasing* (P3), refers to consider environmental concerns along with other traditional factors in purchasing a product from the suppliers [28]. The terms green purchasing and green procurement are used interchangeably [29]. With reference to the attention paid to the practices included in this category from the point of view of both the number and the year-wise distribution of the works performed so far (cf. Appendix), it can be stated that these practices are well-established as their importance have been long discussed in literature as support in achieving SSCM.

| Sustainable Supplier Management [upstream] | Sustainable Operation and Risk Management [Focal Company] | Pressure & Incentives Management [Downstream] |
|---|---|---|
| P1. Supplier Assessment (9.6%)<br>P2. Supplier Collaboration* (1.9%)<br>P3. Green Purchasing* (4.9%)<br>P4. Material and Product Recycling (2.4%) | P5. Green Design* (2.9%)<br>P6. Green Packaging (2.5%)<br>P7. Green Production* (4.9%)<br>P8. Green Manufacturing (4.6%)<br>P9. Product Recovery and Remanufacturing (5.2%)<br>P10. Integration of Environmental Management Systems* (7.4%) | P11. Inventory Management (1.2%)<br>P12. Green Warehousing (1.8%)<br>P13. Green Shipping and Distribution (4.3%)<br>P14. Reverse Logistics (1.8%)<br>P15. Corporate Green Image Management (0.1%) |

| Transversal Practices | *Collaborative practices (9.0%)* |
|---|---|
| P16. Green Product Innovation and Design (1.1%) | P20. Collaborative Supply Chain Planning |
| P17. Corporate Social Responsibility programs (9.6%) | P21. Strategic Supply Collaboration |
| P18. Green Human Resource Management* (1.9%) | P22. Supply Chain Integration System |
| P19. Adoption of Standard and Certifications* (5.1%) | P23. Adoption of Information and Communication Technologies* (6.5%) |

**Fig. 4.** Sustainable supply chain management practices, based on [25].

## 4.2 Sustainable Operations and Risk Management (Focal Company)

From the focal company's point of view, the main practices implemented to achieve SD are *green design* (P5), *green packaging* (P6), *green production* (P7), *green manufacturing* (P8) and integration of *environmental management systems* (P10). Their final aim is to reduce the environmental burden of products and/or processes, preserve the external environment and increase the operational efficiency of the company. The focus is on energy, water and soil conservation and management and animal welfare. All these green operations are supported by the deployment of green technologies [30]. Moreover, establishing key performance indicators helps to achieve a sustainable system [31], as well as the development of lean manufacturing solutions [2]. In addition, the life cycle thinking approach is used in order to quantify the impacts on the three axes of sustainability and it helps to analyze where resources are used. It is worth noticing that green production and manufacturing practices have gained more attention in recent years with respect to the others.

## 4.3 Pressure and Incentives Management (Downstream)

Pressures and incentives, downstream the focal firm, include *inventory management* (P11), *green warehouse* (P12), *green shipping and distribution* (P13), *reverse logistics* (P14) and *corporate green image management* (P15). The first four practices can be conceptualized under the term eco- or green- logistics i.e., "*plan the purchasing and consolidation of raw materials by the strategic and operative prospective, distribution towards final consumers/customers, reverse flow of packages due to post life treatments in agreement with shelf-life constraints, taking into consideration the impact on the environment in addition to the costs*" [2]. P14 could lead to the creation of Closed-Loop SC [32]. Nowadays, it is essential for firms to implement green practices in their operations to sustain the competition in the market. The deployment of green activities of a firm from the point of view of various stakeholders makes up the concept of green image [29].

### 4.4 Transversal Practices

Practices involving the entire SC consist of *green product innovation and design* (P16) i.e., any activities that results in new ideas or improvement addressing some specific sustainability targets [33], *Corporate Social Responsibility programs* (P17), *green human resource management* (P18), *adoption of standard and certifications* (P19), a set of three collaborative practices (P20-P22) and *the exploitation of information and communication technologies* (P23).

By observing the yearly papers distribution, not surprisingly P17 appear to be one of the first discussed in the literature. Corporate Social Responsibility concept describes the set of voluntary initiatives carried out by a company to address social or environmental challenges in their own operations or in neighboring communities [34]. In fact, an initial step toward achieving holistic sustainability objectives lies in a corporation's orientation toward SD. Furthermore, within a company, P18 seeks to spread green values within a company, and it is a mechanism that can be employed by a firm to enhance its sustainability commitment [35]. In addition, a company specifies its engagement toward the SD by setting up standards (P19) which commonly comprise statements and policies to comply with legal requirements, by including also aspects that exceed regulatory concerns [36]. Any party within the SC that does not comply with them might jeopardize the image of a firm. P19 is a key point across the whole SC as it is used as a demonstration that products or processes respect environmental and social criteria.

Collaboration is a common way for companies throughout the SC to share information, make strategic alliances, and reduce overall costs, also in terms of sustainability [37]. In addition, collaboration is a practice historically adopted by farmers. The formalization of their collaboration is achieved by establishing agricultural cooperatives [38]. Thus, collaborative practices involve but it is not limited to *collaborative supply chain planning* (P20), *strategic supply collaboration* (P21) and *supply chain integration system* (P22).

Also, the adoption of Information and Communication Technologies (P23) has a significant impact on SSCM and appear to be a very recent field of study in the food industry. Economically, P23 allows to reduce costs and increase productivity. The positive impacts related to the environmental dimension can be ascribed to lower the consumption of resources, to reduce emissions and food losses and waste. Concerning the social aspect, P23 improves traceability, food safety, transparency, communication and coordination among actors [39]. Furthermore, the importance of e-commerce is often mentioned. Especially for Small and Medium Enterprises it might be an opportunity for supporting their business, reducing the cost and enhancing the demand [40]. In addition, it is recognized as one of best practices in gaining access to the market, also considering the restrictions due to COVID-19 pandemic [41].

## 5 Conclusion and Future Research Directions

The key objective of this research is to provide an overview of the recent developments in SSCM and related practices in the food industry via a systematic literature review. To date, the food industry industry has not yet been analyzed in depth compared to other sectors. In fact, the first study found through the queries is dated 2008. Moreover, during the pandemic, along with the drug industry, the food industry gained crucial importance worldwide. Thus, it deserves specific studies and analysis. Therefore, 224 relevant research papers are analyzed from Scopus and ScienceDirect databases. Based on the description of the theories underpinning the Sustainable Development concept, the findings reveal an increasing interest of research. The implications of this work are relevant for academics as they enlarge the body of knowledge on the adoption of sustainability practice in the food industry. From a practical point of view this study proposes an overview of the most common and adopted practices that can be implemented in order to achieve Sustainable Development in the food industry. In this sense, this work might be used as a framework for companies that are willing to assess their level of sustainability practices implementation. It provides a novel SCM practices model obtained via a systematic literature review as a precise approach methodology able to identify the most important research trends. This paper it is also a first attempt to assess the best practices that companies might implement to be aligned with the sustainability requirements. The framework can be compared with the industrial world as a preliminary standard by considering operational perspectives implications (Fig. 4).

## Appendix

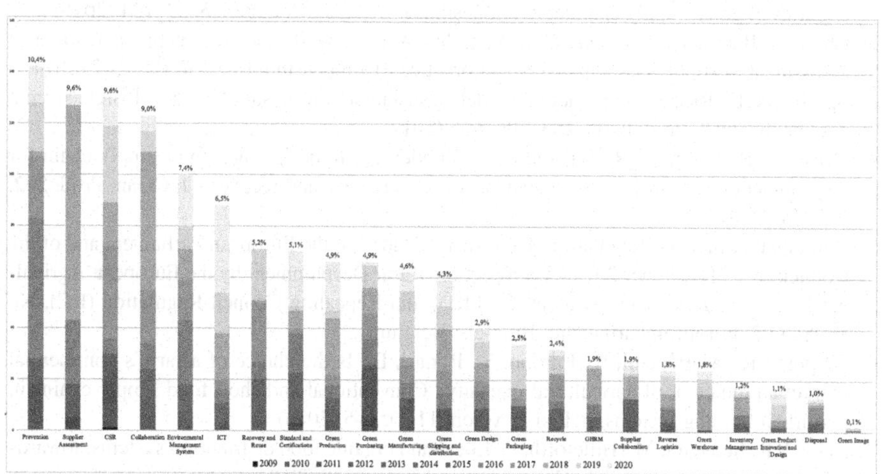


**Fig. 5.** Year-wise distribution of the practices with their relative importance.

## References

1. Rohmer, S.U.K., Gerdessen, J.C., Claassen, G.D.H.: Sustainable supply chain design in the food system with dietary considerations: a multi-objective analysis. Eur. J. Oper. Res. **273**, 1149–1164 (2019)
2. Manzini, R., Accorsi, R.: The new conceptual framework for food supply chain assessment. J. Food Eng. **115**, 251–263 (2013)
3. Nosratabadi, S., Mosavi, A., Shamshirband, S., Kazimieras Zavadskas, E., Rakotonirainy, A., Chau, K.W.: Sustainable business models: a review. Sustainability **11**(6), 1663 (2019)
4. Khan, S.A.R., Yu, Z., Golpîra, H., Sharif, A., Mardani, A.: A state-of-the-art review and meta-analysis on sustainable supply chain management: future research directions. J. Clean. Prod., 123357 (2020)
5. Emamisaleh, K., Rahmani, K.: Sustainable supply chain in food industries: drivers and strategic sustainability orientation. Cogent Bus. Manag. **4**(1), 1345296 (2017)
6. Elkington, J.: Partnerships from cannibals with forks: the triple bottom line of 21st-century business. Environ. Qual. Manag. **8**(1), 37–51 (1998)
7. Tidy, M., Wang, X., Hall, M.: The role of supplier relationship management in reducing greenhouse gas emissions from food supply chains: supplier engagement in the UK supermarket sector. J. Clean. Prod. **112**, 3294–3305 (2016)
8. Genovese, A., Acquaye, A.A., Figueroa, A., Koh, S.L.: Sustainable supply chain management and the transition towards a circular economy: evidence and some application. Omega **66**, 344–357 (2017)
9. Pohlmann, C.R., Scavarda, A.J., Alves, M.B., Korzenowski, A.L.: The role of the focal company in sustainable development goals: a Brazilian food poultry supply chain case study. J. Clean. Prod. **245**, 118798 (2020)
10. Kalmykova, Y., Sadagopan, M., Rosado, L.: Circular economy–from review of theories and practices to development of implementation tools. Resour., Conserv. Recycl. **135**, 190–201 (2018)
11. Lee, L.S., Misni, F.: A review on strategic, tactical and operational decision planning in reverse logistics of green supply chain network design. J. Comput. Commun. **5**, 83–104 (2015)
12. Chardine-Baumann, E., Botta-Genoulaz, V.: A framework for sustainable performance assessment of supply chain management practices. Comput. Ind. Eng. **76**, 138–147 (2014)
13. Sgarbossa, F.: Russo, I: a proactive model in sustainable food supply chain: Insight from a case study. Int. J. Prod. Econ. **183**, 596–606 (2017)
14. Krishnan, R., Agarwal, R., Bajada, C., Arshinder, K.: Redesigning a food supply chain for environmental sustainability–An analysis of resource use and recovery. J. Clean. Prod. **242**, 118374 (2020)
15. European Parliament. Regulation (EU) No 1305/2013 of the European Parliament and of the Council of 17 December 2013 on Support for Rural Development by the European Agricultural Fund for Rural Development (EAFRD) and Repealing Council Regulation (EC), No 1698/2005, European Parliament, Brussels, Belgium
16. Filippini, R., Marraccini, E., Lardon, S., Bonari, E.: Is the choice of a farm's commercial market an indicator of agricultural intensity? Conventional and short food supply chains in periurban farming systems. Italian J. Agron. **11**(1), 1–5 (2016)
17. Baez, Y.P., Sequeira, M., Hilletofth, P.: Local and organic food distribution systems: towards a future agenda. Oper. Supply Chain Manag. **13**, 336–348 (2020)
18. Chan, H.Y., Abdul Halim-Lim, S., Tan, T.B., Kamarulzaman, N.H., Jamaludin, A.A., Wan-Mohtar, W.A.A.Q.I.: Exploring the drivers and the interventions towards sustainable food security in the food supply chain. Sustainability **12**(19), 7890 (2020)

19. Wohlin, C.: Guidelines for snowballing in systematic literature studies and a replication in software engineering. In: 18th International Conference on Evaluation and Assessment in Software Engineering, EASE'2014, London, England, pp. 1–10 (2014)
20. Gunasekaran, A., Gawankar, S., Kamble, S.S.: Achieving sustainable performance in a data-driven agriculture supply chain: a review for research and applications. Int. J. Prod. Econ. **219**, 179–194 (2020)
21. Hox, J.J., Boeije, H.R.: Data collection, primary vs secondary. Ency. Soc. Manag. **1**, 593–599 (2005)
22. Gustavsson, J., Cederberg, C., Sonesson, U.: Global food losses and food waste—extent, causes and prevention. FAO, Rome, Italy (2011)
23. FoodDrink Europe. https://www.fooddrinkeurope.eu/uploads/publications_documents/FoodDrinkEurope_-_Data__Trends_2020_digital.pdf. Accessed 13 Jan 2021
24. Monteiro, C.A.: A new food classification based on the extent and purpose of industrial food processing. In: 8th International Conference on Diet and Activity Methods, FAO, Rome (2012)
25. Zimon, D., Tyan, J., Sroufe, R.: Drivers of sustainable supply chain management: practices to alignment with UN sustainable development goals. Int. J. Qual. Res. **14**(1), 219–236 (2019)
26. Papargyropoulou, E., Lozano, R., Steinberger, J.K., Wright, N., Ujang, Z.: The food waste hierarchy as a framework for the management of food surplus and food waste. J. Clean. Prod. **76**, 106–115 (2014)
27. Mangla, S.K., Rich, N., Luthra, S., Kumar, D., Rana, N.P., Dwivedi, Y.K.: Enablers to implement sustainable initiatives in agri-food supply chains. Int. J. Prod. Econ. **203**, 379–393 (2018)
28. Govindan, K., Kadziński, M., Sivakumar, R.: Application of a novel PROMETHEE-based method for construction of a group compromise ranking to prioritization of green suppliers in food supply chain. Omega **71**, 129–145 (2017)
29. Luthra, S., Raut, R.D., Narkhede, B.E., Mangla, S.K., Gardas, B.B., Priyadarshinee, P.: Examining the performance oriented indicators for implementing green management practices in the Indian agro sector. J. Clean. Prod. **215**, 926–943 (2019)
30. Boye, J. I., Yves. A.: Current trends in green technologies in food production and processing. Food Eng. Rev. **5**, 1–17 (2013)
31. Makinde, O., Mowandia, M.T., Michael, A.: Performance evaluation of the supply chain system of a food product manufacturing system using a questionnaire-based approach. Procedia Manuf. **43**, 751–757 (2020)
32. Accorsi, R., Baruffaldi, G., Manzini, R., Pini, C.: Environmental impacts of reusable transport items: a case study of pallet pooling in a retailer supply chain. Sustainability **11**(11), 3147 (2019)
33. Nemecek, T., Kulak, M., Frossard, E., Gaillard, G.: Eco-efficiency improvement by using integrative design and life cycle assessment. The case study of alternative bread supply chains in France. J. Clean. Prod. **112**, 2452–2461 (2016)
34. Wiese, W., Toporowski, A.: CSR failures in food supply chains – an agency perspective. Br. Food J. **115**(1), 92–107 (2013)
35. Jaaron, A.A., Zaid, A.A., Bon, A.T.: The impact of green human resource management and green supply chain management practices on sustainable performance: an empirical study. J. Clean. Prod. **204**, 965–979 (2018)
36. Grimm, J.H., Hofstetter, J.S., Sarkis, J.: Exploring sub-suppliers' compliance with corporate sustainability standards. J. Clean. Prod. **112**, 1971–1984 (2016)
37. Azevedo, S.G., Silva, M.E., Matias, J.C., Dias, G.P.: The influence of collaboration initiatives on the sustainability of the cashew supply chain. Sustainability **10**(6), 2075 (2018)
38. Lutz, J., Smetschka, B., Grima, N.: Farmer cooperation as a means for creating local food systems—potentials and challenges. Sustainability **9**(6), 925 (2017)

39. El Bilali, H., Allahyari, M.S.: Transition towards sustainability in agriculture and food systems: role of information and communication technologies. Inf. Process. Agri. **5**, 456–464 (2018)
40. Kummer, S., Milestad, R.: The diversity of organic box schemes in Europe—an exploratory study in four countries. Sustainability **12**(7), 2734 (2020)
41. Mihailović, B., Jean I. R., Popović, V., Radosavljević, K., Krasavac, B.C., Bradić-Martinović, A.: Farm differentiation strategies and sustainable regional development. Sustainability **12**(7223) (2020)

# Getting Collaborative Networks Sustainable: Drivers and Barriers Within a Digital Laboratories Network

Valentin Kammerlohr[1,2](✉), Heiko Duin[3], Jannicke Baalsrud Hauge[3,4], and Nadera Sultana Tany[5]

[1] Hochschule für Technik Stuttgart, Stuttgart, Germany
Valentin.Kammerlohr@hft-stuttgart.de
[2] Auburn University College of Business, Auburn, USA
[3] BIBA – Bremer Institut Für Produktion Und Logistik GmbH, Bremen, Germany
[4] KTH-Royal Institute of Technology, Södertälje, Sweden
[5] University of Bremen, Bremen, Germany

**Abstract.** Rapid technology changes and the transition to digitalised production and education pose significant challenges to engineering education. Hands-on experimentation requires access to new technologies, often in a lab setting. Cross-organisational collaboration and resource sharing can reduce costs and increase utilisation. Success depends on trust, practical resource management, smooth service delivery, and performance. This paper presents an initial evaluation of a resource management approach using an online lab booking process, considering stakeholders' various roles and needs. In addition, we gathered external inputs through two surveys targeting industry and students as potential customers and interviews with professionals working in collaborative working environments to assess drivers and barriers to network success using SCOR metrics. These findings are essential inputs for lower-level design decisions, such as designing the underlying business models, the relationship between education and research for the labs, the rules of use, and how to motivate collaborators.

**Keywords:** Collaborative network · Trust · Sustainability · Digital laboratories · Shared resources · Adaptability

## 1 Introduction

Sharing economies have a strong traditional practice on the one hand side; on the other hand, we see several new digitalised shared economies that would not work without technological advances [1, 2]. The concept of a sharing economy can also be applied to digital laboratories (lab). Digital labs outline a solution and describe virtual and remote labs, where personal presence in the lab is not required but accessible via the internet. This reduces entry barriers, allows worldwide access, and enables the application towards sharing economy. Advantages of virtual labs can be safety, scalability, remote access,


Published by Springer Nature Switzerland AG 2021
L. M. Camarinha-Matos et al. (Eds.): PRO-VE 2021, IFIP AICT 629, pp. 31–38, 2021.
https://doi.org/10.1007/978-3-030-85969-5_3

higher utilisation, and cost-efficiency. A more detailed explanation of how labs get digitalised and the different variations like access to the resource (local/remote), nature of lab (real/virtual), or involved organisations (one/multiple) can be found in [3]. However, virtual labs cannot fully replace real/physical lab environments, as different knowledge is required and encouraged when manipulating real hardware [4].

One of the biggest challenges for the growth of a sharing economy is establishing trust [2, 5, 6], including the different stakeholders' understanding of trust [5, 7–9]. In the scope of a sharing economy, the actors need to know and trust on: *"(1) states (conditions) of shareable assets regarding the capacity, presence and (idle time), capability; (2) previous experience in the sharing of the same resource; (3) restrictions and compensation; (4) level of behavioural congruence of actors participating in the sharing; (5) regulatory issues and dispute resolution"* [10]. Furthermore, the relevance and what is considered relevant vary in the literature, both depending on the field of application and the phase of the networked organisation. For shared lab environment, factors related to elements of virtual enterprises [7], role-based trust, interpersonal and inter-organisational trust, institutional-based trust [11], static and dynamic trust factors [9], and the elements of service relationships incl. personal trust [6, 12] apply [10]. Trust problems are gathered by Daudi [13] and are the complexity of the sharing network structure, uncertainties of the logistics processes, and behaviour of the partners.

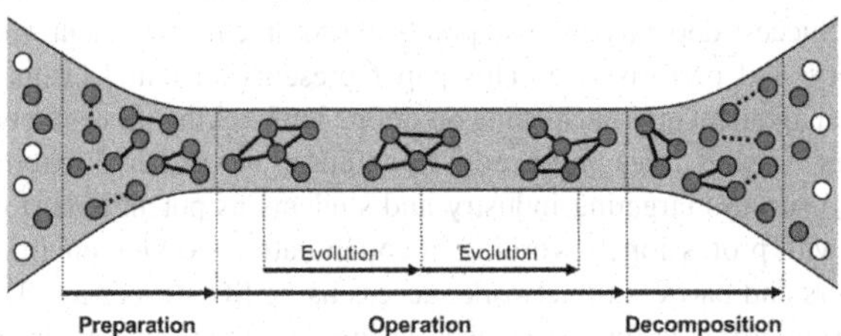


**Fig. 1.** From virtual organisations to long-term collaboration

The success of operating shared resources in a collaborative network over a longer time depends not only on the trust but also on the business considerations and the needs of all stakeholders. Figure 1 above illustrates how a virtual organisation's setup and evolution operates over time. The stakeholders go through the phases of preparation in which the relationships between stakeholders are formed, operation in which the evolution of the virtual organisation takes place, and decomposition in which the virtual organisation dissolves. Many research projects can be seen as virtual organisations where the typical customer is the funding organisation. The common goal and vision are stated in the project proposal and work description [14]. These have a temporary character ending when the funding ends. If such collaboration continues to exist after a funding period (which would be an evolutionary step in the figure above), mutual interest and a business model fitting the different stakeholders' needs and preferences need to be developed. Each stakeholder gets an added value higher than what each organisation can achieve alone, both in the medium and long term. Based on these considerations, we have identified three research questions:

1. Do the identified metrics match people's experience having years of experience working both in collaborative research projects and establishing long-term collaborations after the project ended? For this purpose, we have interviewed experienced people, and currently, the analysis of 4 of these are included here.
2. Related to existing stakeholders in the collaboration (i.e., the virtual, temporary one)- to what extent do they feel that the developed process model fits their needs and requirements. For this, each stakeholder was asked to fill in a feedback template.
3. The current business model foresees that the consortium gets funding and thus, at the moment, does not need to look into the return-on-investments. However, this funding will not last for long, and a stable and solid long-term collaboration regarding shared resources needs to generate income at least matching their costs. For investigating this, two online surveys have been designed and distributed to two potential user groups: a) students b) companies that could be interested in using the educational offer for the life-long training of their employees.

The rest of the paper is structured as follows: Sect. 2 describes the research methodology, while Sect. 3 outlines the current setup and the intended future structure of the network. Section 4 presents the interviews, the feedback forms, and the online surveys, while Sect. 5 discusses the findings and the contribution to the research questions. Section 6 concludes the paper and outlines further research steps.

## 2 Research Methodology

This paper investigates factors that contribute to a successful transition from a project-based collaboration as a virtual organisation towards a long-term partnership in a collaborative network. To address related questions, we have used a blended research method consisting of:

- Two semi-structured online surveys (open & closed questions) to gather requirements and demands for the shared laboratory network. One online survey to understand the purpose of the students and one for understanding the industry by surveying Italian companies. The survey for students contained 25 questions, while the survey for companies included 23 questions.
- Expert Interviews were used for investigating the operationalisation factors of the cognitive trust model. We used semi-structured interviews with four pre-defined questions. The interview time varied between 45 min and three h. Currently, we have analysed the results of four interviews.
- A feedback survey with participants representing all stakeholder types currently involved. These have validated the process flow of future collaborative services.

## 3 Collaborative Network of Shared Laboratories

The public-funded cross-institutional research project DigiLab4U intends to provide a digitalised lab environment that enables a learning marketplace for digital lab facilities [3]. The goal is to develop an integrated, hybrid learning and research environment consisting of a variety of lab technologies for a digital offering that can be used by any student, from undergraduate to graduate, anywhere. The research consortium consists of four German and one Italian academic institution working on digitalising and sharing their education, training and research labs. The DigiLab4U learning marketplace consists of digital labs from various providers on the one hand and users accessing the labs on the other. The cooperation between universities, research institutions, and industry makes it possible to bundle the providers' resources so that users, such as learners and researchers, have access to a greater variety of digital courses based on different labs. A critical step in the project is to increase the number of participants on both sides (providers and buyers) to increase the platform's value, the so-called network effect [15, 16]. An important starting point for sustainable development prospects of the marketplace is to strengthen the trust of suppliers, users, and marketplace providers [16, 17].

To ensure sustainability after research funding ends, a multi-sided platform is to be used as a business and collaboration model for sharing these labs. The multi-sided platform is a hub or intermediary for exchanging value between interested parties and providers from two or more markets [16]. In the case of a digital lab network, the interested party includes students, professors/lecturers/teachers, researchers, industry companies, and research institutes (collectively referred to as buyers). The suppliers are universities, research institutes, and industry companies (or vendors, collectively referred to as suppliers), as shown in Fig. 2. The marketplace aims to bring together the supplier of the labs with the buyer [16]. The challenges of a multi-sided platform, according to Henseling et al. [17], are: (1) building user trust, (2) further developing marketplace offerings, and (3) attracting new user groups.

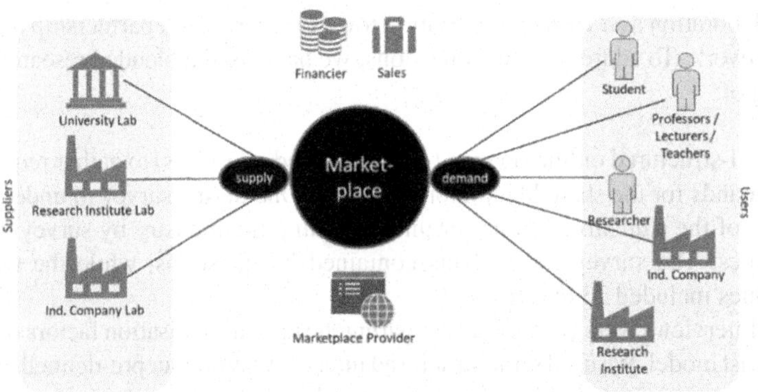


**Fig. 2.** Stakeholders of the digital lab marketplace

As the temporary collaborative lab network is to be transformed into a sustainable long-term collaboration, the stakeholders' goals might change from collaboratively ensure the fulfilment of the funder's requirement towards goals that fits into the long-term company strategy. In some cases, it will hardly be any changes in the goals. In some cases, partners will have such different purposes that they will leave the collaboration. However, the corresponding business model will change since the revenue streams will change as the stakeholder Funding Institution has to be replaced with another type of customer. To address how different factors influence the transition of the collaboration and the need to identify new revenue streams, the next section will present the expert interviews and surveys results.

## 4 Evaluation Results

For evaluation purposes, four streams have been followed. Two online surveys in February through April 2021 have been conducted concerning the service's customer side, including students and industrial companies. Another survey addressed the processes for resource booking among the current members of the virtual labs' network. Finally, semi-structured interviews with external experts have been conducted to verify the metrics and key performance indicators for success.

### 4.1 Understanding Potential Customers: Student and Company Survey

93 students participated in the survey (43% female). The majority of students were already aware of digital labs before our survey, and 12% used digital labs in their academic curriculum/practice. The experienced students are under the explicit conditions of adding value to the learning experience. Participants who had no prior experience expect digital labs to provide valuable content (70%), ease of use (67%), affordability (48%), otherwise inaccessible materials and equipment (59%), and customer support (39%). And what would keep them from using the digital labs are technology (65%) (effectiveness of the service), organisation (55%) (management of the service), and safety or security (26%). The feedback on the willingness to pay and thus the financial maintenance of digital labs is controversial. The majority expect universities to pay (54%), followed by government (35%), students (6%), and the rest from a mixture. Finally, students expect a clear added value from the marketplace compared to regular classes at the university. Twenty-one entrepreneurs and practitioners (18 managers or heads of technical departments) from the Northern Italy area participated in the survey to better understand industrial customers' interest in the supply and demand side of the multi-sided platform. The results show that industry customers have a strong interest in using digital labs as customers; examples given were solutions for mechanics, electrics, and electronics. None of the participants has yet used a digital lab. Nevertheless, 67% say they see digital labs as applicable for continuously improving business practices or the portfolio of offerings to customers. Limitations are found in the cost-benefit ratio, unique value proposition, data security, and the risk of losing intellectual property. Especially for small and medium-sized companies, digital labs represent an economical and flexible alternative to direct experimentation possibilities. Another possible motivator mentioned the current travel restrictions, with digital labs enabling remote testing and experimentation. Regarding the financial sustainability of digital labs and marketplaces, 67% of respondents believe they can be considered fee-based service offerings.

### 4.2 Cognitive Model of Trust, Expert Interviews

Four expert interviews have been carried out and analysed to assess the operationalisation of the cognitive trust model. A semi-structured interview approach was used, where the questions were defined in advance. The main supporting factors for successful collaboration are around open communication. Interviewees said that knowing each other from previous projects helps and being open-minded, talking the same language (in terms of professional jargon), transparency, and visibility. Monetary and resource-based aspects do complicate collaboration. Delays caused by not following the defined procedures and processes and not communicating them, and/or following an own hidden agenda are critical for the success of the collaboration. Another inhibiting factor is territorial behaviour. The common goals and a clear vision need to be in place. A common understanding of how the results are exploited after the project-based collaboration ends needs to be defined before the long-term collaboration starts. The critical success factors for the long-term sustainability of collaboration are ROI (Return on Investment), market opportunities, reliability, responsiveness, balanced relationships, and resource provision. Concerning the SCOR Level 1 Metrics, all interviewees agree that Perfect Order Fulfilment is most important in both respects, internal (within the collaboration) and external (towards the customer of the collaboration). Other important metrics include Order Fulfilment Cycle Time, Upside Supply Chain Flexibility, Upside Supply Chain Adaptability, and Downside Supply Chain Adaptability. Cost and related financial metrics are considered not particularly important.

### 4.3 Stakeholders' Feedback on Booking Process Model

The evaluation of the resource usage process is based on the (TO-BE) digital lab booking process model developed in an earlier phase of the project. Five different groups of potential users, depending on their role in the partner organisation lab facilities, have been identified and surveyed: Professors, Lab Managers, Lab Operators, Researchers, and Students (as Learners). The evaluation process consisted of presenting a process model involving their role followed by a simple questionnaire. A total of 32 responses have been collected, of which three are from professors, two from lab managers, six from lab operators, seven from researchers, and 14 from students.

Out of 32 responses, 29 respondents agreed that their roles are reflected in the proposed process model, two disagreed, and another did not respond. One participant argues that the "Student" role and the "Researcher" role do not differ in the process. Unless additional features are included or excluded from one of these roles, combining them into one "Lab User" role is more meaningful. The other participant wants to have access to things that are more aligned with their research interest. 15 participants want to see possible changes in the system. 16 participants found the process model adequate, and one did not respond. The critical feedback of the third question includes: Users want to have an option to do a test of the lab setup or a chance to apply for an examination of the lab setup before the teaching start. We see that 88% of the participants from different action roles find that their role is positively reflected in the process model. 81% of the participants think that the processes necessary to their specific function are addressed in the process model. And finally, 50% of the participants do not want to change the process model presented to them; 47% want to have changed in the system from the other half. This shows that the process model can cater to the role-specific needs of users even though there is room for improvement.

## 5 Discussion

For sustainable participation in a digital lab marketplace by industrial companies, a cost-benefit ratio, a unique selling proposition of the solutions, data security, and intellectual property protection is essential. From the perspective of these, fee-based service offerings for digital labs are conceivable as financial sustainability, relying on market regulation. In contrast, students expect valuable content, ease of use, affordability, otherwise inaccessible materials and equipment, and customer support. A problematic issue is the willingness to pay; traditionally, education in Europe is free. Students accept that the effort of a digital lab has to be paid for, but there is a significant dispute whether the state should pay this, the university or the student himself. The cost-benefit discussion is also reflected in the trust model: the cognitive model of trust shows that trust-related factors dominate collaboration success. This includes a common understanding of objectives and processes and appropriate and collaborative behaviour among partners. Therefore, it is not astonishing that Perfect Order Fulfilment is the central metric to measure a collaboration's success combined with metrics addressing flexibility and adaptability. A majority of the participants from the evaluation survey of the booking process provide a positive response to the presented process model. Those participants think that these processes are essential and that their specific role is addressed in the model. Half of the participants do not want to change the process model presented to them; the other half requested changes to the system. This shows that there is room for improvement.

Returning to the research questions, we can conclude that the identified metrics match people's experience having years of experience working both in collaborative research projects and establishing long-term collaborations. Existing stakeholders in the collaboration feel that the developed process model fits their needs and requirements despite identifying improvement needs. Future users are willing to pay, but there is no common sense of who should do it.

## 6 Conclusion and Outlook

This paper has investigated different factors that influence the transformation from a temporarily (virtual) organisation towards a long-term networked collaboration as well as the possibility to replace one type of customer (funding organisation) with a different kind (students and companies willing to use shared labs). The expert interviews show that long-term collaboration depends very much on trust factors like reliability, order fulfilment, and response time. Variations are depending on whether the organisations have common previous experience and not. The two surveys conclude that these respondents assess the access to shared laboratory resources as positive, even if quite a few have experience in using remote and virtual labs. In the next step, we will need to improve the booking process and investigate if this collaboration can be seen as a product-service system and then explore what services will contribute to a sustainable collaboration that can act smart in a dynamic field.

**Acknowledgements.** This work has been funded by the German Federal Ministry of Education and Research (BMBF) through the project DigiLab4U (No. 16DHB2112 and 16DHB2113).

## References

1. Belk, R.: Why not share rather than own? Ann. Am. Acad. Pol. Soc. Sci. **611**, 126–140 (2007)
2. Behrendt, S., Henseling, C., Scholl, G. (eds.) Digitale Kultur des Teilens. Mit Sharing nachhaltiger Wirtschaften. Springer Fachmedien, Wiesbaden (2019). https://doi.org/10.1007/978-3-658-21435-7
3. Kammerlohr, V., Pfeiffer, A., Uckelmann, D.: Digital laboratories for educating the IoT-generation heatmap for digital lab competences. In: Auer, M.E., May, D. (eds.) REV 2020. AISC, vol. 1231, pp. 3–20. Springer, Cham (2020). https://doi.org/10.1007/978-3-030-52575-0_1
4. Nedic, Z., Machotka, J., Nafalski, A.: Remote laboratories versus virtual and real laboratories. In: Frontiers in Education, T3E_1–6. IEEE, Westminster, CO, USA (2003)
5. Goudin, P. (ed.): The Cost of Non-Europe in the Sharing Economy. Economic, Social and Legal Challenges and Opportunities. European Parliamentary Research Service, Brussels (2016)
6. Johnson, D.S., Grayson, K.: Sources and dimensions of trust in service relationships. In: Handbook of Service Relationship, pp. 357–370 (2000)
7. Fladnitzer, M., Grabner-Kräuter, S.: Vertrauen als Erfolgsfaktor virtueller Unternehmen. Grundlagen, Rahmenbedingungen und Maßnahmen zur Vertrauensbildung. Deutscher Universitäts-Verlag, Wiesbaden (2006)
8. Mayer, R.C., Davis, J.H., Schoorman, F.D.: An Integrative model of organizational trust. Acad. Manage. Rev. **20**, 709 (1995)
9. Daudi, M.: Trust in Sharing Resources in Logistics Collaboration. Bremen (2018)
10. Baalsrud Hauge, J., Kammerlohr, V., Göbl, B., Duin, H.: Influence of trust factors on shared laboratory resources in a distributed environment. In: Camarinha-Matos, L.M., Afsarmanesh, H., Antonelli, D. (eds.) PRO-VE 2019. IAICT, vol. 568, pp. 624–634. Springer, Cham (2019). https://doi.org/10.1007/978-3-030-28464-0_55
11. Bachmann, R., Inkpen, A.C.: Understanding institutional-based trust building processes in inter-organisational relationships. Organ. Stud. **32**, 281–301 (2011)
12. Johnson, D., Grayson, K.: Cognitive and affective trust in service relationships. J. Bus. Res. **58**, 500–507 (2005)
13. Daudi, M., Hauge, J.B., Thoben, K.-D.: Behavioral factors influencing partner trust in logistics collaboration: a review. Logist. Res. **9**(1), 1–11 (2016)
14. Seifert, M.: Collaboration formation in virtual organisations by applying prospective performance measurement, Aachen (2009)
15. Eisenmann, T.R., Parker, G., van Alstyne, M.W.: Strategies for Two-Sided Markets, October 2006, pp. 1–12. Harvard Business Review (2006)
16. Abdelkafi, N., Raasch, C., Roth, A., Srinivasan, R.: Multi-sided platforms. Elec. Markets **29**, 553–559 (2019)
17. Henseling, C., Hobelsberger, C.: Entwicklungsperspektiven für die Geschäftsmodelle des peer-to-peer sharing. In: Behrendt, S., Henseling, C., Scholl, G. (eds.) Digitale Kultur des Teilens: Mit Sharing nachhaltiger Wirtschaften, pp. 95–118. Springer Fachmedien Wiesbaden, Wiesbaden (2019). https://doi.org/10.1007/978-3-658-21435-7_7

# Sustainability via Digitalization

# Towards a Sustainable Collaborative Distribution Network 4.0 with Blockchain Involvement

Nassim Mrabti[1(✉)], Mohamed Amine Gargouri[1,2], Nadia Hamani[1], and Lyes Kermad[2]

[1] Laboratory of Innovative Technology, University of Picardie Jules Verne, 80025 Amiens, France
{nassim.mrabti,nadia.hamani}@u-picardie.fr, mohamed.amine.gargouri@etud.u-picardie.fr

[2] QUARTZ Laboratory, University of Paris 8, 93200 Saint-Denis, France
l.kermad@iut.univ-paris8.fr

**Abstract.** This paper addresses the problem of designing a collaborative 4.0 distribution network using blockchain to ensure coordination between partners and the secure transfer of transactions. In this study, we compare the performance of horizontal collaboration and that of non-collaboration in terms of sustainability. The economic level is considered by the reduction of the logistics costs, while the environmental level is evaluated by the reduction of $CO_2$ emissions from vehicles through their use and depreciation as well as those from the hubs' operation and construction. The social level is addressed by maximizing the created job opportunities and by reducing the accident risk and the noise level. Both mono and multi-objective optimization approaches are proposed to solve the problem of exact and meta-heuristic optimization using the Genetic Algorithm (GA) and the Non-dominated Sorting Genetic Algorithm-II (NSGA-II). The obtained results show that horizontal collaboration is more efficient and promising at all levels.

**Keywords:** Horizontal collaboration · Blockchain · Distribution network design problem · Multi-objective optimization

## 1 Introduction

The consideration of sustainability in the distribution network design problem is becoming a necessity for companies to participate in the social life and the preservation of a habitable planet. In economic terms, distribution costs and customer demands are increasingly high. On the other hand, in environmental terms, companies are becoming obliged to participate in the protection of the environment, particularly by reducing the greenhouse gas emissions generated by their distribution activities. Indeed, a carbon report may be required for some companies, which affects their brand image. In social terms, the distribution of goods, particularly by road, produces significant noise pollution and results in a large number of road accidents. Companies cannot overcome


Published by Springer Nature Switzerland AG 2021
L. M. Camarinha-Matos et al. (Eds.): PRO-VE 2021, IFIP AICT 629, pp. 41–52, 2021.
https://doi.org/10.1007/978-3-030-85969-5_4

these challenges alone, hence the importance of collaboration. In the literature, there are two main types of collaboration, namely Vertical Collaboration (VC) and Horizontal Collaboration (HC). The first type is between partners of the same supply chain and is mainly limited to the information sharing. However, the second type takes place between partners of different supply chains [1]. The majority of studies focused on vertical collaboration whose performance can be further improved with HC [2]. The horizontal collaboration, also called "pooling", consists in sharing means and resources. It not only reduces costs, but also helps to find a trade-off between sustainability considerations and competitive priorities. In this paper, we focus on the collaborative distribution network design problem under sustainability consideration.

The rest of this paper presents the literature review, in Sect. 2. Section 3 contains the problem description, while Sect. 4 presents the resolution approaches. Section 5 provides a brief conclusion and some perspectives.

## 2 Literature Review

Collaborative distribution network design problem aims at reorganizing or modelling a pooled network by sharing means and resources between partners. It is one of the decision-making strategies that concerns the general direction of the company and involves long-term decisions. Its main objective is to consolidate the logistics flows of different supply chains. Despite its importance, collaborative network has been rarely studied in the literature [1, 2].

The collaborative distribution network design problem aims at finding the optimal locations of hubs, assigning nodes to hubs, determining the links between hubs and routing flows through the network. Verdonck [3] considered the two-echelon distribution network that includes depots, distribution centers and customers. The problem was modelled in mixed integer linear programming (MILP). It consists in opening a subset of the distribution centers (DCs) associated with the cooperating partners and determining the optimal assignments between the different nodes. This was achieved by minimizing the costs of transport and operations in the DCs. In addition, Tang et al. [4] examined the same problem over a multi-period horizon. The authors proposed a MILP to minimize the costs of transporting goods and handling regional DCs. They demonstrated that as the number of facilities increased, the transportation cost decreased. This conclusion is not valid when installation costs are considered. Furthermore, Hacardiaux et al. [5] introduced a mixed integer conic quadratic programming (MICQP) to examine the collaborative location inventory problem (LIP). The model aims at determining the number and locations of the shared DCs, assigning nodes and specifying the size of shipments and inventory levels. These objectives were achieved by minimizing the costs of transport, storage, ordering and installation of DCs as well as by reducing $CO_2$ emissions from transport. Moreover, Fernández and Sgalambro [6] addressed the collaborative location routing problem (LRP) by proposing a MILP to minimize the freight distribution costs. The obtained results showed that more significant savings can be achieved, compared to the traditional non-cooperative strategies. In the same context, Ouhader and El kyal [7] considered the 2E-LRP in a collaborative context by minimizing the costs and $CO_2$

emissions of freight transport. Furthermore, Mrabti et al. [8] studied the design of a two-echelon distribution network by evaluating logistic costs, $CO_2$ emissions, accident risk and noise level. Recently, Aloui et al. [9] investigated the collaborative location inventory routing problem (LIRP) by developing a MILP to reduce costs and $CO_2$ emissions in a two-echelon distribution network.

In summary, most studies have focused on the economic dimension through the reduction of logistics costs, especially those generated by freight transport. Recent studies have started to take into consideration the environmental level by reducing $CO_2$ emissions due to transportation. Unlike recent studies, this paper focuses on the collaborative distribution network design problem by considering the three dimensions of sustainability. The economic sustainability is performed by the reduction of logistic costs caused by transportation, storage, hubs opening, handling and penalty due to delivery delay. At the environmental level, we do not limit ourselves to the reduction of $CO_2$ emissions due to transport, but we also minimize the $CO_2$ emissions due to the depreciation of vehicles and those due to the operation and construction of hubs. At the social level, the distribution of goods has a positive impact on the creation of new jobs. Therefore, we maximize the created job opportunities. In addition, we minimize the negative effects on the inhabitants, especially the accident risk and the noise level.

## 3 Problem Description

In this section, we describe the model objectives, the importance of using blockchain, the discussed scenarios and the evaluated indicators.

### 3.1 Objectives of Mathematical Models

The envisaged distribution network consists of suppliers who collaborate to deliver their products to retailers through shared hubs: warehouses and distribution centers. The objectives are to determine the number, locations and capacities of hubs as well as to establish the links between the distribution network nodes. The developed models help also determining the quantities delivered in each period in the three parts (upstream, midstream and downstream), the inventory levels in the warehouses, the delayed quantities as well as the number and type of the used vehicles. In this paper, the performance of a collaborative scenario (see Fig. 1) is compared to that of a non-collaborative scenario where each supplier is independent of the other in transportation and storage.

To ensure economy of scale, delivery is performed by a heterogeneous fleet of vehicles. This is consistent with the same approach used in [10]. On the other hand, this choice is beneficial for both scenarios because it helps choosing the appropriate type of vehicle for each shipment, which allows improving the fill rate and consequently reducing the total travelled distance. Furthermore, we assume that the retailers' demands are planned over a time horizon (weeks) because several researchers demonstrated the relevance of multi-period planning over static planning [11].

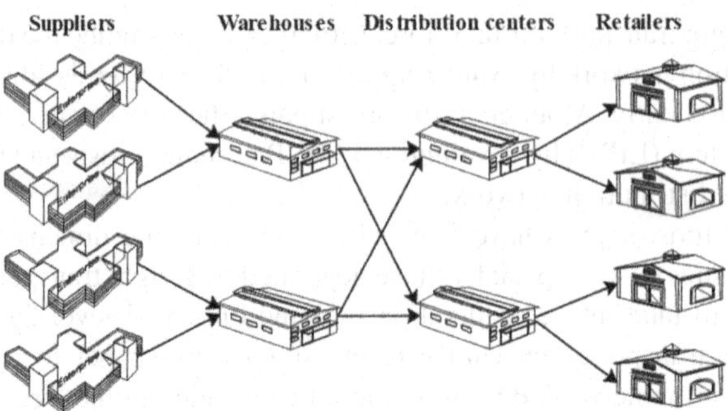


**Fig. 1.** Examined collaborative scenarios.

### 3.2 Importance of Using Blockchain

One of the main obstacles that prevents the success of the horizontal collaboration is the coordination between competing partners, especially information sharing. Typically, the partners use electronic data interchange (EDI) systems to exchange information. However, this data is frequently transmitted in batches rather than in real time. It is therefore likely that a shipment may disappear or not be updated. It is also possible that some collaboration partners may not receive this information till the release of the next EDI package. The use of the blockchain helps overcoming this problem as the information will be updated regularly and can be quickly distributed to all the involved entities.

The blockchain is a decentralized database which represents a powerful solution for all members of the collaborative network to access in a secure and fast way. The use of blockchain enables real-time traceability throughout the collaborative distribution network. The blockchain ensures a secure exchange of monetary values and information, leading to a new cooperation between supply chain entities along the delivery chain [12]. This represents a way to provide customers with additional information about products and processes. Information transparency becomes a source of competitive advantage that allows companies to differentiate themselves from their competitors and build a responsible and trustworthy brand reputation [13].

Sustainability is becoming a key factor in efficiency and profitability. The use of blockchain promotes sustainable practices within distribution networks. At the economic level, the use of blockchain allows trading while avoiding fraud or opportunistic behavior [14]. Blockchain solves several problems such as: real-time communication, fast payment with reduced product costs, and reduced delivery times. In addition, improved transparency allows for better resource management by minimizing waste and thus reducing distribution costs. Blockchain is a great way to manage inventory, accounting, asset scheduling and customer transactions. At the environmental level, tracing products from their origin to the end consumer reduces carbon footprints and unsustainable practices. Indeed, it will be possible to identify in real time the vehicles that emit the highest quantities of $CO_2$ emissions, which facilitates the implementation of sudden measures. In addition, driver behavior can cause adverse impacts on the environment. According to [15], using token-based blockchain to reward eco-driving can encourage the driver to anticipate and protect the environment. Furthermore, drivers are usually only paid when they travel specific distances, resulting in unsustainable practices caused by acceleration. It is possible to combine blockchain with smart contracts to pay the driver in real time, which motivates him to maintain his performance [15]. Blockchain also allows for the control of dangerous waste, distributing responsibility to system participants. At the social level, blockchain can help respect human rights. Indeed, the transparency of blockchain is a way to control companies in violation of working hours limits, child labor and inhumane working conditions. By combining IoT (Internet of Things) and blockchain, it is possible to analyze data that relates to workplace health and safety, namely lighting, temperature, humidity, noise and ventilation. This data can be used to improve the working condition and comfort of workers.

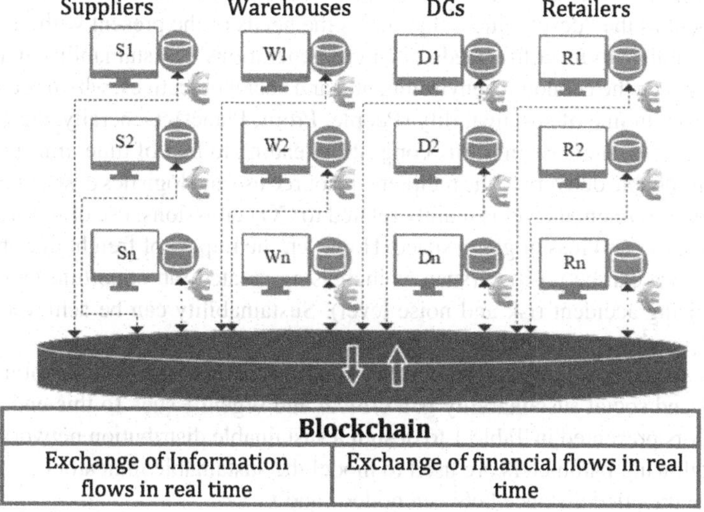


**Fig. 2.** Implication of blockchain in the collaborative distribution network.

In this sense, we assume that information flows and financial flows are managed by the blockchain (see Fig. 2). It allows the transition from the traditional distribution network to the distribution network 4.0 by exchanging data and managing monetary transactions.

### 3.3 Examined Scenarios

As noted above, in this study we examine two scenarios:

**Non-collaborative Scenario (NCS):** It refers to the initial situation, without collaboration between suppliers. In this scenario, each supplier delivers its goods to its own retailer through a warehouse and a distribution center.

**Collaborative Scenario (CS):** In the collaborative scenario, suppliers deliver their goods to the shared warehouses. Flows are massified in the warehouses and distribution centers, which makes it possible to optimize the vehicle fill rates by grouping goods. In this scenario, we assume that each supplier and each retailer are assigned to a single warehouse and a single distribution center, respectively. This assumption reduces the shipping costs as it is less expensive to ship a larger quantity to a single hub than to ship smaller ones to more than one hub. It also facilitates warehouse management. To ensure the flow of all products throughout the distribution network, we assume that a warehouse is assigned to several distribution centers and vice versa.

### 3.4 Sustainability Indicators

The sustainability is now among the top ten unresolved global concerns and still attracts much attention. It was first described by the World Commission on Environment and Development as the "development that meets the needs of the present without compromising the ability to meet the needs of future generations". Sustainability maintains a balance between the economic, environmental and social objectives, which is also called the triple bottom line of sustainability (People, Profit, Planet). Generally, the economic level concerns the increase in traffic congestion leading to loss of time, transport inefficiencies, unreliable delivery to the recipient, resource use and logistics costs. On the other hand, the environmental level is mainly related to $CO_2$ emissions, use of non-renewable resources, waste and loss of green space. However, the impact of freight distribution on the social level can be positive (such as increasing created job opportunities) or negative (e.g. rising accident risk and noise level). Sustainability can be achieved only by considering and combining all three dimensions.

In this sense, designing a collaborative distribution network with economic, environmental and social sustainability is a critical and urgent issue. To this end, we used the indicators presented in Table 1 to design a sustainable distribution network.

The following parameters are used to model the sustainable indicators

$d_{i,j}$: the travelled distance between nodes $i$ and $j$.

$C_{ov}$, $C_{qv}$: the unit costs of transport by an empty and fully loaded vehicle $v$, respectively

$E_{qv}$, $E_{ov}$: the unit $CO_2$ emissions due to transport by an empty and fully loaded vehicle $v$, respectively

$Q_v$: the vehicle capacity $v$

$q_{i,j,p,v,t}$: the quantity of product $p$ transported between two nodes $i$ and $j$ by the vehicle $v$ in the period $t$

$ME_v$: the $CO_2$ emissions due to the manufacturing of the vehicle $v$

$SL_v$: the service life of the vehicle $v$

$N_m$: the number of needed jobs to handle 100 pallets

$TC_{i,j,v,t}$, $TE_{i,j,v,t}$: the costs and $CO_2$ emissions caused by transport between two nodes $i$ and $j$ through a vehicle $v$ in period $t$, respectively

$JO_{m,t}$: the created job opportunities by the opening of hub $m$ in period $t$

The economic level is ensured by reducing the costs of freight transport, storage, handling, delivery delay and the establishment of the hubs. Minimizing the transportation cost guarantees the massification of flows. Indeed, it allows choosing the type of vehicle to be used as well as the quantity of goods to be delivered in each period and assigning the non-hubs nodes to the hubs [8]. The transportation cost is given by Eq. (1) adapted from [16]. It depends on the travelled distance $d_{i,j}$ between nodes $i$ and $j$, the unit transport costs $C_{qv}$ and $C_{ov}$, the vehicle capacity $Q_v$, the quantity of transported goods $q_{i,j,p,v,t}$ and the number of vehicles multiplied by two to consider the empty return. The reduction in the storage cost allows not only minimizing the stock itself, but also decreasing the storage risk, resource management and the operation of hubs. In addition, it means frequent delivery of goods, which improves the service level.

**Table 1.** Evaluated sustainable indicators.

| Economic level | Environmental level | Social level |
|---|---|---|
| - Transportation cost<br>- Storage cost<br>- Handling cost<br>- Penalty cost<br>- Establishment cost | - $CO_2$ emissions dues to vehicles : transportation and depreciation<br>- $CO_2$ emissions due to hubs : operation and construction | - Created job opportunities<br>- Accident risk<br>- Noise level |

In fact, the fixed handling cost includes the costs related to sorting, loading and unloading of goods. The penalty cost is imposed in case of delay in delivering the requested quantity at the right time. The last evaluated cost is that of establishing hubs. The reduction of this cost ensures not only the reduction in the number of hubs but also the adjustment of the surface of each built hub.

Regarding the environmental level, we do not limit our study to $CO_2$ emissions due to the freight transport, unlike previous studies. But, we evaluate those generated by the depreciation of vehicles, the operation and the construction of hubs. The $CO_2$ emissions due to transport is given by Eq. (2) that is similar to that of the transport cost by replacing unit costs by unit emissions $Eqv$ and $E_{ov}$. The $CO_2$ emissions caused by the depreciation of vehicles are given by Eq. (3). They depend on the total travelled distance multiplied by the emissions due to the manufacturing of the vehicle $ME_v$ and divided by its service life $SL_v$.

Socially sustainable goal is also an indispensable criterion that has received insufficient attention in previous studies. In this paper, it is attained by maximizing the created job opportunities and reducing the accident risk and the noise level caused by the freight distribution. Indeed, the automation of hubs affects negatively the created employment opportunities. On the other hand, high unemployment can lead to social instability and a negative multiplier influence. This indicator, given by Eq. (4), depends mainly on the quantities of goods entering each hub and the number of needed jobs $N_m$ to handle 100 pallets. This number depends, in turn, on the type of hub (automated, semi-automated and fully automated). Indeed, the number of created jobs decreases with the increase in the number of automated hubs. In addition, the distribution of goods has negative effects on the human health and road safety that should be reduced.

$$TC_{i,j,v,t} = d_{i,j} \cdot \left( \frac{C_{qv} - C_{ov}}{Q_v} \cdot \sum_{p \in P} q_{i,j,p,v,t} + 2 \cdot C_{ov} \cdot \left\lceil \frac{\sum_{p \in P} q_{i,j,p,v,t}}{Q_v} \right\rceil \right) \quad (1)$$

$$TE_{i,j,v,t} = d_{i,j} \cdot \left( \frac{E_{qv} - E_{ov}}{Q_v} \cdot \sum_{p \in P} q_{i,j,p,v,t} + 2 \cdot E_{ov} \cdot \left\lceil \frac{\sum_{p \in P} q_{i,j,p,v,t}}{Q_v} \right\rceil \right) \quad (2)$$

$$DE_{i,j,v,t} = 2 \cdot d_{i,j} \cdot \left\lceil \frac{\sum_{p \in P} q_{i,j,p,v,t}}{Q_v} \right\rceil \cdot \frac{ME_v}{SL_v} \quad (3)$$

$$JO_{m,t} = N_m \cdot \frac{\sum_{p \in P, v \in V, i \in N} q_{i,m,p,v,t}}{100} \quad (4)$$

## 4 Optimization Approaches

The developed mathematical models were applied on a distribution network of France and solved, in an exact way, for small size problems and, by metaheuristics, for large size problems.

### 4.1 Exact Optimization

The exact optimization was performed by the CPLEX solver. First, the mono-objective optimization was carried out by minimizing the logistic costs and the $CO_2$ emissions as well as by maximizing the created job opportunities. Second, to find a good compromise between the three objectives, the ε-constraint method was used. It consists in optimizing one of these objectives by putting the others under constraints. In addition to its simplicity, this method does not require imposing additional variables on the mathematical model. Furthermore, it does not require a common scaling since it allows each objective function to be represented by its own scale.

In our study, the economic level was considered as the objective, while the other two levels were treated as constraints. This choice is justified by the fact that this level takes into account more indicators than the other two levels. The accident risk and the noise level were evaluated after the resolution of models.

The considered case study concerns a distribution network in France containing a list of suppliers who collaborate to satisfy their customers through shared hubs. The Fig. 3 represents an example of a distribution network obtained by minimizing $CO_2$ emissions. This network includes 7 suppliers, 7 warehouses, 7 distribution centers and 13 retailers.

### 4.2 Meta-heuristic Optimization

Exact resolution is a critical issue when dealing with a large problem. For this reason, both GA and NSGA-II were developed to perform mono-objective and multi-objective model optimization.

**Mono-objective Optimization.** The choice of the genetic algorithm (GA) is justified by the fact that it has shown excellent performance in solving various optimization problems. This algorithm allows to obtain efficient solutions in terms of gap.

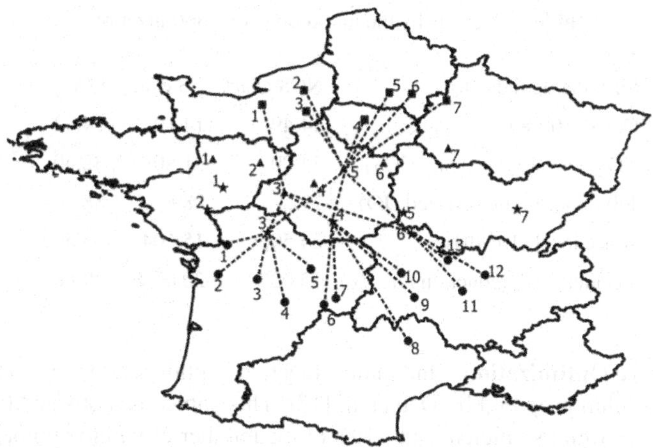

Fig. 3. Example of a distribution network (minimization of $CO_2$ emissions).

The GA imitates three genetic operations on a certain base population such as selection, mutation and crossover. The first operation plays an important role in determining the quality of the new generations. The selection can be done by tournament, roulette wheel or uniformly. The mutation operator allows the GA to better browse the search space by inflicting a modification in a gene. The crossover operator aims to increase the diversity of the population by manipulating the structure of the chromosomes.

The efficient implementation can be ensured and the enhancement of GA can be achieved only by the well choosing the optimal parameters of this algorithm. For this reason, this algorithm was run several times by varying its parameters. The best size of population for this algorithm is 150 that gave the best results in terms of cost (see Fig. 4). The results of the population size parameterization $\mathbf{n_{pop}}$ in the collaborative scenarios were obtained for multi-point crossover and swap mutation probabilities equal to **pc = 0.85 and pm = 0.3**, respectively. The results of the economic mono-objective resolution are represented in Table 2. The latter shows that the horizontal collaboration led to significant reduction in costs and $CO_2$ emissions and an increase in created job opportunities. The noise level and the accident risk are also improved compared to the non-collaborative scenario.

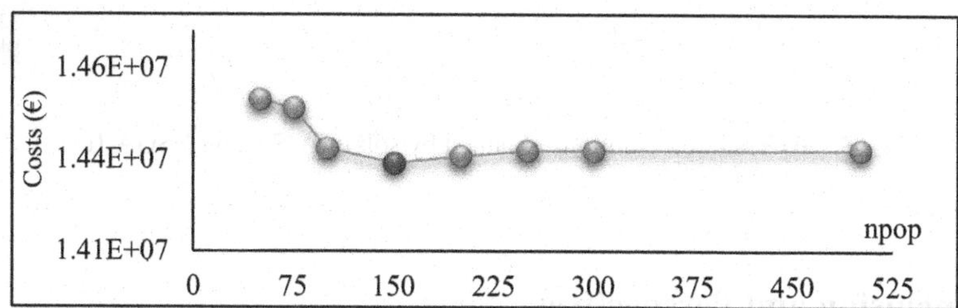


Fig. 4. Variation of costs according to the number of generated populations (CS).

**Table 2.** Results by the mono-objective optimization.

| Sustainable indicators | NCS exact | CS exact | GA |
|---|---|---|---|
| Costs ($10^6$ €) | 14.49 | 14.19 | 14.32 |
| $CO_2$ emissions ($10^5$ kg $CO_2$) | 34.00 | 31.80 | 32.40 |
| Job opportunities created (JO) | 792 | 889 | 881 |
| Noise level ($10^3$ dB) | 24.506 | 15.604 | 15.562 |
| Accident risk reduction rate (%) | 15.02% | 20.03% | 19.88% |

**Multi-objective Optimization.** In multi-objective optimization, we applied the NSGA-II algorithm proposed by Deb et al. [17]. This choice is motivated because this algorithm has proven its efficiency in terms of the number of pareto optimal solutions. It is a fast and elitist non-dominated sorting algorithm that manipulates a population of individuals and uses an explicit diversity preservation mechanism.

Its objective is to randomly generate a population P0 of N solutions (or individuals) and rank them according to the dominance principle. Figure 5 shows the multi-objective results obtained in the collaborative scenario. As the result of the created job opportunities is comparable in the two scenarios, we presented, by a color scale, the results obtained using NSGA-II to minimize logistic costs, $CO_2$ emissions, noise level and accident risk. Each point on the graph represents a solution to the multi-objective problem. However, choosing a solution that offers a particular optimal trade-off is not a trivial task, and interpreting a 3D Pareto front is very difficult. Nevertheless, the points in the middle of the graph turn out to correspond to the optimal solutions that offer a good compromise between the four objectives. On a practical level, decision makers can choose one of these solutions by negotiating among themselves.

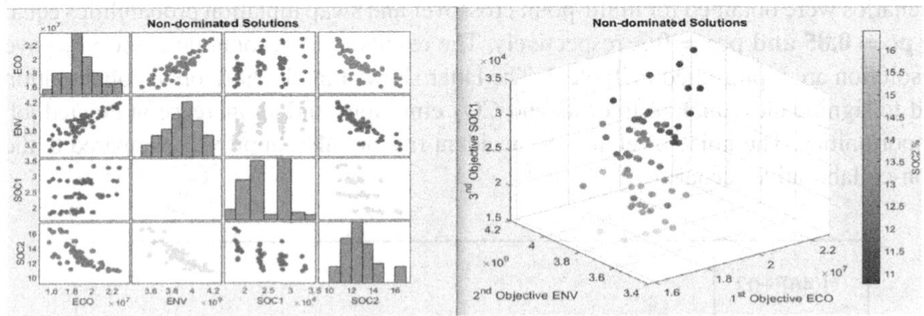


**Fig. 5.** 3D Trade-off solutions obtained by solving CS using NSGA-II.

## 5 Conclusion and Perspectives

In this study, we addressed the collaborative distribution network 4.0 design problem under sustainability considerations. Based on a list of economic, environmental and social sustainability indicators, we compared the performance of collaborative scenario to that of the non-collaborative scenario. Mono-objective solving was performed by the CPLEX solver and the genetic algorithm, while multi-objective resolution was done using the ε-constraint method and the NSGA-II algorithm for large problems. To address the challenges of implementing collaboration, we assumed that information exchange and monetary transactions are carried out through the blockchain. The obtained findings showed that horizontal collaboration achieved notable results, compared to the non-collaborative scenario. As a perspective, we will present a framework on the involvement of blockchain and IoT in collaborative distribution networks. We will also combine multi-criteria analysis methods with metaheuristics to select solutions offering a good compromise between different objectives.

## References


1. Mrabti, N., Hamani, N., Delahoche, L.: A sustainable collaborative approach to the distribution network design problem with CO2 emissions allocation. Int. J. Shipping Transp. Logist. (2021). https://doi.org/10.1504/IJSTL.2021.10037013
2. Aloui, A., Hamani, N, Derrouiche, R., Delahoche, L.: Systematic literature review on collaborative sustainable transportation: overview, analysis and perspectives. Transp. Res. Interdiscip. Perspect. **9**, 100291 (2021). https://doi.org/10.1016/j.trip.2020.100291
3. Verdonck, L., Beullens, P., Caris, A., Ramaekers, K., Janssens, G.K.: Analysis of collaborative savings and cost allocation techniques for the cooperative carrier facility location problem. J. Oper. Res. Soc. **67**(6), 853–871 (2016). https://doi.org/10.1057/jors.2015.106
4. Tang, X., Lehuédé, F., Péton, O., Pan, L.: Network design of a multi-period collaborative distribution system. Int. J. Mach. Learn. Cybern. **10**(2), 279–290 (2017). https://doi.org/10.1007/s13042-017-0713-5
5. Hacardiaux, T., Christof, D., Jean-Sébastien, T., Lotte, V.: Balancing partner preferences for logistics costs and carbon footprint in a horizontal cooperation. Maastricht University, Graduate School of Business and Economics (2020).https://doi.org/10.26481/umagsb.20002
6. Fernández, E., Sgalambro, A.: On carriers collaboration in hub location problems. Eur. J. Oper. Res. **283**(2), 476–490 (2020). https://doi.org/10.1016/j.ejor.2019.11.038
7. Ouhader, H., El Kyal, M.: Assessing the economic and environmental benefits of horizontal cooperation in delivery: performance and scenario analysis. Uncertain Supply Chain Manag. **8**(2), 303–320 (2020). https://doi.org/10.5267/j.uscm.2019.12.001
8. Mrabti, N., Hamani, N., Delahoche, L.: The pooling of sustainable freight transport. J. Oper. Res. Soc. 1–16 (2020). https://doi.org/10.1080/01605682.2020.1772022
9. Aloui, A., Hamani, N., Derrouiche, R., Delahoche, L.: Assessing the benefits of horizontal collaboration using an integrated planning model for two-echelon energy efficiency-oriented logistics networks design. Int. J. Syst. Sci.: Oper. Logist. 1–22 (2021). https://doi.org/10.1080/23302674.2021.1887397
10. Hu, L., Zhu, J.X., Wang, Y., Lee, L.H.: Joint design of fleet size, hub locations, and hub capacities for third-party logistics networks with road congestion constraints. Transp. Res. Part E: Logist. Transp. Rev. **118**, 568–588 (2018). https://doi.org/10.1016/j.tre.2018.09.002
11. Alumur, S.A., Nickel, S., Saldanha-da-Gama, F., Seçerdin, Y.: Multi-period hub network design problems with modular capacities. Ann. Oper. Res. **246**(1–2), 289–312 (2015). https://doi.org/10.1007/s10479-015-1805-9
12. Chen, J. et al.: A Blockchain-driven supply chain finance application for auto retail industry. Entropy **22**(1) (2020). https://doi.org/10.3390/e22010095

13. Macchion, L., Furlan, A., Vinelli, A.: The implementation of traceability in fashion networks. In: Camarinha-Matos, L.M., Afsarmanesh, H., Fornasiero, R. (eds.) PRO-VE 2017. IAICT, vol. 506, pp. 86–96. Springer, Cham (2017). https://doi.org/10.1007/978-3-319-65151-4_8
14. Tan, B.Q., Wang, F., Liu, J., Kang, K., Costa, F.: A Blockchain-based framework for green logistics in supply chains. Sustainability **12**(11), 4656 (2020). https://doi.org/10.3390/su12114656
15. Varriale, V., Cammarano, A., Michelino, F., Caputo, M.: The unknown potential of blockchain for sustainable supply chains. Sustainability **12**(22), 9400 (2020). https://doi.org/10.3390/su12229400
16. Pan, S., Ballot, E., Fontane, F.: The reduction of greenhouse gas emissions from freight transport by pooling supply chains. Int. J. Prod. Econ. **143**(1), 86–94 (2013). https://doi.org/10.1016/j.ijpe.2010.10.023
17. Deb, K., Pratap, A., Agarwal, S., Meyarivan, T.: A fast and elitist multiobjective genetic algorithm: NSGA-II. IEEE Trans. Evol. Computat. **6**(2), 182–197 (2002). https://doi.org/10.1109/4235.996017

# Using Fuzzy-Based Approaches on Partner's Selection to Promote Sustainability on Collaborative Networks

Ricardo Santos[1,2(✉)], João Matias[2], Jose Soares[3], Pedro Carmona Marques[1,4], and Victor Anes[5]

[1] ISEL-Instituto Superior de Engenharia de Lisboa, Instituto Politécnico de Lisboa, Lisbon, Portugal
ricardosimoessantos84@ua.pt
[2] GOVCOPP - University of Aveiro, Aveiro, Portugal
[3] ADVANCE, ISEG, Universidade de Lisboa, Lisbon, Portugal
[4] EIGeS, Universidade Lusófona, Lisbon, Portugal
[5] IDMEC-IST-UL, Lisbon, Portugal

**Abstract.** Collaborative Networks (CN) are well-known by the literature, has a mean to achieve multiple innovations, resulted from the collaboration with a broad variety of partners to access different types of knowledge and skills.

Despite its establishment, even in academia and in the corporate world, its implementation, constitutes a challenge, mainly when concerning to select the suitable partners to promote sustainable CN that attends the three dimensions of sustainability, regarding new product development's (NPD) projects. The lack of decision support frameworks, as well as the subjectivity around CN's manager's perception concerning this issue, motivates the development of this work.

Thus, this paper presents a soft computing-based approach to support CN's managers on partner's selection, regarding the NPD's projects on CN's context. The robustness of the approach developed here, will be assessed and validated through a case study, regarding the development of a green product.

**Keywords:** Sustainability · Collaborative networks · New product development · Partner's selection · Soft computing approaches

## 1 Introduction

Finding suitable partners regarding several knowledge areas, is essential to obtain success with innovation in a collaborative environment [1]. In the last years, researchers have mainly focused their research on social environment effects, over the innovation levels, and regarding everyone [2, 3]. For example, some works have highlighted the importance of providing some autonomy to the SMEs employees, when forming a teamwork from individuals with several competencies to achieve favorable work environments and high innovation levels from SME's employees [4]. Furthermore, the development of social


Published by Springer Nature Switzerland AG 2021
L. M. Camarinha-Matos et al. (Eds.): PRO-VE 2021, IFIP AICT 629, pp. 53–64, 2021.
https://doi.org/10.1007/978-3-030-85969-5_5

networks in the SMEs, has provided their individuals with some sense of collectively, by sharing information with other SMEs to develop specific skills or even some expertise [5, 6].

Additionally, some studies found on literature (e.g. [7]), states that innovation, achieved from collaborative networks (CN), can lead toward to an efficient allocation of assets, improving at the same time the performance of an organization.

Several studies, with focus on partner selection methods for CN context, has been performed, in order to support managers on coordination of their CN to increase their innovative performance, with most of them, examining CN on behalf of different perspectives such as knowledge relevance (e.g. [8]), key CN positions (e.g. [9]), external available resources (e.g. [10]), external cooperation by creating new knowledge or competences on behalf of new product development context (e.g. [11]), among others.

Some studies use Social Networks (SN) to locate the required external assets/resources for SMEs (e.g. [4]) while others, use SN to reach expert individuals (e.g. [3, 10]).

All these studies highlight the importance of partner selection, as a purpose to support managers on coordination of their CN to increase their innovative performance.

The latest developments, regarding information systems, have created many available applications for professional use, with most of them, used by human resource (HR) professionals to search adequate partners for team building [8].

However, and due to the increasing requirements within SMEs on behalf of sustainable development, such as social and environment responsibilities, there are a few limited approaches to support managers on partner's assessment-based criteria, on behalf of the three dimensions of sustainability (Economic, Social and Environmental) [12].

Furthermore, the existence of some subjectivity within manager's perception, regarding the assessment of different partners, based on a set of criteria pre-established, is another issue to be accounted, since that the subjectivity increases with the number of managers/decision-agents on CN to perform the same evaluation. The inclusion of fuzzy logic-based methods, could also minimize such effects.

Thus, we intend to fill a gap on the literature, by presenting a model that integrates all these issues into a single approach, to promote sustainable CN's, through partner's selection and that answers to the following research question: what kind of soft computing-based approach to support CN's managers on partner's selection, regarding NPD's projects is possible to be achieved on a CN context?

The robustness of the proposed model, will be evaluated through a case study, based on a project developed on CN context, to create "green" energy to an industry. This case study will highlight some benefits achieved from this method, and some limitations as well, by pointing some future research to overcome them.

Therefore, this paper is organized as follows; Sect. 2, proposes the CN's model for assessing and choosing suitable partners, from a set of candidates to integrate the same network. Section 3, pretends to present the case study used here to assess method's robustness and the discussion of results. Then Sect. 4, ends this work with the conclusions and some future research remarks.

## 2 Research Method

### 2.1 Proposed Approach

Following what was referred before, a Collaborative Network (CN), normally arises to conceive specific products/systems, by allocating different resources and competences, from a set of partners, to reach high levels of innovation at a lower cost. However, the partner's selection for the same CN, arises multiple challenges, especially when it's intended to promote sustainability within the CN itself on developing such products/systems.

According to [12, 13], sustainable development actions, can be divided into three main groups or dimensions; Economic, Social and Environmental.

From the literature, and regarding the criteria, normally used on partner's selection for CN, we have found a set of criteria, which we have categorized, according to the three dimensions defined before, i.e.:

- Economic: Concerns all the criteria, that might impact the CN's economic and financial viability, which includes issues, mainly related with the organization's economic well-being [4, 6], namely; facility's location, supply chain's channels (distribution points, transportation modes, etc.), scale (available) of operations, operation costs, financial situation and credibility, capacity of facilities, reliability of feedstock supply, among other criteria.
- Social: Concerns all the criteria, that might impact the CN's social viability, which can include issues mainly related with the organization's social wellbeing with its stakeholders [6, 13], as well as reputation and share of knowledge/information issues, i.e.; social responsibility actions (e.g. employees' family members, health insurance, local population, etc.),work conditions, availability to share knowledge and information, knowledge relevance, reputation, number of partnerships firmed with other organizations, among other criteria.
- Environmental: Concerns all the criteria, that might impact the CN's environmental viability, which includes issues, mainly related with the organization's environmental responsibility [3, 5], namely; Self-energy Greenhouse Gas (GHG) emissions, soil and water quality, circular economy policies, environment standards accreditation, among other criteria.

Based on those criteria, it was performed a framework to evaluate each partner's potential, as a candidate to be integrate in a CN. Thus, on Fig. 1, it's presented an example of the same framework, considering a set of criteria, categorized according to the dimensions of sustainability, referred before.

Thus, and based on criteria presented on Fig. 1, it can be defined an attribute $x$, which belongs to an alternative (potential partner) $i$, regarding to a sub criteria $j$, which is related to a dimension/criteria $g$, resulting therefore in $\left(x_{ij}^{g_j}\right)$. For each criterion $i$, related each one to a dimension of sustainability, corresponds to a set of sub criteria, which is then applied to assess each candidate's potential, by using Multi Attribute Value Theory (MAVT). Therefore, there is a dimension/criteria $g$, regarding to a specific sub criteria $j$, used here ($g_j$), which can be represented as follows; A – Economic, B-Social

| Criteria | Attributes/Score Subcriteria | 0% Not Preferable | 25% Low Preferable | 50% Reasonable Preferable | 75% Preferable | 100% Highly Preferable |
|---|---|---|---|---|---|---|
| A - Economics | Financial situation and credibility<br>Available assets<br>Facility's location<br>Supply chain's channels<br>Scale (available) of operations<br>Operation costs | | | | | |
| | Total | 0, 5, 10 | 15, 20, 25, 30, 35 | 40, 45, 50, 55, 60 | 65, 70, 75, 80, 85 | 90, 95, 100 |
| B - Social | Company's Reputation (Transparency)<br>Knowiege relevance<br>Work conditions<br>External available resources (social network)<br>Social responsibility | | | | | |
| | Total | 0, 5, 10 | 15, 20, 25, 30, 35 | 40, 45, 50, 55, 60 | 65, 70, 75, 80, 85 | 90, 95, 100 |
| C - Environment | Industry's energy dependence level from fossil fuels)<br>Compliance with legal requirements regarding environment<br>Circular economy policies<br>Environmental standards (accreditation) | | | | | |
| | Total | 0, 5, 10 | 15, 20, 25, 30, 35 | 40, 45, 50, 55, 60 | 65, 70, 75, 80, 85 | 90, 95, 100 |
| Total Score | | 0, 5, 10 | 15, 20, 25, 30, 35 | 40, 45, 50, 55, 60 | 65, 70, 75, 80, 85 | 90, 95, 100 |

**Fig. 1.** Adopted criteria and pay-off table, used as a 1st approach to define the model

and C-Environmental. In general, each attribute $x_{ij}^{g_j}$ can be defined, i.e.:

$$x_i = \{x_{i1}, x_{i2}, x_{i3}, .., x_{in_g}\} \wedge n_g = \{n_A, n_B, n_C\} \wedge n_A, n_B, n_C, i, j \in \mathbb{N} \tag{1}$$

$$g_j \in \{\{A_1, A_2, .., A_j, ..A_{n_A}\} \cup \{B_1, B_2, .., B_j, .., B_{n_B}\} \cup \{C_1, C_2, .., C_j, ..C_{n_C}\}\} \tag{2}$$

Thus, each attribute $\left(x_{ij}^{g_j}\right)$ considered here, can be aggregated in just one pay-off table (Table 2 a)). Since that each attribute $\left(x_{ij}^{g_j}\right)$, works with different scales and units, the correspondent attribute values, were then converted by using MVAT, to its correspondent value $\left(v_{ij}^{g_j}\left(x_{ij}^{g_j}\right)\right)$, by using the "worst" and "better" results, obtained through a set of alternatives, and related to each criteria $g_j$, i.e.:

$$x_{ij}^{(g_j)} \longrightarrow \left( \frac{\left| x_{ij}^{(g_j)} - x_{ij(worst)}^{(g_j)} \right|}{\left| x_{ij(better)}^{(g_j)} - x_{ij(worst)}^{(g_j)} \right|} \right) \longrightarrow v_{ij}^{(g_j)}(x_{ij}^{(g_j)}) \tag{3}$$

The new values, referred to each $v_{ij}^{(g_j)}\left(x_{ij}^{(g_j)}\right)$, have originated a new pay-off table, which is the result of the conversion of Table 2 a), to Table 2 b), by using (3) (Fig. 2).

Through the attributes previously defined, and by using fuzzy logic techniques, it was achieved the correspondent value functions $V_i^A(x_i^A)$, $V_i^B(x_i^B)$ and $V_i^C(x_i^C)$, regarding each sustainability's dimension. Then, and by using an additive model, based on MAVT approach, it was achieved a unique expression to aggregate all dimensions, to assess each alternative/potential partner. This function is then weighted by a weight factor$(\omega_g)$, expressing thus, the relative importance given to the dimension of each sustainability, resulting therefore in the final assessment function, i.e.:

$$V_i(X_i) = V_i\left(V_i^A\left(x_i^A\right), V_i^B\left(x_i^B\right), V_i^C\left(x_i^C\right)\right) = \omega_A.V_i^A\left(x_i^A\right) + \omega_B.V_i^B\left(x_i^B\right) + \omega_C.V_i^C\left(x_i^C\right) \tag{4}$$

With $\omega_A$, $\omega_B$, $\omega_C$, being achieved by using Analytical Hierarchical Process (AHP) method, as it presented and described on following sections.

| $x_{ij}^{gj}$ | A1 | A2 | ... | $An_A$ | B1 | B2 | ... | $Bn_B$ | C1 | C2 | ... | $Cn_C$ |
|---|---|---|---|---|---|---|---|---|---|---|---|---|
| $X_1$ | $x_{11}^{A1}$ | $x_{12}^{A2}$ | ... | $x_{1}^{An_A}$ | $x_{11}^{B1}$ | $x_{12}^{B2}$ | ... | $x_{1}^{Bn_B}$ | $x_{11}^{C1}$ | $x_{12}^{C2}$ | ... | $x_{1n_C}^{Cn_C}$ |
| $X_2$ | $x_{21}^{A1}$ | $x_{22}^{A2}$ | ... | $x_{2n_A}^{An_A}$ | $x_{21}^{B1}$ | $x_{22}^{B2}$ | ... | $x_{2n_B}^{Bn_B}$ | $x_{21}^{C1}$ | $x_{22}^{C2}$ | ... | $x_{2n_C}^{Cn_C}$ |
| ... | ... | ... | | ... | ... | ... | ... | ... | ... | ... | ... | ... |
| $X_n$ | $x_{n1}^{A1}$ | $x_{n2}^{A2}$ | ... | $x_{nn_A}^{An_A}$ | $x_{n1}^{B1}$ | $x_{n2}^{B2}$ | ... | $x_{nn_B}^{Bn_B}$ | $x_{n1}^{C1}$ | $x_{n2}^{C2}$ | ... | $x_{nn_C}^{Cn_C}$ |

a)

| $v_{ij}^{gj}(x_{ij}^{gj})$ | A1 | A2 | ... | $An_A$ | B1 | B2 | ... | $Bn_B$ | C1 | C2 | ... | $Cn_C$ |
|---|---|---|---|---|---|---|---|---|---|---|---|---|
| $x_1$ | $v_{11}^{A1}(x_{11}^{A1})$ | $v_{12}^{A2}(x_{12}^{A2})$ | ... | $v_{1n_A}^{An}(x_{1}^{An_A})$ | $v_{11}^{B1}(x_{11}^{B1})$ | $v_{12}^{B2}(x_{12}^{B2})$ | ... | $v_{1}^{Bn_B}(x_{1}^{Bn_B})$ | $v_{11}^{C1}(x_{11}^{C1})$ | $v_{12}^{C2}(x_{12}^{C2})$ | ... | $v_{1n_C}^{Cn_C}(x_{1n_C}^{Cn_C})$ |
| $x_2$ | $v_{21}^{A1}(x_{21}^{A1})$ | $v_{22}^{A2}(x_{22}^{A2})$ | ... | $v_{2n_A}^{An}(x_{2n_A}^{An_A})$ | $v_{21}^{B1}(x_{21}^{B1})$ | $v_{22}^{B2}(x_{22}^{B2})$ | ... | $v_{2n_B}^{Bn_B}(x_{2n_B}^{Bn_B})$ | $v_{21}^{C1}(x_{21}^{C1})$ | $v_{22}^{C2}(x_{22}^{C2})$ | ... | $v_{2n_C}^{Cn_C}(x_{2n_C}^{Cn_C})$ |
| ... | ... | ... | | ... | ... | ... | ... | ... | ... | ... | ... | ... |
| $x_n$ | $v_{n1}^{A1}(x_{n1}^{A1})$ | $v_{n2}^{A2}(x_{n2}^{A2})$ | ... | $v_{nn_A}^{An_A}(x_{nn_A}^{An_A})$ | $v_{n1}^{B1}(x_{n1}^{B1})$ | $v_{n2}^{B2}(x_{n2}^{B2})$ | ... | $v_{nn_B}^{Bn}(x_{nn_B}^{Bn})$ | $v_{n1}^{C1}(x_{n1}^{C1})$ | $v_{n2}^{C2}(x_{n2}^{C2})$ | ... | $v_{nn_C}^{Cn_C}(x_{nn_C}^{Cn_C})$ |

b)

**Fig. 2.** Pay-off table, used to define model's criteria: (a) $x_{ij}^{(g_j)}$; (b) $v_{ij}\left(x_{ij}^{(g_j)}\right)$.

## 2.2 Model's Architecture, Fuzzy Modelling and Linguistic Variables

The proposed architecture, intends to integrate all the issues, referred before with fuzzy inference systems, to support managers into the development of a product on behalf of Collaborative Networks (CN) (Fig. 3). Additionally, the integration of Fuzzy Systems, has the purpose of incorporating the ambiguity and subjectivity, related with human perception on assessing each potential partner, according to a set of criteria previously defined.

The proposed approach is presented on Fig. 3.

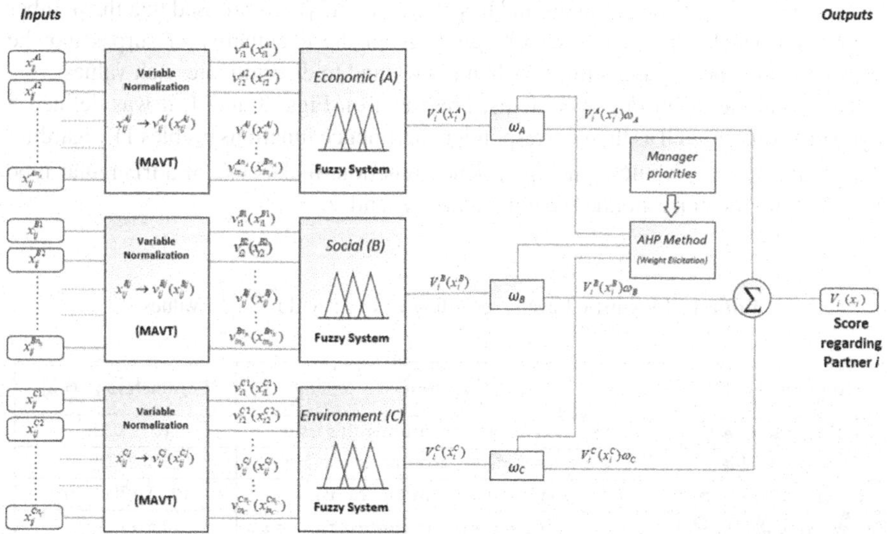


**Fig. 3.** Proposed model.

Based on Fig. 3, each alternative/potential partner *i*, has a set of individual scores $v_{ij}^{gj}(x_{ij}^{gj})$, which are correspondent, each one, to a given criteria/dimension (*g*), related to each sub criteria j, which is then used as an input regarding for each correspondent Fuzzy System (related each one to a specific dimension/criteria). By using a fuzzy inference mechanism, and through a set of inference rules, regarding a sentence from the type of "If…And…Then", it is obtained the overall score of each criterion, regarding each alternative/potential partner *i* ($V_i^g(x_i^g)$).

Therefore, each $V_i^g(x_i^g)$, regarding the dimensions considered here (A,B and C), are achieved, by using a set of functions, based on the inputs $v_{ij}^{gj}(x_{ij}^{gj})$, i.e.:

$$V_i^g(x_i^g) = v_{i1}^{g1}(x_{i1}^{g1}) \cap v_{i2}^{A2}(x_{i2}^{g2}) \cap \ldots . \cap v_{ij}^{gj}(x_{ij}^{gj}) \cap \ldots . \cap v_{in_g}^{gn_g}(x_{in_g}^{gn_g}) \tag{5}$$

Thus, and through $V_i^A(x_i^A)$, $V_i^B(x_i^B)$ and $V_i^C(x_i^C)$, it is achieved an expression to assess each alternative/potential partner *i*, i.e.:

$$V_i(x_i) = V_i\left(V_i^A\left(x_i^A\right), V_i^B\left(x_i^B\right), V_i^C\left(x_i^C\right)\right) = \omega_A . V_i^A\left(x_i^A\right) + \omega_B . V_i^B\left(x_i^B\right) + \omega_C . V_i^C\left(x_i^C\right) \tag{6}$$

With $\omega_A$, $\omega_B$, $\omega_C$, be achieved by using Analytical Hierarchical Process (AHP) method, and satisfying the following condition:

$$\omega_A + \omega_B + \omega_C = 1 \tag{7}$$

## 2.3 Linguistic Variables

Concerning the linguistic variables and based on ([13, 15]) it is advised that the number of linguistic levels should not surpass nine, given the eventuality of surpassing the decision-agent's perception's limits, when it's wanted to discriminate such values.

Thus, and based on Fuzzy Systems, presented on Figs. 3 and 4, it was defined 5 linguistic levels, as well as their correspondent pertinence functions (Tables 1), regarding $v_{ij}^{gj}(x_{ij}^{gj})$ and $v_i^{gj}(x_i^{gj})$ values. Each pertinence function, makes use of a triangular type function, with the correspondent parameters $\gamma$, $\beta$ and $\alpha$.

**Table 1.** Linguistic Levels, regarding $v_{ij}^{gj}(x_{ij}^{gj})$ and $v_i^{gj}(x_i^{gj})$ values

| Linguistic Levels | Description | Parameters [γ,β,α] |
|---|---|---|
| Not Preferable | There is no evidence, accounting this issue. | (0 ,0 ,0.25) |
| Low Preferable | There is some evidence, accounting this issue. | (0 ,0.25,0.50) |
| Reasonble Preferable | There is evidence, accounting this issue. | (0.25,0.50,0.75) |
| Preferable | There is a strong evidence, accounting this issue. | (0.5,0.75,1.0) |
| Highly Preferable | There is a clear evidence, accounting this issue. | (0.75, 1, 1) |

Thus, and based on the parameters presented on Table 1, it's converted the linguistic values into a numerical format, by establishing a set of intervals, to be further aggregated, by using expression (8).

## 2.4 Fuzzy Deployment and Software's Implementation

Based on Fig. 3, each Fuzzy System, was deployed by using Matlab® software (version R2018a), which has included the membership functions and the inference rules previously defined (Table 1).

As it stated before, and regarding each Fuzzy Systems defined here, it was adopted triangular functions, with the correspondent parameters, being obtained from Table 1. The inference rules, were deployed by using Mamdani's inference mechanism (Fig. 4), given its intuitive method, which is well-suited to the human inputs and its widely acceptance on literature [15].

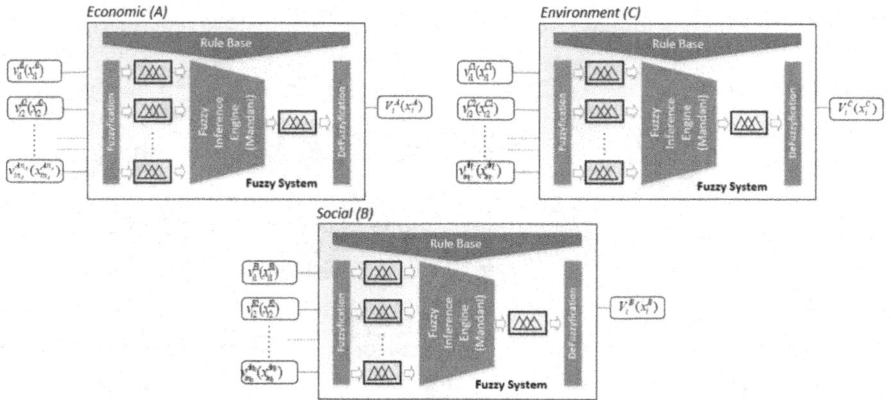


**Fig. 4.** Fuzzy Systems, regarding $V_i^A\left(x_i^A\right)$, $V_i^B\left(x_i^B\right)$ and $V_i^C\left(x_i^C\right)$ values

Regarding the defuzzification method for each FS's, it was adopted centroid approach, mainly due its widely acceptance in other works existed on literature [15].

# 3 Case Study

For model's validation, we have used a case study based on a CN, which was created to develop a system, to produce green electric energy to an industry, with the purpose of being $CO_2$ free emissions, regarding its energy consumption.

This system allows to an industry to produce its own energy, by integrating photovoltaic, with hydrogen systems. The CN's purpose, is to make this system an integrated product, to be launched to the market, to be further deployed in industries, with an installed power, with valued, ranged between 50–100 kW.

In a 1st stage, this system, was tested in a prototype version, by feeding a small industry of 70 kW, to be self-sufficient from the electric public grid. The system itself is formed by a set of components, where besides the PV System, with its main components (the converter and PV panels), its formed by the main components regarding hydrogen systems (e.g., Fuel Cell, $H_2$ and $O_2$ tanks, and Electrolyze) and the other components, needed to perform the supervision, control and data acquisition of the system. Each part/component of the system, is developed/produced by a unique organization (partner), or even a set of them. The organization can have several types, which means that it can be public or even private (R&D, University, Company, etc.).

All the partners involved, contributes each one to the development part of a system, by exchanging resources and competencies (as depicted in Fig. 5). In this case, the Collaborative Network (CN) has 12 partners, which have different nature, and they come from different sectors.

For the modelling of different resources and competencies exchanged on this CN, between the different CN partners, we have used the framework proposed by [13], to manage enterprises' innovation in open innovation contexts (Fig. 5).

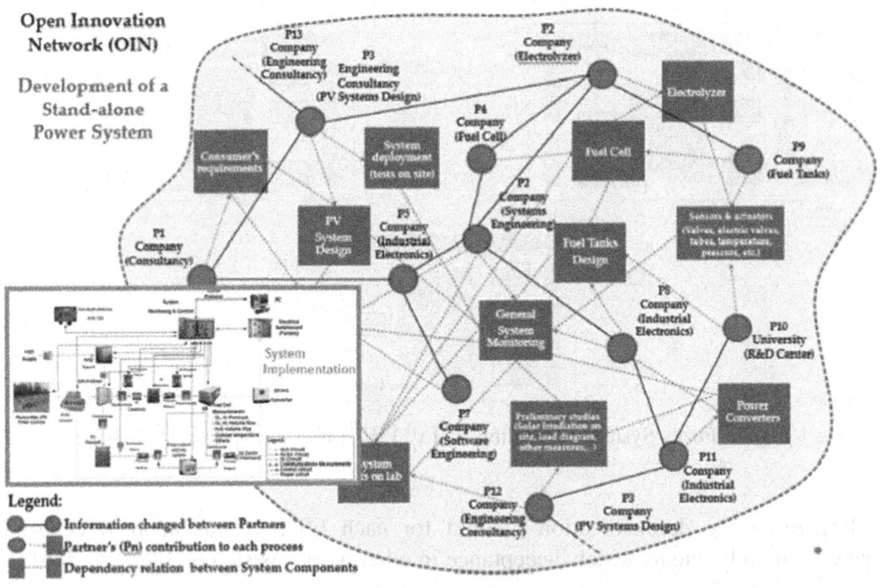


**Fig. 5.** CN regarding the developed system [13]

By following the same approach, and based on the network presented on Fig. 5, we can systematize the resources and competencies exchanged between the partners involved, by defined as a contribution from each partner to each process, which are regarded to each system part under development, as well as the relationship between each part/component of the system.

Such contribution can be better understood by presenting an example on Table 2, where it can be observed some of the processes of the system under development, followed by the description of partners/actors involved.

**Table 2.** Some of the processes, used on behalf of the system under development.

| Process Reference | Description | Partners |
|---|---|---|
| … | … | … |
| K02Pr3 | PV System design | P3, P12 |
| … | …. | …. |
| K01Pr6 | Human Machine Interface (HMI) | P6 P? P? |
| K02Pr5 | Systems tests on lab | P2,P6 e P12 |
| K02Pr5 | General System Monitoring and Control | P6, P7, P10 |
| … | … | … |

To apply the model presented here, we have selected from Table 2, the process, with Process Reference K01Pr6 (Human Machine Interface (HMI)), where the Chief Technology Officer, as well as the CN's board of managers, wants to select two more partners to join to the existence one, already established (Partner P6). The purpose is to increase the goal of innovation level regarding the HMI to be developed, which was previously defined by the CN's management.

Therefore, a group of managers, have made use of the model's inputs, and based on the three dimensions of sustainability, already defined.

They have contacted a group of potential partners, to be further assessed as candidates, to fulfill the two available places of partners to be added to the CN defined here. By using the Fuzzy Systems approach, proposed on Figs. 3 and 4, as well as the linguistic variables defined on Table 1, and according to a set of rules, we have achieved the correspondent outputs, regarding each partner to be assessed (Table 3).

The weights, corresponding each one to a sustainability's dimension, where then defined by using the Analytical Hierarchical Process (AHP) method.

**Table 3.** Model's inputs and the correspondent outputs

| | | | | Partner's Score $(V_i(x_i))$ | | | | | | | | | | | | | | | | | |
|---|---|---|---|---|---|---|---|---|---|---|---|---|---|---|---|---|---|---|---|---|---|
| Process Reference | Partners required | Partner (s) Candidate (s) | | A $\left(v_{ij}^{Aj}(x_{ij}^{Aj}) \rightarrow v_{ij}^{Aj}\right)$ | | | | | | B $\left(v_{ij}^{Bj}(x_{ij}^{Bj}) \rightarrow v_{ij}^{Bj}\right)$ | | | | | C $\left(v_{ij}^{Cj}(x_{ij}^{Cj}) \rightarrow v_{ij}^{Cj}\right)$ | | | | $\left(V_i^g(x_i^g) \rightarrow V_i^g\right)$ | | |
| | | Name | Organization | $v_{i1}^{A1}$ | $v_{i2}^{A2}$ | $v_{i3}^{A3}$ | $v_{i4}^{A4}$ | $v_{i5}^{A5}$ | $v_{i6}^{A6}$ | $v_{i1}^{B1}$ | $v_{i2}^{B2}$ | $v_{i3}^{B3}$ | $v_{i4}^{B4}$ | $v_{i5}^{B5}$ | $v_{i1}^{C1}$ | $v_{i2}^{C2}$ | $v_{i3}^{C3}$ | $v_{i4}^{C4}$ | $V_i^A$ | $V_i^B$ | $V_i^C$ |
| K02Pr3 | 3 (with 1 already existed (P4)) | "A" | Public - University | | | | | | | | | | | | | | | | | | |
| | | "B" | Private - Company | | | | | | | | | | | | | | | | | | |
| | | "C" | Private - Company | | | | | | | | | | | | | | | | | | |
| | | "D" | Private - Company | | | | | | | | | | | | | | | | | | |
| | | "E" | Public - R&D Center | | | | | | | | | | | | | | | | | | |
| | | "F" | Public - R&D Center | | | | | | | | | | | | | | | | | | |
| | | "G" | Private - Company | | | | | | | | | | | | | | | | | | |
| | | "H" | Private - Company | | | | | | | | | | | | | | | | | | |
| | | "I" | Public - University | | | | | | | | | | | | | | | | | | |

**Legend (Linguistic variable):**

| Not Preferable ([0,1]) | Low Preferable ([1,2]) | Reasonble Preferable ([2,3]) | [illegible] | [illegible] |
|---|---|---|---|---|

The results, presented on Table 3, were obtained by using the fuzzy inference systems, referred before (Fig. 3), where, and based on a set of linguistic values, it was then converted into quantitative ones, through the deployment of a series of intervals, in order to achieve the score of each one of the 9 (potential/candidate) partners considered here, regarding each one, to one of the three sustainability's dimensions. Then, and by applying the correspondent weights, previously achieved, it was achieved the overall score, regarding each one of the 9 partners considered here (Table 4).

**Table 4.** Overall results, regarding each candidate (potential partner) to be selected.

| Process Reference | Partners required | Partner (s) Candidate (s) | | | | | | | | | | Partner(s) Selected (order of preference) | | | |
|---|---|---|---|---|---|---|---|---|---|---|---|---|---|---|---|
| | | Nr. | Name | Organization | $V_i^A$ | $V_i^B$ | $V_i^C$ | $\omega_A$ | $\omega_B$ | $\omega_C$ | $V_i$ | Rank | Name | Organization | $V_i$ |
| K02Pr3 | 3 (with 1 already existed (P4)) | 1 | "A" | Public - University | 0,2 | 1,1 | 1,9 | 0,27 | 0,21 | 0,52 | 1,27 | 1st | "D" | Private - Company | 3,36 |
| | | 2 | "B" | Private - Company | 1,3 | 1,8 | 3,6 | 0,36 | 0,14 | 0,50 | 2,52 | 2nd | "E" | Public - University | 3,22 |
| | | 3 | "C" | Private - Company | 2,1 | 2,7 | 1,5 | 0,30 | 0,22 | 0,48 | 1,94 | 3rd | "I" | Public - University | 3,14 |
| | | 4 | "D" | Private - Company | 3,1 | 2,8 | 3,8 | 0,39 | 0,17 | 0,44 | 3,36 | 4th | "H" | Private - Company | 2,56 |
| | | 5 | "E" | Public - University | 2,1 | 3,7 | 3,6 | 0,27 | 0,21 | 0,52 | 3,22 | 5th | "B" | Private - Company | 2,52 |
| | | 6 | "F" | Private - Company | 0,7 | 1,8 | 0,9 | 0,36 | 0,14 | 0,50 | 0,95 | 6th | "C" | Private - Company | 1,94 |
| | | 7 | "G" | Private - Company | 2,9 | 1,4 | | 0,30 | 0,22 | 0,48 | 1,18 | 7th | "A" | Public - University | 1,27 |
| | | 8 | "H" | Private - Company | 2,5 | 2,1 | 2,8 | 0,39 | 0,17 | 0,44 | 2,56 | 8th | "G" | Private - Company | 1,18 |
| | | 9 | "I" | Public - University | 3,2 | 2,4 | 3,4 | 0,27 | 0,21 | 0,52 | 3,14 | 9th | "F" | Private - Company | 0,95 |

**Legend (Preference degree):** 1st 2nd 3rd 4th 5th

After the score of each partner took place, it was re-ordered the candidates according to its overall score (Table 4), to define the order of preference. Therefore, and according to Table 4, the 2 candidates, needed for process K02Pr3 with more preference degree, are the private company "D", followed by the public university "E".

We can also select the candidate with more score related to a specific dimension of sustainability, which can be useful when we want to prioritize the candidates according to a specific dimension. We can also consider the next candidates to fulfill the CN needs, and in case of a contingency occur (e.g., private company "D" has quitted after the negotiations took place), which allows to select the next candidate with the highest score (in this case will be the private company "D"). Additionally, if we want to add just one partner, the selected partner would be the partner with the highest rank i.e., the private company "D", or if we want to select three more partners (instead of two), the candidates would be the first 3 (i.e., organizations "D", "E" and "I") and so on.

## 4 Conclusions of the Work

The approach presented here was developed to answer the proposed research question, thus presenting a new soft model, that support CN's management on partner's selection, regarding NPD and the three sustainable dimensions (Economic, Social and Environmental) by assessing a set of potential partners, assessing and prioritizing them.

Besides by the assessment and prioritization of each candidate, according to its attributes, it was also possible to perceive in which sustainability's dimension, each candidate is more "stronger" (suitable), according to the CN's objectives, which is defined by the priorities, which are established by the CN's managers, through AHP method.

Furthermore, it is even possible to face eventual contingencies from one or more partners (e.g., unavailability of selected partner after negotiations takes place), by selecting other partners with the next highest score.

The integration of Fuzzy Logic methods, also allows to reduce the ambiguity, related with the subjectivity around CN's manager perception on defining the attributes, needed to preform each assessment.

However, the limitations found with this model, allows to establish some future work, which will be then used to perform some enhancements, such as the addition of neural networks to predict CN's manager priorities, regarding sustainability's dimensions, or even additional sub criteria, more related with social networks.

## References

1. Mansor, N., Yahaya, S.N., Okazaki, K.: Risk factors affecting new product development (NPD). Int. J. Recent Res. Appl. Stud. **27**(1), 18–25 (2016)
2. Obradović, T., Vlačić, B., Dabić, M.: Open innovation in the manufacturing industry: a review and research agenda. Technovation **102**, 102221 (2021), ISSN 0166-4972. https://doi.org/10.1016/j.technovation.2021.102221
3. Hameed, W.U., Nisar, Q.A., Wu, H.: Relationships between external knowledge, internal innovation, firms' open innovation performance, service innovation and business performance in the Pakistani hotel industry. Int. J. Hosp. Manage. **92**, 102745 (2021). https://doi.org/10.1016/j.ijhm.2020.102745
4. Guertler, M.R., Sick, N.: Exploring the enabling effects of project management for SMEs in adopting open innovation – a framework for partner search and selection in open innovation projects. Int. J. Project Manage. 102–114 (2021). ISSN 0263-7863. https://doi.org/10.1016/j.ijproman.2020.06.007
5. Goyal, S., Ahuja, M., Kankanhalli, A.: Does the source of external knowledge matter? Examining the role of customer co-creation and partner sourcing in knowledge creation and innovation. Inf. Manage. **57**(6), 103325 (2020). ISSN 0378-7206. https://doi.org/10.1016/j.im.2020.103325
6. Santamaría, L., Nieto, M.J., Rodríguez, A.: Failed and successful innovations: the role of geographic proximity and international diversity of partners in technological collaboration. Technol. Forecast. Soc. Change **166**, 120575 (2021). ISSN 0040-1625. https://doi.org/10.1016/j.techfore.2021.120575
7. Grace, M.F., Leverty, J.T., Phillips, R.D., Shimpi, P.: The value of investing in enterprise risk management. J. Risk Insur. **2**(82), 289–316 (2015)
8. Wei, F., Feng, N., Yang, S., Zhao, Q.: A conceptual framework of two-stage partner selection in platform-based innovation ecosystems for servitization, J. Cleaner Prod. **262**, 121431 (2020). ISSN 0959-6526. https://doi.org/10.1016/j.jclepro.2020.121431
9. Li, E.Y., Liao, C.H., Yen, H.R.: Co-authorship networks and research impact: a social capital perspective. Res. Policy **42**(9), 1515–1530 (2013)
10. Markovic, S., Bagherzadeh, M., Vanhaverbeke, W., Bogers, M., Managing business-to-business open innovation: a project-level approach. Ind. Market. Manage. **94**, 159–163 (2021). ISSN 0019-8501. https://doi.org/10.1016/j.indmarman.2021.02.009
11. Coscia, M., Rossetti, G., Pennacchioli, D., Giannotti, F.: You know because i know: a multi dimensional network approach to human resources problem. In: ACM International Conference on Advances in Social Networks Analysis and Mining, pp. 434–441 (2013)

12. Dias, A.S.M.E., Abreu, A., Navas, H.V.G., Santos, R.: Proposal of a holistic framework to support sustainability of new product innovation processes. Sustainability **12**, 3450 (2020). https://doi.org/10.3390/su12083450
13. Santos, R., Abreu, A., Dias, A., Calado, J.M.F., Anes, V., Soares, J.: A framework for risk assessment in collaborative networks to promote sustainable systems in innovation ecosystems. Sustainability **12**, 6218 (2020). https://doi.org/10.3390/su12156218
14. Uren, V., Miller, T., Da Campo, R., Dadzie, A.-S.: A model for partner selection criteria in energy from waste projects. J. Cleaner Prod. 279, 123582 (2021). ISSN 0959-6526. https://doi.org/10.1016/j.jclepro.2020.123582
15. Abreu, A., Santos, R., Calado, M.F., Requeijo, J.: A fuzzy logic model to enhance quality management on R&D units. KnE Eng. **5**(6), 285–298 (2020). https://doi.org/10.18502/keg.v5i6.7047

# Product-Service Systems Delivered by SMEs During Building Use Stage: Sustainability Criteria Framework

Davide Gamba[1](✉) and Elena Malakhatka[2]

[1] Department of Management, Information and Production Engineering, University of Bergamo, Bergamo, Italy
davide.gamba@unibg.it

[2] KTH Royal Institute of Technology, Stockholm, Sweden
elenama@kth.se

**Abstract.** The building use stage offers the opportunity to provide valuable and sustainable product-service systems (PSS) that enhance the buildings' value for the end-users. Many of them are delivered by networks of stakeholders that actively involve small and medium enterprises (SMEs). We have combined an existing literature review with the multiple stakeholders' feedback to identify several problems and define the main hypothesis: diverse and presented in a structural way information about PSS can contribute to a better understanding of the added value by multiple stakeholders. We have co-created a list of criteria, which were formed into the sustainability multi-criteria framework. The proposed framework also supplements PSS-specific criteria, such as PSS type, PSS collaborative partnership networks type, and PSS integration type. A list of findings related to the topic was declared to help further develop the study, such as the correlations between PSS-related and PSS sustainability-oriented criteria.

**Keywords:** Product-service system (PSS) · SMEs · Collaborative partnership networks · Sustainability criteria · Building use stage

## 1 Introduction

Achieving sustainable competitive advantage based upon product-service systems (PSS) provision is often claimed to be viable for businesses. There has, however, been little evidence captured on the application of aspects of servitization in general and developing well-functioning integrated solutions within real estate development in particular [1]. Integrated solutions refer to the PSS concept, as they are defined as bundles of physical products, services, and information, seamlessly combined to provide more value than the parts alone, that address customer's needs concerning a specific function or task in their business system [2]. However, PSS seems far to be methodically applied by real-estate industry's firms, especially small and medium enterprises (SMEs). SMEs represent 99% of all non-financial businesses in the EU, providing two-thirds of the total private sector employment [3].


Published by Springer Nature Switzerland AG 2021
L. M. Camarinha-Matos et al. (Eds.): PRO-VE 2021, IFIP AICT 629, pp. 65–77, 2021.
https://doi.org/10.1007/978-3-030-85969-5_6

Literature has primarily concentrated efforts on large companies [4] even though servitization occurs in all types of supply chains, including the ones that involve SMEs. Literature has devoted few efforts about servitized collaborative partnerships that involve SMEs [5, 6], concentrating on the manufacturing industry and neglecting the real estate. This highlights a clear research gap. On the other hand, collaborative partnerships with and between SMEs represent a strategic opportunity even for buildings owners that can enhance the value of their assets during the operating use phase. In fact, recent research [7] involving 340 international companies shows that partnerships with SMEs are expected to impact their total revenues by up to 19% in the three years following the start of the collaboration. While there are numerous collaborative partnerships and alliances in the real estate sector between established players, many industry experts highlight a need to include SMEs in their business ecosystems.

In this paper, we primarily focus on the use stage of the building – which is also named as operation stage in many professional literatures – emphasizing on end-users related PSS. Grounded on all the above, we concluded that the topic of PSS delivered by SMEs through collaborative partnership to the building use stage is relevant and requires profound and comprehensive research. This study is the first step towards understanding this complex and interdisciplinary field developing a framework that attempts to bridge through a sustainable perspective SMEs' PSS collaborative partnerships networks implemented to deliver value to stakeholders with the real one perceived from the latter. We identified gaps from the overlap of literatures about real estate and building use stage, PSS business model innovation, and role of SMEs in the business ecosystem. Hence, based on the available general knowledge about PSS and qualitative data from the interviews with actors representing building industry, SMEs, and end customers, we developed the main hypothesis: more structured and diverse information about PSS can help to assess its potential and contribute to the more sustainable implementation of PSS delivered by SMEs for the building use stage. Built on the multi-actors' feedbacks, we have created a list of criteria, which were identified as necessary to a better understanding of the added value of the PSS. These criteria were compared and supplemented by the criteria already existing in academic practice and formed into the sustainability multi-criteria framework. The proposed framework also supplements PSS-specific criteria, such as PSS type, PSS partnership type and PSS integration type. This study is explorative and has some limitations, which are listed in the final part.

## 2 Research Methodology

This research's design follows the schema traced in Fig. 1. The first stage is the observation phase: the research object is interpreted, while gaps and research questions are detected. In addition, we have added the experts' feedback to align the process with market knowledge. We identified the problem during the second phase, based on the existing literature review and experts' feedback collected. Last, the third phase – namely theory building and tool development – was carried out to create a tool for evaluating added value of PSS from the point of three dimensions of sustainability and general PSS characteristics.

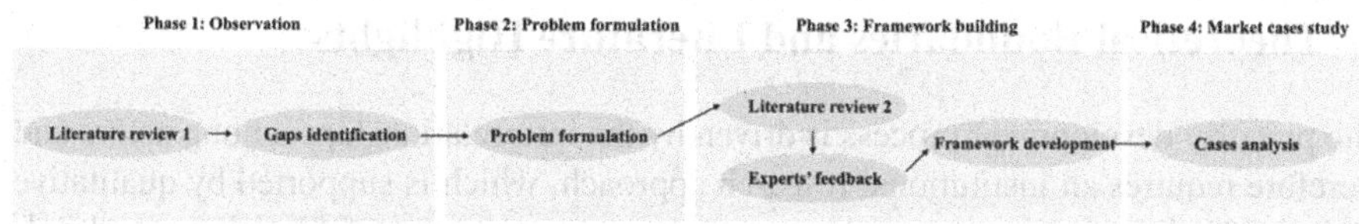


**Fig. 1.** Research design and methodology.

The experts' feedback is based on a mixed-method approach [8], that combines semi-structured expert interviews and quantitative survey. We interviewed KTH Live-in-Lab's 12 key actors in in real estate innovation arena from Sweden, Germany, and France[1]. The key issues in the interviews were an evaluation of general relationship with PSS business model and different sustainability dimensions. Their potential and actual courses of action and strategies towards using more PSS. We analysed the interviews by applying a category system derived from network theory and frame analysis [21] to identify the members of the network and their respective priorities for use of PSS in the buildings. The list of experts and their roles are presented in Table 1.

**Table 1.** Participants of the feedback sessions.

| Actor category | Role | Background |
|---|---|---|
| *Property related* | Director | Large Scandinavian property development firm |
| | Property manager | Large Scandinavian property development firm |
| | Chief of Innovation | Large Scandinavian property development firm |
| | Facility manager | Building IT firm |
| | Main architect | Large European architecture bureau |
| | Project manager | Large European architecture bureau |
| | Head of Smart Home | Furniture producer |
| | Innovation manager | Home appliances firm |
| *SME* | CEO | Last meter services |
| | CTO | Smart water metering |
| | Founder | Home energy management |
| | IT Chief | Smart thermostats |
| *End-user* | Tenant at student apartment | Age group 20–25 |
| | Tenant of newly built property | Age group 35–50 |
| | Tenant of retrofit | Age group 55+ |

[1] See www.liveinlab.kth.se.

## 3 Theoretical Boundaries and Literature Highlights

The property development process is driven by the interrelationships among actors and therefore requires an institutional research approach, which is supported by qualitative analysis [9]. A further institutional approach know as structures of provision was developed by [10–12], suggesting that the production and consumption (i.e., provision) of buildings is a physical and social process guided by economic interests [13].

In this study our focus will be on the building use stage (i.e., provision), as we see that this stage is the least regulated and most dynamic in terms of innovation and relevance from several points of view. First, during the use of the building, we directly deal with the use of different kinds of resources, which creates an opportunity to influence various consumers' choices and create a prerequisite for changing the building use in a more environmentally sustainable manner. Secondly, during the building use stage, we touch on the topic of everyday life of the end-users and their wellbeing and health, which can bring us the opportunity to increase overall social sustainability and can contribute to the more sustainable future of the whole society. Thirdly, the use stage of the building has the highest potential for implementing smart home solutions, more of which are PSS. The latter indicates *"marketable systems of products and services capable of fulfilling a user's demand"* [14] and a strong relationship with users enhances the market competitiveness of a company. Smart home scenarios [15] suggests that service elements are important for fulfilling user needs and offering values. As developing the high technology for smart home providing various services are realized through partnership, synergies among stakeholders from diverse areas are required. In this context, PSS development methodology can encourage cooperation among various stakeholders. Constructing multi-dimensional collaborative partnership allows stakeholders to take advantage of professional knowledge, advanced technology and high-quality products or services of other companies and lower system costs at the same time [16]. PSS development tools or methods to analyze stakeholders' needs and to help their communication and involvement can contribute to PSS development involving a variety of stakeholders.

It is a matter of fact that transition towards smarter home and more PSS applications requires not only new design methodologies of the buildings and products that support our everyday life, but also need to redesign business models towards through circular and pro-environmental approaches. That is why the next theoretical pillar in PSS is a new approach for an environmentally oriented business model.

This study is interdisciplinary and lies at the junction of three different fields (Fig. 2): real estate (building use stage), business model innovation (PSS model), and business ecosystem (collaborative partnership networks with and between SMEs). At the initial stage of the study, it is important to prioritize which sub-divisions in the selected areas may have practical knowledge. Based on the initial research of these fields, we decided to create some theoretical boundaries within each major field. Considering the overall complexity of the context (i.e., real estate business), we need to expand the business ecosystem and bring new players into the game. SMEs demonstrated the ability to quickly respond to different challenges and deliver value to the end-users through collaborative networks, which makes us focus on them in this study. We will delve deeper into each of these areas in the next chapter.

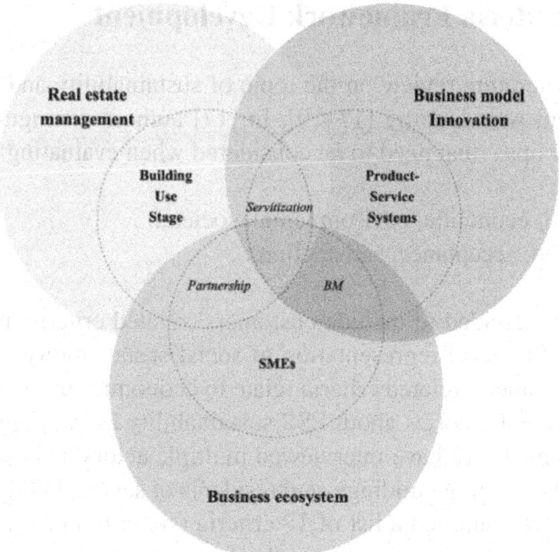


**Fig. 2.** Research's theoretical boundaries.

# 4 Problem Formulation

Based on theoretical gaps highlighted in the previous chapter from the literature review and the first experts' feedback sessions, Table 2 identified a few systematic problems related to the PSS delivery to the end-user of the building by SMEs and the related domain.

**Table 2.** Identified problem summary by multiple actors.

| Identified problems | Problem domain | Problem owner |
|---|---|---|
| Lack of PSS integration mechanisms for SMEs | ICT Infrastructure | Property owner, SME |
| Lack of understanding of PSS delivery mechanism | Tool and methods | Property owner, SME |
| Lack of understanding of PSS added value | Knowledge | Property owner, SME, end-user |

All three problems are significant and deserve to be researched, but due to the specific focus on the end-user perspective, we will focus on the third one (i.e., lack of understanding of general PSS added value). Following the problem formulation, we have designed a working research question for this explorative study: *Which criteria explain PSS added value in the best possible way to each actor?*

In addition, we have added two sub questions:

*SRQ1: Which information about PSS would be relevant for each actor?*

*SRQ2: Which sustainability-oriented criteria could be relevant for each actor?*

## 5 PSS Multi-criteria Framework Development

A comprehensive literature review on the topic of sustainability and value assessment in PSS development was done by [17–19]. In [17] authors distinguish five aspects – clustered in two groups – that need to be considered when evaluating a PSS:

- Provider oriented: economic, environmental, societal.
- Customer oriented: acceptance, satisfaction.

In this study, we decided to include customers' related criteria into social sustainability as an individual level representation of social sustainability, even if we clearly understand that customers' related criteria relate to economic sustainability as well.

To align the general theories about PSS sustainability assessment with the context of the built environment, we have interviewed multiple actors: building owners, SMEs delivering PSS to the existing buildings, and residents of several buildings. Based on the literature analysis, we compiled a list of 18 criteria (six criteria for each sustainability dimension). Then, we provided this list in the form of a survey (google form) to our experts to prioritize the criteria. Different actors gave preference to different criteria according to their needs. Table 3 shows a generalized summary of criteria from different actors' perspectives and correlation of each criteria with sustainability dimension is shown.

**Table 3.** PSS sustainability criteria identified by multiple actors.

| Actor | Prioritized criteria | Sustainability dimensions |
|---|---|---|
| Property owner | Cost optimisation<br>Resource consumption<br>Innovation | Economic<br>Environmental<br>Economic |
| SME | Market size<br>ROI<br>Customer satisfaction | Economic<br>Economic<br>Societal (individual level) |
| End-user | Price category<br>Overall experience<br>Environmental impact | Economic<br>Societal (individual level)<br>Environmental |

Based on this knowledge, we have created an overall PSS sustainability multi-criteria framework, which can help to pre-evaluate different PSS cases and understand how well they are addressing their added values from different sustainability perspectives.

Environmental dimension of sustainability is represented by resource efficiency criteria, eco materials criteria and circularity criteria. Economical sustainability is represented by market size criteria, cost optimisation criteria and ROI criteria. Social sustainability is represented by social wellbeing (societal level), needs fulfilment and overall experience (individual level). Due to the nature of the overall assessment and multivariate data for each criterion we have decided to use a radar chart as a method for comprehensive evaluation.

Because this exploratory study is addressed to the early decision-making stage, we propose to carry out an assessment using a scale-based assessment method using three main categories: low, medium, and high scores. Thus, we have a simplified system for evaluating each criterion without having a large number of different types of data. Of course, this approach is generalized and requires a subsequent more detailed qualitative assessment as the next step. But at this stage, this approach is sufficient to have grounds for further, more in-depth study of both the criteria themselves and the reasons why specific criteria have a particular value.

**Table 4.** PSS sustainability multi criteria assessment guidance.

| Score | Economic | | | Social | | | Environmental | | |
|---|---|---|---|---|---|---|---|---|---|
| | *Market size (EUR)* | *Cost optimisation* | *ROI* | *Overall experience* | *Needs Fulfilment* | *Societal Wellbeing* | *Resources Efficiency* | *Eco materials* | *Circularity* |
| Low: 1-2 | < 100 000 | Not part of value prop. | < 5 | Mostly negative feedbacks | - | Not part of value prop. | Not part of value prop. | Not part of value prop. | Not part of value prop. |
| Medium: 3-5 | 100 000 - 1000 000 | Indirect value prop. | 5-10 | Slightly more positive feedbacks | - | Indirect value prop. | Indirect value prop. | Indirect value prop. | Indirect value prop. |
| High: 6-8 | > 1000 000 | Direct value prop. | > 10 | Mostly positive feedbacks | - | Direct value prop. | Direct value prop. | Direct value prop. | Direct value prop. |

## 6 Market Cases Analysis

To apply newly generated knowledge into practice, we decided to select several market cases and analyse them from the point of the proposed framework (Table 5). Due to the scope of this paper, the analysis was made empirically. The main selection criteria of SMEs for this case study were:

- representing different types of PSS.
- end-user oriented (B2C or B2B2C).
- EU based.

Data were collected from secondary sources.

**Table 5.** Market SMEs' PSS cases from building use stage (B2C/B2B2C).

| Name | Brief description | Product component | Service component |
|---|---|---|---|
| Sangalli (Italy) | Sangalli Technologies focuses on project consultancy, technical assistance and maintenance for sound systems, video, lighting and digital signage | Sound systems, video, lighting and digital signage | Project consultancy, technical assistance, and maintenance |
| Standard Access (Ireland) | Standard Access focuses on building's access management through Sonic Handshake, a technology that allows to eliminate keys and cost associated with locks changing | Smart access system (e.g., door lock) | Digital platform for access systems remote set-up and management |
| Olimpia Splendid (Italy) | Olimpia Splendid is an Italian company that designs, produces and sells products for building air conditioning, heating, air treatment | Air conditioning system | Product total care business model |
| FM Mattsson (Sweden) | FM Mattsson is a Swedish IoT-based water mixer that facilitates the operation of water in the public and private environments | Water tap, integrated smart water sensors | Water management app |
| Tado° (Germany) | Tado° is a technology company and manufacturer of home thermostats and air conditioning controls. Besides reducing energy consumption and increasing savings the thermostat also considers the residents' overall comfort | Smart thermostat, Tado internet bridge | Tado app |

(*continued*)

**Table 5.** (*continued*)

| Name | Brief description | Product component | Service component |
|---|---|---|---|
| Tibber (Sweden) | Tibber is a digital platform, which buys the cheapest available electricity per hour and also doing hourly analytics of electricity consumption on the individual level (via plugged-in smart products) | Diverse smart home devices ecosystem (partnership) | Tibber electricity management app |

# 7 Results and Discussion

## 7.1 PSS Related Criteria

Selected market cases were associated with value constellations (i.e., collaborative partnership network) identified by [5], namely the configuration of firm's direct network relationships into distinct, specific, and integrated structures to create value. In addition, the taxonomy used [20] to cluster PSS allow to classify them among product oriented (PO) PSS, use oriented (UO) PSS, and result oriented (RO) PSS. PO PSS highlights vertical integration partnerships, while UO vertical ones. On the other hand, RO PSS mixes both horizontal and vertical integration types. Results from empirical cases analysis is shown in Table 6.

**Table 6.** PSS related criteria summary.

| Name | PSS type | Partnership type | Service component |
|---|---|---|---|
| Sangalli | Product-oriented (PO) | System integration | Vertical |
| Standard Access | Use-oriented (UO) | Specialist externality | Horizontal |
| Olimpia Splendid | Result-oriented (RO) | Dual customer contact partnership | Horizontal and vertical |
| FM Mattsson | Product-oriented (PO) | Competence co-location | Vertical |
| Tado° | Use-oriented (UO) | Specialist externality | Horizontal |
| Tibber | Result-oriented (RO) | System integration | Vertical |

The partnership network for each PSS case is presented on the Fig. 3. Based on summary result presented in Table 6, we can find the following correlations. Product-oriented PSS show mostly vertical integration of service components among involved actors, rather than use-oriented and result-oriented ones. The latter are characterized by horizontal integration forms, which explain a smaller number of partners but with more robust relationships. From the other side, the vertical integration opens opportunity for many partners to join the collaboration network in an open and easy way. One of the cases selected (i.e., Tibber) in a outlier due to its deservitization approach [22].

The next logical step is to analyse each case in a more profonde way by applying PSS sustainability multi criteria assessment framework proposed in Sect. 5. It is important to analyse each case from different dimensions to reach an objective vision of each case performance. That is why we propose to examine each case from three sustainability dimensions: economic, social, and environmental.

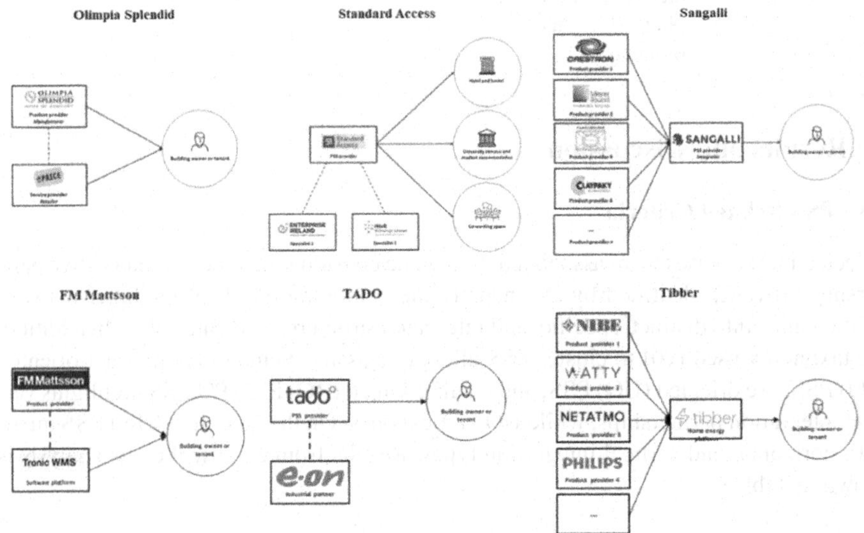


**Fig. 3.** Collaborative partnership network of each of six cases: Olimpia Splendid, Standard Access, Sangalli, FM Mattsson, TADO, and Tibber.

## 8 PSS Sustainability Related Criteria

Based on the available data about each of six cases the proposed in Sect. 5 PSS sustainability multi criteria assessment was organized. The results of the analysis are presented in the form of radar charts, which are a useful way to display multivariate observations with an arbitrary number of variables (Fig. 4). For this stage of the study, we just assume that all criteria will be considered equally important to reflect the general view of each case study. We clearly understand that the proposed list of PSS sustainability multi-criteria is just a first attempt to create an objective framework and have a lot of limitations and assumptions, which will be discussed in the discussion part of this report.

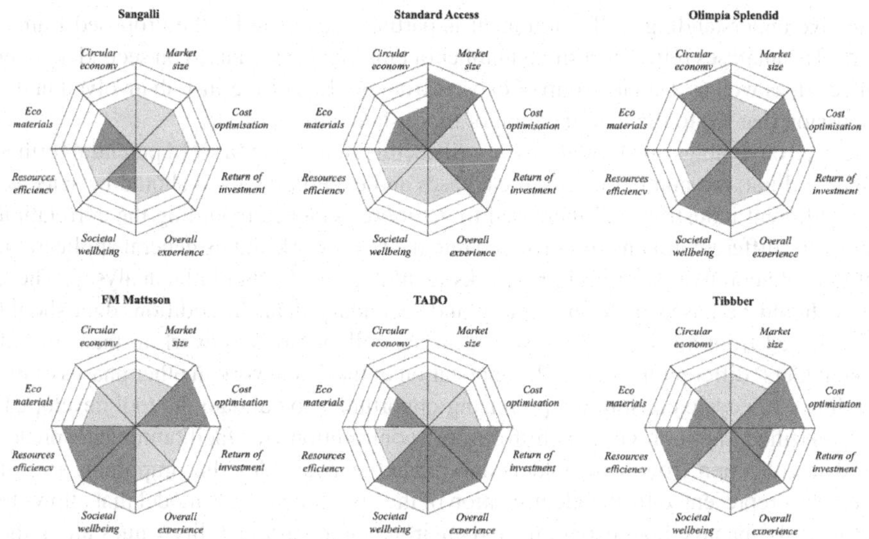


**Fig. 4.** PSS sustainability related criteria summary for each market cases.

## 9 Conclusions

In this section, we summarise findings, limitations, and further research opportunities of this study highlighting the role of SMEs' collaborative partnership networks.

This study explores the role of SMEs network for PSS delivery in the real estate industry's operations stage, which it has never been used to describe servitized SMEs in literature to the best of our knowledge. We have developed a framework that attempts to bridge through a sustainable perspective SMEs' PSS collaborative partnerships networks implemented to deliver value to stakeholders with the real one perceived from the latter. This framework represents a tool for practitioners – both managers and entrepreneurs from SMEs – that aims to properly design and understand the added value transfer to end-users. Despite multi-actors have different priorities, KTH Live-in-Lab's expert discussions and empirical cases preliminary analysis suggests correlations between PSS related criteria and sustainability-oriented criteria. For instance, selected use-oriented PSS cases are delivered through a specialist externalities collaborative partnership network, which highlights the return on investment as a critical dimension for stakeholders. Again, selected result-oriented PSS cases show that cost optimization dimension is an important value perceived by stakeholders, arising from the fact that economic sustainability is more prior for PSS SMEs then environmental sustainability, which can make us conclude that it is not an easy task to balance a high performance of both.

This paper is not exhaustive, and it presents a set of limitations. Due to the uniqueness of the field, the findings already mentioned cannot be fully generalized. In addition, the framework is based on authors' personal choices about both PSS related and sustainability criteria. In fact, literature has defined different classifications for PSS, SMEs' collaborative networks, and sustainability criteria. This means that the proposed framework represents just a point of view over added values perceived by stakeholders: an objective understanding of the argument is partially achieved by the proposed framework. The analyses relied on a small number of empirical cases based on secondary data collected, as well as a small group of experts from the KTH Live-in-Lab involved in the discussion that led to the identification of the sustainability criteria.

Based on findings and limitations described, this study opens a set of potential further research. First, the number of empirical cases and experts involved should be selected from different industries and increased to get more evidence regarding the correlation among the different dimensions involved into the framework and its general application. All the collaborative partnership networks identified by [5] should be analysed. Then, cases should be based both on primary and secondary data. In addition, data should be collected from all the actors involved in the collaborative network to take care of stakeholders' different interests. The application of the framework in other phases of the building's life cycle constitute a promising opportunity to validate the tool developed. Once certified, the tool will benefit from ICT contributions for facilitating and spreading data collection from stakeholders and related analysis. Another important area of research is represented by the identification of the optimal business model that allows to successfully manage both economic and environmental sustainability values along the collaborative network. In this direction, a deeper understanding of SMEs' unique sees and network mechanisms is needed.

## References


1. Zighan, S., Bamford, D.: Sustainable competitive advantage through servitization: an investigation into servitization strategy in the real estate development sector. In: 22nd EurOMA Conference (2015)
2. Brax, S.A., Jonsson, K.: Developing integrated solution offerings for remote diagnostics: a comparative case study of two manufacturers. Int. J. Oper. Prod. Manage. **29**, 539–560 (2009)
3. European Commission – EASME: Annual Report on European SMEs (2019)
4. Adrodegari, F., Saccani, N., Kowalkowski, C., Vilo, J.: PSS business model conceptualization and application. Prod. Planning Control **28**, 1251–1263 (2017)
5. Kowalkowski, C., Witell, L., Gustafsson, A.: Any way goes: identifying value constellations for service infusion in SMEs. Ind. Market. Manage. **42**, 18–30 (2013)
6. Lelah, A., Mathieux, F., Brissaud, D., Vincent, L.: Collaborative network with SMEs providing a backbone for urban PSS: a model and initial sustainability analysis. Prod. Planning Control **23**, 299–314 (2012)
7. McHale, J.: StartUps and their Impact on Smart Buildings 2021. Memoori Research AB (2021)
8. Hollstein, B.: Mixed methods social networks research: an introduction. In: Mixed Methods Social Networks Research: Design and Applications, vol. 1 (2014)
9. Adams, D., Dunse, N., White, M.: Conceptualising state-market relations in land and property: the growth of institutionalism. In: Planning, Public Policy and Property Markets (2005)
10. Ball, M.: Housing Policy and Economic Power: The Political Economy of Owner-Occupation. Methuen, London (1983)
11. Ball, M.: Coming to terms with owner-occupation. Capital Class **16**, 15–44 (1985)
12. Ball, M.: Housing analysis: time for a theoretical refocus. Hous. Stud. **1**, 147–166 (1986)
13. Gore, T., Nicholson, D.: Models of the land-development process: a critical review. Environ. Planning **23**, 703–730 (1991)

14. Brezet, J.C., Bijma, A.S., Ehrenfeld, J., Silvester, S.: The design of eco-efficient services. In: Methods, Tools and Review of the Case Study Based "Designing Eco-Efficient Services" Project (2001)
15. Kim, S., Baek, J.S.: Diagnosis of current smart home appliance development process for application of PSS design methodology. In: DS 77: Proceedings of the DESIGN 2014 13th International Design Conference (2014)
16. Tukker, A., Tischner, U.: Product-services as a research field: past, present, and future. Reflections from a decade of research. J. Clean. Prod. **14**, 1552–1556 (2006)
17. Nakada, T., Sholihah, M.A., Mitake, Y., Shimomura, Y.: Toward the development of a comprehensive product-service system (PSS) evaluation method. Procedia CIRP **93**, 802–807 (2020)
18. Bertoni, M.: Multi-criteria decision making for sustainability and value assessment in early PSS design. Sustainability **11**, 1952 (2019)
19. Sundin, E., Nässlander, E., Lelah, A.: Sustainability Indicators for small and medium-sized enterprises (SMEs) in the transition to provide product-service systems (PSS). Procedia CIRP **30**, 149–154 (2015)
20. Baines, T., Ziaee Bigdeli, A., Bustinza, O.F., Shi, V.G., Baldwin, J., Ridgway, K.: Servitization: revisiting the state-of-the-art and research priorities. Int. J. Oper. Prod. Manage. **37**, 256–278 (2017)
21. Borgatti, S.P., Halgin D.S.: On network theory. Organ. Sci. **22**, 1168–1181 (2011)
22. Kowalkowski, C., Gebauer, H., Kamp, B., Parry, G.: Servitization and deservitization: overview, concepts, and definitions. Ind. Market. Manage. **60**, 4–10 (2017)

# Analysis and Assessment of Business Ecosystems

# Exploring Performance Assessment Scenarios in Collaborative Business Ecosystems

Paula Graça[1,2](✉) and Luís M. Camarinha-Matos[1](✉)

[1] Faculty of Sciences and Technology and Uninova CTS, NOVA University of Lisbon, Campus de Caparica, 2829-516 Caparica, Portugal
paula.graca@isel.pt, cam@uninova.pt

[2] Instituto Superior de Engenharia de Lisboa, Instituto Politécnico de Lisboa, Rua Conselheiro Emídio Navarro 1, 1959-007 Lisbon, Portugal

**Abstract.** Sustainability of collaboration in a business ecosystem is a significant concern for organizations to survive in an increasingly competitive marketplace. This study addresses this concern contributing with a performance assessment and influence mechanism to measure the performance and induce more sustainable collaboration behaviours in a Collaborative Business Ecosystem. The level of collaboration can be measured if the ecosystem's manager adopts appropriate performance indicators that, at the same time, can help influencing the behaviour of the organisations as they try to improve their position according to the assessment metrics. A simulation model is designed to evaluate the proposed approach, and a simulation scenario discussed, showing some of the achieved results.

**Keywords:** Collaborative networks · Business ecosystem · Performance indicators · Sustainable collaboration · Simulation

## 1 Introduction

The possibilities offered by new information and communication technologies are changing business strategies and innovation capabilities [1]. With increasing competition in the market and the acute need for sustainability, it is crucial for organisations to build long-term relationships with their "*supply-chain*" and other partners through sustainable collaboration [2]. Participation in collaborative processes brings benefits to the involved entities, including the opportunity of "survival capability" in the occurrence of market turbulence and the possibility of better achieving common goals [3]. However, an important challenge is to keep members of the collaborative network engaged, thus ensuring the sustainability of collaboration in the long-term. This study addresses these concerns for Collaborative Business Ecosystems (CBEs), under the assumption that the performance indicators adopted to assess the ecosystem can have an influence on the behaviour of its members and thus affect collaboration sustainability. As such, we present some foundations and propose a set of performance indicators to assess collaboration performance. Furthermore, a model of the influence of these performance indicators in the behaviour


Published by Springer Nature Switzerland AG 2021
L. M. Camarinha-Matos et al. (Eds.): PRO-VE 2021, IFIP AICT 629, pp. 81–91, 2021.
https://doi.org/10.1007/978-3-030-85969-5_7

of the CBE's organisations and the evolution of behaviour towards better performance is described, thus contributing to the sustainability of the ecosystem.

The remaining sections of this paper are organised as follows: section two identifies the benefits of collaboration, highlighting the most important ones for a CBE and presenting the considered research questions; section three briefly explains the structure of a CBE, the profile of organisations, the performance assessment to evaluate the level and status of collaboration and the influence mechanism; section four presents the performance assessment and adjustment model and discusses an example of a simulation scenario; the last section concludes the work, identifying limitations of the study, and ongoing and future work.

## 2 Collaboration Benefits in a CBE

It is widely accepted that collaboration brings benefits to the involved players, allowing divergent thinking to develop new understandings, which can facilitate the design of new products and services [4], and reduce or remove conflicts [5].

Moreover, multi-stakeholder collaboration optimises financial and human capital, provides organisations with valuable information, access to markets and knowledge, induces creativity due to the diversity of players' backgrounds, helps prevent confrontation, and shortens the time to achieve objectives [6]. Most literature on collaborative networks offers long lists of potential benefits of collaboration. For instance, works on benefits analysis [7] and value systems for sustainable collaboration [3] have highlighted several collaboration advantages: share and reduce costs, share risks, reduce the level of dependence on third parties, increase innovation capacity, defend a position in the market, increase flexibility, increase agility, increase specialisation, establish proper regulations and share social responsibility.

Inspired by Moore's [8] business ecosystem and by Camarinha-Matos and Afsarmanesh's collaborative networks developments [9, 10], the concept of Collaborative Business Ecosystem was introduced in [11], representing a kind of long-term strategic collaborative network that aims to help its members to be prepared to rapidly engage in collaborative business opportunities.

Despite the identified and often mentioned collaboration benefits for collaborative networks in general and CBEs in particular, there is not much concrete work on collaboration assessment and adequate performance indicators to assess these benefits. Therefore, after the literature review, the motivation for the present work is led by the research questions and hypotheses shown in Fig. 1.

## 3 Performance Indicators for a CBE and Influence Mechanism

As mentioned, a CBE is a business environment of organisations that collaborate, creating relationships. This CBE structure can be modelled as a network of weighted interconnected nodes, whose links refer to the number of collaboration opportunities that the organisations exchange when responding to market opportunities.

According to [12], network structures are described as social capital, for which, in line with the inter-organisational view of [13], ties' weight can mean, for instance, trust

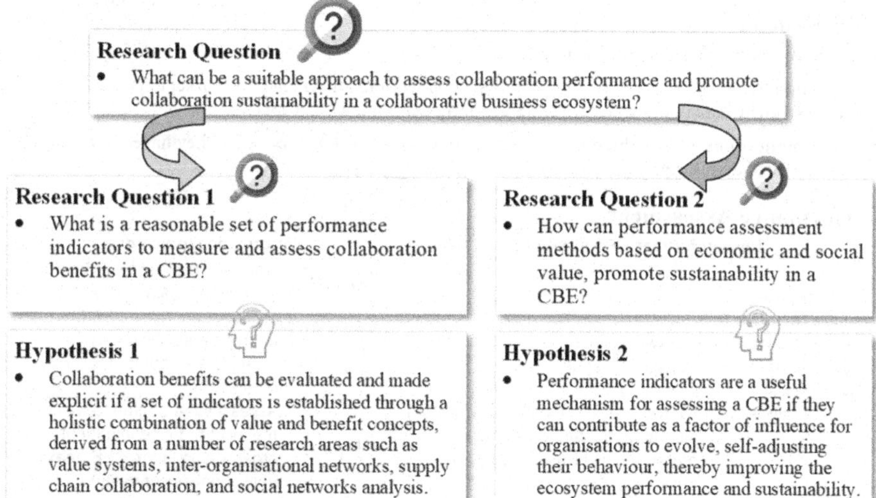


**Fig. 1.** Research questions and hypotheses to assess and influence a CBE expecting to improve its performance and collaboration sustainability.

and power, and nodes' centrality and network status are associated with their performance. The strength of a tie may also be determined by the frequency of interactions among organisations [14]. According to an inter-organisational network perspective, more measurement efforts can be found in [15] and in complex networks [16]. Taking into account such foundations and inspired by measures and indicators coming from the areas of Social Networks Analysis (SNA) [17, 18] and Collaborative Networks (CNs) [7, 19, 20], we propose a set of performance indicators tailored for CBEs as briefly summarized in Fig. 2.

The choice of the performance indicators is mainly related to the network structure, to assess the benefits that collaboration can bring to the individual organisations and the CBE as a whole.

Considering the measurements at the level of organisations:

- **Contribution Indicator** ($CI_i$)**:** The number of collaboration links between organisations, taking into account the links' strength, gives a measure of the value created by the organisations, considering as benefits, increased access to markets and knowledge, increased creativity and capacity for innovation, increased flexibility, agility and specialisation, optimised financial and human capital, shared social responsibility, reduction of conflicts, and shorter time to achieve objectives [3–7, 13]. This indicator is calculated by the weighted degree centrality;
- **Prestige Indicator** ($PI_i$)**:** The topology of the collaboration links, taking into account the links' strength, shows the most prominent/influential organisations signifying power, performance and ability to generate social capital [13]. This indicator is calculated by the weighted betweenness centrality;

**CBE Structure**

- A **network** of organisations (the **nodes**)
- The **nodes** are connected by relationships (the **connections**) that mean the market opportunities they share by collaborating, called collaboration opportunities (CoOps)
- The **connections** are **weighted** by the number of CoOps (#CoOps) in which they have participated during a period

**Performance Assessment**

| Research Areas / Foundations | | Performance Indicators | |
|---|---|---|---|
| - Clarify how to measure centrality considering a node or the network as a whole in Social Network Analysis (SNA) [17] | - **Network** structures are described as social capital [12] | $CI_{CBE}in$ $CI_{CBE}out$ | Assesses the degree to which the most popular/active organisation in the CBE (max degree centrality in/out) exceeds the contribution of the others |
| - Define measures of centrality and clustering in SNA [18] | "Network level" - measures of density, centrality, clusters of connected organisations [15] and complex networks [16] | $PI_{CBE}$ | Assesses the degree to which the most prominent/influent organisation in the CBE (max betweenness centrality) exceeds the contribution of the others |
| | | $II_{CBE}$ | Ratio of innovation of the organisations in the CBE, weighted by the correlation due to collaboration |
| - Identify benefits in Collaborative Networks (CNs) combined with metrics of SNA [7] and propose performance indicators for CNs [19] | - "Ego level" (**node**) - high degree centrality of organisations is positively related to their performance; structural holes and closure generate social capital; and network status explains organisational performance [13] | $CI_i in$ $CI_i out$ | Assesses the contribution of organisation $O_i$ in terms of accepted/created #CoOp (in/out) |
| | | $PI_i$ | Assesses the prominence/influence of organisation $O_i$ in terms of the #CoOp |
| - Propose indicators to measure social capital in CNs inspired by SNA [20] | - "Dyadic level" (**connections**) – strong ties among organisations increase trust and generate future ties; high trust lowers transaction costs and increases benefits; and the most requested partner is the one with the most power [13] | $II_i$ | Ratio of the number of new products/services/patentes of the organisation $O_i$ by the total portfolio |

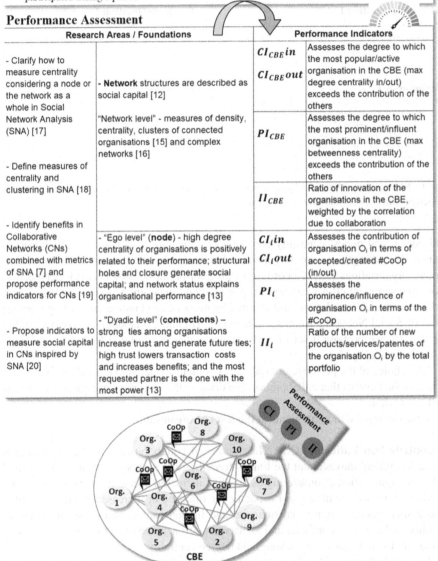

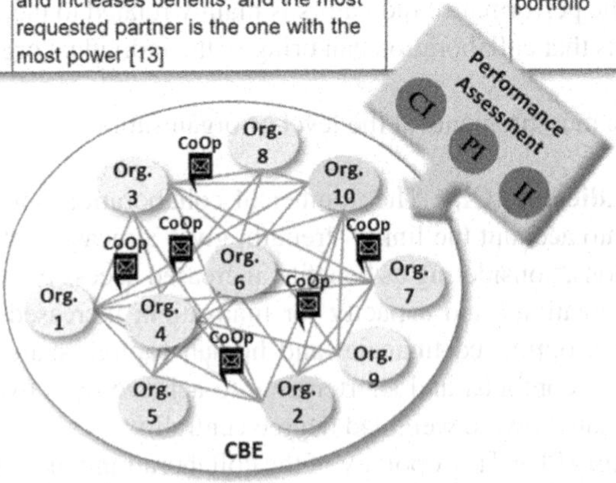

Performance Assessment
CI
PI
II

Org. 8
CoOp
Org. 3
Org. 10
CoOp
CoOp
CoOp
Org. 6
Org. 7
CoOp
Org. 1
Org. 4
CoOp
Org. 9
Org. 5
Org. 2
CBE

**Fig. 2.** Foundations and inspiration for a proposal of performance indicators for CBEs.

- **Innovation Indicator** ($II_i$)**:** The number of collaboration links between organisations that involve innovation when creating products, patents or services, gives a measure of the innovation capacity. This indicator is related to the CI and is calculated by the ratio between the number of new products, patents or services by the organisations' portfolio.

Considering the measurements at the level of the CBE:

- **Contribution Indicator** ($CI_{CBE}$) and **Prestige Indicator** ($PI_{CBE}$)**:** These indicators assess the equilibrium of collaboration in the CBE, measuring to what extent the organisations with the highest $CI_i$ and $PI_i$ are ahead of the others. The goal is to achieve a more uniform collaboration to assure the sustainability of all the organisations in the CBE;
- **Innovation Indicator** ($II_{CBE}$)**:** This indicator assesses the innovation capacity in the CBE by correlating the $II_i$ with collaboration.

It is expected that the proper measurement of collaboration using performance indicators will motivate organisations to evolve towards better performance, thus contributing to the sustainability of the ecosystem. In other words, the choice of indicators and corresponding weights in an assessment framework can strongly influence the evolution of behaviour of the CBE members.

Some authors have studied how inter-organisational relations influence organisational learning and innovation [14]. These relationships form structures capable of influencing organisations' behaviours, including organisational change, by promoting or constraining their access to information, physical, financial, and social resources [14]. However, organisations manifest different collaborative behaviours in response to market opportunities. As such, in Fig. 3, we propose a composition of classes of collaboration willingness to characterize the organisations' behaviours in terms of willingness to invite others to collaborate (*Contact rate*), the readiness to accept invitations (*Accept rate*), and the tendency to accept opportunities related to innovation (*New products rate*).

The ways social networks influence organisations to change, as found in [14], can help understand the influence on the network structure of a CBE. On the other hand, the micro-foundations and micro-dynamics principles discussed in [21] also help understand network evolution dynamics based on the different profiles of organisations.

Based on the assumption that the choice of indicators and corresponding weights can influence the behaviour of CBE members, we propose an influence mechanism through which the CBE manager may vary the weights attributed to each performance indicator Fig. 4 in order to analyze behavioural changes. These weights are associated with the attributes of the classes of collaboration willingness, i.e. the *Contact rate* is related to the *CI*, the *Accept rate* to the *PI* and *New products rate* to the *II*. As such, given a factor of influence ($\%FI$), the improvement in the organisations' profile is calculated by adding the calculated factor plus an exogenous/random positive or negative influence ($\pm F_e$). This factor can be used in the simulation model, for example, to induce collaboration into organisations that do not accept or invite others, or it can be used to decrease collaboration in cases where it deteriorates and fails.

**Organisations Profile**

- The CBE organisations have different profiles categorised into classes of collaboration willingness, which characterize their collaborative behaviour in response to market opportunities

**Classes of Collaboration Willingness**

- **Contact rate:** Willingness to invite others to collaborate
- **Accept rate:** Readiness to accept invitations
- **New products rate:** Tendency to accept opportunities related to innovation

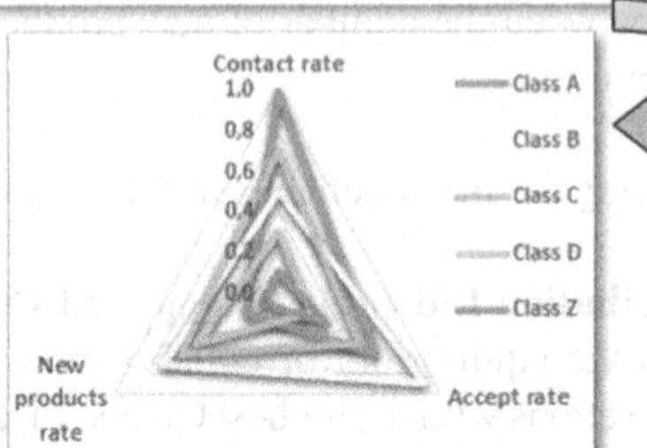


- Identify five ways in which social networks **influence** organisations changes [14]

| The Role of Social Networks in Organisational Change | |
|---|---|
| **Ways of Influence** | **Description** |
| Innovation | An organization in a denser organizational network is likely to have more frequent innovations driving organizational change |
| Imitation | An organization in a denser organizational network is likely to experience change through imitation |
| Inertia | An organization in a denser network is likely to take a longer period of time to implement and complete change |
| Structural equivalence | An organization's actions for change are likely to be influenced by those of a structural equivalent |
| Structural positioning | A more central organization is likely to change more frequently and more successfully |

**Note**. Source: Adapted from Ferreira and Armagan, 2011 [14]

- Identify four primary **micro-foundations** as the fundamental drivers to explain the genesis and **evolution** of networks operating through **micro-dynamics** to form, dissolve or maintain ties [21]

| | | Micro-foundations | | | |
|---|---|---|---|---|---|
| | | **Agency** | **Opportunity** | **Inertia** | **Exogenous** |
| **Micro-dynamics** | Nodal assortativity driven | Homophily, heterophily, prominence attraction | Proximity, common goals, common identity | Habits, networking propensity, collaborative expertise | Network structures may result from exogenous factors or from simple random processes |
| | Tie pattern driven | Brokerage, closure | Transitivity, repetition, referral | Dense clusters, low connectivity | |

**Note**. Source: Adapted from Ahuja et al. 2012 [21]

**Fig. 3.** Organisations profile and foundations to explain the network influence and evolution.

As a result of the influence mechanism applying the formulas of Fig. 4, the *Contact rate*, *Accept rate* and *New products rate* are recalculated, causing organisations to self-adjust their behaviour in the direction of the evaluation criteria, the same way as individuals, thus improving their profile and that of the CBE.

**Influence Mechanism**

- The significance (**weight**) given by the CBE Manager to each **performance indicator**, is expected to influence the behaviour of the organisations
- Organisations react differently according to their classes of collaboration willingness
- The assumption is that, as with individuals, organisations tend to perform according to the way they are evaluated, improving their profile and that of the CBE

| Formulas to calculate the factors of influence | | | | |
|---|---|---|---|---|
| **Classes of Collaboration Willingness** | **Related to** | **P. Ind** | **Wgt** | **Factor of Influence (FI %)** |
| Contact rate | It is related to activity | *CI* | *wCI* | $Contact_{rate} += Contact_{rate} * wCI * \frac{FI}{wCI + wPI + wII} \pm F_e$ |
| Accept rate | It is related to prominence/influence | *PI* | *wPI* | $Accept_{rate} += Accept_{rate} * wPI * \frac{FI}{wCI + wPI + wII} \pm F_e$ |
| New prods rate | It is related to innovation | *II* | *wII* | $New\ prods_{rate} = New\ prods_{rate} * wII * \frac{FI}{wCI + wPI + wII} \pm F_e$ |

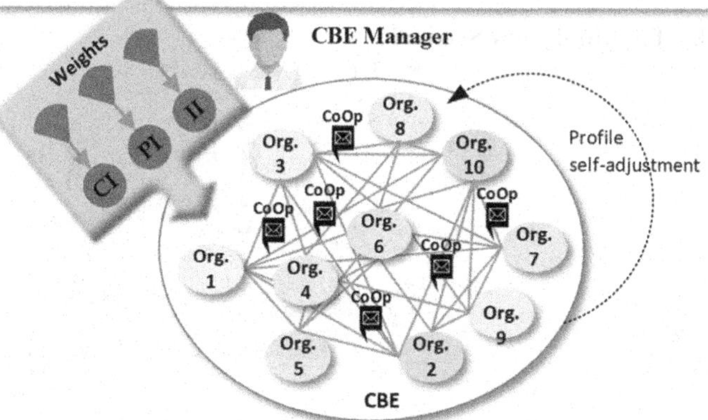


**Fig. 4.** Proposal of an influence mechanism.

# 4 Performance Assessment and Adjustment Model

For the experimental evaluation of the proposed CBE model, we designed a Performance Assessment and Adjustment Model (PAAM) using the AnyLogic tool [22], as summarized in Fig. 5. Due to the lack of historical concrete collaboration data from the organisations, PAAM is used for the establishment of several simulation scenarios representing different cases of CBEs (simulation environment), populated with different organisations of different classes (the agents), sending and receiving collaboration opportunities (the links or ties) to accomplish business opportunities.

This study uses a simulation study parameterised using actual data to achieve more realistic scenarios. These data represent one year of activity of IT industry organisations operating in the same CBE, consisting of the number of human resources, number and duration of market opportunities received, and number and duration of collaboration

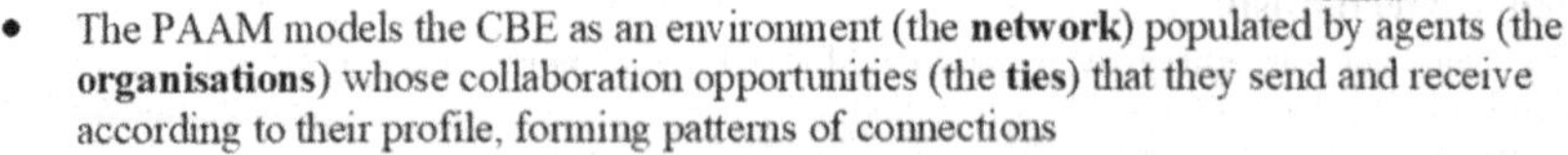

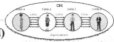

**Performance Assessment and Adjustment Model (PAAM)**

- The PAAM models the CBE as an environment (the **network**) populated by agents (the **organisations**) whose collaboration opportunities (the **ties**) that they send and receive according to their profile, forming patterns of connections

- In order to explore the **network dynamics**, the architecture can be conceptualised in terms of the **nodes** that compose it, the **ties** that connect the nodes, and the patterns that result from those connections [21]

**PAAM Main Parameters**

**Resources**
- Total (persons/day)
- Consulting (% Total)
- R. & D. (% Total)
- Inner Tasks (% Total)

**Market Opps**
- Duration [min..max] (days/person)

**Collaboration Opps**
- Units [min..max] (% Duration)

**Classes of Co. Willingness**
- Contact rate [0..1]
- Accept rate [0..1]
- New products rate [0..1]

**Example of a Simulation Scenario**
- Organisations: Class A – 5; Class B – 5; Class C – 5; Class D – 5

classA_Agents ClassA_Agent [5]
classB_Agents ClassB_Agent [5]
classC_Agents ClassC_Agent [5]
classD_Agents ClassD_Agent [5]
Classes of Collaboration Willingness
CLASS A
CLASS B
CLASS C
CLASS D
CBE Organisations

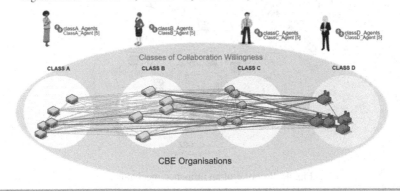

**Fig. 5.** A scenario of simulation using the performance assessment and adjustment model.

opportunities created and accepted. This latter data also makes it possible to establish different classes of collaboration willingness.

Some results of the simulation scenarios are illustrated in Fig. 6 using a graphical view [23]. The figures represent each organisation's performance measures before and after influencing the CBE by the CBE manager, varying the weights attributed to each performance indicator. The achieved measures correspond to the contribution indicator *CI_in* (accepted collaboration opportunities), *CI_out* (collaboration opportunities created by inviting other organisations), and the prestige indicator *PI* (prominence/influence of organisation in the network).

The variation of the indicators' weights increased the value of *wCI* (related to the collaboration activity of the organisations) and decreased the value of *wPI* (related to

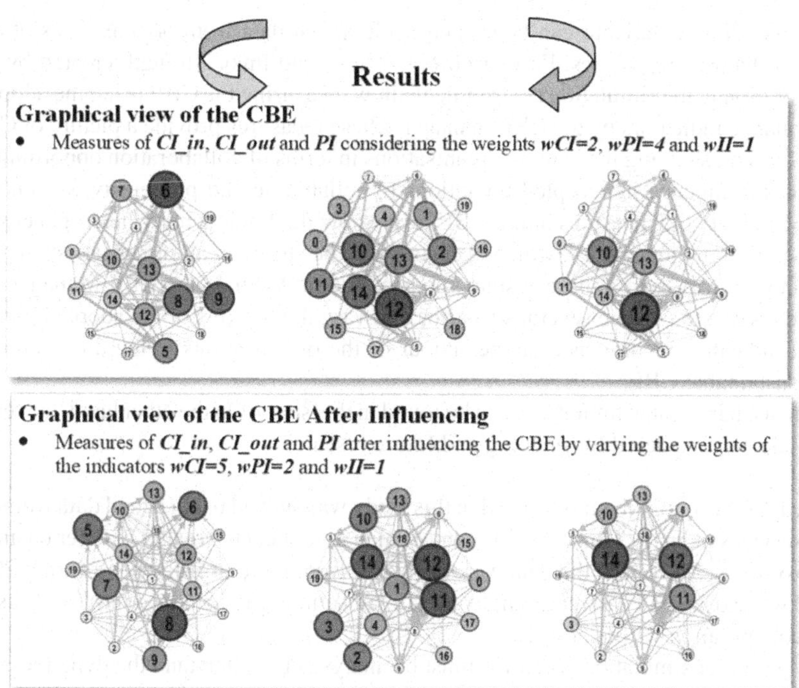


**Fig. 6.** Results of a scenario of simulation presenting the measures *CI_in*, *CI_out* and *PI*, before and after influencing the CBE by varying the weights of the performance indicators.

the prominence/influence of the organisations). As a result, there was a strengthening (although not very marked) in the CI indicators and a relief in the PI.

The results presented in Fig. 6 illustrate a simulation scenario before and after influencing the CBE by varying the weights of the performance indicators. The nodes' size is correlated with the indicators' measures, and the links' strength is correlated with the number of collaboration opportunities exchanged by the organisations.

The results show that the CBEs' managers might have a set of performance indicators and corresponding weights that can help them measure collaboration and adopt those that can lead to more sustainable ecosystems. Varying the weights, CBEs managers can also analyse several simulation scenarios seeking the best configurations towards the desired behaviour.

## 5 Conclusions

Sustainable collaboration in a business ecosystem is a significant concern to survive in an increasingly competitive market context. Given the importance of this objective, this study attempts to provide appropriate performance indicators, contributing not only to measure but also to influence organizations towards more effective collaboration.

Due to the lack of actual collaboration data, a simulation model has to be used for the evaluation of the proposed model. Nevertheless, the model can hold any number of agents whose behaviour can be shaped using actual data from organisations of different collaboration profiles. Furthermore, the links and links' strength created by the collaboration in the simulation environment allow measuring the CBE using the adopted performance indicators by the CBE manager. These measures provide a picture of CBE collaboration, showing the leading organisations in terms of collaboration opportunities created, prominence in accepted invitations to collaborate and propensity for innovation. Moreover, the measures at the CBE level show the homogeneity/heterogeneity of collaboration in the network, which is desirable to be strong in all organisations so that they thus contribute to a more sustainable ecosystem. As such, the CBE Manager can use the PAAM to explore several scenarios and vary the weights of the adopted performance indicators to influence the behaviour of the organisations in the direction of a more sustainable CBE.

On one hand, some limitations can be found in this study. On the other hand, however, a few can be considered for ongoing and future research:

- The PAAM simulation model used in this study was shaped using actual data from the IT services industry. However, this context may not reflect the reality of other business ecosystems. Moreover, the data were collected from three organisations during 2019 and was extrapolated to represent twenty organisations characterised into four classes of collaboration willingness.
- Several other simulation scenarios must be analysed to understand the dynamics of a CBE to improve the influence mechanism towards better collaboration performance and sustainability.
- This study proposes a set of performance indicators for a CBE based on measures of centrality inspired by SNA and measures of innovation correlated with collaboration. For future research, other indicators based on metrics of density and clustering can be considered to assess collaboration sustainability.
- In this study, the CBE model is considered a network of organisations (the nodes) connected by relationships (the ties) that represent collaboration opportunities weighted by the number of times they collaborate. Future research can support different value types (economic, social, and environmental) with different weights.

**Acknowledgements.** This work was funded in part by Fundação para a Ciência e Tecnologia through the program UIDB/00066/2020, and the European Commission (project DiGiFoF).

## References

1. Chen, L., Zhao, X., Tang, O., Price, L., Zhang, S., Zhu, W.: Supply chain collaboration for sustainability: a literature review and future research agenda. Int. J. Prod. Econ. **194**, 73–87 (2017)
2. Govindan, K., Dhingra Darbari, J., Kaul, A., Jha, P.C.: Structural model for analysis of key performance indicators for sustainable manufacturer-supplier collaboration: a grey-decision-making trial and evaluation laboratory-based approach. Bus. Strategy Environ. **30**(4), 1702–1722 (2021)

3. Abreu, A., Camarinha-Matos, L.M.: On the role of value systems to promote the sustainability of collaborative environments. Int. J. Prod. Res. **46**(5), 1207–1229 (2008)
4. Denise, L.: Collaboration Vs. c-three cooperation, coordination, and communication. Innovating **7**(3), 1–6 (1999)
5. Lozano, R.: Collaboration as a pathway for sustainability. Sustain. Dev. **15**(6), 370–381 (2007)
6. Fadeeva, Z.: Promise of sustainability collaboration-potential fulfilled? J. Clean. Prod. **13**(2), 165–174 (2005)
7. Abreu, A., Camarinha-Matos, L.M.: A benefit analysis model for collaborative networks. In: Camarinha-Matos, L.M., Afsarmanesh, H. (eds.) Collaborative networks: Reference modeling, pp. 253–276. Springer US, Boston, MA (2008). https://doi.org/10.1007/978-0-387-79426-6_18
8. Moore, J.F.: Predators and prey: a new ecology of competition. Harv. bus. rev. **71**(3), 75–86 (1993)
9. Camarinha-Matos, L.M., Afsarmanesh, H.: Collaborative networks: a new scientific discipline. J. Intell. Manuf. **16**(4–5), 439–452 (2005)
10. Camarinha-Matos, L.M., Afsarmanesh, H.: On reference models for collaborative networked organizations. Int. J. Prod. Res. **46**(9), 2453–2469 (2008)
11. Graça, P., Camarinha-Matos, L.M.: The need of performance indicators for collaborative business ecosystems. In: Camarinha-Matos, L.M., Baldissera, T.A., Di Orio, G., Marques, F. (eds.) DoCEIS 2015. IAICT, vol. 450, pp. 22–30. Springer, Cham (2015). https://doi.org/10.1007/978-3-319-16766-4_3
12. Burt, R.S.: The network structure of social capital. Res. Organ. Behav. **22**, 345–423 (2000)
13. Zaheer, A., Gözübüyük, R., Milanov, H.: It's the connections: the network perspective in interorganizational research. Acad. Manag. Perspect. **24**(1), 62–77 (2010)
14. Ferreira, M.P., Armagan, S.: Using social networks theory as a complementary perspective to the study of organizational change. BAR-Braz. Adm. Rev. **8**, 168–184 (2011)
15. Provan, K.G., Fish, A., Sydow, J.: Interorganizational networks at the network level: a review of the empirical literature on whole networks. J. Manag. **33**(3), 479–516 (2007)
16. Barabási, A.L., Albert, R.: Emergence of scaling in random networks. Science **286**(5439), 509–512 (1999)
17. Freeman, L.C.: Centrality in social networks conceptual clarification. Soc. Netw. **1**(3), 215–239 (1978)
18. Jackson, M.O.: Social and Economic Networks. Princeton University Press, Princeton (2008)
19. Camarinha-Matos, L.M., Abreu, A.: Performance indicators for collaborative networks based on collaboration benefits. Prod. Plan. control **18**(7), 592–609 (2007)
20. Abreu, A., Camarinha-Matos, L.M.: An approach to measure social capital in collaborative networks. In: Camarinha-Matos, L.M., Pereira-Klen, A., Afsarmanesh, H. (eds.) PRO-VE 2011. IAICT, vol. 362, pp. 29–40. Springer, Heidelberg (2011). https://doi.org/10.1007/978-3-642-23330-2_4
21. Ahuja, G., Soda, G., Zaheer, A.: The genesis and dynamics of organizational networks. Organ. Sci. **23**(2), 434–448 (2012)
22. Borshchev, A.: The big book of simulation modeling: multimethod modeling with anyLogic 6. AnyLogic North America (2013)
23. Bastian, M., Heymann, S., Jacomy, M.: Gephi: An open source software for exploring and manipulating networks. In: Third international AAAI Conference on Weblogs and Social Media (2009)

# Platform-Based Business Ecosystems - A Framework for Description and Analysis

Christoph H. Wecht[1](✉), Mike Demuth[2], and Frank Koppenhagen[3]

[1] New Design University, Mariazeller Strasse 97a, 3100 St. Pölten, Austria
christoph.wecht@ndu.ac.at

[2] University of St. Gallen, Dufourstrasse 50, 9100 St. Gallen, Switzerland
mike.demuth@student.unisg.ch

[3] Hamburg University of Applied Sciences, Berliner Tor 21, 20099 Hamburg, Germany
frank.koppenhagen@haw-hamburg.de

**Abstract.** Value creation is increasingly driven by digital or semi-digital business models. Platforms offer the necessary backbone for such highly profitable business models. Our research centers on the questions how platforms are created, which drivers are behind this development and how platforms are successfully implemented. We analyzed various business ecosystems and their underlying platforms to understand the various roles companies can take in platform-based business ecosystems. Based on our results we propose a framework to describe business ecosystems as well as a canvas to analyze their underlying platforms, the acting companies' roles, and the applied business models. One case study illustrates this tool. Our results will (1) help to understand why companies bet on platforms to establish business ecosystems, (2) analyze the processes and methods behind successful business ecosystems, and (3) reflect about the dominant and still growing importance of platform-based business ecosystems.

**Keywords:** Business ecosystem · Platform · Multi-sided platform · Platform-based business ecosystem · Ecosystem framework · Business model · Innovation · Two-sided market

## 1 Introduction

Value creation is increasingly driven by digital or semi-digital business models utilizing network effects. Namely platforms have received increasing interest from scholars in management research, particularly in general management [e.g. 1, 2], organizational studies [e.g. 3, 4] and innovation management [e.g. 5, 6]. Besides, the topic also became subject to multiple publications of practitioner-oriented periodicals [e.g. 7, 8] underlining the importance of platforms in management practice. However, even though the body on platform literature is growing rapidly many aspects are still in need for better specification. One of these aspects is the understanding how platform business models in combination with an innovation ecosystem work and get innovated [6, 9, 10]. Multi-sided platforms have ecosystems where participants are organized in lose networks [11] and


Published by Springer Nature Switzerland AG 2021
L. M. Camarinha-Matos et al. (Eds.): PRO-VE 2021, IFIP AICT 629, pp. 92–100, 2021.
https://doi.org/10.1007/978-3-030-85969-5_8

innovation from outside a company gets attracted based on technological interfaces and modularization [12]. This innovation activities occur in two different forms, as complementary co-innovation, whereby the focal firm can complement its offering, or in form of an open innovation approach [13]. This is also reflected in their respective business models, which describe interdependent activities of the focal firm and partners [14]. Moreover, the environment of platforms and their ecosystems is usually very volatile due to the fast technological progress and the constant change of market conditions in platform economies [15].

## 2 Platforms, Ecosystems, and Business Models

So far, platform business models have been explained in a mainly economic-driven context of two-sided market platforms [e.g. 16, 17] and in terms of antecedents for a successful platform business model [e.g. 18]. Nevertheless, research did not emphasize how platforms, business ecosystems, and business models are linked. Hence, we address this gap in our research in order to (a) strengthen the promising link between business model and platform research and to (b) gain a better insight how the roles of companies in platform-based ecosystems influence their business models.

In theory, despite a growing number of research especially on multi-sided platforms [e.g. 19, 20, 13], the platform concept still lacks of a deeper theoretical foundation [cf. 6]. By combining the platform literature with the business model (innovation) stream, we deliver new insights on the phenomenon and subsequently contribute to its rootedness in the management literature.

### 2.1 Platforms

Building on the former, mainly engineering driven publications on platforms [e.g. 21], a new platform notion emerged focusing on rather business-driven platform types, which allow agents to connect and exchange in an efficient way and even create completely new markets [e.g. 22, 23]. These platforms are built in a modular fashion with a stable technical core and periphery components, which can be innovated by independent, external developers [1, 6, 12]. Each platform has a platform leader, platform users, and independent innovators. These entities form the platform ecosystem [11, 24].

### 2.2 Business Ecosystems

Ecosystem as a management theory was originally introduced by Moore [25] stating that the key success factor for generating sustainable, competitive advantages is to out-innovate the existing industry competition. Using the analogy of a biological ecosystem, the notion business ecosystem is presented as a collaborative network of companies that co-evolve around innovation [25]. Despite the increasing significance of ecosystems in the business practice, the term has been used with no unanimous definition or sound theoretical backing [26]. For the sake of this analysis Teece's ecosystem definition is used: "Organizations, institutions, and individuals that impact the fate of the focal firm and its customers and suppliers, including complementors, suppliers, regulatory authorities, standard setting bodies, the judiciary, and educational and research institutions" [27]. In a platform ecosystem, the platform leader takes a special role as important governance functions are performed by this company [cf. 28]. Hence, decisions on the technological core and interfaces as well as the platform business model have to be elaborated well.

### 2.3 Business Models

Our research centers on the questions how platforms are linked to business models, which drivers are behind the ecosystem development and how platform-based ecosystems are successfully implemented. The business model literature aims to answer the question how companies create value. Despite the fast growing body of literature, there is still a very vivid debate on the theoretical foundation and the conceptualization of business models [e.g. 14]. Zott, Amit and Massa [29] argue that no theory fully describes the value creation through business models, while different domains of the topic developed independently, resulting in various concepts and definitions. Nevertheless, a basic agreement amongst researches was achieved as the elements value creation, value delivery and value capturing are widely regarded as describing parts of a business model [30, 31]. The business models need to be correspondingly and continuously innovated in order to maintain competitive advantages.

## 3 Platform-Based Ecosystem Framework

We analyzed various business ecosystems and their underlying platforms to understand the underlying business models and differentiate the various roles companies can take in those ecosystems. Platform-based ecosystems are based on the mechanism of network effects [32, 33]. Strong network effects are an important value driver for platforms as they might create "winner-take-all" situations amongst competing platforms [6, 34]. Another stream of research identifies the key strengths of managerial ecosystems as the potential to create synergy caused by complementary relationships. Jacobides, Cennamo and Gawer [35] argue that ecosystems create non-generic complementary relationships both on the production as well as on the consumer side and that there is no need of vertical integration. The emphasis on complementarities of ecosystems leads to this description: "An ecosystem is a set of actors with varying degrees of multilateral, non-generic complementarities that are not fully hierarchically controlled" [35]. Even though the authors still anticipate that an ecosystem consists of one orchestrator and multiple participants, the power and control within an ecosystem is not centralized by the orchestrator. Participants within an ecosystem keep residual control over the services or products they offer to the customers via the ecosystem.

### 3.1 Roles in the Framework

A company that wants to enter ecosystems has several strategic positioning opportunities as described in the following part leading to our proposed framework. Based on our results we propose a framework to describe and analyze business ecosystems, their underlying platforms and the applied business models. The ecosystem in the narrower sense consists of the platform leader, its partner(s), the users/customers, and its complementors. Adding politics/law, technology, competitors and culture leads to the ecosystem in a wider sense (Fig. 1). The core ecosystem is therefore led by the platform leader, the focal firm in the ecosystem, the orchestrating party [cf. 20]. According to Adner [36], the key responsibility of an orchestrator is to determine the value proposition of the ecosystem, to select suitable members and to secure the position among other ecosystems in the future.

A platform leader can be supported by an ecosystem partner, who is responsible for the ecosystem as well. The role of the partner is to support the platform leader, which can be technological support like the provision of the platform, or strategic support such as being the main shareholder. The orchestrator relies on complementors in the ecosystem to deliver their contribution to the strategically defined product or service. Complementors are bound together through an interdependency, e.g. by adhering to certain regulation or governance principles [35].

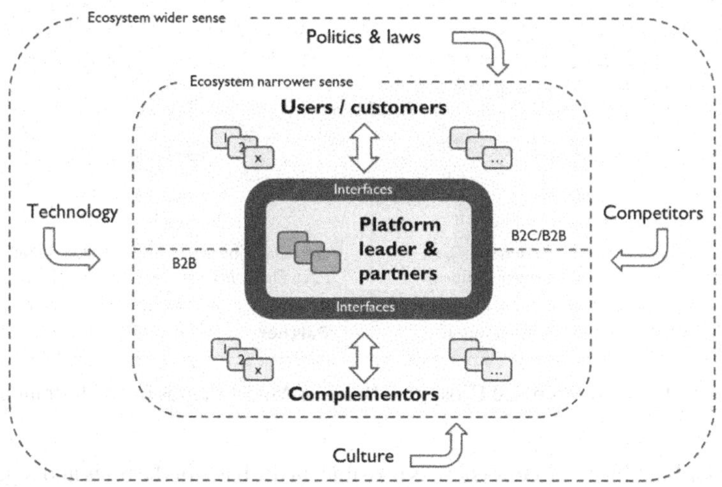


**Fig. 1.** The Platform-based Ecosystem Framework (own illustration)

In order to realize the focal value proposition, product and service offerings are contributed by the ecosystem complementors [25]. As mentioned by Teece [27] the idea is using the core competencies of the complementors to enhance the overall value proposition of an ecosystem. This requires a complementary relationship between the platform leader and the complementor itself. The last actor within an ecosystem is the user or customer. Ecosystems are designed from a customer-centric perspective, and the core idea is to create a product or service system that responds to a fundamental need of the customer [35].

### 3.2 Linking Ecosystem Framework and Business Models

According to Täuscher and Laudien, there is a need to understand holistically how platform business models work and how their possible manifestations and approaches can look like [37]. Business models can be described by answering four questions: (1) Who is the target customer? (2) What is offered to the customer? (3) How is the value proposition created? (4) Why does the business model generate profit? [38]. This approach is combined with the Platform-based Ecosystem Framework to derive at the canvas depicted in Fig. 2. This Platform-based Ecosystem Business Model Canvas is used to evaluate and understand such platform business models by examining value streams between the platform actors and analyzing their interrelationships. This helps to understand how the actors interpret their role and benefit from the ecosystem.

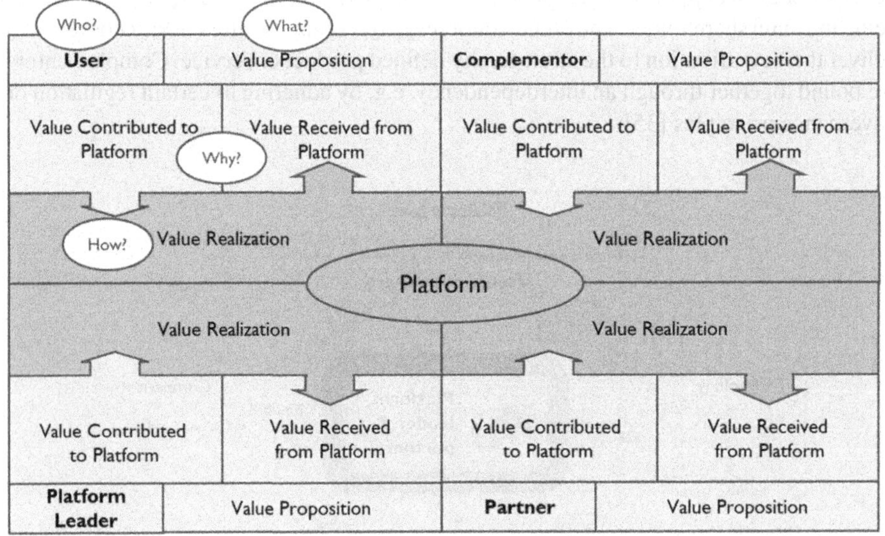


**Fig. 2.** The Platform-based Ecosystem Business Model Canvas (own illustration)

The coordination of the ecosystem is possible on the basis of the rules and regulations set [39]. Ecosystem rules can be strictly defined, especially in the case of technology-based platforms, but can also be just a set of unexpressed expectations. The rules and standards can govern various aspects, such as entry to the ecosystem, participation level and behavior [35]. According to Pauli et al. [40] a platform firm's success depends on their "ability to leverage an ecosystem of actors who contribute to the platform in various ways".

## 4 Case Study MoneyPark

We applied this canvas to more than 20 ecosystems in the DACH region over the last five years. MoneyPark is an example for a developing business ecosystem in the Swiss real estate market. In 2012, MoneyPark created a platform for mortgage comparisons thereby increasing product choice and price comparability for customers at the same time. In combination with desk research, interviews with four different ecosystem actors were conducted, analyzed and compared, namely the platform provider MoneyPark, the partner Helvetia and the two complementors Mobiliar and Credit Suisse. Our case study focusses on certain aspects of this mortgage "sub ecosystem" as shown in Fig. 3. Over time, the initial platform evolved in a network with more than 150 complementors. The mortgage broker business centered on Mobiliar and Credit Suisse as key complementors is still the core of MoneyPark's ecosystem. Financing as first area of activities enabled the expansion towards additional services with added value for the customers. In order to capture network effects that push the rapid growth of the platform-based ecosystem they focused initially on the actions and mechanisms that drive value creation to reach the critical network mass. Following the platform-based ecosystem idea MoneyPark set-up win-win situations with its partners and complementors. Once this step was reached, the platform started to focus on securing parts of the value creation for itself. [cf. 41].

Findings suggest that Money Park's customer-centric approach tackles major customer pain points along the journey of a real estate purchase, such as the low price comparability and the high time expenditure around mortgages. In addition, ecosystem complementors are able to gain customer access and thereby gather customer data without facing initial acquisition costs.

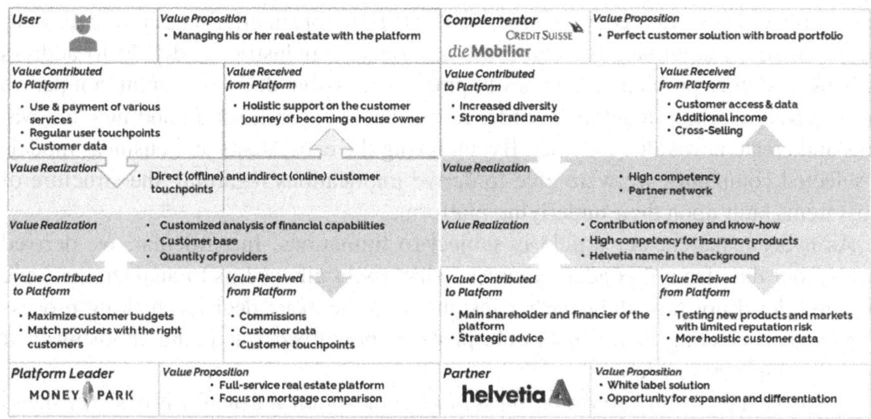


**Fig. 3.** Sector of the MoneyPark ecosystem (own illustration)

The platform-based ecosystem around MoneyPark is based upon multilateral value creation in collaborative networks. The constellation of users, platform leader, partner and complementors results in distinct value streams within the ecosystem. While matching insurance companies with insurance-seeking customers might be viewed as a rather transactional value creation by the platform provider (reduction of acquisition costs for complementors and creation of price advantages for users), other contributions have a more profound value potential. Provided by the ecosystem users themselves, the customer data represents such a component whose underlying value goes beyond the scope of a single business. While the platform provider MoneyPark uses a customer's property information to create additional digital services that involve building projects in the surrounding neighborhood, the complementor Mobiliar plans to make use of the same customer data by creating tailored marketing initiatives in combination with its subsidiaries. Therefore, the ecosystem MoneyPark fits into Moore's notion of business ecosystems as it co-creates potential for further innovations, like the forming of additional services that extend the scope or intensify the depth of the user journey as it is addressed today.

According to Adner [36], every member has to set up its own strategy and secure its own role in a competitive ecosystem. Therefore, the use or non-use of the underlying value potentials discussed above can be partly attributed to the individual strategies of the ecosystem actors. Especially for ecosystem complementors, the sole capturing of additional revenue streams appears to constitute a sufficient motive to participate in the ecosystem MoneyPark. Being satisfied with their role, the complementors positively influence the overall product variety for ecosystem users. With every new complementor in the ecosystem there is an increasing likelihood that customers find a provider meeting their requirements in terms of quality, location, or price, thus creating positive network effects.

## 5 Conclusion and Paths for Future Research

Platform-based business ecosystems play an important role in offering a complete, well-integrated set of solutions that can cross a variety of industries and help to address pressing customer problems. This development is possible due to different companies cooperatively working together in order to co-evolve capabilities around new innovations and create new value together. By analyzing the ecosystems and business models of selected companies we were able to derive implications regarding the structure of ecosystems built upon their underlying platforms.

As every research, our article is subject to limitations. In particular, we derived most of our data from secondary sources, which only allowed us to analyze the topic on a high level not providing further insights into the exact decision making process of managers selecting their roles in the platform-based ecosystem and choosing their respective business model.

However, the combination of business model innovation and platform-based business models promises some fruitful paths for future research. While this paper addresses how platform-based ecosystems require different roles and business models future research could investigate how connections between different business models of an ecosystem are established and what patterns they follow. Additionally, it could be of interest how managers identify threats and chances for their platforms, for instance by applying the attention-based view on this research topic.

Our results will help to understand why companies bet on platform-based business models to establish business ecosystems, analyze the processes and methods behind successful business ecosystems, and reflect about the dominant and still growing importance of collaborative network aspects in today's business world.

**Acknowledgments.** We thank Madeleine Horgby, Laura Raschle, Léonie Leser, and Samuel Schweizer for their contribution to this study.

## References


1. Thomas, L., Autio, E., Gann, D.: Architectural leverage: putting platforms in context. Acad. Manage. Perspect. **3015**(1), 47–67 (2015)
2. Zhu, F., Iansiti, M.: Entry into platform-based markets. Strateg. Manage. J. **106**(May), 88–106 (2012)
3. Boudreau, K.J.: Let a thousand flowers bloom? An early look at large numbers of software app developers and patterns of innovation. Organ. Sci. **23**(3), 1409–1427 (2012)
4. Gawer, A., Phillips, N.: Institutional work as logics shift: the case of Intel's transformation to platform leader. Organ. Stud. **34**(8), 1035–1071 (2013)
5. Frattini, F., Bianchi, M., De Massis, A., Sikimic, U.: The role of early adopters in the diffusion of new products: differences between platform and nonplatform innovations. J. Prod. Innov. Manage. **31**(3), 466–488 (2014)
6. Gawer, A., Cusumano, M.A.: Industry platforms and ecosystem innovation. J. Prod. Innov. Manage. **31**(3), 417–433 (2014)
7. Accenture: Technology vision 2015. https://www.accenture.com/us-en/_acnmedia/Accenture/Conversion-Assets/Microsites/Documents11/Accenture-Technology-Vision-2015.pdf. Accessed 21 Dec 2015
8. Deloitte: Business ecosystems come of age (2015). https://www2.deloitte.com/content/dam/insights/us/articles/platform-strategy-new-level-business-trends/DUP_1048-Business-ecosystems-come-of-age_MASTER_FINAL.pdf
9. Tucci, C.L., Chesbrough, H., Piller, F., West, J., Fe, E.P.: When do firms undertake open, collaborative activities? Introduction to the special section on open innovation and open business models. Ind. Corp. Change **25**(2), 283–288 (2016)
10. Vanhaverbeke, W., Chesbrough, H., West, J. (eds.): Surfing the new wave of open innovation research. In: New Frontiers in Open Innovation, pp. 281–294. Oxford University Press (2014)
11. Adner, R., Kapoor, R.: Innovation ecosystems and the pace of substitution: re-examining technology S-curves. Strateg. Manage. J. **37**(4), 625–648 (2015)
12. Chesbrough, H.W., Van Alstyne, M.: Permissionless innovation. Commun. ACM **58**(8), 24–26 (2015)
13. Mancha, R., Gordon, S.: Multi-sided platform strategies for organizations: transforming the business model. J. Bus. Strategy (2021)
14. Amit, R., Zott, C.: Crafting business architecture: the antecedents of business model design. Strateg. Entrep. J. **9**(4), 331–350 (2015)
15. Nambisan, S., Baron, R.A.: Entrepreneurship in innovation ecosystems: entrepreneurs' self-regulatory processes and their implications for new venture success. Entrep. Theory Pract. **37**(5), 1071–1097 (2013)
16. Brousseau, E., Penard, T.: The economics of digital business models: a framework for analyzing the economics of platforms. Rev. Netw. Econ. **6**(2), 81–114 (2007)
17. Hagiu, A., Wright, J.: Multi-sided platforms. Int. J. Ind. Organ. **43**, 162–174 (2015)
18. Chesbrough, H.W.: Open innovation: where we've been and where we're going. Res.-Technol. Manag. **55**(4), 20–27 (2012)
19. Bivona, E., Cosenz, F.: Designing a multi-sided platform business model assessment framework: a dynamic performance management perspective. Syst. Res. Behav. Sci. **38**(1), 93–107 (2019)
20. Hou, H., Shi, Y.: Ecosystem-as-structure and ecosystem-as-coevolution: a constructive examination. Technovation **100**, 102193 (2021)
21. Baldwin, C.Y., Clark, K.: Managing in an age of modularity. Harv. Bus. Rev. **75**(5), 84–93 (1997)
22. Armstrong, M.: Competition in two-sided markets. Rand. J. Econ. **37**(3), 668–691 (2006)

23. Hagiu, A., Spulber, D.: First-party content and coordination in two-sided markets. Manage. Sci. **59**(4), 933–949 (2013)
24. Mäkinen, S.J., Kanniainen, J., Peltola, I.: Investigating adoption of free beta applications in a platform-based business ecosystem. J. Prod. Innov. Manage. **31**(3), 451–465 (2014)
25. Moore, J.F.: Predators and prey: a new ecology of competition. Harv. Bus. Rev. **71**(3), 75–86 (1993)
26. Tsujimoto, M., Kajikawa, Y., Tomita, J., Matsumoto, Y.: A review of the ecosystem concept – towards coherent ecosystem design. Technol. Forecast. Soc. Change **136**, 49–58 (2018)
27. Teece, D.J.: Explicating dynamic capabilities: the nature and microfoundations of (sustainable) enterprise performance. Strateg. Manage. J. **28**(13), 1319–1350 (2007)
28. Scholten, S., Scholten, U.: Platform-based innovation management: directing external innovational efforts in platform ecosystems. J. Knowl. Econ. **3**(2), 164–184 (2012)
29. Zott, C., Amit, R., Massa, L.: The business model: recent developments and future research. J. Manage. **37**(4), 1019–1042 (2011)
30. Casadesus-Masanell, R., Ricart, J.E.: From strategy to business models and onto tactics. Long Range Plan. **43**(2–3), 195–215 (2010)
31. Winterhalter, S., Zeschky, M.B., Gassmann, O.: Managing dual business models in emerging markets: an ambidexterity perspective. R D Manage. **46**(3), 464–479 (2016)
32. Cusumano, M.A.: The evolution of platform thinking. Commun. ACM **53**(1), 33–35 (2010)
33. Parker, G.G., Van Alstyne, M.: Two-sided network effects: a theory of information product design. Manage. Sci. **51**(10), 1494–1504 (2005)
34. Eisenmann, T., Parker, G.G., Van Alstyne, M.: Strategies for two-sided markets. Harv. Bus. Rev. **84**(10), 91–101 (2006)
35. Jacobides, M.G., Cennamo, C., Gawer, A.: Towards a theory of ecosystems. Strateg. Manage. J. **39**(8), 2255–2276 (2018)
36. Adner, R.: Ecosystem as structure. J. Manage. **43**(1), 39–58 (2017)
37. Täuscher, K., Laudien, S.M.: Understanding platform business models: a mixed study of marketplaces. Eur. Manage. J. **36**(3), 319–329 (2018)
38. Gassmann, O., Frankenberger, K., Csik, M.: The Business Model Navigator: 55 Models That Will Revolutionise Your Business. Pearson (2014)
39. Pidun, U., Reeves, M., Schüssler, M.: BCG. Do you need a business ecosystem? (2019) https://www.bcg.com/publications/2019/doyou-need-business-ecosystem. Accessed 5 Nov 2020
40. Pauli, T., Marx, E., Dunzer, S., Matzner, M.: Modeling platform ecosystems. In: CEUR Workshop Proceedings, vol. 2716 (2020)
41. Jacobides, M.G., Sundararajan, A., Van Alstyne, M.: Platforms and ecosystems: enabling the digital economy. In: Briefing Paper World Economic Forum, Cologny/Geneva, pp. 1–32 (2019)

# Organizational Maturity Assessment Model for Collaborative Networks

Fernando Zatt Schardosin[1,2](✉) and Carlos R. De Rolt[2]

[1] Federal University of Frontier Border (UFFS), 405 Br 158, Laranjeiras do Sul, PR 85301-970, Brazil

[2] Superior School of Management and Business, Santa Catarina State University, Florianopolis, SC, Brazil

**Abstract.** This paper aims to propose an organizational maturity assessment model for taking part in collaborative networks, aiming to contribute to the theory on this topic. It uses the mixed research method, with a qualitative approach, using systematic research and focus group techniques, to highlight the theoretical gaps and the establishment of evaluation criteria, and a quantitative approach with the use of the multicriteria decision-making method, to assign the importance of each criterion and establish the level of maturity of an organization. The result was an assessment instrument composed of eight dimensions and fifty-five categories, with the organization's positioning in indicators according to the four possible levels for each category.

**Keywords:** Preparedness · Readiness · Multicriteria decision-making method · Capability · Ability

## 1 Introduction

The ecosystems evaluate ideas, projects, and business plans of established or emerging companies, to make the activities feasible. Once inserted in these environments, organizations are encouraged to develop with the formation of collaborative networks, establishing a process of preparation to integrate networks among organizations for sharing resources and competencies.

There is a perception that networks are fragile, and participants need to be mobilized and involved to maintain collaborative networks, whose organizational maturity facilitates this participation [1]. For example, the development of vaccines against covid-19 by organizations: Pfizer and Biotech; Oxford and AstraZeneca; Modern and NIAID. This shows the importance of networks to counter the disease very quickly with the maturity to share skills and resources.

The higher the organization's maturity, the lower the need for preparation, to maintain or enter into networks. A conscious assessment of maturity conditions provides clarity for understanding the organization's conditions. Thus, the organization will be able to self-evaluate to know how to improve, to become a member of collaborative networks.


Published by Springer Nature Switzerland AG 2021
L. M. Camarinha-Matos et al. (Eds.): PRO-VE 2021, IFIP AICT 629, pp. 101–110, 2021.
https://doi.org/10.1007/978-3-030-85969-5_9

The challenges for this study include, among others, integration and interconnection of formal knowledge, development of rules of cooperation, the establishment of trust and recognition among members [2], training, preparation, awareness, commitment, and resilience [3].

Therefore, it is a process that involves many dimensions and decision-making, after all, a network can fail in its objectives, if all aspects are not considered already in the selection stage [4]. Thus, we have the research question: What is the maturity assessment model applicable to organizations for taking part in collaborative networks?

This paper aims to propose a model for assessing organizational maturity for taking part in collaborative networks, providing elements that enable a conscious business analysis.

## 2 Literature Review

The organizational maturity assessment to take part in collaborative networks considers the type of network being composed, permanent networks such as Virtual Breeding Environment (VBE) and temporary networks such as Virtual Enterprise (VE).

These networks are discussed together because of dependence between them, thus, the study refers to different analyzes for each type of network, although it considers this interdependence.

VBE is an association of organizations with a long-term cooperation agreement, supported by common infrastructure and operating principles, to increase their readiness to collaborate in potential goal-oriented temporary alliances [5], such as VE.

### 2.1 Organizational Readiness for Collaborative Networks

The relationship between organizations is one of the factors considered to identify the ability of organizations to compose collaborative networks, such as technological compatibility (structural element) and relationships of affection and empathy (relational element) [6]. Partner characteristics, market knowledge, intangible assets, capabilities, complementary and aptitude [4]. These are principles for identifying the characteristics of organizations and aligning them to the suitable level.

The working principles in the VBE can be described from five perspectives [7]: the organizational perspective, VBE structure, governance rules and statutes; the business process perspective; the resource perspective; the value system and business model perspective; and interaction perspective.

Many of the concepts discussed diverge among the authors, some alignments are presented and analyzed, this divergence of concepts contributed to the heterogeneity of the topic.

Some papers use the concept of virtuality [8, 9], others use the concept of preparation [10] as a pre-condition for entry into the VBE-type ecosystem. Others claim that preparation is a process internal to the organization, while readiness refers to the organization's relationship with its external environment [11].

In another concept, preparation is a stage, preceded by character and character-related preparation conditions, while readiness combines preparation, willingness to collaborate, aptitude for competence, and affective and empathetic relationships [12], in this case, preparation is a precondition for readiness. The preparation was further studied, in two ways, as a pre-condition for participation in ecosystems, and post-adhesion to be part of temporary networks [13].

### 2.2 Organizational Maturity Assessment Models

There are many different models for assessing readiness in a collaborative network, whether it is decision making for admitting network partners [14], or for organizations, following an individualized assessment guide [7].

Establishing criteria is important in this assessment for organizations to become members of collaborative networks, with guidelines to continually improve their readiness for collaboration. Competence assessment, past performance, market, processes, resources, organization, information, knowledge, and culture [7, 10], behavior patterns, character and disposition [12], network cooperation, integration, trust, and use of ICT [9], are some of the individual criteria.

There are criteria for aligning readiness with a business strategy such as strategic needs and required capabilities [8], strategic, operational, cultural, and commercial synergies [15], motivation, and interoperability [16], partnership structure, information system architecture, process architecture, and coordination [17].

Competency profiles are dynamically determined according to requirements. These definitions represent a sequence of steps based on some opportunity for collaboration, to adjust the competencies of each organization and those necessary to meet expectations [18].

These criteria, instruments, methods, and studies were engaged in analyzing the problems related to maturity to compose collaborative networks. There is no predominant study or even replication of studies, some authors deployed the models, others also applied them empirically. These studies helped to make the basis for the development of this paper.

## 3 Research Methodology

This research uses a mixed research method, which enables a better understanding of a research problem or question [19]. Qualitative data represent attributes of some object and these can be quantified [20].

The research was divided into two phases (1. qualitative research and 2. quantitative research). Phase one was subdivided into two steps, step 1 consisted of a systematic review of the literature, with planning, execution, and reporting [21], the following search string was used in four databases (Scopus, WoS, Ebsco, and Science Direct):

- ("virtual network*" OR "virtual organi?ation*" OR "virtual corporation*" OR "virtual entreprise*" OR "collaborative network*") AND ("readiness" OR "preparedness" OR "maturity").

After applying the filters in the research, 95 papers remained, which were analyzed individually to identify theoretical gaps regarding the topic. Step 2 of the qualitative approach consisted of research with a focus group, which is a convenient way to collect data, such as beliefs, opinions, and views of several people simultaneously, whose group interaction is part of the method [22]. This group was composed of 12 members (2 moderators and 10 members), characterized as market professionals, with training in the areas of administration, accounting, electrical and chemical engineering, with experience in managing public and private organizations.

The objective was to establish the criteria for evaluating the organizational maturity to compose collaborative networks, the information generated by the systematic research was presented, familiarizing the members with the subject, and instructing about the research interests, each member suggested criteria according to their area of knowledge and contributed to the debate with the other criteria suggested by the other members.

Next, phase 2 of the research (quantitative approach) consists of establishing scales of importance for the dimensions, categories that make up the dimensions, and the four levels in each category.

These scales are established based on the multicriteria decision-making method that considers more than one aspect in the analysis, in which each criterion represents a mathematical function, and measures the performance of the aspect concerning the others, enabling the simultaneous optimization and transitivity established by the order of preference among the criteria [23], that is, it allows defining a road map for the organization, which intends to improve its general level of maturity.

The four levels in the categories follow a linear scale of importance, placing each organization based on indicators for each level. The actors present in the environment in which the networks are formed jointly determine the scales of the criteria, based on the judgment of the importance that each one has on a scale from 0 to 10. The grades given by the actors are converted into percentages of model explanation, based on Eq. 1. Where x represents the percentage rate, n is all grades assigned by the actors, and $n_i$ is the criterion grade to be converted into a percentage rate.

$$x = \frac{ni}{\sum_{n}^{i=1} n} \times 100 \tag{1}$$

Thus, it is possible to measure the maturity of an organization to take part in collaborative networks, whose indicator will be established by Eq. 2 [23].

$$V(a) = W_1.V_1(a) + W_2.V_2(a) + W_3.V_3(a) + \ldots + W_n.V_n(a) \tag{2}$$

Where V(a) corresponds to the maturity index, $V_1(a), V_2(a), \ldots, V_n(a)$, correspond to the values of the organization's positioning levels for each criterion, and $W_1, W_2, \ldots, W_n$, refers to the percentages established for each criterion.

## 4 Results

For this study, the focus group was defining the criteria for assessing organizational maturity for participation in collaborative networks, these were subdivided into dimensions, and these were subdivided into categories. The dimensions identified were: 1. assets; 2. knowledge; 3 people; 4. trust; 5. finances; 6. innovation; 7. marketing; and 8 connectivity.

The complementarity, sharing, and coupling of "assets" is a factor in the development of partnerships among companies, contributing to the use of idle capacity and risk dilution, whose management is a crucial factor [24].

The exchange of "knowledge" between organizations contributes to collaborative networks, familiarizing partners with the information that companies have, accessing different bases, improving knowledge of the organization, and contributing to the knowledge of the network, increasing collective knowledge [25].

"People" are considered a very valuable organizational resource, they are responsible for carrying out projects, processes, and routines in companies. Aspects such as experience, flexibility, innovation, knowledge management, mobilization, and internationalization of the people who make up companies can favor the formation of networks among organizations [26].

The "trust" dimension refers to the aspects present in the company's environment and in the relationships among organizations that enable the exchange of information, sharing of resources, and collaboration. That limits opportunistic attitudes, reduces costs, facilitates problem-solving, contributes to the construction of flexible and efficient partnerships [27].

About "finance", participation in collaborative networks favors access to funding sources, investment sharing, cost savings, and increased revenue, mediated by transparency [8].

The "Innovation" turns new ideas into opportunities that have a wide practical use, capturing value from them. Through collaborative networks, companies seek partnerships to complement resources and skills to innovate, sharing the risks of these initiatives [28].

"Marketing" manages relationships and involves customers in business, aiming to attract, maintain and increase the number of customers, delivering value and satisfaction, understanding their needs, developing, distributing, and promoting products and services to the market with value and prices suitable [29].

The "connectivity" dimension represents processes, norms, and agreements that enable connections among organizations in a collaborative network, such as interoperable infrastructure, sharing, interaction, operating rules, cooperation agreements, and appropriate trust level [30]. From these eight dimensions, the categories were established, a total of fifty-five categories were identified, as shown in Table 1.

The complete model is accessible from the link: http://bit.ly/organizationalmodel. The criteria established in Table 1 are applied to the actors present in the ecosystems to identify the importance of each criterion for the formation of collaborative networks, whose grades of importance are converted into percentages, as mentioned in the methodology. Then, companies are classified in this model in one of four levels for each of the categories, as shown in Fig. 1, according to indicators.

The gathering of all the categories calculated according to Eq. 2, showing in the methodology, will form the organization's maturity, which for the hypothetical example in Fig. 1, the resulting index is 0.595425.

This analysis will make it possible to identify the main points in which the company needs to improve, constituting a road map to collaborative networks preparedness, among the different areas of improvement, which would have the greatest impact and should

**Table 1.** Criteria for organizational maturity assessment for participation in collaborative networks

| Dimension | Category | Cod |
|---|---|---|
| Assets | Production capacity | A001 |
| | Idle capacity | A002 |
| | Reliability | A003 |
| | Asset control | A004 |
| | Depreciation, amortization, and depletion | A005 |
| | Operational availability | A006 |
| | Flexibility | A007 |
| | Asset management in the strategic plan | A008 |
| | Maintenance | A009 |
| | Monitoring | A010 |
| | Asset system | A011 |
| | Lifetime | A012 |
| Knowledge | Organizational learning | B001 |
| | Knowledge management | B002 |
| | Schema | B003 |
| | Gatekeepers | B004 |
| People | Learning and innovation | C001 |
| | Coupling capacity | C002 |
| | People management | C003 |
| | Processes | C004 |
| | Results | C005 |
| | Systems | C006 |
| Trust | Commitment | D001 |
| | Trust signals | D002 |
| | Governance | D003 |
| | Reputation | D004 |
| Finance | Funding | E001 |
| | Financial management | E002 |
| | Economic and financial planning | E003 |
| | Transparency (visibility of Financial Statements (FS's)) | E004 |

(*continued*)

**Table 1.** (*continued*)

| Dimension | Category | Cod |
|---|---|---|
| Innovation | Strategy | F001 |
| | Dynamics | F002 |
| | Adaptive interfaces | F003 |
| | Promote new products, services, or processes | F004 |
| Marketing | Analysis of the quality of products or services concerning the competition | G001 |
| | Uncertainty assessment | G002 |
| | Search for opportunities | G003 |
| | Competitors | G004 |
| | Strategy/business model | G005 |
| | Competition analysis | G006 |
| | Product customization study | G007 |
| | Norms and rules study | G008 |
| | Portfólio and roadmap | G009 |
| | Target segments of activity | G010 |
| Connectivity | Network access | H001 |
| | Easy access to the supply chain | H002 |
| | Product collaboration with customers, suppliers, competitors, research institutions, test institutes, Universities | H003 |
| | Sharing competencies with other organizations | H004 |
| | Sharing organizational goals | H005 |
| | Forming permanent alliances and partnerships | H006 |
| | Forming temporary alliances and partnerships | H007 |
| | Promotion of multiple internal and external communication channels | H008 |
| | Promotion of work in physically distant teams | H009 |
| | Promotion of work in physically close teams | H010 |
| | Prospection | H011 |

undergo intervention first. For example, should it improve first, from level 1 to level 3 in category 3 of dimension B or category 1 of dimension C?

In the first case, the resulting index would be 0.695925 and in the second case, the index is 0.7311, in this case, there would be a maturity gain of approximately 5% with the best choice, the other interventions can follow the order of impacts, from the biggest to the smallest. However, certain organizations may have greater restrictions to promote changes and some criteria, in which case they can opt for changes in other criteria with less impact, but which does not negatively affect the organization.

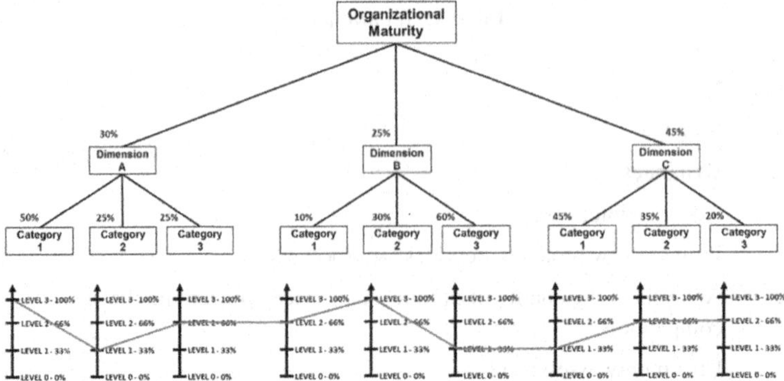


**Fig. 1.** Hypothetical example for assessing organizational maturity.

Managers and brokers will have criteria to select and advise the necessary improvements in the companies. However, the collaborative networks formed will be supported by scientific and practical criteria aiming at the success of these intentions.

## 5 Conclusions and Further Research

This paper aimed to propose an organizational maturity assessment model for participation in collaborative networks, providing elements that enable a conscious business analysis, exploring all the benefits existing in these types of business arrangements.

The literature review showed the existence of many studies on the subject, however, it also showed many differences between them, resulting in scientific gaps.

This paper proposed a different model, scientific and practical, supported by organizational, physical, human, organizational, and technological resources that are integrable and shareable among organizations that are part of the network.

To measure organizational maturity, the multicriteria decision-making method was used, which establishes an index for each company, the higher the index, the more prepared it will be to participate in collaborative networks.

This study presents an advance in the subject, to contribute with researchers and practitioners in the establishment of organizational maturity assessment. New research is needed for the application of the instrument among ecosystem actors to establish measures evaluation for each criterion based on its importance degree, and application in companies to determine its maturity assessment, based on the criteria showing in this study.

**Acknowledgment.** This study receives a scholarship subvention from the Fundação de Amparo à Pesquisa e Inovação de Santa Catarina (FAPESC) and was developed at UDESC and UFFS universities in Brazil.

## References

1. Durugbo, C.: Collaborative networks: a systematic review and multi-level framework. Int. J. Prod. Res. **54**, 3749–3776 (2016)

2. Da Silva, J.M.V.B., De Almeida, I.D.: Collaborative networks as incubators of dynamic virtual organisations: A case study of the emerging MAP sector. Int. J. Manuf. Technol. Manage. **31**, 192–216 (2017)
3. Gimenez, R., Labaka, L., Hernantes, J.: Building city resilience through collaborative networks: A literature review. In: Díaz, P., Bellamine Ben Saoud, N., Dugdale, J., Hanachi, C. (eds.) ISCRAM-med 2016. LNBIP, vol. 265, pp. 131–142. Springer, Cham (2016). https://doi.org/10.1007/978-3-319-47093-1_12
4. Polyantchikov, I., Shevtshenko, E.: Partner selection criteria for virtual organization forming. In: 9th International Conference of Daaam Baltic, Industrial Engineering, Daaam-Baltic, pp. 163–168 (2014)
5. Graça, P., Camarinha-Matos, L.M.: Performance indicators for collaborative business ecosystems - literature review and trends. Technol. Forecast. Soc. Chang. **116**, 237–255 (2017)
6. Appio, F.P., Martini, A., Massa, S., Testa, S.: Collaborative network of firms: antecedents and state-of-the-art properties. Int. J. Prod. Res. **55**, 2121–2134 (2017)
7. Romero, D., Galeano, N., Molina, A.: Mechanisms for assessing and enhancing organisations' readiness for collaboration in collaborative networks. Int. J. Prod. Res. **47**, 4691–4710 (2009)
8. Jackson, P., Klobas, J.: Aligning goals, virtuality and capability: a virtual alignment model. In: Klobas, J.E. (eds.) Becoming Virtual. Contributions to management science, pp. 11–21. Springer (2008). https://doi.org/10.1007/978-3-7908-1958-8_2
9. Moeini, A., Farahani, A.F., Ravasan, A.Z.: The consistency of virtual organizations enabling capabilities and improvements in knowledge management performance. Int. J. Enterp. Inf. Syst. **9**, 20–43 (2013)
10. Baldo, F., Rabelo, R.J.: Guidelines to transform industry clusters in virtual organization breeding environments - a case study. In: Cellary, W., Estevez, E. (eds.) Software Services for e-world, vol. 341, pp. 161–172 (2010)
11. Gall, P., Burn, J.: Strategies aligning in the virtual organisation. In: Proceedings of European and Mediterranean Conference on Information Systems, vol. 61, pp. 1–13 (2007)
12. Rosas, J., Camarinha-Matos, L.M.: An approach to assess collaboration readiness. Int. J. Prod. Res. **47**, 4711–4735 (2009)
13. Rajper, N.J., Reiff-Marganiec, S., Nizamani, Q.U.A.: Towards a gamified approach for enhancing VBE preparedness for establishing virtual collaborations. In: Afsarmanesh, H., Camarinha-Matos, L.M. Soares, A.L. (eds.) Collaboration in a Hyperconnected World, vol. 480, pp. 165–177 (2016)
14. Durugbo, C., Riedel, J.C.K.H.: Readiness assessment of collaborative networked organisations for integrated product and service delivery. Int. J. Prod. Res. **51**, 598–613 (2013)
15. Bititci, U., Turner, T., MacKay, D., Kearney, D., Parung, J., Walters, D.: Managing synergy in collaborative enterprises. Prod. Planning Control **18**, 454–465 (2007)
16. Cannas, V., Lancia, G., Conte, M., Santoro, R., Da Bormida, M.: Establishing a collaborative cluster in the Lazio aerospace district. In: IEEE International Technology Management Conference (ICE), pp. 1–8 (2007)
17. Bukhsh, F.A., Daneva, M., Weigand, H.: Understanding maturity of collaborative network organizations by using B-ITa processes. In: Bajec, M., Eder, J. (eds.) CAiSE 2012. LNBIP, vol. 112, pp. 580–591. Springer, Heidelberg (2012). https://doi.org/10.1007/978-3-642-31069-0_48
18. Rosas, J., Macedo, P., Camarinha-Matos, L.M.: Extended competencies model for collaborative networks. Prod. Planning Control **22**, 501–517 (2011)
19. Creswell, J.W.: Research Design: Qualitative, Quantitative, and Mixed Methods Approaches. 4th edn, Thousand Oaks, California. SAGE Publications (2014)
20. Cheptulin, A.: A dialética materialista: categorias e leis da dialética. São Paulo, Alfa Omega (1982)

21. Tranfield, D., Danyer, D., Smart, P.: Towards a methodology for developing evidence-informed management knowledge by means of systematic review. Br. J. Manage. **14**, 207–222 (2003)
22. Kitzinger, J.: Qualitative research: Introducing focus groups. BMJ Clin. Res. Ed. **311**, 299–302 (1995)
23. Ensslin, L., Montibeller Neto, G., Noronha, S.M.: Apoio à decisão - Metodologia para estruturação de problemas e avaliação multicritério de alternativas. Insular. Florianópolis (2001)
24. Powell, W.W., Koput, K.W., Smith-Doerr, L.: Interorganizational collaboration and the locus of innovation: networks of learning in biotechnology. Adm. Sci. Q. **1**, 116–145 (1996)
25. Abreu, A., Urze, P.: An approach to measure knowledge transfer in open-innovation. In: 3rd International Conference on Operations Research and Enterprise Systems, Icores 2014. Loire Valley, Angers, pp. 183–189 (2014)
26. Berthod, O., Grothe-Hammer, M., Sydow, J.: Network ethnography: a mixed-method approach for the study of practices in interorganizational settings. Organ. Res. Methods **20**, 299–323 (2017)
27. Msanjila, S.S., Afsarmanesh, H.: FETR: a framework to establish trust relationships among organizations in VBEs. J. Intell. Manuf. **21**, 251–265 (2010)
28. Franco, C., Wanke, P.F.: On building partnership networks in an innovation context. Manage. Res. **16**, 179–196 (2018)
29. Kotler, P., Armstrong, G.: Principles of Marketing, 17 edn. Person Higher Education, Hoboken (2018)
30. Expósito-langa, M., Tomás-miquel, J.V., Molina-morales, F.X.: Innovation in clusters: exploration capacity, networking intensity and external resources. J. Organ. Chang. Manage. **28**, 26–52 (2015)

# Human Factors in Collaboration 4.0

# Antecedents of Constructive Human-AI Collaboration: An Exploration of Human Actors' Key Competencies

Thomas Süße(✉), Maria Kobert, and Caroline Kries

Faculty of Engineering and Mathematics, Bielefeld University of Applied Sciences, Gütersloh Campus, Langer Weg 9 a, 33332 Gütersloh, Germany
thomas.suesse@fh-bielefeld.de

**Abstract.** Artificial intelligence (AI) has become an integral element of modern machines, devices and materials, and already transforms the way humans interact with technology in business and society. The traditionally more hierarchical interaction, where humans usually control machines, is constantly blurring as machines become more capable of bringing in their own (intelligent) initiatives to the interaction with humans. Thus, nowadays it is more appropriate to consider the interactive processes between humans and machines as a novel form of interdependent learning efforts between both sides, where processes such as critical discourses between humans and machines may take place (hybrid intelligence). However, these developments demand a shift in the understanding about the role of technology at work and about specific competencies required among human actors to collaborate constructively and sustainably with AI systems. This paper seeks to address this issue by identifying human actors' key competencies, which enable a more constructive collaboration between humans and intelligent technologies at work.

**Keywords:** Artificial intelligence · Human-AI collaboration · AI-related competencies

## 1 Introduction

The opportunities and capabilities of interconnected intelligent technologies foster the further emergence of smart and sustainable collaborative networks and enable more integrative forms of interaction as well as resource, knowledge or information exchange between a greater variety of heterogeneous actors and artificial agents perceived as increasingly intelligent. These developments also result in changes on the micro level of human-machine interaction and directly affect the way work processes are performed. Interconnected agents based on artificial intelligence (AI) in modern work environments, for instance, increasingly assist human actors by taking on standardized tasks and recently also tasks of limited complexity to support or enable more collaborative


Published by Springer Nature Switzerland AG 2021
L. M. Camarinha-Matos et al. (Eds.): PRO-VE 2021, IFIP AICT 629, pp. 113–124, 2021.
https://doi.org/10.1007/978-3-030-85969-5_10

communication, information, decision-making or production processes [1–4]. Some typical applications are chatbots that take over routine interactions with customers [5], algorithms that support the selection of new employees [6], medical diagnoses [7, 8], predictive maintenance of machines [9] or intelligent robots that are able to work safely alongside humans in factories, where they take on highly repetitive and exhausting tasks [9]. The company Hyundai, for example, recently introduced wearable robotic devices which can adapt quickly to various tasks, contexts and workers in order to perform jobs "with superhuman endurance and strength" [10]. Moreover, such intelligent agents or machines can be trained by employees during the working process [3, 5, 9, 11]. Thus, the human can be regarded as a trainer or educator of machines and the latter as a human's trainee. As soon as these machines are sufficiently trained, they can possibly take on the role of the trainer for new or inexperienced colleagues. Thus, the roles between human and machine are becoming more interchangeable in modern work environments [3, 9].

Based on these examples, it is evident that intelligent technologies are transforming traditional human-machine interaction. The ability of AI-enabled technology to learn independently, interpret context, make its own decisions and communicate these to humans and, thus, influence human decision-making and actions ensures that it is viewed by humans increasingly as a colleague, teammate or even a buddy [1, 3, 9, 12]. Though these developments are currently in their early stages and machines' rudimentary intelligent capabilities are only partially comparable to those of humans, an understanding towards a human-AI collaboration has evolved [1, 2, 8, 13]. On the one hand obvious benefits are seen in achieving higher efficiency and quality by humans and machines complementing each other [3, 14], on the other hand the absence of acceptance and understanding on the part of employees towards the new technology, entails new challenges [15].

One important step to overcome these challenges is seen in further training and development of employees' competencies [16]. Consequently, the question of which competencies humans need or will need in the future to be able to work effectively and sustainably with AI-based technologies arises [9, 11]. In practice, it has already been shown that AI-related competencies of employees represent a particularly critical success factor for the actual unfolding of smart technologies' potentials [11, 17–19]. However, so far, particularly IT, mathematical, leadership and social skills have been discussed as essential elements or partial aspects of AI skills in current research [20]. Furthermore, occupational fields were mainly examined in which predominantly academics are active, but employees who collaborate with AI systems in the workplace and are only indirectly involved in the introduction or basic development of AI have so far received less attention [13, 21]. However, intelligent technologies are increasingly present across many working areas – from production to administration or social professions [11, 19].

The objective of this work is to explore and systematize the competencies humans working in different industry sectors and positions may need to not only be able to introduce, monitor or use but rather to constructively collaborate with more intelligent technologies at work. To derive the competencies we applied an iterative and reflexive approach. We performed literature research on recent technical and social developments as well as challenges in the field of human-AI collaboration. We validated and refined the findings in workshops and ongoing conversations with experts on human-AI applications from science and business. In this article, the final findings are presented.

We consider the systematization of key competencies as an important initial step in the derivation of an AI-related competencies framework. The framework shall provide an important contribution to a more specific understanding in science and business about the key enablers for human-AI collaboration and mutual learning between human and technology at work.

## 2 Related Work and Conceptual Background

The term "artificial intelligence (AI)" was first coined by John McCarthy in 1956 [22] and is still not clearly defined. A very popular definition from Nils J. Nilsson [23] reads: "Artificial Intelligence is that activity devoted to making machines intelligent, and intelligence is that quality that enables an entity to function appropriately and with foresight in its environment." Kaplan and Haenlein [15] state that AI is "a system's ability to correctly interpret external data, to learn from such data, and to use those learnings to achieve specific goals and tasks through flexible adaptation." According to the first definition, AI has the potential to be comparable or even superior to human intelligence [14]. However, up to now, scientists have outlined that a so-called strong or general AI, which can be applied to any problem and is, therefore, comparable to human intelligence, does not exist yet but is an important issue in current research [24]. Furthermore, the so-called super AI, which is even supposed to be superior to human intelligence, is so far only a philosophical speculation [25]. Thus, we argue that the definition given above by Kaplan and Haenlein [15] describes the current perception and understanding about existing and widely used AI as narrow AI more appropriately. In fact, narrow AI is defined as insentient and typically focused on a narrow, very specific task or area of applications [26].

Today's most common narrow AI technique is machine learning or, more precisely, a class of it, the so-called deep learning. As the name already indicates, deep learning neural networks learn from data by extracting complex structures and creating calculation models. These are composed of several processing layers and can thus create different levels of abstraction [27]. With this technique, intelligent machines are able to understand written or spoken language, pictures or videos, to draw conclusions on this basis independently as well as interact or communicate with their environment [26]. The latest developments even show that robots equipped with such AI techniques are able to detect, respond and display emotions [28].

Even though, as already indicated, today's intelligent machines are based on weak AI and are far from being as intelligent as humans, they tend to ascribe certain 'human traits' to an AI system. As a result, the interaction between humans and AI-based agents can transform itself into a collaboration and cooperation 'at eye level'. Thus, the AI-related technological enhancements and their dissemination contribute to the emergence of new forms of human-machine interaction. Whereas previously it was primarily the human being who took the initiative and largely specified what the machine had to work on, this hierarchical relationship is increasingly being transformed by AI-related capabilities. As AI-enabled agents become increasingly capable of making their own decisions, performing simple or repetitive tasks and improving more independently over time [9, 11], these agents are constantly developing towards artificial colleagues or teammates for their human counterparts at work [1, 12]. As a result, human-machine interaction is transforming to a more integrative level, the human-AI collaboration [1, 3, 13]. In essence, this means that AI and humans will work and learn increasingly 'hand-in-hand' and mutually integrative in the future to achieve higher levels of performance [1, 3, 29]. This is what we refer to as *constructive* human-AI collaboration. In the context of human-AI collaboration, the term hybrid intelligence has also recently been introduced [2], which is defined as the combination of artificial and human intelligence. The benefit of the integration of the latter is seen in the capability of solving increasingly complex problems faster and more efficiently than if only one of them had been involved. A central aspect of hybrid intelligence is that over time, not only the socio-technical system as a whole but also the human and the machine themselves improve through the experiences gained in solving problems collaboratively and by learning in a mutual beneficial way [2].

In practice, it has already been shown that a closer collaboration between humans and technology can be very beneficial [3, 9], for example, humans can be released from dangerous, hazardous, physically demanding or monotone tasks and are, therefore, enabled to take over more cognitively challenging or creative tasks [3, 11]. Nevertheless, from employees' point of view there are fundamental reservations and challenges, such as the fear of being replaced by the machine teammate or the lack of transparency and understanding about its functionality, preventing the new technology's further dissemination. Many attempts to overcome these problems focus on the design of AI-systems to be more explainable, transparent or applicable to humans [30, 31]. However, holistic approaches focusing on the human counterpart are also required. One main aspect in this context is that job profiles, roles and working conditions are changing [15]. For example, humans will rather have to train machines in order to enable them to take over repetitive tasks or understand and explain technology's decisions or outcomes [3, 9]. Thus, the aim is to enable employees to take on new or 'higher-quality' tasks, on the one hand, and to work together with AI systems more effectively, responsibly and sustainably, on the other hand [1, 3, 11]. This leads to the question about which specific competencies are indispensable for a constructive and responsible human-AI collaboration [26, 32]. Research to date has revealed that an essential prerequisite for a successful introduction and sustainable performance of AI-based systems can be seen in the existence of specific human actors' competencies for collaborating with AI technologies [11, 19]. However, further systematizations and conceptualizations of the competencies demanded are still rare and fragmented.

We refer in this article to competencies as behavioral repertoires that people carry out at the job, for example, coping with job-related tasks [33]. This means that competencies should not be mixed up with performance outcomes, such as effectivity or quality, but should, instead, be considered as crucial enablers for successful job performance. Consequently, we refer to competencies as actual "dimensions of behavior which are related to superior job performance" [33]. These behavioral dimensions of human actors' competencies can further be systematized by the three interdependent clusters of *cognitive*, *emotional* and *social* competencies [34]. Cognitive competencies include elements such as systems thinking or pattern recognition. Emotional competencies refer to self-awareness and self-management or emotional self-control. Social competencies include elements such as social awareness or relationship management, for example, empathy, teamwork or inspiration. We find this systematization of competencies, which refers explicitly to the outstanding performance of human actors at work, highly applicable for the development of a framework of competencies demanded for human-AI collaboration, as we showed above that AI-based systems trigger profound changes in work processes and human job roles.

## 3 Towards a Framework of AI-Specific Demands of Human Actors' Competencies

In the following, a set of human actors' competencies supporting constructive human-AI collaboration is presented. These competencies were identified by an extensive literature research on the latest developments as well as challenges in intelligent technologies' application areas. The research was complemented with ongoing dialogues with experts applying or implementing AI-based systems.

There are already some very fruitful AI-related investigations about competence and skill demands in literature. The conceptualization of "AI literacy" introduced by Long and Magerko [21] holds 17 skills that humans need to work effectively and sustainably with and critically evaluate AI technologies. Another study by Pfeifer [35] outlines the potential of applying AI in the context of predictive maintenance and consulting-intensive clerical work. An important conclusion from this study is that employees have to understand the potentials and limitations of AI-based systems and should be able to place them and their results in the professional context as well as the situational requirements in order to quickly exploit the potential of the technology in the company [35]. A further examination of job advertisements for the fields of data science, software and business development, and sales, combined with a literature review, reveals that technical competence, leadership and soft skills are required for the usage of AI [20].

These works focus predominantly on the introduction of intelligent technologies in a narrow field of work environments and on higher qualified positions. Namely, the identified competencies are rather basic or technical and may be applied to humans developing and supervising AI-systems, rather than to humans who are actually collaborating with such systems. However, in the near future a penetration of various employment fields with more interactive AI technologies is expected. Thus, while previous research provides a great basis for further systematization of AI-related human competencies, there is a lack of a sufficient and holistic behavioral framework about human actors' competencies demanded for a constructive human-AI collaboration in organizations. The framework presented below shall provide an important starting point for closing this gap.

During our research we found it fruitful and highly applicable to refer to the clustering dimensions of cognitive, emotional and social competencies [34] in order to provide a more comprehensive and systematic framework. Based on our analysis and investigations, nine distinct dimensions of human actors' competencies are revealed to be essential elements of an AI competencies framework (see Table 1). We label these dimensions as: (1) Context-specific understanding and interpretation of AI impulses; (2) expressing oneself comprehensibly towards the AI colleague; (3) evaluating the intelligence and capabilities of AI agents; (4) dealing with AI systems in a reflective manner; (5) engaging oneself in a constantly constructive discourse; (6) handling sensitive data critically; (7) constantly upholding ethical and moral standards; (8) showing an awareness of an AI agent as a sort of virtual colleague; and, finally, (9) negotiating one's own recovery phases with AI agents. Table 1 shows a clustering of these nine dimensions allocated to the three clusters cognitive, emotional and social. We are aware that a clear allocation of all AI-related competencies to one unique cluster is rather challenging. Thus, we marked only that cluster for each AI-related competence with an "x" which we find shows the strongest suitability based on our investigations.

**Table 1.** Clustering of AI-related competencies (AI competencies framework)

| | Clustering | | |
|---|---|---|---|
| AI-related competencies | Cognitive | Emotional | Social |
| 1. Context-specific understanding and interpretation of AI impulses | x | | |
| 2. Expressing oneself comprehensibly towards the AI colleague | | | x |
| 3. Evaluating the intelligence and capabilities of AI agents | x | | |
| 4. Dealing with AI systems in a reflective manner | x | | |
| 5. Engaging oneself in a constantly constructive discourse | | | x |
| 6. Handling sensitive data critically | x | | |
| 7. Constantly upholding ethical and moral standards | | | x |
| 8. Showing an awareness of an AI agent as a sort of virtual colleague | | x | |
| 9. Negotiating one's own recovery phases with AI agents | | x | |

The nine AI-related competencies can be described in more detail as follows.

**1. Context-specific understanding and interpretation of AI impulses**

One major challenge in human-AI collaboration is that humans often cannot understand how or why an AI system arrives at a specific conclusion or decision. Clinical decision support systems that are able to, for example, detect cancer and assist clinicians to inspect clinical cases are difficult to integrate into practice because clinicians do not understand how their potential machine teammates draw their conclusions and make decisions and, thus, have difficulty trusting them [8]. This circumstance is often referred to as 'black box' in science [31]. There have already been attempts in research to overcome the AI's black box system by developing explainable AI (XAI); this should be more transparent or able to explain or justify its behaviors and decisions [12, 31, 36]. However, in such cases where systems are based on complex deep neural networks, not even data scientists or software developers have yet been able to consistently understand the underlying decision rules [37]. Nevertheless, an essential demand to be able to work constructively with intelligent systems, to use them as a basis for one's own decisions and actions, or to explain their conclusions to others is that humans have to be able to understand and interpret AI-based technology's decisions and impulses regarding the specific context.

**2. Expressing oneself comprehensibly towards the AI colleague**

From the perspective of the AI-based learning algorithms, researchers and practitioners have revealed that a common challenge is that AI often fails to understand humans as well. This is particularly known from communicating with virtual assistants, which frequently tend to misunderstand human actors due to various reasons, such as different perceptions or interpretations of constructs, dynamic situations or ambiguous problems. There is a prominent example for Apple's Siri, which took the request "Call me an ambulance!" as a request to name its user "Anne Ambulance" [38]. It is also important in working situations, for example, to receive certain information from the AI system or give it an instruction, that the AI-based agent understands and interprets the request correctly in order to initiate appropriate actions [3]. Thus, humans have to be able to express themselves in a way that is comprehensible for the technology. This contributes to the (re)creation of a shared meaning of key concepts between human and AI.

**3. Evaluating the intelligence and capabilities of AI agents**

Humans can also tend to place too much confidence in AI technology or rely completely on its judgment because AI can be very good in some specific areas and can even outperform humans in speed, scalability and quantitative capabilities [14, 28]. Instead, humans should know how to combine their distinctive human skills with those of a smart technology [3]. To be more precise, intelligent machines are, for example, able to generate new combinations, classify things or take over repetitive activities. Humans, as counterparts, can come up with unique or original ideas, be emphatic or bring in human judgement [1, 14]. When building a vehicle, for example, an AI-based machine can take over simple, repetitive tasks, such as checking parts for quality or lifting heavy parts, but, in some cases, it is still more challenging for machine-like robots to perform dexterity tasks, such as assembling a gear motor [3]. The AI-based systems are usually trained for a specific purpose using data currently available and not necessarily covering all possible cases. Exemplarily, an AI-medical device was recently developed to predict the risk of cardiovascular heart disease [7]. However, the clinician who collaborates with this technology has to be aware that there is a risk that it could draw inaccurate predictions for patients of various ethnicities based on the fact that this AI system was trained with patients' data from three hospitals in a particular geographical area in Germany [7]. Moreover, AI systems are usually not able to transfer or generalize their ability or knowledge as easily as humans do [15]. Each new task requires a lot of data and extensive training. Consequently, it might not be immediately possible to teach an AI that has been trained to visually examine pictures or objects to recognize noises [9]. If the demands for AI agents change over time, then retraining might be required with the help of appropriate training data [39]. Thus, it is necessary for humans to be able to evaluate the suitability of an AI agent's capabilities concerning the execution of specific tasks and the complementarity to the human counterparts.

**4. Dealing with AI systems in a reflective manner**

As has already been indicated, nearly all AI algorithms are based on statistical or probabilistic methods. Therefore, it is usually impossible to train them to be 100% accurate and, thus, they can, similar to humans, make errors in specific cases [39]. This can be illustrated by an incident in Australia in 2016 where an AI-based system assigned with verifying the legality of social benefit payments was introduced. The technology detected those cases wrongly receiving unemployment benefits or social assistance and then automatically sent reminder letters to the relevant people. There was, in fact, no basis for the refunds claimed by it in 7,000 of 200,000 dunning letters sent by the software [40]. To prevent such incidents from happening, humans have to deal more reflectively and critically with the AI agent's conclusions or suggestions to be able to identify possible errors or incorrect decisions before they can harm or affect other people. In fact, this competence is an important prerequisite for constructively providing the AI-based technology with appropriate feedback that is comprehensible to it so that it can learn from mistakes and improve over time [40]. Such evolutionary progression is hardly possible if the system, for example, receives exclusively one-sided feedback, e.g. no feed-back regarding the fact that an individual denied credit was actually able to repay [40].

**5. Engaging oneself in a constantly constructive discourse**

Researchers and practitioners argue that learning processes should take place in both directions, from the AI agent to the human being and vice versa. The humans, for example, can receive feedback from their digital assistant on how a specific task was conducted regarding quality or performance indicators. This provides humans with more specific information where and possibly how to improve their own work processes or competencies [1, 2]. Regarding a constructive collaboration with AI systems in the workplace, this means that employees must be able to constructively absorb the impulses of the AI system and interpret them as support for their own ongoing learning processes and constant improvement. Consequently, humans should be more aware of an AI agent in its role as a helpful sparring partner in critical situations, during task performance or problem solving processes [14, 40]. Thus, a key demand of humans' competencies can be seen in behavioral patterns of constantly constructive discourse and dialogue between them and the AI.

**6. Handling sensitive data critically**

It is well known that most AI algorithms are based on personal and, therefore, often highly sensitive private data. Chatbots in customer care, for instance, are trained using personal data of customers. Search engines, recommender systems or digital assistants learn constantly from humans who engage with them [42]. The AI agents in production systems are very often based on data of high economic value for business organizations. Although the goal of intelligent technologies is to provide their human counterpart with optimal and personalized services, critical data gathering can compromise privacy, anger customers, endanger the competitive advantages of businesses and run afoul of the law [3]. Therefore, a further important competence demand for humans is to be able to handle sensitive data critically and with all required caution [42, 43].

**7. Upholding ethical and moral standards**

In 2014, a hiring AI system, which has been assigned to select suitable applicants for technical jobs, was developed and introduced by Amazon. However, it preferred male applicants over women, since, based on the data it was given, it learned that more men than women work in technological fields [44]. One can see from this example and many others, e.g. credit approving AI agents, which are known to be able to discriminate against people in certain groups [3, 38] that AI systems also have the potential to make biased decisions. This circumstance causes many controversies in society and there have already been attempts in politics and science to overcome this problem. Some governments, for example, have introduced principles and guidelines for AI developers [45]. Thus, AI researchers are working on developing trustworthy AI (TAI) that should be unbiased and just [7, 46]. However, because, in practice, AI systems are increasingly learning from direct interaction with humans, orientation to ethical and moral standards and values represent crucial requirements for humans who constantly collaborate with AI systems [40, 47].

**8. Showing an awareness of an AI agent as a sort of virtual colleague**
Human-AI collaboration can also be particularly challenging if the AI only has a virtual appearance, on the one hand, but, on the other hand, is to be attributed traits of a great teammate, for example, for joint task processing in stressful situations [28, 48].

**9. Negotiating one's own recovery phases with AI agents**
Finally yet importantly, it has to be considered that AI systems, in comparison to humans, require no or possibly other types of recovery phases. This needs to be negotiated and taken into account in the future between AI agents and humans in a similar way as between humans. The humans should be highly aware of their own physical and psychological limitations and must interpret signs of exhaustion correctly in order to insist on recovery phases and detachment from work [49].

## 4 Conclusion and Outlook

Our results reveal that the competencies demanded from the AI-based agent's counterpart, the human actor, cannot be covered completely by IT and mathematical skills, context competencies or leadership and social competencies. We suggest, instead, that there are additional cognitive, emotional and social competencies of humans that should be considered to enable a constructive human-AI collaboration. Our framework, shown in Table 1, introduces nine key competencies, which can be regarded as rather independent of specific tasks or problem situations at work but should be understood as general behavioral patterns that humans might be able to perform or learn when collaborating with AI-based agents at work. It also shows that there are certain interrelationships between the nine competencies identified so far; for example, competencies of dealing with AI in a reflective manner (4) might be interrelated with competencies of handling sensitive data critically (6) or competencies of upholding ethical and moral standards (7). In addition, we assume that there might be rather context and job specific configurational types of the set of introduced competencies (compositions) showing different levels of importance or relevance of each competence dimension in relation to the other competencies identified.

Thus, we expect that specific configurations or compositions of these AI-related competencies might enable a greater number of employees from various fields and professions to collaborate more constructively with AI. Furthermore, we argue that human actors holding these competencies will be able to participate and engage more constructively in the further development of AI-based systems as AI development should not only be a question of appropriate techniques and algorithms but has to deal much more with the transformational changes of work and society.

Concerning the framework deduced, we seek to initiate and contribute to further discussion and progress regarding the understanding and knowledge about transforming work environments, the changing role of employees and, consequently, the shift of job demands and challenges for the human actor in increasingly collaborative and interconnected work environments.

We invite future research to take up this framework in order to develop it further towards a scientifically sound model of human's AI-related competencies. Therefore, more qualitative and quantitative empirical field research seems to be necessary to evaluate, validate and adjust the results produced by our research. We argue that an empirically evaluated AI competence model is a key prerequisite for specific competence evaluation and development of humans within future work environments. This may also mean that in areas such as human resource management, researchers and practitioners should better understand the distinct capabilities and types of interaction of various AI-based agents in order to relate those to challenges for human actors during collaborative processes. Thus, research and practice may benefit from more interdisciplinary research and development approaches in this area.

## References

1. Seeber, I., et al.: Machines as Teammates: A Collaboration Research Agenda, vol. 10 (2018). https://doi.org/10.24251/HICSS.2018.055.
2. Dellermann, D., Calma, A., Lipusch, N., Weber, T., Weigel, S., Ebel, P.: The future of human-AI collaboration: a taxonomy of design knowledge for hybrid intelligence systems. In: Presented at the Hawaii International Conference on System Sciences (2019). https://doi.org/10.24251/HICSS.2019.034
3. Wilson, H.J., Daugherty, P.R.: Collaborative intelligence: humans and AI are joining forces. Harv. Bus. Rev. **96**, 114–123 (2018)
4. Süße, T.: Digital citizenship behavior in organization as indicator for actors' co-creative problem-solving in ecosystem-oriented work environments. In: Ahram, T., Taiar, R., Colson, S., Choplin, A. (eds.) IHIET 2019. AISC, vol. 1018, pp. 675–681. Springer, Cham (2020). https://doi.org/10.1007/978-3-030-25629-6_105
5. Hildesheim, W., Michelsen, D.: Künstliche Intelligenz im Jahr 2018 – Aktueller Stand von branchenübergreifenden KI-Lösungen: Was ist möglich? Was nicht? Beispiele und Empfehlungen. In: Buxmann, P., Schmidt, H. (eds.) Künstliche Intelligenz, pp. 119–142. Springer, Heidelberg (2019). https://doi.org/10.1007/978-3-662-57568-0_8
6. Upadhyay, A.K., Khandelwal, K.: Applying artificial intelligence: implications for recruitment. Strateg. HR Rev. **17**(5), 255–258 (2018). https://doi.org/10.1108/SHR-07-2018-0051
7. Zicari, R.V., et al.: Z-Inspection®: a process to assess trustworthy AI. IEEE Trans. Technol. Soc. 1 (2021). https://doi.org/10.1109/TTS.2021.3066209.

8. Cai, C.J., Winter, S., Steiner, D., Wilcox, L., Terry, M.: "Hello AI": uncovering the onboarding needs of medical practitioners for human-AI collaborative decision-making. Proc. ACM Hum. Comput. Interact. **3**, 1–24 (2019)
9. Ahlborn, K., et al.: Technologieszenario "Künstliche Intelligenz in der Industrie 4.0". Bundesministerium für Wirtschaft und Energie (BMWi) (2019)
10. Hyun, D.J., Bae, K., Kim, K., Nam, S., Lee, D.-H.: A light-weight passive upper arm assistive exoskeleton based on multi-linkage spring-energy dissipation mechanism for overhead tasks. Robot. Auton. Syst. **122**, 103309 (2019). https://doi.org/10.1016/j.robot.2019.103309
11. PLS - Plattform Lernende Systeme: Arbeit, Qualifizierung und Mensch-Maschine- Interaktion. acatech Deutsche Akademie der Technikwissenschaften, München (2019)
12. Wanner, J., Herm, L.-V., Janiesch, C.: Countering the fear of black-boxed AI in maintenance: towards a smart colleague. In: Proceedings of the 2019 Pre-ICIS SIGDSA Symposium, vol. 8 (2019)
13. Wang, D., et al.: Human-AI collaboration in data science: exploring data scientists' perceptions of automated AI. Proc. ACM Hum. Comput. Interact. **3**, 1–24 (2019). https://doi.org/10.1145/3359313
14. Othman, A., Eriksson, Y., Chirumalla, K.: Mapping artificial intelligence (AI) capabilities around human competences: an explorative study, 82 (2019)
15. Kaplan, A., Haenlein, M.: Siri, Siri, in my hand: who's the fairest in the land? On the interpretations, illustrations, and implications of artificial intelligence. Bus. Horiz. **62**, 15–25 (2019). https://doi.org/10.1016/j.bushor.2018.08.004
16. Weber, D.M.: Künstliche Intelligenz Wirtschaftliche Bedeutung, gesellschaftliche Herausforderungen, menschliche Verantwortung. Bitkom e. V., DFKI, Berlin, Kaiserslautern (2017)
17. Bundesministeriums für Arbeit und Soziales (BMAS): Begleitband des Bundesministeriums für Arbeit und Soziales, 356 (2020)
18. Wangermann, T.: KI in KMU: Rahmenbedingungen für den Transfer von KI-Anwendungen in kleine und mittlere Unternehmen. Konrad Adenauer Stiftung (2020)
19. Rammer, C., Bertschek, I., Schuck, B., Demary, V., Goecke, H.: Einsatz von Künstlicher Intelligenz in der Deutschen Wirtschaft: Stand der KI-Nutzung im Jahr 2019. ZEW-Gutachten und Forschungsberichte (2020)
20. Anton, E., Behne, A., Teuteberg, F.: The human behind artificial intelligence - an operationalisation of AI competencies. In: Proceedings of the 28th European Conference on Information Systems (ECIS), pp. 19–36 (2020). https://aisel.aisnet.org/ecis2020_rp/141
21. Long, D., Magerko, B.: What is AI literacy? Competencies and design considerations. In: Proceedings of the 2020 CHI Conference on Human Factors in Computing Systems, Honolulu, pp. 1–16. ACM (2020). https://doi.org/10.1145/3313831.3376727
22. Ashby, W.R., et al.: Automata Studies (AM-34). Princeton University Press (1956)
23. Nilsson, N.J.: The Quest for Artificial Intelligence: A History of Ideas and Achievements. Cambridge University Press, Cambridge (2009). https://doi.org/10.1017/CBO9780511819346.
24. Butz, M.V.: Towards Strong AI. KI - Künstliche Intelligenz **35**(1), 91–101 (2021). https://doi.org/10.1007/s13218-021-00705-x
25. Schneider, S.: Superintelligent AI and the Postbiological Cosmos Approach. In: Losch, A. (ed.) What is Life? On Earth and Beyond, pp. 178–198. Cambridge University Press, Cambridge (2017). https://doi.org/10.1017/9781316809648.011
26. Massmann, C., Hofstetter, A.: AI-pocalypse now? Herausforderungen Künstlicher Intelligenz für Bildungssystem, Unternehmen und die Workforce der Zukunft. In: Fürst, R.A. (ed.) Digitale Bildung und Künstliche Intelligenz in Deutschland. AUE, pp. 167–220. Springer, Wiesbaden (2020). https://doi.org/10.1007/978-3-658-30525-3_8

27. Wick, C.: Deep Learning. Informatik-Spektrum **40**(1), 103–107 (2016). https://doi.org/10.1007/s00287-016-1013-2
28. Schmitt, B.: Speciesism: an obstacle to AI and robot adoption. Mark. Lett. **31**(1), 3–6 (2019). https://doi.org/10.1007/s11002-019-09499-3
29. Brynjolfsson, E., McAfee, A.: The business of artificial intelligence, 20 (2017)
30. Zhang, R., McNeese, N.J., Freeman, G., Musick, G.: "An Ideal Human": Expectations of AI Teammates in Human-AI Teaming. Proc. ACM Hum.-Comput. Interact. 4, 1–25 (2021). https://doi.org/10.1145/3432945
31. Adadi, A., Berrada, M.: Peeking inside the black-box: a survey on explainable artificial intelligence (XAI). IEEE Access **6**, 52138–52160 (2018). https://doi.org/10.1109/ACCESS.2018.2870052
32. Brock, J.K.-U., von Wangenheim, F.: Demystifying AI: what digital transformation leaders can teach you about realistic artificial intelligence. Calif. Manage. Rev. **61**, 110–134 (2019). https://doi.org/10.1177/1536504219865226
33. Woodruffe, C.: What is meant by a competency? Leadersh. Org. Dev. J. **14**, 29–36 (1993). https://doi.org/10.1108/eb053651
34. Boyatzis, R.E.: Competencies in the 21st century. J. Manage. Dev. **27**, 5–12 (2008). https://doi.org/10.1108/02621710810840730
35. Pfeiffer, S.: Kontext und KI: Zum Potenzial der Beschäftigten für Künstliche Intelligenz und Machine-Learning. HMD Praxis der Wirtschaftsinformatik **57**(3), 465–479 (2020). https://doi.org/10.1365/s40702-020-00609-8
36. Ehsan, U., Tambwekar, P., Chan, L., Harrison, B., Riedl, M.O.: Automated rationale generation: a technique for explainable AI and its effects on human perceptions. In: Proceedings of the 24th International Conference on Intelligent User Interfaces, Marina del Ray California, pp. 263–274. ACM (2019). https://doi.org/10.1145/3301275.3302316.
37. Zweig, K.A.: Algorithmische Entscheidungen: Transparenz und Kontrolle, 16 (2019)
38. Yampolskiy, R.V., Spellchecker, M.S.: Artificial intelligence safety and cybersecurity: a timeline of AI Failures, 12 (2016)
39. Brynjolfsson, E., Mitchell, T.: What can machine learning do? Workforce implications. Science **358**, 1530–1534 (2017). https://doi.org/10.1126/science.aap8062
40. Zweig, K.A., Lischka, K.: Wo Maschinen irren können: Verantwortlichkeiten und Fehlerquellen in Prozessen algorithmischer Entscheidungsfindung. Arbeitspapier Algorithmenethik (2018). https://doi.org/10.11586/2018006.
41. Van Aartrijk, M.L., Tagliola, C.P., Adriaans, P.W.: AI on the Ocean: the RoboSail project. In: ECAI, pp. 653–657 (2002)
42. Conrad, C.S.: Künstliche Intelligenz—Die Risiken für den Datenschutz. Datenschutz und Datensicherheit - DuD **41**(12), 740–744 (2017). https://doi.org/10.1007/s11623-017-0870-4
43. Gausling, T.: KI und DS-GVO im Spannungsverhältnis. Künstliche Intelligenz, pp. 11–53. Springer, Wiesbaden (2020)https://doi.org/10.1007/978-3-658-30506-2_2
44. Dastin, J.: Amazon scraps secret AI recruiting tool that showed bias against women (2018). https://www.reuters.com/article/us-amazon-com-jobs-automation-insight-idUSKCN1MK08G
45. Smuha, N.A.: The EU approach to ethics guidelines for trustworthy artificial intelligence. Comput. Law Rev. Int. **20**, 97–106 (2019). https://doi.org/10.9785/cri-2019-200402
46. Thiebes, S., Lins, S., Sunyaev, A.: Trustworthy artificial intelligence. Electron. Markets **31**, 447–464 (2020) https://doi.org/10.1007/s12525-020-00441-4
47. Hagendorff, T.: The ethics of AI ethics: an evaluation of guidelines. Mind. Mach. **30**(1), 99–120 (2020). https://doi.org/10.1007/s11023-020-09517-8
48. Baylor, A.L.: Promoting motivation with virtual agents and avatars: role of visual presence and appearance. Philos. Trans. R. Soc. B Biol. Sci. **364**, 3559–3565 (2009). https://doi.org/10.1098/rstb.2009.0148
49. Sonnentag, S., Kuttler, I., Fritz, C.: Job stressors, emotional exhaustion, and need for recovery: a multi-source study on the benefits of psychological detachment. J. Vocat. Behav. **76**, 355–365 (2010). https://doi.org/10.1016/j.jvb.2009.06.005

# Collaborative Plan to Reduce Inequalities Among the Farms Through Optimization

Ana Esteso[1(✉)], M. M. E. Alemany[1], Angel Ortiz[1], and Rina Iannacone[2]

[1] Research Centre on Production Management and Engineering (CIGIP), Universitat Politècnica de València, Camino de Vera S/N, 46022 València, Spain
{aesteso,mareva,aortiz}@cigip.upv.es

[2] ALSIA-Metapontum Agrobios Research Center, S.S. Jonica 106, Km 448,2, 75012 Metaponto, MT, Italy
rina.iannacone@alsia.it

**Abstract.** The crop planning problem consists in defining the crop and acreage to be planted at each farm. There are several centralized mathematical programming models to support crop planning in literature. However, centralized solutions often produce economic unfairness among the members of the supply chain, being especially relevant among the farmers in the agri-food sector. To solve it, this paper tries to answer the following research question: is it possible to reduce inequalities among the farmers through a collaborative plan? A centralized multi-objective mathematical programming model to support crop planning and the next decisions up to the sale of vegetables through a collaborative plan is proposed to answer this question. To show the validity of the proposed collaborative plan, results obtained are compared against those obtained without collaboration. The analysis of results shows that inequalities among the supply chain members can be highly reduced in a centralized decision-making approach by implementing the proposed collaborative plan, reducing a bit the supply chain profit.

**Keywords:** Agri-food supply chain · Crop planning · Collaboration · Optimization

## 1 Introduction

Farmers decide what crops to plant at their farms and the acreage dedicated to each of the selected crops through the crop planning process [1]. The mathematical programming has proved its validity to support the crop planning process [2, 3]. Proof of this is the large number of models to support the crop planning in the literature (e.g. [4–7]). However, most of these models propose centralized approaches in which one single user makes decisions for the entire supply chain (SC).

Centralized decisions lead to the best solution for the SC, however, it produces inequalities in the profits perceived by each SC member, leading to the unwillingness to cooperate among them [8]. Farmers are often the most vulnerable actors in the chain because they tend to have fewer business-related skills, however collaboration can be


Published by Springer Nature Switzerland AG 2021
L. M. Camarinha-Matos et al. (Eds.): PRO-VE 2021, IFIP AICT 629, pp. 125–137, 2021.
https://doi.org/10.1007/978-3-030-85969-5_11

used to improve their results [9]. In view of given situation, this paper tries to answer the following research question: Is it possible to reduce inequalities among the farmers through a collaborative plan?

To answer this question, a multi-objective mathematical programming model to support the crop planning problem through a collaborative plan is proposed. Its results are compared to the equivalent model not considering the collaborative plan. This model not only defines the crop planning but anticipates decisions related to the harvest, storage, distribution, sale, and clearance sale of vegetables. It considers two objectives: the maximization of SC profits, and the minimization of the unfairness among farmers.

The proposed collaborative plan is based on the three dimensions of collaboration: information sharing, decision synchronization, and incentive alignment [10]. The information on the demand for each vegetable and the available area for planting is shared with all members of the SC and each of them is assigned the demand that should satisfy according to its available area. Decisions are synchronized since a centralized model is used that simultaneously plans the planting, harvesting, storage, and distribution of vegetables. An incentive alignment is carried out since, with the sharing of demand, risks are redistributed among all members of the SC. In addition, by minimizing the unfairness among farmers, the benefits obtained are also shared.

Therefore, the contributions of this paper are the proposal of a new collaborative plan to reduce the inequalities among farmers, the mathematical modelling of the distribution of information among the members of the supply chain, and the modelling of the possibility of clearing vegetables at retailers to reduce waste.

The rest of the paper is structured as follows. Section 2 describes the problem under study and the proposed collaborative plan. Section 3 formulates the multi-objective model to support the crop planning with the established collaborative plan. Section 4 implements the model and applies it to the Argentinean tomato case study, identifying the effect of implementing the proposed collaborative plan. Finally, Sect. 5 outlines the main conclusions and future research lines.

## 2 Problem Description

This proposal focuses on the crop planning problem which consists in selecting the crops to be planted in a farm and the area allocated to each selected crop [1]. To balance the supply and demand of vegetables at markets it is necessary to anticipate the impact that such crop planning will have on the production and distribution of vegetables [11].

Because of that, this paper focuses on an entire SC and on processes carried out from the planting of vegetable plants to their sale to end consumers. The SC under study is composed of farms, cooperatives, and retailers Fig. 1, and commercializes vegetables with an annual planting (such as tomatoes or peppers), which shelf life is limited.

Farmers are responsible for the planting and harvest of vegetables, their storage, and their transport to the cooperative with which the farm is associated. Farms can only be associated with one cooperative. Farmers can also waste vegetables when their shelf life is consumed, being the vegetables unfit for human consumption. Cooperatives act as a consolidator of vegetables received by their associated farms. Therefore, cooperatives can store vegetables, transport them to retailers, or waste them in case they deteriorate.

Finally, retailers sell the vegetables received to end consumers. Storage is not allowed at retailers to avoid the need of collecting the fresh vegetables from shelves at the end of each day, store them in a refrigerated warehouse located at the retailer, and putting back vegetables on their shelves at the beginning of the next day. In this way, fresher vegetables are sold to consumers, and costs related to the refrigerated warehouse and laboring dedicated to those handling tasks are avoided. Therefore, all vegetables available at retailers should be sold in the same period of their arrival. Otherwise, vegetables should be wasted. To facilitate the sale of the oversupply of vegetables and reduce the waste that can be generated at this point, it is possible to clear some vegetables at a lower price.

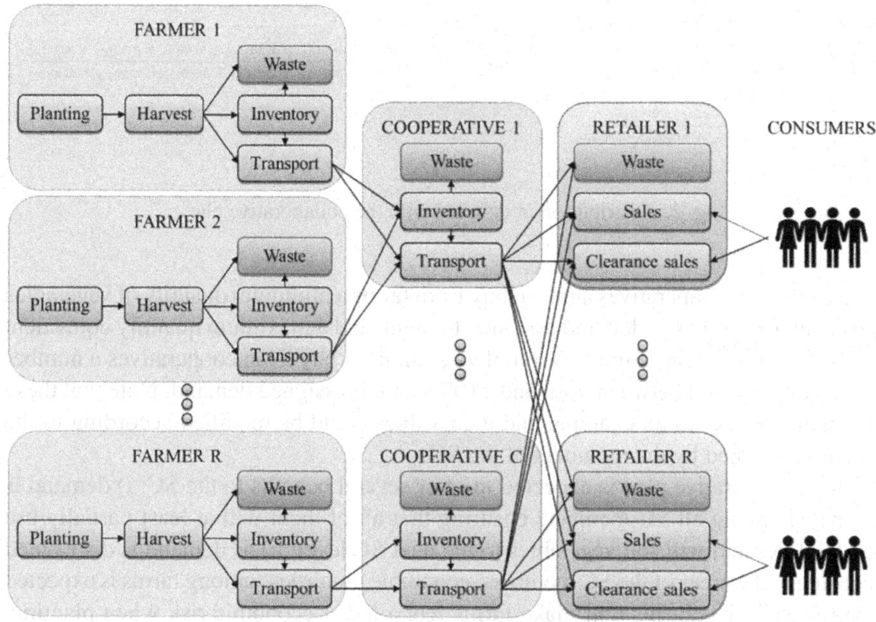


**Fig. 1.** SC configuration and decisions.

In this paper, we also propose to establish a collaborative plan between the different levels of the SC, being the main contribution of this paper. This collaborative plan is based on minimum information sharing, and more concretely the sharing of the demand for each vegetable and of the area available for planting at each location. In this way, retailers share the information on their demand for each vegetable among the cooperatives in such a way that the demand is distributed among cooperatives according to the total area of farmers affiliated with the cooperative. Once cooperatives know the demand for each vegetable that they should meet, they break down said demand among their members according to their areas. So, the demand for each vegetable is distributed among the SC members according to their available area for planting (Fig. 2) with the aim of adjusting the supply to the demand as much as possible, and reduce inequalities among the members of the supply chain.

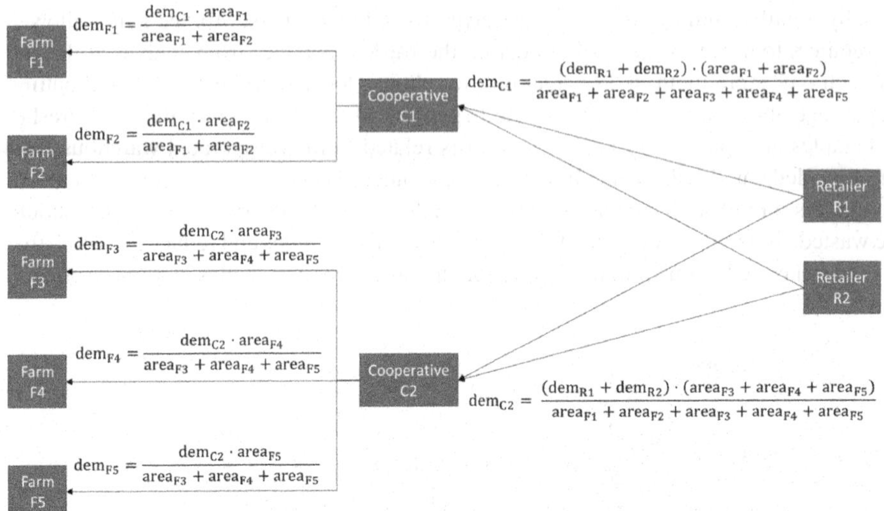


**Fig. 2.** Distribution of demand with the collaborative plan.

In exchange, cooperatives agree to buy from farms a minimum quantity of vegetables equivalent to 90% of the demand assigned to them, and a maximum quantity equivalent to 110% of the demand. Similarly, retailers commit to buy from cooperatives a number of vegetables ranged between 90% and 110% of their assigned demand. Note that these percentages are set as an example and their values could be modified according to the agreement reached by the members of the SC.

This collaborative plan is expected to offer several benefits to the SC: i) demand is distributed among all SC members ensuring that all of them will at least partially use their facilities and will sell vegetables to the next SC level; ii) as demand is distributed according to the areas of the SC members, economic unfairness among farms is expected to be reduced; iii) all this will make farms feel a lower economic risk when planting, being more inclined to implement the crop planning centrally defined.

## 3 Multi-objective Model Formulation

Table 1 exposes the nomenclature used to formulate the model, where $f$ refers to farms, $c$ to farms cooperatives, $r$ to retailers, $v$ to vegetables, $p$ to planting periods, $h$ to harvest periods, $t$ to time periods comprising the planning horizon, $FC_c$ to the set of farms $f$ belonging to the cooperative $c$, $P_v$ to the set of planting periods $p$ in which vegetables $v$ can be planted, and $PH_{vp}$ to the set of harvest periods $h$ in which vegetables $v$ planted in period $p$ can be harvested.

**Table 1.** Nomenclature.

| Parameters | |
|---|---|
| $ap_f$ | Available area for planting in farm $f$ |
| $ac_c$ | Available area for planting in all farms belonging to cooperative $c$ |
| $am_v$ | Minimum area to be planted with vegetable $v$ when it is decided to plant it |
| $y_v^{ph}$ | Yield of vegetable $v$ planted at $p$ and harvested at $h$ |
| $de_{vr}^t$ | End consumers' demand of vegetable $v$ at retailer $r$ at period $t$ |
| $e_{vr}^t$ | Percentage of demand of vegetable $v$ that can be sold at retailer $r$ at a clearance sale price at period $t$ |
| $mdc_c$ | Percentage of demand that farms should meet when serving cooperative |
| $Mdc_c$ | Percentage of demand that farms can oversupply when serving cooperative |
| $mdr_r$ | Percentage of demand that cooperatives should meet when serving retailers |
| $Mdr_r$ | Percentage of demand that cooperatives can oversupply when serving retailers |
| $sp_{vc}^t$ | Selling price of one kg of vegetable $v$ to cooperative $c$ at period $t$ |
| $mp_{vr}^t$ | Market price of one kg of vegetable $v$ at retailer $r$ at period $t$ |
| $gp_{vr}^t$ | Clearance sale price of one kg of vegetable $v$ at retailer $r$ at period $t$ |
| $uc_{vr}^t$ | Penalty cost for not meeting one kg of vegetable $v$ demand at retailer $r$ at period $t$ |
| $wc_v^t$ | Penalty cost for wasting one kg of vegetable $v$ at period $t$ |
| $pc_v$ | Planting, cultivation, and harvest cost per hectare planted with vegetable $v$ |
| $tcf_{vfc}$ | Cost of transporting one kg of vegetable $v$ from farm $f$ to cooperative $c$ |
| $tcc_{vcr}$ | Cost of transporting one kg of vegetable $v$ from cooperative $c$ to retailer $r$ |
| $hc_v$ | Holding cost for vegetable $v$ |
| $sl_v$ | Shelf life of vegetable $v$ after harvest |
| $msl_v$ | Minimum required shelf life of vegetable $v$ at sale |
| $ml_v$ | Minimum service level for each vegetable $v$ |
| **Decision variables** | |
| $A_{vf}^p$ | Area planted in farm $f$ with vegetable $v$ at planting period $p$ |
| $H_{vf}^h$ | Quantity of vegetable $v$ harvested at farm $f$ in period $h$ |
| $IF_{vf}^{ht}$ | Quantity of vegetable $v$ harvested at farm $f$ in period $h$ stored at period $t$ |
| $WF_{vf}^{ht}$ | Quantity of vegetable $v$ harvested at farm $f$ in period $h$ wasted at period $t$ |
| $TF_{vfc}^{ht}$ | Quantity of vegetable $v$ harvested at farm $f$ in period $h$ transported to cooperative $c$ at period $t$ |

(*continued*)

**Table 1.** *(continued)*

| Decision variables | |
|---|---|
| $DF^t_{vfc}$ | Demand of vegetable $v$ at cooperative $c$ that should be met by farm $f$ in period $t$ |
| $IC^{ht}_{vc}$ | Quantity of vegetable $v$ harvested in period $h$ stored at period $t$ at cooperative $c$ |
| $WC^{ht}_{vc}$ | Quantity of vegetable $v$ harvested in period $h$ wasted at period $t$ at cooperative $c$ |
| $TC^{ht}_{vcr}$ | Quantity of vegetable $v$ harvested in period $h$ transported from cooperative $c$ to retailer $r$ at period $t$ |
| $DC^t_{vcr}$ | Demand of vegetable $v$ at retailer $r$ that should be met by cooperative $c$ in period $t$ |
| $WR^{ht}_{vr}$ | Quantity of vegetable $v$ harvested in period $h$ wasted at period $t$ at retailer $r$ |
| $S^{ht}_{vr}$ | Quantity of vegetable $v$ harvested in period $h$ sold at retailer $r$ at period $t$ |
| $G^{ht}_{vr}$ | Quantity of vegetable $v$ harvested in period $h$ cleared at retailer $r$ at period $t$ |
| $B^t_{vr}$ | Quantity of unmet demand of vegetable $v$ at retailer $r$ at period $t$ |
| $D_f$ | Difference between the region and farm f margin per area (absolute value) |
| $YP^p_{vf}$ | Binary variable that takes value equal to one when farm $f$ plant vegetable $v$ at period $p$ |

### 3.1 Objectives

The model takes into account two objectives: the maximization of the SC profits, and the minimization of the economic unfairness perceived by farmers.

SC profits ($Z_E$) are composed of sales, clearance of vegetables, costs related to the planting, cultivation, and harvest of vegetables, their storage and transport between the nodes of the SC, and economic penalties for waste and unmet demand. In this way, this objective is not only promoting the economic sustainability of the SC, but also the environmental and social sustainability by including penalties for waste and unmet demand respectively, thus promoting their reduction (1).

$$\begin{aligned} Z_E = {} & \sum_v \sum_r \sum_h \sum_t S^{ht}_{vr} \cdot mp^t_{vr} + \sum_v \sum_r \sum_h \sum_t G^{ht}_{vr} \cdot gp^t_{vr} - \sum_v \sum_f \sum_{p \in P_v} A^p_{vf} \cdot pc_v \\ & - \sum_v \sum_f \sum_h \sum_t IF^{ht}_{vf} \cdot hc_v - \sum_v \sum_c \sum_h \sum_t IC^{ht}_{vc} \cdot hc_v \\ & - \sum_v \sum_f \sum_c \sum_h \sum_t TF^{ht}_{vfc} \cdot tcf_{vfc} - \sum_v \sum_c \sum_r \sum_h \sum_t TC^{ht}_{vcr} \cdot tcc_{vcr} \\ & - \sum_v \sum_f \sum_h \sum_t WF^{ht}_{vf} \cdot wc^t_c - \sum_v \sum_c \sum_h \sum_t WC^{ht}_{vc} \cdot wc^t_c - \sum_v \sum_r \sum_h \sum_t WR^{ht}_{vr} \cdot wc^t_c \\ & - \sum_v \sum_r \sum_t B^t_{vr} \cdot uc^t_{vr}. \end{aligned} \tag{1}$$

The perception of economic unfairness among farms ($Z_U$) is calculated as the difference in absolute value of the margin per hectare obtained by farm and the average margin per hectare obtained by all farmers (2). $PF_f$ indicates the margin obtained by farm f and is calculated as the difference of the sale of vegetables to cooperatives and costs related to planting, cultivation and harvest of vegetables, their transport to cooperatives, and the penalty for waste in the farm (3)

$$Z_U = \sum_f \left| \frac{PF_f}{ap_f} - \frac{\sum_f PF_f}{\sum_f ap_f} \right| \tag{2}$$

$$PF_f = \sum_v \sum_c \sum_h \sum_t TF_{vfc}^{ht} \cdot \left( sp_{vc}^t - tcf_{vfc} \right) - \sum_v \sum_{p \in P_v} A_{vf}^p \cdot pc_v - \sum_v \sum_h \sum_t IF_{vf}^{ht} \cdot hc_v - \sum_v \sum_h \sum_t WF_{vf}^{ht} \cdot wc_c^t \quad \forall f \tag{3}$$

### 3.2 Constraints

The model is subjected to the following constraints. The area planted with all vegetables throughout the planning horizon at each farm cannot exceed its available area (4).

$$\sum_v \sum_{p \in P_v} A_{vf}^p \leq ap_f \quad \forall f \tag{4}$$

Due to technical reasons, a minimum area should be planted for each vegetable when it is decided to do so (5), and the maximum area is limited to the available area at farm.

$$YP_{vf}^p \cdot am_v \leq A_{vf}^p \leq YP_{vf}^p \cdot ap_f \quad \forall v, f, p \in P_v \tag{5}$$

The quantity of vegetables to be harvested depends on the planted area and the yield of plants (6). It is assumed that all matured vegetables at the plant should be harvested.

$$H_{vf}^h = \sum_{p \in PH_{vp}} A_{vf}^p \cdot y_v^{ph} \quad \forall v, f, h \tag{6}$$

Once harvested, vegetables can be stored at farm, transported to cooperative, or wasted (7). Vegetables can be stored until their remaining shelf life gets lower than the required by consumers (8). Thus, the inventory for vegetables with lower remaining shelf lives should be equal to zero (9).

$$IF_{vf}^{ht} = H_{vf}^h - \sum_c TF_{vfc}^{ht} - WF_{vf}^{ht} \quad \forall v, f, h, t = h \tag{7}$$

$$IF_{vf}^{ht} = IF_{vf}^{ht-1} - \sum_c TF_{vfc}^{ht} - WF_{vf}^{ht} \quad \forall v, f, h, h < t \leq h + sl_v - msl_v \tag{8}$$

$$IF_{vf}^{ht} = 0 \quad \forall v, f, h, t \geq h + sl_v - msl_v \tag{9}$$

Each farm should transport to the cooperative a quantity of vegetable within the range agreed with the cooperative (10). This forces all farms to plant all vegetables.

$$DF_{vfc}^t \cdot mdc_c \leq \sum_{h \leq t} TF_{vfc}^{ht} \leq DF_{vfc}^t \cdot Mdc_c \quad \forall v, c, f \in FC_c, t \tag{10}$$

Once vegetables arrive to cooperatives can be stored, transported to retailer, or wasted (11). Vegetables can be stored until their remaining shelf life gets lower than the required by consumers (12)

$$IC_{vc}^{ht} = IC_{vc}^{ht-1} + \sum_f TF_{vfc}^{ht} - \sum_r TC_{vcr}^{ht} - WC_{vc}^{ht} \tag{11}$$

$$\forall v, c, h, h \leq t \leq h + sl_v - msl_v.$$

$$IC_{vc}^{ht} = 0 \quad \forall v, f, h, t \geq h + sl_v - msl_v \tag{12}$$

Each cooperative should transport to retailers a quantity of vegetable within the range agreed with the retailer (13).

$$DC_{vcr}^{t} \cdot mdr_r \leq \sum\nolimits_{h \leq t} TC_{vcr}^{ht} \leq DC_{vcr}^{t} \cdot Mdr_r \quad \forall v, c, r, t \tag{13}$$

Once vegetables reach the retailer, it must be sold in the same period of its arrival. If there is an excess of supply, vegetables can be cleared or wasted (14).

$$\sum\nolimits_{c} TC_{vcr}^{ht} = S_{vr}^{ht} + G_{vr}^{ht} + WR_{vr}^{ht} \quad \forall v, r, h, h \leq t \leq h + sl_v - msl_v \tag{14}$$

The quantity of vegetables to be cleared is limited by a percentage of demand (15).

$$\sum\nolimits_{h \leq t} G_{vr}^{ht} \leq e_{vr}^{t} \cdot de_{vr}^{t} \quad \forall v, r, t \tag{15}$$

If there is not enough vegetable at retailer to meet demand, unmet demand is produced (16).

$$\sum\nolimits_{h \leq t} S_{vr}^{ht} + B_{vr}^{t} = de_{vr}^{t} \quad \forall v, r, t \tag{16}$$

A minimum service level should be met at each retailer in the planning horizon (17).

$$\sum\nolimits_{h} \sum\nolimits_{\substack{t \geq h \\ t \leq h + sl_v - msl_v}} S_{vr}^{ht} \geq \sum\nolimits_{t} ml_v \cdot de_{vr}^{t} \quad \forall v, r \tag{17}$$

Retailer distributes its demand between cooperatives according to the available area of the farms belonging to cooperatives (18).

$$DC_{vcr}^{t} = \frac{de_{vr}^{t} \cdot ac_c}{\sum_c ac_c} \quad \forall v, c, r, t \tag{18}$$

Cooperatives distributes its assigned demand between farms belonging to the cooperative according to the available area for planting at each farm (19).

$$DF_{vfc}^{t} = \frac{\sum_r DC_{vcr}^{t} \cdot ap_f}{ac_c} \quad \forall v, c, f \in FC_c, t \tag{19}$$

The nature of decision variables is defined (20).

$$\begin{array}{ll} A_{vf}^{p}, H_{vf}^{h}, IF_{vf}^{ht}, WF_{vf}^{ht}, TF_{vfc}^{ht}, DF_{vfc}^{t}, IC_{vc}^{ht}, WC_{vc}^{ht} & CONTINUOUS \\ TC_{vcr}^{ht}, DC_{vc}^{rt}, WR_{vr}^{ht}, S_{vr}^{ht}, G_{vr}^{ht}, B_{vr}^{t} & \\ Y_{vt}, YP_{vf}^{p} & BINARY \end{array} \tag{20}$$

### 3.3 Resolution Methodology

Equation (2), which corresponds to the minimization of economic unfairness perceived by farmers, should be linearized. To do this, it is replaced by Eqs. (21)–(23), in which the variable $D_f$, that represents the unfairness perceived by the farmer, is forced to acquire the absolute value for the difference between the margin per hectare obtained by the farmer and the average margin per hectare obtained by all farmers.

$$Z_U = \sum_f D_f \tag{21}$$

$$D_f \geq \frac{PF_f}{ap_f} - \frac{\sum_f PF_f}{\sum_f ap_f} \quad \forall f \tag{22}$$

$$D_f \geq \frac{\sum_f PF_f}{\sum_f ap_f} - \frac{PF_f}{ap_f} \quad \forall f \tag{23}$$

The weighted sum method is used to solve the multi-objective model. Through this method weights are distributed among the objectives ensuring that the weight assigned to all of them adds up to one ($w_E + w_U = 1$). In addition, the values for the objectives need to be scaled to acquire values between zero and one. For that, each objective is divided by an estimation of the highest value they can acquire ($MZ_E$ for objective $Z_E$, and $MZ_U$ for objective $Z_U$). The multi-objective model used to carry out experimentation is:

$$Max\ Z = w_E \cdot \frac{Z_E}{MZ_E} - w_U \cdot \frac{Z_U}{MZ_U} \tag{24}$$

subject to: (1), (3), (4)–(23).

## 4 Application to the Argentinean Tomato Case Study

The model is validated through its application to the Argentinean Tomato Case Study extracted from [12], in which ten farms from La Plata region in Argentina should decide the crop planning for three types of tomato: round, pear, and cherry. Farms are grouped into two cooperatives and one retailer is considered. Demand and prices for the three types of tomato are obtained from the Buenos Aires Central Market webpage (www.mercadocentral.gob.ar/). The planning horizon is composed of 52 weeks, which is equivalent to one year. The calendar for the planting and harvest of plants is shared by the three types of tomato and is displayed in Fig. 3.

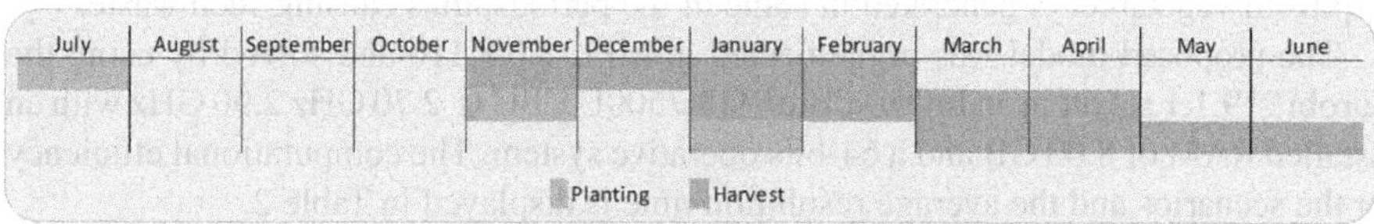


**Fig. 3.** Planting/Harvest calendar.

Through the collaborative plan, it is considered that farmers should serve the cooperatives an amount of product that represents between 90 and 110% of the assigned demand for each type of tomato. The same happens between cooperatives and retailers so that cooperatives must serve between 90 and 110% of the demand for each type of tomato assigned to them by the retailers.

The proposed model is solved for six scenarios characterized by different distribution of weights between the objectives: maximization of profits and minimization of economic unfairness among farms (set CPP). These same scenarios are executed for a situation in which the proposed collaborative plan is not considered (set NCP). For that, constraints (10), (13), (18), and (19) are avoided.

The solutions for all sets and scenarios are compared in terms of SC profits, economic unfairness perceived by farms, the percentage of harvest wasted, and the percentage of unmet demand (Fig. 4).

The results show that the scenarios in which the collaborative plan is implemented obtain less SC profits chain than when the collaborative plan is not implemented. However, SC profits are reduced between 12% and 22%, being this acceptable if other indicators, such as the unfairness perception by farms, are highly improved.

In fact, in those scenarios in which the weight assigned to the objective of minimizing the economic unfairness between farms is ranged between 0% and 60%, it is observed that, when applying the collaborative plan, the economic unfairness among farms can be drastically reduced. In this way, reducing the economic unfairness perceived by farms from 90% to 95% only implies a worsening of the SC profits by approximately 20%.

These results are of great interest since the reduction of unfairness makes the members of the SC more involved when implementing the crop planning obtained centrally. On the contrary, trying to implement a crop planning obtained centrally without a collaborative plan provides great unfairness among the SC members and can cause some of these members, usually the most disadvantaged, not to jointly participate in the crop planning but to take their individual decisions. This would be a great inconvenience for the entire SC, which would see its profits diminished due to the imbalance between supply and demand generated by farmers who individually decide their crop planning without taking into account the rest of the members of the chain.

On the other hand, the impact of implementing the collaborative plan can be observed on environmental aspects, such as the percentage of harvest wasted along with the SC, and social aspects, such as the percentage of unmet demand (in addition to the unfairness among farms). In this sense, waste increases between 1 and 10% when implementing the collaborative plan, while the unmet demand is reduced by up to 100%. This is because, when implementing the collaborative plan, an average of two more hectares are planted in all scenarios, thus obtaining more vegetables that are dedicated to serving such demand. As the pattern followed by the plant's yield is not similar to the patterns of demand, a surplus of vegetables is generated in some of the periods, thus causing such waste.

The proposed model was implemented in MPL 5.0.8.116 and solved by using the Gurobi™ 9.1.1 solver in an Intel® Core™ i7-7500U CPU @ 2.70 GHz 2.90 GHz with an installed RAM of 8.00 GB and a 64-bits operative system. The computational efficiency for the scenarios and the average resolution time is displayed in Table 2.

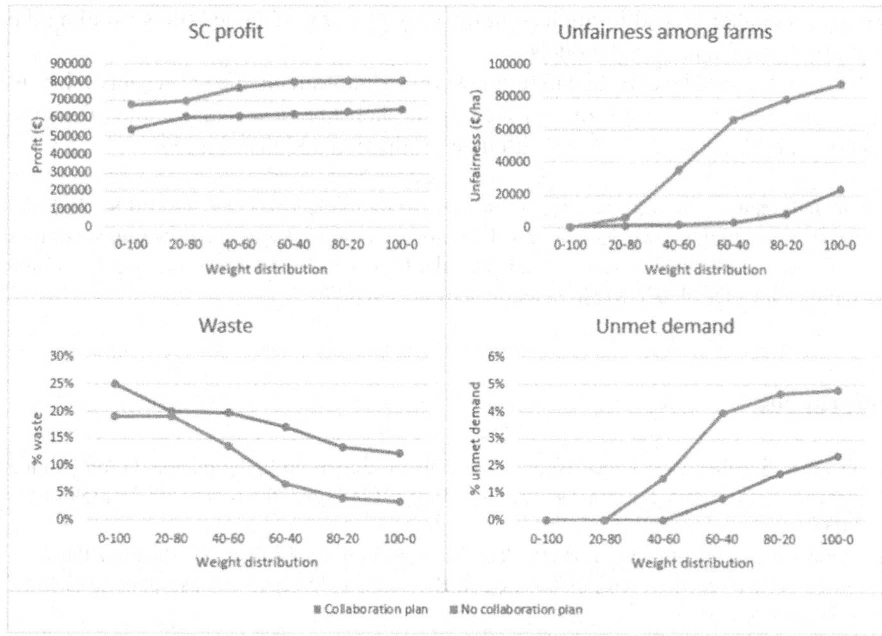


**Fig. 4.** Results for the SC profits, unfairness among farms, waste, and unmet demand.

**Table 2.** Computational efficiency.

| Scenario | Constraints | Continuous variables | Binary variables | Resolution time |
|---|---|---|---|---|
| CPP | 194,371 | 25,271 | 90 | 1.4 s |
| NCP | 187,195 | 23,399 | 90 | 0.7 s |

## 5 Conclusions and Future Research Lines

This paper proposes a multi-objective mathematical programming model to centrally define the crop planning of an agri-food SC while implementing a collaborative plan to reduce the economic unfairness perceived by farmers. Results obtained by this model are compared with the ones of an equivalent centralized model not considering the collaborative plan. Results are compared in terms of SC profits, economic unfairness among farms, percentage of harvest wasted, and percentage of unmet demand for six scenarios characterized by different weight distribution between objectives.

Results show that implementing the collaborative plan would highly reduce the unfairness perceived by farmers while reducing the SC profits. Implementing the proposed collaborative plan can therefore be very beneficial for agri-food SC since it allows drastically reducing the unfairness perception of its members without this supposing a great economic loss for the SC. This reduction in the unfairness makes farmers more willing to collaborate and to implement the crop planning obtained, thus avoiding the main problem of centralized models.

This study could be extended in future works by introducing the uncertainty inherent to the agri-food sector in parameters such as the shelf life of vegetables, their demand, and prices, or the costs associated with their production and distribution.

**Acknowledgments.** We acknowledge the support of the project 691249, RUCAPS: "Enhancing and implementing knowledge based ICT solutions within high risk and uncertain conditions for agriculture production systems", funded by the European Union's research and innovation programme under the H2020 Marie Skłodowska-Curie Actions.

## References

1. Dury, J., Schaller, N., Garcia, F., et al.: Models to support cropping plan and crop rotation decisions. rev. Agron. Sustain. Dev. **32**, 567–580 (2012). https://doi.org/10.1007/s13593-011-0037-x
2. Handayati, Y., Simatupang, T.M., Perdana, T.: Agri-food supply chain coordination: the state-of-the-art and recent developments. Logist. Res. **8**(1), 1–15 (2015). https://doi.org/10.1007/s12159-015-0125-4
3. Esteso, A., Alemany, M.M.E., Ortiz, A.: Conceptual framework for designing agri-food supply chains under uncertainty by mathematical programming models. Int. J. Prod. Res. (2018). https://doi.org/10.1080/00207543.2018.1447706
4. Flores, H., Villalobos, J.R., Ahumada, O., et al.: Use of supply chain planning tools for efficiently placing small farmers into high-value, vegetable markets. Comput. Electron. Agric. **157**, 205–217 (2019). https://doi.org/10.1016/j.compag.2018.12.050
5. Sinha, D.K., Singh, K.M., Ahmad, N., et al.: Natural resource management for enhancing farmer's income: An optimal crop planning approach in Bihar. Indian J. Agric. Sci. **88**, 641–646 (2018)
6. Ahumada, O., Rene Villalobos, J., Nicholas Mason, A.: Tactical planning of the production and distribution of fresh agricultural products under uncertainty. Agric. Syst. **112**, 17–26 (2012). https://doi.org/10.1016/j.agsy.2012.06.002
7. Esteso, A., Alemany, M.M.E., Ortiz, A., Liu, S.: Optimization model to support sustainable crop planning for reducing unfairness among farmers. Cent. Eur. J. Oper. Res. (2021). https://doi.org/10.1007/s10100-021-00751-8
8. Stadler, H.: A framework for collaborative planning and state-of-the-art. In: Meyr, H., Günther, H.-O. (eds.) Supply Chain Planning, pp. 3–28. Springer, Heidelberg (2009). https://doi.org/10.1007/978-3-540-93775-3_1
9. Ammirato, S., Felicetti, A.M., Ferrara, M., et al.: Collaborative organization models for sustainable development in the agri-food sector. Sustainability **13**, 2301 (2021). https://doi.org/10.3390/su13042301
10. Esteso, A., Alemany, M.M.E., Ortiz, A.: Conceptual framework for managing uncertainty in a collaborative agri-food supply chain context. In: Camarinha-Matos, L.M., Afsarmanesh, H., Fornasiero, R. (eds.) PRO-VE 2017. IAICT, vol. 506, pp. 715–724. Springer, Cham (2017). https://doi.org/10.1007/978-3-319-65151-4_64

11. Esteso, A., Alemany, M.M.E., Ortiz, Á.: Impact of product perishability on agri-food supply chains design. Appl. Math. Model **96**, 20–38 (2021). https://doi.org/10.1016/j.apm.2021.02.027
12. Alemany, M., Esteso, A., Ortiz, A., del Pino, M.: Centralized and distributed optimization models for the multi-farmer crop planning problem under uncertainty: application to a fresh tomato Argentinean supply chain case study. Comput. Ind. Eng., 107048 (2020). https://doi.org/10.1016/j.cie.2020.107048

# Working Beside Robots: A Glimpse into the Future

Paula Urze[1,2](✉), João Rosas[1,3], and Luis M. Camarinha-Matos[1,3]

[1] School of Science and Technology, NOVA University of Lisbon, Caparica, Portugal
pcu@fct.unl.pt

[2] Interuniversity Center for the History of Science and Technology (CIUHCT), Lisbon, Portugal

[3] Center of Technology and Systems (CTS), UNINOVA, Caparica, Portugal
{jrosas,cam}@uninova.pt

**Abstract.** Automation throughout history has caused profound changes in employment dynamics. With the advent of the fourth industrial revolution, a new threat may affect employability, as robots and AI-based processes can now assume tasks considered exclusive to humans. This position paper aims to motivate the study of the effects of AI and automation on employability, extending it into a collaborative network perspective. The problem is firstly observed from a historical perspective. The collaboration aspects are considered through the analysis of two case studies. Results suggest that a latent element of collaborative networks, complexity, may have effects in terms of employability.

**Keywords:** Employability · Artificial intelligence · Automation · Collaborative networks

## 1 Introduction

Since the end of the 19th century, humanity has witnessed several technological disruptive events with such a magnitude characterized as industrial revolutions. Now, it is said that we are currently going through the fourth industrial revolution (Industry 4.0). Meanwhile, there was progressive innovation with profound effects of technological, economic, and social nature, namely, the developments in the areas of Robotics and Artificial Intelligence. One of such profound effects was the transference of jobs between cross-industrial sectors, as many jobs were killed in some sectors, and new jobs were created in other ones. In this regard, researchers and history tell us that fears of job loss are unfounded, at least after some adaptation period, after which jobs transference succeeds. However, this time, things might be different, as Robots and Artificial Intelligence (AI) might effectively take a more significant proportion of our jobs at a faster speed. Or at least the impacts during the adaptation period might reach a different scale.

Two attitudes towards employability (or professional occupation) persist due to advances in automation and AI. In the 1980s, most publications were optimistic about technology and employment, and best-selling books announced the increasing amount of


Published by Springer Nature Switzerland AG 2021
L. M. Camarinha-Matos et al. (Eds.): PRO-VE 2021, IFIP AICT 629, pp. 138–147, 2021.
https://doi.org/10.1007/978-3-030-85969-5_12

qualified work. Today, the vision is mostly pessimistic: job shedding, the rise of robotics and technological systems as synonym for the replacement of human workers; predictions of a dystopian future based on the aforementioned replacement and mass unemployment are now often put forward, as well as "intelligent machines" being considered driving forces in the dehumanization of work or the development of a cyber-proletariat [1].

In contrast with the gradual or linear evolution typical of previous technological revolutions, the fast diffusion of the digital economy represents an enormous challenge due to its intrinsic complexity, unpredictability, and dematerialization of processes, products, goods, and services [2]. In some way, it is predicted that information technology, robotics, and AI will have a dominant role in society. More recent forecasts even indicate that some "non-routine cognitive tasks" may be developed by robots, and that the service sector is subject to a widespread risk [3, 4]. For technological determinists, the question of whether machines will displace human labor "*will be answered by the nature of the technology that arrives in the future*" [5, 6]. Technological determinism regards technology as the key force shaping society and determining social change and progress. This notion of progress is therefore centered around technological growth and the conception that the problems of the social whole are solved by technological advances. There are, however, divergent approaches on the future of work that argue that there will not only be job distribution, but that new professions will also emerge from the process of social and technical transformation. Also, some traditional professions might be recreated and gain a new scope. In turn, from the social construction of technology's perspective, technology is socially constructed, and its trajectory is dependent on several social elements and pertinent social groups.

In this **position paper**, the two perspectives, the optimistic and the pessimistic, concerning the dynamics of Artificial Intelligence and Robotized Automation over employability/professional occupation are addressed. In addition, this problem is also addressed from the "collaborative networks" perspective. Since this is a position paper, our aim is not to present conclusive results but rather to provide arguments supported by existing evidence for the proposed problem and motivate inter-disciplinary discussion between social sciences and engineering.

## 2 The Impact of Innovation on Employability

In the past, automation was associated with machines and robots performing repetitive tasks in factories. Currently, thanks to the combination with certain disruptive technologies, such as AI, Robotics, Robotic Process Automation (RPA), and Machine Learning (ML), among others, machines are now able to perform operations that were previously unique to humans, for example, driving a car, landing a plane, writing news, predicting our behavior, and so on.

This capacity for machines/systems to now perform tasks known to be exclusive of humans has raised fears that automation could lead to a significant loss of jobs. As mentioned in a study from McKinsey in 2017 regarding the impacts of AI, Automation and Robotics on employability, 50% of existing activities are technically automatable [7].

From a historical perspective, whenever an industrial revolution occurred, there was subsequent massive destruction of jobs that became obsolete in some sectors. However, contrary to the fears and social unrest felt at those times, after a while job destruction was compensated by the creation of other jobs in new sectors. Figure 1 illustrates the phases of employment transfer to other sectors.

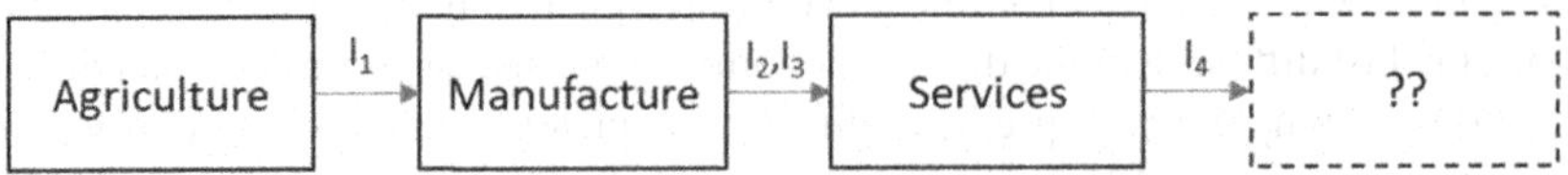


**Fig. 1.** Jobs displacement during industrial revolutions.

Instead of the feared jobs' loss during these transformation periods, there was a significant shift of employment to other sectors, briefly:

- **I1:** Transference of jobs from agriculture to manufacturing due to mechanization, steam power, …
- **I2:** Transference of jobs from manufacture to services due to electrical energy, mass production, assembly lines, …
- **I3:** More jobs transference due to automation, computers, and electronics, …
- **I4:** Due to Robots, AI, and other paradigms, many activities from the services sector can be taken by smart robots/smart systems. Will those lost jobs be transferred to other activities? Which ones?

More recently, society has benefited from the emergence of disruptive technologies, such as the Internet of Things (IoT)/Cyber-Physical Systems (CPS), Intelligent Robotics, and Artificial Intelligence/Machine Learning, which have allowed a deeper level of automation and robotization. By applying AI/ML algorithms, machines have been able to assume various roles and jobs that were previously exclusive to humans, e.g., non-predictable tasks requiring creative or intellectual effort. Therefore, contrary to previous disruptive events, these jobs' appropriation might be more challenging or even threatening, as it occurs across several activities sectors, including services, and encompassing non-repetitive, non-structured, more intellectual, and more creative tasks.

As stated by the authors of the study "*A Future that works: Automation; employment, and productivity*" [7], it is predicted that "50% of current work activities are technically automatable by adapting currently demonstrated technologies" and that "6/10 current occupations have more than 30% of activities that are technically automatable" [7]. According to the same authors, "Up to 375 M workers globally may need to transition to new occupational categories by 2030" [7]. Thus, there is increasing uncertainty about what might occur in terms of employability/professional occupation in the future. Still, as mentioned before, there are two types of attitudes or perspectives, optimistic and pessimistic, regarding the progressive innovation brought in by these technologies.

### 2.1 The Optimistic Perspective

Many researchers from several areas are optimistic that society will adapt to the higher levels of robotization and automation. Jobs' loss in some sectors will eventually be complemented by creating new work in other sectors. It happened before, it will happen now. They maintain that "*It is easy to see which jobs are being destroyed by technology, but difficult to imagine which jobs will be created by it*" [7]. As happened before, "*history would suggest that such fears may be unfounded: over time, labor markets adjust to changes in demand for workers from technological disruptions*" [7].

In fact, an optimist perspective could foresee:

- ***Recreation of professions in traditional sectors.*** Several sectors (e.g., agriculture and fisheries) have suffered a marked loss of interest on the part of the new generations, even when they offer job opportunities. This is due to the harshness of traditional activities in these sectors and the low social prestige associated with them. The introduction of robotization and intelligent systems in these areas will make it possible to recreate the nature of the functions to be performed by humans, now more focused on planning, creativity (new products), management and participation in value chains. This naturally requires other levels of qualification and will likely lead to an increase in social prestige.
- ***Establishment of new professions and functions.*** Robotics and its integration with intelligent networked systems will allow the emergence of new professions or a considerable extension of human capabilities (sensory, acting and telepresence) in areas such as support for active aging, security, entertainment, education, and training. It is also important to take advantage of such technological advances to compensate for the natural decline in capacities that comes with aging, allowing for a better integration in the socio-economic activities of the elderly and people with special needs.
- ***Promotion of new models of inter-generational collaboration.*** The current and predictable demographic evolution requires new approaches for effective inter-generational dialogue and collaboration. Robotization, namely in terms of service robotics and extension to human sensory and action capabilities, should be used as a catalyst for collaboration between different age groups. In addition, AI and the growing hyperconnectivity of society, interconnecting organizations, people, and objects in the physical world (IoT/CPS) can enhance new network business models, where it is important to find suitable models of inter-generational integration.
- ***Enhance collaboration between humans and intelligent systems.*** Human-machine collaboration (e.g., ongoing developments in collaborative robotics) and human-systems collaboration, namely exploring new forms of interface, computational models of emotions and creativity, etc., should lead to a redefinition of functions. This should allow not only a better use of the cognitive, creative, and emotional capacities of humans, but also an improvement in their professional achievement.

As mentioned in [8] and [9], "*alarmism is not justified, as the diffusion of artificial intelligence and robotics will not be as fast and accelerated as advertised. However, computers will replace routine tasks. But tasks requiring problem-solving, adaptability, flexibility, and creativity are the most resistant to innovation. Despite advances, there are limitations of current technology to perform non-routine tasks.*" However, that statement was made more than five years ago. Progress and innovation run fast in areas like AI, robotics, ML, among others.

### 2.2 The Pessimistic Perspective

Until recently, robots were relatively limited, typically applied in routine and predictable tasks. However, as said by Elan Musk, "There will be fewer and fewer jobs that a robot cannot do better" [10]. Now, intelligent systems can take on increasingly complex tasks. An illustrative example is a system called Watson (IBM) which, supported by several AI functions, can beat humans in such a games as complex as "Jeopardy" [11]. AI-based processes and machines can now drive cars, write news, do trading in financial markets, impersonate humans in call centers as agents or chatbots, among others.

Around the beginning of the century, it was stated about the future of automation that activities, such as autonomous driving or natural language processing, would be quite challenging to perform by a computer [12]. However, such predictions were wrong. Some researchers believe that it is different this time. Intelligent processes and robots supported by AI and ML will be increasingly empowered to replace humans in a broader range of activities. As machines become more capable and sophisticated, there will be fewer and fewer tasks that they cannot do better.

AI and ML may therefore eliminate many jobs due to their unlimited potential for automating tasks. Any task can be the object of automation even faster than before, even if it involves complex work requiring human effort [13]. In addition, ML models can be replicated and reused at no cost, increasing this effect of eliminating human jobs. This certainly requires further multi-disciplinary discussion.

## 3 A Collaborative Networks Perspective

The influence of automation, robotics, and AI on employability can be addressed from a collaborative networks' perspective. For this, we will start by referring to the concept of network effects and the Metcalfe's Law. Then, for illustrative purposes, we describe two cases obtained from new media sources. The first one describes a system that can organize and coordinate a collaborative project involving a network of freelancers. The second case involves a supply chain dedicated to the manufacture of a "smart product."Afterward, we hypothesize that the determining factor for collaborative networks, versus robotics and AI, versus employability is related to the complexity of collaborative networks.

### 3.1 Network Effects

The "network effect" or "network externality" or "demand-side economies of scale" consists of the phenomenon by which the value or utility of a product is dependent on the number of users using that product or other compatible ones [14]. A network effect manifests, in a direct way, when the number of users increases, the value of the product also increases. It also manifests indirectly, as when the utility of the product for one group increases, the utility for other groups also increases. For instance, when people started to drive cars, road construction, gas stations, service areas, and other sectors became more important.

Metcalfe's law can characterize network effects [15]. This classical law establishes that the value of the network grows in proportion to the square number of elements participating in the network. The cost of a network increases directly proportionally to the size of a network. However, when a product reaches a critical number of users, network effects drive the subsequent growth of the network until it achieves a stable balance. From a certain point, due to saturation or congestion issues, which affect the network's ability to grow [16].

Some researchers have proposed more conservative formulations for Metcalfe's law in determining the value of a network [17]. In general, this law has been correct to explain the growth in telephone networks, faxes, web applications, social networks [18], and even Bitcoin [19]. Many companies began the transition from a traditional "business economy" to a "networked economy" to benefit from the strategic value of network effects.

### 3.2 Case-Studies

The following two cases serve as an illustration and inspiration for the discussion that will be made afterward. The description of the cases is reduced to the minimum considered necessary for our purposes. The reader should consult the corresponding bibliography for more insights.

**Freelancers' Collaborative Projects.** We start with an example regarding collaborative projects management involving teams of freelancers. For the management of projects, a software called iCEO is used. "*iCEO is a virtual management system that automates complex work by dividing it into small individual tasks*" [20]. This software can significantly reduce project costs. This reduction is done in two ways. On one hand, the software eliminates and replaces "middle management". On the other hand, over the various projects, it tries to automate the tasks carried out by freelancers [20].

When the system is used in a new project, it firstly decides which jobs can be automated and which ones require human effort. Then, the system searches online for freelancers with the necessary skills. The system then distributes the tasks and manages the execution of the project. For this purpose, the system monitors every single task being developed by each freelancer. Meanwhile, it collects massive amounts of data, providing enough information to understand how each freelancer developed his/her tasks. Afterwards, ML algorithms begin to run through the collected data, obtaining models for task automation. What is happening is that the freelancers are effectively teaching the system how to perform their tasks.

Although the software eliminated the manager's role, in a first stage it helped create work for freelancers, which could be considered positive. However, as the system is used in posterior projects, it can significantly reduce freelancers' participation.

**Supply-Chain Network.** This case encompasses a company in a supply chain for assembling a "smart-product" [21]. It eloquently illustrates how network effects arise within a collaborative network.

The smart product brand company focuses on its core competencies (design, assembling, sales to the public). It outsources the other stages of product construction to better-qualified suppliers (manufacture, distribute, install, servicing). A generic representation of this network, expressing direct and indirect network effects in the supply-chain is illustrated in Fig. 2. To ensure product quality, the company needs to control critical logistics processes [21]. This requires a high-level of collaboration, which allows monitoring the product being manufactured at all stages, sharing demand plans, communicating changes in product design. That must be done in real-time. But as the customer base at the demand-side increases, there is a consequent increase in pressure and greater complexity of coordination on the supply-side. This happens in contexts where supply-chains can grow up to a global scale. According to Metcalfe's law, a level of congestion in the chain can be reached. To deal with the resulting complexity, it is necessary to automate chain coordination progressively. As described in the next section, this poses potential effects on employability.

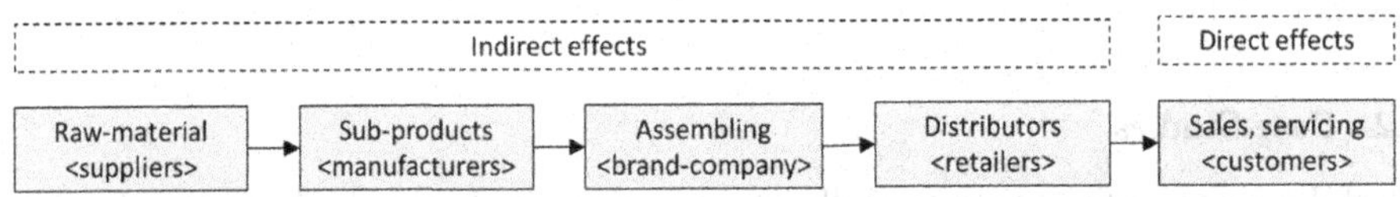


**Fig. 2.** Representation of the supply-chain focusing on the network effects.

### 3.3 Discussion

Regarding the described cases, the first one refers to an example of a system, which eliminates "middle-management" in collaborative projects. Eventually, using ML with data taken from freelancers' tasks monitoring, the system can even automate many of their tasks, reducing their need in subsequent projects. The case takes place in the context of networks. If there is a growing trend towards using this type of software for managing collaborative projects by itself, it poses a threat in terms of employability.

The second case is more interesting. When a supply chain comprises a small number of trustworthy suppliers, it can be managed and operated by humans and standard management processes. As the number of participants on the demand-side increases, supply-chain complexity also increases [22]. At a certain level, network growth can be hampered, not by lack of capacity, but by management complexity [23, 24]. As such, many companies started to automate supply-chain management with Robotic Process Automation [25].

In this regard, the supply-chain automation with RPAs is accompanied by the digitalization of the entire chain, which, similarly to the previous case, allows recording massive amounts of data. That data is fed into Machine Learning algorithms to obtain mechanisms that improve network management. With this level of visibility, non-deterministic tasks performed by humans are subject to automation, which can free the human from repetitive tasks, but might also take jobs [25, 26].

Meanwhile, while finding the best suppliers, the RPAs try to identify the ones with the best price, quality, and delivery time. Eventually, the chosen ones might comprise suppliers who are involved in automation strategies on their own (as they were identified as the best ones). We can therefore stipulate, this self-organizing effect towards suppliers with more level of automation effects on employability.

From a taxonomic viewpoint, the first case resembles the PVC/VT network types. The second one comprises a supply chain. From related research, we know that complexity is a feature in collaborative networks [27]. We could therefore generalize this line of thinking to the other existing collaborative network forms. We could consider the utilization of RPA-based to implement, e.g. *X*-planners and *X*-managers, in which *X* belongs to {VE, VO, Extended Enterprise, …}, to deal with network complexity, as suggested in [28].

As mentioned before, since this is a position paper, our purpose is not to present definite research results but rather to present arguments to consider a new line of research or added concerns for current research streams. In this case, our hypothesis addresses the effects of AI and automation on employability from a collaborative networks' perspective. Having said that, we consider the hypothesis illustrated in Fig. 3.

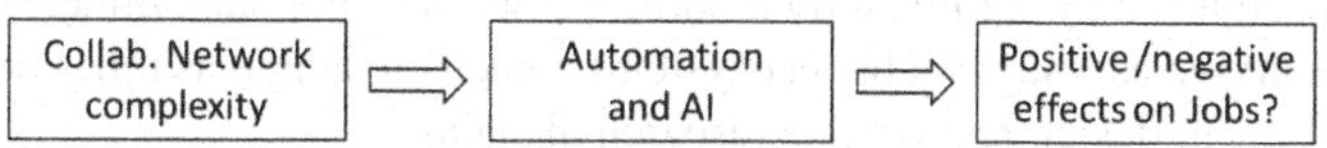


**Fig. 3.** CN Complexity and effects on jobs.

Therefore, we propose the hypothesis that collaborative networks complexity may pose positive or negative effects on employability. Further research work is necessary to confirm or refute this research premise and to devise promising directions for sustainable technological development. As this problem is complex and broad, other perspectives could be taken in consideration [29]. For instance, a more skeptical viewpoint could assume that complexity is a feature of many things and certainly would affect employability. Even considering the risks of this "unknown territory", it is the responsibility of researchers to also devise strategies that turn those risks into opportunities. As such, it is necessary to include such concerns in the research agenda. For instance, we could consider questions such as:

- What is an appropriate methodology to study the link between AI/ML/Robotics and employability, from a collaborative network perspective?
- Which socio-technical models for the development and integration of robotics and intelligent systems, complemented with organizational models in collaborative networks/business ecosystems, can enhance the recreation of professions and new functions in traditional sectors?
- How to explore and develop new technological possibilities to extend the human capacities, opening opportunities for new forms of professional occupation?
- How to explore and develop new collaborative models, contributing to peace, sustainability, and quality of life, including professional occupation?

Such challenges naturally require an interdisciplinary and socio-technical approach to research. The growing precariousness of labor relations, accentuated by some current socio-economic models, may constitute an obstacle to the social acceptance of new technologies. In addition to a strategy to raise awareness of new opportunities, it is also important to develop research into new models of "social security" for the "network economy" in a highly technological society.

## 4 Conclusions

This research work addressed the effects of AI, Robotics and automation on employability from a collaborative networks' perspective. We began addressing this issue from a historical perspective, looking at the effects of automation on job dynamics throughout the most significant disruptive events. Then, the perspective of collaboration was established, starting from two case studies, towards reaching our research hypotheses established in the previous sections. The question of whether AI and Robotics will lead to the loss of jobs is now even more uncertain. From a historical perspective, we most likely should not worry in the medium term. But things might be different now. The nature of innovation in the information age is different from what has happened before. This time, machines may significantly assume the work of humans. Either way, for the economy to survive as a sustainable ecosystem, it needs to adapt, as it has done before. And this calls us to design appropriate research agendas.

The next step, as future work, is to incorporate more aspects to the proposed research hypothesis. The problem is worth being addressed from a collaborative networks' perspective.

**Acknowledgments.** This work has also been partially funded by the Center of Technology and Systems (CTS) – UNINOVA, and the Portuguese FCT Foundation project UIDB/00066/2020, and by Interuniversity Center for the History of Science and Technology (CIUHCT) and the Portuguese FCT Foundation project UIDB/00286/2020.

## References

1. Huws, U.: Labor in the Global Digital Economy: The Cybertariat Comes of Age. NYU Press (2014)
2. Marques, A.P., Chaves, M., Serra, H., Urze, P.: Introdução-Imaginar "futuros" do trabalho, contextos e vivências subjetivas. Configurações [Online], 24 | 2019. https://doi.org/10.4000/configuracoes.7620
3. Marien, M.: The second machine age: work, progress, and prosperity in a time of brilliant technologies. Cadmus **2**, 174 (2014)
4. Frey, C.B., Osborne, M.A.: The future of employment: how susceptible are jobs to computerisation? Technol. Forecast. Soc. Chang. **114**, 254–280 (2017)
5. Virgillito, M.E.: Rise of the robots: technology and the threat of a jobless future. Labor Hist. **58**, 240–242 (2017)
6. Boyd, R., Holton, R.J.: Technology, innovation, employment and power: does robotics and artificial intelligence really mean social transformation? J. Sociol. **54**, 331–345 (2018)
7. Manyika, J., et al.: Jobs Lost, Jobs Gained: Workforce Transitions in a Time of Automation, p. 150. McKinsey Global Institute (2017)

8. David, H.: Why are there still so many jobs? The history and future of workplace automation. J. Econ. Perspect. **29**, 3–30 (2015)
9. McGuinness, S., Pouliakas, K., Redmond, P.: Skills-displacing technological change and its impact on jobs: challenging technological alarmism? Econ. Innov. New Technol., 1–23 (2021)
10. Vox: The big debate about the future of work, explained. https://www.youtube.com/watch?v=TUmyygCMMGA. Accessed 15 Jan 2021
11. Ferrucci, D., Levas, A., Bagchi, S., Gondek, D., Mueller, E.T.: Watson: beyond jeopardy! Artif. Intell. **199**, 93–105 (2013)
12. Levy, F., Murnane, R.J.: The New Division of Labor: How Computers are Creating the Next Job Market. Princeton University Press (2004)
13. McKendrick, J.: Artificial intelligence will replace tasks, not jobs. Forbes (2018). https://www.forbes.com/sites/joemckendrick/2018/08/14/artificial-intelligence-will-replace-tasks-not-jobs
14. Shapiro, C., Carl, S., Varian, H.R., et al.: Information Rules: A Strategic Guide to the Network Economy. Harvard Business Press (1998)
15. Metcalfe, B.: Metcalfe's law after 40 years of ethernet. Computer **46**, 26–31 (2013)
16. Evans, D.S., Schmalensee, R.: Failure to launch: Critical mass in platform businesses. Rev. Netw. Econ. **9**, 1–34 (2010)
17. Briscoe, B., Odlyzko, A., Tilly, B.: Metcalfe's law is wrong-communications networks increase in value as they add members-but by how much? IEEE Spectr. **43**, 34–39 (2006)
18. Hendler, J., Golbeck, J.: Metcalfe's law, web 2.0, and the semantic web. J. Web Semant. **6**, 14–20 (2008)
19. Peterson, T.: Metcalfe's law as a model for bitcoin's value. Altern. Investment Anal. Rev. **7**(2), 9–18 (2018)
20. Fidler, D.: Here's How Managers Can Be Replaced by Software. https://hbr.org/2015/04/heres-how-managers-can-be-replaced-by-software. Accessed 15 Jan 2021
21. Howells, R.: How the network effect enables a global supply chain. Forbes, 16 February 2021
22. Potts, J., Mandeville, T.: Toward an evolutionary theory of innovation and growth in the service economy. Prometheus **25**, 147–159 (2007)
23. Yang, B., Yang, Y.: Postponement in supply chain risk management: a complexity perspective. Int. J. Prod. Res. **48**, 1901–1912 (2010)
24. Serdarasan, S.: A review of supply chain complexity drivers. Comput. Ind. Eng. **66**, 533–540 (2013)
25. Hartley, J.L., Sawaya, W.J.: Tortoise, not the hare: digital transformation of supply chain business processes. Bus. Horiz. **62**, 707–715 (2019)
26. Ageron, B., Bentahar, O., Gunasekaran, A.: Digital supply chain: challenges and future directions. Supply Chain Forum Int. J. **21**, 133–138 (2020)
27. Scherrer-Rathje, M., Arnoscht, J., Egri, P., Braun, E., Csáji, B.C., Schuh, G.: A generic model to handle complexity in collaborative networks. In: PICMET'09-2009 Portland International Conference on Management of Engineering & Technology, pp. 271–287. IEEE (2009)
28. Urze, P., Osório, A.L., Afsarmanesh, H., Camarinha-Matos, L.M.: A balanced sociotechnical framework for collaborative networks 4.0. In: Camarinha-Matos, L.M., Afsarmanesh, H., Ortiz, A. (eds.) PRO-VE 2020. IAICT, vol. 598, pp. 485–498. Springer, Cham (2020). https://doi.org/10.1007/978-3-030-62412-5_40
29. Wong, A.: The laws and regulation of AI and autonomous systems. In: Strous, L., Johnson, R., Grier, D.A., Swade, D. (eds.) Unimagined Futures – ICT Opportunities and Challenges. IAICT, vol. 555, pp. 38–54. Springer, Cham (2020). https://doi.org/10.1007/978-3-030-64246-4_4

# Maintenance and Life-Cycle Management

# Supporting Predictive Maintenance in Virtual Factory

Go Muan Sang(✉), Lai Xu, and Paul de Vrieze

Faculty of Science and Technology, Bournemouth University, Poole, Dorset, UK
{gsang,lxu,pdevrieze}@bournemouth.ac.uk

**Abstract.** In Industry 4.0 manufacturing collaborative network, product design processes, manufacturing processes, maintenance processes should be integrated across different factories and enterprises. The collaborative manufacturing network 4.0 allows the amalgamation of manufacturing resources in multiple organizations to operate processes in a collaborative manner for reacting to the fast changes of markets or emergencies. In this paper, we propose a predictive maintenance service as a part of a virtual factory, a form of collaborative manufacturing network. Data-driven predictive maintenance service is built-in FIWARE, an industry 4.0 framework. To optimize predictive maintenance services based on different criteria within a virtual factor, such as geographical locations, similar types of machinery, or cost/time efficiency, etc., we provide our design and implementation to deal with providing better maintenance services and data exchanging across different collaborative partners with different requirements and modularizing of related functions.

**Keywords:** Virtual factory · Predictive maintenance · Maintenance schedule · Industry 4.0 · Collaborative networks 4.0

## 1 Introduction

Traditional monolithic manufacturing usually involves physical machines, buildings, etc., and setting the manufacturing process is generally slow and expensive [1]. Thus, it cannot deal with the challenges of dynamic market demands, competitions and short product lifecycle [2]. To overcome the challenges, modern collaborative industry is shifting towards the concept of Collaborative Networks 4.0 [2–4].

Virtual factory as one implementation of collaborative networks 4.0 and a foundational concept to future manufacturing, allows the flexible integration of manufacturing resources from different multiple organizations using emerging technologies such as cloud, sensors, IoT, etc. [3, 5, 6]. Traditional monolithic factory heavily relies on its own capabilities e.g. internal functions, physical machines, buildings, etc., whereas virtual factory allows the integration of diverse capabilities from a network of specialized domains and experts across industries collaboratively, flexibly and inexpensively regardless of their physical locations [3, 5]. This enables the collaborative network better dealing with constant demands i.e. market, productivity, etc., since each partner firm


Published by Springer Nature Switzerland AG 2021
L. M. Camarinha-Matos et al. (Eds.): PRO-VE 2021, IFIP AICT 629, pp. 151–160, 2021.
https://doi.org/10.1007/978-3-030-85969-5_13

focuses on what it does best within the network [1, 6]. To facilitate virtual factory, a flexible platform is required [3, 5].

Effective maintenance is essential to the factory collaborative network as it can impact on the collaborative network i.e. integrated processes, value and cost associated with downtime, faulty products, etc. [7, 8]. Data generated by the various processes, systems/machine equipment tools across factories operation and production offer opportunities such as data-driven analytics e.g. predictive maintenance to the collaborative network [9–12]. Flexible collaboration with other businesses is an important aspect of a virtual factory [5]. In this context, a network partner, as a service provider can offer data-driven predictive maintenance across the collaborative network i.e. manufacturers, factories, etc.

We look at how to support predictive maintenance in a collaborative network virtual factory complying Industry 4.0 standards using FIWARE and IDS, which leads to supporting flexible collaboration among different enterprises facilitating transparent data exchange and modularizing of related functions. The contributions of this work are: a) to investigate a predictive maintenance for supporting virtual factory networks, b) to present a predictive maintenance schedule using data-driven approach for virtual factory, and c) using the proposed solution to apply with a manufacturing case.

The paper is structured as follows. In Sect. 2, we present related work in collaborative manufacturing network 4.0 and related technologies. In Sect. 3 we describe the design of a reference architecture for a virtual factory with predictive maintenance service. In Sect. 4 and 5, we present the scheduling approaches and implementation of the predictive maintenance service in a virtual factory. The future work and conclusion are provided in Sect. 6.

## 2 Related Work

In this section, the relationship between collaborative networks 4.0 and virtual factory is described in Sect. 2.1. FIWARE industry 4.0 platform is an important industry 4.0 implementation platform. Section 2.2 presents the FIRST virtual factory reference architecture, which is adapted for our implementation. International data space is an important data storage for implementing industry 4.0 applications. IDS is introduced in Sect. 2.3. General work on predictive maintenance is evaluated in Sect. 2.4.

### 2.1 Collaborative Networks 4.0 and Virtual Factory

Collaborative networks 4.0 is driven by the amalgamation of different processes, partners, third parties, advanced analytics and machines spanning across different enterprises and organizations for collaborative value creations. Industry 4.0 drives the focus of modern manufacturing system design [2, 13]. It facilitates collaborative processes across different factories and enterprises for complex manufacturing processes. Essentially Industry 4.0 enables better control and operations to adapt in real time and in response to constant demands [14].

The concept of virtual factories derives from the expansion of virtual enterprises in the context of manufacturing [3]. Virtual factory can be seen as one of implementation of collaborative networks 4.0 in the context of Industry 4.0, and it allows the flexible integration of manufacturing resources in multiple organizations to manage (i.e. model, simulate, test) factory layouts and processes in a virtual environment with the support of emerging technologies such as cloud, IoT, etc. This enables the simulation of a desired factory before committing to investment and creating the actual factory in shorter time with demand-driven product lines [3].

### 2.2 FIWARE Virtual Factory

FIWARE virtual platform reference architecture in Fig. 1 maximizes cloud technology to offer smart manufacturing and digital marketplaces, especially for virtual enterprises and cross-organizations [15]. The virtual platform promotes a business ecosystem framework which supports GEs (genetic enabler components), digital asset sharing and enterprise collaboration/interoperability. These different components are the foundation of a higher-level software layer.

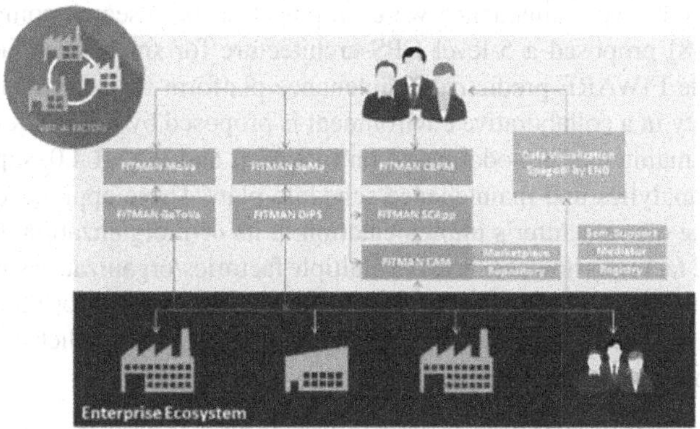


**Fig. 1.** FIWARE virtual factory reference architecture [15]

The collaborative assets can be managed by FITMAN CAM which supports the virtualization and management of digital assets as a platform. The supply chain and business ecosystem are supported by FITMAN SCApp. It supports digital assets such as scheduling and building processes. Collaborative business processes can be managed by FITMAN CBPM. It supports the design and execution of semantically-annotated business processes in a web environment [15]. Data interoperability can be facilitated by FITMAN DIPS. It is a platform based on open standards such as WSMO, WSMX and supports semantic-based web service interoperability. Data mappings such as metadata and ontologies semantic matching with different OWL-based ontologies and XML schemas, can be supported by FITMAN SeMa [15].

### 2.3 Industrial Data Space (IDS)

The Industrial Data Space (now International data space) is a virtual data space that facilitates data exchange and association in business ecosystems using common standards and governance models [16]. Digital sovereignty of data owners is a key part of IDS, and it provides a basis for the creation and utilization of smart services and business processes [16]. It is also the important block of building a virtual factory or building a co-design and co-creation product platform [5]. The Reference Architecture Model is based on common system architecture models and standards. It utilizes a five-layer structure which states several stakeholders' concerns and viewpoints at different levels of granularity [16].

### 2.4 Predictive Maintenance

Predictive maintenance facilitates advance detection of pending failures and enables timely pre-failure interventions, using different prediction tools based on various data i.e. historical operation, condition, etc., and different machine/deep learning approaches [8, 17]. Predictive maintenance model typically involves data collection i.e. machine tools operation/condition, data processing and modeling i.e. predictive model, and maintenance analytics i.e. maintenance schedule plan and decision making [8]. Different Industry 4.0 predictive maintenance were proposed in the research community [7, 8, 11, 18, 19]. [18] proposed a 5-level CPS architecture for smart manufacturing solutions. A flexible FIWARE predictive maintenance platform for supporting modularity and transparency in a collaborative environment is proposed by [7]. [8] designed a flexible predictive maintenance model based on FIWARE and RAMI 4.0, supporting both online/offline analytics and maintenance schedule plan. These approaches are mostly designed for the manufacturer's implementation in its own organization. Collaborative network virtual factories however involve multiple factories/organizations/partners operating in a collaborative network. Thus, a new approach is needed for the collaborative network virtual factories whereas a firm/company can provide predictive maintenance services in a modular manner.

## 3 Predictive Maintenance Service Provider in a Virtual Factory

In this paper, we present how a predictive maintenance service can be provided in a collaborative network. Predictive maintenance as a new service can collect all related data through the collaborative network as well as some data from IDS. In this section, we present a reference architecture based on FIWARE in Sect. 2.2, an industry 4.0 platform, which serves a base of the virtual factory or a collaborative network.

A reference architecture for supporting predictive maintenance service in a collaborative network or a virtual factory is established as presented in Fig. 2. In the virtual factory network, different enterprises, and partners (i.e. numbers of various collaborative partners such as the shopfloor, suppliers, designers, logistics, insurance, etc.) across the industry can join the network with their own services for common business objective using the FIWARE virtual factory GE components described in Sect. 2.2. And the virtual factory network can be expanded as different needs or innovative services arise.

In the reference architecture, the predictive maintenance acts as a collaborative network partner which provides predictive maintenance services to the network. Thus, it has expert knowledge and skills in big data, advanced analytics, AI, machine learning, etc., and has access to the required data such as machine operation, condition, maintenance, etc. via the network accommodated by IDS. IDS is utilized for data movement and access to gain data transparency, ownership as well as monetization. Flexibility and capabilities of big data analytics are essential aspects of operating predictive maintenance [7, 11]. Thus, our previous work [7] is adopted for flexible FIWARE predictive maintenance, related big data analytics, functions and data model.

In the context of complex collaborative virtual network, predictive maintenance is essential to operating factories operation and assisting in creating effective maintenance schedule plan for decision making [7, 8, 11]. The proposed solution described in the next section addresses the consideration of data-driven approach for complex systems for optimal predictive maintenance schedule plan in virtual factories as it is still not addressed by most existing approaches [7, 8, 11, 18, 20–24].

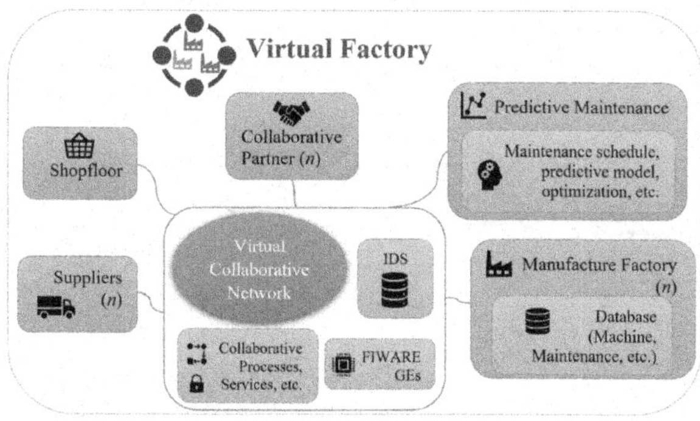


**Fig. 2.** A reference architecture for a virtual factory with a predictive maintenance service

## 4 Scheduling for the Predictive Maintenance in Collaborative Network

Monitoring status of different machines and different components in a machine in a collaborative network or a virtual factory is a similar activity as monitoring machines in a factory, which the related work is reviewed in Sect. 2.4. In this section, we focus on a schedule plan of predictive maintenance service in a collaborative network and the detailed procedure of maintenance schedule is discussed.

In general, predictive maintenance scheduling is described as an optimization process that is driven by data-driven predictions i.e. predictive model and related data i.e. maintenance, machine component, to assign the resources over time regarding the maintenance activities. This must satisfy a set of constraints which reflect the temporal relationships between the maintenance activities and the capacity limitations of the shared resources in a collaborative network [25]. The objective is to find optimal schedule in which a timeslot on the machines or machine components that minimizes the defined goal, is allocated for the maintenance task(s) [25].

To manage predictive maintenance scheduling in a complex collaborative context such as a maintenance service company as a part of the virtual factory, different important factors need to be considered. These factors are derived from the nature of the Industry 4.0 collaborative manufacturing setting, which includes: multiple organizations with similar machines, multiple machine components within an organization or in the collaborative network, as well as the maintenance task associated with cost and availability, which is especially for providing maintenance services within a collaborative network. The objective of data-driven optimal maintenance is to provide a maintenance schedule plan driven by predictive model incorporating with related factory maintenance data, which minimizes the overall cost related to conducting the required maintenance and thereby reducing downtime and cost. Considering the identified factors for an optimal maintenance schedule, the following procedure is established for assisting in maintenance decision process.

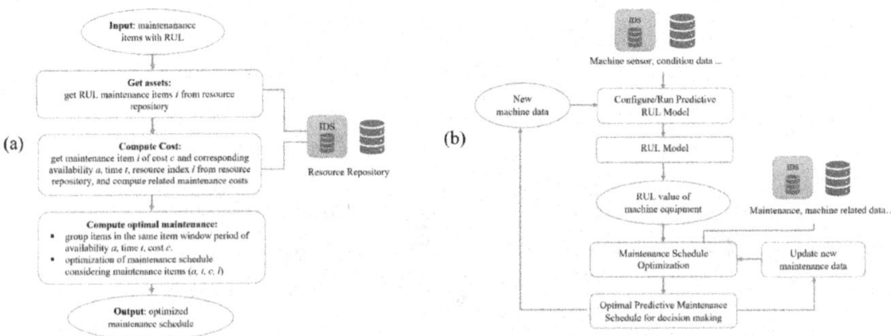


**Fig. 3.** (a) Algorithm 1: optimal maintenance schedule (b) Procedure of maintenance schedule process

Algorithm 1 in Fig. 3(a) illustrates the optimal maintenance schedule processing considering multiple machine components driven by data-driven predictive RUL value. The input parameter, maintenance items with RUL is provided through running the predictive model. The prediction of machine equipment for remaining useful life (RUL) is considered from our previous work [7]. The input RUL value of the machine component refers to specific maintenance item with a predicted value e.g. 5 days etc.

In addition to the input maintenance items with RUL, a resource repository is used to support multiple machine component maintenance by getting any outstanding items required for maintenance within the same time window period. The resource repository accommodated by the data model from [7] is adopted. The resource repository stores the machine components and maintenance related information such as maintenance cost and availability, as well as collaborative data derived from IDS. Upon the acquisition of outstanding maintenance items, maintenance availability, time and cost are processed by checking any pre/plan or existing production and maintenance schedule from the resource repository against the outstanding maintenance items.

After the maintenance availability and cost are determined, maintenance items are grouped into the same time window period for optimization. Then the optimal maintenance schedule is computed using Python Pulp Optimization, and then an optimized maintenance schedule is then available for the maintenance operator/engineer assisting decision making. Section 5 provides the results with related information e.g. maintenance item, schedule, cost, in this work.

To support the dynamic nature of collaborative networks i.e. different business requirements or changes, etc., the proposed solution supports handling new data i.e. machine, maintenance, etc. as illustrated in the Maintenance Schedule Process in Fig. 3(b). This is achieved by using new machine data, setting the RUL model, and adjusting appropriate optimization model parameters to get new RUL values. Subsequently, new maintenance schedule can be made. The next section presents the details about maintenance scenario and dataset with the corresponding results.

## 5 Implementation

In this section, a set of data are using to verify Algorithm 1 (Fig. 3(a)). Section 5.1 explains different data related to predictive maintenance for a flexible manufacturing collaborative network and Sect. 5.2 presents the scheduling results based on Algorithm 1 and a predictive maintenance case in Sect. 5.1.

### 5.1 Maintenance Case

A maintenance case from flexible manufacturing [7] is applied for evaluating the proposed algorithm for multiple machine/component schedule plan. For example, there are three same machines in two different factories within a collaborative network. In this work, we considered 21 components from one of CNC machines of flexible manufacturing in [7]. Sensor measurement data such as temperature, vibration, energy consumption and condition (health status) of machine components, are considered as input features for the predictions [7]. The RUL values of the machine component derived from the prediction are then processed for maintenance schedule.

The maintenance dataset includes multiple factory machine components, resource index, maintenance task, timestamps, and related cost. These different data are currently collected from different sources, for analyzing the proposed maintenance schedule plan. With the proposed predictive maintenance model and maintenance schedule in Sect. 3 and Sect. 4, the different data can be easily integrated, processed, and used for different analyses after it is fully implemented.

The scenario from the case study is described in Fig. 4(a). RUL values i.e. predicted value in day of the machine components are identified over a time window of 6 days period. Maintenance schedule should be planned and allocated to 6 different days period for the maintenance activities. In this scenario, 4 repairs and 1 replacement maintenance are considered. The maintenance activity i.e. repair, or replacement can also be decided by a maintenance engineer based on the predicted RUL information and other related maintenance information.

In the case of constraints, all the machine components are scheduled within their RUL period to avoid substantial maintenance and related costs such as downtime, setup, etc. The costs extracted from the case data for this model are presented in Fig. 4(b). RUL values of the machine components are mostly utilized for the scheduling as the cost of

RUL is relatively less. Group maintenance i.e. time window over 6 days with 2 available maintenance slots per day, and optimizations such as location-based based on resource index i.e. factory location/dependency are applied to reduce high value of setup/location cost. This enables the model to minimize the number of set-ups with associated other costs including location maintenance.

(a)

| RUL | 14 | 16 | 19 | 20 |
|---|---|---|---|---|
| Comp4 | | | $M$ | |
| Comp7 | | | | $M$ |
| Comp13 | $M$ | | | |
| Comp16 | | $M_{Rp}$ | | |
| Comp18 | | | $M$ | |

RUL = predicted value in day, Comp n = machine component, M = maintenance repair, $M_{Rp}$ = maintenance renew or replacement

(b)

| Maintenance | Item | Cost |
|---|---|---|
| Repair | 4 | 4672.35 |
| Replacement | 1 | 5291.65 |
| Group (setup, engineer, etc.) | | 3187.00 |
| | *Total* | 13151.00 |

**Fig. 4.** (a) Machine components with RUL identified for Predictive Maintenance (b) Maintenance machine components with associated cost

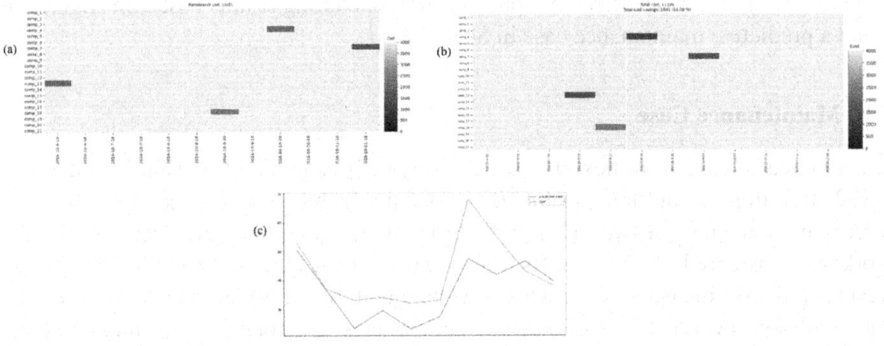

**Fig. 5.** Maintenance schedule with group maintenance over 6 days period (a) without optimization (b) with optimization over 14% cost saving (c) predicted cost comparison between the optimal cost and actual cost

## 5.2 Scheduling Result

The results of the proposed model are presented in Fig. 5. The subfigure (a) illustrates the normal maintenance schedule without optimization whereas the subfigure (b) represents the optimal maintenance schedule. The maintenance costs include the individual cost (repair or replacement) and setup cost which covers the engineer, downtime of each group. The optimal maintenance schedule can save over 14% of the expected cost based on the 6 days period window. Moreover, the maintenance prediction in subfigure (c) shows cost saving can be made over the period if maintenance activity is performed as the optimal approach suggests. Ultimately the maintenance engineer or operator can make appropriate maintenance decision based on the business needs.

## 6 Conclusion

Most predictive maintenance research focus on monitoring and scheduling maintenance tasks within one organization. Collaborative Networks 4.0 such as virtual factories are complex, dynamic and face different challenges such as a flexible platform with optimal predictive maintenance. We proposed a predictive maintenance service within a collaborative manufacturing network that offers flexible and modular components for optimizing maintenance service. A manufacturing case is used to demonstrate that predictive maintenance service can be integrated using a modular fashion into FIWARE framework and maintenance schedule plans can be created by accessing distributed data in the collaborative network. In the future, optimized models for different scenarios in different industrial sectors will be assessed.

**Acknowledgments.** This research is part of the FIRST project which has received funding from the European Union's Horizon 2020 research and innovation programme under the Marie Skłodowska-Curie grant agreement No. 734599.

## References

1. Upton, D., McAfee, A.: The Real Virtual Factory. Harv. Bus. Rev. (1996)
2. Koren, Y., Gu, X., Guo, W.: Reconfigurable manufacturing systems: principles, design, and future trends. Front. Mech. Eng. **13**(2), 121–136 (2017). https://doi.org/10.1007/s11465-018-0483-0
3. Debevec, M., Simic, M., Herakovic, N.: Virtual factory as an advanced approach for production process optimization. Int. J. Simul. Model. **13**, 66–78 (2014). https://doi.org/10.2507/IJSIMM13(1)6.260
4. Xu, L., et al.: Overview of existing interoperability of virtual factories, D1.3, First EU project H2020-MSC-RISE-2016 Ref. 6742023. Technical report. EC (2019)
5. Xu, L., de Vrieze, P., Yu, H.N., Keith, P., Bai, Y.: Interoperability of virtual factory: an overview of concepts and research challenges. Int. J. Mechatron. Manuf. Syst. **13**, 3–27 (2020)
6. Sang, G.M., Xu, L., de Vrieze, P.: Mid-sized companies in virtual factories a strategy for growth? IM&IO, 72–75 (2020)
7. Sang, G.M., Xu, L., de Vrieze, P., Bai, Y.: Towards predictive maintenance for flexible manufacturing using FIWARE. In: Dupuy-Chessa, S., Proper, H.A. (eds.) CAiSE 2020. LNBIP, vol. 382, pp. 17–28. Springer, Cham (2020). https://doi.org/10.1007/978-3-030-49165-9_2
8. Sang, G.M., Xu, L., de Vrieze, P., Bai, Y.: Applying predictive maintenance in flexible manufacturing. In: Camarinha-Matos, L.M., Afsarmanesh, H., Ortiz, A. (eds.) PRO-VE 2020. IAICT, vol. 598, pp. 203–212. Springer, Cham (2020). https://doi.org/10.1007/978-3-030-62412-5_17
9. Thoben, K.-D., Wiesner, S., Wuest, T.: "Industrie 4.0" and smart manufacturing – a review of research issues and application examples. Int. J. Autom. Technol. **11**(1), 4–16 (2017). https://doi.org/10.20965/ijat.2017.p0004
10. Sang, G.M., Xu, L., de Vrieze, P.: Simplifying Big Data analytics systems with a reference architecture. In: Camarinha-Matos, L.M., Afsarmanesh, H., Fornasiero, R. (eds.) PRO-VE 2017. IAICT, vol. 506, pp. 242–249. Springer, Cham (2017). https://doi.org/10.1007/978-3-319-65151-4_23

11. Sang, G.M., Xu, L., de Vrieze, P., Bai, Y., Pan, F.: Predictive maintenance in Industry 4.0. In: Proceedings of the 10th International Conference on Information Systems and Technologies, pp. 1–11. ACM, New York (2020). https://doi.org/10.1145/3447568.3448537
12. Sang, G.M., Xu, L., de Vrieze, P.: A reference architecture for big data systems. In: 2016 10th International Conference on Software, Knowledge, Information Management & Applications (SKIMA), pp. 370–375. IEEE (2016). https://doi.org/10.1109/SKIMA.2016.7916249
13. Zezulka, F., Marcon, P., Vesely, I., Sajdl, O.: Industry 4.0 – an Introduction in the phenomenon. IFAC-PapersOnLine **49**(25), 8–12 (2016). https://doi.org/10.1016/j.ifacol.2016.12.002
14. Porter, M.E., Heppelmann, J.E.: How smart, connected products are transforming competition (2014)
15. FIWARE: FIWARE virtual factory reference architecture. https://www.fiware4industry.com/virtual-factory-reference-architecture/. Accessed 15 Apr 2021
16. Otto, B., Steinbuß, S., Teuscher, A., Lohmann, S.: Reference architecture model Version 3.0. International Data Space Association (2019)
17. Mobley, R.K.: An Introduction to Predictive Maintenance, 2nd edn. (2002).https://doi.org/10.1016/B978-075067531-4/50018-X
18. Lee, J., Bagheri, B., Kao, H.-A.: A Cyber-Physical systems architecture for Industry 4.0-based manufacturing systems. Manuf. Lett. **3**, 18–23 (2015). https://doi.org/10.1016/j.mfglet.2014.12.001
19. Wang, L.: Machine availability monitoring and machining process planning towards Cloud manufacturing. CIRP J. Manuf. Sci. Technol. **6**, 263–273 (2013). https://doi.org/10.1016/j.cirpj.2013.07.001
20. Wang, H.: A survey of maintenance policies of deteriorating systems. Eur. J. Oper. Res. **139**, 469–489 (2002). https://doi.org/10.1016/S0377-2217(01)00197-7
21. Chan, G.K., Asgarpoor, S.: Optimum maintenance policy with Markov processes. Electr. Power Syst. Res. **76**, 452–456 (2006). https://doi.org/10.1016/j.epsr.2005.09.010
22. Nicolai, R.P., Dekker, R.: A review of multi-component maintenance models. In: Proceedings of the European Safety and Reliability Conference 2007, ESREL 2007 - Risk, Reliability and Societal Safety (2007)
23. Dekker, R., Wildeman, R.E., Van Der Duyn Schouten, F.A.: A review of multi-component maintenance models with economic dependence. Math. Methods Oper. Res. **45**, 411–435 (1997). https://doi.org/10.1007/BF01194788
24. Van Horenbeek, A., Pintelon, L.: A dynamic predictive maintenance policy for complex multi-component systems. Reliab. Eng. Syst. Saf. **120**, 39–50 (2013). https://doi.org/10.1016/j.ress.2013.02.029
25. Pinedo, M.L.: Scheduling. Springer, Cham (2016). https://doi.org/10.1007/978-3-319-26580-3

# Reconfigurable Supply Chain Performance: A Bibliometric Analysis

Slim Zidi[1,2](✉), Nadia Hamani[2], and Lyes Kermad[1]

[1] University of Paris 8, 140 rue de la Nouvelle France, 93100 Montreuil, France
slim.zidi02@etud.univ-paris8.fr

[2] University of Picardie Jules Verne, 48 Rue d'Ostende, 02100 Saint-Quentin, France

**Abstract.** Market disruptions and changes make the assessment process of supply chain performance more complex. Hence, the implementation of key indicators to evaluate the ability of the supply chain to cope with these disruptions has received increasing attention. Reconfigurability provide the ability to quickly change supply chain structure and functions by increasing its responsiveness and flexibility to deal with disruptions. This paper aims to analyze the contributions of researchers in the field of performance evaluation under supply chain disruption. A bibliometric analysis is conducted to identify publications dealing with performance evaluation under supply chain disruption field. The analysis started with the selection of articles using the following keywords (Reconfigurability, Evaluation, Supply Chain). Then, the selected articles were analyzed based on the criteria of the bibliometric analysis. The paper aims to capture the current research and potential research related to the evaluation of performance in reconfigurable supply chain under disruption.

**Keywords:** Reconfigurable supply chain · Performance evaluation · Supply chain disruption · Bibliometric analysis

## 1 Introduction

The need to adapt to market changes requires the implementation of new supply chain redesign strategies. Market disruptions and changing customer requirements are causes that drive managers and decision makers to restructure their supply chains. Reconfiguration of supply chains presents an effective solution to meet new market needs [1, 2]. The reconfigurable supply chain is a flexible chain able to change its structure with minimum resources [3]. It refers to changing the structure and functionality of the supply chain in a cost-effective, responsive, sustainable and resilient manner [4]. The reconfigurability assessment is an important phase to measure the ability of the supply chain to cope with disruptions and meet new market requirements [5].

Several concepts have been discussed in the literature that refer to the ability of the supply chain to adjust its structure and functions with new market needs such as agility, flexibility, etc. [3] consider agility and flexibility as advantages of implementing


Published by Springer Nature Switzerland AG 2021
L. M. Camarinha-Matos et al. (Eds.): PRO-VE 2021, IFIP AICT 629, pp. 161–169, 2021.
https://doi.org/10.1007/978-3-030-85969-5_14

a reconfigurable supply chain. Reconfigurability is characterized by modularity, convertibility, integrability, diagnosability, scalability and customization that reduce the effort of reconfiguration. These characteristics can be considered as performance indicators to evaluate the reconfigurability of supply chains [5]. Nevertheless, the lack of works elaborated in the area of reconfigurability evaluation in the network/supply chain level leads us to study the different aspects and concepts that can be addressed in the process of reconfigurable supply chain evaluation. The aim of this paper is to study the concepts addressed in the context of the evaluation of reconfigurable supply chains and to analyze the differences between them and to respond to the following question:

- *What are the criteria that can be considered to evaluate supply chain performance in the context of reconfiguration?*
- *How can the supply chain's ability to cope with disruptions be assessed?*

Answering this question provides a way for managers and decision makers to have visibility into the ability of their supply chain to resist and cope with disruptions. Indeed, it requires an in-depth study of the performance indicators that can be used to better evaluate the performance of the supply chain in the context of reconfiguration.

For this purpose, a bibliometric analysis has been conducted in order to gather the concepts used in the context of the above problematic and to identify the most relevant performance indicators that provide managers the possibility to evaluate and improve the performance of their supply chain in a context of disruption.

The rest of the paper is organized as follows. In Sect. 2, we present a definition of the reconfigurability evaluation. The research methodology is described in Sect. 3. Section 4 presents the analysis and the obtained results of the bibliometric analysis. Section 5 concludes the paper.

## 2 Reconfigurability Evaluation

The evaluation of the ability of the supply chain to change its current configuration by reducing the effort of reconfiguration is called the "Reconfigurability Evaluation". Reconfiguration can be a strategy for improving supply chain performance [6]. The concept of supply chain reconfiguration is defined as the structural and functional change of the supply chain. It concerns the change of supply chain configuration that is considered as a set of nodes and connections. The need for reconfiguration can be triggered by a disruptive event that forces decision makers to quickly react to ensure the functioning of the supply chain, or by a decision made by decision makers to ensure the continuous improvement of their supply chain. The need for reconfiguration is generally due to a hazard or disruptive event that causes a supply chain failure. Then the reconfiguration can be deployed within the innovation strategy to improve the operational and organizational performance of the supply chain without being affected by an external event. Reconfiguration is linked to several levels of application (network, system, plant and machine) [7, 8]. Indeed, each level of application has its own parameters and attributes allowing to judge their degree of reconfigurability and to choose the best configuration that changes its structure and functions easily and quickly. The reconfigurability characteristics (modularity, integrability, convertibility, diagnosability, scalability and customization) can be relevant indicators for the evaluation of supply chain reconfigurability [5], thanks to their effective roles in reducing the reconfiguration effort [9, 10]. Several indicators have been used to measure the degree of reconfigurability in the different previously mentioned levels such as lead time, reconfiguration time and cost, reliability, productivity, etc. Several concepts can describe this ability, such as agility, flexibility, adaptability, alignment, etc. The performance of the supply chain is significantly dependent on the ability to adapt to the dynamic environment [11]. These can be indicators to measure the ability of the supply chain to cope with market disruptions.

## 3 Research Methodology

Bibliometric analysis is defined as a research collection technique that studies a specific research area quantitatively using mathematical and statistical methods [12–17]. Also, it is the quantification of bibliographic information for use in analysis [18]. It is used particularly in analyzing publications' content and network [19]. The bibliometric has advantages in predicting future trends of disciplines [20]. The Scopus database is used for our literature search. As indicated in [21], it is "the largest abstract and citation database of peer-reviewed literature: scientific journals, books and conference proceedings". First, a set of keywords was used to determine the application domains of the reconfigurability concept and to select the words indicating the reconfigurability evaluation indicators. Secondly, this search was restricted by using the "title, abstract, keywords" search in Scopus database to determine the most important aspects related to the evaluation of the supply chain reconfigurability. The initial search yielded 2325 articles. The minimum number of occurrences of a keyword was set at 10. Only 88 of the 6500 keywords reached this threshold. The keywords "Reconfigurable", "Supply Chain", "Evaluation" and "Performance" were used to obtain a first list of articles using them. The second search was more precise and found 1149 papers using "Supply chain", "Reconfigurability" and "Criteria" as keywords. Only 101 keywords reached the 5 keyword threshold out of a total of 3324. The VOSviewer software is used to visualize and explore maps based on network data obtained. The steps of the proposed approach are presented in Fig. 1.

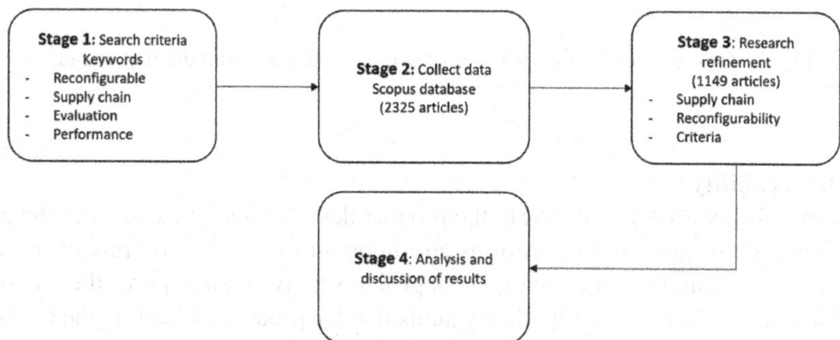


**Fig. 1.** Research methodology

# 4 Results and Analysis

## 4.1 The Obtained Results

The first research aims to identify the concepts used in the literature in the context of supply chain performance evaluation. This analysis allowed to identify 6 clusters that indicate the 5 aspects referring to the ability of the supply chain to resist and cope with disruptions. Then, by including the keyword "criteria", our first search was consistent with the results of the second search, which allowed to identify 5 relevant indicators to evaluate the performance of the supply chain in the context of reconfiguration. The first search results generated six clusters as shown in Fig. 2. This clustering groups all the selected keywords into clusters that designate mainly the domain of application and the aspects related to reconfigurability. The clusters in red and light blue concern the first aspect called "changeability" which is related to product development and sustainability. The second aspect called "Resilience & Robustness" relates to the cluster in green. The cluster in blue represents the third aspect called "Reliability". The fourth aspect is deduced from the yellow cluster and is called "Flexibility". The last cluster in purple is the fifth aspect called "Agility".

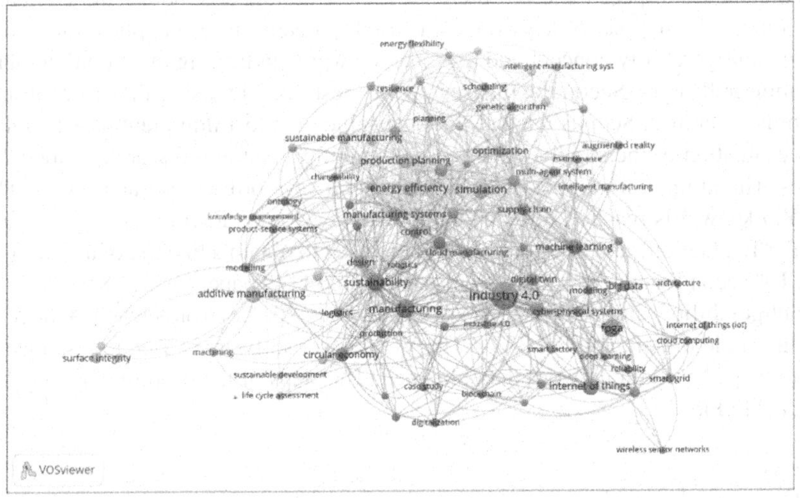


**Fig. 2.** Co-occurrences of keywords of evaluated papers from the first search

**The Changeability**

The Changeability aspect is related to the product development at the level of the manufacturing system. Indeed, production is an important enabler to ensure a changeable supply chain. The implementation of a changeable supply chain requires the coordination of production capacities [22]. The dynamism of the production leads to the necessity of a changeable organization and the differentiation of the products to ensure the sustainability [23]. The implementation of a changeable system provides flexibility and reconfigurability [24]. In fact, the changeability allows to evaluate the ability to change the production capacity to quickly and economically adjust to the new requirements.

**The Resilience & Robustness**

The Resilience & Robustness aspect designates the ability of the supply chain to resist and avoid change and succeed after failure. [25] consider that resilience and avoidance are the two dimensions that allow to judge the degree of robustness of the supply chain. The ability of the supply chain to succeed after a failure refers to resilience [26], which means that the supply chain is able to change and reconfigure its structure and resources to achieve the expected functions [27]. Resilience & Robustness can be created to mitigate threats to organizational performance caused by market disruptions [28]. From a reconfiguration perspective, Resilience and Robustness are important indicators because they allow judging the ability of the supply chain to withstand or avoid failures (before the failure occurs) or to return to its normal state with minimal delay (after a failure occurs).

**The Reliability**

The Reliability aspect refers to the ability of the supply chain to meet the needs of customers within the required conditions. Reliability is a key indicator for quantifying risks and uncertainties in the supply chain [29]. It unifies the fuzzy and random meaning in a dynamic environment [30]. [31] consider reliability as a key indicator in the performance evaluation of reconfigurable systems as it has a positive impact on responsiveness. In the process of evaluating the reconfigurability of supply chains, reliability increases the visibility of the supply chain as well as the quality of service with customers. The implementation of new technologies, especially those of digitalization, allows to improve the reliability of the supply chain, especially the reliability related to the information flows.

**The Flexibility**

The flexibility aspect designates the ability of the supply chain to quickly respond to changing customer requirements. It is considered as an advantage of reconfigurable supply chain [3]. Flexibility allows to deal with market uncertainty [32]. The flexible supply chain is defined as the ability to correctly and quickly react to changes by restructuring the chain cost-effectively to cope with market disruptions and uncertainties [33–35]. In reconfigurable supply chains, as flexibility can be considered as an advantage of reconfigurability, it is necessary to measure the ability of the supply chain to respond to new customer requirements in an uncertain environment to improve reconfigurability.

**The Agility**

The agility aspect is closely related to the flexibility aspect. This aspect is defined as the ability to quickly react to short-term changes in demand or supply [36]. Responding quickly to new requirements requires the integration and sharing of information within collaboration strategies between all actors in the supply chain [37–39]. Agility is seen as a benefit of the reconfigurable supply chain through new technologies that allow engagement with innovative supply chain partners [3]. [37] consider that without flexibility, the supply chain cannot be agile. As part of reconfiguration, the measurement of agility allows to assess the ability of the supply chain to survive with new challenges and engage in new market opportunities.

## 4.2 Discussion

Evaluating the performance of a reconfigurable supply chain essentially requires measuring its degree of reconfigurability. This measurement consists of assessing the ability of the supply chain to change its structure and functions to cope with market disruptions and meet new customer requirements. The results of the bibliometric analysis showed several elaborated concepts that designate the supply chain's ability to adapt to new market needs (Changeability, Resilience & Robustness, Reliability, Flexibility and Agility). Furthermore, a more precise research was developed to verify the concepts related to the evaluation of the reconfigurability of supply chains as explained in the previous section as shown in Fig. 3.

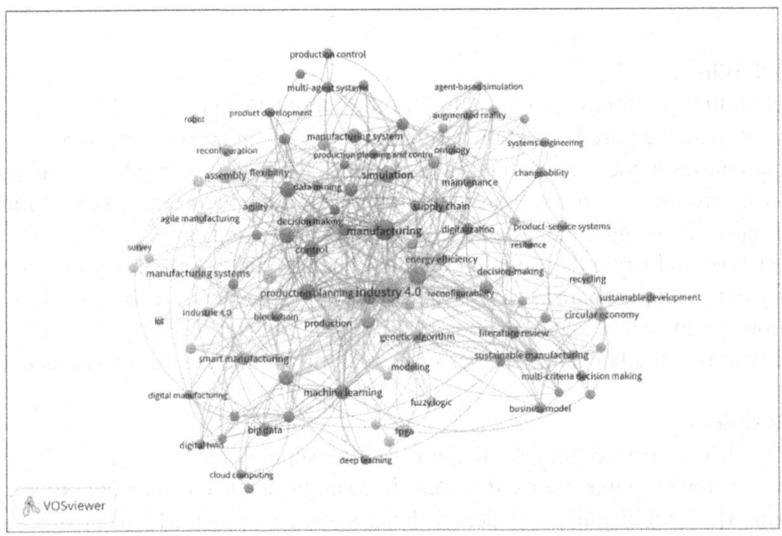


**Fig. 3.** Co-occurrences of keywords of evaluated papers from the restricted search

The results of this research gave the same concepts found in the first research. This shows the importance of the aspects previously mentioned in the evaluation process of the reconfigurable supply chain by integrating the different levels such as the manufacturing system, the machine, the product, etc. In the last few years, these concepts have been addressed in the context of new technologies such as industry 4.0, digitalization, cyber physical systems, machine learning, artificial intelligence. The 5 aspects found also showed the importance of sustainability in improving the reconfigurability of supply chains.

The assessment of the supply chain's ability to cope with disruptions and change its configuration to adapt to new changes requires the consideration of indicators to judge this ability. The main changes are related to the implementation of new technologies. Although our analysis shows the relevance of the 5 aspects found, it will be interesting to study how these aspects can be ensured and improved by integrating Industry 4.0 technologies. Indeed, the parameters for evaluating the supply chain's ability to change must include the characteristics of Industry 4.0 and digitalization, namely the reduction of truck time, the time between the need for reconfiguration and its realization, the increase in visibility of information, promoting adaptation with new changes, etc. On the other hand, it is recommended to integrate the concept of sustainability and its aspects in the parameters of performance evaluation of the supply chain under disruption. Indeed, the improvement of changeability, resilience & robustness, reliability, flexibility and agility must include other aspects, in this case the aspects of Industry 4.0 and its positive impact on sustainability while promoting the possibility of easy reconfiguration.

## 5 Conclusion

In this article, a study of the aspects and concepts treated within the context of the evaluation of reconfigurable supply chains was elaborated. Based on a bibliometric study, an analysis has been carried out through two searches of papers dealing with the evaluation of reconfigurable supply chains.

The first study gave the results of five essential aspects related to the evaluation of reconfigurability (Changeability, Resilience & Robustness, Reliability, Flexibility and Agility). These aspects allow an effective assessment of the supply chain's ability to cope with disruptions and meet new market requirements. The second, more precise research validated the five aspects identified above. This study showed the crucial role and the high dependence between these aspects and Industry 4.0 technologies in the supply chain reconfiguration strategy, as it is the most common keyword found in the researches elaborated. Thus, the latter must integrate the concept of sustainability to meet its requirements. Thus, the guarantee of the six characteristics of reconfigurability (modularity, convertibility, integrability, diagnosability, scalability and customization) provides a reconfigurable supply chain and has a crucial role in ensuring changeability, resilience & robustness, reliability, flexibility and agility.

The proposed approach has two main limitations. First, the lack of detail on the parameters and metrics allowing to quantitatively measure the five aspects previously mentioned. Secondly, it is recommended to consider the interrelationships between these five aspects in order to better optimize the model of evaluation and improvement of the supply chain's ability to cope with disruptions.

As a perspective, we propose to study the evaluation of reconfigurable supply chains in the area of Industry 4.0.

## References

1. Zidi, S., Hamani, N., Kermad, L.: Proposition d'une approche de reconfiguration des processus métiers de la chaîne logistique, vol. 2. Génie industriel et productique (2019)
2. Zidi, H., Hamani, N., Laajili, C., Benaissa, M.: A reconfiguration approach for a supply chain tracking platform. Int. J. Shipping Transp. Logistics (2021, in press). Inderscience Editor. https://doi.org/10.1504/IJSTL.2021.10037168

3. Chandra, C., Grabis, J.: Supply Chain Configuration. Springer, New York (2016). https://doi.org/10.1007/978-1-4939-3557-4
4. Dolgui, A., Ivanov, D., Sokolov, B.: Reconfigurable supply chain: the X-network. Int. J. Prod. Res. **58**, 4138–4163 (2020)
5. Zidi, S., Hamani, N., Kermad, L.: New metrics for measuring supply chain reconfigurability. J. Intell. Manuf. (2021). https://doi.org/10.1007/s10845-021-01798-9
6. Bin Ma, Xia, L.X.X., Lim, R.: Modeling supply chain's reconfigurability using fuzzy logic. In: 2007 IEEE Conference on Emerging Technologies and Factory Automation, EFTA 2007, Patras, pp. 234–241. IEEE (2007)
7. Napoleone, A., Pozzetti, A., Macchi, M.: Core characteristics of reconfigurability and their influencing elements. IFAC-PapersOnLine **51**, 116–121 (2018)
8. Wiendahl, H.P., Heger, C.L.: Justifying changeability. A methodical approach to achieving cost effectiveness. J. Manuf. Sci. Prod. **6**(1–2), 33–40 (2004). https://doi.org/10.1515/IJMSP.2004.6.1-2.33
9. Koren, Y., Shpitalni, M.: Design of reconfigurable manufacturing systems. J. Manuf. Syst. **29**, 130–141 (2010)
10. Napoleone, A., Pozzetti, A., Macchi, M.: A framework to manage reconfigurability in manufacturing. Int. J. Prod. Res. **56**, 3815–3837 (2018)
11. Vanderhaeghe, A., De Treville, S.: How to fail at flexibility. Supply Chain Forum Int. J. **4**, 64–73 (2003)
12. Bellis, N.D.: Bibliometrics and Citation Analysis: From the Science Citation Index to Cybermetrics. Scarecrow Press (2009)
13. Ding, Y., Chowdhury, G.G., Foo, S.: Bibliometric cartography of information retrieval research by using co-word analysis. Inf. Process. Manage. **37**, 817–842 (2001)
14. Godin, B.: On the origins of bibliometrics. Scientometrics **68**, 109–133 (2006)
15. Merigó, J.M., Muller, C., Modak, N.M., Laengle, S.: Research in production and operations management: a university-based bibliometric analysis. Glob. J. Flex. Syst. Manag. **20**(1), 1–29 (2018). https://doi.org/10.1007/s40171-018-0201-0
16. Pourkhani, A., Abdipour, K., Baher, B., Moslehpour, M.: The impact of social media in business growth and performance: a scientometrics analysis. Int. J. Data Netw. Sci. **3**, 223–244 (2019)
17. Pritchard, A.: Statistical bibliography or bibliometrics? J. Documentation **25**, 348–349 (1969)
18. Garfield, E., Malin, M.V., Small, H.: Citation data as science indicators (1978)
19. Ellegaard, O., Wallin, J.A.: The bibliometric analysis of scholarly production: how great is the impact? Scientometrics **105**(3), 1809–1831 (2015). https://doi.org/10.1007/s11192-015-1645-z
20. Wang, Q., Su, M.: Integrating blockchain technology into the energy sector—from theory of blockchain to research and application of energy blockchain. Comput. Sci. Rev. **37**, 100275 (2020)
21. Elsevier: About | Elsevier Scopus Blog. https://blog.scopus.com/about
22. Niemann, J., Seisenberger, S., Schlegel, A., Putz, M.: Development of a method to increase flexibility and changeability of supply contracts in the automotive industry. Procedia CIRP **81**, 258–263 (2019)
23. Wiendahl, H.-P., et al.: Changeable manufacturing - classification, design and operation. CIRP Ann. **56**, 783–809 (2007)
24. Francalanza, E., Borg, J., Constantinescu, C.: Deriving a systematic approach to changeable manufacturing system design. Procedia CIRP **17**, 166–171 (2014)
25. Durach, C., Wieland, A., Machuca, J.: Antecedents and dimensions of supply chain robustness: a systematic literature review. Int. J. Phys. Distrib. Logistics Manag. **45**, 118–137 (2015)

26. Zhang, W.J., van Luttervelt, C.A.: Toward a resilient manufacturing system. CIRP Ann. **60**, 469–472 (2011)
27. Zhang, W.J., Lin, Y.: On the principle of design of resilient systems–application to enterprise information systems. Enterp. Inf. Syst. **4**, 99–110 (2010)
28. Brandon-Jones, E., Squire, B., Autry, C.W., Petersen, K.J.: A contingent resource-based perspective of supply chain resilience and robustness. J. Supply Chain Manag. **50**, 55–73 (2014)
29. Ha, C., Jun, H.-B., Ok, C.: A mathematical definition and basic structures for supply chain reliability: a procurement capability perspective. Comput. Ind. Eng. **120**, 334–345 (2018). https://doi.org/10.1016/j.cie.2018.04.036
30. Miao, X., Yu, B., Xi, B.: The uncertainty evaluation method of supply chain reliability. Transport **24**, 296–300 (2009)
31. Mittal, K.K., Jain, P.K.: An overview of performance measures in reconfigurable manufacturing system. Procedia Eng. **69**, 1125–1129 (2014)
32. Zhong, Y.: Flexibility assessment and management in supply chain : a new framework and applications (2015)
33. Kumar, V., Fantazy, K.A., Kumar, U., Boyle, T.A.: Implementation and management framework for supply chain flexibility. J. Enterp. Inf. Manag. **19**, 303–319 (2006)
34. Wadhwa, S., Ducq, Y., Saxena, A., Prakash, A.: Supply chain as a flexible system: a KM focused competence. Glob. J. Flex. Syst. Manag. **9**(2–3), 15–30 (2008). https://doi.org/10.1007/BF03396540
35. Tachizawa, E.M., Gimenez, C.: Supply flexibility strategies in Spanish firms: results from a survey. Int. J. Prod. Econ. **124**, 214–224 (2010)
36. Lee, H.L.: The Triple-A Supply Chain, the-triple-a-supply-chain (2004)
37. Swafford, P.M., Ghosh, S., Murthy, N.: Achieving supply chain agility through IT integration and flexibility. Int. J. Prod. Econ. **116**, 288–297 (2008)
38. Dwayne Whitten, G., Green, K.W., Zelbst, P.J.: Triple-A supply chain performance. Int. J. Oper. Prod. Manag. **32**, 28–48 (2012)
39. Green Jr., K.W., Whitten, D., Inman, R.A.: The impact of timely information on organisational performance in a supply chain. Prod. Plan. Control **18**, 274–282 (2007)

# A MILP Model for Reusable Containers Management in Automotive Plastic Components Supply Chain

Eduardo Guzman(✉), Beatriz Andres, and Raul Poler

Research Centre on Production Management and Engineering (CIGIP), Universitat Politècnica de València (UPV), Calle Alarcón, 03801 Alcoy, Alicante, Spain
eguzman@cigip.upv.es

**Abstract.** The automotive sector operates under the just-in-time (JIT) approach, but variations in demand mean that first-tier suppliers generate an accumulation of stocks at second-tier suppliers. Second-tier suppliers have a limitation of storage space, reason to limit their production to the size of the warehouse, but always attending the first-tier demand plan. A further limitation of the second-tier supplier is the number of empty reusable containers that the first-tier supplier delivers to the second-tier supplier and that are used to package the injected plastic components. The reusable filled containers are returned to the first-tier supplier, according to the plastic components demand plan. Thus, a closed-loop logistic is carried out between first and second-tier suppliers. This study proposes, from the second-tier perspective, a mixed integer linear programming (MILP) model for fleet sizing decisions of the cardboard containers in a production system. The model determines the number of cardboard containers that second-tier supplier has to use when the production is higher than the number of available reusable containers.

**Keywords:** Lot-sizing · Scheduling · Supply chain · Mixed integer linear programming · Closed-loop supply chain · Sustainability

## 1 Introduction

An increasing trend for companies is to work towards meeting environmental and economic requirements and reducing the environmental and social impact of their activities. There is also a rapidly growing interest in reusable packaging, such as wooden pallets and plastic crates and others. Several companies sell products in packaging that can be reused. Returnable transport items (RTI), which represent a specific type of reusable packaging material, including pallets, plastic boxes, or containers (air and maritime), are used today in various industries, for example, in the food sector, in the automotive industry or in the consumer goods industry [1].

The use of reusable packaging is justified by the benefits it can generate, such as the amortization of the price of packaging over its useful life [2]. The literature provides several studies showing the environmental benefits associated with reusable containers


Published by Springer Nature Switzerland AG 2021
L. M. Camarinha-Matos et al. (Eds.): PRO-VE 2021, IFIP AICT 629, pp. 170–178, 2021.
https://doi.org/10.1007/978-3-030-85969-5_15

[3]. Glock and Kim [1] argued that the use of reusable packaging materials rather than single-use packaging materials has the significant contribution of reducing global $CO_2$ emissions from production and transportation, and can significantly minimize the gross energy consumption and the waste generation from transportation.

The difficulty of the reusable container management problem is to have an appropriate supply of empty containers to meet the customer demand. Part of this supply is the result of returns of previously issued containers. A challenging factor is that, during the lead time, the same container may be emitted, returned, re-emitted, etc.

The aim of this research is to investigate the production and fleet-sizing of cardboard containers decisions of a production system when reusable containers are utilized. This model has applicability to the automotive industry, which uses reusable containers to protect and transport plastic parts produced by the second-tier supplier and shipped to the first-tier supplier. The focus of our model is to determine the optimal levels of production and storage rate to minimize the setup times and the quantity of cardboard containers to be purchased when reusable containers, which are property of first-tier supplier, are insufficient to store the parts produced by the second-tier supplier.

The structure of the paper is as follows. Section 2 provides an overview of related work. Section 3 develops a mixed integer linear programming (MILP) model for Reusable Containers Management and contains numerical and negotiation examples. Section 4 concludes the article and offers suggestions for future research.

## 2 Literature Review

This section provides a literature review of relevant contributions in the related research field. The literature focuses on packaging costs and emissions as a target to optimize the use of packaging. Most relevant studies are presented next. Accorsi et al. [4] propose a mixed-integer linear programming (MILP) model to address the use of reusable packaging in the food industry. The model establishes the number of available packaging and forces to meet the demand for packaging over the planning horizon by encouraging reutilization and recycling. Rajae et al. [2] present a MILP model that addresses the problem of reusable containers in a reverse supply chain, in a multi-tiered network and under a carbon emission constraint. Goudenege et al. [5] developed a generic reverse logistics management model focused on investing in and managing reusable packaging at the lowest cost in order to reduce the amount of cardboard used by the company under study. Glock et al. [1] examine a supply chain consisting of a single supplier and several retailers that use returnable transportation items, such as containers or boxes, to facilitate the shipment of products from the supplier to the retailers. The paper presents two mathematical models used to determine the cycle time, container size, individual retailer order quantities, and shipping sequence with the intention of minimizing the average total system costs. Park and Kim [6] present an analytical model for fleet-sizing of containers that are used for the protection (storage of finished parts), transportation and storage of parts between a component plant and multiple assembly plants. Atamer et al. [7] analyse the pricing and production decisions of a manufacturer selling a single product when using reusable containers with stochastic customer demand, and two supply scenarios are analysed: (1) new containers and (2) containers returned by customers.

In our paper we consider different characteristics addressed in the literature, with the novelty that integrates the decisions of production scheduling and sequencing to determine the optimal use of reusable containers and cardboard containers required to store and send plastic components. The problem modelled adjusts to a real problem that have transmitted to us the first and second-tier supplier of an automotive supply chain.

## 3 Problem Definition

We consider a second-tier supplier that produces plastic components for its assembling in the first-tier supplier. The second-tier supplier produces the parts in moulds that are assembled on injection machines. The machine setup has a high cost associated; therefore, production is constrained by the number of moulds changed in a specific period and the amount of periods that the mould must be mounted within the machine. The main aim is to minimize the costs of production, storage, and machine setups, without incurring in backorders on the first-tier demand plan. Once the second-tier supplier has produced the plastic components, according to its optimal production plan, the parts are sent to the first-tier supplier in reusable containers, which are of its property. Reusable containers are limited in capacity and number, when the second-tier supplier produces more parts than he can store in the reusable containers, he has to store in temporary cardboard containers, until empty plastic containers arrive. The use of cardboard containers implies that the second-tier supplier must incur handling costs because they must put the parts in the cardboard containers and then switch to the reusable containers. In addition, the manufacturer must purchase the cardboard containers. Figure 1 shows the closed loop of reusable containers.

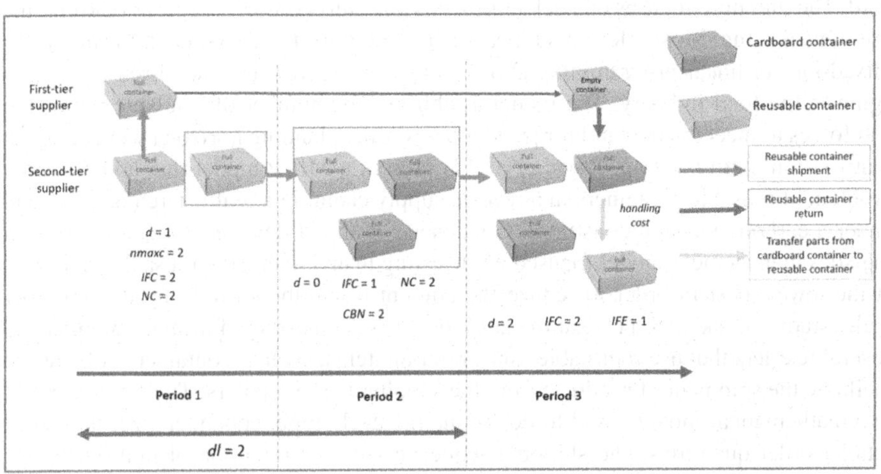


**Fig. 1.** Closed loop of reusable containers scheme.

The optimization of the second-tier supplier production and scheduling plan, results in grouping production in batches and thus having to stock products. If there are sufficient reusable containers, the produced parts are stored and wait in the warehouse to be delivered to the first-tier supplier, and after a lead time the reusable containers re-circulate and are returned to the second-tier supplier. When there are not sufficient reusable containers, second-tier supplier stores the parts in the cardboard containers.

### 3.1 A MILP Model for Reusable Containers Management

This study proposes, from the second-tier perspective, a Mixed Integer Linear Programming (MILP) model for the production, lot-sizing, and scheduling of automotive plastic components, which takes into consideration the number of reusable containers in circulation throughout the closed-loop logistic. Moreover, the model also determines the number of cardboard containers that second-tier supplier has to use when the production is higher than the number of available reusable containers. This model allows to determine the optimal number of reusable containers that should be bought by the first-tier supplier in order not to incur in extra costs due to the use of cardboard containers, which will increase the price of plastic components produced in the second-tier supplier, compromising the supply chain sustainability. This information is useful for both first and second-tier suppliers since with this data both suppliers in the supply chain can negotiate the final price of plastic components, which is contractually dependent on the number of returnable containers delivered by the first-tier supplier to the second-tier supplier (Table 1).

**Table 1.** Nomenclature for Reusable Containers Management model

| **Index** | |
|---|---|
| *T* | time period index $t \in \{1, \ldots, T\}$ |
| **Data** | |
| *Ch* | handling cost of cardboard container |
| *Cb* | purchase cost of the cardboard container |
| *Cc* | container capacity |
| *Cs* | setup cost of preparing tool |
| *Cap* | warehouse volume storage capacity |
| $d_t$ | demand of containers at period t |
| *inv0* | initial inventory of reusable containers |
| *Dl* | delay between sending a full reusable container to the first-tier supplier and returning an empty reusable container to the second-tier supplier |
| $invp_0$ | initial inventory of parts |
| $invec_0$ | initial inventory of empty reusable containers |
| $invfc_0$ | initial inventory of filled reusable containers (filed of plastic parts) |
| *Nmaxc* | maximum number of reusable containers |

(*continued*)

**Table 1.** (*continued*)

| | |
|---|---|
| $nc_t$ | number of mould changes permitted during time period t |
| $x_t$ | number of parts that the machine is able to produce during time period t |
| $V$ | volume of containers |
| **Decision variables** | |
| $CBN_t$ | number of cardboard containers |
| $INV_t$ | inventory of parts at the end of time period t |
| $IEC_t$ | inventory of empty reusable containers |
| $ICF_t$ | inventory of filled reusable containers |
| $NC_t$ | number of containers required |
| $SA_t$ | 1 when the mould is set up on machine during period $t$, 0 when mould is set up on machine during period $t-1$ |
| $S_t$ | 1 when the mould is set up on machine during period $t$, 0 otherwise |
| $Xn_t$ | number of parts to produce during period t |

The MILP model formulation for managing the availability of reusable containers in automotive plastic components supply chain is represented below. The objective function minimizes total costs, which comprise setup costs, and investment and handling cost of reusable containers.

$$Min\, z = \sum_t cs \cdot SA_t + \sum_t ch \cdot cb \cdot CBN_t \tag{1}$$

Subject to:

***Sequence and Setup Constraints***

$$S_t \leq 1 \; \forall t \tag{2}$$

$$SA_t \geq S_t - S_{t-1} \; \forall t \tag{3}$$

$$SA_t \leq nc_t \; \forall l, t, \tag{4}$$

Constraint (2) guarantees that one or neither mould could be set up in production during each period $t$. Constraint (3) guarantees the first tool setup on the machine in period $t$. Constraint (4) guarantees the number of tool changes allowed during period $t$.

***Production Constraint***

$$Xn_t \leq S_t \cdot x_t \; \forall t \tag{5}$$

Constraint (5) determines the number of parts produced during time period *t*.

***Inventory Constraints***

$$INV_t = invp_0 + Xn_t - d_t * cc \; \forall t = 1 \tag{6}$$

$$INV_t = INV_{t-1} + Xn_t - d_t * cc \; \forall t > 1$$

$$NC_t = INV_t / cc \; \forall t \tag{7}$$

$$IFC_t = invfc_0 - d_t \; \forall t = 1 \; if \; NC_t > invec_0 \tag{8}$$

$$IFC_t = NC_t - d_t \; \forall t = 1 \; if \; NC_t \leq invec_0 \tag{9}$$

$$IFC_t = IFC_{t-1} + IEC_{t-1} - d_t \; \forall t > 1 \; if \; NC_t > IEC_{t-1} \tag{10}$$

$$IFC_t = NC_t - d_t \; \forall t > 1 \; if \; NC_t \leq IEC_{t-1} \tag{11}$$

$$IEC_t = invec_0 \; \forall t = 1 \; if \; NC_t > invec_0 \tag{12}$$

$$IEC_t = invec_0 - IFC_t \; \forall t = 1 \; if \; NC_t \leq invec_0 \tag{13}$$

$$IEC_t = d_{t-dl} \; \forall t > 1 \; if \; NC_t > IEC_{t-1} \tag{14}$$

$$IEC_t = IEC_{t-1} - d_{t-dl} \; \forall t > 1 \; if \; NC_t \leq IEC_{t-1} \tag{15}$$

$$CBN_t = NC_t - invec_0 \; \forall t = 1 \; if \; NC_t > invec_0 \tag{16}$$

$$CBN_t = 0 \; \forall t = 1 \; if \; NC_t \leq invec_0 \tag{17}$$

$$CBN_t = NC_t - IEC_{t-1} \; \forall t > 1 \; ifNC_t > IEC_{t-1} \tag{18}$$

$$CBN_t = 0 \; \forall t > 1 \; if \; NC_t \leq IEC_{t-1} \tag{19}$$

$$v \cdot (IEC_t + IFC_t + CBN_t) \leq cap \; \forall t \tag{20}$$

$$nmaxc \geq IEC_t + IFC_t + d_t \; \forall t \tag{21}$$

Constraint (6) defines the inventory level of parts that have not been packaged and delivered in a reusable container, i.e., it determines the inventory of overproduction due to the batch sizes. Constraint (7) establishes the required number of reusable and cardboard containers needed for packaging plastic parts. Constraints (8 to 11) manage the inventory of filled reusable containers and control the allocation of plastic parts to reusable and cardboard containers. Constraints (12 to 14) control the inventory of empty reusable containers. Constraints (16 to 19) determine the allocation of parts that have been packaged in cardboard containers, due to the fact that there are missing empty reusable containers reusable containers on the second-tier supplier side. It is determined that after a delay time a filled reusable container sent to the first-tier supplier is released as empty reusable container to the second-tier supplier. Constraint (20) is referred to as the storage capacity constraint, which guarantees that the reusable and cardboard container inventory in the warehouse in period t is always less than the capacity of the manufacturer's warehouse. Constraint (21) limits the number of filled and empty reusable containers, since there is a limited number of reusable containers delivered from the first-tier supplier to the second-tier supplier.

***Bound and Nature Variables***

$$SA_t,\ S_t \in \{0, 1\}\ \forall t \tag{22}$$

$$INV_t, ICF_t, IEF_t, CBN_t, NC_t, Xn_t \in \mathbb{Z}\ \forall t \tag{23}$$

Constraint (22) denotes the binary character of the variables $S_t$ and $SA_t$. Constraint (23) specifies the integer character of the variables represented.

### 3.2 Numerical Experiment

The model is formulated in Python and solved with Gurobi. The data in this case study has been generated randomly. Table 2 shows the solutions that arrive at one of the generated instances, in this case we have considered 6 periods, in this scenario as can be seen in Table 2 the second level supplier has to use cardboard containers ($CBN_t$) in several periods causing it to incur handling costs. Gurobi takes a few seconds to find the optimum solution on a computer configured with 11th Gen Intel(R) Core (TM) i7-1165G7 @ 2.80 GHz processors and 16 GB of RAM.

### 3.3 Collaboration Scheme

Figure 2 depicts the process of negotiating the price of plastic components produced by the second-tier supplier. The price of the plastic components is determined by (i) the number of reusable containers that the first-tier supplier delivers to the second-tier supplier; (ii) the number of cardboard containers that the second-tier supplier has to buy (if the number of empty reusable containers is insufficient to store the plastic components produced by the second-tier supplier); (iii) and the costs associated with the plastic components production process, setup costs.

**Table 2.** Results of MILP model for Reusable Containers Management.

| $t$ | $CBN_t$ | $IEC_t$ | $IFC_t$ | $INV_t$ | $NC_t$ | $S_t$ | $SA_t$ | $Xn_t$ |
|---|---|---|---|---|---|---|---|---|
| 1 | 0 | 1 | 0 | 60 | 15 | 1 | 1 | 32 |
| 2 | 9 | 15 | 0 | 40 | 10 | 1 | 0 | 20 |
| 3 | 0 | 10 | 2 | 60 | 15 | 1 | 0 | 72 |
| 4 | 3 | 13 | 0 | 52 | 13 | 1 | 0 | 44 |
| 5 | 4 | 13 | 0 | 68 | 17 | 1 | 0 | 84 |
| 6 | 6 | 17 | 0 | 76 | 19 | 1 | 0 | 84 |

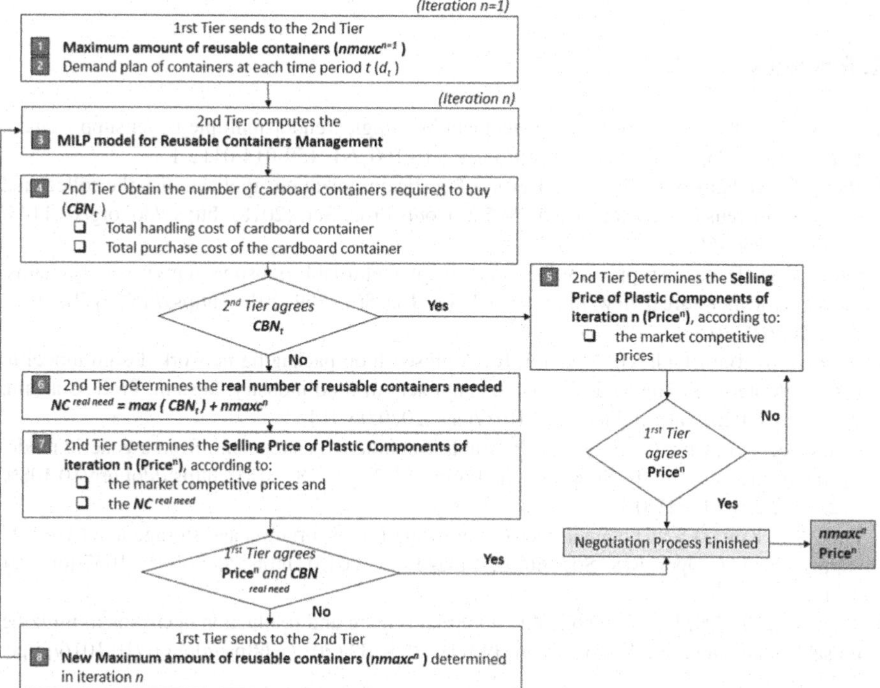


**Fig. 2.** Flow chart of negotiation process

## 4 Conclusions

In this paper, we provide an integrated approach to help companies consider options when managing their reusable containers. This paper proposes a MILP model for optimizing the scheduling of automotive plastic components, which takes into account the use of reusable containers that are required for the protection and transportation of finished products from a second-tier manufacturer to a first-tier supplier. It also determines the number of cardboard containers to be purchased by the second-tier supplier when reusable containers are not available, so the second-tier supplier must incur handling costs to store the parts in cardboard containers until reusable containers are available. Future research lines are led to (i) include in the model the carbon emissions derived from the transport of reusable containers; (ii) the consideration of backorders penalization in the objective function; (iii) and the algorithm implementation of the proposed collaboration scheme, in order to determine the optimal number of reusable containers and the competing price of plastic components.

**Acknowledgments.** Funding for this work has been provided by the Conselleria de Educación, Investigación, Cultura y Deporte - Generalitat Valenciana for hiring predoctoral research staff with Grant (ACIF/2018/170) and European Social Fund with Grant Operational Program of FSE 2014-2020, the Valencian Community.

## References

1. Glock, C.H., Kim, T.: Container management in a single-vendor-multiple-buyer supply chain. Logist. Res. **7**(1), 1–16 (2014). https://doi.org/10.1007/s12159-014-0112-1
2. Rajae, E., Mohamed, B., Tarik, Z.: Reverse logistic optimization: application to the collect and the reuse of reusable containers. ACM Int. Conf. Proc. Ser. (2018). https://doi.org/10.1145/3230905.3230966
3. Glock, C.H.: Decision support models for managing returnable transport items in supply chains: a systematic literature review. Int. J. Prod. Econ. **183**, 561–569 (2017). https://doi.org/10.1016/j.ijpe.2016.02.015
4. Accorsi, R., Baruffaldi, G., Manzini, R.: A closed-loop packaging network design model to foster infinitely reusable and recyclable containers in food industry. Sustain. Prod. Consum. **24**, 48–61 (2020). https://doi.org/10.1016/j.spc.2020.06.014
5. Goudenege, G., Chu, C., Jemai, Z.: Reusable containers management: from a generic model to an industrial case study. Supply Chain Forum **14**(2), 26–38 (2013). https://doi.org/10.1080/16258312.2013.11517313
6. Park, S.J., Kim, D.S.: Container fleet-sizing for part transportation and storage in a two-level supply chain. J. Oper. Res. Soc. **66**(9), 1442–1453 (2015). https://doi.org/10.1057/jors.2014.111
7. Atamer, B., Bakal, I.S., Bayindir, Z.P.: Optimal pricing and production decisions in utilizing reusable containers. Int. J. Prod. Econ. **143**(2), 222–232 (2013). https://doi.org/10.1016/j.ijpe.2011.08.007

# End-of-Life Product Recovery Optimization of Disassembled Parts Based on Collaborative Decision-Making

Elham Jelodari Mamaghani(✉) and Xavier Boucher

Mines Saint-Etienne, Univ Clermont Auvergne, CNRS, UMR 6158 LIMOS, Institut Henri Fayol, Saint-Etienne, France
{Elham.jelodari,Xavier.boucher}@emse.fr

**Abstract.** Greenhouse gas emissions are a major problem for the environment. One of the vital activities to reduce the emissions is including the circular economy (CE) approaches like reuse and remanufacture in disassembled products to recovering End-of-life products. In this paper, we consider CE in the disassembly of products not only to reduce $CO_2$ emissions but also to reducing cost and improving fairness among operators. To obtain this goal, collaborative decision-making with three decision-makers (DMs) is considered to set sustainability via choosing the best EOL recovery options in the disassembly of products. Industrial managers, human resource managers, and environmental managers are three decision-makers who will collaborate to improve three indicators, which are cost, setting fairness among operators, and reducing $CO_2$ emissions. To implement this collaboration, a mixed-integer multi-objective mathematical model is proposed and solved by Ɛ-constraint. According to the results, DMs can select the best recovery options of parts to have a trade-off among indicators.

**Keywords:** Disassembly planning · Circular economy · Collaborative decision-making · End-of-life product recovery · Ɛ-constraint

## 1 Introduction and Related Works

Increased greenhouse gases leads to global warming, climate change, and has visible effects such as sea level rise [1]. In 2015, each member of (COP 21) by participating in Paris agreement, adopted to prevent global temperature rising by taking urgent actions to protect planet [1]. One of the important strategies to GHG reduction is in the supply chain of a product assembly and recovery stage [2]. In fact, it is an alternative for manufacturing to produce new products and using new materials. Hence, recovery is an opportunity to the lack of natural resources [3]. To recover assembled products, there are major strategies that we call hereafter end of life (EOL) options. These options are recycling, reusing, and remanufacturing [4]. They can have high effects to save energy and prevention of GHG emissions compared to new products [5]. These approaches are known in the new type of economy called circular economy for waste prevention and resource efficiency [4]. In


L. M. Camarinha-Matos et al. (Eds.): PRO-VE 2021, IFIP AICT 629, pp. 179–187, 2021.
https://doi.org/10.1007/978-3-030-85969-5_16

this type of industry, through reuse, remanufacturing or recycling at the end of life cycle, products components and materials can be get in the second life cycle. To implement these strategies, disassembly of the products is required, which is the systematic approach to separate a product into its manufactured parts [6]. Although disassembly process is costly, it can generate value (and money) by reusing, recycling or remanufacturing to prevent buying new components or materials. Furthermore, the approaches applied in disassembly process are more environmental friendly approaches can help to set the environmental axes of sustainability in the manufacturing system [4, 7]. Hence, disassembly process is inseparable function in implementing different strategies of CE. There are many methods for disassembly such as petri nets, metaheuristics algorithms, or disassembly graphs [8, 9].

Disassembly papers can be classified to papers with and without life cycle option. In other words, some studies like [10, 11] have considered life cycle option while [12] did not study the life cycle subject. The authors only focused on reduction of disassembly costs and solving the presented mathematical model with a metaheuristics algorithm. Due to the effect of GHG emissions in environment, it can be observed there are studies that have focused on the impact of life cycle option on GHG emissions in product disassembly problems [13, 14]. Multi partial disassembly by including cost, revenue, and environmental impacts was proposed by [13]. [14] proposed mixed integer mathematical model for disassembly sequence while selecting of the parts was done in terms of life cycle option. The authors considered reduction of $CO_2$ emission in besides reduction of disassembled costs. Concerning applications for the industrial world, decision processes for End-of-life (EOL) product recovery via disassembly planning of products and circular economy approaches have been sometimes implemented on real cases like in [15, 4]. Some other researches like [16] assumed not real case but special product. The reason to include CE in industry is not only reducing GHG emissions, but also it is a new sustainability paradigm [17], which can provide the axes of sustainability like economy and environment. In order to increase the industrial added-value, the current paper proposes two advances: (i) to consider not only two but the three dimensions of sustainability by including human factors (indicator of fairness among operators) besides the environmental and economic factors; (ii) to take in consideration the necessary collaboration among several decision makers when choosing the most suitable recovery option. We consider in this paper collaboration among three decision makers; collaboration among human-resource manager, environmental manager, and industrial manager, with their distinct points of view: fairness among operators, $CO_2$ emission reduction, and cost reduction in the recovery process sequentially. This collaborative decision making problem is modelled by a mixed integer multi-objective mathematical model and solved by $\varepsilon$-constraints. According to obtained solutions, decision makers can make decision considering the values of all indicators. The reminder of the paper is structured as follows. Section 2 is describes the problem definition and presenting mathematical model. Section 3 is presenting the results of mathematical model based on a set of benchmark results. In that section, the collaborative decision-making is explained. Conclusion and future research propositions are summarized in Sect. 4.

## 2 Problem Description and Research Model

The research problem in this paper is making a decision by collaboration among three decision makers to determine the most suitable recovery operation (remanufacturing, reusing or disposal) for the disassembled products of EOL product by considering the quality information of EOL products. Actually, three decision makers (industrial manager, human resource manager, and environmental manager) collaborate to make the most appropriate recovery operations to achieve a minimum recovery cost and high saving rate of $CO_2$ emissions besides setting fairness of time among operators. Hence, a mixed integer mathematical programming model is proposed to assign a recovery operation to the parts of a product to satisfy time fairness among operators, cost minimization and saving $CO_2$ emissions. Additionally, at the end of execution, the presented model, for each disassembled part, the most suitable operations (remanufacturing, reusing or disposal) is proposed (according to constraints 8–13). Furthermore it will be determined an operation of each part is implemented by which operator. Finally, an allocation execution time for each operator is determined at the end of model's execution.

There are variety of factors with impacts on EOL strategy. In the following, a set of assumptions has been made to build the research model and the parameters and decision variables applied in the mathematical model are summarized in Table 1 and Table 2:

1. Disassembly sequence is the order of removal parts. In this paper, the optimal disassembly directions and the sequence of parts are deterministic. There is a disassembly precedence graph that is given is advance and all the nodes of the graph are indivisible nodes.
2. Remanufacturing, reusing and disposal are studied in this paper. One of the important assumptions is all of the EOL components are recoverable and one of the most suitable recovery operation (remanufacturing, reusing or disposal) is allocated to each disassembled component.
3. To simplify the mathematical model, economic information (process cost), process information (method of disassembly and its time), and quality information are presented in advance.
4. There are sufficient market demands for the products recovered by the operations (CE operations).
5. Each part of products has to be assigned to one operator to implement one operation.

In the following, the proposed mixed integer multi-objective mathematical programming model is presented. The constraints 8–20 are described at Appendix A.

In first objective function (adopted from [4] due to limited page readers can refer to that paper), all costs like disassembly cost and the cost of recovery operations (reuse, disposal, and remanufacturing) are minimized. This objective function is an indicator, which an industrial manger makes decision about it.

$$\min Z_2 = C_{max} \tag{1}$$

Objective function (1) besides Eq. (7) guarantee the time fairness among operators. Thus, this is an indicator considered by a human resource manager. This function,

**Table 1.** Sets and parameters of the proposed model

| Symbols | Description |
|---|---|
| I | Set of parts |
| P | Set of operators |
| K={1,2,3} | Set of operations (1.Recycling 2. Reuse 3.Remanufacture) |
| $H_i$ | Set of predecessors for part i∈I |
| $o_i$ | Quality of part i∈I after operation |
| $\alpha_i$ | Importance (weight) of part i in the final quality of product |
| $q_i$ | Quality of part i∈I before operation |
| $qm$ | Minimum acceptance quality of a part after operation |
| $l_i^1$ | Maximum quality value required for disposal of part i∈I |
| $l_i^2$ | Minimum quality value required for reuse of part i∈I |
| $l_i^3$ | Minimum quality value for remanufacturing part i∈I |
| s | Usage year |
| $f_i$ | Life expectancy of part i∈I |
| $e_i$ | $CO_2$ saving rate of part i∈I |
| $d_i$ | Treatment and disposal cost of part i∈I |
| $cr_i$ | Reuse cost of part i∈I |
| $cn_i$ | Remanufacturing cost of part i∈I |
| $cd_i$ | Disassembly cost of part i∈I |
| $t_{ipk}$ | Processing time of operation k∈K on part i∈I by operator p∈P |

**Table 2.** Decision variables of the proposed model

| Symbols | Description |
|---|---|
| $x_{ipk}$ | 1,if and only if operation k∈K is done by operator p∈P on the part i∈I; 0, otherwise |
| $y_{ijp}$ | 1, if and only if operator p∈P operates on part i∈I then part j∈I; 0,otherwise |
| $u_i$ | Starting time of an operation on part i∈I |
| $C_{max}$ | Variable used to balance the operation time of operators |

together with Eqs. (4)–(7), can determine the starting time of operation by each operator on each part of the disassembled product.

Objective function (3) adopted from [4], associated to the environmental manager, maximizes the saving rate of $CO_2$ produced in remanufacturing and reusing process. Constraints are:

Equations (4) adopted from [4] induce that, on each part of disassembled product, an operator implements one operation.

$$2 \times \left(y_{ijp} + y_{jip}\right) \le \sum_{k \in K} \left(x_{ipk} + x_{jpk}\right) \qquad \forall i, j \in I, i \ne j, \forall p \in P \tag{2}$$

$$\left(y_{ijp} + y_{jip}\right) \ge \sum_{k \in K} \left(x_{ipk} + x_{jpk}\right) - 1 \qquad \forall i, j \in I, i \ne j, \forall p \in P \tag{3}$$

Equations (2) and (3) indicate that an operator cannot work simultaneously on a part and its predecessor (two operations cannot be done by an operator).

$$u_j \ge u_i + \sum_{p \in P} \sum_{k \in K} t_{ipk} x_{ipk} \qquad \forall j \in I, \forall i \in H_j \tag{4}$$

Constraints (4) show the starting time of an operation on a part and its predecessor part.

$$u_j \ge u_i + \sum_{k \in K} t_{ipk} x_{ipk} - M\left(1 - y_{ijp}\right) \qquad \forall i, j \in I, i \ne j, \forall p \in P \tag{5}$$

$$u_i \ge u_j + \sum_{k \in K} t_{jpk} x_{jpk} - M\left(1 - y_{jip}\right) \qquad \forall i, j \in I, i \ne j, \forall p \in P \tag{6}$$

Constraints (5) and (6) are working together and show the starting operation time of an operator on the allocated parts according to the position of each part.

$$C_{max} \ge u_i + \sum_{k \in K} t_{ipk} x_{ipk} \qquad \forall i \in I, \forall p \in P \tag{7}$$

Constraints (7) point to the maximum of working time for each operator.

## 3 Experimental Results

The proposed model that is mixed-integer linear programming is solved by Ɛ-constraints method. Since real disassembly enterprises are small, it is not needed to solve the model with heuristics or metaheuristics algorithms even though the problem is NP-hard [16]. In fact, the firms need to solve easily the problem in their business by common commercial solvers instead of complicated algorithms. Data applied to solve the problem are chosen from [4] and adjust according to the considered problem. The solution approach is Ɛ-constraints method that is implemented by GAMS 12.6. The results have been illustrated in Table 1, Fig. 1 and Fig. 2 as the first figure shows the relation between costs and rate of saving $CO_2$ emission and in the second figure costs and time fairness of operators has been depicted. According to Fig. 1, industrial manager and environmental manager can make decision about the impact of increasing (or reducing) costs and saving rate of $CO_2$ emission. As it can be understood from the figure, the saving rate of $CO_2$ emission increases when more money is spent. It means that, selection of remanufacturing operation or reusing operation can reduce GHG emission. Therefore, the two managers can make decision about the costs and the saving rate of $CO_2$ emission. To observe the effect of costs on the time fairness of operators, Fig. 2 can be used. It is clear that when the number of operators is increased the time fairness is improved while the value of cost is increased. Table 1 shows the assignment of operators and operations to each parts. Hence, this model gives an idea to industrial manager and human resource manager how they can handle time of operators and total costs of recovery operations (Table 3).

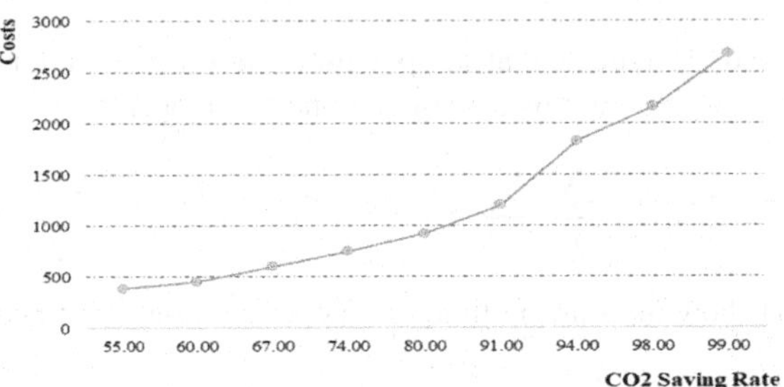


**Fig. 1.** Behaviors of the disassembly parts selection of $CO_2$ saving rate and recovery cost

**Table 3.** Recovery operation on each parts of [4]

| Number of a part | Operation | Operator |
|---|---|---|
| 1 | 3 | 1 |
| 2 | 3 | 2 |
| 3 | 1 | 1 |
| 4 | 2 | 1 |
| 5 | 2 | 1 |
| 6 | 2 | 2 |
| 7 | 2 | 2 |
| 8 | 1 | 1 |
| 9 | 2 | 1 |
| 10 | 2 | 1 |
| 11 | 2 | 1 |
| 12 | 2 | 1 |
| 13 | 2 | 2 |
| 14 | 2 | 1 |

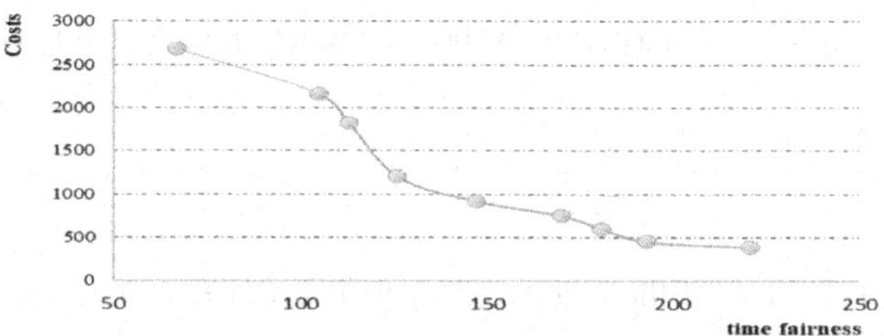


**Fig. 2.** Behaviors of the disassembly parts selection in terms of recovery cost and time fairness

## 4 Discussion and Conclusion

*Discussion on Collaborative Decision-Making*

This study suggested a life cycle option selection of disassembly parts by collaborative decision-making. Each part is selected for disposal, reuse or remanufacturing and decision makers by collaboration can make decision to minimize cost, maximize $CO_2$ saving rate, and maximize the fairness among operators. In case of convergence between these criteria, the sustainability in the disassembly part selection can be achieved. In other words, by including collaboration among three decision makers, three aspects of sustainability (providing economic concept, environmental issues, and social factors) can be satisfied. A first perspective is thus to further model and study collaborative decision process. Through collaboration each decision makers could become aware of the effect of each objective function's value on the other objection functions. In addition, by analyzing the increase and reduction of the respective values of each function, decision makers could study the impacts on the choice of an appropriate recovery operation.

*Conclusion and Perspectives*

In this paper, a mixed integer multi-objective mathematical model was proposed to recovery of a product parts after disassembly through circular economy operations. The objective is to minimize all the costs besides increasing $CO_2$ emission rate, and maximization of fairness among operators (in terms of time). The problem was solved by Ɛ-constraints method to obtain the most suitable recovery operations. However, there are a number of limitations that should be considered in the future works. The first limitation is not considering reliability of each part, while the reliability should be included in the usage years. Second proposition is solving the problem for large size instances with metaheuristics algorithms. Finally, quality manager as a next decision maker can be cooperated in the decision-making process to maximize the total quality of by choosing of the most suitable operations at the EOL.

## Appendix A

$$\sum_{p \in P} q_i x_{ip1} \leq l_i^2 \qquad \forall i \in I \tag{8}$$

Equations (8) confirm that a part with above a predetermined quality is not candidate to be disposed.

$$\sum_{p \in P} q_i x_{ip2} \geq l_i^3 \qquad \forall i \in I \tag{9}$$

Equations (9) indicate if the quality of a part is lower than a certain quality level, that part cannot be reused.

$$\sum_{p \in P} q_i x_{ip3} \geq l_i^4 \qquad \forall i \in I \tag{10}$$

$$\sum_{p \in P} q_i x_{ip3} \leq 1 \qquad \forall i \in I \tag{11}$$

Equations (10) and (11) define the quality of a part that has can be candidated to remanufacturing recovery operation.

$$o_i = \sum_{p \in P} q_i x_{ip2} + 1 - \sum_{p \in P} x_{ip2} \qquad \forall i \in I \tag{12}$$

Equations (12) imply to the quality of a part after reuse operation.

$$\sum_{i \in I} o_i \alpha_i \geq qm \qquad \forall i \in I \tag{13}$$

Equations (13) confirm the total obtained quality should be bigger than minimum acceptable quality.

## References

1. United Nations (2015). https://sustainabledevelopment.un.org/topics/climatechange. Accessed 30 Apr 2018
2. Kokubu, K., Itsubo, N., Nakajima, M., Yamada, T.: Low Carbon Supply Chain Management. Chuokeizai-sha Inc., Tokyo (2015)
3. Ilgin, M.A., Gupta, S.M.: Remanufacturing Modeling and Analysis. CRC Press, Boca Raton (2012)
4. Hasegawa, S., Kinoshita, Y., Yamada, T., Bracke, S.: Life cycle option selection of disassembly parts for material-based $CO_2$ saving rate and recovery cost: analysis of different market value and labor cost for reused parts in German and Japanese cases. Int. J. Prod. Econ. **213**, 229–242 (2019)
5. Inoue, M., et al.: Quantitative estimate of $CO_2$ emission reduction from reuse of automobile parts in Japan. Int. J. Supply Chain Manag. **6**(4), 110–117 (2017)
6. Lambert, A.J.D., Gupta, S.M.: Disassembly Modeling for Assembly, Maintenance Reuse, and Recycling. CRC Press, Boca Raton (2005)
7. European Commission (2015). https://ec.europa.eu/clima/policies/international/negotiations/paris_en. Accessed 10 May 2018
8. Ren, Y., Tian, G., Zhao, F., Yu, D., Zhang, C.: Selective cooperative disassembly planning based on multi-objective discrete artificial bee colony algorithm. Eng. Appl. Artif. Intell. **64**, 415–431 (2017)

9. Wang, H., Penga, Q., Zhangb, J., Gub, P.: Selective disassembly planning for the end-of-life product. Procedia CIRP **60**, 512–517 (2017)
10. Igarashi, K., Yamada, T., Gupta, S.M., Inoue, M., Itsubo, N.: Disassembly system modeling and design with parts selection for cost, recycling and $CO_2$ saving rates using multi criteria optimization. J. Manuf. Syst. **38**, 151–164 (2016)
11. Smith, S., Hsu, L.Y., Smith, G.C.: Partial disassembly sequence planning based on cost-benefit analysis. J. Clean. Prod. **139**, 729–739 (2016)
12. Hasegawa, S., Kinoshita, Y., Yamada, T., Inoue, M., Bracke, S.: Disassembly reuse Part Selection for recovery rate and cost with lifetime analysis. Int. J. Autom. Technol. **12**(6), 822–832 (2018)
13. Rickli, J., Camelio, J.A.: Partial disassembly sequencing considering acquired end-of-life product age distributions. Int. J. Prod. Res. **52**(7), 496–512 (2014)
14. Riggs, R.J., Jin, X., Hu, J.: Two-stage sequence generation for partial disassembly of products with sequence dependent task times. Procedia CIRP **29**, 698–703 (2015)
15. Jun, H.B., Cusin, M., Kiritsis, D., Xirouchakis, P.: A multi-objective evolutionary algorithm for EOL product recovery optimization: turbocharger case study. Int. J. Pro. Res. **45**, 18–19 (2007)
16. Meng, K., Lou, P., Peng, X., Prybutok, V.: An improved co-evolutionary algorithm for green manufacturing by integration of recovery option selection and disassembly planning for end-of-life products. Int. J. Pro. Res. **54**(18), 5567–5593 (2016)
17. Geissdoerfer, M., Savaget, P., Bocken, N.M., Hultink, E.J.: The circular economy–a new sustainability paradigm? J. Clean. Prod **143**, 757–768 (2017)

# Policies and New Digital Services

# Analysis Model to Identify the Regional "Strategic Bets" of Startup Porto's Network

Claudio Roth[1(✉)], Carla Pereira[2,3(✉)], Rafael Pedrosa[4(✉)], and Maria Roth[5(✉)]

[1] DE - Department of Education, CTISM - Industrial Technical College of Santa Maria, Federal University of Santa Maria, Santa Maria 97105-900, Brazil
claudiowroth@ctism.ufsm.br

[2] CIICESI - Center for Research and Innovation in Business Sciences and Information Systems, ESTG - School of Technology and Management, Polytechnic of Porto, 4610-156 Felgueiras, Portugal
cpereira@estg.ipp.pt

[3] INESC TEC - Institute for Systems and Computer Engineering of Porto, 4200-465 Porto, Portugal

[4] PORTIC - Porto Research, Technology and Innovation Center, Polytechnic of Porto, 4200-374 Porto, Portugal
rafael.pedrosa@sc.ipp.pt

[5] DDI - Department of Individual Sports, CEFD - Physical Education and Sports Center, Federal University of Santa Maria, Santa Maria 97105-900, Brazil
ddicefd@gmail.com

**Abstract.** The economic development process associated with entrepreneurial ecosystems comprises different approaches and its understanding is vital for regional growth. The Polytechnic Institute of Porto is boosting its entrepreneurial ecosystem, to reinforce its action as an agent of economic and social development in the regions where it operates. The objective of the work was to propose the criteria for the construction of an analysis model that allows the identification of regional "strategic bets" that will support the development of proposals for the provision of support services that integrate with the regional business base and incorporate "Decision Intelligence" to performance of the "Entrepreneurial Regional Observatory of the Porto Startup Network." The methodology used was an exploratory research and, at the end, the initiatives taken and the results are presented.

**Keywords:** Economic development · Entrepreneurial ecosystems · Decision intelligence

## 1 Introduction

The process of economic growth and development associated to entrepreneurial ecosystems, has been on the agendas of politicians, businessmen, academia and citizens with different approaches, both from a conceptual point of view and from its use [1].


Published by Springer Nature Switzerland AG 2021
L. M. Camarinha-Matos et al. (Eds.): PRO-VE 2021, IFIP AICT 629, pp. 191–198, 2021.
https://doi.org/10.1007/978-3-030-85969-5_17

The European Commission defines entrepreneurship as the process of improving economic activity in an organization, when it takes risks, it is creative, innovative and has a capable management system.

And as an entrepreneur, the Commission considers a person who is constantly looking for an opportunity to create value and who is never satisfied with the existing condition [2].

The Polytechnic Institute of Porto (P.Porto) is boosting its entrepreneurial ecosystem, to reinforce its actions as an agent of economic and social development in the regions in which it operates.

To this end, it is supported by the creation of the "Regional Observatory of Entrepreneurial Ecosystems of the Startup Porto network", which includes its two hubs: Porto and Felgueiras, in order to characterize these ecosystems, providing information to understand their evolution.

This paper presents a proposal for an analysis model that allows the identification of regional "strategic bets" that will support the development of proposals for the provision of support services that integrate with the regional business base of the entrepreneurial ecosystem of Startup Porto's network.

The analysis model is based on consensus criteria that can determine the level of achievement of organizations and incorporate "Decision Intelligence" into the performance of the "Regional Observatory of Entrepreneurial Ecosystems of the Startup Porto network".

The specific objectives of this work are:

- Define consensus criteria to determine the level of achievement of organizations
- Apply the proposed criteria to objectively quantify the results achieved
- Compare the results achieved with the pre-established goals and the respective performance levels.

## 2 Systemic Context

The constitution of an ecosystem that encourages entrepreneurship has among its essential purposes the creation of a dynamic context, characterized by the continuous flow of information, resources and knowledge that enhance innovation.

A more systemic view of the concept of these ecosystems, called entrepreneurial ecosystems, allows public policy makers to trace a new and distinct path to understanding the heterogeneous nature of these ecosystems and, through them, to promote regional economic and social development [3].

Although there is some interest at the national level, an entrepreneurial ecosystem is primarily understood as taking place in a local environment or, at most, regions, using their assets and resources, from the regional business base and the local cooperation networks [4].

The insertion, therefore, of a company in an entrepreneurial ecosystem has a strategic character, because, acting in environments in continuous mutation, where decisions and strategies must be implemented quickly, being an active participant in this ecosystem represents the possibility of sharing competences, investments and creation of value.

For an entrepreneurial ecosystem to function fully, it is necessary that three pillars are fully active, namely: nonconformed entrepreneurs wishing to solve problems, knowledge necessary to solve these problems and investors with the necessary capital to transform ideas into practice and to take the business to a higher level.

Since the European Union's reformed cohesion policy for 2014–20, European regions have been promoting research and innovation strategies for intelligent specialization as a way to create technological capacity, strengthen regional innovation systems and increase the "related variety" among the existing economic activity policies [5].

Introduced in the discussion of territorial development strategies, smart specialization is based on local endowments, international network orientation and the regions' potential for excellence.

Regional governments can align innovative actions and economic development strategies, allowing decision makers to be encouraged to adopt location-based policies, ensuring thematic prioritization and concentration to foster innovation, growth and entrepreneurship [6].

This large-scale European experience provides a new type of industrial policy, especially geared towards the modernization of traditional industrial sectors, which in itself does not bring anything new, but which is innovative in the way it proceeds [7].

The overarching idea of the smart specialization strategy is that regions can identify their innovation activities based on evidences and try to combine them into new ways of providing products and services that are attractive in the global market [8].

Some risks of bottlenecks to the application of this smart specialization strategy are observed, such as the non-coincidence between functional and administrative regions, the inability of insertion in the global value chains or the low capacity for absorption of knowledge by part of the business community associated with academic actors of regional scope.

The perception of these risks makes it possible to identify that, in order to apply the smart specialization strategy in these regions, it is necessary to focus on greater interregional and transnational articulation and on overcoming the difficulty of defining priorities due to the contrast between the internal realities of the regions [9].

The operationalization of the smart specialization policy has been quite limited, as diversification through more complex technologies can be attractive, but difficult to fulfill by the regions of the European Union.

Regions can overcome this diversification dilemma by developing new technologies that are based on related local resources, highlighting the potential risks and rewards for regions in adopting competing diversification strategies [10].

The understanding of how the regions develop new trajectories of growth and economic development and why they differ in this ability, goes through the perception that they have different possibilities to restructure their economies in the long run [11].

Regional diversity can result in benefits for the productivity of companies due to the recombination of knowledge, which allows greater opportunities to imitate, share and recombine ideas [12].

The principle of related variety then defines that economic development is driven by interactions between sectors of regional economies that are related in terms of technology or industry.

These complementary skills can improve the dissemination of knowledge and can also affect significant externalities in a region, thus contributing to the growth of an industry and a region [13].

In this context, a sustainable option will be to seek the diversification of the regional economy in new fields that take advantage of the development capacity of the regional business base and entrepreneurial ecosystem and that adhere to the existing analytical and symbolic knowledge base in the region [14].

In this sense, the study of the different regional, temporal and social configurations presents itself as an extremely current topic in the assessment and monitoring of the impact of these ecosystems as mechanisms responsible for economic development, and may, in some cases, even be presented as vital factors for the growth of the regions.

Today, the regional business base is constantly confronted with revolutionary technological advances, new emerging markets, fluctuations in demand or unexpected movements in the competition, leading companies to seek to incorporate "Decision Intelligence" in their processes and management.

Thousands of information, vertical and horizontal, flow and play an important role within companies and evaluating the efficiency of each one is an extremely critical task.

In response to that, companies are increasingly evaluating their tools to practice decision intelligence in conducting their business [15].

"Decision Intelligence" is a new concept that integrates the best of applied data science, mathematics, statistics, social and behavioral sciences and strategic management principles, unified in this nascent methodology.

The idea behind "Decision Intelligence" is to use the data in an integrated and organic way, which contains at its *core* the attributes of Artificial Intelligence, Machine Learning and the intensified use of algorithms combined with other structural methodologies.

A very effective approach to achieve the objective of adding "Decision Intelligence" to management is to define "strategic bets" [16], options that allow companies to test the possibilities presented and build their experience. If they fail, these options are likely to give up, but if they succeed, they can position organizations to capitalize valuable opportunities.

The complexity of the business environment and the amount of information available for decision-making, can lead companies to lose focus on the most relevant information. In this sense, organizations must use and benefit from the information services that can be offered by an observatory [17].

This need for useful information to assist in choosing the best decisions shows to be old, since to manage any process we need to detect trends and analyze possibilities that facilitate the decision to be made.

The construction of a "Regional Observatory of Entrepreneurial Ecosystems of the Startup Porto network" is, therefore, an important initiative, which consists of the assessement and analysis of information whose main objective is to characterize and monitor the regional entrepreneurial ecosystems, thus making known subsidies that allow understanding and monitoring their evolution [18].

In creating the observatory, P.Porto believes that it will identify regional "strategic bets" and that it will be an opportunity for the development of proposals for the development of entrepreneurial projects, oriented to the provision of support services and applied innovation, which reinforce and integrate the regional business base.

This study aimed to propose the criteria for the construction of an analysis model to enable the identification of regional "strategic bets", the first stage for the implementation of the observatory, giving reach to the vision of the future outlined for the region.

## 3 Identification of Startup Porto's "Strategic Bets"

For the creation of the "Regional Observatory of Entrepreneurial Ecosystems in the Startup Porto network", seven stages were defined, namely, the Identification of Strategic Bets, the Combination of Technologies and Related Markets, the Survey of Ideas for the Provision of Support Services, Systematization, Public Calls, Presentation of Proposals for the Provision of Support and Monitoring Services.

This work is about the first stage, the identification of the "strategic bets" of the Startup Porto network.

In this stage, the aim is to propose an analysis model based on criteria that allow gathering data from the analytical and symbolic knowledge bases and the capacities for business development and the entrepreneurial ecosystem.

This information will allow the identification of regional "strategic bets", which will subsidize the development of proposals for the provision of support services that integrate with the regional business base, as shown in Fig. 1.

| Regional Observatory of Entrepreneurial Ecosystem of the StartUP Porto |
|---|
| Stage 01: Identify Regional "Strategic Bets" |
| **Technological Assets and Resources** Analytical and Synthetic Knowledge Base |
| **Non-Technological Assets and Resources** Symbolic Knowledge Base |
| **Entrepreneurship** Entrepreneurial Ecosystem |
| **Regional Industrial Base** Development Capacity |
| **Strategic Analysis** Analysis of Internal and External Environments |
| **Strategic Matrix Analysis** Combined Analysis of Internal and External Environments |

**Fig. 1.** Stage 01 Identify Regional "Strategic Bets" of the Startup Porto Network

The collection of these basic data is made through different ways, such from questionnaires, interviews, data analysis, among others, involving public and private entities,

entities related to entrepreneurship and education and research institutions and through research of publications of governmental and private organizations, as shown in Fig. 2.

The objective of this process is the characterization of the potential impact of PPorto in the regional economic development, to support the definition of the strategic bets.

This characterization will be done according three complementary dimensions of analysis: PPorto R&D Centers, Entrepreneurial Ecosystem and Regional Industrial Base.

The characterization of the R&D Centers is important to define the level of proximity of the research made in the P.Porto regarding the industry.

The characterization of the Entrepreneurial Ecosystem is based on the analysis of its Determinants, Results and Impacts and the Economic Performance of Entrepreneurship.

Finally, the characterization of the Regional Industrial Base is determined by the analysis of indicators that reveal the intensity of its action for technological innovation and its industrial performance.

These dimensions will be evaluated under three validated methods, namely:

a) Technological Readiness (TRL), which indicates the ability to identify and create technology concepts and test prototypes in a laboratory environment,
b) Business Readiness (CRI), which demonstrates the ability to propose a hypothetical business model for a technology concept;
c) Commercial Readiness (BRL), which demonstrates the ability to define the potential market value of a technology concept.

The integrated application of these methods will allow to obtain, to which of the above mentioned perspectives/dimensions, a certain level of readiness aligned with Innovation, Economic and Social results and impacts and Partnerships with the productive sector.

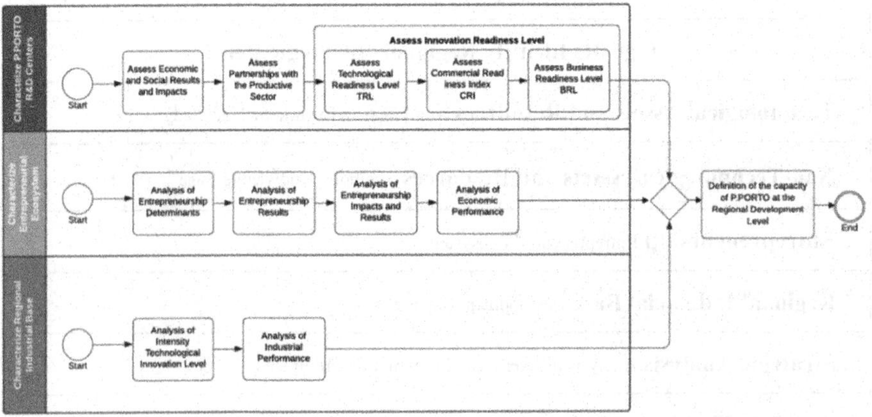


**Fig. 2.** Diagram of the capacity of P.Porto at the regional development level

These isolated data are not sufficient to express something and should be processed and translated into performance indicators so that they can measure regional performance.

The information obtained represents the factors that will provide the basis for the strategic analysis, using the scenario analysis tool "SWOT Matrix", of the internal and external environments of the entrepreneurial ecosystem of Startup Porto's network, corresponding to the identification of resources, skills, strengths and weaknesses of the region.

Then, after determining exactly what are the opportunities, weaknesses, strengths and threats of the entrepreneurial ecosystem of Startup Porto network, we proceed with the analysis of how external factors interfere in the possibility of interns happening.

A complementary analysis of the results of the strategic analysis "SWOT Matrix", with the objective of identifying which actions should be taken to improve the situation, can be carried out through the tool called "Cross Analysis of the SWOT Matrix", which consists of confronting the elements of the Matrix.

Depending on the elements of the SWOT Matrix that you confront, it can establish four types of strategies called: Offensive Strategy; Reinforcement Strategy; Confrontation Strategy; and Defensive Strategy, which can be adopted and converted into regional "strategic bets", producing intense synergy.

In the end, it is important to ensure that this self-assessment and the strategy that results from it are shared and appropriated widely by the region.

## 4 Conclusions

From the emergence of the initiative to implement the "Regional Observatory of Entrepreneurial Ecosystems of the Startup Porto network", this work dealt with the proposal of criteria for use in an analysis model that allows the identification of regional "strategic bets".

From this proposal of criteria, it was possible to preliminarily analyze the history of fundraising and socioeconomic impact of collaborative projects between P.Porto and the regional industry.

In a step to follow, internal forum will be held for the presentation and discussion of the results of the most recent research and projects in execution.

For future work, the criteria for collecting primary and secondary data related to Assets and Technological and Non-Technological Resources, Regional Business and Basis of Entrepreneurship will be proposed.

It is worth mentioning that this work starts a first proposition of criteria, which should be further developed and improved for future analysis, and that other criteria can also be proposed.

Finally, it was observed that, from the proposition of these criteria, there was a demonstration of interest from the academic community to the theme and, mainly, to the suggestion of new analysis criteria.

## References

1. Valente, F., Dantas, J., Brito, M.M.: Ecossistemas empreendedores: estudo de caso. Jornadas Hispano Lusas de Gestión Cientifica, Osuna, Espanha (2019)

2. Santos, H., Sá Marques, T., Ribeiro, P., Torres, M.: Especialização inteligente: as redes de projetos europeus H2020 com ancoragem em Portugal. In: Teresa Sá Marques, Helder Santos & M. Pilar Alonso Logroño (Coord.), VIII Jornadas de Geografía Económica: La Geografía de las Redes Económicas Y la Geografía Económica en Rede, Livro de Atas, Porto, pp. 13–35, Faculdade de Letras da Universidade do Porto, Asociación de Geógrafos Españoles (2018)
3. Brown, R., Mason, C.: Looking inside the spiky bits: a critical review and conceptualisation of entrepreneurial ecosystems. Small Bus. Econ. **49**(1), 11–30 (2017). https://doi.org/10.1007/s11187-017-9865-7
4. Malecki, E.J.: Entrepreneurship and entrepreneurial ecosystems. Geogr. Compass. **12**, e12359 (2018)
5. Pinto, H., Nogueira, C., Sampaio, F., Sá, A.F.: 26th APDR Congress. Redes de inovação e especialização inteligente no brasil: algumas lições da experiência ris3 em Pernambuco (2019). ISBN 978-989-8780-07-2
6. Săftescu, R., Paul, C., Simion, E., Mitroi, M.: Governance of smart specialisation: experiences of four Europeans regions. Europolity Continuity Change Eur. Governance **10**(2), 1–17 (2016)
7. Foray, D.: Smart specialisation strategies and industrial modernisation in European regions - theory and practice. Camb. J. Econ. **42**(6), 1505–1520 (2018)
8. Mäenpää, A., Teräs, J.: In search of domains in smart specialisation: case study of three Nordic regions. Eur. J. Spat. Develop. **68**, 1–20 (2018)
9. Maroufkhani, P., Wagner, R., Wan Ismail, W.K.: Entrepreneurial ecosystems: a systematic review. J. Enterp. Communities People Places Glob. Econ. **12**(4), 545–564 (2018)
10. Balland, P.A., Boschma, R., Crespo, J., Rigby, D.L.: Smart specialization policy in the European Union: relatedness, knowledge complexity and regional diversification. Reg. Stud. **53**(9), 1252–1268 (2019)
11. Santos, G.O.: Caminhos para a construção de uma nova trajetória de desenvolvimento: Uma abordagem evolucionária do Sistema Regional de Inovação do Estado do Rio de Janeiro. Tese (Doutorado em Políticas Públicas, Estratégias e Desenvolvimento) – Instituto de Economia, Universidade Federal do Rio de Janeiro, Rio de Janeiro (2020)
12. Santos, G.O.: Caminhos para a construção de uma nova estratégia de desenvolvimento: Uma Abordagem Evolucionária do Sistema Regional de Inovação do Estado do Rio de Janeiro. Universidade Federal do Rio de Janeiro: June 2020 (2020)
13. Melkas, H., Uotila, T., Tura, T.: Policies of related variety in practice: the case Innovation Session Method. Eur. Plan. Stud. **24**(3), 489–510 (2016)
14. Boschma, R.: Evolutionary Economic Geography and its Implications for Regional Innovation Policy. OECD, Paris (2009)
15. Kahraman, C., Kaya, I., Çevikcan, E.: Intelligence decision systems in enterprise information management. J. Enterp. Inf. Manage. **24**, 360–379 (2011). ISSN 1741-0398
16. Stalk, G., Iyer, A.: How to Hedge Your Strategic Bets: Make short-term investments to test opportunities. Harvard Bus. Rev. **94**, 80–86 (2016)
17. Vieira, J.K.M., Moura, H.P., Farias Jr., I.H.: Um Modelo de Observatório para Projetos. In: Workshop de Teses e Dissertações (WTDSOFT) - Congresso Brasileiro de Software: Teoria e Prática (CBSOFT), 2019, Salvador. Anais [...]. Porto Alegre: Sociedade Brasileira de Computação, pp. 38–46 (2019). ISSN 2177-9384
18. Rosa, F.L., Jung, C.F., Von Mengden, P.R.: Um Modelo para Avaliação do Potencial Estratégico de Projetos de P&D de Inovação Tecnológica. Produção Online - Revista Científica Eletrônica de Engenharia de Produção, v. 13, n. 3 (2013). ISSN 1676-190

# Behavior Data Collection in Collaborative Virtual Learning Environments

Tianqi Wu[1], Juanqiong Gou[1](✉), Wenxin Mu[1], and Zhe Wang[2]

[1] School of Economic and Management, Beijing Jiaotong University, Beijing, China
{20120614,Jqgou,wxmu}@bjtu.edu.cn
[2] Shanghai Siye Network Technology Co., Ltd., Shanghai, China

**Abstract.** Educational Data Mining has gained a variety of attention. It describes students' cognitive needs through data mining, and provides individualized knowledge support for cognitive differences. Although the application of data mining algorithms is relatively mature, the data pre-processing based on data collection still suffers from high costs. The paper focus on a research question: how to effectively collect behavior data in virtual learning environments? "Effectively" in the sense of ensuring that value-intensive behavior data on decision-making can be accurately collected which reflects the students' cognitive. Therefore, the paper presents a method to achieve the object. The method comprises six steps, including extraction, transformation, determination, design, trigger and store. Based on the fact that all behavior data generated by the interaction is objective, identifying the collection points on the trigger event matches the granularity level of behavior data. Considering the related platforms and intelligent applications, the method can be used, providing behavior data support for the research of knowledge services.

**Keywords:** Behavior data collection · Virtual learning environments · Educational Data Mining

## 1 Introduction

There are two types of virtual learning environments available: one is the learning management system represented by MOOC, which is mainly in the form of online teachers teaching knowledge to students and students internalizing it through learning. The other type is the gamified learning platform represented by serious games, where achievement is mainly addressed the results of the game. The disadvantage of the former is that traditional teaching methods don't allow for personalized teaching, while the latter's disadvantage is that students focus more on the game itself than on knowledge. Therefore, a focus on both "learning" and "practicing" is necessary to achieve knowledge collaboration in a virtual learning environment, as shown in Fig. 1.


L. M. Camarinha-Matos et al. (Eds.): PRO-VE 2021, IFIP AICT 629, pp. 199–211, 2021.
https://doi.org/10.1007/978-3-030-85969-5_18

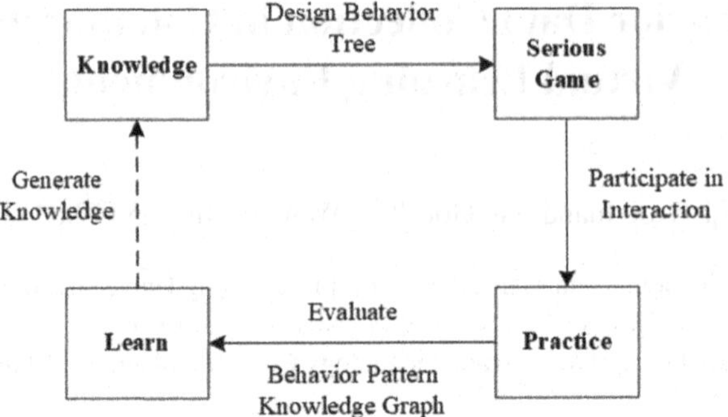


**Fig. 1.** Knowledge collaboration in virtual learning environments

Educational Data Mining (EDM) is a special area [1], accompanied by discovering valuable and potential information from the vast amount of data available in educational settings [2]. One of core objectives of EDM is to offer more personalized, interactive learning environments based on students' cognitive needs [1, 3]. Although there has been much work on mining algorithms [4], substantial work has been done related with data collection [2]. Furthermore, data collection plays a vital role as it provides the foundation for EDM [2]. According to the background mentioned above, the research is conducted by a main question:

*How to effectively collect student behavior data in virtual learning environments for behavior data mining?*

Therefore, the paper needs to achieve the following objectives:

1) To reduce the cost of subsequent pre-processing by designing a structured format.
2) To ensure that value-intensive data can be collected accurately.

The structure of the paper is as follows: Sect. 1 introduces the main question of the paper. Section 2 presents an overview of behavior data collection. Section 3 describes a method of behavior data collection. In order to better illustrate the method, Sect. 4 describes a case study. Research prospects will be presented by Sect. 5.

## 2 Related Works

### 2.1 Data Collection and Data Pre-processing for EDM

In many cases, data collection is categorized as the first step in data pre-processing, which is the first step in the data mining process [5]. Figure 2 shows the main pre-processing steps with educational data [6]. It is not difficult to find that most studies define the data collection phase as the collection of raw data and separate out the stages of cleaning, identifying and filtering of raw data as other stages of data pre-processing. However, the data pre-processing stage essentially consumes 60–90% of the time, resources and efforts in the whole data mining process, remains a challenge that needs to be addressed [6].

Many researchers have proposed solutions to the high cost of data pre-processing, mainly by converting manual data pre-processing to automated data pre-processing [5, 7, 8], while others have argued for a standardized data format starting with data collection [2, 3, 6, 8]. In this paper we focus on the data collection itself. [2] proposed a framework for collecting educational data based on data needs, but with a wide range of data sources and no guidance for data collection in virtual learning environments. [6] raised the need to collect data from multiple types of virtual learning environments, arguing that a collected data set with its own educational benchmark eliminates the need for pre-processing. [8] believed that one of the future research directions could focus on standardizing the format of data collected in virtual learning environments in order to shorten the most time-consuming pre-processing. In general, the solution of relying on educational data collection itself to improve the efficiency of data pre-processing is still at a preliminary stage, mainly because most objective data collected comes from system log files [7]. The raw data in these log files can't be easily made to change and therefore can only be collected indiscriminately.

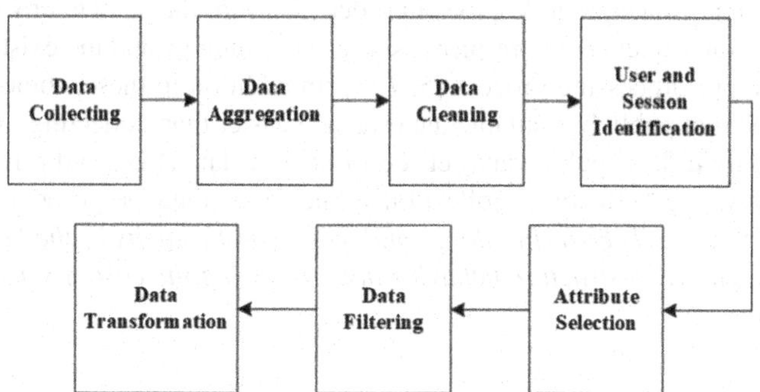


**Fig. 2.** The main pre-processing steps with educational data [6]

## 2.2 Behavior Data Collection in Virtual Learning Environments

First, learning environments can store large amounts of data from multiple sources, such as interactions between students, teachers and virtual platforms, administrative data, statistics, student affectivity and so on [9]. So, it is important to determine the level of granularity at which behavior data is collected [10]. Figure 3 depicts different granularity levels and their relationship to the amount of data, from the smallest (Events) to the largest (Courses) [9], which implies different collection frequencies and corresponding data set sizes [6]. The level of granularity chosen for the behavior data described in the paper is the smallest level. Therefore, the data collected can be characterized by whether event actions are captured, and the status of the event feedback [10].

Secondly, it is essential to understand how behavior data is currently collected in virtual learning environments. In the beginning, many case studies focused on questionnaires and continued to quantify their indicators in the hope of increasing accuracy

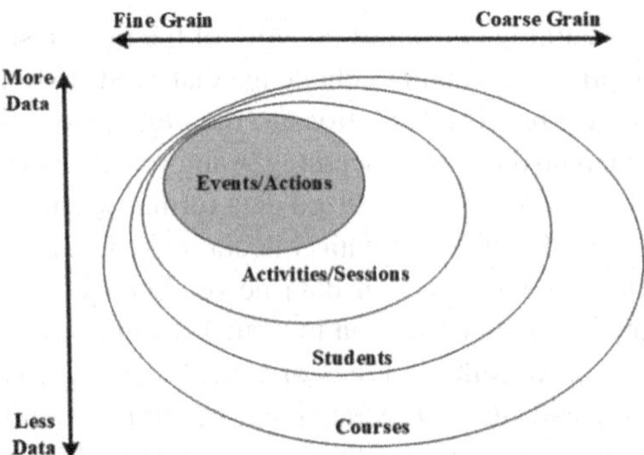


**Fig. 3.** Different granularity levels and their relationship to the amount of data [9]

[11, 12]. However, as questionnaires are strongly subjective in nature [11], it was gradually replaced by log files represented by Moodle [7, 8, 13, 14]. Log files are based entirely on student interactions with the platform [8]. The granularity of behavior data is also at the event level [6], but as mentioned in the previous section, it is difficult for researchers to make changes to log files in order to ensure the authenticity of raw data. So, the cost of subsequent data pre-processing is very high [5]and the existing solution is to automate pre-processing process [5, 7, 8]. In addition to these, some researchers have suggested that publicly available data sets are easier than collecting own behavior data [9], but only if these public data sets don't involve data ethics and privacy [6, 9].

In summary, the "effective" collection of behavior data proposed in this paper involves two objects: *(I) Ensuring the granularity and objectivity of the behavior data itself. (II) Attempting to structure behavior data, reducing the cost of subsequent data pre-processing.*

## 3 Method of Behavior Data Collection

As shown in Fig. 4, the method comprises six stages: extraction, transformation, determination, design, trigger and store, which are further explained below.

**(I) Extraction**

The behavior of students interacting with the platform depends on the rules of the platform [15]. Therefore, the first stage is to extract the logic rules of the platform applied by the configuration platform. These rules are the core basis for the subsequent construction of behavior logic model. There are two methods of extraction, one is based directly on the documents provided by platform developers and the other is based on the whole interactions with the platform, generating rule documents.

**(II) Transformation**

Once we have the required logic rules, we need to transform them into the behavior logic model. In order to achieve the goal of logic clarity and visualization, the paper refers to Behavior Tree theory. Behavior Tree (BT) is a formal modeling language. Its concept

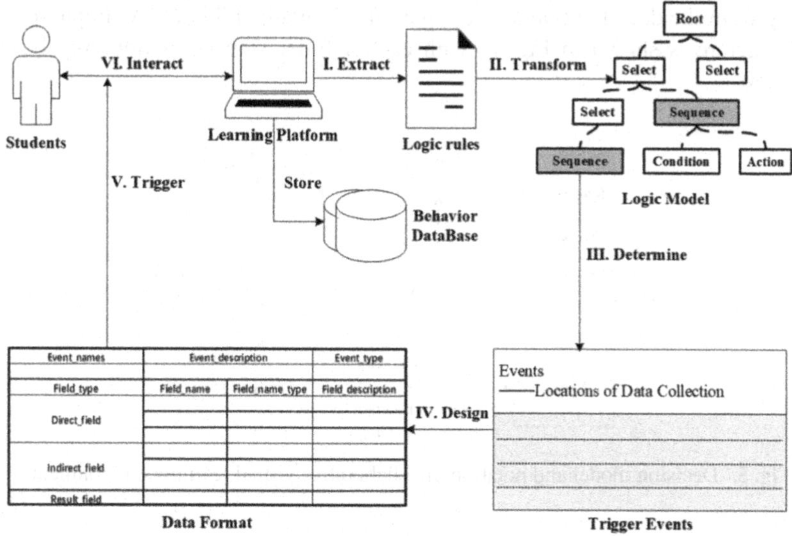


**Fig. 4.** A method of behavior data collection in virtual learning environments

was developed by Dromey in 2001 [16]. Behavior Tree has been widely applied on behavior decision-making of intelligent object NPC (Nonplayer Character) in interactive simulation applications [17]. The basic idea of Behavior Tree is to decompose individual behaviors into multiple levels. The nodes of logic model in Fig. 4. can be divided into the following types according to BT: **(1)** Select node (Select, SEL), a node that describes the interactive selection of students on the virtual learning platform. Its parent node is the root or a select node and its child nodes are select or sequential nodes. **(2)** Sequence node (Sequence, SEQ), a node that describes decision-making, usually containing a set of decision conditions and actions. Its parent node is a select node and its child nodes are a few condition nodes and action nodes. **(3)** Condition node (Condition, CON), is the leaf node to determine whether to execute or jump out of the sequence node. Its parent node is a sequence node. **(4)** Action node (Action, ACT), is a leaf node that represents the student's operational behavior. Its parent node is a sequence node.

**(III) Determination**

The logic model enables modularity and independence of individual behaviors through transparent logic encapsulation. It can not only help researchers to identify the location of behavior data collection points, but also help platform operators to control the interaction logic more clearly. The decision points are a part of the student's behavior that occurs when interacting with the platform–"mouse click" [18].

From the perspective of decision making in collaborative networks, the logic model we constructed is in fact a decision model of students in collaborative virtual learning environments, as shown in Fig. 5. In Decision Model, the output data is determined from the input data, other sub-decisions and pre-defined business logic rules [19]. In the logic rule-based transformed logic model, we decouple students' decision points into multiple possible sub-decision points that correspond to different necessary conditions and actions resulting from the decision (Detail examples are shown in Table 2). A simple decision model diagram is shown in Fig. 6, with each sub-decision point implying business knowledge.

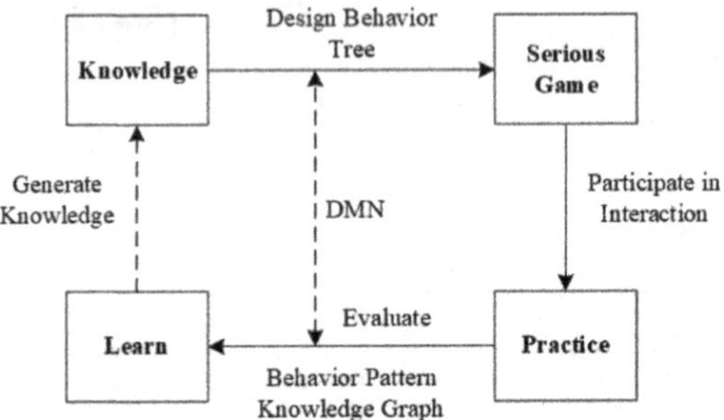


**Fig. 5.** Decision model and notation in collaborative virtual learning environments

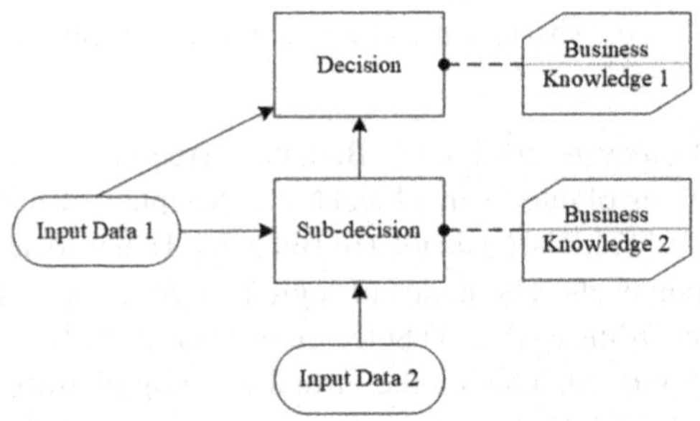


**Fig. 6.** Decision model and notation in collaborative networks [19]

Therefore, those sub-decision points are the part of behaviors that contains the most valuable behavior data, including information about students' cognitive and behavior patterns to be mined later. This precise data collection improves the efficiency of data pre-processing and ensures the quality of data compared to the full collection of raw data such as log files. So how to collect these behavior data? The first issue is to determine the location of behavior data collection points. In the logic model, the point at which a student makes a decision is represented by a sequential node. In addition, the leaf nodes in the logic model - the condition node and the action node - describe the trigger conditions and the corresponding actions that result when the event is triggered. Therefore, all sequence nodes in the logic model are the behavior data collection points we need to determine. They need to be extracted and stored as trigger events.

**(IV) Design**

Once the behavior data collection points have been identified, the collection can usually begin. However, before this can be done, a structured data format needs to be developed for the behavior data in order to make it more "effective". This paper designs a structured data format based on event triggering, including event name, event description, event type, field type, field name, field data type and field description. Of these, the field types are divided into three categories: direct fields, indirect fields and result fields. We design direct fields as behavior data that can be captured directly based on the event trigger. Indirect fields can be collected indirectly through pre-defined procedures. Based on the above two types of fields, the system can output judgement results through the result fields and trigger corresponding actions.

**(V) Trigger**

The location of behavior data collection points has been determined and the structured data format has been designed. The next stage is to trigger the event and collect the corresponding behavior data. Unlike the data collection of log files, the paper uses a front-end event monitoring mechanism, which is explained as follows: when an interaction decision is made between a student and the platform, the front-end event monitoring mechanism collects the relevant fields according to the structured data format. The collection is real-time. The mechanism will feed the trigger results (result fields, actions, etc.) back to the students.

**(VI) Store**

Finally, the platform stores collected data in a dedicated behavior database to facilitate subsequent data mining research. In addition, social data of students outside the platform, for example, can be correlated with the behavior data to analyze the impact of the environment, social and other factors on students' behaviors.

We try to make the data collection achieve two goals mentioned in Sect. 2. Based on the fact that all behavior data generated by the interaction is objective, identifying the collection points on the trigger event matches the granularity level of behavior data.

## 4 Case Study

A case study was conducted on a New Retail Business Simulation Platform to better illustrate the application of the method described in Sect. 3.

The New Retail Enterprise Simulation Platform is based on business simulation, game theory and other technologies, aiming at the needs of enterprise operation and management courses. Students are exposed to various situations such as purchasing, marketing and warehousing, they implement enterprise activities based on financial management, inventory management and some other multidimensional knowledge. Therefore, behavior data generated by interaction between students and the platform contains intensive individualized cognitive needs, and the main form of which is individual interaction decision-making. The purpose of the case study is to acquire these interactive behavior data for the related research of data mining such as individualized decision-making difference analysis.

**1. Extraction**

According to the documents provided by the platform developer, a comprehensive logic rule for the New Retail Enterprise Simulation Platform is shown in Fig. 7. This is only an overview, there are also specific logic rules for each part. These extracted logic rules are the core basis for the next stage in constructing a behavior logic model.

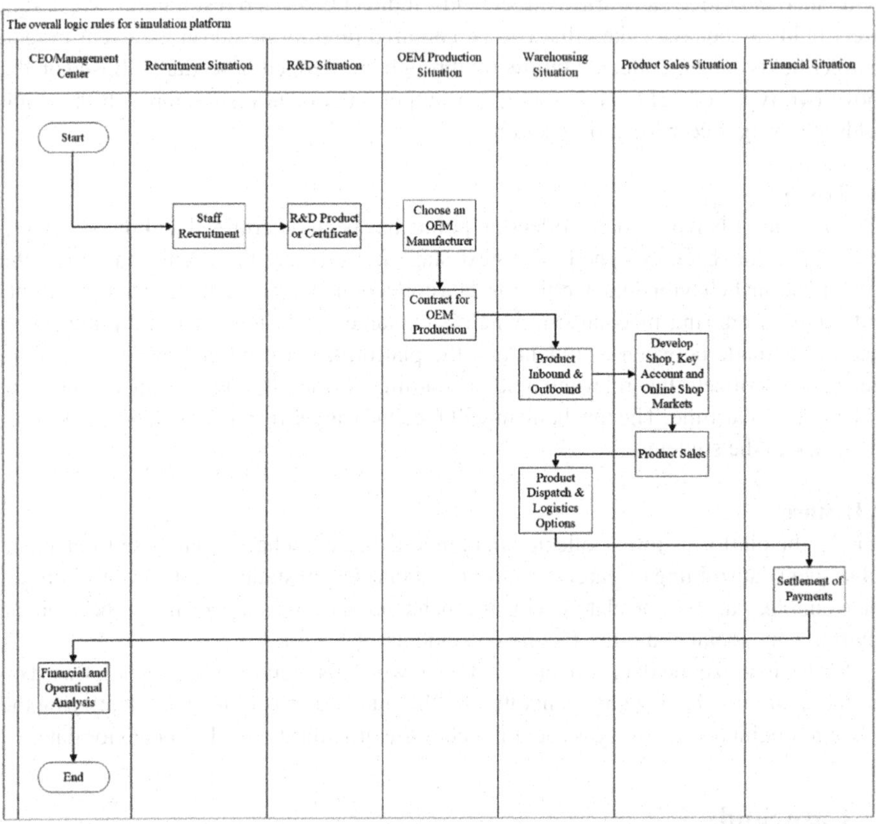


**Fig. 7.** The overall logic rules for new retail enterprise simulation platform

**2. Transformation**

The logic rules are transformed into a behavior logic model as shown in Table 1 referring to Behavior Tree theory. Due to space limitations, only two of these situations are shown here: key account market and warehouse. The logic model consists of five types of nodes: select node, sequence node, behavior node, and condition node. The logic model provides a clear view of all decision points, and these are trigger events we will determine in the next stage.

**Table 1.** Part of the logic model for New Retail Enterprise Simulation Platform.

| Key Account Market | SEL: market operation | SEQ: develop a new market | CON: development costs<=corporate funds | |
|---|---|---|---|---|
| | | | CON: have the certificate required: YES | |
| | | | ACT: develop a new market | |
| | | SEL: R&D qualification certificate | SEQ: research and develop the certificate | CON: development costs<=corporate funds |
| | | | | CON: have the certificate required: NO |
| | | | | CON: number of R&D personnel >=2 |
| | | | | ACT: research and develop a certificate |
| | | | SEQ: recruit R&D personnel | CON: development costs<=corporate funds |
| | | | | CON: have the certificate required: NO |
| | | | | CON: number of R&D personnel<2 |
| | | | | ACT: recruit R&D personnel |
| | SEL: order operation | SEQ: win an order | ACT: select a developed market | |
| | | | CON: number of marketing specialists available>0 | |
| | | | ACT: choose the order | |
| | | SEQ: accept an order | ACT: obtain the information of the order | |
| | | | ACT: accept the order | |
| | | SEL: wrap up an order | SEQ: complete the order | CON: complete the delivery: YES |
| | | | | ACT: confirm completed |
| | | | SEQ: break a contract | CON: complete the delivery: NO |
| | | | | ACT: break the contract |
| Warehouse | SEL: put in storage | SEQ: raw material inventory | ACT: select the warehousing order | |
| | | | CON: inventory required< remaining stock capacity | |
| | | | ACT: put the raw materials in storage | |
| | | SEQ: commodity warehousing | ACT: select the incoming batch | |
| | | | CON: inventory required> remaining stock capacity | |
| | | | ACT: put merchandise in storage | |
| | SEQ: put out storage | ACT: select the outbound order | | |
| | | CON: procurement costs < corporate funds | | |
| | | ACT: expel merchandise from warehouse | | |

**3. Determination**

At this stage, we extract all sequence nodes from the logic model, some of which are shown in Table 2. This stage actually determines the location of behavior data collection points and they are also triggering events. These events contain the conditions that must be met for the trigger and all associated trigger actions. After storing the trigger events, we can design the corresponding data format for each event.

**4. Design, Trigger and Store**

The determination stage focuses on reducing the cost of data pre-processing through accurate the location of valuable behavior data. The design stage, on the other hand, is about designing a structured data format to improve the efficiency of collection and pre-processing. When we start data collection, we mainly use front-end monitoring mechanisms to collect behavior data in real time based on students' interactions with the platform. The platform stores the collected data to a back-end behavior database for behavior data mining. Taking the sequence node 'win an order' described in Table 2 as an example. Table 3 shows the structured format design of the data acquisition for the 'win an order' event. When a student makes a decision to win an order, the event 'Market Win Order' in Table 3 will be triggered to collect the relevant behavioral data. Among them, 'Direct Field' can be collected directly according to the order and the status of the enterprise. 'Indirect Field' can be obtained through the preset program of the system. Finally, according to 'Direct_Field' and 'Indirect Field', the system can calculate and output the judgement result through 'Result Field'.

**Table 2.** Part of the locations of data collection determined.

| Trigger events—locations of data collection points |
|---|
| SEQ: develop a new market |
| SEQ: research and develop the certificate |
| SEQ: recruit R&D personnel |
| SEQ: win an order |
| SEQ: accept an order |
| SEQ: complete the order |
| SEQ: break a contract |
| SEQ: view supplier information |
| SEQ: sign purchase order |
| SEQ: cancel the signed order |
| SEQ: raw material inventory |
| SEQ: commodity warehousing |
| SEQ: put out storage |

This case describes the process of behavior data collection. Extraction is to extract logic rules of the New Retail Enterprise Simulation Platform. Transformation is to transform complex logic rules into a clear and transparent logic model. Determination is to initially reduce the cost of pre-processing through accurate collection points. Design is to further reduce the cost by designing a structured data format. Finally, students interact to trigger events for data collection. The data stored in behavior database can be exported in .TXT or .XLS file format for subsequent behavior data mining by researchers. At the same time, whether students have access to their behavior data source is a matter for discussion, but they can certainly review their behavior patterns through behavior data visualization.

**Table 3.** Structured data format triggered by 'win an order' event.

| **Event_names** | **Event_description** | | **Event_type** |
|---|---|---|---|
| Market_WinOrder | The marketing specialist wins an order | | Decision trigger |
| **Field_type** | **Field_name** | **Field_name_type** | **Field_description** |
| **Direct_field** | Order_MarketType | int | The ID of the market category in which the order belongs |
| | Order_Avil_Person | int | The number of key account specialists currently available |
| | Account | int | The cash in hand |
| | Time | int | The current number of months from the start of the game |
| | GoodinStock_All | int | Total current stock |
| | Order_GoodType | int | The cargo type ID of the order |
| | GoodinStock_Use | int | Current inventory occupancy |
| **Indirect_field** | Order_Have_Amount_1 | int | The quantity of Order_GoodType to be delivered in the next month |
| | Order_Have_Amount_2 | int | The quantity of Order_GoodType to be delivered in the next two months |
| **Result_field** | Expected_Performance | tinyint | 1 is expected to perform, 0 is expected to default |

## 5 Conclusion

To collect value-intensive behavior data that reflects cognitive characteristics of students, the paper proposed a method for data collection. The presented method consists of six processes: extraction, transformation, determination, design, trigger and store. Achieving knowledge collaboration in virtual learning environments is a core goal of behavior data mining. Future works will focus on evaluating behavior patterns of students through behavior data mining, enabling students to move from "practicing" to "learning" based on personalized knowledge support.

There are some noted limitations in the research. Due to complex logic rules, the transformation of behavior logic rules still requires artificial participation. Therefore, future research will focus on the automatic transformation of behavior logic models.

Another noted limitation is that empirical studies on more types of simulation learning platforms are also needed to support the presented method. The situation in which data collected for the case study was in the individual mode. However, the students' individual behavior patterns will be subjected to decisions of others when they collaborate in team mode. Differences in behavior patterns arising from different collaboration modes are also the focus of future research.

**Acknowledgments.** The presented research works have been supported by "the National Natural Science Foundation of China" (61972029).

## References

1. Aldowah, H., Al-Samarraie, H., Fauzy, W.M.: Educational data mining and learning analytics for 21st century higher education: a review and synthesis. Telematics Inform. **37**, 13–49 (2019). https://doi.org/10.1016/j.tele.2019.01.007
2. Mahanama, B., Mendis, W., Jayasooriya, A., Malaka, V., Thayasivam, U., Thayasivam, U.: Educational data mining: a review on data collection process. Presented at the 1 September (2018). https://doi.org/10.1109/ICTER.2018.8615532
3. Romero, C., Ventura, S.: Educational data mining: a review of the state of the art. IEEE Trans. Syst. Man Cybern. Part C Appl. Rev. **40**, 601–618 (2010). https://doi.org/10.1109/TSMCC.2010.2053532
4. Romero, C., Ventura, S.: Educational data mining: a survey from 1995 to 2005. Exp. Syst. Appl. **33**, 135–146 (2007). https://doi.org/10.1016/j.eswa.2006.04.005
5. Feldman-Maggor, Y., Barhoom, S., Blonder, R., Tuvi-Arad, I.: Behind the scenes of educational data mining. Educ. Inf. Technol. **26**(2), 1455–1470 (2020). https://doi.org/10.1007/s10639-020-10309-x
6. Romero, C., Romero, J.R., Ventura, S.: A survey on pre-processing educational data. In: Peña-Ayala, A. (ed.) Educational Data Mining. SCI, vol. 524, pp. 29–64. Springer, Cham (2014). https://doi.org/10.1007/978-3-319-02738-8_2
7. Kolekar, S.V., Pai, R.M., Manohara Pai, M.M.: XML based pre-processing and analysis of log data in adaptive e-learning system: an algorithmic approach. In: Vincenti, G., Bucciero, A., Vaz de Carvalho, C. (eds.) eLEOT 2015. LNICSSITE, vol. 160, pp. 135–143. Springer, Cham (2016). https://doi.org/10.1007/978-3-319-28883-3_17
8. Munk, M., Drlík, M., Benko, L., Reichel, J.: Quantitative and qualitative evaluation of sequence patterns found by application of different educational data preprocessing techniques. IEEE Access **5**, 8989–9004 (2017). https://doi.org/10.1109/ACCESS.2017.2706302
9. Romero, C., Ventura, S.: Educational data mining and learning analytics: an updated survey. WIREs Data Min. Knowl. Discov. **10**, e1355 (2020). https://doi.org/10.1002/widm.1355
10. Ihantola, P., et al.: Educational data mining and learning analytics in programming: literature review and case studies. Presented at the 4 July (2015). https://doi.org/10.1145/2858796.2858798
11. Angeli, C., Howard, S.K., Ma, J., Yang, J., Kirschner, P.A.: Data mining in educational technology classroom research: can it make a contribution? Comput. Educ. **113**, 226–242 (2017). https://doi.org/10.1016/j.compedu.2017.05.021
12. Munoz-Organero, M., Munoz-Merino, P.J., Kloos, C.D.: Student behavior and interaction patterns with an LMS as motivation predictors in e-learning settings. IEEE Trans. Educ. **53**, 463–470 (2010). https://doi.org/10.1109/TE.2009.2027433

13. Cerezo, R., Sánchez-Santillán, M., Paule-Ruiz, M.P., Núñez, J.C.: Students' LMS interaction patterns and their relationship with achievement: a case study in higher education. Comput. Educ. **96**, 42–54 (2016). https://doi.org/10.1016/j.compedu.2016.02.006
14. McCuaig, J., Baldwin, J.: Identifying successful learners from interaction behaviour. International Educational Data Mining Society (2012)
15. Domagk, S., Schwartz, R.N., Plass, J.L.: Interactivity in multimedia learning: an integrated model. Comput. Hum. Behav. **26**, 1024–1033 (2010). https://doi.org/10.1016/j.chb.2010.03.003
16. Dromey, R.G.: From requirements to design: formalizing the key steps. In: Cerone, A., Lindsay, P. (eds.) Proceedings of the 1st International Conference on Software Engineering and Formal Methods, pp. 2–11 (2003). https://doi.org/10.1109/SEFM.2003.1236202
17. Subagyo, W.P., Nugroho, S.M.S., Sumpeno, S.: Simulation multi behavior NPCs in fire evacuation using emotional behavior tree. In: 2016 International Seminar on Application for Technology of Information and Communication (ISemantic), pp. 184–190 (2016). https://doi.org/10.1109/ISEMANTIC.2016.7873835
18. Papamitsiou, Z., Economides, A.: Learning analytics and educational data mining in practice: a systematic literature review of empirical evidence. Educ. Technol. Soc. **17**, 49–64 (2014)
19. Biard, T., Le Mauff, A., Bigand, M., Bourey, J.-P.: Separation of decision modeling from business process modeling using new "decision model and notation" (DMN) for automating operational decision-making. In: Camarinha-Matos, L.M., Bénaben, F., Picard, W. (eds.) PRO-VE 2015. IAICT, vol. 463, pp. 489–496. Springer, Cham (2015). https://doi.org/10.1007/978-3-319-24141-8_45

# Collaborative Trusted Digital Services for Citizens

A. Luis Osório[1(✉)], Luis M. Camarinha-Matos[2], Adam Belloum[3], and Hamideh Afsarmanesh[3]

[1] ISEL - Instituto Superior de Engenharia de Lisboa, Instituto Politécnico de Lisboa, and POLITEC&ID, Lisbon, Portugal
lo@isel.ipl.pt

[2] School of Science and Technology, NOVA University of Lisbon and CTS-UNINOVA, Caparica, Portugal
cam@uninova.pt

[3] University of Amsterdam (UvA), Amsterdam, The Netherlands
{a.belloum,h.afsarmanesh}@uva.nl

**Abstract.** In modern society, citizens aspire to get trusted and reliable digital services to authenticate theirs to payments. With the COVID-19 crisis, online shopping's fast growth has led citizens to increase registration in different systems. The registration is typically done without any guarantee that the involved business entity is trusted and that private data is managed adequately, namely according to the General Data Protection Regulation (GDPR). There are cases where online business adopts a federated authentication mechanism based on the existing and extensively adopted service providers, e.g., Facebook, and Google. With the European authorities' complacency, this de facto trend seems to contribute to a dangerous unregulated digital services model. While avoiding the centralization risks, a possible alternative is to pursue the concept of regulated and competing digital online shops or services offered under a single collaborative model across Europe. Citizens aspire to get simple mechanisms based on a single provider for authentication and pay anywhere, even with some associated costs. In this direction, we propose a model that considers regulated providers managing citizens' access to any online business in Europe, avoiding, in this way, the spreading of personal data across (business) organizations, thus decreasing the risk of personal data leaks. A collaborative network is foreseen to logically tie committed regulating authorities, providers, and digital online service providers. The proposed approach is ground on our previous research on systems integration, collaborative network infrastructure, and unified mobility payment services. This position paper offers a digital strategy for citizens, designated by Digital Person Ecosystem (DPE), which relies on Collaborative Networks concepts and centered on public authority leadership.

**Keywords:** Complex informatics system of systems · Distributed systems · Collaborative networks · Blockchain · Distributed ledger


Published by Springer Nature Switzerland AG 2021
L. M. Camarinha-Matos et al. (Eds.): PRO-VE 2021, IFIP AICT 629, pp. 212–223, 2021.
https://doi.org/10.1007/978-3-030-85969-5_19

## 1 Introduction

There is a growing awareness of the unbalanced concentration of digital services offered by quasi-unique providers. Examples range from social networks led by Facebook, electronic commerce conducted by Amazon, Google search engine, and payments concentrated on VISA and PayPal. A table with the largest global companies in 2018 [31] from the European Parliamentary Research Service includes the first three examples in the top five companies. One main concern is that we depend on and trust that these entities do not interrupt service provision, neither do they share our private data with others [4]. Yet, the case of exploring without consent the personal data of eighty-seven million Facebook users by Cambridge-Analytics is a critical privacy failure [17]. A more recent case where Facebook banned the account of a President of one of the largest countries on the planet raises questions about the power of such private companies. In [14], the authors question the potentially harming our democracy from the current self-regulated social media. While not directly suggesting the need for public regulation, the mentioned publication somehow raises the Regulation topic. Although our research is not about political sciences, we consider being our responsibility to research collaborative models giving policymakers proper tools to act.

Our research is founded on the ISoS [24] and ECoNet [26] framework models and the collaborative mobility service provider concept [27]. The primary motivation for adopting ISoS is establishing a multi-supplier or multi-vendor technology landscape and reducing the vendor lock-in risks. Furthermore, based on ISoS, a specialized informatics system, the enterprise collaboration management system is responsible for formalizing collaboration contexts to manage interactions among organizations. Based on these technology and modeling structuring approaches, we propose a paradigm shift from the current unregulated digital business to a regulated model where Regulation Authorities play a moderation role on behalf of citizens. This paper presents and discusses the proposed change from Central Unregulated to a Decentralized Regulated model, as depicted in Fig. 1.

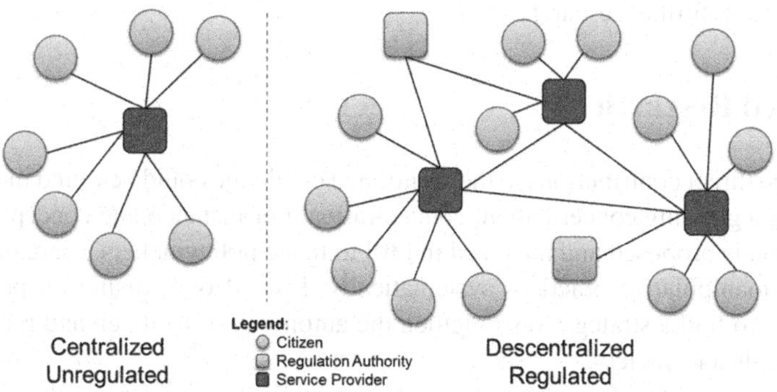


**Fig. 1.** Centralized and decentralized models

Evolving from the notion of collaborative mobility service provider [27], we add to the proposed provider a broader role. In other words, we assume an extension of the provider's responsibilities with an authentication service that allows citizens to log in to any regulated digital service. The idea goes beyond adopting a federated authentication as the one already offered by larger digital service providers. In our approach, the citizen uses his/her (unique) digital services provider's authentication to access any digital business, solving the current need to disperse personal data among untrusted places. We name the proposed model Digital Payment Ecosystem (DPE).

A DPE provider manages data on behalf of citizens and so the owner of the data. The provider is responsible for the technology artifacts necessary to guarantee that the citizen can maintain transaction data. Beyond controlling personal data, the objective is to eliminate the need for specific citizen accounts spread across digital providers. Federated authentication is an emerging model already adopted by private and large public digital providers, e.g., Google, Facebook. However, even if contributing to reducing accounts' spread, the existing model does not establish a generic and regulated mechanism.

While computer science and engineering theoretically have solutions making the endeavor technically feasible, the challenge is to "induce" the market towards the proposed model. There is a need for a "third force" and a convergence effort of companies and research organizations to compel consensus, what [2] calls collaborative governance. Collaborative governance defines as the mode of governance joining competing stakeholders and public agencies "*to engage in consensus-oriented decision making.*" There is also a need for a novel approach to structure technology artifacts since service-oriented architectures (SOA) and, more recently, the microservices trend has been revealed to be insufficient.

Another challenge is to articulate technology artifacts involved in collaborative processes. Defining collaborative processes and activities operationalized by technology artifacts in different organizations requires coordinating execution, making transparent the heterogeneous distribution [23, 26].

The remaining of this paper is organized as follows: Sect. 2 presents related research work and industry contributions for the proposed endeavor. Section 3 introduces the proposed strategy for a Digital Payment Ecosystem (DPE). Section 4 describes the ISoS framework's adoption and the interactions among organizations. Finally, Sect. 5 presents conclusions and further research.

## 2 Related Research

Although no direct contributions to the mentioned challenge could be found in literature, we can find a growing concern about concentration. For instance, the concept of online manipulation is proposed and analyzed in [30] to make policymakers aware of the need to address manipulative practices systematically. Instead of focusing on privacy, the challenge is to find a strategy to strengthen the autonomy of a citizen and reduce harm for individuals and society.

The concentration of power around large technology providers is also a concern. The guidelines on outsourcing arrangements [11] published by the European Banking Authority (EBA) are discussed by Microsoft in terms of the suggested multi-cloud provider strategy, arguing that concentration already exists with on-premises mainframes [21]. Microsoft discusses the potential risks of adopting a multi-cloud approach for cloud services in the financing sector, arguing by strengthening the similarity with mainframes and the advantages of adopting a single cloud provider. Based on state of the art in complex integrated informatics systems, Microsoft might have a point here. However, the question is to weigh the risks and invest in open standards and conforming products supervised by some Competition Regulatory Authority. Our understanding is that existing dependencies are not of industry responsibility but instead of policymakers. The case of the European Court of Justice (ECJ), judgment of the Court of First Instance (CFI) process T-201/04 - Microsoft vs. Commission where "*Decision finding infringements of Article 82 EC - Refusal of the dominant undertaking to supply and authorize the use of interoperability information*", is discussed in [18]. The interoperability issue seems to be a clear message to European policymakers to impose open standards and force European public procurement to strict conformity.

Some research works advocate that the solution for these issues is open-source. The example of Munich's municipality moving from Microsoft to Linux in 2005, named LiMux, resulted in a return to Microsoft in 2013, as reported in [19]. The report does not give any clue towards a reasonable scientific or technical explanation for the failure, and only in the article "The rise and fall of LiMux" [13] from a talk of Matthias Kirschner, President Free Software Foundation Europe (FSFE), management issues are evidenced. The retention of upgrades in some municipality departments resulted in some already corrected matters that did not become accessible to users. The question is if the suggestion of the president of FSFE appealing for lawmakers to "*implement legislation requiring that publicly financed software developed for the public sector be made publicly available under a Free and Open Source Software license*" is the right approach.

Moreover, the question is if open-source software is an adequate path to reduce concentration and at the same time contribute to the development of a competing market. The survey about free/open-source software (FOSS) developed by the Linux Foundation's Core Infrastructure Initiative (CII) shows an increase in contributors paid by their employers [16]. The trend means that companies see open source as a shared collaborative platform to value their product developments. On the other hand, the growing integration requirement makes their products better prepared to incorporate or interact with elements of other informatics systems.

While collaborative strategies to develop software libraries to incorporate as parts of systems are essential, the question is how to organize and structure enormous heterogeneous contributions consistently and reliable. Moreover, the question is how to cope with architectural complexity since companies have developed their architecture practices pulled by a fast-evolving integration pressure imposed by digitalization [20]. As a strategy to cope with architectural complexity, Fig. 2 depicts an alternative view of the five architectures' suggested examples (Information, Process, Product, Application, and Technical). In addition, we consider the ISoS framework [24] and runtime architecture, denoting the trend for a balanced adoption of a hybrid on-premises/cloud strategy.

The authors suggest the need for a bottom-up integration of architectural domains, each with its specific language for structuring software components. In this direction, the ISoS framework unifies the diversity of architectures under the Service concept as explored in Sect. 4, aligned with the microservices trend [10].

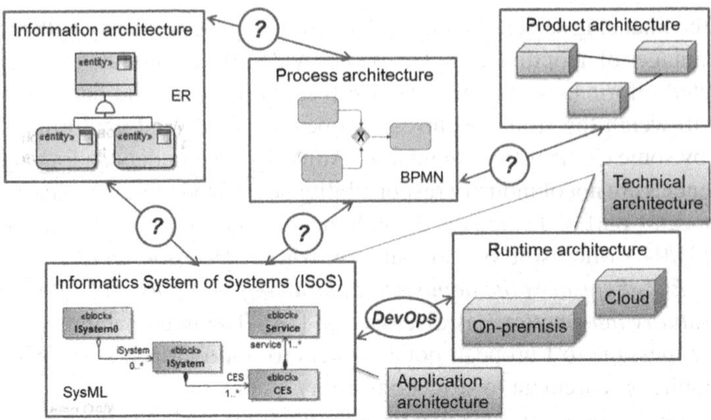


**Fig. 2.** The heterogeneous architecture domains adapted from [20]

Figure 3 illustrates three specific technology architectures conceptualized, modeled, developed and deployed, maintained, and evolved under complex and critical coordination of multidisciplinary teams, commonly associated with the development and operations (DevOps) concept [32]. Despite the potential of contributing to a decentralized integration, as demonstrated in the SITL-IoT project [27], the well-known business-IT alignment remains problematic [20]. One example is the difficulty of decoupling business process logic hard-coded into applications and evolving to a business process-oriented approach adopting a standard such as BPMN [29]. Despite research efforts to adopt a complete declarative business process management system, most successful products are proprietary, e.g., the successful Outsystems[1] platform. However, there would be a clear benefit in adopting BPMN instead of a proprietary process definition language for the links marked with question marks in Fig. 2 to be removed.

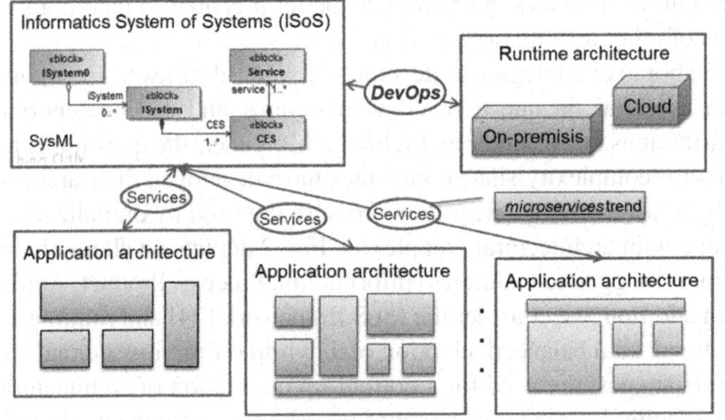


**Fig. 3.** ISoS hiding application architecture diversity through microservices

[1] www.outsystem.com

In the following, we present and discuss the Digital Personal Ecosystem (DPE) model, hypothesizing a modeling and technology development strategy able to contribute to a shift from the current predominantly centralized approach to decentralized digital services.

## 3 Model Towards a Trusted and Democratic Digital Services

The risks of citizens' control over their data is not a new concern as expressed in [8] "*... the content and software applications are only accessible online, users have no longer control over how they can access their data ...*". The strategy followed by current large centralized providers that "*... have built successful business models around the realization that, instead of getting money in exchange for a service, it is often more valuable to provide services for free ...*" is paradigmatic. Such strategy allowed them to get the network effect necessary to scale up, e.g., Google search engine, Facebook social network, or Amazon online shopping. A communication from the European Commission to the European Parliament recognizes that the fast rise of digital services, a consequence of COVID, generated dependency "*... the crisis also exposed the vulnerabilities of our digital space, its increased dependency on critical, often non-EU based, technologies ...*". This sentence confirms the need for a new strategy promoting a shift from the current "concentration" to a decentralized model, involving the European industry actively, from start-ups to large corporations, in fair competition on the open global market.

A challenging question is how to address the European Commission's concern regarding the "*often non-EU based, technologies*". Previous research on a mobility payment service based on collaborative open systems defended that we need public leadership to "impose" open standards to the industry [27]. The suggestion is consistent with the US national or federal public investments to pull for consensus, motivated by integration. An example is an investment of the US Department of Defense to "*ensure a common unifying approach for the commands, military services, and defense agencies to follow in describing their various architectures*", the DoDAF/C4ISR Architecture Framework [20].

**Data Ownership in DPE.** The proposal introduces federated authentication and citizen's ownership of the data as core services. Beyond generalizing to a pan-European payment system to pay for any digital service, a citizen would remain the data owner. To this extent, we propose adopting the distributed ledger supported by blockchain technology [4] in addiction with encryption as a strategy to manage the data generated and utilize the offered services. Moreover, the citizen maintains the prerogative of moving across providers, maintaining a continuum of access to digital services and access to private data. We name these integrated core digital services Digital Payment Ecosystem (DPE) and the regulated providers as DPE Providers.

At the start, we are concerned with payment and federated authentication (FA) services since they establish a minimal core that can contribute to revert the current concentration and give citizens the trust to access and use digital services. As discussed in previous research, the mobility service providers case was an opportunity to "impose" some convergence mechanisms led by European authorities to facilitate the development of reliable underlying technology artifacts and streamlining the integration of new services, which is still not achieved. The proposed DPE concept goes further by offering the citizen a unified mechanism to access any online service. Instead of adopting proprietary federated authentication as provided by Facebook and Google to login into any adherent site, the idea would be to restrict such service offerings to authorized DPE providers. Companies such as Facebook, Google, and any other could apply for being DPE providers and maintain their offerings. However, to get a DPE statute, they would have to comply with EU regulations imposing that a citizen client of any $DPE_X$ can log in to any of their systems with his/her authentication mechanism. In this formulation, a citizen has a unique digital identification managed by his/her selected DPE provider and can log in to any authorized (regulated) digital service by selecting his/her DPE provider among the listed ones. In this way, the online business only has access to data from the citizen (client) necessary for the business transaction. For example, a citizen with an identification managed by the $DPE_X$ provider would log in to Amazon online shop by simply selecting $DPE_X$ from the list of authorized providers listed in the online shop. After selecting check-out, the payment and access to the delivery address are under the control of his/her DPE provider. This model means that citizens have a single digital identity provider that manages their data instead of spreading registration data across multiple online businesses.

**Data Coordination/Exchange in DPE.** Furthermore, we could envisage that a DPE provider, through collaboration, could extend its core services. Adding new services requires a tight collaboration among participating business stakeholders to guarantee reliable data and coordination. Consider the example of a citizen logging in to a digital business that fails because his/her DPE provider fails for some technical reason, depending on a third party, e.g., a failure in a cloud provider, resulting in a loss. In that case, the question is which participating stakeholder shall be accountable for the potential damage.

**Figure 4** depicts the main stakeholders participating in the envisioned collaborative trusted digital services for citizens.

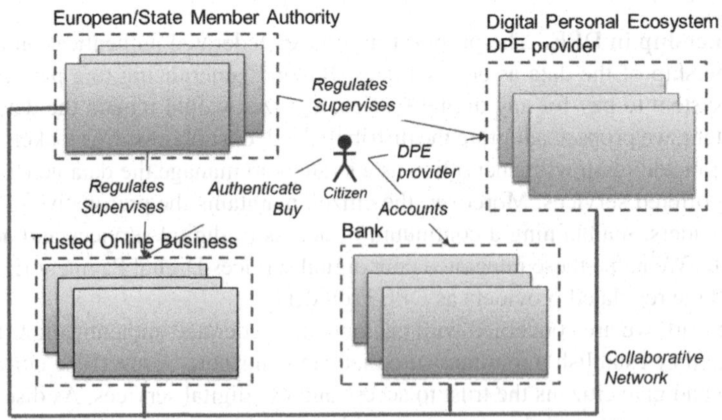


**Fig. 4.** The Digital Personal Ecosystem (DPE) main stakeholders

We assume that the participating organizations exchange data and coordination information through a collaborative network infrastructure. Some of the risks mentioned earlier associated with the proposed model are managed and resolved based on formal business agreements. For instance, if a login operation fails, the respective DPE provider can solve the problem. It is important to note that the model needs to be prepared to scale up. If considering only the European inhabitants, the technology artifacts need to be ready to scale up to five hundred million, based on the EU population. Engineering such networked systems are challenging since many peer businesses, and authority nodes need to reliably handle large volumes of business transactions and events per second.

The DPE provider, beyond payment that can be operationalized based on SEPA/PSD2 open specifications [12], includes federated authentication and data owned by the citizen. Federated authentication does not raise research challenges except for integration issues due to the diversity of existing single sign-on (SSO) schemes, about fourteen according to [1]. However, the mechanisms to guarantee that only the DPE customer's citizen "sees" or authorizes third parties to access parts of his/her private data raise a more complex challenge. Furthermore, the violation risk is related to the probability of potential tampering based on the robustness of the used encryption algorithm.

**Data Privacy and Protection in DPE.** In current digital services offering [15], privacy relies on the efficiency (and willingness) of providers to protect data, which can raise risks like Analytica's case [17]. Even if assuming that a provider makes the best efforts to protect data, risks depend on service providers' technology and security strategies. A possible approach considers a set of design principles known as privacy by design, as proposed in [5] and extended in [7], introducing tactics as a privacy pattern. However, given the heterogeneity and the lack of well-delimited responsibilities for the technology landscape, operations, and maintenance procedures, the proposed strategy is challenging and risky in data privacy.

Blockchain technology opens new development paths towards data privacy strategies when complemented with privacy techniques [35]. In a simplified characterization, blockchain is the glue of a distributed ledger, where linked blocks store the transactions, and peer nodes maintain a consistent replica. The addition of a new block consensus among the participating peer nodes and since the application domain is not a fiat currency but rather services for citizens, the cost of generating a block doesn't involve the concept of a miner as adopted in the bitcoin system [22]. The digital personal environment (DPE) and digital business service (DBS) providers could establish blockchain/distributed ledger to maintain business transactions. The authorities (Auth) responsible for supervising the fulfillment of regulations might also set blockchains to manage regulation/auditing events. The citizens are clients of both DPE and DBS providers and do not participate directly as blockchain nodes. However, citizens can access auth to register any complaint about any provider or access formal information about both DPE and DBS, e.g., about the accredited fact that the offered online services are authorized and supervised. The authority's role for the specialized digital business is vital for citizens to trust online digital business.

An approach to data owned by citizens could get hints from [33], which suggests a Resource Server accessed by a service provider (SP) on behalf of the End-User. The SP corresponds in our model to the DPE provider and the End-User to the citizen. We assume that blockchain infrastructures for different application domains might be heterogeneous based on different coordination strategies to persist immutable data. For example, one application domain could be the mobility payment events [27], where a mobility infrastructure agrees with dpe providers a distributed ledger store and share mobility payment events. Since the application domains refer to authorized nodes by one or more European member state authorities, the model considers the adoption of permissionless blockchains [28]. One interesting research question is how to manage the coexistence of heterogeneous blockchain implementations. The research in [28] addresses the issue of heterogeneity "*... there are a lot of frameworks, and all of them are slightly different in terms of consensus protocols ...*" suggesting the need for benchmarking existing platforms. However, based on the ISoS model [18], our strategy is to assume technology diversity to make possible heterogeneous technology elements and new technologies to be adopted. Contributions to combining diverse blockchain infrastructures as the heterogeneous multi-chain Polkadot [4], the cross-blockchain communication [34], and related technologies [3] need evaluation. Beyond adopting blockchain to support distributed immutable business data, it must be guaranteed that such data are secure and available for business operation and auditing. The review [9] identifies a strong relationship between privacy and anonymization and application techniques for its implementation. However, the main research challenge is to reliably articulate organizations with their own technology culture, assuming that heterogeneity is a fact.

## 4 Adopting ISoS and ECoNet

The DPE model requires a reliable, complex distributed system made of heterogeneous nodes (organizations), each with its processes and technology systems. Based on a previous mobility services provider model [27], we further consider federated authentication in payment based on SEPA/PSD2 open specifications [12]. This approach is supported by the experience of 'wrapping' legacy computing technology systems, configuring a company's product portfolio under the ISoS framework. In our ISoS model, the *Service* concept models the executive elements. The *ISoS Service* concept is naturally based on the traditional Service Orientation (SOA) architecture pattern and incorporates the more recent microservice terminology. An empirical study in [10], based on industry practices in migrating legacy systems, discusses the lack of microservices architecture (MSA). One main problem is the diversity of semantics associated with Service in SOA and the more recent Microservice. While [6] argues that the microservice trend differentiates from Service/SOA, "*.. tendency can be given to the ability of independent service deploy and elastic scalability ...*", the ISoS/Service has for long evolved with reliability and quality concerns. Our prior research considers reliable, collaborative mobility services as independent computing entities running on-premises or on the cloud [25]. The ISoS Service concept abstracts reliability mechanisms as an independent computing entity.

As discussed in Sect. 2, one possibility is to assume that the enterprise architecture of a DPE stakeholder follows the ISoS framework as depicted in Fig. 5.

Any computing or communication element is modeled as a service that is part of some ISystem/CES. This simple model "unifies" the specific technology architectures,

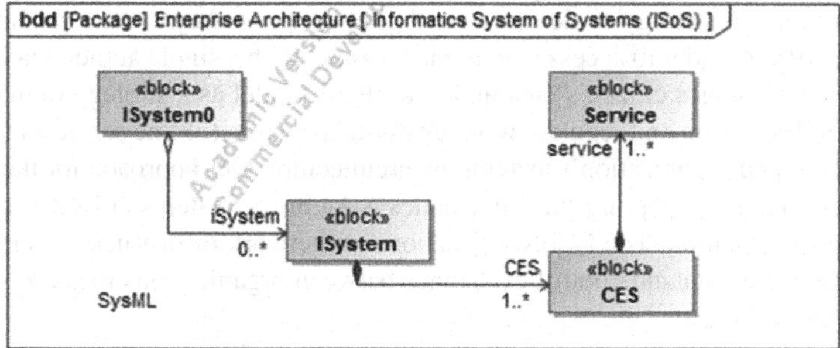


**Fig. 5.** The Informatics System of Systems (ISoS) framework

'constructed' under diverse software development projects. Current approaches derive the architecture guided by an individual perspective of mapping problem domain requirements and technology structuration decisions. Different architects arrive for sure at different structuration of technology elements, making the resulting artifact unique. The experience of migrating an enterprise's system in the SITL-IoT project [27] suggests adopting the ISoS services framework for adapting legacy systems in the DPE context. The executive entities (Services) are, in this way, grouped in CES abstractions. Any Access to a Service entity goes through the interface zero ($I_0$) of the meta-informatic system ISystem$_0$. For example, to access a Service$_i$, a peer service lookups ISystem$_0$ based on a path to /Isystem$_i$/CES$_i$/Service$_i$ entity with the meta-data required to access the implemented functionalities. The Service instance can be running anywhere from on-premises to a cloud provider.

The results from the SITL-IoT project make us suggest a similar approach to the DPE stakeholders. Accessibility from inside or outside the organization to every Service "computational responsibility" can go through the $I_0$ of System$_0$. The current reference implementation of ISoS, the ISystem$_0$, adopts a REST interface accessible at isos. <organization domain>:2058 endpoint. An authorized peer computing service can access the $I_0$ REST interface and any implemented service through its ISystem/Ces/Service path. In other words, the ISystem$_0$ functions as a services registry, making authorized computational clients lookups for and access services.

Following a similar approach to mobility payment service, the interactions between organizations can take advantage of using the ECoNet Infrastructure [26] as formalized in [27]. For example, participation in a blockchain can be formalized as a collaboration context to share low-level secure interaction, secure communication layers, and multitenant virtual collaboration contexts.

## 5 Conclusions and Further Research

This position paper discusses the risks of centralizing digital services that got crescent attention by society and the research community since the Analytica/Facebook case. The "concentration" of services is related to a lack of standardization of technology systems that can reduce the risks of developing competing digital service providers and make them more accessible for authorities to supervise. The Digital Business Ecosystem

(DPE) concept is a strategy to decentralize digital services. Any citizen can subscribe to a single DPE provider to access any online business with a single authentication. The DPE provider manages citizen's data under a 'blind' model as a strategy to make data safe. The authorization and regulation of any digital business (online services) motivate 'impose' a unified organization's technology architecture. Our approach for the needed unification considers adopting the Informatics System of Systems (ISoS) framework as an open specification. The ECoNet collaborative network infrastructure is proposed as a base to make data and control exchanges between organizations to share standard collaboration services.

**Acknowledgments.** The research conducted by GIATSI/ISEL/IPL develops in collaboration with the SOCOLNET scientific network and its ARCON-ACM initiative. The ANSR/SINCRO, BP/HORUS, and FORDESI/SITL-IoT-PT-2020 projects partially support the research. Partial support also from the Center of Technology and Systems – UNINOVA, and the Portuguese FCT Foundation (project UIDB/00066/2020), and the European Commission (project DiGiFoF).

## References

1. Alaca, F., van Oorschot, P.C.: Comparative analysis and framework evaluating web single sign-on systems. CoRR, abs/1805.00094 (2018)
2. Ansell, C., Gash, A.: Collaborative governance in theory and practice. J. Public Admin. Res. Theo. **18**(4), 543–571 (2007)
3. Borkowski, M., Frauenthaler, P., Sigwart, M., Hukkinen, T., Hladký, O., Schulte, S.: Cross-blockchain technologies: review, state of the art, and outlook (2019)
4. Burdges, J., et al.: Overview of Polkadot and its design considerations, May 2020
5. Cavoukian, A.: Operationalizing privacy by design: a guide to implementing strong privacy practices. Commun. ACM **55**(9), 7 (2012)
6. Cerny, T., Donahoo, M.J., Pechanec, J.: Disambiguation and comparison of SOA, microservices and self-contained systems. In: Proceedings of the International Conference on Research in Adaptive and Convergent Systems, RACS 2017, pp. 228–235, New York, NY, USA. Association for Computing Machinery (2017)
7. Colesky, M., Hoepman, J., Hillen, C.: A critical analysis of privacy design strategies. In: 2016 IEEE Security and Privacy Workshops (SPW), pp. 33–40, May 2016
8. De Filippi, P., Mccarthy, S.: Cloud computing: centralization and data sovereignty. Eur. J. Law Technol. **3**(2) (2012). https://ejlt.org/index.php/ejlt/issue/view/9
9. de Haro-Olmo, F.J., Varela-Vaca, Á.J., Álvarez Bermejo, J.A.: Blockchain from the perspective of privacy and anonymisation: a systematic literature review. Sensors **20**(24), 7171 (2020)
10. Di Francesco, P., Lago, P., Malavolta, I.: Migrating towards microservice architectures: an industrial survey. In: 2018 IEEE International Conference on Software Architecture (ICSA), pp. 29–2909 (2018)
11. EBA. Final report oneba guidelines on outsourcing arrangements. web, February 2019.
12. EBF: Guidance for implementation of the revised payment services directive- psd2 guidance, December 2019
13. Edge, J.: The rise and fall of limux, November 2017
14. Eisenstat, Y.: How to hold social media accountable for undermining democracy. Web, January 2021

15. EuParliament: General data protection regulation (EU) 2016/679 (GDPR). Web, April 2016
16. Lifshitz-Assaf, H., Ham, H., Hoffman Frank Nagle, J.L., Wheeler, D.A.: Report on the2020 FOSS contributor survey the linux foundation & the laboratory for innovation science at Harvard, December 2020
17. Margaret, H.: Cambridge analytica's black box. Big Data Soc. **7**, 8 (2020)
18. Kerber, W., Schweitzer, H.: Interoperability in the digital economy. JIPITEC **8**(1), 39–58 (2017)
19. KPMGtoEC: Study on open source software governance at the European Commission and selected other European institutions (2020)
20. Lankhorst, M.: Enterprise Architecture at Work: Modelling, Communication and Analysis, 4th edn. Springer, Heidelberg (2017). https://doi.org/10.1007/978-3-642-29651-2
21. Microsoft: Concentration risk: Perspectives from Microsoft, September 2020
22. Narayanan, A., Bonneau, J., Felten, E., Miller, A., Goldfeder, S.: Bitcoin and Cryptocurrency Technologies: A Comprehensive Introduction. Princeton University Press, USA (2016)
23. Osorio, A., Camarinha-Matos, L.: Towards a distributed process execution platform for collaborative networks. In: Information Technology for Balanced Manufacturing Systems, vol. 220 of IFIP, pp. 233–240. Springer, Boston (2006)https://doi.org/10.1007/978-0-387-36594-7_25
24. Osório, A.L., Belloum, A., Afsarmanesh, H., Camarinha-Matos, L.M.: Agnostic informatics system of systems: the open ISoS services framework. In: Camarinha-Matos, L.M., Afsarmanesh, H., Fornasiero, R. (eds.) PRO-VE 2017. IAICT, vol. 506, pp. 407–420. Springer, Cham (2017). https://doi.org/10.1007/978-3-319-65151-4_37
25. Osório, A.L., Camarinha-Matos, L.M., Afsarmanesh, H., Belloum, A.: On reliable collaborative mobility services. In: Camarinha-Matos, L.M., Afsarmanesh, H., Rezgui, Y. (eds.) PRO-VE 2018. IAICT, vol. 534, pp. 297–311. Springer, Cham (2018). https://doi.org/10.1007/978-3-319-99127-6_26
26. Osório, L.A., Camarinha-Matos, L.M., Afsarmanesh, H.: ECoNet platform for collaborative logistics and transport. In: Camarinha-Matos, L.M., Bénaben, F., Picard, W. (eds.) PRO-VE 2015. IAICT, vol. 463, pp. 265–276. Springer, Cham (2015). https://doi.org/10.1007/978-3-319-24141-8_24
27. Osório, A.L., Camarinha-Matos, L.M., Afsarmanesh, H., Belloum, A.: Towards a mobility payment service based on collaborative open systems. In: Camarinha-Matos, L.M., Afsarmanesh, H., Antonelli, D. (eds.) PRO-VE 2019. IAICT, vol. 568, pp. 379–392. Springer, Cham (2019). https://doi.org/10.1007/978-3-030-28464-0_33
28. Polge, J., Robert, J., Le Traon, Y.: Permissioned blockchain frameworks in the industry: a comparison. ICT Express **7**, 229–233 (2020)
29. Stiehl, V.: Process-Driven Applications with BPMN. Springer, Switzerland (2014). https://doi.org/10.1007/978-3-319-07218-0
30. Susser, D., Roessler, B., Nissenbaum, H.: Technology, autonomy, and manipulation. Internet Pol. Rev. **8**(2), 6 (2019)
31. SzczepaÅ" ski, M.: Is data the new oil? Competition issues in the digital economy, January 2020
32. Taibi, D., Lenarduzzi, V., Pahl, C.: Continuous architecting with microservices and DevOps: a systematic mapping study. CoRR, abs/1908.10337 (2019)
33. Binh Truong, N., Sun, K., Myoung Lee, G., Guo, Y.: GDPR-compliant personal data management: a blockchain-based solution. CoRR, abs/1904.03038 (2019)
34. Xiao, X., Yu, Z., Xie, K., Guo, S., Xiong, A., Yan, Y.: A multi-blockchain architecture supporting cross-blockchain communication, pp. 592–603 (2020)
35. Zhang, R., Xue, R., Liu, L.: Security and privacy on blockchain. ACM Comput. Surv. **52**(3), 1–34 (2019)

# Safety and Collaboration Management

# Collaborative Safety Requirements Engineering: An Approach for Modelling and Assessment of Nuclear Safety Requirements in MBSE Context

Emir Roumili[1,2](✉), Jean-François Bossu[1](✉), Vincent Chapurlat[2](✉), Nicolas Daclin[2](✉), Robert Plana[1](✉), and Jérôme Tixier[2](✉)

[1] Assystem, Paris, France
{eroumili,jfbossu,rplana}@assystem.com
[2] Laboratoire Des Sciences Des Risques (LSR), IMT Mines Alès, Alès, France
{emir.roumili,vincent.chapurlat,nicolas.daclin, jerome.tixier}@mines-ales.fr

**Abstract.** The nuclear safety demonstration aims to demonstrate that a Nuclear Facility respects all the requirements specified in standards from safety authorities, which is a key objective for the licensing of a nuclear installation. It requires, firstly, supporting the necessary collaborative work involving various stakeholders. Secondly, it should be able to use a common and shared requirements repository. However, it is still the so-called "classic" working methods that are put forward. Almost all the documents are in written form. Due to the complexity of the Nuclear Facility of interest, it is proposed to move from this document-oriented system engineering to a model-based system engineering approach which would improve the performance, delay, and qualities of the engineering processes. Models would allow a better cognition and sharing without ambiguities of information by the engineering teams. Subject of this paper is a hybrid MBSE/AI approach facilitating collaborative work on nuclear safety demonstration processes.

**Keywords:** System Engineering · Collaborative work · Nuclear Safety Demonstration · Requirements · Information Research · Information extraction · MBSE · Licensing · Machine Learning · NLP

## 1 Introduction

It is understood that Nuclear Power Plant (NPP) projects are becoming increasingly complex. If we take the example of a nuclear reactor, there are more than 50 buildings, 500 km of piping, 500,000 components and more than 100 million units of data (requirements, reports, schemes, etc.). The nuclear safety demonstration is at the heart of the nuclear industry. It is the most important element and remains a limiting factor for all nuclear activities. Globally, nuclear safety represents the sine qua non condition for the licensing of installations. Indeed, even though nuclear energy is very low-carbon and


Published by Springer Nature Switzerland AG 2021
L. M. Camarinha-Matos et al. (Eds.): PRO-VE 2021, IFIP AICT 629, pp. 227–236, 2021.
https://doi.org/10.1007/978-3-030-85969-5_20

represents 72% of the total electricity production in France in 2019, it remains an energy that worries the public opinion. [1] It is therefore important that all nuclear activities are fully controlled from a safety point of view. To ensure that all operations are carried out safely, a validation of the demonstration of safety is mandatory to obtain the license to build, operate, dismantle, etc.

The demonstration of safety is defined as follows: "*Assessment of all aspects of a practice that are relevant to protection and safety; for an authorized facility, this includes siting, design and operation of the facility.*" [2].

In this context, any demonstration of safety is part of an industrial project and is therefore a balance between different constraints of scope, schedule, budget, quality, resources, etc. [3].

The nuclear safety engineer calls upon the various disciplines present in the project to jointly carry out the safety demonstration of the installation. This safety demonstration is based on iterative and collaborative processes. Despite the difficulty in terms of collaboration, efficiency and productivity, a classic document-oriented approach is used to achieve this demonstration of safety. We propose a digital-based approach, which could be complementary to the work on documents. This approach draws its strengths from Artificial Intelligence (AI) and from the use of system engineering/MBSE. This paper illustrates the MBSE contribution in the whole safety demonstration methodology. Readers interested by AI contributions can have a look on [3].

We will first present the problematic that underlies our work. The second section discusses our proposed contribution in the context of this problem. The last section proposes a concrete case to illustrate our approach.

## 2 Problematic and SoA

The nuclear safety demonstration is at the interface of several disciplines and constitutes the argument presented to the nuclear safety authorities justifying that the installation is, in its various phases of its life cycle (design, operation, decommissioning etc.), a safe facility. It represents a real challenge of collaboration between actors from different fields, with different levels of responsibilities and since the begin of the whole design and development project. Obviously, all of these actors must have a minimum level of understanding of the safety issues relating to the installation they are designing as part and all along their project. In the design phase of the project, they have to collaborate, define, trace rigorously and confidently all the requirements, architectural choices, intermediate results of evaluation and analysis, decisions, tests to be carried out for commissioning, etc. This work is carried out, as in many areas of engineering, through a document-oriented approach. These documents are not read then interpreted by all actors in the same way, some will read them completely, others partially, and still others will not read them at all. Indeed, this represents a time commitment, and time is often lacking in projects. Even for those with a full reading of the safety-related documents, the biases of their own experience and reflection will be mixed with the written information, the latter leave more or less room for subjective interpretation. This could have an impact on the cognition of these complex subjects in terms of information gathering and processing, as well as the possibility of using more often heuristics in their judgement on certain items. [4] In this way, system engineering (SE) [5] allows these actors to take more attention and manage more efficiently the complexity of both the so-called system of interest to be designed and built, here considered a Nuclear facility, and the so-called system used to engineer, i.e. the project itself. So, SE based on systemic principles, proposes more suitable processes and promotes particularly modelling activities and models handling in opposition to documents management. In this sense, as stated during INCOSE Symposium in 2007 [6] Model Based System Engineering (MBSE) "*enhances the ability to capture, analyze, share, and manage the information*" This engineering approach that inherits from SE allows a better cognition and information sharing between engineering teams with less ambiguities by using models, highlighting the following benefits:

- Improved communications.
- Increased ability to manage system complexity.
- Improved product quality.
- Enhanced knowledge capture.
- Improved ability to teach and learn systems engineering fundamentals.

The MBSE approach is more and more used and well known in the nuclear world [7, 8]. However the elements related to the demonstration of nuclear safety remain poorly considered, and there is then a problem in the appropriation of the modelling way usages and analysis of models, by nuclear engineers.

As detailed in Sect. 3, the classic approach to the demonstration of safety is described in IAEA (International Atomic Energy Agency) documents such as the GSR (general safety requirements). For Nuclear Power Plants, the SSR-2/1 describes this process and presents the main safety principles and concepts that must be fulfilled throughout the facility lifecycle. [9] The hazards to be addressed are then declined in lower level safety guides.

Driven by the Environmental law, the French regulation adds more general principles to those technical concepts. For instance, it is based on the responsibility of the owner of the plant and on the performance obligation rather than the obligation of means.

The French nuclear facility decree of 7 February 2012 is the one put forward in our work, allowing engineers to model more naturally, to use and to be confident with modelling activities and models. [10] We will see in the next section the operational approach and the concepts put forward by the safety authorities to move towards the safety demonstration.

## 3 Contribution

In our work, we consider the possibility of achieving this demonstration of safety being based on the principles of systems engineering: 1) by using systemic principles, 2) by following SE main processes that are collaborative and iterative throughout the project, and 3) by promoting the intensive use of models.

With regards to SE processes, two ways are used to establish and promote multi-actors collaboration during a project:

1. The classic approach of having milestones and reviews. When the milestones are reached, a review is carried out of the work and a decision is made whether as to validate the proposed design.
2. Refocus and share continuously an up to date requirements repository between all stakeholders of the project: engineers, business actors, customer, operator and authorities representatives at least.

Thus, to improve the level of demonstration, the proposed method does not oppose these two paths. However, it focuses on a requirements repository that would have the 'right' properties, i.e. composed of SMART requirements. This implies making available a formalized requirement modelling language as proposed in various works, allowing actors: to trace, assume the completeness and coherence of requirements, but also to refine, decompose, rewrite any requirement in a semantically equivalent way for the needs of certain domains by adapting to the domain vocabulary.

Thus, the elements quoted previously of the classical approach to safety demonstration have all been assimilated to requirements because they constitute a "contract" between the operator and the safety authority. [11] Indeed, a requirement is a *"statement that translates or expresses a need and its associated constraints and conditions"* [12].

Our analysis of the expected safety demonstration leads us to consider the following elements:

- **Interests Protection Functions** (formally denoted as "FPI" in french litterature): functions that, if compromised, could result in radioactive releases or damage to the environment, the public or employees (referred to as "interests" in french regulation [13])
  - o Here we will have an identification, based on an initial design, of the types of risks that may affect the facility, which could compromise an FPI. We will then select from a list of generic FPIs the one that applies to the facility of interest, based on the risks identified.

- **Safety Requirements** (formally denoted as "EX" in french litterature): for each type of risk, definition of the safety requirements to be taken into account for conducting the risks analyses and design: these are general design principles, "primary" safety requirements (e.g., "absence of dissemination in the event of an earthquake"), which serve as input data for the safety analyses.
- **Expected Characteristics** (formally denoted as "CA" in french litterature): performance of design based risk analyses (iterative process with the technical design engineers) and the safety requirements. CA are "second level" requirements. They are the result of the risk analyses. They are broken down by technical batch and are thus directly applicable by the technical design engineers. A "primary" safety requirement generally generates several CAs.
- **Defined Requirement** (formally denoted as ED in french litterature): in an iterative way with the previous point, the design is carried out by the technical trades based on the CAs. These are the technical measures proposed by the technical design engineers

to meet the CAs. An ED applies to a system or sub-system. Thus, several EDs may be required to meet a CA.

An FPI requirement will give rise to several EXs. An EX will give rise to several CAs and so on.

The terms used in our description of the safety demonstration are related to the regulatory semantics of nuclear power. [10] A parallel was made with the corresponding concepts in system engineering in working groups comparing the semantics/concepts of nuclear safety engineering and system engineering. It was considered more interesting to link all the elements introduced to the notion of requirements. The types of requirements, the relationships between requirements, the allocation relationships between requirements and functions or components allow great flexibility in the correct conceptualisation and specification of these ones considering the nuclear safety demonstration objectives.

As explained, considering these elements as "requirements" provides a great flexibility in the links that can be chosen to describe, for example, the transition from a CA to an ED. The literature on requirements engineering and recent work allow judicious choices to be made on these points in order to be as close as possible to the spirit intended by this division and this hierarchy intended by the nuclear safety domain.

Following this discussion, [14] proposes various relationships between requirements. Three of them are of particular interest to us:

- Decomposition: this consists of decomposing a requirement into several requirements in order to reduce its complexity, possibly making of different natures, both functional and non-functional, appear.
  - o Relationship between: FPI to EX and EX to CA.
- Derivation: this relationship allows a new requirement set to be derived from a requirement set in order to specify the behaviour or state of a system when it is in a particular configuration. This relationship allows the abstraction level of the requirements to be changed.
  - o Relation between a higher level ED and a lower level ED.
- Refinement: the purpose of requirement refinement is to add detail to a requirement, often in cases where the abstraction of a requirement is too strong. This requests then allows a set of requirement of the same nature as those that being refined to appear.
  - o Relation between CA and ED.

Figure 1 shows a simplified version of the main concepts and relationships between concepts that are presented in the text. This is a part of a global metamodel that allows us to formalise, structure and detail all the concepts, attributes and relationships that will be used in order to bridge the gap between MBSE domain and Safety demonstration domain.

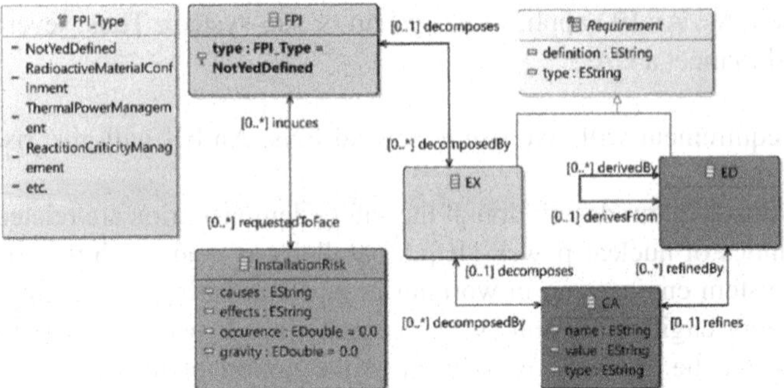


**Fig. 1.** Meta model of the method (partial view).

## 4 Illustrative Case

In SE, a viewpoint model is a "*representation of a whole system from the perspective of a related set of concerns.*" [15] With this method we try to provide a safety view to the architecture models of new or ongoing projects.

This method is currently being implemented within an application project. We will present in this section the first elements of this method presented before. Prior on testing the approach, many exchanges with experts in the field of safety have been requested to understand the main processes that compose it.

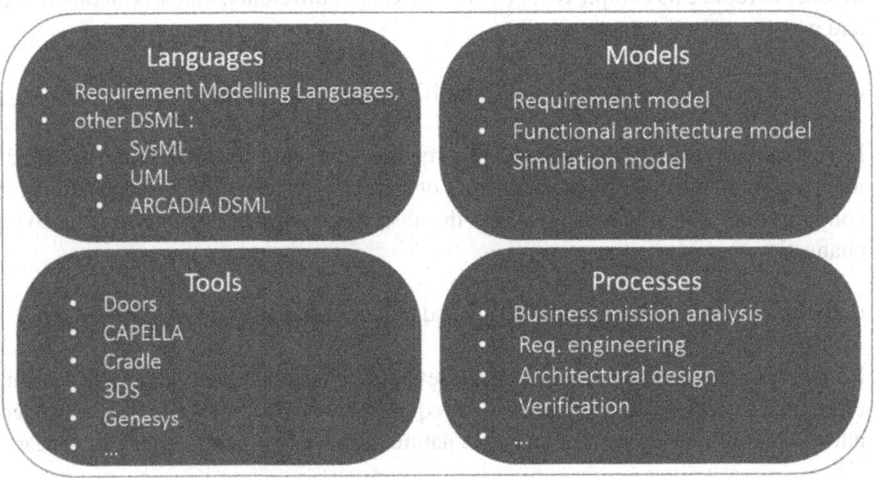


**Fig. 2.** MBSE Pilars

Also, in order to have research work that will be valued and put into practice in our projects we make sure to have a coherent development around the four pillars of MBSE (see Fig. 2) i.e. to have a research which covers these 4 pillars with a reflection on the models, on the processes which will allow their implementation, on the language used as wèll as the selected tool. These reflections must allow the proposal to be adapted to real application cases.

It was therefore necessary to observe the current state of the MBSE approach within the compagny in order to develop a safety view, integrated with the multiple views offered by the MBSE approach, which could be adapted to the habits already present among our engineers. For several reasons, it is the Capella tool [15] from Thales that is the most used within the group. It is therefore around this software, the Arcadia method [16] and the Arcadia DSML language [15, 16] that we are integrating our current research to move towards the demonstration of safety.

Our work focuses in particular on processes, with a proposed methodology for integrating nuclear safety into the proposed installations models. Of course, the methodology may have software limitations that prevent the implementation of the new methodological elements provided. This could be overcome by modifications to the software, which is made possible by the open source nature of this software (i.e. Capella).

Figure 3 shows an example of a requirements decomposition structure diagram that allows us to trace the origin of a particular requirement in our model while respecting the requirements types (see meta model in Fig. 1) specific to nuclear safety as presented above.

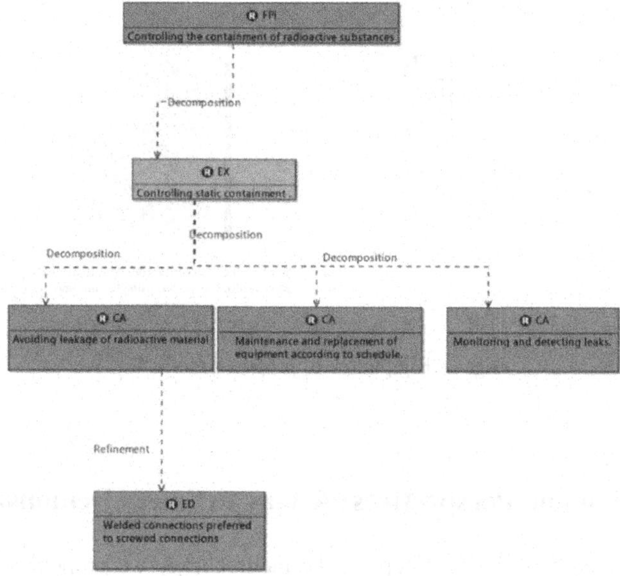


**Fig. 3.** RBS

This method, illustrated in Fig. 4, is a part of our proposed methodology in a MBSE context for nuclear safety demonstration. As shown in our big picture, the collaborative aspect is intrinsic to the work related to nuclear safety demonstration. This collaboration, if well conducted, allows each discipline to contribute its expertise in the best possible conditions in order to provide an optimal safety of the installation. The work of the nuclear safety engineer is not done alone but in interaction with all field of competencies. Moreover, projects in nuclear industry involve the nuclear safety engineer from start to end. In collaboration with the project manager and the technical manager, he must be able to check that each of the design proposals of the installation will ensure the protection of interests (security, public health and safety, protection of nature and the environment) [13].

Our proposal attempts to bring to the conduct of these projects the benefits of a Model-Oriented methodology rather than a Document-Oriented one. In order to achieve this, our work focuses on finding solutions to take into account nuclear safety in these models. These models constitute the common basis for collaboration between these different fields of expertise.

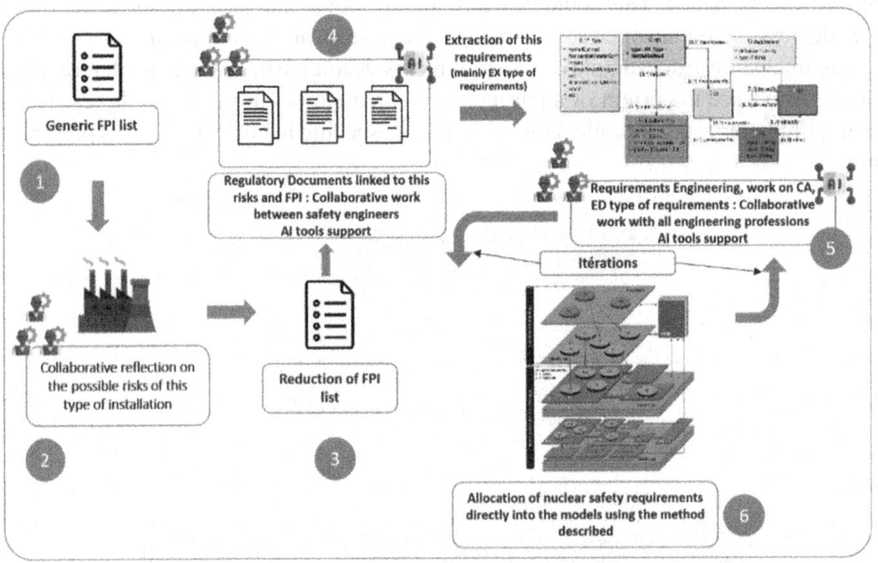


**Fig. 4.** Big picture of proposed method

## 5 Conclusion and Perspectives: A Way to Safety Demonstration

We have presented here the first steps of the methodology we propose on the way to the demonstration of nuclear safety. A deep understanding of both engineering (nuclear safety and systems engineering) is necessary to propose the coherent concepts of the former for application to the latter.

The demonstration of safety, as the name implies, involves demonstrating to the safety authority that the installation is safe for the outside world, the environment, and the workers. To demonstrate this, it is necessary to rely on consistent evidence, which is contained in the safety requirements in relation to the systems and activities they specify. The next step is to propose the methodology for moving from this evidence to the demonstration itself. The elements we find of interest to exploit are the notions around evaluation criteria, technical indicators including measures of effectiveness (MOE) and performance indicators (MOP). [17] These elements could be coupled with our CA type requirements which includes expected characteristics from systems.

It is essential that the stakeholders grasp the issues and understand the elements of the demonstration, which makes it a collaborative work by excellence with a strong objective: to obtain the licence allowing the installation commissioning. There is no doubt that this highly collaborative work is facilitated using models.

Although we did not mention it in this paper as it was not the purpose, the model-based approach is complemented by the use of AI on safety demonstration tasks that can be learned from the data. It is applied in those tasks of the safety demonstration that lend themselves to the inductive approach to facilitate the work of engineers. (automatic extraction of requirements for example [3]).

In the end, it is a set of processes brought together in a tool-based methodology that will enable more productive collaboration of stakeholders in projects that include a nuclear safety demonstration.

## References


1. Statista: L'énergie nucléaire en France - Faits et chiffres (2017). https://fr.statista.com/themes/2752/l-energie-nucleaire-en-france
2. IAEA: Safety Glossary STI/PUB/1290, International Atomic Energy Agency (2007)
3. PMI: Project Management Body of Knowledge (PMBOK GUIDE) 5th edn, Project Management Institute (2013)
4. Baron, J.: Thinking and Deciding. Cambridge (2007)
5. ISO: ISO/IEC 15288 Systems and software engineering—System life cycle processes, ISO (2008)
6. Friedenthal, S., Griego, R., Sampson, M.: INCOSE model based systems engineering (MBSE) initiative. In: INCOSE 2007 Symposium, San Diego (2007)
7. Navas, J., Tannery, P., Bonnet, S., Luc Voirin, J.: Bridging the gap between model based systems engineering methodologies and their effective practice – a case study on nuclear power plants systems engineering. In: INSIGHT, vol. 21, no. 1 (2018)
8. Zhuang, M., Zhao, X., Siqiao, Z.: Study on the NPP general operation strategy design method based on MBSE. In: Proceedings of the 27th International Conference on Nuclear Engineering (ICONE-27) (2019)
9. IAEA: Safety of Nuclear Power Plants: Design, Vienna (2007)
10. Légifrance: Arrêté du 7 février 2012 fixant les règles générales relatives aux installations nucléaires de base, France (2012)
11. INCOSE: INCOSE SE Terms Glossary (1998)
12. ISO, ISO/IEC/IEEE 29148 (2011)
13. Légifrance: Article L. 593-1 du code de l'environnement (2012)
14. Lori, L.: Conception d'un système avancé de réacteur PWR (2018)
15. ISO/IEC: ISO/IEC 10746-1, Information technology—Open Distributed Processing—Reference model: Overview, ISO/IEC (2009)
16. Roques, P.: MBSE with the ARCADIA Method and the Capella Tool. In: 8th European Congress on Embedded Real Time Software and Systems (ERTS 2016), Toulouse (2016)
17. Thalès: ARCADIA - Méthode pour l'ingénierie des systèmes soutenue par son langage de modélisation conceptuel - Description Générale, AFNOR (2018)

18. Lo, M.: Contribution à l'évaluation d'architectures en Ingénierie (2013)
19. AIEA: Licensing Process for Nuclear Installations (SSG-12), Vienne (2010)
20. Roumili, E., et al.: Requirements engineering enabled by natural language processing and artificial intelligence for nuclear safety demonstration. In: 11th Complex Systems Design & Management (CSD&M) Conference (2020)

# A Model to Manage Organizational Collaborative Networks in a Pandemic (Covid-19) Context

Marco Nunes[1](✉), António Abreu[2,3](✉), and Jelena Bagnjuk[4](✉)

[1] Department of Industrial Engineering, University of Beira Interior, 6201-001 Covilhã, Portugal
marco.nunes@ubi.pt

[2] Department of Mechanical Engineering, Polytechnic Institute of Lisbon, 1959-007 Lisbon, Portugal
ajfa@dem.isel.ipl.pt

[3] CTS Uninova, 2829-516 Caparica, Portugal

[4] Project Management Department, UKE (University Medical Center Hamburg-Eppendorf), Martinistraße, 20251 Hamburg, Germany
j.bagnju@uke.de

**Abstract.** The pandemics situation has brought unforeseen challenges to all organizations at a global scale. While some strongly profit from it, others thrive to survive or already died. In such times the bulk of leadership and management related skills, gains a disproportional importance especially for organizations where most of their workforce strongly depends on remote collaboration. Being aware of the difficulties to manage collaboration within and between teams in "normal times", the "still" ongoing situation has only brought more complexity to organizations in that aspect. In this work is proposed a model to manage organizational remote collaborative networks in order to identify collaboration extremes (lack of collaboration, or collaborative overload) which emerges as people work together in projects or operations, developed based in three pillars (collaborative networks, social network analysis, and business intelligence). A real case study is presented to illustrate the functioning principles of the model.

**Keywords:** Collaborative networks · Business intelligence · Social network analysis · Pandemics (Covid-19) · Organizational inclusion and performance

## 1 Introduction

The abrupt change in the way people around the world interact due to the pandemics, has profoundly changed. The impacts the future human relationships are far from being known [1, 2]. In these times, organizations face unexpected challenges in several dimensions. For example, the need of immediate implementation of complex measures to prevent the spread of the pandemics within their internal structures (in order to protect their workforce), overloaded many organizations in financial and human resources.


Published by Springer Nature Switzerland AG 2021
L. M. Camarinha-Matos et al. (Eds.): PRO-VE 2021, IFIP AICT 629, pp. 237–246, 2021.
https://doi.org/10.1007/978-3-030-85969-5_21

Simultaneously, the need of keep running the business in order to survive, demanded their employees to do the "extra-mile running" while using imagination and flexibility to keep the business as usual. In such scenario, effective and efficient collaboration within and between organizations has never been so important [3]. It is often argued that to organizations achieve sustainable competitive advantages they must excel in performance and innovation [4]. However, research shows that one of the most efficient ways to achieve sustainable competitive advantages, is by partnering with other organizations, such as institutes, universities, or even competitors, engaging in controlled collaborative environments that enable the creation of unique value, that otherwise would not be possible [5]. Still according to research, the lack of models to manage collaborative initiatives is the major obstacle that prevented organizations back in "normal times" to engage in such partnerships with a higher frequency [5, 6]. In these "new times", for the obviously reasons, it became worst [7, 8]. Latest research shows that organizational collaborative trends are deviating from the center - characterized by a balanced collaboration type -, towards the extremes [8], which may strongly negatively impact an organization's performance and innovation capacities [5, 6]. Such extremes (known as behavioral and ambiguity risks [5, 6]), where in one side is characterized by the evolution of collaboration towards an *overload collaborative status* and in another side characterized by *poor or lack of collaboration status*, is in line with research regarding organization collaboration tendencies, which argues that negative external factors (also called external noise) - as the case of the pandemics in these "new times" -, are dangerous to organizations [9]. Research shows also that such behavioral risks can only be properly addressed by first understanding the underlying reasons, and later apply generated knowledge to future similar situations - in other words, lessons learned [5]. To contribute with a solution to the mentioned emerging and growing problem, is introduced in this work a model to support the management of organizational collaboration (also known as organizational collaborative networks), to bring collaboration trends out from the extremes towards a balanced status. The proposed model supported by three pillars (1-collaborative networks (which gives the model the theoretical background that defines collaboration within and between organizations), 2-social network analysis (which gives the model the tools and techniques to perform a quantitative analysis), and 3-business intelligence (which gives the model the capacity to operate in an autonomous (automatic) way), will analyze how organization's employees remotely collaborate in the "new times" by analysing their dynamic interactions in four interrelated dimensions.

## 2 Literature Review

### 2.1 Collaborative Networks

Collaborative networks represent different entities, such as people, or organizations that share resources to achieve common and compatible goals, exchange information, adjust and plan activities [10]. Collaboration means working together in a shared creation approach [10]. It comprises the sharing of responsibilities, risks, and rewards, as participants mutually engage to solve a problem or challenge [10]. Collaboration is for example when experts from different organizations or departments, work together to develop a new service or product in an environment where natural coordination exists, and also a continuously seeking process of new ideas and insights, fueled with psychological safety and meaningful discussions, rather than only working under a perfect balanced environment [10]. Factors such as reciprocity (feedback regarding a particular subject), trust, and interlocking directorates are part of collaboration [10, 11]. Research shows that efficient collaboration contributes to better adapt to change, enables to create strategic inter-organizational networks, and increases flexibility to better face disruptive changes [12]. In the model presented in this work collaboration is assumed the "joint work level" existing between organizations employees.

## 2.2 Social Network Analysis

Social network analysis (SNA) studies social structures applying a variety of SNA centrality metrics (CM) enabling to the understand how they emerge and evolve in the environment where they exist [13]. SNA centrality metrics (SNAcm) can be applied in organizations to quantitatively analyze collaborative patterns, talent shortages, cultural fit, information exchange, unethical behaviors, employee turnover, fraud, and so on [14]. SNAcm play a fundamental role in understanding the importance of organizational social capital, and therefore is being continuously incorporated into organizational human resources processes and frameworks, as well in organizational risk management departments [15, 16]. Literature shows that the application of SNAcm enabled to identify three critical informal networks ((1) communication – uncovering who interacts with whom, (2) advice- uncovering who gives or asks advice, and (3) trust - uncovering who trusts whom) that exist in any organization regardless of type or size, and play an important role in performance and innovation [17]. SNAcm enables the identification of key informal roles, such as central connectors (people who play a central role within an organizational network), peripheral people (people who either intentionally or not, are not integrated within an organizational network), brokers (people who connect different organizational departments or organizations), and energizers (people who positively influence others around them) that exist in organizations [18]. In project management SNAcm can identify project critical success factors regarding the dynamic behavior of project people across the phases of a project lifecycle [16]. SNAcm such as in-degree, out-degree, closeness, betweenness, are applied to identify organizational hidden behavioral patterns, and growing in popularity [16]. Research shows that such CM are often correlated with an entity's importance, prestige, and influence, and can be an index of a network's potential activity, communication, control and spreadness [16, 18–21]. In this work the application of SNAcm enables to quantitatively measure the amount of informal behavioral patterns within an organizational network.

## 2.3 Business Intelligence

Business intelligence (BI) are strategies, frameworks, processes, tools, technologies and concepts employed by organizations to analyze business data, to accelerate and optimize the decision-making processes [22–24]. A typical BI architecture collects row data (data from different applications or platforms in several formats) from several sources, such as finance, engineering, human resources, sales, or other. Then, collected data is cleaned and organizing by a process called ETL (extract, load and transform) which normalizes collected data into readable and editable form. Then, data will be analyzed - usually by the application of mathematical and statistical tools and techniques. Finally analyzed data is displayed in visual meaningful representations (usually called data dashboarding), such as graphs, tables, or line trends (usually in the form of critical success factors and key performance indicators), so that organizations can perform the decision-making process in a more data-informed way (also known as a less biased way). Incorporating a BI into an organization's structure may provide unique benefits regarding the measuring, understanding, and correlation of past events with outcomes (usually known as descriptive analysis), and how these can help manage ongoing situations (usually known as predictive analysis), while parallelly identifying future business trends and suggesting strategical moves (usually known as prescriptive analysis) [23–25]. In this work the proposed model to manage organizational collaborative networks includes the incorporation of an organizational BI architecture to provide all the above-mentioned benefits to organizations regarding the overall data analysis process.

## 3 Development and Implementation of the Proposed Model

The proposed model in this work illustrated in Fig. 1 was developed based on three pillars and will analyze how organization's employees remotely collaborate to accomplish organization´s tasks and activities.

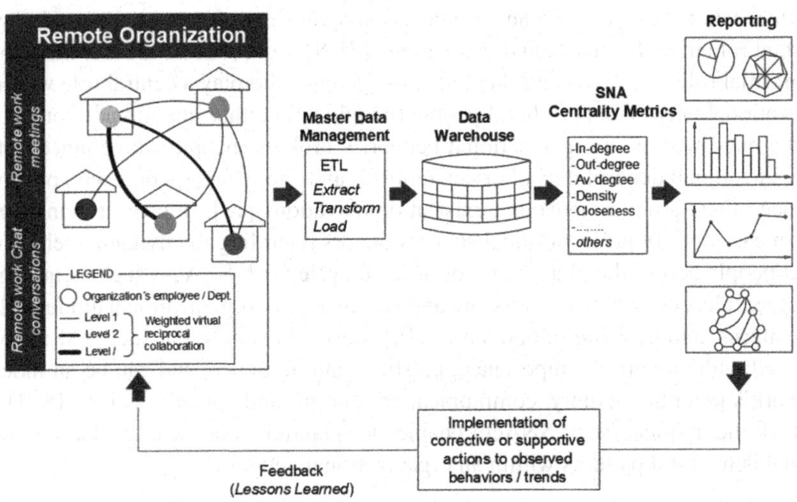


**Fig. 1.** Proposed model implementation framework and application methodology.

The model illustrated in Fig. 1 will analyze how remote dynamic interactions emerge and evolve across time by measuring four different but interrelated dimensions ((1) attendance degree in work-remote meetings, (2) amount of time spoken in work-remote meetings, (3) number of communicated people through work-chats conversations, and (4) the respective amount of time spent in work-chats conversations). Such dimensions were chosen because most of them represent the core of dynamic interactions between employees of an organization in a remote context. The implementation and application of the propose model follows the following methodology: First, data from two different sources ((1) remote work meetings), and (2) remote work chats conversations) will be collected and prepared (extracted, transformed, and loaded) to be stored into a master data warehouse. Then, data will be quantitatively measured by the application of SNAcm. Then, analyzed data will be outputted in graphic or tabular form o be properly interpreted and extracted hidden behavioral patterns that may put at risk collaboration and thus threaten the organizations goals and objectives. Finally, accurate quantitatively measures can be applied to adjust or support uncovered behavioral patterns. To quantify the amount of dynamic remote interaction between employees of an organization, SNAcm will be applied as illustrated in Table 1.

**Table 1.** Proposed model SNAcm

| Sources | SNA centrality Metrics & Description |
|---|---|
| Remote work meetings | Objective 1: Measure the attendance degree in work-remote meetings. Objective 2: Measure the amount of time spoken in work-remote meetings. Data: In each remote work meeting record the number of participants and the respective spoken time. SNAcm: For objective 1 the simple sum (recorded attendance) will be applied. For objective 2 the CM weighted in-degree [19] (1) will be applied.<br>$I_{DW}(n_i) = \sum_j x_{ji}$ (1)<br>Where:<br>$I_{DW}$= weighted in-degree of an organization employee regarding remote working meetings attendance. Weights are classified in 3 levels (Level 1, 2, and 3). n = total number of work remote meetings for i = 1…, n. *xji* = number of links from entity *j* to entity *i*, where $i \neq j$, which represents the direct attachment from a given employee to a given remote work meeting. |
| Remote work-chat conversations | Objective 1: Measure the number of communicated people through work-chats conversations. Objective 2: Measure the respective amount of time spent in work-chats conversations. Data: In each remote chat conversation record the number of different conversations and the respective chatted time. SNAcm: For objectives 1 and 2 the simple sum (in-degree) [19] will be applied. Additional: To characterize the remote work social network's structure the SNAcm average in-degree will be applied [19] (2).<br>$I_{Av}(N) = \frac{\sum_{i=1}^{n} x_{ji}}{n}$ (2)<br>Where:<br>$I_{Av}$= average in-degree of given social network (remote work social network).<br>n = total number of participants in remote chat work conversations for i = 1…, n<br>*xji* = number of links from entity *j* to entity *i*, where $i \neq j$, and vice-versa. *N* = all elements of a remote work social network. |

### 3.1 Real Case Application of the Proposed Model in This Work

A food & beverage market leader organization (named as organization A due to legal and anonymous reasons) applied the propose model in this work to understand how collaboration in the "new times" affected by the still ongoing pandemics, has been evolving across their 16 elements of the engineering department. For this matter organization A implemented the proposed model into a BI architecture as illustrated in Fig. 1, and collected data according to Table 1 between March and May of 2020. All 16 elements agreed to participate in the study complying with the general GDPR (General Data Protection Regulation at https://gdpr-info.eu/) rules. Within the mentioned period of time 12 work meetings (coined as virtual weekly *coffee-breaks*) have been accomplished to discuss organizational matters and to promote the interaction between employees who were exclusively working remotely. In Table 2 are illustrated the results regarding the dimension remote work meetings between March and May 2020 by applying the simple sum and (2) according to Table 1.

**Table 2.** Results for virtual work meetings between March and May 2020

| *E* | *1* | *2* | *3* | *4* | *5* | *6* | *7* | *8* | *9* | *10* | *11* | *12* | *13* | *14* | *15* | *16* |
|---|---|---|---|---|---|---|---|---|---|---|---|---|---|---|---|---|
| *VM* | 9 | 8 | 12 | 10 | 11 | 12 | 9 | 12 | 11 | 8 | 7 | 12 | 9 | 11 | 11 | 8 |
| *ST* | 1 | 1 | 1 | 1 | 1 | 1 | 1 | 3 | 3 | 2 | 2 | 2 | 1 | 1 | 1 | 1 |

In Table 2 *E* stands for employee number, *VM* stands for total number of attended work virtual meetings, and *ST* stands for spoken time level. There are 3 *ST* levels (L1 (yellow): 0–50 min, L2 (green): 51–100 min, and L3 (orange): > 101 min). According to Table 2, 70% of the 16 engineers only spoke a total time between 0 and 50 min, while 13% spoke > 101 min in all remote meetings. Such values represent an unbalanced social network regarding collaboration measured in work spoken time. Such results suggest a deeper analysis to better understand how such collaborative behavior emerged and evolved across time. This is illustrated in Fig. 2.

In Fig. 2 is illustrated the evolution of spoken time in each remote work meeting *vm(i)*, (virtual meeting) for elements 2, 15, 4 and 9, which correspond to the highest values observed in Table 2 (element 9) and to the lowest values observed in Table 2 (elements 2, 4, and 15). As it can be seen in the upper side of Fig. 2 element 9 had a total of 241 spoken minutes, contrasting with the 27 spoken minutes of elements 2, 15, 4 together. In Fig. 2, can also be seen that from *vm3* to *vm4* there has been an abrupt change in the behaviors of elements 2, 4, and 15, which simultaneously coincides with the almost exponential growth of element 9, specially from *vm5* onwards. These behaviors may represent a risk of collaboration between the 16 engineers of organization A, which if not properly managed it may evolve either to an overload collaborative status (namely by most participative elements, such as element 8 and 9) or to a poor or even a lack of collaboration status (namely by less participative elements such as 2, 4, and 15). If such observed trend keeps evolving across time, it still may evolve to collaborative bottlenecks (emerging in elements with disproportional participative levels) or even lead to the emergence of organizational silos (weak collaborative group *vs* high collaborative

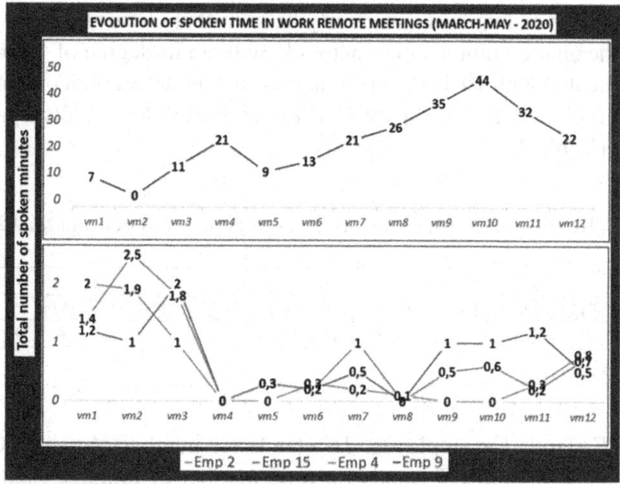


**Fig. 2.** Spoken time longitudinal evolution in virtual meetings for employees 2, 15, 4 and 9.

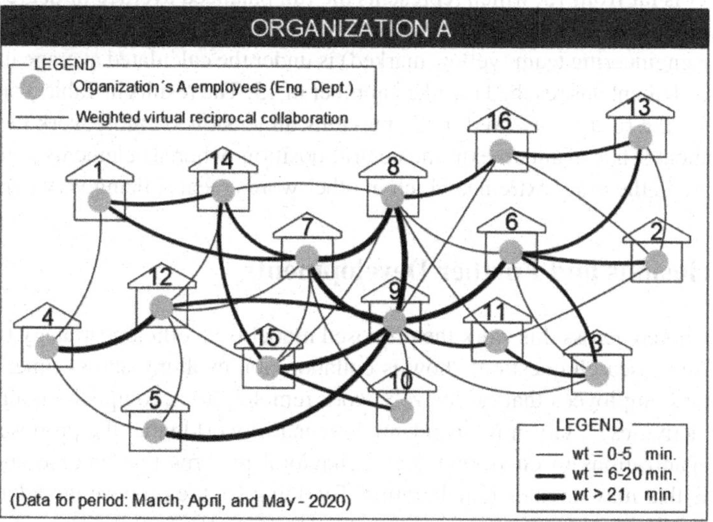


**Fig. 3.** Chat communication network between March and May 2020.

group). In Fig. 3 are illustrated the results regarding the second dimension (remote work-chat conversations), by the application of the simple sum and (2), according to Table 1.

In Fig. 3 is illustrated the chat communication network between the 16 engineering elements of organization A, that took place between March and May 2020. As it can be seen in the legend of Fig. 3, the weighted lines that connect the different 16 elements of organization A, represent who chatted with who (given by the lines between any give two elements), and how much it communicated (represented by the thickness of the respective lines). For example, it can clearly be seen that element 9 is by far the most central within the chat communication network, with an in-degree of 10 (which means that he communicated with 10 different elements), and a total amount of communicating time (wt, which is essentially writing) of 458 min. The individual results regarding Fig. 3, are illustrated in Table 3.

**Table 3.** Results for virtual chat conversations between March and May 2020.

| *E* | *1* | 2 | *3* | *4* | *5* | *6* | *7* | *8* | *9* | *10* | *11* | *12* | *13* | *14* | *15* | *16* |
|---|---|---|---|---|---|---|---|---|---|---|---|---|---|---|---|---|
| *TC* | 3 | 5 | 4 | 3 | 3 | 7 | 7 | 7 | 10 | 2 | 4 | 6 | 3 | 5 | 6 | 4 |
| *CT* | 32 | 21 | 36 | 48 | 68 | 212 | 254 | 198 | 458 | 28 | 19 | 68 | 56 | 97 | 208 | 77 |

In Table 3 *E* stands for employee, *TC* stands for number of people chatted to in virtual communication, and *CT* stands for total number of minutes chatted in virtual communications. The average in-degree (applying (2)) for this network is 5, which means that in average each element had communicate with 5 different colleagues. However, this number is far from 15, which represents the full balanced average in-degree of each element if all elements had communicated among themselves. It can also be seen that 50% of the engineering team (yellow marked) is under the calculated average in-degree, and that no element has reached the ideal number of 15. The results in Table 3 are clearly aligned with the results observed in the previous dimension - remote work meetings -, where element 9 has again an extreme central position, whereas elements 2 and 4, but not only, are in the other extreme, which in other words means, being very peripheral.

## 4 Conclusions and Further Developments

As demonstrated across this work the proposed model is an efficient strategy to answer the following research question: "how is collaboration evolving across time, between organizations employees that exclusively work remotely to accomplish organizational tasks and activities?". Given the pandemic's scenario worldwide, the proposed model enables organizations to uncover hidden behavioral patterns that emerge and evolve across time that may threaten collaboration. By doing so, the propose model addresses behavioral and ambiguity risk types, as suggested by [5, 6, 16, 26, 27]. The model enables organizations to quantify past collaborative evolutions which allows them to learn how dynamic behaviors can be correlated with outcomes - in other words, lesson learned. This in turn, enables organizations to in a more data-informed way, identify critical success and failure collaborative factors, which they later can use to guide and monitor future collaborative initiatives. The implementation of the proposed model in organizations implies first to create the necessary "virtual space" to enable an efficient functioning in all model's stages (data collection, transforming, analyzing and dashboarding). This step (implementation of a BI architecture), translates a boost in the digital transformation process, in transferring many of the manual organization operations and procedures into digital ones. This step also enables organizations to perform according to GDPR guidelines - and for the propose model itself - it enables a non-invasive, and full bias-free data treatment, by opposition to traditional performance management systems, such as pulse surveys conducted by organizations to evaluate collaboration and satisfaction levels. The proposed model positively contributes to the sustainability triple bottom line (economic, social, and environmental), by enabling organizations to minimize or eliminate risks regarding collaboration in formal and informal organizational networks, which in turn contributes to optimize and improve resources usage, leading to leaner organizational business strategies. Nevertheless, the implementation and application of the proposed model requires organizations to be flexible and open to adopt a new way of working. This may become a challenge to organizations, due to the power that resistance to change may offer, usually hidden in organizational informal networks. The proposed model does not capture all interactions between organization's employees, such as those that happen in work email exchange and phone calls. Therefore, new SNA centrality metrics - but also dispersion- should be developed, and other existing SNA metrics should be applied in order to better mold a 360 approach towards the identification of risk collaborative behavioral patterns. In order to clear identify the differences between "now and then" (in covid-19 rimes and after covid-19 times) regarding collaborative initiatives, is suggested that organizations apply the proposed model in "both times". This will lead to better understand the impacts that covid-19 has in collaborative initiatives. Finally, because some employees might not agree with such vast analysis of relational data, further research should be conducted in finding ways to capture such employee's relational data without going against employees legal and privacy aspects.

## References


1. Harris, T.F., Yelowitz, A., Courtemanche, C.: Did COVID-19 change life insurance offerings? IZA Discussion Paper No. 13912. https://ssrn.com/abstract=3743136. Accessed 08 Mar 2021
2. Marois, G., Muttarak, R., Scherbov, S.: Assessing the potential impact of COVID-19 on life expectancy. PLoS ONE **15**(9), e0238678 (2020)
3. Hamouche, S.: COVID-19 and employees' mental health: stressors, moderators, and agenda for organizational actions. Emerald Open Res. **2**, 15 (2020)
4. Friar, J.: Competitive advantage through product performance innovation in a competitive market. J. Prod. Innov. Manage. **12**, 33–42 (2003)
5. Nunes, M., Abreu, A.: Managing open innovation project risks based on a social network analysis perspective. Sustainability **12**, 3132 (2020)
6. Nunes, M., Abreu, A.: A model to support OI collaborative risks applying social network analysis. In: Camarinha-Matos, L.M., Afsarmanesh, H., Ortiz, A. (eds.) PRO-VE 2020. IAICT, vol. 598, pp. 324–335. Springer, Cham (2020). https://doi.org/10.1007/978-3-030-62412-5_27
7. Tannenbaum, S.I., Traylor, A.M., Thomas, E.J., et al.: Managing teamwork in the face of pandemic: evidence-based tips. BMJ Qual. Safe. **30**, 59–63 (2021)
8. Kaushik, M., Guleria, N.: The impact of pandemic COVID -19 in workplace. Eur. J. Bus. Manage **12**(15) (2020). https://iiste.org/Journals/index.php/EJBM/article/view/52883. Accessed 25 Mar 2021
9. Cross, R., Rebele, R., Grant, A.: Collaborative overload. Harv. Bus. Rev. **94**, 74–79 (2016)
10. Camarinha-Matos, L.M., Afsarmanesh, H.: Collaborative networks. In: Wang, K., Kovacs, G.L., Wozny, M., Fang, M. (eds.) PROLAMAT 2006. IIFIP, vol. 207, pp. 26–40. Springer, Boston, MA (2006). https://doi.org/10.1007/0-387-34403-9_4

11. Rindfleisch, A.: Organizational trust and interfirm cooperation: an examination of horizontal versus vertical alliances. Mark. Lett. **11**, 81–95 (2000)
12. Schalk, R., Curşeu, P.: Cooperation in organizations. J. Manage. Psychol. 25, 453–459 (2010)
13. Abreu, A., Nunes, M.: Model to estimate the project outcome's likelihood based on social networks analysis. KnE Eng. **5**(6), 299–313 (2020)
14. Blacker, K, McConnell, P.: People Risk Management: A Practical Approach to Managing the Human Factors That Could Harm Your Business. Kogan Page Publishers, CPI Group (UK), Ltd, Croydon (2015)
15. Krivkovich, A., Levy, C.: Managing the people side of risk. McKinsey Global Institute (2015). https://www.mckinsey.com/business-functions/risk/our-insights/managing-the-people-side-of-risk. Accessed 15 Feb 2019
16. Nunes, M., Abreu, A.: Applying social network analysis to identify project critical success factors. Sustainability **12**, 1503 (2020)
17. Krackhardt, D., Hanson, J.: Informal Networks the Company behind the Charts. Harvard College Review, Massachusetts (1993). https://www.andrew.cmu.edu/user/krack/documents/pubs/1993/1993%20Informal%20Networks.pdf. Accessed 5 Mar 2018
18. Cross, R., Parker, A.: The Hidden Power of Social Networks: Understanding How Work Really Gets Done in Organizations. Harvard Business School Press, Boston (2004)
19. Wasserman, S., Faust, K.: Social network analysis in the social and behavioral sciences. In: Social Network Analysis: Methods and Applications. Cambridge University Press, Cambridge, pp. 1–27 (1994). ISBN 9780521387071.
20. Liaquat, H., Wu, A., Choi, B.: Measuring coordination through social networks. In: Proceedings of the ICIS 2006 Proceedings, Milwaukee, Wisconsin, USA, 10–13 December 2006
21. Freeman, L.: Centrality in social networks conceptual clarification. Soc. Netw. **1**, 215–239 (1979)
22. Rouhani, S., Asgari, S., Mirhosseini, V.: Review study: business intelligence concepts and approaches. Am. J. Sci. Res. 50, 62–75 (2012). ISSN 1450-223X
23. Rad, R.: Microsoft SQL Server Business Intelligence Development Beginner's Guide. Packt Publishing, Birmingham (2014)
24. Dedić, N., Stanier, C.: Measuring the success of changes to existing business intelligence solutions to improve business intelligence reporting. In: Tjoa, A.M., Xu, L.D., Raffai, M., Novak, N.M. (eds.) CONFENIS 2016. LNBIP, vol. 268, pp. 225–236. Springer, Cham (2016). https://doi.org/10.1007/978-3-319-49944-4_17
25. Ponnambalam, K.: Business analytics foundations: descriptive, exploratory, and explanatory analytics (2020). https://www.linkedin.com/learning/business-analytics-foundations-descriptive-exploratory-and-explanatory-analytics/stages-of-business-analytics?u=77012418. Accessed 29 Mar 2020
26. Nunes, M., Abreu, A., Saraiva, C.: Identifying project corporate behavioral risks to support long-term sustainable cooperative partnerships. Sustainability **13**, 6347 (2021)
27. Nunes, M., Abreu, A., Saraiva, C.: A model to manage cooperative project risks to create knowledge and drive sustainable business. Sustainability **13**, 5798 (2021)

# Measuring Complexity for Collaborative Business Processes Management

Youssef Marzouk[1], Omar Ezzat[2], Khaled Medini[2](✉), Elyes Lamine[3], and Xavier Boucher[2]

[1] Mines Saint-Etienne, 42023 Saint- Etienne, France
[2] UMR 6158 LIMOS, Mines Saint-Etienne, University Clermont Auvergne, CNRS, Institut Henri Fayol, 42023 Saint- Etienne, France
khaled.medini@emse.fr
[3] Department of Industrial Engineering, Toulouse University, IMT Mines Albi, Route de Teillet, 81013 Cedex 9 Albi, France

**Abstract.** Organizations are increasingly working on business processes improvement to meet stakeholders' requirement. Process engineering and improvement projects are challenged by identifying proper metrics to guide improvement efforts and mitigate process complexity. This latter is intuitively related to factors such as usability, modularity, reliability and maintainability. A process that is too complex is more likely to fail and produce costly quality problems. In a context of collaborative decision-making, complexity management must consider the expectations of several stakeholders, and the definition/use of suitable metrics is the starting point. The current paper identifies and uses a set of metrics to enable the evaluation of process models. The proposed metric system is used within a case study highlighting the key role of modularity in mitigating process complexity. More generally, the results show how using the metric system can support complexity mitigation and therefore performance improvement in (re)engineered processes.

**Keywords:** Business process · Modelling · Collaboration · Complexity · Performance · Metrics · Project

## 1 Introduction

The literature witnesses the importance of sufficiently expressive and formal process modelling languages, which are easily understandable by end-users and not only by experts in the field. A collaborative business process is composed of a set of activities, tasks or services brought together to achieve a final objective [1]. Process complexity can be defined as the degree to which a process is difficult to understand, explain, analyse or manage. When the complexity of a process increases, it can lead to poor quality and difficult reorganization [2]. According to authors such as Dumas et al. [1] and Chinosi & Trombetta [3], there is a need to study process complexity as a distinct factor


Published by Springer Nature Switzerland AG 2021
L. M. Camarinha-Matos et al. (Eds.): PRO-VE 2021, IFIP AICT 629, pp. 247–254, 2021.
https://doi.org/10.1007/978-3-030-85969-5_22

influencing processes. As a matter of fact, high process complexity can lead to misunderstandings, errors, defects, and exceptions, which means that processes need more time to be developed, tested and maintained. Currently, organizations have not adopted complexity measures as part of their process management practices [4]. As a result, even simple processes can be designed in a complex manner. A means to characterize process complexity is business process measurement, described as an empirical and objective measurement of various business processes properties, in order to characterize them rigorously [5]. A complexity measure could be used to identify existing processes that are good candidates for improvement and simplification, or even complete re-engineering [6, 7]. A measure could also be used to predict the effort required to manage and complete a new instance of a process or to select a process manager with an appropriate level of competency.

The current paper identifies and uses a set of metrics to enable the evaluation of process models. The proposed metric system is used within a case study highlighting the key role of modularity in mitigating process complexity. More generally, the results show how using the metric system can support complexity mitigation and therefore performance improvement in (re)engineered processes. The remainder of this paper is organized as follows: Sect. 2 identifies and selects a set of metrics for measuring the complexity associated with business process models. Section 3 presents an illustrative case study to measure process complexity in two different scenarios, modelled using BPMN. Section 4 discusses paper results. Conclusions and perspectives are summarized in Sect. 5.

## 2 Complexity Metrics

Collaborative business processes describe how organizations operate thorough providing a global view of the interactions between several actors to achieve common business goals [8, 9]. These processes span across complex and dynamic environments, within one or multiple organizations. The complexity induced by such environment heavily impacts on process performance [10]. Therefore, improving process performance and reducing its complexity is undoubtedly a driver to meet stakeholders' expectations. To this end, identifying suitable metrics for measuring complexity is a key step.

The metrics presented in this paper were identified using a specific approach involving two stage: (i) metrics collection and structuring, and (ii) metrics selection. During the first stage (i), several metrics were collected from the literature and grouped according to their types (discrete or direct metrics, with or without operationalization). Direct metrics use simple and effective formulas that provide a quick measure of complexity. Discrete measures are applied to the detailed structure of the model and allow a thorough calculation of its complexity, by evaluating its resources. Both metrics are used to evaluate complexity of business process models from structural perspective [5, 6]. From a behavioural perspective, the behaviour of process elements within a business process model can be defined by describing how they interact throughout the structure of the process. During the second stage (ii), based on collected metrics from stage one, metrics were selected according to measurability and relevance for complexity measurement and performance improvement. The selected metrics are detailed in Table 1.

**Table 1.** Metrics used for the evaluation

| Metric | Definition | Objective |
|---|---|---|
| Number of activities | Measures the number of activities in a given process | Helps evaluating complexity, cost and time of the process |
| Number of human resources types | Measures the number of resource types for a given process | Helps evaluating complexity, cost of the process and the organizational impact |
| Control-flow Complexity | Evaluates the number and complexity of gateways in a given process | Helps evaluating process complexity |
| Longest path of the process (Diameter) | Measures the longest path between the first and last nodes in a given process model | Measures the longest lead time for each process |
| Percentage of multi- skilled human resources | Measures the percentage of the multi- skilled resources of the total human resource for a given process | Helps evaluate organizational impact, cost, lead time and complexity |
| The flow between activities from different lanes | Calculates the number of sequence flow between different lanes of a given process | Helps evaluating process complexity |
| Number of clusters (modules) | Measures the total number of formed modules for each process model | Helps evaluating organizational impact of each process |
| Coefficient of Network Complexity (CNC) | Measures the complexity of a network (the ratio of arcs to nodes) | Helps evaluating process complexity |
| Process users | Measures the number of employees involved in a given process | Helps evaluating organizational impact |
| Workload | Measures the number of products or services handled per employee/resource type | Helps evaluating organizational impact |

Process complexity management influences how efficiently and economically processes are planned, managed, and executed. Cicmil et al. [11], Dao et al. [12] identified complexity as a factor that helps determine planning and control practices, a factor that hinders the identification of goals and objectives, or a factor that influences the time, cost and quality of a business process. According to [5], there is no single measure that can be used to evaluate process complexity. Four main perspectives of complexity can be identified: activity complexity (the number of activities in a process), control flow complexity (divisions, junctions, loops, and start and end points), complexity of data flow (complexity of data structures, number of formal activity parameters, and the correspondence between activity data), complexity of resources (a resource is defined as any entity required by an activity for its execution, such as a database, external application or role). These perspectives were also noted through the literature review recently conducted by [7]. Complexity is closely related to process performance as it impacts process output accuracy and its capacity of handling changes. More generally performance may refer to process efficiency, effectiveness and flexibility.

## 3 Case Study

In this section, we present a concrete example of manufacturing a cleaning robot, which is inspired by real industrial companies, to show how complexity and performance metrics can support collaborative business process improvement and can be helpful in such business. The case company manufacture automate agents, composed of different modules: battery, energy, cleaning and body modules. Different resources are needed for the

**Table 2.** Human resource types related to each product/service

| Product or service element | | Module reference | Human resource |
|---|---|---|---|
| Products | Battery L/H/M (*) | E1,2,3 | Electrical Engineer; |
| | Microcontroller | E4 | Electrical Engineer; |
| | Security | E5 | Electrical Engineer; |
| | Body L/S/M | E6,7,8 | Design and mechanical engineer; |
| | Cleaning 1,2,3 | E9,10,11 | Electrical Technician; Engineer |
| | Energy System 1,2,3 | E12,13,14 | Electrical Technician |
| Services | Battery Maintenance | E15 | Maintenance Engineer; Electrical Technician |
| | Cleaning module maintenance | E16 | Maintenance engineer; |
| | Cleaning the robot | E17 | Technician; |
| | Displacement maintenance | E18 | Maintenance engineer; Mechanical technician |
| | Upgrade | E19 | Electrical Engineer; Technician |
| | Consulting service | E20 | Consulting Engineer; Electrical Engineer |
| | Equipment Test execution | E21 | Electrical engineer; Maintenance engineer; Consulting Engineer |

**L = long lifespan battery, H = low life span, M = medium life span*

execution of the service or assembly of the product, e.g. electrical, design and mechanical engineers for design and manufacturing, technicians for cleaning, highly qualified operators for maintenance activities (maintenance engineers, qualified technicians…), qualified personnel for after-sales services and training. Human resources as a grouping criterion can heavily influence the generation of different modularity scenarios mixing product and service in consistent modules [13]. Table 2 briefly illustrates the human resource type related to each element of product and service.

In this case study, the reduction of process complexity can be addressed through the development of modularity concerning both product and service operations. By combining products and services, modules can be formed to mitigate the whole process complexity by combining products and services (E'x'). A module can be defined as a block of multiple products or services. Each module is formed by respecting the logical sequence of robot manufacturing. For example, a module composed of battery and upgrade cannot be considered, as the process of upgrade concerns the whole robot, not only the battery. In order to conduct this study, we made two different scenarios to illustrate how modularity affects the complexity of the process. The two scenarios result from different clustering methods and parameters but they share the same input elements: scenario 1 is based on modules containing no more than two components each (product and/or service): {E1, E12}, {E9}, {E6}, {E15}, {E16}, {E18}, {E20,E21}, {E5,E4}, {E17}, {E19}, scenario 2 relies on clusters made from several products and services: {E1,E12,E6,E9}, {E15,E16,E18}, {E20,E21}, {E4,E5}, {E17, E19}. For deeper discussion on how to build and generate different product and service modularity scenarios, the reader can report to the full study in [13].

ADONIS software for business process management was used to model and visualize the above scenarios consistently with BPMN standard. As an example, Fig. 1 shows a representation of the collaborative processes supplying module 8, in the first scenario. This module is composed of two products, microcontroller (E4) and security (E5). In Fig. 1 processes related to each of the modules are highlighted with dashed lines.

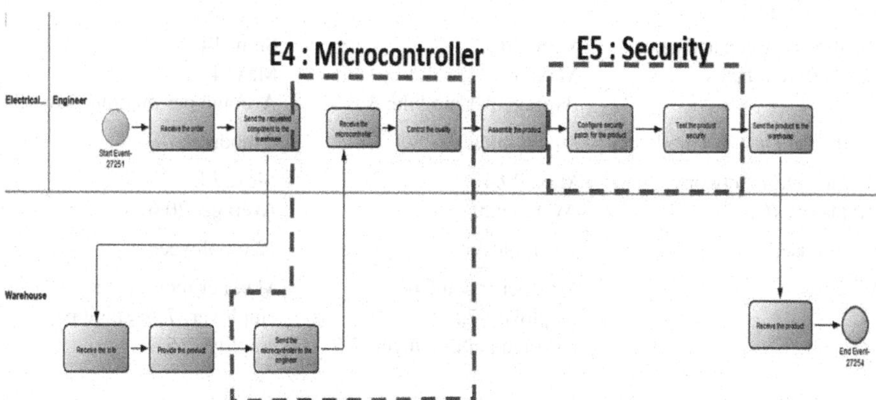


**Fig. 1.** Example showing module 8 for scenario 1

### 3.1 Complexity Evaluation and Discussion

Business process models and the identified metrics are used to evaluate the complexity of the scenarios described above. Table 3 summarizes the assessment results of the two modelled scenarios. These indicators are relevant to measure structural complexity. They can be easily calculated based on relatively simple process models, and thus they can be applied to various industrial contexts. This induces that this complexity approach could certainly be easily applicable in industrial environment.

The results show a significant difference between the two scenarios. It is worth noticing that the lower the value of the metric, the less complex the process is. In general, almost all the metrics show that the second scenario tends to have better scores. This confirms that this scenario exhibits lower level of complexity than the first one. The final choice between these different alternative solutions (scenarios) also depends on the costs and difficulties of process management.

**Table 3.** Process models evaluation results

| Metrics | Scenario 1 evaluation results | Scenario 2 evaluation results |
|---|---|---|
| Number of activities | 151 activities | 84 activities |
| Number of human resources types | 10 different resources types with average of 1 per module | 6 different resources types with average of 1.2 per module |
| Control-flow Complexity Metric | CFCabs(P) = 33 | CFCabs(P) = 17 |
| Longest path of the process (Diameter) | Longest: 25<br>Average: 17.2–18 per module | Longest: 22<br>Average: 16.6–17 per module |
| Percentage of multi-skilled human resources | 0% | 33% |
| The flow between activities from different lanes | Sum: 30<br>Max: 4<br>Average per module: 3 | Sum: 14<br>Max: 4<br>Average per module: 2.8 ~ 3 |
| Number of clusters (modules) | 10 modules | 5 modules |
| Coefficient of Network complexity (CNC) | Max: 29.4<br>Average:20 | Max: 27<br>Average: 20.6 |
| Process users | 26 employees | 12 employees |
| Workload | Max per module per employer: 7.5<br>Average per employer: 5.5 | Max per module per employer: 7 Average per employer: 5.4 |

## 4 Discussion

The case study is considered a theoretical approach tested with industrial data. We can add it as a future perspective, to validate the approach on larger industrial case studies, for companies with complex processes (such as offering both product and services or offering varieties of products). This case study shows the real opportunity offered by measuring the complexity of different scenarios, to lead to (re)engineer processes towards more straightforward and easily manageable organization. As a matter of fact, the complexity metrics enables process managers and administrators to calculate the complexity of processes generated by process owners. Designers can analyse the complexity of a process in development; consultants could also contribute with new process components for complexity analysis of the proposed solutions.

The outcome of our study does not seem unpredictable. Indeed, this result is in line with previous research in relation to modularity, seen as a driver for mitigating system complexity [2, 14]. Such a system (e.g. business process, organizational structure) is deconstructed into independent units (modules in our case). The modules should be able to exist independently from each other, but the system can only function as an integrated structure. Our results suggest the use of a reduced number of modules, each of them with more integrated elements, in order to create fewer complex processes, thus reducing the time spent for understanding and managing processes in order to remove failures or adapt the organization to changing requirements.

There are however rooms for improvement. For example, no single complexity metric can be considered superior to the others, which may represent some limitation for the work. For better results, one option could involve combining several metrics into an aggregated score. Furthermore, metrics can be extended to cover both structural and behavioural perspectives of process complexity. This can be achieved by use of simulation of collaborative business processes. The complexity assessment could also be extended in the future to consider the collaboration mechanisms spanning over several organizations. A potential area to investigate is the mass customization in the healthcare sector.

## 5 Conclusion

The goal of finding a measure for the structural complexity of business processes is ultimately to improve the processes, so that they can produce more value for their stakeholders: customers, owners and work forces. A complexity measure could point out a direction for the process improvement efforts, especially when it's consistent and computable like we have seen in the past sections.

With a measure of complexity, we can make compromise between process complexity and other process properties, such as lead time or resource requirements. At some point, adding additional resources or decreasing the complexity of a process is likely to become counterproductive, even though the lead time should in principle decrease, as too much complexity or too costly resources can have negative effects. When improving business processes, there are usually various possibilities to reorganize the process. The structural complexity of these scenarios should be a factor to consider. Several questions still need to be addressed such as, what would be an ideal complexity measure?

And does a measure have a unique and clear interpretation? This answer will only be given based on empirical results when organizations have successfully implemented complexity assessment in their process development projects.

**Acknowledgements.** This work is supported by Région Auvergne Rhône Alpes (AURA) through VARIETY project (https://perma.cc/6QM4-VLPJ).

## References

1. Dumas, M., La Rosa, M., Mendling, J., Reijers, H.A.: Fundamentals of Business Process Management. Springer, Berlin, Heidelberg (2018)
2. Medini, K., et al.: Highlights in customer-driven operations management research. Procedia CIRP **86**, 12–19 (2019)
3. Chinosi, M., Trombetta, A.: BPMN: an introduction to the standard. Comput. Stand. Interfaces **34**(1), 124–134 (2012)
4. Mentzas, G., Halaris, C., Kavadias, S.: Modelling business processes with workflow systems: an evaluation of alternative approaches. Int. J. Inf. Manage. **21**(2), 123–135 (2001)
5. Cardoso, J.: Business process control-flow complexity. Int. J. Web Serv. Res. **5**(2), 49–76 (2008)
6. Latva-Koivisto, A.M.: Finding a Complexity Measure for Business Process Models. Technical report Mat-2.108, Helsinki University of technology, Finland (2001)
7. Polančič, G., Blaž, C.: Complexity metrics for process models – a systematic literature review. Comput. Stand. Interfaces **51**, 104–117 (2017)
8. Villarreal, P.D., Lazarte1, I., Roa1, J., Chiotti, O.A.: Modeling approach for collaborative business processes based on the UP-ColBPIP language. Int. Conf. Bus. Process Manage., 318–329 (2009)
9. Hachicha, M., Fahad, M., Moalla, N., Ouzrout, Y.: Performance assessment architecture for collaborative business processes in BPM-SOA-based environment. Data Knowl. Eng. **105**, 73–89 (2016)
10. Barcelona, M.A., García-Borgoñón, L., Escalona, M.J., Ramos, I.: CBG-Framework: a bottom-up model-based approach for collaborative business process management. Comput. Ind. **102**, 1–13 (2018)
11. Cicmil, S., Cooke-Davies, T., Crawford, L., Richardson, K.: Exploring the complexity of projects: implications of complexity theory for project management practice. Project manage. J. **40**(3), 84 (2009)
12. Dao, B., Kermanshachi, S., Shane, J., Anderson, S., Hare, E.: Identifying and measuring project complexity. Procedia Eng. **145**(1), 476–482 (2016)
13. Ezzat, O., Medini, K., Boucher, X., Delorme, X.: A clustering approach for modularizing service-oriented systems. J. Intell. Manuf. https://doi.org/10.1007/s10845-020-01668-w (2020)
14. Reijers, H., Mendling, J.: Modularity in process models: review and effects. In: Dumas, M., Reichert, M., Shan, M.-C. (eds.) BPM 2008. LNCS, vol. 5240, pp. 20–35. Springer, Heidelberg (2008). https://doi.org/10.1007/978-3-540-85758-7_5

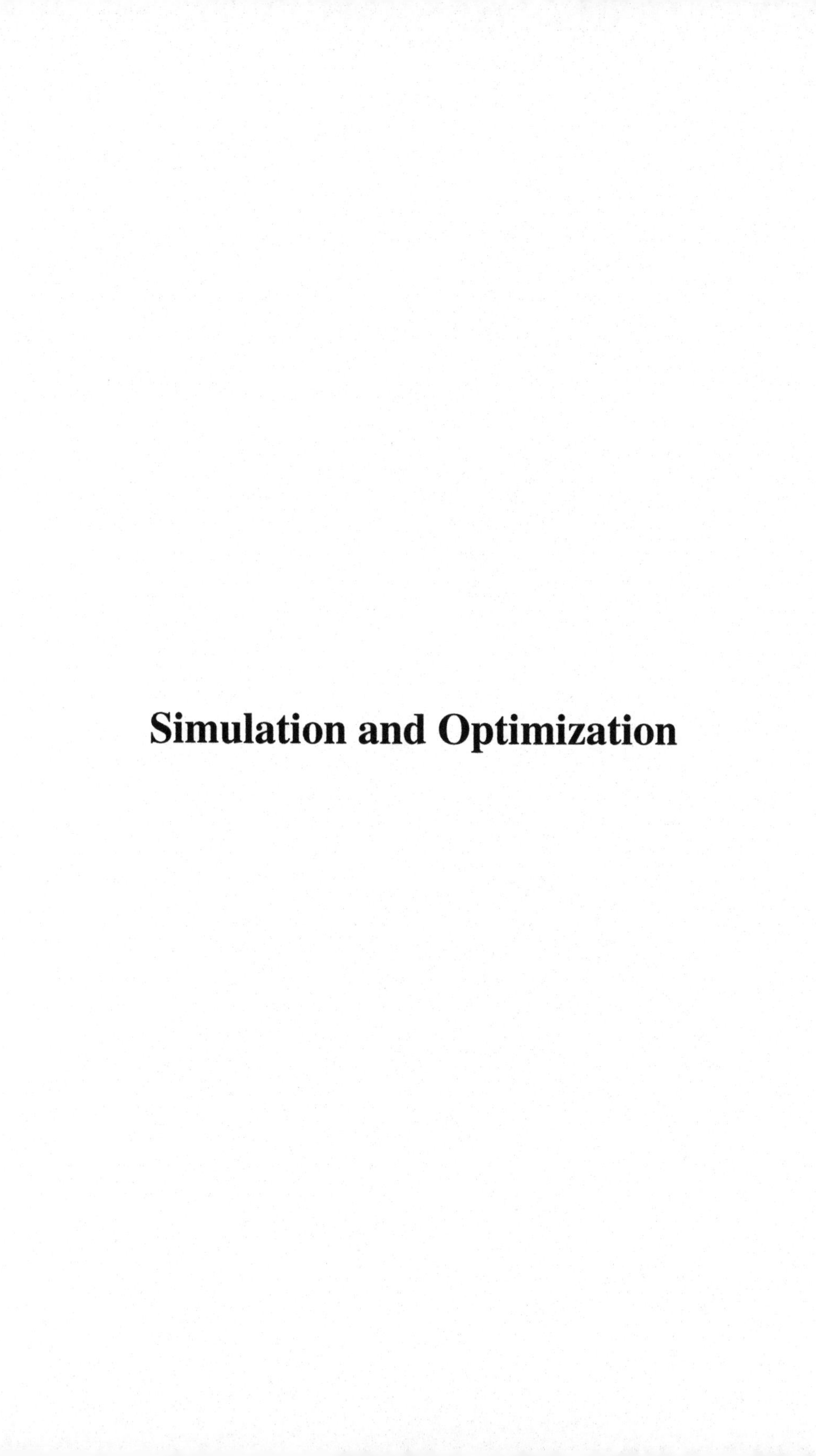

# Simulation and Optimization

# Research on Configuration Framework of Simulation Rules Based on Existing Simulation Teaching Platform

Wenqiang Li[1], Juanqiong Gou[1](✉), Shuyao He[1], and Zhe Wang[2]

[1] School of Economic and Management, Beijing Jiaotong University, Beijing, China
{20120606,jqgou}@bjtu.edu.cn
[2] Shanghai Siye Network Technology Co., Ltd., Shanghai, China

**Abstract.** Virtual simulation can help students and enterprise employees to understand the company systematically and gain insights into the complexity and uncertainty of the enterprise's digital innovation. The design focus of the virtual simulation teaching platform needs to base on the business and data of the enterprise. Considering authenticity and interest, the simulation rules are designed to adapt to the simulation needs of different business situations of various enterprises in a more flexible way. Therefore, this paper proposes a three-layer framework and implementation Methodology for extracting and configuring simulation rules, which can realize simulations of different business quickly and provide support for teachers in teaching. The implementation methodology of rule configuration serves for the three-layer framework. The paper takes rule configuration of a virtual simulation as a case to illustrate the proposed framework and methodology.

**Keywords:** Simulation rule · Simulation platform · Simulation teaching · Rule configuration

## 1 Introduction

Currently, the global digital infrastructure including social media, the Internet of Things, digital business platforms, and other digital networks and ecosystems is gradually being improved. It enables people, technologies, processes, and organizations complete hyper-connections and interdependence with each other, which intensifies the complexity of the entire digital world. The nonlinearity, self-organization, co-evolution, bifurcation and other characteristics of the entire complex socio-technical system inevitably has led to an unpredictable state which is called uncertainty [1].

In the discipline of Information Management, the intersection and integration of management and technology are difficulties. The complexity and uncertainty in digital innovation has further exacerbated the dilemma of students' learning and innovation, which brings challenges to the teaching of Information Management and other subjects. In regard to the teaching in college, how to help students better understand enterprise business and gain insight into the complexity and uncertainty of enterprise digital innovation has become more and more important [2].


L. M. Camarinha-Matos et al. (Eds.): PRO-VE 2021, IFIP AICT 629, pp. 257–266, 2021.
https://doi.org/10.1007/978-3-030-85969-5_23

Virtual simulation can inject people into virtual core roles through enabling, decision-making, communication, etc. [3]. Specifically, business simulation uses the same variables, relationships and events in the business world to simulate business reality. Through designing basic rules, relationships and market dynamics in enterprise business, simplifying the complexity of real companies and highlighting content and rules, the students can better understand enterprise business, personally experience enterprise decision-making behavior [2], and face the uncertainties in the process of business operations. Also, students can deeply experience the business of different companies through "immersive learning". Therefore, the simulation teaching can improve students' comprehensive implementation ability, comprehensive strategy ability, innovation ability, and cultivate students' sense of cooperation and team spirit [4]. However, the cost of developing simulation teaching platforms for different companies is relatively high. Also, it cannot meet the teaching tasks of different disciplines. Faced with the demands for mass customization, product configuration design is a key technology for rapid design and rapid response to the market demands [5]. Therefore, for the diversified needs of business simulation, a configuration platform is needed. Based on predefined components and constraint relationships, product configuration design can quickly form a personalized product BOM (Bill of Materials, BOM), which can meet the diverse needs of customers [6].

Product configuration design includes four aspects: components, product structure, configuration rules and constraints [6]. Specifically, configuration rules are important parts of product configuration design [5]. Because the primary task of product configuration is to translate customer knowledge into engineering knowledge. The bridge between these two knowledge domains is achieved by configuration rules [6]. Simulation rules are defined as the mapping relationship between simulation platform operation and enterprise business. Some institutions have begun to pay attention to the accumulation, organization, management and reuse of simulation models [7], but there are few researches on the configuration of simulation rules. Simulation analysis generates a lot of data, which hides a lot of useful knowledge [8]. This knowledge contains a large number of simulation rules. Extracting and reconfiguring these rules can help to improve an existing simulation teaching platform, or configure a new simulation teaching platform quickly which is similar and has a certain of differences with the existing business simulation platform. Under this context, this paper proposed following main question:

*How to extract the simulation rules of the simulation teaching platform, enable this platform to achieve flexible iterative update based on this rule, and enable the platform to meet other business extension requirements based on the configuration of simulation rules.*

The paper is structured as follows: Sect. 1 introduces the research issues. Then, Sect. 2 provides an overview of simulation research. Section 3 describes the three-layer framework for configuration of simulation rules based on the simulation teaching platform, which includes the extraction of rules, and gives specific implementation methodology. Section 4 provides a short case to help illustrate the framework and methodology. Finally, Sect. 5 gives conclusions and opportunities for further work.

## 2 Related Works

Simulation is not a new tool and used in many fields. For example, simulation is applied to supply chain configuration [9]. Also, many business decisions and process can be supported by various types of simulation platforms. Business domain simulation has been developed for decades and widely used in different fields, such as setup, planning and control [10]. Virtual simulation improves the conversion speed from theory to practice, and helps learners understand enterprise business more quickly to save time and cost [11]. Virtual simulation has been proved to be conducive to the understanding of theoretical knowledge, and can enhance the cognition of enterprises. In 2008, Hancock and others defined virtual simulation as a simulation that injects people into the virtual core role through enabling, decision-making, communication and other aspects [12]. Therefore, virtual simulation can help students to understand the complexity and uncertainty of enterprise.

Simulation teaching is an important part of realizing the information construction of higher education through the cross collaboration of multiple technologies. Simulation teaching platform can be divided into technology teaching and ability teaching through teaching objectives. Specifically, technology teaching is to realize the cognition of things or processes through virtual simulation, which is mainly applied to the teaching of medicine and nursing, engineering machinery, chemical biology and so on. Simulation teaching in medical care is particularly important after COVID-19 [13]. In addition to the construction of medical nursing virtual environment, in order to enhance students' cognition of medical and nursing knowledge, more and more researches on the simulation of patients' feelings [12]. Ability teaching is to form relevant consciousness or idea through virtual simulation teaching, so as to establish the ability to solve related problems. It is mainly applied to humanities and social sciences. For example, schools set up "training company" games to cultivate students' ability to communicate and solve communication problems [14].

Game simulation teaching has the characteristics of good interest [2], good interaction and strong creativity [15]. Therefore, the concept of serious game is brought into the virtual simulation teaching, so that students can feel the sense of competition, control and belonging in the simulation. Game simulation can stimulate students' internal needs and make them study actively. The game is a complex but intuitive system [16], including multimedia and simulation technology, as well as story interaction. Students' learning in game simulation teaching is a kind of self behavior. It is believed that the internal needs and emotions of drive are the motivation sources of self-determination behavior.

Virtual simulation has many applications in the field of teaching, including medical teaching, engineering teaching, business teaching, etc., and even adds the concept of game to increase the fun of simulation. This research is mainly about the teaching in the business field. When designing the simulation teaching platform, it is inevitable to embed the business process in the simulation. Faced with diversified business, we should establish a product configuration platform, in which rule configuration is an important content [5]. There are many studies researched about simulation teaching applications and simulation model reuse, but few of them focused on Rules. There are a lot of rules in simulation. Based on this, this paper focuses on the rule extraction of existing simulation platform and configuration of simulation rules.

## 3 Configuration Framework of Simulation Rules

In the design of simulation teaching platform, different types of business have different processes, so we need a flexible way to realize the simulation teaching platform to meet different business needs. At present, some organizations focusing on simulation teaching have implemented the configuration of simulation platform for different businesses, but the rule configuration process is difficult to be understood by others, and cannot complete the rule configuration quickly and flexibly.

In order to meet the requirements of configuration of simulation rules, a three-layer configuration framework and configuration implementation methodology is proposed in this section, which can extract simulation rules and configure simulation rules from simulation teaching platform that is a problem-oriented platform.

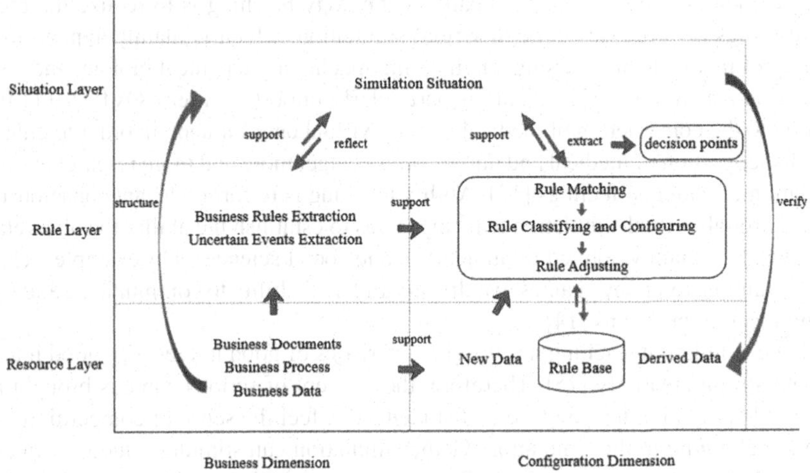


**Fig. 1.** Configuration framework

As shown in Fig. 1, the proposed configuration framework includes two dimensions: (1) business dimension, (2) configuration dimension; and three layers: (1) situation layer, (2) rule layer, (3) resource layer.

**Situation Layer:** The configuration dimension and business dimension of this layer are represented as simulation situations. From the simulation situations, the decision points of collaborative situations can be extracted, which is the embodiment of simulation rules in the simulation situations.

**Rule Layer:** In the business dimension, it is represented by the extraction of business rules and uncertain events which are needed to support the rule configuration process.

In the configuration dimension, it is shown as the matching of simulation rules, the classification and configuration of rules, and the adjustment of rules. The configuration rules are divided into three parts: (1) basic data, which are directly from the data of the enterprise and do not need to be changed; (2) Rules Based on actual data, which are from the data of the enterprise but need to be adjusted; (3) Rules Based on simulation knowledge, which are designed because of the need of simulation [6].

**Resource Layer:** In the business dimension, it represents the business documents, business processes and business data of the target enterprise. In the configuration dimension, it is the rule base of the corresponding business simulation, the new data which can support rule configuration and the derived data generated in the process of new virtual simulation. The data in the business dimension supports the newly constructed data in the configuration dimension.

In the business dimension, the business rules and uncertain events are extracted through the business documents, business processes and business data in the resource layer. The simulation situations are initially constructed. The simulation situations have no rules, but can be compared with the simulation template to select the appropriate simulation model. In the configuration dimension, the collaborative situation decision points are extracted from the selected simulation situations, and the collaborative situation decision points are matched with the corresponding rules of the simulation situations. This step mainly solves the problem of understanding rules. Then the rules are classified, configured and adjusted. The newly generated rules are stored in the rule base. The rationality of the new simulation rules is verified by the derived data generated by the new simulation teaching platform.

The above framework illustrates the whole process of rule configuration. In order to further illustrate the most important process of rule layer of the configuration dimension, the implementation methodology of configuration of simulation rules is proposed. The process involves multi-role and multi-agent cooperation, so the methodology is designed based on the metamodel for collaborative situations [17]. As shown in Fig. 2, the methodology includes five main parts: collaborator, behavior, rule, objective and resource.

Rules are co-configured by partners. The configuration steps are as follows: (1) Mining collaborative situation decision points in simulation template based on simulation platform. (2) Based on the simulation data, the rule base is matched with the decision points of the collaborative scene. (3) New rules are classified and configured based on business resources and simulation data. (4) The rules after configuration are adjusted based on business resources and simulation data.

The decision points of collaborative situation are represented by behavior tree. The concept of behavior tree and corresponding application in the system was first proposed by Dromey in 2001 [18]. Based on the behavior tree, this paper redefines its traversal rules to illustrate the decision-making behavior in virtual simulation.

The behavior tree has four nodes: Select Node, Sequence Node, Condition Node and Action Node. (1) Select node: no matter whether the execution of the child node is successful or failed, all the child nodes will be executed in sequence, and success will be returned. Select node has the concept of LOOP (n), which means to repeatedly execute

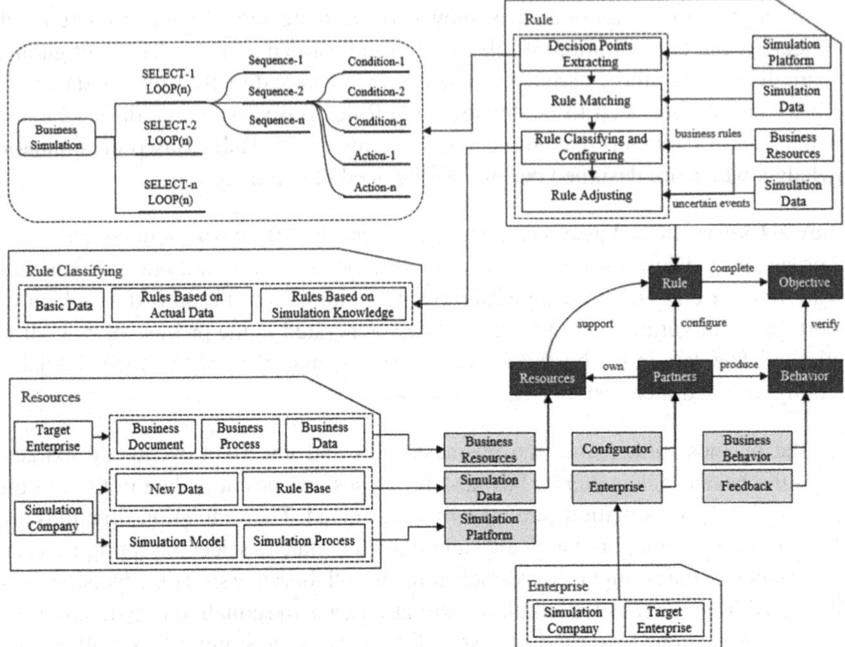


**Fig. 2.** Implementation method based on configuration framework

select node n times. (2) Sequence node: all the child nodes are executed in sequence, all of them succeed and return success. One node fails and stops traversing and returns failure. (3) Condition node: judge the condition, and the configuration rules correspond to the Condition node. (4) Action node: execute action according to the result of Condition node, which is the user's operation in the simulation platform.

The implementation methodology is goal-oriented methodology. In order to achieve the configuration goal, the configurator configures the rules according to the resources provided by the enterprise. After completing the new simulation teaching platform, business behavior and feedback are carried out to verify the rationality of the configuration rules.

## 4 Case of Simulation Rule Configuration

To better illustrate how the framework and implementing method described in Sect. 3 should be applied in real situations, a brief case of rule configuration was conducted in a business simulation rule configuration. In order to highlight the specific process of rule configuration, this case mainly illustrates the operation process of configuration dimension and simplifies the process of business dimension based on implementation methodology.

The background of this case is the simulation of the sales business of an outdoor products company. The following example calls the enterprise the target enterprise, which provides the business process of sales business, sales data, commodity information and supplier information. The cooperative enterprise of this example also includes a simulation company which has a simulation configuration platform. The platform can meet most of the requirements of business simulation configuration. However, the configuration of simulation rules is cumbersome, and it is difficult for people outside the company to understand.

By investigating the relevant business documents and processes of the target company's sales business, it is found that the sales business to be simulated by the target company is similar to the new retail simulation. Simulation company provides necessary resources. Based these resources and the representation method of the decision points of collaborative situations proposed in Sect. 3, the decision points of new retail simulation are sorted out, some of which are shown in Fig. 3.

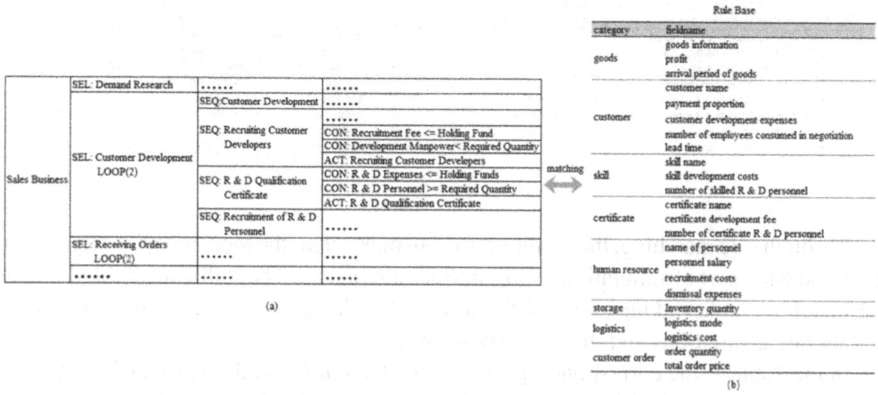

| | | | |
|---|---|---|---|
| Sales Business | SEL: Demand Research | …… | …… |
| | SEL: Customer Development LOOP(2) | SEQ:Customer Development | …… |
| | | SEQ: Recruiting Customer Developers | …… |
| | | | CON: Recruitment Fee <= Holding Fund |
| | | | CON: Development Manpower< Required Quantity |
| | | | ACT: Recruiting Customer Develepers |
| | | SEQ: R & D Qualification Certificate | CON: R & D Expenses <= Holding Funds |
| | | | CON: R & D Personnel >= Required Quantity |
| | | | ACT: R & D Qualification Certificate |
| | | SEQ: Recruitment of R & D Personnel | …… |
| | SEL: Receiving Orders LOOP(2) | …… | …… |
| | …… | …… | …… |

(a)

matching

Rule Base

| category | fieldname |
|---|---|
| goods | goods information<br>profit<br>arrival period of goods |
| customer | customer name<br>payment proportion<br>customer development expenses<br>number of employees consumed in negotiation<br>lead time |
| skill | skill name<br>skill development costs<br>number of skilled R & D personnel |
| certificate | certificate name<br>certificate development fee<br>number of certificate R & D personnel |
| human resource | name of personnel<br>personnel salary<br>recruitment costs<br>dismissal expenses |
| storage | Inventory quantity |
| logistics | logistics mode<br>logistics cost |
| customer order | order quantity<br>total order price |

(b)

**Fig. 3.** Decision points based on collaborative situations

Figure 3(a) shows any situations of the new retail sales business. (1) Demand Research is used to find suitable customers for the enterprise. (2) Customer Development is used to develop the selected customers. (3) Customer Order is used to receive orders. SEL is Select Node. Seq is the Sequence Node. Con is Condition Node. Act is Action Node. The relationship between nodes and node traversal rules are based on the definition in Sect. 3. The attribute of LOOP (2) is given to customer development to complete the operation of customer development.

Condition Node in the figure is the premise of Action Node operation. For example, in the "SEQ: R & D Qualification Certificate" node, the premise of "ACT: R & D Qualification Certificate" is "CON: R & D Expenses < = Holding Funds" and "CON: R & D Personnel > = Required Quantity". If any of the conditions is not met, the "ACT: R & D Qualification Certificate" cannot be issued. The next process is to traverse the "SEQ: R & D Personnel Recruitment". After completion, because "SEL: Customer Development" has the attribute Loop (2), it is necessary to traverse this SEL node again. The rule corresponds to the Condition Node.

After the extraction of the decision points of collaborative situations, configuration rules need to be matched. Figure 3(b) shows the related rules in the rule base. These existing rule tables are goods, customer, skills which is needed to sell or process a commodity, certificate which is provided by the enterprise for selling products, human resource, warehouse, logistics and customer order.

**Table 1.** Simulation rule matching

| Decision Point | | Category | Rule Information |
|---|---|---|---|
| Con: the profit of needed goods meets the expectation | >> | goods | Goods information |
| Con: the profit of needed goods meets the expectation | >> | goods | profit |
| Con: customer lead time meets expectations | >> | customer | Lead time |
| Con: customer lead time meets expectations | >> | customer | Customer name |
| Con: customer payment ratio meets expectations | >> | customer | Payment proportion |
| Con: the delivery period of goods meets the demand of delivery period | >> | goods | Arrival period of goods |
| Con: Sales / processing skills | >> | skill | Skill name |
| Con: development cost < = capital held | >> | skill | Development cost |
| Con: R & D personnel > = required quantity | >> | skill | Number of R & D personnel |
| Con: recruitment fee < = holding fund | >> | human resources | R & D personnel recruitment costs |
| Con: recruitment fee < = holding fund | >> | human resources | Cost of R & D personnel dismissal |
| Con: the salary of R & D personnel meets the expectation | >> | human resources | Salary of R & D personnel |
| Con: development cost < = capital held | >> | customer | Development cost |
| Con: own R & D certificate corresponding to the market | >> | certificate | Certificate name |
| Con: the number of employees needed to develop the market | >> | human resources | Employee name |
| Con: development manpower < required quantity | >> | human resources | Market developer |
| Con: R & D expenses < = holding funds | >> | certificate | Development cost |
| Con: R & D personnel > = required quantity | >> | certificate | Number of R & D personnel |
| Con: item stock > = scheduled quantity | >> | storage | Inventory quantity |
| Con: mode of transportation > target expectation (cost + timeliness) | >> | logistics | Logistics mode |
| Con: mode of transportation > target expectation (cost + timeliness) | >> | logistics | Logistics cost |
| Con: delivery time < = deadline | >> | customer | Lead time |
| Con: delivery time < = deadline | >> | order | Order quantity |

Through rule matching, the configurator can make clear the meaning of configuration rules and what part of simulation configuration rules act on. The following Table 1 shows the matching table (taking some of them for example) between the decision points of collaborative situations and the simulation rules.

In the Table 1, the corresponding rules in the Condition Node are extracted. Among them, the information in the black dotted circle is the Condition Node and the corresponding rules in the example of decision points given above. A condition may correspond to one or more rules.

Rule Classifying and Configuring

| category | fieldname | value |
|---|---|---|
| basic data | Commodity information | pizex |
| | Customer name | China Mobile |
| | Name of personnel | Key Account Manager |
| Rules Based on actual data | Arrival period of goods | 1 |
| | Cost of goods | 1071.14 |
| | Selling price | 1969.54 |
| | Lead time | 3 |
| | Payment proportion | 30%,50%,20% |
| | Development cost | 120000 |
| | Personnel salary | 6000 |
| | Recruitment costs | 15000 |
| | Dismissal expenses | 9000 |
| | Inventory quantity | 5000 |
| | Logistics mode | Air transport |
| | Logistics cost | 1000 |
| | Number | 275 |
| | Total price | 541475 |
| Rules Based on simulation knowledge | Skill development costs | 9000 |
| | Customer development expenses | 9000 |
| | Number of skilled R & D personnel | 2 |
| | Certificate name | Quality management system certification |
| | Skill name | Construction of environmental management system |
| | Number of certificate R & D personnel | 1 |
| | Name of personnel | R & D management |

(a)

Rule Adjusting

<table>
<tr><th>Fieldname</th><th>Adjustment</th></tr>
<tr><td>Payment proportion</td><td>30%,50%,20%|40%,40%,20%</td></tr>
<tr><td>range of demand quantity</td><td>250-300</td></tr>
<tr><td>range of demand price</td><td>89%-100%</td></tr>
</table>

(b)

**Fig. 4.** Rules configuration and adjustment

As shown in Fig. 4, the sorted rules are classified and configured. Figure 4(a) shows the classification of rules. Rules are designed based on the business data provided by the target company. Figure 4(b) shows the adjustment of rules based on uncertain events. The payment proportion of customers is random, so two payment proportions of "30%, 50%, 20" and "40%, 40%, 20%" are set. For the users of the platform, less initial payment from customers may lead to the rupture of the enterprise cash chain. There may be differences in the quantity and price of goods that customers need in different periods. Therefore, the value of demand quantity and demand price is set as interval value to simulate the real situation.

This case illustrates the three-layer framework and the implementation methodology of rule configuration by configuring the sales business of a target enterprise (the sales business of the target enterprise is similar to the sales business of the simulation company's new retail simulation). Configurators can meet the requirements of rule configuration in a more flexible way.

## 5 Conclusion

Faced with the simulation requirements of multiple businesses, configuration of simulation rules is particularly important. A rule configuration framework and corresponding configuration implementation methodology are proposed. It can meet various learning tasks such as cognition of operation and management complexity, reverse engineering of demand analysis and design, design and configuration of intelligent industrial interconnection system, and data analysis of operation and management behavior.

The main innovation of this paper is to extract the decision points of collaborative situations from the simulation platform, and find the rule source of the simulation platform on this basis. Combined with the three-layer framework and configuration methodology, it provides a reference idea for rapid configuration of rules. The future work will focus on the design of components and constraints of configuration platform and the development of configuration platform.

**Acknowledgements.** The presented research works have been supported by "the National Natural Science Foundation of China" (61972029).

## References

1. Benbya, H., Nan, N., Tanriverdi, H., Yoo, Y.: Complexity and information systems research in the emerging digital world. MIS Q. **44**(1), 1–17 (2020)
2. Borrajo, F., et al.: SIMBA: a simulator for business education and research. Decis. Support Syst. **48**, 498–506 (2010)
3. Foronda, C.L., Fernandez-Burgos, M., Nadeau, C., Kelley, C.N., Henry, M.N.: Virtual simulation in nursing education: a systematic review spanning 1996 to 2018. Simul. Healthc. **15**(1), 46–54 (2020)
4. Zhang, L.: Design and practice of virtual simulation experiment teaching center for modern enterprise business operation. In: Deng, D. (ed.) ACSS 2015. Advances in Social and Behavioral Sciences, vol. 15, pp. 65–70. Singapore Management and Sports Science Institute, Paris (2015)

5. Ren, B., Zhang, S.: Knowledge acquisition from simulation data to product configuration rules. Adv. Mater. Res. **308–310**, 77–82 (2011). https://doi.org/10.4028/www.scientific.net/AMR.308-310.77
6. Chen, Z., Wang, L.Y.: Adaptable product configuration system based on neural network. Int. J. Prod. Res. **47**, 5037–5066 (2009). https://doi.org/10.1080/00207540802007571
7. Song, X.: Reusability implementation method of large-scale simulation model architecture. Mod. Navig. **7**(2), 131–136 (2016)
8. Yin, J.L., Li, D.Y., Peng, Y.H.: Knowledge acquisition from metal forming simulation. Int. Adv. Manuf. Technol. **29**, 279–286 (2006)
9. Fornasiero, R., Macchion, L., Vinelli, A.: Supply chain configuration towards customization: a comparison between small and large series production. IFAC-PapersOnLine **48**(3), 1428–1433 (2015)
10. Jahangirian, M., Eldabi, T., Naseer, A., Stergioulas, L.K., Young, T.: Simulation in manufacturing and business: A review. Eur. J. Oper. Res. **203**, 1–13 (2010)
11. Musselwhite, C.: University executive education gets real. Training and Development Magazine **6**, 57–59 (2006)
12. Thompson, J., White, S., Chapman, S.: Virtual patients as a tool for training pre-registration pharmacists and increasing their preparedness to practice: A qualitative study. PLoS One **15**(8) (2020). https://doi.org/10.1371/journal.pone.0238226
13. Sahi, P.K., Mishra, D., Singh, T.: Medical education amid the covid-19 pandemic. Indian Pediatr. **57**(7), 652–657 (2020). https://doi.org/10.1007/s13312-020-1894-7
14. Gareyeva, E.A., Dubinina, E.: The ⟨Training Firm⟩ as a Way of Implementing a System- and Activity-Based Approach to Teaching in Higher Education Institutions. Tomsk State Univ. **457**, 175–186 (2020)
15. Hamalainen, R.: Designing and evaluating collaboration in a virtual game environment for vocational learning. Comput. Educ. **50**(1), 98–109 (2008)
16. Sauve, L., Renaud, L., Kaufman, D., Marquis, J.S.: Distinguishing between games and simulations: A systematic review. Educ. Technol. Soc. **10**(3), 247–256 (2007)
17. Benaben, F., Li, J., Koura, I., Montreuil, B., Lauras, M., Mu, W., et al.: A tentative framework for risk and opportunity detection in a collaborative environment based on data interpretation. In: Proceedings of the 52nd Hawaii International Conference on System Sciences, pp. 3056–3065. ScholarSpace, Hawaii (2019). http://hdl.handle.net/10125/59742.
18. Dromey, R.G.: From requirements to design: formalizing the key steps. In: Cerone, A. and Lindsay, P. (eds.) First International Conference on Software Engineering and Formal Methods, Proceedings. pp. 2–11 (2003)

# A Federated Simulation Framework for Cross-organisational Processes

Rushan Arshad(✉), Paul Ton de Vrieze, and Lai Xu

Department of Computing and Lnformatics, Faculty of Science and Technology, Bournemouth University, Talbot Campus, Bournemouth B12 5BB, UK
{arshadr,pdvrieze,lxu}@bournemouth.ac.uk

**Abstract.** Simulation is a significant tool that can be used to evaluate, monitor and enhance the processes and to predict the behaviour of a system in a particular scenario. Collaborative processes involving multiple organisations are becoming important in the changing landscape of the manufacturing industry towards industry 4.0. Simulating these processes require an independent and distributed execution because of the privacy concerns of partner organisations and the reusability of existing simulators. In this paper, we propose a simulation framework based on a federated approach for the simulation of collaborative processes. The federated approach enables the simulation of parts of the processes from multiple organisations by combining independent simulators through a common interface. The common interface is responsible for the synchronisation of all the simulators within the federation. The framework will be evaluated using an industrial case study of textile manufacturing using Virtual Organisations.

**Keywords:** Industry 4.0 · Simulation · Federated Simulation · Collaborative Processes

## 1 Introduction

The modern industry 4.0 enabled landscape provides for a rich and complex organisation of business. For some products, the design may be done by one organisation, and the production by another, where distribution and marketing are managed by yet two other organisations. At the same time, the customer's experience should be of the same quality as if interacting with only one organisation. While the resulting collaborative networks may be able to handle dynamic market conditions better, the networks themselves are more complex to understand. This is exacerbated by the independence of the organisations making up the collaboration.

Where monitoring of key performance indicators is a key tool in the management of processes [1], it is only a post-hoc tool. Instead, simulation of the processes can allow for a prediction of the indicators ahead of time. The use of simulation tools takes various forms and complexities, from anomaly detection to a 'what-if' analysis [2, 3]. All without disrupting the actual system that is in place.


Published by Springer Nature Switzerland AG 2021
L. M. Camarinha-Matos et al. (Eds.): PRO-VE 2021, IFIP AICT 629, pp. 267–279, 2021.
https://doi.org/10.1007/978-3-030-85969-5_24

In the case of industrial systems, simulation requires specialist knowledge that is sometimes only available to the manufacturer of the devices involved. In other cases, the simulation is provided in relation to a Manufacturing Execution System (MES) that coordinates the manufacturing process. When looking at the broader business, the business processes surrounding manufacturing would also need to be simulated. Such simulation is not provided by a machine manufacturer or the MES. Given the complexity and variability involved in managing the different simulation models, it is not realistic to have this simulation done in a monolithic way. Instead, multiple simulators are likely to need to cooperate in simulating business processes involving manufacturing aspects.

Cross-organisational processes introduce an increased complexity. In addition to this, the desire to keep a local control of processes would likely increase the frequency of change to the processes. Overall, this leads to processes that are harder to make, keep correct and be optimised. Simulation can help in addressing this complexity and variability by identifying any errors and anomalies before deployment. After deployment, a comparison of the simulation results with actual performance can be used to identify potential process issues.

Cross-organisational processes involve independent actors with independent, but integrated, processes. To be able to accurately simulate such integrated processes, it is important that the simulation is able to simulate the integrated processes in addition to the integration. At the same time, for various reasons (technical or business), it is desirable or unavoidable to have processes simulated independently. This combines with the need to have multiple simulators for the different process aspects for individual organisations. The solution to both issues is to use a federated simulation approach that allows for coordinating simulators to simulate the integrated outcomes in parallel with the integration of the actual processes.

For example, in the case of a just-in-time production chain, including a supplier of parts, an end manufacturer and a shipping provider, various processes would be involved in the production of a single end product. In the case of a sudden surge in the demand of the end product, the ability to produce the products is (also) limited by the production of the part, as well as by the shipping considerations. In part production, the pure production line capacity comes into play, but also staffing, maintenance and supply considerations. Overall, to determine how the potential increase in production could be realised and with what time frame would require simulating the business and manufacturing processes of all three parties in a way that mirrors the coordination present in the actual production process.

Federated simulation has been used in various contexts, and, in particular, it has been explored by the US armed forces in a military context [4]. A later example can be found [5] in the context of multi-modal transportation. While this clearly shows that federated simulation is feasible and valuable, the work is limited in genericity. In this paper, we address this by proposing, from the context of collaborative industry 4.0 processes, a generic framework for federated simulation.

In contrast to the existing approaches, the proposed framework is capable of simulating collaborative processes involving multiple organisations using existing simulators. The simulators are a part of a federation and a simulation coordinator is used to synchronise and facilitate the communication between the simulators. This enables interoperability while also maintaining the maximum confidentiality of the data being shared between the simulators.

## 2 Related Work and Simulation Requirements

The design of the federated simulation framework requires an understanding of simulation approaches (especially when applied in industry and business process contexts); the purposes of the simulation; collaborative manufacturing; and existing federated simulation approaches. These will be discussed below.

### 2.1 Approaches to Simulation

Simulation is used for various purposes. Depending on these purposes, different techniques to simulation are the most effective. For example, physical processes, such as weather prediction, are often best simulated using *System Dynamics*. For other problems, techniques, such as Discrete Event Simulation (DES), Discrete Time Step (DTS) and Agent Based Techniques (ABS), are used.

DES simulates a system based on discrete events that occur at different time intervals (which can vary for each event), whereas, in DTS, the time interval is fixed. On the other hand, ABS consist of Agents which are programmed to do specific tasks by modelling their behaviour. Agents can also interact with other systems and can respond to the dynamic changes to their environment [6].

In both the manufacturing process and business process contexts, the most commonly used technique is Discrete Event Simulation. In manufacturing it is used in almost every stage, starting from facility design and general system design [7, 8] to the material handling stage [9, 10]. As DES is fundamentally a detail-oriented simulation paradigm, it has also been used for operational scheduling (resources, tasks) [11].

Discrete Event Simulation differs from the other techniques in the fundamental way that it is based upon a sequential processing of events in the simulation context. In contrast, the other approaches tend to use computation resources linearly with the simulated time duration. As such, discrete event simulation can be more efficient where it is appropriate. More significantly, the other approaches can, with some restrictions, be mapped to allow for integration with an event-based approach.

### 2.2 Simulation Evaluation

Simulation models and frameworks are developed to model a system's behaviour and to predict the performance of a system in a specific scenario. Simulation results and their analysis determine how a system is expected to perform in a particular point in time. Hence, the accuracy of such a simulation model is significant.

A simulation model or framework answers particular questions about a problem or application. The purpose of the evaluation or validation is to find out whether or not the simulation model is capable of answering these questions with a reasonable accuracy (which should be determined prior to the development of the model). If the simulation model answers the questions reasonably accurately, then it is said to be acceptable.

Expert opinions can be used from a third party, called Independent Verification and Validation (IV and V), to evaluate a simulation model. The models are evaluated under different parameters by the independent experts. A simulation framework is then applied on the case studies from industry to evaluate its accuracy and applications in real-world scenarios. Usually, a diverse set of case studies is used from different backgrounds to make the evaluation accurate [12].

Another approach being used in the evaluation of simulations is the structural walkthrough. In a structural walkthrough traces of events and states in a specific use case are also used to show that the logic and structure of a framework are valid. The logical and structured walkthrough of a conceptual model consists of a formal explanation and field experts can then check the model correctness. The traces of a conceptual model depict the step-by-step process of the execution and then the correctness of the logic is determined [12].

There are other validation techniques like computerised model verification, operational validity, comparison with other models, statistical validation (type I and type II errors), predictive validation and the Turing Test etc. [12].

### 2.3 Simulation in Collaborative Manufacturing

In terms of collaborative manufacturing, simulation is used in scheduling in order to optimise production schedules and resource utilization [13]. Supply chain management involving multiple organizations also uses simulation to enhance the production and delivery times [14] and to predict the behaviour of the system under varying demands. DES is commonly used to simulate such systems and these simulations are mostly used to optimise specific parts of the processes, for example production lead time, resource cost etc., and does not entirely focus on a complete simulation of parts of the processes that are involving multiple organisations [15].

In collaborative manufacturing, the coordination of the parts of the processes with time is significant because, otherwise, constituent simulators would be running at different times – any communication about the state or events would be invalid and the data and operations would be inconsistent. Traditional (non-federated) simulations do not focus on the coordination mechanism that helps in enhancing the communication and integration of various parts of the processes. This integration results in improving the accuracy of the simulation and the enhancement of the processes.

The requirements for simulation in different organisations can vary. For example, to simulate a specific part of a collaborative process, details, such as the resource cost, are not required but in another part of the process, it is necessary to simulate the resource cost. Therefore, different simulators with multiple simulation techniques must be used. Moreover, the data that is being used by multiple organisations can be heterogeneous, and thus it would not be feasible for a monolithic simulation model to incorporate this data.

Traditional simulation techniques, like DES, Agent Based Simulation (ABS) and System Dynamics (SD) and their applications in the industry, are largely based upon monolithic models. As such, they have inherent limitations when it comes to cross-organisational processes. The different simulation models need to be integrated in such a way that simulators from different organisational boundaries can communicate with each other and share results so that the overall simulation becomes reliable and complete.

### 2.4 Existing Approaches in Federated Simulation

Federated Simulation enables the combination of more than one simulation model and incorporates the feedback loops of simultaneously executed simulations [5]. It also enables the communication of operational characteristics and functions of one model with another where there is a probability of any dependency, making the overall simulation more accurate. Federated simulation is preferred because existing simulators can be used to simulate different types of functions/processes.

High Level Architecture (HLA) is a standard [16] that has been developed for simulation interoperability between different simulators by the US Military [4]. HLA consists of some basic rules that govern the interaction of the components of the HLA federation. The components include simulators (federates) and the interface that is responsible for an efficient communication between the federates.

The HLA allows different simulators to be combined in a federation where each simulator has its own data and configurations. A common interface is used to provide communication between these simulators to achieve a simulation objective. For example, multiple simulators using discrete event and discrete time step simulation are combined in a federation to simulate a transportation system [5].

One of the goals of the framework is to support the validation of processes through simulation. Where the processes using a single-instance are long-lived and complex, rather than those using many small instances, and they require simulating processes using a monte-carlo simulation approach on the level of the federation (not only for individual simulators). There are many ways in which component simulators can be adjusted, requiring the framework to be designed accordingly.

## 3 Simulation Framework

A generic framework based on federated simulation (Fig. 1) consists of a federated simulation runtime that includes different simulators as part of a federation. These simulators are equipped to simulate various processes, connected through a generic component which is named the simulation coordinator. Each simulator has a local data normalisation component which handles the data interoperability between the simulators. Each of the components within the federation is provided with initial configurations, and, at the end of a simulation run, the data collation module combines the data from the simulators for a comprehensive analysis for the decision support. The working of individual components of the framework is described in the subsequent parts of this section.

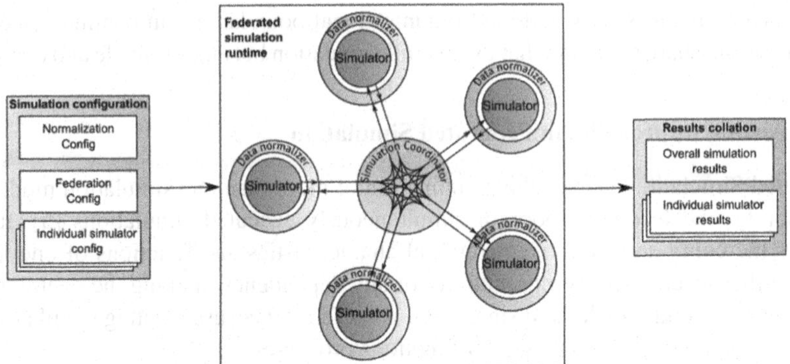


**Fig. 1.** Conceptual framework for federated simulation

### 3.1 Top Level Design

Core components of the proposed framework include the initial configuration, simulation coordinator, and the simulators consisting of event and state sharing through the coordinator.

There are three types of configurations: Normalization Configuration, which provides data for the data normalizer to execute its tasks. This is specified through the *initial configuration*. As an example, the common format in which all data needs to be converted before transmission. Federation Configuration provides instructions for the simulation Coordinator whereas individual simulators are also provided with data and instructions to execute their own tasks. These instructions and configurations initiate the simulation process.

The *simulation coordinator* is responsible for the synchronisation of the federated simulators. The queries related to the state of one simulator over another simulator go through the simulation coordinator. Any change in an event or the state of any simulator triggers the simulation coordinator. For example, if a simulator wants to know the status of a resource from the Resource Status simulator (an example simulator), then it sends a query to the simulation coordinator and then the simulation coordinator communicates with the required simulator to get the result (Fig. 1).

*Synchronisation* is an important part of the simulation framework. Synchronisation is responsible for synchronising the time and state of every simulator within the federation. This helps in maintaining an accurate behaviour of the simulation at a particular time. The synchronisation of simulators enables consistency in the time and state of each simulator and individual simulators are consistent with the time of the coordinator. After the execution of certain events, each simulator time is jumped forward to match the coordinator.

**Framework Assumption**

Each simulator has its own state and time which can be forwarded to any point in time for its synchronisation.

**Algorithm 1** describes how the synchronisation works for the framework given in Fig. 1. For each simulator (S), an initial state is initialised as $s_i$ and the time taken for each event to occur is represented by $t$.

$S$ represents the set of simulators. If there is an event(s) $E$ available to execute, then the event, which is the earliest in the queue to be executed, will be preferred and the execution of that event will start. After one event, the next event in the queue will be executed. There can be multiple types of events, for example Information Event, Query Event, Notification Event etc. If the event that is to be executed is an Information Event, then the subscribed simulators to that event will be notified and updated with the data from that particular event. Similarly, the simulator generating the query event will be updated with relevant data.

After a certain time T, the simulators are synchronised to the same time by the coordinator. All the simulators within the federation are forwarded to a common point in time. When a process or a part of the processes is executed, the state of the simulator is changed as well. The states of the simulators are also updated after each event.

The synchronisation in a simulation coordinator plays a vital role in the whole simulation scenario. The consistency, accuracy and completeness of a simulation depend on how well the simulators are synchronised; otherwise, the prediction of the working of a system at a particular point in time will not be accurate.

The simulators within the federation *share state and event* data based on the type of communication that is required at a particular time. This data is shared through the simulation coordinator.

The simulators can share the events with each other depending on their respective requirements. *Event sharing* is important in the case where one simulator's execution is dependent on an event from another simulator. A Publish-Subscribe mechanism provides a suitable solution for event sharing because simulators can subscribe to events from a particular simulator based on its requirements. Each simulator has a list of events that it has a subscription for; for example, one simulator is subscribed to all events from another one, whereas it also has a subscription for all the events related to the order of delivery from another simulator.

**Algorithm 1**: Working of Simulation Coordinator

```
S: A set of Simulators
T: Current Time
E: Event Types
while True do
  events: (T,E),S) = ∪_s^S(s.nextEvent, s)
  if events = ∅ then
    ((nextT, nextE), nextS) = events.firstBy(t ← ((t, e), s))
  end if
  messages = [];
  for s ∈ S do
    if s = nextS then
      messages = s.execute(nextE)
    else
      s.progressTo(nextT)
    end if
  end for
  for message ∈ messages do
    if message ∈ Queries then
      message.source.queryResult(message.dest.query(message))
    else if message ∈ Notifications then
      message.dest.notify(message)
    else if message is Broadcast then
      for d ∈ destinationsFor(message) do
        d.notify (message)
      end for
    else if message is Subscribe then
      message.dest.subscribe(message)
    end if
  end for
end while
```

The simulators are also able to *share states* with each other through the simulation coordinator. When a simulator wants to know the state of another simulator, for example, due to the inter-dependencies between them, it can make a request through the simulation coordinator and the resultant state value is provided to the corresponding simulator through the simulation coordinator (Algorithm 1).

*Data Normalization* supports the exchange of the data between the simulators and also combines the data in a common format (for example XML). Whenever data is transferred from a simulator, it goes through the data normalizer to convert it into a format which is consistent throughout the system. This enables the communication of data between different parts of the federation.

The *results collation* module collects the data from individual simulators and produces the results based on the analysis of the individual as well as the combined reports. The results produced provide support for dynamic scheduling, machine performance and decision support to enhance the processes and system within the industry 4.0 framework.

### 3.2 Framework Refinements

The proposed simulation framework is equipped with refinements like the publish and subscribe mechanism and cross-simulator resource allocation. These refinements are significant improvements in the implementation of the overall simulation system.

A *publish and subscribe* mechanism is used to share the events and data between the simulators. A simulator can subscribe to a set of events from different simulators based on the requirements. A simulator can also publish the events which are required by the other simulators within the federation.

*Allocation of resources* is an important part of collaborative manufacturing where resources are being shared by multiple organisations or between different departments within the same organisation. State Object (Vacant or Busy) can be used to allocate resources. If a resource is required, the status of the resource is checked through the simulation coordinator and then the resource is allocated accordingly. A complete simulator for this purpose is not necessary.

## 4 Evaluation of Simulation Framework

To evaluate the proposed federated simulation framework, a case study from literature is used. Section 4.1 describes this case, after which Sect. 4.2 applies the framework to the case.

The proposed federated simulation framework is evaluated in this section using an industrial case study derived from the literature. The business case, as well as the details of an application of the simulation framework in context of the use case in consideration, is discussed.

### 4.1 Description of the Case Study

The case study to evaluate the framework is derived from [17] with some modifications. The case in consideration involves two companies (Company A and Company B for anonymity) which collaborate to deliver an order for thousands of school uniforms. Both companies belong to the textile industry. Company A specialises in women's clothing and fabrics with the state-of-the-art facility for sample production and highly customised products. Company A also has a broader value chain consisting of modelling, design, production and delivery. Company B specialises in generic clothing fabrics (particularly synthetic fibre fabrics) and is one of the largest exporters to the USA.

There are two types of product that are produced. One is Engineered to Order (ETO) and the other is Customised to Order (CTO). ETO is based on specific customer requirements with particular design and production specifics, whereas CTO refers to mass customisation; for example, a type of product ordered by a number of companies.

## 4.2 Applying Framework to a Case Study

The two companies, Company A and Company B reach an agreement to form a Virtual Organisation (VO) in which each partner has separate responsibilities. Company A has expertise in ETO, and so the highly customised orders are fulfilled by company A and for mass customisation, like the uniform, orders are executed by company B.

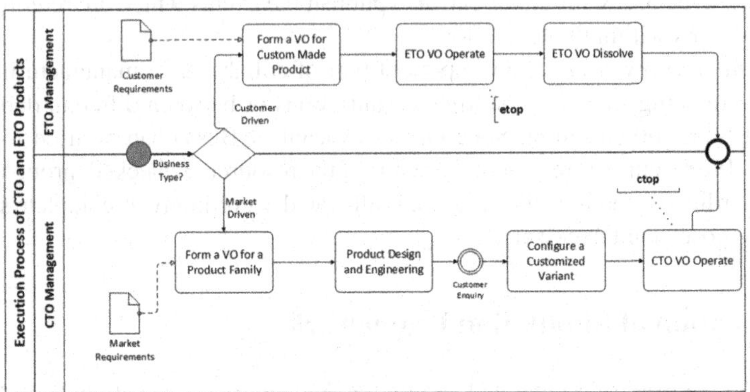


**Fig. 2.** Case study process

Two separate simulators are used within a federated simulation environment to simulate the processes in both companies. One simulator deals with the ETO products and the other simulates the production of the CTO products. The communication between the simulators is done through the simulation coordinator. An example of the process for this case, depicting the execution of CTO and ETO, is depicted by Fig. 2.

Events, states and data are shared between the simulators at different stages as required by the processes. For example, data regarding the customisations for a part of the order is shared between the simulators and then when the customisations are finished, the state and events data regarding this process is also shared between the simulators through the coordinator. State transitions within a simulation run are shown in Table 1.

The *events* that are executed by *Actors* are *cbt* (check business type), *ctop* (CTO Process), *etop* (ETO Process), and *start*. The time $\cdot t_i$ s is used for time just before *t*, whereas $t_i \bullet$ is used for a time just after *t*. Each simulator has its own time and after a certain time period (execution of events), the local time of simulators is synchronised with the coordinator time.

The transitions of state and time in Table 1 show the step by step execution of different parts of processes. Simulator 1 (*s1*) is responsible for executing ETO, whereas CTO processes are executed by Simulator 2 (*s2*). These step by step transitions show that the proposed framework is applicable to the case in consideration.

**Table 1.** Transition of states

| Time C | Events | Actor | Action | time $s_1$ | time $s_2$ |
|---|---|---|---|---|---|
| $\cdot t_0$ | | C | Init | $\cdot t_0$ | $\cdot t_0$ |
| $\cdot t_0$ | $(t_0, s_1, start), (t_0, s_2, start)$ | C | first | $\cdot t_0$ | $\cdot t_0$ |
| $\cdot t_0$ | | $s_1$ | *start* | $t_0\cdot$ | ... |
| $\cdot t_0$ | $(t_1, s_1, cbt), (t_0, s_2, start)$ | C | first | ... | ... |
| $\cdot t_0$ | | $s_2$ | *start* | ... | $t_0\cdot$ |
| $t_0\cdot$ | | C | Sync | ... | ... |
| $t_0\cdot$ | $(t_1, s_1, cbt), (t_5, s_2, ctop)$ | C | First | $t_0\cdot$ | $t_0\cdot$ |
| $\cdot t_1$ | | $s_1$ | *cbt* | $t_1\cdot$ | ... |
| $t_1\cdot$ | – | C | Sync | ... | $t_1\cdot$ |
| $t_1\cdot$ | $(t_2, s_1, etop), (t_6, s_2, ctop)$ | C | First | $t_1\cdot$ | $\cdot t_1$ |
| $t_1\cdot$ | $(t_2, s_1, etop), (t_6, s_2, ctop)$ | C | first | $t_1\cdot$ | $\cdot t_1$ |
| $\cdot t_2$ | | $s_1$ | *etop* | $t_2\cdot$ | $\cdot t_2$ |
| $t_2\cdot$ | – | C | Sync | ... | $t_2\cdot$ |
| $t_2\cdot$ | $(t_3, s_1, cbt), (t_7, s_2, ctop)$ | C | First | $t_2\cdot$ | $t_2\cdot$ |
| $\cdot t_2$ | | $s_1$ | *etop* | $t_2\cdot$ | $\cdot t_2$ |
| $t_2\cdot$ | – | C | Sync | ... | $t_2\cdot$ |
| $t_2\cdot$ | $(t_3, s_1, cbt), (t_7, s_2, ctop)$ | C | First | $t_2\cdot$ | $t_2\cdot$ |
| $\cdot t_3$ | | $s_1$ | *cbt* | $t_3$ | ... |
| $t_3\cdot$ | – | C | Sync | ... | $t_3\cdot$ |
| $t_3\cdot$ | $(t_4, s_1, etop), (t_8, s_2, ctop)$ | C | First | $t_3\cdot$ | $\cdot t_1$ |
| $\cdot t_4$ | | $s_2$ | *ctop* | $t_3\cdot$ | $t_4\cdot$ |
| $t_4\cdot$ | – | C | Sync | $t_4\cdot$ | ... |
| $\cdot t_5$ | | C | End | $\cdot t_5$ | $\cdot t_5$ |

## 5 Conclusion and Future Challenges

Simulation is a significant tool to detect errors at design time and is used to predict the behaviour of a system at a specific point in time. In the context of modern industrial systems, especially those processes that are involve multiple organisations, simulation becomes more challenging due to the heterogenity of processes and the data involved. We propose a generic simulation framework based on a federated simulation, which allows for simulating different parts of the process in separate but distributed simulators in parallel. This federation helps an organisation to share only the necessary details with other simulators, protecting the confidentiality of the data of the different organisations that are involved in the execution of the processes. A simulation coordinator is responsible for coordinating the data exchanges and the synchronisation of the simulators.

An industrial case study of a textile sector was used to demonstrate the function of the working of the framework.

While, overall, the framework is sufficient to support a coordinated simulation there are also limitations. While information sharing can be atomic, based upon a full order of events, the ordering of events is not defined by the coordinator. As such, different simulations of the same configuration could be ordered differently and have different results. The framework can apply various optimisations, in particular, for a repeated simulation of the same scenario. In addition, resources would benefit from special handling.

**Acknowledgements.** This research is partially funded by the State Key Research and Development Program of China (2017YFE0118700) and it is part of the FIRST project which has received funding from the European Union's Horizon 2020 research and innovation programme under the Marie Skłodowska-Curie grant agreement No. 734599.

## References

1. Dumas, M., La Rosa, M., Mendling, J., Reijers, H.A.: Fundamentals of Business Process Management. Springer, Heidelberg (2018). https://doi.org/10.1007/978-3-662-56509-4
2. Vieira, A.A.C., Dias, L.S., Santos, M.Y., Pereira, G., Oliveira, J.A.: Setting an industry 4.0 research and development agenda for simulation – a literature review. Int. J. Simul. Model. **17**, 377–390 (2018)
3. Rodi, B.: Industry 4.0 and the new simulation modelling paradigm. Organizacija **50**, 193–207 (2017)
4. Sung, C., Kim, T.G.: Framework for simulation of hybrid systems: interoperation of discrete event and continuous simulators using HLA/RTI. In: 2011 IEEE Workshop on Principles of Advanced and Distributed Simulation, pp. 1–8. IEEE (2011)
5. Wall, T.A., Rodgers, M.O., Fujimoto, R., Hunter, M.P.: A federated simulation method for multi-modal transportation systems: combining a discrete event-based logistics simulator and a discrete time-step-based traffic microsimulator. Simulation **91**, 148–163 (2015)
6. Büth, L., Broderius, N., Herrmann, C., Thiede, S.: Introducing agent-based simulation of manufacturing systems to industrial discrete-event simulation tools, pp. 1141–1146 (2017)
7. Greasley, A.: Using simulation for facility design: a case study. Simul. Model. Pract. Theory **16**, 670–677 (2008)
8. Jagstam, M., Klingstam, P.: A handbook for integrating discrete event simulation as an aid in conceptual design of manufacturing systems, vol. 2, pp. 1940–1944 (2002)
9. Durieux, S., Pierreval, H.: Regression metamodeling for the design of automated manufacturing system composed of parallel machines sharing a material handling resource. Int. J. Prod. Econ. **89**, 21–30 (2004)
10. Hao, Q., Shen, W.: Implementing a hybrid simulation model for a Kanban-based material handling system. Robot. Comput.-Integr. Manuf. **24**, 635–646 (2008)
11. Koh, S.C.L., Saad, S.M.: MRP-controlled manufacturing environment disturbed by uncertainty. Robot. Comput.-Integr. Manuf. **19**, 157–171 (2003)
12. Sargent, R.G.: Verification and validation of simulation models. J. Simul. **7**, 12–24 (2013)
13. Holweg, M., Disney, S.M., Hines, P., Naim, M.M.: Towards responsive vehicle supply: a simulation-based investigation into automotive scheduling systems. J. Oper. Manag. **23**, 507–530 (2005)

14. Jung, J.Y., Blau, G., Pekny, J.F., Reklaitis, G.V., Eversdyk, D.: A simulation based optimization approach to supply chain management under demand uncertainty. Comput. Chem. Eng. **28**, 2087–2106 (2004)
15. Liotta, G., Kaihara, T., Stecca, G.: Optimization and simulation of collaborative networks for sustainable production and transportation. IEEE Trans. Ind. Inform. **12**, 417–424 (2014)
16. IEEE Standard for Modeling and Simulation (MS) High Level Architecture (HLA)– Framework and Rules. IEEE Std 1516-2010 (Revision of IEEE Std 1516-2000), pp. 1–38 (2010)
17. Carneiro, L., Shamsuzzoha, A.H.M., Almeida, R., Azevedo, A., Fornasiero, R., Ferreira, P.S.: Reference model for collaborative manufacturing of customised products: applications in the fashion industry. Prod. Plan. Control **25**, 1135–1155 (2014)

# Robust Optimization for Collaborative Distribution Network Design Problem

Islem Snoussi[1], Nadia Hamani[1(✉)], Nassim Mrabti[1], and Lyes Kermad[2]

[1] University of Picardie Jules Verne, 48 Rue d?Ostende, 02100 Saint Quentin, France
islem.snoussi@etud.u-picardie.fr, {nadia.hamani, nassim.mrabti}@u-picardie.fr

[2] University of Paris 8, 2 Rue de la Liberté, 93200 Saint-Denis, France
l.kermad@iut.univ-paris8.fr

**Abstract.** Collaboration is an interesting solution adopted to improve the levels of sustainability by massifying flows. In this study, we present a new design of a distribution network under uncertainties at two levels in a collaborative context. The proposed network includes suppliers who collaborate to deliver their products to retailers through common platforms. On the other hand, uncertainty is treated in terms of two parameters, namely demands and unit transportation costs. The different used models are validated and analysed by a case study. Computational results provided by the robust model and those given by the deterministic one are compared to evaluate the importance of uncertainty. The effects of uncertainty level on the optimal network configuration are also highlighted.

**Keywords:** Hub location problem · Horizontal collaboration · Sustainability · Robust optimization · Budget of uncertainty

## 1 Introduction

Nowadays, faced with high customer's demands, increasing transport costs and the drawbacks of Covid-19 health crisis on the market, companies find themselves in complex situations. Therefore, they must optimize their logistics operations by opting for a strategy that creates an efficient logistics system. According to [1, 2] and [3], the best solution that should be adopted to solve these problems is the integration of collaboration. In the literature, the latter can be Vertical (VC) or Horizontal (HC) [4]. Besides, [5] asserted that vertical collaboration takes place between partners who belong to the same logistic chain and are not at the same level. This type of collaboration is mainly limited to the sharing of information between partners, while in horizontal collaboration, also named ''pooling'', means and resources are shared between partners who are at the same level and do not belong to the same logistic chain [6]. In fact, most of the existing studies focused on

The original version of this chapter was revised: the order of authors has been corrected. The correction to this chapter is available at https://doi.org/10.1007/978-3-030-85969-5_76


Published by Springer Nature Switzerland AG 2021
L. M. Camarinha-Matos et al. (Eds.): PRO-VE 2021, IFIP AICT 629, pp. 280–288, 2021.
https://doi.org/10.1007/978-3-030-85969-5_25

VC. However, its performances can be improved only by pooling. HC involves massification of flows through concentrating certain flows on the same site to optimize the supply and distribution circuits. It allows increasing the frequency of delivery, augmenting service rate, improving the vehicle fill rate and, thus, reducing the logistics costs and the greenhouse gas (GHG) emissions. An important issue that arises while treating a Distribution Network Design Problem is how to cope with data uncertainty because the parameters of the logistic system are variable. For this reason, the deterministic approach is unfavourable to achieve the mission, such as for long-term strategic decisions like the location of hub facilities related to some parameters (e.g. demands, transportation costs, etc.). In cases where these parameters can be estimated, their probability distributions are determined by using stochastic programming techniques. However, in cases where the only available information is the specification of intervals containing the uncertain values of these parameters, the solution is the robust optimization techniques that can perform well even in the worst-case scenarios [7]. In this paper, we focus on the collaborative distribution network design problem incorporating demand and unit transportation costs uncertainties when the only available information is an interval of uncertainty.

The remainder of the paper is structured as follows. Section 2 is a literature review. Section 3 represents the problem description. Section 4 shows the results produced by each model. Finally, Sect. 5 is dedicated to the conclusion and our perspectives.

## 2 Literature Review

The distribution network design problem is known as the "Hub Location Problem" (HLP) or "Hub Median Problem" (HMP) [8]. The combination between this problem and the horizontal collaboration is still underdeveloped in the literature [6].

To our knowledge, only [1] dealt with this combination under uncertainties. They studied a robust capacitated hub location problem under the uncertainty of installation costs for two distribution networks. Their objective was to reduce the costs generated by transportation and hub installations treating three cases of collaboration and four cost-sharing strategies. Moreover, [9] examined the robust capacitated single allocation and multiple allocation hub location problems under the uncertainty of fixed setup cost and the capacity of each hub using a minimax regret model. The latter is used to minimize the setup and transportation costs. The authors showed that neglecting uncertainty can cause large losses and expenses. Furthermore, [7] introduced robust counterparts for uncapacitated multiple allocation HLP employing a budget uncertainty model. They presented three different cases of uncertain parameters, namely demands, and transportation costs. The third case was solved using a branch-and-cut algorithm implemented on a commercial solver. Also, [10] investigated the same problem and proposed a new approach to quantify the robustness of a solution in the presence of uncertainties as it is the case of uncertain demands. So, the approach developed by [11] is, now, considered as a special case. The research work aimed at minimising the transportation costs in the presence of uncertain flows and the model was solved using a heuristic approach which is the VNS (Variable Neighbourhood Search). However, [12] studied a modelling framework for stochastic Capacitated Multiple Allocation Hub Location Problem with multi-period, dealing with uncertain demands to minimize logistics costs. [13] proposed a robust optimization for multiple allocation hub location problem with uncertain demand flows and fixed setup costs. In their study, the level of conservatism was adjusted by an uncertainty budget. Authors also evaluated the transportation and setup costs and used benders decomposition and a hybrid heuristic approach to solve large scale problems. In addition, [14] introduced a robust uncapacitated multiple allocation hub location problem with uncertainty of demands, hub establishment fixed cost and inter hub flow discount factor by applying an uncertainty budget model employed to assess the costs generated by transportation and establishing hubs. The same problem was treated by [15], but with only uncertain demands by using a set of scenarios and assigning for each one a probability of occurrence. The problem was formulated as a nonlinear stochastic optimization problem to reduce the hub installation costs, expected transportation costs, and estimated absolute deviation of transportation costs. Besides, two Benders Decomposition strategies were suggested to solve the obtained mathematical model and then, results were compared to each other. Yet, [16] introduced a heuristic procedure for stochastic Uncapacitated r-Allocation p-Hub Location Problem under demand and cost uncertainties. They also developed a heuristic approach for the deterministic part. The objective of the study was to minimize the total cost by reducing the allocation and the transportation costs. [17] suggested a methodology for the stochastic design problem of two-stage distribution networks by integrating demand uncertainty.

In summary, most studies dealing with the uncertain distribution network design problem focused on the economic objective, by reducing logistics costs, and evaluated uncertainties related to the latter and the flows. In this paper, we examine the distribution network design problem with robust optimization to evaluate not only the economic dimension, but also the environmental one under demand and unit transportation costs uncertainties.

## 3 Problem Description

We cite, in the following sub-section, the objectives of the deterministic mathematical model and explain the uncertainty parameters.

### 3.1 Objectives of the Deterministic Model

The mathematical model proposed by [6] uses a three-echelon pooled distribution network represented in Fig. 1. This distribution network consists of suppliers who collaborate to deliver their products to retailers through shared warehouses and distribution centers. Two objective functions are investigated: the economic function, which minimizes logistics costs, and the environmental one that reduces $CO_2$ emissions from vehicles and hubs. The economic objective function, represented by (1), aims to lowering the various logistical costs related to transportation *CT*, storage *CS*, late delivery penalties *CD*, opening hubs *CO*, and handling CH. The transportation cost $CT^v{}_{ijt}$, represented by (2), depends on the quantity of product *p* transported between the origin *i* and the destination *j* ($q_{ijt}{}^{pv}$), the type of vehicle (capacity $Q^v$, unit costs of empty vehicles $C_0{}^v$ and full vehicles $C_q{}^v$), the travelled distance $d_{ij}$ and the number of the required vehicles or trips $N_{ijt}{}^v$. It is important to consider the delay in delivery when designing a pooled distribution network. Indeed, this delay directly affects the service rate and the retailer loyalty. In some above-mentioned studies, the opening cost was predefined since there is a list of capacity choices. However, in this research work, the cost of installing a hub *m* (*CWm*) depends on its area Am and the unit opening cost. It is given by Eq. (3). The area of the hub *m*, depending on the capacity of the hub *Cm*, the unit area of a pallet *AP* and a coefficient $\alpha$, is obtained by (4).

$$F_1 = CT + CS + CD + CO + CH. \tag{1}$$

$$CT^{v}_{ijt} = d_{ij}\left(\frac{Q^{v}.C^{v}_{q} - C^{v}_{o}}{Q^{v}}.\sum_{p} q^{pv}_{ijt} + 2.\,C^{v}_{o}.N^{v}_{ijt}\right); \forall t \in T_2, v \in V, (i,j) \in A. \tag{2}$$

$$CW_m = A_m.\, Cw_m; \forall m \in H. \tag{3}$$

$$A_m = \alpha.AP.C_m; \forall m \in H. \tag{4}$$

The environmental objective function, represented in (5), is applied to minimize the $CO_2$ emissions due to vehicles *EV* (caused by their manufacturing, use/depreciation and freight transportation) and to hubs operation (resulting from their constructions *EC*, operations *EO*, heating, cooling, ventilation and auxiliaries, production of domestic hot water, lighting of premises, as well as upkeep and maintenance).

$$F_2 = EV + EO + EC \tag{5}$$

In this study, we consider the collaborative scenario shown in Fig. 1. We assume that each supplier is assigned to a single warehouse and that this warehouse can serve multiple distribution centres, while each retailer can only be served by a single distribution centre.

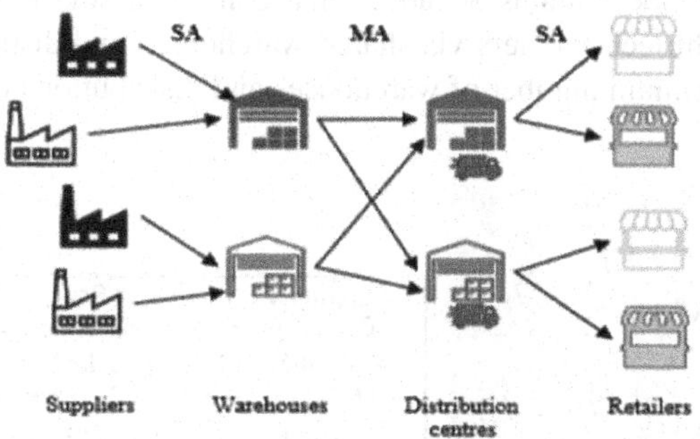


**Fig. 1.** Example of a collaborative distribution network.

## 3.2 Robust Proposed Uncertainties

Giving that the weaknesses of the stochastic programming make it inadequately used to deal with problems where there is no information about the parameter's distributions, we opt for the robust approach already used in several works [9, 10] and [14] to design a collaborative distribution network that can operate in worst-case scenarios. Our model incorporates several uncertainty levels to face the different variations caused by hazards, especially in this period of health crisis caused by COVID-19.

Nowadays, customer's demands cannot be estimated since, during this epidemic, the demands of some companies changed considerably (decrease or increase in sales). Indeed, unit transportation costs vary according to the price of fuel which is very sensitive to several external factors such as geopolitical tensions, epidemics and global growth. Thus, we study the two cases for which the parameters are subject to interval uncertainty. We choose the budget model already applied by [7, 13] and [18] as it offers a certain flexibility to decision-makers to choose more or less efficient solutions through the uncertainty budget that determines the maximum used number of demand (or unit transportation costs). This budget is defined as uncertain parameter. As a result, each uncertain parameter is assumed to have an interval of uncertainty. Demands are defined as $W_{jt}^{p} \in \left[W_{jt}^{pL}, W_{jt}^{pL} + W_{jt}^{p\Delta}\right]$ where $W_{jt}^{pL}$ and $W_{jt}^{p\Delta} \geq 0$ are their nominal and deviation values, respectively. In addition, unit transportation costs are defined as $C_{q}^{v} \in \left[C_{q}^{vL}, C_{q}^{vL} + C_{q}^{v\Delta}\right]$ for the full-loaded vehicles and $C_{0}^{v} \in \left[C_{0}^{vL}, C_{0}^{vL} + C_{0}^{v\Delta}\right]$ for empty vehicles where $C_{q}^{vL}, C_{q}^{v\Delta} \geq 0$, $C_{0}^{vL}$, and $C_{0}^{v\Delta} \geq 0$ are their nominal and deviation values for each case, respectively. Designing a collaborative distribution network under the mentioned uncertainties causes the nonlinearity of the mathematical models. As a solution, the dual procedure should be used to linearise them and provide a mixed integer linear programming (MILP) optimization problem for each robust counterpart.

## 4 Computational Experiments

In this section, we examine a case study of a French distribution network represented in Fig. 2. This network contains 34 nodes that consist of seven suppliers delivering seven products to thirteen retailers via shared warehouses and distribution centres for six weeks. The maximum number of warehouses and distribution centres to be opened

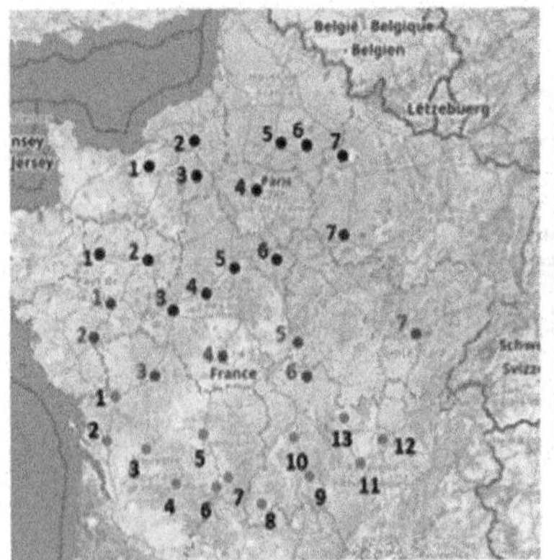

- **Suppliers:** 1: Lisieux, 2: Rouen, 3: Evreux, 4: Paris, 5: Compiègne, 6: Soissons, 7: Reims
- **Warehouses:** 1: Laval, 2: Le Mans, 3: Tours, 4: Blois, 5: Orléans, 6: Montargis, 7: Troyes
- **Distribution centres:** 1: Angers, 2: Cholet, 3: Poitiers, 4: Châteauroux, 5: Nevers, 6: Moulins, 7: Dole
- **Retailers:** 1: Niort, 2: Saintes, 3: Angoulême, 4: Périgueux, 5: Limoges, 6: Brive-la-Gaillarde, 7: Tulle, 8: Aurillac, 9: Brioude, 10: Clermont-Ferrand, 11: Saint-Étienne, 12: Lyon, 13: Roanne

**Fig. 2.** Set of selected nodes on the map of France.

**Table 1.** Summary of the results of uncertain demands and unit transportation costs cases.

| Sustainability indicators | Demands case | | | | | | Unit transportation costs case | | | | | |
|---|---|---|---|---|---|---|---|---|---|---|---|---|
| | Fixed deterministic | | Robust | | Gap (%) | | Fixed deterministic | | Robust | | Gap (%) | |
| | S.eco | S.env | S.eco | S.env | S.eco | S.env | S.eco | S.env | S.eco | S.env | S.eco | S.env |
| Costs ($10^7$ €) | 1.449 | 1.616 | 1.476 | 1.667 | 1.86 | 3.16 | 1.354 | 1.578 | 1.483 | 1.666 | 9.53 | 5.58 |
| $CO_2$ emissions ($10^9$ g $CO_2$) | 3.005 | 2.987 | 3.269 | 3.202 | 8.79 | 7.20 | 2.907 | 2.883 | 3.184 | 3.147 | 9.53 | 9.16 |

is seven for each set. The number of hubs and their storage capacities are determined by the employed model. The resulting MILP formulations are solved exactly using CPLEX and we use 5% of the uncertain parameters as the initial value of the uncertainty budget. Besides, the latter limits the number of uncertain parameters allowed to deviate from their nominal values. This behaviour is justified by the fact that the case where all parameters deviate from their nominal values are rare.

Table 1 presents a comparative study of the robust optimization results and the fixed deterministic findings using the gap between them. The fixed deterministic case means that the used parameter values are those found in the worst case [14]. Therefore, the values of these parameters are equal to the nominal ones plus the deviations obtained by solving the robust model. The S.eco and S.env are the economic and environmental objective scenarios, respectively.

We note that when 5% of the uncertain parameters can take their worst-case values, the total logistics cost of the robust approach is higher than that of the deterministic one with an average of 2.51% with uncertain demands and 7.56% with uncertain unit transportation costs. Moreover, the robust $CO_2$ emissions have higher values with an average of 8% for demands uncertainty and 9.35% for costs uncertainty. We can conclude that the uncertainty does not result in big changes in the costs and $CO_2$ emissions.

In Table 2, we compare fixed deterministic and robust problems in terms of total capacities of hubs. Considering uncertain demands, results show an average increase of 10.19% and a maximum increase of 12.55%. Similarly, capacities of hubs are subject to an average increase of 12.78% and a maximum increase of 14.80%, when dealing with uncertain unit transportation costs. Therefore, we can explain the rise of hubs' capacities by the fact that uncertainty improves the filling rate of vehicles.

Figure 3 demonstrates that, by presenting more opened warehouses, the optimal configuration obtained in the S.eco scenario for the uncertain demands case is different from the costs case. This behaviour is due to the use of more resources when demands increase.

**Table 2.** Summary total capacities of hubs.

| Parameter | Approach | Scenario | Total capacity of hubs | |
|---|---|---|---|---|
| | | | Upstream hubs | Downstream hubs |
| Demands | Robust | S.eco | 3050 | 3050 |
| | | S.env | 3028 | 3259 |
| | Fixed deterministic | S.eco | 2710 | 3014 |
| | | S.env | 2808 | 3168 |
| Unit transportation costs | Robust | S.eco | 3040 | 3219 |
| | | S.env | 3029 | 3226 |
| | Fixed deterministic | S.eco | 2745 | 2804 |
| | | S.env | 2651 | 2898 |

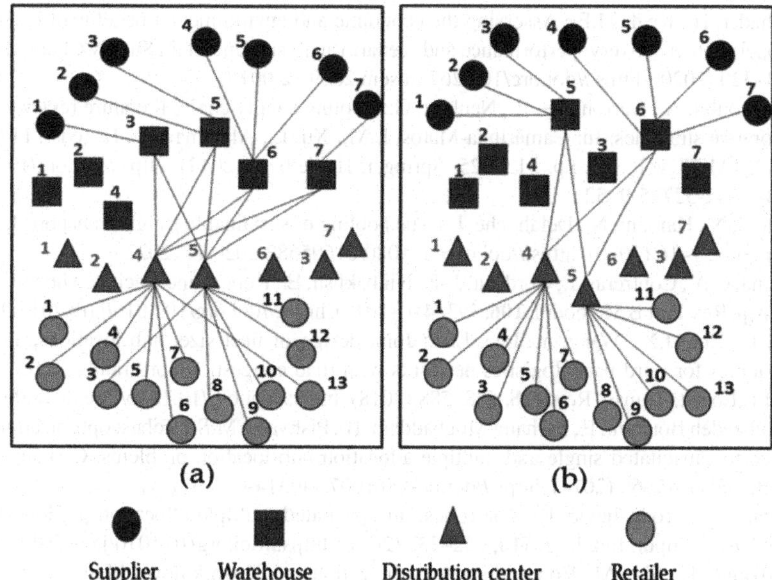


**Fig. 3.** Optimal network configurations of the S.eco scenario.

## 5 Conclusion and Perspectives

This study introduced a collaborative distribution network design problem under uncertainties of demands and unit transportation costs. It minimizes logistics costs and $CO_2$ emissions. A case study was examined via a distribution network in France. The obtained results show that the robust optimization improves the filling rate of vehicles and solutions are conservative and tolerant of the fixed deterministic ones in terms of costs and $CO_2$ emissions. However, solving the problem exactly with CPLEX limits its size. Thus, it is preferable, in this case, to provide a heuristic method for the resolution of larger instances. We also intend to propose, in our future works, a robust counterpart that considers the uncertainty of the maximum number of vehicles in use and another case that combines demand, unit transportation costs and maximum number of vehicles in use uncertainties.

## References

1. Habibi, M.K.K., Allaoui, H., Goncalves, G.: Collaborative hub location problem under cost uncertainty. Comput. Ind. Eng. **124**, 393–410 (2018). https://doi.org/10.1016/j.cie.2018.07.028
2. Ferrell, W., Ellis, K., Kaminsky, P., Rainwater, C.: Horizontal collaboration: opportunities for improved logistics planning. Int. J. Prod. Res. **58**, 4267–4284 (2020). https://doi.org/10.1080/00207543.2019.1651457
3. Aloui, A., Hamani, N., Derrouiche, R., Delahoche, L.: Systematic literature review on collaborative sustainable transportation: overview, analysis and perspectives. Transp. Res. Interdiscip. Perspect. **9**, 100291 (2021). https://doi.org/10.1016/j.trip.2020.100291

4. Ouhader, H., Kyal, M.E.: Assessing the economic and environmental benefits of horizontal cooperation in delivery: performance and scenario analysis. Uncertain Supply Chain Manag., 303–320 (2020). https://doi.org/10.5267/j.uscm.2019.12.001
5. Moutaoukil, A., Derrouiche, R., Neubert, G.: Pooling supply chain: literature review of collaborative strategies. In: Camarinha-Matos, L.M., Xu, L., Afsarmanesh, H. (eds.) PRO-VE 2012. IAICT, vol. 380, pp. 513–525. Springer, Heidelberg (2012). https://doi.org/10.1007/978-3-642-32775-9_52
6. Mrabti, N., Hamani, N., Delahoche, L.: The pooling of sustainable freight transport. J. Oper. Res. Soc., 1–16 (2020). https://doi.org/10.1080/01605682.2020.1772022
7. Zetina, C.A., Contreras, I., Cordeau, J.-F., Nikbakhsh, E.: Robust uncapacitated hub location. Transp. Res. Part B Methodol. **106**, 393–410 (2017). https://doi.org/10.1016/j.trb.2017.06.008
8. Hu, L., Zhu, J.X., Wang, Y., Lee, L.H.: Joint design of fleet size, hub locations, and hub capacities for third-party logistics networks with road congestion constraints. Transp. Res. Part E Logist. Transp. Rev. **118**, 568–588 (2018). https://doi.org/10.1016/j.tre.2018.09.002
9. Habibzadeh Boukani, F., Farhang Moghaddam, B., Pishvaee, M.S.: Robust optimization approach to capacitated single and multiple allocation hub location problems. Comput. Appl. Math. **35**(1), 45–60 (2014). https://doi.org/10.1007/s40314-014-0179-y
10. Talbi, E.-G., Todosijević, R.: The robust uncapacitated multiple allocation p -Hub median problem. Comput. Ind. Eng. **110**, 322–332 (2017). https://doi.org/10.1016/j.cie.2017.06.017
11. Bertsimas, D., Sim, M.: Robust discrete optimization and network flows. Math. Program. **98**, 49–71 (2003). https://doi.org/10.1007/s10107-003-0396-4
12. Correia, I., Nickel, S., Saldanha-da-Gama, F.: A stochastic multi-period capacitated multiple allocation hub location problem: formulation and inequalities. Omega **74**, 122–134 (2018). https://doi.org/10.1016/j.omega.2017.01.011
13. Martins de Sá, E., Morabito, R., de Camargo, R.S.: Benders decomposition applied to a robust multiple allocation incomplete hub location problem. Comput. Oper. Res. **89**, 31–50 (2018). https://doi.org/10.1016/j.cor.2017.08.001
14. Rahmati, R., Bashiri, M.: Robust Hub Location Problem with Uncertain Inter Hub Flow Discount Factor, 10 (2018)
15. Lozkins, A., Krasilnikov, M., Bure, V.: Robust uncapacitated multiple allocation hub location problem under demand uncertainty: minimization of cost deviations. J. Ind. Eng. Int. **15**(1), 199–207 (2019). https://doi.org/10.1007/s40092-019-00329-9
16. Peiró, J., Corberán, Á., Martí, R., Saldanha-da-Gama, F.: Heuristic solutions for a class of stochastic uncapacitated P-Hub median problems. Transp. Sci. **53**, 1126–1149 (2019)
17. Ben Mohamed, I., Klibi, W., Vanderbeck, F.: Designing a two-echelon distribution network under demand uncertainty. Eur. J. Oper. Res. **280**, 102–123 (2020). https://doi.org/10.1016/j.ejor.2019.06.047
18. Hamaz, I.: Méthodes d'optimisation robuste pour les problèmes d'ordonnancement cyclique. Université Paul Sabatier, Toulouse III, France (2018)

# Simulating Impact of Smart Product-Service Systems

Christian Zinke-Wehlmann[1](✉), Sebastian Frericks[2], and Andreas Kluge[2]

[1] InfAI e.V., Group Service- and Knowledge Management, Goerdelerring 9, 04109 Leipzig, Germany
zinke@infai.org

[2] University Computer Centre, Group Research and Development, Leipzig University, Augustusplatz 10, 04109 Leipzig, Germany

**Abstract.** Waves of digitalization and Industry 4.0 currently boost research and development activities for smart product-service systems. The usage of information technology within products (e.g., IoT) and services as well as processing big data leads to the development of novel product-service bundles like functional sales. One of the main barriers of smart PSS innovation is missing information on possible economic (cost/revenue) and ecological (environmental) impacts. This paper presents a novel simulation approach to overcome the named barrier. Methodologically, the paper is based on design science research to develop an appropriate approach. Our simulation model will be able to enhance transparency about the different forms and power of impact of smart PSS. Furthermore, the core of the new approach is the possible low threshold integration of existing data on business model and process model layers into the simulation. Finally, an existing use case demonstrates how the approach can be applied.

**Keywords:** Smart product-service system · Simulation · Business model innovation

## 1 Introduction

The number of product-service systems (PSS) in various sectors of the economy is rising. The trend of 'servitization' is supported by using smart technology to recognize and address customer needs and create new smart PSS [1]. Thus, the rapid development of technology (e.g., Internet of Things - IoT) and the steadily increasing ability to process big data lead to this 'smartification' of PSS [2]. The technological developments towards smart PSS enhance stakeholders' digital integration and facilitate highly customized product-service bundles for customers – driven by their needs.

Besides customization, there is also a growing demand for sustainable, eco-friendly, and ethically tenable solutions [3]. Novel approaches of transparency and business model innovations are needed to cover these societal and individual customer demands. The potentials of sustainable business models driven by PSS, e.g., through functional sales,


Published by Springer Nature Switzerland AG 2021
L. M. Camarinha-Matos et al. (Eds.): PRO-VE 2021, IFIP AICT 629, pp. 289–297, 2021.
https://doi.org/10.1007/978-3-030-85969-5_26

have already been discussed in the respective research, e.g., [4]. Using the new wave of 'smartification' [2], driven by digitalization, Industry 4.0, and IoT, PSS business models, have reached the next evolution stage. However, the switch from classical product selling business models to 'smart' and service-oriented models, like functional sales, is non-trivial and complex. To evaluate and recreate a business model in a sustainable way, the whole product lifecycle must be considered. Further, novel services must be designed, developed, and maintained. Moreover, rapidly changing technologies (e.g., IoT, web technologies) have to be included in the product and service life cycle. In addition, many competencies must be combined within the innovation and business development process. Thus, the business development of smart PSS is complex, risky with mostly unknown components and costs. As [5] stated out "Costs of PSS can be high when compared to the production of only one product, which includes labor and transaction costs, since a PSS is usually delivered by a group of companies, resulting in hiring and more complicated revenue-sharing scheme" [5]. Therefore, the major obstacle within this innovation process in collaborative networks is the difficulty of estimating the possible future impact of the novel business model - the economic impact for both customers and the businesses and the ecological impact. There is a significant gap in supporting PSS development processes, e.g., business model development, by easily simulating possible PSS scenarios based on business model information (e.g., key resources, revenue structure) and target process descriptions (e.g., key processes and activities) to calculate its possible impacts. However, simulation of PSS solutions is not a novel approach. One highly relevant but still missing detail of the currently used simulations is simple compatibility with existing business development processes (e.g., business model canvas, process management standards) in the companies and a low usage threshold. A novel smart PSS simulation approach is needed to customize and configure smart PSS and predict potential benefits and risks to overcome this gap. Thus, we want to approach the main research questions: How can a simulation approach support smart PSS business innovation processes? How to combine basic information of the target business model and business processes to enable a simulation and predict possible revenues, costs, and environmental KPIs?

## 2 Methodology

The method chosen in the present case is based on the design science research approach (DSR) described by [6] and [7]. These are I: Identify and describe the problem, II: Develop objectives for a solution, III: Design and develop artifact, VI: Demonstrate and V: Evaluate, as well as VI: Communicate. The process described is continuous and multi-stage. The paper presents the results of our research's first steps, given by a real-world scenario of our industrial partners. The scenario will be introduced in Sect. 4. We are currently working within stage III to design and implement a simulation environment. While the work is still in progress, the results enrich the current state of the art of simulation approaches for smart and collaborative PSS development. Although design science research's strength lies in its practicality, various DSR models simultaneously propose elaborating a clear state of the art of the given problem to ensure scientific rigor [6, 8]. Therefore, in the present paper, a thorough state of the art is presented first.

## 3 Simulation of Smart Product-Service Systems – The State of the Art

First, the term of smart product-service systems (smart PSS) will be introduced. The combination of tangible products and intangible services is referred to in the literature as product-service systems [9]. Smart PSS are combining products, services, and ICT services into smart packages and customizable solutions [10]. With the rise of sensors and IoT, mobile devices and other products start to collect data, IT services process them to information, and platform services bring them into use for customers or providers. While the benefits of smart PSS for customer and provider are the reduction of costs, the reduction of environmental impact, as well as efficient use of the equipment, one of the significant risks is the difficulty in measuring results as well as the question of revenue streams and success conditions [5]. Thus, the paper will develop a simulation model to overcome these challenges. The next part will briefly introduce the current simulation approaches within the (smart) PSS domain.

Simulation is a very broad concept, with and without information technology, to replicate real-world processes and situations for various purposes [11]. This paper only refers to IT-based (computer-based) simulation approaches, esp. for Industry 4.0, smart manufacturing, and PSS. A lot of work has been done within the domain of process and (IT) service simulation, e.g., for the model-driven service engineering approach [12] or smart manufacturing orchestration approaches [13]. These approaches are fruitful for business process design, e.g., optimize time and costs of (IT) services and sustainable KPIs [14], but hard to use for ICT-based product-service systems. Further, Jaghbeer et al. [15] conclude "that current tools and methods extensively focus on manufacturing, especially sustainable manufacturing, while less attention is given towards other life cycle phases" [15]. The challenges which came with other life cycle phases are demonstrated by Goodall et al., who create a simulation model for data-driven re-manufacturing service [16] in Industry 4.0 environments. They demonstrate how end-of-life services (also given for PSS) can be integrated into planning and manufacturing processes. In addition, Angelopoulou et al. simulate the human factor to predict the human error probability in Industry 4.0 [17]. With Industry 4.0, manufacturing processes and IT services are getting highly digitalized, and this opens space for simulation approaches to optimize its impact (economically and ecologically). Further, Rondini et al. give a brief overview about the PSS simulation approaches [18] and summarize "that some attempts to evaluate the performance perceived by the customers, the company efficiency and the PSS environmental performance through BPS [Business Process Simulation] already exist, and that simulation techniques can potentially help to gather the dynamics of a PSS provision process." [18]. This analysis shows different simulation approaches (discrete, agent-based, system dynamics) that can be used or combined for different focusses in PSS development: Focusing on customer (behavior and interaction), on efficiency and resources as well as on environmental impact. While the combination of all methods is recommendable, this paper concentrates on the 'smartification' of PSS business model innovation towards smart and collaborative systems, exemplary on simulation of 'smart' functional sales to predict economic and ecological impact (e.g., compared to classical product sales and service delivery).

## 4 Results – Supporting PSS Development by a Simulation Approach

One of the most prominent business cases for PSS business models is functional sales, where the functions are sold. A simplified use case from our industrial partners is the development of "drilling services", where no tangible product (professional drillers) is sold to the customer (product-oriented PSS with additional service), but the function "drilling" is sold (smart PSS) - see Business Model comparison as part of the economical layer following Joyce and Paquin [19] in Table 1[1]. To develop these services from the existing manufacturing model, the driller producer needs to 'smartifice' and 'servitize' its products by including novel technologies, integrating them on a digital platform, and building new business processes/partnerships for maintenance, repair, and re-manufacturing. Besides these developments of value proposition and value creation processes, the producer needs to define the value capturing model – revenue and cost structure.

**Table 1.** Product-oriented vs. Smart PSS on drilling example

| Drilling example | Product-oriented PSS | Smart product-service system |
|---|---|---|
| Revenue (Value Capturing) | One-time payment | Pay-per-drill |
| | Number of sold drillers | Number of drills |
| (Key) Resources | Materials and Store | Smart Driller (with IoT) and a platform (drilling activities, contract details, state of the machine, etc.) |
| Value Propositions (Product) | Driller, Maintenance | Drilling |
| (Key) Activities | Manufacturing (Supply Chain) and Selling | Customer Services (e.g., maintenance, platform services), manufacturing and re-manufacturing (supply chain) |
| Costs | Materials, Manufacturing, Marketing | (re-)Manufacturing, Customer Services, Service platform (IT-Services), Marketing |

The switch from product and service selling to 'smart' functional sales as described is complex, and besides the challenges of customer acceptance, decision-makers must estimate possible impacts. While on product-oriented PSS, product and services are loosely coupled, for example, in its revenue and cost structure, in smart PSS, the product/function

[1] Customer Relationship, Segments and Channels have not been mentioned, because it is not focus of the used simulation approach – we will argue later on why. Further we concentrate on economical layer, and will give a brief introduction later on the other layer.

are closely tied. Therefore, the revenue of smart PSS depends on well-designed services and resources. This paper aims to develop a simulation model for such smart product-service Systems to support decision-makers on business model innovations towards smart PSS.

A starting point for the simulation was deciding what kind of simulation is suitable for the given problem. We choose a process-based discrete event simulation (DES) approach because:

- Services (smart drilling service) are realized when the respective functions are used (drilling),
- Functions are measurable and discrete variables (count of drilling),
- Services are processes where resources (driller, platform, and customer) get integrated (in a range of time) and
- Resources (driller) have functions (drilling) and other measurable performance indexes (costs per time, C02-footprint, energy costs).

Other approaches, like agent-based approaches, may also be successful adapted for our purpose, but more likely for cooperation [20] and customer acceptance [21]. While integrating these approaches has been shown in [18], we concentrate on a novel generic way to simulate smart PSS from the provider's business model innovation perspective. Further, DES is mainly based on three concepts: the events, the objects' activities, and the process. While an event triggers the object's activities through changing object states, the object's activities are defined as a time interval mostly between two object states, and the processes refer to the sum of activities and states for an object or the simulation [22]. The concept that processes a set of activities is quite similar to process models (like BPMN), the problem is that, for example, BPMN is not suitable for real automated transformation in simulation models, like [23] stated out, "that there are quite a few ambiguous elements, missing concepts, and redundant elements in BPMN" [23]. This is one of the major gaps in the modeling and interconnection of objects and resources [24] within process models. Our approach uses existing terms from business models (resources, processes) and business processes (activities, gates, lanes) to integrate the information into our simulation and predict business model impact (revenue and cost structure as well as ecological impact [19]). An overview is given in Fig. 1 below.

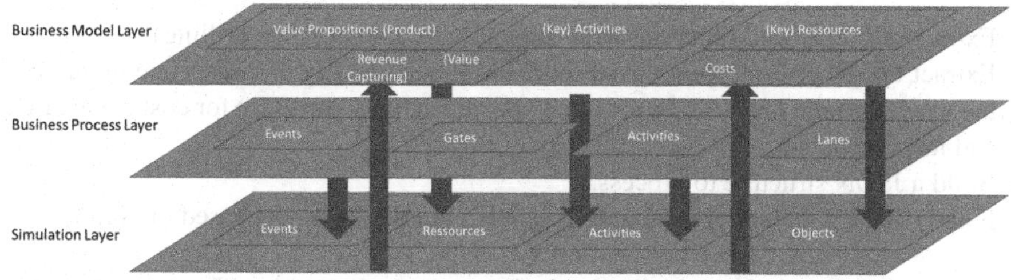


**Fig. 1.** Integration from business model and business process to simulation

The transmission of information from the business model canvas over business processes to simulation and back implies (practical) difficulties because each level includes different granularities of information. To overcome these difficulties, we suggest the following steps: (1) Define the (key) resources, processes, and activities for the business model (e.g., through business model canvas); (2) Define the selling functions and bring them into relation with the (key) resources; (3) Develop process models for key processes. Define customer, supplier, and company activities and processes in a standardized way, e.g., described with the help of BPMN (4) Define cost, revenue, and environmental (or other) indexes for function, activities, and sub-processes.

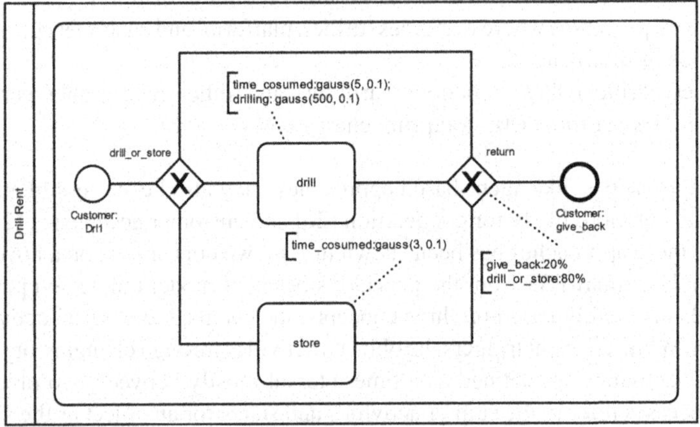


**Fig. 2.** Key drilling process

The definitions of step 1 can be found above in Table 1. In step 2, we define the value proposition "drilling", which is linked to key-resource driller (remember it is an oversimplified case). For step 3, we developed a process model for our simulation approach. The smartified subprocess as a simplified BPMN is shown in Fig. 2. We also include the cost structure as comments to demonstrate step 4. There is a fixed cost for keeping the drill and a dynamic cost for using the drill in this scenario. To bridge all the information and bring them into a simulation approach, we do follow:

- Extract resources and functions from Business Modell (Driller, drilling)
- Extract the process elements from the BPMN and classify and associate them with the used resource (drill) and a resource-specific activity (drilling) for cost calculation and its descendants.
- Build a JSON structure to process.
- Finally, the JSON model is fitted to a generic simulation model based on Simply.

Thus, resources will be initialized as well as gates and activities. The start function is decided based on the first function following the process source and is either a gate or an activity. The current generic model is limited to exclusive gates, which are only moving the process state, based on statistical distribution, to the next activity and activities which calculate the costs or any other KPI and time of the process.

We demonstrate how to combine data for smart PSS development with this prelimited model and process, like functional sales. The simulation enables a flexible PSS business development by estimating the cost, revenue, generic KPIs, and environmental impact of given value propositions, key resources, and key activities/processes. Thus, better decisions, flexible pricing models, as well as bonus program options can be made. Information about economic and ecological impacts may also trigger re-design and robustness of products, novel development of end-of-life services, and other activities to enhance efficiency of the provided PSS, in terms of functional sales. Finally, the digital simulation (as an online service) enables cross-organizational development of business model innovation by combining different developers' and departments' information. Thus, decision-makers obtain a more valid basis for sustainable business innovations.

## 5 Discussion and Conclusion

The evolution of smart PSS is one way to a more sustainable economy both economical and ecologically. Walking over the edge to new business models without intense consideration of risks and chances takes companies into jeopardy. The approach proposed in this paper enriches the arsenal of a suitable methodology for smart business model innovation by a new integrated simulation model. Our approach gives the opportunity to test hypothetical business models' ideas within a sandbox environment as a digital twin. It contributes to the field of smart PSS simulation mainly by giving the possibility to transform common business model notations into a for simulation usable format without enormous effort.

The required data is generated from existing business model layers as well as business process layers. The threshold of supplying the simulation with the named data is low, as the data is usually already stored in the company. Looking forward, the model will be developed further to find a way to not only test hypothetical models but evaluate business models and give input in smart innovation processes on product-service systems. However, there are still a lot of limitations. First, the model and the simulation tool are still under development. The first real PSS innovation simulations and first real proof of usability are planned within the next year. Second, the model still concentrates on specific aspects of the sustainable Business Model Innovation Canvas [19]. There will be a high demand to include agent-based simulation approaches to integrate the customer-side and the social and supply dimension of business development, which we need to consider.

## References


1. Zheng, P., Wang, Z., Chen, C.-H., et al.: A survey of smart product-service systems: key aspects, challenges and future perspectives. Adv. Eng. Inform. **42**, 100973 (2019). https://doi.org/10.1016/j.aei.2019.100973
2. Schuh, G., Zeller, V., Hicking, J., et al.: Introducing a methodology for smartification of products in manufacturing industry. Procedia CIRP **81**, 228–233 (2019). https://doi.org/10.1016/j.procir.2019.03.040

3. Scholz, U., Pastoors, S., Becker, J.H., Hofmann, D., van Dun, R. (eds.): Praxishandbuch Nachhaltige Produktentwicklung. Springer, Heidelberg (2018). https://doi.org/10.1007/978-3-662-57320-4
4. van Halen, C.J.G., te Riele, H.R.M.: Product Service systems, Ecological and Economic Basics (1999)
5. Moro, S., Cauchick-Migue, P.A., Mendes, G.H.S.: Product-service systems benefits and barriers: an overview of literature review papers. Int. J. Ind. Eng. Manag. **11**, 61–70 (2020). https://doi.org/10.24867/IJIEM-2020-1-253
6. Peffers, K., Tuunanen, T., Rothenberger, M.A., et al.: A design science research methodology for information systems research. J. Manag. Inf. Syst. **24**, 45–77 (2007). https://doi.org/10.2753/MIS0742-1222240302
7. Hevner, A., Chatterjee, S.: Design Research in Information Systems, vol. 22. Springer, Boston (2010). https://doi.org/10.1007/978-1-4419-5653-8
8. Hevner, A.R.: A three cycle view of design science research. Scand. J. Inf. Syst. **19**, 4 (2007)
9. Baines, T.S., Lightfoot, H.W., Evans, S., et al.: State-of-the-art in product-service systems. Proc. Inst. Mech. Eng. Part B J. Eng. Manuf. **221**, 1543–1552 (2007). https://doi.org/10.1243/09544054JEM858
10. Valencia, A., Mugge, R., Schoormans, J., et al.: The design of smart product-service systems (PSSs): an exploration of design characteristics. Int. J. Des. **9**, 13–28 (2015)
11. Simões-Marques, M.J.: Modeling and simulation in system life cycle. Procedia Manuf. **3**, 785–792 (2015). https://doi.org/10.1016/j.promfg.2015.07.331
12. Boyé, H., Ducq, Y., Zacharewicz, G., et al.: SLMToolBox: enterprise service process modelling and simulation by coupling DEVS and services workflow. IJSPM **11**, 453 (2016). https://doi.org/10.1504/IJSPM.2016.10001547
13. Gorecki, S., Possik, J., Zacharewicz, G., et al.: A multicomponent distributed framework for smart production system modeling and simulation. Sustainability **12**, 6969 (2020). https://doi.org/10.3390/su12176969
14. Rocca, R., Rosa, P., Sassanelli, C., et al.: Integrating virtual reality and digital twin in circular economy practices: a laboratory application case. Sustainability **12**, 2286 (2020). https://doi.org/10.3390/su12062286
15. Jaghbeer, Y., Hallstedt, S.I., Larsson, T., et al.: Exploration of simulation-driven support tools for sustainable product development. Procedia CIRP **64**, 271–276 (2017). https://doi.org/10.1016/j.procir.2017.03.069
16. Goodall, P., Sharpe, R., West, A.: A data-driven simulation to support re-manufacturing operations. Comput. Ind. **105**, 48–60 (2019). https://doi.org/10.1016/j.compind.2018.11.001
17. Angelopoulou, A., Mykoniatis, K., Boyapati, N.R.: Industry 4.0: the use of simulation for human reliability assessment. Procedia Manuf. **42**, 296–301 (2020). https://doi.org/10.1016/j.promfg.2020.02.094
18. Rondini, A., Tornese, F., Gnoni, M.G., et al.: Hybrid simulation modelling as a supporting tool for sustainable product service systems: a critical analysis. Int. J. Prod. Res. **55**, 6932–6945 (2017). https://doi.org/10.1080/00207543.2017.1330569
19. Joyce, A., Paquin, R.L.: The triple layered business model canvas: a tool to design more sustainable business models. J. Clean. Prod. **135**, 1474–1486 (2016). https://doi.org/10.1016/j.jclepro.2016.06.067
20. Campos, P., Brazdil, P., Mota, I.: Comparing strategies of collaborative networks for R&D: an agent-based study. Comput. Econ. **42**, 1–22 (2013). https://doi.org/10.1007/s10614-013-9376-9
21. Lieder, M., Asif, F.M.A., Rashid, A.: Towards Circular Economy implementation: an agent-based simulation approach for business model changes. Auton. Agent. Multi-Agent Syst. **31**(6), 1377–1402 (2017). https://doi.org/10.1007/s10458-017-9365-9

22. de Lara, J., Guerra, E., Boronat, A., Heckel, R., Torrini, P.: Domain-specific discrete event modelling and simulation using graph transformation. Softw. Syst. Model. **13**(1), 209–238 (2012). https://doi.org/10.1007/s10270-012-0242-3
23. Guizzardi, G., Wagner, G.: Can BPMN be used for making simulation models? In: Barjis, J., Eldabi, T., Gupta, A. (eds.) EOMAS 2011. LNBIP, vol. 88, pp. 100–115. Springer, Heidelberg (2011). https://doi.org/10.1007/978-3-642-24175-8_8
24. Enstone, L.J., Clark, M.F.: BPMN and Simulation. Lanner Group Limited (2006)

# Complex Collaborative Systems and Ontologies

# Compliance Checking of Collaborative Processes for Sustainable Collaborative Network

Oyepeju Oyekola(✉), Lai Xu(✉), and Paul de Vrieze(✉)

Computing and Informatics, Bournemouth University, Poole, Bournemouth B12 5BB, UK
{ooyekola,lxu,pdvrieze}@bournemouth.ac.uk

**Abstract.** Coronavirus pandemic has changed our lives and is likely to have a lasting impact on our economic development, i.e., industry and services. Most organisations must change their businesses and services to comply with the strategies and rules published by the governments of different countries for providing agility, sustainability, and resilience in the current situation. Non-compliance can result in an organisation paying a considerable sum of money in fines and litigation. In Collaborative Networks 4.0 (CN4.0), the importance of compliance is even more evident as its issue becomes more complicated when it involves collaborative processes due to its design principles for decentralized decision-making. The Collaborative Processes in CN 4.0 imply the collaborative business process and their relevancy in industry 4.0, i.e., the collaborative processes through Enterprise Resource Planning (ERP) and Manufacturing Execution System (MES). In this paper, we adopt two motivating use cases, define some of the regulatory requirements that govern the execution of each process, and then evaluate each process with the current compliance checking approaches. Based on this, we identify the challenges of compliance checking of collaborative processes, formalized as requirements needed to support the compliance checking of collaborative processes at design and running time, respectively. This paper further explores how the FIWARE architecture supports the automated compliance checking solution of collaborative processes in industry 4.0.

**Keywords:** Collaborative processes · Collaborative networks · Compliance · FIWARE · Business process · Industry 4.0

## 1 Introduction

Compliance is a big deal in today's business world, costing organizations a considerable sum of money in fines or litigation in case of non-compliance. As a result, compliance checking has become an inevitable step for organizations. The term compliance checking in this paper means the process of checking whether a business process complies with applicable policies and regulations [1]. The importance of compliance checking is even more evident as its issues become more complicated when it involves collaborative processes. The Collaborative Processes in CN 4.0 imply collaborative business processes and collaborative processes in the context of industry 4.0. The current trend in


Published by Springer Nature Switzerland AG 2021
L. M. Camarinha-Matos et al. (Eds.): PRO-VE 2021, IFIP AICT 629, pp. 301–310, 2021.
https://doi.org/10.1007/978-3-030-85969-5_27

digital transformation and market demand has presented an environment where organizations establish business collaboration between diversified and geographically distributed organizations to achieve a shared goal quickly and cost-effectively [1]. This concept has also created an environment for Small and Medium Enterprises (SMEs) to collaborate and compete with top-rated organisations. Achieving compliance in such a dynamic and networked environment is complex and challenging due to its design principle for decentralized decision-making. For instance, Collaborative processes present a unique attribute, such as the need to conform with security and privacy requirements, the need to comply with the regulatory requirement as a cross border process, the need to support data flow among partners, as well as the need to conform to the frequent changes in policies and regulations continuously, presents a unique challenge.

Most works on compliance checking are mainly structured for a single organisation process using different approaches and techniques. In contrast, compliance checking for collaborative processes is still sparse in the literature. Few works like [2, 3] that address the compliance checking of collaborative processes still lack full support to address the different phases of the process life cycles, i.e., control, data, time, and resource perspectives at both designs and run time [1]. Considering this, we justify the need to support the automated compliance checking of collaborative processes with varied regulatory requirements at all phases of the process life cycle at both design and runtime. Having such an automated compliance solution helps to reduce cost, avoid starting from scratch, wasting time and resources in creating new processes each time policies or regulations change.

To achieve compliance in such a dynamic environment, first, this paper adopts two motivating use cases to interpret the concept and complexities of the current compliance approaches in supporting compliance checking in collaborative processes. Second, we identify the challenges as requirements needed to support compliance checking of collaborative processes at both design and running time. Third, since the paper considers the compliance of collaborative processes in industry 4.0, we propose designing the compliance checking solution based on FIWARE architecture.

The rest of the paper is described as follows: Sect. 2 presents two motivating use cases and their applicable policies and regulations. Section 3 uses the motivating use cases to explain some challenges in expressing compliance rules in collaborative processes. Finally, in Sect. 4, a conceptual architecture is provided to design a solution that incorporates the identified challenges based on FIWARE.

## 2 Motivating Use Cases

This section presents two motivating use cases and their applicable policies and regulations that include internal policies, external regulations, and contractual obligations among partners. Section 2.1 describes the Collaborative Business Process (car insurance case), and Sect. 2.2 describes the collaborative process between the business process and manufacturing processes in the context of industry 4.0 (Car Assembly case).

### 2.1 Car Insurance Case

The car insurance case is adapted from the original work [4]. The collaborative business process involves five different partners, as shown in Fig. 1. The process starts with the policyholder who owns the insurance policy and reports any damage to the issued car. Euro Assist is the company that registers the claim received from the policyholder via the telephone and encourages approved garages. AGFIL is the insurance company that underwrites the car policy and decides whether the reported claim is valid or not. If the claim is valid, AGFIL will make payment to all parties involved. Lee Consulting Services (CS) works on behalf of AGFIL and manages the day-to-day emergency service operation. Lee CS access and determine whether the car requires an assessor after the assigned Garage estimated the repair cost, i.e., an assessor would be assigned to assess the damage of the car only when the repair cost exceeds a certain amount. They control how quickly garages will receive payment, as all invoices received from the Garage are sent through Lee CS, and further present the invoice to AGFIL to process the payment while ensuring that repair figures align with industry norms. The approved garages are then responsible for repairing the car after Lee CS has agreed upon the repair. The repair work must be carried out quickly and cost-effectively.

Table 1 summarizes related policies and different requirements reflect in the car insurance case. For each requirement mentioned in Table 1, we analyzed what the current compliance checking approach could potentially address and its limitations in expressing some of the requirements.

**Table 1.** Policy requirement for car insurance

| ID | Compliance requirement | Sources | Categories |
|---|---|---|---|
| Rq.1 | The Garage must receive payment for all invoices within a specific period | Contractual Obligation | Control, process time |
| Rq.2 | AGFIL must check the policy's validity, and if it is invalid, it must be left a void | Internal policy, Contractual Obligation | Control, Data |
| Rq.3 | Each partner process must conform to the principle of privacy, and data access must be granted only on a justifiable need to complete a specific task | GDPR, Contractual Obligation | Data |

### 2.2 Car Assembly Case

The car assembly process case is adapted from [5]. The assembly process of these cars requires a collaborative process involving mixed actor types (human and robot) to produce different types of cars with different configurations based on each customer preference assembled in the same production line. Compared to conventional factories, where

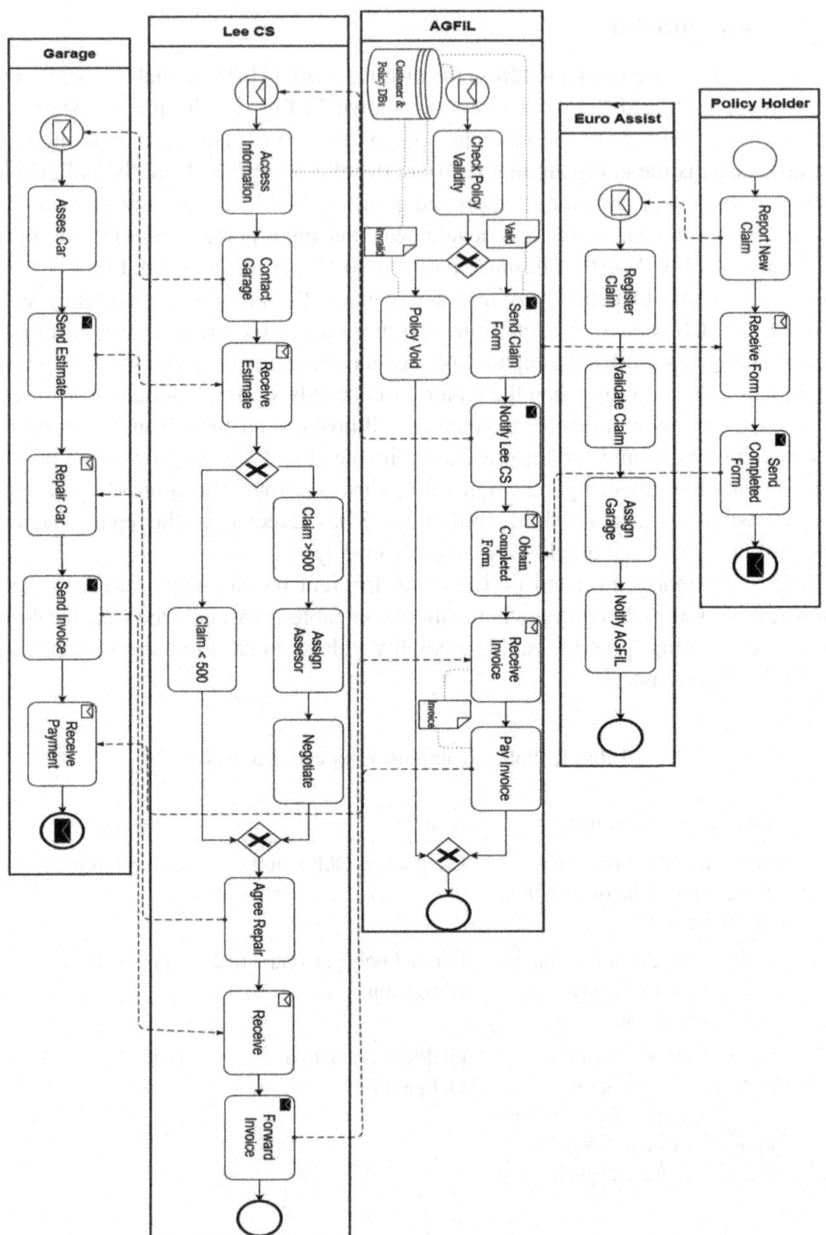


**Fig. 1.** Car insurance case

humans and robots are separated in workspaces to prevent humans from entering a hazardous area, the robotic system's operating state could pose a danger to humans [6]. The process has significantly changed with technological advancement in achieving flexible, efficient, and intelligent manufacturing, i.e., the concept of Industry 4.0, bringing about new forms of collaborative networks. This change has brought about humans and robots working together on the same production line, where the safety situation on the shopfloor is controlled by sensors and possibly signals in a dangerous situation. The car assembly process must comply with several rules and regulations. These include the organization's internal policy and industry regulations, such as the International Standard ISO 10218 that incorporate safety in industrial robotic environments described in Table 2.

**Table 2.** Policy and regulatory requirement for car assembly case

| ID | Compliance requirement | Sources | Categories |
|---|---|---|---|
| Rq.4 | The process must comply with the safety standards and regulations | External Regulations - ISO 10218 | Control, Resources |
| Rq.5 | The process must meet up customer demands within a specified time | Internal policy | Control, process time |

## 3 General Findings and Idea

This section uses the motivating use cases described in Sect. 2 to further interpret the concepts and complexities of the compliance checking of collaborative processes. For each requirement mentioned in Table 1 and Table 2, we analyze what the exciting compliance checking approach could potentially address and its challenges in expressing some of the compliance rules in collaborative processes.

**Car Insurance Requirement**

For **Rq1,** since the collaborative processes involve multi partners, activities in such a process involve a high level of dependency and response between each partner activity. Any break in the precedence and response between activities is a violation. For example, if Garage does not receive the payment within the set time, then it is ideal to know which partner(s) is(are) the potential violator during the process execution. The compliance requirements require the activities of the different partners in the collaboration, which becomes impossible to check as each partner's private activity cannot be viewed. And as a result, identifying the potential violator, in this case, might be tricky as any of the partners could be the potential violator. Expressing this type of rule is challenging as we cannot envisage that this violation will occur or when it will occur at runtime until it happens. The existing approaches do not support the preliminary specification of the future state of an action.

**Rq.2**, the existing compliance checking approach can check the conformance of this rule using data flow rules and conditional rules [7]. The requirement can be described such that the activity "Policy void" will only be executed when the data object "Policy" is in the state "Invalid" as a result of the execution of activity "Check policy validity."

Thus, it ensures that a specific condition must always hold at the time an activity is executed.

**Rq3** involves regulations with GDPR (General Data Protection Regulation) that require compliance with data privacy and addresses data transfer within the EU area. In the car insurance case, policyholder data is being accessed and processed between different partners. The reality is that each partner in the collaboration can be in different countries within the EU, and their ways of treating and managing customer data may be different. This means the same business function process can be specified in various forms in different countries. Conforming to privacy requirements in such instances remains challenging. The current work on access control and authorization mechanism [8–10] does not adequately address the existing complex and dynamic privacy requirements in collaborative processes environment. Therefore, checking data accessibility compliance needs to be context-aware. For example, at design time, the collaborative processes should be modeled as of which capabilities an actor should have to perform the task, which rights to access the data, how long the data can be access, what can be accessed when it can be accessed, and which part of the database can be accessed. At runtime, the roles should not allow access to specific data when they do not perform the activity. For instance, Lee CS should only be granted access to a single record per session of time a policyholder's details are needed to execute their tasks. This idea is a fundamental change from the traditional access control and authorization mechanisms that grant and authorize more access beyond what may be required and violate the data privacy principle.

**Car Assembly Requirement**

For **Rq.4,** since tasks are assigned to both humans and robots, it is necessary to check whether the assigned task to each actor is the right decision considering the safety, viability, or resource accessibility. For instance, when a task is scheduled to be executed by a human and robot simultaneously, a complete detailed description of the machine's condition and environment must be specified at design time and constantly monitored during execution, i.e., at runtime.

For **Rq.5,** each actor in the car assembly process can execute different tasks. These tasks must follow a strict schedule that must work flawlessly to meet customer demands on time. The delay in delivery schedule can tarnish the company's reputation and long-term customer relationship. Delay in delivery schedule can arise for different reasons. For instance, in a situation where the human actor assigned to complete a task is unavailable or in the event of machine failure, a task meant to be executed by a robot actor is passed to a human actor to perform manually. As such, there is a possibility that the completion time will take longer than already planned, resulting in unplanned downtime and costs for the entire production line.

Based on **Rq**1–5, supporting collaborative process variability is essential and required; it makes it challenging to specify compliance constraints and collaborative process models. So, at design time, we can specify necessary and sufficient conditions for triggering certain activities. This implies that several deviations from the abstracted process can be specified at design time and allow the process model to be instantiated at the running time.

Also, time compliance needs to consider process variants i.e., dependency of activities, access rights, and different roles. The time compliance for the different process instances cannot always be constant. For example, when actors suddenly become unviable or safety conditions are not satisfied, the time compliance needs to be reflected. Accessibilities of resources may also be specified as temporal rules to support the control flow of the collaborative process model.

## 4 Proposed Solution Based on FIWARE Architecture

With industry 4.0, business processes are collaborated among different factories and organizations to achieve flexible and effective handling of demands and the entire production life cycles. The collaborative processes are executed in a process execution environment, an integration system among the activities of ERP systems (i.e., ordering, inventory…), and MES (i.e., production planning, production) or other manufacturing systems [11, 12]. The process integration and collaboration through MES and ERP system require checking the compliance of predefined processes at design time, i.e., designing each process to comply with different rules before execution and continuously monitor process instances during execution. And since FIWARE offers scalable, flexible, and simple architecture that effectively manages dynamic collaborations, cost, product, and production life cycle [13, 14]. Then, to achieve compliance in industry 4.0, FIWARE architecture is adopted for the proposed compliance checking solution. The conceptual architecture describes how FIWARE could be extended to support the compliance checking of collaborative processes in industry 4.0, incorporating both design and runtime compliance checking, respectively.

The proposed Collaborative Process Compliance Checking solution based on FIWARE architecture is presented in Fig. 2, consisting of three main layers. The lower layer entails the information systems, i.e., Manufacturing Execution Systems (MES), ERP system, design-time compliance checking module, CPS system, robots, equipment, (IoT) sensors in the shop floor. The second layer consists of the FIWARE Generic Enablers modules such as the FIWARE context broker, IDM & Access Control, IDAS IoT agents, Real-time media processing, different adapters, shopfloor map, mashup platform, runtime execution monitoring, database, and 3rd organizations. Lastly, the top layer includes the interfaces and dashboards for real-time monitoring.

The proposed compliance check module (see the dashed box at the lower layer of Fig. 2) is designed to handle the design time-related compliance checking and running time authorization before and during execution. The compliance checking module will be part of the process engine for integrating business management (ERP) and manufacturing operations (MES).

At design time, there are three primary modules involved in achieving compliance. The first module is the **Modeling and Specification module** and is further divided into three sub-modules. **(i)** The modeling of the manufacturing processes integrating the ERP system, MES, shop floor, and human interface using BPMN 2.0 populated by humans and various automated systems at the lower layer. This will include specifying several deviations from the abstracted process **(ii)** the elicitation and specification of compliance requirements sourced from internal and external regulations as well as contractual obligations among partners; then formalize these requirements into compliance constraints

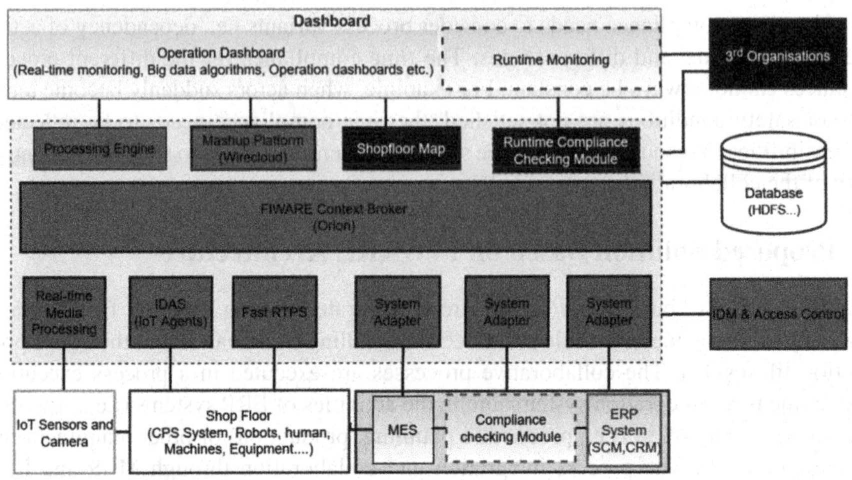


**Fig. 2.** Collaborative process compliance checking architecture based on FIWARE.

using a formal language that is expressive enough to capture all the requirements correctly. **(iii)** The compliance verification supports the process model and constraints; it serves as inputs for constraints and process models during the verification and storing verification results and feedback. The second module is the **Verification Service module** invoked during verification by submodule **(iii)** through an API. The Verification Service module consists of a process verification engine which employs different techniques and mechanism, like the simulation technique, compliance verification algorithms and the Process-Driven Access Control and Authorization (PDAC) mechanism [15]. The third module is the **Feedback and Reporting module**, which involves giving intelligent, appropriate, and comprehensible feedback to the end-user if any violations are detected.

After compliance has been checked at design time, the complaint process will start to initiate process instances as defined by the ERP, and MES then sends instructions to the shop floor as specified in the process model. But there is no certainty that the corresponding running process instance will be compliant during this time due to human and machine-related errors [1]. This implies that after checking the compliance at design time and the actual execution of a process is initiated, it is crucial to constantly monitor the running process to detect any inconsistencies or deviant behavior. Therefore, a dedicated process engine will be used to track the system's behavior and occurrences of specific events during the process execution; The Runtime compliance checking module (see the dashed box at the middle layer of Fig. 2) checks and identifies the undesired process behavior by comparing the actual behavior of the process instance with the expected behavior and alerts the end-users for any violations. The identified violations will then be displayed on the dashboard (see the dashed box at the top layer of Fig. 2). The end-users then take appropriate measures actions to rectify the violations in case any violation is detected.

## 5 Conclusion and Future Works

Collaborative network 4.0 provides a rich concept to reshape industry digitalization. In this paper, the requirements to achieve compliance with collaborative processes at both design and running time are identified. The conceptual architecture for collaborative process compliance checking is presented. The development and implementation of our compliance checking solution are based on the FIWARE architecture and provides a service for Industry 4.0. Despite the different approaches of checking compliance in the literature, existing approaches are not sufficient enough to support the requirements imposed by the challenges of collaborative processes. Our ongoing work includes formalizing the process model and regulatory requirements using formal languages that are expressive enough to capture all the required requirements described in Sect. 3 correctly. Then use techniques such as process simulation, algorithms, and PDAC to check for compliance. Lastly, we plan to implement the proposed compliance checking solution at both design and running time.

**Acknowledgments.** This research is part of the FIRST project that has received funding from the European Union's Horizon 2020 research and innovation programme, the Marie Skłodowska-Curie grant agreement No. 734599.

## References

1. Oyekola, O., Xu, L.: Verification and compliance in collaborative processes. In: Camarinha-Matos, L.M., Afsarmanesh, H., Ortiz, A. (eds.) PRO-VE 2020. IAICT, vol. 598, pp. 213–223. Springer, Cham (2020). https://doi.org/10.1007/978-3-030-62412-5_18
2. Bischoff, F., Fdhila, W., Rinderle-Ma, S.: Generation and transformation of compliant process collaboration models to BPMN. In: Giorgini, P., Weber, B. (eds.) CAiSE 2019. LNCS, vol. 11483, pp. 462–478. Springer, Cham (2019). https://doi.org/10.1007/978-3-030-21290-2_29
3. Fdhila, W., Rinderle-Ma, S., Knuplesch, D., Reichert, M.: Change and compliance in collaborative processes. In: IEEE International Conference on Services Computing, pp. 16–169 (2015)
4. Xu, L.: A multi-party contract model. In: SIGecom Exchange, pp. 13–23 (2004). https://doi.org/10.1145/1120694.1120697
5. Vanderfeesten, I., Grefen, P.: Business process management technology for discrete manufacturing. BETA publication: working papers, Technische Universiteit Eindhoven (2015)
6. Robla-Gómez, S., Becerra, V.M., Llata, J.R., Gonzalez-Sarabia, E., Torre-Ferrero, C., Perez-Oria, J.J.I.A.: Working together: a review on safe human-robot collaboration in industrial environments. IEEE Access **5**, 26754–26773 (2017)
7. Awad, A., Weidtich, M., Weske, M.: Specification, verification and explanation of violation for data-aware compliance rules. In: Service-Oriented Computing, 7th International Joint Conference, ICSOC-ServiceWave, pp. 24–27 (2009)
8. Wolter, C., Schaad, A.: Modeling of task-based authorization constraints in BPMN. In: Alonso, G. , Dadam, P., Rosemann, M. (eds.) BPM 2007. LNCS, vol. 4714, pp. 64–79. Springer, Heidelberg (2007). https://doi.org/10.1007/978-3-540-75183-0_5
9. Gautam, M., Jha, S., Sural, S., Vaidya, J., Atluri, V.: Poster: constrained policy mining in attribute-based access control. In: Proceedings of the 22nd ACM on Symposium on Access Control Models and Technologies (2017)

10. Jin, X., Krishnan, R., Sandhu, R.: A unified attribute-based access control model covering DAC, MAC and RBAC. In: IFIP Annual Conference on Data and Applications Security and Privacy (2012)
11. Erasmus, J., Vanderfeesteen, I., Traganos, K., Grefen, P.: The case for unified process management in smart manufacturing. In: IEEE 22nd International Enterprise Distributed Object Computing Conference (2018)
12. Jaskó, S., Skrop, A., Holczinger, T., Chován, T., Abonyi, J.: Development of manufacturing execution systems in accordance with Industry 4.0 requirements: a review of standard-and ontology-based methodologies and tools. Comput. Ind. **123**, 103300 (2020)
13. Sang, G., Xu, L., de Vrieze, P., Bai, Y.: Towards predictive maintenance for flexible manufacturing using FIWARE. In: Dupuy-Chessa, S., Proper, H.A. (eds.) CAiSE 2020. LNBIP, vol. 382, pp. 17–28. Springer, Cham (2020). https://doi.org/10.1007/978-3-030-49165-9_2
14. FIWARE Catalogue: FIWARE (2020). https://www.fiware.org/developers/catalogue/. Accessed 12 Apr 2021
15. Kasse, J., Xu, L., de Vrieze, P., Bai, Y.: Process driven access control and authorization approach. In: Yang, X.-S., Sherratt, S., Dey, N., Joshi, A. (eds.) Fourth International Congress on Information and Communication Technology. AISC, vol. 1041, pp. 313–322. Springer, Singapore (2020). https://doi.org/10.1007/978-981-15-0637-6_26

# Identification of Service Platform Requirements from Value Propositions: A Service Systems Engineering Method

Onat Ege Adali(✉), Baris Ozkan, Oktay Turetken, and Paul Grefen

School of Industrial Engineering, Eindhoven University of Technology, PO Box 513, 5600 MB Eindhoven, The Netherlands
{o.e.adali,b.ozkan,o.turetken,p.w.p.j.grefen}@tue.nl

**Abstract.** Digital service platforms are the facilitators of value co-creation within service ecosystems. They are instrumental in the design of compelling value propositions. Despite the substantial amount of contributions for the conceptualization of digital service platforms, the methodological contributions concerning the engineering of service platforms are scarce. In this paper, we adopt a service systems perspective and present a method for the identification of digital service platform requirements. The method is driven by the value propositions that are based on the capabilities of the actors in service exchange networks. In the paper, we demonstrate the method by applying it to an international Mobility-as-a-Service platform development project.

**Keywords:** Service systems engineering · Service platform · Requirements engineering

## 1 Introduction

In today's increasingly interconnected world, organizations' understanding of business is shifting away from delivering value in isolation to co-creating value in collaboration with other actors in service ecosystems [1, 2]. Digitalization is taking various roles in this transition not only through increasing connectedness beyond spatio-temporal constraints but also by influencing the way value is co-created and experienced [3–6]. Thus, businesses are increasingly adopting digital service platform business models which allow various actors to engage with one another for mutual benefit [7–9].

As with any business, value propositions are the key determinants of the success and the level of engagements between the actors over digital service platforms [5, 10]. Offering a vast amount of possibilities for effective and efficient resource mobilization [5, 11], digital service platforms provide the means for multiple actors to integrate and configure their competent resources in service systems and design compelling and complete value propositions [12–14]. Many digitally-enabled value proposition and service system examples can be given from successful online marketplaces, car sharing, or


Published by Springer Nature Switzerland AG 2021
L. M. Camarinha-Matos et al. (Eds.): PRO-VE 2021, IFIP AICT 629, pp. 311–322, 2021.
https://doi.org/10.1007/978-3-030-85969-5_28

streaming media platforms, which reflect the multi-actor and integrative characteristic of businesses around digital service platforms well [14, 15].

Despite the opportunities, the design of a service platform involves many challenges regarding the identification of platform system requirements [16]. In particular, the derivation of platform requirements from value propositions is a complex task as each value proposition involves the design of a network of activities (i.e., service system functionality) and the capabilities of the service system actors thereof [9, 17]. The identification of platform system functionality in a way that supports the activities of all platform actors and in alignment with their capabilities is crucial for the realization of the value propositions and the intended value cocreation over the platform [8, 9, 18]. While there is a considerable number of contributions for the conceptualization of digital service platforms, only a few studies propose methodological guidance for deriving requirements from the value propositions to be supported by the platform.

The objective of this research is *to design a method for the identification of platform requirements from value propositions in the form of use case descriptions*. To design our method, we adopt a service system view on value proposition design [14, 15] and follow a situational method engineering approach [19]. More specifically, we extend the Value-Proposition driven Business Service Identification Method (VP-BSIM) [17] with the Service Requirements Engineering Method (SREM) for a Digital Service Ecosystem [16]. We demonstrate our method by applying it in a real Mobility as a Service (MaaS) digital platform development business case.

The remainder of the paper is structured as follows. Section 2 presents the related work. Section 3 elaborates on the research design followed. Section 4 introduces the proposed method and Sect. 5 demonstrates the application of the method in a business case. Finally, Sect. 6 concludes the paper with a discussion of the limitations of our approach and the opportunities for future work.

## 2 Related Work

The identification of the software requirements in a multi-actor socio-technical system context has been an interesting field of research for decades [20]. A significant number of papers followed the conventional goal-oriented approaches [21] and proposed requirements identification methods to bridge the business-level and software-level understandings of what a software system should do. However, only a few studies in the literature explicitly account for value propositions in the requirements identification process. Lessard et al. [18] adopted a service system view on value proposition design and proposed a service systems metamodel and a graphical Goal-oriented Requirement Language profile for modelling service systems. In addition, they proposed a heuristic to guide the elicitation of requirements for the service systems based on their metamodel. Immonen et al. [16] defined ecosystem members, ecosystem infrastructure, ecosystem capabilities, and digital services as the elements of a digital service ecosystem. They proposed a service requirement engineering method to support the development of a digital service in a digital ecosystem. In the design of their method, they used Use Case Analysis for the elicitation and specification of the requirements.

However, to our best knowledge, no methods exist in the literature yet that account for service system actors' resources (i.e., capabilities) and guide the translation of value propositions into platform requirements. Hence, the present study addresses this gap in the context of digital service platforms.

## 3 Research Design

In the design and development of our method, we followed a Situational Method Engineering (SME) approach [19]. SME proposes three distinct method construction strategies: "*1. from scratch strategy", "2. extension-based strategy", and "3. paradigm based strategy*". Respectively the strategies relate to the construction of a novel method (1) from scratch, (2) by extending an existing *base method*, and (3) by abstracting a given model or instantiating a meta-model [19]. As our research objective relates to the extension of a base method, we followed the *extension-based strategy*. Accordingly, we considered the VP-BSIM as our base method and adapted it into a method that guides the identification of platform requirements from value propositions in the form of use case descriptions.

The base method, the VP-BSIM, guides *an actor* in a service system to transform their value propositions into contextualized, standardized, and modular resource re-configurations represented by business services [17, 22]. Accordingly, the business services that the VP-BSIM yields describe the functionality of the overall service system but not in the form of software requirements that can be used in the design of a software system (i.e., a digital service platform in our context). Therefore, we extend the VP-BSIM with the means to guide the translation of service system functionality that is captured as business services into platform requirements.

In finding the right method for the extension, we searched Google Scholar (https://scholar.google.com/) for requirements engineering methods designed for service systems and/or ecosystems. Accordingly, we entered the search query ("service system" OR "service ecosystem") AND "requirements engineering method" which returned a total of 88 studies. After reviewing the title, abstract, and keywords of the studies, we selected [16] which proposes the SREM. The SREM consists of three steps and the final step: *Requirements analysis, negotiation and specification* relates to the translation of services defined for a service system into requirements for a service platform. The first two steps of the SREM relate to the definition of services and since the base method already includes the means to do that, we excluded the first two steps from our extension. As such, we added the procedure of the third step (i.e., method chunk) at the end of the VP-BSIM (i.e., Extended VP-BSIM) as shown in Fig. 1. As such, the added method chunk takes in business service descriptions as input and transforms them to use case descriptions that describe how the digital services interact and cooperate to provide the required end-to-end digital services [16].

## 4 Method Description

In this section, we describe the Extended VP-BSIM (Fig. 1) by briefly introducing the three original steps of the VP-BSIM and presenting in detail the added in the scope of our extension. For the detailed description of the three steps of the original VP-BSIM, we refer the reader to [17].

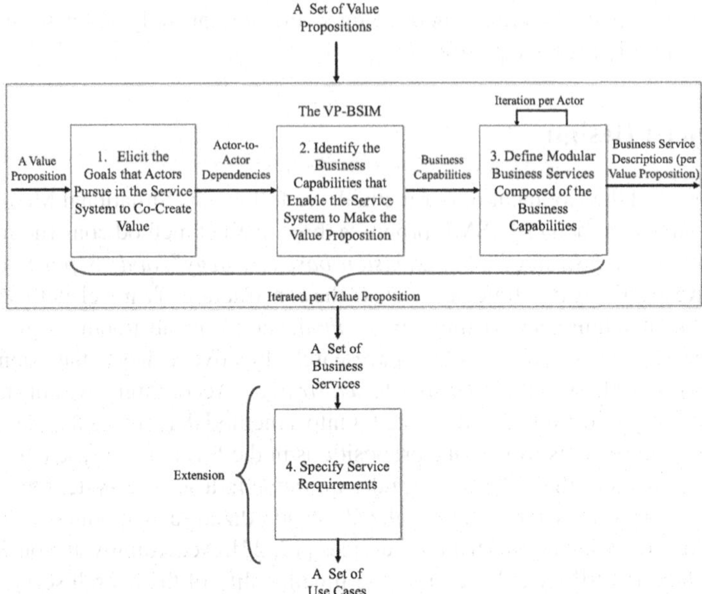


**Fig. 1.** The extended VP-BSIM

**Step 1: Elicit the Goals that Actors Pursue in the Service System to Co-create Value**
The first step of the Extended VP-BSIM constitutes a value proposition-driven analysis to make sure that the business services to be identified enable the co-creation of value as outlined by the value proposition inputted into the method. This step uses *Strategic Dependency (SD) and Strategic Rationale (SR) Modelling* from i* framework [23, 24] to dissect value propositions into intentional and strategic interdependencies among actors in a service system, along with the underlying motives that each actor has in place in pursuit of these interdependencies. The outputs of this step are SD and SR Models that define the strategic and intentional relationships between the actors involved in the service system.

**Step 2: Identify the Business Capabilities that Enable the Service System to Make the Value Proposition**
The second step of the Extended VP-BSIM focuses on identifying the business capabilities that actors need to apply and integrate within their service system to co-create value. This step uses *Capability-Business Service Domain Mapping* [25] to identify the business capabilities that fulfil the intentional and strategic interdependencies defined in Step 1. To identify the business capabilities, first, service domains (i.e., a collection of tasks called service operations that are under the control of an actor [26]) are defined. Then, each service operation under a service domain is matched with a business capability that facilitates the service operation in question. The output of this step is a set of

business capabilities that enable the actors in the service system to co-create value as outlined by a value proposition.

**Step 3: Define Modular Business Services Composed of the Business Capabilities**
The third step focuses on defining modular business services, that describe the functionality of the service system. Furthermore, it formalizes each identified service with a description. This step uses *Service Analysis with Feature Binding Technique* [27] to compose the business capabilities identified in Step 2 into modular business services. This technique considers a modular service to be *Self-Contained* (meaning that a service should not need a service feature of another service), *Stateless* (meaning that a service should not require context or state information of another service), and Representative of a *Domain Specific Service* (meaning that a service should provide an autonomous and unique business function) [27]. The composition of the business capabilities into business services is done by following these three properties.

It should be noted while the scope of the method is the whole service system in Steps 1 & 2, in Step 3 the scope changes to a single actor (i.e., the actor utilizing the Extended VP-BSIM to identify its business services). Therefore, this step should be repeated for every actor (as shown with the arrow on top of Step 3 in Fig. 1) to identify business services for the complete service system. The output of this step is a list of business services that describe the business functions that the service system should provide.

**Step 4: Specify Service Requirements**
The fourth step of the Extended VP-BSIM transforms the business service descriptions produced in Step 3 into use case descriptions that describe the behaviour of the service platform. This step uses the service system requirements engineering technique that *SREM's Requirements analysis, negotiation and specification* step proposes. There are two activities to be performed in this step:

*Activity 4.1: Service Requirements Analysis and Negotiation*
The purpose of this activity is to determine the business services that will be used for requirements specification. As such, the business services identified in Step 3 are selected and prioritized. This requires active collaboration between stakeholders such as IT managers and business analysts to discuss and address various concerns regarding the scope of the requirements specification [16]. The third step of the VP-BSIM ensures that each business service is unique and has business potential (i.e., relates to a value proposition). Therefore, there is no need to identify and merge similar services or reject business services without business potential as the SREM originally suggests [16]. However, the stakeholders can still prioritize certain business services based on factors such as feasibility. The output of this step is a list of business services that are selected for requirements specification.

*Activity 4.2: Service Requirements Specification*
The purpose of this activity is to specify service requirements in a textual or graphical format that is complete, understandable, and useful [16]. This requires several rounds of use case analysis that together transform business service descriptions into use case descriptions. This is assured in the Extended VP-BSIM by considering each business

service description as a use case and the business service operations listed in each business service description as the steps of the happy flow of the use case. The outcome of this activity is a set of use case descriptions that describe the behaviour of the service platform.

## 5 The Application of the Method

We applied our method in a real-life business case originating from the mobility domain [28] to demonstrate its validity (i.e., its ability to guide practitioners in the specification of requirements for a service platform). Below, we first introduce the business case in detail and explain the application of the method in it.

**Business Case: Seamless, Optimized, & Customized Mobility Service Provisioning** In the face of ever-expanding modes of transportation and the number of transport operators, travellers have a hard time choosing the travel itinerary that complies with their needs and expectations. Besides, travellers are usually left to their own devices when passing through the different interfaces that exist between the mobility services of different transport operators. These travel management issues are even more present for international travels due to the barriers that relate to policy and language. Recognizing these issues, a European Innovation and Technology (EIT) project consortium has been focusing on the development of collaborative solutions to offer seamless, optimized, and customized mobility solutions to travellers. To do so, the consortium has envisioned a solution that integrates the resources of actors in the mobility domain, such as mobility service providers (e.g., transport operators), government bodies (e.g., cities, municipalities), traffic authorities, financial transaction providers and enhancing service providers (e.g., insurance providers). The consortium has organized a set of value proposition design workshops to realize this vision. To represent the value propositions, the SDBM Radar technique (Fig. 2) is used [29, 30].

The resulting value proposition revolves around a service platform that enables mobility service providers to register and offer their transport services (i.e., Mobility as a Service - MaaS platform) [31]. Furthermore, the value proposition involves the inclusion of enhancing services such as insurance within the service platform. By using the platform, travellers can input their travel itinerary along with travel preferences and receive a set of recommended mobility and enhancing services that satisfies their itinerary and preferences. When travellers confirm the recommended set of transport services, the platform handles the payment and management of the tickets, and then presents all the tickets to travellers on a single application. Accordingly, the *Traveller* is the main beneficiary in the value proposition, who experiences the *Seamless, Optimized, & Customized Mobility Service*. The initiator of the value proposition is the Service Platform Operator, who is responsible for the integration of various services. The service system is further composed of *Mobility Service Providers*, who provide their transport services on the platform, *Enhancing Service Providers*, who provide services such as insurance on the platform, *Traffic Authorities*, who provide traffic data used to enhance transport services, *Government Bodies*, who set policies to support the value proposition, and *Financial Transaction Provider*, who manages and secures the transactions between service providers.

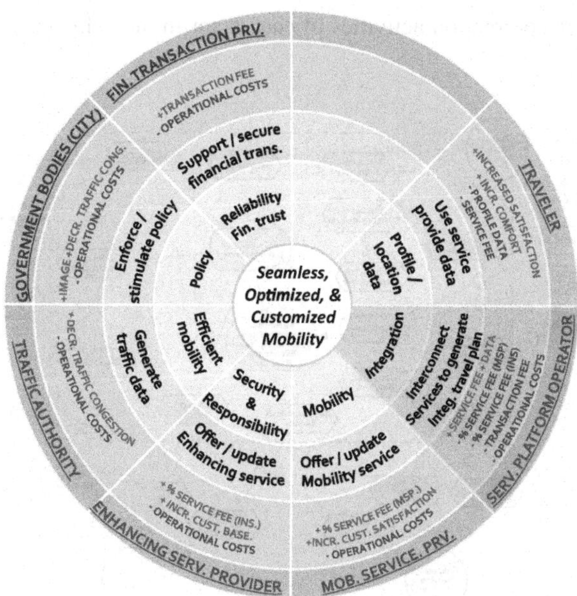


**Fig. 2.** The value proposition: seamless, optimized, & customized mobility service provisioning

**Application of the Method to the Business Case**

In the application of the method, we considered the Service Platform Operator as the actor (i.e., platform owner) that wants to use the method to identify its business services. Being the owner and operator of the platform, the Service Platform Operator represents the actor that orchestrates all the interactions between all the other actors in this service system. Because of this, the business services to be identified for the Service Platform Operator relate to facilitating these interactions and are directly coupled to and provisioned on the service platform. Thus, specific to our case, the business services to be identified for the Service Platform Operator represent the overall functionality that the service platform should support. This means that our case does not require iterating the third step of the method for all the actors of the service system. In general, we suggest applying the third step of the method solely for the actor that is the owner and/or the operator of the service platform as this results in the identification of business services that cover all the service system functionality. However, in the cases where a service platform is owned and/or operated by multiple actors, we suggest iterating the third step for all actors. In the following, we present the application of the method by taking the Service Platform Operator as the platform owner for the method.

**Application of Step 1**

We translated the value proposition design (Fig. 2) into an SR model -including also an SD model- (Fig. 3) that captures the goals that actors pursue in the service system. We depicted every actor in the value proposition as an actor in the SR model as well. Furthermore, for every actor in the SR model, we defined a high-level goal (highlighted in blue in Fig. 3) based on the actor's contribution to the value proposition. Lastly, we depicted the value co-creation activities of each actor in the value proposition as tasks in the SR model.

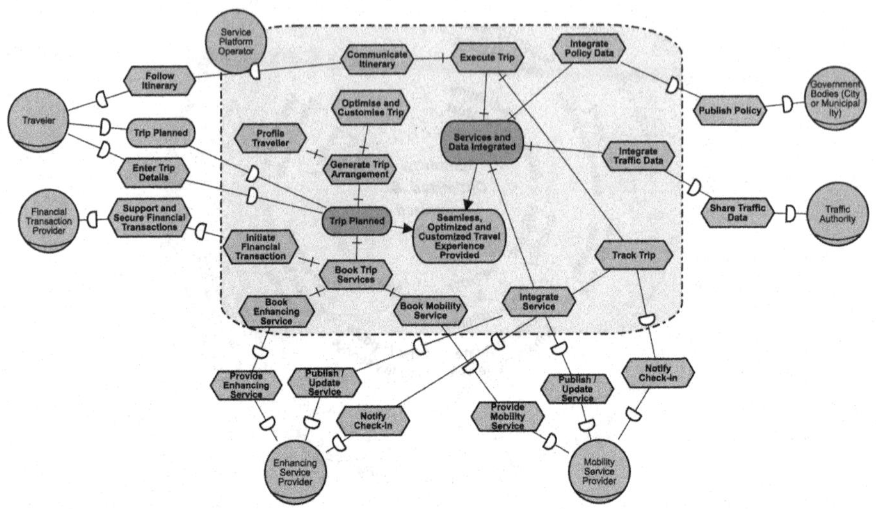


**Fig. 3.** SD-SR model of the value proposition

**Application of Step 2**

Prior to matching the business capabilities to service operations, we defined the business capabilities of the actors through interviews with relevant stakeholders. The resulting list of business capabilities was validated by the same stakeholders (provided at shorturl.at/bjxFH). After defining the business capabilities, we created a service domain for each high-level goal defined in the SR model along with service operations for every task that resides under the high-level goals. We put the defined business capabilities, service domains, and service operations in a Service Domain - Business Capability Matrix as shown in Fig. 4. In the matrix, service domains and operations are placed as rows and business capabilities, and the actors owning them are placed as columns. A cell in the matrix is marked with an 'X' if the business capability corresponding to the cell facilitates the service operation corresponding to the same cell.

**Application of Step 3**

After identifying the business capabilities, we composed them into business services that are (1) Self-Contained, (2) Stateless, and (3) Representative of a Domain Specific Service. As it is the platform owner of our business case, we focused on the business capabilities of the Service Platform Operator as shown with the red-dashed rectangle in Fig. 4. We considered each business capability of the Service Platform Operator as a candidate business service, and we evaluated whether they rely on (1) features or (2) information that reside in another business service and whether they (3) represent a domain specific service. Our evaluation shows that the candidate business services do not need further composition as they are each self-contained, stateless, and representative of a domain specific service. As shown in Fig. 4, each coloured cell on the matrix

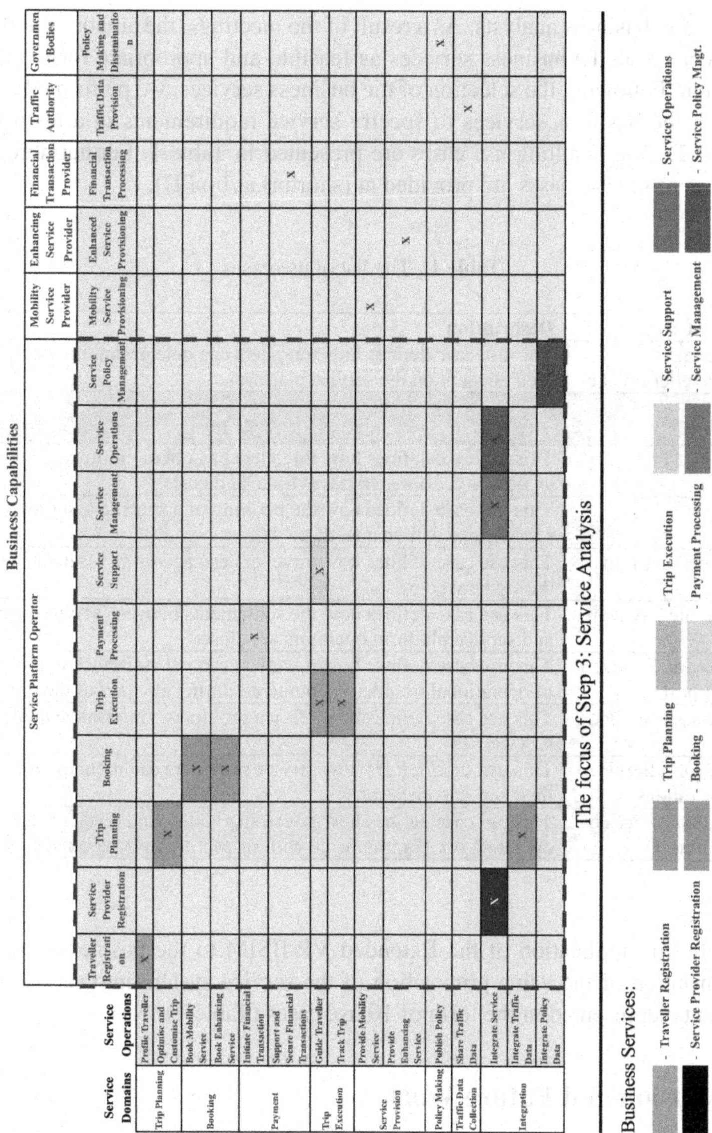


**Fig. 4.** Service domain – business capability matrix and business services

represents a business service that we identified, and the coloured rectangles below the matrix present the names of these business services.

**Application of Step 4**

After the identification of the business services, we arranged three online meetings with the stakeholders from the Service Platform Operator to select the business services for requirements specification (Activity 4.1). The stakeholders included software platform developers and business analysts. As a result of the meetings, the authors and the stakeholders deemed all 10 business services as feasible and appropriate for requirements specification. Following the selection of the business services, we performed a use case analysis on the business services to specify service requirements in a textual format (Activity 4.2). The resulting use cases are presented in Table 1. Furthermore, the full descriptions of the use cases are provided at (shorturl.at/bjxFH).

**Table 1.** The list of use cases

| ID | Use Cases | Description |
|---|---|---|
| 1 | Manage Traveller Profile | This use case defines how travellers can delete, sign-up, or log in to their account on the service platform. |
| 2 | Manage Serv. Provider Profile | This use case defines how service providers can delete, sign-up, or log in to their account on the service platform. |
| 3 | Plan a Trip | This use case defines how travellers can obtain information about availability, estimated travel time, and costs. |
| 4 | Book a Trip | This use case defines how the booking of a specific asset for a specific place, time, and date. |
| 5 | Execute a Trip | This use case defines how travellers can access an asset and a trip during booked period. |
| 6 | Handle Payment | This use case defines how the settlements between service providers and service platform operators are closed. |
| 7 | Provide Service Support | This use case defines how travellers can get assistance in the solution of operational troubles encountered during any part of the process. |
| 8 | Manage Service | This use case defines how service providers can manage their services. |
| 9 | Perform Service Operations | This use case defines how service providers can monitor and manage their service operations. |
| 10 | Manage Service Policy | This use case defines how governing bodies and service platform operators can communicate with respect to service policies. |

Overall, our application of the Extended VP-BSIM to the business case resulted in the translation of the value proposition of the service system into service platform requirements represented in the form of 10 use cases (Table 1).

## 6 Conclusion and Future Work

In this paper, we have proposed a method designed to guide the identification of platform requirements from value propositions in the form of use case descriptions. Using an SME approach [19], we have constructed the proposed method by extending an existing method. In addition, we have demonstrated the validity of the method by applying it to a business case, where the focus was on the identification of platform requirements based on a service system value proposition. The results of our demonstration show that our method guides the derivation of platform requirements from the value propositions. Hence, our study contributes to filling the gap of methodological guidance for the identification of platform requirements from the value propositions in the context of a service system.

Our study is subject to limitations rooted in the demonstration strategy we have followed. As such, we have applied our method to a single business case to demonstrate that it can support what it is designed to do (i.e., validity). Additional applications in different business cases and domains are needed to strengthen the evidence with respect to the method's validity. Furthermore, the perceived usefulness of our method (i.e., utility) by its intended users (e.g., business analysts and requirements engineers) remains to be evaluated. Therefore, additional applications should focus on obtaining user feedback on the utility of the method in addition to its validity.

Finally, our method's application to the presented business case should be followed by a longitudinal study that aims at validating that the service platform that is designed by following the service platform requirements defined with our method is operational.

## References

1. Ng, I., Wakenshaw, S.: Service ecosystems: a timely worldview for a connected, digital and data-driven economy. In: The Sage Handbook of Service-Dominant Logic, pp. 199–213. Sage, London (2018)
2. Vargo, S.L., Lusch, R.F.: Service-dominant logic 2025. Int. J. Res. Mark. **34**(1), 46–67 (2017). https://doi.org/10.1016/j.ijresmar.2016.11.001
3. Breidbach, C.F., Maglio, P.P.: Technology-enabled value co-creation: an empirical analysis of actors, resources, and practices. Ind. Mark. Manag. **56**, 73–85 (2016). https://doi.org/10.1016/j.indmarman.2016.03.011
4. Engel, C., Ebel, P.: Data-driven service innovation: a systematic literature review and development of a research agenda, p. 20 (2019)
5. Lusch, R.F., Nambisan, S.: Service innovation: a service-dominant logic perspective. MIS Q. **39**(1), 155–175 (2015). https://doi.org/10.25300/MISQ/2015/39.1.07
6. Turetken, O., Grefen, P., Gilsing, R., Adali, O.E.: Service-dominant business model design for digital innovation in smart mobility. Bus. Inf. Syst. Eng. **61**(1), 9–29 (2019). https://doi.org/10.1007/s12599-018-0565-x
7. Breidbach, C.F., Brodie, R.J.: Engagement platforms in the sharing economy: conceptual foundations and research directions. J. Serv. Theory Pract. **27**(4), 761–777 (2017). https://doi.org/10.1108/JSTP-04-2016-0071
8. Fehrer, J.A., Woratschek, H., Brodie, R.J.: A systemic logic for platform business models. J. Serv. Manag. **29**(4), 546–568 (2018). https://doi.org/10.1108/JOSM-02-2017-0036
9. Smedlund, A.: Value cocreation in service platform business models. Serv. Sci. **4**(1), 79–88 (2012). https://doi.org/10.1287/serv.1110.0001
10. Chandler, J.D., Lusch, R.F.: Service systems: a broadened framework and research agenda on value propositions, engagement, and service experience. J. Serv. Res. (2014). https://doi.org/10.1177/1094670514537709
11. Normann, R., Ramirez, R.: From value chain to value constellation: designing interactive strategy. Harv. Bus. Rev. **71**(4), 65 (1993)
12. Blaschke, M., Haki, K., Aier, S., Winter, R.: Capabilities for Digital Platform Survival: Insights from a Business-to-Business Digital Platform, p. 17 (2018)
13. Böhmann, T., Leimeister, J.M., Möslein, K.: Service systems engineering. Bus. Inf. Syst. Eng. **6**(2), 73–79 (2014). https://doi.org/10.1007/s12599-014-0314-8
14. Maglio, P.P., Spohrer, J.: A service science perspective on business model innovation. Ind. Mark. Manag. **42**(5), 665–670 (2013)

15. Maglio, P.P., Vargo, S.L., Caswell, N., Spohrer, J.: The service system is the basic abstraction of service science. Inf. Syst. E-Bus. Manag. **7**(4), 395–406 (2009). https://doi.org/10.1007/s10257-008-0105-1
16. Immonen, A., Ovaska, E., Kalaoja, J., Pakkala, D.: A service requirements engineering method for a digital service ecosystem. SOCA **10**(2), 151–172 (2015). https://doi.org/10.1007/s11761-015-0175-0
17. Adali, O.E., Türetken, O., Ozkan, B., Gilsing, R., Grefen, P.: A multi-concern method for identifying business services: a situational method engineering study. In: Nurcan, S., Reinhartz-Berger, I., Soffer, P., Zdravkovic, J. (eds.) BPMDS/EMMSAD -2020. LNBIP, vol. 387, pp. 227–241. Springer, Cham (2020). https://doi.org/10.1007/978-3-030-49418-6_15
18. Lessard, L., Amyot, D., Aswad, O., Mouttham, A.: Expanding the nature and scope of requirements for service systems through service-dominant logic: the case of a telemonitoring service. Requirements Eng. **25**(3), 273–293 (2020). https://doi.org/10.1007/s00766-019-00322-z
19. Ralyté, J., Deneckère, Rébecca., Rolland, C.: Towards a generic model for situational method engineering. In: Eder, J., Missikoff, M. (eds.) CAiSE. LNCS, vol. 2681, pp. 95–110. Springer, Heidelberg (2003). https://doi.org/10.1007/3-540-45017-3_9
20. Yu, E.S.K. (ed.): Social Modeling for Requirements Engineering. MIT Press, Cambridge (2011)
21. Horkoff, J., et al.: Goal-oriented requirements engineering: an extended systematic mapping study. Requirements Eng. **24**(2), 133–160 (2017). https://doi.org/10.1007/s00766-017-0280-z
22. Adali, O.E., Ozkan, B., Türetken, O., Gilsing, R.A., Grefen, P.: A method to transform value propositions of a service system into business services. ECIS 2021 Research Papers, vol. 77 (2021)
23. Dalpiaz, F., Franch, X., Horkoff, J.: iStar 2.0 Language Guide. CoRR, abs/1605.0 (2016)
24. Yu, E.: Modelling strategic relationships for process reengineering. University of Toronto (1995). https://doi.org/10.1007/11603412
25. Kohlborn, T., Korthaus, A., Chan, T., Rosemann, M.: Identification and analysis of business and software services-a consolidated approach. IEEE Trans. Serv. Comput. **2**(1), 50–64 (2009). https://doi.org/10.1109/TSC.2009.6
26. Jones, S.: Toward an acceptable definition of service [service-oriented architecture]. IEEE Softw. **22**(3), 87–93 (2005). https://doi.org/10.1109/MS.2005.80
27. Lee, J., Muthig, D., Naab, M.: An approach for developing service oriented product lines. In: 2008 12th International Software Product Line Conference, pp. 275–284 (2008). https://doi.org/10.1109/SPLC.2008.34
28. Gilsing, R., et al.: Evaluating the design of service-dominant business models: a qualitative method. Pac. Asia J. Assoc. Inf. Syst. **13**(1), 2 (2021)
29. Luftenegger, E.R.: Service-Dominant Business Design. Eindhoven University of Technology (2014). https://doi.org/10.6100/IR774591
30. Turetken, O., Grefen, P.: Designing service-dominant business models. In: ECIS 2017 Proceedings, vol. 2017, pp. 2218–2233 (2017). http://aisel.aisnet.org/cgi/viewcontent.cgi?article=1140&context=ecis2017_rp
31. Coconea, L., Mizaras, V., Turetken, O., Dovinola, G., Grefen, P.: Insights on traffic management in the MaaS value chain. In: 13th ITS European Congress, June 2019, pp. 3–6 (2019)

# A Modular Ontology Framework for Building Renovation Domain

Prathap Valluru[1](✉), Janakiram Karlapudi[1], Teemu Mätäsniemi[2], and Karsten Menzel[1]

[1] Institute of Construction Informatics, Technische Universität Dresden, Dresden, Germany
{Prathap.Valluru,Janakiram.Karlapudi, Karsten.Menzel1}@tu-dresden.de

[2] VTT Technical Research Centre of Finland Ltd., Espoo, Finland
Teemu.Matasniemi@vtt.fi

**Abstract.** Building renovation is a complex collaborative process requiring the interaction between planners, architects, civil engineers, energy experts, and managers of (pre-)manufacturing plants supplying building elements, components of energy supply and distribution systems "just in sequence" to densely used urban spaces – where the majority of buildings under renovation are located. Therefore, the availability of a complete, comprehensive Building Information Model, amalgamating current and future product and process models is of outstanding importance. Approaches, suggesting so-called "monolithic" building information models did not deliver the expected "value for money" since the efforts required to set up and maintain such digital models requested more resources than available. Therefore, the authors present in this paper an alternative approach to information, knowledge management, and sharing in the AECO-sector, i.e. modular ontologies. The flexible and dynamic approach to combine new and available modules of information addresses more responsively the needs of the AECO sector. Furthermore, such BIM models overcome limitations in adaptability, extensibility, etc. of current "openBIM models". Due to this the shift towards using semantic web technologies for knowledge base and semantic interoperability has been increased in the AECO industry. The work presented in the paper introduces a recently developed linked data, an ontology-based framework that harmonizes and orchestrates ontologies recently developed for the construction domain. It studies inter-model and inter ontology relationships to address concepts that are currently absent from "building ontologies". The developed framework can be used to support collaborative environments in the engineering and manufacturing sector supporting the efficient sharing of information between architects, engineers, manufacturing plants, and assembly crews on the construction site.

**Keywords:** Ontology composition · Renovation process · Information sharing/exchange · Collaborative networks · Collaborative manufacturing


L. M. Camarinha-Matos et al. (Eds.): PRO-VE 2021, IFIP AICT 629, pp. 323–334, 2021.
https://doi.org/10.1007/978-3-030-85969-5_29

## 1 Introduction

The building renovation process involves stakeholders throughout the life cycle. The stakeholders of the Architecture, Engineering, Construction, and Operations (AECO) industry exchange heterogeneous information among multiple stakeholders, using tools and datasets of different nature [1]. The heterogeneous information includes as-built BIM models, energy information, images, documents, plans, etc. However, the identification of critical information, its management along with the efficient collaboration, and communication between the participants in the project are some barriers in the traditional building construction process [2].

The development of Collaborative Networks (CNs) allows effective collaboration between the teams [3, 4] and there is a need to improve the data sharing and management in CNs [5]. The specifications of shared vocabulary can play an important role where knowledge-based systems are expensive to build, test, and maintain [6]. Research work by L.M. Camarinha-Matos et al. explained that ontology engineering is a potential domain that can contribute to the information/knowledge management in Collaborative Networks (CNs) [7]. Also, the usage of ontologies in CNs is supported in several research efforts [8–10]. However, the ontologies that can cover construction management data are not available on the web, and also, some existing ontologies cover limited data. There is a need to fill the gaps for entities, construction information, construction activities, stakeholders, level of details, materials, occupants, etc.

In the BIM4EEB[1] project, several ontologies (Digital Construction Ontologies[2] - DICon) are developed to support the renovation data modeling/sharing and act as a resource to the collaborative system called BIM management system (BIMMS[3]). The development of ontologies was carried out by using Web of Data (WoD) technologies. The semantic web and Linked data are two sources of WoD [11]. The semantic web technologies have Resource Description Framework (RDF[4]) model for data interchange, Web Ontology Language (OWL[5]) to represent complex knowledgebase, and Simple Protocol and RDF Query Language (SPARQL[6]) to run the queries across the data sets. Linked Data[7] is to identify things using URIs, look up the name of things using HTTP URIs, add information to the things using semantic web technologies, and link the information to add more context or semantics to existing information.

To make the developed or existing ontologies to be useful, two objectives must be met, as per Barry Smith and Mathias Brochhausen 2008 [12]. First, it is essential to align/match existing ontologies by harmonization process. Secondly, it is necessary to find ways to evaluate ontologies transparently. In this paper, we discussed the first part and developed a framework to harmonize the ontologies by modularization approaches.

---

1 https://www.bim4eeb-project.eu/.

2 https://digitalconstruction.github.io/v/0.5/index.html.

3 https://bim4eeb.oneteam.it/BIMMS/Default.aspx.

4 https://www.w3.org/RDF/.

5 https://www.w3.org/OWL/.

6 https://www.w3.org/TR/sparql11-query/.

7 https://www.w3.org/DesignIssues/LinkedData.

## 2 Ontology Modularization

Modularization of ontologies will make user easier to understand, extend, reuse, maintain and reason the ontologies [13, 14]. However, the concept of modularization is not well defined in the context of ontologies compared to software engineering. A single approach for modularization does not match every situation since people tend to have various ideas in the development of ontologies. Several various approaches appeared in the field of ontology modularization. These approaches are mainly categorized into "ontology separation" and "ontologies composition" and are shown in Fig. 1. These two main approaches are sub-categorized into ontology partition, ontology module extraction, ontologies integration, and ontologies mapping respectively [15].

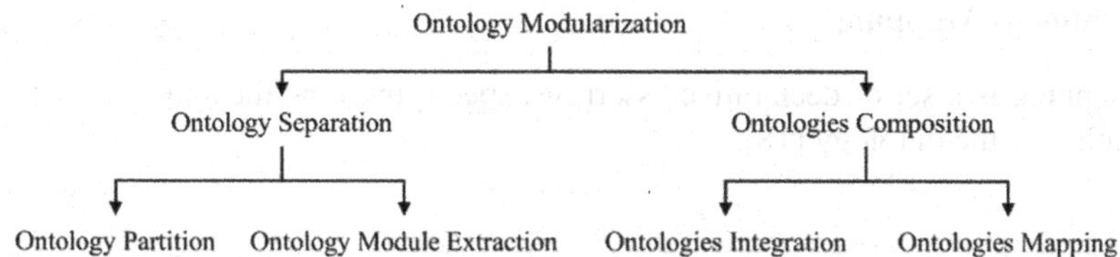


**Fig. 1.** Ontology modularization approaches

The ontology separation approach is mainly useful to make large-scale ontology into small-scale ontologies to use for narrower use cases. But, in the ontologies composition approach small ontologies will be integrated to make a large ontology by maintaining its modularity. The DICon ontologies cover different domain gaps (e.g. entities, occupant comfort, lifecycle, materials…etc.). To make it useful for broader domain use cases, ontologies modularization applied on DICon ontologies by using the ontologies composition approach.

### 2.1 Ontology Integration

Ontology integration is the process of forming a new ontology by using one or more ontologies without changing their original concepts, if possible, they are extended [16]. Integrate $(O_1, O_2, A) = O_1$, where O1 is the target ontology into which the source ontology O2 will be integrated and A is the alignment expressed in the same logical language as ontologies O1 and O2 [17]. Ontology alignment may be seen as a pre-step for detecting where the involved ontologies overlap and can be connected. This approach is especially interesting if given ontologies differ in their domain. Through integration, the new ontology can cover a bigger domain in the end.

In the integration process, two approaches are primarily considered and shown in Fig. 2. The ontologies $O_1$, $O_2$, and alignment $O_1$-$O_2$ are considered to discuss these approaches. The Ontology $O_1$, alignment module $O_1$-$O_2$, are imported to ontology $O_2$ in the first approach, few required concepts from $O_1$ are redefined in the ontology $O_2$. In the second approach, required concepts from ontology $O_1$ are redefined in ontology $O_2$, alignment module $O_1$-$O_2$ imports ontologies $O_1$, $O_2$ to extend the scope of usage of ontologies. In this paper, the second approach is considered to develop an ontology framework.

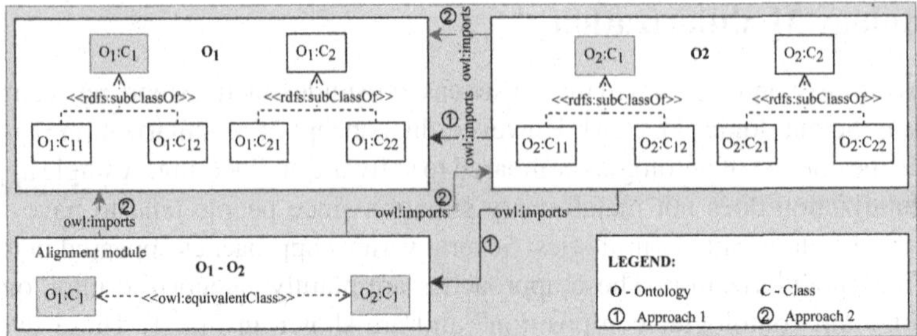


**Fig. 2.** Ontology integration methods

## 2.2 Ontology Mapping

The mapping is a set of declarative assertions specifying how the sources in the data layer relate to the ontology [18].

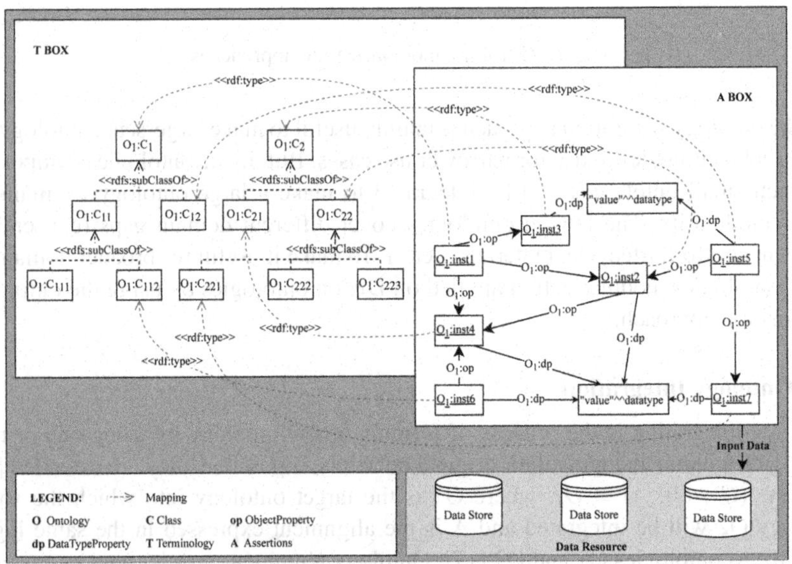


**Fig. 3.** Ontology mapping concept

An ontology mapping represents a function between the ontologies. The original ontologies are not changed, but the additional mapping axioms describe how to express concepts, relations, or instances in terms of the second ontology. They are stored separately from the ontologies themselves [16]. Figure 3 represents the ontology mapping concept. Three concepts called Terminology Box (T-BOX), Assertion Box (A-BOX), Data sources are considered to explain the ontology mapping process. T-BOX is an ontology with classes, properties, and A-BOX is individual data that comes from the data sources. The individual data that comes from the data sources are mapped with

T-BOX data and a knowledge base will develop. The axiom rdf:type is used to relate an individual for a class.

## 3 Collaborative BIM Environments and Knowledge Base

For several years, several research initiatives have been focused on the creation and operation of collaborative processes in the construction sector [19]. However, the lack of effective collaborative processes tools, information management of heterogeneous data, and sharing it among the actors are still barriers in AECO sector. Also, lack of tools with integrated Common Data Environments (CDE) [5, 20]. The BIMMS is a collaborative environment developed in the BIM4EEB project. BIMMS is a platform built around a common data environment (CDE) that stores all the data and information gathered through different sources and along the whole building lifecycle, acting as a single source of truth (SSOT) [21].

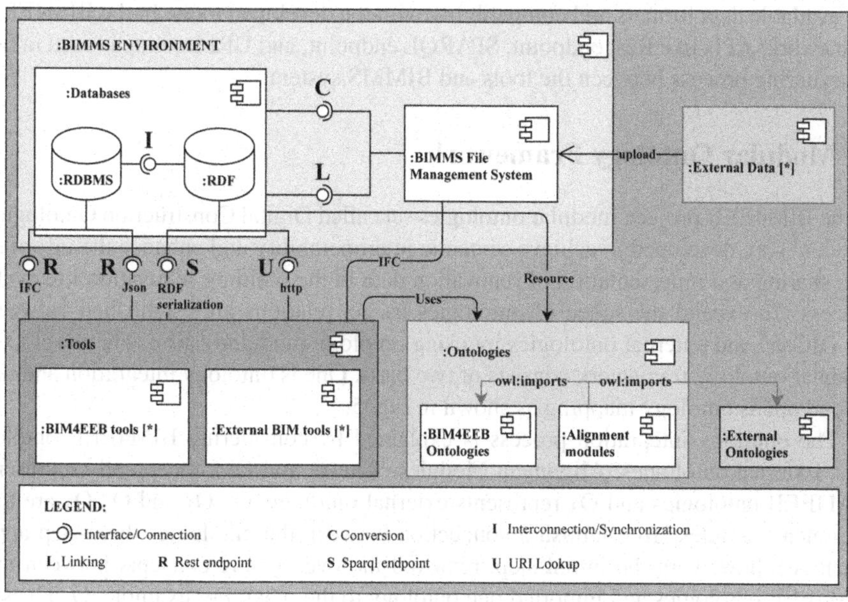


**Fig. 4.** Usage of modular ontologies in a collaborative environment

The aim of this BIMMS is the effective management of information produced in the renovation processes along with the establishment of efficient communication between the involved tool kits. This process supports the storage of information in various formats (ontologies, models, diagrams, etc.) and manages the information by enabling the links between them. This section intends to explore the ontology-based information management facilities within the BIMMS platform.

A component diagram represented in Fig. 4 comprehensively illustrating the adopted BIM4EEB framework. The involved components in this framework are 1) Ontologies,

2) BIMMS environment, 3) BIM4EEB tools, and finally, 4) external data (images, files, models, sensor data, etc.). As shown in the figure, the ontology component describes a set of developed ontologies as part of the BIM4EEB project and their alignments to external ontologies in terms of alignment modules. This ontology component is further integrated into BIMMS environment and supports the representation of the BIM model information and other resource information. In specific, the BIMMS system enables this representation by converting the resource data in the File management system into Linked data (RDF data) and Relational Database (RDBMS). It also provides the linkage between these data models or data formats to synchronize the updates or changes effectively. The use of ontologies and linked data in the tools is a promising solution to explore dynamic and heterogeneous data [22].

The last component in the framework is the tool-set, which is used for the progressive and successful implementation of the renovation process. This tool component is equipped either with BIM4EEB tools and/or external tools. The data stored in BIMMS system is effectively shared to these tools based on the required interface connections. In general, there are many interface connections but their application is only dependent on the available data formats and compatibility with the developed tools. In the BIM4EEB framework, APIs like Rest endpoint, SPARQL endpoint, and URI Lookup is used in the data sharing process between the tools and BIMMS system.

## 4 Modular Ontology Framework

In the BIM4EEB project, modular ontologies set called Digital Construction Ontologies (DICon[8]) are developed to achieve semantic interoperability and enhance the information sharing and representation of renovation data in the building renovation life cycle process. To expand the scope of ontologies usage, relations are established between the DICon[8] and external ontologies by using ontology modularization. The developed modular ontology framework consists of two parts. One is ontology integration and the second one is ontology mapping as shown in Fig. 5.

The ontology integration process is explained by considering BIM4EEB ontologies, External ontologies, Alignment Modules. The $O_1$ and $O_2$ conceptually represent BIM4EEB ontologies and $O_3$ represents external ontology, $O_1$-$O_3$ and $O_2$-$O_3$ are the alignment modules. To establish a connection between the ontologies three-step approach is followed. In the initial step, removed the overlapping concepts between the BIM4EEB ontologies and imported one ontology to the other. For example, $O_1$:$C_1$ is a class in $O_1$ and the same class is defined in the ontology $O_2$ with the URI of $O_1$. This approach helps to avoid redundancy and the ontology merging process will be easier. In the second step, alignment modules are developed between the BIM4EEB ontologies and external ontologies and kept as separate files. In the last step, aligned ontologies are imported into its alignment module, which extends the scope of the ontologies. The modular ontologies developed using this integration process are published on the GitHub page https://digitalconstruction.github.io/v/0.5/index.html.

In the second part ontology mapping developed using the concept of "Ontology-Based Data Access (OBDA) [23]". The idea behind OBDA is to use a DL ontology as

[8] https://digitalconstruction.github.io/v/0.5/index.html.

a means to access a set of data sources, to mask the user from all application-dependent aspects of data, and to extract useful information from the sources based on a conceptual representation of the domain, expressed as a T-Box in a suitable DL [24]. The ontologies $O_1$, $O_2$, and $O_3$ are ontology T Box data, inst:Individual1, inst:Individual2, inst:Individual3, inst:Individual4 are the assertions (A Box data) or data stored in the data resource layer or from the tool. The T-Box data and A-Box data are mapped together using the axioms to form a complete Knowledge Base (KB).

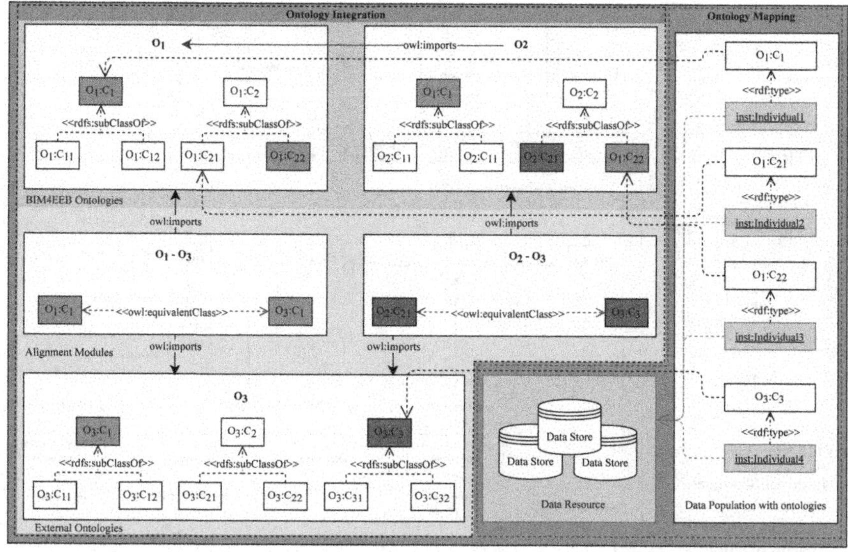


**Fig. 5.** Modular ontology framework using ontologies composition approach

## 5 Proof of Concept and Result

The developed use case is based on the BIMeaser (BIM Early Stage Energy Scenario tool) tool. The BIMeaser was developed for the early phase evaluation of residential building refurbishment designs. This tool able to download BIM models from the BIMMS and Renovation scenarios are defined for simulation, computes the indicators of building energy performance. These indicators are then compared with reference requirements, the Owner's Project Requirements (OPRs). However, the modular ontologies framework is used to establish a relation between the ontologies used to store BIMeaser OPRs. Finally, OPRs calculated with BIMeaser are uploaded into BIMMS in the triple store. Ontologies have been developed and integrated, mapped with the BIMeaser OPRs to develop complete KB. In this process, BIM4EEB ontologies entities (DICI), Contexts (DICC), Variable (DICV), Information (DICI), Materials (DICM), and Energy (DICES) are used. Also, the vocabulary Units (DICU) used. The external ontologies Building Topology Ontology (BOT), Quantities, Units, Dimensions and Types (QUDT[9]), QUDT

[9] http://www.qudt.org/pages/QUDToverviewPage.html.

UNITS (see footnote 9), Data Catalog Vocabulary (DACT[10]), PROV Ontology (PROV-O[11]), QUDT Quantity Kind (see footnote 9). The ontologies are aligned and imported to their respective align modules as shown in Fig. 6. Therefore, BIMeaser provides an effective collaboration tool for experts with different backgrounds in the design team and can speed up decision-making in building refurbishment projects [25].

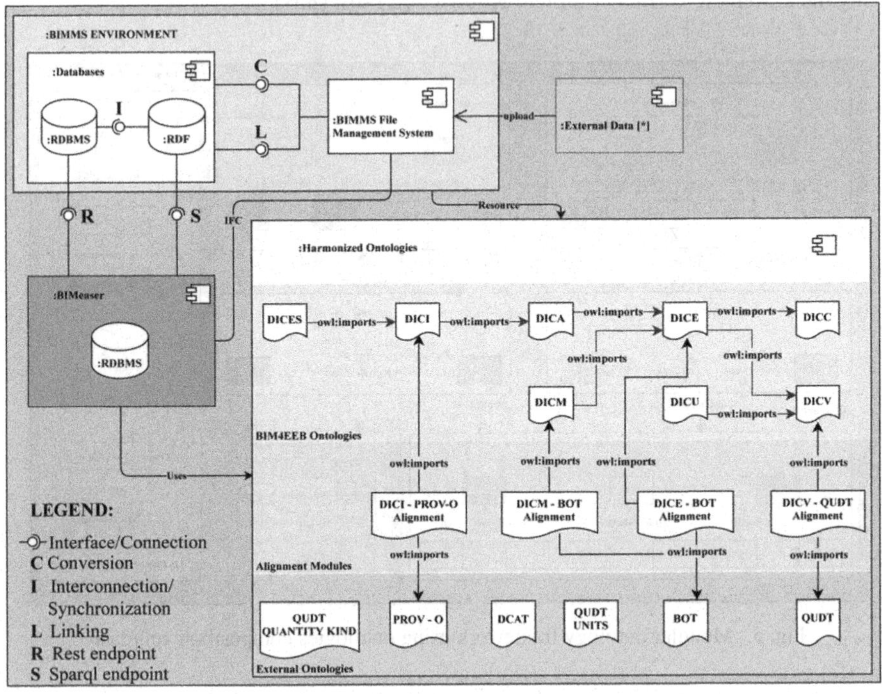


**Fig. 6.** Usage of modular ontologies in BIMeaser tool

The OPRs for the baseline (no investment cost) and different scenarios are considered and listed in the table below. Each renovation scenario is specified by renovation measures to change building structures or technical systems. The impact of these measures is presented in the terms of Owners Project Requirements (OPR) indicators. The OPR's -e.g. operational energy cost, the payback time of renovation, and summer thermal comfort are an important part of the performance-based building design process, which assumes that design selections are validated against the OPR's in each design stage before moving to the following design stage. The design team will handle the detailed technical energy selections affecting the OPR's using the tool as part of the collaborative work. OPR indicators are computed after detailed building energy simulations based on localized data (e.g. energy and investment cost data). After all, OPRs have been prepared the scenarios can be compared. In a conclusion, BIMeaser presents the impact of each

[10] https://www.w3.org/TR/vocab-dcat-2/.

[11] https://www.w3.org/TR/prov-o/.

renovation scenario and also baseline results in terms of Owners Project Requirements (OPR). The most important OPR values are calculated to support the performance-based building design process and validation of design decisions.

**Table 1.** An example of scenario and OPR results presented in BIMeaser tool

| Scenario | Operational energy cost €/floor-m², a | Investment €/floor-m² | RES share % | Heating kWh/m², a | Cooling kWh/m², a | Electricity kWh/m², a | Summer thermal h/year, zone (Tindoor > 27 °C) |
|---|---|---|---|---|---|---|---|
| S1 | 14.87 | 0.00 | 0.01 | 123 | 0.0 | 35 | 1763 |
| S2 | 13.39 | 46.41 | 0.01 | 97 | 0.0 | 35 | 2045 |
| S3 | 12.89 | 11.25 | 5.55 | 123 | 0.0 | 26 | 1763 |
| S4 | 13.88 | 16.00 | 0.01 | 106 | 0.0 | 35 | 1763 |
| S5 | 13.60 | 72.18 | 0.01 | 101 | 0.0 | 35 | 1875 |
| S5 | 9.55 | 145.84 | 8.89 | 64 | 0.0 | 26 | 2284 |

The OPR results are enriched with the classes of the ontologies in BIMeaser tool. These results are converted into an RDF file for data sharing. An example of the OPR data with the ontologies shown in Fig. 7.

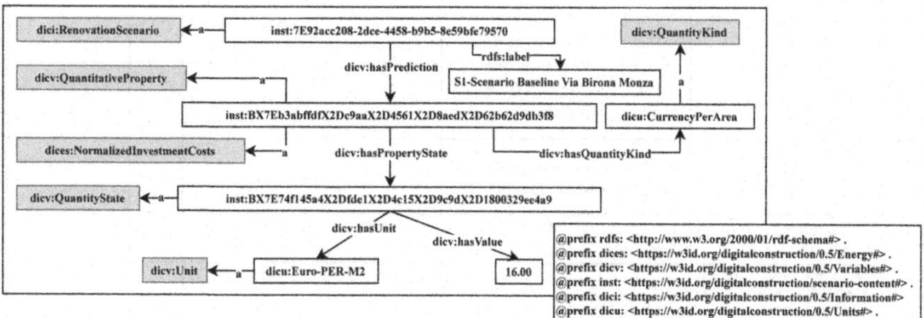


**Fig. 7.** An example of OPR data in RDF notation

These RDF will be stored in the BIMMS containing links to the IFC model used in the simulation. The linking of OPR's and the BIM model in the BIMMS enables tracking of the building energy performance during the evolution of the renovation design, which is an important part of the performance-based design approach. Also, BIMMS system allows the stakeholder to query and get the required information using the SPARQL Endpoint. For example, the OPR data of heating energy consumption for all renovation scenarios can get from the BIMMS by using the SPARQL query.

**SPARQL Query**

```
prefix dicv: <https://w3id.org/digitalconstruction/0.5/Variables#>
prefix dices: <https://w3id.org/digitalconstruction/0.5/Energy#>
prefix dicu: https://w3id.org/digitalconstruction/0.5/Units#
prefix inst: <https://w3id.org/digitalconstruction/scenario-content#>
SELECT ?scenarioName ?Property ?PState ?Value ?Unit
FROM <https://w3id.org/digitalconstruction/scenario-content-opr>
WHERE { ?scenario dicv:hasPrediction ?Property .
?scenario rdfs:label ?scenarioName .
?Property dicv:isPropertyFor dices:hasNormalizedHeatingEnergyConsumption .
?Property dicv:hasPropertyState ?PState .
?PState dicv:hasValue ?Value .
?PState dicv:hasUnit ?Unit . }
```

**SPARQL Query Results**

Figure 8 shows the query results which are shown by the SPARQL Endpoint in BIMMS. These results are validated with the OPR data (Table 1) presented in BIMeaser tool.

| scenarioName | Property | PState | Value | Unit |
|---|---|---|---|---|
| "S2-Scenario Insulation~211a3c72-67df-4f5d-ae45-11c3ae8e6c73" | inst:BX7E02748d58X2Dfa92X2D4f02X2Daad9X2D4dc5cd3522ea | inst:BX7Eee4a6369X2D0ea4X2D45ccX2D999aX2D97ef026943bf | 97.0 | dicu:KiloW-HR-PER-M2-YR |
| "S1-Scenario Baseline Via Birona Monza" | inst:BX7Ea0a2d9fcX2D3888X2D4595X2D9bd9X2Dd30d0e51a55c | inst:BX7E0fa86f9fX2D73dfX2D46dcX2Db614X2D7e13c65c0b9d | 123.0 | dicu:KiloW-HR-PER-M2-YR |
| "S5-Scenario Replacing the windows~6438aeaf-578b-4d3f-9934-68705cdadbe9" | inst:BX7E60b57d94X2D2d96X2D4fd2X2Dab7dX2De4e9e50f7b9f | inst:BX7E89a150a7X2D1743X2D42e6X2Da2d9X2De174ca256935 | 101.0 | dicu:KiloW-HR-PER-M2-YR |
| "S3-Scenario Solar PV panels~4aee83d0-5df5-4edb-a3ee-1a93b0a75477" | inst:BX7Ef22acff9X2Ded7bX2D4274X2D9730X2D3179481bbb80 | inst:BX7E71b4ccfbX2D86dfX2D4393X2D99b8X2D6a31bef47748 | 123.0 | dicu:KiloW-HR-PER-M2-YR |
| "S6-Scenario~7634d9d3-0a94-4c7a-a2cd-f00ea2890a70" | inst:BX7Eb939fb70X2D4771X2D4072X2D8653X2D7b397ccffbaa | inst:BX7E7ae930edX2D5b6eX2D4ab3X2D9f0dX2D581190637c06 | 64.0 | dicu:KiloW-HR-PER-M2-YR |
| "S4-Scenario New condensing gas boiler~92acc208-2dce-4458-b9b5-8e59bfe79570" | inst:BX7Efc2ac50dX2D3826X2D49aaX2Da837X2De67e0c07c3fd | inst:BX7E98d48f7eX2D8735X2D42e9X2Da971X2D084824999ca9 | 106.0 | dicu:KiloW-HR-PER-M2-YR |

**Fig. 8.** SPARQL query results for scenario and OPR data

## 6 Conclusion

The building renovation is a complex process, requires the intervention of stakeholders throughout the renovation. The efficient Collaboration Networks (CNs) equipped with Common Data Environments (CDE) can play a crucial role in the collaboration between the stakeholders in the project. The developed framework will enhance the interoperability between the stakeholders and tools. Ontologies composition approaches have been used to develop the framework. The developed harmonized shared vocabulary will be a resource to the collaboration system and it can be used in the renovation tools for data mapping and representation. A small use case of BIMeaser tool is considered to apply the ontology framework and discussed.

In the future more detailed demonstration of ontologies mapping, data transfer of the other tools using the ontologies, and validation is carried out.

**Acknowledgement.** This research is carried out as a part of BIM4EEB project (BIM based fast toolkit for the Efficient rEnovation of Buildings). The BIM4EEB project has received funding from European Union's H2020 research and innovative programme under grant agreement N.820660. The content of this publication reflects author view only and the commission is not responsible for any use that may be made of the information it contains. Finally, we would like to thank Seppo Törma and all partners in the BIM4EEB project for their valuable inputs.

## References

1. Mirarchi, C., Lucky, M.N., Ciuffreda, S., Signorini, M., Lupica Spagnolo, S., Bolognesi, C., et al.: An approach for standardization of semantic models for building renovation processes. Int. Arch. Photogramm. Remote Sens. Spatial Inf. Sci. **XLIII-B4-2020**, 69–76 (2020). https://doi.org/10.5194/isprs-archives-XLIII-B4-2020-69-2020
2. Valluru, P., Karlapudi, J., Menzel, K., Mätäsniemi, T., Shemeika, J.: A semantic data model to represent building material data in AEC collaborative workflows. In: Camarinha-Matos, L.M., Afsarmanesh, H., Ortiz, A. (eds.) PRO-VE 2020. IAICT, vol. 598, pp. 133–142. Springer, Cham (2020). https://doi.org/10.1007/978-3-030-62412-5_11
3. Camarinha-Matos, L.M., Afsarmanesh, H.: Collaborative networks. In: Wang, K., Kovacs, G.L., Wozny, M., Fang, M. (eds.) PROLAMAT 2006. IIFIP, vol. 207, pp. 26–40. Springer, Boston (2006). https://doi.org/10.1007/0-387-34403-9_4
4. Camarinha-Matos, L.M., Afsarmanesh H.: Classes of collaborative networks. In: IT Outsourcing: Concepts, Methodologies, Tools, and Applications. IGI Global, pp. 364–370 (2009). https://doi.org/10.4018/978-1-60566-770-6.ch021
5. Sousa, C., Pereira, C.: Sharing through collaborative spaces: enhancing collaborative networks interoperability. In: Camarinha-Matos, L.M., Afsarmanesh, H. (eds.) PRO-VE 2014. IAICT, vol. 434, pp. 481–488. Springer, Heidelberg (2014). https://doi.org/10.1007/978-3-662-44745-1_48
6. Thomas, R.G.: A translation approach to portable ontology specifications. Knowl. Acquis. **5**(2), 199–220 (1993). https://doi.org/10.1006/knac.1993.1008
7. Camarinha-Matos, L.M., Afsarmanesh, H.: Collaborative networks in industry and services: research scope and challenges. IFAC Proc. Volumes **40**(1), 33–42 (2007). https://doi.org/10.3182/20070213-3-CU-2913.00007
8. Pagoropoulos, A., Andersen, J.A.B., Kjær, L.L., Maier, A., McAloone, T.C.: Building an ontology of product/service-systems: using a maritime case study to elicit classifications and characteristics. In: Camarinha-Matos, L.M., Afsarmanesh, H. (eds.) PRO-VE 2014. IAICT, vol. 434, pp. 119–126. Springer, Heidelberg (2014). https://doi.org/10.1007/978-3-662-44745-1_11
9. Antonelli, D., Bruno, G.: Ontology-based framework to design a collaborative human-robotic workcell. In: Camarinha-Matos, L.M., et al. (eds.) PRO-VE 2017, IFIP AICT 506, pp. 167–174 (2017)
10. Rachman, A., Ratnayake, R.C.: Ontology-based semantic modeling for automated identification of damage mechanisms in process plants. In: Camarinha-Matos, L.M., et al. (eds.) PRO-VE 2018, IFIP AICT 534, pp. 457–466 (2018)

11. Törmä, S.: Web of building data – integrating IFC with the Web of Data. In: Mahdavi, A., Martens, B., Scherer, R.J. (eds.) EWork and eBusiness in Architecture, Engineering and Construction. Proceedings of 10th European Conference on Product and Process Modelling (ECPPM 2014), Vienna, Austria, 17–19 September 2014. CRC Press, Boca Raton, pp. 141–147 (2015)
12. Barry, S., Mathias, B.: Establishing and harmonizing ontologies in an interdisciplinary health care and clinical research environment (2008)
13. Bernardo, G., Ian, H., Yevgeny, K., Uli, S.: A logical framework for modular integration of ontologies. In: Proceedings of the 20th International Joint Conference on Artificial Intelligence (IJCAI-07) (2007)
14. d'Aquin, M., Schlicht, A., Stuckenschmidt, H., Sabou, M.: Criteria and evaluation for ontology modularization techniques. In: Stuckenschmidt, H., Parent, C., Spaccapietra, S. (eds.) Modular Ontologies. LNCS, vol. 5445, pp. 67–89. Springer, Heidelberg (2009). https://doi.org/10.1007/978-3-642-01907-4_4
15. Sarra, B.A., Andreas, S., Thomas, M., d'Aquin, M.: Characterizing modular ontologies. In: CEUR Workshop Proceedings, vol. 875 (2012)
16. Marc, E.: Ontology Alignment. Bridging the Semantic Gap. (Semantic Web and Beyond, Computing for Human Experience), vol. 4. Springer, Boston (2007). https://doi.org/10.1007/978-0-387-36501-5
17. Inès, O., Sadok, B.Y., Gayo, D.: Ontology integration: approaches and challenging issues. Inf. Fusion **71**, 38–63 (2021). https://doi.org/10.1016/j.inffus.2021.01.007
18. Di Pinto, F., de Giacomo, G., Lembo, D., Lemzirini, M., Rosati, R.: Acquiring ontology axioms through mappings to data sources. Future Internet **11**(12), 260 (2019). https://doi.org/10.3390/fi11120260
19. Keller, M., Katranuschkov, P., Menzel, K.: Modelling collaborative processes for Virtual Organisations in the building industry. In: eWork and eBusiness in Architecture, Engineering and Construction, pp. 417–431. Balkema Publishers (2004)
20. Alreshidi, E., Mourshed, M., Rezgui, Y.: Factors for effective BIM governance. J. Build. Eng. **10**, 89101 (2017)
21. Alessandro, V., Davide, M., Jacopo, C., Diego, F.: The BIM management system: a common data environment using linked data to support the efficient renovation in buildings. In: Proceedings, vol. 65(1), p. 18 (2020). https://doi.org/10.3390/proceedings2020065018
22. Shafahi, M., Bart, H., Afsarmanesh, H.: BioMed Xplorer - exploring (Bio)medical knowledge using linked data. In: Proceedings of the 9th International Joint Conference on Biomedical Engineering Systems and Technologies - BIOINFORMATICS, (BIOSTEC 2016) (2016). ISBN 978-989-758-170-0, ISSN 2184-4305, pp. 51–62 (2016). https://doi.org/10.5220/0005700300510062
23. Calvanese, D., Giacomo, G., de Lembo, D., Lenzerini, M.: Ontology-based database access. In: SEBD 2007 (2007)
24. Di Pinto, F., Giacomo, G., de Lenzerini, M., Rosati, R.: Ontology-based data access with dynamic TBoxes in DL-Lite. In: The AAAI Conference on Artificial Intelligence, vol. 26(1) (2012). https://ojs.aaai.org/index.php/AAAI/article/view/8223
25. Shemeikka, J., Vesanen, T., Hasan, A., Mätäsniemi, T.: Early stage energy refurbishment assessment tool for buildings using high-end BIM data: benefits and challenges. In: Proceedings, vol. 65(1), p. 28 (2020). https://doi.org/10.3390/proceedings2020065028

# Value Co-creation in Digitally Enabled Ecosystems

# Value Co-creation in the Context of Digitally-Enabled Product-Service Systems

Oliver Stoll[1], Wenting Zou[2], Eugen Rodel[3], and Shaun West[1](✉)

[1] Institute of Innovation and Technology Management, Lucerne University of Applied Sciences and Arts, 6048 Horw, Switzerland
{oliver.stoll,shaun.west}@hslu.ch

[2] Industrial Engineering and Management, Aalto University, 00076 Aalto, Finland
wenting.zou@aalto.fi

[3] Thingminds, 8853 Lachen, SZ, Switzerland
er@thingminds.ch

**Abstract.** This paper describes the development of a conceptual framework to support the identification of value co-creation within the context of digitally-enabled Product-Service Systems (PSS). The framework was developed based on five themes. It considers how and where value co-creation occurs and also the translation of data into information that can become knowledge for individuals and organizations within the digitally-enabled PSS context. The model brings together the different actors and beneficiaries with a governance process that focuses on supporting value co-creation by integrating the information with data. The framework supports new innovation and improvements to existing PSS.

**Keywords:** Value co-creation · Product-service system · Digitalization · Servitization · Lifecycle · Service-dominant logic

## 1 Introduction

As servitizing activities proliferate within industries, the research focusing on Product-Service System (PSS) advances in line with the research on service-dominant (S-D) logic [1, 2]. Manufacturing firms with servitization strategies are moving to PSS-based business models to gain more stable income [3]. Prior studies demonstrate that successful PSS strategies can fulfill diverse customer needs and enhance resource efficiency by extending product lifecycles [4].

Despite these potential benefits, adopting PSS proves complex for firms for designing and implementing successful service strategies [5]. This is because PSS provides a complex environment consisting of multiple actors, stakeholders, and beneficiaries in the context of servitization [6] and the machines within the system. A paradox is developing that hinders exploitation of digitally-enabled solutions in PSS [7]; it is due to the transformational aspects of digitally-enabled PSS and servitization [8]. A lifecycle perspective is useful when considering data and information flows and how they can assist


Published by Springer Nature Switzerland AG 2021
L. M. Camarinha-Matos et al. (Eds.): PRO-VE 2021, IFIP AICT 629, pp. 337–344, 2021.
https://doi.org/10.1007/978-3-030-85969-5_30

value creation [9]. Value co-creation has been identified as a complex process in this context and requires further investigation. This study aims to explore this in digitally-enabled Product-Service Systems (PSS) along the lifecycle. It provides initial input into a framework that supports value co-creation in digitally-enabled PSS, which will then be developed further.

## 2 Research Framework and Methodology

PSS and servitization are mature fields that are closely tied to lifecycle management and value co-creation. The application of S-D logic is a core tenet of servitization, notably within the definition of advanced services [1–3]. The concept of value (identification, creation and capture) in digitally-enabled PSS in industry however, remains poorly researched over the lifecycle. The literature remains generally fragmented, with limited integration from different research fields. For this reason, an integrative literature review has been chosen as the most appropriate approach, bounded by the concept of PSS in an industrial context, the product lifecycle, and value co-creation, allowing the integration of knowledge from other disciplines [10]. The review outcome will be a theoretical framework that can be applied, tested, and improved in the future. The literature has primarily been selected from the Web of Science. Selection of relevant and insightful literature was initially based on keywords, title and abstract: "*value co-creation*" OR "*value creation*" OR "*value propositions*" AND "*manufact**".

## 3 Integrative Literature Review

Based on the thematic content analysis investigating the aspects of value co-creation, papers were analyzed into five categories: value creation processes, lifecycle governance of value co-creation, PSS based value propositions, value creation and advanced services, and value creation in the digitally-enabled PSS. The literature is summarized in Table 1 segmented based on these five categories. The number of papers identified is given, along with the key references used to build up the sub-sections in this literature review. They support building an initial framework that supports value co-creation over the lifecycle of PSS. 157 papers were found initially, before the final selection in Table 1, where the papers used in each critical review are listed,

**Table 1.** Overview of the literature

| Theme | Papers | Cross-related to themes |
|---|---|---|
| Value creation processes | 11 | 7 |
| Lifecycle governance of value co-creation | 8 | 0 |
| PSS based value propositions | 6 | 1 |
| Value creation and advanced services | 15 | 13 |
| Value creation in digitally-enabled PSS | 15 | 9 |

### 3.1 Value Creation Processes

To create value, two actors must be involved in a service ecosystem [11]. The value co-creation process is based on the integration of their explicit and tacit knowledge to develop a solution [12], the ecosystem is important because many actors and machines can be involved in the value creation process [13]. Shedroff [14] applies aspects of interaction design to understand value co-creation in terms of control/feedback, productivity and adaptability, this is in line with SD logic [15]. Value co-creation is not a single event, Grönroos [16] expanded on this along the product lifecycle with a focus on the beginning of life and the middle of life [17]. Bertoni et al., [18] visualized the links between value in use and value in exchange. Journey mapping can also be used to investigate the value co-creation processes [19, 20]. Describing value (i.e., financial, tangible, intangible, etc.) to parties who are involved demonstrates the outcomes to the stakeholders and the beneficiaries [21].

### 3.2 Lifecycle Governance of Value Co-creation

Value co-creation in an advanced service agreement occurs over the product's whole lifecycle providing opportunities to create value, which is described as 'sharing pains and gains' in some contexts [1, 22]. Advanced service providers are dependent on the ecosystem's resources to achieve the desired performance [23, 24]. Changes to laws and partner behaviors, technologies, or markets may shift the equilibrium of value co-creation and require a realignment to achieve a new win-win position [25]. Institutional arrangements are necessary to support the re-alignment and hence governance of the value co-creation and resource integration [26]. Generally, the more successful forms of contact were longer-term oriented and reflected collaborative working [27]. However, role ambiguities were identified as key challenges in the servitization process.

### 3.3 PSS Based Value Propositions

Servitization strategies may be delivered by a firm through PSS, as it enables them to create more value for customers and has aspects of SD logic embedded within [3]. The approach (together with digital servitization) provides customer integration and models that focus on value co-creation and capture [7]. The classification of the value propositions within a PSS context has been developed to support the understanding of the services (revenue model and nature of the value proposition) [28]. For digitally-enabled PSS a model has been proposed that provides additional insights into the value propositions [7]. This work agrees with others that describe new digitally-enabled value co-creation in PSS contexts [29, 30], where value capture can be problematic as firms fail to change business models [31].

### 3.4 Value Creation and Advanced Services

Advanced services focus on the outcomes delivered through the product's performance [31, 33]. These outcomes are based on explicit and tacit knowledge being exchanged among different actors. Digitalization can support the exchange of information to increase perceived ‘customer value’ [31]. The delivery of advanced services requires many actors to deliver the expected performance, and value is often co-delivered for the beneficiary [34]. The development of digitally-enabled PSS takes place with the customer through a process of value co-creation [16]. As a company moves towards advanced services, the product becomes a distribution mechanism for the services as the firm shifts into SD logic from goods-based logic [2, 15]. Advanced services require a firm to reframe its position within the value creation process over the whole lifecycle, reinforcing the SD logic [2, 12]. The integrator’s role to moderate interactions for value co-creation in industrial settings has been investigated [35, 36]. Within SD logic, value co-creation is supported by integrators (or moderators) applying resources along the life-cycle to help customers in their own value-creation processes [2, 12, 15]. Information and interaction design can be supported with digital tools, supporting the integrator to transform data into knowledge [14]. The interrelationship between data, information, knowledge, and wisdom, are explored in the literature [37–39].

### 3.5 Value Co-creation in the Digitally-Enabled PSS

Data alone cannot create value [40]. The difference between data and information is not structural but functional [38]; visualization makes it meaningful [18]. Data can be considered information only if organized, presented as relevant, usable, significant, or meaningful answers [41]; only then can knowledge be built up through multiple interactions [42]. Knowledge originates from information integration and exchange, which in turn generates experience [39]. According to the literature [2, 15], value in PSS delivery is continuously created through interactions between multiple actors, who act as the resource integrators, forming ecosystems of service offerings and exchanges [43]. It is co-generated through the reciprocal application of resources by the integrators to benefit a receiving entity [2]. The system integrator orchestrates the ecosystem in such a configuration allowing actors to contribute actively [44]. Value co-creation can be achieved by establishing different types of participant engagement; value capture needs the active involvement of at least two actors in the service ecosystem [45].

## 4 Framework for Value Co-creation in Digitally-Enabled PSS

In this study, the framework developed (Fig. 1), based on the literature, supports value co-creation in digitally-enabled PSS in an industrial context. In many cases, the operational life of the equipment is tens of years. This is a limitation on the framework, although, it provides a clear set of boundaries be later validate. The framework builds upon the five thematic blocks, providing an initial framework to support value co-creation. The framework is based on dyadic relationships as this is simpler than triadic (or more). The framework supports and promotes the exchange of explicit and implicit knowledge to be integrated into a solution delivering the value co-creation process for the beneficiaries [12]. The framework applies feedback between the parties, supporting productivity, and adaptability from integration design, to aid build knowledge (within and between different life cycle phases).

The integration of the actors at each phase of the lifecycle and between each phase, needs orchestration to ensure two-way flows [9]. Each touchpoint or transaction between

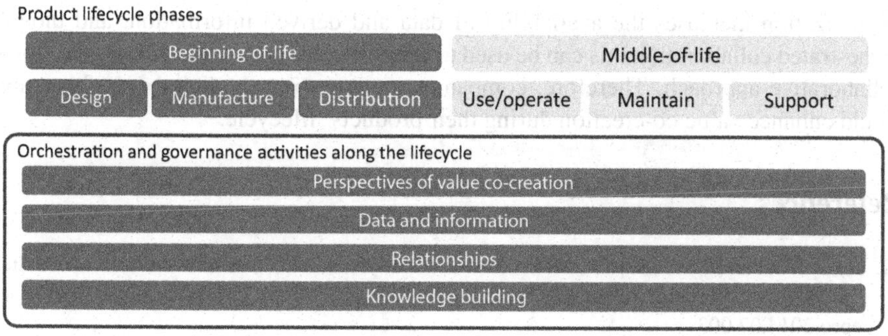

Product lifecycle phases

Beginning-of-life | Middle-of-life

Design | Manufacture | Distribution | Use/operate | Maintain | Support

Orchestration and governance activities along the lifecycle

Perspectives of value co-creation

Data and information

Relationships

Knowledge building

**Fig. 1.** Framework to supporting value co-creation along the product lifecycle

actors provides an opportunity for value co-creation. Starting from the beginning of life, value co-creation is possible, although in PSS there is a tendency for a good-dominant logic approach to apply. During the middle of life, there are many situations where value co-creation and co-delivery can occur, and the impulse may be from people, operational, or technology changes. Here it is necessary to adapt to maximize the value co-creation and value capture opportunities and share the lessons with the installed base and to the team focused on the beginning of life phase. To achieve value co-creation across the lifecycle, four aspects identified from the literature form the basis of the framework: i. perspectives of value co-creation; ii. data and information; iii. relationships between actors; and iv. knowledge building. The connections between the beginning of life and middle of life must be actively supported and encouraged (orchestrated via the support of a resource integrator).

Building long-term relationships, based on institutional structures (e.g., contracts), between the actors in the ecosystem is essential to support the orchestration and governance of value co-creation (via a moderator/resource interrogator) [19, 20]. Value is generally co-created through in-depth interactions and intensive capability integration between the actors. These interactions are based on exchanging data, information, and knowledge between many actors who are in effect participating in value co-creation over the lifecycle for a range of beneficiaries. Moderators/resource interrogators support the relationship between different actors in the ecosystem and are in effect "*valuable bridges, as they give one actor access to the resources of another*" [46, p. 68].

## 5 Conclusions and Recommendations

The integrative literature review unifies different research themes from different academic perspectives and creates a framework to support value co-creation over the PSS lifecycle. This is particularly important where there is a digital aspect to the system. The framework created needs to be tested and refined, while further research is needed in the multidisciplinary area.

The framework supports value co-creation along the PSS lifecycle. It confirms that firms need to determine new approaches for collaboration to improve value co-creation and co-delivery processes and allow them to adapt over the full life cycle of the PSS.

Digitalization increases the availability of data and derived information, and though orchestrated collaboration this can be used to support value co-creation through a closer collaborative approach. Therefore, companies moving towards digital transformation would enhance value co-creation during their products' lifecycle.

## References

1. Reim, W., Parida, V., Örtqvist, D.: Product-service systems (PSS) business models and tactics - a systematic literature review. J. Clean. Prod. **97**, 61–75 (2015). https://doi.org/10.1016/j.jclepro.2014.07.003
2. Vargo, S.L., Lusch, R.F.: From goods to service(s): divergences and convergences of logics. Ind. Mark. Manage. **37**(3), 254–259 (2008). https://doi.org/10.1016/j.indmarman.2007.07.004
3. Baines, T.S., Lightfoot, H.W., Benedettini, O., Kay, J.M.: The servitization of manufacturing: a review of literature and reflection on future challenges. J. Manuf. Technol. Manag. **20**(5), 547–567 (2009). https://doi.org/10.1108/17410380910960984
4. Tukker, A.: Eight types of product–service system: eight ways to sustainability? Experiences from SusProNet. Bus. Strateg. Environ. **13**(4), 246–260 (2004). https://doi.org/10.1002/bse.414
5. Zou, W., Brax, S.A., Rajala, R.: Complexity in product-service systems: review and framework. Procedia CIRP **73**(1), 3–8 (2018). https://doi.org/10.1016/j.procir.2018.03.319
6. Kuijken, B., Gemser, G., Wijnberg, N.M.: Effective product-service systems: a value-based framework. Ind. Mark. Manage. **60**, 33–41 (2017). https://doi.org/10.1016/j.indmarman.2016.04.013
7. Kohtamäki, M., Parida, V., Oghazi, P., Gebauer, H., Baines, T.: Digital servitization business models in ecosystems: a theory of the firm J. Bus. Res. **104** 380392 (2019). https://doi.org/10.1016/j.jbusres.2019.06.027
8. Tronvoll, B., Sklyar, A., Sörhammar, D., Kowalkowski, C.: Transformational shifts through digital servitization. Ind. Mark. Manage. **89**, 293–305 (2020). https://doi.org/10.1016/j.indmarman.2020.02.005
9. Wuest, T., Wellsandt, S., Thoben, K.-D.: Information quality in PLM: a production process perspective. In: Bouras, A., Eynard, B., Foufou, S., Thoben, K.-D. (eds.) PLM 2015. IAICT, vol. 467, pp. 826–834. Springer, Cham (2016). https://doi.org/10.1007/978-3-319-33111-9_75
10. Snyder, H.: Literature review as a research methodology: an overview and guidelines. J. Bus. Res. **104**, 333–339 (2019). https://doi.org/10.1016/j.jbusres.2019.07.039
11. Raja, J.Z., Frandsen, T., Kowalkowski, C., Jarmatz, M.: Learning to discover value: value-based pricing and selling capabilities for services and solutions. J. Bus. Res. **114**, 142–159 (2020). https://doi.org/10.1016/j.jbusres.2020.03.026
12. Valtakoski, A.: Explaining servitization failure and deservitization: a knowledge-based perspective. Ind. Mark. Manage. (2017). https://doi.org/10.1016/j.indmarman.2016.04.009
13. Payne, A.F., Storbacka, K., Frow, P.: Managing the co-creation of value. J. Acad. Mark. Sci. **36**(1), 83–96 (2008). https://doi.org/10.1007/s11747-007-0070-0
14. Shedroff, N.: Information interaction design: a unified field theory of design. Inf. Des. 267–292 (1999)
15. Vargo, S.L., Lusch, R.F.: Evolving to a new dominant logic for marketing. J. Mark. **68**(1), 1–17 (2004). https://doi.org/10.1509/jmkg.68.1.1.24036
16. Grönroos, C.: Value co-creation in service logic: a critical analysis. Mark. Theory (2011). https://doi.org/10.1177/1470593111408177

17. Terzi, S., Bouras, A., Dutta, D., Garetti, M., Kiritsis, D.: Product lifecycle management - from its history to its new role. Int. J. Prod. Lifecycle Manage. (2010). https://doi.org/10.1504/IJPLM.2010.036489
18. Bertoni, A., Bertoni, M., Isaksson, O.: Value visualization in product service systems preliminary design. J. Clean. Prod. **53**, 103–117 (2013). https://doi.org/10.1016/j.jclepro.2013.04.012
19. Lemon, K.N., Verhoef, P.C.: Understanding customer experience throughout the customer journey. J. Mark. **80**(6), 69–96 (2016). https://doi.org/10.1509/jm.15.0420
20. Paiola, M., Gebauer, H.: Internet of things technologies, digital servitization and business model innovation in BtoB manufacturing firms. Ind. Mark. Manage. **89**, 245–264 (2020). https://doi.org/10.1016/j.indmarman.2020.03.009
21. Kambanou, M.L., Lindahl, M.: A literature review of life cycle costing in the product-service system context. In: Cavalieri, S., Ceretti, E., Tolio, T., Pezzotta, G. (eds.) Product-Service Systems across Life Cycle, vol. 47, pp. 186–191. Elsevier Science Bv, Amsterdam (2016)
22. Hou, J.C., Neely, A.: Investigating risks of outcome-based service contracts from a provider's perspective. Int. J. Prod. Res. **56**(6), 2103–2115 (2018). https://doi.org/10.1080/00207543.2017.1319089
23. Kim, S.-H., Cohen, M.A., Netessine, S.: Performance contracting in after-sales service supply chains. Manage. Sci. **53**(12), 1843–1858 (2007). https://doi.org/10.1287/mnsc.1070.0741
24. Story, V.M., Raddats, C., Burton, J., Zolkiewski, J., Baines, T.: Capabilities for advanced services: a multi-actor perspective. Ind. Mark. Manage. **60**, 54–68 (2017). https://doi.org/10.1016/j.indmarman.2016.04.015
25. Chesbrough, H., Schwartz, K.: Innovating business models with co-development partnerships. Res. Technol. Manag. **50**(1), 55–59 (2007). https://doi.org/10.1080/08956308.2007.11657419
26. Frost, R.B., Cheng, M., Lyons, K.: A multilayer framework for service system analysis. In: Maglio, P.P., Kieliszewski, C.A., Spohrer, J.C., Lyons, K., Patrício, L., Sawatani, Y. (eds.) Handbook of Service Science, Volume II. SSRISE, pp. 285–306. Springer, Cham (2019). https://doi.org/10.1007/978-3-319-98512-1_13
27. Kowalkowski, C., Ulaga, W.: Service Strategy in Action: A Practical Guide for Growing Your B2B Service and Solution Business. Service Strategy Press, Scottsdale (2017)
28. Sjödin, D.R., Parida, V., Wincent, J.: Value co-creation process of integrated product-services: effect of role ambiguities and relational coping strategies. Ind. Mark. Manage. **56**, 108119 (2016). https://doi.org/10.1016/j.indmarman.2016.03.013
29. Kristensen, H.S., Remmen, A.: A framework for sustainable value propositions in product-service systems. J. Clean. Prod. **223**, 25–35 (2019). https://doi.org/10.1016/j.jclepro.2019.03.074
30. Paschou, T., Rapaccini, M., Adrodegari, F., Saccani, N.: Digital servitization in manufacturing: a systematic literature review and research agenda. Ind. Mark. Manage. **89**, 278292 (2019). https://doi.org/10.1016/j.indmarman.2020.02.012
31. Gebauer, H., Fleisch, E., Lamprecht, C., Wortmann, F.: Growth paths for overcoming the digitalization paradox. Bus. Horiz. **63**(3), 313–323 (2020). https://doi.org/10.1016/j.bushor.2020.01.005
32. Calabrese, A., Levialdi Ghiron, N., Tiburzi, L.: 'Evolutions' and 'revolutions' in manufacturers' implementation of industry 4.0: a literature review, a multiple case study, and a conceptual framework. Prod. Plan. Control **32**(3), 213227 (2020). https://doi.org/10.1080/09537287.2020.1719715
33. Naik, P., Schroeder, A., Kapoor, K., Ziaee Bigdeli, A., Baines, T.: Behind the scenes of digital servitization: actualizing IOT-enabled affordances. Acad. Manag. Proc. **89**, 232–244 (2019). https://doi.org/10.5465/ambpp.2019.12804abstract

34. Grubic, T., Jennions, I.: Do outcome-based contracts exist? The investigation of power-by-the-hour and similar result-oriented cases. Int. J. Prod. Econ. **206**, 209–219 (2018). https://doi.org/10.1016/j.ijpe.2018.10.004
35. Hertog, P.D.: Knowledge-intensive business services as co-producers of innovation. Int. J. Innov. Manag. **4**(4), 491–528 (2000). https://doi.org/10.1142/s136391960000024x
36. Kohtamäki, M., Partanen, J.: Co-creating value from knowledge-intensive business services in manufacturing firms: the moderating role of relationship learning in supplier-customer interactions. J. Bus. Res. **69**(7), 2498–2506 (2016). https://doi.org/10.1016/j.jbusres.2016.02.019
37. Liew, A.: Understanding data, information, knowledge and their inter-relationships. J. Knowl. Manage. Pract. **8**(2), 1–16 (2007)
38. Aven, T.: A conceptual framework for linking risk and the elements of the data–information–knowledge–wisdom (DIKW) hierarchy. Reliab. Eng. Syst. Saf. **111**, 30–36 (2013)
39. Bagheri, S., Kusters, R., Trienekens, J.: The customer knowledge management lifecycle in PSS value networks: towards process characterization. In: Massaro, M., Garlatti, A. (eds.) Proceedings of the 16th European Conference on Knowledge Management, pp. 66–77 (2015)
40. Lee, J., Kao, H.A., Yang, S.: Service innovation and smart analytics for Industry 4.0 and big data environment. Procedia CIRP **16**, 38 (2014). https://doi.org/10.1016/j.procir.2014.02.001
41. Rowley, J.: The wisdom hierarchy: representations of the DIKW hierarchy. J. Inf. Sci. **33**(2), 163–180 (2007). https://doi.org/10.1177/0165551506070706
42. Choo, C.W.: The knowing organization: how organizations use information to construct meaning, create knowledge and make decisions. Int. J. Inf. Manage. **16**(5), 329–340 (2007). https://doi.org/10.1016/0268-4012(96)00020-5
43. Sklyar, A., Kowalkowski, C., Sörhammar, D., Tronvoll, B.: Resource integration through digitalisation: a service ecosystem perspective. J. Mark. Manag. **35**, 974–991 (2019). https://doi.org/10.1080/0267257X.2019.1600572
44. Kindström, D., Kowalkowski, C.: Service innovation in product-centric firms: a multidimensional business model perspective. J. Bus. Ind. Mark. **29**(2), 151–163 (2014)
45. Anderson, J.C., Narus, J.A., Van Rossum, W.: Customer value propositions in business markets. Harv. Bus. Rev. **84**(3), 2–10 (2006)
46. Harland, C.M.: Supply chain management: relationships, chains and networks. Br. J. Manag. **7**(S1), S63–S80 (1996)

# Selling the Value of Complex Data-Based Solution for Industrial Customers

Tuija Rantala[1(✉)], Tiina Valjakka[2], Kirsi Kokkonen[3], Lea Hannola[3], Mira Timperi[3], and Leo Torvikoski[4]

[1] VTT Technical Research Centre of Finland Ltd., P.O. Box 1306, 33101 Tampere, Finland
Tuija.Rantala@vtt.fi

[2] VTT Technical Research Centre of Finland Ltd., P.O. Box 1000, 02044 VTT, Espoo, Finland
Tiina.Valjakka@vtt.fi

[3] LUT University, P.O. Box 20, 53851 Lappeenranta, Finland
{Kirsi.Kokkonen,Lea.Hannola,Mira.Timperi}@lut.fi

[4] Eurostep Oy, Metsänneidonkuja 12, 02130 Espoo, Finland
Leo.Torvikoski@eurostep.com

**Abstract.** Selling complex data-based solutions is multifaceted as ecosystem actors perceive the value differently during the product lifecycle. The purpose of this paper is to study data-based solution sales in business ecosystems by presenting findings from nine recent interviews with manufacturing industry professionals. The results are demonstrated in two categories: 1) challenges in sharing, selling and buying data, and 2) the value of data for different actors in an ecosystem-like business environment. The managerial implications consist of clarifying the scattered viewpoints for selling data-based solutions and value formulation for different actors in an ecosystem. Theoretical contributions provide important aspects for the gap between business and sales research of data-based solutions, as current literature mainly focuses on the technical aspects.

**Keywords:** Data-based service · Data-based solution · Business-to-business sales · Business ecosystem · Customer value · Manufacturing industry

## 1 Introduction

Developing business with this constantly increasing amount of *data* raises growing interest in manufacturing companies. Alongside the fast development of digital technologies as well as companies' transition from traditional, product-centred dominant logic to service-centred dominant logic (cf [1]), the data solutions are increasingly composed by several technology components from different providers, and the value of the solution is created via different use cases for several different utilisers along the product lifecycles. Thus, the data-based solutions become more and more complex, both from the standpoint of technology and of utilisation. These *complex data-based solutions*, such as digital twins and product lifecycle data management services, are also complex to sell


Published by Springer Nature Switzerland AG 2021
L. M. Camarinha-Matos et al. (Eds.): PRO-VE 2021, IFIP AICT 629, pp. 345–353, 2021.
https://doi.org/10.1007/978-3-030-85969-5_31

and buy, and require a new approach to sales. In value-based selling, it is important that both the buyer and the salesperson are active participants in the two-way communication mapping the buyer's value creation potential. *Understanding value and selling value are* two of the primary components related to selling complex data-based solutions. During the product lifecycle, the value for the buyer can be formulated in different phases, such as design, production or maintenance.

The complexity of data-based solutions demands that companies increasingly adopt ecosystem-based thinking in the development and utilisation of data (e.g., [2]; [3]); the solutions are increasingly provided and utilised in large ecosystem-like environments consisting of several actors, such as OEMs, subcontractors, suppliers, service providers and end customers. In addition, there may be a totally new kind of actor, such as companies, for selling content-related services. All these actors have different needs for the data, and the data also has different impacts on their businesses. Therefore, the sales of complex data-based solutions is multifaceted, while the value may be different for different actors (e.g., [4]; [5]) and thus, there may appear challenges to identify the parties or persons who should, or are willing to pay for the data-based solution or persons who actually initiate the decision-making process.

Current literature related to data-based solutions, for example, digital twins, mainly focuses on the technical aspects and technology or the development of the solution. There is a gap related to the business and especially on sales and customer value aspects concerning data-based solutions. The purpose of this paper is to fill this gap by studying data-based solution sales, especially in a business ecosystem, focusing on customer needs, challenges and value creation. The aim of this paper is to clarify how complex data-based solutions can create value from a B2B sales perspective. We explore the theme by presenting findings from nine recent interviews with data-based solution providers and utilisers from the manufacturing sector. The results are demonstrated related to two categories 1) challenges in sharing, selling and buying data, and 2) the value of data for different actors in ecosystem-like business environment, which is an important viewpoint in selling the data-based solution with proper emphasis on each actor.

The main research question of the study is: *How can complex data-based solutions create value from the B2B sales perspective?* Two sub-questions of the study are as follows:

1. *What kind of challenges emerge when selling complex data-based solutions?*
2. *What kind of industrial needs are there for data-based solutions in a digitally enabled business ecosystem?*

## 2 Literature Review

### 2.1 Business Ecosystems and the Role of Data

Digitalisation is increasingly triggering the development of and transition to ecosystem-based business [6, 7]. In the so-called 'digitally-enabled business ecosystems' (e.g., [7]), companies are simultaneously searching for a technological fit of solutions, but are also increasingly aligning their interests, business models and processes in order to co-create value for the end customer, i.e., adopting ecosystem-based thinking (e.g., [1, 3]).

One essential element in the growth of these business ecosystems is the data. The continuous innovations in digital technologies have enabled explosive growth in data resources and use cases (e.g., [8, 9]). For example, in the manufacturing sector, various data in the entire product lifecycles and production processes can be obtained, and developing business with this data raises increasing interest in manufacturing companies [9, 10]. Companies are increasingly developing and utilising solutions for enabling convergence between a physical system and its digital counterpart, which connect data-driven intelligence and physical knowledge into one model. The level of complexity of these solutions varies a lot, from digital models of a single piece of equipment, to complex and intelligent manufacturing systems utilising digital twins and artificial intelligence [4]. The more complex the data-based solution is, the more likely it is created and utilised among a bunch of different organisations [2]. Complex data-based solutions have a lot of business potential at the ecosystem level (e.g. [9]). However, there exist several challenges to tackle, such as how to take over and keep control on the vast amount of data, which can be isolated and fragmented [10]. Another great challenge is that companies' understanding and needs for data-based solutions vary a lot; for example, the definition of a "digital twin" and the needs for its utilisation are highly dependent on the company in question [4, 5]. Thus, development and utilisation of complex data-based solutions require the concretisation of the *value* of each company involved.

## 2.2 Selling Value from Data-based Solutions

Profiting from data utilisation is still relatively new for many companies. In addition, digital business models in several companies are not structured [11]. There are several theories in the literature related to making profit from data utilisation, e.g., data monetisation [12]. Data monetisation can have several different meanings for researchers and practitioners, such as:

- selling data as a new source for earning in business
- productivity leap by using data
- utilising data in decision-making
- achieving better customer awareness [13]

Fred [14] concluded in her study that data monetisation is divided into two main categories: indirect and direct monetisation. Indirect data monetisation is about creating information-based products and services or data wrapping as a primary or supplementary offering. Direct data monetisation is related to data samples, data packaging or data wrapping as a primary or supplementary offering. However, recent literature is still quite theoretical without practical aspects for earning money from data utilisation, especially in business-to-business (B2B) companies. Our study will provide a practical aspect for selling complex data-based solutions while including an ecosystem perspective.

Selling data-based solutions is about selling value to the customer. These kinds of solutions require understanding of customers' businesses in order to realise the value for the customer. Value-based sales are usually not about the customer's expressed needs, but rather about finding the offering's most valuable benefit for the customer's business [15]. When selling complex data-based solutions, such as digital twins, value to a specific customer needs to be recognised and created together with the customer, and the understanding of customers' business and the solution itself is crucial [16, 17]. With respect to complex data-based solutions, however, the B2B sales perspective is not properly studied in previously published research. Our study will provide new perspectives on a less researched topic, selling complex data-based solutions in digitally enabled business ecosystems.

## 3 Methodology

A qualitative case study was employed as the research methodology in this paper. The case study is suitable for situations and processes containing complex and multiple variables and, therefore, is suitable for this study as well [18]. A case study can be used as an empirical study for examining a phenomenon, e.g., the digital twin concept, especially, with a volatile boundary of phenomenon and real-life contexts [18]. In our study, eight cases were selected where the concept of a complex, data-based solution was examined from a sales point of view. The qualitative data were collected in March 2021 from nine semi-structured theme interviews held with 10 representatives from 8 different large, industrial companies (Table 1).

**Table 1.** Interviewees

| Case company | Industry solutions | Number of interviewees |
|---|---|---|
| A | For conveying passengers | 1 |
| B | For the marine industry | 1 |
| C | For the refining industry | 1 |
| D | For automation and electric power technology | 1 |
| E | For the marine and energy industry | 1 |
| F | For production machinery | 3 |
| G | For lifting loads | 1 |
| H | For wood processing | 1 |

The case companies all operate in B2B markets and they can be both providers and utilisers of data-based solutions. They were selected because they are actively developing and taking into use complex data-based solutions, such as digital twins. In addition, they are all established, industrial companies, whose main offering is a big investment for their customers. The case companies are not from one specific business ecosystem but are giving their experiences from several different business environments and ecosystems.

The interviews were recorded and comprehensive notes were taken during each interview by several interviewers. The duration of a typical interview was 1–1.5 h, and each involved 1–4 interviewers. The main source of empirical material was semi- structured theme interviews, because the study is partly explorative in nature. The area of industrial data-based solutions including ecosystem development and complex data utilisation, is evolving, and the definition of concepts such as complex data-based solutions needed to be negotiated with the interviewees. The interviews went beyond the sale of data-based components of solutions to cover a broad range of themes, such as the current utilisation of digital twins, their advantages and challenges, ecosystemic development and customer value and understanding. The approach for analysing the data was content analysis. In several researcher meetings, the primary emerging themes were grouped and analysed.

## 4 Findings

The primary results of the interviews are summarised in Table 2. The first column specifies the interviewed company (A–H). The second column indicates which kind of challenges and risks emerge when companies are sharing, selling and buying data, and the third column summarises the value of data for different actors in an ecosystem-like business environment.

One of the main challenges was that data can be highly sensitive and cannot be shared in too exact a form. It can cause risks in privacy, cybersecurity, ownerships, or fear of losing information to competitors. However, one interviewee responded that it is more about the safety aspect than a fear of competitors, but the sensitivity side can be seen as a threat as well. Further challenges mentioned were the problems with information flows, especially when there are long subcontractor chains involved. Sometimes it is challenging to correctly interpret the data received from subcontractors. Data is also often fragmented and there is no general view available, thus it becomes hard to process and analyse it. In addition, the vast amount of data causes difficulties to utilise it properly without automation. Equipment tracking and co-scaling of data were also mentioned to be difficult as the product range is wide, lifecycles are long and the equipment may come from different decades. Additionally, storing all the data that keeps building up was seen as a challenge.

The results of the interviews also revealed several industrial needs and the value of data for different actors in an ecosystem-like business environment. The company representatives indicated needs for data-based solutions especially in the middle of the product lifecycle phase, i.e., installed space data for maintenance and modernisation, proactive maintenance and process monitoring data. Further, data about equipment usage was needed, especially concerning how the devices are run, for how long they are run and how large the loads are; this would help design a device that exactly meets the relevant needs. Equipment usage data and "black box"-type information behind fault situations were seen as valuable. However, data needs to be up-to-date and contain a complete product structure of equipment.

The different actors' views in various fields of business highlighted that a clear win-win situation in data sharing has not yet been seen. However, customers have been interested in integration opportunities and exchange of information between systems. One interviewee from the automation and electric power technology industry pointed out that selling data in a standard form could be useful for others as well. Another interviewee saw that easily accessible data would be valuable for subcontractors and logistics operators as well. Further, data exchange between the equipment of different actors would be useful. In general, customers have different data needs; some customers produce their products with mass production, others create expensive, customised and high-quality products.

**Table 2.** Challenges and value of data when selling complex data-based solutions.

| | Challenges of sharing, selling and buying data | Needs for data and data value for different actors in business ecosystem |
|---|---|---|
| A | Irregular information flow; Data privacy risks | Easily accessible data for subcontractors and logistics operators |
| B | Processing and utilising a vast amount of data; Finding an appropriate level of data sharing | Usability of data for predictive maintenance with long life cycle equipment; System integration and data exchange between systems |
| C | Providers' minor role in their customers' business; Equipment tracking: due to a wide product range and long lifecycles; Irregular information flow in long subcontractor chains | Installed base data for maintenance and modernisation; Process reliability data; Data-based tools for distributors related to efficient selling and maintenance |
| D | Highly sensitive data; Fragmented data | Selling data in a standard form for others; Simulation models for customers |
| E | Cyber security; Access to data | Equipment usage data and a "black box" type of information; Life cycle costs from customers' perspectives |
| F | Sensitive core business data and technological know-how; Interpreting challenges of subcontractor data | Equipment location data; Highlighting win-win situation in sharing |
| G | Data variety from old to new equipment; Getting access to usage data | Equipment usage data |
| H | Comprehensive utilisation of physics-based digital twin; Fragmented data; Varying principles for data sharing | Data exchange between equipment of different providers; Customers' varying data needs |

Based on the interviews, the business ecosystem from, i.e., the data providers and utilisers are the conventional parties that are involved in design, production, installation, use and maintenance of the equipment. In new product development, the first version of a data-based solution, for example, a digital twin of the physical product, is born, and if a product is very tailored it represents a single physical product which is a long-term investment for the customer company. Suppliers and subcontractors providing systems and subsystems are important data providers in the design and manufacturing phases of the case companies' products, and the part of the ecosystem where the needed data is quite readily available.

The vast amount of data is seen as an asset, and the case companies were actively looking for a means of monetising this asset. In all cases, the monetisation was indirect: the case companies have, or are planning to have, data-based business in optimisation of customers' production processes, proactive maintenance or modernisation.

When equipment or machinery is installed and handed over to the customer, there are typically more barriers for data sharing and utilisation, and the parties become more protective of the data they have. When the data is available, in several cases, the main utiliser of data collected from installed base was found in the firm's own R&D and design department. The data were utilised in designing the next generations of products to better fulfil the customer's needs and requirements.

The data of the installed base is mainly customers (equipment owners, or even their customer) property. The customers typically need a wider view to their production or operations than data related to a single piece of equipment. To gain a systemic view, they need to combine and process data from different manufacturers and service providers. Here the customers can utilise third parties that analyse and process the data. The ecosystem involved is more dynamic at this phase, since, e.g., maintenance partners or suppliers of spare parts can change.

## 5 Discussion

From a data-based solution sales point of view, there is a need for collaboration and partnership where data is shared, and value is co-created among several actors over the product life cycle (cf [1]). The increased complexity demands companies to see the "big picture" and the value of data in a larger ecosystem. However, the companies often see the data as their own property, as they don't recognise the preferable partners and collaboration opportunities at the ecosystem level. The benefits of business ecosystems are still difficult to perceive, as they demand companies to balance between maximising the ecosystem value, and at the same time, growing their own sales volume (e.g., [19]). The companies seem to be in a phase where the value of the data still needs to be clarified from their own business viewpoint. After that, they can expand the examination of the components of value of other actors and emerging business opportunities of data-based solutions.

Selling data-based solutions is challenging for the interviewed companies, as it requires selling value and understanding the customers' business (e.g., [15, 16]). As one interviewee mentioned, the value is different to different persons in the customer company. Therefore, the data-based solution could be divided into pieces in order to clarify the value from different perspectives and reach out to different buyers in the customer company. In addition, the negotiation position is affecting the data-based solution sales and value sales. When the share of the customer's total solution is small (like 5%), their negotiation position is very small. The situation will be totally different, if the provider's share of the customer's total solution is high (like 60%). In the future, business models will change and the possibility to sell, e.g., capacity instead of physical products can be easier. Thus, the requirements for data collection and utilisation will increase.

The interviewees shared the opinion that if the customer's operation or usage data were available and combined with the data from previous phases, the companies would be able to offer more value to the customer. Third parties that analyse and process data further are still rare in the ecosystem.

## 6 Conclusions

The managerial implications of this study are for clarifying the scattered concepts around selling complex data-based solutions. This study will help practitioners to benchmark practices in other companies and to give feedback to managers for developing their B2B sales function successfully in practice. Theoretical contributions indicate how data-based solution sales is multifaceted, requires understanding of customer's business and needs, as well as the buying process. Regarding the eco-systemic aspects related to complex, data-based solution sales, the companies are still practising and trying to understand the related ecosystems and their prerequisites, opportunities and challenges.

Our research findings present several practical examples of challenges and value creation related to selling complex data-based solutions. However, our qualitative data is collected from eight large industrial companies and, the interviews were mainly related to their solutions and their customers. In addition, our interviewees occupied more technological positions than on sales positions. For gathering a more thorough understanding of the value of data-based solutions from the perspective of customers, the research could be broadened by interviewing, e.g., actual buyers of the solutions.

**Acknowledgments.** The authors would like to thank the Digibuzz (Towards Commercial Exploitation of Digital Twins) project and all its parties, as well as Business Finland (the Finnish government organisation for innovation funding and trade, travel and investment promotion) for their support.

## References

1. Yang, M., Evans, S.: Product-service system business model archetypes and sustainability. J. Clean. Prod. **220**(March), 1156–1166 (2019)
2. Bolton, R.N., et al.: Customer experience challenges: bringing together digital, physical and social realms. J. Serv. Manag. **29**(5), 776–808 (2018)
3. Clarysse, B., Wright, M., Bruneel, J., Mahajan, A.: Creating value in ecosystems: crossing the chasm between knowledge and business ecosystems. Res. Policy **43**(7), 1164–1176 (2014)
4. Kritzinger, W., Karner, M., Traar, G., Henjes, J., Sihn, W.: Digital twin in manufacturing: a categorical literature review and classification. IFAC-Pap. On Line **51**(11), 1016–1022 (2018)
5. Meierhofer, J., West, S., Rapaccini, M., Barbieri, C.: The digital twin as a service enabler: from the service ecosystem to the simulation model. In: Nóvoa, H., Drăgoicea, M., Kühl, N. (eds.) IESS 2020. LNBIP, vol. 377, pp. 347–359. Springer, Cham (2020). https://doi.org/10.1007/978-3-030-38724-2_25
6. Parida, V., Sjödin, D., Reim, W.: Reviewing literature on digitalization, business model innovation, and sustainable industry: past achievements and future promises. Sustainability **11**(2/391), 1–18 (2019)
7. Senyo, P.K., Liu, K., Effah, J.: Digital business ecosystem: literature review and a framework for future research. Int. J. Inf. Manage. **47**, 52–64 (2019)
8. Li, X., Cao, J., Zhenggang, L., Luo, X.: Sustainable business model based on digital twin platform network: the inspiration from Haier's case study in China. Sustainability **12**(3), 936–962 (2020)

9. Olaf, J.M., Hanser, E.: Manufacturing in times of digital business and industry 4.0 - the industrial internet of things not only changes the world of manufacturing. In: Hloch, S., Klichová, D., Krolczyk, G.M., Chattopadhyaya, S., Ruppenthalová, L. (eds.) Advances in Manufacturing Engineering and Materials. LNME, pp. 11–17. Springer, Cham (2019). https://doi.org/10.1007/978-3-319-99353-9_2
10. Tao, F., et al.: Digital twin-driven product design framework. Int. J. Prod. Res. **57**(12), 3935–3953 (2019)
11. Ulander, M., Ahomäki, M., Laukkanen, J.: The future of European companies in data economy. Sitra 2019. www.sitra.fi/en/publications/the-future-of-europeancompanies-in-data-economy/ (2019)
12. Hanafizadeh, P., Harati Nik, M.R.: Configuration of data monetization: a review of literature with thematic analysis. Glob. J. Flex. Syst. Manag. **21**(1), 17–34 (2019). https://doi.org/10.1007/s40171-019-00228-3
13. Wixom, B.H.: Cashing in on your data. Center for Information Systems Research, Sloan School of Management, Cambridge: Massachusetts Institute of Technology. Research Briefing, vol. XIV, no. 8, August (2014)
14. Fred, J.: Data Monetization – How an Organization Can Generate Revenue With Data?, 66. Master of Science Thesis, Tampere University of Technology (2017)
15. Terho, H., Haas, A., Eggert, A., Ulaga, W.: It's almost like taking the sales out of selling' – towards conceptualizing value- based selling in business markets. Ind. Mark. Manag. **41**(1), 174–185 (2012)
16. Rantala, T., Kokkonen, K., Hannola, L.: Selling digital twins in business-to-business markets. In: Ukko, J., Saunila, M., Heikkinen, J., Semken, R.S., Mikkola, A. (eds.) Real-time Simulation for Sustainable Production: Enhancing User Experience and Creating Business Value, Routledge Advances in Production and Operations Management, p. 242 Routledge (2021)
17. Vargo, S.L., Lusch, R.F.: Institutions and axioms: an extension and update of service- dominant logic. J. Acad. Mark. Sci. **44**, 5–23 (2016)
18. Yin, R.K.: Case Study Research: Design and Methods (5th ed.). Sage Publications, Thousand Oaks (2014)
19. Kokkonen, K., Hannola, L., Rantala, T., Ukko, J., Saunila, M., Rantala, T.: Digital twin business ecosystems: preconditions and benefits for service business. Presented in 21st International CINet Conference, 20–22 Sept 2020 (2020)

# The Use of Goal Modelling for the Analysis of Value Co-creation in Collaborative Networks

Garyfallos Fragidis(✉)

Faculty of Economics and Business, International Hellenic University, Terma Magnisias Campus, 62124 Serres, Greece
gary.fragidis@ihu.gr

**Abstract.** Collaborative networks engage their members in sharing resources, competencies and responsibilities in order to attain advanced results or common goals. This paper studies the relationship between these two key concepts in collaborative networks, goals and collaborative value creation. Goal achievement can be seen as a value creation behavior and as a value co-creation procedure since it is based on the collaboration and the interdependencies between actors. Therefore, goal modelling can be used for the analysis of value co-creation in collaborative settings. The paper develops a goal meta-model that describes the key concepts of value co-creation. The proposed goal meta-model can serve to the better understanding of the value creation process, the analysis of value co-creation in real-world cases and the design and implementation of digital systems that enable value co-creation.

**Keywords:** Goal model · Requirement analysis · Requirement engineering · Value creation · Value co-creation · Collaborative network · Service design

## 1 Introduction

Business organizations collaborate with partners and quite often form collaborative networks in order to acquire information, knowledge, competencies and resources that exist out of their boundaries. There are different forms of collaborative networks that can have various objectives, such as sharing information among their members, seeking the alignment of their activities and operations in order to achieve improved efficiency and engaging their members in sharing resources, competencies and responsibilities in order to attain advanced results or common goals [1]. In general, businesses participate in collaborative networks and collaborate with others in order to serve better their goals or pursue mutual benefits and common goals.

Two key concepts in the study of collaborative networks are the attainment of the goals of their members and the collaboration in the creation of value – that could be termed also 'value co-creation'. Participation in collaborative networks absolutely serves the achievement of certain goals of their members, either their common goals or individual goals. The attainment of goals and the collaborative value creation are closely


Published by Springer Nature Switzerland AG 2021
L. M. Camarinha-Matos et al. (Eds.): PRO-VE 2021, IFIP AICT 629, pp. 354–361, 2021.
https://doi.org/10.1007/978-3-030-85969-5_32

related to each other as the goals have or bring value to the members of the network and/or their stakeholders and their attainment is certainly a collaborative procedure. In particular, value creation is a direct collaborative procedure when the members collaborate and coordinate their activities for the creation of value in concert, while it is an indirect collaborative procedure when they exchange or share resources and information so as to enable their partners to create value.

In this paper we focus on these two key concepts in collaborative networks, goals and value creation, in order to study their relationship and suggest a method for the analysis of value co-creation as a goal attainment procedure. In this realm, the paper describes how goal modelling techniques can be applied for the analysis of value creation in collaborative networks and presents a meta-model that integrates goal attainment and value creation in the same analytical framework. The proposed meta-model can serve as a general pattern both for the study of the relationships between actors and the various interdependencies that are present in value creation in collaborative networks and for the development of particular goal models that describe value co-creation in particular cases and settings.

The research approach employs methods from goal-oriented requirements engineering (GORE) for the analysis of goals and the modelling of goal structures in collaborative networks. For the requirements of the value creation procedure, we use the contemporary literature of service management, which regards value creation as a collaborative procedure that puts emphasis on the role of the service customer/user.

The paper aims at the development of a goal modelling approach for the analysis of collaborative value creation. Goal modelling is appropriate for this because it emphasizes on the intentions and the motivation of the actors and highlights the interdependencies between their goals and their practices [2]. Hence, it can describe the sharing of goals and resources and the need for collaboration between the different actors and their stakeholders. Goal modelling, as an early-phase requirement engineering method, aims at the clarification and the better understanding of the domain knowledge, emphasizes on business concepts and can support the analysis of business concerns in the analysis and design of collaborative processes and systems.

## 2 Value Co-creation in Collaborative Networks

The concept of value and the process of value creation has gained great interest in the literature of collaborative networks. Collaborative networks can be seen as 'value networks' in which a group of organizational entities work together to co-create different forms of value [3]. Preeminent in the literature is the study of value creation in collaborative networks in the industrial setting [1]. Some studies have also paid attention to the role of the customer, especially with regard to mass customization, personalization, customer integration and open innovation [3]. In general, collaborative networks can create value propositions that can address the needs of their shareholders, the end-customer, their members and the external markets [4].

In this paper we build on the contemporary literature of service management that regards service value as a collaborative procedure that features the key role of the customer. We wish to fertilize the research field in collaborative networks with the introduction of concepts that reveal the underpinnings of the value creation procedure and introduce a customer-oriented perspective that draws attention to the use of service as the critical stage in value creation. Notice that in the recent years collaborative networks have been applied beyond manufacturing to become relevant to a variety of business settings. For instance, collaborative networks are present in e-commerce since many years with the development of collaborative commerce (c-commerce) [5], while recently social commerce has emerged as a new type of e-commerce model that includes also the consumers, who participate in collaborative procedures with service providers and other partners for the co-creation of content, services and value [6].

Major contribution derives from the Service Dominant (SD) Logic [7, 8]. Value co-creation is defined as a resource-integrating, reciprocal-service providing process among actors who co-create value through holistic, meaning-laden experiences in nested and overlapping service ecosystems, governed and evaluated through their institutional arrangements [8]. It is notable that providers do not create and deliver value by themselves, but they support their customers in their value creating processes. Therefore, service providers can only make value propositions and provide service as input to the value co-creation process with the customers. If the proposition is accepted, value is co-created in concert with the customer and in the customer's context [7]. Hence, value is defined as value 'value-in-use' and 'value-in-context'/'value-in-social-context' [8].

Another prevalent approach, Service Logic [9], suggests value can take place in three spheres: a) the provider's sphere, where the firm produces resources and performs processes for the customers and, thus, facilitates customer's value creation, b) the customer sphere, where the customer creates value as value-in-use, independently of the provider, by integrating resources and adding self-resources, and c) the joint or co-creation sphere, where the customer interacts with the provider for the co-creation of value. Hence, value creation is the customer's process of extracting value from the use of service and value co-creation refers to the direct collaboration between the customer and the provider for the creation of value.

The customer-oriented perspective is further stressed in Customer-Dominant (CD) Logic [10] that regards services as embedded in customer's life practices and shifts the focus to what the customers are doing with services and how they involve services in their daily life practices. Value is driven by customer activities and is influenced/facilitated by the actions of other actors (providers, other customers, friends, etc.). The 'customer ecosystem' augments a service ecosystem with the dimensions of the social reality and the physical and mental identity of the customer.

In sum, these approaches enlighten different aspects of service roles and interactions and allow developing a global understanding of service systems in order to create successful business models and architectures. Basic difference between the SD Logic and the Service Logic is the divergent conception of service interactions: while SD Logic zooms out and studies the relationships between actors that share service flows in service ecosystems, Service Logic zooms into the dual relationship between the customer and the provider and aims to provide a managerial perspective. CD logic, on the other hand, refocuses and places the interest on the customer, rather than on the service itself, the provider or the service system, and suggests seeing service interactions from the point of view of the customer.

## 3 Goal-Oriented Requirements Engineering

Requirements engineering (RE) is the initial phase in the process of system engineering that refers to the definition and the analysis of the needs a system has to fulfil. Goal-oriented requirements engineering (GORE) uses 'goals' as the basic conceptualization in order to elicit, model, and analyze requirements [11]. In the recent years the interest for GORE has increased and goal modelling has been incorporated into several RE frameworks [12], because the ultimate criterion for the evaluation of the success of a system is that it can meet the goals and address the concerns of the users and other stakeholders [13]. The key question in GORE is therefore 'why' something is happening, while the key objective is to understand the motivations, intentions and rationales of the system's users and stakeholders. Such an approach enables also revealing conflicts and identifying alternative solutions.

There are several approaches in GORE [12]. In this paper we use i-star (i*) [13] because it is a well-established and widely-practiced approach [12] that can fit well to and accommodate several characteristics of the value co-creation literature.

The central role in i-star is the Actor and the central concept is his/her Goals. Actors depend on others for the fulfilment of their goals – but they may also fall short in their intentions because other actors (partners) may fail to deliver the necessary outcomes. Actors are considered as 'strategic' and 'social' [13] because they seek opportunities and aim at rearrangements of their environment that could serve better their interests and they operate (interact) in social structures (e.g. organizations, markets, collaborative networks) that are governed by social conventions/institutions.

The i-star framework captures requirements by analyzing the strategic relationships between actors. It uses two types of models [13]: a) Strategic Dependency (SD) models, and b) Strategic Rationale (SR) models. SD models address the early-phase requirements analysis; they focus on the dependency between actors, i.e. what actors require from other actors in order to achieve their goals, and represent thus a network of intentional dependencies, which belong in four types: goal, softgoal, task and resource dependencies. SR models proceed with the systematic refinement of goals identified in SD models to explore ways for achieving them, a task that is addressed in later phases of requirements analysis. There are three types of relationships: a) task-decomposition, b) means-end, and c) contribution. A means-end relationship indicates a relationship between an end (it can be a goal or a softgoal, a task to be performed or a resource to be produced) and a means for attaining it; a task decomposition relationship analyses a task into its subcomponents; a contribution relationship shows the positive or negative effect of softgoals to the achievement of goals or the execution of tasks.

## 4 A Goal Meta-model for Value Co-creation

GORE and the i-star modelling methodology are appropriate for the analysis of value co-creation. GORE aims at understanding the motivations, intentions and rationales of the actors and stakeholders in the way they pursue their goals. Goals are related to value, as the achievement of a goal certainly brings value to the actor. The relationship between goals and value was also discussed elsewhere in this paper.

Goal models in i-star can highlight the structural, strategic and interactive aspects of collaborative networks. In particular, SD models can a) accommodate the various actors and roles that participate in a collaborative network, and b) represent and analyze the interdependencies in their efforts to achieve their goals. SR models on the other hand can emphasize on the analysis of the dependencies on the tasks and resources and highlight the procedural rationale and the requirements for the achievement of goals and the creation of value.

With regard to value co-creation in service research, the basic conceptualization of service as activities performed in order to bring benefit to somebody else [7] and the premise that the service user, as beneficiary, is always co-creator of value reveals that the service user interacts with and depends on the service provider and other social actors [8, 10] for receiving the expected service benefit. In i-star the focus is on the analysis of dependency relationships, while the notion of softgoals can express the preferences and qualitative requirements of the actors and therefore the idiosyncratic aspects of value [7]. Therefore, goal models can be used for the general representation of the value co-creation procedure.

In Fig. 1 we present a goal meta-model of the major concepts of value co-creation. It includes five types of actors: the Service User/ Customer, the Service Provider, the Provider's Partners, the Social Actors and the Institutions that govern service ecosystems. We adopt the ecosystemic approach of SD logic [8] and go beyond the direct relationship between the Customer and the Provider to include also the Customer's ecosystem [10], with the inclusion of the Social Actors, as well as the Provider's business ecosystem, in order to indicate that service development takes place in complex value chains and networks. Institutions are included as an abstract actor that provides the institutional framework for the operation of the service ecosystem by creating the necessary Institutional Arrangements [8].

The central relationship is between the Customer and the Provider. Each actor has a major goal in this relationship, the achievement of which depends on the other actor. The goal of the Customer is to Create Service Value, that is value through the use of service received from the Provider. The goal of the Provider is to have his Value Proposition Accepted by the Customer, which is prerequisite for selling service to the Customer and, thus, achieving other more basic business goals (e.g. making revenue).

The Customer and the Provider depend on each other also for the Service Co-creation (it is a task, not a goal in itself), that is the participation of the Customer in the procedures of the Provider for the development of the service. Figure 1 shows that the Customer depends on the Provider, meaning that the customer wishes to participate in the service development procedure; however, the relationship could be reverse when the Provider requires the participation of the Customer in the procedure.

The major goal of the Customer in service interactions is to Create Service Value. It occurs as a result of Use of Service (task), which is a procedure performed in the customer context. Hence, Value Creation has the characteristics of value-in-use and value-in-context. Value creation depends on the Provider only in a general/abstract way, as it is not directly related to any particular function, task or resource of the Provider. This way we denote the role of the Provide in value co-creation is universal [8], while his contribution can be direct or indirect [9].

The Use of Service can potentially require to Co-create/ Co-produce Service in close collaboration with the Provider and thus it depends on the Provider's Service Development process. The Use of Service by the Customer is a particular way of Integrating Resources in order to Create Service Value and address the needs and requirements of the daily life practices. In particular, the Use of Service refers to case that service is acquired from Providers to be used for the Creation of Service Value. The Customer can integrate other resources as well that he/she owns, such as his/her experience and personal knowledge and skills. As the Customer operates in a social context, he/she can integrate and use also Resources (e.g. supplementary services, information, knowledge, competencies, comments, suggestions, etc.) received from Social Actors (family members, friends, colleagues, peers), in a similar way that receives and uses service (as a resource) from Service Providers. In sum, the Customer attains the goal of Service Value Creation by Integrating Resources and Service Value Creation requires the Use of Service among the resources to be integrated.

The Customer has two additional goals, to Appraise Service Value and to Perform Life Practices. The Customer Appraises Service Value being based on the personal Preferences and the Social Norms (attitudes, beliefs, trends, etc.) that prevail in the social environment and govern the operations of the Social Actors; hence, service value is manifested as value-in-social-context [8]. The Customer performs the daily Life Practices according to his/ her Needs, while depends on the Social Norms and the Institutional Arrangements that govern and guide the personal life practices and the social life practices.

The major goals of the Service Provider are to Develop Service and to Make a Value Proposition (of the service) that will be accepted by the Customer. These goals refer to the basic function of business organizations to produce and sell, respectively. Both these goals get operationalized by various Business Practices. The acceptance of the Value Proposition depends on the degree it meets the Needs and Preferences of the Customer. Once the Value Proposition is accepted, the Provider facilitates, directly or indirectly, the value creation process of the Customer. For instance, a particular method for the direct facilitation of the Customer is to Co-Produce service, which is depicted in Fig. 1. There can be additional ways for the Customer facilitation in the use of service, either directly or indirectly [9].

The Provider collaborates with Business Partners in order to Develop Services. The Provider is also a resource integrator in performing his mission and in creating business value [8]. Here we focus on the value creation process for and with the Customer and do not get in details in the collaboration between the Provider and his Business Partners for the performance of the Business Practices. The Value Proposition and in general the business and marketing practices of the Provider are shaped and affected by Institutional Arrangements.

Certain key concepts of the literature, such as value co-creation, value-in-use and value-in-context, are not depicted in the goal meta-model. The reason is that a goal model emphasizes on the actor's goals and their dependencies. These concepts are not explicit goals, but they occur as the result of the interaction, the interdependencies and the collaboration of the actors. For instance, in the proposed goal meta-model, value co-creation occurs as a result of the interaction between the Customer and the

Provider to achieve their particular goals, i.e. Creating Service Value and having the Value Proposition Accepted respectively.

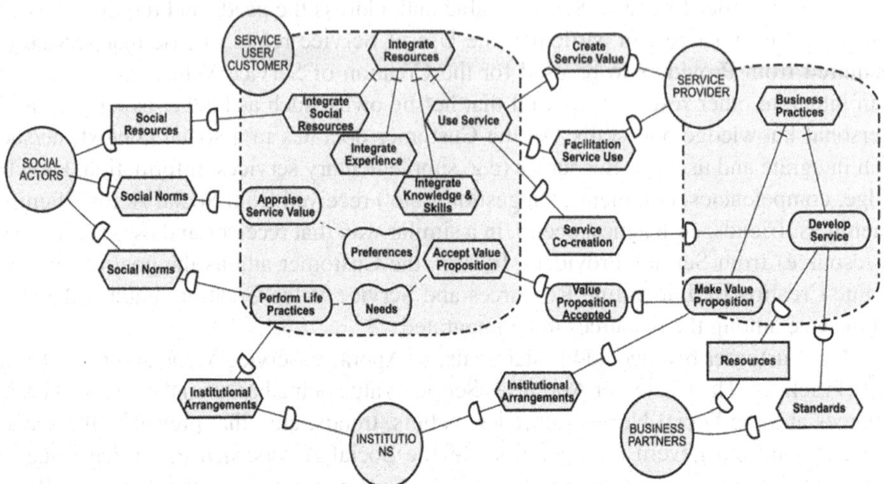


**Fig. 1.** A goal meta-model of value co-creation

## 5 Conclusions

The concept of value co-creation has been extensively discussed in the literature, but mostly in an abstract way that does not explicate several practical aspects. Hence, it is not clear how does value co-creation take place, under what circumstances, who does contribute and in what way, when it succeeds or fails, why it succeeds or fails, what alternatives can be pursued, etc. Moreover, value co-creation has not been addressed by requirements analysis and especially by formal modelling techniques. This paper addressed these shortcomings in the literature by attempting to apply the goal modelling technique for the analysis of value co-creation.

Goal modelling can be a promising method for the analysis of value co-creation because it can accommodate many key notions of the literature of value co-creation: it is based on the concept of the goal that is pertinent to the concept of value as the goal carries intrinsic value, it emphasizes on the goal achievement of the actors and especially on the interactions and the interdependencies between the actors during their goal seeking behavior, and it recognizes the role and the contribution of several actors and stakeholders that may have a role in the design and the function of complex structures, such as service ecosystems and collaborative networks. Hence, goal modelling can provide the baseline for the requirements analysis and design of service systems. In this paper we suggest the behavior and the operation of the actors in order to achieve their goals can be seen as a value creation behavior and moreover it can be seen as a value co-creation procedure, since the goal achievement is based on the collaboration and the interdependencies between the actors.

The paper proposes a goal meta-model of value co-creation in collaborative networks that can serve to the better understanding of value co-creation and the analysis of value co-creation procedures in real world situations. As an early-phase requirements engineering method, goals models can be used for the analysis of the needs and the business requirements of digital systems that support value co-creation. Goal models can be supplemented with other modelling techniques for the design and implementation of procedures and services in collaborative business architectures in e-business and in e-commerce that require and support value co-creation procedures (e.g. collaborative commerce, or social commerce).

## References


1. Camarinha-Matos, L.M., Afsarmanesh, H., Galeano, N., Molina, A.: Collaborative networked organizations: concepts and practice in manufacturing enterprises. Comput. Ind. Eng. **57**(1), 46–60 (2009). https://doi.org/10.1016/j.cie.2008.11.024
2. Yu, E., Mylopoulos, J.: Why goal-oriented requirements engineering. In: Proceedings of 4th International Workshop on Requirements Engineering, vol. 15, pp. 15–22 (1998)
3. Romero, D., Molina, A.: Collaborative networked organisations and customer communities: value co-creation and co-innovation in the networking era. Prod. Plann. Control **22**(5–6), 447–472 (2011)
4. Bititci, U.S., Martinez, V., Albores, P., Parung, J.: Creating and managing value in collaborative networks. Int. J. Phys. Distrib. Logist. Manag. **34**(3/4), 251–268 (2004)
5. Hartono, E., Holsapple, C.: Theoretical foundations for collaborative commerce research and practice. IseB **2**(1), 1–30 (2004)
6. Huang, Z., Benyoucef, M.: From e-commerce to social commerce: a close look at design features. Electron. Commer. Res. Appl. **12**(4), 246–259 (2013)
7. Vargo, S.L., Lusch, R.F.: Service-dominant logic: continuing the evolution. J. Acad. Mark. Sci. **36**(1), 1–10 (2008)
8. Vargo, S.L., Lusch, R.F.: Institutions and axioms: an extension and update of service-dominant logic. J. Acad. Mark. Sci. **44**(1), 5–23 (2016)
9. Grönroos, C., Ravald, A.: Service as business logic: implications for value creation and marketing. J. Serv. Manag. **22**(1), 5–22 (2011)
10. Heinonen, K., Strandvik, T.: Customer-dominant logic: foundations and implications. J. Serv. Mark. **29**(6/7), 472–484 (2015)
11. Van Lamsweerde, A.: Goal-oriented requirements engineering: a guided tour. In: Proceedings of 5th IEEE International Symposium on Requirements Engineering, pp. 249–262 (2001)
12. Horkoff, J., et al.: Goal-oriented requirements engineering: an extended systematic mapping study. Requirements Eng. **24**(2), 133–160 (2019)
13. Yu, E.: Towards modeling and reasoning support for early-phase requirements engineering. In: Proceedings of RE-97, 3rd International Symposium on Requirements Engineering, Annapolis, pp. 226–235 (1997)

# Towards Sustainable Manufacturing Through Collaborative Circular Economy Strategies

Leila Saari[1(✉)], Vafa Järnefelt[2], Katri Valkokari[3], Jorge Tiago Martins[2], and Federica Acerbi[4]

[1] VTT Technical Research Centre of Finland Ltd., Kaitoväylä 1, Oulu, Finland
Leila.Saari@vtt.fi

[2] VTT Technical Research Centre of Finland, Tekniikantie 21, 02150 Espoo, Finland
{Vafa.Jarnfelt,Jorge.Martins}@vtt.fi

[3] VTT Technical Research Centre of Finland, Visiokatu 4, 33720 Tampere, Finland
Katri.Valkokari@vtt.fi

[4] Department of Management, Economics and Industrial Engineering, Politecnico di Milano, Piazza Leonardo da Vinci 32, 20133 Milan, Italy
Federica.Acerbi@polimi.it

**Abstract.** The principles of a circular economy (CE)—social, economic and environmental—could enhance the sustainability of the manufacturing sector, but radical transitions and collaboration are required in order to fully engage with this paradigm change. This study is based on the assumption that, through collaborative strategies, a CE could transform the inefficiencies of linear value chains into novel competitive advantages for manufacturing companies. This conceptual paper presents a framework that integrates the identified inefficiencies of linear manufacturing value chains and an assessment model describing the five maturity levels of CE. At the lowest level—linearity—there is no collaboration; at the next—industrial piloting—experiments are conducted with discrete pilot projects within supply-chain partners. The third level—systemic material management—cannot be achieved without close collaboration and fair data exchange, while the next level—CE thinking—envisages a closed-loop supply chain. The highest level—full circularity—contributes not only to environmental, but also to economic and social sustainability. This paper argues that the identification of novel value circles and the co-creation of value with a variety of partners are crucial aspects for enabling the CE transition.

**Keywords:** Circular economy · Connected factories · Collaboration · Manufacturing companies · Digitalisation · Supply chain

## 1 Introduction

The manufacturing industry—as, increasingly, with all industries—is faced with the challenging requirements of a transition to sustainability, which, in the literature, is discussed mainly from an environmental perspective, while the social and economic


Published by Springer Nature Switzerland AG 2021
L. M. Camarinha-Matos et al. (Eds.): PRO-VE 2021, IFIP AICT 629, pp. 362–373, 2021.
https://doi.org/10.1007/978-3-030-85969-5_33

dimensions are often neglected [1]. Despite the term being widely used, the definition of CE is rather vague, and most of the literature has focused on one specific region or on a specific CE-related application [2]. A broader formulation of consistent CE strategies therefore remains a challenge [1, 3]. In line with the collaborative networks approach, we highlight the system perspectives and use Korhonen *et al.*'s definition: '*CE is an economy constructed from societal production-consumption systems that maximizes the service produced from the linear nature-society-nature material and energy throughput flow. This is done by using cyclical materials flows, renewable energy sources and cascading type energy flows. Successful CE contributes to all the three dimensions of sustainable development. CE limits the throughput flow to a level that nature tolerates and utilises ecosystem cycles in economic cycles by respecting their natural reproduction rates*' [4].

In this paper, we present a CE matrix for the manufacturing sector, which aims to assist in i) identifying the level of CE at which a company operates and ii) the needs for improvements and collaboration that would enable the next maturity level of circularity to be achieved. The CE matrix seeks to translate the maturity levels of CE to help in conceptualising the sustainability vision of a company and to provide a conceptual framework for an elaborated roadmap to that vision's realisation.

## 2 Relationship with Existing Theories and Research

The principles characterising CE are a great driver for sustainable industrial systems—especially for the manufacturing sector [5], where it is called circular manufacturing [6]. In the context of the manufacturing industry, the regeneration of resources happens through different strategies, which, if adopted concurrently, support the sustainable development of manufacturing firms. Thus, there remains a clear need to identify novel, promising innovations to shift from linear business models to circular ones [7].

There are two main cycles typically identified within CE concepts: biological and technical [8]. In parallel with a sustainable transition, a digital transition disrupts ways of doing business, enabling, by the flow of information, more effective product and material circulation [9, 10]. CE implies not only decreasing one's own environmental footprint within the take–make–dispose model, but also interacting with the supply chain to optimise the entire materials loop. Thus, collaboration is a crucial enabler of sustainability [11] that can be practically implemented using Industry 4.0 technologies [12] and is necessary to enable interaction and fair data exchange between companies [13].

The CE provides opportunities to turn the inefficiencies of linear value chains (unsustainable materials, underutilised capacity, prematurely ended product lives, wasted end-of-life value and unexploited customer engagement [Fig. 1] [14]) into business value. However, due to production and consumption often taking place in different countries, supply chains may need to be reorganised to facilitate reuse and remanufacturing, and product lifetimes can be extended by upgradeability [15]. Collaborative incentives throughout the supply chain are needed for companies to actively consider sustainable materials, durability and reparability.

To overcome inefficiencies along the manufacturing value chain, deeper investigation is needed of the distinct points at which the different levels of CE strategies can

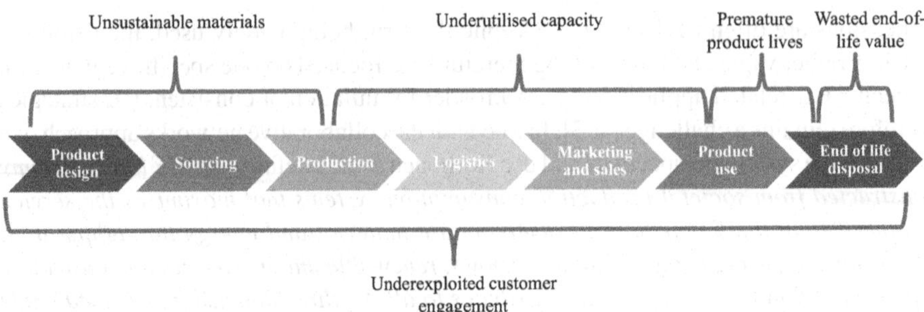


**Fig. 1.** Substantial inefficiencies may occur in all parts of the manufacturing value chain. Adapted from [14].

be implemented. Collaborative strategies are needed to enable meta- and macro-level transitions [16]—that is, to broaden the approach from the concept of sustainable islands [17] towards a green transition—and the environmental challenge calls for commitment from and collaboration by companies, industries and authorities [18].

However, companies face difficulties in deciding how to examine and proceed with the sustainability transition [19], and various methods and tools have been developed to guide them in their CE transformation journeys. For example, Blomsma et al. [20] created the Circular Strategies Scanner, a tool to support the visualisation of circular-oriented innovation, to make the CE concept more tangible, to map ongoing circular initiatives and to generate new ideas for circularity. Unal and Shao [21] provided a taxonomy of strategies for CE implementation; according to the authors, despite common assumptions, companies cannot make simultaneous improvements to all CE practices simply by emphasising them equally, and need to select a CE collaboration strategy such as trade-off, cumulative model or threshold model.

Organisational sustainability readiness can be assessed with tools that are based on capability maturity models [22–24], and the ManuMaturity tool has been highlighted as an example of an implemented maturity tool that includes the sustainability dimension [25]. Its sustainability dimension has two questions: "How are resources used?" and "How are environmental impacts considered?" Applicable tools are included in the CE playbook for Finnish SMEs [14], including ecosystem partner identification and technology maturity assessment.

The CE pathway developed in the Connected Factories 2 (CF2) project raises awareness and highlights the importance of the CE paradigm for the sustainability of the manufacturing sector. The CE maturity levels are i) linearity, ii) industrial CE piloting, iii) systemic material management, iv) CE thinking and v) full circularity. Each level is described in more detail in Table 1 [26].

## 3 Research Methods

The aim of this paper is to identify collaborative CE strategies that can boost the transition towards a sustainable manufacturing industry. Through the lens of design science [27], the goal of exploratory researchers is to develop a 'means to an end'—an artefact to solve a practical problem. In our study, the practical managerial challenge and the research question were distilled to 'How can collaborative CE strategies enhance the transition towards sustainable manufacturing industry?' The conceptual framework for sustainable industrial systems was constructed through a literature review that combined the relevant streams of literature: circularity in value chains, collaborative (CE) strategies and CE maturity assessment. Based on this preliminary framework, a matrix combining value chain analyses and CE maturity assessments was configured.

**Table 1.** CE maturity level descriptions.

| Level | Description |
|---|---|
| Full circularity | Company has achieved full circularity of products, processes and operations, which are sustainable on the environmental, social and economic levels. This is accomplished by a broad understanding of value flows (such as synergies among forward and reverse logistics, local value chains and zero-waste manufacturing) and the co-creation of new value circles within manufacturing networks (such as flexible remanufacturing networks, upgrading of products and on-demand production) as a key managerial practice |
| CE thinking | Eco design and circularity are an essential part of new products and the deployment of new services. The company is internally able to re-purpose industrial materials, but further opportunities are found externally. In particular, the exchange of resources with third parties is promoted through the creation of an industrial symbiosis network, and an attempt to establish a closed-loop supply chain is envisaged |
| Systemic material management | The adoption of CE is extended to the whole company to identify and exploit all the emerging opportunities, at least from an internal perspective. The 'R-cycles' of industrial materials have become standard practice adopted by the company in order to systematically identify possibilities to reuse, refurbish, recycle and remanufacture materials |
| Industrial CE piloting | Senior management has pushed pilot projects for some strategies that seek resource sufficiency either internally or by exchange with external industrial actors |
| Linearity | Senior management of a manufacturing company is stuck in the traditional linear concept of make–take–dispose. Legal requirements for recycling, waste management and other environmental obligations are met, and the company's performance is monitored only to ensure no additional costs rather than to find new opportunities |

The framework building and testing was conducted in collaboration with CF2 research practitioners [28]. The preliminary framework was presented and tested in the *Pathways to Digitalisation of Manufacturing and Associated Use Cases* webinar on Wednesday 24th March 2021, organised by the European Factories of the Future Research Association (EFFRA). Out of 77 people registered, 55 attended the webinar; three represented associations or standardisation organisations, seven consultancies, 14 industrial companies and 31 research organisations. Feedback was collected in an interactive session via an online collaborative whiteboard platform, the Miro board. Information on the pilot projects was also gathered during the workshop, particularly case examples of the different development pilots of companies seeking to solve identified value chain inefficiencies at each CE maturity level. The input from workshop—the development pilots illustrating the CE strategies and readiness of companies in the context of the manufacturing industry [22]—was analysed, and the matrix was finalised by the researchers.

Instances of collaboration were identified in the solutions implemented in CF2 projects, see Table 2.

**Table 2.** Collaboration in the solutions of CF2 projects.

| Level | Instance of collaboration | Projects and solutions |
|---|---|---|
| Linearity | No collaboration, prevalence of make–take–dispose paradigm | No instances among CF2 projects |
| Industrial CE piloting | Collaboration and experimentation with external industrial actors, with an emphasis on production and logistics | QU4LITY: quality pilots on the reduction of unnecessary scrap material and augmented reality (AR) demos to support the maintenance<br>European Factory Platform: logistics traceability via blockchain |
| Systemic material management | Integrated concerns with opportunities to reuse, refurbish, recycle and remanufacture materials | Kyklos: automatic product design for a personalised 3D-printed wheelchair with AR manuals<br>TRICK: tracing 'from sheep to shop' via blockchain<br>European Factory Platform: digital marketplace with automated B2B matchmaking and new market opportunities<br>AI.SOV: AI-based solution to forecast and optimise spare parts production |

(*continued*)

**Table 2.** (*continued*)

| Level | Instance of collaboration | Projects and solutions |
|---|---|---|
| CE thinking | Commitment to an industrial symbiosis network in which the ultimate goal is to leverage a closed-loop supply chain | Kyklos: in addition to the web-based configuration tool (a digital twin), the IoT is embedded in the product, enabling predictive maintenance<br>European Factory Platform: smart waste management with connected factories, real-time data analytics and blockchain |
| Full circularity | Aspirational goals reflecting a broad understanding of value flows and the co-creation of new value circles within manufacturing networks | None to date |

The co-development of the framework to integrate the CE maturity levels and the analysis of the value chain processes together entailed the identification—by the participating companies—of solutions to the challenges encountered at each self-assessed stage of maturity and how they intersect with the various stages of the value chain: product design, sourcing, production, logistics, marketing & sales and product use.

## 4 Preliminary Conceptual Framework for a Sustainable and Circular Manufacturing Industry

Our framework combines the linear value chain [14] and the maturity levels of the CE pathway [26] into a matrix in which the value chain appears as rows and the maturity levels as columns, as shown in Table 3. The illustration of the embodiment and performance of the company in each cell guides both the assessment and identification of further steps in developing sustainable manufacturing.

**Table 3.** CE maturity levels mapped with the linear value chain.

| Linear value chain | Linearity | Industrial CE piloting | Systemic material management | CE thinking | Full circularity |
|---|---|---|---|---|---|
| Product design | Product design does not consider durability, upgradeability, circularity or sustainability | Company considers transition from the use of unsustainable and hazardous substances to sustainable raw materials. Company has piloted the repair or reuse of products | Durability and upgradeability of products is promoted and applied. Personalisation of products is driven by demand and purpose | Environmental impact assessment is a driving force of product development (eco design). Products are designed to avoid loss and premature end-of-life | Products are fully circular by design, enhancing purpose-based durability during the life-cycle and enabling multiple reuse, repair, remanufacturing and regenerative recycling at end-of-life |
| Sourcing | No actions to reduce the consumption of energy and/or materials are being implemented. Materials are sourced based on performance and price | Company seeks to minimise inputs of energy and materials. Material sourcing is being shifted from unsustainable to sustainable raw materials | Sourcing is based on code of conduct guidelines for circularity and the sustainability of materials. The amount of waste is minimised and side streams are utilised | Raw materials are sourced mainly from known and monitored secondary markets and through reverse logistics. Social impacts are considered in the sourcing process | Full circularity is enabled by sustainable materials that have less environmental impact (on biodiversity, climate change, acidification, etc.) than traditional counterparts |

(*continued*)

**Table 3.** *(continued)*

| Linear value chain | Linearity | Industrial CE piloting | Systemic material management | CE thinking | Full circularity |
|---|---|---|---|---|---|
| Production | Operations of the company meet environmental regulations, but R-cycles are not considered | The minimisation of virgin raw materials, water and energy has been piloted at machine, process and company levels | Production-on-demand allows the company to limit inputs and to reduce outputs, avoiding unnecessary use of raw materials, water and energy | Circular production scheduling considers stocks on different levels | Production is environmentally sound, which is enabled by close monitoring of the environmental impacts of production processes |
| Logistics | Company has no goal to optimise logistics | Logistics optimisation pilots are taking place | In addition to deliveries, logistics covers raw materials and waste | Linear and reverse logistics are considered with partners. Traceability of products is implemented | Value chains are localised, and closed loops are implemented. Transparency of products, production and logistics is enabled |
| Marketing and sales | Company has not included CE sustainability views in their marketing activities | Communication of CE piloting activities is planned as part of strengthening the company's image | Materials origins, work force and locations are communicated transparently | Proactive demonstrations of sustainability activities on the environmental, social and economic levels are capitalised | Product-as-a-service and X-as-a-service approaches are implemented |
| Product use | Products are not reused or repaired during their life-cycles | Pilots are undertaken for reuse and for the recovery of materials from used products | Production plans are based on an analysis of multisource product usage data | Understanding customer behaviour and needs enables a prolonged life-cycle, upgrades and repairs to products | Sharing economy business models provide novel alternatives for product usage |

*(continued)*

**Table 3.** (*continued*)

| Linear value chain | Linearity | Industrial CE piloting | Systemic material management | CE thinking | Full circularity |
|---|---|---|---|---|---|
| End-of-life | At end-of-life, the product is treated as waste | Pilots are undertaken that upgrade materials or products for reuse | Reuse of products, side flows and waste is implemented | Environmental, social and economic impacts of end-of-life products are known | The next life-cycle of a product is known, with its environmental, social and economic impacts |

## 5 Conclusions and Future Work

In this paper, we presented a matrix that combines the CE maturity levels defined in the CF2 project with the linear value chain. The readiness (or maturity) assessment enables capability-building and a sustainable manufacturing strategy, which is made visible via solutions and development pilots that decrease environmental impact and increase collaboration along the supply chain. The collaboration viewpoint emerges when moving from the linearity level towards full circularity. Collaboration also indicates data exchange along the supply chain, which was a key enabling element in the CE solutions presented in the webinar.

At the linearity level, no collaboration takes place, while industrial piloting indicates some goals, trials and pilots around production and logistics that remain discrete and do not flow through material management processes. Systemic material management invites R-cycles, like the reuse, refurbishment, recycling and remanufacturing of materials. The CE thinking level envisions the closed-loop supply chain, and the highest level—full circularity—contributes not only to environmental, but also to economic and social sustainability, but is not possible without collaboration.

Companies need methods and tools to guide them in their CE transformation strategy and journey. The proposed preliminary framework enables the assessment of CE maturity along the manufacturing value chain and seeks to upgrade that maturity level, contribute to the CE strategy of the company and provide options to proceed with both collaboration and digital solutions that require data exchange.

Critically, the linear model is insufficient to the transition towards a sustainable industry because it neglects the values and interests of other actors in the value chain, and sustainability needs to be approached through collaboration and jointly set goals, steps and practices. Collaboration can leverage the CE by turning the inefficiencies of linear value chains into novel competitive advantages for the manufacturing industry. Potential approaches, such as circular supply chain and product-as-a-service, require strategic collaboration within both business models and solution development.

In the next paper, we will present the results of assessments of company pilots; validation will be done with pilots from the CF2 project.

**Acknowledgements.** This work has been supported by funding from the European Union's Horizon 2020 research and innovation programme under grant agreement 873086 (Connected Factories 2) as part of the Factories of the Future Public–Private Partnership initiative.

## References

1. Bjørnbet, M.M., Skaar, C., Fet, A.M., Schulte, K.Ø.: 'Circular economy in manufacturing companies: a review of case study literature. J. Clean. Prod. **294**, Article no. 126268 (2021)
2. Alnajem, M., Mostafa, M.M., ElMelegy, A.R.: Mapping the first decade of circular economy research: A bibliometric network analysis. J. Ind. Prod. Eng. **38**(1), 29–50 (2021)
3. Kirchherr, J., Reike, D., Hekkert, M.: Conceptualizing the circular economy: an analysis of 114 definitions. Resour. Conserv. Recycl. **127**, 221–232 (2017)
4. Korhonen, J., Honkasalo, A., Seppälä, J.: Circular economy: the concept and its limitations. Ecol. Econ. **143**, 37–46 (2018)

5. Geissdoerfer, M., Savaget, P., Bocken, N.M.P., Hultink, E.J.: The circular economy – a new sustainability paradigm? J. Clean. Prod. **143**, 757–768 (2017)
6. Acerbi, F., Taisch, M.: A literature review on circular economy adoption in the manufacturing sector. J. Clean. Prod. **273**, Article no. 123086 (2020)
7. Garza-Reyes, J.A., Salomé Valls, A., Peter Nadeem, S., Anosike, A., Kumar, V.: A circularity measurement toolkit for manufacturing SMEs. Int. J. Prod. Res. **57**(23), 7319–7343 (2019)
8. Ellen MacArthur Foundation: Towards a Circular Economy: Business Rationale for an Accelerated Transition. Ellen MacArthur Foundation, Cowes (2015)
9. Valkokari, P., Tura, N., Ståhle, M., Hanski, J., Ahola, T.: Advancing Circular Business. Tampere University, Tampere (2019)
10. Kristoffersen, E., Blomsma, F., Mikalef, P., Li, J.: The smart circular economy: a digital-enabled circular strategies framework for manufacturing companies. J. Bus. Res. **120**, 241–261 (2020)
11. Mishra, J.L., Chiwenga, K.D., Ali, K.: Collaboration as an enabler for circular economy: a case study of a developing country. Manag. Decis. (to appear)
12. Rajput, S., Singh, S.P.: Connecting circular economy and industry 4.0. Int. J. Inf. Manage. **49**, 98–113 (2019)
13. Parikka, H., Härkönen, T., Sinipuro, J.: A Fair Data Economy is Built Upon Collaboration. Sitra, Helsinki (2021)
14. Sitra, Technology Industries of Finland, and Accenture: Circular Economy Business Models for the Manufacturing Industry: Circular Economy Playbook for Finnish SMEs. Sitra, Technology Industries of Finland, and Accenture, Helsinki (2020)
15. Khan, M.A., Wuest, T.: Upgradable product-service systems: implications for business model components. Procedia CIRP **80**, 768–773 (2019)
16. Romero, D., Molina, A.: Green virtual enterprise breeding environments: A sustainable industrial development model for a circular economy. In: Camarinha-Matos, L.M., Xu, L., Afsarmanesh, H. (eds.) PRO-VE 2012. IAICT, vol. 380, pp. 427–436. Springer, Heidelberg (2012). https://doi.org/10.1007/978-3-642-32775-9_43
17. Wallner, H.P., Narodoslawsky, M.: The concept of sustainable islands: cleaner production, industrial ecology and the network paradigm as preconditions for regional sustainable development. J. Clean. Prod. **2**(3–4), 167–171 (1994)
18. Paloneva, M., Takamäki, S.: Summary of Sector-Specific Low-Carbon Roadmaps. Ministry of Economic Affairs and Employment, Helsinki (2021)
19. Rizos, V., et al.: Implementation of circular economy business models by small and medium-sized enterprises (SMEs): barriers and enablers. Sustain. **8**(11), 1212 (2016)
20. Blomsma, F., et al.: Developing a circular strategies framework for manufacturing companies to support circular economy-oriented innovation. J. Clean. Prod. **241,** 118271 (2019)
21. Ünal, E., Shao, J.: A taxonomy of circular economy implementation strategies for manufacturing firms: analysis of 391 cradle-to-cradle products. J. Clean. Prod. **212**, 754–765 (2019)
22. Barletta, I., Despeisse, M., Hoffenson, S., Johansson, B.: Organisational sustainability readiness: a model and assessment tool for manufacturing companies. J. Clean. Prod. **284**, Article no. 125404 (2021)
23. Teichert, R.: Digital transformation maturity: A systematic review of literature. Acta Univ. Agric. Silvic. Mendelianae Brun. **67**(6), 1673–1687 (2019)
24. Kuusisto, O., Kääriäinen, J., Hänninen, K., Saarela, M.: Towards a micro-enterprise–focused digital maturity framework. Int. J. Innov. Digit. Econ. **12**(1), 72–85 (2020)
25. Saari, L., Kuusisto, O., Häikiö, J.: ManuMaturity – the maturity tool for manufacturing companies to reach beyond Industry 4.0. VTT Technical Research Centre of Finland, Oulu, Finland (2021)

26. Acerbi, F., Taisch, M.: Information flows supporting circular economy adoption in the manufacturing sector. In: IFIP International Conference on Advances in Production Management Systems 2020, pp. 703–710 (2020)
27. Peffers, K., Rothenberger, M., Tuunanen, T., Vaezi, R.: Design science research evaluation. In: Peffers, K., Rothenberger, M., Kuechler, B. (eds.) DESRIST 2012. LNCS, vol. 7286, pp. 398–410. Springer, Heidelberg (2012). https://doi.org/10.1007/978-3-642-29863-9_29
28. Acerbi, F., Järnefelt, V., Martins, J.T., Saari, L., Valkokari, K., Taisch, M.: Developing a qualitative maturity scale for circularity in manufacturing. In: Presented at Advances in Production and Management Systems 2021 IFIP International Conference, Nantes, France, 5–9 September 2021

# Collaborative Networks in Person-Related Services – Designing Humane and Efficient Interaction Processes in Childcare

Julia Friedrich[1(✉)], Vanita Römer[1], Kristin Gilbert[2], Christian Zinke-Wehlmann[1], Anne Steputat-Rätze[2], and Ulrike Pietrzyk[2]

[1] Research and Development Department, University of Leipzig, University Computer Center, Augustusplatz 10, 04109 Leipzig, Germany
{julia.friedrich,vanita.roemer, christian.zinke-wehlmann}@uni-leipzig.de

[2] School of Science, Faculty of Psychology, TU Dresden, Arbeitsgruppe Wissen-Denken-Handeln, 01063 Dresden, Germany
{kristin.gilbert,anne.steputat-raetze, ulrike.pietrzyk}@tu-dresden.de

**Abstract.** Collaborative networks are becoming increasingly important in production and product-service-systems. By linking cooperation partners along the value chain, they offer the opportunity to make the product-related value creation process efficient and transparent. In addition, collaborative networks facilitate the work of employees by improving social and organizational working conditions. Driven by digitalization and its efficiency and work facilitation potential, providers of person-related services are also increasingly using collaborative networks. This raises the question of how collaborative networks must be (re)designed in the context of social services to support the core of work and value creation, the personal interaction between people. To answer this question, a novel social service engineering approach is applied that combines methods of work science with those of service engineering and design to address the specifics of designing person-related services. The potentials of the approach are exemplified by the concrete use case of childcare.

**Keywords:** Social service engineering · Collaborative network · Person-related services · Interaction

## 1 Introduction

Person-related services are defined as services that create value through the interaction (value-in-use) of the service provider and the service recipient [1], for example medical or care services but also educational or cosmetic services.

In Germany, childcare, as a type of person-related service, is anchored in law to provide all children the opportunity of early childhood education and care and enable


Published by Springer Nature Switzerland AG 2021
L. M. Camarinha-Matos et al. (Eds.): PRO-VE 2021, IFIP AICT 629, pp. 374–381, 2021.
https://doi.org/10.1007/978-3-030-85969-5_34

both parents to pursue a professional career [2]. Therefore, every child has a legal right to a childcare place in a "Kindertagesstätte" (Kita), a facility that provides care for children from the age of one until they start school. The partnership between Kita, child, and parents or legal guardians[1] is as individual as the expectations and requirements of those involved. The value proposition associated with the service of childcare in Kitas focuses on promoting personal development, creating equal opportunities with regard to the future school career of the children, and providing protected space for playing and learning in a community of peers. It cannot be successful without trustful and transparent cooperation between parents and educators, describable as educational partnership. This term reflects a particularity and challenge of the childcare service, in which not only the child assumes the role of a value co-creator, but also its parents.

The use of collaborative networks in a Kita offers an opportunity to foster efficient communication channels between those involved in the child's care and therefore creates time for the core of the value creation process – the interaction with children and families. Designing "humane" digital networks might also contribute to the employability and health of service providers, e.g. by relieving them of monotonous routine tasks, providing opportunities for learning on the job, and fostering improved social relationships [3]. To achieve these goals, the requirements of all actors involved in the value network must be considered. A mere focus on technical innovation falls short and does not do justice to the demands of person-related services and the actors' roles as interaction partners and value co-creators. Therefore, a novel methodology is required.

The main objective of this paper is to answer the following research question:

How can collaborative networks in Kita settings help improve the quality of person-related services while addressing all stakeholders' needs equally? For this purpose, the technology-driven, economic and customer-oriented approach of service engineering and the employee-oriented view of work science are combined in an approach we call Social Service Engineering.

## 2 Collaborative Networks in Person-Related Service and Care Systems

Collaborative networks are used for the exchange of information between a variety of people and organizations that are "largely autonomous, geographically distributed, and heterogeneous in terms of their operating environment, culture, social capital and goals" [4]. Network examples in person-related services include clinical information systems used for structured collection and use of patient and administrative information [5] and expert networks to connect and share knowledge between science and practice experts [6]. In the context of childcare, studies on how to implement collaborative networks in Kitas are rare, and the existing studies only look at the process partially, as, e.g., in [7]. Scientific literature that deals with technology use in childcare facilities often focus exclusively on media usage concepts, media education, and media literacy [8]. Increasingly, collaboration technologies are coming into focus, not only to facilitate interaction between educators and children, but also to improve interaction processes with external parties, e.g., through digital documentation (ibid.).

[1] For better readability, only the term "parents" is used in the following.

Still, collaborative networks need to be subject of further research in order to realize their full potential for improving person-related service quality. Therefore, it is necessary to develop a methodological framework and tools for the development, implementation and evaluation of collaborative networks in childcare facilities. Neither classical service engineering nor labor science alone provides the theoretical and methodological framework required for the analysis and design of a collaborative network in this particular field of work. For improving the quality of interaction for both, the service provider (work quality) and the receiver (service quality), an interdisciplinary methodological approach is needed, as proposed by [9] for the topic of collaborative networks in general.

Therefore, the study combines two significant perspectives on services, namely (I) the design of good work as aimed at by the methods and models of labor science and (II) the engineering of efficient and customer-oriented services as aimed at by service engineering.

## 3 Methodology

We applied an iterative design science research approach as suggested by Peffers [10], combined with a work analysis based on criteria for evaluating the extent of human-centered work design [11]. For this paper, only the steps problem analysis, objective description and design & development will be considered, as they represent the current status of the research.

The study was conducted in two Kitas of different sizes, one with 280 children and 45 educators, the other with 140 children and 21 educators. The larger Kita is divided into three administrative units in three buildings for children of different age groups. Both Kitas are divided into different care areas: nursery (for children under three years) and kindergarten (for children three years and older).

To identify the requirements for the design and implementation of a collaborative network in the daycare setting, the current situation of collaboration and communication was analyzed. For this purpose, nine qualitative semi-structured interviews with educators and the daycare management staff were conducted in the two Kitas. Process flows and framework conditions of the Kita work were determined concerning daily documentation, communication and administration processes, as well as the subjective perception of working conditions and all aspects of the interaction between the stakeholders involved. Additionally, two quantitative online surveys were conducted. The first one was about the current satisfaction with communication processes, the second asked about the work design as perceived by the employees. Furthermore, 160 documents were reviewed, of which 47 were coded and analyzed in terms of work design. From the service engineering perspective, a process and interaction analysis were combined with customer journeys and touchpoint and stakeholder analysis. From a labor science perspective, analyses were carried out on working conditions, information flow, and occupational health and safety, based on the German alliance criteria or occupational safety and health (Gemeinsame Deutsche Arbeitsschutzstrategie – GDA) [11].

While the analysis was performed separately by experts from each scientific discipline, the methods were combined for the service design phase. Ten design dimensions were identified as fields of action for joint design activities, namely idea and change management, occupational health and safety, cooperation with parents, social relations within the team, work demands in the Kitas, process design, childcare ratio, qualification and training, feedback, design of information flows, and documentation.

## 4 Results

The results of the analysis indicate complex and interconnected communication processes in the two childcare facilities.

**Analysis:**

The stakeholder map in Fig. 1 gives an overview of the large variety of stakeholders and co-producers involved: The child as primary service recipient, its educators and family (parents, grandparents resp. other guardians) represent the core actors within the childcare service. They interact with each other and exchange information. External stakeholders like teachers from cooperating schools, therapists (e.g., speech therapists) or external service providers (e.g., photographers) are also involved in the childcare service, interacting with the child and exchanging information with educators and families.

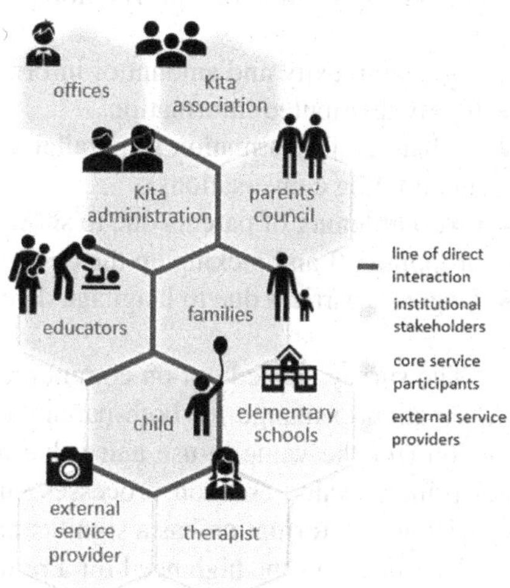


**Fig. 1.** Stakeholder map Kita network

They can be understood as part of the extended childcare network. The Kita administration does not interact with the child but with its parents and educators. The administration interacts and exchanges work- and child-related information with the parents' council, the Kita association and official bodies such as youth welfare offices which thereby frame and influence the provision of the person-related service. In the following, we focus on the internal communication within the core group (blue in Fig. 1) as a starting point for implementing a collaborative network.

Families and Kita exchange a wide range of information on a daily base such as information about the emotional state of a child, events, or special occurrences. As the touchpoint analysis showed, the communication channels for the information exchange between parents and educators are primarily personal conversations but also notice boards, flyers, or even small notes in the children's wardrobe compartment.

The analysis revealed that the informational needs of both the parents and the educators could not be satisfied in the current situation. Approval rates show that parents in the two Kitas do not feel sufficiently informed about the daily pedagogical work with the children (35%/46%) and the individual development of the child (37%/67%). Likewise, educators expressed the desire for better structured, daily updated and accessible information about their children as well as the work organization.

We saw in both Kitas that internal information flows were quite complex and partly confusing. For example, in one case, more than 50 paper lists were stored and used to transfer information between educators or educators and the Kita administration. The numerous lists included information about the children (e.g., attendance, allergies, napping time behavior, pick-up authorization), contractual matters (e.g., exceedance of contractual care hours), and the Kita (e.g., educators' areas of responsibilities and contact information).

The Kitas face several information-sharing challenges, leading to insufficient exchange of information, information overload or missing information, including:

- high complexity and amount of information for all internal stakeholders
- highly distributed information
- exchange of information in parallel with other activities (e.g., supervising children and holding conversations)
- Overburdening of parents due to short time windows for receiving information when dropping off and picking up the child
- language barriers due to language diversity of parents

The survey carried out on communication satisfaction showed that the insufficient information exchange for both parents and educators lead to frustration and dissatisfaction (for the value-in-use and value-in-work). Although information processes are not primary value creation processes but supporting processes in value creation, the provision of information has a significant impact on job and service satisfaction.

Herein shows the high need for a re-design and digitization of existing communication processes, which creates time for interaction between child, educator, and family by shifting some of the (mainly administrative and organizational) information into the digital space.

**Design of an Interaction Environment:** With the aim of improving the current situation by digitizing information flows and support documentation activities in the Kita network, a platform architecture was designed. As shown in Fig. 2, the Kita network is composed of three functional blocks (modules).

At the center of the platform is the administration module, supporting internal collaboration between the educators or the educators and the administration by bundling information and enabling it to be communicated and accessed regardless of time and place. It allows collecting all child-related information, from documentation of the child's development to the daily activities to organizational aspects such as check-in and check-out times. The module also supports the information logistics on group level and care area the children belong to. It is open to the educators via tablet in each Kita room to access and enhance information about the children.

The second module, the external communication module, enables digital communication between the Kita and the children's families. Information can be distributed individualized so that families are only provided with relevant information or relate to their child. In this way, parents can participate in their children's everyday life at the Kita. Vice versa, families can communicate information regarding their children directly and easily to the Kita, e.g. cancel their child's visit due to illness. The digital availability of a sick note, in turn, makes it easier for the Kita to plan the day. An optimized exchange of information creates transparency and contributes to the realization of the legally anchored ideal of educational partnership. Integration of a translation service allows information to be exchanged across language barriers.

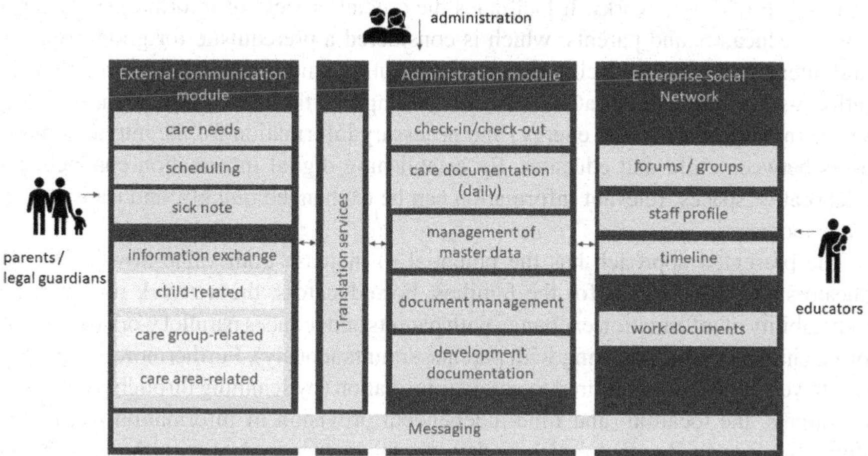


**Fig. 2.** Stakeholder map Kita network

The third module is an enterprise social network (ESN). An ESN combines various advantages of Web 2.0 and hereby allows its users to exchange ideas, organize, share information, and network [12]. Characteristic functions are user profiles, group chats and video conferences, micro-blogging, media sharing, screen sharing, and functions for tagging, rating, or marking (bookmarks) of content (contributions or comments). In the Kita context, an ESN allows educators and administration staff to document and reflect on their pedagogical work. This creates an opportunity for mutual feedback and recognition. Besides, the digital exchange of work documents within the Kita or between different Kitas of the same Kita association simplifies work processes, since the documents can be retrieved from any location and can be structured and displayed individually (e.g., via timeline) according to one's priorities (e.g., via subscriptions to channels).

## 5 Discussion and Conclusion

In person-related services, value-creation takes place in the interaction of the persons involved. Mutual understanding and trust are of great importance in this regard. Therefore, the design of service processes must consider the needs of both, the service provider (Kita staff), in order to experience value-in-work, and the service recipients (children and parents), in order to benefit from value-in-use. Currently, there are few established and validated methods for such an approach. We have chosen a balanced and structured interdisciplinary approach that considers work design on an equal footing with customer experience. This approach combined methods for analyzing and designing services from labor science, such as psychological risk assessment, work observations, employee surveys, and from service engineering, including process analysis, stakeholder mapping, and touchpoint analysis. Subsequent research will expand the application areas of the approach and improve person-related services in other fields of action.

The results from the design phase show that the approach of digital collaboration is promising for Kita networks. It facilitates the crucial process of information exchange between educators and parents, which is considered a prerequisite for good educator-child interaction [13]. By facilitating communication among the Kita stakeholders, the platform-supported collaborative network can improve the work in the Kita, primarily by creating capacities (time, energy) and necessary information for the interaction processes between child and educator. By establishing digital information channels and collaborative spaces, relevant information can be exchanged quickly, and transparency can be increased.

The presented approach has the potential to increase both value-in-work for the educators and value-in-use for the families. For educators, the network improves the predictability of information exchange with parents and reduces parallel work (e.g., monitoring children communicating with parents, simultaneously). Furthermore, employees are relieved of the effort required to obtain information (by scanning through paper lists). For parents, the location- and time-independent provision of information can reduce information overload and stress since they get the chance to deal with the information at a time and place of their choosing. In addition, by using digital communication tools, it can be ensured that information reaches its intended recipient (such as the child's primary educator). Moreover, collaborative networks can facilitate communication by incorporating translation tools to remove language barriers.

The presented results are limited to the analysis and design of a collaborative network in the childcare context of two Kitas. Implementation and evaluation of the platform in the Kita are still pending. Evaluation should consider the perspectives of all stakeholders. The use of network technology must not lead to wrong expectations on the part of the parents (e.g., permanent availability of the educators and immediate response to questions) or increased pressure or stress on the part of the employees (e.g. disruption due to incoming messages). As part of further design loops, it will be necessary to examine how other stakeholders from the network, such as external service providers or the Kita association, can be integrated beneficially.

In conclusion, implementing a collaborative network is a promising approach in person-related services. However, sharing information on a collaborative platform has its limitations when it comes to sharing non-verbal (e. g., facial expressions) or non-verbalizable (tacit) information [13]. This can only succeed if the use of technology in the context of interaction work is seen for what it is, namely an enabler for interaction. The process of digital information transfer supports the actual core of person-related service work, the interaction, but never replaces it.

**Acknowledgments.** This research and development project are funded by the German Federal Ministry of Education and Research (BMBF) within the "Innovations for Tomorrow's Production, Services, and Work" Program (funding number 02L18A182) and implemented by the Project Management Agency Karlsruhe (PTKA). The authors are responsible for the content of this publication.

## References


1. Lattemann, C., Robra-Bissantz, S., Ziegler, C.: HMD Praxis der Wirtschaftsinformatik **57**(4), 639–654 (2020). https://doi.org/10.1365/s40702-020-00638-3
2. KiTa-Qualitäts- und -Teilhabeverbesserungsgesetz - KiQuTG. In: Bundesgesetzblatt Teil I Nr. **49**, 2696–2699 (2018)
3. Wang, B., Liu, Y., Parker, S.K.: How does the use of information communication technology affect individuals? a work design perspective. ANNALS (2020). https://doi.org/10.5465/annals.2018.0127
4. Camarinha-Matos, L.M.: Collaborative networks in industry trends and foundations. In: Cunha, P.F., Maropoulos, P.G. (eds.) Digital Enterprise Technology, pp. 45–56. Springer, Boston (2007). https://doi.org/10.1007/978-0-387-49864-5_5
5. Islam, M.M., Poly, T.N., Li, Y.-C.J.: Recent advancement of clinical information systems: opportunities and challenges. Yearb. Med. Inform. (2018). https://doi.org/10.1055/s-0038-1667075
6. Lannon, C.M., Peterson, L.E.: Pediatric collaborative networks for quality improvement and research. Acad. Pediatr. (2013). https://doi.org/10.1016/j.acap.2013.07.004
7. Yost, H., Fan, S.: Social media technologies for collaboration and communication: perceptions of childcare professionals and families. Australas. J. Early Childhood (2014). https://doi.org/10.1177/183693911403900206
8. Knauf, H.: Kita 2.0. Potenziale und Risiken von Digitalisierung in Kindertageseinrichtungen. Aus Politik und Zeitgeschichte **69**, 36–41 (2019)
9. Camarinha-Matos, L.M., Afsarmanesh, H.: Collaborative networks: a new scientific discipline. J. Intell. Manuf. **16**, 439–452 (2005). https://doi.org/10.1007/s10845-005-1656-3
10. Peffers, K., et al.: The design science research process: a model for producing and presenting information systems research. In: Proceedings of First International Conference on Design Science Research in Information Systems and Technology DESRIST, pp. 83–106 (2006)
11. GDA: Arbeitsschutz in der Praxis. Empfehlungen zur Umsetzung der Gefährdungsbeurteilung psychischer Belastung. Bundesministerium für Arbeit und Soziales
12. Wehner, B., Ritter, C., Leist, S.: Enterprise social networks. A literature review and research agenda. Computer Networks (2017). https://doi.org/10.1016/j.comnet.2016.09.001
13. Haab, H., Bieber, D., Elfert, P.: Zwischen Interaktionsarbeit und Service-Engineering – Auf dem Weg zu einem integrativen Ansatz in der Dienstleistungsforschung. In: Stich, V., Schumann, J.H., Beverungen, D., Gudergan, G., Jussen, P. (eds.) Digitale Dienstleistungsinnovationen, vol. 10, pp. 49–71. Springer, Heidelberg (2019)

# Physical Prototypes to Foster Value Co-creation in Product-Service Systems Conceptual Design: A Case Study in Construction Equipment

Alessandro Bertoni(✉) and Ryan Ruvald

Department of Mechanical Engineering, Blekinge Institute of Technology, 37179 Karlskrona, Sweden
{alessandro.bertoni,ryan.ruvald}@bth.se

**Abstract.** The paper presents the experience collected in a case study in the construction equipment concerning the use of physical prototypes for the development of product-service systems (PSS) enabled by new digital technologies. The paper firstly presents how a scaled physical prototype has been deployed to foster value co-creation with customers about the cross-disciplinary opportunity of the transition toward autonomous and electrical construction sites. Secondly, the paper presents the lessons learned during the empirical study.

**Keywords:** Product-service systems · Digitalization · Prototypes · Design thinking · Co-creation · Value · Case study · Construction equipment

## 1 Introduction

Engineering design and systems engineering practices are centered around the collection of the customers' needs followed by a series of activities that culminate in the creation of prototypes to validate and test a final solution (e.g. [1]). The use of early prototyping for quick learning circles through trial and error is a recurrent topic in the literature on design thinking [2]. Traditionally design thinking has been related to the human-centered and creative part of the design, slightly in contrast with the established analytical approaches for systems engineering [3]. In addition to this, the digitalization of manufacturing industries is increasingly seen as an opportunity to differentiate and create customer value. Digital technologies have been identified as a major instrument to build knowledge about product-service systems (PSS) solutions that could drive innovation from both a business strategy and an engineering capabilities perspective [4]. However, PSS brings new challenges for those design teams that have been historically predominantly built with mechanical engineering competencies at their core. The research presented in this paper focuses on the early design stage of the PSS and builds on the potential synergies in using design thinking principles in systems engineering to address design complexity by recognizing systems interdependences and interactions [5]. In particular, the research


Published by Springer Nature Switzerland AG 2021
L. M. Camarinha-Matos et al. (Eds.): PRO-VE 2021, IFIP AICT 629, pp. 382–389, 2021.
https://doi.org/10.1007/978-3-030-85969-5_35

focused on how can physical prototypes facilitate customer co-creation and transdisciplinary collaboration in the early phases of PSS design in the context of a traditional manufacturing industry transitioning from pure product to PSS provision.

The paper presents the findings from a case study in the construction equipment industry featuring the use of physical prototypes in PSS conceptual design as an instrument to foster customer value co-creation. The PSS context is introduced by the transition toward autonomous and electrical construction sites that forces construction equipment companies to consider the possibility to retain the ownership of the physical products along its life to grant data accessibility and hardware and software updates. The paper presents how a scaled physical prototype has been deployed with customers to investigate the uncertainties in customer value creation and to co-define opportunities and challenges of the PSS. Finally, the paper describes the lessons learned from the empirical study reflecting on their generalizability and on the opportunity for future research.

## 2 Research Approach

The research presented in this paper has been performed in the frame of the Model-Driven Development and Decision Support Research Profile at Blekinge Institute of Technology. The research was performed through a combination of participatory action research and case study analysis partially in collaboration with an industrial partner operating in the construction equipment industry.

During participatory action research, data were gathered by means of open-ended and semi-structured interviews, company presentations, and concurrent development of demonstrators. During the case study, data were qualitative and were collected through interviews and observations that were later triangulated with surveys. The data collection about value co-creation and prototyping was supported by the use of a physical replica of a construction site (described in Sect. 3.1). Data from potential customers about emerging needs and expectations of future solutions were collected on the occasion of a national exhibition at the university facilities and 3 international exhibitions in the US, China, and India sponsored by the partner company.

## 3 Case Study: Context, Focus, and Limitation

The case study focused on the transition toward autonomy and electromobility in the construction equipment industry. Such a future scenario raised several challenges in the design that goes beyond machine development, stressing the need for the re-design of a whole PSS with a related supporting ecosystem [7]. The new PSS solution aims at drastically reducing air pollutants, increase workers' safety, and create value for customers by reducing the cost of operations. However, while the possibility to drive fully electrically and autonomously on a single machine is nowadays a reality, there is still a low understanding of the implications of scaling this innovation up to a network of machines and a large collaborating system. Among those uncertainties the results presented in this paper focus on two aspects: the uncertainty of the customer perception of such innovation and the uncertainties introduced by the increased availability of machines and ecosystem data.

To clarify the positioning of the case study in relation to the current literature, the work can be seen as targeting the technology trade-off phase in the Product Innovation Process framework proposed by Kennedy et al. [8]. Such a framework describes the innovation process as divided into a knowledge value stream and a product value stream. The knowledge value stream represents the capture and reuse of knowledge about markets, customers, technologies, products, and manufacturing capabilities, which is general across projects and organizations. The product value stream is instead specific for each project and consists of the flow of tasks, people, and equipment needed for creating, for example, drawings, bills of materials, and manufacturing systems. This model is increasingly proposed as a lean enabler for systems development and has been further contextualized by Isaksson et al. [9] as a framework to support value and sustainability decision models, with different needs observable progressing along the two streams. The main activities along the value streams can be summarized as:

- Concept/technology Screening (Scoping): when possible solutions need to be screened quickly and with limited effort and time, typically in the order of hours.
- Concept/technology trade-off: where a set of the most promising solutions is selected for further analysis. Here the solution space is more limited but the trade-off is still driven by simple models with low maturity and dependent on variable input.
- Emerging Design (product commitment): here decisions are made to enable the design team to confine the design space and down select a limited number of concepts from the previous set.
- Concept development: here the knowledge value stream is abandoned to commit to a specific product value stream. Product and process definitions are refined to minimize risks and costs.

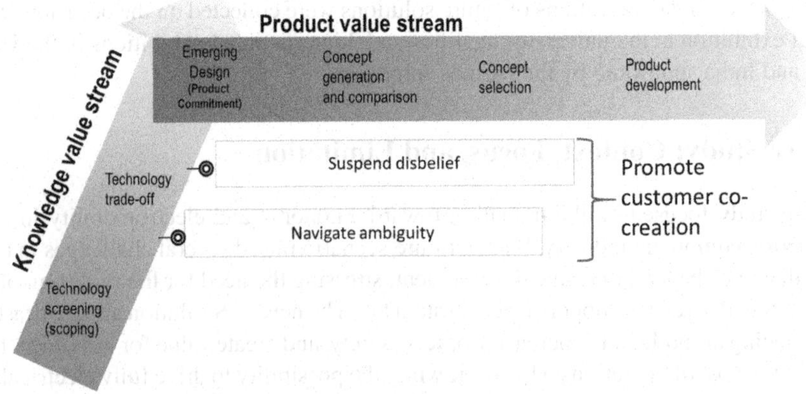


**Fig. 1.** The focus of the case study in promoting customer co-creation framed in the Product Innovation Process (adapted from [8])

As shown in Fig. 1 the research performed in the case study targeted specifically the role of physical prototyping as support for value co-creation limited to the technology trade-off stage, that is, when preliminary ideas of the most promising PSS solutions were already identified, but uncertainties about different dimensions of customers and stakeholders' value were still present.

## 3.1 The Physical Prototype - The Small Scale Site

The physical prototype deployed in the case study, and named "small-scale site", is a concept centered around generic scenarios that could be relevant for a broad audience of potential customers and engineers. The small-scale site consisted of a 5 m × 5 m scaled-down site including two autonomous haulers in loading and dumping interactions (Fig. 2) typical of a quarry or mine operation. The machines were 1:14 scale remote control versions of electric excavator and hybrid wheel loader concepts, with the addition of the prototype autonomous haulers. To best reflect the reality of the current transition period from manual operation to a fully autonomous future, loading machines (excavator and wheel loader) were left as remotely (human) controlled machines, while the haulers were fitted with sensors, control boards, and communication devices to enable an autonomous experience for the user. Alongside the site, a prototype of an augmented reality interface was created capable of voice and gesture commands to control the autonomous machines as well as displaying basic information about the machine. Such a feature was initially introduced as an add-on to the physical prototype to attract customer attention to it.

**Fig. 2.** The small scale site during a loading operation with autonomous wheel loader [6]

## 3.2 Findings of the Case Study

Physical prototypes are at the core of traditional product development, validation and testing activities are run both internally and with customers to test verify e.g., functionalities, aesthetics, and systems integrations. Customer needs and "first-impressions" are often gathered through prototyping to improve the final product before production and ramp-up. Modern innovative product development processes stress the importance of creating tangible prototypes for their ability to communicate complexity, enable rapid feedback and provide guidance on design changes in the early stages of the process [6].

In the case study, the physical prototype was meant to be used as an effective tool for engaging relevant stakeholders in meaningful dialog around small details or the entire physical system, ultimately expanding the focus of the conceptual design activities to operational questions that might not be directly visible for the company developing the new PSS. In such a context the small-scale site was used to convey information and raise discussion and understanding about the new PSS. The scaled site provided tangibility to the feasibility claims about the full-scale operation and engage customers in conceptual value co-creation design activities. Here customers could raise concerns, evaluations, and wishes about the future PSS.

The collection and post-analysis of customers feedback and interactions allowed for the formalization of new needs and expectation that not only concerns product features (e.g. dimensions and or productivity of a machine) but encompass general reflection of the PSS system as a whole with the related support infrastructure and physical and digital ecosystem, In the case study, the co-creation activities with customers generated design feedback related to operational changes, flexibility, availability, and feasibility of the systems, while the same activities run internally at the development company focused more on technology readiness, technology bleed, and manufacturability of the machines (results also presented in [6]). In relation to the aim of the research two main benefits from the case study concerning the use of physical prototypes for customer co-creation of PSS were identified and are summarized as follows.

**The Physical Prototype Provided a Sense of Full-Scale Feasibility.** The small-scale site worked effectively in suspending customer disbelief in the new technologies encouraging explorative enquiring. For instance, customers started inquiring how other machines could be designed differently rather than arguing about the feasibility of the presented solution.

*The Physical Prototype Worked as Boundary Objects for a Shared Experience.* The value of the functional site as a boundary object was multilayered from the individual machines to the overall solution. On the system level, it provided an easily comprehensible overview of how the system components will interact to provide the functional result. Stakeholders from different groups were able to inquire in a meaningful way on the impacts compared to their current solutions building empathy around the future scenario concept, resulting from both a shared cognition of the system and the subjective impact on their disciplinary context.

In addition to such results, the use of an augmented reality interface emerged as an interesting source of qualitative data concerning human-autonomous machine interaction and trust. The qualitative observation suggested that:

*The Augmented Reality Interface Helped to Build Trust in Human-Autonomous Machine Interaction.* This happened because envisioning the future scenario of autonomous machines sharing the same worksite as humans raised several questions. One of those concerned how humans would trust their autonomous counterparts on the worksite, given traditional communication methods were absent due to the loss of the (human) machine operator. The prototype of the augmented reality interface integrated into the small-scale site allowed to create a contextualized experience for users and customers and gather additional feedback on new the new PSS concepts including individual perceptions and personal trust in the technology.

## 4 Discussion

While in traditional product development, customer needs are translated into functional requirements mainly focusing on the product as a physical entity, in a PSS context, the physical entity is only a part of the complete solution, thus, more inferences can be made about the PSS by analyzing the behaviors in its surrounding. Both PSS and systems engineering literature (e.g. [10]) highlight the challenge in identifying the impact of a change in a design variable at the sub-system level on the *performance requirements* of the overall system. When it comes to the design of smart PSS that will operate in a digital ecosystem it is not straightforward to define what corresponds to such *performance requirements*, mainly because needs and expectations for a system that is not yet existing are poorly defined.

The case study focused on the opportunities linked to the use of physical prototypes of a PSS, and related ecosystems, to collect the customer needs concerning both the configuration of the future PSS solutions and the potential value added by digitalization and data acquisition from the PSS operations. In the context of the new PSS, the small-scale site was used to convey information and raise discussion and understanding. Besides the findings described in Sect. 3.1. lessons learned gathered during the work can be summarized as follows:

*Lesson Learned 1.* We as humans experience the world as a series of events so it makes sense to have live prototypes, especially in the PSS context. These new products will interact, move and communicate in unexpected ways. Providing all relevant stakeholders with the ability to comprehend and inquire about the system solution at multiple layers of the concept, enables designers to collaborate more effectively with customers and other stakeholders up and down the value chain.

*Lesson Learned 2.* In the process of design, enabling informed decisions early has shown to greatly impact the value of the final solution. The fidelity level of the scale site elements and system shown in the case study reflects the needs of the designers at that stage, as such this is not generally applicable to all situations. Zooming out we see the site concept as part of a larger framework for rapidly growing impossible ideas into nearly improbable solutions. To generate the desired level of feedback and input from stakeholders a concerted effort must be expended in the decisions of the designers to convey the uniqueness in a clear and interactive experience.

*Lesson Learned 3.* By creating a physical representation to capture the complexity of a PSS we capture people's desire to feel and touch the future in a way that videos or 3D models cannot. There is a threshold that allows the observer to properly suspend disbelief enough to engage in generative questions that otherwise are less likely to occur or seem relevant based on the horizon distance of the new technology. New PSS solutions that utilize unrecognizable technology benefit by finding ways of conveying their possibility to potential users to find partners for case studies of deeper applications.

## 5 Conclusion, Generalization, and Future Research

The paper has presented the rationale, the setting, the findings, and the lessons learned of a case study run in the construction equipment industry with the intent to promote customer value co-creation in the conceptual design stage of the development of a PSS featuring a future scenario based on machine autonomy and electromobility. The findings presented in this paper concerned the experimentation of the use of a physical prototype in conceptual PSS design to capitalize on potential synergies in using design thinking principles in a system engineering setting, by supporting the recognition of systems interdependencies and interactions.

The prototype showed to be useful as a boundary object for cross-disciplinary communication, giving at the same time a sense of system feasibility and building trust in the interaction between the human and the autonomous machine. However, the data collection concerning customer co-creation might suffer from intrinsic biases given the context in which the feedback from the customers was collected, that is, on the occasion of events sponsored by the partner company under the partner company brand. Based on this the generalizability and validity of the findings cannot be confirmed and further validation activities need to be run in future research. Similarly, the lessons learned collected would benefit from further verification in contexts other than construction equipment. This calls for future research concerning the definition of case studies with multiple industrial partners. Based on the experience emerged while integration augmented reality in physical prototyping, future research will focus on recreating more advance augmented reality setting with a larger capability of interaction with the physical machines. Concurrently, further validation on the benefits of using physical prototypes for early PSS design will need to be performed by comparing those with the use of 3D models in a virtual reality setting. Although the latter not being currently at a level of maturity to be used for comparison, it can be expected that virtual reality solutions will soon be available to a degree that will allow comparative research evaluating the benefits and the drawbacks of the two different settings.

**Acknowledgment.** The authors would like to acknowledge the industrial partners and Swedish Knowledge and Competence Development Foundation for providing financial support through the Model-Driven Development and Decision Support research profile at Blekinge Institute of Technology.

## References

1. Ulrich, K.T., Eppinger, S.D.: Product design and development (2008)

2. Brown, T., Katz, B.: Change by design: how design thinking transforms organizations and inspires innovation, vol. 20091. HarperBusiness, New York (2019)
3. Greene, M.T., Gonzalez, R., Papalambros, P.Y.: Measuring systems engineering and design thinking attitudes. In: Proceedings of the Design Society: International Conference on Engineering Design, 1, 1, pp. 3939–3948. Cambridge University Press (2019)
4. Pirola, F., Boucher, X., Wiesner, S., Pezzotta, G.: Digital technologies in product-service systems: a literature review and a research agenda. Comput. Ind. **123**, 103301 (2020)
5. Greene, M.T., Gonzalez, R., Papalambros, P.Y., McGowan A.M.: Design thinking vs. systems thinking for engineering design: what's the difference? DS 87–2. In: Proceedings of the 21st International Conference on Engineering Design (ICED 17) 2 (2017)
6. Ruvald, R., Bertoni, A., Askling, C.J.: A role for physical prototyping in Product-Service System design: case study in construction equipment. Procedia CIRP **83**, 358–362 (2019)
7. Frank, M.: A step towards the design of collaborative autonomous machines: a study on construction and mining equipment. Licentiate diss., Blekinge Tekniska Högskola (2019)
8. Kennedy, M., Harmon, K., Minnock, E.: Ready, set, dominate - Implement Toyota's Set-Based Learning for Developing Products and Nobody Can Catch You. The Oaklea Press, Richmond (2008)
9. Isaksson, O., Bertoni, M., Hallstedt, S., Lavesson, N.: Model based decision support for value and sustainability in product development. In: 20th International Conference on Engineering Design (ICED), Milan. The Design Society (2015)
10. Isaksson, O., et al.: Value-driven design–a methodology to link expectations to technical requirements in the extended enterprise. INCOSE International Symposium **23**(1), 803–819 (2013)

# Digitalization Strategy in Collaborative Enterprises Networks

# Open and Collaborative Micro Services in Digital Transformation

A. Luis Osório[1(✉)], Luis M. Camarinha-Matos[2], Tiago Dias[1], Carlos Gonçalves[1], and José Tavares[3]

[1] ISEL - Instituto Superior de Engenharia de Lisboa, Instituto Politécnico de Lisboa, and POLITEC&ID, Lisbon, Portugal
lo@isel.ipl.pt, {tiago.dias,carlos.goncalves}@isel.pt

[2] School of Science and Technology, NOVA University of Lisbon and CTS-UNINOVA, Caparica, Portugal
cam@uninova.pt

[3] FORDESI, Informatics Systems, and Solutions Company, Lisbon, Portugal
jose.tavares@fordesi.pt

**Abstract.** The ongoing digital transformation raises the need to address the evolution of legacy systems in response to integration requirements. One challenge is integrating sensors and actuators (and their controllers), modeled as IoT elements, and linking them to data analytics, management, and operations decision support functions or processes. Since legacy technology systems follow proprietary architectures, their integration into open service-oriented architectures (SOA) requires a strategy that maintains a high degree of reliability. This paper presents the strategy adopted to integrate legacy software in an open SOA to manage an agri-food silos infrastructure. This approach follows the Informatics System of Systems (ISoS) idea and is based on the ISoS framework. A reference implementation concept is used to validate the (re)construction of legacy systems and make them ready for collaboration with agro-industry business partners considering their Enterprise Resource Planning.

**Keywords:** Collaborative networks · Internet of Things · Systems integration · Cyber-physical systems · Distributed systems

## 1 Introduction

Today, several strategies are already available to implement the digital transformation processes. However, the support for a coordinated and collaborative effort for participative contributions is still lacking. Furthermore, a significant challenge is the need to update legacy systems while maintaining their proven reliable features. Whenever the changes required to migrate legacy systems compromise the system's quality, alternative strategies must be adopted. In this context, the SITL-IoT project [16] develops an open technology infrastructure for the industry agri-food sector adopting a System of Systems (SoS) framework that integrates Internet of Things (IoT) elements (a kind of IoT Bus).


Published by Springer Nature Switzerland AG 2021
L. M. Camarinha-Matos et al. (Eds.): PRO-VE 2021, IFIP AICT 629, pp. 393–402, 2021.
https://doi.org/10.1007/978-3-030-85969-5_36

Extensive work has been done regarding IoT and its corresponding platforms at different levels. One pragmatic perspective relates to connecting simple sensors through radio frequency links based on protocols like Sigfox, LoRa, and NB-IoT, popularized as low-power wide-area networks (LPWAN) [11]. More recently, the LPWAN networks got the attention of cellular phone networks and Internet providers to establish a unified WAN for connecting any device with sensor/actuator, computing, and communication capabilities. Communication between things based on limited resources often adopts LPWAN and machine-to-machine (M2M) connection, complemented by 4G LTE technologies. Lately, 5G seems to show a convergence between M2M IoT device communications and personal communications with enhanced quality [6]. This unification seems essential for cases where things cross local LAN domains, and public communication infrastructure is necessary. An extensive survey on 5G IoT [10] confirms the trend of highly available and reliable 5G wireless communications connecting IoT devices or systems. However, the IoT devices or systems do not exist in isolation, and there is a need for some framing strategy, making clear the responsibility for their lifecycle management.

The focus of our research is how to get things to be "plugged" as elements of a computing system, rather than IoT connections or the convergence between wide and local networks. Following a similar direction, the Ethernet Time-Sensitive Networking (TSN), as discussed in [7], emphasizes the convergence of Information Technology (IT) and Industrial Operations Technology (OT) as a trend-making towards open data exchange between the operations field and the enterprise systems, which is referred to as Industrial IoT (IIoT). There is some tendency to establish the concept of an IoT Bus as a facilitator to seamlessly merging specific protocols, e.g., OPC-UA, towards a symbiotic industrial technology landscape, which can be modelled as a system of systems where IoT devices plug as services. As suggested by other authors [7], both legacy communications and legacy systems need to evolve in such a way that current "*manufacturer lock-in*" conditions do not force the acquisition of new devices.

This paper presents a strategy to represent IoT devices in the cyber-space as services and their application to the migration of an existing legacy system named FORSIL. Under the proposed approach, the FORSIL system evolves to a combination of two systems: (1) the ISysFORSIL-PROC, responsible for the silos processes automation, and (2) the ISysFORSIL-MON, responsible for monitoring the ISysFORSIL-PROC services. The migration strategy is based on the ISoS framework [15] and consisted of revisiting the legacy FORSIL architecture towards a new modular structure. One important motivation for adopting the ISoS framework was its readiness to support collaboration processes between the silos infrastructure and its business agro-food industry partners. As any informatics system (Isystem) in the ISoS framework can be accessed both from inside and outside the organization, based on a canonical interface named I0, collaborative exchanges can go through direct invocation of the ISystem services. In other words, without the need for heavy changes, implementing service abstraction enables wrapping the legacy technology and make it evolve to comply with the ISoS pattern and, in this way, participate or plug to the adaptive IoT Bus.

The paper is organized as follows. Section 2 presents and discusses the SITL-IoT challenge for an open IoT Bus for the agro-food silo infrastructure. In Sect. 3, we clarify the IoT Bus design in the context of the ISoS model. Section 4 extends the discussion into a collaborative space, where networked organizations need to access services for business collaborations. Finally, Sect. 5 presents the main conclusions of our research work and outlines the open research challenges.

## 2 Collaboration Challenges in the SITL-IoT Industry Case

Current approaches to structure computing artifacts do not follow any kind of common and generic reference model or strategy. As a result, products developed by different companies usually adopt custom solutions that quite often result in proprietary architectures. The legacy FORSIL product from the FORDESI company also followed this approach. FORSIL is an enterprise software system composed of technical parts organized within a computing responsibility. Such monolithic technology solutions present fuzzy "responsibility borders", which makes it difficult to establish accountability decisions. Those less clear responsibility borders make IT governance a complex endeavour. Such modular monolithic systems, even if agile and possible to integrate with any other system, require the development of specific adapters.

The SITL-IoT project was motivated by the will of the FORDESI company to make FORSIL evolve towards an open IoT Bus, combined with cloud services [16]. The challenge was to (re-)structure the legacy FORSIL to make its functionalities available to other enterprise systems, both from internal and external business partners. It is interesting to identify that depending on the viewpoint of the researchers, adopted approaches emphasize either what is known as enterprise systems or the production infrastructure, where the notion of "things" prevails. An example of the second perspective is the proposal of an IoT platform as a *"piece of software that works like a kind of "glue" to combine platforms and orchestrate capabilities that connect devices, users and applications/services in a "cyber-physical world"* [18]. Such an idea is quite similar to the Enterprise Service Bus (ESB) concept since it combines a suite of adapters to integrate microservices [4]. However, adopting a centralized integration strategy, either an IoT platform or an ESB as an integration hub, leads to dependencies from a single responsibility or single vendor. Therefore, the proposal in [4] considers a Service Oriented Architecture (SOA) and microservices under a similar rationale. Commonly both SOA services and microservices are widely discussed as capable of abstracting independent computing entities. At the same time, the microservice concept often tends to be associated with the cloud.

When the goal is to achieve integrated process automation in complex heterogeneous collaborative contexts, one major challenge is establishing a systemic structuring strategy capable of incorporating multi-vendor and/or multi-supplier contributions while maintaining confidence in the system as a whole. Like other application domains, the SITL-IoT project addresses a critical scenario where the adopted technology arrangement needs to be reliable, as discussed in [17]. Any failure potentially harming a business function needs to be accountable for direct responsibility. However, the association of accountabilities is not simple to determine in the current diversity of technology structuration approaches since they are based on mappings between specific architectures. When integration is required, the inclusion of diverse technology architectures faces the lack of a "unified model" where independent contributions still lead to a consistent system. More than its parts, such a uniform system requires a suitable strategy to manage the various heterogeneous contributions under the same coordination and operation model. Research on integrating heterogeneous models [2] suggests the implementation of five phases: (1) pre-integration assessment, (2) preparation of models for integration, (3) orchestration of models during simulation, (4) data interoperability, and (5) testing, addressing both the physical world and enterprise business processes. Often, the discussion of interoperability does not seem to cope with the integration pressure of the digital transformation. As suggested in [12], "*… we need formalization of interoperability grounded in the general system theory: the Ontology of Interoperability (OoI) …*", for instance, based on the CEN/ISO-11354 Framework for Enterprise Interoperability standard.

To contribute to this open challenge, we suggest an alternative approach that considers that, even when maintaining diversity, we need some kind of "reference framework" to model the resulting transformed system. Hence, our approach is focused on finding a balanced model for the "digitally transformed system" where independent computing responsibilities collaborate under pre-established conditions, preferably based on open standards. The strategy for such collaboration among sub-systems shall be similar, both when addressing the physical world or the automation of enterprise business processes.

## 3 The ISoS Model and the Open IoT Bus

To tackle the above issues in the context of the SITL-IoT project, we adopted the ISoS framework [15] as a "glue", nonintrusive, integration reference model. The ISoS abstraction plays the role of a registry for the enterprise informatics systems (ISystems). A particular $\text{ISystem}_0$ operationalizes the registration of any enterprise ISystem. The ISystem concept is simply a composition of Service elements, and these are, in fact, the executive entities. The Service concept refers to an independent and possibly autonomous computing entity, representing some computational responsibility. By computational responsibility, we mean the answer to the functional and the non-functional requirements through a set of capabilities. If other Service entities need to access some Service computing capabilities, the interoperability realization is in the associated metadata.

Therefore, the ISoS concept aims to establish a unified model for the enterprise system's architecture. By adopting the ISoS framework, we unify what [9] calls Application Architecture specific for each enterprise system supplier or integrator. The heterogeneous application domains comprise computing-related technology ranging from enterprise systems, which we model as an ISystem, to IoT devices with minimal computing capabilities, which we mimic as a Service entity. For example, when an IoT device is a simple sensor or actuator with minimal computing capabilities, the Service entity can be the gateway responsible for the communication with the device.

Figure 1 depicts a simplified view of the validation case with a Silos located in Leixões (SDL). Two cyber-physical systems (CPS) comprise a programmable logic controller (PLC) coordinating temperature sensors in the silos and truck weighing bridges. The CPS computational parts (a kind of digital twin) are modelled as a Service registered into the $\text{ISystem}_0$ as SerTemperature for the temperature subsystem and SerWeighingBridge for the weighing bridges. Both SerTemperature and SerWeighingBridge are computational wrappers abstracting the interactions with the legacy physical equipment since they do not yet embed the ISoS Service entity.

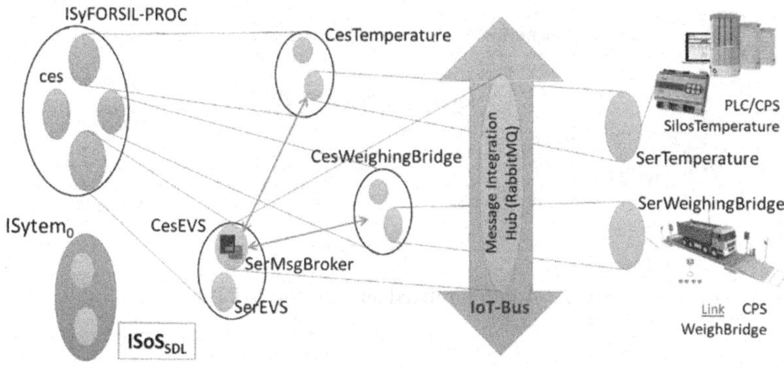


**Fig. 1.** A centralized approach to IoT Bus

Furthermore, Fig. 1 refers to a centralized approach to integrating IoT services. The model considers a classic technique where a kind of Enterprise Service Bus (ESB) manages the access to the IoT services [5]. The centralized IoT Bus is operationalized by a message broker service, in this case, implemented by the message-oriented middleware (MOM) RabbitMQ[1] and the events management SerEVS. It is worth mentioning that (i) the message broker (CesEVS) and its services, and (2) the IoT services, all must be registered at the $\text{ISystem}_0$. Any Service entity registered at $\text{ISystem}_0$ makes us question the need for the intermediary CesEVS. Depending on the problem domain constraints, e.g., if a reliable messaging mechanism is necessary because IoT events cannot be lost, having an "intermediary" approach is an option. However, an alternative is to embed the IoT service with messaging capability and enhance the implementation with event subscriptions and other features, thus avoiding intermediary entities. Instead of adopting such a decentralized architecture, if IoT shares some advanced features, then the CesEVS mediator must be considered. A mediation strategy is also proposed in [14] for predictive streaming data processing for real-time context-aware microservice actions. Within ISoS, such mediation services can be grouped as part of a CES in a similar organization of the implemented CesEVS.

To clarify the architectural options to structure the technology artifacts that are ISoS-enabled, in Fig. 2, we depict the approach that considers reliable IoT services embedding messaging middleware features. The CesEVS component is removed, and the services SerTemperature and SerWeighingBridge are enhanced with messaging and event management features.

It is worth mentioning that depending on the application domain, the possibility of changes to legacy systems, and reliability or dependability issues, among other aspects, the ISoS architect can decide by alternative options. Furthermore, the ISoS model accommodates offering services under both centralized and decentralized models.

[1] Message Oriented Middlware (MOM) RabbitMQ - https://www.rabbitmq.com/.

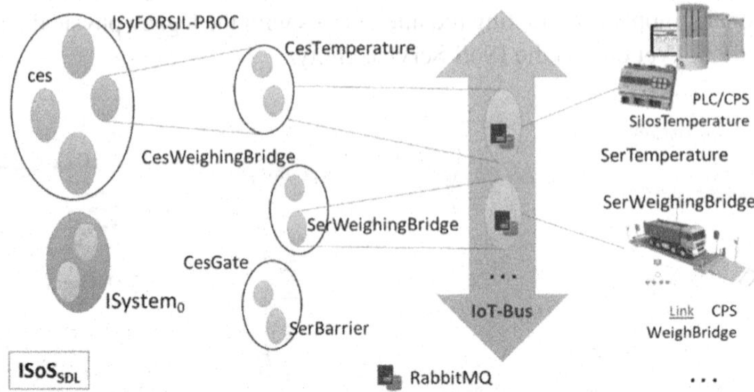


**Fig. 2.** A decentralized approach to IoT Bus

According to the ISoS model, everything is an abstract ISystem, an abstract CES, or a specific Service implemented in any technology. The Service artifact models any computational entity regardless of its complexity or size. Compared to a microservice, the ISoS Service concept does not imply any size or complexity restriction nor imposes an interaction protocol. A primary challenge addressing legacy systems is to make them evolve for multi-supplier technology composites, reducing vendor lock-in problems [13]. The ISystem, CES, and Service are the ISoS constructs where a Service abstracts a single computational responsibility regardless of its size.

## 4 The SITL-IoT Collaborative Contexts

The Silos of Leixões (SDL) organization collaborates with agro-industry factories (denoted as FACT), managing the trucks transporting the cereals from the silos to their infrastructures. The coordination of such transports requires the ERP at a factory to interoperate with the ISyFORSIL-PROC at SDL. This kind of interdependency is growing fast as organizations move to digital and automate their business processes, i.e., internal processes and those managing actions or events from business partners. These interdependencies, typically addressed under the Collaborative Networks perspective, are challenging since the state of such interactions relies on specific adapters that are difficult to maintain and evolve [3, 17].

To address the SITL-IoT collaboration needs, we consider two complementary strategies. The currently implemented approach considers the ISoS $I_0$ interface offered by the ISystem$_0$ of any ISoS enabled organization to access any implemented service. A complementary approach considers the adoption of the ECoNet collaborative network infrastructure introduced in [17]. We first discuss the direct access through the ISoS $I_0$ meta-services, followed by adopting ECoNet.

**Collaboration Through the ISoS $I_0$ Meta-service.** Internal services of an organization implementing the ISoS framework access the meta-service $I_0$ to locate other services. Furthermore, any business partner organization can also access the meta-service $I_0$ with the required authentication to access authorized internal services. In the current reference implementation, the ISoS $I_0$ meta-service is located at the address endpoint isos. <organization domain>:2058 as a simple REST interface. However, even without adopting ISoS, any organization can access a computational service of an ISoS enterprise with $\text{ISystem}_0$ running on the isos. <organization domain> server, by default at port 2058. Figure 3 depicts the SITL-IoT case where an ERP from a business partner we identify as FACT (some agro-factory) needs to access services at SDL.

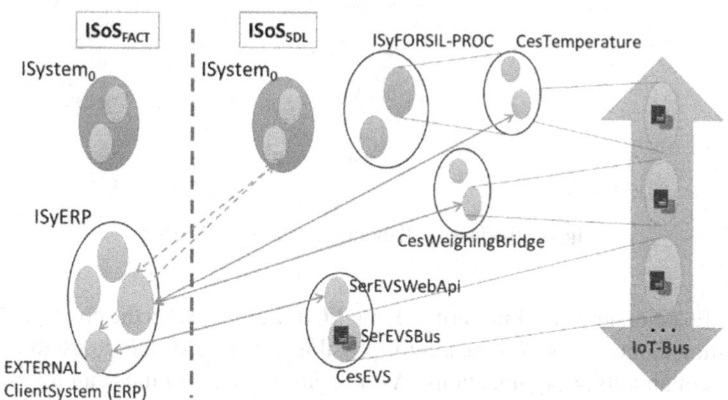


**Fig. 3.** Business collaborations between SDL and FACT organizations

The advantage concerning the current point-to-point specific adapter interactions where the client computing service needs to know a priori the location of the peer service does not happen with ISoS. In the current approach, if, for some reason, the target service location changes, the calling business partner might face a failure if business partners did not update the new endpoint. As depicted in Fig. 3, a service of ISyERP accessing, e.g., the SerEVSWebAPI, first lookups for the service at SDL $\text{ISystem}_0$ ($\text{ISy}_0$) and retrieved meta-data to access the target service. We assume that at SDL, any change that occurs in any internal service the $\text{ISy}_0$ updated.

It is worth mentioning that $\text{ISystem}_0$ tends to play technology landscape operations and governance roles. Therefore, the model considers any independent or atomic computational entity, the Service concept, to behave according to ISoS principles.

**Collaboration by Adopting ECoNet.** The SITL-IoT collaboration needs could also be successfully fulfilled by adopting the ECoNet Collaboration infrastructure [17]. However, using this infrastructure requires centralized coordination of the data and control exchanges. As depicted in Fig. 4, there is a single direct interaction between services in both organizations in this alternative approach, likewise in the implemented solution illustrated in Fig. 3. However, with ECoNet, the interactions occur exclusively through a special ISystem responsible for all the collaboration processes - the Enterprise Collaboration Manager (ECoM) - and its specific application domain, Collaboration Contexts (CoC).

Compared to the first approach, where interactions go through the I0 interface of ISystem0, low-level communication and security protocols and mechanisms are shared

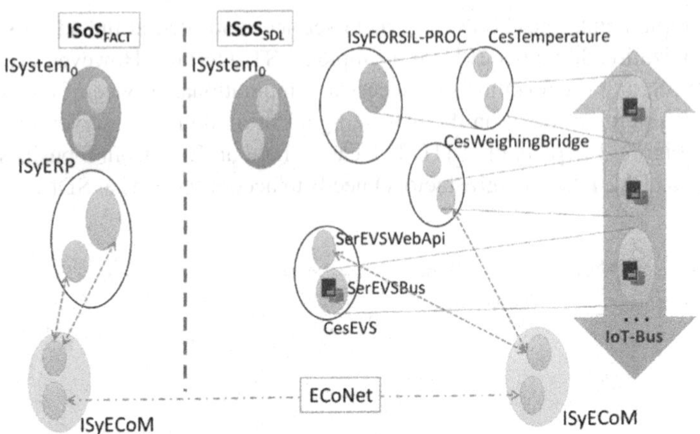


**Fig. 4.** Business collaborations through ECoNet

across the ECoNet network. Furthermore, the ECoM implements the concept of Virtual Collaboration Contexts (VCC), making it possible for any ISystem to establish virtual groups of collaborating organizations. As a result, Service entities can access ECoM services to create or join a VCC and manage through CoC, multi-tenant collaboration spaces, for data and control exchanges. The advantage of adopting the CoC concept is that data exchanges in the same specific application context, e.g., transport management of agro-products from/to silos infrastructure, can be shared by an ERP, invoice management, or other informatics systems.

The migration of the legacy FORSIL product to the ISoS framework demanded the (re)thinking of its original monolithic architecture. Tightly coupled parts must be reorganized as independent Service elements. Structuring FORSIL as a composite of Service elements demonstrates the advantage of supporting the coexistence of alternative implementations for accessing implemented functionalities. As discussed, the mediation implemented by the CesEVS services composite and the integration of the mediated services as part of the IoT Bus introduced alternative interoperability mechanisms for the internal and partner organizations' informatics systems. Another significant result of the SITL-IoT project is the practical demonstration of the added value of the ISoS concepts in constructing an agile and adaptive IoT Bus made of independent Service elements managed through the $\text{ISystem}_0$.

## 5 Conclusions and Further Research

In this work, we present and discuss a strategy to address the open IoT Bus formulated by the SITL-IoT research project in a partnership with the FORDESI company. From simple sensors and actuators through devices with computing capabilities and cyber-physical components to enterprise systems or (applications), different perspectives of the IoT concept are discussed towards a definition for the SITL-IoT project. Accordingly, the adoption of the ISoS framework is presented and discussed, following the evaluation of integration strategies for multi-supplier heterogeneous computing artifacts. Finally, the adoption of ISoS also considers the validation of a reference implementation for the ISystem0 of the SDL organization as a strategy to validate services developed by FORDESI and incorporating their FORSIL-PROC product.

The collaboration dimension considers the adopted approach based on direct interactions between Services in the involved organizations, which are accessed through the $ISystem_0$ canonical $I_0$ interface. While presenting the advantages of this approach compared to the commonly used point-to-point interactions supported on specific adapters, the adoption of the ECoNet collaborative infrastructure is also discussed.

Although the migration of the FORSIL product to comply with the ISoS framework was revealed to be quite promising, further research is necessary to consolidate the adoption of the proposed adaptive integration framework by other companies. The adoption of the ECoNet also needs further research, in particular the use of the ECoM ISystem for managing virtual collaboration contexts supporting critical business processes.

**Acknowledgments.** This work has partial support from the SINCRO/ANSR research project, from the PT2020 project SITL-IoT promoted by the FORDESI company, and from BP Portugal through the research project HORUS. Partial support also from the Center of Technology and Systems - UNINOVA and the Portuguese FCT Foundation (project UIDB/00066/2020). We also thank research fellow Bruno Serras for his valuable contributions to the experimentation/validation work.

## References

1. Afsarmanesh, H., Camarinha-Matos, L.M., Ermilova, E.: Vbe Reference Framework. In: Camarinha-Matos, L.M., Afsarmanesh, H., Ollus, M. (eds.) Methods and Tools for Collaborative Networked Organizations, pp. 35–68. Springer US (2008). https://doi.org/10.1007/978-0-387-79424-2_2
2. Belete, G.F., Voinov, A., Laniak, G.F.: An overview of the model integration process: from pre-integration assessment to testing. Environ. Model. Softw. **87**, 49–63 (2017)
3. Camarinha-Matos, L.M., Fornasiero, R., Afsarmanesh, H.: Collaborative networks as a core enabler of industry 4.0. In: Camarinha-Matos, L.M., Afsarmanesh, H., Fornasiero, R. (eds.) PRO-VE 2017. IAICT, vol. 506, pp. 3–17. Springer, Cham (2017). https://doi.org/10.1007/978-3-319-65151-4_1
4. Cerny, T., Donahoo, M.J., Pechanec. Disambiguation and comparison of soa, microservices and self-contained systems. In: Proceedings of the International Conference on Research in Adaptive and Convergent Systems, RACS 2017, pp. 228–235. Association for Computing Machinery, New York (2017)
5. Chappell, D.: Enterprise Service Bus: Theory in Practice. O'Reilly Media, July 2004
6. Chaudhari, B.S., Zennaro, M., Borkar, S.: Lpwan technologies: Emerging application characteristics, requirements, and design considerations. Future Internet, 12(3) (2020)
7. Smith, N., Wheeler, D.M., Cheruvu, S., Kumar, A.: Connectivity technologies for IoT in: demystifying internet of things security. In: Demystifying Internet of Things Security. Apress, Berkeley (2020)
8. Gigli, M., Koo, S.: Internet of things: Services and applications categorization abstract. Adv. Internet Things **1**, 27–31 (2011)
9. Lankhorst, M.: Enterprise Architecture at Work: Modelling, 4th edn. Communication and Analysis. Springer Publishing Company, Incorporated (2017)

10. Li, S., Da Li, X., Zhao, S.: 5g internet of things: a survey. J. Ind. Inf. Integr. **10**, 1–9 (2018)
11. Mekki, K., Bajic, E., Chaxel, F., Meyer, F.: A comparative study of lpwan technologies for large-scale IoT deployment. ICT Express (2018)
12. Naudet, Y., Latour, T., Guedria, W., Chen, D.: Towards a systemic formalisation of interoperability. Comput. Ind. **61**(2), 176–185 (2010). Integration and Information in Networked Enterprises
13. Opara-Martins, J., Sahandi, R., Tian, F.: Critical review of vendor lock-in and its impact on adoption of cloud computing. In: 2014 International Conference on Information Society (i-Society), pp. 92–97, November 2014
14. Ortiz, G., Caravaca, J.A., García-de Prado, A.: Fràncisco Chavez de la O, and Juan Boubeta-Puig. Real-time context-aware microservice architecture for predictive analytics and smart decision-making. IEEE Access **7**, 183177–183194 (2019)
15. Osório, A.L., Belloum, A., Afsarmanesh, H., Camarinha-Matos, L.M.: Agnostic informatics system of systems: the open isos services framework. In: Camarinha-Matos, L.M., Afsarmanesh, H., Fornasiero, R. (eds.) PRO-VE 2017. IAICT, vol. 506, pp. 407–420. Springer, Cham (2017). https://doi.org/10.1007/978-3-319-65151-4_37
16. Osório, A.L., Camarinha-Matos, L.M., Dias, T., Tavares, J.: Adaptive integration of IoT with informatics systems for collaborative industry: the SITL-IoT case. In: Camarinha-Matos, L.M., Afsarmanesh, H., Antonelli, D. (eds.) PRO-VE 2019. IAICT, vol. 568, pp. 43–54. Springer, Cham (2019). https://doi.org/10.1007/978-3-030-28464-0_5
17. Osório, A.L., Camarinha-Matos, L.M., Afsarmanesh, H., Belloum, A.: On reliable collaborative mobility services. In: Camarinha-Matos, L.M., Afsarmanesh, H., Rezgui, Y. (eds.) PRO-VE 2018. IAICT, vol. 534, pp. 297–311. Springer, Cham (2018). https://doi.org/10.1007/978-3-319-99127-6_26
18. Trilles, S., González-Pérez, A., Huerta, J.: An IoT platform based on microservices and serverless paradigms for smart farming purposes. Sensors **20**(8), 2418 (2020)

# Collaboration Through Digital Integration – An Overview of IT-OT-Integration Use-Cases and Requirements

Jan Hicking, Max-Ferdinand Stroh(✉), and Sebastian Kremer

FIR, Institute for Industrial Management at RWTH Aachen University, Campus-Boulevard 55, 52074 Aachen, Germany
{Jan.Hicking,Max-Ferdinand.Stroh, Sebastian.Kremer}@fir.rwth-aachen.de

**Abstract.** Digitalization and Industry 4.0 continue to shape our industrial environment and collaboration. For many enterprises, a key challenge in moving forward in this matter is the integration of their shop-floor systems (hard- and software) with their office-floor systems to harvest the full potential of industry 4.0. A multitude of different technologies and respective use-cases available on the market leave many companies startled. This paper presents a set of use-cases for IT-OT-Integration to bring transparency into a company's digital transformation. Additionally, a technical requirements profile for integrating IT- and OT-Systems based on the use cases is presented. Both, use-cases and their requirements, guide companies in selecting the digitalization measures that fit their current situation and help in identifying technical challenges that need to be addressed in the transformation process.

**Keywords:** Industry 4.0 · IT-OT-Integration · Digitalization

## 1 Introduction

Industry 4.0 together with digital transformation pose great innovation opportunities for many different industries and enterprises [1]. A majority of Industry 4.0 use-cases require integrating shopfloor systems, so called OT systems, with an enterprise's office floor systems (IT systems) [2, 3]. Being a central component of Industry 4.0, the integration of IT and OT also becomes a main component for collaborative networks, enabling to harvest their full potential [4].

However, realizing IT-OT-Integration is a main challenge for companies, especially for the limited budgets of SMEs [5–7]. Furthermore most enterprises' IT-OT-Landscape, meaning the existing IT-Systems, OT-Systems and interfaces, are very heterogeneous and companies are lacking transparency [8]. In addition, suitable methods for approaching a structured IT-OT-Integration process are missing [9, 10].

To address the issue the authors have developed a systematic approach for IT-OT-Integration based on the as-is assessment of an IT-OT-Landscape as well as a selection


Published by Springer Nature Switzerland AG 2021
L. M. Camarinha-Matos et al. (Eds.): PRO-VE 2021, IFIP AICT 629, pp. 403–410, 2021.
https://doi.org/10.1007/978-3-030-85969-5_37

of Industry 4.0 utility potentials. Thus, combining a company's digitalization goals with the as is assessment of its infrastructure.

After a brief introduction into IT-OT-Integration and utility potentials, this paper presents an overview of industry 4.0 (utility) potentials forming the base for a structured IT-OT-Integration process. Next to that, an IT-OT-Integration profile prototype for assessing the status-quo of an IT-OT-Landscape as well as the matching process with the utility potentials is presented.

## 2 Developed IT-OT-Integration Methodology

To tackle the challenges of IT-OT-Integration, both the potential digitalization use-cases that are of relevance for a company's digital transformation as well as the existing IT-OT-Landscape need to be considered. This ensures the alignment of a company's strategic goals with its current situation. *IT-OT-Integration* refers to the interconnection of IT- and OT-Systems [10, 11]. The term, *IT-System* refers to the office floor systems of an enterprise such as: ERP (Enterprise Resource Planning) or Customer Relationship Management (CRM) [10, 12]. *OT-System* refers to the shop floor systems such as machines, scales, scanners and sensors, but also the software included for controlling them, such as MES (Manufacturing Execution System) [10, 12]. For structural reasons, MES is considered as an IT-System in terms of the methodology presented in this paper.

In their previous work the authors presented a methodology for strategically selecting different digitalization measures [10]. Based on this work, this paper presents the next building blocks within the developed general IT-OT-Integration process. Figure 1 gives an overview of this process.

In the beginning, potential digitalization measures, the so called utility potentials, are selected. In this paper, the term utility potential is used to describe business benefits (utility) in combination with their digitalization measure (potential) [10]. The selection process is covered in detail in [10]. In Sect. 3 the authors present a list of predefined utility potentials for industrial application, also providing orientation in the process of the digital transformation.

After that, a company's or a certain environment's (such as a disctinct manufacturing line) IT-OT-Landscape is assessed. The methodology uses a morphological box as profile for assessing the as is status of the IT-OT-Landscape. For every system that is part of the assessment a profile is filled and stored for later assessment. Section 4 of this paper gives a detailed description of the assessment profile.

Step three uses the same profile for the matching process. In that process, the profiles from the assessment are compared with the profiles filled with the requirements of the utility potentials, revealing, which of the potentials can be easily fulfilled and which require further integration effort.

Finally, the matching results are combined with a set of action recommendations for starting the integration process. From there on, a company can take individual steps in realizing their IT-OT-Integration potentials.

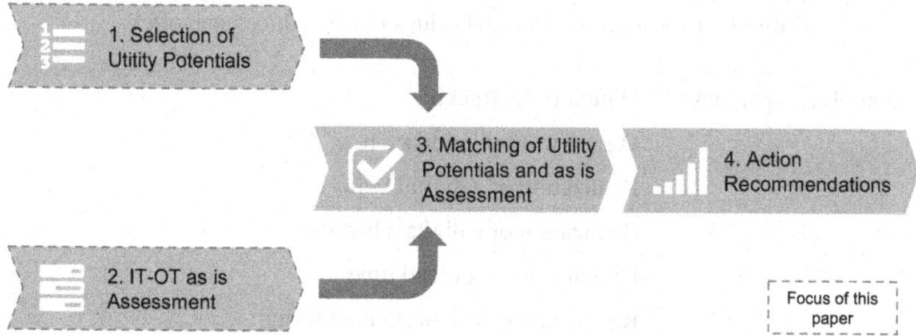


**Fig. 1.** Overview of developed methodology

## 3 Industry 4.0 Utility Potentials

The presented list of Industry 4.0 utility potentials was developed within a research project which forms the basis for this research. The potentials are derived from both literature research as well as expert interviews and were verified with the members of the user committee of the research project. The main literature sources include [13–18]. The expert interviews yielded individually applicable use cases and their respective analysis in the context of utility potentials.

Utility potentials map to general benefits to be achieved in production, consisting of cost reduction, optimization of process time, enhancement of the product's quality and flexibility of production. They describe specific measures that are classifiable into the categories *promotion of transparency*, *decision support* and *active production adaption* (compare Table 1).

The category *promotion of transparency* includes measures, in which data is collected to visualize operational conditions and further allow the analysis of simple causalities between process parameters and the product.

The *support of decision-making* builds on top of the enhanced transparency, by utilizing further data sources and active analysis to generate insights into production, forecasts and detect necessary actions.

The final category, *active production adaption*, usually adds onto the previous decision-making, by actively reacting to available information. The adaption takes the form of automatic decision-making and regulation of the process or system. In contrast to the perceived complexity, the measures implementing active adaption can also represent a simple functionality such as the automatic configuration of machines in response to an order command.

The identified utility potentials were each analyzed to determine the required functionalities and architecture within the construct of IT components, OT components and their corresponding connectivity. This analysis was supported by modelling the expected data flow, to demonstrate the individually required system in a network of general IT and OT components, as shown in Fig. 2. The model allowed an intuitive translation of the utility potentials into the proposed IT-OT-Integration Profile.

**Table 1.** List of utility potentials clustered into three categories

| | |
|---|---|
| Promotion of transparency | Digital order tracking |
| | Digital worker guidance (e.g. AR) |
| | Realization of a digital twin |
| | Realization of a digital shadow |
| | Digital capture of lead time |
| | Realization of condition monitoring |
| | Automatic process quality documentation |
| | Automatic collection of production KPI |
| | Data-based derivation of actual process cost |
| | Order status transparency in production |
| Decision support | Predictive maintenance |
| | Dynamic pricing in production |
| | Realization of a production's digital show |
| | Automatic quality evaluation with data analytics/Machine learning |
| Active production adaption | Reduction of machine downtime |
| | Production process optimization with data analytics/Machine learning |
| | Optimization of process duration |
| | Active energy management using data analytics |
| | Adaptive production adjustment for errors and downtimes |
| | Automatic machine configuration based on the order |

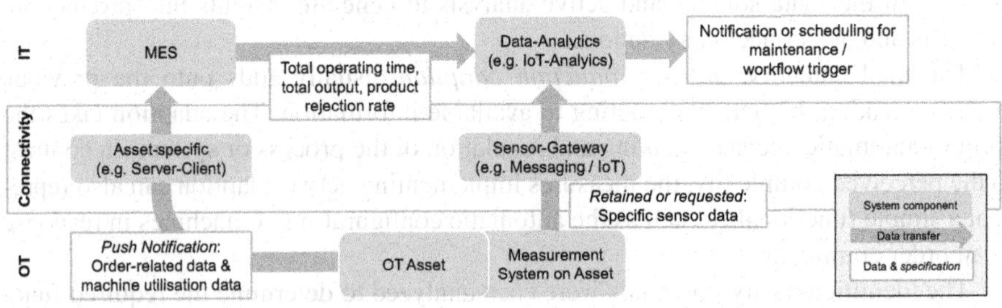


**Fig. 2.** Requirements on the IT-OT-architecture for the utility potential "Predictive Maintenance"

## 4 Prototype of IT-OT-Integration Profile

The matching of a production's IT-OT as is assessment to the determined utility potentials requires a unified IT-OT-integration profile. The goal is to establish a generalized framework that allows a representation of both actual, specific production systems/architectures and the diffuse requirements of a utility potential, without dictating definitive solutions and technologies. Furthermore, the as is and the proposed architecture need to be comparable to derive technical measures that are required to fulfill the utility potentials requirements.

The proposed profile divides the underlying architecture into OT-components, IT-components and interfaces, whereas each specific component in an actual production is represented as its own instance within either of these sections. An ERP-System for example is represented as an IT-component, a production machine as an OT-component and their interconnection as an interface component. The whole structure including the list of options for the components' attributes is shown in Table 2 (table is split into three segments due to print formatting). The structure and attributes were derived and developed in expert interviews. The profiles are used to capture the specification of a component, by selecting relevant options of a given attribute.

The OT profile comprises the general type of exchanged data (namely order data, process data and environment data), the technical nature of the interfaces, regarding physical ports and data protocols, and the capabilities of the data transfer. It represents the digital capabilities and functionalities of the OT system under consideration, including all its applied additions e.g. sensors and retrofits.

The IT profile comprises the type of IT system at hand, the implemented communication protocols, the exchanged data (similarly to the OT system) and the general functionality extended by eventual data analytics capabilities. The exchanged data is further divided into required and provided data.

Interfaces between each one or more IT and OT systems are defined by its communication protocol, its configurability and the characteristic of the data transfer regarding directionality, format and bandwidth. Additionally, the interface references the IT and OT systems it is connecting. Multiple interfaces of similar nature, e.g. a one-to-many connection, can easily be summarized within one interface instance by referencing multiple IT or OT components.

The generalized requirements of a utility potential are summarized in exactly three components, one of each type. The specific attributes of each component are disregarded (marked in gray), as they dictate a technical solution. This approach was chosen to allow for a general evaluation of multiple and vastly different specific production architectures. In fact, disregarded attributes only serve to evaluate possible interconnections of components and eventually the difficulty of achieving such. The matching of a production's as-is assessment to the utility potentials is demonstrated in Table 3.

By assessing an attribute's delta to the desired utility potential and evaluating its difficulty of solving the delta, using the specific attributes (in grey), an appropriate measure can be derived. Similarly the interfaces, the IT-systems and the interconnectivity is handled. The overall assessment then allows for an identification of critical measures and their respective difficulties, e.g., solvable by using Retrofits, to achieve the utility potential.

**Table 2.** Unified OT-, Interface- and IT-profiles with corresponding attributes and their respective list of options (gray attributes are not defined by utility potentials)

| **OT** | | | | |
|---|---|---|---|---|
| **Attribute** | **Value Options** | | | |
| Exchanged Data | Process data | Order data | Environment data | |
| Push-Capabilities (Data out) | Real-time | < once per day | < once per hour | |
| | Events only | None | | |
| Pull-Capabilities (Data out) | On request / polling | Short-time buffered | | |
| | Real-time | Historical | None | |
| Access Permissions | Read | Write | Execute | None |
| Hardware Interface | None | Analog / parallel IO | Basic serial IO | |
| | RJ45 | Profibus | <custom> | |
| Avl. Communication Protocols | None | HTTP(S) | MQTT | |
| | OPC-UA | Profibus | <custom> | |
| System Modifiability | Proprietary | Proprietary, but unlockable | Open | |
| **IT** | | | | |
| **Attribute** | **Value Options** | | | |
| Required Data | Process data | Order data | Environment data | |
| Provided Data | Process data | Order data | Environment data | |
| Avl. Communication Protocols | None | HTTP(S) | MQTT | |
| | OPC-UA | Profibus | <custom> | |
| Type | ERP | MES | IoT-Platform | |
| | Database | Dashboard | PLM | <custom> |
| Functionality (data-) | Acquisition (from OT) | Acquisition (from IT/user) | | |
| | Preprocessing | Enrichment | Virtualization | |
| | Distribution | Storage | Analytics | |
| | Delivery | Visualization | | |
| Data Analytics | None | Target vs. actual | | |
| | Generate visibility | Transparency & diagnostics | | |
| | Forecast | Adaption & decision automation | | |
| **Interface** | | | | |
| **Attribute** | **Value Options** | | | |
| Communication Protocol | HTTP(S) | MQTT | OPC-UA | |
| | Profibus | <custom> | | |
| Configurability | Proprietary | Programmable | | |
| | Static configuration | Low-code / No-code | | |
| Roles of the IT System | Server | Client | | |
| Transfer Format | Stream | Database | File | |
| | Request/transaction | Manual | <custom> | |
| Transfer Volume | Low | Medium | High | |
| Connected Systems | <OT references> | <IT references> | | |

**Table 3.** Attribute-wise matching of as-is assessment (crosses) and chosen utility potential (circles) in an exemplary OT profile

| OT | | | | |
|---|---|---|---|---|
| Exchanged Data | Process data | ⊗ Order data | ○ Environment data | |
| | | | | → *Environment data ist not handled: Sensor are to be fitted* |
| Push-Capabilities (Data out) | Real-time | ○ < once per hour | × < once per day | |
| | Events only | | None | |
| | | | | → *Push rate is too low: Proprietary modifialbility dictates Retrofit* |
| Pull-Capabilities (Data out) | On request / polling | × Short-time buffered | | |
| | Real-time | Historical | ○ None | |
| | | | | → *No Requirements by utility potential* |
| Access Permissions | ⊗ Read | × Write | × Execute | None |
| | | | | → *Requirements are met* |

## 5 Outlook and Conclusion

Mastering the IT-OT-Integration process is a challenge for many companies, especially SMEs. Therefore, this paper presents a set of utility potentials as well as an IT-OT-Integration profile to structure and assist the integration process.

In the beginning, the developed IT-OT-Integration approach is presented and put into the context of previous research activities. Afterwards a set of utility potentials to select in the beginning of an IT-OT-Integration project is shown. Subsequently, an Integration profile with the categories IT, OT and Interface to assist the structured as is assessment of an IT-OT-Landscape is introduced. Finally, the matching process between the selected utility potentials and the as is assessment of the IT-OT-Landscape is explained.

Future research will further explore the presented approach to prove its validity. Additionally, the methodology will be assisted by a web-based application to facilitate the access to IT-OT self-assessments.

**Acknowledgements.** The IGF project 20768 BG of the Research Association FIR e. V. at the RWTH Aachen University is funded via the AiF within the framework of the programme for the funding of cooperative industrial research (IGF) by the Federal Ministry of Economics and Energy (BMWi) on the basis of a resolution of the German Bundestag.

## References

1. Vogel-Heuser, B., Bauernhansl, T., Ten Hompel, M. (eds.): Handbuch Industrie 4.0 Bd.2. SRT, Springer, Heidelberg (2017). https://doi.org/10.1007/978-3-662-53248-5
2. Bildstein, A., Seidelmann, J.: Migration zur Industrie- 4.0-Fertigung. In: Vogel-Heuser, B., Bauernhansl, T., Hompel, M. ten (eds.) Handbuch Industrie 4.0 Bd. 1. Produktion, pp. 227–242. Springer, Berlin (2017) https://doi.org/10.1007/978-3-662-45279-0_44
3. Schlick, C. (ed.): Megatrend Digitalisierung - Potenziale der Arbeits- und Betriebsorganisation. GITO, Berlin (2016)

4. Camarinha-Matos, L.M., Fornasiero, R., Afsarmanesh, H.: Collaborative networks as a core enabler of industry 4.0. In: Camarinha-Matos, L.M., Afsarmanesh, H., Fornasiero, R. (eds.) PRO-VE 2017. IAICT, vol. 506, pp. 3–17. Springer, Cham (2017). https://doi.org/10.1007/978-3-319-65151-4_1
5. Henke, N., et al.: The age of analytics. Competing in a data driven world (2016)
6. Saam, M., Viete, S., Schiel, S.: Digitalisierung im Mittelstand. Status Quo, aktuelle Entwicklungen und Herausforderungen. Frankfurt (2016)
7. Pettey, C.: When IT and Operational Technology Converge. CIOs and IT leaders will drive significant competitive advantages with this integration (2017)
8. Urbach, N., Ahlemann, F.: Die IT-Organisation im Wandel. Implikationen der Digitalisierung für das IT-Management. HMD Praxis der Wirtschaftsinformatik **54**, 300–312 (2017)
9. Lara, P., Sánchez, M., Villalobos, J.: Bridging the IT and OT worlds using an extensible modeling language. In: Comyn-Wattiau, I., Tanaka, K., Song, I.-Y., Yamamoto, S., Saeki, M. (eds.) ER 2016. LNCS, vol. 9974, pp. 122–129. Springer, Cham (2016). https://doi.org/10.1007/978-3-319-46397-1_10
10. Schuh, G., Hicking, J., Jordan, F., Stroh, M.F., Saß, S.-A.: Strategic target system to select digitalization measures in manufacturing companies. In: Camarinha-Matos, L.M., Afsarmanesh, H., Ortiz, A. (eds.) Boosting Collaborative Networks 4.0, pp. 227–237. Springer, Cham (2020) https://doi.org/10.1007/978-3-030-62412-5_19
11. Garimella, P.K.: IT-OT integration challenges in utilities. In: October 25th - 27th, 2018, Kathmandu, Nepal : an IEEE Nepal Sub Section Conference. IEEE, Piscataway, NJ (2018)
12. Noronha, A., Moriarty, R., O'Connell, K., Villa, N.: Attaining IoT Value: How To Move from Connecting Things to Capturing Insights. Gain an Edge by Taking Analytics to the Edge. https://www.cisco.com/c/dam/en_us/solutions/trends/iot/docs/iot-data-analytics-white-paper.PDF
13. Goto, S., Yoshie, O., Fujimura, S.: Industrial IoT business workshop on smart connected application development for operational technology (OT) system integrator. In: IEEE IEEM 2017 : 10–13 December, Singapore. IEEE, Piscataway, NJ (2017)
14. Global Lighthouse Network:. Insights from the Forefront of the Fourth Industrial Revolution (2019)
15. Reinhart, G. (ed.): Handbuch Industrie 4.0. Geschäftsmodelle, Prozesse, Technik. Hanser, München (2017)
16. Kleinemeier, M.: Von der Automatisierungspyramide zu Unternehmenssteuerungs-Netzwerken. In: Vogel-Heuser, B., Bauernhansl, T., Hompel, M. ten (eds.) Handbuch Industrie 4.0 Bd. 1. Produktion, pp. 219–226. Springer, Berlin (2017) https://doi.org/10.1007/978-3-662-45279-0_43
17. Lechler, A., Schlechtendahl, J.: Steuerung aus der Cloud. In: Vogel-Heuser, B., Bauernhansl, T., Hompel, M. ten (eds.) Handbuch Industrie 4.0 Bd. 1. Produktion, pp. 61–74. Springer, Berlin (2017) https://doi.org/10.1007/978-3-662-45279-0_27
18. Pelino, M., Hewitt, A.: The Forrester Wave™: IoT Software Platforms, Q4 2016. The 11 Providers That Matter Most And How They Stack Up (2016)

# A Collaborative Cyber-Physical Microservices Platform – the SITL-IoT Case

Carlos Gonçalves[1(✉)], A. Luís Osório[1(✉)], Luís M. Camarinha-Matos[2(✉)], Tiago Dias[1(✉)], and José Tavares[3(✉)]

[1] ISEL – Instituto Superior de Engenharia de Lisboa, IPL – Instituto Politécnico de Lisboa, and POLITEC&ID, Lisbon, Portugal
{carlos.goncalves,tiago.dias}@isel.pt, lo@isel.ipl.pt

[2] School of Science and Technology, NOVA University of Lisbon and CTS-UNINOVA, Caparica, Portugal
cam@uninova.pt

[3] FORDESI, Informatics Systems, and Solutions Company, Lisbon, Portugal
jose.tavares@fordesi.pt

**Abstract.** Managing heterogeneous software and hardware artifacts from multiple suppliers is a complex and challenging process. The integration of sensors, actuators, and their controllers, modeled as IoT elements, also presents significant challenges. Typically, a vendor supplies one or more parts, each one with its proprietary interface, which may raise vendor lock-in and supplier dependencies that can compromise the replacement of some of the artifacts by equivalent ones from competing vendors. The research presented in this paper addresses such challenges in the context of the SITL-IoT project aiming at transforming an industrial agri-food environment towards an open, integrated system-of-systems. We present and discuss a reference implementation of a collaborative platform to simplify the management of different artifacts, supplied by alternative suppliers, modeled as services. More specifically, the concepts of *ISystem (Informatic System), CES (Cooperation Enabled Service)*, and *Service* are used to manage the different elements that compose an agri-food environment transparently and uniformly. We argue that the adopted model simplifies the collaboration among technology suppliers along the life cycle maintenance and evolution of their enabled products.

**Keywords:** Internet of things · Systems integration · Collaborative networks · Cyber-physical systems · Microservices · Distributed systems

## 1 Introduction

Organizations that use different software or hardware elements face challenging problems when updating or upgrading their technological infrastructures. Typically, each technology solution or product is provided by a different supplier with its own proprietary protocols, which quite often makes it very difficult and expensive to replace a


L. M. Camarinha-Matos et al. (Eds.): PRO-VE 2021, IFIP AICT 629, pp. 411–420, 2021.
https://doi.org/10.1007/978-3-030-85969-5_38

given element with an equivalent one from a competing supplier. On the other hand, the Internet of Things (IoT) enables industries to manage their existing sensors and actuators as elements that exist on their local networks or WAN. However, because collaborating suppliers deliver sensors and actuators using different protocols and Application Programming Interfaces (APIs), the integration of such technology artifacts results in complex and demanding processes both in terms of the development and maintenance cycles. Indeed, competing suppliers source elements under technology diversity, raising risks of vendor lock-in or supplier dependencies. Such dependencies compromise the replacement of artifacts, being an obstacle to sustainable innovation.

This paper presents and discusses a reference implementation of an Informatics System of Systems (ISoS) platform [8] that contributes to the Model-Driven Open Systems Engineering (MDEOS) and promotes an open market competitive technology landscape for organizations. The ISoS model establishes a system-of-systems where each system might have market competitors able to provide possible substitutions. The main objective is to make a system, or elements of a system, replaceable by an equivalent technology artifact from an alternative supplier. The notion of Cooperation Enabled Services (*CES*) is adopted as part of the strategy to attain partial substitutability, a challenging endeavor to achieve. The ISoS model comprises three abstraction layers: i) *ISystem,* establishing a coarse computational and cooperation responsibility border; ii) *CES,* as a composite of *Services*; and iii) *Service,* as the operating element that can be a pure software artifact or a cyber-physical element, e.g., an IoT sensor/actuator, as the finer-grained computational responsibility border. By ISoS reference implementation, we mean the instantiation of an operating *ISystem*, named $ISystem_0$, aiming to validate and certify the compliance of all the *ISystem/CES/Service* products.

This work expands further the initial approach of the SITL-IoT project [12], aiming to evolve an industrial agri-food environment towards an agri-food ecosystem supported by an open, integrated system-of-systems. We present the first ISoS reference implementation and discuss its utilization for simplifying the management of artifacts supplied by alternative vendors. Such ISoS reference implementation is the first effort to deliver an actual implementation of the ISoS model, thus allowing organizations to be ISoS enabled. As a case study, we demonstrate the *ISystem, CES,* and *Services* instances developed within the SITL-IoT project devoted to structure and manage the agri-food silos environment transparently and uniformly.

The remainder of this paper is organized as follows. Section 2 briefly presents the ISoS background, while Sect. 3 reviews the SITL-IoT project and its strategies to integrate the ISoS reference implementation. Finally, Sect. 4 presents the conclusions and discusses future work.

## 2 Enterprise Architecture with ISoS Background

By adopting the ISoS framework [8], an enterprise platform architecture is based on three core modeling elements: *ISystem, CES,* and *Service.* Furthermore, to be ISoS enabled, an organization needs to instantiate the meta-*ISystem,* i.e., an instance of the $ISystem_0$, an *ISystem* with the unique role of managing the ISoS landscape. Figure 1 depicts the primary elements that make an ISoS organization using a SysML Block Definition

Diagram. The ISoS abstraction is a composite of exactly one $ISystem_0$ and zero or more *ISystems*. Each *ISystem* is composed of one or more *CES*, which are composed of one or more *Services*. The ISoS elements model the technology artifacts through a set of properties, e.g., name, version, supplier, or description. In the case of a *Service*, the modeling element instance has associated the meta-data required for a peer *Service* to access the implemented functionalities.

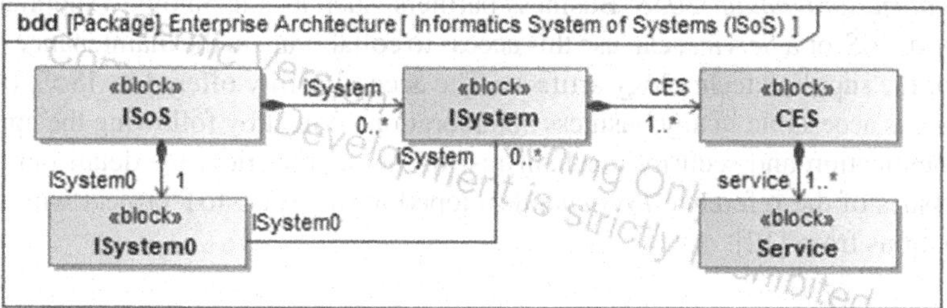


**Fig. 1.** The simplified SysML block definition diagram of the ISoS model

The ISoS model considers a meta-*element* with management or coordination roles at the ISoS, *ISystem*, and *CES* levels, respectively $ISystem_0$, $CES_0$, and $Service_0$. A primary role of the $ISystem_0$ is to act as a directory service managing the metadata of the ISoS elements that exist within an organization. In the current version of the ISoS reference implementation, the $ISystem_0$ relies on Apache Zookeeper [4]. Figure 2 depicts the internal structure of the $ISystem_0$ linked to the ISoS Znode, the children nodes $ISystem_0$, $ISystem_1$,…, $ISystem_N$, the corresponding children *CES*, and, for each $CES_J$, the children *Services*. $ISystem_0$ has a $CES_0$ composed by $Ser_0$ and $Ser_1$. The ISoS administration user interface has a $CES_{UI}$ composed of $Ser_0$ and $Ser_{UI}$ that makes possible the navigation across ISoS instance elements, facilitating introspection of its properties.

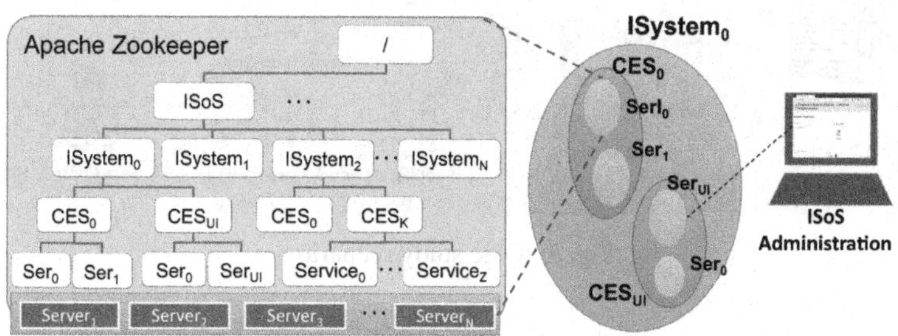


**Fig. 2.** The internal organization of the $ISystem_0$

The adoption of the open-source Zookeeper system is motivated by $ISystem_0$ being a critical system since the other *ISystems* depend on its availability. If configured in redundancy mode, the Zookeeper system maintains a consistent replica in N independent servers, preferably based on separate hardware. The approach follows the strategy proposed in [10], considering a reliable $ISystem_O$ dependent on the fault-tolerant configuration of the Zookeeper, implementing the Zab distributed coordination algorithm [3, 4]. Furthermore, beyond the fault-tolerance and distributed coordination strategies [6], the $ISystem_O$ implementation is prepared to scale several *Service* instances through the Observer nodes concept to speed up read-only service lookup operations [5].

One important feature of the ISoS is its capability to make any *Service* instance accessible both inside and outside the organization. The $ISystem_O$ is accessible at *isos.organizationDomain:2058*. Business partners, such as a technology supplier of an *ISystem*, a *CES*, or a *Service*, can use this access to collaborate in the maintenance or evolution of the supplied technology artifacts. The access facility offered by ISoS, through $ISystem_O$, is accessible in any business collaboration context by following the appropriate authentication and security mechanisms. In the next section, we detail implementation issues of the reference $ISystem_O$ developed in the SITL-IoT project with further contributions from [12].

## 3 The SITL-IoT Project Case Study

The SITL-IoT research and development project aims at developing an open IoT Bus for cyber-physical elements modeled as *Services*. The project answers the research question of how to evolve towards an open multi-supplier technology landscape. In this section, we show how the ISoS model was used to structure the computing elements that compose the SITL-IoT project.

### 3.1 The SITL-IoT Base Scenario

Figure 3 depicts a simplified view of an agri-food company located nearby the seaport of Leixões in the north of Portugal, identified as Organization A.

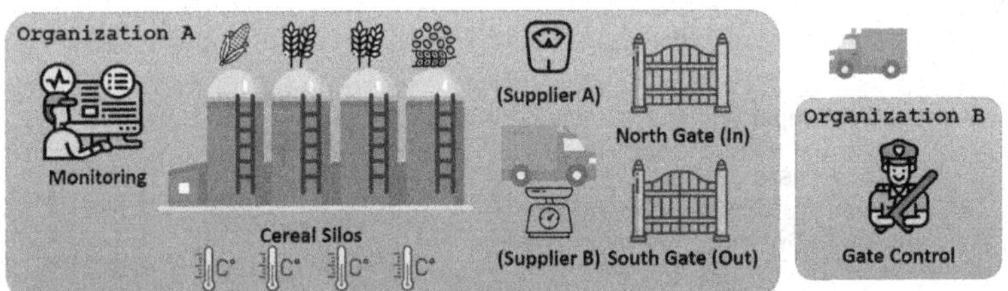


**Fig. 3.** Case study scenario

In this scenario, we consider only a subset of the elements necessary for loading and unloading cereals to/from trucks for reasons of simplicity. For truck control, access to the industrial facilities is done using two gates: North for inbound and South for outbound. Moving agri-food barges inside the seaport requires an authorization issued by the Port Authority, represented by Organization B. The purpose of the gate in Organization B is to control the trucks discharging the bulk-carrier ships from the seaport area. This area is the Portuguese and EU border with customs and border-police control. As such, the movement of products between the seaport and the agri-food organization requires drivers to authenticate and validate its transport. As shown in Fig. 3, trucks are weighed both inbound and outbound using industrial scales from different suppliers with its own specific weigh controller technology and interfaces. The silos include several temperature sensors that are used to manage the temperature at regularly spaced levels of its structure. This weighing bridge infrastructure, the temperature sensor elements, and other cyber-physical systems of Organization A are modelled as IoT devices. Each IoT device is a *Service* element of the ISoS framework. All *ISystem, CES,* and *Service* elements may have an associated synoptic panel for the monitoring and operating of the physical elements. For the visualization of interrelated technology elements, from *ISystems* to *Service*, a generic Synoptics of Things framework is being developed to simplify central supervision interfaces [13].

### 3.2 The SITL-IoT Project Structure and Elements

The ISoS reference implementation groups the artifacts into specialized projects as Application Programing Interface and Model Elements (APIM), Operations Elements (OPE), Deployment and Operations Elements (DOE), and Monitoring Elements (MOE). This approach aims to facilitate the integration of complex technology landscapes, complying to the reference structure and following the guidelines suggested by the Collaborative Enterprise Development Environment (CEDE) [7]. Figure 4 shows the ISoS reference implementation structure with the $ISystem_0$ and the corresponding *CES* and *Service* elements. The elements *ISystem* and *CES* are organized using the above-mentioned specialized projects (modules) DOE and MOE, since the APIM and OPE are exclusive of the *Service* elements.

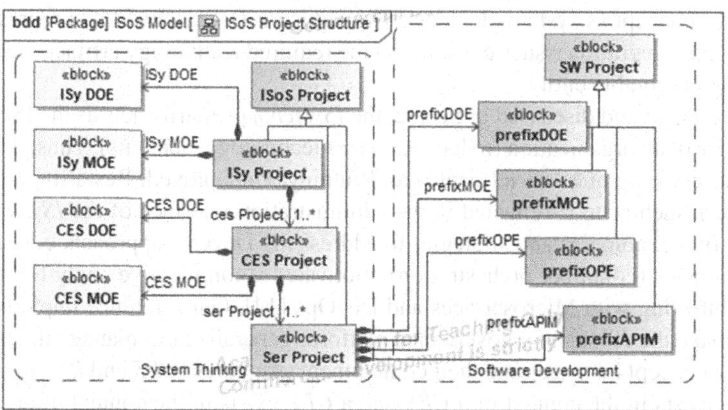


**Fig. 4.** ISoS reference implementation project structure (CEDE concerns)

The DevOps approach inspires the DOE project incorporating the mechanisms to coordinate the development and instantiation of executive parts of ISoS [1]. The MOE aims to deal with the monitoring mechanisms, e.g., by adopting the Simple Network Management Protocol (SNMP) with the respective Management Information Base (MIB) to model the instrumentation of *Service* elements. The technology selection can also use the Java Management Extension (JMX) protocol and the respective instrumentation modeling using Mbean to be managed by JMX agents. The monitoring of technology artifacts is of paramount importance to achieve reliable integrated systems, as discussed in the ISoS framework reliability [11]. OPE organizes the computational logic making a *Service* entity. The project of a *Service* also includes: i) the APIM module, to define interfaces and models specific to the *Service*; ii) the MOE module, to support the implemented monitoring elements; iii) the DOE module, responsible for deploying the *Service*. An alternative is to associate the *CES* DOE module responsible for deploying the composing *Service* elements. Another option is to consider an integrated deployment of an *ISystem* done by its DOE project element. In the current *ISystem* deployment, the strategy is to invoke the DOE projects of the *ISystem* or *CES* composites recursively. For each *CES*, the element executes the deployment logic until the leaf *Service* elements.

The ISoS reference implementation was developed based on the Java ecosystem, using Apache Maven to structure the project, manage the dependencies, and generate isolated and composed artifacts. Nevertheless, very similar principles can be used to develop an ISoS reference implementation using any other technological ecosystem.

As discussed in [7], while ISoS aims to contribute to the substitutability of technology artifacts (*Service*, *CES*, or *ISystem*), technology independence needs to be completed by a unified development environment for unique technology artifacts. Accordingly, the ISoS reference implementation establishes a separation between *ISystems*, *CES*, and *Service* elements as concepts, what we refer to as system thinking to enforce technology independence. The realization of *Services* in some technology and executed within the organization (on-premises) or on the cloud refers to software and deployment/management issues. Figure 4 depicts *System Thinking* and *Software Development* dotted boxes. The *System Thinking* dotted box represents the ISoS *ISystem*, *CES*, and the *Service* concept as system elements. The *Software Development* box represents the software and integration issues considering the required technology artifacts making the *Service* an executable entity.

As presented and discussed in Sect. 2, the $ISystem_0$ primarily acts as the ISoS directory service of an organization (to locate *Service* technology elements). Thus, depending on the current state of *Service* (Deployed, Running, Undeployed, Restarting, Shutting-down, etc.), such state is reflected in the administration interface of the $ISystem_0$. The diversity of technologies and strategies to address the DevOps approach, e.g., Ansible, and Kubernetes (container orchestration), motivated a comparative study for a continuous architecting with Microservices and DevOps [14]. Our reference implementation aims to make the $ISystem_0$ a governance platform generalized to manage the life cycle of *Service* concept instances and their containment structures (*CES* and *ISystems*). Since a *Service* exists in the context of a *CES* and a *CES* exists in the context of an *ISystem*, we can consider the registering of a *Service* within the ISoS landscape involving the following steps:

a. Create (or update) the meta-information of the corresponding *ISystem*;
b. Create (or update) the meta-information of the corresponding CES(s);
c. Create (or update) the meta-information of the *Service*(s);
d. Start the OPE and MOE modules of the *Service*(s).

As a result, the ISoS reference implementation includes i) a generic *ISystem* DOE capable of implementing step a; ii) a generic *CES* DOE capable of implementing step b; and iii) a generic *Service* DOE capable of implementing steps c and d. Furthermore, since in this case study the Java ecosystem was used as the base for the ISoS reference implementation, the above artifacts are made available as independent JAR files. This approach allows us to change the implementing artifact by a competing one (substitutability). Although the discussion presented in this work is focused on the Java ecosystem, the proposed concepts can be extended to other ecosystems. In fact, that extension can be a very straightforward process that consists only in the configuration of the above mentioned JAR files to execute native Operating System processes rather than Java processes.

For an *ISystem* reference implementation, the DOE project module is a Java command-line tool (CLI) that receives two XLM files as arguments. The *ISystem* metadata is specified with the argument *-d isystemDef.xml*. The list of configuration elements used to start all the *CES* included in this *ISystem* is set with the argument *-c cesCfg.xml*. Each configuration element has the location of: i) the *CES* DOE module; ii) the file containing the *CES* metadata; and iii) the file containing the configuration of the services included in the *CES*. All file paths in the configuration elements are relative to a base directory, specified as an attribute in the configuration file. Additionally, the configuration file has two attributes to specify the path of the Java Virtual Machine (JVM) and the base working directory of the modules to start.

The *CES* reference implementation considers that the DOE module follows a similar approach to the one used in the *ISystem* DOE module. It is a Java CLI application that receives as arguments the name of the XML file containing the metadata of the *CES* (*-d cesDef.xml*) and the name of the XML file containing the configuration of the *Service* elements that compose the *CES* (*-c serviceCfg.xml*).

The file used to define the *Service* configuration has all the information to start a *Service,* including the DOE, OPE, and MOE modules and the corresponding arguments. Please note that the OPE and MOE modules are the only ones committed to specific functionalities, represented using a darker blue in Fig. 4. The ISoS reference implementation offers a default DOE module, assuming that the OPE and MOE *Service* modules are JAR files receiving their arguments in the command line.

## 3.3 The ISoS Administration User Interface for the SITL-IoT Case

An administrator can use the ISoS user administration interface to register the different *Services* that compose the ISoS landscape organization using only the OPE and MOE modules of each *Service* and a set of configuration files, as discussed in the previous section. The fulfillment of the ISoS interface with the tree *ISoS/ISystem/CES/Service* is, therefore, a quite straightforward task, as a result of the reference implementation discussed in the previous sections.

It is worth mentioning that advanced abstractions are under evaluation, namely the use of container orchestrations, e.g., the Kubernetes automated container deployment, scaling, and management toolset. However, our approach does not aim exclusively for the cloud. In fact, we strive for a balanced strategy for the organization's computing technology landscape that can be deployed either on-premises or on the cloud, depending on resource allocation needs and the most advantageous options that can change dynamically. The vendor lock-in risks motivated the proposal of a "… *overlay layer that provides users with an inter-operable and visibility-supported environment for MSA-based IoT-Cloud service composition over the existing multiple clouds*" [2]. Nonetheless, the proposed layer seems to introduce additional complexity. The DOE project structuring element can manage the deployment issues in our approach, eventually providing alternative implementations to cope with cloud provider's heterogeneity.

### 3.4 Revisiting the SITL-IoT Scenario Under a Collaborative Perspective

The ISoS implementation described in the previous sections also enables to analyze the SITL-IoT scenario presented in Sect. 3.1 under the collaborative network perspective. As discussed above, every time a truck needs to enter the agri-food area located on-premises of Organization A, it is necessary to obtain inbound access issued by Organization B. Using the ISoS model and its associated reference implementation, the collaboration between the two organizations is a straightforward process. Each of the gates shown in Fig. 3 is running a *Service*, denoted as *ServiceA*, performing the following actions:

1. Collect the driver and truck identification;
2. Contact the ISoS landscape of Organization B (*isos.organizationB:2058*) to get an instance of its $ISystem_O$, denoted as $ISystem_OB$;
3. Using $ISystem_OB$, *ServiceA* performs a lookup operation to obtain the *Service* responsible for granting the entry access, denoted as *ServiceGateB*;
4. *ServiceA* uses *ServiceGateB* to authenticate the driver and the truck;
5. If the authentication is successful, the truck can access the agri-food area.

This simple example shows that the presented ISoS reference implementation allows establishing collaboration among two different organizations, each with well-identified responsibilities, without knowing the internal details of the involved organizations. However, the example can be extended to more complex scenarios involving several organizations. The only requirement is that the involved organizations can access the ISoS landscape of each other, i.e., access the involved $ISystem_O$. One main problem is that for *ServiceA* of Organization A to access *ServiceGateB* of Organization B, there is a need for *ServiceA* to know a priori the path $ISystem_i/CES_j/ServiceGateB$ and with it obtain the *ServiceGateB* meta-data. This problem can be resolved using ISoS. With the *ServiceGateB* metadata, the *ServiceA* client from Organization A can get the necessary data to configure the client proxy to access the implemented functionalities properly.

The collaboration infrastructure offered natively by the ISoS framework can be enhanced by adopting the ECoNet collaborative infrastructure [9]. In this case, *ServiceA* of Organization A used its ECoM *ISystem* to have access to a collaboration context shared with Organization B, that provides the required interaction with *ServiceGateB* using an ECoM instance in Organization B. The advantage of collaboration through the ECoM *ISystems* is that domain application *ISystems* share low-level communication, security mechanisms, and higher-level virtual collaboration contexts multi-tenant groups.

## 4 Conclusions and Further Research

This paper presents and discusses a reference implementation of the ISoS framework, which models the computing technology landscape of an organization. The Java ecosystem adopting the Apache Zookeeper and other open-source projects supports the validation of the framework in the context of the SITL-IoT project. Beyond the $ISystem_0$ as a core technological element for any ISoS enabled organization, we present and discuss a project structure to avoid dependency from subcontracted developments. Furthermore, we discuss a modeling schema for the automatic management of ISoS concept instances. Also, we demonstrate how this approach enables configuring operating system services to automatically register an ISoS *Service* and the corresponding *ISystem* and *CES* when the computer (physical or virtual) supporting the *Service*'s execution starts.

We further discuss a monitoring strategy based on SNMP agents operationalized by the ISoS *Service* concept and managed by the MOE project structuring element. The association of monitoring *Service* agents to domain application *Services* requires further research considering the need to abstract legacy protocols, following the adaptive ISoS Service interoperability mechanism.

For software solution providers like Fordesi, ISoS is a tool that brings industrial IoT solutions to the transport and logistics sector. The modularity and decoupling strategies used by the framework enables a quick-wins project management approach that leads to time and cost-effective solutions.

Concerning collaboration issues, the proposed approach based on the ISoS framework offers collaboration support facilities, since services from collaborative organizations can mutually find each other and interoperate based on the $I_0$ canonical entry point and ISoS metadata facilities. In addition, we discuss the alternative ECoNet using the collaborative contexts and virtual collaboration contexts as shared infrastructure elements. While the collaboration mechanisms offered by ISoS proved to be sufficient for the current business case, further research will validate the adoption of ECoNet infrastructure as a more general approach.

**Acknowledgments.** The research conducted by GIATSI/ISEL/IPL was developed in collaboration with the SOCOLNET scientific network and its ARCON-ACM initiative. The ANSR/SINCRO, BP/HORUS, and FORDESI/SITL-IoT-PT-2020 projects partially supported this research. Partial support also from the Center of Technology and Systems – UNINOVA, and the Portuguese FCT Foundation (project UIDB/00066/2020), and the European Commission (project DiGiFoF). We also recognize the excellent contributions from Bruno Serras as a research fellow.

## References

1. Balalaie, A., Heydarnoori, A., Jamshidi, P.: Microservices architecture enables DevOps: migration to a cloud-native architecture. IEEE Softw. **33**(3), 42–52 (2016)
2. Han, J., Park, S., Kim, J.: Dynamic overcloud: realizing microservices-based IoT-cloud service composition over multiple clouds. Electronics **9**(6), 969 (2020)
3. Hunt, P., Konar, M., Junqueira, F.P., Reed, B.: ZooKeeper: wait-free coordination for internet-scale systems. In: Proceedings of the 2010 USENIX Conference on USENIX Annual Technical Conference, USENIX Association (2010)

4. Junqueira, F.P., Reed, B., ZooKeeper: Distributed Process Coordination. 1st edition, O'Reilly Media, Inc., Beijing (2013)
5. Junqueira, F.P., Reed, B., Serafini, M.: Zab: high-performance broadcast for primary-backup systems. In: Proceedings of the 2011 IEEE/IFIP 41st International Conference on Dependable Systems & Networks, pp. 245–256. IEEE Computer Society (2011)
6. Lamport, L.: Paxos made simple. ACM SIGACT News (Distributed Computing Column) **32**, 51–58 (2001)
7. Osório, A.L.: Towards vendor-agnostic IT-system of IT-systems with the CEDE platform. In: Afsarmanesh, H., Camarinha-Matos, L.M., Lucas Soares, A. (eds.) PRO-VE 2016. IAICT, vol. 480, pp. 494–505. Springer, Cham (2016). https://doi.org/10.1007/978-3-319-45390-3_42
8. Osório, A.L., Belloum, A., Afsarmanesh, H., Camarinha-Matos, L.M.: Agnostic informatics system of systems: the open ISoS services framework. In: Camarinha-Matos, L.M., Afsarmanesh, H., Fornasiero, R. (eds.) PRO-VE 2017. IAICT, vol. 506, pp. 407–420. Springer, Cham (2017). https://doi.org/10.1007/978-3-319-65151-4_37
9. Osório, L.A., Camarinha-Matos, L.M., Afsarmanesh, H.: ECoNet platform for collaborative logistics and transport. In: Camarinha-Matos, L.M., Bénaben, F., Picard, W. (eds.) PRO-VE 2015. IAICT, vol. 463, pp. 265–276. Springer, Cham (2015). https://doi.org/10.1007/978-3-319-24141-8_24
10. Osório, A.L., Camarinha-Matos, L.M., Afsarmanesh, H., Belloum, A.: On Reliable Collaborative Mobility Services. In: Camarinha-Matos, L.M., Afsarmanesh, H., Rezgui, Y. (eds.) PRO-VE 2018. IAICT, vol. 534, pp. 297–311. Springer, Cham (2018). https://doi.org/10.1007/978-3-319-99127-6_26
11. Osório, A.L., Camarinha-Matos, L.M., Afsarmanesh, H., Belloum, A.: Liability in collaborative maintenance of critical system of systems. In: Camarinha-Matos, L.M., Afsarmanesh, H., Ortiz, A. (eds.) PRO-VE 2020. IAICT, vol. 598, pp. 191–202. Springer, Cham (2020). https://doi.org/10.1007/978-3-030-62412-5_16
12. Osório, A.L., Camarinha-Matos, L.M., Dias, T., Tavares, J.: Adaptive integration of IoT with informatics systems for collaborative industry: the SITL-IoT Case. In: Camarinha-Matos, L.M., Afsarmanesh, H., Antonelli, D. (eds.) PRO-VE 2019. IAICT, vol. 568, pp. 43–54. Springer, Cham (2019). https://doi.org/10.1007/978-3-030-28464-0_5
13. Serras, B., Gonçalves, C., Dias, T., Osório, A.L.: Synoptics of things (SoT): an open framework for the supervision of IoT devices. In: 5th International Young Engineers Forum on Electrical and Computer Engineering. IEEE Xplore digital library, (2021)
14. Taibi, D., Lenarduzzi, V., Pahl, C.: Continuous architecting with microservices and DevOps: a systematic mapping study. In: Muñoz, V.M., Ferguson, D., Helfert, M., Pahl, C. (eds.) CLOSER 2018. CCIS, vol. 1073, pp. 126–151. Springer, Cham (2019). https://doi.org/10.1007/978-3-030-29193-8_7

# Pathways and Tools for Digital Innovation Hubs

# Experimentation of Cross-Border Digital Innovation Hubs (DIHs) Cooperation and Impact on SME Services

Margherita Volpe[1(✉)], Omar Veledar[2], Isabelle Chartier[3], Isabelle Dor[3], Fredy Ríos Silva[4], Jure Trilar[5], Csaba Kiraly[6], Gabriele Gaffuri[1], and Sabine Hafner-Zimmermann[4]

[1] Zabala Innovation Consulting, Brussels, Belgium
mvolpe@zabala.eu
[2] AVL List GmbH, Graz, Austria
[3] Université Grenoble Alpes, CEA, Leti, 38000 Grenoble, France
[4] Steinbeis Europa Zentrum, Karlsruhe, Germany
[5] University of Ljubljana, Ljubljana, Slovenia
[6] Digital Catapult, London, UK

**Abstract.** As digital transformation imposes cultural changes in terms of how value is delivered, continual experimentation helps define optimal solutions for key stakeholders. From the DIH perspective, the hunt is on for the most impactful and financially sustainable services that lend themselves to practical customisation against target group needs. Among these, fostering cross-border collaboration amongst themselves and between SMEs is also a desirable, albeit challenging strategy to be pursued by DIHs. We present the approach of DigiFed (European Commission funded project), which relies on a network of 12 DIHs and Research Technology Organisations (RTOs) to design and experiment with novel innovation support mechanisms for SMEs across Europe. We analyse the currently implemented cross-border cooperation instruments and their preliminary results and describe additional instruments under ongoing experimentation. We also elaborate on prospects to generalise these instruments for adoption by other DIH networks.

**Keywords:** DIH network · Collaborative methods · Innovation support · Application Experiments · Cross-border collaboration · SMEs

## 1 Introduction

The experimentation of tools and collaborative services that are offered by DIHs is a matter of interest at the national and European level. The offered support occasionally benefits from the opportunities presented by European Commission's (EC) R&I funding programmes. This is the case of DigiFed - *Digital Innovation Hubs (DIH) federation for large scale adoption of digital technologies by European SMEs*, which


Published by Springer Nature Switzerland AG 2021
L. M. Camarinha-Matos et al. (Eds.): PRO-VE 2021, IFIP AICT 629, pp. 423–432, 2021.
https://doi.org/10.1007/978-3-030-85969-5_39

is currently experimenting with different pathways to foster cross-border collaborative innovation, primarily among SMEs. The paper discusses the currently implemented cross-border cooperation instruments and their preliminary results, as a contribution to the investigation of collaborative services and success stories among DIHs.

To maximise the benefits of digital innovations for European industries, the EC is realising its Digitising European Industry (DEI) Strategy [1]. It focuses on upgrades of assets and processes, and business models adaptation to the digital age. This calls for the full integration of digital innovations across all economic sectors. One of DEI's key elements is DIH. These hubs support Small and Medium Enterprises (SME), start-ups and mid-caps in boosting their competitive advantage by fostering the adoption of the latest digital technologies. Acting as a one-stop-shop, they provide access to digital technologies and competence, infrastructure to test digital innovations, training to develop digital skills, financing support, market intelligence and networking opportunities. The EC invests in EU-wide collaboration across the network of DIHs. What started in 2013 with the ICT Innovation for Manufacturing SMEs (I4MS) initiative [2], was followed by the Smart Anything Everywhere initiative (SAE) in 2015 [3]. The SAE covers different projects, involving DIHs throughout Europe, in several technology areas, including Cyber-Physical Systems (CPS) and Embedded Systems. All projects offer so-called cascade funding to SMEs and mid-caps to enhance their assets through the inclusion of innovative digital technologies. The expectation is for the selected projects to achieve technical maturity worthy of sustainable introduction to the market, as also reported by others [4]. By improving digital maturity levels, DigiFed also leverages created solutions to enable new use cases and services in an industrial context. Hence, the focus is placed on successfully formulating and implementing go-to-market strategies based on expressed customer needs. Such an approach is critical for customer-driven innovation [5].

EC has financed 16 projects under the umbrella of SAE. Besides aiding industrial digitalisation, these projects open new markets enabled by CPS and embedded systems. One of those projects is DigiFed, which was launched in January 2020. Its objectives include supporting the digitalisation of companies, enhancing DIH services offer, improving collaboration among DIHs and experimenting with new funding schemes to support the digital transformation of European companies. The consortium currently gathers the following DIHs: Minalogic, France; Ikerlan, Spain; Digital Catapult, UK; and Steinbeis, Germany. All DIHs work with and enhance cooperation within established ecosystems, expanding and linking with other networks to create an EU-wide Federation of DIHs. These DIHs offer sustainable cross-border services and partnerships between relevant European innovation stakeholders (e.g. research & technology organisations (RTOs), Universities, Accelerators, etc.). To that purpose, the project implements 3 interrelated innovation pathways: Application Experiment (AEs), Generic Experiment and Digital Challenge.

AEs are at the core of DigiFed. This pathway attracts companies with varying digital maturity levels. Those with low digital maturity are supported in upgrading existing products and skills with dedicated services, tools and solutions. Digitally mature companies are offered further innovative technology integration and access to potential customers, including large industrial stakeholders. AEs have proven their worth through several initiatives, especially in the cases of I4MS and SAE.

This paper contributes to the research question "*How DIHs can effectively foster cross-border collaboration among each other and between private companies?*" by describing the toolbox of services implemented within DigiFed project and by analysing the evaluation results and success rate of collaborative projects (TWIN AE) against those that are originating from individual organisations (SINGLE AE) at the application stage. The analysis facilitates the assessment of the potential of such supporting instruments to effectively promote and foster cross-border collaboration. The paper also attempts to identify if DigiFed's support infrastructure could serve as a portable example of DIH collaboration to foster similar cross-border partnerships between SMEs and midcaps across Europe to achieve increasing returns through innovation enticed by cross-border cooperation, as reported in [6].

**Open Calls for Application Experiments.** AE is a cascade funding pathway that selects and finances SMEs and mid-caps to develop CPS solutions based on existing or to-be-developed prototypes and products. The selection process is initiated via public open calls and obeys the EC's principles of transparency, confidentiality, equal treatment, and avoidance of conflict of interests. Applicants may apply via two different configurations:

- *Single AE*: a company requests funding (maximum €55k) for an exclusive collaboration with one cross-border DigiFed technical partner, which is selected by the applicant based on a portfolio of technological offerings.
- *Twin AE*: two SMEs or mid-caps jointly apply for maximum funding of €55k per applicant, while respecting the cross-border eligibility criteria.

The experience acquired through innovation actions, such as EuroCPS [7] and FED4SAE [8], suggests that the SINGLE AE type is better adapted to the needs of organisations that are already engaging digital technologies or wish to integrate new digital technologies and increase digital maturity. TWIN AE is already tested in a slightly different form by other SAE innovation actions, such as Tetracom [9] or Tetramax [10]. While also open to companies with a high digital maturity level, TWIN AE attracts "non-digital" applicants that wish to create the first product/service demonstrator based on digital technologies. TWIN AE fosters the collaboration of companies that aim to further CPS-based innovation and have a clear market vision but lack expertise to validate the concept with companies that bring the complementary expertise to realise the prototype or directly access the market.

The two AE types are evaluated through the same evaluation process using the same scoring criteria (i.e. business development potential, excellence, impact and quality of implementation). They are also ranked in a unified evaluation list. The top-scoring applications are selected for financing. To ensure the maximum possible transparency and equal treatment of all applicants, each proposal is evaluated in parallel by 3 external independent experts and a panel of DigiFed internal evaluators, generating an aggregated scoring list. Considering that no AE type is favoured (i.e. there is no minimum guaranteed number of SINGLE or TWIN AEs to be funded), the emerging results from two open calls (OC) provide insights into the success of each AE type.

## 2 Support Provided by DIHs to Open Call Applicants

The described OC organisation and management is complemented by specific actions aimed at supporting AEs in their creation, application, implementation and sustainable exploitation. The crucial support at the creation phase often helps to form the basis for sustainable collaboration. The initial support considers two basic aspects:

- *The eligibility criteria* are clarified to potential applicants at the start of the process.
- *Proposal creation-* support guidance identification of the project's crucial aspects and their mapping to the requirements of the proposal. Aside from the benefit for the applicants to gain experience with the proposal writing, this process also fosters improvement in the realistic estimation of the project's scope, time and budget.

This support takes several forms, including self-service materials (e.g. guide for applicants, detailed application template), an online application platform (including Frequently Asked Questions, information helpdesk), and interactive sessions. As concerns the latter, the following formats have been implemented:

- *Webinars* with a focus on specific application aspects are also recorded and provided as a YouTube video reference for further self-help. An example includes business pitch video guidelines. The pitch replaces the originally planned short interviews with the applicants. In order to optimise the effectiveness of the process and reduce the time needed to process the relevant amount of applications expected and actually received, the pitch enables the applicants to present their value creation concisely.
- *Bootcamps* represent an opportunity to discover DigiFed's technology and innovation management offer, while also enabling applicants to meet prospective partners (i.e., a form of matchmaking).

The support is geared towards the creation of structured proposals through dialogue that encourages applicants to question their own ideas. Thus, the selection process distinguishes the most promising AEs. Further support aids the creation of TWIN projects through several matchmaking opportunities for the prospective partners. Where applicable, DigiFed also facilitates dialogue between those partners to perfect a common offer. The complete process, together with the monitoring of the selected AEs, aims at the sustainable success of the generated assets in the post-AE phase.

## 3 Application Experiment Analysis and Discussion

The effectiveness of the DigiFed AE pathway is based on statistical evaluation (basic distribution and dispersion analysis) of the results achieved so far. the outcome of the analysis is interpreted using the direct experience of the authors in the implementation of the DigiFed project and interaction with the involved beneficiaries, in a living-lab-like approach. OC1 (active from March to June 2020) received 72 eligible proposals, submitted by 94 companies from 26 (EU and associated) countries. They ranged from start-up to mid-cap size, with an expected prevalence of smaller applicants, i.e. start-up and SMEs up to 10 employees representing 72% of applicants. After the implementation of the selection process, OC1 resulted in 14 projects selected for funding and 22 companies receiving a total of over €1.1 million for digital innovation. OC1 served as an experiment to assess the reception and application capability of EU companies concerning different collaboration requirements of SINGLE and TWIN AEs. These instruments were well received as OC1 resulted in over 90 companies applying and a total of 48 Single AE and 24 TWIN AE proposals received.

OC2 (launched in September 2020 and closed in December 2020) received a total of 75 proposals from 96 companies originating from 25 EU and associated states. The application rate per AE type was again fairly – and even better- balanced, with 32 SINGLE AE and 43 TWIN AEs eligible for evaluation. Once again, there was a clear prevalence of applicants from smaller companies (i.e. 28% start-up, 48% SME 1–10 employees), confirming the trend observed in OC1. OC2 resulted in 16 proposals selected for funding, which involved a total of 25 companies.

These initial data on application rates raised two indications:

- AE is confirmed to be particularly appealing to smaller companies,
- Despite being in its experimental stage, the cross-border aspect of the TWIN AE type is confirmed to be an interesting approach for collaboration amongst peers in the framework of a financed research & innovation project.

Upon confirming the appeal of the TWIN AE, the following step was to understand whether the TWIN AE proposals were also successful in the selection process. The evaluation process data indicate not only that TWIN AEs were equally represented among selected AE, but their evaluation scores were also on average higher than those of SINGLE AEs. Table 1 displays the comparison of the TWIN and SINGLE AE success rates for both OCs, with 14 and 16 proposals being selected, respectively. The initial observation is that the final proposal ranking for both OCs generates a fairly balanced ratio between the two AE types.

**Table 1.** Success rate at the application stage

| | TOTAL SELECTED | TWIN AE | SINGLE AE |
|---|---|---|---|
| OC1 | 14 (100%) | 6 (43%) | 8 (57%) |
| OC2 | 16 (100%) | 7 (44%) | 9 (56%) |

Yet, to define the relevance of these data or their bias by a higher application rate in one or the other cluster, the number of selected proposals was compared to the number of applications submitted per each AE type to determine the actual success rate, corresponding to the ratio between awarded and submitted proposals per type. This resulted in divergent trends between two OCs, as the success rate per AE type was:

- OC1 → Twin AE 33% success rate vs. Single AE 13% success rate
- OC2 → Twin AE 16% success rate vs. Single AE 26% success rate

Nevertheless, further data analysis (Table 2) suggests that smaller companies had a consistently higher success rate when applying within the TWIN AE configuration rather than in a SINGLE AE; suggesting that this instrument is particularly apt to aid the major target audience and smaller companies (as per DIH mission).

**Table 2.** Success rate with respect to the company size

| | *Start-ups* | | *SME 1–10 employees* | |
|---|---|---|---|---|
| | TWIN AE success rate | SINGLE AE success rate | TWIN AE success rate | SINGLE AE success rate |
| OC1 | 23% | 25% | 16% | 5% |
| OC2 | 35% | 13% | 24% | 14% |

The analysis of the evaluation scores per AE type is visualised in Fig. 1. The distribution of the scores of all the applicants in each of these categories per OC shows a general tendency of a higher scoring of TWIN over SINGLE AEs, albeit without a strong dominance. If focusing only on the call winners, the dispersion of the scores is reduced. However, a soft dominance of TWIN AEs is present.

The total score per application is also analysed. The score is obtained by simply adding the scores in the four criteria. A clearer dominance of TWIN AE is observable, especially if only focusing on the winners of OC2. A difference is also observed in TWIN AEs between the two OCs. In this case, the dispersion of the scores drastically increases for winners, as well as overall applicants. A possible explanation could be related to the fact that SINGLE proposals were being more comprehensively guided by the DigiFed technical partners, hence containing the dispersion of scores. The in-depth investigation of this aspect exceeds the scope of this paper and will be the object of further analysis.

Hence, the analysed data suggest that the TWIN AE was an effective tool to boost cross-border collaboration among peers, and, mostly among smaller companies, in line with the mission of DIHs. Further information elaborated at the qualitative level suggests added relevant impacts. First, it has been noticed that TWIN AEs were particularly suitable to promote the participation of low digital companies. Indeed, based on the direct interactions that the DigiFed monitoring partners had with the applicants during the OC1 implementation phase and during the helpdesk sessions, a qualitative trend of low digitalised companies' participation predominantly in TWIN AEs was appreciated. For this reason, a first assessment tool was introduced in OC2, based on a single question asked to all the applicants during the registration phase (for preliminary characterisation of the applicant population). The results of this test confirmed the fact that, among low digital maturity companies (13% of the total OC1 and OC2 applicants), two thirds applied as TWIN AE. Indeed, the number of applicants with low digital maturity has been twice as high in TWIN AEs than in SINGLE AEs. Based on the preliminary evidence, DigiFed is experimenting in its third OC with a specific AE type aimed at increasing the participation of low digital maturity companies and is working in parallel on an extended structure of digital maturity assessment and impact estimation (see Sect. 4). The complex issues of assessing the maturity level of SMEs [11] is simplified to the level adequate for implementation within DigiFed. Secondly, based on a brief online survey addressed to all awarded TWIN AE beneficiaries, it has been noted that this AE type is also functional to support the business of the applicants. Most respondents (66,7%) confirmed that the TWIN AE allowed them to consolidate ongoing collaboration partnerships and that the expected benefits of this collaboration encompass the complementarity of competences, the consolidation of long-lasting collaborations and the possibility to enter new markets.

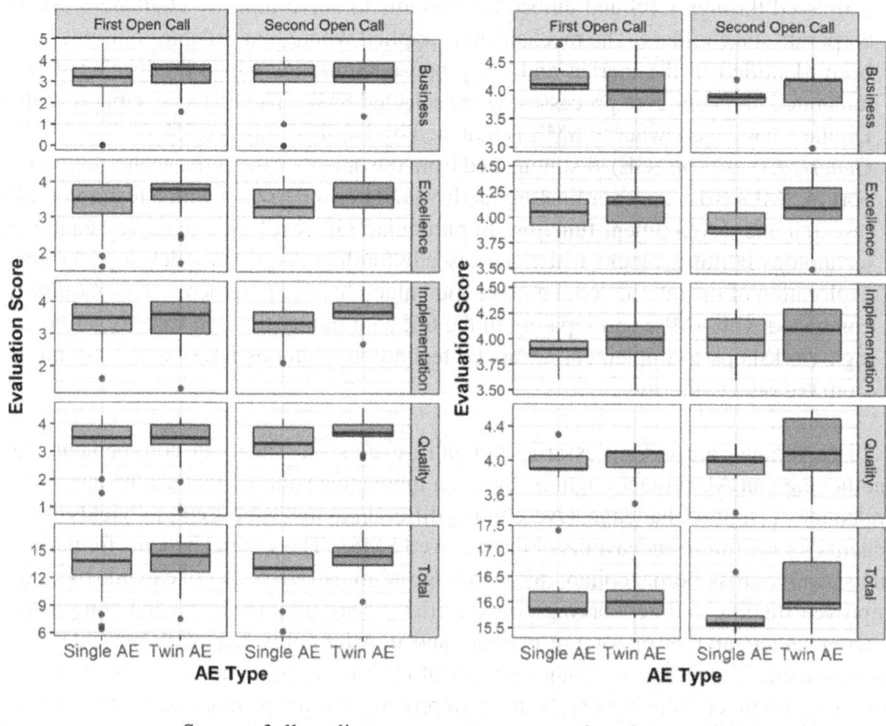


a. Scores of all applicants    b. Scores of the winners

**Fig. 1.** Distribution of the scores of applicants and winners of both DigiFed OCs according to the different evaluation criteria and the total score

## 4 Other Collaborative Actions

Although the TWIN AE instrument is the key mechanism of fostering cross border [12, 13] technical and business innovation amongst SMEs [14] through cascade funding-supported projects, DigiFed is experimenting with other variants of similar engagement. The other variants are not presented in detail here, but we will further explore recognisable topological features of these instruments to provide improved understanding and potential reuse in DIHs and collaborative scenarios.

Three other instruments had been developed to foster the close-knit cross-border cooperation, taking a different angle on how the projects could be formed:

- *Low-digital TWIN AE* (conceived based on the evidence discussed above) targeting asymmetric scenarios with one SME as a technology provider that integrates innovative concepts into the environment of a low digital maturity SME in another country. Funding up to €50k is offered for each applicant.
- *Digital Challenge* is another asymmetric scheme, where a large enterprise (Digital Challenge Owner) acts as an early adopter seeking cutting-edge digital solutions to a defined challenge. The purpose is to highlight attractive market needs to be addressed through CPS and embedded systems to solve industry challenges set by corporate stakeholders. The mechanism is applied where no available solutions have been identified in the market and the proposed solutions are to be developed and integrated into their core processes by the selected SME. The financial support of the Digital Challenge Owner to SME is matched by DigiFed (up to €55k).
- *Generic Experiment* (GE), distinguished from the others by the active technology support to SMEs from the coordinating facility (DIH or otherwise) with a technological research and development function. In particular, GE revolves around key-enabling technology building blocks which the cascade funding coordinator develops through exploration of the international market and value-chain requirements. This inquiry is conducted with SMEs participating in the GE community through various activities, e.g., workshops to implement advanced technology demonstrators with co-funding from regional authorities.

The variants are not necessarily mutually exclusive. They can complement one another e.g.; an AE project might result in an innovative solution that can be later integrated into a Digital Challenge. Overcoming differences in business culture yields direct benefits for the future endeavours of the involved SMEs. The general benefits for participants involve cross-border collaboration through administrative rules of cascade funding, improved funding and networking opportunities, access to knowledge and equipment, a better understanding of foreign markets and transferability potential, possible staff exchange etc. There is also a major benefit of customised schemes of co-funding and scale of funding coordinator involvement to provide distinct results based on resources and objectives of DIHs. European DIHs strive to engage more actors to increase coverage of industrial sectors and widen own networks for future opportunities [15]. Thus, quick transferability and replicability are essential for paced implementation to support these common goals [16]. In our assessment, the AE cascade funding instrument with a focus on cross-border cooperation is portable to other ecosystems. Sustainability potential, transferability in other DIH potential, adaptability to context variation and common approaches, balancing flexibility and control, external collaboration [17] within new and established innovation mechanisms, are to be further investigated in a longer and more diversified scenario.

## 5 Conclusion

DigiFed is on the lookout to create the most impactful mechanism to aid the creation of value and competitive advantage for European SMEs and mid-caps. The analysis of the proposal for the Application Experiment (AE) facilitates the portability assessment for the innovation pathway. While TWIN AE was tested by other initiatives in the past, its relatively recent appearance allows further experimentation in a quest to optimize this instrument according to target stakeholders' needs. In DigiFed's case, the experimentation focuses on fostering cross-border collaboration, which has had limited coverage in the past involvement of DIHs, which are typically working on a regional level. Two recent open calls have created a balanced portfolio of AE types (SINGLE vs TWIN). The smaller companies (1–10 employees) had a consistently higher success rate in terms of proposal application to TWIN AE type. Equally, companies with lower digitalisation maturity level are more likely to apply to the collaborative AE (TWIN). The future investigations will consider AEs' implementation progress and sustainable exploitation, as well as the evolution of the funding mechanisms. Authors consider that there is a need for a deeper understanding of the DIH impact and their improved collaboration for the benefit of innovation and digitalisation in Europe's SMEs.

**Acknowledgement.** The presented work has received funding from the European Union's Horizon 2020 Research and Innovation program under grant agreement No 761708 (DigiFed). This work was supported by the French National Research Agency in the framework of the "Investissements d'avenir" program (IRT Nanoelec, ANR-10-AIRT-05).

## References

1. Digitising European Industry. Reaping the full benefits of a Digital Single Market, Brussels, 19.4.2016 COM(2016) 180 final. https://eur-lex.europa.eu/legal-content/EN/TXT/PDF/?uri=CELEX:52016DC0180&from=EN.Accessed 6 Apr 2021
2. ICT Innovation for Manufacturing SMEs (I4MS). https://i4ms.eu/. Accessed 6 Apr 2021
3. Smart Anything Everywhere. https://smartanythingeverywhere.eu/. Accessed 6 Apr 2021
4. Cecchi, F., Dario, P.: The experiment instrument in ECHORD++: cascade funding for small-scale research projects for facilitating the introduction of robotics technology into industry. In: Grau, A., Morel, Y., Puig-Pey, A., Cecchi, F. (eds.) Advances in Robotics Research: From Lab to Market. STAR, vol. 132, pp. 13–28. Springer, Cham (2020). https://doi.org/10.1007/978-3-030-22327-4_2
5. Armengaud E., Peischl B., Priller P., Veledar O. (2019) Automotive meets ICT—enabling the shift of value creation supported by European R&D. In: Langheim, J. (eds) Electronic Components and Systems for Automotive Applications, in Mobility. pp. 45–55. Springer, Cham https://doi.org/10.1007/978-3-030-14156-1_4
6. Raposo, M.L., Ferreira, J.J.M., Fernandes, C.I.: Local and cross-border SME cooperation: effects on innovation and performance. Cooperación local y transfronteriza de las PYME: Efectos sobre la innovación y el desempeño **23**(4), 157–165 (2014)
7. EuroCPS project. https://www.eurocps.org/. Accessed 6 Apr 2021
8. FED4SAE program. https://fed4sae.eu/ Accessed 6 Apr 2021
9. Tetracom project. https://www.tetracom.eu/. Accessed 6 Apr 2021
10. Tetramax project. https://www.tetramax.eu/. Accessed 6 Apr 2021
11. Borštnar, M.K., Pucihar, A.: Multi-attribute assessment of digital maturity of SMEs. Electronics **10**(8), 885 (2021). https://doi.org/10.3390/electronics10080885
12. European Union Countries. https://europa.eu/european-union/about-eu/countries_en. Accessed 6 Apr 2021

13. European Commission- Directorate-General for Research & Innovation https://ec.europa.eu/research/participants/data/ref/h2020/grants_manual/hi/3cpart/h2020-hi-list-ac_en.pdf. Accessed 6 Apr 2021
14. European Commission - Internal Market, Industry, Entrepreneurship and SMEs: SME definition. https://ec.europa.eu/growth/smes/sme-definition_en. Accessed 6 Apr 2021
15. Crupi, A., et al.: The digital transformation of SMEs – a new knowledge broker called the digital innovation hub. J. Knowl. Manag. **24**(6), 1263–1288 (2020)
16. Hinings, B., Gegenhuber, T., Greenwood, R.: Digital innovation and transformation: an institutional perspective. Inf. Organ. **28**(1), 52–61 (2018)
17. Mastering the Digital Innovation Challenge, MIT Sloan Management Review, 07-Mar-2017. https://sloanreview.mit.edu/article/mastering-the-digital-innovation-challenge/. Accessed 6 Apr 2021

# Problematizing the Service Portfolio of Digital Innovation Hubs

Fredrik Asplund[1], Hugo Daniel Macedo[2], and Claudio Sassanelli[3](✉)

[1] KTH Royal Institute of Technology, 100 44, Stockholm, Sweden
fasplund@kth.se

[2] Aarhus University, Finlandsgade 22, 8000 Aarhus, Denmark
hdm@ece.au.dk

[3] Politecnico Di Milano, Piazza Leonardo da Vinci, 32, 20133 Milan, Italy
claudio.sassanelli@polimi.it

**Abstract.** Digital innovation hubs (DIHs) are a strategic means to drive European Small and Medium Enterprises (SMEs) digital transition. The European Commission has envisioned four main functions characterizing DIHs' service portfolios ("Test before invest"; "Support to find investments"; "Innovation ecosystem and networking"; and "Skills and training"). However, DIHs target different functions, e.g. focusing on helping launch novel digital technologies to market, or directing investment opportunities. DIHs are also at different maturity levels, interact with different actors and exist in regions with different conditions for innovation. There might not be an equal need for all four functions, and they might not be equally well served. This study aims to explore and derive implications for the deployment of the four main functions by DIHs. It builds on the activities of DIHs involved in the DIH initiative through several innovation actions, including FED4SAE and HUBCAP.

**Keywords:** Digital innovation hubs · Service portfolio · Innovation ecosystems

## 1 Introduction

Digital innovation hubs (DIHs) are entities that support European companies in the ongoing digital transformation of society. This support is provided in the form of services related to four "functions" [1]: (a) "Test before invest" (services related to technical expertise and experimentation); (b) "Support to find investments" (services related to brokerage between firms and funding organisations); (c) "Innovation Ecosystem and Networking" (services related to finding and supporting connections that enable or make innovation more effective); and (d) "Skills and training" (services related to ensuring that firms can access the training or adequately trained professionals they require for pursuing digitalisation). The European Commission (EC) has supported the establishing of DIHs since 2014, primarily through funding innovation actions. DIHs form the nucleus in a growing number of public-private innovation ecosystems, i.e., interconnected production


Published by Springer Nature Switzerland AG 2021
L. M. Camarinha-Matos et al. (Eds.): PRO-VE 2021, IFIP AICT 629, pp. 433–440, 2021.
https://doi.org/10.1007/978-3-030-85969-5_40

and user side organisations of both public and private character that, directed by a lead organisation, focus on value creation [2, 3].

While innovation ecosystems are gaining increasing attention, the concept itself [4], their genesis [5], and the associated implications of public-private cooperation [3] are understudied. Which actions public actors should take during ecosystem genesis to ensure that an innovation ecosystem thrives is unclear. The four functions relate to activities necessary for successful ecosystem growth that typically fall under the responsibility of different roles, such as the provision of advice by experts ("Test before invest") and the forging of partnerships by ecosystem leaders ("Innovation Ecosystem and Networking"). Different DIHs will strive to fill different roles, either by choice or to ensure a fit with their current capabilities. DIHs might thus, rightfully, not strive to address all four functions, and they should possibly also address them differently.

This paper aims to problematize the DIH deployment of services according to the four functions, exploring difficulties for DIHs in providing services in one or several of the functions. More specifically, this study probes such difficulties to identify implications for public innovation ecosystem leadership.

## 2 Related Work

Organisations participate in innovation ecosystems for different reasons [6, 7]. Depending on whether they are public or private, they often enter into innovation ecosystems from central positions either in knowledge or business ecosystems [8, 9]. That said, many areas that used to be the responsibility of either public or private organisations have become shared [10], and the increased public-private collaboration in innovation ecosystems is a part of enabling this shift.

However, this collaboration is not without friction. Firstly, the basic culture and character of the work outputs of firms and academia usually differ, introducing problems when cooperating [11, 12]. Secondly, the reasons for participating in an innovation ecosystem can also mean that organisations choose to take on specific roles. Focusing on a leadership, direct value creation, value creation support or entrepreneurial ecosystem role [5] will both provide and remove opportunities. Thirdly, the governance of innovation ecosystems is often supported by platforms that constrain the evolution of technology and services [13]. The control of such platforms, and associated non-pricing instruments, can be critical to avoid innovation ecosystem failure [14]. Ultimately, the success of ecosystem genesis also depends on the characteristics of the people that form the collaborative network(s) within an ecosystem. Over time, this should select for relationships with little initial knowledge overlap [15], and between narrowly focused academia and firms focusing on technology recombination [16].

## 3 Methodology

This paper builds on the activities of several DIHs that have cooperated over several years. Each of the functions mentioned in the introduction is approached using data sets gathered by the authors during Horizon 2020 innovation actions associated with the

DIH initiative. This section discusses the associated data gathering, data analysis, and associated validity concerns.

The "Test before invest" function is analysed using three data sets from the HUBCAP [17] innovation action, which started in 2020 to facilitate the use of model-based design technology for cyber-physical systems (CPS) by bringing together an innovation ecosystem around a collaboration platform[1]. The collaboration platform provides a web application that features a collaboration environment (consisting of an enterprise social software) enhanced with a sandbox (a cloud-based solution catering tools and models in a ready to use virtual environment). The first data set comes from a survey integrated on the collaboration platform to obtain initial feedback from users on its usability and limitations. Responses were gathered from a population of small and medium-sized enterprises (SMEs). The second data set comes from the 8 DIHs in HUBCAP, and consists of a summary of the most important innovation support services they provide. A central member from each DIH listed their most important services. Then the types and descriptions of the services were harmonized by a single investigator. The result was reviewed by two independent investigators to identify mistakes during the harmonization.

The "Support to find investments" function is analysed using two data sets. The second data set used for the "Test before invest" function is used again. Furthermore, the contacts providing funding opportunities to the 8 DIHs were also collected. This information was gathered through iterations with several members of each DIH and constituted: (a) the organisations that are part of their ecosystem; (b) their relationships; and (c) the associated learning, networking and funding opportunities. 7 ecosystems were mapped out with enough quality to be useful for comparative purposes.

The "Innovation ecosystem and networking" function is analysed using data from the effort of the HUBCAP project to build a more tightly connected network of DIHs. To foster the ecosystem building and networking HUBCAP set up an open call programme with multiple trickle-down funding calls. Before each call a number of open workshops and Q&A sessions brought SMEs together, creating opportunities for new partnerships. The data set for this function was collected by asking each DIH in the network which of the SMEs that were funded by first two open calls that were also new to the ecosystem.

The "Skills and training" function is analysed using data from the FED4SAE innovation action, which between 2017 and 2021 aimed to lower the technical and business barriers for innovative companies in the CPS and embedded systems markets. As part of this project 8 DIHs were asked to provide details on the organisations in their public-private innovation ecosystems, their relationships, and their ways of upskilling their employees. After networks maps for the knowledge and training relationships had been established, the firms seeking to join the DIH innovation ecosystems through FED4SAE were approached for interviews. Out of a 100 such firms, 20 were interviewed for about 20 min each by two interviewers. An interview script focusing on learning opportunities and the skill set of SME employees were used to ensure a coherent coverage across all interviews. As both the questions and number of interviewees were limited, the interviewers created summaries of the replies for each question during the interviews. These summaries were then used to discuss each question in separation when all interviews had been concluded.

[1] https://dihiware.eng.it/dihwelcome/

## 4 Results

The detailed results from the survey on the initial HUBCAP industry experience[2] and the summary of innovation support services[3] are available in separate reports.

### 4.1 Test Before Invest

Survey respondents were overall satisfied with the platform. Nonetheless, 40 percent declared that the platform limits features of the asset deployed to it, as a cloud-based/virtual machine always has limits that a physical machine does not have in terms of hardware, software, or licensing. In some cases, only part of the features of the assets provided by the initial population of SMEs were feasible to deploy.

In regard to the summary of available services, Table 1 describes the number of "Test before invest" services provided by the DIHs. These services aimed at providing (a) physical, exceptional testing and validation equipment, (b) demonstration facilities, (c) insights and training on novel technology, and (d) collaborative research.

**Table 1.** Testing and funding – DIH functions

| DIH | Testing services | Funding services | Ecosystem funding opportunities |
|---|---|---|---|
| 1 | 2 | 1 | 13 |
| 2 | 0 | 1 | 9 |
| 3 | 2 | 0 | 14 |
| 4 | 3 | 0 | 1 |
| 5 | 1 | 1 | 5 |
| 6 | 1 | 3 | 12 |
| 7 | 1 | 2 | 11 |
| 8 | 1 | - | - |

The most important "Test before invest"' services identified by the DIHs are centred on the DIHs themselves. They involve firms collaborating with DIHs through a hub-and-spoke collaboration model. i.e., a network design where the DIH as a central organisation (a hub) is connected to firms which themselves (mostly) lack direct connections. In contrast, the HUBCAP collaboration platform enables point-to-point collaboration between firms. One of the most important aspects of a central platform is that it allows innovation ecosystem leaders, by constraining technology and services, to avoid low quality that might turn away potential users. It is then noteworthy that survey respondents mentioned that only part of the features of some platform assets were feasible to deploy. This might lead to users becoming frustrated with the digital format. Successful quality control by

[2] https://www.hubcap.eu/assets/res/files/D3_2.pdf.

[3] https://www.hubcap.eu/assets/res/files/D2.1_DIH-Services.pdf.

ecosystem leadership rests on them being prepared for actively using non-pricing instruments, such as legal agreements, licenses, and oversight. Therefore, even if the services provided by firms are only intended to *demonstrate* the functionality of their products, *DIHs* must ensure this is framed correctly to give users the right impression.

### 4.2 Support to Find Investments

Table 1 also describes the number of funding services provided by the investigated DIHs, and the funding opportunities that they perceive in their ecosystem. 7 DIHs, which were possible to map with a good enough quality, are included. These DIHs provided funding services aimed at (a) helping other organisations write competitive research proposals, (b) providing direct financial support in e.g. open calls, and (c) building business and innovation skills.

Many funding services in the innovation ecosystems, and especially those focused on enabling firms to *separately* apply for funding, were not emphasised by the DIHs. The culture and character firms and academia differ, most likely making DIHs as ecosystem leaders lean towards funding opportunities that firms can explore in synergy with the research focus of academia. However, SMEs are often very focused on identifying funding to grow opportunities from early discovery to sustainable business. This suggests that DIHs should increase their emphasis on brokering funding that targets also higher technology readiness levels.

### 4.3 Innovation Ecosystem and Networking

Table 2 describes (a) the number of proposals that were accepted in the two calls, and (b) how many of the associated SMEs were already known to the involved DIHs.

**Table 2.** Networking and open calls

| Open call | Number of accepted proposals | Previously known SMEs |
|---|---|---|
| #1.1 | 21 | 4 |
| #1.2 | 14 | 3 |

The results suggests that the open calls enabled many new SMEs to enter the DIH innovation ecosystems. Unfortunately, this is not only positive. DIHs might be unable to collaborate smoothly with firms they are not familiar with, since they can for instance be active in application domains unknown to the DIHs[4].

An online collaboration platform, like that of HUBCAP, could possibly ease such collaboration difficulties: as collaboration is built upon point-to-point relationship, such platforms can allow networking firms to tie other DIHs to their original innovation

[4] This was the case in this data set, as shown in https://www.hubcap.eu/assets/res/files/D2.2_Ecosystem_Building.pdf.

ecosystem. In other words, these platforms can allow SMEs to build networks of DIHs able to jointly support their specific needs.

### 4.4 Skills and Training

The network maps indicated that the learning opportunities deemed most important by the FED4SAE innovation ecosystem participants could be divided into preparatory and continued education. The former preparing professionals for employment, and the latter meant to provide upskilling during their careers. Important preparatory education was carried out by the (primarily academic) partners in the innovation ecosystem nucleus. However, important continued education was almost exclusively provided by peripheral organisations or initiatives that were only open to paying members. The interviews probed the implications of the network maps, as these indicated that SMEs would struggle to access advanced continued education. However, most SMEs indicated that they had a close relationship with academic institutions, for instance through founders that were formerly, or even currently, employed within academia. Through these informal relationships they were able to access both knowledge, learning opportunities and experiment facilities related to advanced state-of-the-art research at low or no cost. In fact, even if continued education would have been accessible through more formal relationships, the SMEs would struggle to pay for it. The solution to accessing necessary skills was thus seldom upskilling, but rather recruiting someone who already possessed the right set of skills.

It is positive that the interviewed SMEs do not have difficulties in accessing the advanced training they need, but not that this access is dependent on personal contacts. DIHs should work towards also formalizing access to training, to ensure that it is provided on a fair and equal basis. However, if not supported by authorities or funding agencies, this could come with a price tag rendering the training inaccessible to most SMEs. One way of overcoming this obstacle could be for DIHs to work towards securing a training budget in other activities that involve novel technology. This could involve other services, such as those within the "Test before invest" function, or the trickle-down funding of open calls.

## 5 Discussion

The results obtained through this research confirm that different DIHs play different roles, addressing specific combinations of the four functions defined by the EC. These differences in emphasis are the prerogative of the individual DIH, as the EC envisions an extended pan-European ecosystem of DIHs – each DIH defined by its own nature, region, and focus regarding industries and digital technologies. As long as the pan-European ecosystem can activate innovation-driven collaboration, any single DIH would not have to strive to concurrently address all of the four functions. However, this emphasis should impel informed choices to ensure ecosystem growth.

This should include recognizing the impact of public innovation ecosystem leadership. We explain the importance attributed to funding services focused on exploiting synergies with research with the leadership of research institutions. Although this is in line with the primary needs of public, especially academic, institutions, such DIHs should not forget to put effort into brokering funding that targets higher technology readiness levels. As funding is often the basis for enabling collaboration this focus on research might also further drive the selection for specific collaboration partners observed in public-private collaboration, i.e., firms focusing on technology recombination. Similarly, we explain the lack of formal pathways to continued education with higher education institutions found in the centre of knowledge ecosystems – actors that might easily become important stakeholders in innovation ecosystems. To avoid a skewed training provision, these DIHs should ensure that such pathways are created, and that these do not incur costs that prohibit SMEs from using them. It should also include recognizing the increased requirements of the new relationships and types of collaboration that the DIH initiative is initializing. The investigated DIHs were focused on a hub-and-spoke collaboration model and were seeing an influx of many SMEs from application domains unknown to them. As small knowledge overlaps can lead to strong relationships centred on knowledge brokering, this initial large knowledge distance could easily force a large effort upon DIHs. Collaborative platforms can help mitigate this difficulty by allowing SMEs to build networks of DIHs ably to jointly support their specific needs, as collaboration can be built on point-to-point relationships rather than the hub-and-spoke collaboration model. However, when moving away from an innovation to a business ecosystem, DIHs must still ensure a collaboration platform with high-quality services and artefacts. This might require the use of non-pricing instruments, such as licensing and oversight. These might not be well understood by DIHs run by research-focused organisations, which suggests that these DIHs should be especially careful when deploying services via digital collaboration platforms. A main limitation of this research is the study of only one particular type of DIH ecosystems, i.e., those focused on the CPS industries and with considerable engagement by public organisations. Other industries or types of innovation ecosystem leadership could have other difficulties. Nevertheless, further research should investigate these difficulties in more detail to provide further guidance to public leadership on how to ensure innovation ecosystem growth.

## 6 Conclusions

The innovation ecosystem literature typically focuses on private innovation ecosystem leadership. This study highlights how public innovation ecosystem leadership could fail to support (all) firms in their innovation ecosystem by providing services for the four functions primarily skewed towards exploiting synergies with their other activities. Addressing associated bias might involve considering the, especially financial, limitations of the typical SME, as well as making use of contemporary technology such as collaboration platforms. The latter could bring further benefit through the additional flexibility brought on by moving innovation ecosystems away from the hub-and-spoke collaboration model, although it could also bring extended requirements on business skills that public organisations might find it difficult to address.

**Acknowledgments.** The work is partially supported by the Horizon 2020 Programme under GA n° 701708 and 872698, and VINNOVA under GA n° 2015–01524.

## References

1. Kalpaka, A., Sörvik, J., Tasigiorgou, A.: Digital Innovation Hubs as policy instruments to boost digitalization of SMEs. EUR 30337 EN, Publications Office of the EU (2020)
2. Autio, E., Thomas, L.: Innovation ecosystems: implications for innovation management. In: The Oxford handbook of innovation management. Oxford University Press, Oxford (2014)
3. Asplund, F., Björk, J., Magnusson, M., Patrick, A.J.: The genesis of public-private innovation ecosystems: bias and challenges. Technol. Forecast. Soc. Change **162**, 120378 (2021)
4. Shipilov, A., Gawer, A.: Integrating research on interorganizational networks and ecosystems. Acad. Manag. Ann. **14**(1), 92–121 (2020)
5. Dedehayir, O., Mäkinen, S.J., Ortt, J.R.: Roles during innovation ecosystem genesis. Technological Forecasting and Social Change **136**, 18–29 (201
6. Oh, D.S., Phillips, F., Park, S., Lee, E.: Innovation ecosystems: a critical examination. Technovation **54**, 1–6 (2016)
7. Ritala, P., Almpanopoulou, A.: In defense of 'eco'in innovation ecosystem. Technovation **60**, 39–42 (2017)
8. Valkokari, K.: Business, innovation, and knowledge ecosystems. Technol. Innov. Manage. Rev. **5**(8), 17–24 (2015)
9. de Vasconcelos, G., et al.: Unpacking the innovation ecosystem construct. Technol. Forecast. Soc. Chang. **136**, 30–48 (2018)
10. Etzkowitz, H.: Innovation in innovation: The triple helix of university-industrygovernment relations. Soc. Sci. Inf. **42**(3), 293–337 (2003)
11. Cyert, R.M., Goodman, P.S.: Creating effective university-industry alliances. Organ. Dyn. **25**(4), 45–58 (1997)
12. Siegel, D.S., Waldman, D., Link, A.: Assessing the impact of organizational practices on the relative productivity of university technology transfer offices. Res. Policy **32**(1), 27–48 (2003)
13. Baldwin, C.Y., Woodard, C.J., et al.: The Architecture of Platforms: a Unified View. Platforms, Markets and Innovation, Edward Elgar Publishing Limited, Cheltenham (2009)
14. Boudreau, K.J., Hagiu, A.: Platform rules: Multi-sided platforms as regulators. Platforms, Markets and Innovation, pp. 163–191. Edward Elgar Publishing Limited, Cheltenham (2009)
15. Bloodgood, J.M.: Acquiring external knowledge: how much overlap is best? Knowl. Proc. Manage. **22**(3), 148–156 (2015)
16. Soh, P.-H., Subramanian, A.M.: When do firms benefit from university-industry R&D collaborations? The implications of firm R&D focus on scientific research and technological recombination. J. Bus. Ventur. **29**(6), 807–821 (2014)
17. Peter Gorm Larsen et al. A Cloud-Based Collaboration Platform for Model-Based Design of Cyber-Physical Systems. In: Proceedings of the 10$^{th}$ SIMULTECH (2020)

# Digital Innovation Hubs: One Business Model Fits All?

Gustavo Dalmarco[1(✉)], Vasco Teles[1], Olivia Uguen[2], and Ana Cristina Barros[1]

[1] INESC TEC - Institute for Systems and Computer Engineering, Technology and Science, Rua Dr. Roberto Frias, 4200 - 465 Porto, Portugal
{gustavo.dalmarco,vasco.b.teles,ana.c.barros}@inesctec.pt
[2] BLUMORPHO 8, rue de l'Isly, 75009 Paris, France
uguen@blumorpho.com

**Abstract.** Digital transformation is critical for the competitiveness of SMEs. Digital Innovation Hubs (DIHs) aim to regionally support companies in the development of new products, processes, or services, providing access to advanced technologies. Since DIHs have to be financially sustainable, it is important to discuss which business models are put forward in such complex arrangements. Our main goal is to analyse how DIHs, specialized in Industry 4.0 technologies and services, create, offer, and capture value. The research was conducted through a documentary analysis of reports about DIHs' Business Models, generated by three European initiatives (encompassing more than 300 DIHs). Results demonstrate that one Business Model does not fit all, since regional characteristics, which vary among different DIH's, are the main drivers to define value creation, offer and capture. This work aims to provide DIH managers insights to help them develop sustainability strategies.

**Keywords:** Business model · Digital transformation · Digital innovation hub · Innovation

## 1 Introduction

The current phase of the digital transformation, described by initiatives such as Industry 4.0, Smart Manufacturing and Industrial Internet of Things (IIoT), among others, is receiving increasing attention from manufacturing industries. Through Industry 4.0, companies aim to reduce operational costs while increasing productivity, quality, and flexible production supported by the intensive use of technologies in production and commercialization processes [1, 2]. Improvements are achieved through the integration of physical and virtual objects that allow a real-time monitoring of people and machinery, adding to the interconnectivity between machines, products, intelligent systems, and interrelated solutions [3, 4]. Supported by different models such as the Reference Architectural Model Industry (RAMI) 4.0, industry 4.0 enables the transfer of the decision-making process down to machine level, deploying a self-regulating production system [5, 6]. The digitalization of products and processes allowed by improvements in sensing and


Published by Springer Nature Switzerland AG 2021
L. M. Camarinha-Matos et al. (Eds.): PRO-VE 2021, IFIP AICT 629, pp. 441–448, 2021.
https://doi.org/10.1007/978-3-030-85969-5_41

communication are key for advanced decision-making processes [7]. The application of digitalization in companies can occur in phases or levels of technology implementation, involving: 1) the digitalization of processes and integration of the value chain; 2) the digitalization of products and services; and 3) the generation of new digital business models [8].

To support companies through its digital transformation, DIHs offer a wide range of services through an ecosystem organization model [9]. DIHs are usually formed by a network of Research and Technology Organizations (RTOs), universities, and technology providers, among others, acting as one-stop-shops to offer customized solutions to companies [10]. DIHs can be considered a Virtual Breeding Environment (VBE) [11], since they represent an association of different organizations with complementary skills and resources. There are currently already 664 DIHs across 39 European countries identified in the European Union (EU) Digital Innovation Hubs Catalogue [12]. The main challenge of DIHs, given its complex arrangement of technologies and agents, is to define a proper business model for their operations.

Business model (BM) is a logical structure to create value for all stakeholders of a business [4] and includes, in general, four main areas of an organization: a) customers, b) value offer, c) infrastructure, and d) financial viability [13]. DIHs, however, usually only stimulate partnerships among the agents of its network and SMEs, while services are offered in a one-to-one relation between the company (demand agent) and the RTO/University/Tech Provider. One of the tools used to portray an organization's business model is the Business Model Canvas [13] which presents a visual structure that allows the presentation of the critical elements for business operation. This tool, however, does not always address all the relevant characteristics of an organization with complex ecosystems such as DIHs. Consequently, other tools, more suitable to accommodate DIHs' BM specificities, had to be identified.

Given this scenario, our objective is to analyse how DIHs, specialized in Industry 4.0 technologies and services, create, offer, and capture value, by identifying business model patterns. This work aims to contribute to the theoretical body of knowledge on business model innovation and provide DIH managers insights to help them better steer their activity. The next section presents the theoretical background about Business Model Analysis and DIHs, followed by the Research Method in Sect. 3. Section 4 presents the main results, followed by the concluding remarks on Sect. 5.

## 2 Literature Review

The main objective of a BM is to define how a company addresses aspects of its business (physical, human, and material resources) to create and deliver value to its customers [14]. In addition, it also describes how to attract clients willing to deliver value to the company (capture value), generating financial results to the company [15]. Here, the business model framework, also known as Business Model Canvas (BMC) [13], presents a visual structure of a BM's basic elements, and its interrelations, thus emphasizing the critical elements of business success. The BMC is represented by nine blocks [4, 13, 16], describing:

- Customer segments: groups or segment of clients the company aims to sell its product / service to;
- Customer relationships: how the company will interact and create loyalty within its clients;
- Revenue streams: company's income sources;
- Key Activities: company's the main activities necessary to deliver its value proposition and implement its business model;
- Key Resources: company's key assets, e.g. exclusive machinery, Intellectual Property, or highly trained employees, necessary to run its key activities;
- Key Partners: company's external partners (suppliers, partnerships, outsourcing) necessary to run its key activities;
- Cost Structure: company's main expenses to run its business model;
- Value Proposition: company's unique solution – either product or service – that will be offered to the market. It should address a problem or create value to company's customer segment.

The BMC presented by [13], however, is mainly suited for companies with one single product, such as start-ups, or companies with independent products. Here, each product has its own business strategy, aiming to maximize its individual rentability. A DIH, however, is a much more complex organization, since on the one hand it has its own technological specialization, according to regional demands, and on the other it orchestrates a set of different actors with different business strategies [17]. DIHs are network organizations, usually managed by public organizations, constituted of regional or national innovation actors. Consequently, DIHs must have a broader strategy to encompass different types of value streams, also addressing social and public impacts.

Therefore, in order to analyse the main characteristics of DIH business models, two other BM Canvases will be jointly used: the Public Private Partnerships (PPP) Canvas [15] and the Service Logic BMC (SLBMC) [18]. Adding to the BM Canvas, the PPP Canvas has four extra blocks describing [19]:

- Extended Beneficiaries: Describes organizations or other type of entities who receive indirect benefits of the DIH's services;
- Impact: Describes how the services offered by the DIH benefits its own region through the creation of social, public, or environmental value;
- Governance: Describes the DIH governance model with its associates;
- Business Ecosystem: Describes how the DIH interacts with regional/national business ecosystems.

On the other hand, the SLBMC is also composed of nine building blocks, just like the original BMC, but here, each block contains two perspectives: the organisation's (as usual) and the customer's. The customer perspective was added to make organisations analyse their business from the perspective of customers' activities, practices and experiences, thus focusing on the services they can provide to the customers [18].

Considering the different ways to analyse and detail a business model, in addition to the specific characteristics of industry 4.0 [20, 21], our analysis will describe and compare how DIHs specialized in Industry 4.0 create, deliver, and capture value to and from its associates and companies served: (1) value creation represents the DIH's main activities, identifying its operation, resources, and relationships with key partners; (2) value offering represents how the services offered by the DIH satisfy customers' needs; (3) finally, value capture refers to how the DIH define and engage with its customers, determine demands and needs, how customers perceive value delivery and what type of relationship the DIH must maintain with the customers served by its associates. A key aspect here is not only analysing the BM elements, but how their interrelation demonstrates the organisation's full strategy.

## 3 Research Method

Following this work's objective, the research question is as follows: What are the relevant characteristics of value creation, offer and capture for DIHs specialized in Industry 4.0 technologies?

The research design was developed through the following steps: first, we reviewed the literature about Business Model Design, Business Model Canvas and PPP Canvas in order to identify the main elements of Business's Value Creation, Value Offer and Value Capture. Second, we carried out an exploratory research based on document analysis [22], mainly based in project reports. Three project reports were analysed: (1) BEinCPPS - Business Experiments in Cyber Physical Production Systems [23], describing 5 DIHs; (2) Smart4Europe2 – Catalysing Digitisation throughout Europe [24], describing 5 DIH networks; and (3) DIH.NET Community [25], presenting survey data of 300 DIHs.

All documents provided rich information about DIH business models, being reports 1 and 2 based on an in-depth analysis of specific DIHs, while report 3 conducted a survey with 300 DIHs. This analysis was combined with DIH's websites and other reports publicly available. In the next sections we present the consolidated analysis of all DIHs, presenting the main characteristics of value Creation, Value Offer, and Value Capture for DIHs specialized in Industry 4.0 technologies and services.

## 4 Research Results

In order to consolidate the data from different documents, our analysis focused on describing the main characteristics of value creation, value offer, and value capture of the different DIHs. As the main objective of DIHs is to support companies in the improvement of their production processes, products or services, using digital technologies [12], the discussion about value creation, offer, and capture aims to foster the development of new DIH, or support existing ones with benchmark analysis.

### 4.1 Value Creation

In order to be competitive and sustainable, a DIH must create value to its region according to local demands and governmental goals. As could be observed, most analysed DIHs create value through five main activities: (1) Ecosystem building, scouting, brokerage, networking - here collaborative platforms such as DIH4Industry, DIHNET and AI4EU, among others, increase DIH's competences; (2) Collaborative Research among companies and DIH's associates; (3) Education and skills development; (4) Concept validation and prototyping; and (5) Testing and validation. These activities, however, do not create value by itself. They should be aligned with different strategic definitions, as described below:

- Regional characteristics and industrial demand;
- Partners and how they complement their resources;
- Legal arrangement;
- Vision, mission and expected impact;
- Main services, technologies and facilities;
- Cost structure.

In addition to these strategic definitions, issues related to the legal structure and *modus operandi* of the DIH emerged. E.g., the main identified DIH strategic decision was to be established through a public or non-profit organization, such as RTOs, thus sharing its facilities and cost structure. This type of organization usually assures high commitment and low cost for companies, as well as high trust for the involved stakeholders. Another form of legal organization is through the DIH network, without a formal structure. Here one organization is defined as lead partner, which officially represents the whole network. In both cases an executive managing team could be arranged among the most active DIH partners, committed by a memorandum of understanding that can also describe the DIH main activities and processes (such as service portfolio, admission process of service providers, governance, dissemination policy, conflict of interests, financing sources, advisory group, etc.).

### 4.2 Value Offer

Although addressing the needs and demands of a specific region, differences in DIHs value offer represents their own competitive advantage. Companies, as clients, have a critical eye when choosing a DIH to partner with. Consequently, geographical proximity does not necessarily mean companies will not look for other DIHs with a better value offer. Therefore, as the value offer of DIH is mainly represented by how the services offered by the DIH satisfy customer needs, the greater the quality of the service, the greater the chance of a certain DIH to attract more clients.

In this sense, the most observed strategy is defined by training services and workshops, where companies can discuss how the services offered by the DIH may address their specific need. The development of training sessions in solutions identified as key to a specific sector shall bring the attention of a specific cluster of companies, opening an opportunity to demonstrate how new technologies work and how could it be applied to other companies. Such training activities, often carried out through hands-on experience in demonstrations labs, may result into future services to implement the technologies presented, thus upgrading company's technology maturity level. In a similar way, workshops open to specific groups of companies may be an opportunity to present certain technologies in a 'test-before-invest' methodology, consolidating the DIH as the reference organization for a particular technology. Consequently, through unique value proposition, DIHs build on new business models for the sustainability of their activities.

### 4.3 Value Capture

Given the current sustainability challenge, DIHs must define strategies to improve value capture. One of the main activities in this sense is to properly disseminate the benefits of the DIH to its region, engaging in dissemination activities. Besides using online platforms, DIHs also offered open seminars, technology demonstration sessions, and workshops to representatives of the different regional industrial sectors, using the opportunity to present its activities, how it could add value to companies, and in which ways companies could engage in activities with the DIH partners. Here the identification of who are the DIH's main clients and industrial sectors, adding to which are the most relevant services offered by the DIH, supports the deployment of a value capture strategy.

Another important issue identified is the definition of the DIH revenue streams, as they should define a proper strategy for its individual sustainability. Although the DIHs main funding sources are still public (either regional, national or European), private funding is one option for half of the DIHs analysed. Here we observed not only the payment of specific services by SMEs, but also periodic fees or subscription taxes payed by the DIH network members (who have the advantage of being part of the network, thus having access to public funding opportunities). Membership services could also be offered to partner companies, who in turn could have access to technology demonstration, dedicated workshops and assessment services. Here the main strategic movement is agility, keeping the DIH updated in a very fast-moving and complex environment, while also remaining in line with the emerging needs of companies and the corresponding answers provided by technology and knowledge.

## 5 Final Remarks

DIHs are public-funded collaborative networks that, guided by an open innovation strategy, support and promote partnerships between SMEs and technological intense organizations towards increasing the digitalization of industry. In recent years, Europe observed a rapid growth in the number DIHs, each one with its own characteristics, technologies, and services. These initiatives are usually led by non-profit organizations as RTOs or universities, mostly regionally anchored to better address the regions' demands and needs. Financial sustainability is a common goal to DIHs to which they develop their own BM.

Based on different BM frameworks, the present study suggests patterns on the way DIHs dedicated to Industry 4.0 implementation create, offer, and capture value. Results demonstrated that DIHs use different BMs to create, offer and capture value. Given their VBE behaviour, which encompasses particular strategies of different organizations, having a clear BM support DIH's to be recognized as an important agent of regional and national innovation system. In this sense, this study was able to show that:

- despite differences in competences, regional contexts, manufacturing sectors, and needs and demands, it is apparent that the value creation is achieved through five

main activities: Ecosystem building, scouting, brokerage, networking; Collaborative Research among companies and DIH's associates; Education and skills development; Concept validation and prototyping; Testing and validation - closely aligned with strategic DIH decisions;
- the value is usually offered by a set of services which aim to capacitate companies through the implementation technological solutions to improve their processes, while increasing their digital maturity, as well as through workshops, demonstrations, and training, which also act as vehicles to better understand those companies' challenges;
- finally, the value is captured as revenues, paid by customers for the services DIHs provide, or e.g., fees giving access to the network's activities, knowledge materials, demonstration installations, etc. These private funding in the form of revenues play a very relevant role toward financial sustainability, since after a ramp-up period, it is expected that the public funding for DIH operation decreases or even ceases.

With this work, we contribute to the body of knowledge about regional DIHs and the way they operate - concerning the way they create, offer, and capture value. These results also support DIH managers and customers to better understand the main patterns emerging from their operation. As questioned by the title if "one business model fits all?", our work concludes that regional characteristics – such as innovation behaviour, collaborative culture, trust, and also funding sources – are the main distinguishing drivers composing each DIH business model. In addition, as DIHs offer a combination of members' individual competences, similarities in their own business models are key to define the DIH business model as a whole. This leads each DIH to be more efficient addressing regional needs and demands while differentiating DIHs from one another in the way they operate. Future research in this field could address the influence of DIHs in wealth creation and contributions to GDP at regional and national level.

**Acknowledgements.** This research received funding from European Union Framework Programme for Research and Innovation Horizon 2020 under Grant Agreement nos. 952003 (AI REGIO), 872111 (Smart4Europe2), and 825640 (DIHNET.EU).

## References

1. Saucedo-Martínez, J.A., Pérez-Lara, M., Marmolejo-Saucedo, J.A., Salais-Fierro, T.E., Vasant, P.: Industry 4.0 framework for management and operations: a review. J. Ambient. Intell. Humaniz. Comput. **9**, 1–13 (2017). https://doi.org/10.1007/s12652-017-0533-1
2. Dalenogare, L.S., Benitez, G.B., Ayala, N.F., Frank, A.G.: The expected contribution of Industry 4.0 technologies for industrial performance. Int. J. Prod. Econ. **204**, 383–394 (2018). https://doi.org/10.1016/j.ijpe.2018.08.019
3. Safar, L., Sopko, J., Bednar, S., Poklemba, R.: Concept of SME business model for industry 4.0 environment. TEM J. **7**, 626–637 (2018). https://doi.org/10.18421/TEM73-20
4. Kiel, D., Arnold, C., Voigt, K.I.: The influence of the Industrial Internet of Things on business models of established manufacturing companies – A business level perspective. Technovation **68**, 4–19 (2017). https://doi.org/10.1016/j.technovation.2017.09.003
5. Hermann, M., Pentek, T., Otto, B.: Design principles for industrie 4.0 scenarios. In: 49th Hawaii International Conference on System Sciences, pp 3928–3937. IEEE (2016)

6. Hernández, E., Senna, P., Silva, D., Rebelo, R., Barros, A.C., Toscano, C.: Implementing RAMI4.0 in production - a multi-case study. In: Almeida, H.A., Vasco, J.C. (eds.) ProDPM 2019. LNME, pp. 49–56. Springer, Cham (2020). https://doi.org/10.1007/978-3-030-29041-2_6
7. Bienhaus, F., Haddud, A.: Procurement 4.0: factors influencing the digitisation of procurement and supply chains. Bus. Process. Manag. J. **24**, 965–984 (2018). https://doi.org/10.1108/BPMJ-06-2017-0139
8. Oztemel, E., Gursev, S.: Literature review of Industry 4.0 and related technologies. J. Intell. Manuf. **31**(1), 127–182 (2018). https://doi.org/10.1007/s10845-018-1433-8
9. Antonopoulos, C.P., Keramidas, G., Tsakanikas, V., et al.: Capacity building among european stakeholders in the areas of cyber-physical systems, IoT & embedded systems: the SMART4ALL digital innovation hub perspective. In: 2020 IEEE Computer Society Annual Symposium on VLSI (ISVLSI), pp. 464–469. IEEE (2020)
10. DEI Digital Innovation Hubs: Mainstreaming Digital Innovation Across All Sectors (2017)
11. Camarinha-Matos, L.M., Afsarmanesh, H., Galeano, N., Molina, A.: Collaborative networked organizations–concepts and practice in manufacturing enterprises. Comput. Ind. Eng. **57**, 46–60 (2009). https://doi.org/10.1016/j.cie.2008.11.024
12. DIH Digital Innovation Hubs Catalogue. https://s3platform.jrc.ec.europa.eu/digital-innovation-hubs-catalogue. Accessed 29 Apr 2021
13. Osterwalder, A., Pigneur, Y.: Business Model Generation: A Handbook for Visionaries, Game Changers, and Challengers. John Wiley & Sons, New Jersey (2010)
14. Morris, M., Schindehutte, M., Allen, J.: The entrepreneur's business model: toward a unified perspective. J. Bus. Res. **58**, 726–735 (2005). https://doi.org/10.1016/j.jbusres.2003.11.001
15. Teece, D.J.: Business models, business strategy and innovation. Long Range Plann. **43**, 172–194 (2010)
16. Trimi, S., Berbegal-Mirabent, J.: Business model innovation in entrepreneurship. Int. Entrep. Manag. J. **8**, 449–465 (2012). https://doi.org/10.1007/s11365-012-0234-3
17. Hervas-Oliver, J.-L., Gonzalez-Alcaide, G., Rojas-Alvarado, R., Monto-Mompo, S.: Emerging regional innovation policies for industry 4.0: analyzing the digital innovation hub program in European regions. Compet. Rev. Int. Bus. J. (2020)
18. Ojasalo J, Ojasalo K (2018) Service logic business model canvas. J. Res. Mark Entrep. **20**, 70–98. https://doi.org/10.1108/JRME-06-2016-0015
19. PPP Lab (2016) PPPCanvas User Guide
20. Müller, J.M., Buliga, O., Voigt, K.I.: Fortune favors the prepared: how SMEs approach business model innovations in Industry 4.0. Technol. Forecast Soc. Change **132**, 2–17 (2018). https://doi.org/10.1016/j.techfore.2017.12.019
21. Müller, J.M., Däschle, S.: Business model innovation of industry 4.0 solution providers towards customer process innovation. Processes **6**, 1–20 (2018). https://doi.org/10.3390/pr6120260
22. Bowen GA (2009) Document analysis as a qualitative research method. Qual Res J
23. BEinCPPS. http://www.beincpps.eu/. Accessed 30 Apr 2021
24. Smart4Europe. https://smart4europe.eu/. Accessed 30 Apr 2021
25. Digital Innovation Hub Networks. https://dihnet.eu/. Accessed 30 Apr 2021

# Business Intelligence and Innovation: A Digital Innovation Hub as Intermediate for Service Interaction and System Innovation for Small and Medium-Sized Enterprises

Florian Maurer(✉)

Department Business Informatics, Vorarlberg University of Applied Sciences, Hochschulstraße 1, 6850 Dornbirn, Austria
florian.maurer@fhv.at

**Abstract.** Digital Innovation Hubs are a policy instrument of the European Commission to keep with the speed of the digital transformation within the European economy (especially small- and medium-sized enterprises, mid-caps). Within this article, the Digital Innovation Hub on Business Intelligence & Innovation within the region of the Federal State of Vorarlberg is presented and a possible network of collaborators and co-creators get introduced. In doing so, the academic discipline of Service Science – Service-Dominant Logic – is presented as theoretical manifestation. The contextual embedment of this article at hand is in the European Commission's Digitising European Industry Strategy (2016) and European Industrial & Digital Strategies (2020). Based on these, a collaborative network of collaborators and co-creators for the Digital Innovation Hub on Business Intelligence & Innovation to increase service interaction and system innovation get introduced.

**Keywords:** Digital Innovation Hub · Business Intelligence & Innovation · Service science · Network collaboration

## 1 Introduction

European economy run the risk to lack the digitization of its systems [1]. As highlighted by the European Commission (2021), around 60% of large industries and more than 90% of small- and medium-sized enterprises lag behind in digital innovation [2]. The willingness of the managers and organizational decision makers to go with the digital transformation, as explored empirically, is high. But also, due to limited resources and missing interorganizational system interaction and service innovation, the organizations run the risk to miss the implementation of the Industry 4.0 technologies into systems [3].

No organization can innovate in isolation and (European) Digital Innovation Hubs (DIH), a policy instrument of the European Commission, play an important role within this field of collaborative innovation. DIHs are designed to build up of structured relationships with, for example, regional authorities, industrial clusters, SME associations,


Published by Springer Nature Switzerland AG 2021
L. M. Camarinha-Matos et al. (Eds.): PRO-VE 2021, IFIP AICT 629, pp. 449–459, 2021.
https://doi.org/10.1007/978-3-030-85969-5_42

incubators, accelerators, chambers of commerce, etc. Their task is to bring together the stakeholders among the supply- and value-chain for open and collaborative innovation, incl. co-creation of value, testing and experimentation.

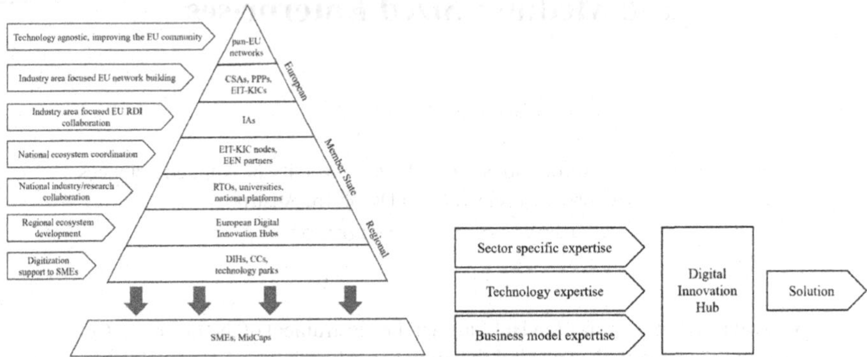


**Fig. 1.** Getting a view on EDIHs and EU-networks (source: [4]; own representation)

**Fig. 2.** Digital innovation hub model (source: [5]; own representation)

As exemplified in Fig. 1 and 2, there are a variety of perspectives to design and develop a network of collaborators and co-creators for a Digital Innovation Hub. This variety motivates and inspires us to develop a regional ontology of co-creators for the Digital Innovation Hub on Business Intelligence & Innovation within the Federal State of Vorarlberg.

The research originates within the guidance of the European Commission: to be a critical actor of the regional/national innovation ecosystem, a DIH needs to establish and maintain partnerships with actors with complementary competencies and specializations on a regional, national and European level [6] and [7].

The structure of this research is built-upon the research question on how a Digital Innovation Hub as intermediate for service interaction and system innovation for small and medium-sized enterprises within the Federal State of Vorarlberg can look like. In particular: who are the (possible) stakeholders of the Digital Innovation Hub on Business Intelligence & Innovation and what are their activities and tasks?

This article is composed of four sections. Section 1 introduces the research problem, research motivation and research question. Section 2 investigates into related works on cooperation and collaboration in networks. This section presents the Service-Dominant Logic as theoretical manifestation and the Digital Innovation Hub initiative (*service science in action*) as contextual embedment. Focus within Sect. 2 is on the activities and tasks out of theoretical manifestation on service science and in the contextual embedment of the Digital Innovation Hub policy initiative. Section 3 investigates into regional, national and European network collaborators and co-creators for the Digital Innovation Hub on Business Intelligence & Innovation. Section 4 concludes the article and provides a future outlook in development of intended DIH for Business Intelligence & Innovation.

## 2 Related Works on Cooperation and Collaboration in Networks

This section investigates into the question on what the activities and tasks of the Hub stakeholders are. As presented in Sect. 2.1, the theoretical manifestation of this article at hand origins in the academic discipline of Service Science. The contextual embedment (c.f. Sect. 2.2) roots in the European Commission's Digitising European Industry Strategy (2016) and European Industrial & Digital Strategies (2020).

### 2.1 The Academic Discipline of Service Science

The academic discipline of Service Science (e.g. [8–10]) is a theory to increase service interaction and value co-creation mechanism among heterogenous system stakeholders. Main streams of research are the Service-Dominant Logic (SDL) (pioneering articles: [11–13]), Service Science, Management, Engineering and Design (SSMED) [14], Viable Systems Approach [15] and Work System Theory [16]. It is an interdisciplinary field of research and is about the science of service, service systems and service ecosystems as well as how service systems interact and co-create value [17]. The general aim of Service Science is to increase customer centricity and to enable enhanced levels of service innovation. It considers (collaborative, open) service innovation (e.g. technological innovation) as most important trigger for service system engineering and evolution. Especially in Germany, service (system) engineering and innovation has a long tradition. For example, the articles of Ganz (2006), the work group "Evaluation Service Science" [19] and Böhmann, Leimeister, and Möslein (2014) could be identified as pioneering works.

The concept of SDL, according to Maglio and Spohrer (2007), builds the philosophical/theoretical foundation for the general theory of Service Science. It was firstly introduced and published by Vargo & Lusch in 2004 [11, 12] and investigates into the shift from Good-Dominant Logic to increased service thinking and thinking systems in service. SDL emphasizes to move forward "ordinary" service management: service can be provided through a good but service are superordinate to goods – not substitutes. Service, in this perspective, are the common dominator of social and economic exchange. Service, in this context, are considered as a "framework for thinking about value creation, rather than a support activity" [22]. SDL has a strong emphasis on service interactions, value co-creation and marketing methods such as, for example, customer relationship management and many-to-many marketing. Core constructs of the SDL are Service, Value, System, Interaction, Resources.

**Service:** SDL associate service (singular) as a (collaborative) process of serving [23] – doing something for and/or with another service system (entities; relationships and collaborations) to create holistic service experience satisfaction.

**Value:** Value co-creation principle is existential part of SDL [23]. Value is always co-created and thus SDL is inherently customer-centric. Value, thus, is assimilated by existing and new knowledge and is influenced by the service environment [23, 24].

**System:** SDL considers service systems as networks of multiple, loosely-coupled and specialized actors that integrate, apply and transform resources. Service systems act in service ecologies – "a spontaneously sensing and responding spatial and temporal structure of largely loosely coupled, value-proposing social and economic actors" [25]. These value-creation networks contribute to value co-creation, co-production and exchange of service offerings.

**Interaction:** SDL bases on service interactions manifested in collaborative communication (among multiple service systems) and learning via exchange (e.g. feedback loops).

**Resources:** "At the heart of Service-Dominant Logic is the transfer and sharing of resources" [23]. If a resource contributes to a specific outcome/benefit, this process then is called resourcing (e.g. resource creation, integration and resistance removal) [23, 26].

### 2.2 Service Science in Action: Digital Innovation Hubs

With this article at hand, a Digital Innovation Hub (DIH) is considered as a special case of a service system. DIHs are to increase collaboration in networks, service interaction and system innovation. A DIH is either a single organization or a coordinated group of organizations (a heterogenous group of actors and constellations [27]) that complement each other with knowledge, best-practice and expertise [1]. A DIH should act as service center of a digital innovation ecosystem and shall provide access to services, facilities and expertise to a wide range of stakeholders [6]. Stakeholders of a DIH, for example, are: public administrations, national and regional authorities, clusters, incubators, chambers of commerce, industry associations, etc. [6].

As presented by the European Commission, DIHs are a policy instrument to support the regional innovation ecosystem in the themes of digital transformation and digitization of existing business and industry [27, 28]. The purposes of DIHs are to bring together industry, businesses and administrations [1]; to foster business growth, to upgrade local suppliers, to export/transfer specialization to SMEs [28]; to better organize the innovation support system in the region, to make the system more transparent, to communicate more clearly to potential beneficiaries [27]). DIHs foster interregional and international cooperation across the European Union (and beyond, e.g. Africa) and can function as co-designers or advisors of local smart specialization strategies [6] by, for example, provision of information and (specialized) knowledge for decision makers [27]. DIHs than facilitate knowledge exchange, learning and share of good practices between European regions and are engaged in benchmarking.

DIHs are diverse organizations and range from regional bodies to clusters or research centers. Their geographical focus can be regional or beyond [28]. Usually a DIH has local functions and European functions [1]: at the local level, DIHs are embedded into local economy and build ecosystems by bringing into contact actors along the value chain; at the European level, DIHs can connect different ecosystems together by identifying innovation opportunities for users and suppliers coming from different regions.

A DIH is a flexible organization and should be based on regional needs and existing capabilities [27] and works with experimentation and co-creation mechanisms [28]. DIHs can also be important partners for strategy development [28]. As depicted in Table

1, DIHs provide four main services and a sub-set of support services for their clients to access knowledge, methods and software, technology platforms, prototyping solutions and testing facilities [1, 6, 29].

**Table 1.** Main services and sub-services of a digital innovation hub (Sources: [1, 6, 29])

| Main services | Sub-services |
|---|---|
| Test before invest | E.g. awareness raising, digital maturity assessment, demonstration activities, visioning for digital transformation, fostering the integration, adaptation and customisation of various technologies, testing and experimentation with digital technologies (software and hardware), knowledge and technology transfer. (software and hardware [6]) |
| Skills & training | E.g. advertising, hosting or providing of training, boot-camps, traineeships, as well as supporting the implementation of the short-term advanced digital skills training courses and job placements [6] |
| Support to find investments | Intermediate: access to follow up finance to bring the results of testing and experimentation to the next phase; e.g. access to financial institutions and investors, supporting the use of InvestEU and other relevant financing mechanisms (e.g. Enterprise Europe Network) [6] |
| Innovation ecosystem & networking | Brokerage function/matchmaking between the needs of organizations and suppliers: provision of structured relationships with regional authorities, industrial clusters, SME associations, business development agencies, incubators, accelerators, EEN, EIT co-location centers, and chambers of commerce [6] |

A DIH, at least, should cover the technology side and the business development side. However, DIHs go beyond borders and supply local industry with highly competitive services [28], connect DIHs from different regions that can provide companies the complementary knowledge they need [27], coordinate the collaboration between actors in the ecosystem and foster networking and matchmaking, either directly by organizing or by participating in events, or through information on the web [27].

## 3 Business Intelligence and Innovation: Network Collaboration

This section investigates into the question on who the (possible) stakeholders are for the DIH on Business Intelligence & Innovation. To better understand the economic system and the ecosystem's stakeholders within the Hub's region, Sect. 3.1 presents the economic demography of the Federal State of Vorarlberg. Sections 3.2, 3.3, 3.4 and 3.5 investigate into the possible network of collaborators and co-creators.

As depicted in Table 2 and presented in the following sections, 57 network collaborators and co-creators within the region of Vorarlberg and beyond could be identified. These stakeholders are clustered among the Quadruple Helix Stakeholders: business & industry, government & public administration, civil society & users and research & education. Furthermore, the stakeholders are assigned to the identified activities and tasks out of the theoretical manifestation and the contextual embedment.

### 3.1 Demography and Economic System of the Federal State of Vorarlberg

The Federal State of Vorarlberg/Austria is embedded into the international region of the Lake of Constance. It is surrounded by the countries of Liechtenstein and Switzerland in

**Table 2.** Activities and tasks assigned to the hub stakeholders (Quadruple Helix Stakeholders)

| | | Hub stakeholders (Quadruple Helix) | | | |
|---|---|---|---|---|---|
| **Dimen-- sion** | **Activities and tasks** | **Business & industry** | **Government & public administration** | **Civil society & users** | **Research & eduction** |
| **Innovation networking** | Cooperation & collaboration | X | (x) | (x) | (x) |
| | Customer relationship management & marketing | X | | | (x) |
| | International cooperation & collaboration | (x) | | | X |
| **Skills & training** | Learning, knowledge sharing, best practice, expertise | (x) | | (x) | X |
| | Resourcing, sharing of resources | X | (x) | | (x) |
| **Innovation ecosystem** | Service system / ecosystem science: Service-Dominant Logic | (x) | | | X |
| | Service environment: customer centricity & requirements | X | | (x) | (x) |
| | Service interaction & (digital) innovaton | (x) | (x) | (x) | X |
| | Value co-creation, service experience & satisfaction | (x) | (x) | (x) | X |
| **Test before invest & investment** | Smart specialization | | X | | (x) |
| | System engineering and evolution | X | (x) | (x) | (x) |
| | Innovation support system | (x) | | | X |
| | Intermediate investments, innovation funding | (x) | X | | (x) |

the West, Germany (Baden-Württemberg, Bavaria) in the North and Tyrol (Austria) in the East. At the cut-off date of 31st March 2020, Vorarlberg was home to 427.758 citizens (398.657 main residences, 29.101 s residences). Vorarlberg count 161.629 dependent employees and 16.915 commuters to Liechtenstein and Switzerland. Vorarlberg is one of the strongest economic regions in Europe. The basis of the economic power is an above-average level of industrialization, coupled with competitive trade and export, numerous innovative enterprises and a strong tourism industry. The export/import quota is positive – Vorarlberg exports more than it imports (10.691 Mio Euro export vs. 7.930 Mio EUR import). Main trade partners are Germany, Switzerland, Italy and France. Vorarlberg is a highly active region in the field of innovation. For example, in 2019, 116 patents out of the region have been filed to the Austrian Patent Office. The Government of the Federal State of Vorarlberg committed itself to five smart specialization strategies that are Smart Textiles, Energy- and Energy Efficiency, Human and Technology, Education and Health and Intelligent Production. In doing so, the Government released several lighthouse projects and innovation projects. Based on a survey about digital transformation in enterprises, 93% of interviewed managers within Vorarlberg expect impacts caused by technological change and digital transformation.

### 3.2 Network Collaborators and Co-creators Out of Business and Industry

**Business- and Industry:** at the level of associations for business and industry relevant stakeholders are the Wirtschaftsstandort Vorarlberg GmbH (WISTO), Chancenland Vorarlberg, the Vorarlberg chamber of commerce and its youth organization (Junge Wirtschaft Vorarlberg) as well as the Vorarlberg federation of industries (IV) and its youth organization (Junge Industrie Vorarlberg). WISTO supports and grants industrial and entrepreneurial innovation projects as well as organizes Chancenland Vorarlberg: a platform to recruit knowledge workers for the Vorarlberg labor market. The Vorarlberg chamber of commerce represents the interests of business and entrepreneurs within the region. The Vorarlberg federation of industries represents the interests of the industry. The Junge Wirtschaft and the Junge Industrie – the youth organizations of the Vorarlberg chamber of commerce and the Vorarlberg federation of industries – represent the interest of young entrepreneurs and start-up organizations within business and industry. For example, an initiative of the Junge Wirtschaft that could be relevant for the Hub is Startupland. It provides a platform for entrepreneurs and start-ups and is active in networking and interest representation. The business association Vorarlberg, the Vorarlberger trade association, the Export Club Vorarlberg and the Marketing Club Vorarlberg could be identified as further stakeholders out of business and industry. These organizations are to support and to lobby for the economic objects of business.

**Thematic Associations:** the Logistic Research Austria, the Verein Netzwerk Logistik, its regional branch Verein Netzwerk Logistik Region West and the platform Industrie 4.0 are identified as network co-creators. Logistic Research Austria is an association composed of universities (*of applied sciences*) within Austria that investigates into the fields of logistics and supply chain management. The Verein Netzwerk Logistik is Austria's largest industrial business network in the field of logistics and supply chain management. It has several branches within Austria (incl. Vorarlberg: Verein Netzwerk Logistik Region West) and beyond (e.g. Switzerland).

**(Private) Initiatives:** there are a variety of (private) initiatives within the region of Vorarlberg. These are, for example, Platform V and the Platform for Digital Initiatives. Platform V aims to provide an industrial platform for collaborative design and engineering of disruptive and digital business models. The Platform for Digital Initiatives is an association for (young) innovators and provides a maker-space for business, industry and society. A further relevant stakeholder could be Interactive West. It is the largest conference on digital transformation within the region of the Lake of Constance. The platform Industrie 4.0 is a national initiative to bring together business, industry, politics and academia and to discuss the emergent trends and technologies within the field of the digital transformation.

### 3.3 Network Collaborators and Co-creators Out of Government and Public Administration

The Government of the Federal State of Vorarlberg could be identified as primary stakeholder from the field of politics and government for the DIH on Business Intelligence

& Innovation. The government is the owner of the Vorarlberg University of Applied Sciences. Based on the "Verordnung des Landeshauptmannes über die Geschäftseinteilung des Amtes der Vorarlberger Landesregierung (ALReg-GE)", departments of special interest are the departments for European Affairs (§2 ALReg-GE Art. c)), Science and Education (§4 ALReg-GE Art. b), Gruppe II) and General Economic Affairs (§8 ALReg-GE Art. a), Gruppe VI). Further important co-creators at governmental level are the Federal Ministries of the Republic Austria for (1) Education, Science and Research, (2) Digital and Economic Affairs and (3) Climate Action, Environment, Energy, Mobility, Innovation and Technology. These ministries enable the connection to a broad variety of accompanied stakeholders from Austria, Europe and Global.

### 3.4 Network Collaborators and Co-creators Out of Civil Society and Users

Newspapers and journals that are relevant for the Hub on Business Intelligence & Innovation are Wirtschaftszeit, Die Wirtschaft and Thema Vorarlberg. These are tailored newspaper for managers, decision makers and accompanied stakeholders out of the field of executive management, marketing, controlling, manufacturing, HR, etc. Furthermore, Die Wirtschaft and Thema Vorarlberg are newspaper of the Vorarlberg chamber of commerce and deal with topics out of business, industry and economy – at both: operational and visionary/philosophical level. NEUE and Vorarlberg Nachrichten are daily newspapers within the region and supply the citizens in Vorarlberg with current news out of politics, economics, technology, environment, social, legislative, culture, etc. Taken together, NEUE and Vorarlberg Nachrichten maintain a market coverage of almost 95%. Relevant for the Hub on Business Intelligence & Innovation are Der Standard and Die Presse too. These are national newspapers and maintain a large section for science and innovation.

**Beyond the Region of Vorarlberg:** relevant stakeholders outside the region, as identified, are the consortium of the Interreg Central Europe projects 4Steps, CEUP, Chain Reactions and ECOS4IN. The consortiums could complement with additional, tailored knowledge, expertise and services. A further important initiative is DIHNET.eu, a project that aims to create a pan-European network of Digital Innovation Hubs. A stakeholder from the European Commissions level is the Smart Specialization Platform. This platform captures the tools and instruments to boost smart specialization in the Union's region, incl. the (European) Digital Innovation Hubs.

### 3.5 Network Collaborators and Co-creators Out of Research and Education

At regional level, the Vorarlberg University of Applied Science (FHV) and its heterogenous departments and institutions, Schloss Hofen and V-Research as well as WIFI Vorarlberg and the Volkshochschule could be identified. The Vorarlberg University of Applied Science is composed of heterogenous research departments and faculties. These are, for example, the research department Business Informatics (*that is the operator of the Hub*), the research department Digital Factory and the faculty Business & Economics as well as the study courses on Digital Innovation (Bachelor), Informatics (Bachelor, Master) and

International Business Management (Bachelor, Master) as well as the formats of Blickpunkt Wirtschaft and Business Summit. Additional stakeholder is FHV's startupstube and FHV's Alumni network. The StartupStube is a support organization for students, scholars, young entrepreneurs and innovators to bring an innovation to the market. The Alumni network consists of people that graduated at the FHV and now are successfully working in business and industry. Schloss Hofen is an education- and training center at academic level. It provides several academic courses for further qualification and specialization (e.g. business and law, human science, health, social, etc.). V-Reserach is a non-university center of excellence for applied research, development and innovation. WIFI Vorarlberg and the Volkshochschule Vorarlberg are providers for vocational education and training. For example, WIFI Vorarlberg offers more than 1.800 courses and seminars within a variety of fields related to management, leadership, business, trade, traffic, etc.

**Scholarly Networks and Conferences:** a primary stakeholder out of the field of scholarly networks with the region of Vorarlberg is the International Bodensee-Hochschule. This is an international network of universities (*of applied sciences*) within the regions of Alpine-Rhine and the Lake of Constance. It enables scientific exchange among the networking universities. A further relevant stakeholder is the Long Night of Research. The Long Night of Research is a tailored event to connect science with stakeholders from politics, society, industry and business.

## 4 Findings and Conclusion

The scientific discipline of Service Science and the European Commission's strategies on Digitising European Industry has been reviewed as basis for the design and development of an ontology of co-creators for the Digital Innovation Hub on Business Intelligence & Innovation. The Hub shall act as intermediate for increased service interaction and system innovation within the regional innovation system. Service Science, as identified, provides the philosophical/theoretical foundation and the European Commission's strategies on Digitising European Industry the pragmatical direction. To increase service interaction and system innovation within the regional innovation ecosystem, as identified in this article, base on a broad variety of activities and tasks that are captured under the dimensions of innovation networking, skills and training, innovation ecosystem and test before invest/investment. To perform the Hub's responsibilities, its activities and tasks, a tight cooperation and collaboration with stakeholders from business & industry, government & public administration, civil society & users and research & education (Quadruple Helix Stakeholders) is key for success. As identified (c.f. Table 2), main stakeholders are business & industry in close collaboration with research & education. The cooperation and collaboration of these stakeholders is of major importance to successfully install the Hub as intermediate for increased service interaction and system innovation within the regional innovation ecosystem, including: the interaction and the sharing of resources (e.g. information and knowledge, pro-active value co-creation and system innovation) for increased value propositions. There are a variety of actions in preparation and range from tight relationship management with the co-creators and the

SMEs, the collaborative organization and conduction of tailored events for digital innovation in SMEs, workshops on technology impact assessment and innovation, digital business modelling, employment patterns until the provision of services within the area of Artificial Intelligence, System/Ecosystem Collaboration and Resilience Engineering.

**Acknowledgments.** This article at hand was made possible by the financial support of Interreg Central Europe research project "4Steps" (Towards the application of Industry 4.0 in SMEs; project number: **CE1492**).

## References

1. European Commission: European Digital Innovation Hubs in Digital Europe Programme, Brussels (Belgium), Programme (2021). [Online]. Available: https://ec.europa.eu/digital-single-market/en/digital-innovation-hubs-dihs-europe
2. European Commission: Shaping Europe's digital future: digital Innovation Hubs (DIHs) in Europe (2021). https://ec.europa.eu/digital-single-market/en/digital-innovation-hubs-dihs-europe
3. Maurer, F.: Business intelligence and innovation: an European digital innovation hub to increase system interaction and value co-creation within and among service systems. In: Proceedings of the 10th International Conference on Operations Research and Enterprise Systems, March 2021, pp. 208–217. [Online]. Available: https://www.scitepress.org/Link.aspx? https://doi.org/10.5220/0010255602080217
4. Butter, M.: DIHNET. Presented at the Opportunities and services provided by CSAs to support DIHs and EDIHs, digital, 2021. [Online]. Available: https://spaces.fundingbox.com/spaces/i4ms-i4ms-news/60587d999bbc1905d0abeb2a
5. Tasig, A.: Roundtable on digitising European industry: mainstreaming digital innovation across all sectors. In: European Commission, Brussels (Belgium), Report of Working Group 1, 2017. [Online]. Available: https://ec.europa.eu/futurium/en/content/report-wg1-digital-innovation-hubs-mainstreaming-digital-innovation-across-all-sectors-final
6. Kalpaka, A., Sorvik, J., Tassigiorgou, A.: ***Digital innovation hubs as policy instruments to boost digitalisation of SMEs. In: European Commission, Brussels, 2020. [Online]. Available: https://ec.europa.eu/newsroom/dae/document.cfm?doc_id=66604
7. Kalpaka, A., Sörvik, J., Tasigiorgou, A., Rissola, G.: Digital Innovation Hubs as policy instruments to boost digitalisation of SMEs. In: European Commission, Brussels (Belgium), JRS Science for Policy Report JRC121604, 2020. [Online]. Available: https://ec.europa.eu/jrc/en/publication/eur-scientific-and-technical-research-reports/digital-innovation-hubs-policy-instruments-boost-digitalisation-smes
8. Chesbrough, H., Spohrer, J.: A research manifesto for services science. Commun. ACM **49**(7), 35–40 (2006). https://doi.org/10.1145/1139922.1139945
9. Chesbrough, H.W.: Toward a new science of services. Harv. Bus. Rev. **83**,16–17 (2005)
10. Spohrer, J., Maglio, P.P., Bailey, J., Gruhl, D.: Steps toward a science of service systems. IEEE Comput. Soc. vol. January 2007, pp. 71–78 (2007). https://doi.org/10.1109/MC.2007.33
11. Vargo, S.L., Lusch, R.F.: Evolving to a new dominant logic for marketing. J. Mark. vol. 68, no. January 2004, pp. 1–17 (2004)
12. Vargo, S.L., Lusch, R.F.: Service-dominant logic: continuing the evolution. J. Acad. Mark. Sci. **36**(1), 1 (2008). https://doi.org/10.1007/s11747-007-0069-6
13. Vargo, S.L., Akaka, M.A.: Service-dominant logic as a foundation for service science: clarifications. Serv. Sci. **1**(1), 32–41 (2009). https://doi.org/10.1287/serv.1.1.32

14. Spohrer, J., Kwan, S.K.: Service science, management, engineering, and design (SSMED): an emerging discipline - outline & references. Int. J. Inf. Syst. Serv. Sect. vol. 1, no. 3, July–September 2009, pp. 1–31 (2009)
15. Barile, S., Polese, F.: Smart service systems and viable service systems: applying systems theory to service science. Serv. Sci. **2**(1–2), 21–40 (2010). https://doi.org/10.1287/serv.2.1_2.21
16. Alter, S.: Work system theory: overview of core concepts, extensions, and challenges for the future. J. Assoc. Inf. Syst. vol. 14, no. 2, Feb. 2013, [Online]. Available: http://aisel.aisnet.org/jais/vol14/iss2/1
17. Vargo, S.L., Maglio, P.P., Akaka, M.A.: On value and value co-creation: a service systems and service logic perspective. Eur. Manag. J. **26**(3), 145–152 (2008). https://doi.org/10.1016/j.emj.2008.04.003
18. Ganz, W.: Germany: service engineering. Commun. ACM **49**(7), 79 (2006). https://doi.org/10.1145/1139922.1139954
19. Satzger, G., et al.: Auf dem Weg zu einer Service Science: Perspektiven, Forschungsthemen und Handlungsempfehlungen aus der Sicht einer interdisziplinären Arbeitsgruppe. Mediendienstleistungen des Fraunhofer Informationszentrum IRB, Stuttgart, 2010. [Online]. Available: https://www.ksri.kit.edu/downloads/WegServiceScience.pdf
20. Böhmann, T., Leimeister, J.M., Möslein, K.: Service systems engineering - a field for future information systems research. Bus. Inf. Syst. Eng. **6**(2), 73–79 (2014). https://doi.org/10.1007/s12599-014-0314-8
21. Maglio, P.P., Spohrer, J.: Fundamentals of service science. J. Acad. Mark. Sci. **36**(1), 18–20 (2007). https://doi.org/10.1007/s11747-007-0058-9
22. Barile, S., Polese, F.: Linking the viable system and many-to-many network approaches to service dominant logic and service science. Int. J. Qual. Serv. Sci. **2**(1), 23–42 (2010)
23. Vargo, S.L., Lusch, R.F., Akaka, M.A.: Advancing service science with service-dominant logic. In: Handbook of Service Science, pp. 133–156. Springer, Boston (2010). https://doi.org/10.1007/978-1-4419-1628-0_8
24. Barile, S., Pels, J., Polese, F., Saviano, M.: An introduction to the viable systems approach and its contribution to marketing. J. Bus. Mark. Manag. **2**, 54–78 (2012)
25. Vargo, S.L., Lusch, R.F.: It's all B2B…and beyond: toward a systems perspective of the market. Ind. Mark. Manag. **40**(2), 181–187 (2011). https://doi.org/10.1016/j.indmarman.2010.06.026
26. Spohrer, J., Anderson, L., Pass, N., Ager, T.: Service science and service-dominant logic. In: Otago Forum 2 (2008) - Academic Papers, Otago, 2008, vol. Paper no. 2. Accessed: 20 Sept 2017. [Online]. Available: http://citeseerx.ist.psu.edu/viewdoc/download?doi=10.1.1.486.3642&rep=rep1&type=pdf
27. Rissola, G., Sörvik, J.: Digital innovation hubs in smart specialization strategies. European Commission, Brussels (Belgium), JRC Technical Reports EUR 29374 EN, 2019. [Online]. Available: https://ec.europa.eu/jrc/en/publication/digital-innovation-hubs-smart-specialisation-strategies
28. Rissola, G., Sörvik, J.: Digital innovation hubs in smart specialisation strategies. European Commission, Brussels (Belgium), JRC113111 (2018)
29. AI DIH network: What are digital innovation hubs (2021). https://www.ai-dih-network.eu/project.html Accessed 25 Mar 2021

# The D-BEST Based Digital Innovation Hub Customer Journeys Analysis Method: A Pilot Case

Claudio Sassanelli(✉), Sergio Gusmeroli, and Sergio Terzi

Department of Management, Economics and Industrial Engineering, Politecnico Di Milano, Piazza Leonardo da Vinci, 32 20133 Milan, Italy
{claudio.sassanelli,sergio.gusmeroli,sergio.terzi}@polimi.it

**Abstract.** Digital Innovation Hubs (DIHs) are ecosystems sustaining European enterprises to overcome innovation hurdles and push Europe as a world leading innovator in the Fourth Industrial Revolution context. They operate as a one-stop-shop, characterized by four main functionalities, i.e., test before invest, support to find investments, innovation ecosystem and networking, skills and training. These functionalities are addressed through the delivery of a set of services, grouped in the five macro-classes of services of the Data-driven Business-Ecosystem-Skills-Technology (D-BEST) model, a reference model able to configure the service portfolios of DIHs and to model collaborative networks in the I4.0 era. The model has been used in the DIH4CPS project to classify the extant service portfolios of the DIHs belonging to the network, to detect which new services should be provided in the future by the network of DIHs, and to identify opportunities for collaboration among DIHs fostering the creation of a pan-European DIH. However, to support an easier codification of such dynamics directly involving companies in the innovative DIHs ecosystems, a Customer Journey (CJ) analysis method has still to be built. This paper presents the D-BEST-based CJ analysis method, identifying typical digital transformation processes for the two main categories of customers of a DIH, Technology Users and Technology Providers.

**Keywords:** Digital innovation hub · Customer journey · Service portfolio · Digital transformation

## 1 Introduction

Digital Innovation Hubs (DIHs) are ecosystems sustaining European enterprises to overcome innovation hurdles and push Europe as a world leading innovator in the Fourth Industrial Revolution context. They operate as a one-stop-shop, characterized by four main functionalities, i.e. test before invest, support to find investments, innovation ecosystem and networking, skills and training (European Commission 2018). Their main scope is to enable companies of different types, sectors, and dimensions to exploit digital innovations for strengthening their solutions portfolios, streamlining their processes and adjust their business models to the digital dimension.


Published by Springer Nature Switzerland AG 2021
L. M. Camarinha-Matos et al. (Eds.): PRO-VE 2021, IFIP AICT 629, pp. 460–470, 2021.
https://doi.org/10.1007/978-3-030-85969-5_43

Among the several projects funded by the European Commission (EC), the DIH4CPS project (DIH4CPS – Digital Innovation Hub for Cyber-Physical Systems 2020) is working to create an embracing, interdisciplinary network of DIHs and solution providers, focussed on cyber-physical and embedded systems (CPES), interweaving knowledge and technologies from different domains, and connecting regional clusters with the pan-European expert pool of DIHs. DIH4CPS innately builds on an extensive existing network, adds value to its existing knowledge transfer capabilities and guarantees the sustainability of the growing DIH network. The project aims at expanding the already existing network and creating an integrated platform for DIHs from different, especially digitally underdeveloped, sectors and regions. The operating context of the DIH4CPS ecosystem is the CPES domain, with the scope of identifying and materialising service-based collaboration processes among a network of DIHs oriented to improving this kind of technologies. So far, the project has developed the Data-driven Business-Ecosystem-Skills-Technology (D-BEST) model, a reference model able to configure the service portfolios of DIHs, modelling collaborative networks in the I4.0 era. The model is the result of an iterative development: conceived originally as the ETB model (Butter et al. 2019), it evolved in the ETBSD model (used in the MIDIH Project (2020)). Finally, it evolved in the D-BEST, used in the DIH4CPS project (2020) (Sassanelli et al. 2020) to classify the extant service portfolios of the DIHs belonging to the network, to detect which new services should be provided in the future by the network of DIHs, to identify opportunities for collaboration among DIHs and their stakeholders to be combined in a pan-European DIH. However, to support an easier codification of such dynamics directly involving companies in the innovative DIHs ecosystems, a Customer Journey (CJ) analysis method has still to be built. The D-BEST-based DIH CJ analysis method (whose need and development has been grounded on the practical experience of several European Commission-funded Innovation Action projects belonging to the I4MS initiative) identifies typical digital transformation processes for the two main categories of DIH customers: Technology Users (TU) and Technology Providers (TP). TUs are those companies using technologies to best perform their business, typically manufacturing companies. Instead, TPs are instead those companies whose business is to develop new technologies, typically digital technologies developers. Starting from the service portfolios of the DIHs mapped through the use of the D-BEST model, this paper aims at outlining how CJs can be analysed and configured in a DIH for both TU and TP, presenting the results of the pilot case of the Politecnico di Milano's (POLIMI) DIH. In this analysis, the D-BEST services composing the DIHs service portfolios are combined towards the implementation of DIHs Unique Value Proposition, building and defining flexible service workflows for DIH customers. The paper is structured as follows. Section 2 presents the research method used to develop the CJ method and introduces the case. Section 3 presents the CJ method and Sect. 4 discusses its role to foster the creation of interdisciplinary networks of DIHs supporting the digital transformation process, presenting limitations and further research.

## 2 Research Method

This section is aimed at describing how the CJs have been built in the DIH4CPS ecosystem, a H2020 project funded by the European Commission. The input of this work has been the result coming from a survey previously conducted in the project, based on the D-BEST model and aimed at obtaining a preliminary configuration of the service portfolios of the DIHs belonging to the project's ecosystem. This paper presents the specific results of the pilot case so far conducted in the project, the DIH of the POLIMI, presenting part of the activities conducted by the Manufacturing Group of the Business School. The main goal is to use the experiment conducted in this pilot case to develop the method to systematically build the CJs of the customers (TU and TP) of a DIH. This methodology will be then extended to the other 10 DIHs belonging to the DIH4CPS ecosystem. Therefore, starting from the result of the survey, the first task conducted has been the organization of a workshop with the representatives of the DIH analysed (Project Manager, Research Coordinator, Business Developer) to obtain the complete overview of the service portfolio. Then, a second workshop with the same users has been organized, with the support of an online collaborative platform, to build the CJs of the TP and TU of the DIH.

## 3 Results

The DIH4CPS project, with the main aim of easing the shift towards digitization of the manufacturing SMEs through the help of DIHs as innovation ecosystems, has to focus on the codification of typical CJs. Indeed, the progressive adoption of new technologies and digital applications strictly depends on the company maturity to employ them in its manufacturing systems. In fact, the digital transformation journey is a constant path, affected by several business areas as the business strategy, the operating model and business model, leading the company to master the Industry 4.0.

Digital transformation entails the support of an innovation ecosystem. The role of a DIH is to support companies (especially SMEs) to achieve a superior digitization level compared to the current one by offering services according to the Digital Transformation pillars. Despite this is a technology-related path, the definition of blueprints, where DIHs' tools and services are allocated to cover a wide range of requirements to foster the digital transformation of manufacturers, are needed. In the following sub-sections, two step-based digital transformation journeys created in the DIH4CPS project are presented: they are the TU CJ (for manufacturing companies) and the TP CJ (for digital developers and providers).

### 3.1 Technology End-User Customer Journey Templates

The TU CJ is composed of five steps (Observation, Awareness, Experimentation, Experience, and Adoption), chaperoning the manufacturers towards a higher level of digital maturity. During Observation manufacturers access to content in a passive way, driven by wonder or by individuals looking for information on the digitization concept, through popular information channels. Then, the Awareness phase follows, once the contact company-DIH has materialized, accessing to this network. In this phase, the company actively looks for targeted information with an open up behaviour to new chances. In this moment, the company needs to know its digital maturity level and plan for a roadmap to be pursued in the following experimentation phase. The DIH provides here technological or informative services as events, webinars, demo rooms, experience centres, courses and basic training on the I4.0. During the Experimentation, the DIH and its own network sews the customized digital dress to the company: new technological solutions and competences are proposed to meet the opportunities and the expected benefits of digital change. Services here support the new digital solutions concepts development, delivering proofs of concepts (PoC) and testing them in provided facilities (max TRL 4–5). In the Experience phase, the technologies are shifted in the company's facility at the structured level, limited at a test/pilot scale. Service provided are here typically training of personnel (upskilling/re-skilling), support for organizational change (operational, decision-making and information management processes), technological development of customized solutions according to the real environment of the enterprise and definition of structured KPIs of the digital transformation. Finally, in the Adoption phase occurs the decision of developing the new solution at the whole company level, flanked by investments in the innovation of the entire company. Services supporting the definition of new business models, together with strategic consulting, support for massive deployment and new project management methods.

### 3.2 TP Customer Journey Template

For TPs, the CJ is a skill-demanding process model going through five main phases leading to the final product market launch (Ideation, Design & Engineering, MVP, Verification & Validation, Go to Market).

During Ideation the business idea is conceived (flanked by preliminary architecture of the solution to be implemented and by the key technical milestones and (functional and non-functional) requirements to be addressed in the following stages), through a creative process (through methods as Brainstorming, Creative thinking, Creative matrix, Wall of idea, etc.). Services offered to TP are workshops/webinars on design thinking, SWOT analysis, idea market positioning, hackathons. Once consolidated the business idea, the Design and Engineering phase starts with the design phase and the specifications for its technical development. Tools that could be useful in this phase are: Technical pills, Dockers, Kubernetes, visual analytics, UX, UI, an assessment about how to validate the solution or customer discovery (validation of the idea to see if the idea has a market). In this phase there could be some deviations from the original business idea since current software components cannot meet the requirements or new functionalities can be added without cost increases. A comprehensive Market Requirements Document (MRD) needs to be prepared in this phase (to articulate the new product plan including customers, buyers, goals, use-cases, requirements, and specification sizing), leading to a more streamlined Minimum Viable Product (MVP) definition, useful for the company to validate products value and growth hypotheses as fast as possible. MVP needs to be experimented to be confirmed or refuted. Tools such as FIWARE Lab, credit from Google/Amazon cloud, 3D Printers, sensors, etc., can be provided in this stage as well as any service to find economical support for subcontracting to realize the final MVP and elaborating the business part programme. Verification and validation are essential parts of the product development process (Ulrich and Eppinger 2012). On one hand, verification (e.g., automated tests, integration tests and code review) checks if the solution confirms the specification and looks for mistakes made in the model. On the other hand, validation assures the satisfaction of user needs and conformity with the solution intended use, involving the revision of the market requirements (e.g., on-site surveys/questionnaires, user interaction monitoring and tracking) and the funds finding. The last phase, Go to market, deals with the commercialization of the product to be launched. Typical activities are the definition of a commercialization strategy (depending on the milestones to be reached and covering issues in the legal domain as IPR protection and management, management of legal aspects), of a communication and marketing plan, with the identification of channels for distribution and the definition of the revenue model.

### 3.3 The Pilot Case: The POLIMI DIH

The D-BEST model was used, through the launch of a survey, to configure the service portfolios of all the DIHs of the DIH4CPS network. In this section, the services composing the Politecnico di Milano DIH portfolio have been allocated on the two five-step CJs to build its unique value proposition for TU (Fig. 1) and TP (Fig. 2). The service portfolio has been fully detailed, going through the five macro-areas of the D-BEST model (Table 1):

**Table 1.** The Polimi DIH service portfolio based on the D-BEST reference model

| Class of service | Service instance | POLIMI's service instance |
|---|---|---|
| Ecosystem | | |
| SME and people engagement and brokerage | Academic conferences and workshops; Training sessions and other events | WMF; Open days; Conferences; Webinar & seminar (Observatory *Transition I4.0*) |
| Technology scouting | Identification of emerging technologies | Research projects results; Reports, articles |
| | Communication of technology related information to organizations | Research projects results; Reports, articles |
| Communication and trend watching | Sharing of best practices experiences | Research projects results; Reports, articles; Webinar & Seminar (Observatory Transition I4.0) |
| | Invitation of experts in business and entrepreneurship, or industry sectors to give talks and interact with (potential) customers and partners | |
| | DIH business model definition and updating through up-to-date information on the trends in the market | |
| | Provision of trend reports | Benchmark from CLIMB/DREAMY maturity models results |
| Ecosystem management | Definition of Intellectual Property (IP) rules | |
| Technology | | |
| Technology concept development/Proof of Concept (PoC) | Proof of concept development | Industry 4.0 lab |

(*continued*)

**Table 1.** *(continued)*

| Class of service | Service instance | POLIMI's service instance |
|---|---|---|
| Access to infrastructure and technological platforms | Provision of access to lab facilities | Industry 4.0 lab |
| Business | | |
| Methods and tools, business operations modelling | Provision of training and development in business skills and entrepreneurship (e.g., formal courses, workshops, seminars) | Courses on value proposition canvas & business model canvas |
| Secondment | Orienting partners to the needed training organization | |
| Development of proposals | Provision of technical assistance in the proposal development process to comply with specific proposal requirements (e.g., for project funding) | Building of consortia; Open calls |
| Skills | | |
| Maturity assessment | Assessment of the maturity companies, e.g.: assessment of company readiness for Industry 4.0 | DREAMY digital maturity assessment model |
| Human skills maturity assessment | Assessment of human skills maturity (e.g., regarding skills in Industry 4.0) | CLIMB/DREAMY maturity assessment models |
| Skills improvement | Definition of educational programs (forming Industry 4.0 employees and workers) | Workshops (e.g., Industry 4.0 overview, predictive maintenance, MOVE TO 4.0)<br>Master's Program in Industrial Engineering and the MBA and Masters' programs about Industry 4.0 |
| Data | | |
| Data analytics | Provision of data analytics services: semantic analysis, data discovery, advanced data analytics (edge analytics, cloud analytics) services | |
| Decision support and development | Provision and development of decision support services: cognition, prediction and prescription, simulation, machine learning, reinforcement, DNNs, formal logics | |
| User experience | Provision of support/consultancy services for user experience, navigation and exploration | Dashboarding and KPIs |

### 3.3.1 Technology End-User Customer Journey

*Observation*: The generic customer journey of a TU starts with the observation step. During this first phase, POLIMI organizes (and participates to) many public events like conferences, webinars, open days and workshops (e.g., of the Observatory *Transition I4.0*) that TUs can access to understand and realize which are the possible application of digital technologies in the manufacturing context. Such events can be focused on specific topics, to provide the extant state of theory and practice to both academics (professors, researchers, students, etc.) and practitioners (manufacturing companies and professionals). A reference example of these events is the World Manufacturing Forum (WMF), a yearly event of general interests in the manufacturing digital domain organized by the *World Manufacturing Foundation* together with POLIMI. The WMF indeed aims to enhance and spread industrial culture worldwide, as a means to ensure economic equity and sustainable development. It promotes innovation and development in the manufacturing sector, with the fundamental goal of improving competitiveness in all nations through dialogue and cooperation among the manufacturing sector's key players. The WMF supports national and international industrial agendas, provides a framework through which its stakeholders can meet and exchange opinions to find innovative solutions, disseminates knowledge through international and regional meetings and publications. This kind of events is also the best opportunity to share best practices experiences coming from research projects and to invite business and entrepreneurship experts/industry actors to give talks and interact with (potential) customers and partners. Always to support the observation phase, POLIMI defines educational programs allowing to attract and form next generation talent (forming I4.0 employees and workers). The main examples are the Master's Program in Industrial Engineering and the MBA and Masters' programs about Industry 4.0 topics.

*Awareness*: For those TUs interested in further collaborating with POLIMI, a maturity model, called DREAMY (Digital REadiness Assessment MaturitY model) is provided. Indeed, in the awareness phase manufacturers need to realise which is their digital *status quo*. DREAMY model assesses a manufacturing company's readiness level to trigger its digital transitioning process and to identify manufacturing company's strengths, weaknesses and opportunities, creating a roadmap for investments in digitisation and transitioning to smart manufacturing. Moreover, manufacturers need to understand and to evaluate how these new digital technologies are used to support their product development process along the entire company. Indeed, to deliver successful solutions in the market, companies can choose among various best practices to apply in their development process. Chaos-low-intermediate-mature-best practice (CLIMB) model (Rossi and Terzi 2017) measures maturity in product development activities. Together with DREAMY, CLIMB provides an evaluation also of the digital skills needed in the organization to better address the digital transformation of a TU. In addition, these services are the starting point for more structured collaborations aimed at increasing TU's digital maturity level through tailored paid projects. In the awareness phase, also Business-related services are provided. Technical assistance in the proposal development process to comply with specific proposal requirements (e.g., for project funding) can be the key to involve TUs in new European projects collaborations. In this phase, also open calls, launched throughout research projects, can be exploited to support the ideation of new technologies (several calls have been launched by POLIMI in the last years thanks to its belonging to different consortia). Finally, ecosystem services (as provision of trend reports, communication of technology related information to organization, and identification of emerging technologies) are provided. They can be provided also during Open Days including demonstrative applications of the Industry 4.0 Lab functionalities. Afterward, the generic TU can have access to specific didactic services, namely

Corporate Education & Training courses encompassing realistic demonstrations of I4.0 applications representing the state-of-the-art of manufacturing.

*Experiment*: In addition to the didactic services offered, companies would be provided with specific services aimed at experimenting applications in their specific fields. In particular, POLIMI makes available the facilities and instruments present in the Industry 4.0 Lab to support manufacturing TU in this sense. Doing this, POLIMI supports the development of proofs of concepts. In addition, strictly related to the technologies experimented, are provided data analysis services, followed by decision support services and user experience/navigation (dashboard and KPIs setting) service. Finally, contacts of POLIMI's ecosystem (secondment) can be provided in this phase.

*Experience:* To prepare the TU to best cope with the adoption phase's issues, POLIMI provides training on business skills and entrepreneurship (e.g., formal courses, workshops, seminars). In addition, secondment services are provided.

*Adoption:* Finally, once the TU has been specifically trained and has both experimented and experienced the technologies needed, POLIMI can provide secondment services to support TU in the very last phase of adoption.

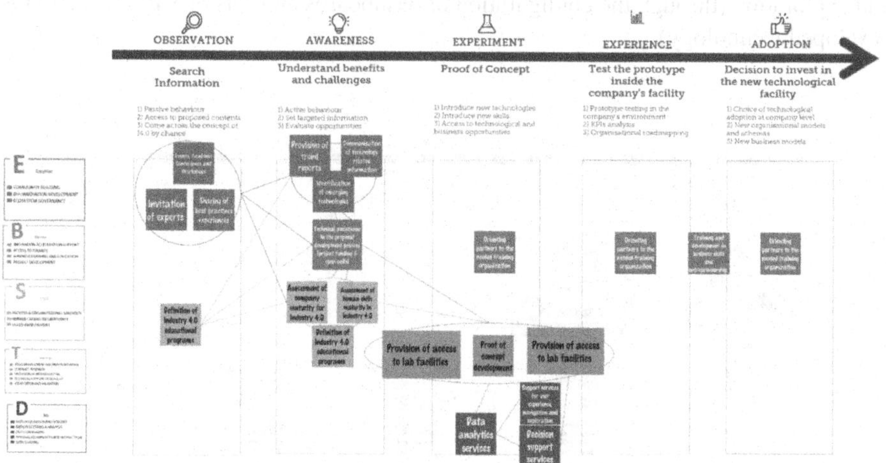


**Fig. 1.** Technology users customer journey: the POLIMI typical path

## 3.3.2 Technology Providers Customer Journey

*Ideation:* The TP CJ starts with the Ideation step. During this first phase, POLIMI organizes (and also participates to) many public events like conferences, webinars, open days and workshops (e.g. of the Observatory *Transition I4.0*) that TPs can access to improve and update their knowledge on digital technologies and to get in contact with TUs. Indeed, such events can be focused on specific topics, to provide the extant state of theory and practice to both academics (professors, researchers, students, etc.) and practitioners (manufacturing companies and professionals). As stated in the TU's journey, one of the main events is the WMF. POLIMI also supports the IPR definition throughout the entire TP journey. Also Business-related services are provided: technical assistance in the proposal development process to comply with specific proposal requirements (e.g. for project funding) can be the key to involve TUs in new project collaborations. From this phase up to the last ones, open calls, launched throughout research projects, can be also exploited to support the ideation of new technologies (several calls have been launched by POLIMI in the last years).

*Design and Engineering*: In this phase, as in the case of TUs, ecosystem services (as provision of trend reports, communication of technology related information to organization, and identification of emerging technologies) are provided, also during dedicated events and Open Days, including demonstrative applications of the Industry 4.0 Lab functionalities. Afterward, the TP can have access to specific didactic services, namely Corporate Education & Training courses that encompass also realistic demonstrations of I4.0 applications (representing the State-of-the-Art of manufacturing). These courses can support TPs in either defining the PoC of the technology to be provided or improving and refining the design and engineering of their solutions. This combined Technology/Training service can be provided by POLIMI from this phase up to the Verification & Validation. In addition, POLIMI provides services for user experience, navigation and exploration (through the configuration of dashboards and sets of KPI related to the developed technology).

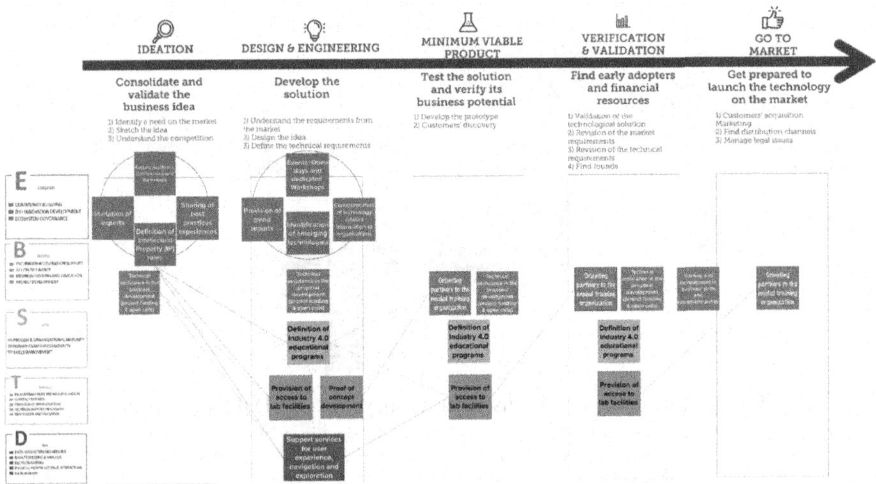


**Fig. 2.** Technology providers customer journey: the POLIMI typical path

*MVP*: The development of an MVP is supported through the provision of secondment services to meet TP's needs. Otherwise, the access to the Industry 4.0 lab is provided to support them. Finally, educational programs in the I4.0 domain and the involvement in consortia and open calls can be catered in this phase.

*Verification & Validation:* The same happens for the Verification & Validation step. In case the Technology/Training services are not suitable to the TP' case, POLIMI provides secondment services. Also, the participation to new project consortia or open calls can be fostered. Finally, before the launch to the market, the generic TP may rely on POLIMI for training on business skills and entrepreneurship.

*Go to Market:* Also in this last step, POLIMI can provide secondment services.

## 4 Discussions, Conclusions, and Future Work

This paper has the aim of introducing the methodology used to build DIHs CJs. It supports the definition of flexible service workflows for DIH customers (i.e. TPs and TUs), by combining the services composing the DIH portfolio, configured through the D-BEST model, towards the implementation of DIHs Unique Value Proposition. Indeed, the method not only assesses the role of DIHs in catalysing the digitalization dynamics of SMEs but could also support the definition of the service pipeline of DIHs. Process gates have been defined along the two digital transformation paths of TU and TP, leading to the definition of the two 5-step paths towards the full digital maturity and awareness of the customer. Moreover, allocating and connecting typical D-BEST services along the two templates, the model demonstrated to be able to develop the two different CJs for the POLIMI DIH pilot case. Typical paths have been created for both TU and TP, revealing a different DIH value propositions per each of the two types of stakeholders. Among the main limitations of the method introduced there is the lack of the blocking points unlocked along the CJs through the support of DIHs. Indeed, although technology offers high potentials and DIHs foster the new technologies exploitation for SMEs, the percentage of companies giving up the CJ before its completion is relevant. For this reason, the CJs need to be enriched with the blocking points that SMEs might have to cope with when going through it. A limitation of this paper is the application of the CJ model only to the pilot case, the POLIMI DIH. From the future extensive use of the method, it is easy to hypothesise that some DIH will be more targeting the development and commercialisation of new CPS technologies, some others are more interested in creating awareness and investments in the demand side of the marketplace. Finally, based on the journeys presented in this paper, where the typical paths between TPs and TUs with the DIH have been indicated, success stories and best cases can be detected and be shared.

**Acknowledgments.** This work has received funding from the European Union's Horizon 2020 research and innovation programme under grant agreement No 872548.

## References

1. Butter, M., Gijsbers, G., Goetheer, A., Karanikolova, K.: Digital innovation hubs and their position in the European, National and Regional Innovation Ecosystems. In: Feldner, D. (ed.) Redesigning Organizations, pp. 45–60. Springer, Cham (2020). https://doi.org/10.1007/978-3-030-27957-8_3
2. DIH4CPS – Digital Innovation Hub for Cyber-Physical Systems (2020). Available at: http://dih4cps.eu/. Accessed 9 May 2020
3. DIH4CPS project (2020) D2 .1: DIH Service Catalogue for Ecosystem , Technology , Business Development - WP2: Network Setup and Management (2020)

4. European Commission (2018) Smart Anything Everywhere - Digital Innovation Hubs - Accelerators for the broad digital transformation of the European industry. Available at: https://ec.europa.eu/digital-single-market/en/news/communication-digitising-european-industry-reaping-full-benefits-digital-single-market. Accessed 4 February 2020
5. MIDIH Project (2020) D3.4 Specifications and Design of DIH/CC Services 2 - WP3 Network of Competence Centers and Pan-EU DIHs in CPS/IoT (2020)
6. Rossi, M., Terzi, S.: CLIMB: maturity assessment model for design and engineering processes. Int. J. Prod. Lifecycle Manag. **10**(1), 20 (2017). https://doi.org/10.1504/IJPLM.2017.082998
7. Sassanelli, C., Panetto, H., Guedria, W., Terzi, S., Doumeingts, G.: Towards a reference model for configuring services portfolio of digital innovation hubs: the ETBSD model. In: Camarinha-Matos, L.M., Afsarmanesh, H., Ortiz, A. (eds.) PRO-VE 2020. IAICT, vol. 598, pp. 597–607. Springer, Cham (2020). https://doi.org/10.1007/978-3-030-62412-5_49
8. Ulrich, K.T., Eppinger, S.D.: Product design and development. Prod. Des. Dev. (2012). https://doi.org/10.1016/B978-0-7506-8985-4.00002-4

# A Framework to Strengthen Collaboration Between Universities and Industrial-Related Entities Towards Boosting Industry 4.0 Adoption and Development

Ricardo J. Rabelo(✉)

UFSC - Federal University of Santa Catarina, Florianopolis, SC, Brazil
ricardo.rabelo@ufsc.br

**Abstract.** Industry 4.0 has become a centerpiece of strategic plans and national policies in many countries. Studies have pointed out the many obstacles for the adoption of Industry 4.0 in larger scale towards such strategic plans, including the lack of skilled people and the low level of companies' innovation. Triple-helix-based innovation models have been proposed to reinforce collaboration between different actors, and it is reasonably clear nowadays "what to do". However, the "how to do" is not so trivial, considering the so many existing differences from region to region, in their culture, and in companies' Industry 4.0 maturity levels. Relying on collaborative networks foundations, this paper presents a framework as a contribution to make those actors working together more effectively and systematically in way to mitigate some of those obstacles. This framework has been gradually implemented during the last two years. This paper presents the framework itself and its main results so far achieved.

**Keywords:** Industry 4.0 · Collaborative networks · Innovation ecosystem

## 1 Introduction

Industry 4.0 has become a centerpiece of strategic plans and national policies in many countries. From an initial vision pretty much focused on manufacturing and on the use of some technologies to provide flexibility and intelligence to industries, the Industry 4.0 vision has evolved since then. It is no longer seen as a final goal, but rather as a means to leverage social, economic, and technological development of countries [1].

Many studies have pointed out the several obstacles for the adoption of Industry 4.0 in larger scale towards such strategic plans. They include the lack of prepared engineers and instructors to understand and to work on the several areas impacted by the Industry 4.0 model; the need to increase the scientific and technological development in the many areas involved; the lack of proper regulations and secure communication infrastructures; the low level of management and technological modernization in the SMEs; the several open points and risks related to ethical and social implications of Industry 4.0; the low


Published by Springer Nature Switzerland AG 2021
L. M. Camarinha-Matos et al. (Eds.): PRO-VE 2021, IFIP AICT 629, pp. 471–481, 2021.
https://doi.org/10.1007/978-3-030-85969-5_44

level of companies' preparedness to be part of larger and more profitable value chains; the low level of innovation initiatives inside the companies to strive their competitiveness; the cost of some technologies and the need for high investments to deploy them sustainably; the risk of investments in 4.0-related initiatives against expected ROI; the lack of innovative business models; among others [2, 3].

Inspired on the classical triple-helix innovation model, diverse actors (such as industrial associations, governments, innovation ecosystems, and universities) have been creating specific Frameworks, dedicated physical spaces, etc., to face those obstacles, nationally and regionally [4]. Despite the benefits being got from this and the intrinsically collaborative vision of the model, practice has been showing the low level of their effectiveness in many cases [5]. These initiatives have not been able to create a systemic innovation culture inside the SMEs, to make them adopt (at least) "less closed" innovation models, and to consider the involvement of universities in such model [4]; or to make companies to get real acquaintance on Industry 4.0 to adopt it more effectively [6]. Several works have highlighted that strengthening collaboration between universities and industrial-related entities considering SMEs reality represents an adequate approach to boost Industry 4.0 adoption and technological development [6, 7]. The underlying research question of this paper refers to how universities can be organized to help in tackling these problems.

In this direction, this paper presents a framework as a contribution to make those actors working together more effectively and systemically. Its ultimate goal is to mitigate some of those obstacles towards a smarter and more sustainable collaborative networked environment. The framework considers those actors as members of an ecosystem of independent organizations that strategically decide to work more collaboratively aiming at reaching better common objectives. It supports most of the many activities/business models involved in education, research, outreach and assistance to companies, in what the needs of Industry 4.0 are concerned.

This paper is organized as follows. Section 1 has introduced the problem and the objectives of the work. Section 2 summarizes the framework's rationale. Section 3 presents the framework. Section 4 lists the business cases implemented with the proposed framework and preliminary results. Section 5 presents some conclusions.

## 2 Development Methodology and Rationale

### 2.1 Existing Pre-conditions

There is a vibrant innovation ecosystem in the Greater Florianopolis City, South of Brazil. It is composed of almost four thousand IT, technology, and automation-based companies and startups, services providers, incubators, innovation hubs, science parks, industrial institutions, and some private and public universities. Complementarily, special regulations and funding mechanisms have been created by local governments and banks to irrigate the ecosystem functioning and growth. Groups of investors complete the list of actors of this ecosystem.

Due to historical factors, there is a long culture of cooperation between industries and local universities, and many startups and companies of the region have emerged from this. Nevertheless, this cooperation does not happen systemically and homogeneously.

Yet, not as intense as it could be given the number of companies and the potentials of all that. It mostly involves the same large companies that come to the university to look for cooperation to carry out research on very sophisticated methods or technologies that they are not fully able to develop alone. SMEs – both Industry 4.0 technology adopters and developers – are not used to working with universities.

About two years ago, some SME companies begun to collaborate with the university as a strategy to leverage their innovation levels. Starting with *ad-hoc* and individual actions, this became more common and new types of cooperation arose. It was then necessary to create a more comprehensive framework, including mechanisms to scale the model and to keep it flexible for newer actions.

## 2.2 Framework's Requirements

Four main drivers have been considered to conceive the framework: the aforementioned obstacles; the diagnostics from the Brazilian policies related to Industry 4.0 and to the lack of stronger cooperation between actors [8]; the local interests and regional priorities looking at future possibilities and trends in Industry 4.0; and the lessons learned from those previous ad-hoc initiatives.

The priorities were: i) SMEs need a very special attention due to their importance in the local and national economies. This includes SME technology adopters and developers. They have a big potential of competitiveness growth, but they are generally limited (mainly in terms of financial and human resources) to adopt and develop new and innovative industry 4.0-related solutions; ii) the regional industrial pressure to cope with Industry 4.0 needs, which demands more and better human resources training and technology development; and iii) the need to increase the level of technological development and of potential market *solutions* (e.g. products, patents, software, algorithms, instrumentation, etc.) for Industry 4.0 by the ecosystem's SMEs, also involving undergrad and graduate students entrepreneurship.

Collaborative Networks [9] has been used as the main foundation for conceiving the framework. In a time where working with higher efficiency, effectiveness and innovation is becoming a must to underpin organizations' sustainability, individual initiatives prevent organizations from the sort of advantages that collaborative actions can provide, such as: the non-duplication efforts when dealing with given demands; the sharing of costs and risks between the members of the collaborative action; the sharing or use of complementary human, technological and knowledge resources; the sharing of infrastructures for research, education, professional training, businesses, etc.; the co-creation of new and less endogenous ideas, solutions, etc., when attending to new business opportunities; and the access to resources and technologies they do not have or even could not hire or buy individually [9].

There are many possible "entry points" to foster the cooperation between universities and companies. One of them refers that several implementation actions related to Industry 4.0 require the deployment of equipment and technologies as well as the assessment of new production methods and more recent ICT by companies. This is too costly and risky (mainly) for SMEs as Industry 4.0 also involves the adoption of new theories and technologies [10]. In this line, the core of the collaborative initiatives of the framework is mostly based on the use and sharing of physical universities' infrastructures and industrial labs. This aims to make them act as different types of *demonstrators*, like testbeds, showcases, living labs, learning factories, and didactic plants [10], depending on their conditions and sophistication.

### 2.3 Methodological Aspects

There are many general frameworks to make universities and industries working more integrated. However, we could not find in the literature neither an existing framework that coped with the needed requirements nor one specifically devised to boost Industry 4.0 adoption. Thus, some frameworks were selected, analyzed, the aspects considered as the most appropriate ones to be applied for Industry 4.0 purposes and local goals were identified, some practices and mechanisms were combined and adapted to the local conditions, and some new actions were added considering the local culture, goals, and pre-existing conditions. To be highlighted four frameworks: *Babson College*, EUA, in the area of entrepreneurship; *Virginia Tech*, EUA, in terms of involvement of companies in the courses' curricula; the *Fraunhofer* institute, Germany, in terms of cooperation between companies and universities for applied research; and the Dual Study initiative from the *MOKSH* German Program, in terms of cooperation between industries and students for integrated internships[1].

The Action-Research methodology [11] was adopted to devise the framework. Adopting a constructivist and evolving approach, this meant that a given artifact (the framework) was gradually, jointly, and interactively built up with its users (the university and the other ecosystem's actors) with the aim of facing the general issues involved in the collaboration endeavor related to Industry 4.0. The framework has been implemented in different paces and phases, depending on the issues to address.

## 3 The Collaboration Framework

The elicited priorities (Sect. 2.2) were decomposed into four very concrete goals to be delivered by the framework:

i. Improving the skills and increasing the number of undergraduate and graduate students trained in Industry 4.0-related subjects to become future workers, entrepreneurs, and instructors/professors;
ii. Increasing the number of works from undergraduate and graduate students whose Final Works and Theses have the potential to be transformed into future Industry 4.0 solutions or as technology transfer artifacts;
iii. Improving the skills and increasing the number of SME managers trained in Industry 4.0-related subjects;
iv. Improving the innovation level of Industry 4.0 technology developers SMEs.

[1] https://www.babson.edu/; https://vt.edu/; https://www.fraunhofer.de/en.html; https://www.moksh16.com/dual-study-opportunities-in-germany/

As part of the constructivist approach, the way these goals were planned has considered the general Teaching, Research, and Outreach dimensions, set up in the university when it was founded 70 years ago.

Figure 1 shows the general framework's elements. One can see it as "yet another collaboration framework between universities and industries", and even less comprehensive than other ones (mentioned in the previous section). Its value proposition is actually grounded on the way the framework's elements work integrately as well as on how the different actors collaborate to achieve the framework's goals considering the local culture.

- *Teaching*: it means training undergraduate and graduate students on topics more directed to Industry 4.0 throughout the several engineering courses and internships. Students will supply the market needs, acting as engineers in the companies, consultants, professors/instructors, or future entrepreneurs.

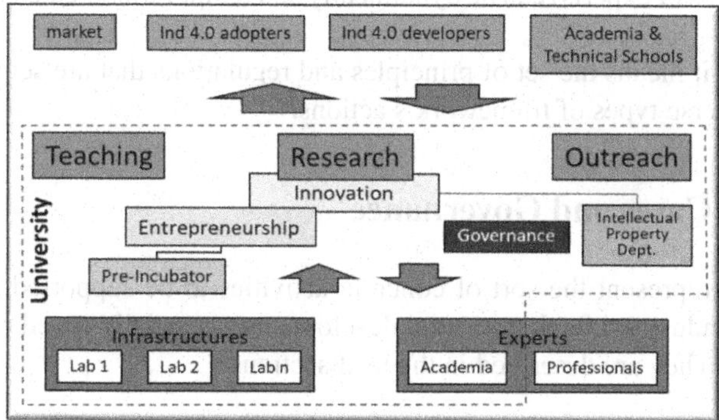


**Fig. 1.** Framework elements

- *Research*: it means investigating and developing new techniques, models, algorithms, prototypes, etc., directed to Industry 4.0 needs. This mostly comes from Industry 4.0 developers and adopters (*tech pull*) based on their needs. By 'needs' it does not mean developing solutions for companies' current problems, but rather proof-of-concept prototypes, technologies assessments, innovations, etc., as bases for future companies' products and services.

*Entrepreneurship* is stimulated. Researchers do works that can either be further interesting to companies (*science push*) or can use their works for launching their future startups or spin-offs. The university offers methodological and mentoring support for that through its *pre-incubator*.

Although innovation is present in the teaching and outreach activities, it is essentially present in research. The way innovations are developed can vary from case to case, requiring a more formal means to manage them. This includes e.g., dealing with *intellectual property rights* when pertinent.

- *Outreach*: it means a set of "services" that universities offer to society. In the context of Industry 4.0, this usually involves specific courses to companies and professionals; consultancy to companies; and technical evaluations, advisory, and technical reports to government/industrial councils.
- *Infrastructures*: considering the focus on Industry 4.0, it refers to the strategy of starting using existing infrastructures that industries (mainly SMEs) do not have to test or develop technologies and solutions on their own. From the business models viewpoint, this means seeing infrastructures as a "platform" over which "services" can be offered and used in different modalities by different "actors".
- *Experts*: it means the group of professionals, both from the academia and the market (including former students who are eager to retribute the training got from the university) that are skilled to help companies in coping with their needs. This group is equivalent to the concept of *Virtual Professional Community* [9], where *Virtual Teams* (i.e., subgroups of experts) can be dynamically and temporarily created to attend those needs.
- *Governance*: it means the set of principles and regulations that are set up to rule and guide the diverse types of framework's actions.

## 4 Business Cases and Governance

Business cases represent the sort of concrete activities to be supported by the framework to boost Industry 4.0 adoption and development, especially based on the existing infrastructures. They are described in the next sections.

### 4.1 A Shop Floor as a Framework's Physical Instance, and Piloting Actors

The current infrastructure is composed of two *FESTO MPS* set of stations placed in two physical locations. These infrastructures are able to communicate with each other, so they can do some integrated work. One, placed at one of the university labs, is constituted by six assembly-related stations, which works sequentially (although they are modular), equipped with *Siemens* PLC series 1200, and that communicate via *wifi* and a *Profinet/OPC* protocols. It includes some IoT devices and sensors, and a SCADA system, via the Siemens *TIA Portal*. The other plant, placed in an industrial training center 5 km far from the university, has three stations and one AGV, equipped with *Siemens* PLC series 1700, which communicate via *wifi* and *Profinet & Fieldbus/OPC-UA* protocols, also having IoT devices and sensors.

An important aspect to use these infrastructures is the adoption of a 'plug and play' & SaaS (Software-as-a-Service) general strategy. Based on a bus integration approach, and given that the infrastructures strongly rely on ICT standards, the developed software solutions (from Industry 4.0 company developers and researchers) are made available as "services", accessed as SaaS, deployed at different clouds. In the case of hardware and equipment, they should be locally deployed (Fig. 2).

The initial implementation of the framework started as a pilot, and new actions have been gradually added as results appear. The main actors involved in the pilot are: UFSC (the department of Automation engineering); some selected professors from other UFSC departments; the computer science department of the State University of Santa Catarina; the Industrial Center for Apprenticeship; and some companies from the manufacturing cluster.

## 4.2 Teaching

The main activities supported by the framework on Teaching are:

- New courses (mostly as elective) at both undergraduate and graduate levels specifically directed to Industry 4.0 foundations (e.g., maturity models, digital transformation, etc.) and enabling technologies (e.g., AI, digital twins, IoT and cyber-physical systems, etc.);
- These courses are flexible to introduce new specific contents, technologies, visits to industries, classes inside companies, talks by entrepreneurs, etc.;
- Some courses' topics are taught by professors from other departments or universities, by specialists on the given topic; and/or by professionals from the market, also experts, but more focused on real problems, practices and commonly used tools or methodologies;
- Strong emphasis on hands-on activities, where students can work on selected Industry 4.0-related problems brought by the ecosystem's own companies. During the scholar semester and following milestones, undergraduate students are mentored by these professionals, together with the professors.
- Some more promising ideas and prototypes developed in such courses have been deepened – also helped by the Pre-incubator – and become initial seeds/MVPs for future products to the market, or technologies that can be incorporated into companies' existing solutions, or themes to be chased in future graduate Theses;
- Adoption of up-to-date tools used in the market, provided by companies, free of licenses, instead of old-versioned or limited academic tools;
- Use of the lab infrastructure to teach the students.

Achieved results of this include: i) increasing the number of trained students on Industry 4.0; ii) according to the piloting companies, students are clearly better prepared to more comprehensively handle problems related to Industry 4.0 projects; iii) companies have saved time and costs in initial training when hiring students as internships or engineers; iv) students' mindset shift in the way they see the potentials of their final works in becoming new solutions for Industry 4.0; v) students are trained about how transforming ideas in potential future businesses; vi) increasing the number of startups and spin-offs created by the undergraduate students in the several areas embraced by Industry 4.0; vii) students are more excited with the university itself, with the courses and related daily activities, and with better potential future jobs.

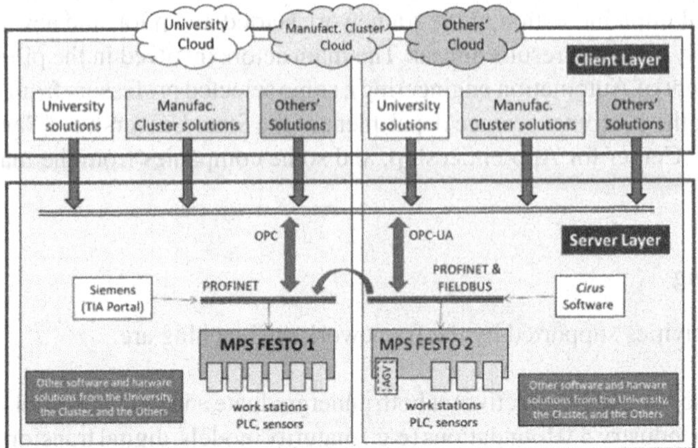


**Fig. 2.** General view of existing infrastructures

### 4.3 Research

The main activities supported by the framework on Research are:

- From a *Tech pull* innovation perspective, MSc and PhD students are presented to problems brought by companies. Problems can be both "infrastructure-related" and about higher-level topics (e.g., Supply Chain, AI-based control, etc.).
- Companies either sponsor students with scholarships or stimulates their employees to pursue a graduate course to research on an agreed theme. Considering the usual restrictions from SMEs in terms of human resources and technologies, this represents a feasible way to outsource their R&D activities;
- From a *Science push* innovation perspective, results from some MSc and PhD students are presented to companies (via *pitches*), showing envisioned benefits of the developed "technology" to companies;
- Solution providers make their products available to students and professors to add some value. This can be subject of IPR and specific business agreements. Some graduate works can become small research projects, funded by companies and/or research funding agencies, and can involve other students (including undergraduate) or professors/researchers.

Achieved results of this include: i) increasing the number of cooperation projects with the industry in the area of Industry 4.0; ii) increasing the number of graduate works with potentials to be exploited at business level; ii) increasing the number of professionals from companies starting their MSc thesis; iv) increasing in the average awareness level of students, professors, and companies about pros and difficulties to work collaboratively in a business-oriented project; v) increasing in the average awareness level of companies about the intrinsic risks, time, and costs of innovation projects; vi) increasing in the average awareness level of companies about the role of the university (that it is not a 'company'); and vii) increasing the number of startups created by the graduate students in the several areas embraced by Industry 4.0.

### 4.4 Outreach

The main activities supported by the framework on Outreach are:

- Professors use the infrastructure to deliver courses and continuous training to industries and professionals about specific subjects related to Industry 4.0;
- Companies (both Industry 4.0 adopters and developers) can use the infrastructures' facilities to evaluate technologies, methods, devices, etc., in near-real environments before deciding to buy them, or as a support for their decisions if they keep investing in some innovation project whose technical feasibility is not well known. This can be subject to fees for the university;
- Companies can make use of the infrastructure as a support for product demonstrations, integrated to a near-real environment, and for training customers on the developed solution. This are subject to fees for the university;
- Use of the infrastructure for teaching students and instructors from other universities and technical schools;
- Formation of Virtual Teams [9] of professors (and eventually also involving professionals) to attend requests from companies and from funding agencies for consultancy in issues related to Industry 4.0.

Achieved results of this include: i) increasing the number of courses and training activities to industries on Industry 4.0 as well as to external students; ii) increasing the number of companies looking at the university to assess some technologies and to make some general tests of their products; iii) increasing the number of companies looking at the university to show how their products can work in real-life; and iv) increasing the number of advisory services to companies in Industry 4.0.

### 4.5 Governance Model and Framework Sustainability

Considering there are: i) different institutions and many possible companies interested in using the available infrastructure and offer their solutions; ii) some equipments (that need maintenance, can break, etc.), technical staff, scheduled classes in the labs, and legal restrictions related to cooperation university: industries; and iii) existing regulations for installing software and hardware at the university, etc.; a governance model had to be devised. In general, it means defining the "rules of the game" for the different business cases and actors involved in each scenario with the aim of mitigating possible conflicts and problems that can bring the framework down.

Inspired in the life cycles of the VBE and VO (Virtual Organization) types of collaborative organizations [9, 12], the governance model is basically composed of a bylaw-like instrument and operating rules. The former generally depicts the main working principles of the network that is formed to cope with the different business cases (e.g., the existence of a common management committee, aspects related to payments, and rules related to sensitive information and to competing companies). The latter comprises the basic rules for a company: i) to be accepted to work with the university under this framework (e.g., rules to make software available, to donate funds and resources, to licensing, etc.); ii) to operate within this framework (e.g., rules to use the infrastructure and other resources, the involvement of professors, technicians and students in research and outreach, etc.); and iii) to leave the framework (e.g., rules to cancel the permission of a company to use the infrastructure under the framework, to remove companies' resources previously installed, etc.).

## 5 Final Considerations

This paper has presented a tailor-made framework developed to boost the adoption and the development of the Industry 4.0 in the Greater Florianopolis City, the South of Brazil. Considering a set of identified obstacles that have been preventing a larger adoption of Industry 4.0, the developed framework was conceived taking advantage of some pre-conditions. In more particular, the existence of a solid innovation ecosystem and a good number of local Industry 4.0 solution developers.

The main motivation for the framework was that universities and companies/industries are not used to cooperate at a large scale, systemically, despite the big potentials. The framework can be seen as a kind of 'answer' from the university to the industrial community, trying to attract companies to work more effectively in terms of generating more concrete and useful results in terms of Industry 4.0 needs.

A set of concrete actions were conceived regarding the way the university is organized, namely in terms of teaching, research, and outreach, also involving innovation, entrepreneurship, and apprenticeship.

The results so far achieved are very promising given the improvements obtained in all the supported dimensions and the specific goals the framework was tailored to. However, there is a long way to go. Especially in terms of measures to increase the level of awareness and general mindset – both from the university and entrepreneurs – related to the initial difficulties and to the learning and evolving process a cooperation between them represents. This also involves some legal obstacles to be overcome as some situations were not explicitly supported by current regulations as some situations were new. Thus, the framework cannot be taken as finished. Instead, it is constantly updated as newer scenarios and better practices appear.

Besides identifying the set of business cases for the diverse cooperation scenarios, a governance model was necessary to be established to regulate the functioning of the framework, and to preserve and reinforce the relations between the involved actors.

**Acknowledgments.** This work has been partially supported by CAPES - The Brazilian Agency for Higher Education Improvement, project PrInt CAPES-UFSC "Automation 4.0".

## References

1. Propris, L., Bailey, D.: Industry 4.0 and Regional Transformations. Francis & Taylor (2020)
2. ACATECH: Industrie 4.0 International Benchmark, Options for the Future and Recommendations for Manufacturing Research (2016). https://en.acatech.de/publications/
3. World Manufacturing Forum: Readiness for the Future of Production (2018). http://www3.weforum.org/docs/FOPReadinessReport2018.pdf

4. Carayannis, E., Grigoroudis, E.: The ecosystem as helix: an exploratory theory-building study of regional coopetitive entrepreneurial ecosystems as Quadruple/Quintuple Helix Innovation Models. R&D Manage. **48**(1), 148–162 (2017)
5. Gray, D., Sundstrom, E.: When triple helix unravels: a multi-case analysis of failures in industry-university cooperative research centres. Ind. High. Educ. **25**(5), 333–345 (2011)
6. European Union: Industry 4.0 Implications for Higher Education Institutions (2017). https://universitiesofthefuture.eu/wp-content/uploads/2019/02/State-of-MaturityReport.pdf
7. OCDE: University-Industry Collaboration - New Evidence and Policy Options (2019). http://www.innovationpolicyplatform.org/www.innovationpolicyplatform.org/system/files/imce/OECD_UniIndCollaboration_FullReport_Website/index.pdf
8. MCTI: Plano de CT&I para Manufatura Avançada no Brasil – ProFuturo (2017). https://antigo.mctic.gov.br/mctic/export/sites/institucional/tecnologia/tecnologias_convergentes/arquivos/Cartilha-Plano-de-CTI_WEB.pdf
9. Camarinha-Matos, L.M., Fornasiero, R., Ferrada, F.: Collaborative networks - a pillar of digital transformation. J. Appl. Sci. **9**(24), 5431 (2019)
10. Damgrave R., Lutters, E.: Smart industry testbed. In: 29th CIRP Design Conference, pp. 387–392 (2019)
11. Reason, P., Bradbury, H.: Handbook of action research. SAGE Editors, London (2001)
12. Rabelo, R.J., Costa, S.N., Romero, D.: A governance reference model for virtual enterprises. In: Camarinha-Matos, L.M., Afsarmanesh, H. (eds.) PRO-VE 2014. IAICT, vol. 434, pp. 60–70. Springer, Heidelberg (2014). https://doi.org/10.1007/978-3-662-44745-1_6

# Socio-Technical Perspectives on Smart Product-Service Systems

# Product-Service System for the Pharmaceutical Industry

Mariusz Salwin[1(✉)], Andrzej Kraslawski[2], Michał Andrzejewski[2,3], and Jan Lipiak[4]

[1] Faculty of Production Engineering, Warsaw University of Technology, 85 Narbutta Street, 02-524 Warsaw, Poland
mariusz.salwin@onet.pl
[2] School of Engineering Science, Lappeenranta University of Technology, P.O. Box 20, 53581 Lappeenranta, Finland
[3] Kalmar-Pac, 38 Oksywska Street, 01-694 Warsaw, Poland
[4] Etigraf Printing House, 52 Głowackiego Street, 05-071 Sulejówek, Poland

**Abstract.** This article presents an industrial workshop on the design of the Product-Service System (PSS) for the pharmaceutical sector. The result of the research is a new PSS solution for high-value machines with advanced technology used in pharmaceutical production. When designing this PSS, the attention was paid to the specific features of the pharmaceutical sector and pharmaceutical production, problems as well as the needs and requirements of a pharmaceutical company. Taking into account all these elements aim to develop a comprehensive solution. The workshops were divided into stages and presented in a very synthetic way. The article illustrates the collaboration between the machine selling company (manufacturer's representative), pharmaceutical company and scientists to co-design effective PSS solutions.

**Keywords:** Product-Service System (PSS) · Pharmaceutical industry · Pharmaceutical machine

## 1 Introduction

Recent decades have brought advances in the design of the Product-Service System (PSS) [1–4]. The researchers' attention is focused primarily on the development of new design methods or the use of already well-known tools in PSS design [5–8]. Much less importance is attached to the co-design of the PSS in order to generate effective solutions. The combination of products and services in PSS opens up a number of opportunities that both producers and users should take advantage of [8–10]. These opportunities often only become apparent when both sides work together. There is therefore a strong need to develop this area of PSS design [11–13]. Nevertheless, the article undertook the co-design of PSS for the pharmaceutical industry in a research workshop. An important element on which the emphasis was placed was the cooperation of the company selling the machines


Published by Springer Nature Switzerland AG 2021
L. M. Camarinha-Matos et al. (Eds.): PRO-VE 2021, IFIP AICT 629, pp. 485–493, 2021.
https://doi.org/10.1007/978-3-030-85969-5_45

(manufacturer's representative), the pharmaceutical company and scientists. This made it possible to generate a specific solution.

The paper is structured as follows: the first part is the introduction. The next part contains the research methodology. The third part presents the literature analysis. The next part presents results. The fifth part is the discussion and conclusions.

## 2 Research Methodology

The aim of this paper is to develop a PSS for the pharmaceutical sector in collaboration with scientists, the machine selling company (manufacturer's representative) and the pharmaceutical company. The following research question was posed in the work:

- Can PSS bring benefits to entities operating in the pharmaceutical sector?

The research carried out in the article emphasizes the role of cooperation and provides suggestions for practitioners regarding the design and use of PSS in the pharmaceutical sector.

This paper adopts the methodology consisting of the following stages:

1. Systematic literature review. At this stage, two parallel literature reviews were carried out. The first focused on the analysis of the PSS found in industry, the second on the analysis of PSS design methods.
2. Analysis of the pharmaceutical industry. On the basis of industry reports, the pharmaceutical industry was characterized at this stage. The focus was on the analysis of users and manufacturers of pharmaceutical machinery.
3. Researching the user of pharmaceutical machines. This stage was carried out in the form of industrial workshops. This study was conducted on manufacturing issues, tablet press needs and requirements, and related services.
4. Product-Service System project. This stage was carried out in the form of industrial workshops. This is the result of cooperation between scientists, the company selling the machines (manufacturer's representative) and a pharmaceutical company. It was developed based on practical knowledge and information obtained at the earlier stages of the research.

## 3 Literature Review

### 3.1 Product-Service System in Industrial Practice and Product-Service System Design

This stage concerned the analysis of the literature related to the PSS used in industry and PSS design methods. The table presents guidelines for a systematic literature review.

The investigated industrial PSS cases were created by large companies operating on the global market. These solutions target many sectors of the economy. Innovation plays an important role in them. Their use is aimed at creating lasting added value for customers. The characteristic features of the analyzed PSS are high value and long service life of the products, the use of advanced technologies and an emphasis on environmental protection. In most cases, the PSS material element is a product composed of many systems and parts. On the other hand, the services that guarantee its continued use constitute an intangible element. The flagship examples of PSS include: Philips Lighting (pay per lux) and Ivchenko-Progress ZMKB (Support serial production. Repair). The industrial PSS cases conducted closely did not demonstrate the use of this solution in the pharmaceutical sector (Table 1).

**Table 1.** Guidelines for Systematic literature review

| | Product-service system in practice | Product-service system design |
|---|---|---|
| Analysis period | 2001–2019 | |
| Information sources | ProQues, Springler Link, Science Direct, Taylor & Francis Online, EBSCOhost, Scopus, Emerald, Insight, Web of Science, Ingenta, Dimensions, Wilma, IEEE Xplore Digital Library and Google Scholar | |
| Keywords | "Product-Service System in industry" or synonyms | "Product-Service System in design" or synonyms |
| Result | 150 works describing PSS functioning in industry | 60 PSS design methods |

The conducted literature study on PSS design provides information on 60 PSS design methods. Out of 60 analyzed methods, 12 were verified in industrial practice, and 21 research projects. The rest are scientists' proposals. Out of 60 methods (Fig. 1), as many as 12 are universal methods that have not been assigned to any industry. The remaining methods were targeted at one or more industries simultaneously. Most of the methods are directed to the mechanical engineering sector. There are: cutting tools, metalworking machines, production machines, valves and tank control systems, heavy machinery for road construction, hoists and elevators, compactors, industrial laser systems, refrigeration equipment, agricultural machinery and aviation. The conducted analysis does not provide information on the PSS in the pharmaceutical sector [6, 7].

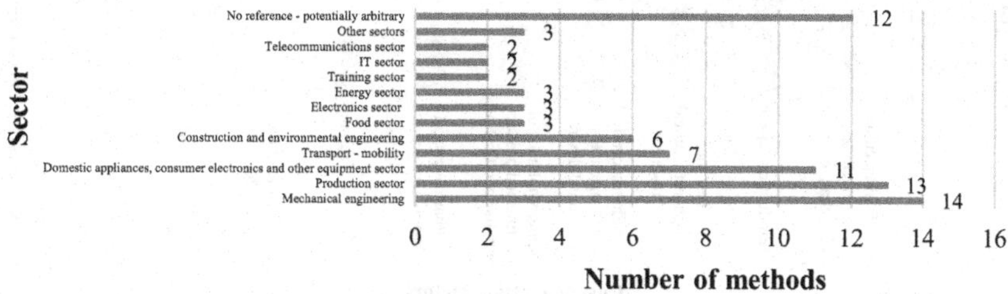


**Fig. 1.** Classification of PSS design methods by sector [7].

### 3.2 Pharmaceutical Industry and Pharmaceutical Machines

The pharmaceutical sector is an innovative branch of the economy that focuses on the development and production of drugs and medical devices. Pharmaceutical products are used to save the health and life of people and animals. Their production is characterized by, among others, meeting strict requirements, high accuracy and cleanliness. Asia, Europe and North America are currently the largest pharmaceutical markets. The pharmaceutical sector of the European Union consists of 4,106 enterprises employing 595,751, and the production value is around 287.89 EUR billion [14–16].

One of the key resources of the pharmaceutical sector is the production machinery (e.g. capsule presses, tablet presses, blister machines). These machines differ significantly in size, level of automation and the way they are operated. The production of the drug in a specific form (e.g. a tablet) can only be carried out on a specific machine equipped with specific format parts (tablet press). Currently, leading manufacturers of machines and lines (for example Norden, Citus Kalix, HAPA) for the production of pharmaceutical products offer machines in various equipment variants. Services, on the other hand, constitute a narrow part of their offer. In 2018, pharmaceutical companies operating in the European Union invested approximately 6.73 EUR billion in production machinery [14–16].

## 4 Results

This part of the paper deals with research workshops carried out with the participation of the company selling the machines (manufacturer's representative), a pharmaceutical company and scientists.

### 4.1 Company Problems and Needs

The aim of this phase of the workshop was to find out what problems the user of pharmaceutical machines is facing. In addition, it was possible to precisely define and what needs related to the said machine.

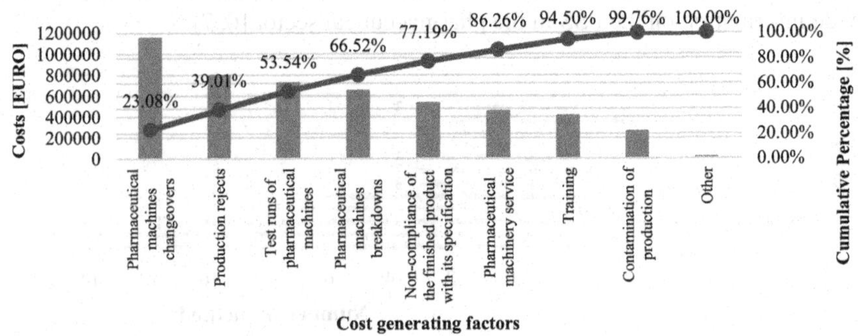


**Fig. 2.** Pareto-Lorenz analysis - problems causing losses for the user of pharmaceutical machines.

Despite its experience and tradition, the pharmaceutical company struggles with many problems during production. The implemented improvements are aimed at reducing losses, but not always these actions bring the expected results. In order to illustrate their diagnosis, the Pareto-Lorenz analysis was used (Fig. 2). The losses presented in the figure are very characteristic of the analyzed sector. The problem with the greatest losses is the retooling of pharmaceutical machines.

The workshops also allowed to identify the needs of the manufacturer of pharmaceutical products related to the machine. The needs relate to four main areas: machine purchase, training, drug production process, and sanitary and hygienic requirements (Table 2).

**Table 2.** The needs of a pharmaceutical company and pharmaceutical machine manufacturer

| | Purchase of the machine | Training | Drug production process | Sanitary and hygienic requirements |
|---|---|---|---|---|
| Pharmaceutical company | Elimination of high purchase costs | Operator training related to new machines | Support for the production process | Meeting the sanitary and hygienic requirements for pharmaceutical production |
| | Full machine service | Training of new employees | Error diagnosis | Adequate protection of production workers |
| Pharmaceutical machine manufacturer | Payment schedule | Information about needed training and schedules | Collection of data on the operation of the machine | Reporting changes |
| | Declaration of the period of use of the machine | Cooperation with human resources | Constant contact with the company | Information about the problems and difficulties of the enterprise |

## 4.2 Interest in Machine User Services and Product-Service System Design for Pharmaceutical Industry

At this stage, the service preferences of the pharmaceutical company were examined. The study covered the company's employees. All the services the machine user is interested in have been sorted and presented in the table below. Preferred services will be an intangible component of the PSS. This is to adjust the designed PSS to the requirements of the machine user. Additionally, it is aimed at complete elimination or reduction of emerging problems. At this stage, the user company confirmed its interest in the PSS with the machine rental option.

Based on the obtained service preferences and suggestions from other participants of the workshops, the PSS was developed (Fig. 3, Table 4). The main material component is a pharmaceutical production machine. The intangible component is a user-preferred service (Table 3).

**Table 3.** Services an enterprise that uses pharmaceutical machinery is interested in.

| Services related to a pharmaceutical machine | Services related to a Drug manufacturing | Services related to health and safety at work | Additional services |
|---|---|---|---|
| Delivery, installation, commissioning | Cleaning and washing format parts | Advice, consultations and training in pharmaceutical law | Audits |
| Diagnostics and troubleshooting | Data visualization on cards and boards | Noise reduction | Disposal of protective materials |
| Financial services | Giving the right shape to products | Optimization of the supply of protective materials | Integration of data visualization on cards and boards |
| Machine software update | OEE analysis and optimization | Optimization of work ergonomics | Lean tools |
| Maintenance and inspection | Optimization and standardization of working time | Optimizing job matching | Optimization and standardization of working time |
| Monitoring, machine operation | Optimization of changeovers of format parts | Safety certificates and sets of standards used in pharmaceutical production | Optimizing the use of utilities (water, air, electricity) |
| Rent | Optimizing the supply of raw materials and materials | Security checks | Take-bake |
| Repair shop equipment | Packing and cost optimization of packaging materials | Sterilization | |
| Service agreement | Quality control of finished products | Training | |
| Supply of spare parts | Training and integration | Waste disposal | |
| Training | Waste disposal | | |
| Updating (reconstruction, modernization) of the machine | | | |
| Warranty | | | |
| Washing and cleaning | | | |

In the developed PSS, the manufacturer retains ownership of the machine that is made available to the user. With the machine, the user receives services tailored to his needs. The manufacturer charges a monthly fee depending on the work performed by the machine. The machine user needs to work with the machine and produce as many products as possible, not to have it. After the agreed period of use, the pharmaceutical production machine will be reconditioned and made available again. The customer also chooses whether he wants to get a new or reconditioned machine.

In this case, the manufacturer obtains financial benefits both on the pharmaceutical machine and the related services. The solution enables the manufacturer to have constant access and analysis of the machine's operation. The data collected thanks to this will be used by the manufacturer in the design of new generations of machines and the regeneration of used machines. In addition, it will allow for the efficient replacement of elements that wear out quickly and do not keep precisely defined parameters.

Thanks to this model, the pharmaceutical company does not spend a lot of money on the machine. It is no longer concerned with service and repair, so she can concentrate on her core business. In addition, thanks to the services throughout the life of the machine,

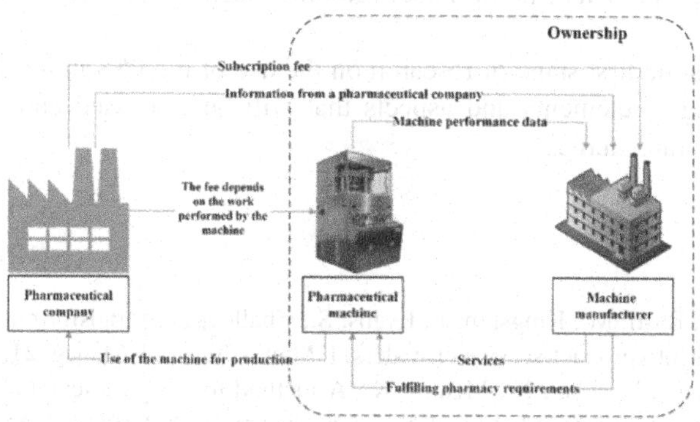


**Fig. 3.** Product-service system concept for the pharmaceutical industry

**Table 4.** Product-service system for the pharmaceutical industry - assumptions

<table>
<tr><td>Ownership</td><td colspan="2">The manufacturer is the owner</td><td colspan="2">The pharmaceutical company is a user</td></tr>
<tr><td>Sale</td><td colspan="4">Subscription depends on the operation of the machine</td></tr>
<tr><td>Services</td><td colspan="2">A set of services tailored to the user's needs</td><td colspan="2">Services divided into packages</td></tr>
<tr><td>Benefits for the producer</td><td rowspan="2">Co-creating solutions and improving relationships</td><td>Machine performance data</td><td>Machine reuse</td><td>Environmental Protection</td></tr>
<tr><td>Customer benefits</td><td>Focus on the development of new drugs</td><td>Elimination of costs related to the purchase and maintenance of the machine</td><td>Faster enterprise development</td></tr>
</table>

it receives technical support regarding the production process and meeting the sanitary criteria set for this industry.

## 5 Discussion and Conclusion

The industrial workshops presented in the paper illustrate the collaboration between a company selling machines (manufacturer's representative), a pharmaceutical company and scientists to co-design effective PSS solutions for the pharmaceutical sector. Cooperation as presented in the article and learning about the requirements and problems of the machine user is an important point that should be taken into account in the design of the PSS.

The developed solution will be an impulse for the development of small and medium-sized pharmaceutical companies, which usually have problems with the purchase of new machines. On the other hand, large enterprises will be able to concentrate on developing new products. The framework of the PSS presented in the article shows close cooperation between enterprises throughout the life of a pharmaceutical production machine. This is an important fact that will be helpful in developing machine usage scenarios in a specific enterprise.

The paper is the first stage of research on the use of the PSS in the pharmaceutical sector. It highlights elements and aspects that will be discussed and analyzed more extensively in future studies.

## References


1. Martinez, V., Bastl, M., Kingston, J., Evans, S.: Challenges in transforming manufacturing organisations into product-service providers. J. Manuf. Technol. Manag. **21**, 449–469 (2010)
2. Andriankaja, H., Boucher, X., Medini, K.: A method to design integrated product-service systems based on the extended functional analysis approach. CIRP J. Manuf. Sci. Technol. **21**, 120–139 (2018)
3. Annarelli, A., Battistella, C., Nonino, F.: Product service system: a conceptual framework from a systematic review. J. Clean. Prod. **139**, 1011–1032 (2016)
4. Baines, T., Lightfoot, H.: Servitization in the aircraft industry: understanding advanced services and the implications of their delivery. In: Lay, G. (ed.) Servitization in Industry, pp. 45–54. Springer, Cham (2014). https://doi.org/10.1007/978-3-319-06935-7_3
5. Salwin, M., Kraslawski, A., Lipiak, J., Gołębiewski, D., Andrzejewski, M.: Product-service system business model for printing houses. J. Clean. Prod. **274**, 122939 (2020).
6. Salwin, M., Kraslawski, A.: State-of-the-art in product-service system classification. In: Ivanov, V., Trojanowska, J., Pavlenko, I., Zajac, J., Peraković, D. (eds.) DSMIE 2020. LNME, pp. 187–200. Springer, Cham (2020). https://doi.org/10.1007/978-3-030-50794-7_19
7. Salwin, M., Kraslawski, A., Lipiak, J.: State-of-the-art in product-service system design. In: Panuwatwanich, K., Ko, C.-H. (eds.) The 10th International Conference on Engineering, Project, and Production Management. Springer Singapore, pp. 645–658 (2020). https://doi.org/10.1007/978-981-15-1910-9
8. Annarelli, A., Battistella, C., Nonino, F.: Competitive advantage implication of different product service system business models: consequences of 'not-replicable' capabilities. J. Clean. Prod. **247**, 119–121 (2020)

9. Li, A.Q., Kumar, M., Claes, B., Found, P.: The state-of-the-art of the theory on product-service systems. Int. J. Prod. Econ. **222**, 107491 (2020). https://doi.org/10.1016/j.ijpe.2019.09.012
10. Vezzoli, C., Kohtala, C., Srinivasan, A., Diehl, J.C.: Product-service system design for sustainability. Green Leaf, Sheffield (2014)
11. Lim, C.-H., Kim, K.-J., Hong, Y.-S., Park, K.: PSS Board: a structured tool for product–service system process visualization. J. Clean. Prod. **37**, 42–53 (2012)
12. Gaiardelli, P., et al.: Product-service systems evolution in the era of Industry 4.0. Serv. Bus. **15**(1), 177–207 (2021). https://doi.org/10.1007/s11628-021-00438-9
13. Medini, K., Boucher, X.: Value chain configuration for PSS delivery – evidence from an innovative sector for sludge treatment. CIRP J. Manuf. Sci. Technol. **12**, 14–24 (2016)
14. European Federation of Pharmaceutical Industries and Associations: The pharmaceutical industry in figures. Key Data 2020 (2020)
15. Top national pharmaceutical markets by revenue 2019. https://www.statista.com/statistics/266469/revenues-of-the-top-10-global-pharmaceutical-markets/. Accessed 27 Jan 2021
16. Eurostat - Data Explorer. https://appsso.eurostat.ec.europa.eu/nui/show.do?dataset=sbs_na_ind_r2&lang=en. Accessed 27 Jan 2021

# Smart Product Service System: Process Value Model in the Framework 3DCE

Thecle Alix[1(✉)] and Gregory Zacharewicz[2]

[1] Arts et Métiers Institute of Technology, I2M Bordeaux, 33400 Talence, France
thecle.alix@ensam.eu

[2] Laboratoire Des Sciences des Risques (LSR), IMT Mines Ales, 6 Avenue de Clavières, 30319 Alès Cedex, France

**Abstract.** The world industrial economy has turned into an economy of service over the past two decades. Evidence can be easily found, such as the shift of more and more manufacturers from traditional product-centered logic towards a service-centered logic. Transactional business models are evolving towards recurring revenue models, which raises questions about the new value proposition to be met. The addition of complementary services to the product to maintain, among other things, the performance of assets throughout the whole PSS life cycle presents both an opportunity and a complexity. To make this integration sustainable, we suggest operationalizing the PSS concept so that the value proposition is customer oriented, considering simultaneously the engineering of the offering, the processes, and the support network. We suggest developing scenarios of new value propositions based on service value process models. Our contribution will present a three-dimensional engineering framework as well as a service process value model.

**Keywords:** Process value model · Smart product service system · Three dimensional concurrent engineering · Customer orientation

## 1 Introduction

Sustainable development has become a priority issue for manufacturing companies since: their commitment to a responsible policy aiming to avoid waste and resources overconsumption, rare and precious metals real criticality consideration, individual and collective awareness to reduce both one's own waste and environmental footprint, etc. Consequently, many challenges raise: which offer for which customer? how to do more with less? how to do better with less globally? how to adapt the offer to individual and collective usage which evolves over time? which business model for which product? how to eco-design? how to increase eco-circularity? etc.

Product Service Systems (PSS) defined as integrated solutions of services and goods based on the sale of a performance in use or a usage and not on the simple sale of goods" [1, 2], linked to modular eco-designed systems supported by specific business model, are a first step to reduce the renewable rate of products/service consumption in


Published by Springer Nature Switzerland AG 2021
L. M. Camarinha-Matos et al. (Eds.): PRO-VE 2021, IFIP AICT 629, pp. 494–505, 2021.
https://doi.org/10.1007/978-3-030-85969-5_46

the society–rather measured at a micro economic level, and for specific sectors. Other strategies, such as the 10 R strategies, are in progress to emphasize circular economy and intensify the use or expand the life of products or material, or recover products [3]. They allow preserving the value of the products. In general, product design needs to be thought in a comprehensive way, encompassing production processes, logistics systems, consumption patterns and lifestyles. The development of IOT and ICT plays in important role in the implementation of the 10 R strategies, enabling the collection of customer behavioral data in real time and thus to renegotiate service level agreement based on real usage or to manage maintenance, etc. [4]. PSS, IOT and ICT association is currently implemented in what is called Smart PSS solutions. While promoting many advantages, Smart PSS still question on their effectiveness to satisfy the sustainable character and thus their design remains prevalent to promote sustainability [4, 5].

PSS design must encompass the compatibility and overlap of some components (subassemblies of the system) addressed to the consumer, and the processes supporting the design, manufacture, and provision of this offer. Both PSS design framework and smart PSS design framework have been proposed in the literature which mostly focus on the offering, sometimes on the coupling process, sometimes on the supporting network organization but rarely on these three dimensions simultaneously [6–8]. Modularity in PSS design is also exploited but only considering the offering dimension and not yet the support organization. To address such concerns, a three-dimensional PSS design framework is proposed in this paper based on a modular approach of products, services, and resources (industrial partners) or production resources used to support the offering production and delivery.

The following section reviews several useful notions and concepts to address the scope of our study. Section 3 reviews the design challenges that guided the key principles of the framework. The implementation and operationalization of the framework is presented in Sects. 4 and 5. Finally, the paper ends with a conclusion that highlights the main points of the proposed framework and the directions for future work.

## 2 Problem Statement

The above-mentioned definition of PSS emphasises the sustainability of a solution developed to satisfy customers' requirements through a high value-added offering that favour companies' profit [1]. The concept of PSS has taken shape through several typologies linked to different coupling between the products and the services and to different business models. The satisfaction mentioned in the definition and primarily linked to the customers has been extended over the years to all stakeholders. The sustainability discussed initially based on environmental concerns has gradually integrated social and economic dimensions and is trying to consider the whole system lifecycle. The potential for added value has been opened to users and all stakeholders of these systems through the development of personalised e-services. All these evolutions, for which the core concepts are outlined hereafter, have a significant impact in the assumptions and structuring of the design framework we propose.

## 2.1 PSS and Smart Typologies and Representation

The first recognized typology distinguishes three types of PSS: product-oriented PSS, use-oriented PSS and result-oriented PSS [9]. The difference between them concerns the offer dominant logic and the associated business model. This typology drawbacks are: first, the unrepresentative of the possibilities found in practice and, second that it is no more representative of the market evolution: customers' requirements and sustainable concerns. The classification proposed by Van Ostaeyen [10] distinguishes PSS based on: the performance orientation of the dominant revenue mechanism and the degree of integration between product and service elements. This typology question the coupling between the product and the service to determine if the service is supported by the product or added to the product or to the service expected by the product as a tangible support. Accordingly, the delivery mode can be constrained and the offering component proper existing conditions challenged. More recently Aas et al. [11] have proposed a typology with eight categories relevant in the digital era delineated in conjunction with the business models relates to the suppliers' ownership of delivered products degree, the smartness of the services provided degree and the performance orientation of contracts degree. This typology is more suitable with Smart PSS, the link to the business model is explicit, and the features of the service are considered. But the product and service coupling that can be a weakness regarding the sustainable concerns.

Smart services can be viewed as the combination of: (1) products: i.e., tangible supports for functional services inherent to the products, that cannot be sold independently; (2) support services: services linked to physical supports/functional services allowing to preserve its initial performance that cannot be sold separately; (3) additional services: pure service existing by themselves that can be sold separately. These services can be online (e-service) or offline. IoT can be used to help users or solution providers to better manage the product (e.g., maintenance) or to optimize its performance (e.g., energy management). It is also possible to imagine helping the system provider to design more reliable systems through, for example, feedback on incidents that have occurred during use. E-services as defined by Casati [12], are an "application accessible via the web, providing a set of functionalities to companies or individuals or viewed as a component provided by an organization to be assembled and reused in a distributed environment on the Internet". For their implementation, product support infrastructures are needed. These infrastructures may be other PSS or smart PSS solutions created to meet other primary needs. IOT + ICT can be used to propose either support or additional service.

Figure 1 summarizes the evolution from product to Smart PSS and the underlying typology.

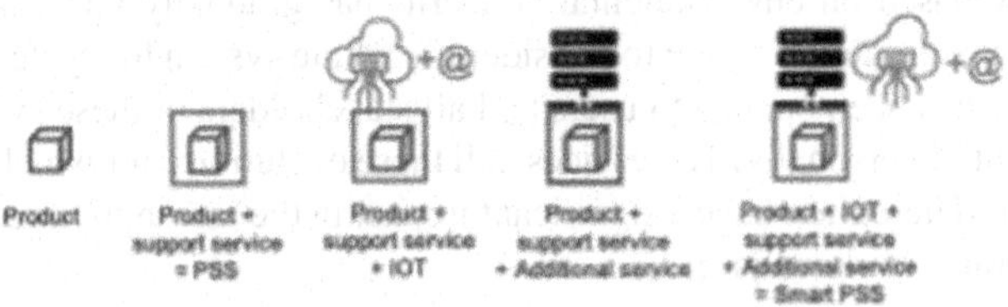


**Fig. 1.** From product to smart PSS.

### 2.2 Smart PSS as a Lever to Respond to Stakeholders' Sustainability Concerns

Smart PSS solution are intended to be sustainable as their predecessors should be, either for customers and providers. Indeed, whatever the business model, customer usage needs satisfaction remains at the heart of the initial offer to which can be added services to ensure the tangible supports for functional services performance preservation if possible (e.g., maintenance). In the latter case, advantage may be: to anticipate failures before they occur and thus reduce the downtime or, to avoid excessive maintenance due to major failures in case he would own the solution. In the case where the owner of the solution is the provider, feedbacks obtained from remote sensors allow, in the case of maintenance, to anticipate or to remain in control operations and thus to replace just what is necessary, or even, for a defective solution that should leave the market, to imagine the R4 to R9 strategies. These strategies show that Smart PSS are high added value solutions for different stakeholders: users, providers, the society, or politicians, regarding their injunctions to reduce waste, minimize the consumption of natural resources and reduce energy consumption.

Smart PSS can be a lever for environmental performance if they are designed considering the potential they represent and if the support infrastructures for their design, production, provision, use and end-of-life treatment exist and are rationalized. To help achieve this objective, several requirements derived from [7] need to be considered (Table 1). As can be seen, the offer reconfigurability to adapt over time to the usage needs and to satisfy the customer in the long term is a common requirement to both the user and the provider of the solution.

**Table 1.** Stakeholder's requirements regarding a Smart PSS offering (derived from 7).

| requirement | customer / user | provider | society | politicians |
|---|---|---|---|---|
| response to functional requirements | X | X | | |
| quality of user experience | X | | | |
| customised offering | X | | | |
| reconfigurable offer | X | X | | |
| market drivers | | X | X | |
| economical dimension | X | X | X | X |
| social dimension | X | X | X | X |
| environemental dimension | X | X | X | X |
| good compromise between cost, quality and time | X | X | | |
| technological innovation | X | X | | |
| e-service proposition | X | X | | |
| safety and reliability | X | X | | |

### 2.3 From Smart PSS to Smart Reconfigurable PSS

Reconfigurable systems have been around for a long time now. The well-known are Reconfigurable Manufacturing Systems (RMS), defined as being able to quickly change their structure, as well as their hardware and software components, to quickly adjust to new production needs. To do so, RMS are designed based on predefined equipment components that can be rearranged, moved and replaced quickly using the following principles: modularity, scalability, integrability, convertibility, reliability, maintainability and customization [13]. Considering the definition and typology of Smart PSS and the requirements set out in Table 1, a Smart PSS can be viewed as a new type of reconfigurable system which must obey the same rules of rapid adaptation to needs, i.e. usage needs and not production needs. In any case, the adaptation must be quick and with the least effort. We thus propose to use modularity, key concept of RMS to design Smart and sustainable PSS [14].

Modularity concept has already been used to design PSS [15, 16]. Here we assume that the design of Smart PSS will be based on the composition of products and services functional units, assembled to obtain a sustainable composition, considering all the requirements above-mentioned. Smart PSS instrumentation allows to consider two different cases: one involved in the design of the initial solution and the other involved in the redesign or adjustment of this solution to the customer's usage needs over time.

In the first case, the choice of products, support services and additional services can be personalized and the whole can be instrumented according to the customer's needs, defined based on the desired uses and the accessible product support infrastructures.

In the second case, since usage information can be collected either through direct interaction with the customer or through direct feedback from sensors integrated into the initial offer, the system can be augmented or reduced in functionality. The use of modularity is, in this case, a key element to increase or decrease the functional scope of the physical part of the PSS and thus improve PSS sustainability as it allows to reach the highest level of the 10 R strategies. Reconfigurability through modularity has an advantage for scalable solution design, able to meet users' needs over the long term, provided that the user can explicit his needs when designing the first offer. For this, we suggest a co-design user-provider of the offer.

## 2.4 User-Provider Smart Reconfigurable PSS Co-design

A customized solution, co-designed by the user and the provider at the outset and adapted to changes in usage throughout the link between the solution and its user, ensures a high value-added solution for these two stakeholders. This is because the system is then adapted to the most demanding requirements and its unused components can be reused by the provider to meet the needs of other customers. This opportunity is part of the Corporate Social Responsibility (CSR) and on the way in which organisations make a PSS offer available to their clients, other objectives such as the search for quick profitability compromise the sustainability of the offers proposed. Several drawbacks emerge in this context: the needs to which the PSS respond are sometimes unclear, the scope of the related service system is poorly defined and the impact of the definition of the service system on its components poorly qualified and quantified. These facts generate problems of mismatch between specifications and needs, service delivered, and service wanted, cost and value, or services offered and uses of services, which negatively impact on the objectives of the companies. This is reinforced in a multi-organisational context because the difficulty is not only to propose a coherent offer, but also to analyse the compatibility of the processes and the logistical network supporting this offer throughout its life cycle, while guaranteeing the satisfaction of all its stakeholders. The co-design user-provider allows to have a customer centric approach recognised by several authors as allowing the delivery of higher service quality and enhancement of customer satisfaction [17].

Based on all the considerations presented in part 2, we propose in the next section the design challenges and principles on which we propose to build the three-dimensional framework for Smart reconfigurable PSS design.

## 3 Design Challenges and Framework

The design framework is based on the simultaneous engineering of product, process and supporting infrastructure. The product is here extended to Smart PSS. The requirements that drive this design are those presented in Table 1. Interaction with the customer is heard throughout the design process, i.e., until the best compromise between all expectations is found. The processes here are the support processes for the design, manufacturing and implementation of the Smart PSS consisting of the product, the supporting and additional services, and the associated technologies. The supporting infrastructure is considered as being made up of all the partners constituting the supply chain required for the design, realization, provision, maintenance in operational conditions and treatment at the end of the product's life (Fig. 2).

The principle of modularity consists in assuming the smart PSS as an arrangement of functional units of products and services. Therefore, as soon as the needs are expressed, an analysis of the functional units of the library formed by solution providers is carried out to see whether units are available. Three scenarios can occur:

- all the necessary units exist without a variant. An analysis then consists in simulating the coupling and comparing the solutions on the basis of criteria classically used in reconfigurability analysis (time, difficulty of coupling, etc.).
- all the necessary units are present with a variant, the analysis then consists of simulating the coupling and comparing the solutions on the basis of criteria classically used in reconfigurability analysis. Once the choice is done, a double analysis of process compatibility and support networks design can be carried out.
- some elements are missing and. In this case, either the requirements must be revised or a solution must be found through innovation.

In case there is no process compatibility or the support network design is not feasible; the offering must be modified (Fig. 3). The metrics proposed to ensure the sustainability of the offer and stakeholders satisfaction, the tools as well as the methods allowing to perform the different sub activities contained in the three main ones are further detailed in [7]. It corresponds to the first case of the initial design of the offer but does not exclude other phases related to the redesign of adapted offers over time. Indeed, it will then be a question of analyzing the additional modules desired or those to be removed and of redesigning the adapted offer by checking the compatibility of the processes and supporting infrastructures as initially. Obviously, a digital twin of the PSS, processes and supporting infrastructures would be useful in carrying out tests, particularly about the complexity of coupling.

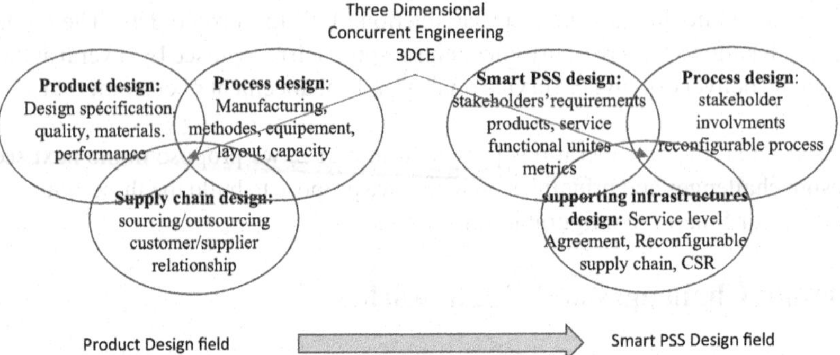


**Fig. 2.** 3DCE Smart reconfigurable PSS principles, adapted from (6).

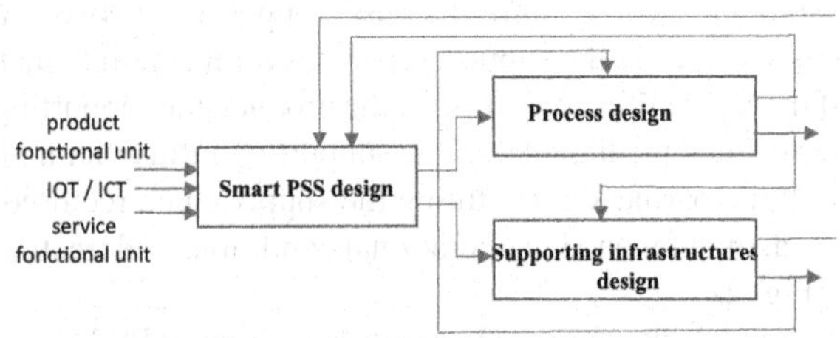


**Fig. 3.** 3DCE dynamic.

# 4 Framework Implementation

## 4.1 Modeling Process Approaches and PSS

In [18], the authors introduce the basic principle of a service delivery, that is an interaction within a service provider/consumer pair oriented from the provider to the consumer. The intensity of the service delivered grows in the same way as a parameter that characterizes the provider/consumer pair. A provider is identified by his function and is noted P. A consumer is characterized by his need. Of course, an object cannot be limited to being a provider or a consumer. Therefore, it is generally considered that objects can behave simultaneously as both. The initial principle presents an object as a single provider or consumer of services. Clearly, a complex object can provide and/or consume several services. Consequently, an object can be a provider/consumer of several services. The service provision relationships then become more complex, i.e., each relationship is defined for a given service. An object is then part of a series of services, linked to another object upstream as a service consumer and to an object downstream as a service provider. The authors proposed to call the "object" providing or demanding the service a "service agent" or, in short, a "sergeant".

## 4.2 Modeling of Behavior, Functions, and Data

Indeed, the service modelling also requires the modelling of the interactions between multiple services; this process can lead very quickly to a significant level of complexity from a static point of view and even more in a dynamic view. Proposed in previous works [19] a first tentative to represent service in simulation. We therefore focus in this paper on the establishing operations for a single service coupling in the G-DEVS formalism [20]. This discrete formalism is selected because of its formal property and its time management capability. We propose to model each service component through a G-DEVS model based on attributes. The model attributes are described from a qualitative and quantitative point of view and all elements (actors and material) that interact within its environment are required. New Smart PSS design and development is based on a strategic analysis whose objective is to define lines of innovation while keeping sustainability as core concern. Most of the time, innovations are incremental -series of small steps -as enterprises find ways to update their products and processes or to integrate basic services. Simulation principle is to analyze the possibility that new functionalities supplement a PSS existing one while receiving benefits, if any, of components already used to fill these existing functionalities. Specifically, the assembly of components can be simulated to measure their capacity to easily interact and to cope with the customers' need and use, with the manufacturers 'profit expectations and with the environmental incentive. The simulation of scenario tests can give clue to manufacturers to develop and set up a win-win strategy with their customers, and environment.

### 4.3 Service Process and Service Process Value Model

Service process is an important part of service as it is the operational workflow for service delivery. The execution of service processes is respecting an SLA between service provider and customer. The SLA specifies the requirements of the customer used to monitor and verify the contract. Under the SLA, the candidate service elements of each service can be divided into different service set, and the service process reaching customer's requirements can be constructed quickly. As described by Zhou in [21], for the same requirement of the customer, under different SLA constraints, the service provider can select different service elements to form different service processes.

According to Zhou [21], Service value is a common metric recognized by the stakeholders of a service, the service requester, and the service providers. System requirements of smart PSS toward customer needs and co-creative value propositions Several parties have to contribute to co-create value in a collaborative production to meet an overall value expectation [4]. However, in general, different PSS actors can have different PSS value expectations [5]. Therefore, value is multidimensional, and an actor's expectation of value may contain only some of these dimensions. Because of the different concerns, each person may define their values from different dimensions. For example, value can be defined from the economic point of view, ownership of the product, the economy of resources used and the customer experience, etc. Three dimensions were used to define service value: time and space, profit, and experience in [21]. The time and space dimension refers to the requirements of creating service value in time and space, which can only be achieved by meeting the requirements. Service value is strongly related to the activities in the service process. Time and space dimension reflects the time consumption and location/status changes in activities.

The profit dimension refers to the different benefits obtained by actors in the service activity, including economic benefits, physical products ownership, information obtained, etc. It is related to the service actors since each actor in the service process, including the customer, benefits from it.

The experience dimension refers to the intangible value or impact of service process or service results, including corporate reputation, social impact, customer satisfaction, experience, and skills, etc. Experience dimension is related to the effect of service process or result.

The sustainability dimension must be considered in the early design phase to reduce potential failure to meet the environmental and social requirements in delivery stage. However, according to [22], the existing PSS evaluation frameworks consider less about characteristics of digitalization and smartness.

In addition, in the design process of smart PSS [23], since the creation of value is inseparable from the use of smart resources, the resources need to be extended to smart objects, tools, materials, products, data, etc. The operationalization of the 3DCE framework in the context of Smart PSS consists in adding the process and value dimensions.

## 5 Framework Operationalization

### 5.1 Smart PSS Value

Smart PSS value includes the profit and usage dimensions that refer to the benefits obtained by actors in the service activity. Since Smart PSS, it adds the sustainability dimension [22] as a core global benefit since it reduces the environmental and social impact. Obviously, it is related to the service actors involved since each actor in the service process must contribute in a sustainable way and/or benefits from it.

Then, the experience dimension refers to the intangible value or impact of service process or service results, including corporate reputation, social impact, customer satisfaction, experience, and skills, etc. Experience dimension is related to the effect of service process or result. The PSS user experience dimension is increasingly important in the service and digital domain (in digital domain it is known as UX, i.e., User Experience). It corresponds to the way a service is perceived by its users or the customers. The user experience includes several criteria that are not yet extensively defined but literature up to now. It can include criteria such as ergonomics, usage, and satisfaction. In addition, in the process of PSS, the creation of value is inextricable from the use of resources. These resources can be human, materials, data, such as described in MDISE [24].

### 5.2 Smart PSS Service Process

In the proposed approach, a smart PSS is composed of different service elements coming either from a library (Fig. 4 top left side), such as described in sergeant approach, which represent specific activities or tasks in the service process or service to be created on demand. Hence, each service process is composed of different activities organized in workflows (Fig. 4 middle left side), which are executed by resources (Fig. 4 bottom left side) to complete the whole service. In the service process described in Fig. 4 right side, each activity needs to be fulfilled by at least one actor that can be human, including customer, service provider and participant and artefact or digital support form IT. By participating in the activities, resources (co-)create value, exchange value, and meet their own value expectations. Workflows are picked from library or created on demand according to the specification of customer needs.

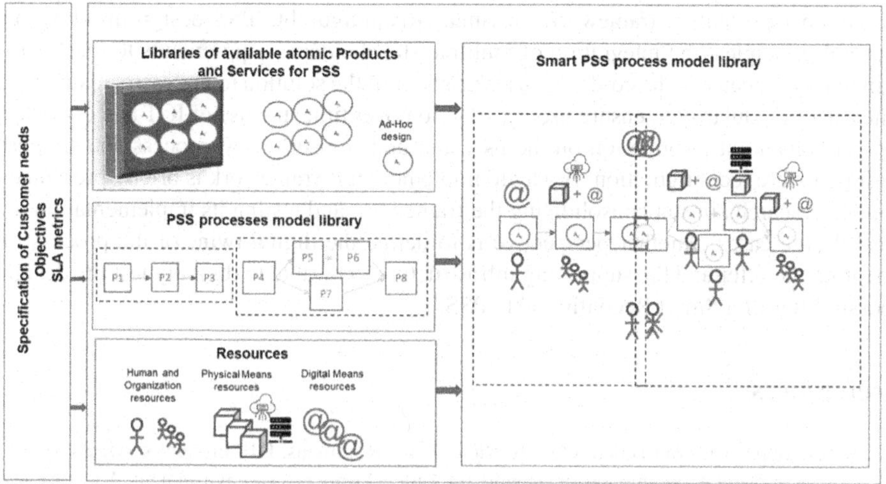


**Fig. 4.** Coupled approach mixing product and service for Smart PSS.

## 5.3 Smart PSS Process Value Model

The user experience and sustainability are central element in mixing product and digital content in the building of Smart PSS process value. The goal is to create the most fluid and frugal pairing possible between the product, service, and user through a PSS and potentially a web-based data collection form IoT for smart PSS such as described in the Fig. 3 right side. The idea is, when pairing process, to limit the overlap between functionalities and resource used at the frontier of PSS subcomponents connection. A fluid connection of services and its smart support generates less consumption of resources and make much easier the smart PSS usage, reduces the impact on the environment and can increase loyalty of customer, as it is the case in buying and using physical products. In a chaotic e-service where it is almost impossible to find, produce and provide what the user is looking for or in slow PSS delivery; the potential customer will not be inclined to proceed to the PSS usage. On the contrary, in an ergonomic and aesthetic service delivery approach, the same customer will be much more likely to spend time there and to proceed to the act of service usage. The main causes of unpleasantness that spoil the user experience are usability issues that prevent from non-expert to use it, bugs that start over the service during run time, non-intuitive usage that slow down the access to the service, information not found that demotivate to reuse the service. Users who leave the e-service support frustrated are unlikely to try again on the same PSS, so they will naturally go to its competitors. Therefore, the contribution proposed will contribute to monitor the user experience on the service delivery process and applications and make it a central element of the PSS digital strategy.

## 6 Conclusion and Future Works

This paper presents a framework for Smart Reconfigurable PSS design that lays on several principles: the integration of multiple stakeholders' requirements to reach sustainability objectives, the co-design user/provider of the solution to increase satisfaction, the use of modularity to ensure user satisfaction over time, the use of IOT and e-service to get behavioral information on the user and update user' SLA, process and support infrastructure reconfiguration. A way to implement this framework is briefly presented. Future research aims at consolidating the framework and testing its implementation on real design cases. Another perspective is to define the digital twins of the process of creating the offer and the supporting infrastructure to be able to digitally test the design possibilities of a Smart Reconfigurable PSS.

## References


1. Goedkoop, M.J., Van Halen, C.J., Te Riele, H.R., Rommens, P.J.: Product service systems, ecological and economic basics. Report for Dutch Ministries of environment (VROM) and economic affairs (EZ), vol. 36, pp. 1–122 (1999)
2. Vuidel, P., Pasquelin, B.: ADEME: vers une économie de la fonctionnalité à haute valeur environnementale et sociale - Synthèse (2017)
3. Potting, J., Hekkert, M.P., Worrell, E., Hanemaaijer, A.: Circular Economy: Measuring Innovation in the Product Chain. PBL Publishers, Sydney (2017)
4. Liu, Z., Ming, X., Qiu, S., Qu, Y., Zhang, X.: A framework with hybrid approach to analyse system requirements of smart PSS toward customer needs and co-creative value propositions. Comput. Ind. Eng. **139**, 105776 (2020)
5. Li, X., Wang, Z., Chen, C.-H., Zheng, P.: A data-driven reversible framework for achieving Sustainable Smart product-service systems. J. Cleaner Product. **279**, 123618 (2021)
6. Watanabe, K., Okuma, T., Takenaka, T.: Evolutionary design framework for Smart PSS: service engineering approach. Adv. Eng. Inform. **45**, 101119 (2020)
7. Guan, H., Alix, T., Bourrieres, J.-P.: An integrated design framework for virtual enterprise-based customer-oriented product-service systems. Procedia CIRP **83**, 198–203 (2019). https://doi.org/10.1016/j.procir.2019.03.143
8. Coba, C.M., Boucher, X., Gonzalez-Feliu, J., Vuillaume, F., Gay, A.: Towards a risk-oriented Smart PSS Engineering framework. Procedia CIRP **93**, 753–758 (2020)
9. Tukker, A.: Eight types of product–service system: eight ways to sustainability? Experiences from SusProNet. Bus. Strateg. Environ. **13**, 246–260 (2004)
10. Van Ostaeyen, J., Van Horenbeek, A., Pintelon, L., Duflou, J.R.: A refined typology of product–service systems based on functional hierarchy modeling. J. Clean. Prod. **51**, 261–276 (2013)
11. Aas, T.H., Breunig, K.J., Hellström, M.M., Hydle, K.M.: Service-oriented business models in manufacturing in the digital era: toward a new taxonomy. Int. J. Innov. Manage. **24**(8), 2040002 (2020)

12. Casati, F., Shan, M.C., Georgakopoulos, D.: Special Issue on E-services. Springer, New York (2001)
13. Koren, Y., Gu, X., Guo, W.: Reconfigurable manufacturing systems: principles, design, and future trends. Front. Mech. Eng. **13**(2), 121–136 (2017). https://doi.org/10.1007/s11465-018-0483-0
14. Sonego, M., Echeveste, M.E.S., Debarba, H.G.: The role of modularity in sustainable design: a systematic review. J. Clean. Prod. **176**, 196–209 (2018)
15. Wang, P.P., Ming, X.G., Li, D., Kong, F.B., Wang, L., Wu, Z.Y.: Modular development of product service systems. Concurr. Eng. **19**, 85–96 (2011). https://doi.org/10.1177/1063293X11403508
16. Sun, J., Chai, N., Pi, G., Zhang, Z., Fan, B.: Modularization of product service system based on functional requirement. Procedia CIRP **64**, 301–305 (2017)
17. Guan, H.: An integrated design framework for Customer-Oriented PSS based on Three-Dimensional Concurrent Engineering (2019)
18. Alix, T., Zacharewicz, G., Vallespir, B.: Service systems modeling and simulation: the sergent distributed approach. In: Mertins, K., Bénaben, F., Poler, R., Bourrières, J.-P. (eds.) Enterprise Interoperability VI. PIC, vol. 7, pp. 357–367. Springer, Cham (2014). https://doi.org/10.1007/978-3-319-04948-9_30
19. Alix, T., Zacharewicz, G.: Product-service systems scenarios simulation based on G-DEVS/HLA: generalized discrete event specification/high level architecture. Comput. Ind. **63**, 370–378 (2012)
20. Zacharewicz, G.: Generalized discrete event system specification: a state-of-the-art study. Simulation 0037549718777626 (2018)
21. Zhou, X., Zacharewicz, G., Chen, D., Chu, D.: A method for building service process value model based on process mining. Appl. Sci. **10**, 7311 (2020)
22. Liu, L., Song, W., Han, W.: How sustainable is smart PSS? An integrated evaluation approach based on rough BWM and TODIM. Adv. Eng. Inform. **43**, 101042 (2020)
23. Zheng, P., Xu, X., Trappey, A., Zhong, R.: Editorial notes: design innovation of smart PSS. Adv. Eng. Inform. **44**, 101069 (2020)
24. Zacharewicz, G., Daclin, N., Doumeingts, G., Haidar, H.: Model driven interoperability for system engineering. Modelling **1**, 94–121 (2020)

# Digital Platforms as Enablers of Smart Product-Service Systems

Henrique Silva[1(✉)] and António Lucas Soares[1,2]

[1] INESCTEC, Campus da FEUP, Rua Dr. Roberto Frias s/n, 4200-465 Porto, Portugal
{henrique.d.silva,antonio.l.soares}@inesctec.pt
[2] Department of Informatics Engineering, Faculty of Engineering, University of Porto, Porto, Portugal

**Abstract.** The impact of digital technologies in manufacturing organizations has been felt for decades. Servitization processes themselves have developed from the traditional Product-Service Systems (PSS) toward new business models infused with digital technologies, paving the way to smart PSS. There is, however, a lack of understanding of how digital platforms (DP) can be leveraged for the offering of smart service offerings. In this paper, we highlight how the emergence of DP traces the evolution of PSS and highlight how a platform-based modular architecture can serve as the reference infrastructure for organizations to deliver smart and highly customized products and services. The architecture of the Transformer 4.0 platform is used to demonstrate how DP can serve as orchestrators for an ecosystem of digital twin-driven smart PSS.

**Keywords:** Smart product-service system · Servitization · Digital platforms

## 1 Introduction

The impact of digital technologies in everyday life has been felt for decades [1] In the industrial realm, the Industry 4.0 (i4.0) phenomenon is proof that information technologies (IT) have changed the nature of products and services. While IT started by influencing internal organizational processes optimizing traditional product and service offerings, business model innovation, the emergence of new technologies, and evolving consumer expectations have pushed IT's place outwardly, encouraging companies towards servitization. Even the servitization process itself, that has impacted manufacturing companies for decades, and changed focuses toward new business models based on the bundling of products and services into Product-Service Systems (PSS) has been infused with digital technologies. Authors such as are now arguing for attention to the interplay between digitalization and servitization and how this connection paves the way for PSS embedding digital technologies into smart PSS.

A similar path can be traced for digital platforms (DP). Tracing their lineage to intraorganizational information systems, digital platforms (DP) have grown to become the infrastructure of digital ecosystems that are at the core of how (1) organizations


Published by Springer Nature Switzerland AG 2021
L. M. Camarinha-Matos et al. (Eds.): PRO-VE 2021, IFIP AICT 629, pp. 506–513, 2021.
https://doi.org/10.1007/978-3-030-85969-5_47

interact in cooperation, coordination and collaboration [2] and (2) in how services are provided to users. Previous studies have begun to suggest how manufacturing firms can leverage a platform approach to overcome some of servitization most common problems. There is, however, a lack of understanding in how digital platforms both support the development and selling of advanced, highly customized, smart product-service offerings and how they structure interactions and data flows between actors of the ecosystem.

In this paper, we highlight how the emergence of DP traces the evolution of PSS, focusing on how platform roles, elements of a platform ecosystem, and a platform-based modular architecture, in general, can serve as the reference infrastructure for organizations to deliver smart and highly customized products and services.

## 2 Theoretical Background

The servitization trend of manufacturing firms that shifted from the focus of industrial products to a strategy that provides a combination of products and services has been ongoing for decades [3]. This shift led to the emergence of new business models based, the so-called Product-Service Systems (PSS). Manufacturing organizations adopt a PSS approach to increase their revenues and enhance customer satisfaction [4] by improving efficiency [5] gaining access to new business opportunities and adding differentiation from competitors.

However, in today's highly competitive i4.0 context, a traditional servitization strategy and PSS-based business models do not automatically increase performance. They can even create obstacles that may lead to diminished revenues [6]. Studies such as [7] and [8] have shown that investment in extending service offerings leads to increased costs but frequently lacks in generating the expected higher returns. In fact, in a 2004 survey achieved, only a small percentage (21%) of firms reached what was considered a financial success after implementing a service strategy, with most companies abandoning their service strategy after a few years. All these factors point to manufacturer's necessity of deploying efficient mechanisms to exploit the benefits of servitization and deliver adapted product and services offerings with a clear strategy and competitive prices while assuring competitive levels of both customization and organizational efficiency.

Recent literature points to how digital technologies help manufacturers improve service offerings and reduce operational costs [9] and in particular, how digitalization and DP allow organizations to configure and deploy service implementations that offer levels of customization at a scale previously not achievable [7]. Although different terms have been used to define what is now more commonly called Smart PSS, a comprehensive definition is presented by [10]. The authors define Smart PSS as "an IT-driven value co-creation business strategy consisting of various stakeholders as the players, intelligent systems as the infrastructure, smart, connected products as the media and tools, and their generated e-services as the key values de-livered, that continuously strives to meet individual customer needs in a sustainable manner". Although, as pointed out by [1] there is still not a commonly agreed conceptual vision and framework for Smart PSS design and implementation, the implied interplay between intelligent digital technologies and service-based business models, is becoming crucial to accomplish a successful servitization model [11].

Although earlier conceptualizations of platform view these modular elements as "software products" [12, 13] (Baldwin et al. 2000; Sanchez and Mahoney 1996), others that analyze DP in manufacturing sectors go further into considering "product platforms" as sets of physical components [14, 15] or service platforms as sets of "service modules" [16]. On a formal level, [17] and [18] describe platform modularity as the decoupling of the platform and its addon functionalities plus the specifications of how these addon systems interact with the platform. This decoupling allows organizations to optimize offerings by: leveraging product and service modules in different offerings [19] allowing for the configuration of several offerings using different combinations of modules [20] and facilitating the creation of pre-defined sets of modules that make up a given service and make the customization process more agile. On the other hand, it is also important to highlight that a modular architecture may also present disadvantages for both the platform and platform-based PSS. On an implementation level, modularity comes at a cost [17], with most of it coming upfront in the platform design stages. This increased difficulty in the architecture design process may lead to significant heterogeneity in offerings [16, 20] and not lead to the expected operational efficiencies [21]. On a business level, the literature points to greater levels of modularity leading to an increased risk of imitation by rivals [22] and imposing additional costs on platform addon developers [17]. This cripples the potential development of the platform's ecosystem, hindering the long-term feasibility of the DP [23].

These factors point to the implementation of successful platform-based smart PSS resting primarily not on the anticipation of all requirements and dependencies to achieve a completely modular system but on finding the right balance of modularization for the offering in question. Research has even high-lighted that intermediate levels of modularity produce the most valuable innovations [24] and that how data and information components are handled is a more critical indicator into the successful implementation of advanced service offerings [4].

## 3 Digital Platforms for Servitization

Recent literature has offered two key insights into understanding how the characterization of the complex servitization process has been lacking. Authors such as [4], supported by [25], highlight how a predominant unidirectional view of the product to service continuum has been sup-planted by the customer's need of a full continuum of products and services. [1] direct attention to the interplay between the fields of servitization and digitalization [26, 27] looking to the bulk of literature on "digital servitization" starting from 2017 and highlight how the unknowns regarding convergence of digitalization and servitization, the linking between digital servitization and ecosystem management, and the DP impact on digital servitization strategies still outweigh what is found in the literature.

Taken together, these two insights provide a first understanding of how a platform-based approach might serve to alleviate some of the tensions that emerge with servitization. [17] summarizes the characteristics that differentiate platform ecosystems into four properties: (i) compressed evolution as the capacity of platforms to shorten the period required to observe different market dynamics; (ii) an evolutionary life cycle process that requires evolution and transformation to survive; (iii) the capacity to harness external disruptions; and (iv) the ability of architecture and governance to shape evolution. As architecture and governance are intrinsically tied in platform environments, shaping the two elements can be leveraged to mold a platform ecosystem's evolution.

The flexibility these four properties embed DP with has positioned them as the preferred infrastructure for developing a new paradigm of business models centered around customers, suppliers, and the developers' aggregation. The resulting ecosystem can generate externalities and synergies where the joint value creation is greater than the sum of the value created by individual businesses [28].

We argue that these four characteristics also play an essential role in implementing business models centered around smart PSS. Taking the perspective of a DP that manages and orchestrates the entire product/service lifecycle, we argue that a com-pressed evolution capacity allows firms to develop, deploy and validate these highly customized offerings with an efficiency that other infrastructures would not allow for. Furthermore, as described above, the power of modularity comes into play by giving the DP the ability to drop or implement different combinations of products and ser-vices according to current business requirements. This allows organizations to harness innovation and constantly develop solutions that can be plugged in with current products and services to improve both returns and efficiency.

The combination of the modularity of physical goods with the layered (and modular) architecture of software gives rise to architectures that, loosely coupled through standardized interfaces, lead to products open for new meanings after manufacture [29, 30]. This, in term, pushes the servitization process forward, further away from its linear continuum to an iterative and flexible process where data is gathered from products and services and further contributes to the improvement of the PSS.

## 4 Digital Twins Powering Smart PSS - the Transformer 4.0 Case

Current power transformer development processes are still traditional in nature, relying on document-based information exchange and a set of product lifecycle management (PLM) and simulation tools that are not interconnected. As such, an opportunity presents itself to implement a digital twin-based DP, which will enable the integration of information and data originating in various sources and offer services that streamline power transformer development and add value to the machine beyond its operation and maintenance. Our vision for the Digital Twin (DT) and the DT Enabled DP will be applied to the Power Transformer lifecycle in a Portuguese enterprise of the energy field, effectively shaping its technologies and processes to Industry 4.0 standards.

Based on [17] software four functional elements, the architecture of the Transformer 4.0 (TFR4.0) DP is divided into four components (Fig. 1): a data layer, that comprises both data storage and access, a tools layer, and an interface layer. Connecting these modular layers three abstraction tools are responsible for the orchestration of all components.

Placed at the core of the DP, the Digital Twin Orchestrator Engine (DTOE) is a crucial component for the management and orchestration of multiple instances of the DT. A direct link between platform services and the DTOE allows for a shorter latency

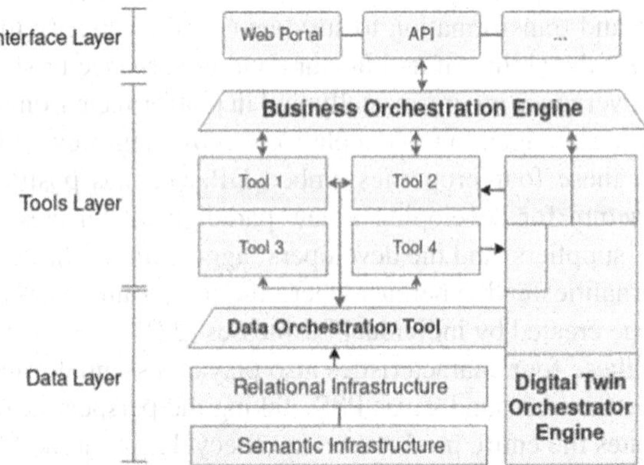


**Fig. 1.** TRF4.0 platform modular architecture

between platform services and the virtual and physical realities of products/services. This direct link benefits the management of the existing products while facilitating the development and prototyping of new products and services based on the twin. The DTOE is responsible for the dual role of: (i) centralizing the management of the DT components by providing the platform with structured interfaces for direct control, and thus influence both virtual and physical components of multiple instances of a product or service; and (ii) interface with the remaining data layer com-ponents to structure and integrate design and operational data and information.

A modular tools layer, built upon the DTOE, leverages the data and information available from the data layer, to deliver the platform's core functionalities. This set of tools ranges from the standard platform services to power the ecosystem, such as user and transaction management, to sets of data-driven tools that fuel the PLM from product development to after-sales servicing. The BOE is responsible for the abstraction and orchestration between the platform's different tools into a coherent set of platform-services. Through the BOE, platform users can leverage and arrange the different modular platform tools into different configurations to test and develop new and innovative, highly customized smart PSS that leverage the full potential of the physical/virtual interaction.

## 5 Conclusion

Although the impacts of technology in the servitization process are not a recent phenomenon, its full extent has not yet been fully realized. The recent focus on digital servitization has started to shed light on how organizations of the future will be able to leverage technology to deal with the growing complexity of requirements for customized products and service offerings.

In this paper, we start from an overview of the current literature on servitization to show that, like how DP have grown in many other sectors of the market, a platform-based approach can improve service-product offerings. Through the modularization of the architecture, a DP can gather loosely coupled value of different services into a set of highly customized offerings that fit better fit for different customers.

Furthermore, we present the TRF4.0 case that leverages the benefits of a modular architecture to develop a DP to support a smart PSS business model that generates added value from the entire lifecycle of power transformers. The platform-based approach plays the dual of (i) orchestrating both the multiple instances of the digital twins and the remaining platform services to provide platform users with the capability of developing new offerings, identifying new combinations of products and services and even identify unmet customer needs and new business opportunities; while (ii) serving as the infrastructure for the establishing and managing of a multi-sided business ecosystem that can foster collaboration and innovation between organizations.

The explosion of the platform model has had a profound impact on established business structures. While information-intensive industries were the first to transition to see its effects, technological and business advances will soon convert many of the remaining industries. The integration of PSS business models and digital twin technologies combined with the managed and orchestrated by platform-provided tools becomes an important research issue as they become the leading enabler for developing smart products and services throughout the entire life cycle.

From an operational perspective, system design issues, data management, and how traditional user roles can be rearranged become critical for efficiently implementing these systems. In contrast, from a business perspective, how a successful DP can be designed toward evolution in a way that a sustainable business ecosystem can develop should still be the focus of research.

**Acknowledgments.** The project TRF4p0 - Transformer 4.0 leading to this work is co-financed by the European Regional Development Fund - ERDF, through COMPETE -Operational Program Competitiveness and Internationalization (POCI) and by the Foundation for Science and Technology under the MIT Portugal Program under POCI-01-0247-FEDER-045926.

## References

1. Pirola, F., Cimini, C., Pinto, R.: Digital readiness assessment of Italian SMEs: a case-study research. J. Manuf. Technol. Manag. **31**(5), 1045–1083 (2020). https://doi.org/10.1108/JMTM-09-2018-0305
2. Cremona, L., Ravarini, A., Sutanto, J.: KMS in a cluster of firms: the role of a digital platform. In: Baglieri, D., Metallo, C., Rossignoli, C., Pezzillo Iacono, M. (eds.) Information Systems, Management, Organization and Control. LNISO, vol. 6, pp. 253–262. Springer, Cham (2014). https://doi.org/10.1007/978-3-319-07905-9_18
3. Beuren, F., Ferreira, M., Miguel, P.: Product-service systems: a literature review on integrated products and services. J. Clean. Prod. **47**, 222–231 (2013). https://doi.org/10.1016/j.jclepro.2012.12.028
4. Cenamor, J., Rönnberg Sjödin, D., Parida, V.: Adopting a platform approach in servitization: leveraging the value of digitalization. Int. J. Prod. Econ. **192**, 54–65 (2017). https://doi.org/10.1016/J.IJPE.2016.12.033.
5. Eggert, A., Hogreve, J., Ulaga, W., Boehm, E.: Revenue and profit implications of industrial service strategies. J. Serv. Res. **17**, 23–39 (2014). https://doi.org/10.1177/1094670513485823

6. Benedettini, O., Swink, M., Neely, A.: Examining the influence of service additions on manufacturing firms' bankruptcy likelihood. Ind. Mark. Manag. **60**, 112–125 (2017). https://doi.org/10.1016/j.indmarman.2016.04.011
7. Ransbotham, S., (Jerry) Kane, G.C.: Membership turnover and collaboration success in online communities: explaining rises and falls from grace in Wikipedia. MIS Q. **35**(3), 613–627 (2011). https://doi.org/10.2307/23042799
8. Gebauer, H., Fleisch, E., Friedli, T.: Overcoming the service paradox in manufacturing companies. Eur. Manag. J. **23**(1), 14–26 (2005). https://doi.org/10.1016/j.emj.2004.12.006
9. Kindström, D., Kowalkowski, C.: Service innovation in product-centric firms: a multidimensional business model perspective. J. Bus. Ind. Mark. **29**(2), 96–111 (2014). https://doi.org/10.1108/JBIM-08-2013-0165
10. Lerch, C., Gotsch, M.: Digitalized product-service systems in manufacturing firms: a case study analysis. Res. Manag. **58**(5), 45–52 (2015). https://doi.org/10.5437/08956308X5805357
11. Eloranta, V., Turunen, T.: Platforms in service-driven manufacturing: leveraging complexity by connecting, sharing, and integrating. Ind. Mark. Manag. **55**, 178–186 (2016). https://doi.org/10.1016/j.indmarman.2015.10.003
12. Baldwin, C.Y., Clark, K.B.: Design rules: the power of modularity, vol. 1. MIT Press, Cambridge (2000)
13. Sanchez, D., Cavero, J., Marcos, E.: The concepts of model in information systems engineering: a proposal for an ontology of models. Knowl. Eng. Rev. **24**(1), 5–21, (2009). http://www.google.com/search?client=safari&rls=en-us&q=The+concepts+of+model+in+information+systems+engineering:+A+proposal+for+an+ontology+of+models&ie=UTF-8&oe=UTF-8
14. Salvador, F.: Toward a product system modularity construct: literature review and reconceptualization. IEEE Trans. Eng. Manag. **54**(2), 219–240 (2007). https://doi.org/10.1109/TEM.2007.893996
15. Huo, B., Zhang, C., Zhao, X.: The effect of IT and relationship commitment on supply chain coordination: a contingency and configuration approach. Inf. Manag. **52**(6), 728–740 (2015). https://doi.org/10.1016/j.im.2015.06.007
16. Voss, C.A., Hsuan, J.: Service architecture and modularity. Decis. Sci. **40**(3), 541–569 (2009)
17. Tiwana, A.: Platform ecosystems: aligning architecture, governance, and strategy. Newnes (2013)
18. Tiwana, A., Konsynski, B., Bush, A.: Platform evolution: coevolution of platform architecture, governance, and environmental dynamics. Inf. Syst. Res. **21**(4), 675–687 (2010). https://doi.org/10.1287/isre.1100.0323
19. Meyer, M.H., Jekowsky, E., Crane, F.G.: Applying platform design to improve the integration of patient services across the continuum of care. Manag. Serv. Qual. An Int. J. **17**(1), 23–40 (2007). https://doi.org/10.1108/09604520710720656
20. Bask, A., Lipponen, M., Rajahonka, M., Tinnilä, M.: The concept of modularity: diffusion from manufacturing to service production. J. Manuf. Technol. Manag. **21**(3), 355–375 (2010). https://doi.org/10.1108/17410381011024331
21. Bask, A., Lipponen, M., Rajahonka, M., Tinnilä, M.: Framework for modularity and customization: service perspective. J. Bus. Ind. Mark. **26**(5), 306–319 (2011). https://doi.org/10.1108/08858621111144370
22. Ethiraj, S., Levinthal, D., Roy, R.: The dual role of modularity: innovation and imitation. Manag. Sci. **54**, 939–955 (2008). https://doi.org/10.1287/mnsc.1070.0775
23. Silva, H.D., Soares, A.L.: From digital platforms to ecosystems: a review of horizon 2020 platform projects. In: Camarinha-Matos, L.M., Afsarmanesh, H., Ortiz, A. (eds.) PRO-VE 2020. IAICT, vol. 598, pp. 111–120. Springer, Cham (2020). https://doi.org/10.1007/978-3-030-62412-5_9

24. Ethiraj, S., Levinthal, D.: Modularity and innovation in complex systems. Manag. Sci. **50**, (2004). https://doi.org/10.2139/ssrn.459920.
25. Baines, T., Lightfoot, H.W.: Servitization of the manufacturing firm. Int. J. Oper. Prod. Manag. **34**(1), 2–35 (2014). https://doi.org/10.1108/IJOPM-02-2012-0086
26. Frank, A.G., Mendes, G.H.S., Ayala, N.F., Ghezzi, A.: Servitization and Industry 4.0 convergence in the digital transformation of product firms: a business model innovation perspective. Technol. Forecast. Soc. Change **141**, 341–351 (2019). https://doi.org/10.1016/j.techfore.2019.01.014
27. Paschou, T., Rapaccini, M., Adrodegari, F., Saccani, N.: Digital servitization in manufacturing: a systematic literature review and research agenda. Ind. Mark. Manag. **89**, 278–292 (2020). https://doi.org/10.1016/j.indmarman.2020.02.012
28. Yablonsky, S.: A multidimensional framework for digital platform innovation and management: from business to technological platforms. Syst. Res. Behav. Sci. **35**(4), 485–501 (2018). https://doi.org/10.1002/sres.2544
29. de Reuver, M., Sørensen, C., Basole, R.: The digital platform: a research agenda. J. Inf. Technol. 1–12 (2017). doi: https://doi.org/10.1057/s41265-016-0033-3.
30. Yoo, Y., Henfridsson, O., Lyytinen, K.: The new organizing logic of digital innovation: an agenda for information systems research. Inf. Syst. Res. **21**(4), 724–735 (2010). https://doi.org/10.1287/isre.1100.0322

# Knowledge Transfer and Accelerated Innovation in FoF

# Implementation of IoT Platform's Dashboards for the Visualisation of Dynamic KPIs: Insights from a Case Study

Marco Venuta[1(✉)], Michela Zambetti[1(✉)], Fabiana Pirola[1(✉)], Giuditta Pezzotta[1(✉)], Piergiorgio Grasseni[2(✉)], Marco Ferrari[2(✉)], and Stefano Salvi[2(✉)]

[1] Department of Management, Information and Production Engineering, University of Bergamo, Viale Marconi, 24040 Dalmine, Italy
{marco.venuta,michela.zambetti,fabiana.pirola, giuditta.pezzotta}@unibg.it

[2] Smigroup, Via C. Ceresa, 24015 San Giovanni Bianco, Italy
{piergiorgio.grasseni,marco.ferrari,stefano.salvi}@smigroup.net

**Abstract.** Nowadays, Internet of Things (IoT) platforms are becoming a huge opportunity for companies to collect data from connected machinery and analyse them to increase efficiency in production, optimize maintenance and introduce personalized service offerings. Specifically, multiple users can monitor real-time data and act based on updated information. Nevertheless, few studies are systematically focused on the implementation of Key Performance Indicators (KPIs) in the IoT environment. Based on an empirical case study, the article presents the implementation of dynamic KPI dashboards for an IoT platform, showing the challenges to face related to the trade-off between user desire and companies' technological readiness.

**Keywords:** KPI · IoT platform · Implementation · Case study

## 1 Introduction

Among the enabling technologies that are at the basis of Industry 4.0 and are transforming the traditional factories into smart factories, a prominent role is played by the Internet of Things (IoT) and its application in industrial contexts (IIoT) [1, 2]. An increasing number of companies are equipping the physical assets within their industrial environment with sensors, connecting devices to the Internet through IoT platform that manage the communication flow between machinery and users and provide application-level capabilities for users to interact with the IoT system [3]. The adoption of IoT platforms enables the collection of a huge amount of data, that allows dynamic visualization of information and, among other metrics, of Key Performance Indicators (KPIs) [4]. Moreover, the implementation of advanced data analytics techniques, such as machine learning (ML) and artificial intelligence (AI) enables to identify future trends and detect potential problems [5]. The adoption of such a technology, therefore, deeply changes


Published by Springer Nature Switzerland AG 2021
L. M. Camarinha-Matos et al. (Eds.): PRO-VE 2021, IFIP AICT 629, pp. 517–525, 2021.
https://doi.org/10.1007/978-3-030-85969-5_48

the role of KPIs and leads to an improvement in the overall performance and services of industrial companies by increasing the production efficiency, optimizing the maintenance interventions, and introducing personalized offerings for customers [6, 7]. In the literature, many studies in the field have focused their research on the development of ML and AI algorithms, while few describe how to implement an IoT platform and how to manage traditional KPIs in this new situation. Based on an empirical case, the paper discusses the path towards defining an IoT platform, focusing on the development of the dynamic KPI monitoring and visualization, showing its usefulness in supporting companies in their decision-making process. KPIs are defined as dynamic due to their dynamic calculation and visualisation, through real-time data acquisition, and their flexibility in calculating targets and thresholds through automatically updated inputs. The article discusses how the implementation phase was undertaken and how it was impacted by the trade-off between specific desired functionalities of the user and actual technological possibilities of the firm. The paper is structured as follows: Sect. 2 presents the theoretical background that motivates the research. Section 3 presents the case study, where the implementation path for the development of dashboards for the visualization of dynamic KPIs. In Sect. 4 challenges and benefits regarding the dynamic KPIs implementation are presented. Finally, Sect. 5 provides conclusions and future development of the study.

## 2 Background

In recent years, companies are continuously looking for production systems characterised by excellent performance in terms of reliability, flexibility, sustainability and productivity [8], and the technologies within the Industry 4.0 paradigm represent an incredible opportunity to achieve these goals [9]. IoT, in particular, enables objects equipped with radio frequency identification, sensors, actuators to interact with each other and cooperate to achieve common goals [1]. Typically, to achieve a business opportunity like this, small and medium-sized enterprises, having limited skills and resources, need to join efforts in collaborative networks (CNs) [10]. A CN structure can provide an appropriate working environment for IoT because in this way different entities can share information in a facilitated way thanks to mutual trust. In this way, IoT assumes a key role in the provision of efficient and effective monitoring combined with an improvement in decision-making related to asset management [11]. Business monitoring is typically supported by an information system that provides information about several KPIs [12], which are powerful tools that relate enterprise data to business goals, enabling managers to guide the analytic process and identify deviations in their strategic plan [13]. The KPIs monitoring process always represented a challenging issue because of different factors:(1) large volumes and high speed of data that needed to be processed and analysed, (2) static calculation based on historical data, (3) not enough flexible visualization to quickly and accurately identify potential problems [6]. The adoption of technological advancements conveyed in IoT platforms allows users to monitor data in real-time (or near real-time) and make decisions based on KPIs calculated and visualized dynamically [14]. IoT platforms also enable to filter massive amounts of data and to parse out information and KPIs according to the different interests of the final users [6, 15]. Moreover, KPIs can be used to investigate the root causes of a problem and eliciting the future behaviour of the production thanks to the adoption of predictive algorithms [16]. An effective way of monitoring and evaluating performance is the selection of appropriate KPIs that strongly depends on the company's strategic intentions and its competitive environment [17, 18]. Several regulations as [19, 20] list the most common KPIs used by companies to monitor production and maintenance areas. The Overall Equipment Effectiveness (OEE) is the main KPI adopted in all the companies to monitor production performance. It identifies production losses [19] and their impacts [21] resulting in better use of available resources and therefore in optimization of production management and a reduction of associated costs. Besides OEE, other KPIs can be used to monitor production such as: Throughput rate, Production pace, Setup rate, etc. As far as maintenance monitoring is concerned, the most important and widely adopted KPIs are Mean Time Between Failures (MTBF), Mean Time To Failures (MTTF), Mean Time To Repair (MTTR). This family of indicators provide a synthetic measure of the expected time between two successive failures of an item, distinguishing between the expected time spent for repairing it and its expected functioning time [19]. Although automated process monitoring tools are accessible and already established performance measurements are available, there is a lack of proper processes to guide the transformation of raw data into applied knowledge [16, 22] and a lack of management tools to guide the process of capturing KPIs [23].

## 3 Case Study

In this paper, a case study methodology has been applied because, as indicated by [24], the intent is to illustrate new and innovative practices that organizations are adopting. The case study has been conducted in an Italian manufacturing company: SMI, one of the world's largest producers of bottling plants and packaging machinery. The company is characterized by a proactive attitude in the innovation field, and in recent years started an IoT project, initially focusing only on one of its machinery: the stretch-blow moulder, which transforms PET preforms into blown bottles. Through this project, SMI aims to collect operating data from all the machinery installed at the customer site and provide continuous real-time monitoring of industrial plants. This will allow them to enhance the decision-making process, improve asset and maintenance management and strategies. Moreover, by exploiting knowledge of the use phase of the machines, other objectives are related to the improvement of product design, customer profiling and service enlargement. All the information has been collected through participatory observation, which involved one of the researchers actively working on the achievement of the IoT solution. To develop this project, SMI has created a goal-oriented CN, characterised by a cooperative environment between different entities - SMI, university, technology providers and reseller, customers - working together to realise the IoT platform project. Thanks to this environment, many companies managers and external experts have been involved through semi-structured interviews and cross-department workshops to consider different points of view, and several established tools as Business Process Model and Notation (BPMN 2.0) and Failure Mode, Effects, and Criticality Analysis (FMECA) have been used to organize all the information collected [25, 26]. During the project collaboration, the researchers have elaborated an implementation path, that can be taken as the model for future IoT implementation works. The path can be divided into four main steps: (1) definition of the platform desired functionalities; (2) re-engineering of the business processes affected by the platform; (3) development of the proof of concept of the platform dashboards (which represents the core of this paper); (4) implementation of the IoT platform with the connection of customer machines. At the beginning of the project, the different departments of the company have been asked to work on the definition of their needs and the desired functionalities that the platform should include (phase 1). This work has also been supported with an analysis of the company business processes (phase 2), to understand the peculiarities of SMI's processes and identify the areas and departments that could mostly be impacted and benefit from the introduction of IoT. Among the desired functionalities, the visualization of metrics related to production and maintenance performance emerged as fundamental to monitor the machinery functioning, but also to define internal business performances and using them to define targets and continuous improvement strategies. The proof of concept of platform dashboards (phase 3) contains all the information, data and KPIs that the end-users want to manage in the platform. To achieve this outcome, several activities have been carried out in this third phase. First, an FMECA on the machine has been carried out to understand the main critical components. Then, based on these results and the functionalities previously defined, the machinery data to monitor has been selected. Particularly, the company has recognised that not only machine-specific telemetry data (e.g. temperature, vibration, peak current, electric consumption) plays a central role in the machine monitoring process, but also production and maintenance KPIs. Indeed, the role and the calculation of traditional KPIs change with the introduction of IoT, shifting from a static and always historical analysis towards dynamic calculation thanks to real-time data and data analytics algorithms. To define which KPIs include in the proof of concept, a literature analysis on most adopted KPIs has been conducted. To this purpose, the most common standards [19, 20] have been taken into account. The KPIs report has been presented to the internal users, who then evaluated each KPI considering the theoretical benefits and all the possible uses in the SMI context.

Before starting the development of the proof-of-concept, a study on how the platform is structured has been performed. The platform is characterized by a recurrent hierarchical structure. Starting from the homepage dashboard, the user can explore the platform in different ways, using the direct link on the dashboard or using the navigation menu with the button "GROUPS". Groups are organized in a hierarchical way and, gradually deepening the analysis into connected subgroups, it is possible to obtain information and statistics related to smaller samples of devices, until the visualization of the dashboards of a single machine. Each machine can be reached by the exploration of all groups since it is assigned to more than one group using a one-to-many logic. This structure combined with the scalability property of the KPIs enables the creation of a realistic proof of concept; it represents several standard dashboards that contain all the information requested by the users and can be applied in all the different hierarchical level of the platform. Based on these characteristics, preliminary proof of concept has been developed. Figure 1 shows an example of a dashboard; it depicts the KPIs and data selected in order to monitor, in the specific case, the aggregate production of the customers. The same dashboard can be used at each level of the hierarchical structure:

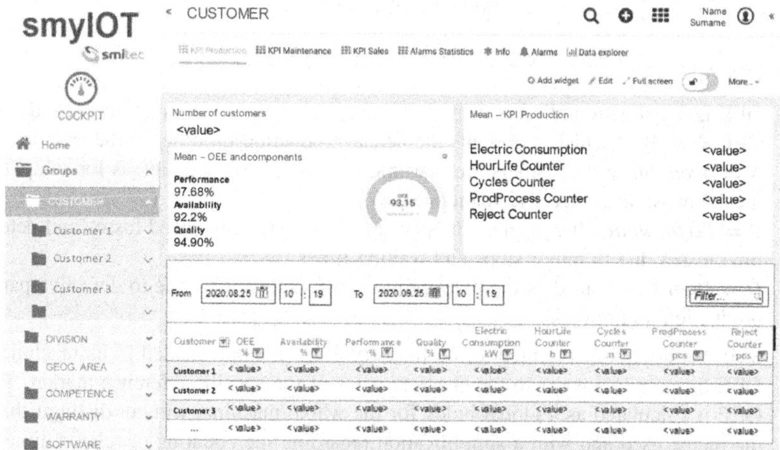


**Fig. 1.** SmyIoT dashboard example with fictitious values

the framework and KPIs will be replicated but their calculated values, targets and thresholds will change depending on the level of aggregation and trends of input data. Before the implementation phase, some important considerations of the prioritisation and feasibility must be done. All the data and the KPIs selected until this point represented the desires of the internal-end users, without considering technological and economical constraints. Thus, through several interviews, the software developers validated the feasibility of the proof-of-concept requests, considering what the company technological readiness permitted and what was feasible. Given the central role of the KPIs, also their implementation feasibility evaluation was crucial. So, four steps have been identified:

1. Theoretical analysis: define how the KPIs are calculated theoretically
2. Analysis of data availability: define what the company already has, and which data is missing
3. Analysis of possible solutions: define how to collect the necessary missing data and its feasibility
4. Definition of the implementation priority: select what should be implemented and in which order, also considering the component FMECA criticality

An explanatory case of the implementation feasibility evaluation is reported in Table 1, considering the OEE.

**Table 1.** OEE analysis

| Steps | Description |
|---|---|
| 1 | OEE is a synthetic indicator of the effectiveness of the work units. Its formula is OEE = AxPxQ which represents the actual production ratio net of the time losses: ***A = Availability*** It considers the plat uptime considering time losses for setup, breakdowns, and corrective maintenance ***P = Performance*** It considers the plat uptime considering speed losses and detects time losses due to minor stops and waiting times ***Q = Quality*** It considers the plat uptime considering losses due to defective parts production and rework |
| 2 | SMI, being already oriented to the Industry 4.0, has implemented in its machines its OEE formula to answer to the characteristics of the specific reference market. The OEE is calculated as a global index for the whole machine, without distinguishing the recipe used and with a simplification regarding the counting of relative times (planned shutdown time, setup time, etc.). Furthermore, at the machinery level, events and times related to shutdowns for maintenance and set-up operations are not detected and classified because such detailed calculations and analysis are typically left to higher-level factory IT applications |
| 3 | This state of the art has indicated the need for specifics enrichments of the current machinery dataset, not only considering the machine level but also all IoT stack. It will be possible to collect and classify data according to the used recipe, link single machine state and alarms to specific machine components and track related occurrences and timing. Furthermore, to collect set-up and maintenance time it will be necessary to define and implement an appropriate IT infrastructure to interact with operators and technicians to collect this information from their feedbacks |
| 4 | SMI decided to improve the current OEE by adding the recipe and components identification, due to its low software development effort and its importance for the internal users. SMI decided to not take into consideration the set-up time, although operators could provide this information with active feedback, currently, they are not engaged in these kinds of activities. Therefore, SMI needs to provide an unfailing system to obtain them, but its costs are high and there is no implementation urgency |

After this analysis, SMI decided to keep the previously defined OEE formula, but improving it, adding the possibility to exploit the scalability potential through the detection of recipes used and components effectiveness. Some of the issues raised for the OEE analysis were also visible in the calculation of others KPIs. In particular, given the actual difficulty of collecting and interpreting in the right way data about maintenance intervention traceability, SMI decided that, at the current state, the MTBF would be considered later. In fact, even if MTBF is a useful KPI, the effort needed to detect maintenance interventions would have slowed down the IoT project excessively. At this point, the software developers had all the information to develop the IoT platform (phase 4). The implementation phase followed an agile approach characterized by flexibility and adaptability principles, to maintain the platform open to modification and extensions, always supported by technology provider personnel. SMI started to collect data to feed the platform from the machines of the showroom and test department allowing the developers to get responsive feedback on their work, and improve the platform features one piece at a time until the ultimate platform version has been installed in a set of SMI machinery.

## 4 Discussion

The development of the IoT platform highlights several challenges that SMI had to face for the successful implementation of dynamic KPI, that can be generalized for other companies too. Overall, it is possible to notice that there are potential issues related to the complete availability of data, since the machine protocol often does not include the necessary data to compute specific metrics. The collection of these data may require software developments, the selection of proxy or the development of a system that enables operators to collect feedbacks. Considering this last choice, the level of confidence in the machine operators is still low, since they are not usually prone to use such solutions, not considering them essential for their daily work; so, it is clear that there is a need to improve a digital culture and a proactive mentality at all levels of CN companies. In particular, this culture must emerge among end-customers, because they are a key part of the data collection; if the customer does not understand the usefulness and importance of this data, it may not be inclined to collaborate effectively. However, once the right data and KPIs are implemented in the platform, they will be accessible in real-time, will increase machine reliability, and will be scalable at different levels, paying back the efforts required for their collection and calculation. The real-time computation will enhance the monitoring of production and the recognition of problems, as well as the definition of the responsibility when a certain KPI lowers under predefined limits. In addition, it will be easy to carry out benchmarking analyses on machine performance, which can be used, among other options, to improve machine design. The chance to access real customer data will enhance the possibility to show the performance of machinery to increment sales, but also to introduce new business models and customized solutions thanks to better customer profiling. Another interesting utilization is the opportunity to compare machinery performance over time and give evidence of the enhancement achieved after maintenance interventions or adopting preventive maintenance approaches.

## 5 Conclusion and Future Research Direction

Thanks to the CN collaboration, SMI was able to quickly develop an IoT platform for the dynamic visualisation of KPIs; having a common goal, the entities cooperated effectively by leveraging the network's expertise to overcome challenges. In future, the CN will be able to exploit the IoT platform to strengthen communication between its parts. However, the work does not come without limitations: even if the proposed work has been proven to be effective for the reference company, multiple applications are recommended to reach a higher level of generalisation. Because of the initial state of activities, the most severe limitation of the project is represented by the absence of numerical data that represent the platform's benefits. In parallel with the continuous development of the platform functionalities future research directions have been defined. First of all, there is the need to define ways to create a digital culture and mentality for the use of platforms, or to improve it where it is already present. Besides the qualitative evaluation of benefits, which may be more attractive for managerial departments rather than the operative users, and traditional training sessions to explain tools and their benefits, one suggestion could be to work on the gamification of specific platform parts, to involve the end-users with real incentives. Moreover, a new way to conduct the development process should be conceptualised and introduced in the industrial setting including both user-centric and technology-driven perspective and competencies, considering the need to understand the technological dimension related to digital components of the machinery, and the user-centric dimension.

**Acknowledgement.** The researchers of the University of Bergamo have been funded by the Erasmus + Knowledge Alliance project DIGIFoF (Digital Design Skills for Factories of the Future - Project Nr. 601089-EPP-1–2018-1-RO-EPPKA2-KA).

## References

1. Dalzochio, J., et al.: Machine learning and reasoning for predictive maintenance in industry 4.0: current status and challenges. Comput. Ind. **123**, 103298 (2020)
2. Schneider, S.: The Industrial Internet Of Things (IIoT): Applications and Taxonomy, 42 (2017)
3. Machorro-Cano, I., Alor-Hernández, G., Cruz-Ramos, N., Sanchez-Ramirez, C., Segura-Ozuna, M.: A brief review of IoT platforms and applications in industry. In: New Perspectives on Applied Industrial Tools and Techniques. Management and Industrial Engineering, pp. 293–324. Springer, Cham (2018). https://doi.org/10.1007/978-3-319-56871-3_15
4. Moens, P., et al.: Scalable fleet monitoring and visualization for smart machine maintenance and industrial IoT applications. Sensors **20**(15), 4308 (2020)
5. Subramaniyan, M., Skoogh, A., Salomonsson, H., Bangalore, P., Bokrantz, J.: A data-driven algorithm to predict throughput bottlenecks in a production system based on active periods of the machines. Comput. Ind. Eng. **125**, 533–544 (2018)
6. Mate, A., Zoumpatianos, K., Mylopoulos, J., Palpanas, T., Koci, E., Trujillo, J.: A Systematic Approach for Dynamic Targeted Monitoring of KPIs, p. 15 (2014)
7. Pauli, T., Lin, Y.: The Generativity of Industrial IoT Platforms: Beyond Predictive Maintenance?, p. 7 (2019)
8. Ante, G., Facchini, F., Mossa, G., Digiesi, S.: Developing a key performance indicators tree for lean and smart production systems. IFAC-PapersOnLine. **51**, 13–18 (2018)
9. Lu, Y.: Industry 4.0: a survey on technologies, applications and open research issues. J. Ind. Inf. Integr. **6**, 1–10 (2017)
10. Camarinha-Matos, L.M., Afsarmanesh, H., Galeano, N., Molina, A.: Collaborative networked organizations – concepts and practice in manufacturing enterprises. Comput. Ind. Eng. **57**(1), 46–60 (2009)
11. Syafrudin, M., Alfian, G., Fitriyani, N.L., Rhee, J.: Performance analysis of IoT-based sensor, big data processing, and machine learning model for real-time monitoring system in automotive manufacturing. Sensors (Basel) **18**(9), 2946 (2018)
12. Parmenter, D.: Key Performance Indicators: Developing, Implementing, and Using Winning KPIs, 4th Edition | Wiley. Wiley.com (2010)
13. Badawy, M., El-Aziz, A.A.A., Idress, A.M., Hefny, H., Hossam, S.: A survey on exploring key performance indicators. Future Comput. Inf. J. **1**, 47–52 (2016)

14. Mörth, O., Eder, M., Holzegger, L., Ramsauer, C.: IoT-based monitoring of environmental conditions to improve the production performance. Procedia Manuf. vol. 45, 283–288 (2020)
15. Mahmoodpour, M., Lobov, A., Lanz, M., Makela, P., Rundas, N.: Role-based visualization of industrial IoT-based systems. In: 2018 14th IEEE/ASME International Conference on Mechatronic and Embedded Systems and Applications (MESA), Oulu, lug, pp. 1–8 (2018)
16. Papacharalampopoulos, A., Giannoulis, C., Stavropoulos, P., Mourtzis, D.: A digital twin for automated root-cause search of production alarms based on KPIs Aggregated from IoT. Appl. Sci. **10**(7), pp. 2377 (2020)
17. Jovan, V., Zorzut, S.: Use of key performance indicators in production management. In: 2006 IEEE Conference on Cybernetics and Intelligent Systems, pp. 1–6 (2006)
18. Hwang, G., Lee, J., Park, J., Chang, T.-W.: Developing performance measurement system for Internet of Things and smart factory environment. Int. J. Prod. Res. **55**(9), 2590–2602 (2017)
19. ISO22400 KPI Manufacturing operations management, Key performance indicator (2011)
20. prEN 15341 Maintenance - Maintenane Key Performance Indicators. BSi (2006)
21. Nakajima, S.: Introduction to TPM: Total Productive Maintenance. Productivity Press (1988)
22. Miller, H., Mork, P.: From data to decisions: a value chain for big data. IT Prof. **15**, 57–59 (2013)
23. Softic, S., Lüftenegger, E., Turcin, I.: Tracking and analyzing processes in smart production. In: Al-Turjman, F. (ed.) Trends in Cloud-based IoT. EICC, pp. 37–50. Springer, Cham (2020). https://doi.org/10.1007/978-3-030-40037-8_3
24. Scapens, R.W.: Researching management accounting practice: the role of case study methods. Bri. Acc. Rev. **22**(3), 259–281 (1990)
25. Voss, C., Tsikriktsis, N., Frohlich, M.: Case research in operations management. Int. J. Oper. Prod. Manage. **22**, 195–219 (2002)
26. Yin, R.K.: Case Study Research: Design and Methods. SAGE Publications (1984)

# BEDe: A Modelling Tool for Business Ecosystems Design with ADOxx

Maria-Sophie Schoder[1(✉)] and Wilfrid Utz[2(✉)]

[1] Faculty of Computer Science, Research Group Knowledge Engineering, University of Vienna, Währingerstraße 29, 1090 Vienna, Austria
maria-sophie.schoder@univie.ac.at
[2] OMiLAB gGmbH, Lützowufer 1, 10785 Berlin, Germany
wilfrid.utz@omilab.org

**Abstract.** In this contribution we explore a design technique for business ecosystem applying conceptual modelling techniques as a means to conceptualize such environments and provide capabilities to explore and analyze its outcomes in a comprehensive manner. The motivation for this work is attributed to the need of methods in the field that support design, collaborations during evaluation/evolution phases of business ecosystems. The requirements are derived from a review of literature and case studies, used as input for a conceptual analysis performed. As an outcome we propose a modelling method and prototype that provides a formal representation of the concepts identified, interaction and sharing capabilities of models and enables domain-specific extension capabilities realized through metamodeling.

**Keywords:** Business ecosystems · Business strategy · Conceptual modelling · Metamodelling · Modelling method engineering

## 1 Introduction and Problem Statement

Today's consumers no longer need standardized products or services, nor goods in harmonized quantities. Instead, they demand integrated and complex solutions that satisfy their specific needs. Consequently, the value-adding processes of a company are not limited to its structural boundaries and require an integrated organizational structure that utilizes resources allocated flexibly and in a cooperative manner.

Considering these trends, interactive and dynamic structures between organizations are required. However, a single organization can no longer meet the above challenges [1, p. 24] in isolation. The alternative for vertically integrated companies is a market with many participants that respond independently to quantity and price. In such markets there is a low level of coordination and no common evolution of specific capabilities. When a common benefit is advantageous and complex knowledge is required, such markets fail; they lack in skills as they are specialized in standardized goods [1, p. 24].


Published by Springer Nature Switzerland AG 2021
L. M. Camarinha-Matos et al. (Eds.): PRO-VE 2021, IFIP AICT 629, pp. 526–535, 2021.
https://doi.org/10.1007/978-3-030-85969-5_49

### 1.1 Business Ecosystems as a Concept

"Business ecosystems" offer a solution to these problems: they are characterized as networks of organizations and individuals who jointly develop skills and coordinate their investments. Assuming the rapidly changing environment, this form of organization offers advantages in the appropriate context to traditionally integrated enterprises. Flexible configuration of the ecosystem enables intelligent offerings based on coordinated activities, and capabilities to respond to unexpected events.

The concept of "business ecosystems is not new and has been under investigation in recent years (e.g. [2, 3], [4, pp. 50–51]), lately experiencing a boom in strategy development [5, p. 2256]. In "The Palgrave Encyclopedia of Strategic Management" [6] Teece assumes that "the concept of ecosystem might now substitute for the industry as a useful domain for performing economic analysis." [6, p. 2]. Reviewing these results published, it can be observed that due to extended definition space, a common understanding of the terminology cannot be derived; conceptual design instruments are required to retrospectively understand and learn from past developments with respect to ecosystems but also provide tools for planning and assessing future designs and their evolution. As such, this contribution aims to clarify and derive systematically a conceptual view of the terminology established, develop a modelling method formalizing the terminology including processing techniques for design interaction and assessments.

### 1.2 Observations and Identified Challenge

Tsujimoto explores in [4] that the focus of research is set to a limited degree on ecosystem dynamics and patterns as well as organizational behavior [4, p. 52]. It is increasingly important to investigate design approaches for business ecosystems and understand how one needs to construct value-creating systems [7, pp. 255–256]. Following Philips and Srai in [8] there has been limited focus on the creation and design of business ecosystems [8, p. 3], further extended by Senyo et al. in [9] arguing that this research trend should be supported by modelling artefacts as a basis for validation [9, p. 58]. Consequently, the research objective underlying the work presented aims to introduce a metamodel for business ecosystem, having its baseline on a conceptual analysis of the terminology used in literature and elevating the formal knowledge representation towards functionality to support the design and evaluation phases systematically, using the representation capabilities of digital model artefacts.

The remainder of the paper is structured as follows: Sect. 2 provides an introduction to related work as input for the concept development performed in Sect. 3.1. Sect. 3.2 presents the BEDe modelling method applying the framework of Karagiannis discussed in [10] and using the design technique discussed in [11]. The paper concludes with a presentation of the resulting prototype in Sect. 3.2 as an evaluation and concluding remarks/further research directions in Sect. 4.

### 1.3 Related Work

This chapter introduces related work within the domain and establishes the foundation for the conceptualization performed.

**Business Ecosystem.** Business ecosystems according to Moore [3] are *"an economic community supported by a foundation of interacting organisations and individuals (…)."* [3, p. 9]. Jacobides et al. see their distinctiveness in complementarity: *"(…) they provide a structure within which complementarities (of all types) in production and/or consumption can be contained and coordinated without the need for vertical integration."* [5, p. 2263]. Adner suggests they are a *"(…) multilateral set of partners that need to interact in order for a focal value proposition to materialise"* [12, p. 42].

We can recognize that "structure" for coordination between nodes is required. This implies that nodes are typed and represent partner relations, which, based on their classification describe the coordination structure. Thus, a distinction can be made based on the classification of a business ecosystem as suggested by Adner in [12, p. 40] into ecosystems-as-structure, focusing on the value proposition and ecosystems-as-affiliation, focusing on communities, sharing a common network and platform. This observation is defined within the proposed metamodel as "views" on the ecosystems, characterized as a network structure, utilizing the concepts for describing them and resulting in a meaningful, human-interpretable visualization. Four types of concepts are recognized from literature:

- Actors: as typed members within the ecosystem,
- Activities: as a classification of interaction,
- Positions: as a classification of actors in the network, and
- Links: defined generically as relationships.

These concepts are considered in the conceptualization specifically focusing on Actors and Relationships as the combination of both aspects result in Activities (tasks performed between actors), Position as the relative position within a concrete ecosystem and Links as the foundation for any relationship established. The related work shows that the semantics of ecosystems is derived from the relationship of actors which define the behavior aspects and domain purpose in the design.

**Actors.** The work of Iansiti and Levien in [2, p. 4] and Moore in [3] identify three types of actors. They are understood as constraints imposed on the generic type of an actor and relate to their prevalence, position as influence, characteristic in the domain, related activities and the role they play in the ecosystem.

Table 1 provides an overview of the findings and the classification based on common characteristics. A dimension that is relevant for the modelling artefact and the design of the metamodel relates to the contextualization of an ecosystem. Context as the domain-specific representation influences the characteristics and their assessment.

**Relationships.** Although relationships in business ecosystems originate with one actor and end with another one, they are also reciprocal and interactive [13, pp. 158–159]. Tsujimoto et al. find that vision sharing and trust are essential elements of business ecosystem relationships [4, pp. 52–55] though literature about business ecosystem relationships offers varying views.

**Table 1.** Actor types and characteristics

| Characteristic | Actor type | | |
|---|---|---|---|
| | Keystone | Niche-player | Dominator |
| Prevalence | Few | Numerous | Numerous/few/none |
| Influence | Powerful | Low | Powerful |
| Task/activity | Regulation, change initiation, guiding | Specialization, expertise | Controlling, destruction, exploitation, value draining |
| Ecosystem supportive | Yes | Yes | No |

Camarinha-Matos and Afsarmanesh see collaborative relations as central and divide them into organised-collaborative and ad-hoc ones. The former are long-term and strategic, the latter are short-term and focused on specific tasks. The existence of organized-collaborative relations makes business ecosystems possible [14, pp. 2464–2465]. Actors and relationships represent the core concepts considered for the design supporting hierarchy and modularity (as discussed in [5, p. 2260]), boundaries (introduced as interdependencies in [15]) and evolution.

**Structural Analysis.** Although literature widely discusses collaboration benefits, there is still no suitable way to measure them [16, p. 238]. Iansiti and Levien aim to find factors of a healthy ecosystem and identify these: productivity, robustness and niche creation [2], extended by reciprocity [13] and value alignment [17].

1. Productivity: This could be measured by evaluating the conversion of technology and materials into reduced costs and new products. A traditional way of measuring this is return on invested capital [2, pp. 3–4].
2. Robustness: Organizations in a robust business ecosystem have relative predictability, and buffer external shocks. A metric is the members' survival rate in relation to benchmark ecosystems [2, p. 4].
3. Niche creation: An ecosystem's ability to create meaningful diversity helps to absorb external shocks. One way to assess niche creation is to measure the application of new technologies in organizations and goods [2, pp. 4–5].
4. Reciprocity: Every actor who invests should receive something in return. It is not purely mathematically, as it is intuition or gut feeling and its analysis examines the ratio between providing and receiving. [13, p. 197].
5. Value Alignment: A quantitative way of analysis is the alignment of the system members. Three areas of analysis are proposed: shared core values, positive impact and potential for conflict [17, p. 416].

For the modelling method design these criteria are considered as evaluation and assessment that operate as model-value functionality on the model artefact and utilizes the design results achieved.

## 2 Modelling Method: BEDe

In this chapter, the conceptual metamodel for the Business Ecosystem Design Environment (BEDe) is introduced based on the related work section above. The concepts identified above are systematically mapped in the Generic Metamodeling Framework introduced in [10], and utilized during various domain-specific modelling method development projects (see [18] for examples). Two areas are considered in the conceptualization: a) the modelling technique (as the metamodel, defining the modelling language and modelling procedure) and b) model-processing algorithms based on the metamodel.

**Modelling Language as the Metamodel.** The modelling language defines the concepts, characteristics and connectors relevant for the domain of business ecosystem design. The language is constituted as the metamodel, defining notation, syntax and semantic of the concepts and their interdependencies in a formal manner.

The conceptual metamodel defining the language capabilities is graphically shown in Fig. 1. Applying the CoChaCo approach as a domain-specific language for metamodel design (introduced in [19] and applied on conceptual structures in [11]). Concepts are depicted as squares, connectors as ellipses and characteristics as dotted boxes. The relations in the metamodel are defined according to core RDF syntax. A specific aspect in CoChaCo is the assessment of the purpose of metamodel elements, depicted as orange edged squares.

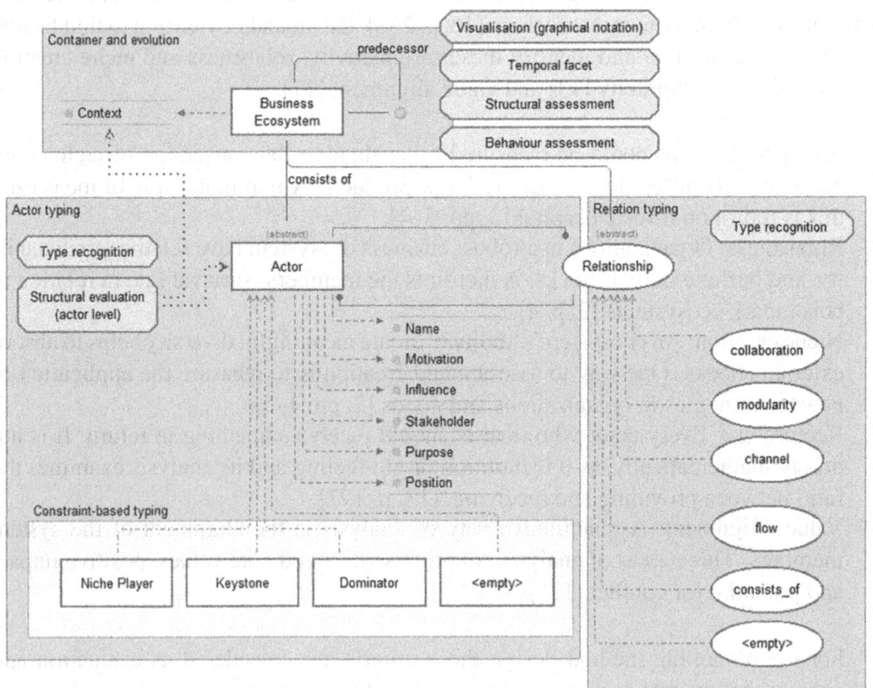


**Fig. 1.** BEDe metamodel design result

The BEDe metamodel considers at this stage the following aspects:

- Temporal/evolution aspect of a business ecosystem: represented using a predecessor relation
- Composition: general composition logic to support the view characteristic (containment relation between abstract actors and relationships)
- Typing: Actors and Relationships are typed by the domain-specific classification. The tying logic operates upon the characteristics and defined constraints on each concrete type
- Network structure: an ecosystem is characterized by a network structure between Actors applying Relationships. Cardinalities in the structure are currently disregarded but would elevate the constraint logic based on their types.

The metamodel is considered a conceptual structure that covers the structural aspects, but also logical representation as a serialization of the design artefact.

**Mechanisms and Algorithms.** Model processing in BEDe is established based on the metamodel introduced in Sect. 3.1. As a means for structural assessment, a continuous evaluation approach is suggested that informs the business ecosystem designer during the modelling task on the artefact's "health" status. The processing logic uses the contextual information (defined in accordance with semantic lifting approaches introduced in [20]) as a flexible technique to elevate the formal representation. The definition of the assessment logic is shown as pseudo-code for the specific case of modularity in the ecosystem.

Modularity calculation in BEDe

```
calculate_modularity_score
  evaluate_constraints
  if (constraints_satisfied)
    ratio_modularity = count (relation_modular)/count(all_relation)
    modularity_weak_threshold = read_context(weak_modularity)
    modularity_moderate_threshold = read_context(moderate_modularity)
    if (ratio_modularity < modularity_weak_threshold)
      update_actor_modularity ("weak")
    elsif (ratio_modularity < modularity_moderate_threshold)
      update_actor_modularity ("moderate")
    else
      update_actor_modularity ("strong")
    endif
    ecosystem_modularity = "WEAK"
    for actor in:actors_in_ecosystem
      position = assess_position(actor)
      weight = apply_position_weighting(actor)
      ecosystem_modularity = calculate_modularity_score
        (actor_modularity, position, weight)
    endfor
  else
    inform_on_violated_contraints
  endif
```

The example shows the implication of the metamodel concepts and characteristics for the purpose of the calculation and provides an assessment of each actor as well as a weighted, position-based calculation of the overall ecosystem design.

**Modelling Procedure.** The modelling procedure on how the modelling language is applied during the phase of model creation, evaluation and assessment is based on the business ecosystem design approach by den Ouden (2012), the following procedure for designing and modelling business ecosystems is defined:

1. Get a clear picture of the value proposition: the value proposition is a characteristic in the context of the business ecosystem
2. Define stakeholders: the actors are defined and typed
3. Define stakeholder interests and roles: describing each actors interest
4. Identify relationships between stakeholder: similar as for stakeholders, the relationships are established and typed
5. Structural analysis: during the design, the structural analysis is continuously performed and provides immediate feedback to the designer. The indicators are defined a) as constraints and b) processing logic for specific types of indicators that can be extended dynamically

The procedure definition is based on the work of den Ouden [13], having informed the metamodel design and processing algorithm specification.

## 3 Evaluation: BEDe Tool Prototype

For evaluation purposes of the modelling method, a prototypical implementation has been performed applying the metamodeling techniques established by the ADOxx platform [21]. From a technical viewpoint, the implementation and deployment represent a proof-of-concept evaluation of the modelling method, elevated by case studies from literature represented with the prototype.

### 3.1 Case Study: Android

Experiments with different ecosystem were conducted to test the prototype for adequacy of its capabilities. As an indicative example, the Android-Google system based on the case-study developed in [22] is presented. The procedure starts with understanding the value proposition of the system, which in the case of Google's Android is universally accessible information of the world through a standardized open mobile platform in the form of an ecosystem. It forms the basis for the second step, which is to select the stakeholders and assign them to the characteristics of the actors defined in the metamodel and position them according to their similarity. The following step serves to identify the interests of the different stakeholders by formulating it for each of them and evaluating it in relation to the value proposition. The next step is to describe the role and function of each stakeholder in the system. The fifth step is to draw connectors between the actors by using the metamodel relationships. Here, several different relations can operate between two actors. Based on the actors, their characteristics and relations among each other, the analysis is carried out, which continuously evaluates whether the system is in a good or bad status. This procedure's result is presented in Fig. 2.

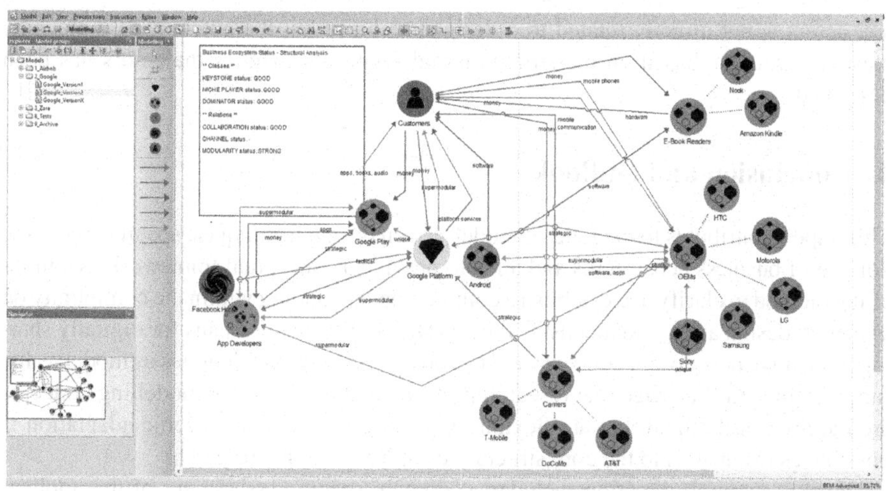


**Fig. 2.** BEDe modelling toolkit: example android case

The implementation results are shown in Fig. 2. The business ecosystem of Android exemplifies the design capabilities (graphical modelling and formal representation), interactive assessment logic (structure performance indicators) and evolutionary aspects (temporal trajectory) of business ecosystems. The implementation follows the programming paradigm of ADOxx as "instantiation" of meta-meta concepts and embedded scripting using the ADOxx language AdoScript for its realization. As a metamodeling technique is applied, the prototype allows for a flexible extension of the base classes of BEDe to capture domain-specific semantics in case required.

### 3.2 Evaluation and Lessons Learned

As an outcome, we can recognize that the conceptualization of business ecosystems in the form of a metamodel supports a common, structured approach for design and evaluation, whereas domain-specific aspects become feasible and are reflected within the design. This is specifically related to the use of metamodeling concepts and consequently results in a knowledge representation that supports the modelling and design aspects in business ecosystems, depending on the purpose of design and assessment. As such, the BEDe metamodel and prototype tool is positioned as a mediation layer (building on conceptual models) to enable the interaction of domain experts and share their knowledge about the domain collaboratively, but also provide input for machine interpretation as model processing algorithms and service invocation are enabled, without excluding the work on tool and concepts from the research community.

An observation related to the explorative assessment performed, relates to the use of concepts and their understanding when applied in a collaborative manner. The semantic assigned to the concepts in the metamodel can potentially lead to an interpretation by the modeler which impacts the model results and their evaluation. Consequently, further work is required in the way how concepts can be communicated, and which constraints and rules might be applied on the metamodel concepts. This means that the typing of e.g. actors is not directly related to a designers choice but the outcome of a machine reasoning process based on the structural and relation semantics the actors has been described.

## 4 Conclusion and Outlook

This paper contributes to the field of model-driven design techniques, specifically in the domain of business ecosystems and aims to provide a conceptual framework as a modelling method to clarify and establish a common understanding within the community on a) how to design and evaluate business ecosystems, b) provide means for digitally sharing innovative new design concepts and c) embed processing techniques as model-value functionality. At this stage, the research performed showcases that modelling concepts are required in the field that are flexible in a sense that domain-specific adaptation is possible as extensions to the core structure established in this research.

Further research direction includes a) domain-specific assessment of the applicability of the proposed concept and comparability/similarity matching techniques, and b) a dynamic assessment of the behavior of business ecosystems. In contrast to the structural aspects demonstrated, behavior view provide means for animating/simulating ecosystems to understand the effects of evolution already during design time utilizing operational data from the system environment as well as behavior definition on actor and relationship level.

## References

1. Williamson, P.J., De Meyer, A.: Ecosystem advantage: how to successfully harness the power of partners. Calif. Manag. Rev. **55**(1), 24–46 (2012)
2. Iansiti, M., Levien, R.: Strategy as ecology. Harv. Bus. Rev. **82**(3), 68–81 (2004)
3. Moore, J.F.: Predators and prey: a new ecology of competition. Harv. Bus. Rev. **71**(3), 75–86 (1993)
4. Tsujimoto, M., Kajikawa, Y., Tomita, J., Matsumoto, Y.: A review of the ecosystem concept — towards coherent ecosystem design. Technol. Forecast. Soc. Change **136**, 49–58 (2018)
5. Jacobides, M.G., Cennamo, C., Gawer, A.: Towards a theory of ecosystems. Strateg. Manag. J. **39**(8), 2255–2276 (2018)
6. Teece, D.J.: Business ecosystem. In: Augier, M., Teece, D.J. (eds.) The Palgrave Encyclopedia of Strategic Management, pp. 1–4. Palgrave Macmillan UK, London (2016)
7. Parker, G., Van Alstyne, M.W., Jiang, X.: Platform ecosystems: how developers invert the firm. MIS Quart. **41**(1), 255–266 (2017). https://doi.org/10.2139/ssrn.2861574
8. Phillips, M.A. Srai, J.S.: Exploring emerging ecosystem boundaries: defining the game. Int. J. Innov. Manag. **22**(8), 1840012 (2018)
9. Senyo, P.K., Liu, K., Effah, J.: Digital business ecosystem: literature review and a framework for future research. Int. J. Inf. Manag. **47**, 52–64, Elsevier Ltd (2019)
10. Karagiannis, D., Kühn, H.: Metamodelling platforms. In: Bauknecht, K., Tjoa, A.M., Quirchmayr, G. (eds.) E-Commerce and Web Technologies. EC-Web 2002. LNCS, vol. 2455. Springer, Berlin, Heidelberg (2002). https://doi.org/10.1007/3-540-45705-4_19
11. Utz, W.: Design of metamodels for domain-specific modelling methods using conceptual structures. Dissertation, University of Vienna, Fakultät für Informatik, Supervisor: Karagiannis, Dimitris (2020). https://doi.org/10.25365/thesis.63113

12. Adner, R.: Ecosystem as structure: an actionable construct for strategy. J. Manag. **43**(1), 39–58 (2017)
13. Den Ouden, E.: Innovation Design: Creating Value for People, Organizations and Society. Springer, London Ltd (2012). https://doi.org/10.1007/978-1-4471-2268-5
14. Camarinha-Matos, L.M., Afsarmanesh, H.: On reference models for collaborative networked organizations. Int. J. Prod. Res. **46**(9), 2453–2469 (2008)
15. Adner, R., Kapoor, R.: Value creation in innovation ecosystems: how the structure of technological interdependence affects firm performance in new technology generations. Strateg. Manag. J. **31**(3), 306–333 (2010)
16. Graça, P., Camarinha-Matos, L.M.: Performance indicators for collaborative business ecosystems — literature review and trends. Technol. Forecast. Soc. Change **116**, 237–255 (2017)
17. Macedo, P., Camarinha-Matos, L.M.: A qualitative approach to assess the alignment of value systems in collaborative enterprises networks. Comput. Ind. Eng. **64**(1), 412–424 (2013)
18. Karagiannis, D., Mayr, H.C., Mylopoulos, J.: Domain-Specific Conceptual Modeling: Concepts, Methods and Tools. Springer, Switzerland (2016). https://doi.org/10.1007/978-3-319-39417-6
19. Karagiannis, D., Burzynski, P., Utz, W., Buchmann, R.A.: A metamodeling approach to support the engineering of modeling method requirements. In: Proceedings - 2019 27th IEEE International Requirements Engineering Conference, pp. 199–210 (2019)
20. Woitsch, R.: Hybrid modelling with ADOxx: virtual enterprise interoperability using meta models. In: Franch, X., Soffer, P. (eds.) CAiSE 2013. LNBIP, vol. 148, pp. 298–303. Springer, Heidelberg (2013). https://doi.org/10.1007/978-3-642-38490-5_28
21. ADOxx.org. ADOxx metamodelling platform. https://www.adoxx.org/live/home. Accessed 22 Mar 2020
22. Bhattacharya, M., Gopal, B.S., Syed, A.S.: Google's Android: A Threat to Mobile Giants? vol. IBS Resear, IBS Research Center (2009, online)

# Successful Knowledge Transfer – A Boost for Regional Innovation

Adrian Florea[1(✉)] and Christoph Meinel[2]

[1] Computer Science and Electrical Engineering Department, Lucian Blaga University of Sibiu (ULBS), 550025 Sibiu, Romania
adrian.florea@ulbsibiu.ro

[2] Digital Engineering Faculty, University of Potsdam/Hasso Plattner Institute (HPI), 14482 Potsdam, Germany
christoph.meinel@hpi.de

**Abstract.** Innovation is the only way the EU can maintain a strong, sustainable and competitive economy. However, at present there are large imbalances between degrees of innovation of EU countries. Statistics of 2018 and 2019 classify Romania as the least innovative country of EU. One solution to mitigate this drawback consists of development of collaborative networks that replicate the best models of innovation from advanced countries and adapt them to underdeveloped countries from Europe. Such a collaborative network was proposed by HPI Potsdam in 2018 to ULBS with the aim to create an active knowledge transfer center between academia and business/society in the Sibiu region. This paper describes how the center contributes to increasing competitiveness in the Sibiu region by creating collaborative networks, digital education and training platforms as well as fostering applied research projects building on HPI's experience in Potsdam, Germany.

**Keywords:** Innovation · Knowledge transfer · Digital education platform

## 1 Introduction

Statistics at European level from 2018 and 2019 show that Romania remains the EU's least innovative country having approx. 31% of the EU average [1]. The country registered 15% diminish of the innovation index compared to 2010. The limited vision of leaders, limited communication and comparison with what is happening only at the local level (within the organization/region/country) and the lack of collaborative activities at the international level, the lack of investments in human resources and scientific research show their long-term effects. For a long time, the gross domestic product (GDP) allocated to education was less than 5%. According to Eurostat in 2019, Romania has the second lowest public expenditure on education among the 27 EU member states with 3.6% of GDP [2].

Figure 1 illustrates the four categories of innovative countries from the EU emphasizing the dishonorable place occupied by Romania. The lack of qualified human resources,


Published by Springer Nature Switzerland AG 2021
L. M. Camarinha-Matos et al. (Eds.): PRO-VE 2021, IFIP AICT 629, pp. 536–546, 2021.
https://doi.org/10.1007/978-3-030-85969-5_50

lack of research investments in both public sector and private companies, lack of any kind of innovation inside small and medium enterprises (SME), difficulties to attract and retaining talents in research centers and universities represent the main problems of innovation in Romania (Table 1).

**Fig. 1.** The 2019 EU map of innovation Source: elaborated by authors using https://mapchart.net/europe.html and data from [1]

**Table 1.** The main problems of innovation in Romania.

| Innovation features | Relative to EU in 2019 [%] |
|---|---|
| SME's Product/Process/Organizational innovations | 0 |
| Lifelong learning | 0 |
| Population with tertiary education | 9.1 |
| Investments in research and development of public sector | 2.9 |
| Enterprises providing ICT training | 5.6 |

After the European summit from 8–9 May 2019 organized at Sibiu, Romania, the participants came with the recommendation and commitment that Europe can shape its future through research and innovation focusing on cutting-edge research and innovation projects materialized in viable projects being able to become a successful global competitor with the other developed economies of the world [3].

The scientific contribution of this paper consists in proposing of an innovative mechanism of Collaborative Network for territorial innovation. First, the characteristics of competitiveness in the Sibiu region are briefly described. Then, the paper arguments how the creation of collaboration networks, digital education and training platforms, industrial clusters and the use of recent concepts in product development like Design Thinking

(DT) and Design Value Creation Process can be considered innovation guidelines in Romania.

Additionally, the paper focuses on the following specific objectives:

**O1:** To prove and emphasize the collaboration for innovation between two institutions (in this case laying the foundations of a Knowledge Transfer Center (KTC) in Romania at ULBS), showing the sustainable impacts and highlighting the importance of a KTC for accelerated innovation in Factories of the Future (FoF).

**O2:** To illustrate the knowledge transfer (i) among universities and industrial companies, but also (ii) among different levels of research and innovation groups within HPI to ULBS, through the re-use of German practices that could be applied in Romania. We illustrate also the steps developed for KTC gaining visibility.

## 2 Fostering Innovation and Knowledge Transfer: State of the Art

### 2.1 Mission of KTC

H. Etzkowitz and L. Leydesdorff used first the concept of "technology transfer center" or "knowledge transfer center" in the 1990s [4], by introducing the "*Triple Helix*" innovation model. Thus, to intensify the interaction between the academic environment (high education institutions - HEIs), industry and government, which favors economic and social development by stimulating innovation, technology transfer centers and industrial parks were proposed. The main role of technology transfer center consists in capitalizing on basic research generated by universities by transferring it to the development of new products, commercial goods, the efficiency of technological processes from industrial companies, following the rules established by, or stimulated by, government through smart specialization strategies, the government also having the role of regulating commercial markets. Thus, the Japanese, well known for aiming the "critical technologies" and knowing that these represent the prerequisites for future industrial growth to a high level, invest in developing their academic research and graduate training capacities [4]. HEIs must confront the transformation from a knowledge-importing economy to a knowledge-generating economy [5]. Furthermore, the new paradigm and methodology for Digital Innovation is called Open Innovation 2.0 [6]. Its core feature is represented by the "*Quadruple Helix*" innovation model where government, industry, academia and civil participants work together in a synergistic and faster way to create structural changes.

### 2.2 Examples/Case Studies for Knowledge Transfer

According to [7] "University-industry knowledge transfer is an important source of wealth creation for all partners; however, the practical management of this activity within universities is often hampered".

Hasso Plattner Institute in Potsdam, Germany, was founded in 1998 with the vision to establish a university excellence center in Germany for mastering digital transformation.

The approach for making this vision reality was - and still is - to combine excellence in research and teaching with providing an ecosystem for innovation while focusing on human needs and the user when developing complex IT systems and software solutions. This combination is the source of value creation at HPI and provides various touch points where knowledge is transferred from the university to external organizations such as enterprises, public institutions or NGO's. The process starts with the design of the study programs which are offered at HPI. All programs include a practice-oriented and research-focused project, called bachelor project and master project or lab, which takes around one to one and a half semester and which is structured as team assignment with the aim to find solutions for real problems posed by external project partners. One example of a successful bachelor's project is the "In-Memory Data Management" project together with SAP in 2008/09[1]. This project resulted in the development of SAP's successful HANA platform. SAP and HPI received the German Innovation Award in 2012 for this joint development.

In many cases, project partners stay in cooperation with the institute in various roles - be it as research partner of HPI's research groups, partner for student projects at the HPI School of Design Thinking[2], executive education customer of HPI Academy[3] or as a speaker and supporter of HPI's conferences. This strong network based on the aim to organize effective knowledge transfer as well as to contribute to the economic development in the region and the country has also led to a diversification of HPI's financial resources (Table 2).

**Table 2.** Third-party funds of HPI in 2020.

| Financial resources | [%] |
|---|---|
| Hasso plattner foundation | 59 |
| Public organizations | 28 |
| Private organizations | 13 |

HPI School of Design Thinking started teaching the innovation method in 2007 as the first in Europe. Since then, DT courses are an integral part of HPI's degree programs. HPI School of Design Thinking identified three core elements of design thinking: multidisciplinary team-based mindset, variable creative workspace and iterative process focused on six phases like understanding, observing, formulate of viewpoint, ideate, prototyping and testing.

The teaching offers are complemented by research on design thinking and innovation which contributes to understanding why and how design thinking works in organizations (improves work culture, makes efficient innovation process, reduces the costs) [8]. Additionally, our research highlighted the importance of prototyping in problem-solving and

[1] https://hpi.de/plattner/projects/project-archive/bachelor-project-hana.html.

[2] https://hpi.de/school-of-design-thinking.html.

[3] https://hpi-academy.de.

innovation processes [9]. This insight comes into play again in research projects with third parties and is a powerful tool of knowledge transfer.

HPI invests significant energy in projects on digital learning for diverse user groups. One of these projects is openSAP[4] - a Massive Open Online Courses (MOOC) platform jointly developed together with SAP with the aim to provide online courses for an audience interested in SAP's solutions. The digital education platform, developed 2011/2012 at HPI, is also used at the World Health Organization[5] which must ensure that front-line health responders have access to lifesaving knowledge anytime and anywhere. This platform saw a tremendous rise in course enrollments with the spread of COVID-19, as did other HPI's online learning platforms (Fig. 2).

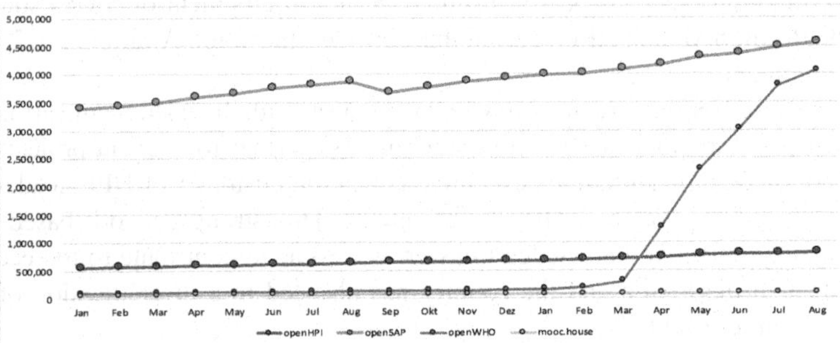


**Fig. 2.** Course enrollments on openHPI, openSAP, openWHO and mooc.house between Jan. 2019 and Aug. 2020 [10]

While MOOC platforms are designed for a large number of users, HPI also supports knowledge transfer on a smaller scale and targeted toward SMEs. In 2016, the German Federal Ministry for Economic Affairs and Energy started a project funding called 'Gemeinsam digital' (Together digital) to support digitalization in German SMEs. For the federal states, Berlin and Brandenburg, HPI became the project partner. Since then has conducted many workshops on topics like digital business models, how to use AI technologies within a company or how to benefit from digital technologies in HR recruiting. The workshop coaches are connected to HPI chairs so that the current research is transferred to German businesses instantly.

Another novel approach to support innovation in Germany is the 'Digital Hub Initiative'[6] also started by the German Federal Ministry for Economic Affairs and Energy. This initiative supports the establishment of focused innovation hubs in Germany. Currently, there are twelve hubs selected, among them being the 'MediaTech Hub Potsdam' leveraging the historically strong film and media industry in Potsdam, Brandenburg. As part of the hub, the University of Potsdam, the Film University and HPI decided to fund

[4] https://open.sap.com/.
[5] https://openwho.org/.
[6] https://www.de-hub.de/en/.

a joint accelerator[7] to support early-stage startup teams in Potsdam in a 6-month structured program. The accelerator complements the universities' own activities to support students interested in founding a company. At HPI, entrepreneurship is supported by the HPI School of Entrepreneurship[8] and the Chair of IT-Entrepreneurship established in 2019. They offer courses, competitions, bootcamp, coaching, mentoring as well as research and support students but also alumni and staff on the path of founding and building up their company. The result of this unique infrastructure has contributed in part to the fact that more than 100 startups have now emerged from the HPI's environment. One of them, Signavio, has been bought by SAP for one billion Euros[9]. Although this may be unusual even for the Berlin startup ecosystem, this acquisition of a company initiated through a student bachelor's project by a multinational enterprise shows the importance of early-on investment in entrepreneurship activities at universities, which may contribute significantly to the regional ecosystem boosting innovation.

## 3 Collaborative Network for Territorial Innovation

The collaborative network between HPI and ULBS is a long-term strategic network [11] with two main actions: creating virtual community targeting excellence in research and education and strengthening the collaboration between academia, business and administration sectors, providing virtual laboratory networks and digital collaboration platforms [12] for academic and industrial use to equip students and employees with skills required by Factories of the Future.

In 2018, understanding the need to create an innovation ecosystem that becomes sustainable, HPI has proposed and financially supported ULBS to create a knowledge transfer center, and, in 2020, supported the development of a Digitalization Hub around KTC HPI-ULBS oriented to build capacities through training, coaching and mentoring as well as digital education to maintain and increase the competitiveness of the Sibiu region. Building strong networks and helping regional stakeholders to benefit from the use of digital technologies fosters innovations and new business models attract talents and contribute toward a responsible society with informed citizens. The HPI support targets:

- Access to organizations and experts in Germany and Europe to support SME's to tackle digital technology challenges
- Access to IT capacities, e.g. HPI's Future SOC (Service-Oriented Computing) Lab
- Knowledge transfer and expertise regarding the promotion of entrepreneurship (e.g., accelerator/incubator/ startup mentoring)
- Potential cooperation in research projects in the fields of security engineering, knowledge engineering and smart city applications

In Sibiu area the industrial sector predominates. The dynamics of the changes generated by digitalization are first found in industrial companies. At the level of 2017,

[7] https://www.mth-potsdam.de/en/accelerator-en/.

[8] https://hpi.de/entrepreneurship/hpi-e.html.

[9] https://www.signavio.com/news/sap-acquisition-signavio/.

economic statistics show that the turnover of all companies in the industrial sector in Sibiu County was 3.93 Billion EUR (up from previous years) out of a total of 7.3 Billion EUR (53.84%). At the country level, Industry was in 2018 the most important economic branch in Romania, with a contribution to the gross added value of 26%, Romania being ranked 4th among the EU countries where the industry fundamentally contributes to the Gross Domestic Product. KTC HPI-ULBS's mission is to contribute to the enhancement of economic competitiveness by stimulating and harnessing the scientific and innovative potential and by assimilating the technological progress in the key areas of ULBS. The objectives are focused on digitalization, innovation, diversity of research teams, cross-fertilization of ideas, and digital transformation with impact on improving the quality of life, economic prosperity, increasing the quality of education and research in Romania (Fig. 3).

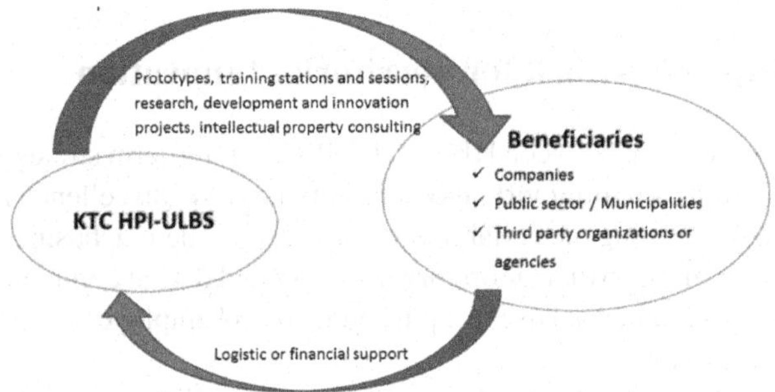


**Fig. 3.** KTC HPI-ULBS value creation process

KTC HPI-ULBS has as main objective the development and promotion of scientific research, know-how transfer, innovative entrepreneurship and building research, development and innovation infrastructures as well as the promotion of scientific and cultural values for consolidating a knowledge-based society. KTC must exploit the economic potential existing in the Sibiu region and the research skills from ULBS.

The overall outputs (key performance indicators) of KTC HPI-ULBS are:

- Information services (e.g. participation to events), Networking activities
- Training activities, innovation labs and hackathons
- Research contracts with companies / Public-Private Partnerships
- Patent applications and awards

## 4 Experimentation and Validation Feedback

KTC HPI-ULBS has implemented in 2019, thanks to HPI Potsdam and, based on collaboration between OMiLAB NPO, ULBS, industrial cluster PrelMet Transylvania and Continental Sibiu company within DigiFoF[10] ERASMUS + KA2 project, a research infrastructure[11] (Fig. 4) as key asset of a digital ecosystem specific to scientific-innovative

[10] https://digifof.eu/.

[11] https://www.omilab.org/nodes/omilab_nodes/ulbs/.

activities [13]. Multidisciplinary working teams formed by researchers, students, masters and doctoral students from ULBS but also from partner companies collaborate for developing innovative products / services, acquiring new skills like Creation of Business Ecosystems, Smart Modeling and Digital Twin Engineering. Through the created infrastructure we have:

- enhanced the industry-academia cooperation fostering knowledge transfer and educating about the benefit of digital technologies in the Factories of the Future
- realized vocational training programs using problem-based learning approach and Design Thinking methods (over 90 MSc students and employees from companies)
- developed innovative teaching and training materials for students and professionals (6 learning modules, 2 software tools and 4 webinars)

**Fig. 4.** KTC HPI-ULBS training and research infrastructure

The digital educational platform and experimental environment serve both to research and training activities related to modelling and simulation methods and tools, digitalization and optimization of business process, AI, image processing, collaborative cyber-physical systems and Internet of Things, robotics and automation, smart city, etc. One of the goals is to provide students and professionals the digital skills required by the Factories of the Future in the context of digitalization and Industry 4.0 society [14]. Considering challenges introduced by COVID-19 pandemic, a solution to mitigate its impact was to redefine training ecosystem proposing online training and changing the ULBS teachers' mindset to use and prepare own MOOCs, developing webinars, thereby enlarging the target audience.

The main success factors of the Romanian-German collaboration were the implementation of the KTC within ULBS, the understanding of the potential activities for territorial innovation performed by it, the transfer of knowledge from the research teams from HPI to ULBS and HPI support for developing a favourable mindset for the innovation process in the Sibiu region. Table 3 illustrates some of the key performance indicators achieved by KTC HPI-ULBS in the period 2019–2020.

Of the lessons learned from the collaboration between HPI and ULBS, at least two are worth highlighting (i) digital transformation and value creation through innovation are prerequisites for sustainable development and, (ii) setting international collaborative networks and the adoption of good practices from advanced countries regarding knowledge transfer can be solutions for boosting the territorial innovation.

We cannot talk about barriers in the collaboration between HPI and ULBS; rather, we can highlight obstacles in the implementation of knowledge transfer to Romanian companies, due to legislative specificity and sometimes, the mentality unwilling to change. It is a reserved attitude of Romanian companies in the use of technology transfer services because of their novelty, the difficulty or cost of changing technology or assembly line, or even from lack of trust in universities and research centers. This fact, also observed after the discussions with companies, is in accordance with certain market studies [15], namely, the degree of use of technology transfer services (4.03%) and product development services (6.71%) is very small, and can be a basis for developing this type of service in Sibiu and in the Central Region of Romania. The KTC HPI-ULBS must invest further in education, especially since the entrepreneurs placed on the 3rd place in the top of the preferences of technology transfer services the training and assistance services regarding innovation.

**Table 3.** The main actions of KTC HPI-ULBS for boosting innovation.

| Actions developed in 2019–2020 at ULBS with the support of HPI Potsdam | Number |
|---|---|
| Developing ULBS Design Thinking school and starting first activities. Connecting with Global Design Thinking Alliance[a] managed by HPI Potsdam | 1 |
| Organizing conferences to increase the visibility of KTC HPI-ULBS: SID[b] | 1 |
| Hackathons / Innovation Labs | 3 |
| Meetings with companies: setting further collaboration activities | 50 |
| Scientific papers based on KTC HPI-ULBS activities | 4 |
| Patent applications | 6 |
| Providing services for/collaborative projects with companies | 21 |
| Investments in R&D grants for building capacities | 6 |
| Investments in infrastructure of existing research centers/create new ones | 21 |
| Providing educational and vocational training | 10 |
| Partnerships with Digitalization HUBs and IT professional cluster | 3 |

[a]https://gdta.org/about-us/member-institutions/#1600250243638-b971147b-bfb5.
[b]The Sibiu Innovation Days 2020 – https://events.ulbsibiu.ro/innovationdays/2020.php.

## 5 Conclusions and Further Work

For boosting regional innovation in Romania a greater collaborative effort is required from clusters, universities and research institutes to position themselves as transfer vectors of technological progress. A top - down approach for boosting innovation should follow the next steps: 1) Romanian government should launch innovation initiatives fostering startups/students interested in founding a company; 2) if this is not possible or feasible, initiatives should be launched at a regional level – supported by digital innovation hubs and collaborative actions between stakeholders; 3) pilot (prototyping) projects between university and third-parties should be showcased at conferences, workshops, or regional networking meetings to serve as 'role models'; 4) learning offers by universities should be jointly developed together with industrial and/or public partners to combine research findings with approaches from practice.

Although the paper presents the HPI-ULBS collaboration aiming territorial innovation in the Sibiu region, this can be considered as innovation pattern that can be applied and extended to other regions or countries, provided it be determined the characteristics of economic competitiveness, the local stakeholders in innovation, both academically and industrially, from the respective region.

As future directions of development, we will carry on with all specified KTC activities, but especially we evaluate the knowledge transfer process in relation to the initially set objectives. Examining the effectiveness of knowledge transfer practices is an ongoing effort that needs to be reviewed as the organization grows.

**Acknowledgments.** This work was partially developed under the ERASMUS+ KA2 project "The FOF-Designer: Digital Design Skills for Factories of the Future", financing contract no. 2018–2553/001–001, project number 601089-EPP-1–2018-1-RO-EPPKA2-KA, web: https://www.digifof.eu/.

## References

1. Hollanders H., Es-Sadki N., Merkelbach I., Khalilova A.: European Innovation Scoreboard 2020, Publications Office of the European Union (2020). ISBN 978-92-76-21528-8
2. Eurostat - statistics explained, Government expenditure on education, data extracted in February 2021. https://ec.europa.eu/eurostat/statistics-explained/index.php. Accessed 1 Mar 2021
3. Commission Proposal for Horizon Europe, Horizon Europe - The Next EU Research & Innovation Investment Programme (2021–2027), May 2019
4. Etzkowitz, H., Leydesdorff, L.: The Triple Helix - University-Industry-government relations: a laboratory for knowledge based economic development. EASST Review **14**(1), 14–19 (1995)
5. Carayannis, E.G., Popescu, D., Sipp, C., Stewart, M.: Technological learning for entrepreneurial development (TL4ED) in the knowledge economy (KE): case studies and lessons learned. Technovation **26**(4), 419–443 (2006)
6. Curley, M., Salmelin, B.: Open Innovation 2.0. The New Mode of Digital Innovation for Prosperity and Sustainability. Innovation, Technology, and Knowledge Management. Springer, Cham (2018)
7. Alexander, A., Martin, D.P., Manolchev, C., Miller, K.: University–industry collaboration: using meta-rules to overcome barriers to knowledge transfer. J. Technol. Transf. **45**(2), 371–392 (2018). https://doi.org/10.1007/s10961-018-9685-1
8. Schmiedgen, J., Rhinow, H., Köppen, E., Meinel, C.: Parts without a Whole? - The Current State of Design Thinking Practice in Organizations (Study Report No. 97), p. 144. Hasso-Plattner-Institut für Softwaresystemtechnik an der Universität Potsdam (2015)

9. Plattner, H., Meinel, C., Leifer, L. (eds.): Design Thinking - Building Innovation Eco-Systems, p. 108. Springer, New York (2013)
10. Meinel, C., Jahresbericht: Fachgebiet "Internet - Technologien und Systeme", Hasso-Plattner-Institut für Digital Engineering gGmbH (2020)
11. Camarinha-Matos, L., Afsarmanesh, H.: Classes of collaborative networks. In: IT Outsourcing: Concepts, Methodologies, Tools, and Applications, pp. 364–370. IGI Global (2010)
12. Nicolaescu, S.S., Palade, H.C., Kifor, C.V., Florea, A.: Collaborative platform for transferring knowledge from university to industry-a bridge grant case study. In: Proceedings of the 4th IETEC Conference, Hanoi, Vietnam, pp. 475–488 (2017)
13. Karagiannis, D., et al.: OMiLAB: a smart innovation environment for digital engineers. In: Camarinha-Matos, L.M., Afsarmanesh, H., Ortiz, A. (eds.) PRO-VE 2020. IAICT, vol. 598, pp. 273–282. Springer, Cham (2020). https://doi.org/10.1007/978-3-030-62412-5_23
14. Florea, A.: Digital design skills for factories of the future. In: MATEC Web of Conferences, vol. 290, p. 14002. EDP Sciences (2019)
15. The demand for research, development, innovation and technological transfer services among SMEs in the Center Region, http://regio-adrcentru.ro/. Accessed Apr 2021

# Interoperability of IoT and CPS for Industrial CNs

# Sustainable Peatland Management with IoT and Data Analytics

Jiun Terng Liew[1](✉), Aduwati Sali[1], Nor Kamariah Noordin[1], Borhanuddin Mohd. Ali[1], Fazirulhisyam Hashim[1], Syamsiah Mashohor[1], Nur Luqman Saleh[1], Yacine Ouzrout[2], and Aicha Sekhari[2]

[1] Wireless and Photonic Networks Research Centre of Excellence (WiPNET), Faculty of Engineering, UPM, Serdang, Malaysia
{liewjt,aduwati,nknordin,borhan,fazirul,syamsiah, nurluqmansaleh}@upm.edu.my

[2] Decision and Information for Production System – DISP, Université Lumière Lyon 2, 86 Rue Pasteur, 69007 Lyon, France
{yacine.ouzrout,aicha.sekhari}@univ-lyon2.fr

**Abstract.** Peatland is important to rural communities' livelihood due to its potential for aquaculture and agriculture. Nonetheless, human activities such as slash-and-burn can greatly increase forest fire risk, which can release a great amount of greenhouse gases and carbon dioxide into the atmosphere. To sustainably manage and restore peatlands, the Internet of Things (IoT) system can incorporate with Cyber-Physical System (CPS) for peatland management. In this study, an IoT system is deployed in the peatland to monitor the ground water level (GWL) and upload it to the server for the machine learning (ML) process. The trend of GWL will be modelled, and the CPS using the developed ML model will control the peatland rewatering process. As a result, the peatland condition can be monitored in real-time, and the risk of forest fire can be mitigated through rewatering automation before the GWL drops to a critical level.

**Keywords:** Machine learning · Peatland · Sustainable · IoT · CPS

## 1 Introduction

### 1.1 Backgrounds

Peatland is the accumulation of partially decayed organic materials due to the water-logged soils causing the anaerobic condition, where the rate of organic matter production exceeds the decomposition rate [1]. As a result, the peatland is a gigantic pool of carbon storage and habitat for many natural wildlife [2]. Peatland is also very important for water management as it can hold water equivalent to 20 times its own weight. Tropical peatland is commonly found in South-East Asia region, covering around 23.6 million hectares which represents 56% of the global tropical peatland.


Published by Springer Nature Switzerland AG 2021
L. M. Camarinha-Matos et al. (Eds.): PRO-VE 2021, IFIP AICT 629, pp. 549–557, 2021.
https://doi.org/10.1007/978-3-030-85969-5_51

For rural communities, peatland is the key to their livelihood due to its potential of aquaculture, agriculture, collection and utilization of forest products. As a result, deforestation rate of peatland reached almost 4% per annum, which is comparatively higher than other forest type [3]. Timber extraction using drainage method often damage the forest with poor recovery and depleted conditions [4]. Furthermore, large scale agriculture development for rice plantation involving slash-and-burn has driven the peat swamp forest loss and leaves the areas susceptible to annual forest fires.

Overall, overexploitation has severely harmed the peatland and increased the risk of forest fire. To make the matter worst, peatlands are the most critical terrestrial carbon sink of the world. The carbon is stored mainly in the peat form and peatlands plays an important role in regulation of climate by absorbing great amounts of carbon dioxide ($CO_2$). Forest fires in peatland not only release the $CO_2$ into the atmosphere, but also two other greenhouse gases, namely methane ($CH_4$) and nitrous oxide ($N_2O$). Therefore, effective method of peatland forest fires management is key to sustainable environment and climate change mitigation.

In this work, a collaborative Internet of Things (IoT) and Cyber-physical System (CPS) system is proposed for sustainable peatland management. IoT system is deployed in the peatland to collect real-time in-situ data to replace the conventional data collection method involving labor-intensive measurement by professional. Data collected by the IoT system is uploaded to the server for data analytic process. The data analytic process helps to predict the trend of Ground Water Level (GWL), which is key to determine the risk of forest risk. Based on the risk projected, CPS conduct the hydrological management using automated water pump facilities. Consequently, the GWL of peatland can be sustainably managed and preventing the occurrence of peatland forest fire.

### 1.2 Related Works

Hydrological management is a proven-effective method in ensuring the peatland ecosystem sustainability and preventing natural fires. During dry season, forest fire is more likely to happen if the GWL of the area is low. Hence, to maintain a high GWL – reduced risk of major fire, blocking of drainage ditches in peatland forest can be conducted. While fires caused by slash-and-burn cannot be exterminated through water management, high GWL can mitigate the spreading of forest fires. For high fire risk areas, rewatering process can be employed by pumping water from nearby rivers and lakes, to ensure the GWL is not more than 20 cm below the surface [5].

Wireless Sensor Network (WSN) or the more advanced IoT network have demonstrated both their flexibility and capability in handling various applications such as fleet management, localization, and healthcare [6–8]. Similarly, CPS has displayed great potential in industrial automation, where a feedback loop is created and integrated with decision making and appropriate response from actuators [9]. In [10], Intelligent predictive management (IPdM) is proposed to achieve zero-defect manufacturing (ZDM) through data-driven CPS. Similarly, [10] explored the architecture of dynamic manufacturing IoT with real-time data collection. Overall, CPS and IoT has shown promising traits that can be used to help manage the peatland.

Due to the ongoing threat of transboundary haze caused by peatland forest fire, peatland management has received a lot of attention in South-East Asia. In [11], an IoT system with piezometers known as AGROMIST is deployed to collect the peatland data in real-time and help improve the water management. Authors of [12] take on a similar approach and improve system by including local atmospheric data into the analysis. To encourage the involvement of stakeholders in the effort of peatland management, [13] used a LoRa-based IoT network to collect the ground parameters and upload to dashboard that is easily accessible.

To fully harness the potential of IoT along with CPS, the author proposed to incorporate IoT with CPS for the peatland management. In this work, an IoT network using LoRa technology is deployed on site to monitor the condition of the peatland, including ground data and atmospheric data. Collected data are uploaded to the server and undergone data analytic process for GWL prediction. Based on the outcome of data analytic, the CPS consists of peatland water pump room will be controlled to automate the peatland rewatering process. Rewatering process commenced is based on the forest fire risk code detailed by the Global Environment Centre to minimize the chance of fire occurrence.

## 2 Methodology

In this section, the architecture and working principle of proposed peatland management system is discussed.

### 2.1 IoT System with CPS

To aid the peatland management, the condition of peatland must be monitored constantly. As such, an IoT system consist of ground sensor nodes (i.e., piezometer), in-situ weather station and LoRa gateway is deployed. The overall architecture of the IoT system is shown in Fig. 1. LoRa communication technology is used for the local sensor nodes' communication due to its low power and low connectivity cost [14]. A reliability test was conducted using the LoRa scanner to verify the packet delivery rate of the network. Subsequently, the spreading factor and data rate of the network are configured for the best performance. At the center of the map, there is an observation tower with the height of approximately 25 m above ground. Weather station and LoRa gateway are installed near the top of the tower to avoid signal distortion by the peatland bushes and trees (around 2 to 10 m of height and of various density). LoRa gateway will aggregate all the data collected by the local sensor node, and upload to the cloud server using 4G cellular communication. The cloud server is located at MIMOS Malaysia, which is also responsible for the development of dashboard for collected data. The dashboard is accessible for local stakeholders for peatland monitoring and promote more efficient management process. Weather station installed is used to collect all the in-situ atmospheric data, including all the Fire Danger Rating System (FDRS) parameters (i.e., wind speed, ambient temperature, relative humidity, accumulated precipitation). Both the weather station and LoRa gateway are solar powered using the solar panel installed on top of the observation tower.

Two ground sensor nodes are installed at forest fire prone area suggested by the forest rangers from Selangor State Forestry Department. Ground data, including soil temperature and GWL or water table are monitored by the sensor nodes. These sensor nodes are battery powered and the battery status along with the Signal to Noise Ratio

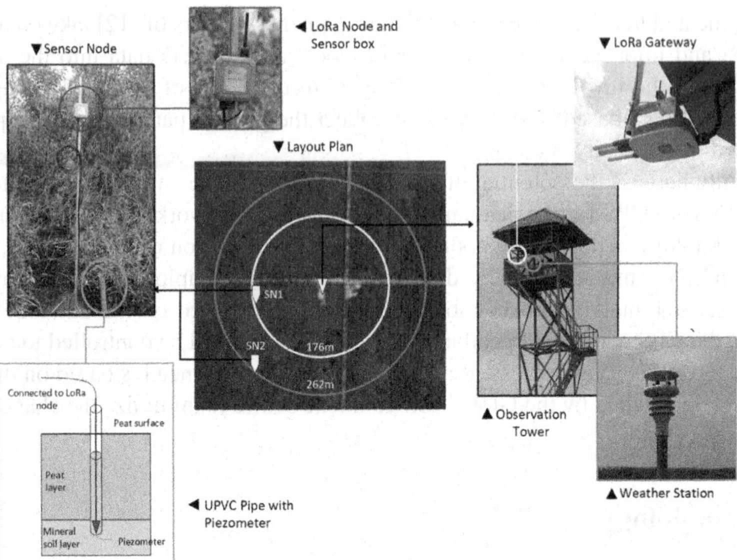


**Fig. 1.** Overall layout plan of the deployed IoT system, with each component highlighted.

(SINR) and collected ground data are transmitted to the LoRa gateway. The location of sensor node 1 (SN1) and sensor node 2 (SN2) are depicted in the Fig. 1.

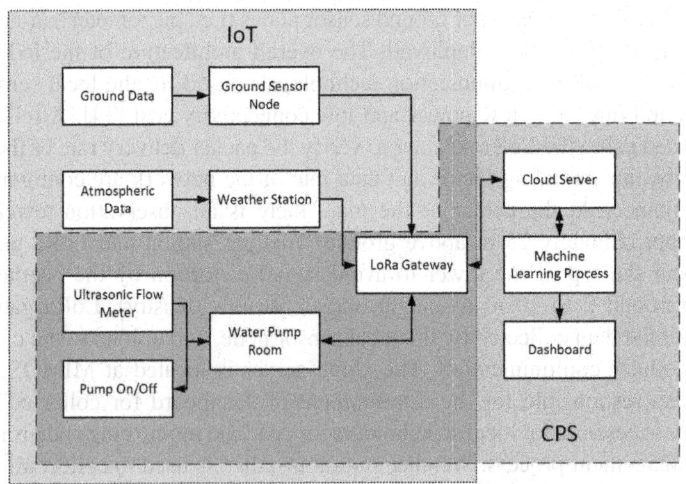


**Fig. 2.** Block diagram of IoT and CPS.

For the CPS, the plan is to integrate the water pump room into the IoT system for automated rewatering process. The block diagram of the collaborative IoT and CPS is illustrated in Fig. 2. The direction of the arrow represents the transmission direction of the data. 1-way arrow means the data is transmitted from source to the destination, whilst 2-way arrow means both uplink and downlink process are involved. Water is pumped from the nearby reservoir and distributed to the peatland using systematically installed water pipes. The water pump room is shown in the Fig. 3, where ultrasonic flow sensor is used to monitor the amount of water pumped to the peatland. The water pump room is also powered by solar panel for sustainable power management. Through the combination of cloud-based data analytic, the CPS can collaborate with the IoT system for automated actuating process and open up the possibility to smarter decision-making using external data.

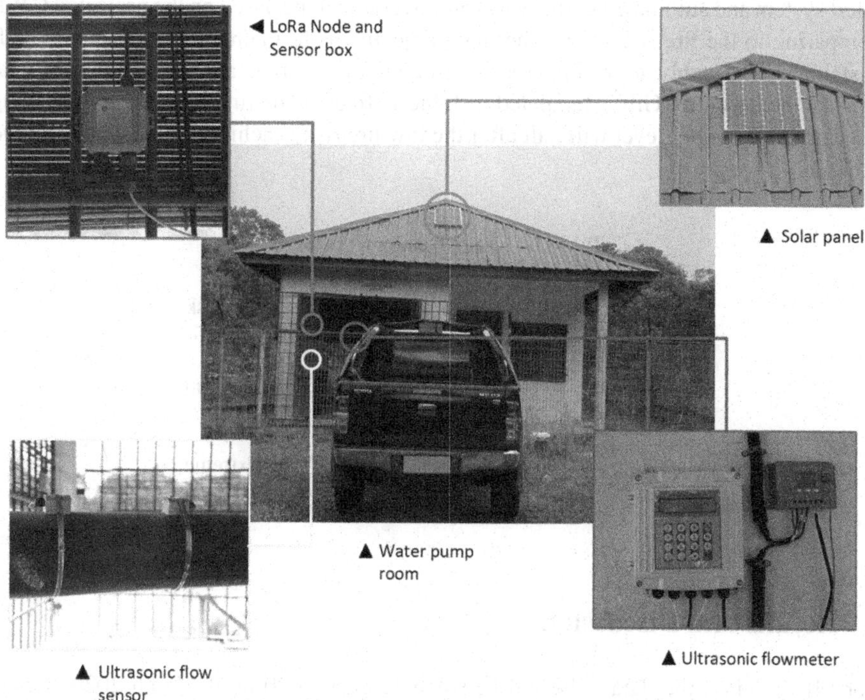


**Fig. 3.** Water pump room and its components.

## 2.2 Data Analytics

Efficient peatland management, especially rewatering method is a time-consuming process. It is benefited to commence the rewatering process early before the GWL drops to a critical level. Therefore, a GWL prediction model is developed using machine learning (ML). The complete process of the ML is depicted in Fig. 4. Prior to the training of ML model, the input data are cleaned and pre-processed. Multivariate regression is used because it encompasses the simultaneous analysis of more than one dependent variable (next-hour SN1 and SN2 GWL, next-day SN1 and SN2 GWL) based on more than one independent variable (FDRS parameters).

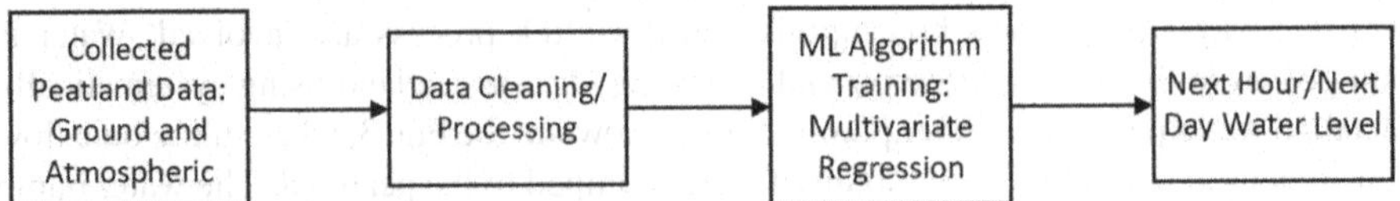


**Fig. 4.** Complete procedure of ML in proposed peatland management.

In this ML model, FDRS parameters and GWL detected by SN1 and SN2 are used as training attributes. The label of the ML model will be next hour and next day GWL. Alert system and automated of the water pump room will be based on the projected GWL comparing to the fire risk code. The main objective is to maintain the peatland GWL sustainably and stably at low fire risk according to the fire risk table provided by Global Environment Centre (GEC), tabulated in Table 1. To avoid disruption to the establishing vegetation, the water level will halt after the low fire risk is achieved, i.e., GWL around 0 mm.

**Table 1.** Fire risk codes from GEC.

| Water table depth range (mm) | Colour code | Fire risk |
|---|---|---|
| 500 to 0 | Blue | Low |
| −500 to 0 | Green | Medium |
| −500 to −700 | Yellow | High |
| −700 to −1000 | Red | Extreme |

## 3 Results and Discussion

For ML training, the data collected between January 2020 until March 2020 is used for the proof of concept. These data are verified, cleaned and subject to pre-processing, including standard scaler and attribute selection. After the cleaning process, 1739 data points are available in total. Following the data splitting, 1391 and 348 data points are used as train set and test set, respectively. GWL is the focus of this study as the CPS involves peatland rewatering process to reduce the risk of peatland forest fire. Figure 5 shows the trend of the GWL over the course of 3 months. The distance of the deployed ground sensor nodes is estimated around 86m, so the recorded GWL is expected to demonstrate similar trend. From the figure, the trend of the GWL recorded is almost identical, with a Pearson Correlation of 0.9695. The difference of the water level is constantly maintained at approximately 200 mm.

Figure 6 illustrated the performance of our ML model in predicting the next hour water level in mm after comparing the predicted values with true values. Blue line plotted on the graph represent the perfect prediction, while the red dots are predicted water level against the true water level. It is obvious that the trained ML model has very good level of

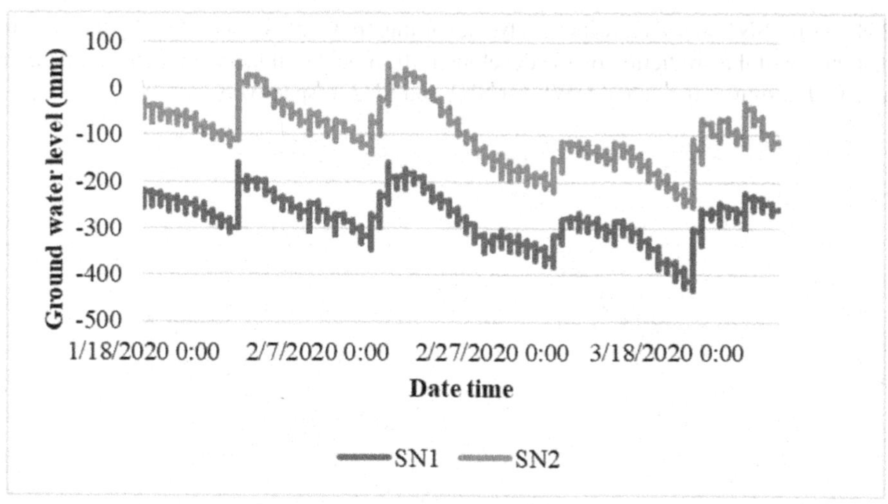


**Fig. 5.** GWL recorded by ground sensor nodes.

performance in terms of predicting the GWL for both SN1 and SN2. Upon analysis, the root mean square errors (RMSEs) of the ML model for next hour water level prediction are 7.2221 and 7.6592 for SN1 and SN2, respectively.

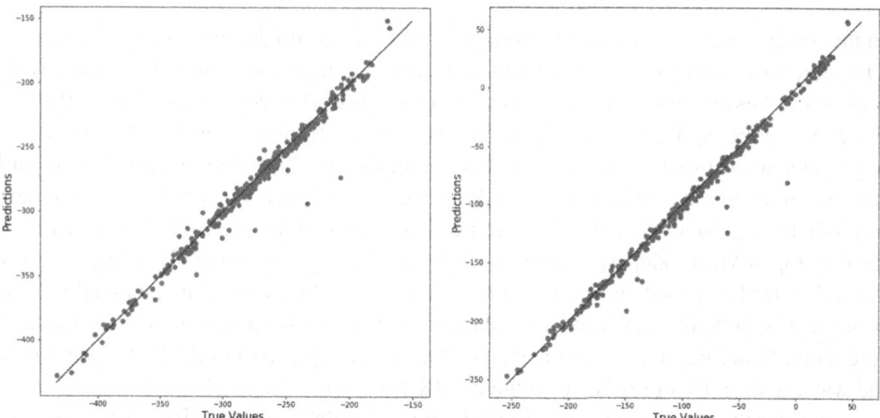


**Fig. 6.** Performance of ML model in predicting next hour GWL, left for SN1, right for SN2.

The ML model for next day water level prediction is also developed as a safety measure in case of any unexpected problem occurred to the water pump room or rewatering process. The performance of the ML model is shown in Fig. 7. Compare the performance of next hour prediction, the performance of ML model in predicting next day GWL has slightly degraded. This observation is reasonable as the relevancy of data at current time degrades heavily over the span of 24 h. Nonetheless, the projected values (red dots) still lie very close to the true values (blue line). The RMSEs of the ML model are 25.1012 and

29.8331 for SN1 and SN2, respectively. According to the 68-95-99 rule [15], this means that 99.7% of the prediction by the developed ML model will fall within the 75.303 mm and 89.499 mm of the actual GWL for SN1 and SN2, respectively.

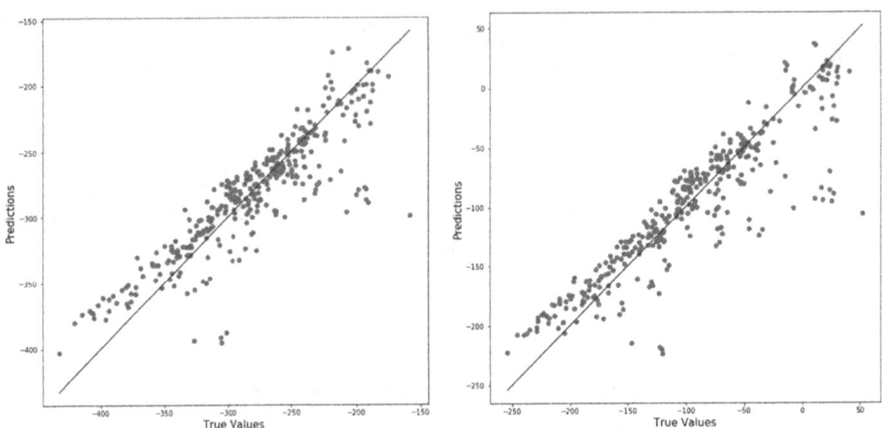


**Fig. 7.** Performance of ML model in predicting next day GWL, left for SN1, right for SN2.

## 4 Conclusion

In this study, a IoT system with CPS is proposed for sustainable peatland management. The reliability of IoT system to collect real-time data from the peatland can effectively reduce the labour cost of peatland management. Wireless communication at the site is established using LoRa technology for cost efficient transmission. Collected data are aggregated at the in-situ LoRa gateway before uploaded to the cloud server for dashboard presentation and data analytic process. ML model is developed using the collected data to predict the ground water level of the peatland in one hour and 24 h. The RMSEs of the developed ML model are averaged at 7.4407 and 27.4672 for next hour and next day ground water level prediction, respectively. The ability to estimate the peatland ground water level enable the stakeholder to take early initiatives in reducing the occurrence of forest fire. Water pump room at the peatland is integrated as part of the CPS to automate the water distribution process from the nearby reservoir.

For future work, the ML model will be trained with more data, including data collected from Meteorological Department Malaysia. Apart from the prediction of GWL, the dashboard of the system will be furnished with calculation of real-time Fire Weather Index. Furthermore, discussion has been held with the regulatory bodies to enhance the system with surveillance system for prevention of illegal slash-and burn activities.

**Acknowledgments.** The authors would like to acknowledge NICT Japan and ASEAN-IVO for funding this project NAPC (Networked ASEAN Peatland Forests Communities), Selangor State Forestry Department (JPNS) for permission to deploy the IoT system, MetMalaysia, LORANET Technologies and Global Environment Centre (GEC) for valuable feedback and validation of peatland data.

## References


1. Craft, C.: Creating and Restoring Wetlands: From Theory to Practice. Elsevier (2015)
2. Harenda, K.M., Lamentowicz, M., Samson, M., Chojnicki, B.H.: The role of peatlands and their carbon storage function in the context of climate change. In: Zielinski, T., Sagan, I., Surosz, W. (eds.) Interdisciplinary approaches for sustainable development goals. GEPS, pp. 169–187. Springer, Cham (2018). https://doi.org/10.1007/978-3-319-71788-3_12
3. Lo, J., Parish, F.: Peatlands and Climate Change in Southeast Asia. ASEAN Secretariat and Global Environment Centre (2013)
4. Istomo, K.E., Tata, H.L., Sumbayak, E.S., Rahma, A.: Evaluation of silviculture systems in peat swamp forest in Indonesia. In: Pusat Penelitian dan Pengembangan Hutan dan Konservasi Alam bekerjasama dengan. ITTO CITES Project. Indonesia (2010)
5. Natural Environment Agency: Asean Guidelines on Peatland Forest Fire Management (2015)
6. Zantalis, F., Koulouras, G., Karabetsos, S., Kandris, D.: A review of machine learning and Iot in smart transportation. Fut. Internet **11**(4), 94 (2019)
7. Paul, A.K., Sato, T.: Localization in wireless sensor networks: a survey on algorithms, measurement techniques, applications and challenges. J. Sens. Actuator Netw. **6**(4), 24 (2017)
8. Dey, N., Ashour, A.S., Shi, F., Fong, S.J., Sherratt, R.S.: Developing residential wireless sensor networks for ECG healthcare monitoring. IEEE Trans. Consum. Electron. **63**(4), 442–449 (2017)
9. Dafflon, B., Moalla, N., Ouzrout, Y.: The challenges, approaches, and used techniques of cps for manufacturing in industry 4.0: a literature review. Int. J. Adv. Manuf. Technol. **113**(7–8), 2395–2412 (2021). https://doi.org/10.1007/s00170-020-06572-4
10. Cheng, L., Wang, T., Hong, X., Wang, Z., Wang, J., Liu, J.: A study on the architecture of manufacturing Internet of Things. Int. J. Model. Ident. Control **23**(1), 8–23 (2015)
11. Ismail, M.E.R., Shukri, I.F.A., Azmi, A., Yahya, Y., Ismail, S.A., Sulaiman, M.S.: Development of agronomist station system for water table management at Peatland. In: 2019 6th International Conference on Research and Innovation in Information Systems (ICRIIS), pp. 1–6. IEEE (2019)
12. Sali, A., et al.: Peatlands monitoring in Malaysia with IoT systems: preliminary experimental results. In: Suhaili, W.S.H., Siau, N.Z., Omar, S., Phon-Amuaisuk, S. (eds.) CIIS 2021. AISC, vol. 1321, pp. 233–242. Springer, Cham (2021). https://doi.org/10.1007/978-3-030-68133-3_23
13. Essa, S., Petra, R., Uddin, M.R., Suhaili, W.S.H., Ilmi, N.I.: IoT-based environmental monitoring system for Brunei peat swamp forest. In: 2020 International Conference on Computer Science and its Application in Agriculture (ICOSICA), pp. 1–5. IEEE (2020)
14. Petäjäjärvi, J., Mikhaylov, K., Pettissalo, M., Janhunen, J., Iinatti, J.: Performance of a low-power wide-area network based on LoRa technology: Doppler robustness, scalability, and coverage. Int. J. Distrib. Sens. Netw. **13**, 3 (2017)
15. Warren, R.M.: Visual intensity judgments: an empirical rule and a theory. Psychol. Rev. **76**, 6 (1969)

# Business Analytics in Production Management – Challenges and Opportunities Using Real-World Case Experience

Andrea Kő(✉) and Tibor Kovács

Corvinus University of Budapest, Fővám tér 8, Budapest, Hungary
{andrea.ko,tibor.kovacs}@uni-corvinus.hu

**Abstract.** Data is a key component of smart manufacturing coming from various sources and in different forms. The amount of data produced in the Manufacturing Data Life Cycle (MDLC) could be vast and remain useless if not processed and mapped into information that is understood by users. Because of the data volume, velocity, variety, and veracity, it is not feasible to expect humans to analyze it using traditional manufacturing tools; business analytics solutions provide more efficient means. In this paper, first, we aim at identifying the latest research areas and trends of business analytics (BA) in the production management (PM) literature using text mining, bibliometric mapping, and visual analytics. We discuss the related research gaps, BA challenges and problems and give suggestions for possible BA applications and future research directions. Second, we selected the performance management and decision-making cluster for presenting a real-world case and we applied MDLC as a framework. The case study presents a big data analytics performance monitoring system from a multi-product refinery.

**Keywords:** Business analytics · Production management · Manufacturing Data Life Cycle · Data-driven decision making · Performance management

## 1 Introduction

Data is a key component of smart manufacturing coming from various sources and in different forms. The amount of data produced in the Manufacturing Data Life Cycle (MDLC) could be vast and remain useless if not processed and mapped into information that is understood by users. Because of the data volume, velocity, variety, and veracity, it is not feasible to expect humans to analyze it using traditional manufacturing tools; business analytics solutions provide more efficient means. The "information age [1]" has laid the foundation of information technologies, that capitalize on manufacturing data for business analytics and process monitoring. Smart manufacturing however delivered the supplementary technologies that were required to handle data in larger quantities, from diverse sources and in disparate formats and to accomplish significantly more complex data transformations and analysis for more responsive decision making. There are numerous challenges related to data driven performance monitoring: vast quantity


Published by Springer Nature Switzerland AG 2021
L. M. Camarinha-Matos et al. (Eds.): PRO-VE 2021, IFIP AICT 629, pp. 558–566, 2021.
https://doi.org/10.1007/978-3-030-85969-5_52

of data, diverse sources, questionable data quality, ongoing use of legacy systems and the absence of strong analytics culture. This latter means that data is not perceived as a core asset of the organization, senior management is not leading the organization to become more data-driven and analytical, and the organization is not using analytical insights to guide strategy [2]. We examine how the new business analytics technologies, and a strong analytics culture could contribute to production management, performance monitoring and performance improvements in the manufacturing environment.

In this paper, we have two goals. First, we aim at identifying the latest research areas and trends of business analytics (BA) in the production management (PM). From methodological aspects we followed the steps of systematic literature review combined with text mining, bibliometric mapping, and visual analytics (we discuss the methodological steps in Sect. 2.1). As a result, we got research areas, clusters, which are worth to investigate. We detail the related research gaps, BA challenges and problems and give suggestions for possible BA applications and future research directions. Second, we selected the performance management and decision-making cluster for presenting a real-world case and we applied Manufacturing Data Life Cycle as a framework. The case study presents a big data analytics performance monitoring system from a multi-product refinery. The contribution of our research is the following: 1) identification the latest research areas and trends of BA in production management based on the literature 2) discussion of research gaps, BA challenges and problems; providing suggestions for possible BA applications and future research directions 3) demonstrate and connect our findings through a real-world case performance monitoring solution.

## 2 Business Analytics in Production Management – Literature Review

The term "business analytics" was introduced to represent the key analytical components of business intelligence in the late 2000s [3]. Chen, Chiang and Storey [4] distinguish 3 phases in the history of business intelligence and analytics (BI&A), denoted as BI&A 1.0, 2.0, and 3.0 according to Gartner BI reports on platforms' core capabilities and the hype cycle. Data management and data warehousing is considered as the foundation of BI&A 1.0, BI&A 2.0 bringing in text and web analytics capabilities for unstructured contents, using web intelligence and the analysis of user-generated content. BI&A 3.0 is opening new opportunities by utilizing data from mobile devices and their complete ecosystems, as well as from sensor-based Internet-enabled devices equipped with RFID, barcodes, and radio tags (the "Internet of Things"). Business analytics covers descriptive analytics (what is happening), predictive analytics (what will happen next) and prescriptive analytics (what is the best course for the future) [5]. Business analytics applies various advanced analytic techniques answering questions or solve problems related to business [6]. Isasi et al. [7] surveyed the literature of big data and business analytics applications in the supply chain using bibliometrics and systematic analysis. Zhang and Chen [8] provides a comprehensive review of the recent research on Industry 4.0, IoT, Blockchain, and Business Analytics.

### 2.1 Literature Review - Methodology and Preliminary Results

Our literature review approach is split into two phases. First, we collected the relevant articles from Scopus to prepare a corpus of BA in PM domain, and analyzed these articles using text mining, bibliometric mapping, and visual analytics. Second, using the results from the first phase and combining it with our own experience in the field, we extended the analysis to potential research challenges, directions and relevant BA solutions using a more detailed and focused discussion.

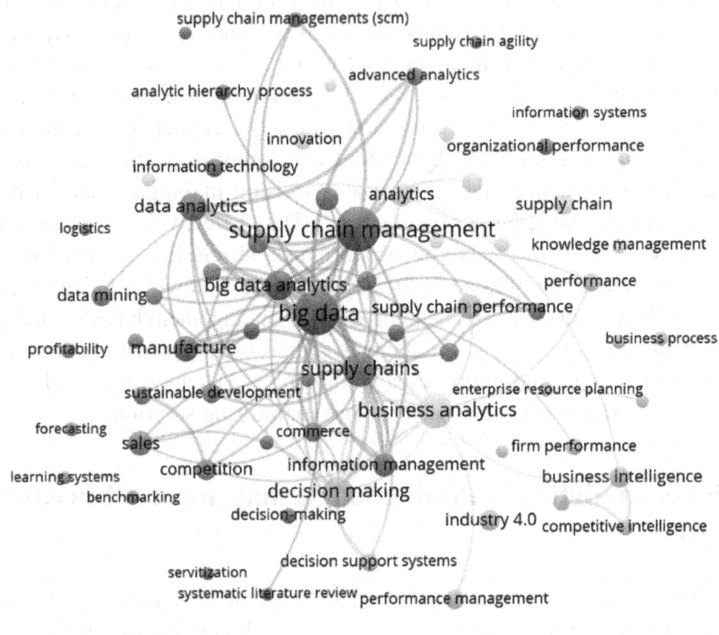


**Fig. 1.** Bibliometric mapping and text mining of business analytics articles with VOSviewer[1]

[1] The Figure is an illustration it doesn't contain all concepts' labels.

Preparing the corpus for text mining, we focused on papers from Scopus with primary keywords of "business analytics" and "production management", resulting to 314 articles (up to December 2020). We tested Web of Science as an alternative source but discarded it due to their limited number of articles (less than 50 papers). To explore the main research areas of BA in PM, we clustered the articles with VOSviewer bibliometric mapping and text mining solution [9] and described the clusters using the most compelling keywords (Fig. 1).

The analysis resulted to five clusters, however due to the similarity of the fourth and fifth clusters, both related to knowledge, information management and business analytics were combined. Table 1 details the research areas defined by the clusters, their domain, and their BA related keywords, as well as the research challenges, directions,

**Table 1.** Research areas/clusters of business analytics in production management corpus

| Research area/cluster name | Keywords describing the research domain | Keywords describing business analytics characteristics | Research challenges, directions and opportunities from BA viewpoints |
|---|---|---|---|
| Sustainable and competitive supply chain | Competition<br>Resource-based view<br>Competitive advantage<br>Sustainability<br>Supply chains<br>Sustainable development | Predictive analytics<br>Data mining<br>Regression analysis<br>Learning systems | How to process unstructured data produced in a supply chain (e.g., log file, image, data from sensors)? This field is usually not included to predictive analytics, but most data produced in this category |
| Performance management and decision making | Supply chain<br>Performance<br>Industry 4.0<br>Performance<br>Firm performance<br>Performance management | Business intelligence<br>Decision support systems<br>Decision making | Which BA tools support problem solving process, cause effect analysis correlation and optimization? |
| Big Data analytics | Supply chain management<br>Industrial research | Big data<br>Big data analytics | Which BA applications to apply, what are the related conditions? |
| Knowledge and information management | Innovation<br>Knowledge management<br>Information management<br>Enterprise resource management | Supply chain analytics<br>Data analytics | How to map and store domain knowledge and which is the way of application of domain knowledge in BA solutions? |

and opportunities from BA viewpoints. Our view is that the key challenges are the following: 1) predictive analytics and data mining require developing methods to process unstructured data produced in a supply chain, 2) business intelligence and decision support systems need developing and implementing BA tools to support the problem solving process, cause effect analysis, correlation and optimization, 3) big data analytics need developing BA applications and that take into consideration production specific conditions, and finally 4) supply chain data analytics poses the challenge of how to map and store domain specific knowledge and which is the way of applying this domain knowledge in BA solutions.

## 2.2 Business Analytics Problems and Challenges in the Manufacturing Data Life Cycle

The aim of this section is to identify the typical BA problems and challenges related to the phases of MDLC. We use MDLC of Tao et al. [1] as a discussion framework to connect the research challenges identified in the literature review, from our experience and the issues revealed from our real-world case (Fig. 2). Data in a manufacturing environment is ***collected*** from numerous ***sources*** in a variety of ways, that can be structured (e.g., databases), semi-structured (e.g., XML documents), or unstructured (e.g., textual information from equipment and error logs) [10]. Data ***processing*** starts with the pre-processing steps of data cleaning and data reduction; it is usually a complex and non-trivial operation. In the manufacturing environment, missing values are common, and they pose a challenge to the application of machine learning algorithms [11].

| Phases of Manufacturing Life Cycle | | Problems and Challenges | Connection to the real-world case |
|---|---|---|---|
| Data sources | Equipment, Product, Management | Diverse data sources, Questionable data quality | Data quality issues: missing data, errors reappearing after initial cleansing |
| Data collection | ETL (Extract, Transform, Load) | Different data sources require different solutions | Skills to handle industrial and business systems as data sources. |
| Data storage | On-site, Cloud | Security concerns and limitations of storing data in the cloud | Real-time data analysis and visualization requires on-site storage |
| Data processing | Data cleaning → Data reduction → Data analysis → Data mining | Model selection Text and process mining | Data reduction required to analyse IoT data over long period. |
| Data visualization | Data visualization | Appropriate selection of visualizations. Interpretation skills | Dashboards to facilitate performance review and problem solving |
| Data application | Design, Decision support, MRO | Lack of BA skills and analytics culture | Driven by KPIs. Broad range from dashboards to Machine Learning models. |

**Fig. 2.** Business analytics challenges using Manufacturing Data Life Cycle MDLC [1].

Data reduction transforms the massive volume of data into ordered, meaningful, and simplified forms, followed by data analysis covering a wide variety of techniques, including machine learning, data mining, time-series analysis, large-scale computing, and the use of forecasting models. Visual analytics and ***visualization*** support the communication with end users, it helps having a clear, user-friendly view of the data and an easy understanding the data processing results [12].

Tao et al. [1] distinguished three types of data applications: The first (design) helps in demand analysis, smart design, and market forecasting through better understanding of customers, competitors, and markets. The second (manufacturing) supports decision making, product quality control and equipment supervision. The third phase (MRO - maintenance, repair, and operations) enriches monitoring operations, fault predictions and smart maintenance. These data applications can lead to informed decisions concerning whether, when, and how to adjust the manufacturing processes and equipment, and how to facilitate the control and improvement of product quality, yield, or energy usage.

## 3 Business Analytics Problems and Challenges from a Real-World Case

We utilize experiences collected in a real-world case to discuss the business analytics problems and challenges in production management. The case is from a large multi-product refinery that has recently implemented a performance monitoring system using big data analytics. Management was driving the implementation to sustain the previously achieved annual performance improvements of over 10% per year in several areas like energy efficiency, yields and volumes; and to make the operation more secure for the long run. The plant applies World Class Manufacturing methodology, of which visual performance management (VPM) is a key component. VPM helps improving internal and external communication, facilitates performance measurement and review, enhances collaboration and supports the cultural change [13]. The system was developed with the desire to use existing data sources, demonstrate compliance to performance standards, visualize performance trends and assist with performance improvement initiatives as a diagnostics tool. The case was specifically selected as the plant possessed large number of Industrial IoT sensors, however the utilisation of data from these sensors were sporadic and ad-hoc. It was therefore interesting to explore how a business analytics system could add value to this installation.

### 3.1 Background on the Case

The plant had high levels of process control with state-of-the-art automation, Industrial IoT process measurement and data storage, recording numerical values of process parameters (e.g. flow rates, temperatures, pressures) and also alarm and error logs. Laboratory results were collected using Excel workbooks, being migrated to a Laboratory Information Management System (LIMS). Maintenance records were stored in a Computerized Maintenance Management System, recording equipment failures, repair and restoration activities as well as predictive maintenance related data. This broad range of separate systems made it difficult the concurrent analysis of data from different sources, limiting process optimisation efforts (Fig. 3).

The project started by reviewing existing key performance indicators and performance metrics, defining new ones, with the desire to get an integrated, holistic view on business performance. Both lead and lag indicators [14] were used in the final set, the former being proactive, preventive and predictive while the latter displaying the final outcome. Process parameters like temperature, pressure, flow rate were often used as lead indicators supporting the process optimisation efforts: setting the optimal parameter values and using process control to ensure the adherence to those set values.

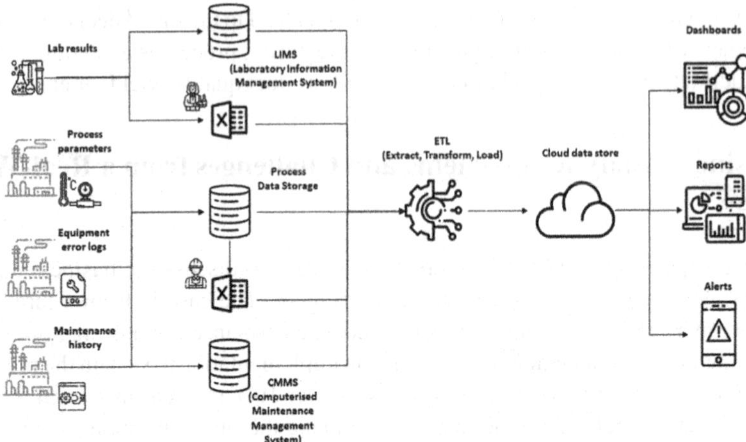


**Fig. 3.** Performance monitoring system architecture using big data.

### 3.2 Challenges to Implement Business Analytics in the Real-World Case

Design science methodology for information systems [15] was used for investigating the problems and challenges of performance monitoring and business analytics solutions in relation to the MDLC phases. The case showed that with the currently available business analytics tools, a performance monitoring solution could be relatively quickly developed, demonstrating the value of data-driven decision making. The amount of data stored in the system was rather a burden than an advantage; finding the appropriate information of process parameters among the ones that were recorded required the thorough knowledge of system. It requires the careful selection of those that objects that are connected to key performance indicators. Data quality poses a serious threat to the success of such projects, often realised only after the project is underway. Structural errors (format errors, typos) could break the data extraction, transformation and load (ETL) process, while missing data and outliers would result to implausible results, making visualizations meaningless. The ETL process therefore must be prepared for both the initial cleansing and the ongoing data quality issues [16]. The benefit of such an automated system over a manual system is enabling real time data processing and alerting, flexible analysis of larger data sets, from desperate sources and better supporting problem solving and decision making by cause and effect analysis. However, the case drew the attention to the fact, that taking advantage of this would require a strong analytics culture. A key success factor of such an initiative is a commitment from management, encouraging the use of analytics and data-driven decision making, and developing the human analytical competence.

## 4 Conclusion

Our investigation of the real-world performance monitoring and business analytics solution in the context of the MDLC of Tao et al. [1] resulted to the following findings: The divers data sources in manufacturing, often with questionable data quality poses some serious challenge to the success of developing a business analytics solution. Missing data and outliers, often related to the unreliability of field equipment makes especially difficult data aggregation, requiring foresight and sound business logic. The data collection requires skills in both industrial and business systems as data sources. Regarding data storage, there are limitations and security concerns of storing data in the cloud. On premises data storage therefore could be a requirement to overcome these problems. The data processing would require the appropriate selection of models, including text mining methods for processing alarm and error logs. The amount of data from IoT sensors would require data reduction, to enable processing it over a longer period. Dashboards should facilitate performance review and problem solving, choosing the right visualizations for different metrics and performance indicators. Finally, Specific business analytics applications should be selected based on key performance indicators that could vary from simple dashboards to complex machine learning models. Our investigation highlighted, that the lack of business analytics skills and analytics culture could be a barrier to success. It needs to be developed simultaneously with the development of the performance monitoring and business analytics solution.

## References


1. Tao, F., Qi, Q., Liu, A., Kusiak, A.: Data-driven smart manufacturing. J. Manuf. Syst. **48**, 157–169 (2018). https://doi.org/10.1016/j.jmsy.2018.01.006
2. Kiron, D., Prentice, P.K., Ferguson, R.B.: The analytics mandate. MIT Sloan Manag. Rev. **55**, 1–25 (2014)
3. Davenport, T.H.: Competing on analytics. Harvard Bus. Rev. **84**, 1–10 (2006)
4. Chen, H., Chiang, R.H.L., Storey, V.C.: Business intelligence and analytics: From big data to big impact. MIS Q. **36**(4), 1165 (2012). https://doi.org/10.2307/41703503
5. Stubbs, E.: The Value of Business Analytics: Identifying the Path to Profitability. Wiley (2011)
6. Trkman, P., McCormack, K., Valadares, M.P., de Oliveira, M., Ladeira, B.: The impact of business analytics on supply chain performance. Decis. Support Syst. **49**(3), 318–327 (2010). https://doi.org/10.1016/j.dss.2010.03.007
7. Isasi, N.K.G., Frazzon, E.M., Uriona, M.: Big Data and business analytics in the supply chain: a review of the literature. IEEE Lat. Am. Trans. **13**(10), 3382–3391 (2015). https://doi.org/10.1109/TLA.2015.7387245
8. Zhang, C., Chen, Y.: A review of research relevant to the emerging industry trends: industry 4.0, IoT, blockchain, and business analytics. J. Ind. Integr. Manage. **05**(01), 165–180 (2020). https://doi.org/10.1142/S2424862219500192
9. van Eck, N.J., Waltman, L.: Software survey: VOSviewer, a computer program for bibliometric mapping. Scientometrics **84**(2), 523–538 (2010). https://doi.org/10.1007/s11192-009-0146-3
10. Gandomi, A., Haider, M.: Beyond the hype: big data concepts, methods, and analytics. Int. J. Inf. Manage. **35**(2), 137–144 (2015). https://doi.org/10.1016/j.ijinfomgt.2014.10.007
11. Pham, D.T., Afify, A.A.: Machine-learning techniques and their applications in manufacturing. Proc. Inst. Mech. Eng. Part B J. Eng. Manuf. **219**(5), 395–412 (2005). https://doi.org/10.1243/095440505X32274
12. Kovács, T., Kő, A.: Machine learning based monitoring of the pneumatic actuators' behavior through signal processing using real-world data set. In: Dang, T.K., Küng, J., Takizawa, M., Bui, S.H. (eds.) FDSE 2019. LNCS, vol. 11814, pp. 33–44. Springer, Cham (2019). https://doi.org/10.1007/978-3-030-35653-8_3

13. Bititci, U., Cocca, P., Ates, A.: Impact of visual performance management systems on the performance management practices of organisations. Int. J. Prod. Res. **54**(6), 1571–1593 (2016). https://doi.org/10.1080/00207543.2015.1005770
14. Anderson, K., McAdam, R.: A critique of benchmarking and performance measurement: lead or lag? Benchmarking Int. J. **11**(5), 465–483 (2004). https://doi.org/10.1108/14635770410557708
15. Wieringa, R.J.: What is design science? In: Design Science Methodology for Information Systems and Software Engineering. Springer, Heidelberg (2014). https://doi.org/10.1007/978-3-662-43839-8_1
16. Marsh, R.: Drowning in dirty data? It's time to sink or swim: a four-stage methodology for total data quality management. J. Database Mark. Customer Strategy Manage. **12**, 105–112 (2005). https://doi.org/10.1057/palgrave.dbm.3240247

# Industrial Collaborative Robotics Platform

Luís Vicente[1], Pedro Lomelino[1], Fernando Carreira[1,3], Francisco M. Campos[1], Mário J. G. C. Mendes[1,2], A. Luís Osório[1], and J. M. F. Calado[1,3](✉)

[1] ISEL – Instituto Superior de Engenharia de Lisboa, Instituto Politécnico de Lisboa, 1959-007 Lisbon, Portugal
{A42292,A43640}@alunos.isel.pt, {fernando.carreira, francisco.campos,mario.mendes,luis.osorio,joao.calado}@isel.pt
[2] CENTEC – Centre for Marine Technology and Ocean Engineering, Lisbon, Portugal
[3] LAETA/IDMEC – Instituto de Engenharia Mecânica, Lisbon, Portugal

**Abstract.** Cyber-physical systems are not designed to integrate an industrial collaborative network when their integration with other systems is required. It is necessary to adopt a strategic model of integration and value creation that allows the interoperability of equipment supported by open technologies, based on the concepts underlying Industry 4.0. To this end, a conceptual information architecture is proposed to manage industrial robotic platforms based on a Cyber Device Bus design. The challenge is to contribute to an open technological framework involving computer systems, cyber-physical systems, and IoT elements in a logic of integration by adaptation without the need for specialized adapters. Adaptation occurs through the adoption of the Informatics System of Systems (ISoS) technological framework, providing an integrated service-oriented (micro-services) view of technology elements and establishing cooperation between computer and cyber-physical systems under different responsibilities and based on a diversity of technological frameworks.

**Keywords:** Interoperability · Industrial collaborative network · Communication platform · Systems of systems

## 1 Introduction

Increasingly, associations seek to increase flexibility and responsiveness to meet the individual requirements of each client. Industry 4.0 has demanded that physical processes interconnect with cyber components, defining cyber-physical systems (CPS), enabling an environment where the physical world merges with the cyber world [1]. From the point of view of information and computer science, new information technologies must be gradually applied on the shop floor, integrating CPS framed into architectures based on the Internet of Things (IoT) as a strategy to create a collaborative environment. The IoT represents a technological revolution where the goal is to connect independent devices (each having its computing and communication parts, technologically differentiated and


L. M. Camarinha-Matos et al. (Eds.): PRO-VE 2021, IFIP AICT 629, pp. 567–576, 2021.
https://doi.org/10.1007/978-3-030-85969-5_53

possibly ownership from different responsibilities) in a network, through the establishment of a global communication system, providing them with the ability to communicate with each other [2, 3].

Currently, any process under the concept of smart factories is carried out using several enterprise information systems (EIS), such as supervisory control and data acquisition (SCADA) systems, manufacturing execution systems (MES), enterprise resource planning systems (ERP), human resource management systems (HRM) and customer relationship management systems (CRM), among others. In this context, it is essential to guarantee the cooperation between EIS and their interoperability in order to achieve an effective management structure of corporate systems. Collaboration between different EIS is hampered by the fact that they are often developed by different suppliers, which creates the need to integrate them into a single collaborative platform [1].

The ability to interconnect systems within a system of systems framework emphasizes the need for an innovative approach to organize the diversity of technological artifacts that may be under the responsibility of different entities. This approach amounts to providing intelligent and communication capabilities to all devices, thus driving automation and monitoring capacity [4]. Currently, the typical EIS framework of organizations is still built on automation islands, as a set of disparate systems for process automation in a given application domain [5].

This paper addresses industrial robotic platforms' management that consists of a collaborative industrial network connecting robots and automated systems. A conceptual information system architecture based on the Informatics System of Systems (ISoS) framework and architectural methodology to achieve that goal is proposed, which guarantees interoperability and allows easy collaboration between different EIS.

This article is organized as follows: Sect. 2 analyses the state of the art of collaborative information architectures; Sect. 3 describes the ISoS methodology; a conceptual information system architecture based on the ISoS approach to achieve a collaborative platform of industrial robots is presented in Sect. 4. Finally, the conclusions and recommendations for future work are summarized in Sect. 5.

## 2 State of the Art

In the last century, the added value for industries came from the development of the mechanical domain. Today, the computer domain made possible through the evolution of information technologies has become the main driver of the development of organizations [6]. The growing mass customization requires that large volumes of data be simultaneously exchanged in real-time between different organizational systems. Thus, the challenge is to achieve direct communication between the Fieldbus and the application layer that promotes interoperability between all software and physical processes. This communication paradigm translates into a communication infrastructure over the internet. Each node represents a computer or CPS within the organization that can communicate with many other nodes (Fig. 1), thereby creating an environment based on collaborative processes. In this interwoven network, machines and applications need to communicate in the same language, coexist in the same infrastructure, and comply with multiple requirements [7].

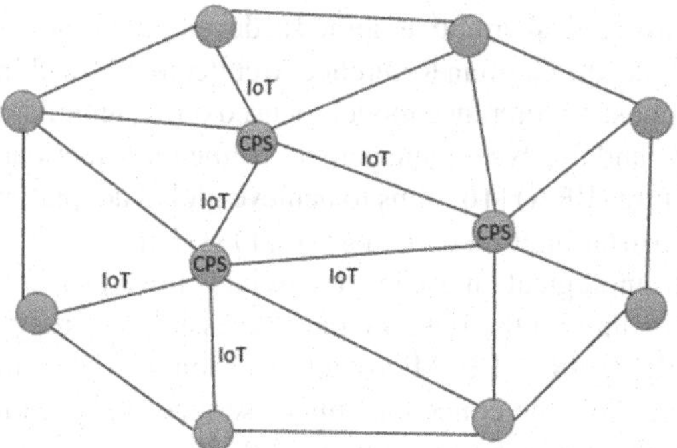


**Fig. 1.** Collaborative information network.

Usually, computers and CPS are not designed to cooperate when the goal is the integration (interoperability) with other systems, potentially from a different business organization, seller, or supplier. When two or more systems under different responsibilities communicate, their managers must agree on the interfaces to use or provide access to a repository (database) through which systems can share data. Despite being a common practice to share information between systems, the access to databases generates strong dependencies between them, reflected in the dependence on changes, which are difficult to manage, e.g., in the face of a change to the database schema [5]. In order to avoid strong dependencies in networks, mediation strategies are adopted involving specialized computer systems to establish "bridges" through the "Hub and Spoke Integration" model [8] or the organization/company service bus (Enterprise Service Bus - ESB) [9, 10]. However, the use of mediation systems, e.g., ESB, contributes to strengthening the technological dependence. Often, these systems centralize dependencies of different technological systems and do not support a more competitive framework of responsibilities, in which exchanging systems or parts of systems would be seamless [11]. From the above, it can be concluded that system diversity hinders traditional systems from achieving the goals of Industry 4.0.

Communication on an industrial network is performed through a cyber platform commonly called Cyber Device Bus. To ensure communication between different systems, a computer systems architecture based on the design of an open Cyber Device Bus is necessary, with the following requirements: provide an open computational platform, ensure collaboration and ensure interoperability between computational entities and/or cyber-physical systems [12]. The design of this platform and the underlying architecture requires a set of non-functional requirements, typical of this type of open and distributed systems, namely: interoperability, transparency in location, fault tolerance, data, and communication security and scalability. In addition to the non-functional requirements, further requirements are needed, such as resilience, performance, portability, and substitutability [13].

In recent years, there has been much research into new collaborative reference architectures for Industry 4.0. However, works on conceptual architectures often lack a physical implementation, and application examples do not typically generalize to other systems [14].

There are currently several initiatives aimed at developing standardized system architectures. As an example, the German Reference Architecture Model Industry (RAMI 4.0) (DIN 2016) [15] proposes a reference model focused on system hierarchy, vertical communication network, and life cycle management, while the American Industrial Internet Reference Architecture (IIRA) [16] aims to achieve global adaptation and collaborative autonomy in an industrial Internet of Things (IIoT) system.

In the current technological landscape, the trend is towards a concentration of functionalities that, depending on the risk, are only accessible to proprietary technological frameworks (SAP, IBM, ORACLE, Microsoft, Amazon, Google, among others). These approaches, which include the concept of micro-services [17], do not convey relevant innovation in the context of a Service-Oriented Architecture (SOA) [18], so they are unlikely to promote integrated approaches that support processes in the digital age. There are currently several approaches to perform interoperability tasks between CPS, but these are proprietary systems. The diversity of techniques means that to perform changes or upgrades in the system, the customer is very dependent on the proprietary organization. Thus, the existing standards do not guarantee the substitutability of systems or elements of a computer system with potentially more competitive alternatives. In other words, the current standards are not complete in the sense of guaranteeing the exchangeability of systems or computer system elements with potentially more competitive alternatives [19]. The lifecycle of a CPS may span decades, depending on its application domain. Thus, it is necessary to ensure those information architectures and their associated support services are available throughout the CPS lifecycle. Current approaches are struggling with the problem of technological dependency, known as the vendor lock-in situation. It is well known that public and private entities experience difficulties developing their innovation processes when they depend on technological devices, from the IoT level to the decision support services [11].

To avoid problems associated with vendor dependency, many companies using CPS have recently chosen to keep the development of their information architecture in-house as a means of avoiding potential risks inherent in commercial architectures. This strategy gave rise to open-source solutions, e.g. Papyrus (2020) [20] and Capella (2020) [21], which allow companies to develop their own customized information architectures. Several open-source initiatives have also been launched, as evidenced by the efforts of NASA, the Japanese Science and Technology Agency, and several consortia of industry and academia in Europe in creating open-source tools to assist in the development of collaborative information architectures [22].

More cooperative EIS environments based on information/knowledge are needed to meet current business demands. The cooperative EIS need contrasts with today's information architectures in most applications, which simply connect devices and can hardly support collaborative optimization for production systems. Other than that, information architectures should promote a relationship chain where all computers and CPSs provide support for knowledge construction, process monitoring, decision support, requirements management, and control [1].

There are currently numerous technological approaches that can be used to build a collaborative information architecture ensuring interoperability between various EIS. However, most of these are proprietary approaches that are difficult to budget and are not based on previously validated models. Most technological artifacts are not based on standard or reference models, which implies that the market does not moderate their cost. Thus, any change to the system, such as an integration requirement, is dependent on the involvement of those responsible for it, at a price that has no reference to be supported [23]. The fact that state-of-art relies on unique computer systems developed as custom software without a formal framework and open modularity foundations has been a barrier to sustainable innovation.

## 3 Informatics System of Systems Approach

Today's industrial challenges have made production structures more complex and require new management and organizational strategies that offer greater flexibility, agility, efficiency, and effectiveness. In order to meet this challenge, remote and intelligent control and monitoring systems must be developed that deal with the distinctive functionalities of sensor and actuator networks, monitor hardware and software, and connect with production management and planning. These smart systems require high automation and information processing levels, allowing for rapid response to shop floor changes. An outcome of coupling smart supervisory with real-time decision support systems is the reduction of lead-times and costs on the shop floor, achieved through flexibility improvement of the production processes and by enhancing management control, which is supported by new decision support tools based on self-learning approaches and smart analytics. Hence, this paper addresses the implementation of a service-oriented *Cooperation Enabled Services* (CES) as a modularity abstraction framework to reduce the technology dependencies and empower the modeling and intelligence capabilities.

The Informatics System of Systems (ISoS) [11] founds an open technological framework and incorporates the concept of Open Adaptive Coupling Infrastructure (OACI) to facilitate interoperability. This framework has been applied in several systems to structure technological artifacts of a company/organization, e.g., the Brisa tolls, speed control network (ANSR/SINCRO), and the automatic payment control in service area networks [23]. In the ISoS framework, a computational or cyber-physical element of *an Informatics System* (Isystem) is structured as the composition of one or more CES. A CES models a composite of Service elements. An innovative aspect of the ISoS model is that a CES is made up of services (computational parts of CPS or computer systems) that can be developed under any technological framework. The ISoS model allows any service belonging to an Isystem to be instantiated as an element of a computer or cyber-physical system. ISoS makes it possible for an organization/company to cooperate with any other Service of a CES from another Isystem without the need for specialized adapters.

The aim of developing ISoS is to contribute to an open technological framework that encompasses computer systems, CPS, and IoT elements and promotes adaptation without special adapters. Instead, adaptation takes place by obtaining meta-data on the service elements and through cooperation between computer systems and CPS under different responsibilities and on the basis of a diversity of technological frameworks [11, 25].

The proposed OACI as a loose coupling strategy based on the CES and Isystems concepts unifies the factory of the future computational infrastructure allowing the separation (decouple) of intelligent processes sharing a common distributed computational infrastructure (coordination, security, scalability, fault tolerance, quality of services reliability, and costs moderation through a multi-supplier framework). The capability of establishing hybrid computational execution environments on-premises and on the cloud, aligned with the microservices dynamics, makes the proposed approach scalable (elasticity) and prone (open) for emerging intelligent services and facilitates business intelligence applications integration.

## 4 Information System Architecture for Collaborative Networking

In the industry 4.0 approach, robot control and supervision system can be considered as a CPS, henceforth referred to as a robotic cyber-physical system (CPS-R). It is essential to reorganize them on a computational platform based on the internet to achieve a global collaborative network that allows covering all EIS, including CPS. The exchange of information between systems creates a collaborative, productive environment. In this work it is defined a system architecture based on the open technological framework ISoS, addressing the use of CPS-R to perform the collaboration and interoperability between CPS and EIS in an industrial plant with robots. Figure 2 shows the context of the adoption of the ISoS framework and the concept of a Cyber Device Bus, forming a computational platform that integrates computational and/or cyber-physical entities. Notice that the presented robot is illustrative only. The information system architecture can be applied to any robot configuration.

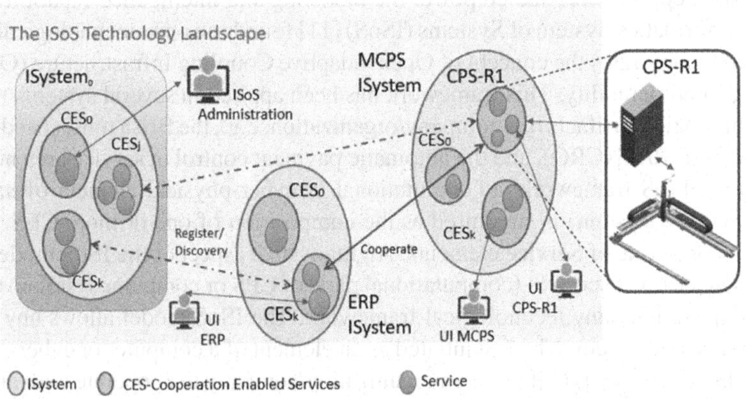


**Fig. 2.** Collaborative network based in the ISoS framework using CPS-R elements.

The framework of the collaborative network represented in Fig. 2 is based on the ISoS system approach, where the ISytem$_0$ meta-system translates the strategy of integration and coordination of the set of technological systems that make up an organization.

In this approach, the CPS-R constitutes a CES that in turn is composed of Services that are constituted as computational elements that guarantee its operation and the availability of functionalities to be accessed by other services, the cyber-physical system, or other computer systems. The CPS-$R_{CES}$ occurs as an element of the ISystem MCPS (A computerized management system for cyber-physical systems). This ISystem may be composed of other CES elements associated with other CPS of industrial robots, which exist or may be added to the organization.

This approach allows you to integrate The CPS with the organization's computer systems, e.g., an ERP computer system can obtain data from a CPS. Each computer system, according to the ISoS approach, will constitute an ISystem, which is in turn composed of CES. In fact, the CES elements are a composition of independent computational elements to which we call the Service. Thus, with this approach, the access of an ERP system modelled by an ISystem is considered as an ISystem to a service of the CPS, as shown in Fig. 2.

Communication in the proposed approach can be carried out between two services, from any CES, even if they are in conformity with different systems. A Service uses the $Isytem_0$ computer meta-system in its management/coordination function to locate each computational element, that is, the information that allows access to a particular service.

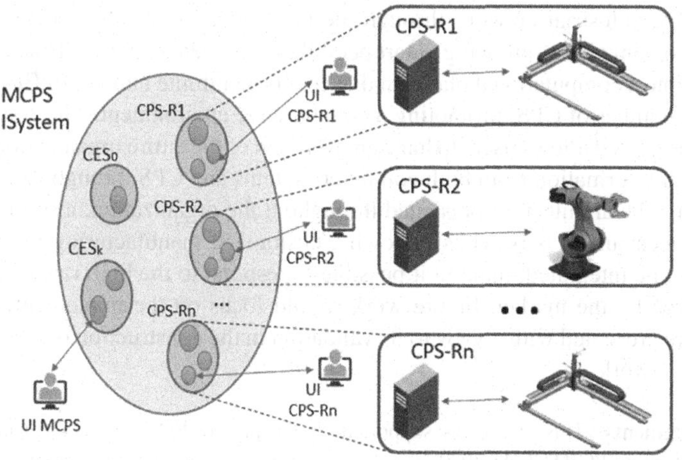


**Fig. 3.** Isystem architectures to perform interoperability with several CPS-Rs.

Additionally, with this architecture may be developed user interfaces (UI), for example, a web interface, from which a person can have access to information from the various services and in specific relevant aspects of the desired CPS.

Usually, processes are performed by several robots that work collaboratively and share data between them or control and supervision systems. Thus, this approach allows to be extended with the creation of new services associated with existing Isystems or new Isystems to take into account the several CPS-R, i.e., with the CPS-R1, CPS-R2, …, CPS-Rn, being n the number of robotic systems that may come to incorporate into the organization (Fig. 3).

This computational platform allows responding to the new service-oriented functionality management paradigm, providing an industrial collaborative network that guarantees interoperability, security, and scalability in accessing and exchanging data. With this computational architecture, an infinite number of computers and CPS can be integrated. At any time, a new service, computer system, or cyber-physical system can be added, integrating it into the organization's collaborative network.

Through the ability to exchange information between services, machine-to-machine communication is promoted, allowing two or more industrial robots to exchange information autonomously with each other, without the need for human intervention, using this computational platform. Because this architecture is internet-based, this allows the integration of all CPS of an organization regardless of their location. In this way, even in different facilities, the CPS can communicate with each other and with all computer systems, thus ensuring a global collaborative network.

## 5 Conclusion

In this article, a conceptual information architecture is proposed to manage industrial robotic platforms based on the design of a Cyber Device Bus, using the ISoS technological framework. The structure of the proposed architecture was built to create a collaborative industrial network through the reorganization of all systems that incorporate an organization, allowing interoperability between systems. This architecture translates into a computational platform that covers an infinite number of EIS, as well as an infinite number of CPS, promoting a collaborative environment. The computational platform presented allows users to have an overview of the entire organization, allowing access to all information from both computer systems and CPS through the various UI. By adopting the architecture presented throughout the organization, a service-oriented colouring mechanism is provided, allowing customers, manufacturing processes, and suppliers to be integrated, making it possible to respond to the high rate of customization required by the market. Future work should focus on the implementation of the architecture presented with a view to its validation in the construction of a collaborative industrial network.

**Acknowledgments.** This work was supported by the project POCI-01-0247-FEDER-039764 under the Program PORTUGAL2020.

## References

1. Wang, J., Xu, C., Zhang, J., Bao, J., Zhong, R.: A collaborative architecture of the industrial internet platform for manufacturing systems. Robot. Comput. Integr. Manuf. **61**, 101854 (2020)
2. Documentos Estratégicos Análise de documentos estratégicos e de boas práticas internacionais com vista à identificação das melhores e mais eficientes praticas e processos no âmbito da Indústria 4.0 (2019). https://hub.pme-digital.pt/wp-content/uploads/2020/08/PMED.089.pdf
3. Malik, P.K., et al.: Industrial Internet of Things and its applications in Industry 4.0: state of the art. Comput. Commun. **166**, 125–139 (2021)

4. Vargas, I.G., Gottardi, T., Teresinha, R., Braga, V.: Approaches for integration in system of systems: a systematic review. In: Proceedings of the 4th International Workshop on Software Engineering for Systems-of-Systems, SESoS 2016, pp. 32–38. Association for Computing Machinery, Inc., New York (2016)
5. Calado, J.M.F., Osório, L.A., Prata, R.: An adaptive IoT management infrastructure for eco-Transport networks. In: Camarinha-Matos, L.M., Bénaben, F., Picard, W. (eds.) PRO-VE 2015. IAICT, vol. 463, pp. 285–296. Springer, Cham (2015). https://doi.org/10.1007/978-3-319-24141-8_26
6. Ding, K., et al.: A cyber-physical production monitoring service system for energy-aware collaborative production monitoring in a smart shop floor. J. Clean. Prod. **297**, 126599 (2021)
7. Coito, T., et al.: A Middleware platform for intelligent automation: an industrial prototype implementation. Comput. Ind. **123**, 103329 (2020)
8. Pels, E.: Optimality of the hub-spoke system: a review of the literature, and directions for future research. Transp. Policy. **104**, A1–A10 (2020)
9. IBM Cloud Education: What is an ESB (Enterprise Service Bus)? | IBM. https://www.ibm.com/cloud/learn/esb
10. Bhadoria, R.S., Chaudhari, N.S., Tharinda, V.: Analyzing the role of interfaces in enterprise service bus: a middleware epitome for service-oriented systems. Comput. Stand. Interfaces **55**, 146–155 (2018)
11. Osório, L.: Collaborative Networks as Open Informatics System of Systems (ISoS), Ph.D. Thesis, University of Amsterdam (2020)
12. Panetto, H., Iung, B., Ivanov, D., Weichhart, G., Wang, X.: Challenges for the cyber-physical manufacturing enterprises of the future. Ann. Rev. Control. **47**, 200–213 (2019)
13. Morel, G., Pereira, C.E., Nof, S.Y.: Historical survey and emerging challenges of manufacturing automation modeling and control: a systems architecting perspective. Annu. Rev. Control. **47**, 21–34 (2019)
14. Biffl, S., Gerhard, D., Lüder, A.: Introduction to the multi-disciplinary engineering for cyber-physical production systems. In: Biffl, S., Lüder, A., Gerhard, D. (eds.) Multi-disciplinary engineering for cyber-physical production systems, pp. 1–24. Springer, Cham (2017). https://doi.org/10.1007/978-3-319-56345-9_1
15. Bousdekis, A., Lepenioti, K., Ntalaperas, D., Vergeti, D., Apostolou, D., Boursinos V.: A RAMI 4.0 view of predictive maintenance: software architecture, platform and case study in steel industry. In: Proper, H., Stirna, J. (eds.) Advanced Information Systems Engineering Workshops, CAiSE 2019. Lecture Notes in Business Information Processing, vol 349. Springer, Cham (2019). https://doi.org/10.1007/978-3-030-20948-3_9
16. Pedone, G., Mezgár, I.: Model similarity evidence and interoperability affinity in cloud-ready Industry 4.0 technologies (2018)
17. Sjödin, D., Parida, V., Kohtamäki, M., Wincent, J.: An agile co-creation process for digital servitization: a micro-service innovation approach. J. Bus. Res. **112**, 478–491 (2020)
18. Niknejad, N., Ismail, W., Ghani, I., Nazari, B., Bahari, M., Hussin, A.R.B.C.: Understanding Service-Oriented Architecture (SOA): a systematic literature review and directions for further investigation. Inf. Syst. **9**, 101491 (2020)
19. Osório, A.L., Camarinha-Matos, L.M., Afsarmanesh, H., Belloum, A.: On reliable collaborative mobility services. In: Camarinha-Matos, L.M., Afsarmanesh, H., Rezgui, Y. (eds.) PRO-VE 2018. IAICT, vol. 534, pp. 297–311. Springer, Cham (2018). https://doi.org/10.1007/978-3-319-99127-6_26
20. Eclipse Papyrus™ Modeling environment. https://www.eclipse.org/papyrus/
21. Model Based Systems Engineering | Capella MBSE Tool. https://www.eclipse.org/capella/
22. Vara, J.L., Ruiz, A., Blondelle, G.: Assurance and certification of cyber–physical systems: the AMASS open source ecosystem. J. Syst. Softw. **171**, 110812 (2021)

23. Osório, A.L., Camarinha-Matos, L.M., Dias, T., Tavares, J.: Adaptive integration of IoT with informatics systems for collaborative industry: the SITL-IoT case. In: Camarinha-Matos, L.M., Afsarmanesh, H., Antonelli, D. (eds.) PRO-VE 2019. IAICT, vol. 568, pp. 43–54. Springer, Cham (2019). https://doi.org/10.1007/978-3-030-28464-0_5
24. Osório, A.L., Camarinha-Matos, L.M., Afsarmanesh, H., Belloum, A.: Towards a mobility payment service based on collaborative open systems. In: Camarinha-Matos, L.M., Afsarmanesh, H., Antonelli, D. (eds.) PRO-VE 2019. IAICT, vol. 568, pp. 379–392. Springer, Cham (2019). https://doi.org/10.1007/978-3-030-28464-0_33
25. Calado, J.M.F., Osório, A.L.: Dynamic integration of mould industry analytics and design forecasting. In: Camarinha-Matos, L.M., Afsarmanesh, H., Fornasiero, R. (eds.) PRO-VE 2017. IAICT, vol. 506, pp. 649–657. Springer, Cham (2017). https://doi.org/10.1007/978-3-319-65151-4_57

# DSRC or LTE? Selecting the Best Medium for V2I Communication Using Game Theory

Evangelos D. Spyrou[1], Afroditi Anagnostopoulou[2], and Chrysostomos Stylios[1](✉)

[1] Laboratory of Knowledge and Intelligent Computing, Department of Informatics and Telecommunications, University of Ioannina, Arta, Greece
stylios@uoi.gr

[2] Centre for Research and Technology Hellas, Hellenic Institute of Transport, Thessaloniki, Greece

**Abstract.** Vehicular communication is a very challenging and essential research area capable of supporting safety and routing decision-making. Vehicle to Infrastructure (V2I) communication often refers to communication between vehicles and Road Side Units (RSU), and recently several technologies have been developed to support it, such as ZigBee, Wi-Fi, GSM, Long Term Evolution (LTE), and 802.11p Direct Short Range Communication (DSRC). In this field, there is a competition between wireless DSRC and cellular LTE to define the most efficient type of communication. This paper aims to analyze the strengths and weaknesses of the DSRC and LTE to evaluate their performances and select the right technology for communication between vehicles and RSUs. Therefore, a vehicle equipped with both LTE and DSRC modules is assumed, and we propose a game-theoretic formulation to select the most efficient type of communication. The proposed formulation results in two equilibria; based on them, the vehicle and the RSU select the same communication module. Here it presents the correlated equilibrium when a trusted source makes the decision, and it discusses the two equilibria as a potential game formulation.

**Keywords:** LTE · DSRC · RSU · Vehicle · Game theory

## 1 Introduction

The automotive industry offers an enormous testbed for new technologies such as vehicular communication, supporting safety, and routing decision-making in the modern environment. Many sensors are embedded in vehicles, and information is exchanged among them, establishing the Vehicle to Vehicle (V2V) communication. Moreover, Vehicle to Infrastructure (V2I) utilizes Road Side Units (RSU) to exchange information, which paves the way for new services.

V2I communication is essentially the exchange of messages or data between a vehicle and an RSU. V2V communication is an ad-hoc network in which vehicles create a Vehicular Ad-hoc Network (VANET), and when two vehicles are within range with each other, they transfer data, or they encapsulate multihop communication [1, 2]. In other


Published by Springer Nature Switzerland AG 2021
L. M. Camarinha-Matos et al. (Eds.): PRO-VE 2021, IFIP AICT 629, pp. 577–587, 2021.
https://doi.org/10.1007/978-3-030-85969-5_54

words, VANET is a form of wireless network, which includes mobility in conjunction with the other properties of the wireless channel. Multiple RSUs, hotspots, and cellular base stations are deployed in the road network. The network infrastructure includes wired devices such as routers or switches and cloud formations [3] or fog computing [4] devices.

Several technologies are available for V2I communication, including ZigBee, GSM [5], DSRC, Wi-Fi [6], LTE, and LTE-V2V [2]. In this field, a competition between wireless DSRC (i.e., 802.11p protocol) and cellular LTE (i.e., 4G telecommunications) has been established to define the most efficient type of V2I communication. If a vehicle includes both technologies in a dual-mode, the most efficient selection is based on the current conditions in the network, such as density, interference, and distance.

This paper aims to analyze the strengths and weaknesses of the DSRC and LTE to evaluate their performances and select the right technology for communication between vehicles and RSUs, which are available at traffic lights. The proper technology should be selected to communicate between vehicles and traffic lights to transfer their data and information. Note that LTE can be substituted by a 5G telecommunication system [7] since it will offer less latency and higher throughput, but this is beyond the scope of this paper since 4G/LTE is a standard technology for vehicular networks, we selected it for this work.

Here, we propose applying a game-theoretic model, whereby the vehicle and the traffic light device must select the same technology. The proposed method reaches an equilibrium of the game, where a central planner chooses the players with respect to the type of messages that will get exchanged. Furthermore, it is proved that this is a potential game that has two Nash equilibria. Finally, it is also proved that the fictitious game learning converges to the two Nash equilibria.

More specifically, in this paper, we show the following contributions:

- We suggest a game-theoretic model for selecting the same network (LTE or DSRC) between a traffic light and a passing vehicle for data transmission.
- We show a correlated equilibrium when a trusted centralized planner selects the choice for both players.
- We propose a modified game as the model for our solution.
- We show that this game is a potential game, which means that it converges to a Nash equilibrium.
- This game has two Nash equilibria in the pure strategies.

The remainder of this paper is as follows: Sect. 2 briefly discusses LTE and DSRC technologies, Sect. 3 provides a brief comparison of the two technologies, Sect. 4 gives a background on game theory and potential games, Sect. 5 describes the derivation of the game-theoretic model, Sect. 6 gives the results and in Sect. 7 conclusions are provided.

## 2 DSRC and LTE

In this section, we provide a summary of the LTE and DSRC technologies for vehicular communications. Our purpose is to show the critical points of each communication medium.

### 2.1 DSRC

Vehicular wireless communication evolved with the emergence of the IEEE 802.11p standard, which results in DSRC. The environment where V2X devices are deployed is quite tricky since interference is high due to buildings infrastructure or other frequencies that act in the area. The DSRC medium offers 75 MHz broadband communication in the 5.850–5925 frequencies [8]. Moreover, DSRC offers high data rates for V2I and V2V communications. The DSRC standard embeds the IEEE 1609.x protocol family and the 802.11p. In particular, the IEEE 1609 resides on top of IEEE 802.11p. It enables the operation of the upper layers from the physical layer and the access control of the MAC layer, across multiple channels, without having information regarding parameters of low-level layers [9].

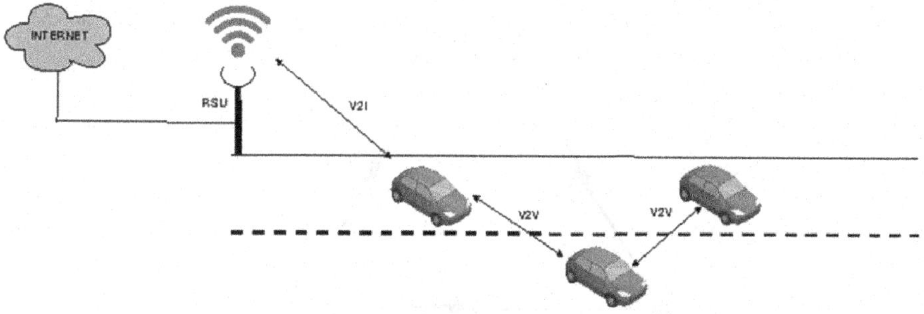


**Fig. 1.** DSRC example

At the PHY layer, DSRC utilizes orthogonal frequency division multiplexing (OFDM) with convolutional coding. The IEEE 802.11p operates in a 10 MHz bandwidth channel and uses doubled OFDM symbol duration and guard interval to counter larger delay spreads. It results in the subcarrier spacing that is halving to 156.25 kHz. Furthermore, IEEE 802.11p introduces improved receiver performance requirements in adjacent channel rejections, handling cross-channel interference. There are defined four spectrum masks utilized in different operations and are more stringent than those demanded of the IEEE 802.11 radios. As for the MAC layer, IEEE 802.11p uses Carrier Sensing Multiple Access with Collision Avoidance (CSMA/CA). In order to improve latency of the Basic Service Set (BSS) procedure, the standard introduces the Wave BSS, whereby vehicles transmit signals without prior association, speeding up the whole process. In order to overcome packet collisions, decentralized congestion control techniques are used, with which adaptation of transmissions concerning congestion of the channel is promoted [10]. Figure 1 presents the DSRC V2X communication structure.

### 2.2 LTE

The LTE standard by the 3rd Generation Partnership Project (3GPP) [11] has come into play, offering excellent performance in throughput and latency. The access network consists of the eNodeBs and the user equipment (UE). The eNodeBs act as centralized base stations, containing a packet programmer, which selects the traffic rate depending on service demands. In theory, LTE can reach a 150 Mbps downlink data rate and a 50 Mbps uplink data rate. In combination with latency less than 5 ms in the user plane, LTE is a strong candidate for vehicular communications.

Moreover, LTE uses orthogonal frequency division multiple access (OFDMA) for downlink and Single Carrier Frequency Division Multiple Access (SC-FDMA) for uplink connections. The width of the channel is from 1.4 to 20 MHz. LTE also supports MIMO giving an advantage in dynamic conditions, such as vehicular applications.

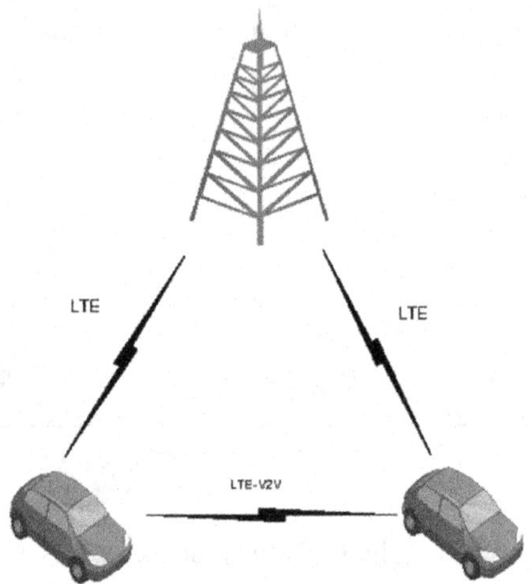


**Fig. 2.** LTE example

The eNodeBs comprise the radio access network (RAN) of the LTE network architecture, responsible for radio control and management functionalities and the communication between the UEs and the LTE core. The eNodeBs relate to the Evolved Packet Core (EPC), which can take care of mobility management quality of service and interoperability with legacy 3GPP or other technologies [12]. An amendment of the LTE is the LTE-A, which offers a more significant bit rate, capacity, and spectrum utilization [13]. Lastly, LTE may offer direct communication between UEs, like DSRC communication, which does not require a base station for its operation. The LTE standard provides broadband communication and enables vehicular applications either by using On-Board Units (OBU) or by smartphone LTE connectivity. Figure 2 presents an essential LTE communication.

## 3 LTE and DSRC Comparison

There is a competition between wireless DSRC and cellular LTE, which defines the most efficient type of communication among vehicular applications. Several research works attempt to find the proper answer. DSRC has been installed in USA cities even though there is an issue with its reliability and efficiency, particularly in high vehicle density applications [14]. The DSRC radio spectrum requires high data traffic demand for in-vehicle Internet access. On the other hand, cellular approaches, such as LTE, offer high capacity, broad coverage, range, and widely existing infrastructure. The main issue with cellular approaches is the centralized means of communication, which may cause problems in the latency between V2V communications. The support of distributed resource management is a significant problem, which is a requirement for allowing V2V operation in the absence of a network infrastructure. Latency may also appear, which is a severe drawback, especially for safety-critical applications. Moreover, a potential problem with using cellular approaches, such as LTE, is the accommodation of V2X data traffic and the increasing data traffic from its legacy users.

Mir and Filali [12] evaluated the IEEE 802.11p and LTE in terms of delay, reliability, scalability, and mobility using different networking conditions and settings. LTE exhibits better network capacity and supports in-vehicle mobility than IEEE 802.11p. Concerning the transmission delays, the authors pointed out that the delay increases with the increase of the network load. On the other hand, IEEE 802.11p exhibited acceptable performance when there is mobility support, and the topologies are sparse. It identifies that IEEE 802.11p performance decreases when it suffers from large vehicle density or traffic load. LTE includes infrastructure-oriented scheduling and access control, as well as it does not contain a vast number of network elements; hence, its performance may surpass the IEEE 802.11p.

Theoretical work shows that in safety-critical vehicular applications, beaconing in LTE is poor due to network overload, even in idealistic conditions [15]. Therefore, the DSRC architecture indeed appears more promising in safety-critical vehicular applications. Based on [16], a combination of the two technologies is the best option. In particular, LTE wins in terms of capacity and communication range, and it does not miss any beacons due to collisions. On the other hand, 802.11p accomplishes better latency due to direct communication.

Overall, the performance of IEEE 802.11p and LTE depend on the conditions even though LTE could be characterized as a better choice in most of the studied cases. Therefore, we may consider "infrastructure" and "passing vehicle" as players that want to select the best communication medium for their data transmission in the proposed methodology on game theory.

## 4 Game Theory and Potential Games

Game theory studies mathematical models of conflict and cooperation between players [17]. The meaning of the term game corresponds to any form of interaction between two or more players. The rationality of a player is satisfied if it pursuits the satisfaction of its preferences through the selection of appropriate strategies. The preferences of a player need to satisfy general rationality axioms, and then its behavior can be described by a utility function. Utility functions provide a quantitative description of the player's preferences, and the main objective is to maximize its utility function.

In this work, we propose strategic non-cooperative games since we consider players to act as selfish players that want to preserve their interests. The intuition behind this is that the players will reach an optimal state without paying the price to maximize their payoffs. The Nash equilibrium [18] is the most crucial equilibrium in non-cooperative strategic form games. It is defined as the point where no node will increase its utility by unilaterally changing its strategy.

In 2008, Daskalakis proved that finding a Nash equilibrium is PPAD-complete [19]. Polynomial Parity Arguments on Directed graphs (PPAD) is a class of total search problems [20] for which solutions have been proven to exist. However, finding a specific solution is difficult if not intractable. The class of Potential Games [21] gained interest since they guarantee the convergence to pure Nash equilibria and best response dynamics.

This class of games consists of the exact, ordinal potential and weighted. This work employs weighted potential games. For the sake of clarity, we mention the necessary conditions for games to be classified as potential. More formally:

A game $\Gamma\langle \mathrm{N}, \mathrm{A}, u\rangle$, with $N$ players, $A$ strategy profiles and $u$ the payoff functions, is an exact potential game if there exists a potential function.

$$V : A \rightarrow \mathbb{R} \tag{1}$$

subject to

$$\forall i \in N, \forall x_{-i} \in A_{-i}, \forall x_i, x_i^{'} \in A_i \tag{2}$$

Where $x_i$ is the strategy of player $i$, $x_i^{'}$ is the deviation of player $i$, $x_{-i}$ is the set of strategies followed by all the players except player $i$ and $A_{-i}$ is the set of strategy profiles of all players except $i$ such as

$$V(x_{-i}x_i) - V\left(x_{-i}, x_i^{'}\right) = u(x_{-i}, x_i) - u\left(x_{-i}, x_i^{'}\right) \tag{3}$$

In terms of an ordinal potential game, the necessary condition for its existence is

$$V\left(x_{-i}, x_i\right) - V\left(x_{-i}, x_i^{'}\right) > 0 \Longleftrightarrow u(x_{-i}, x_i) - u\left(x_{-i}, x_i^{'}\right) > 0 \tag{4}$$

A game $\Gamma$ is a weighted potential game [21] if there exists a vector of positive numbers $w = (w_1, \ldots, w_n) \in \mathbb{R}_{++}^2$ and a real-valued function $V : A \rightarrow R$ is a weighted potential if for every $i \in N$ and for every $x_{-i} \in A_{-i}$, for every $x_i, x_i^{'} \in A^i$

$$u\left(x_{-i}, x_i\right) - u\left(x_{-i}, x_i^{'}\right) = w_{-i}(V\left(x_{-i}, x_i\right) - V\left(x_{-i}, x_i^{'}\right)) \tag{5}$$

Also, we provide a formal description of the correlated equilibrium [22]. We denote players as $p = 1, 2, \ldots, n$. Each player has a strategy $A_p$ and we define the strategy profile as $S = \prod_{p=1}^{n} A_{-p}$, where $A_{-p}$ is the profile for all players except p. We define as y the distribution on A where for $x \in A_{-p}$ we denote by $y_{i,x}$ the probability that a player p chooses strategy I when all the other players choose $\overline{x}$. The payoff to player p, $u_{i,\overline{x}}^{p}$ for selecting strategy $i \in A$ when everyone selects to play x. The distribution y is a correlated equilibrium if and only if conditioned on player p accepting the recommended strategy $i$

$$\sum\nolimits_{\overline{x} \in A_{i-p}} u_{i,\overline{x}}^{p} y_{i,\overline{x}} \geq \sum\nolimits_{\overline{x} \in A_{i-p}} u_{j,\overline{x}}^{p} y_{i,\overline{x}}, \forall i, j \in A_p \tag{6}$$

## 5 Game-Theoretic Communication Selection

Here, we assume that a passing vehicle and the traffic light ahead of it have two communication mediums, an LTE and a DSRC module. In order to accomplish communication, both the vehicle and the traffic light need to select the same medium. The selection is made based on the density of the network and the type of communication, namely safety-critical messages or multimedia download. Any of the two players could select a medium that suits the most. LTE example shows only the communication from the vehicle to the traffic light. Direct communication between the traffic light and the vehicle can achieve using LTE-V; however, we only take the situation where the base station serves the data. As for the DSRC, direct communication is at play.

Here, we propose using the Battle of the Sexes game model, and similarly, we design a payoff matrix. There are two Nash equilibria in the specific game model in pure strategies, which occurs when both the two players make the same choice (DSRC, DSRC) or (LTE, LTE). Furthermore, there is a mixed strategy equilibrium, when player one is choosing LTE with probability 2/3 and DSRC with probability 1/3 and player two is choosing LTE with probability 1/3 and DSRC with 2/3. The utility will be (2/3, 2/3), which ensures fairness but exhibits lower than the worst outcomes of the Nash equilibria in the pure strategies.

It is suggested at [23] to have a centralized trusted authority that informs the players to select the same outcome. Based on the type of messages exchanged by the players, we see that the players do not have an incentive to change their strategies since it will be worse. The advantage of this process is that the expected rewards are higher (3/2, 3/2) comparing to the Nash equilibrium in the mixed strategies. Formally, we can say that this game has a correlated equilibrium. This suits to the current problem under investigation since we want the two players to select the appropriate strategy depending on the message type.

In the absence of a centralized authority, we formulate the Battle of the Sexes as a potential game, with the potential being:

| | LTE | DSRC |
|---|---|---|
| LTE | 2 | 1 |
| DSRC | 0 | 2 |

The revenues and costs do not rise with a different selection in this model. On the other hand, there is a good revenue in the same selection by our two players.

## 6 Results

We use the game formulation in [24] for our scenario. The strategies of the players are {DSRC, LTE}, which can be reflected by the utility function values. Each player has her own payoff from a function involving revenues and respective costs. When both players select LTE the revenues are assumed to be (10, 10) and the respective costs (1, 3). If the two players select DSRC the revenues are (10, 20) and the costs (2, 5). If the players select different means, they incur only costs. Note that this could be addressed by the necessity of communication in practical scenarios, i.e., if it is a safety message or a video streaming. The payoff matrix of the proposed game is given below:

| Player 2 | | | |
|---|---|---|---|
| Player 1 | | LTE | DSRC |
| | LTE | **(9, 7)** | (−1, −5) |
| | DSRC | (−2, −3) | **(8, 15)** |

This game is a weighted potential game with the weights being 1 for player 1 and 3/2 for player 2. The values of the potential are given below:

| | LTE | DSRC |
|---|---|---|
| LTE | 11 | 3 |
| DSRC | 0 | 12 |

Player 1 wants to select (LTE, LTE) while player 2 wants (DSRC, DSRC) depending on the type of communication and density, as has been described in a previous section. In particular, when there is knowledge of the players regarding the type of message required, the game will converge to the respective equilibrium.

Furthermore, this game has the finite improvement property whereby no improvement path can be larger than 2 in length. The finite improvement property is based on Theorem 2.15 given in [24]. It refers to a two-player game with two strategies and two equilibria. If a player deviates from a common choice, then the other player will follow by selecting the same strategy (medium), as shown in Fig. 3.

Here player two (the traffic light) selects DSRC and sends the message to player one. Player 1 (the vehicle) could also select DSRC and reach one equilibrium state. However, Player one changes its action to LTE since it requires video transmission, and player two responds by selecting LTE, giving her a higher payoff than if she remained to her DSRC choice. Regardless of the messages, we observe that improvement gets accomplished with two moves. It is pretty easy to see the exchange of messages and the convergence when the vehicle begins the communication first, i.e., Player 1.

Additionally, every potential game has the fictitious play property and converges to equilibrium [25]. This means that there will be two equilibrium points according to the beliefs of the players.

We also produced the set of correlated equilibria. As we can see in Fig. 4, three equilibria are found, namely the two Nash equilibria (9,7) and (8,15) as well as another equilibrium (3.5,3) for Players one and two, respectively. Note that every Nash equilibrium is a correlated equilibrium [26]; hence we see that the two equilibria described previously appear on the graph.

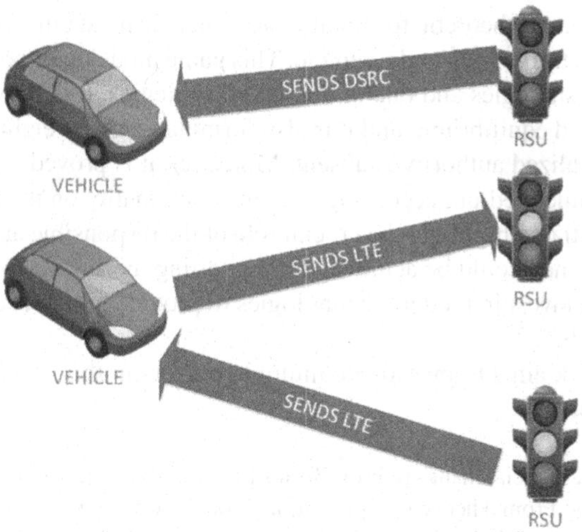


**Fig. 3.** LTE selection example of the game

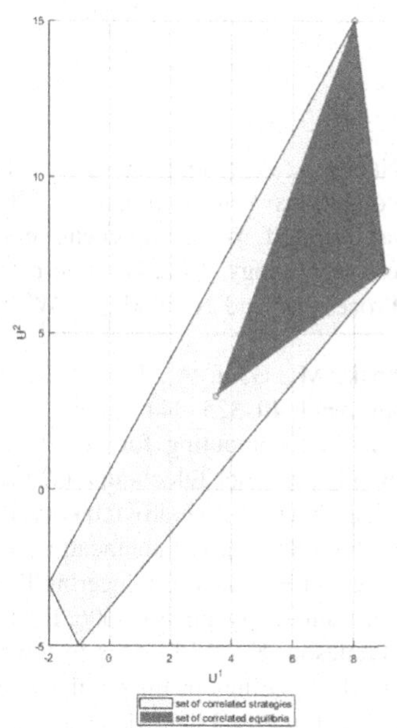


**Fig. 4.** Set of correlated strategies and correlated equilibria [27]

## 7 Conclusions

This paper discusses the DSRC and LTE technologies, and it highlights their strengths and weaknesses for ensuring communication among V2I and RSU. An interesting problem is a proper selection between the two technologies.

We propose a game-theoretic formulation to select the most efficient type of communication between a traffic light and a vehicle. This game model has two Nash equilibrium points in the pure strategies and one in the mixed strategies. It is proved that this game exhibits a correlated equilibrium, and it is also formulated as a weighted potential game whereby the centralized authority is absent. Moreover, it is proved that the two players converge to the same medium according to their functionality on the road segment.

It is also essential to highlight the crucial role of the responsible authority in practice since higher efficiency could be achieved by supporting the sustainable development of modern cities that invest in modern technologies to provide higher accuracy, safety, and better quality of life.

Our future work aims to investigate multiple players in this game and examine the behavior of our model.

**Acknowledgments.** Special thanks to Prof. Bruno Tuffin, author of the book Telecommunication Network Economics: From Theory to Applications, for the valuable conversation regarding the game model approach. This work is funded by the project: "Enhancing research activities of Laboratory of Knowledge and Intelligent Computing" of the Research Committee of the University of Ioannina.

## References

1. Singh, P.K., Nandi, S.K., Nandi, S.: A tutorial survey on vehicular communication state of the art, and future research directions. Veh. Commun. **18**, 100164 (2019)
2. Nshimiyimana, A., Agrawal, D., Arif, W.: Comprehensive survey of V2V communication for 4G mobile and wireless technology. In: 2016 International Conference on Wireless Communications, Signal Processing and Networking (WiSPNET), pp. 1722–1726. IEEE (2016)
3. Whaiduzzaman, M., Sookhak, M., Gani, A., Buyya, R.: A survey on vehicular cloud computing. J. Netw. Comput. Appl. **40**, 325–344 (2014)
4. Kai, K., Cong, W., Tao, L.: Fog computing for vehicular adhoc networks: paradigms, scenarios, and issues. J. China Univ. Posts Telecommun. **23**(2), 56–96 (2016)
5. Chumkamon, S., Tuvaphanthaphiphat, P., Keeratiwintakorn, P.: The vertical handoff between GSM and ZigBee networks for vehicular communication. In: ECTI-CON2010: The 2010 ECTI International Conference on Electrical Engineering/Electronics, Computer, Telecommunications and Information Technology, pp. 603–606. IEEE (2010)
6. Song, Z., Shangguan, L., Jamieson, K.: Wi-Fi goes to town: rapid picocell switching for wireless transit networks. In: Proceedings of the Conference of the ACM Special Interest Group on Data Communication, pp. 322–334 (2017)
7. Shah, S.A.A., Ahmed, E., Imran, M., Zeadally, S.: 5G for vehicular communications. IEEE Commun. Mag. **56**(1), 111–117 (2018)
8. IEEE Standards Association: Draft Standard for Wireless Access in Vehicular preamble Environments (WAVE)-Multi-channel Operation. IEEE Std 1609.4–2010 (2010)
9. Jiang, D., Delgrossi, L.: IEEE 802.11 p: Towards an international standard for wireless access in vehicular environments. In: VTC Spring 2008-IEEE Vehicular Technology Conference, pp. 2036–2040. IEEE (2008)
10. Shimizu, T., Lu, H., Kenney, J., Nakamura, S.: Comparison of DSRC and LTE-V2X PC5 mode 4 performance in high vehicle density scenarios. In: Proceedings of the ITS World Congress, pp. 1–7 (2019)

11. 3GPP: Overview of 3GPP Release 8. (2008). http://www.3gpp.org/. Retrieved 24 Mar 2014
12. Mir, Z.H., Filali, F.: LTE and IEEE 802.11 p for vehicular networking: a performance evaluation. EURASIP J. Wirel. Commun. Netw. **2014**(1), 1–15 (2014)
13. Araniti, G., Campolo, C., Condoluci, M., Iera, A., Molinaro, A.: LTE for vehicular networking: a survey. IEEE Commun. Mag. **51**(5), 148–157 (2013)
14. Abboud, K., Omar, H.A., Zhuang, W.: Interworking of DSRC and cellular network technologies for V2X communications: a survey. IEEE Trans. Veh. Technol. **65**(12), 9457–9470 (2016)
15. Vinel, A.: 3GPP LTE versus IEEE 802.11 p/WAVE: Which technology is able to support cooperative vehicular safety applications? IEEE Wirel. Commun. Lett. **1**(2), 125–128 (2012)
16. Xu, Z., Li, X., Zhao, X., Zhang, M. H., Wang, Z.: DSRC versus 4G-LTE for connected vehicle applications: a study on field experiments of vehicular communication performance. J. Adv. Transp. **2017** (2017).
17. Von Neumann, J., Morgenstern, O., Kuhn H. W.: Theory of games and economic behavior (commemorative edition). Princeton university press. (2007).
18. Nash Jr, J.F.: The bargaining problem. Econometrica: J. Econ. Soc. **18**(2), 155–162 (1950)
19. Daskalakis, C., Goldberg, P.W., Papadimitriou, C.H.: The complexity of computing a Nash equilibrium. SIAM J. Comput. **39**(1), 195–259 (2009)
20. Papadimitriou, C.H.: On the complexity of the parity argument and other inefficient proofs of existence. J. Comput. Syst. Sci. **48**(3), 498–532 (1994)
21. Monderer, D., Shapley, L.S.: Potential games. Games Econ. Behav. **14**(1), 124–143 (1996)
22. Saberi, A.: Correlated Equilibria. Lecture Notes, Stanford (2009)
23. Tardos, E.: Correlated Equilibria. Lecture Notes (2004)
24. Maillé, P., Tuffin, B.: Telecommunication network economics: from theory to applications. California University Press, Berkeley (2014)
25. Ewerhart, C., Valkanova, K.: Fictitious play in networks. Games Econ. Behav. **123**, 182–206 (2020)
26. Hart, S., Mas-Colell, A.: A simple adaptive procedure leading to correlated equilibrium. Econometrica **68**(5), 1127–1150 (2000)
27. Iskander (2021): Correlated equilibria (https://github.com/ikarib/ce/releases/tag/1.3), GitHub. Retrieved 9 June 2021

# Sentient Immersive Response Network

# Toward Resilient and Efficient Maintenance Planning for Water Supply Networks

Marine Dubillard[1](✉), Guillaume Martin[1], Matthieu Lauras[1], Xavier Lorca[1], and Jean Cantet[2]

[1] University of Toulouse – Mines Albi, Industrial Engineering Department, Albi, France
{marine.dubillard,guillaume.martin,matthieu.lauras, xavier.lorca}@mines-albi.fr

[2] Veolia Eau France Région Sud-Ouest, 22 avenue Marcel Dassault, 31506 Toulouse, France
jean.cantet@veolia.com

**Abstract.** Every day, the water supply network evolves to fix or prevent leaks or contaminated drinking water, and hook-ups to buildings are set up or removed. Most technical interventions are planned in advance, but emergencies can abruptly disturb the planning. This work intends to propose a methodology to evaluate various planning strategies in order to maximize the resilience and efficiency of the water supply network scheduling. An industrial application is developed on a large French water management company. The baseline of this case is the existing planning process observed in the field. Then, based on a literature analysis, a set of alternative planning processes when removing some constraints. The proposed methodology allows to compare the existing solution to these alternatives. Finally, as the research is in its infancy, the paper develops avenues for future research through a specific research agenda.

**Keywords:** Water supply maintenance · Planning under uncertainty · Computer modelling · Robust planning

## 1 Introduction and Problem Statement

Population increases in both developed and developing countries around the world constantly puts a greater stress on the needs for amenities. Tap water is one of the most vital of these. However, providing reliable access to it proves to be an increasingly complex task, both by creating new water networks and maintaining the older ones. This paper deals with the latter and especially with the routing of maintenance teams to planned or spontaneous tasks. Maintaining water supply networks calls for three types of actions: (i) first, the evolution of the network with new buildings to hook up, (ii) second, preventive maintenance such as sample collection and proactive leak search and (iii) reactive maintenance when failures occur in the network. While the first two types are predictable, the last is composed of emergencies, thus creating uncertainties in the planning. On top of these, real intervention times and real transportation times in a wide area add more


Published by Springer Nature Switzerland AG 2021
L. M. Camarinha-Matos et al. (Eds.): PRO-VE 2021, IFIP AICT 629, pp. 591–600, 2021.
https://doi.org/10.1007/978-3-030-85969-5_55

sources of uncertainty to the problem. Both these types of uncertainty can be considered as a stochastic phenomenon, for data analysis and field expertise can provide the grounds for a probability distribution, rendering them predictable to a degree. In this study, we focus on the French regional scale. Consequently, we must consider both the effectiveness of the service provider, defined as the capability to deliver the expected service, and the efficiency, defined as the capability to limit the costs of operations, in the wake of the increasing concurrency of providers. In the meantime, the uncertainties in our problem warrant the construction of resilient and robust plans. We define a robust planning as a planning that is not significantly impacted by hazardous events. A resilient planning strategy is a strategy with a high capacity to go back to an acceptable state after having been impacted by a hazardous event. These definitions follow the works of [1]. A vast part of the literature analysing water network maintenance focuses on predictive algorithms that help to decide which canalizations are the most susceptible to fail and should be changed. For example, [2] compare various statistical models to evaluate the failure risk of pipes, using the history of pipe breaks and [3] review state-of-the-art models to use in order to predict the remaining useful life of individual pipes. But producing a proper estimate of the demand (maintenance operations) is only a part of the problem. The other part consists in using these estimates to feed optimized maintenance planning systems, able to better manage disruptions and cost-effectiveness. In such a context, our research question is the following: how to challenge and improve the maintenance planning strategies for water supply networks? To solve this issue, we share an applied methodology to improve this maintenance by considering the optimization of water production and distribution network maintenance planning in an uncertain environment. We start by reviewing the literature on dynamic planning problems. Section 3 then details our methodology to quantitatively compare different planning alternatives and dynamic routing approaches, while looking for resilient, efficient and robust options. Section 4 elaborates the first steps of this applied to a French regional case, along with specificities of their processes, and we conclude with avenues for future research.

## 2 Smart and Collaborative Dynamic Routing Problems

At its core, our maintenance planning problem has two components. It is a capacitated vehicle routing problem (CVRP) with water provider workers having to optimize their maintenance planning. It must also deal with planning uncertainty, rendering it dynamic, with emergency repairs appearing during the day.

**Solving the Capacitated Vehicle Routing Problem.** CVRP problems were first defined in [4] with the intention of finding optimal routes for several fuel vehicles to refill multiple stations. The capacity aspect of the problem is often represented as variable demands of customers, but it may also view task and travel time as consuming the vehicle capacity. The static version of the problem is most often posed as a set of customers with coordinates and varied demands, along with a number of available vehicles. Over the years, several varieties of the CVRP have been formulated: including time windows to fill customer requests (VRPTW in [5]), taking profit into account and allowing customers to be left out of the routes (CVRPP in [6]) or even adding pickup and delivery aspects in between customers (VRPPD in [7]). Interested readers may look for further details in the transformation of VRP problems to job shop scheduling problems in [8], a paper that can have implications in solving the problem in alternative ways. For a survey on heuristics and exact methods on how to solve VRPs and its variants, the reader may turn to [9]. An updated review, but only for exact methods, is also available in [10].

**Dynamic Workforce Routing in Uncertain Environments.** Dynamic vehicle routing problems (DVRP) are a variation on the classic vehicle routing problem where requests (usually in the form of new customers, but equivalent to emergencies in our case) pop up while vehicles are executing their route [11]. The 'dynamic' refers to the fact that these new requests (i) were not part of the starting set of requests and (ii) must be considered in the reconstruction of an updated route. Several methods are used in order to deal with these problems, as for example in the review of [11] and the use of periodic or constant re-optimization. The same authors, along with [12] for example, also consider tackling the problem by identifying the stochastic nature of customer appearance ahead of time. The literature mentions several ways to solve DVRP problems, such as [13] with a greedy random search procedure if the problem is viewed with the scheduling paradigm. Other approaches are available in a series of works from W. Kool and his co-authors, represented in [14]. In this recent paper, they train a reinforcement learning agent to dynamically adapt vehicle routes, thus leveraging the power of deep neural networks. Other meaningful resolution methods are found in [15] and the coupling of simulation software to metaheuristics. We must also mention recent advances in [16] and [17] using multiple stages algorithms implying a clustering of clients to visit for the DVRP. Several use cases were recently documented with the sharp increase of highly connected supply chains with contributions like [18] who consider dynamic optimization of supply chains. Other hyper connected network cases exist with the works of [19] and smart transportation management systems. The different cases of DVRP give rise to various types of uncertainties in the planning like in [20] or [21]. At that point, literature on the DVRP shows many alternatives to both model and solve different variants of the problem. In our case of water supply maintenance, we aim to evaluate if, and to what extent, the existing approaches fit our needs. Consequently, we wish to bridge the gap between statistical methods for predictive maintenance in water networks and dynamic routing of teams in a structured design of experiments. In parallel, by measuring performance against efficiency, resilience and robustness criteria, we should be able to conclude on our problem. The next section details our proposed methodology to answer this question.

## 3 Proposed Research Methodology

Our methodology is summarized by Fig. 1. The first step consists in gathering the maximum amount of information on the existing model: what are the roles of each stakeholder, what are their constraints, how do they cooperate in planning routes with or without emergencies. The end goal of this first step is three-fold: (i) establish the meaningful rules and mechanisms governing the problem at hand, while getting rid of noise in order to build the simulation with the correct degree of precision, (ii) describe the static and dynamic planning methods already used in our use case, that should act as a comparison baseline and (iii) use the data we collected to tune our simulation model to reality, a step also called model calibration. The choice of using (discrete) simulation is motivated by its ability to model the necessary degrees of complexity [22]. Model calibration is an essential part of using simulations for decision-making (see also [22] for further details). The next step of the methodology is to build a list of alternative planning processes, either from the literature, or with new contributions. It must be noted that, for each alternative process, there may be variants due to hyper-parameters or sets of constraints. These two aspects are taken into account by simulating different versions, much similar to a design of experiments. Lastly, each simulation run is evaluated against several performance criteria. We consider two sets of criteria: one coming from the use case, in order to link our results to business expectations, and one tied to resilience and efficiency aspects.

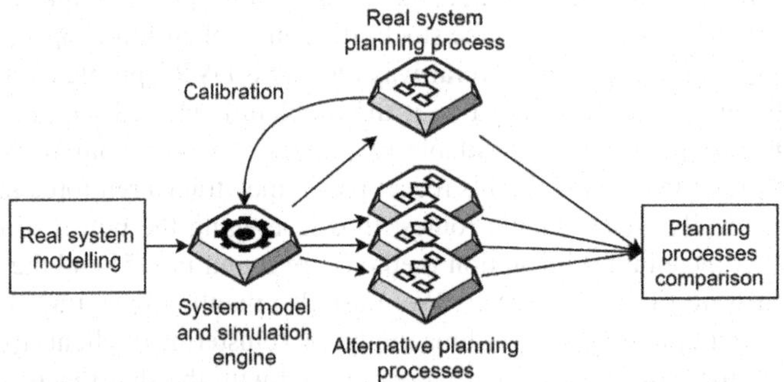


**Fig. 1.** Methodological steps to compare planning alternatives

**Real System Modelling.** In order to establish a baseline, we started by conducting a series of interviews with the water maintenance actors. We asked two series of questions, one for each planning processing method: predictive scheduling (before the occurrence of disturbance during the execution) and reactive (after disturbance) scheduling. 5 people, each with a different role in the general planning and routing process were interviewed. Interviews contained semi-opened questions in order to guarantee a common base but still allow for a possibility to gather supplementary information [23]. In addition, we gathered historical planning data from planning tools over 2019 and 2020. Data covers planning and real execution. We also built a mathematical model of the problem, transforming data into tasks, and the information retrieved into resources and constraints, while staying as close as possible to the use case reality. Finally, we completed the model by concatenating the information into synthetic business processes (using the Business Process Model Notation).

**Simulation Engine Building.** Having only modelled the problem and the baseline process is not sufficient. More steps are needed in order to build the simulation engine. Each experiment we will carry will run on a parallel instance of the problem based on our data collection. As a result, we start by implementing a representative instance generator by fitting its probabilities of intervals and gravity to field data, as well as a failure generator simulating two kinds of uncertainties: the occurrence of an emergency intervention and the real processing time of each intervention.

**Real System Planning Process.** Next the real system processes are implemented based on their previous modelling and can be run on the instance previously generated. Simulation calibration is then done by iterating over the model until behaviours match to a satisfying degree, by comparing output signals.

**Alternative Planning Processes.** Each alternative is either extracted from the literature or built by modifying the constraints of the baseline use case. More details in Sect. 4. We remind that each alternative must be fed with the same instance of the problem in order to give general conclusions.

**Process Performance Comparison.** Possible performance criteria to compare to outputs of real system and alternative processes include inverse schedule tardiness or inverse miss rate [24]. Other metrics follow a statistical approach, such as the standard deviations of routes, the entropy generated or the lateness likelihood of routes ([25, 26]). Feedback from the use case allows to add time spent on maintenance tasks over total working time, time and distance travelled and degree of unforeseen operations in a given time window. The result of these different steps is threefold as they will lead to (i) an exhaustive understanding of real field processes, (ii) a calibrated evaluation tool validated on a real basis, (iii) performance indicators reference values opening the way for improvement.

## 4 Application Case: Veolia EAU Sud-Ouest

**Description of the Ongoing Application Case Specific Problem.** The application case is the water production and distribution network maintenance activity managed by the company Veolia Eau in 18 departments in the southwest of France. The planning problem consists in a set of interventions to execute, each having a precise location, a due date, a predictive processing time and a set of skills needed to intervene. The resources necessary are a set of agents, each having a specific set of skills, working hours and an agency location, which determines their position in the beginning and end of each work shift. The material resources issues are set aside as we consider that each agent has a car available at all times, and small intervention material available. The decision variables considered are the agent and the date associated with each intervention. The problem constraints are the following: for each intervention the due date has to be respected, and the agent in charge must have every skill needed. For each agent, the working hours have to be respected, and of course, time and space consistencies have to be preserved. This planning problem is rendered dynamic with the arrival of emergency interventions randomly popping and intervention times taking less or more time than expected.

**Planning Processes in the Ongoing Application Case.** The complexity of this general problem is reduced with some additional organizational constraints specific to Veolia Eau: the planning processes are executed in small geographic areas, and each executing team composed of 5 to 10 agents has its own interventions set to handle. Moreover, the planning processes are executed each week with a weekly horizon, and each agent is allocated to a specific type of intervention every week. Finally, the interventions on emergencies are only added to an agent's schedule with no re-planning process, and if an

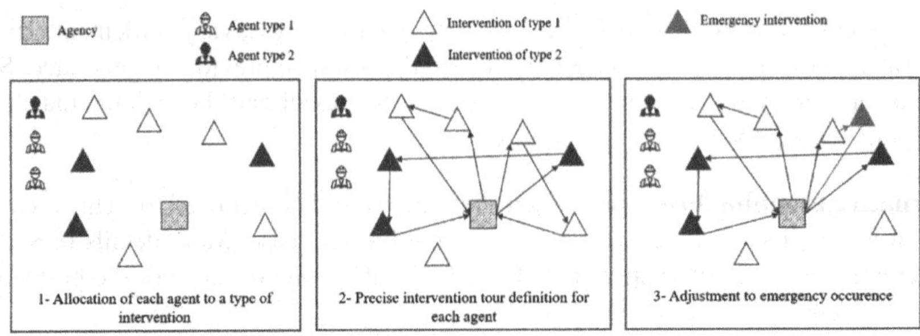


**Fig. 2.** Planning decision steps in Veolia Eau

intervention lasts longer than expected, the remaining interventions in the schedule are just shifted in consequence. This organization makes the planning problem small enough to be handled by human intelligence and divides it into three subproblems depicted by Fig. 2: (i) the allocation of each agent to a specific type of intervention, (ii) the intervention tour definition for each agent, consisting in selecting the interventions to execute and their order, (iii) the choice of an agent to handle an emergency occurring during the intervention tour.

All these steps are executed manually, with practice field intelligence. The allocation of agents to intervention types is made according to the general volume of each intervention type. The intervention tour is decided for each agent, one at a time, in the form of an ordered list of interventions to execute, with the objective of filling their schedules with the maximum number of interventions, while prioritizing time-sensitive interventions. When emergencies occur during the execution of interventions, one agent is chosen according to a geographic criterion and interrupts his tour to intervene. When the emergency is fixed, he executes the other planned interventions in the same planned order, with the risk of not being able to execute the last interventions of the day.

The representation of these processes in a computer tool requires only simple algorithms and a CVRP resolution on a small number of interventions and one agent. The results are not expected to be consequently better than human scheduling and their quality will be considered as a baseline for the further alternative processes.

According to the proposed research methodology, the organization established in Veolia Eau to provide such planning processes was synthetized in Business Process Model Notation (BPMN). The main planning actors are the operations manager of each executing team as well as dedicated schedulers in charge of designing the intervention tours of a certain category of agents. These agents are those allocated to particular types of intervention, characterized by their high quantity and their small processing time, such as water meter reading interventions. Such intervention types generate a more combinatorial dimension to the tour definition. Depending on the intervention type, schedules proposed by dedicated schedulers are directly applied by agents or are reviewed by operations managers before their final application. This organization is depicted in Fig. 3.

The dedicated schedulers also maintain a continuous watch for emergencies. When an emergency occurs, they are the first informed and have the responsibility of calling the appropriate agent and provide him with all the necessary information. Meanwhile each agent intervenes according to his planned schedule, until a hazardous event occurs: a call for emergency, the impossibility to execute an intervention… At the end of each intervention, weather it is correctly achieved or not, the agent reports the time and result into a tracking tool.

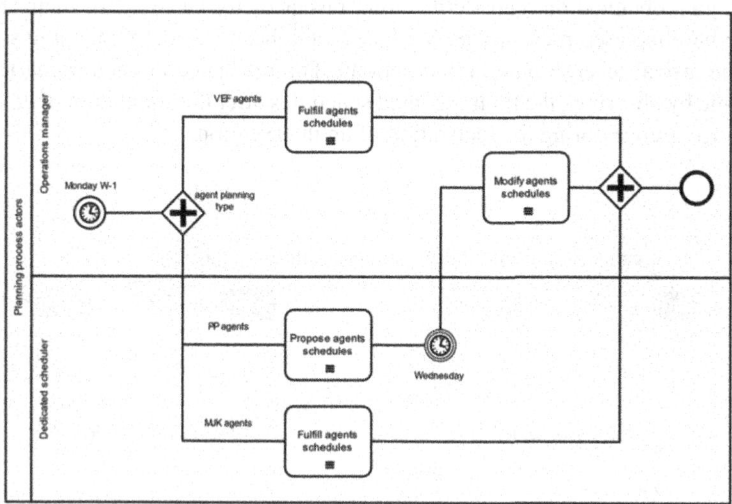


**Fig. 3.** Scheduling organization in Veolia Eau

**Alternative Planning Processes Scenarios**

All the organizational constraints added to the general problem allow to find reasonable solutions to the planning problem manually, but they consequently narrow the field of planning solutions, and as a consequence probably diminish the quality of the adopted schedules. Relaxing such constraints in the planning problem requires the use of a computer tool embedding CVRP algorithms inspired from the literature integrating our specific additional constraints. To estimate the gain obtained by removing each constraint, one scenario will be built for each of them, namely (i) small geographic boundaries, (ii) pre-allocation of agents to specific types of interventions, (iii) planning horizon of one week. Figure 5 illustrates with basic fictional examples the potential limits induced by each of these constraints. In this figure, interventions are represented by circles and arrows of the same colour represent the intervention tour of an agent. In the first illustration, blue and orange areas represent two distinct geographic territories, for which the schedules are presently planned separately. Removing this separation could save transportation costs, especially for interventions located near the boundaries. In the second illustration, blue and orange circles are interventions of two different types, and we assume that the two agents in this figure have the skills to intervene on both of them. Again, transportation time can be saved by removing the constraint of one specific type of interventions for every agent. The dotted blue arrows in the last illustration is a tour executed the week after the tour represented in orange arrows, with the remaining interventions. It shows that anticipation over several weeks can degrade the quality of the first week schedules but improve the global planning in the long term.

The first alternative scenarios to develop are the relaxation of these three organizational constraints, while keeping the same comparative baseline presently used in Veolia EAU. The methodology presented in Sect. 3 will allow us to compare objectively the potential gain obtained on realistic planning instances for each one of them. Keeping the same baseline used presently by Veolia Eau implies to work on planning strategies before the arrival of emergency interventions. The resilience of each scenario is still measurable by observing the final executed schedules after the simulation of emergency or delay occurrence during the realization of an intervention.

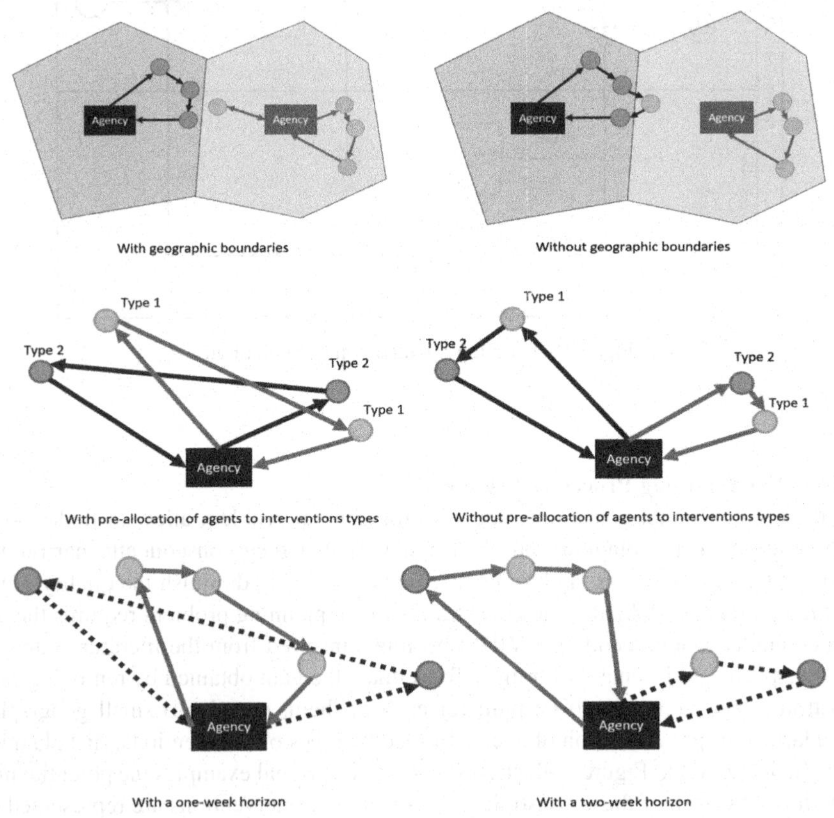


**Fig. 5.** Limits induced by organisational constraints

## 5 Conclusion and Further Research

The research project presented in this paper is in its infancy. If the real field planning water supply maintenance processes applied in Veolia Eau have already been described and modelled, the other steps described in the proposed research methodology remain to accomplish in order to provide answers to our core question: how to challenge and improve the maintenance planning strategies for water production and distribution network in an uncertain environment? The first planning alternative strategies presented in this study are tightly attached to the real field planning processes, in order to measure the cost (in terms of loss of efficiency and resilience) induced by changing a complex theoretical CVRP into a simplified and practical manually resolvable problem. However, other potential research avenues are considered with the integration of more sophisticated re-planning strategies, for a better consideration of the dynamic aspect of the problem.

## References

1. Capano, G., Woo, J.J.: Resilience and robustness in policy design: a critical appraisal. Policy Sci. **50**(3), 399–426 (2016). https://doi.org/10.1007/s11077-016-9273-x
2. Yamijala, S., Guikema, S.D., Brumbelow, K., et al.: Statistical models for the analysis of water distribution system pipe break data. Reliab. Eng. Syst. Saf. **94**(2), 282–293, févr. (2009)
3. Ana, E.V., Bauwens, W.: Modeling the structural deterioration of urban drainage pipes: the state-of-the-art in statistical methods. Urban Water J **7**(1), 47–59, févr. (2010)
4. Dantzig, G.B., Ramser, J.H.: The Truck Dispatching Problem . Manag. Sci. **6**(1), 80–91 (1959)
5. Kallehauge, B., Larsen, J., Madsen, O.B.G., Solomon, M.M.: Vehicle routing problem with time windows. In: Column Generation, Desaulniers, G., Desrosiers, J., Solomon, M.M., et al. (ed.) Boston, MA, pp. 67–98. Springer US (2005). https://doi.org/10.1007/0-387-25486-2_3
6. Archetti, C., Speranza, M.G., Vigo, D.: Chapter 10: vehicle routing problems with profits. In: Vehicle Routing, Society for Industrial and Applied Mathematics, pp. 273–297 (2014)
7. Subramanian, A., Uchoa, E., Pessoa, A.A., Ochi, L.S.: Branch-and-cut with lazy separation for the vehicle routing problem with simultaneous pickup and delivery. Oper. Res. Lett. **39**(5), 338–341 (2011)
8. Beck, J.C., Prosser, P., Selensky, E.: Vehicle routing and job shop scheduling: what's the difference? In: Proceedings of the Thirteenth International Conference on Automated Planning and Scheduling, pp. 267–276 (2003)
9. Toth, P., Vigo, D., (éd.): The Vehicle Routing Problem. Philadelphia: Society for Industrial and Applied Mathematics (2002)
10. Baldacci, R., Mingozzi, A., Roberti, R.: Recent exact algorithms for solving the vehicle routing problem under capacity and time window constraints. Eur. J. Oper. Res. **218**(1), 1-6, avr. (2012)
11. Pillac, V., Gendreau, M., Guéret, C., Medaglia, A.L.: A review of dynamic vehicle routing problems. Eur. J. Oper. Res. **225**(1), 1–11 (2013)
12. Clement, A., Kamissoko, D., Marmier, F., Gourc, D.: The robustness of the round planning face to risks of road freight transport. In: 2018 4th International Conference on Logistics Operations Management (GOL), pp. 1–7, avr. 2018
13. Bent, R., Van Hentenryck, P.: Online stochastic and robust optimization. In: Advances in Computer Science - ASIAN 2004. Higher-Level Decision Making, Berlin, Heidelberg, pp. 286–300 (2005). https://doi.org/10.1007/978-3-540-30502-6_21
14. Kool, W., van Hoof, H., Gromicho, J., Welling, M.: Deep Policy Dynamic Programming for Vehicle Routing Problems, ArXiv Cs Stat (2021)
15. Juan, A.A., Faulin, J., Grasman, S.E., Rabe, M., Figueira, G.: A review of simheuristics: extending metaheuristics to deal with stochastic combinatorial optimization problems. Oper. Res. Perspect. **2**, 62–72 (2015)

16. Abdirad, M., Krishnan, K., Gupta, D.: A two-stage metaheuristic algorithm for the dynamic vehicle routing problem in Industry 4.0 approach. J. Manag. Anal. **8**(1), 69–83 (2002)
17. Abdirad, M., Krishnan, K., Gupta, D.: A Three-Stage Algorithm for the Large Scale Dynamic Vehicle Routing Problem with an Industry 4.0 Approach. ArXiv200811719 Cs Math, October 2020
18. Chibani, A., Delorme, X., Dolgui, A., Pierreval, H.: Dynamic optimisation for highly agile supply chains in e-procurement context. Int. J. Prod. Res. **56**(17), 5904–5929 (2018)
19. Schoen, Q., Lauras, M., Truptil, S., Fontanili, F., Anquetil, A.-G.: Towards a hyperconnected transportation management system: application to blood logistics. In: Collaboration in a Hyperconnected World, Cham (2016)
20. Lei, H., Laporte, G., Guo, B.: A generalized variable neighborhood search heuristic for the capacitated vehicle routing problem with stochastic service times. TOP **20**(1), 99–118 (2012)
21. Li, J.-Q., Mirchandani, P.B., Borenstein, D.: The vehicle rescheduling problem: model and algorithms. Networks **50**(3), 211–229 (2007)
22. Law, A.M., Law, A.M., Kelton, W.D.A., Kelton, W.D., Kelton, D.M.: Simulation Modeling and Analysis. McGraw-Hill, New York (2000)
23. Patten, M.L., Newhart, M.: Understanding Research Methods: An Overview of the Essentials. Taylor and Francis, Abingdon (2017)
24. Shi, Z., Jeannot, E., Dongarra, J.J.: Robust task scheduling in non-deterministic heterogeneous computing systems. In: 2006 IEEE International Conference on Cluster Computing, pp. 1–10, September 2006
25. Canon, L.-C., Jeannot, E.: A comparison of robustness metrics for scheduling DAGs on heterogeneous systems. In: 2007 IEEE International Conference on Cluster Computing, pp. 558–567, September 2007
26. Canon, L.-C., Jeannot, E.: Evaluation and optimization of the robustness of DAG schedules in heterogeneous environments. IEEE Trans. Parallel Distrib. Syst. **21**(4), 532–546 (2010)

# Atomic Supply Chain Modelling for Risk Management Based on SCOR

Thibaut Cerabona[1(✉)], Matthieu Lauras[1,2], Jean-Philippe Gitto[3], Benoit Montreuil[2], and Frederick Benaben[1,2]

[1] Centre Génie Industriel, IMT Mines Albi, Campus Jarlard, CT Cedex 09, 81013 Albi, France
{thibaut.cerabona,matthieu.lauras, frederick.benaben}@mines-albi.fr

[2] ISyE, H Milton Steward School of Industrial and Systems Engineering, 755 Ferst Drive, Atlanta, GA 30332, USA
benoit.montreuil@isye.gatech.edu

[3] Scalian, Batiment Pythagore, 17 Avenue Didier Daurat, 31700 Blagnac, France
jean-philippe.gitto@scalian.com

**Abstract.** At the time of instability becomes the norm (climate changes, natural disasters, epidemic, etc.) the management of collaborative networks, such as supply chains, is becoming more and more complex and critical. This instability only adds to the complexity of an already very complex system. Thus, supply chain managers have to adapt to multi-dimensional complex situations. Dealing with instability is a key expectation for these managers. One tool to help managers make decisions in this unstable environment is simulation. This article introduces some first results on an "atomic" reconfigurable supply chain simulation model based on Supply Chain Operations Reference (SCOR) model. This simulation tool will be used to apply an innovative physics-based approach of risk and opportunity management, that designs disturbances by forces moving the considered supply chain within its performance framework. This approach enables managers to monitor supply chain's performance trajectory by viewing and merging the impact of risks and opportunities.

**Keywords:** SCOR · Supply chain management · Risk management · Performance measurement · Physics and system modeling

## 1 Introduction

At the times of climate changes, natural disasters and pandemics, instability becomes the norm. Supply chains as a very common collaborative network, do not escape and are strongly subjected to this instability. They operate in a dynamic, uncertain and risky environment. This instability increases the complexity of a system that is already very complex due to its network organization, which brings together various interdependent entities interconnected by the flow of money, goods and information. According to [1], the growth of supply chain complexity is accelerated by the following factors:


Published by Springer Nature Switzerland AG 2021
L. M. Camarinha-Matos et al. (Eds.): PRO-VE 2021, IFIP AICT 629, pp. 601–610, 2021.
https://doi.org/10.1007/978-3-030-85969-5_56

globalization, sustainability, customization, outsourcing, innovation and flexibility. [2] identifies the eight most common sources generating this complexity: network, process, range, product, customer, supplier, organizational and information. Thus, supply chain managers have to analyze and adapt to more and more multi-dimensional complex situations. Dealing with instability is a key expectation for supply chain managers, whose purpose is to try to benefit from instability or at least, not to suffer from it. To be able to take advantage of this instability and manage such a complex system, managers need knowledge about the network organization and the business aspects of network operations [3]. But also, to identify and understand the causes of this instability and determine their consequences on all the activities of the supply chain [4]. Many tools and approaches exist to manage this complexity and help managers in their decision making. The solution chosen in this study is simulation. Indeed, according to [5], simulation is a favorable tool for the analysis and study of complex and dynamic systems such as supply chain networks. It allows decision makers to obtain accurate results [4]. However, the more complex the system is, the more difficult it is to model, and the more expensive it is in terms of time, resources and energy. According to [6], the development time of the simulation model represents about 45% of the total effort of a simulation project. The analysis and understanding of the cause and effect relationships of a disturbance and its impact on the performance of such a system become hard to obtain. Therefore, the use of standard reference models such as SCOR model (Supply Chain Operations Reference model) should make possible to create simulation models more quickly (especially for the conceptualization and modeling phases), by introducing understandable and standard processes and metrics [3].

**The aim of this paper is to introduce our preliminary work on a modular reconfigurable supply chain model based on SCOR and its use as a decision support tool by serving as an input to a physics-based approach of risk and opportunity management, called Physics of Decision.**

The remainder of the paper is organized as follows: Sect. 2 presents the supply chain operations reference model. Section 3 introduces preliminary work on our "atomic" supply chain model and its application as decision support tool. The last section concludes on some perspective points, defining a roadmap to make this model and the innovative risk management approach presented functional.

## 2 Supply Chain Operations Reference Model

### 2.1 SCOR Scope

The SCOR model is a process reference model, that provides methodology, standard process definitions, metrics, diagnostic and benchmarking tools in order to improve supply chain processes and performance [7]. SCOR allows to link all these elements into a unique framework [7]. Since its introduction in 1996 by the Supply Chain Council, this model has been constantly reviewed and updated to consider all changes and developments in supply chain business practices. As mentioned in [8], SCOR is composed of three major parts. First, it is a modeling tool that uses and defines standard processes as building blocks for supply chain processes. By breaking down the processes of a supply chain into (re)/configurable process blocks [9], this model can be used to describe and model simple or very complex supply chains. This block breakdown gives a balanced horizontal (inter-process) and vertical (hierarchical) view compared to traditional process decomposition models [9]. The objective of this process structuration is to improve and support the understanding of all supply chain processes and best practices in order to improve the effectiveness of the supply chain management and its overall performance. Second, it defines a set of performance indicators called metrics. Third, it is a benchmarking tool that allows companies to compare with other companies, by comparing their performance indicators.

The two following sub-sections summarize the structure of the SCOR model based on information and materials from [7].

## 2.2 SCOR Processes and Levels

The SCOR model develops standard process divided into four hierarchical levels [3], as illustrated in Fig. 1. Level 1 defines the six major and macro management processes: *Source*, *Make*, *Deliver* and *Return* for the goods and information flows, *Enable* for supply chain management activities and to support the others processes, and *Plan* to coordinate the five others processes [3]. Table 1 describes and defines these six major processes.

**Table 1.** Definitions of SCOR's major processes.

| Major process | Definition |
|---|---|
| Plan | Balances the demand and supply of goods and resources in the other processes in order to develop actions correlated to business objectives [9] |
| Source | "Contains processes that procure goods and services to meet planned or actual demand" [9] |
| Make | Describes the activities consisting of the transformation of raw materials or products to a finished state |
| Deliver | Consists of processes that provide finished products or services to meet customer demand [9] |
| Return | Deals with the activities associated with the reverse flow of defective products [9] |
| Enable | Describes all the activities associated with the supply chain management [7]. Enable processes support the others processes |

These processes are decomposed into process categories in the level 2 depending on the type of business and strategies of the considered supply chain: make-to stock (MTS), make-to-order (MTO) and engineer-to-order (ETO). This level offers more details and simplifies the supply chain. For this level, SCOR model proposes a tool kit of 32 process categories. Thus, from this tool kit, each supply chain configuration can be modeled. Level 3 divides the identified processes of level 2 into generic and standard process elements. These process elements represent the steps of each process. Once these steps are assembled and performed in a certain order, they enable supply chain activities to be planned, materials to be sourced, products to be manufactured, goods and services to be delivered and product returns to be managed. Level 4 describes the detailed tasks for each of the level 3 activities. These tasks, and their interactions, are specific to each company. This level is not considered in our study, because it focuses on the process specific to each company.

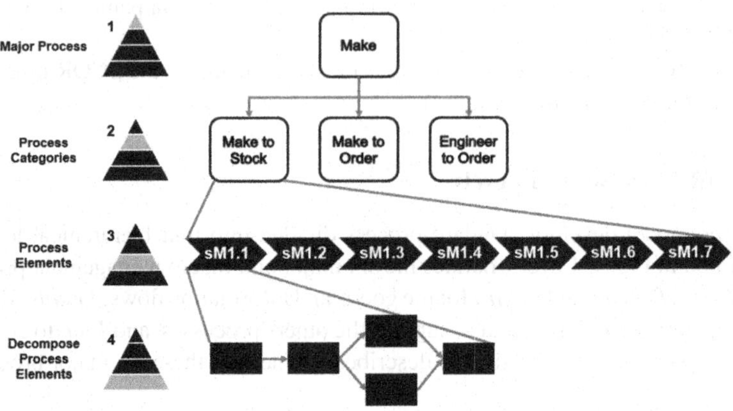


**Fig. 1.** SCOR process levels

### 2.3 SCOR Metrics

In order to evaluate and diagnose the performance of a supply chain, SCOR proposes an approach based on three elements: performance attributes, key performance indicators and best practices [7]. Performance attributes represent the strategic performance characteristics on which the performance of the considered supply chain must be aligned to be still with the business strategy. SCOR defines two types of performance attributes: customer and internal focused attributes. SCOR associates several key performance indicators, called metrics, with each of these performance attributes. These metrics are organized according to a hierarchical structure, i.e. at each level (level 1, 2 or 3) a metric is associated to evaluate the process. This decomposition of the metrics allows an analysis of the supply chain performance according to root-causes. For example, the analysis of the performance of level 2 metrics can explain the gaps in performance of level 1 metrics. As mentioned in [8], each process is associated with a list of best practices to improve the metrics.

## 3 Proposal: Atomic Reconfigurable Supply Chain Model

### 3.1 Background

Currently, supply chain simulation is an integral part of discrete event simulation applications [10]. [11] mentions that the SCOR model can be used to build powerful simulation models based on discrete event simulation. In [11], the authors aim to create supply chain simulation models using the SCOR model, in order to facilitate the construction of these models and to create reusable components from a software allowing discrete event simulation. [12] proposes a comparison and evaluation of several modeling techniques. In this paper, the authors compare three simulation tools: Witness (a commercial simulation software), iGrafx Process (a process modelling and analysis tool) and e-SCOR (a supply chain simulator based on SCOR and developed by GenSym) through the modeling of the same use case. They concluded from their experiments that SCOR-based simulation tools offer advantages over other simulation tools. In particular, by using standard processes and performance indicators, these tools make it possible to build faster and easier to understand models (especially for people familiar with the SCOR model). The disadvantages of this kind of model are the lack of flexibility and the risk of simplifying and transforming certain strategies in order to fit the definitions of the SCOR model and thus modify the reality. In [13] another SCOR-based simulation model is introduced, IBM SmartSCOR that develops an integrated platform to support supply chain transformation by using several simulation and optimization techniques. [14] and [4] develop ontologies, that integrate different models based on SCOR framework and views using Integrated DEFinition (IDEF) suite. Supply chain ontology allows to capture the required knowledge about the supply chain. Their approach generates automatically supply chain models based on a set of predefined modules, derived from the level three of SCOR. [3, 8 and 10] offer SCOR Template model, that allows to model a supply chain by assembling bricks based on the level 2 or 3 of SCOR according to the versions and designed in Arena simulation software.

Based on all this work, it is clear that SCOR occupies an important place in the simulation of supply chains.

### 3.2 Physics of Decision

This atomic simulation model introduced in the next sub-section will be used to apply the Physics of Decision (POD) approach presented in [15]. Indeed, according to [11], simulation models are very interesting as a decision support and performance prediction tool. Simulation is an increasingly important methodological approach to theory development in the strategy and organization literature [16]. The POD approach is based on analogies with physical principles to support decision-making processes and help managers to navigate in unstable environment. To navigate in this kind of environment, managers need a tool that gives them access to information on the following three points, as mentioned in [17] and [15]: (1) the comprehension of the considered system and its environment, (2) understanding the possible consequences of different changes and (3) the mechanisms for selecting the different options available.

To answer the first point, POD approach develops two modelling spaces: the description space and the performance space. In a supply chain context, the **description space** is dedicated to the description of the considered supply chain and its environment. It represents the supply chain's location within its attribute dimensions (for instance customer demand, capacity, number of employees, etc.). It is illustrated in Fig. 2. The value of its attributes changes as a result of the decisions taken by the managers. The degree of liberty for each attribute is set by the control space. It is a subspace in continuous change representing supply chain constraints and in which the supply chain is able to move freely (blue shape). The context characteristics represent a zone in this description space, where the supply chain is more susceptible to certain disruptions and potentials that may impact it (orange shape). There are four types of potentials:

- Environment: all potentials created by the system environment (e.g. new tax on imports of coarse metals from outside the European Union, etc.),
- Charges: mandatory system costs (e.g. wages, process times, etc.),
- Innovations: measures taken to improve the system (e.g. buy new machine, etc.),
- Interactions: represent all the potential generated by the relationships between the network's actors (e.g. customer request, flow of products, etc.).

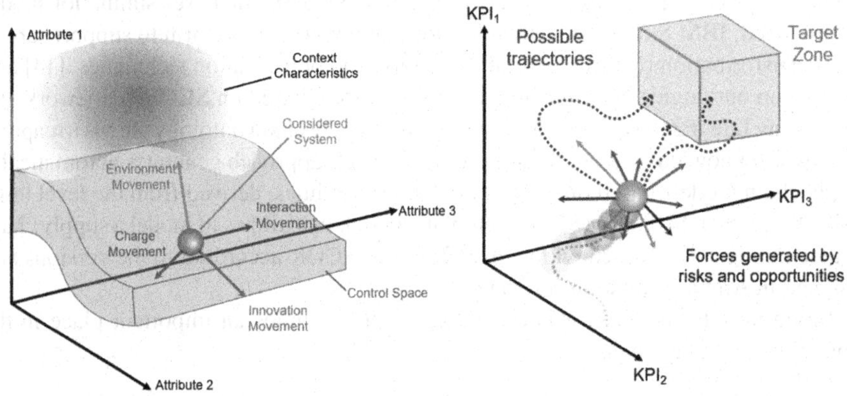


**Fig. 2.** Description (left) and Performance (right) spaces (Color figure online)

The **performance space** describes the performance of the supply chain. This performance space is illustrated in Fig. 2. The first trajectory modeled in this framework is the inertia trajectory (dotted orange line). It represents the nominal performance trajectory of the observed system without any perturbation. It will serve as a reference in the analysis of the impact of risks and opportunities on the supply chain's performance. In this multi-dimensional key performance indicators (KPIs) framework, forces model and reflect the impact of risks and opportunities on the system (color vectors) [18]. Thus, the evolution of the supply chain's performance (schematically its position in the framework) is due to the achievement of risks or opportunities. As mentioned in [15], the main interest of the performance space is to obtain the performance trajectory of the supply chain, which is considered as a way to analyze the evolution of its performance over time. Moreover, as mentioned in [18], this framework is used as a decision support for managers, in particular by studying the best options to choose in order to reach the target area at lower "cost" (which will be modeled as a multi-objective function whose objective is to minimize the effort, i.e. at least the time and money, to reach this target subspace). Schematically, that means defining the best combination of forces to select in order to reach the target zone (the purple possible trajectories). The target zone is an area of the performance space designing the performance objectives of the considered supply chain (green parallelepiped). Its shape is still under study.

### 3.3 Atomic Modelling Vision

This POD approach allows to control and monitor the evolution of the global performance of the supply chain, by assessing the impact of macro risks and opportunities. However, with this approach, it is currently very difficult to evaluate and analyze the micro-consequences generated by the identified risks and opportunities. Especially, their impacts on certain actors or components of such a complex supply chain network. To resolve this problem, our idea is to develop a modular, "atomic", reconfigurable simulation model based on the SCOR model. This model is based on SCOR to take advantage of all the metrics, standard processes and meshes defined in this model. But also, to be able to develop a model accepted by the supply chain community, the only model widely accepted and shared by this community is the SCOR model (according to [14]). SCOR will also be used to define the level of decomposition of a supply chain network from which to build the atoms. Thus, atoms will be created from the 32 processes of level 2 of the SCOR model. In this first version of the model, only the *Source*, *Make* and *Deliver* processes for MTS and MTO products will be modeled. Thus, six atoms are necessary as summarized in Table 2. Each atom is a reconfigurable micro-model, modeling a main function of the supply chain. To be able to fulfill their duties, atoms will carry out actions corresponding to the steps and process elements defined in SCOR level 3. Figure 3 illustrates how the atoms are positioned in the SCOR framework.

**Table 2.** List of required atoms.

| Major process | Atom | Atom Id | Inputs | Outputs |
|---|---|---|---|---|
| Source | MTS | S1 | M1<br>D1-suppliers | M1 |
| | MTO | S2 | M2<br>D2-suppliers | M2 |
| Make | MTS | M1 | S1 | D1 |
| | MTO | M2 | S2 | D2 |
| Deliver | MTS | D1 | M1 | S1-customers |
| | MTO | D2 | M2 | S2-customers |

Each atom should be as configurable as possible, which means that each atom must be parametrizable and change its components (the value of its attributes) in order to adapt to the considered supply chain, its disturbances and decisions made by its managers. As mentioned in the previous subsection, this atomic model will be used to apply the POD approach. To do so, each atom will have its own description and performance spaces, in order to observe the micro-consequences of risks and opportunities on these atoms.

In order to maintain a root-cause analysis of performance, the KPIs measured at the global supply chain level will be calculated using aggregation functions defined from the indicators measured at the atom level. Analogies with the properties of electrical voltage will be studied, for example if the network follows a "series connection" type structure, is the impact of the disturbance equal to the sum of the impacts of its micro-consequences.

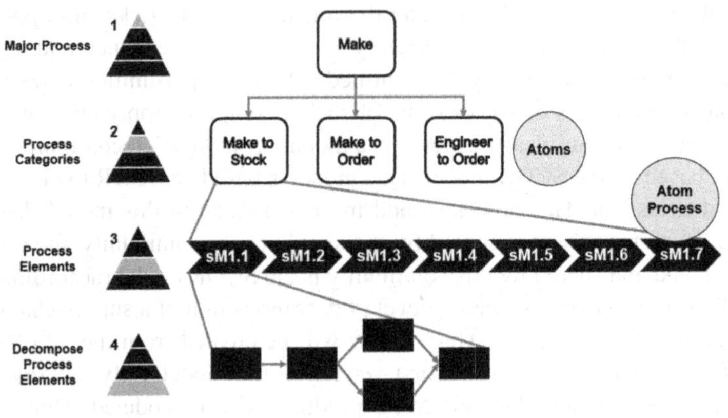


**Fig. 3.** Position of atoms in the SCOR framework

### 3.4 A Simple Illustrative Example

Let's consider a simple example to illustrate this approach, taking the case of the supply chain of a company A. Company A produces plastic bottles and sells them to its only customer, Company B. To produce its bottles, A buys polyethylene terephthalate (PET) granulate from C and recycled PET flake from D. All these products follow a make to stock strategy. With this atomic approach, this supply chain will be modeled from the atoms of type: S1, M1 and D1. Each atom process will be modeled using Anylogic© simulation software using the *Process Modeling Library*. Figure 4 gives an overview of the modeling of this supply chain with the approach presented in this article.

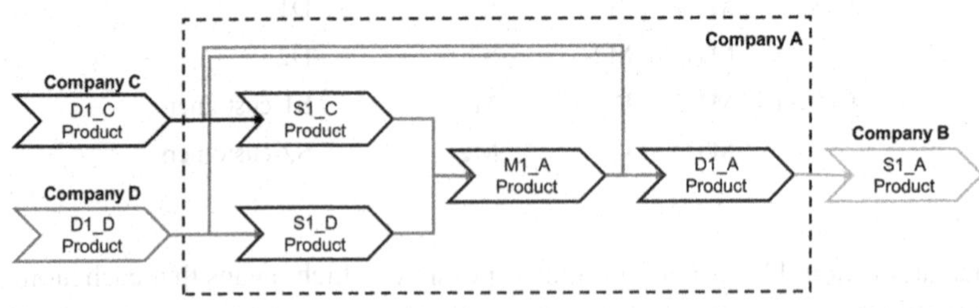


**Fig. 4.** Atomic model of this supply chain

This example illustrates how, starting from a simple case, it is possible to build brick by brick a supply chain and thus to model it, thanks to the atoms developed in this first version and their potential links (presented in Table 2). Once the block arrangement has been made, all these blocks must be parameterized according to the properties and values of the attributes of the studied supply chain. This example also illustrates the potential of this approach, particularly in the study of supply chain reconfiguration following the occurence of risks or opportunities. Studying different implementation of a supply chain, according to several configurations of building blocks allows to compare different obtained performance, resistance to disruption and resilience. The last step consists in implementing the set of performance indicators specific to each atom onto the simulation models of each of these atoms, and applying the POD approach presented in Subsect. 3.2. The objective of this approach is to provide an intuitive and immersive decision support tool, with which managers, following a "what if" reasoning, will be able to analyze the impact of disruptions but also micro-impacts on the key processes of their system. This tool can also be used to visualize and analyze the effectiveness of the corrective actions implemented.

## 4 Conclusion and Perspectives

This article introduces the first works carried out on this modular vision of the supply chain, the following perspectives define a roadmap to make that approach a functional practice. The first one consists in conducting simulation campaigns and sensitivity analyses to cover the widest range of values of the considered supply chain parameters and thus cover as much of the potential accessible description space as possible. The purpose of these simulations and analyses is to generate the volume of data necessary to study the sensitivity and fragility of the supply chain in the face of certain identified risks or opportunities, and thus define the associated forces. Then in a second step, these simulations and analyses aim to generate a sufficient amount of data to feed and train neural networks. They will forward replace atoms, as they offer a more reactive and even more scalable arrangement. Indeed, once trained correctly, neural networks will offer the possibility to study and predict the sensitivity and variability of the supply chain to a wide range of risks and opportunities. The second avenue concerns one of the key points to turn that model functional and suitable, the connectivity between atoms. The objective is to develop compatible bonds between atoms in order to allow them to interact with each other and to be able to build networks of atoms and so model supply chain networks. In particular, by taking inspiration from what has been achieved within the Physical Internet, particularly in the way it manages interfaces and interconnectivity of the developed logistics system.

## References

1. Serdarasan, S.: A review of supply chain complexity drivers. Comput. Ind. Eng. **66**(3), 533–540 (2013). https://doi.org/10.1016/j.cie.2012.12.008
2. Christopher, M.: Logistics & Supply Chain Management. Financial Times Prentice Hall, Harlow (2011)
3. Persson, F.: SCOR template—A simulation based dynamic supply chain analysis tool. 7 (2011)

4. Cope, D., Fayez, M., Mollaghasemi, M., Kaylani, A.: Supply chain simulation modeling made easy: an innovative approach. In: 2007 Winter Simulation Conference, pp. 1887–1896. IEEE, Washington, DC, USA (2007). https://doi.org/10.1109/WSC.2007.4419816
5. Towill, D.R.: Supply chain dynamics. Int. J. Comput. Integr. Manuf. **4**(4), 197–208 (1991). https://doi.org/10.1080/09511929108944496
6. Mackulak, G.T., Lawrence, F.P.: Effective simulation model reuse: a case study for AMHS modeling. In: Proceedings of the 1998 Winter Simulation Conference (1998)
7. Council, S.-C.: Supply-Chain Operations Reference-Model, Scor Version 12.0, Supply-Chain Council (2017)
8. Persson, F., Araldi, M.: The development of a dynamic supply chain analysis tool—Integration of SCOR and discrete event simulation. Int. J. Prod. Econ. **121**(2), 574–583 (2009). https://doi.org/10.1016/j.ijpe.2006.12.064
9. Huang, S.H., Sheoran, S.K., Keskar, H.: Computer-assisted supply chain configuration based on supply chain operations reference (SCOR) model. Comput. Ind. Eng. **48**(2), 377–394 (2005). https://doi.org/10.1016/j.cie.2005.01.001
10. Persson, F., et al.: Supply chain dynamics in the SCOR model - a simulation modeling approach. In: Laroque, C., Himmelspach, J., Pasupathy, R. (eds.) Winter Simulation Conference Proceedings (2012)
11. Hermann, J.W., Lin, E., Pundoor, G.: Supply chain simulation modeling using the supply chain operations reference model. In: Volume 1: 23rd Computers and Information in Engineering Conference, Parts A and B, pp. 461–469 ASMEDC, Chicago, Illinois, USA (2003). https://doi.org/10.1115/DETC2003/CIE-48220
12. Albores, P., Love, D., Weaver, M., Stone, J., Benton, H.: An evaluation of SCOR modelling techniques and tools. In: Proceedings of the EuroMot 2006 Conference (2006)
13. Dong, J., et al.: IBM SmartSCOR - A SCOR based supply chain transformation platform through simulation and optimization techniques. In: Proceedings of the 2006 Winter Simulation Conference, pp. 650–659 IEEE, Monterey, CA, USA (2006). https://doi.org/10.1109/WSC.2006.323142.
14. Fayez, M., Rabelo, L., Mollaghasemi, M.: Ontologies for supply chain simulation modeling. In: Proceedings of the Winter Simulation Conference, 2005, pp. 2364–2370. IEEE, Orlando, FL, USA (2005). https://doi.org/10.1109/WSC.2005.1574527
15. Benaben, F., et al.: Instability is the norm! a physics-based theory to navigate among risks and opportunities. Enterprise Inf. Syst. 1–28 (2021). https://doi.org/10.1080/17517575.2021.1878391
16. Davis, J.P., Eisenhardt, K.M., Bingham, C.B.: Developing theory through simulation methods. Acad. Manag. Rev. **32**(2), 480–499 (2007)
17. Simon, H.A.: A behavioral model of rational choice. Quart. J. Econ. **69**(1), 99–118 (1955)
18. Cerabona, T., Lauras, M., Faugère, L., Gitto, JP., Montreuil, B., Benaben., F.: A physics-based approach for managing supply chain risks and opportunities within its performance framework. In: Camarinha-Matos, L.M. et al. (eds.) Boosting Collaborative Networks 4.0, pp. 418–427. Springer International Publishing, Cham (2020). https://doi.org/10.1007/978-3-030-62412-5_34

# Towards a Collaborative and Open Supply Chain Management Operating Services Platform

Matthieu Lauras[1,2], Raphaël Oger[1(✉)], Jiayao Li[1], Benoit Montreuil[2], Markus Kohl[3], Andreas Habl[3], and Julien Lesbegueries[1]

[1] Centre Génie Industriel, IMT Mines Albi, University of Toulouse, Albi, France
{matthieu.lauras,raphael.oger,jiayao.li, julien.lesbegueries}@mines-albi.fr

[2] Physical Internet Center, ISYE School, Georgia Institute of Technology, Atlanta, USA
benoit.montreuil@isye.gatech.edu

[3] Chair of Materials Handling, Material Flow, Logistics, Technical University of Munich, Munich, Germany
{makus.kohl,andreas.habl}@tum.de

**Abstract.** Supply Chain (SC) uncertainty perspectives must now be translated into practice. SC entities must accept crises and catastrophes as normal situations and increase significantly their culture of SC risk management. They should adapt their decision-support systems to be able considering disruptions as regular inputs, whether small, large or huge. Collaboration should not be limited to few entities of a SC, but to the whole SC. Concrete tools allowing entities to share vital information to give visibility, ensure synchronization of the material flows, align management of emergencies and use of critical resources must be developed and used. That is the purpose of this paper. Practically, a framework for SC risk and opportunity management and a Collaborative and Open Supply Chain Management Operating Services (COSMOS) platform are presented. An illustrative case is developed to highlight the potential benefits of the proposal on one service example.

**Keywords:** Supply chain management · Collaborative information systems · Decision support systems · Uncertainty · Risk management

## 1 Introduction

Current Supply Chains (SCs) have never been so vulnerable to unexpected disruptive events along with the increased complexity of highly dynamic business environment. Recently, as COVID-19 pandemic reveals, an unprecedented disruption in supply and demand is caused that affects numerous both global and local availability of SC activities [1]. It's a fact that today's SCs have demonstrated during this crisis, a poor ability to make efficient and responsive decisions to supply on time and in-full vital, but also


Published by Springer Nature Switzerland AG 2021
L. M. Camarinha-Matos et al. (Eds.): PRO-VE 2021, IFIP AICT 629, pp. 611–620, 2021.
https://doi.org/10.1007/978-3-030-85969-5_57

basic, necessities. As illustrated in [2], the pandemic necessitates SCs and tools coping with enormous uncertainties as a new normal, but the knowledge of an effective and efficient way of recovering from the disturbance is still quite limited. Certainly, COVID-19 amplifies the needs for agility and resilience for SCs.

With a long-term view, effective decision-making has a significant impact on resilient capabilities of collaborative networks [3]. However, such a situation has led to great pressure on stakeholders to make prudential decisions, especially in the face of multitude uncertainties and decision options. Developing a Decision Support System (DSS) is obviously a good way to provide a better visibility and understanding of available options, which enables an optimal decision-making for SCs [4]. But most of current decision-support tools fail to act beyond legacy SC management dogmas and practices [5]. So far, neither in research nor in practices there exist effective and efficient tools that help with overcoming the stated challenges on a long-term perspective, due to a lack of methodological foundation and necessary requirements.

Consequently, it is pivotal to develop suitable tools for both researchers and practitioners that provide reliable guidance for decisions in order to create and maintain stable SCs to support company recovery. What is more, it is crucial that those tools not only recreate economic growth, but also that they support a sustainable long-term business strategy and decision processes under the new circumstances by assuring SC flexibility and resilience in a way that suits the new normal.

In this context, the paper presents an innovative Collaborative and Open Supply chain Management Operating Services (COSMOS) platform that is dedicated to management of uncertainties, variabilities and disruptions in SCs. The COSMOS platform aims to provide actors in the SC with a range of tools that could help them to better manage the huge variabilities they may face in the months and years ahead. In order to achieve the objective, two building blocks are designed and developed, including a software portfolio with open online software services and a knowledge hub with a set of documents and methodological tools relevant for managing the new normal. The remainder of the paper is organized as follows. A brief review of the related works is summarized before introducing the core proposal of the COSMOS platform. Then, an illustrative showcase for one service example embedded in the platform are presented before concluding and opening avenues for future research.

## 2 Background and Related Work

As the COVID-19 crisis reveals, uncertainty-driven SC management is already the new normal. Regarding the definition of SC uncertainty, as given by [6], the term is used to depict decision-making situations that lacks information to accurately predict the effect of SC behaviors or simply lacks appropriate response solutions. Given that SC uncertainty and risk are usually utilized indiscriminately in the literature of SC management, some authors suggest that SC risk mainly reflects negative impacts, while uncertainty may both have positive and negative impacts on SC performance [7]. The article also holds this vision of SC uncertainty that the term can be used to contain the issues of risk to some extent.

During the past decades, many uncertainty-driven SC management techniques have been developed for dealing with disruptions and instabilities. For instance, simulation has been widely used in SC risk modeling, which contributes to the understanding of the impact of interactive factors from a systematic perspective [8]. Besides, stochastic programming and multi-criteria decision making have been effectively utilized to analyze or assess SC uncertainties. Although various approaches for uncertainty-driven SC management have been widely discussed within the literature, they are mainly dedicated to risk identification, assessment, and modeling. It is worth to mention that there is a limited formal solution on how to support decision-making processes from a long-term practical perspective for managing uncertainties.

Regarding the current DSS used for SC management, numerous technologies and systems have been set up for SC collaboration, such as EDI (Electronic Data Interchange), CPFR (Collaborative Planning, Forecasting and Replenishment) or VMI (Vendor Managed Inventory) for instance [9]. With regard to the need of SC planning, it relates to a series of forward-looking decisions in terms of coordinating information from supplier to customer, optimizing product delivery and service. The associated systems include MRP (Material Requirements Planning), MRPII (Manufacturing Resources Planning), ERP (Enterprise Resource Planning) or APS (Advanced Planning and Scheduling).

To sum up, without any doubt, the development of the above-mentioned tools has been conductive to satisfying the needs of business in the context of nominal SCs. However, they are now obsolete as they have been designed to optimize performance in a stable and deterministic world. Even though many studies point out the importance of uncertainty-driven SC management in the current complex and dynamic SC environment; few of DSS in the literature can provide the decision-makers with sound solutions for the purpose of managing uncertainties. Moreover, opportunity-driven SC management will soon be the new normal. Since SCs have become more flexible and open, as presented in [10], the new state "hyperconnectivity" may bring many available opportunities for SC stakeholders. Consequently, the deep insight and reliable guidance for seizing opportunities will be clearly needed, while neither in research nor in practices is unable to support the ambition.

## 3 Proposal

In order to solve the problem statement previously described, we develop in this section our core proposal composed of two main components. First, a theoretical framework dedicated to the management of risks and opportunities in SC Management context is developed. Second, considering the previous framework, a Collaborative and Open Supply chain Management Operating Services (COSMOS) platform is presented.

### 3.1 COSMOS Theoretical Framework

Uncertainty management relates definitively to the management of risks and opportunities, which might be past, present or future ones. In we refer to the ISO 31000, risk management process could be defined as formulated by [11] and exposed on Fig. 1. This process starts with the identification of disruption trigger event(s) (risks or opportunities in our context) and moves to the criticality assessment (defined as a combination of occurrence probability and impact potentiality). Then, decision-makers have to imagine a set of potential solutions or options allowing to avoid or limit the risk incidence, or to catch potential opportunities. All these options must be evaluated in terms of benefits and costs (accessibility) to select the most appropriate one. Finally, through a usual risk management perspective, the most well-balanced solution might be chosen, implemented and followed along the time.

If this approach has demonstrated some benefits in the past, it seems a bit obsolete regarding the new normal described in the previous sections of this paper. Notably, this risk and opportunity management lifecycle should now be focused not only the assets as it is usually the case but also on the business processes which are used to manage and execute the system under study. The new risk and opportunity management status must include its self-ability to make a situation better or worse. In addition, the considered trigger disruption events should be past, live and future to better manage the expected risk and opportunity management capabilities. As a consequence, the set of actionable options and creative solutions to manage risks and opportunities should be able simultaneously to:

- learn from past to avoid reproducing previous mistakes and errors: this step should consist in understanding bad behaviors and decisions regarding past risks or opportunities. This should allow defining efficient mitigation plans based on past data gathered from historical database.
- react live to reduce bad impacts of an ongoing situation: this step should consist in reacting on-the-fly to some real-time data gathered from legacy systems, open-data sources, IoT devices, etc. This should allow defining some alleviating plans, not to avoid risks but to reduce their immediate impacts or at the opposite to benefit from short-term unexpected opportunities.
- proact ahead to prevent potential short-term issues: this step should consist in assuming (through simulation techniques for instance) what should be the status of the SC in the near future according to the existing situation and to a set of challenged assumptions. This should allow designing some sidestep plans able to avoid future disruptions or at least to reduce their impact significantly. Same approach might also be used to take advantages of some in-coming situations.
- prepare future to secure long-term perspectives regarding large set of scenarios: this step should consist in predicting a set of potential futures regarding ongoing or potential demand, supply or internal variabilities in order to support a large, qualitative and quantitative "what-if" perspective. This should allow defining dynamic, wide and effective contingency plans.

This new vision of the risk management lifecycle might be formulated as on Fig. 2. From this, we suggest developing a dedicated platform able to receive and expose concrete technical solutions able to support parts of the functionalities presented in the SC risk and opportunity management framework. This platform is presented in the following section.

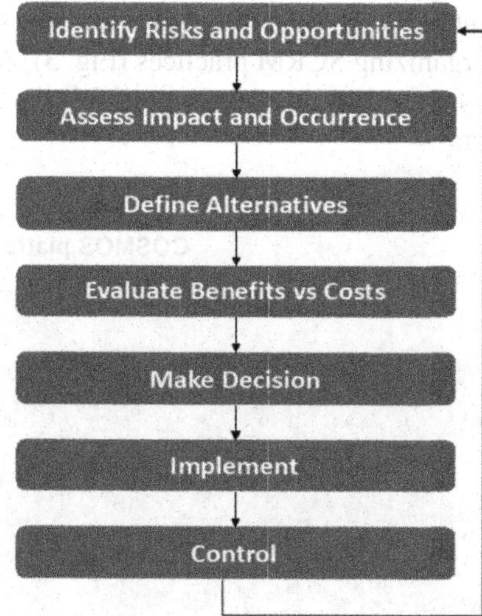


**Fig. 1.** Risk and opportunity management process [11]

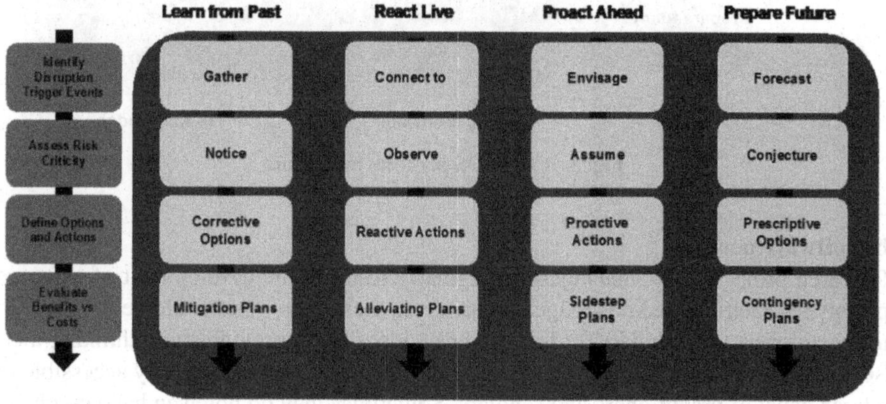


**Fig. 2.** A framework for SC risk and opportunity management

## 3.2 COSMOS Platform

**a) Big picture**

The objective of the COSMOS platform is to provide SC practitioners and scholars with openly accessible resources they can use to foster new ideas for improving and rethinking their SC management practices and knowledge.

The COSMOS platform is composed of two building blocks:

- First, a software portfolio to provide open online software services.
- Second, a knowledge hub to provide a structured knowledge that can be used to better understand the SC new normal and its stakes.

From the business point of view, both building blocks are designed according to the proposed framework for organizing SCRM practices (Fig. 3). At this stage, most of the research efforts have been focused on the software portfolio, which is the focal point of the remaining of this paper.

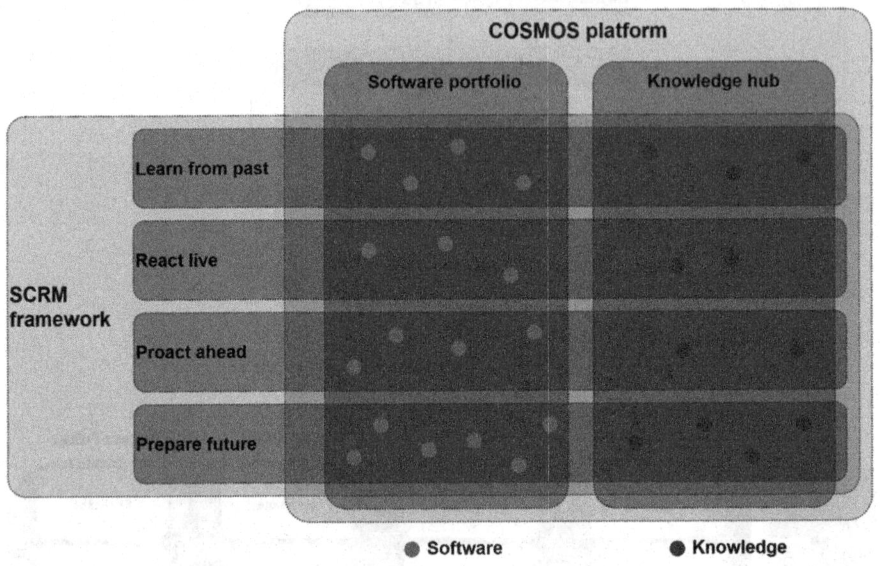


**Fig. 3.** COSMOS platform big picture

**b) Software portfolio**

Research projects in SC management regularly result in the development of software prototypes. Getting the knowledge and access to these prototypes could be a huge help to practitioners and scholars for fostering new ideas for improving and rethinking their SC management practices. However, these prototypes are not often easily accessible to a large panel of practitioners and scholars. Sometimes they do not even have graphical user interfaces. Therefore, the software portfolio has been designed with the objective of making these prototypes, resulting from research projects, openly accessible.

With that objective in mind, the software portfolio has been developed as a cloud-based platform accessible at the following URL: https://cosmos-portal.mines-albi.fr/portal/. Its architecture, from both the user and technical points of view, is illustrated in Fig. 4.

From the user point of view, it is composed of the following two components: first, a homepage organizing the software prototypes according to the SCRM framework introduced in the previous subsection. This homepage provides information about the prototypes as well as links towards their web interface. Second, for each prototype, a web interface to use it. From the technical point of view, the web interfaces are divided in two categories. First, the internally hosted one, mainly used for prototypes that did not had web interfaces. Second, the externally hosted one, for prototypes that already had web interfaces. Then, each internally hosted software web interface relies on the use of software portfolio services, including a single sign-on service as well as a software services proxy. The latter enables web interfaces to use software services by calling the corresponding REST APIs.

A first selection of software to be included in the software portfolio homepage has been made. At this moment, the ones that appear are resulting from research projects undertaken by IMT Mines Albi and some of its partners. For example, the "SC mapper" and "advanced sales and operations planner" are resulting from a research project undertaken by [12, 13]. Another example is the "collaborative plans manager" resulting from a research project undertaken by [14]. Most of these software prototypes were not thought to be available online, therefore an effort is made to create web interfaces so they can be used on the COSMOS platform. Their integration is at different stages, so all currently displayed ones are not accessible yet.

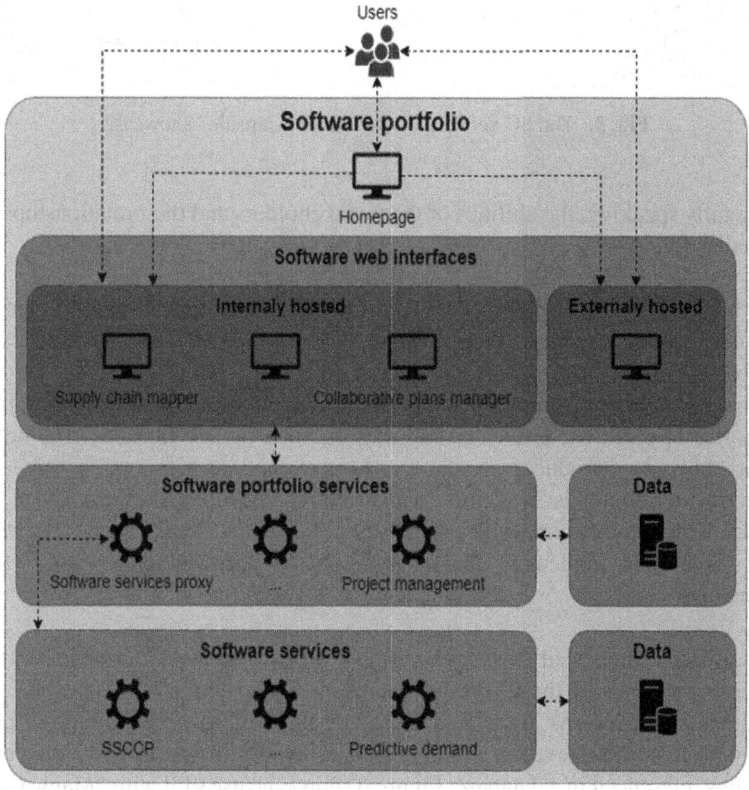


**Fig. 4.** Software portfolio architecture principles

## 4 Example of Service

For the purpose of illustrating the use of software services of COSMOS platform, a simple showcase is designed in a scenario of pharmaceutical supply chain. The case concerns the production and distribution activity of a pharmaceutical product named as "Magic Capsule", as shown in Fig. 5, several stakeholders involve in the considered SC network.

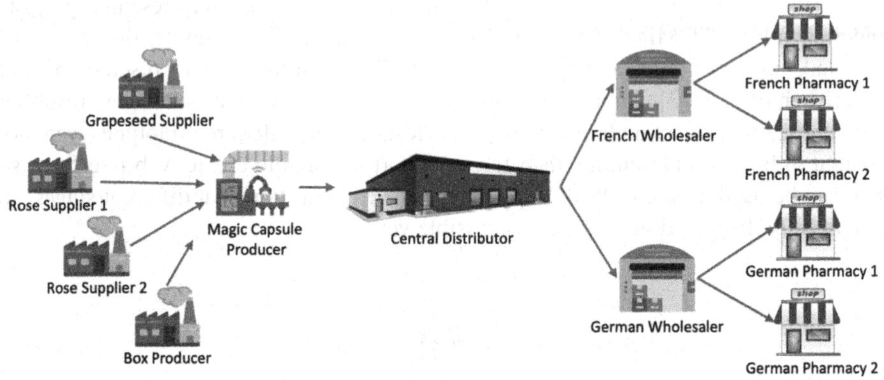


**Fig. 5.** The SC network of the "Magic Capsule" showcase

Generally speaking, the abilities of these stakeholders and their relationships can be described as follows:

- Two main raw materials (grapeseed and rose) are needed to produce the magic capsules, which are respectively provided by a grapeseed supplier and two rose suppliers.
- When the production of magic capsule is finished, those ones will be packed into two categories of products: box of 10 capsules and box of 100 capsules. The boxes are provided by a box producer.
- A central distributor is in charge of distributing the final products into a French wholesaler and a German wholesaler.
- The wholesalers implement the delivery to the corresponding country of two pharmacies.

According to the stated showcase, various software services can be instantiated to show the capabilities of the COSMOS platform. For example, "SC mapper", one of applications that concerns automated discovery of a SC map containing all possible SC options, which is based on an algorithm using information of SC stakeholders' capabilities referenced in a database. Figure 6 shows the use of it with "Magic Capsule" showcase. A potential SC map can be deduced by importing a set of company-specific configuration files. The result map is able to help companies to identify SC alternatives and then to support SC design decisions. What is more, it also enables other software to take advantage of this SC map for additional decision-support features.

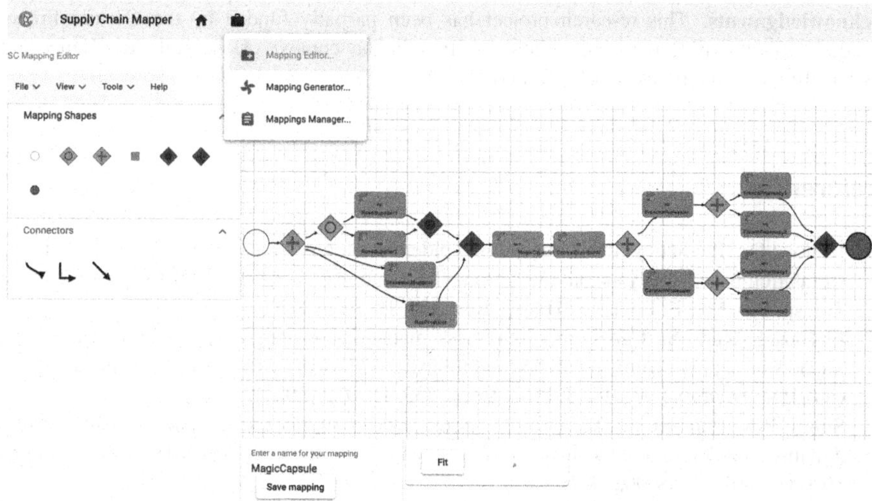


**Fig. 6.** The use of "SC mapper" with "Magic Capsule" showcase

## 5 Conclusion and Future Works

The first two sections of this paper have highlighted that SCs are dealing with a highly uncertain, opportunistic, and dynamic environment that challenges their ability to maintain their performance at satisfying levels. Companies driving these SCs lack knowledge, tools, and processes to efficiently make effective decisions in this context. As an answer to these difficulties faced by SC stakeholders, this paper makes two proposals in the third section that are then illustrated in the fourth section: first, a framework for SC risk and opportunity management that structures SCRM activities according to both a risk management lifecycle dimension and a temporality dimension (Fig. 2). Second, a platform dedicated to providing SC practitioners and scholars with openly accessible resources they can use to enhance their SC management practices and knowledge. This platform, called Collaborative and Open SC Management Operating Services (COSMOS), is organized according to the proposed SCRM framework, and composed of two building blocks: a software portfolio and a knowledge hub (Fig. 3). Finally, this paper fosters several avenues for future research. First, the consolidation of the COSMOS portal by making all already identified software prototypes accessible, intensifying the efforts for developing the knowledge portfolio, and enhancing the user experience so it can really become a platform that fosters new ideas for improving and rethinking SC management practices. A second avenue for future research is about identifying additional existing solutions that would be relevant to highlight according to the proposed SCRM framework. A third and broader one is about structuring current SC management challenges and identifying the ones that require research and development for designing new technological solutions to overcome these challenges.

**Acknowledgments.** This research project has been partially funded by the German-French Academy for the Industry of the Future (GFA) in the context of the call "Resilience and Sustainability for the Industry of the Future".

## References

1. Ivanov, D.: Predicting the impacts of epidemic outbreaks on global supply chains: a simulation-based analysis on the coronavirus outbreak (COVID-19/SARS-CoV-2) case. Transp. Res. Part E: Logistics Transp. Rev. **136**, 101922 (2020)
2. El Baz, J., Ruel, S.: Can supply chain risk management practices mitigate the disruption impacts on supply chains' resilience and robustness? Evidence from an empirical survey in a COVID-19 outbreak era. Int. J. Prod. Econ. **233**, 107972 (2021)
3. Singh, R.K., Modgil, S., Acharya, P.: Assessment of supply chain flexibility using system dynamics modeling. Global J. Flexible Syst. Manage. **20**(1), 39–63 (2019). https://doi.org/10.1007/s40171-019-00224-7
4. Wang, X., Wong, T.N., Fan, Z.-P.: Ontology-based supply chain decision support for steel manufacturers in China. Expert Syst. Appl. **40**, 7519–7533 (2013)
5. Ribeiro, J.P., Barbosa-Povoa, A.: Supply Chain Resilience: Definitions and quantitative modelling approaches – a literature review. Comput. Ind. Eng. **115**, 109–122 (2018)
6. van der Vorst, J.G.A.J., Beulens, A.J.M.: Identifying sources of uncertainty to generate supply chain redesign strategies. Int. J. Phys. Distrib. Logistics Manage. **32**, 409–430 (2002)
7. Simangunsong, E., Hendry, L.C., Stevenson, M.: Supply-chain uncertainty: a review and theoretical foundation for future research. Int. J. Prod. Res. **50**, 4493–4523 (2012)
8. Ghadge, A., Dani, S., Kalawsky, R.: Supply chain risk management: present and future scope. Int. J. Logist. Manag. **23**, 313–339 (2012)
9. McCarthy, T.M., Golicic, S.L.: Implementing collaborative forecasting to improve supply chain performance. Int. J. Phys. Distrib. Logistics Manage. **32**, 431–454 (2002)
10. Montreuil, B.: The physical internet: a conceptual journey, keynote presentation. In: 2nd International Physical Internet Conference (IPIC), Paris, France (2015)
11. Ben Taleb, R., Dahan, M., Montarnal, A., Lauras, M., Miclo, R.: Toward an innvative risk- and opportunity- oriented system for SMEs' decision-makers. In: Presented at the Conférence Internationale en Génie Industrie QUALITA, Grenoble, France (2021)
12. Oger, R., Lauras, M., Montreuil, B., Benaben, F.: A decision support system for strategic supply chain capacity planning under uncertainty: conceptual framework and experiment. Enterprise Inform. Syst. 1–45 (2020)
13. Oger, R., Benaben, F., Lauras, M., Montreuil, B.: Making strategic supply chain capacity planning more dynamic to cope with hyperconnected and uncertain environments. In: Proceedings of the 54th Hawaii International Conference on System Sciences, p. 2057, Hawaii (2021)
14. Tiss, S., Lamothe, J., Thierry, C.: Collaborative supply chain distribution planning under uncertainty. In: ILS 2020 - 8th International Conference on Information Systems, Logistics and Supply Chain, pp. 260–267. Austin, United States (2020)

# Digital Tools and Applications for Collaborative Healthcare

# Fostering the Collaboration Among Healthcare Stakeholders with ICF in Clinical Practice: EasyICF

Daniele Spoladore[1,2(✉)], Atieh Mahroo[1], and Marco Sacco[1]

[1] Institute of Intelligent Industrial Technologies and Systems for Advanced Manufacturing (STIIMA), National Research Council of Italy (CNR), 23900 Lecco, Italy
{daniele.spoladore,atieh.mahroo,marco.sacco}@stiima.cnr.it

[2] Department of Pure and Applied Sciences, Computer Science Division, Insubria University, 21100 Varese, Italy

**Abstract.** The International Classification of Functioning, Disability and Health (ICF) is a standard framework organized as a top-down taxonomy composed of categories allowing to describe a person's functioning within an environment (physical and social context). ICF aims at helping different clinical professionals and health stakeholders to adopt a common conceptual basis and standard definitions for the description of disabilities and impairments, thus easing the collaboration and clinical information exchange among different actors. ICF is not universally adopted in clinical practice: this is caused mainly by a lack of understanding of ICF and of the operative knowledge to qualify impairments. This work introduces EasyICF, an application designed to facilitate the use of ICF in defining wheelchair users' health conditions for vocational therapists and clinical personnel. EasyICF takes into account the restrictions foreseen in the framework and is designed to support the definition of ICF categories for clinicians with little or no knowledge of the classification and its structure. The application was developed with the help of medical personnel and physical therapists, in a collaborative effort to develop a tool for daily clinical practice in the context of Return to Work.

**Keywords:** ICF · Return to work · Clinical stakeholders collaboration

## 1 Introduction

This International Classification of Functioning, Disability and Health (ICF) is a World Health Organization (WHO) standard classification aimed at providing a description of an individual's health condition, taking into account functional aspects, body structures, activities and environmental factors. ICF serves as a conceptual standard basis for the definition of disabilities and impairments and focuses on the person and the context surrounding him/her: the functioning of the individual in specific domains derives from the interactions between the person's health condition and the physical and social environment in which he/she acts [1]. The classification is organized into four main components,


L. M. Camarinha-Matos et al. (Eds.): PRO-VE 2021, IFIP AICT 629, pp. 623–631, 2021.
https://doi.org/10.1007/978-3-030-85969-5_58

which should be completed by a fifth component that – to date – has not been developed yet (Personal factors):

- *Body functions* describe the psychophysiological functions of the body;
- *Body structures* identify the anatomical parts of the human body and their components;
- *Activities and participation* describe, respectively, the execution of tasks in life and the individual's involvement in specific situations;
- *Environmental factors* provide the means to describe the physical and social context in which the person lives, identifying facilitators and barriers.

Each component involves different health domains and is structured into categories, which constitute the atoms of the classification. The categories are identified by a prefix letter ("b" for Body functions, "s" for Body structures, "e" for Environmental factors, "d" for Activities and Participation) and are further detailed by adding digits: the longer is the number of the digits, the more detailed is the category; contrariwise, the lesser is the number of the digits following the letter, the more general is the health-concept represented by the category. Categories can therefore be structured in a hierarchical taxonomy in which the categories with fewer digits contain those with more digits (Fig. 1 illustrates this concept with an excerpt of ICF).

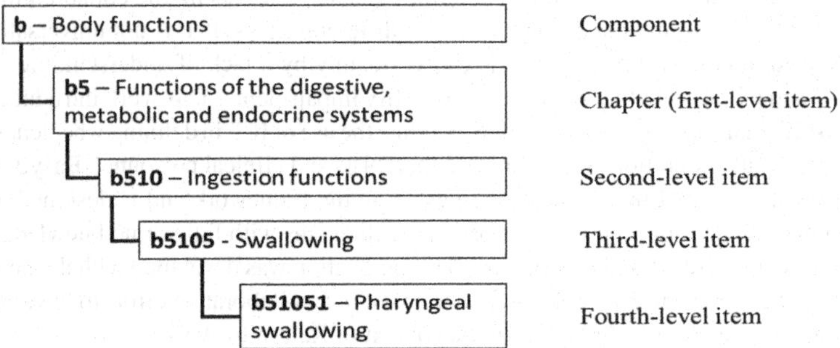


**Fig. 1.** An excerpt of the ICF classification highlighting its hierarchical structure.

The total number of categories amounts to 1454 and they allow the conceptualization of several domains involved in the definition of an individual's functioning and disability. Each category is provided with a text providing unambiguous definitions of the item (e.g.: b51051 – Pharyngeal swallowing is defined as "Function of clearing substances through the pharynx at an appropriate rate and speed"). The definition also provides examples of what can be considered within the range of the category (inclusion) and what is excluded (e.g.: b51051 has as "Inclusions: functions of production and quality of voice; functions of phonation, pitch, loudness and other qualities of voice; impairments such as aphonia, dysphonia, hoarseness, hypernasality and hyponasality", while indicates as "Exclusions: b167 – Mental functions of language; b320 – Articulation functions; b340 – Alternative vocalization functions").

To quantify the severity of impairment, each item is associated with one (or more) qualifier(s), integer numbers following the item and separated from it by a "." (e.g.:

b51051.3): the number of qualifiers an item can accept is determined by its type [2]. For instance, *Body functions* accepts only one qualifier (called "generic qualifier") whose values range from 0 to 4 (0 = "no impairment", 1 = "mild", 2 = "moderate", 3 = "severe", 4 = "complete"), with the addition of 8 (qualifier "not specified") and 9 (qualifier "not applicable"). However, the component *Body structures* accepts up to three qualifiers (the second indicating the nature of the change happened in a body structure, the third describing the location of the impairment in the body, all using integers from 0 to 9 to indicate different causes and locations of the impairment), while *Environmental factors* makes use of the generic qualifier, preceded by " +" to indicate a facilitator (e.g.: e5400.3 indicates a very relevant facilitator in "Transportation services") or without sign to indicate a barrier (e.g.: e410.1 suggests a mild barrier in the "Individual attitudes of immediate family members"). *Activities and participation* dedicate the first and fourth qualifier to describe the *performance*, which is the activity conducted in the individual's current environment, while the second and third describe the *capacity*, which identifies a person's ability to execute a task in a "standardized" environment (like a laboratory or clinical setting); *with/without assistance* indicates whether or not the individual executing the task is evaluated in his/her performance or capacity while using an assistive device or personal assistant (e.g.: glasses, wheelchair, etc.) [3]. Table 1 summarizes the possible qualifiers applicable to ICF items and their meanings.

**Table 1.** A summary of possible qualifiers applicable for each ICF component.

| Component | 1st qual. | 2nd qual. | 3rd qual. | 4th qual. |
|---|---|---|---|---|
| b | Generic qualifier | – | – | – |
| s | Generic qualifier | Nature of the change | Localization of the impairment | – |
| d | Performance (with assistance) | Capacity (without assistance) | Capacity (with assistance) | Performance (without assistance) |
| e | Generic qualifier (+ for facilitators) | – | – | – |

Together with a conceptual framework for the description of disability, ICF was developed as a tool to ease the communication among health-stakeholders (clinicians, therapists, bioengineers, designers of assistive solutions, etc.), since it provides an unambiguous vocabulary. During the early 2000s, ICF gathered a lot of attention and was progressively adopted in many health-related fields (e.g.: frameworks for the rehabilitation [4, 5], Electronic Health Records [6], assessing factors hindering the social participation of people with disabilities [7], etc.).

However, although some solid examples of ICF applications exist, the adoption of ICF in clinical practice is still limited. ICF is a very wide classification, and there exist some barriers in its adoption that prevent healthcare professionals in using the standard as a common language. In this work, we propose to overcome some of the barriers by using an application – namely EasyICF – that allows clinical personnel to build individuals' health condition descriptions using the ICF. We argue that the possibility to rely on an application can significantly reduce the need of specialized training and can support healthcare professionals in selecting categories and qualifiers. Therefore, we argue that to foster cooperation among stakeholders the use of ICF as a "common language" can be made easier by relying on digital tools that can help clinicians and health professionals to overcome some of barriers in the adoption of this standard.

The reminder of this paper is organized as follows: we investigate some of the major barriers hindering ICF adoption in clinical practice (Sect. 2). Within the context of Return to Work (RTW) [8], we developed an application aimed at providing a possible solution (Sect. 3), for which a brief overview of the underlying technology is provided (Sect. 4). Finally, Conclusions summarize the main outcomes of this work.

## 2 Major Issues in the Adoption of ICF in Clinical Practice

Although ICF is universally recognized as a standard able to foster professional and non-professional health stakeholders' information exchange, its actual application in clinical practice and rehabilitation is very limited. The first well-known problem is related to the adoption of ICF in its complete form: as pointed out in many studies [9] ICF structure does not allow for an agile adoption of all its categories, and therefore *Core sets* – subsets of ICF categories providing a comprehensive description of specific health issues – were developed to ease the adoption of ICF in clinical practice [10]. Nevertheless, the use of the framework within clinical contexts remains limited: different studies have analyzed the reasons behind the underutilization of ICF, which can be summarized in:

a. Need of specific training to increase the actual knowledge of ICF and its underlying conceptual model [11];
b. Significant difficulties in the implementation in some fields, including rehabilitation [12] and underestimation of the time and resources necessary for the implementation [13];
c. Lack of standard methods for the selection of the proper qualifiers [14];
d. The necessity to adapt ICF to the individual territories and clinical realities adopting it into their clinical practice [9];

These problems may significantly hinder the adoption of ICF in clinical and rehabilitation contexts, thus undermining the cooperation among different health professionals and stakeholders. In particular, for multi-domain interventions in fields requiring the collaboration of different professionals (e.g.: Ambient Assisted Living [15], Continuity of Care [16], RTW, etc.), the issues a. and b. may result in the inability to deliver tailored solutions to patients.

## 3 EasyICF: Fostering the Adoption of ICF in RTW Contexts

EasyICF was developed to tackle those issues related to the necessity of training to increase the actual knowledge of ICF and to reduce the difficult implementation of ICF-based solutions in clinical practice. This problem emerged in the context of research project dedicated to RTW, but its underlying questions and findings are common for any discipline that foresee the adoption of ICF at different levels.

### 3.1 The Rientr@ Project

EasyICF is one of the results of an Italian research project aimed at fostering the RTW of novice wheelchair users (WU) [8]: the Rientr@ project, promoted by the Italian National Institute for Insurance against Accidents at Work (INAIL). In Rientr@, the patients follow a RTW evaluation process that foresees a multidisciplinary evaluation of their abilities to understand the extent of their disability and to infer which professions they can still perform according to their health condition. In this context, many health professionals are involved: clinicians, physical therapists, biomedical engineers and vocational therapists need to cooperate to tailor the RTW process to the individual's specific needs – therefore they need to "speak the same language". Working in close collaboration with these professionals from INAIL, we were able to identify that problems related to actual knowledge of ICF and time-related issues hindered the adoption of the ICF as a tool in clinical practice, although some training on the ICF was already administered to INAIL personnel. Leveraging on meetings and test cases (i.e. a set of real health conditions of WUs) and adopting a methodology derived from collaborative engineering of knowledge bases [17], INAIL personnel was able to identify the problems described above, thus allowing us to developed a tailored solution in the form of an application: in fact, an application based on ICF serves as a promising solution to reduce the time necessary to formalize a health condition, and to minimize the necessity of training. The application, named EasyICF, was based on those ICF Core sets, which correspond to the main causes that force persons on a wheelchair (Spinal Cord Injury, Traumatic Brain Injury, Stroke); the Core set for Vocational Rehabilitation was added to better address the description of concepts related to WUs' work reintegration.

### 3.2 EasyICF Development

EasyICF was developed as an application that helps clinical professionals in inserting and/or updating a WU's health condition, by selecting the appropriate ICF categories from those composing the Core sets and guiding the clinicians in selecting the appropriate code. Considering the specific case of RTW, we decided to focus our attention on the Body functions component and Activities and participation (offering the possibility to insert the qualifiers for *performance* and *capacity* both *with assistance*, considering that the wheelchair is necessary for performing any task in any environment).

EasyICF is designed and developed exploiting Java programming language Standard Edition and Swing toolkit for Graphical User Interface components. This software is designed to be a standalone application, easily installed on computer platforms where health stakeholders are able to insert and/or modify the WU's health condition – thus, updating and manipulating the information on the ICF. Due to the complex structure of ICF, compiling its categories for each patient is an involute procedure that requires a learning and training phase for the health professionals. However, EasyICF can provide a simple and easy-to-use interface for health stakeholders with limited or no knowledge of ICF and helps them in compiling the ICF codes with minimum time and effort. The application provides step-by-step guidelines and instructions on choosing the correct ICF code and proper qualifiers while hiding the complexity of the ICF structure from the users. It is also capable of checking the quality of data inserted and warning the user in case of incorporating unacceptable values.

### 3.3 Use Case: Inserting a New Health Condition for a Wheelchair User

The EasyICF application consists of a set of sequential windows displaying information from ICF in which the user is guided and supervised to compile the correct ICF codes for each patient. The process of inserting the health condition of a WU initiates where EasyICF displays the list of WUs that have been saved within a database (in this case, a semantic database as described in [18]). Health professional can select the WU for which they want to insert or modify the health condition (Fig. 2). EasyICF then invites the health professional to choose the proper ICF Core set which coincides with the main reason that forced the person on a wheelchair, (spinal cord injury, traumatic brain injury, or stroke, as illustrated in Fig. 2).

After choosing the proper core set, the application provides a list of ICF categories – which composes the selected Core set – together with their names and complete descriptions, and for each code it highlights inclusions and exclusions (Fig. 3).

Finally, EasyICF helps the operator in defining the qualifiers for all the ICF codes chosen in the previous step with hints on acceptable values and data quality checks (according to Table 1) to ensure the inserted qualifier is a valid ICF qualifier digit (Fig. 4). In the end, all the ICF codes and associated qualifiers are stored in a database – hence the WU's health condition is inserted.

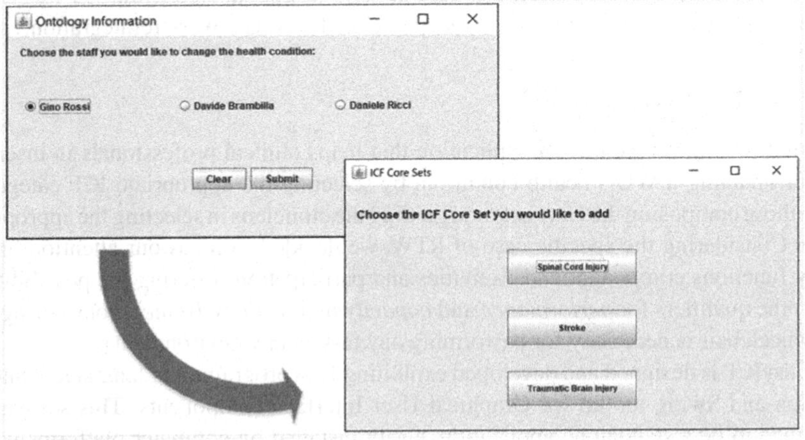


**Fig. 2.** Screenshots of EasyICF to choose the WU (left) and the ICF Core set (right) corresponding to the main cause of WU's impairment.

The application proposes a description of the category to be selected and highlights the inclusion and exclusion, thus helping the compiler (i.e. a health professional) to get a comprehensive view on the definition of the category. Moreover, by selecting a specific category that excludes others, the compiler can significantly reduce the time he/she needs to model a health condition, as the main references and indications to use the categories are provided by the application. In this way, the personnel adopting ICF can increase their level of confidence in using the ICF as a tool, thus reducing the necessity of intensive training to get a comprehensive grasp on the classification (as underlined in the first problem reported in Sect. 2).

Also, by allowing clinical personnel to select the Core set adopted as a reference to model a health condition, the risks connected to incurring in a time-consuming activity for health condition modelling are reduced (second problem proposed in Sect. 2). As other Core sets can be added to EasyICF, this feature can also help mitigating the issues related to ICF adoption in particular fields – such as rehabilitation – by using specific Core sets describing the problem(s) that need to be treated.

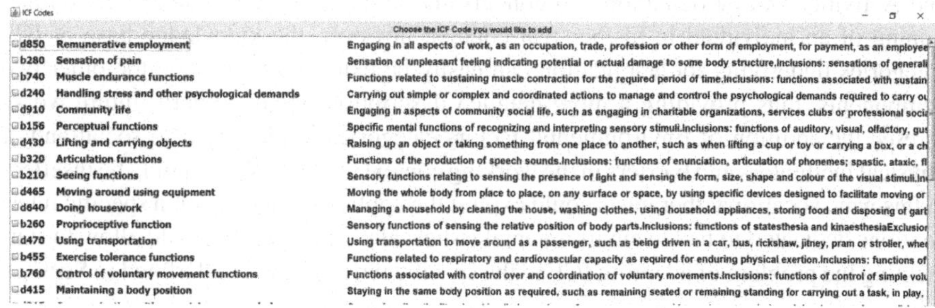


**Fig. 3.** Screenshot of EasyICF displaying the ICF categories, their names, and complete descriptions to help the operator selecting all the codes to describe the WU's health condition.

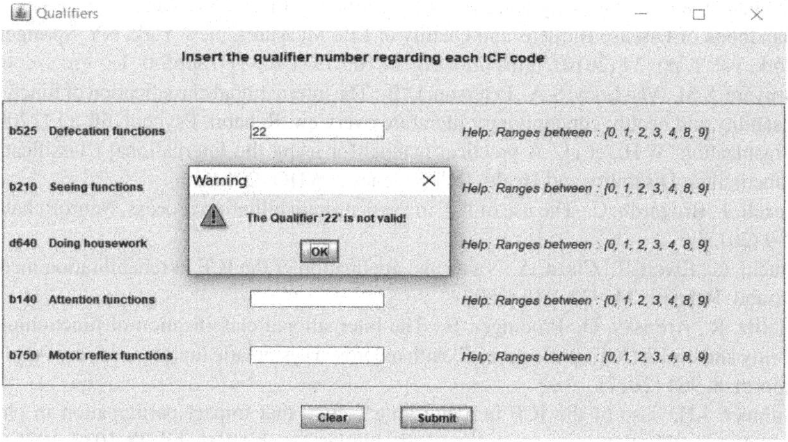

**Fig. 4.** A screenshot of EasyICF illustrating checks on qualifiers' insertion to guide the operator in the correct compiling of WU's health condition.

## 4 Conclusion and Future Works

EasyICF makes a universal environment that can be exploited by different clinical stakeholders who are not necessarily experts in ICF: the possibility to rely on the same classification to exchange health-related information can enhance RTW services provided to WUs through the active collaboration among various healthcare organizations. The application presented is still in its prototypical form and needs to be validated by experts: in particular, to support the hypothesis that EasyICF is able to reduce the time necessary to model a WU's health condition and to reduce the necessity of ICF-specific training sessions, the application will be delivered to social workers (with a very basic knowledge of ICF) involved in the RTW process of novice WUs to be assessed. Although EasyICF was developed specifically for RTW [18], its core idea can be extended to other ICF Core sets to help health stakeholders in describing several health conditions.

From a technical perspective, EasyICF prototype involves only the Body functions and Activities and participation components due to the necessity to describe the functioning of an individual in his/her real context: however, the knowledge base of ICF categories underlying the application can easily be extended to include the other two components, thus providing a more detailed description. In this regard, future works foresee the addition of Environmental factors categories to identify also social and/or physical facilitators and barriers in the working context in which WUs should be inserted: in this way, vocational therapists could exploit the application also to plan specific interventions dedicated to tackle environmental issues: also, this feature would allow to start tackling the problem of adapting ICF to the specific territories (as underlined in Sect. 2).

## References

1. Stucki, G., Kostanjsek, N., Cieza, A.: The international classification of functioning, disability and health: a tool to classify and measure functioning. In: Preedy, V.R., Watson, R.R. (eds.) Handbook of Disease Burdens and Quality of Life Measures, New York, NY. Springer New York, vol. 1, pp. 34 (2010). https://doi.org/10.1007/978-0-387-78665-0_1
2. Bruyère, S.M., Van Looy, S.A., Peterson, D.B.: The international classification of functioning, disability and health: contemporary literature overview. Rehabil. Psychol. **50**, 113 (2005)
3. Organization, W.H., et al.: A practical manual for using the International Classification of Functioning, Disability and Health (ICF), Geneva: WHO (2013)
4. Lexell, J., Brogårdh, C.: The use of ICF in the neurorehabilitation process. NeuroRehabil. **36**, 5–9 (2015)
5. Stucki, G., Ewert, T., Cieza, A.: Value and application of the ICF in rehabilitation medicine. Disabil. Rehabil. **24**, 932–938 (2002)
6. Maritz, R., Aronsky, D., Prodinger, B.: The International classification of functioning, disability and health (ICF) in electronic health records: a systematic literature review. Appl. Clin. Inform. **8**, 964 (2017)
7. Rimmer, J.H.: Use of the ICF in identifying factors that impact participation in physical activity/rehabilitation among people with disabilities. Disabil. Rehabil. **28**, 1087–1095 (2006)
8. Spoladore, D.: Ontology-based decision support systems for health data management to support collaboration in ambient assisted living and work reintegration. In: Working Conference on Virtual Enterprises, pp. 341–352. Springer (2017). https://doi.org/10.1007/978-3-319-65151-4_32

9. Maini, M., Nocentini, U., Prevedini, A., Giardini, A., Muscolo, E.: An Italian experience in the ICF implementation in rehabilitation: preliminary theoretical and practical considerations. Disabil. Rehabil. **30**, 1146–1152 (2008)
10. Yen, T.-H., Liou, T.-H., Chang, K.-H., Wu, N.-N., Chou, L.-C., Chen, H.-C.: Systematic review of ICF core set from 2001 to 2012. Disabil. Rehabil. **36**, 177–184 (2014)
11. Pernambuco, A.P., Lana, R. de C., Polese, J.C.: Knowledge and use of the ICF in clinical practice by physiotherapists and occupational therapists of Minas Gerais. Fisioterapia e Pesquisa. **25**, 134–142 (2018)
12. Escorpizo, R., Stucki, G., Cieza, A., Davis, K., Stumbo, T., Riddle, D.L.: Creating an interface between the international classification of functioning, disability and health and physical therapist practice. Phys. Ther. **90**, 1053–1063 (2010)
13. Wiegand, N.M., Belting, J., Fekete, C., Gutenbrunner, C., Reinhardt, J.D.: All talk, no action?: The global diffusion and clinical implementation of the international classification of functioning, disability, and health. Am. J. Phys. Med. Rehabil. **91**, 550–560 (2012)
14. Rauch, A., Cieza, A., Stucki, G.: How to apply the international classification of functioning, disability and health (ICF) for rehabilitation management in clinical practice. Eur. J. Phys. Rehabil. Med. **44**, 329–342 (2008)
15. Spoladore, D., Mahroo, A., Trombetta, A., Sacco, M.: DOMUS: a domestic ontology managed ubiquitous system. J. Ambient Intell. Humanized Comput. 1–16 (2021). https://doi.org/10.1007/s12652-021-03138-4
16. Spoladore, D., Arlati, S., Colombo, V., Modoni, G., Sacco, M.: A semantic-enabled smart home for AAL and continuity of care. In: IoT in Healthcare and Ambient Assisted Living, pp. 343–371. Springer (2021). https://doi.org/10.1007/978-981-15-9897-5_17
17. Spoladore, D., Pessot, E.: Collaborative ontology engineering methodologies for the development of decision support systems: case studies in the healthcare domain. Electronics **10**, 1060 (2021)
18. Arlati, S., et al.: Analysis for the design of a novel integrated framework for the return to work of wheelchair users. Work **61**, 603–625 (2018)

# Collaborative Design Approach for the Development of an Ontology-Based Decision Support System in Health Tourism

Daniele Spoladore[1,2](✉), Elena Pessot[1], Michael Bischof[3], Arnulf Hartl[3], and Marco Sacco[1]

[1] Institute of Intelligent Industrial Technologies and Systems for Advanced Manufacturing, (STIIMA) National Research Council of Italy, Milan, Italy
{daniele.spoladore,elena.pessot,marco.sacco}@stiima.cnr.it
[2] Department of Pure and Applied Sciences, Insubria University, Varese, Italy
[3] Paracelsus Medical University, Institute of Ecomedicine, Salzburg, Austria
{michael.bischof,arnulf.hartl}@pmu.ac.at

**Abstract.** Evidence-based Health Tourism (EHT) is a branch of general tourism foreseeing tourists to travel with the aim of receiving healing treatments or enhancing a specific mental, physical or spiritual health condition through medically-proven offers. EHT competitiveness is increasingly linked to the sustainability and exploitation of unique natural resources of tourism destinations, which often lack the access to knowledge and networks of stakeholders to improve their offerings, even by the use of digital tools. This study illustrates a Collaborative Design approach for the development of an ontology-based Decision Support System for modelling the relationships between the available natural resources, the value offerings and the target groups of EHT destinations in the Alpine region. The Collaborative Design approach foresees the involvement of end-users (i.e. EHT destinations, stakeholders and tourists) as both sources of knowledge and validators of the ontology and its outputs, aiming to inform decision-making processes in a shared knowledge model.

**Keywords:** Health tourism · Evidence-based health tourism · Collaborative design · Ontology-based decision support system · Collaborative ontology engineering methodology · Alpine region

## 1 Introduction

Evidence-based Health Tourism (EHT) is a branch of general tourism foreseeing tourists to travel with the aim of receiving healing treatments or enhancing a specific mental, physical or spiritual health condition through medically-proven offers [1, 2]. EHT competitiveness is increasingly linked to the sustainability and exploitation of unique natural resources of tourism destinations. Natural healing resources as waterfalls, Alpine


Published by Springer Nature Switzerland AG 2021
L. M. Camarinha-Matos et al. (Eds.): PRO-VE 2021, IFIP AICT 629, pp. 632–639, 2021.
https://doi.org/10.1007/978-3-030-85969-5_59

herbs and peculiar mountain microclimates offer proven health-promoting effects [3–5]. As central components of EHT products, they are a strong unique selling proposition and also increase the authenticity of these Alpine offerings. This opens up numerous approaches for involving different regional actors (e.g. tourism and medical service providers, agriculture, crafts) into the value chain [2], especially the more collaborative ones. Nevertheless, tourism destinations often lack the access to knowledge and networks of stakeholders to improve their offerings and exploit the synergic combination of possible EHT sources and activities [6]. There is the need to identify and adopt solutions that facilitate the connection among key actors by exchanging evidence-based data and systematizing knowledge and local experiences in a collaborative effort. Along with this line, several digital tools are revolutionizing healthcare sectors, including the development of solutions based on Artificial Intelligence and Semantic Web that can help cross-national interactions, redefining competitive EHT services and delivering better management strategies [7]. This work aims to develop a DSS for the creation of a shared knowledge base among EHT destinations, to support them in understanding the potentialities of their territory and to suggest them on which services and natural resource to invest [8]. Specifically, it addresses the destinations delivering healing solutions for tourists in Alpine regions, which are characterized by a high range of natural health resources and high environmental quality, but are still not sufficiently integrated in value chains to properly face the demanding market of health travelers [2]. In particular, the high demand for knowledge from different disciplines as well as the necessary involvement of numerous different actors makes it difficult for these destinations to further develop evidence- and nature-based health tourism and exploit related opportunities.

The result of this work is an ontology-based DSS that leverages the collaborative efforts of different key stakeholders of EHT as part of the HEALPS2 project, which aims at developing and improving framework conditions and tools for a better utilization of Alpine-specific natural health resources for the development of innovative tourism products and service chains. It connects academia, different business sectors such as the health sector, tourism and local service providers, as well as innovation and transfer agencies to jointly implement new business models that improve value creation across sectors in Alpine destinations. This transnational and transversal approach is built on unique Alpine natural health resources and strengthens the Alpine territorial innovation capacity. The project involves six Alpine countries (five from the EU): Austria, Italy, Germany, France, Slovenia and Switzerland, with representatives from both the academia, management bodies of mountain areas, non-governmental associations of Alpine space, thermalism and governmental Alpine networks. The development of the ontology underlying the DSS takes advantage of a collaborative design approach through the adoption of a collaborative ontology engineering methodology that involved all the stakeholders of the project.

The reminder of this work is organized as follows: Sect. 2 highlights a few studies adopting ontologies in health or medical tourism contexts, while Sect. 3 delves into the specific cooperative ontology engineering methodology and process adopted for the cooperative development of the HEALPS2 knowledge base underlying the DSS. Finally, the Conclusions summarize the main outcomes of this work.

## 2 Related Work

The use of Semantic Web technologies – in particular, ontologies – for the development of DSSs in the tourism industry is widely documented in scientific literature. Also, the value of cooperation in ontology engineering – especially in health-related fields – is also widely established [9, 10]. However, there are very few examples of ontology-based DSSs specifically dedicated to the fields of health and medical tourism.

Chantrapornchai et al. [11] developed an ontology dedicated to gather and organize health tourism information for the Hua Hin area in Thailand; the ontology was developed using a waterfall methodology and evaluated by eliciting domain experts opinion at the end of the development phase through questionnaires. In the field of tourist destination recommender systems, Khallouki et al. [12] adopted a domain ontology for the description of touristic context, while Frikha et al. [13] exploited ontologies to enhance user-based recommendations in the field of Tunisian medical tourism. Information regarding facilities and services in medical storage can be formalized and managed through ontologies: Lee et al. [14] proposed a smart orchestrator leveraging semantic models to formalize knowledge from the medical tourism, general tourism and medical treatment domains.

Differently from other approaches, this work introduces an ontology-based DSS able to formalize natural resources, services provided and activities based on available natural resources, stakeholders' cooperation efforts and tourism data. The ontology is developed by a methodology that foresees the involvement of various stakeholders of health tourism value chain in a cooperative effort and in multiple rounds of knowledge exchange. Thus, it relies on collaborative ontology engineering methodologies as a way to improve the correct understanding on domain knowledge in contexts characterized by many stakeholders [15], and tested in different collaborative projects [16, 17]. In this work, the adoption of a collaborative and agile methodology is presented as a key enabler for designing (and thus developing) the DSS's ontology.

## 3 Collaborative Design Approach

This Section deepens into the collaborative approach adopted for the identification of the knowledge to be formalized, its elicitation, conceptualization and formalization with ontological languages. Through this process, informal and formal methods were conveniently adopted to ease achieving specific goals, such as identifying the most relevant bits of knowledge, produce an accessible and shared conceptual model and develop its ontological representation.

HEALPS2 research project fosters the cooperation among various stakeholders in the health tourism values chain, therefore stakeholders' involvement in the phases of knowledge elicitation and conceptualization covers a pivotal role. Stakeholders' ideas, opinions and knowledge were elicited through six national stakeholders' meetings (with the average participation of 15 stakeholders) and one international stakeholders meeting (with the participation of over 50 stakeholders). The aim of the meeting was to select the domains of interest and the relevant pieces of information for each of them. With the support of Project Partners, data collected were transformed in quantifiable KPIs, which were later used to provide a shared conceptualization and, finally, to formalize the ontological model. Figure 1 sketches the process starting from stakeholders' involvement and finishing with the delivery of the ontology.

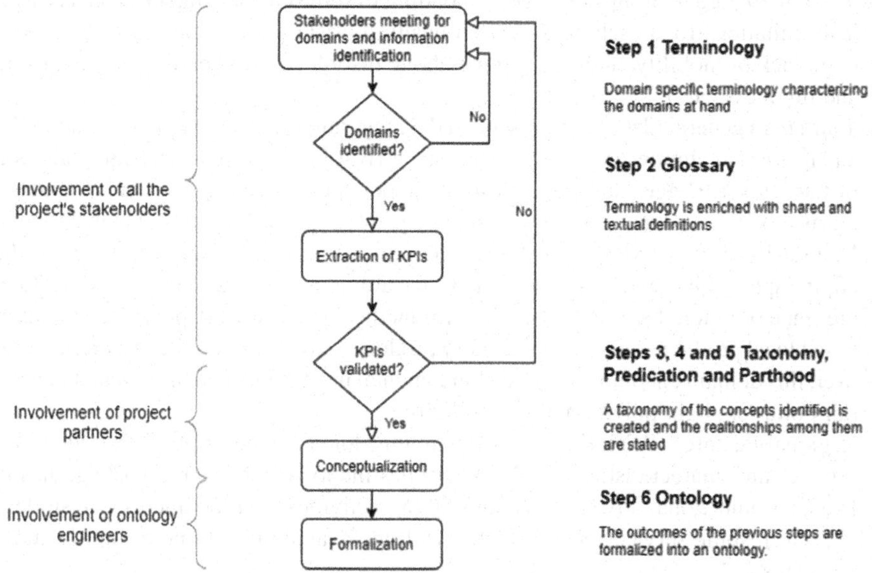


**Fig. 1.** The flowchart representing the collaborative approach process. On the right, the six step composing the UPONLite methodology are represented along the different phases of the process.

The ontology engineering methodology selected for the HEALPS2 project was a collaborative and agile one, namely the UPONLite methodology [18], which foresees non-experts in the field of Semantic Web to adopt common tools to provide a conceptualization of different domains of knowledge. This methodology has proven efficient in different ontology-based development processes [15]. Also, the significant number of stakeholders involved in the early phases of design, required a non-rigid structure for knowledge elicitation and subsequent conceptualization. The formalization phase – which involved mostly partners with experience in ontology development – adopted Resource Description Framework (RDF) [19], Ontology Web Language (OWL) [20] and Semantic Web Rule Language (SWRL) [21] as W3C-endorsed development languages.

### 3.1 Multi-stakeholder Knowledge Elicitation Process

The domains involved in the knowledge elicitation process were different: from a healthcare point of view, the focus was on identifying the main groups of patients who could benefit from nature-based health tourism in the Alpine space. Likewise, from a medical point of view and from a health economic and tourism perspective, it is important to know which natural resources can be used and how, together with the services tourism destinations can provide. Furthermore, quantitative indicators regarding the tourists' arrival, stay and provenance are also fundamental to provide a measurement of the tourism inflow in a specific area. The domains elicited by stakeholders and project partners, and for which knowledge needed to be specified were:

- A list of 19 Target Groups (TG) corresponding to some chronic impairments or physical limitations for which nature-based health tourism activity can provide benefits (e.g.: lack of mobility, diabetes and metabolic disorders, skin conditions, exhaustion and tiredness, etc.).
- Tourism in general (TiG): in this domain data regarding a specific tourism destination and its touristic inflow are detailed (tourists' arrivals, their country of origin, duration of stays, tourists' age and gender, destination population density, economic impact of tourism on the destination – tourism intensity, overnight stays per 1,000 inhabitants).
- Natural Resources (NRs): this domain identifies the main natural resources in the Alpine space (blue spaces, forests, waterfalls, altitudes, protected areas, specific flora, presence of radon that can be exploited for medical purposes and presence of nature-based local products such as Alpine dairy products, farm products, honey, etc.); moreover, this domain encompasses three fundamental indicators of environmental metrics (air pollution, light pollution, noise pollution).
- Regional Features (RFs): the knowledge in this domain is descriptive, as it identifies services and characteristics a health tourist destination can have or offer (e.g.: health manager, nutritional advice, mountain hiking activities, spa treatments, physiotherapy, etc.); some services are correlated with the availability of one or more natural resources.
- Cooperation and Networking (CN): stakeholders recognized the role of cooperation in the success of tourism destination. In particular, they identified being part of a network (regional, national or international) as a success factor.

Together with the identification of the domains and their features, the results from the collaborative efforts of stakeholders, further informed by scientific literature, allowed to identify KPIs for each of the domain features, with the aim of making quantifiable the main features for tourist destination and their services. The consortium identified an array of data types ranging from integers for the impact that tourism destinations' features can have on a specific TG and for environmental metrics indicators, Boolean values for the existence, use and exploitation of NRs, as well as for the presence of specific services (RFs) and cooperation activities (CN). Quantification of TiG features required different data types, including strings, integers and decimal. This step allowed to set a shared vocabulary and to specify the meaning of each terms (Steps 1 and 2 of UPONLite).

### 3.2 Agile Cooperative Methodology for Conceptualization

Once the relevant pieces of information were identified, the conceptualization phase – following the instruction from the UPONLite methodology – was conducted using conceptual maps and spreadsheets, as this kind of tools are more familiar for ontology non-experts. The result of this process further refined the elicited knowledge into a conceptual model in which each bit of information is labelled and linked to others through mathematical relationships. These relationships constitute the basis for the inference of new facts in the ontology, since they specify how a concept should change (in its classification and/or in the values it can assume) according to specific value-driven conditions. A taxonomy of concepts (Step 3) was generated using a spreadsheet and those concepts necessary to qualify others were defined as properties (Step 4), while part-whole relationships among concepts where also formalized (Step 5).

### 3.3 Development

The conceptual model containing the mathematical relationships among concepts were translated into an ontology with the use of Protégé ontology editor [22] and using RDF and OWL to represent the concept hierarchy and SWRL to formalized relationships into rules. The HEALPS2 ontology encompasses more than 85 classes, 9 object properties, 57 datatype properties and includes 1075 individuals (for a total of 7265 axioms, including SWRL rules). Figure 2 shows an excerpt of the developed ontology.

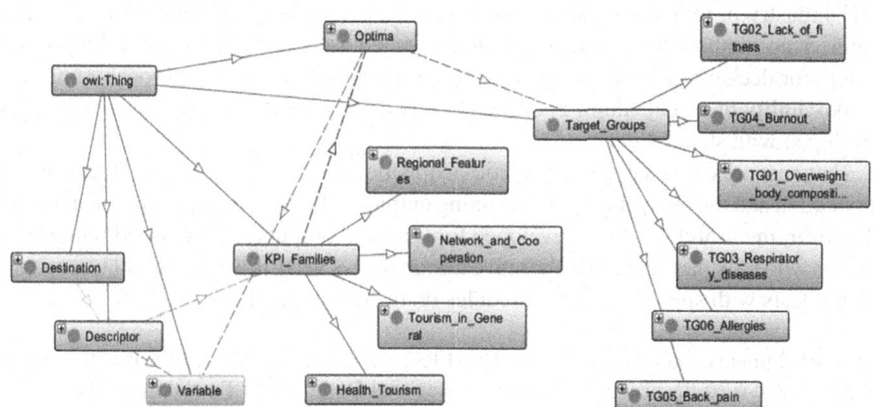


**Fig. 2.** A graphical representation of the main concepts represented in the HEALPS2 ontology and their relationships.

To validate the consistency of the ontology, the Pellet reasoner [23] was selected, as it is one of the few reasoners able to process SWRL built-in functions (necessary to state mathematical relationships among concepts).

### 3.4 Validation of the Ontology and Its Outputs

The HEALPS2 methodology was presented and discussed in a second round of meetings with the key stakeholders. To populate the ontology and test the rules, stakeholders where asked to provide some information. Specifically, five national stakeholders' meetings (with the average participation of 15 stakeholders) and one international stakeholders' meeting (with the participation of over 70 stakeholders) were organized in order to collect data in input, to collect feedbacks on the base of knowledge available and to test the effectiveness of the tool. The DSS was tested with data from four Alpine destinations to check the consistency of the ontological model and the results of the reasoning process. The DSS was able to calculate the distances occurring between the predefined optimum values of KPIs and the real values of the destinations for each target group, thus contributing to identify those natural resources and/or services worth investing on. Also, in this phase the collaborative approach was judged fundamental to gain insights on the further developments of the ontology-based DSS as a reference tool for Alpine regions EHT destinations.

## 4 Conclusions and Future Works

This work developed an ontology-based DSS to support ETH destinations in innovating and enriching their product offerings based on local natural resources, and the systematic sharing of knowledge among key stakeholders to support decisions in management practices. Firstly, it contributes to the growing debates on exploiting the potentialities of digital tools in healthcare industries and the need to identify proper solutions to grow EHT industry in regional value chains. Secondly, it leverages a collaborative ontology engineering methodology to develop an evidence-based and effective ontology-based system for decision-making. In particular, the collaborative design approach reinforces the possibility of actual adoption of the DSS, and encourages the reuse of the ontology developed with stakeholders.

Future works foresee the automatic acquisition of data from stakeholders via an application and the presentation of reasoning outputs in both textual and graphical forms. Moreover, the usability of the developed tools and its outputs will be tested with stakeholders who took part in the collaborative design phase, and further users will be engaged in pilot tests with specific training modules on the developed DSS.

**Acknowledgments.** Acknowledgments. HEALPS2 started in October 2019 and will run until June 2022 and is co-financed by the European Regional Development Fund through the Interreg Alpine Space Programme.

## References

1. Chang, L., Beise-Zee, R.: Consumer perception of healthfulness and appraisal of health-promoting tourist destinations. Tourism Rev. **68**(1) (2013). https://www.emerald.com/insight/content/doi/10.1108/16605371311310066/full/html
2. Steckenbauer, G.C., Tischler, S., Hartl, A., Pichler, C.: Destination and product development rested on evidence-based health tourism. The Routledge handbook of health tourism, pp. 315–331 (2017)
3. Grafetstätter, C., et al.: Does waterfall aerosol influence mucosal immunity and chronic stress? A randomized controlled clinical trial. J. Physiol. Anthropol. **36**, 1–12 (2017)
4. Pieroni, A., Giusti, M.E.: Alpine ethnobotany in Italy: traditional knowledge of gastronomic and medicinal plants among the Occitans of the upper Varaita valley piedmont. J. Ethnobiol. Ethnomed. **5**, 1–13 (2009)
5. Prossegger, J., et al.: Effects of moderate mountain hiking and balneotherapy on community-dwelling older people: a randomized controlled trial. Exp. Gerontol. **122**, 74–84 (2019)

6. Pessot, E., Spoladore, D., Zangiacomi, A., Sacco, M.: Natural resources in health tourism: a systematic literature review. Sustainability **13**, 2661 (2021)
7. Wong, B.K.M., Hazley, S.A.S.: The future of health tourism in the industrial revolution 4.0 era. J. Tourism Futures **7**(2) (2020). https://www.emerald.com/insight/content/doi/10.1108/JTF-01-2020-0006/full/html
8. Spoladore, D., Pessot, E., Sacco, M.: HEALPS 2: tourism based on natural health resources for the development of alpine regions. ERCIM News **123**, 41 (2020)
9. Spoladore, D.: Ontology-based decision support systems for health data management to support collaboration in ambient assisted living and work reintegration. In: Working Conference on Virtual Enterprises, pp. 341–352. Springer (2017). https://doi.org/10.1007/978-3-319-65151-4_32
10. Spoladore, D., Sacco, M.: Towards a collaborative ontology-based decision support system to foster healthy and tailored diets. In: Working Conference on Virtual Enterprises, pp. 634–643. Springer (2020). https://doi.org/10.1007/978-3-030-62412-5_52
11. Chantrapornchai, C., Choksuchat, C.: Ontology construction and application in practice case study of health tourism in Thailand. SpringerPlus **5**(1), 1–31 (2016). https://doi.org/10.1186/s40064-016-3747-3
12. Khallouki, H., Abatal, A., Bahaj, M.: An ontology-based context awareness for smart tourism recommendation system. In: Proceedings of the International Conference on Learning and Optimization Algorithms: Theory and Applications, pp. 1–5 (2018)
13. Frikha, M., Mhiri, M., Gargouri, F., et al.: A semantic social recommender system using ontologies based approach for Tunisian tourism (2015)
14. Lee, H.J., Park, S.Y., Jin, H.R., Sohn, M.: A smart orchestrator of ecosystem in medical tourism. In: Proceedings of the 18th Annual International Conference on Electronic Commerce: e-Commerce in Smart connected World, pp. 1–8 (2016)
15. Spoladore, D., Pessot, E.: Collaborative ontology engineering methodologies for the development of decision support systems: case studies in the healthcare domain. Electronics **10**, 1060 (2021)
16. Kotis, K.I., Vouros, G.A., Spiliotopoulos, D.: Ontology engineering methodologies for the evolution of living and reused on-tologies: status, trends, findings and recommendations. Knowl. Eng. Rev. **35**, 1–34 (2020). https://www.cambridge.org/core/journals/knowledge-engineering-review/article/ontology-engineering-methodologies-for-the-evolution-of-living-and-reused-ontologies-status-trends-findings-and-recommendations/7A2D8D844EE0369C24967E156910AB50
17. Simperl, E., Luczak-Rösch, M.: Collaborative ontology engineering: a survey (2014)
18. De Nicola, A., Missikoff, M.: A lightweight methodology for rapid ontology engineering. Commun. ACM **59**, 79–86 (2016)
19. Pan, J.Z.: Resource description framework. In: Handbook on Ontologies, pp. 71–90. Springer (2009). https://doi.org/10.1007/978-3-540-92673-3_3
20. Antoniou, G., Van Harmelen, F.: Web ontology language: OWL. In: Handbook on Ontologies, pp. 67–92. Springer (2004). https://doi.org/10.1007/978-3-540-24750-0_4
21. Horrocks, I., Patel-Schneider, P.F., Boley, H., Tabet, S., Grosof, B., Dean, M., et al.: SWRL: a semantic web rule language combining OWL and RuleML. W3C Member Submission **21**, 1–31 (2004)
22. Tudorache, T., Noy, N.F., Tu, S., Musen, M.A.: Supporting collaborative ontology development in protégé. In: Sheth, A., et al. (eds.) ISWC 2008. LNCS, vol. 5318, pp. 17–32. Springer, Heidelberg (2008). https://doi.org/10.1007/978-3-540-88564-1_2
23. Sirin, E., Parsia, B., Grau, B.C., Kalyanpur, A., Katz, Y.: Pellet: a practical OWL-DL reasoner. J. Web Semant. **5**, 51–53 (2007)

# Analyzing Hospital Sterilization Service Vulnerabilities Using a Risk-Aware Business Process Modeling Method

Rafika Thabet[1(✉)], Maria Di-Mascolo[1], Elyes Lamine[2,3], Ghassen Frikha[4], and Hervé Pingaud[5]

[1] CNRS, Grenoble INP (Institute of Engineering Univ. Grenoble Alpes), G-SCOP, University of Grenoble Alpes, 38000 Grenoble, France
rafika.thabet@inp-toulouse.fr, maria.di-mascolo@grenoble-inp.fr
[2] ISIS, Institut National Universitaire Champollion, Toulouse University, Rue Firmin-Oulès, 81104 Castres, France
elyes.lamine@univ-jfc.fr
[3] IMT Mines Albi, Department of Industrial Engineering, Toulouse University, Route de Teillet, 81013 Cedex 9 Albi, France
[4] National School of Engineers of Sfax, Sfax University, Route de la Soukra, 3038 Sfax, Tunisia
ghassen.frikha@enis.tn
[5] CNRS-LGC, Institut National Universitaire Champollion, Toulouse University, Place de Verdun, 81012 Cedex 9 Albi, France
herve.pingaud@univ-jfc.fr

**Abstract.** Healthcare processes, such as sterilization, are extremely dynamic, complex, and multidisciplinary, making risk management in healthcare facilities particularly challenging. Risk-aware business process management is a new paradigm for better understanding such processes by identifying and evaluating the risks that go along with them. This paper focuses on analyzing the vulnerability of a hospital sterilization service through the use of a new framework, called *e-BPRIM*, which consists of the digitalization of the Business Process-risk management - Integrated Method (*BPRIM*). The *e-BPRIM* framework promotes and supports risk-aware process management with *AdoBPRIM*, a modeling environment using the ADOxx meta-modeling platform. The main *e-BPRIM* components will be introduced and then used to study the robustness of a given sterilization process taking into consideration several potential risks.

**Keywords:** *BPRIM* · Risk-aware business process management · Modeling method · ADOxx · Sterilization service

## 1 Introduction

In terms of risk analysis, the hospital sterilization service is one of the most significant services. Because of the high-level risk structure and the potential of contagion, managing sterilization services is complex. These services collaborate with other hospital services


Published by Springer Nature Switzerland AG 2021
L. M. Camarinha-Matos et al. (Eds.): PRO-VE 2021, IFIP AICT 629, pp. 640–651, 2021.
https://doi.org/10.1007/978-3-030-85969-5_60

and serve as a focal point in the fight against germs and infections, which is critical to make the service safe. Any risk that this service may face is critical since it affects all of the hospital's other services [1, 2]. Sterilization services are in charge of producing sterile medical devices. The organization of this process may differ from one hospital to another but in general, we find common steps, which are crucial to the functioning of the service [3, 4]. Each step could be a source of risk. Therefore, it is imperative for health facilities to manage the ensuing vulnerability to deal with hazardous situations.

Risk management (RM) is recognized as a relevant method to mitigate process vulnerability by a holistic understanding of the causality of risks and reducing the likelihood of their occurrences and their consequences. In the healthcare domain, there are multiple risk management methods [5].

These techniques, however, do not consider the complexity of risks, their close relationship to process activities, and therefore the effect of organizational and human aspects. Given these findings, healthcare facilities should really study novel risk management techniques that incorporate all-risk concepts and their interdependence with process activities. To fill the gap of existing approaches, in this paper we propose to explore the potential of a Risk-aware Business Process Management (R-BPM) approach [6, 7] to address risks associated with the complicated sterilization service.

The present work is organized as follows. First, in Sect. 2, we provide an overview of healthcare risk management methods and a brief review of related work on R-BPM. In Sect. 3, we present the adopted framework. Section 4 is devoted to illustrating the use of this framework to study various potential risks that might arise from a particular sterilization process. Finally, the paper concludes with some directions for further research.

## 2 Background and Related Work

### 2.1 Healthcare Risk Management

A risk in the healthcare domain can have serious and long-term repercussions, including death [3, 8]. Such risks must be controlled using risk management principles. The goal of the RM approach is to protect healthcare providers from adverse events. In this way, RM contributes significantly to reducing uncertainties and creating rich opportunities for various healthcare sectors. The development of RM helps healthcare facilities reduce harm due to the likely occurrence of faulty processes through error identification, rooting, and strategy development. Implementation of RM in healthcare facilities improves healthcare resource allocation, process management, decision making, reduced organizational losses, patient safety, continuous quality improvement, customer satisfaction, organizational performance, hospital reputation, and creating a better community [9, 10].

Risk management is one among the emerging approaches in management systems, and various papers have examined risk management in healthcare facilities. In [2, 11, 12], a comparative analysis of the most relevant risk management approaches currently in use in the healthcare field is provided.

However, this sector lags far behind other sectors of the industry in the use of these techniques. Today, in the healthcare sectors, there is a consensus that the knowledge, experience, and expertise of other industries in RM can improve the quality of services provided by the healthcare sectors [9]. Therefore, it seems essential to review the choice of RM techniques. These tools need to be customized according to the complexity of the healthcare system and the causes of events that affect the sector [9]. In consequence, in order to improve patient safety, healthcare facilities need to implement effective policies to detect, prevent and control risks associated with the complex processes of healthcare. To address this issue, we advocate exploring new research fields, notably integrated risk within business process management.

### 2.2 Risk-Aware Business Process Management

For several years, a major research focus has been on the merging of the two traditionally distinct areas of risk management and business process management into a single concept known as Risk-aware Business Process Management (R-BPM) [6]. This integration helps to improve the efficiency of risk identification, detection, and evaluation in business processes [6, 7].

One of the key methodologies in the R-BPM field is the Business Process-Risk Management Integrated Method (BPRIM) [7]. The method emphasizes the need for risk management throughout the business process management (BPM) lifecycle. BPRIM proposes a three-pronged integrative approach: (1) a conceptual unification of risk and business process based on the coupling between the ISO /DIS 19440 conceptual model and a new conceptual model for risk, (2) a common modeling notation of risk and business process that extends the Event-driven Process Chains notation, and (3) a synchronized lifecycle based on the coupling between BPM and RM lifecycles.

## 3 Adopted Framework Description

In this work, we adopt a framework based on the *BPRIM* method, called *e-BPRIM*. The latter consists of the digitalization of *BPRIM*. The *e-BPRIM* framework promotes and supports risk-aware process management with *AdoBPRIM*, a modeling environment based on the *ADOxx* meta-modeling platform [13]. An overview of the adopted framework is given in [11, 14]. The *e-BPRIM* framework suggests three main components: a *modeling procedure*, a *modeling language*, and *mechanisms & algorithms*. These latter form, according to [15], the main components of a modeling method.

In the following subsections, we present a short description of the *e-BPRIM* modeling method and the *AdoBPRIM* modeling tool.

### 3.1 *e-BPRIM* Modeling Method

**e-BPRIM Modeling Procedure.** As mentioned before, BPRIM [7] proposes an integration of the two lifecycles of business process management and risk management. The BPRIM lifecycle distinguishes between four main phases (1-Contextualize, 2-Asses, 3-Treat and 4-Monitor), each of which is divided into steps. Considering information exchanged between the first three steps, a set of eleven viewpoints was identified. The e-BPRIM modeling procedure introduces then the sequence to be applied while creating

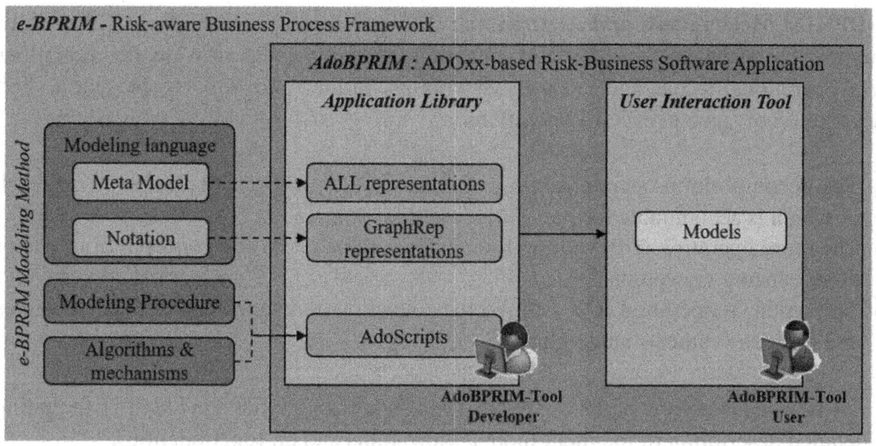


**Fig. 1.** e-BPRIM framework overview

and working with these multiple viewpoints. The complete modeling procedure can be found in [11, 14].

- The contextualization phase starts with the establishment of a "Process Landscape" viewpoint which specifies the value-added processes of the system under study. Next, the "Organizational Chart" viewpoint is defined which aims to identify roles and expectations, thereby establishing a greater understanding of the organization's structure. This definition serves firstly to produce the "Context" viewpoint and secondly to establish the "Business Process" viewpoints.
- The Assessment phase starts with the creation of the "Risk Taxonomy" viewpoint which serves to generate the "Risk-extended Business Process" viewpoints which assign previously identified risks to individual activities of the "Business Process" viewpoints. Next, the "Risk Analysis", "Risk" and "Risk Relationship" viewpoints are defined to analyze each previously identified risk. This analysis serves to evaluate and list the analyzed risks in a two-dimensional risk matrix forming the "Risk Mapping" viewpoint.
- The Treatment phase aims to identify critical risks and treat them by defining control mechanisms in "Risk Treatment" viewpoints.

**e-BPRIM Modeling Language.** As shown on the left side of Fig. 1, the *e-BPRIM* modeling language is composed of abstract and concrete syntax. The abstract syntax is described by a meta-model based on the *BPRIM* conceptual model, called *e-BPRIM* meta-model. The concrete syntax is based on the *BPRIM* modeling notation and describes the graphical representation of each *e-BPRIM* meta-model concept, called *e-BPRIM* notation. It needs to be noted, that the *e-BPRIM* meta-model can be divided into eleven meta-models corresponding to the eleven viewpoints of *e-BPRIM*. A comprehension description of them all of them can be found in [11, 14].

**e-BPRIM Mechanisms and Algorithms.** The e-BPRIM mechanisms & algorithms support the steps of the e-BPRIM modeling procedure and provide functionalities (i.e. operations) to use and evaluate viewpoints. In the following, we present a short description of some e-BPRIM operations:

- The decomposition operation *($Op_1$)* divides a system into smaller subsystems, each of which is accountable for part of the problem domain.
- The reuse operation *($Op_2$)* allows the reusing of one or several concepts from one or more existing viewpoints.
- The synthesis operation *($Op_3$)* allows the collection of data from several perspectives and create a synthesis viewpoint.

A detailed overview of the e-BPRIM framework can be found in [11, 14], including a detailed description of the meta-model, viewpoints and all functionalities.

### 3.2 *AdoBPRIM* Modeling Tool

For realizing a software prototype dedicated to the *e-BPRIM* modeling method, called *AdoBPRIM*, we have resorted to meta-modeling platforms that strongly support the implementation of a modeling method as a tool with little programming effort while providing an environment for storage, user interaction, and model creation automatically [15, 16]. A comparative survey of existing meta-modeling platforms can be found in [7, 11].

In our case, the ADOxx [13] meta-modeling platform was chosen to implement the prototype, as it has been successfully used in research and practical projects for more than 15 years [16]. ADOxx enables the easy definition of modeling languages, their graphical representations and required mechanisms and algorithms. For this purpose, ADOxx provides a number of domain-specific languages for implementing modeling methods. In our case, we used: (a) ADOxx Library Language to specify *e-BPRIM* viewpoints meta-models, (b) GraphRep Language to define the graphical representation of *e-BPRIM* meta-model concepts, and (c) ADOScript language to implement mechanisms & algorithms working on *e-BPRIM* viewpoints.

In order to realize an ADOxx-based software prototype dedicated to the *e-BPRIM* modeling method, the *AdoBPRIM* tool developer uses the generic concepts and languages of ADOxx. Afterwards, the tool environment is set up for *AdoBPRIM* users to create *AdoBPRIM* models (see the right side of Fig. 1). The *AdoBPRIM* modeling tool has been developed as a project within the Open Models Laboratory [16], where a free download and further information can be found[1].

## 4 Case Study: A Hospital Sterilization Service

In this section, we present the application of the *e-BPRIM* framework on a given hospital sterilization service to analyze its robustness. The sterilization delivery process made

[1] *e-BPRIM* project space within OMiLAB [online]: https://austria.omilab.org/psm/content/BPRIM, last visited: 14.04.2021.

the subject of several works aiming to provide a deeper understanding of the functioning of the process and identifying the best practices [3, 4, 17].

Sterilization service plays a prominent role in healthcare facilities. In the medical field, it is an indispensable process. Nonetheless, this process is fraught with risks. Transmission of infectious diseases such as Creutzfeldt-Jakob disease, human immunodeficiency viruses, hepatitis C, and hepatitis B are among these risks. Contamination of medical devices (MD) during surgical procedures and poor sanitation of these MD are the causes of this transmission [4].

The purpose of this section is to demonstrate the usage and the capabilities of the *e-BPRIM* modeling method with the *AdoBPRIM* modeling tool for understanding the sterilization process and analyzing related risks. To this end, the following presentation focuses to demonstrate how an *AdoBPRIM* user should address the environment tool to create models (i.e. instances of *e-BPRIM* viewpoints). For greater clarity, we exclusively work on selected *e-BPRIM* viewpoints namely the "Process Landscap", "Business Process", "Risk Taxonomy", "Risk-extended Business Process", "Risk Analysis", and "Risk Mapping" viewpoints.

It also needs to be noted, that to build *AdoBPRIM* models, we based ourselves on the works of Di Mascolo et al. [2–4, 18]. In these works, a real case study was carried out in the sterilization service of the University Hospital of Grenoble. In their research, the authors looked at documents from the French and international standards on the sterilization process, as well as medical documents on sterilization best practices and the findings of a survey done in the Rhône-Alpes region on sterilization services.

### 4.1 *AdoBPRIM* Modeling Tool

Following the *e-BPRIM* modeling procedure, an *AdoBPRIM* user starts with the contextualization phase by creating:

**A "Process Landscape -- (PL)" Model** (i.e. instance of the "Process Landscape" *e-BPRIM* viewpoint). The latter aims to describe an overview of the value-added processes of the system under study. In our case study, this model describes the sterilization process. In the top of Fig. 2, we illustrate the organization of a hospital sterilization process according to the works carried out in [2–4, 18]. We can then identify eight sub-processes of the hospital sterilization process namely: (1) Pre-disinfect and transfer MD, (2) Rinse MD, (3) Wash MD, (4) Dry MD, (5) Pack the MD, (6) Sterilize MD groups, (7) Transfer MD to the surgical block, and (8) Store the groups of MD.

**A "Business Process – (BP)" Model** (i.e. instance of the "Business Process" *e-BPRIM* viewpoint). The latter aims to provide a deeper understanding of the functioning of each identified sub-process in the PL model. This model depicts a collection of interconnected and collaborative activities that produce a particular service or product. Data and organizational elements can also be introduced. This model can provide a full overview of the system as well as process improvement. In our case study, each identified hospital sterilization sub-process can be described by a BP model. For example, at the bottom of Fig. 2, the "Wash medical devices" process is described in greater detail. This up-down description is ensured through the decomposition operation *($Op_1$)* provided by the *AdoBPRIM* modeling tool functionalities (see Fig. 2).

(a) Process Landscape of the « Sterilization process »

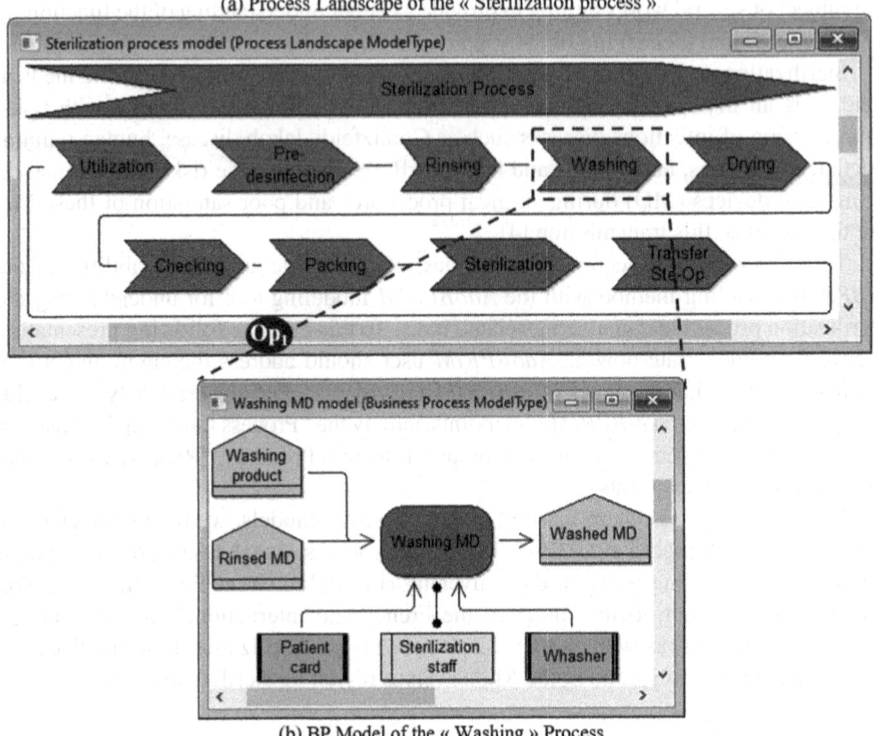


(b) BP Model of the « Washing » Process

**Fig. 2.** Sterilization process mapping (Screenshot from *AdoBPRIM*)

## 4.2 Assessment Phase of a Sterilization Service

After the first phase of the *e-BPRIM* modeling procedure, the *AdoBPRIM* user can then start the assessment phase by creating:

**A "Risk Taxonomy – (RT)" model** (i.e. instance of the "Risk Taxonomy" *e-BPRIM* viewpoint). The latter aims to provide an inventory of potential risks. In our case study, to identify and classify risks that can appear in the sterilization service, we refer to the works carried out in [2–4, 17, 18]. These works used a risk classification inspired by the Ishikawa method. They then differentiate between five risk classes namely: (1) Equipment Risk, which includes all risks associated with the equipment used during the manufacturing process (washer-autoclave-dryer-sink), (2) Entity Risk, which includes all the risks associated with MD, (3) Human Risk, which includes risks associated with the personnel working in the sterilization service, (4) material risk, which includes risks associated with the materials used to ensure the correct functioning of the activities (washing, packaging, etc.), and (5) Environment Risk, which includes risks associated with the system's indoor environment, such as the work area, and the risks associated with the system's external environment. In regards to the Entity Risk class, five main risks can be identified namely: Non-functional MD, Deteriorated MD, MD non-compliant,

Mixing of MD, and Contaminated MD. In the left side of Fig. 3, we illustrate this classification through an RT model.

**A "Risk-extended Business Process – (R-BP)" model** (i.e. instance of the "Risk-extended Business Process" *e-BPRIM* viewpoint). The latter aims to assign individual activities of the BM model to potential risks from identified risks in the RT model. This model ensures the identification of: (1) process activities that are exposed to risks, and (2) Risk factors and situations that can influence the likelihood and/or the severity of a risk. In our case study, as shown on the right side of Fig. 3, we can assign the "Contaminated MD" risk (identified in the RT model) to the "Washing MD" activity. The reuse of an object in different models is ensured through the operation ($Op_2$) provided by the *AdoBPRIM* modeling tool functionalities (see Fig. 3).

**A "Risk Analysis – (RA)" model** (i.e. instance of the "Risk Analysis" *e-BPRIM* viewpoint). The latter aims to analyze each identified risk in the RT model. For this purpose, the model enables: (1) definition of the risk scenario by describing potential risk causes and consequences, and (2) risk level calculation using a qualitative risk analysis method, specifically the Bowtie method [19].

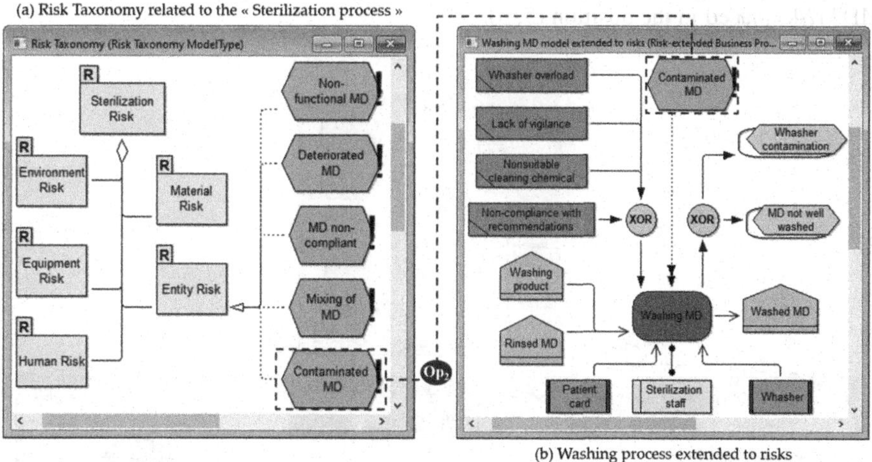


**Fig. 3.** Washing process extended to risks (Screenshot from AdoBPRIM)

In the RA model, a risk event is expressed by three elements: Likelihood (L), Severity (S), and Risk level (R). With:

- *Likelihood* describes the occurrence probability level of risk situations and risk events. To propagate and calculate the likelihood of a risk event, we based our work on the qualitative approach of the Bowtie method [19] and used the qualitative scales as presented in [20].
- *Severity* describes the impact level of a risk event on values and stakeholders of the system under study.

- *Risk level* is calculated in Eq. (1) as the product of likelihood and severity levels.

$$\text{Risk level (R)} = \text{Likelihood (L)} * \text{Severity (S)} \quad (1)$$

In our case study, we focus the analysis on the "Contaminated MD" risk (identified in the RT model). The analysis result is given at the bottom of Fig. 4. In this model, the risk event likelihood of "Contaminated MD" is the result of previous risk situations and factors. The risk factors: "Non-suitable cleaning chemical", "Non-compliance with recommendations", "Lack of vigilance" and "Washer overload", influence directly the likelihood of risk situations: "MD not well washed" and "Washer contamination". The final risk event is impacting two values namely: "Human and social" and "Well-being" values. These two values are of interest for two stakeholders "Healthcare facility" and "Patient".

**A "Risk Mapping – (RM)" model** (i.e. instance of the "Risk Mapping" *e-BPRIM* viewpoint). The latter aims to produce a two-dimensional risk matrix that shows the risk level of each analyzed risk. The risk position in the matrix will be according to likelihood and severity levels as calculated in its RA model. For our case study, Fig. 5 illustrates the mapping of different analyzed risks. For example, according to the analysis result, provided in Fig. 4, we can see the risk "R2" (corresponding to the "Contaminated MD" risk) placed in the position (5, 3).

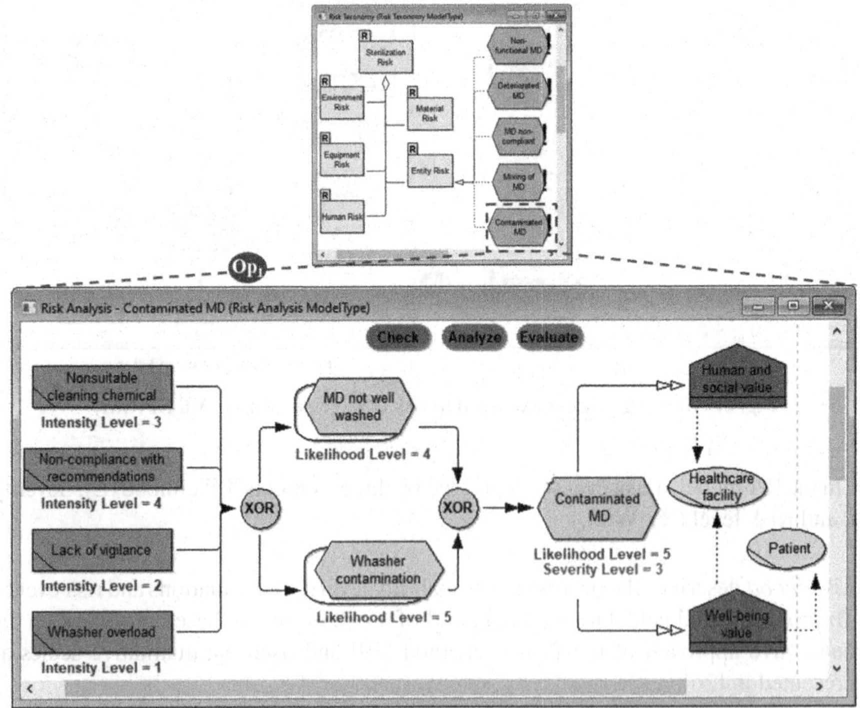


Fig. 4. Analysis of the "Contaminated MD" Risk (Screenshot from *AdoBPRIM*)

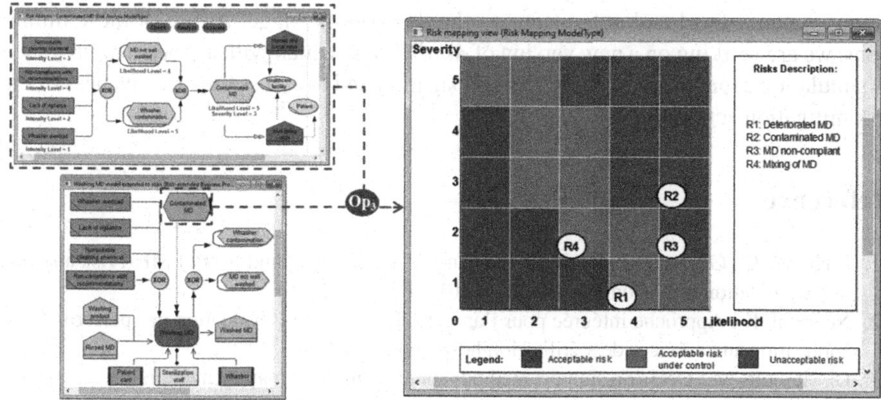


**Fig. 5.** Some risk mapping of the Sterilization process (Screenshot from *AdoBPRIM*) .

## 5 Conclusion

Addressing the vulnerability of hospital sterilization service is at the heart of guardianships in healthcare facilities due to the contagious nature of their environment which could affect the safety of patients and staff. In order to support healthcare professionals in moving forward on this issue, several risk management methods are proposed. Investigations and literature analysis that we conducted on some of them, shows a statement of their limits. Indeed, none of them qualifies the dynamics of risk, any more than the detailed explanation of the contexts generating the latter.

To progress towards a more efficient approach, we present, in this work a new R-BPM framework called *e-BPRIM*, which is a recent achievement of our long-term research in this area. It consists of the digitalization of the *BPRIM*, an R-BPM approach based on the coupling of two typically separate approaches – risk management and business process management – to improve the risk-awareness of an organization's business processes.

To assess the usefulness and relevance of this framework, we analyzed the vulnerability of a hospital sterilization service through the use of *AdoBPRIM*, the dedicated tool for *e-BPRIM*. Thanks to this later, a completed risk map is given with a reliable basis for risk assessment and the investigation of each of the identified risks. This comprehensive map gives us valuable insights into the hospital sterilization service. All developed models enable to improve a hospital's understanding of its risk profile, clarify thinking on the nature and impact of risks taking into consideration both, the organization as a whole, and the context of the risk situation and its relationship to the activities of the sterilization service. This allows vulnerability to be mitigated or coped with more effectively.

Our study has thus shown that R-BPM approaches can overcome some of the limitations of conventional methods. Obviously, *e-BPRIM* framework is not limited to analyzing hospital sterilization service vulnerabilities, it could be used to investigate other healthcare processes which are vulnerable to risks such as the medication-use process. The generic character of the *e-BPRIM* meta-model gives it a wider potential of use, even in other sectors such as the financial services industry or the energy industry. At this stage, it is worth mentioning that the current version of *AdoBPRIM* is of a relatively young maturity level and is focusing on the design-time stage. Aware of these limitations, we are working on a new version of *AdoBPRIM*, which will add new features such as simulation capabilities to study risk propagation and to assess the effectiveness of the risk mitigation activities.

## References


1. Dağsuyu, C., Göçmen, E., Narlı, M., Kokangül, A.: Classical and fuzzy FMEA risk analysis in a sterilization unit. Comput. Ind. Eng. **101**, 286–294 (2016)
2. Negrichi, K.: Approche intégrée pour l'analyse de risques et l'évaluation des performances: application aux services de stérilisation hospitalière (2015)
3. Di Mascolo, M.: Decision support methods for efficient flow management in medical device sterilization departments. In: Health Efficiency, pp. 39–60. Elsevier (2018)
4. Di Mascolo, M., Flaus, J.-M., Daadaa, M.: A new integrated approach for risk analysis and performance evaluation of a hospital sterilization service. In: 9ème Conférence Francophone en gestion et ingénierie des systems hospitaliers, GISEH 2018 (2018)
5. Malicki, J., et al.: Patient safety in external beam radiotherapy, results of the ACCIRAD project: current status of proactive risk assessment, reactive analysis of events, and reporting and learning systems in Europe. Radiother. Oncol. **123**, 29–36 (2017)
6. Suriadi, S., et al.: Current research in risk-aware business process management - overview, comparison and gap analysis. Commun. AIS CAIS. **34**, 52 (2014)
7. Lamine, E., Thabet, R., Sienou, A., Bork, D., Fontanili, F., Pingaud, H.: BPRIM: an integrated framework for business process management and risk management. Comput. Ind. **117**, 103199 (2020)
8. Amantea, I.A., Di Leva, A., Sulis, E.: A simulation-driven approach in risk-aware business process management: a case study in healthcare. In: SIMULTECH, pp. 98–105 (2018)
9. Ferdosi, M., Rezayatmand, R., Taleghani, Y.M.: Risk management in executive levels of healthcare organizations: insights from a scoping review (2018). Risk Manag. Healthc. Policy **13**, 215 (2020)
10. Senna, P., Reis, A., Santos, I.L., Dias, A.C., Coelho, O.: A systematic literature review on supply chain risk management: is healthcare management a forsaken research field? Benchmarking- Int. J. **28**, 926–956 (2021)
11. Thabet, R.: Ingénierie dirigée par les modèles d'un pilotage robuste de la prise en charge médicamenteuse (2020)
12. Thabet, R., Boufaied, A., Lamine, E., Bork, D., Korbaa, O., Pingaud, H.: AdoBPRIM: towards a new healthcare risk-aware business process management tool. In: 13th International Conference on Health Informatics (HEALTHINF 2020), pp. 498–505 (2020)
13. ADOxx.org: Official homepage of the ADOxx meta-modeling platform (2020)
14. Thabet, R., Bork, D., Boufaied, A., Lamine, E., Korbaa, O., Pingaud, H.: Risk-aware business process management using multi-view modeling: method and tool. Requirements Eng. **26**, 1–27 (2021). https://doi.org/10.1007/s00766-021-00348-2
15. Karagiannis, D., Kühn, H.: Metamodelling platforms. In: Bauknecht, K., Tjoa, A.M., Quirchmayr, G. (eds.) EC-Web 2002. LNCS, vol. 2455, pp. 182–182. Springer, Heidelberg (2002). https://doi.org/10.1007/3-540-45705-4_19
16. Fill, H.-G., Karagiannis, D.: On the conceptualisation of modelling methods using the ADOxx meta modelling platform. Enterp. Model. Inf. Syst. Archit. EMISAJ. **8**, 4–25 (2013)
17. Talon, D.: Gestion des risques dans une stérilisation centrale d'un établissement hospitalier: apport de la traçabilité à l'instrument (2011)

18. Di Mascolo, M., Flaus, J.-M., Barkaoui H.: Simulation in degraded mode of sterilization services. In: 12th Conference on Stochastic Models of Manufacturing and Service Operations (SMMSO 2019) (2019)
19. Alizadeh, S., Moshashaei, P.: The Bowtie method in safety management system: a literature review. Sci. J. Rev. **4**, 133–138 (2015)
20. Blondel, P., Brunel, C.: Etude et hiérarchisation du risque infectieux nosocomial selon la criticité: nouvelle approche. Risques Qual. En Milieu Soins. **3**, 17–23 (2004)

# Designing a Collaborative Personal Assistance Model for Persons with Disabilities: The Portuguese Independent Living Case

Patrícia Macedo[1,2(✉)], Filipa Ferrada[1,2,3], Ana Inês Oliveira[1,3], and Rui Neves Madeira[2,4]

[1] Uninova Institute, Centre of Technology and Systems (CTS), Caparica, Portugal
{faf,aio}@uninova.pt
[2] Sustain.RD Center, ESTSetúbal, Instituto Politécnico de Setúbal, Campus do IPS, Setúbal, Portugal
{patricia.macedo,rui.madeira}@estsetubal.ips.pt
[3] Faculty of Sciences and Technology, NOVA University of Lisbon, Caparica, Portugal
[4] NOVA LINCS, FCT, NOVA University of Lisbon, Caparica, Portugal

**Abstract.** This paper presents an ongoing research work that aims to develop governance models and ICTs to enable and empower persons with disabilities according to the orientations settled in the Convention on the Rights of Persons with Disabilities. Starting from the study of the current model of Independent Living Support adopted in Portugal and its practical limitations, we propose a model based on the collaborative networks scientific discipline. This new model aims to guarantee an environment in which all the involved participants can improve and combine their contributions toward providing Personal Assistance to persons with disabilities. The paper also presents a Web platform (SEU - Services to Empower yoU) designed to support offline services acquisition, providing a user interaction adapted to different types of disabilities. Furthermore, we propose an update to the platform SEU to be compliant with the proposed collaborative model.

**Keywords:** Persons with disabilities · Independent living · Personal assistant · Collaborative networks · Offline services · Digital accessibility

## 1 Introduction

With the 2030 Agenda for Sustainable Development adoption, Member States pledged to leave no one behind, including Persons with Disabilities (PwD). This political commitment is in line with the United Nations Convention on the Rights of Persons with Disabilities (CRPD) that was ratified by 177 states in March 2019. Moreover, CRPD recognizes the critical role of information and communication technologies (ICTs) in enabling and empowering PwD and ensuring that they fully enjoy human rights and fundamental freedoms [1]. However, ICTs are not the only critical enablers, as several


Published by Springer Nature Switzerland AG 2021
L. M. Camarinha-Matos et al. (Eds.): PRO-VE 2021, IFIP AICT 629, pp. 652–662, 2021.
https://doi.org/10.1007/978-3-030-85969-5_61

initiatives worldwide have shown that collaborative projects had a positive impact on supporting PwD [2].

The CRPD considers that one of the pillars of the Independent Living Movement is providing personal assistance (PA) based on individual needs assessment and the life situation of each individual. Most European countries have developed policies and specific legislation to guarantee access to PA for persons with disabilities [3]. In Portugal, just in 2017, the government launched the Independent Life Support Model (MAVI) for people with severe physical or mental limitations, providing funds for pilot projects. The model is based on three dimensions agents: (i) PwD who benefits from PA; (ii) PwD; and (iii) Support Center for Independent Living (CAVI). The Support Center is the entity that is responsible for selecting candidates and giving them the necessary and possible support according to the available funding and the existing conditions [4]. There are not yet available studies and data about the effectiveness of this organization model; however, there are two important issues that have been informally raised from interviews with some agents involved. First, how to provide ICT solutions adapted to these persons' specific characteristics, which would facilitate the process of managing the personal assistance needed? Second, how collaborative models can be integrated to provide personalized services?

This paper presents an undergoing exploratory research work where a new model, based on collaborative networks, is proposed as a promising approach for supporting collaboration among all the involved entities that provide Independent Living for PwD. This exploratory research work is part of the funded project called Services to Empower yoU (SEU) - Exploring Interfaces for people with disabilities [5], where a Web Platform for offline services acquisition with accessible interfaces was designed and developed using Participatory Design. During the participatory design process, some partners identified the difficulties they had in efficiently managing the allocation of personal assistants. Therefore, it raised a question regarding how the platform SEU could be adapted to address the identified issue as it provides accessible interfaces for different types of PwD.

The research work presented in this paper adopted the design science research methodology [6], in which a set of artifacts (models) supports more efficiently Independent Living of PwD. These artifacts were developed grounded in the corpus of knowledge of Collaborative Networks (CN) [7]. The paper presents how they can be used in practice, adapting the platform SEU to instantiate them in order to validate the practical relevance of the proposed models.

## 2 Background and Related Work

The right to live independently and be included in the community is set out in Article 19 of the CRPD. In this line, countries worldwide have been preconizing different actions to give effective support to PwD, combining various environmental and individual factors that allow PwD to control their own lives [1]. In Europe, policy actions like the Strategy for the Rights of Persons with Disabilities 2021–2030 [8] are devoted to achieving further progress in ensuring the full participation of persons with disabilities by building new guiding actions based on past achievements. Social and community movements like

ENIL [9] or Independent Living [10] have also played an impressive role by promoting self-determination, equal opportunities, and self-respect for PwD.

The inclusion of Personal Assistance (PA) in PwD is essential to support living and inclusion in the community and prevent isolation. The concept was proposed by Ratzka [11] in Sweden and is now present in many countries worldwide. PA can be defined as the necessary assistance required by a disabled person to ensure that s/he can participate as a full and equal member of society [12]. The individual manages this assistance to guarantee the right choice and control, presupposing adequate support, and it can be adapted to different circumstances both within and outside the home. It can include support with personal care, help with household tasks and administration duties, facilitating attendance at work or college, as well as enabling social activities and participation in community life. Nevertheless, and despite the efforts, PA is still not widely available, and a large number of persons with a disability are still segregated in institutions [13].

In Portugal, via a governmental law[1] in 2017, the MAVI program has been established, allowing PA to PwD to perform a set of activities that they cannot accomplish alone. The implementation of the MAVI is done through the Centers for Supporting Independent Life (CAVI) since they are the structures responsible for providing personal assistance to PwD. CAVIs are created as autonomous units of Non-Governmental Organisations for PwD. Their mission is to assume management, coordination, and support functions of the PA services within the scope of independent living. Each CAVI is responsible for managing the requests of PwD for PA service and recruiting assistants to satisfy the demands. Any citizen can apply to be a PA in a CAVI. There is a personal assistants database with the contacts and availability information of people who have signed up to work as a PA.

There are several types of services that can be requested, and there are also some services that can require more than one PA at the same time (e.g., a person with overweight may need two people at the same time to help with the bathing). A PA service can be characterized in two dimensions: categorization of service (e.g., personal care, travel support, education, etc.) and time (duration, time of the day, days of the week, etc.). However, the PwD is who decides how many PAs s/he needs and selects them. An individual document is drawn up in which the hours, activities and other specific details relating to PA are recorded.

It is easy to understand that for a PwD to fully benefit from PA services is needed an organizational structure that supports collaboration and coordination between operational assistants. Currently, many networks worldwide work in the disability field, supporting and promoting independent living and empowering full participation of PwD in society via PA (e.g., ENIL, ILMI, IEDisabilities, NDIS, among others). However, most of them lack grounded models for collaboration between PwD and PA regarding the organization, governance, and service planning and management. The CN model presented in this paper proposes a potential solution to solve these problems.

Regarding Web platforms explicitly designed to facilitate the acquisition of offline services for PwD, only a few initiatives are known. A pioneering project developed in Taiwan, where a platform called Eden was developed, aimed to provide point-to-point

[1] https://dre.pt/web/en/home/-/contents/108265124/details/normal.

transit services by connecting elderly and disabled passengers to drivers [14]. However, there is no reference that the mobile app developed for the passengers has adapted user interfaces to support specific needs. A case study conducted in Australia [15] of a Web-based platform, which works similarly to Trip Advisor by providing a means through which disability service users can share information about their experiences that can inform subsequent choices, has shown the importance of this kind of solutions to empower PwD. The adaptation of the Web platform SEU to support the CN model, as proposed in this work, envisages allowing better PA services, providing, at the same time, accessible interfaces for different types of PwD.

## 3 Collaborative Personal Assistance Model for Persons with Disabilities

The service being provided by a Personal Assistance Network results from the specific requirements of each individual (PwD) and, therefore, completely customized and personalized to her/ his needs. Given the potential specificity of each service, it might often be necessary to create a new service based on the composition of services [16, 17] provided by several PAs, building a team that will typically dissolve after the service is provided. Nevertheless, depending on the nature of the service, this duration may vary.

Hence, collaboration among PA and PwD introduces some aspects that should be considered in terms of organization, governance and service planning and management. Therefore, it is crucial to understand the nature of these networks and how they can be modeled. In this line, and considering the core context, the collaborative personal assistance (CoPA) model integrates three kinds of networks: independent living model network, independent living support network, and PA network. As such, Fig. 1 illustrates the different networks involved in the provision of services to PwD, focusing on their interactions.

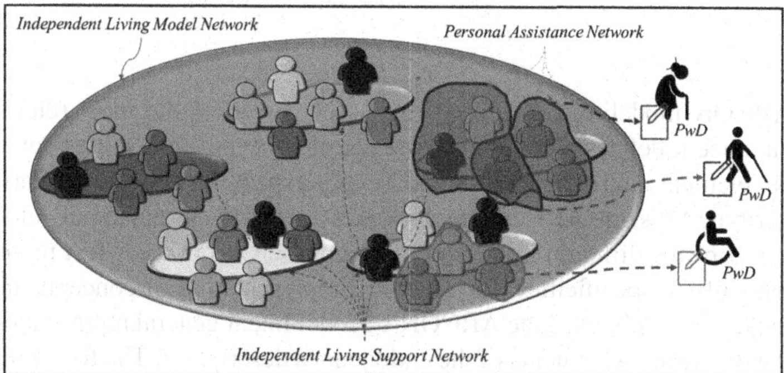


**Fig. 1.** Different networks involved in the provision of services to PwD.

Being the provision of services a collaborative process to support all the involved stakeholders, a CN can be instantiated by combining the different characteristics that these networks have, such as network typology, duration, membership, members from different networks, etc. Thus, it is aimed to model an environment that nurtures collaboration amongst all entities that are involved in services provision to PwD. In this direction, the scientific discipline of collaborative networks [7, 18] introduces some concepts and models that cope with the demanding requirements for such environment, namely virtual organizations breeding environments (VBEs), professional virtual communities (PVCs), virtual organizations (VOs), and virtual teams (VTs) [19]. On the one hand, the VBEs and PVCs increase the level of preparedness of organizations and individuals in succeeding in collaboration; on the other hand, VOs and VTs are temporary consortiums of organizations or individuals, supported by computer networks, which join their competencies to strategically and adequately accomplish a common goal [19]. Considering these concepts, Table 1 includes a description of the proposed networks for the CoPA model.

**Table 1.** Description of involved collaborative networks in the CoPA model.

| Network | Description |
|---|---|
| Independent living model network | Long-term alliance, with the main characteristics of a VBE, that involves the governing, regulation and certification of different types of entities that are willing to provide independent living support, namely the *Independent Living Support Networks* |
| Independent living support network | Long-term alliance, with the characteristics of a PVC, that involves distinct supporting PAs, with different competences, in a defined region, that are willing to collaborate in order to provide a customized and personalized independent living service to PwD |
| Personal assistance network | Temporary consortium, with the characteristics of a VT, involved in the provision of customized and personalized services to PwD |

The ARCON modeling framework [18] is perceived as the most relevant in the CN domain once it defines a comprehensive set of concepts and entities covering both endogenous elements and exogenous interactions perspectives of CNs. Similarly to other works describing CNs, the ARCON framework was used to systematically and comprehensibly describe the different aspects of the proposed CNs in the CoPA model. In this case, despite all the specificities, for a general representation of concepts and related relationships, it was only used the ARCON's Model Intent general representation layer, combined with the main elements of the endogenous description. The following characterization (see Table 2 and Table 3) focuses on the independent living support network and personal assistance network, considering the operation phase of the lifecycle of the networks. In contrast, the Independent Living Model Network will be characterized in further works since its characteristics will emphasise the governing and certification for independent living support networks.

## 4 Adaptation of SEU to Support the CoPA Model

The platform SEU (Services to Empower You) [5], as explained before, was developed in the scope of a larger project and intended to respond to the needs raised by PwD when they wish to acquire services through the Web. Services platforms are usually grouped into three categories [20], according to what they facilitate: (i) transportation; (ii) offline services; (iii) online services. The SEU platform falls into the second category as it is geared to support services that are local and rely on the physical presence of the service provider. The Web platform SEU integrates the following features (see Fig. 2): (i) various customer and service acquisition models; (ii) validation of customers and service providers; (iii) use of adapted digital resources, allowing the automatic provision of adapted interfaces. The need for the supervisor role stands out, allowing the existence of supervised PwD, where the acquisition of a service will require the authorization of her/his supervisor to protect users with cognitive impairment. Sometimes, or due to the characteristics of the PwD, there is a need for a third person to acquire the service; hence, the introduction of the third type of client, the caregiver.

**Table 2.** Characterization of independent living support network.

| Independent living support network | |
|---|---|
| Endogenous elements | |
| Subspace: Structural | |
| Roles | **Administrator** can be performed by a PA responsible for the network governance (can be assisted by a board of directors). All **members** are PAs willing to collaborate to provide customized services to PwDs. The **potential customers** are PwD that request a service |
| Relations | **Control Supervision** ensured by the administrator. All members are responsible for **cooperation and collaboration, and exchange and sharing** of information, and establishing **Trusting** mechanisms |
| Network | Long-term alliance that involves the network governance |
| Subspace: Componential | |
| ICT resources | A software platform to support the independent living support network collaboration and management, allowing the registration of new members, their profiles information and the requests from potential customers (PwD). This platform can be part of the platform used by independent living model network |
| Human resources | Member of the independent living model network |
| Knowledge resources | Detailed profile of members; information about potential customers; network profile data; main common ontologies for common understanding; shared resources repository; value system; governance principles; etc. |

The specified user registration model also foresees that all registrations are subject to approval by the platform manager to ensure that all service providers are validated,

**Table 3.** Characterization of personal assistance network.

| Personal assistance network | |
|---|---|
| Endogenous elements | |
| Subspace: Structural | |
| Roles | **Planner** is responsible for the creation of a PA network; the **Coordinator** is responsible for the coordination of the PA network during its duration; the **Partner** represents all the PAs involved in the provision of the service to the PwD |
| Relations | **Control Supervision** under the responsibility of the Coordinator; **Collaboration, Exchanging and Sharing** between all partners; The constant **trust** establishment among partners is essential |
| Network | Virtual team involved in the provision of a composed service to PwD |
| Subspace: Componential | |
| ICT resources | A software platform to support the creation and management of the personal assistance network. This platform can be part of the platform used by independent living support network |
| Human resources | Different partners can be allocated to specific services provided to the PwD |
| Knowledge resources | Shared resources; Templates with models or reference documents to be instantiated for a specific use case; Main common ontologies used to facilitate the common understanding among the network partners; etc. |

and that client information is valid. It is also proposed that the platform manager has the role of introducing the digital components that will allow the information about a service to be available in an accessible way, which can be, for instance, the introduction of a video with the description of a service in LGP (Portuguese Sign Language).

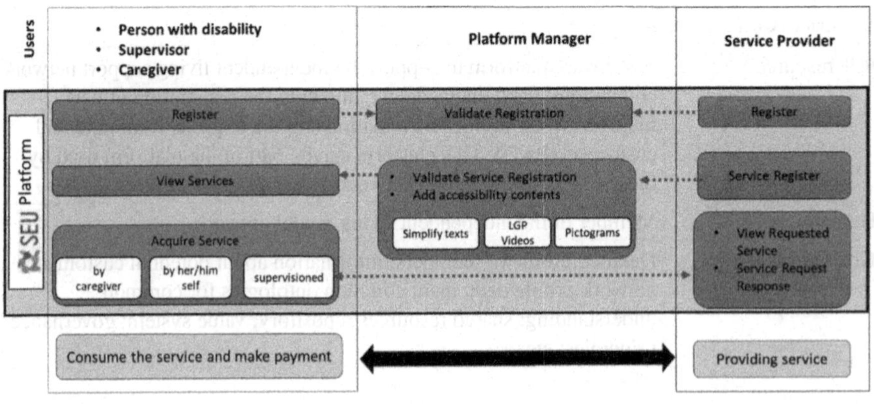


**Fig. 2.** SEU platform: Conceptual model.

The platform has a client-server architecture based on RESTful Web services. MongoDB is used to implement the data repository, Node.JS and the Express.JS framework are the technologies used for the implementation of the server and services logic layer, with Vue.JS being used to support the client layer development. The user interaction is adapted according to the user profile (see Fig. 3A), and each service description has specific information about the types of available adaptations (see Fig. 3B).

Since the platform already has an accessible interface to support users with distinct disabilities (visual, auditory, cognitive, physical), and implements all the components required to support multiple types of clients and services providers, it is presented how it can be adapted to support the CoPA model presented in Sect. 3.

(A) Auditory Adaptation

(B) Services View-Target Group is indicated

**Fig. 3.** Platform SEU: Examples of accessibility adaptation and information adaptation.

The SEU's Conceptual Model supports three user groups: Client; Platform Manager; and Service Provider. In the scope of the CoPA model, the role of the service provider is replaced by the role of PA, which is the one that provides the service directly to the PwD. Since PAs integrate Independent Living Networks, and these integrate an Independent Living Network, both user roles must be supported by the platform SEU. Figure 4 presents the conceptual model Collaborative-SEU (C-SEU), representing the primary users of the platform and the main operations allocated to each one, in the scope of providing integrate plans of personal assistance in the scope of Independent Living Models Networks.

Another important feature that should be designed and implemented is the possibility of service composition. A client should be able to apply for a set of services that the same PA cannot provide. So, the C-SEU should propose a plan of services according to the requirements of the client and the PAs available on the Independent Living Networks to which the client belongs. This coordination of services to build a personalized assistance plan is one of the challenges identified in the C-SEU model for the platform. According to the model proposed, this personalized assistance plan will be executed by a temporary virtual network of personal assistants created with that purpose.

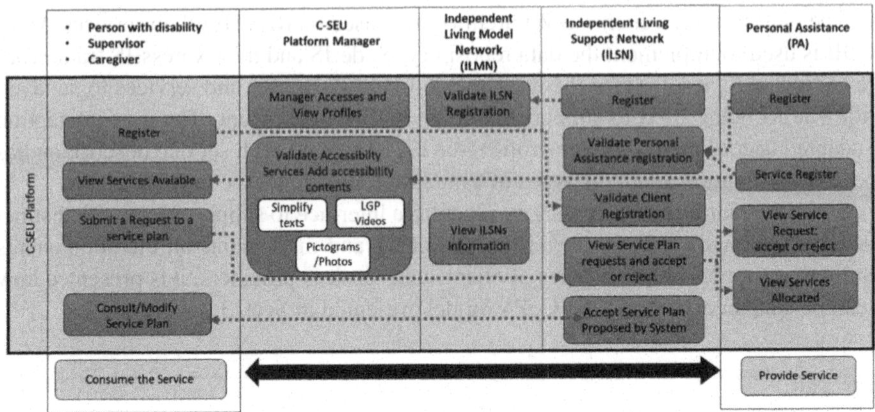


**Fig. 4.** Conceptual model C-SEU.

## 5 Conclusion and Future Work

This paper presents ongoing research aiming to develop governance models and ICTs to enable and empower PwD according to the orientations settled in the Convention on the Rights of Persons with Disabilities. Two main contributions were achieved: i) the CoPA model – a governance model supported by a collaborative network paradigm that aims to guarantee an environment in which all the involved participants can improve and combine their contribution for the provision of Personal Assistance to PwD; ii) a conceptual model for a Web platform, based on SEU as the case study, which supports the acquisition of offline services and presents a user interaction adapted to diverse types of disabilities, in order to be compliant with the CoPA model.

Two main aspects must be carried out concerning the CoPA model. Firstly, each of the three proposed networks must be further characterized within the scope of the ARCON reference model. Secondly, the model that serves to support the Portuguese Personal Assistance governance model known as MAVI needs to be validated next to the institutions that run CAVIs.

According to the research methodology adopted, the validation of the conceptual models proposed comprises the practical relevance of the proposed models. The partners of the research project SEU, Portuguese institutions that work with PwD (APPDA-Setubal, Health School of Alcoitão, and Accessible Portugal), have expertise in Personal Assistance and will be involved in the evaluation of the proposed artifacts, validating our solution against the identified problem.

**Acknowledgements.** Project funded by the Polytechnic Institute of Setúbal, through the internal Research Support Program and by the Portuguese "Fundação para a Ciência e Tecnologia" "Strategic program UIDB/00066/2020" (UNINOVA-CTS project).

## References

1. United Nations: United Nations Convention on the Rights of Persons with Disabilities. https://www.un.org/disabilities/documents/convention/convention_accessible_pdf.pdf. Accessed 28 Apr 2021
2. Cheng, L.R.L., Levey, S.: Collaborative approaches to the support of people with disabilities: the underserved and unserved. Folia Phoniatrica et Logopaedica. **71**(2-3), 62–70 (2019). https://doi.org/10.1159/000492530
3. Nally, D., Moore, S.S., Gowran, R.J.: How governments manage personal assistance schemes in response to the United Nations Convention on the Rights of Persons with Disabilities: a scoping review. Disabil. Soc. (2021). https://doi.org/10.1080/09687599.2021.1877114
4. Silva, J.M.: The Portuguese independent living support model (MAVI). Iris J. Nurs. Care. 2, 1–2 (2020). https://doi.org/10.33552/ijnc.2020.02.000550
5. Macedo, P., Miranda, P., Alburqueue Santos, P., Ferrada, F., Paquete, P., Castro, C.: Plataforma de Serviços SEU – Estudo de Interfaces de Utilizador para Pessoas com Deficiência ou Incapacidade. In: VI CONFERÊNCIA INTERNACIONAL PARA A INCLUSÃO, pp. 237–247 (2020)
6. Peffers, K., Tuunanen, T., Rothenberger, M.A., Chatterjee, S.: A design science research methodology for information systems research. J. Manag. Inf. Syst. **24**, 45–77 (2007). https://doi.org/10.2753/MIS0742-1222240302
7. Camarinha-Matos, L.M., Afsarmanesh, H.: Collaborative networks: a new scientific discipline. J. Intell. Manuf. **16**, 439–452 (2005). https://doi.org/10.1007/s10845-005-1656-3
8. Commission, E.: Strategy for Rights of Persons with Disabilities 2021–2030. https://ec.europa.eu/commission/presscorner/api/files/document/print/en/qanda_21_813/QANDA_21_813_EN.pdf. Accessed 20 Apr 2021
9. ENIL – European Network on Independent Living: European Network on Independent Living Personal Assistance Services in Europe 2015-Report. http://www.enil.eu/wp-content/uploads/2012/06/Personal-Assistance-Service-in-Europe-Report-2015.pdf (2016)
10. Independent Living Institute (ILI). https://www.independentliving.org/. Accessed 23 Apr 2021
11. Westerberg, B.: Personal assistance: a revolution for people with disabilities. In: 7th International Conference on Social Work in Health and Mental Health, Southern California, Los Angeles (2013)
12. Center for Independent Living: National Leader Forum Personal Assistance Services Report. https://ilmi.ie/wp-content/uploads/2018/07/Personal-Assistance-Report-2016-.pdf. (2016)
13. Mladenov, T.: What is good personal assistance made of? Results of a European survey. Disabil. Soc. **35**, 1–24 (2020). https://doi.org/10.1080/09687599.2019.1621740
14. Wu, Y.J., Liu, W.J., Yuan, C.H.: A mobile-based barrier-free service transportation platform for people with disabilities. Comput. Human Behav. **107**, 105776 (2020). https://doi.org/10.1016/j.chb.2018.11.005
15. McLoughlin, I., McNicoll, Y., Beecher Kelk, A., Cornford, J., Hutchinson, K.: A 'Tripadvisor' for disability? Social enterprise and 'digital disruption' in Australia. Inf. Commun. Soc. **22**, 521–537 (2019). https://doi.org/10.1080/1369118X.2018.1538382.
16. Camarinha-Matos, L.M., Ferrada, F., Oliveira, A.I., Rosas, J., Monteiro, J.N.: Integrated care services in ambient assisted living. In: 15th IEEE International Conference on e-health Networking, Applications and Services (IEEEHealthcom 2013), Lisbon (2013). https://doi.org/10.1109/HealthCom.2013.6720666
17. Baldissera, T.A., Camarinha-Matos, L.M.: SCoPE: service composition and personalization environment. Appl. Sci. **8**, 2297 (2018). https://doi.org/10.3390/app8112297

18. Camarinha-Matos, L., Afsarmanesh, H.: Collaborative Networks: Reference Modeling. Springer, Boston (2008). https://doi.org/10.1007/978-0-387-79426-6
19. Camarinha-Matos, L.M., et al.: VO creation assistance services. In: Methods and Tools for Collaborative Networked Organizations, pp. 155–190. Springer, Boston (2008). https://doi.org/10.1007/978-0-387-79424-2_6
20. Fabo, B., Beblavý, M., Kilhoffer, Z., Lenaerts, K.: An Overview of European Platforms: Scope and Business Models. Publications Office of the European Union, Brussels (2017)

# Collaborative Networks and Open Innovation in Education 4.0

# Diagnostic Instrument of the Level of Competencies in Cloud Computing for Teachers in Education 4.0

Gloria Concepción Tenorio-Sepúlveda[1](✉), Katherine-del-Pilar Muñoz-Ortiz[2], Cristóbal-Andrés Nova-Nova[3], and María-Soledad Ramírez-Montoya[4]

[1] Computer Systems Engineering, Tecnológico Nacional de México/TES de Chalco, Carretera Federal México-Cuautla S/N, La Candelaria Tlapala, Chalco, Estado de México, Mexico
gloria_cts@tesch.edu.mx

[2] Corporación Educacional Nagüilán, Michimalonco 3855, San Pedro de la Paz, Concepción, Chile
katherine.munozortiz@colegiopaulofreirespc.cl

[3] Liceo Bicentenario de Excelencia Domingo Ortiz de Rozas, Héroes de la Concepción 342, Coelemu, Ñuble, Chile
cristobal.nova@liceobicentenariocoelemu.cl

[4] Tecnologico de Monterrey, School of Humanities and Education, Institute for the Future of Education, Avda. Garza Sada 2501 Sur; Col. Tecnológico, Monterrey, Nuevo León, Mexico
solramirez@tec.mx

**Abstract.** Universities face a paradigmatic educational challenge, driven by Industry 4.0 technologies such as Cloud Computing, producing the need to develop new teaching competencies. The question arises: How can we diagnose the level of Cloud Computing competencies that teachers have in the context of Education 4.0? To address this question, the objective was to design a valid and reliable instrument to measure these competencies. A literature review and expert collaboration were carried out. For validation, it was submitted to expert judgment and Kendall's W concordance coefficient was calculated; for reliability, a pilot test was carried out with teachers of the Computer Systems Engineering career and the KR20 (Kuder-Richardson) was used. The result was an instrument with 23 items capable of measuring seven competencies identified by the collaborative network Industry 4.0 Node. This instrument contributes as a guideline for educational institutions, bridging the gap between technological progress and formal education.

**Keywords:** Teaching competencies · Education 4.0 · Educational innovation · Cloud computing · Higher education

## 1 Introduction

During the last decade the use of technologies related to Industry 4.0 has grown exponentially, the World Economic Forum after applying surveys to business leaders in 25


Published by Springer Nature Switzerland AG 2021
L. M. Camarinha-Matos et al. (Eds.): PRO-VE 2021, IFIP AICT 629, pp. 665–673, 2021.
https://doi.org/10.1007/978-3-030-85969-5_62

countries states that the adoption of technologies such as Cloud Computing, Big Data and E-Commerce are a sustained trend [1], this implies that every day a greater number of jobs require people who have developed competencies aimed at addressing them. The disruptive emergence of various technologies has led to the need to develop new skills and even rethink new careers at the educational level or adapt curricula to meet these new challenges [2], this has been identified by various agencies, such is the case of the Government of the State of Mexico (GEM), one of the 32 states of the country Mexico.

The GEM, with the vision of preparing its higher education students in cutting-edge technologies, formed a collaborative network called Industry 4.0 Node composed of teachers and researchers specialists of Higher Education Institutions (HEI) of state control that offer undergraduate and graduate academic programs with profile in these technologies, this network aims to determine through a structured methodology, the competencies aligned to Industry 4. 0 that are required in a local, national and global context to implement them in the curricula of these HEIs [3], this implementation brings with it several challenges, one of them is education 4.0.

### 1.1 Education 4.0

It arises in response to the challenges presented by the disruptive innovations of the Industrial 4.0 [4], it is an education characterized by the use of digital technology in the process of multiple and flexible learning independent of time and place [5–7]. The use of Information and Communication Technologies (ICT) allows students to learn on the move through blended and virtual learning [8]. Learning is built around students in terms of where and how to learn and the tracking of their performance is done through data-driven personalization [5], in other words, education 4.0 redefines the educational landscape by placing the learner at the center of the ecosystem and shifting the focus from teaching to active learning [9].

Likewise, education 4.0 produced a new way of solving problems and new methods of thinking [6], this paradigm shift allows the creation of collaborative networks, in which teachers assume the role of learning facilitators [5], which implies on the part of teachers a great commitment so that they also develop certain competencies, this is important because they are responsible for the training of future generations [10], therefore, the teacher of education 4.0 has to be a facilitator, possess soft skills, have a human sense and must manage the new technology [11].

The challenge of education 4.0 in universities is that these competencies go beyond digital literacy, exerting on teachers and the school an increase in the expectations that society places on them [12]. Regarding the mastery of emerging technologies, some universities have taken significant steps in this direction, for example, Wester Sydney University, in 2017 published some guidance on its curricular reform, projected advances in alternative credentials oriented to future work and new curricula [13].

Following this inertia, the Industry 4.0 Node, in order to impact the curricula of its institutions, after an analysis in economic units at the State of Mexico, national and international level, identified 15 Industry 4.0 technologies, the first of these technologies is Cloud Computing (CC) [3], which is the focus of this work.

## 1.2 Cloud Computing

There is currently no single definition for CC as there are variations depending on the services and applications, which can range from educational to business [14], however the most widely used is the one outlined by the National Institute of Standards and Technology "NIST" which states that CC is a model that allows ubiquitous, convenient and personalized access to a set of computing resources that can be configured according to the need or demand of the user, among which are: applications, networks, servers and storage. Differentiating three service models: Software as a Service (SaaS), Platform as a Service (PaaS) and Infrastructure as a Service (IaaS) [15].

CC, can be seen as a group of interconnected computers where there is a wide range of users with different requirements for access to applications and data provided from anywhere, be these applications information or storage space, such as Dropbox or Google Drive [16, 17]. This has caused it to become a very popular and required tool within organizations to manage ICT workloads [18] allowing the use of applications or software without the need to know technical details, offering in turn the possibility of implementing large-scale projects without having to rely on qualified personnel or infrastructure experts [19], with variable costs depending on what is needed at a given time.

CC is also being widely required in the educational field and with great force due to the Covid-19 pandemic contingency, since it allows improving organizational efficiency [20], increasing collaborative work favoring not only learning, but also research, giving students access to knowledge efficiently and at a lower cost, being able to provide a wide range of benefits by offering academic resources, high-performance computing services, a large amount of storage, research applications and various tools for use in favor of learning [21], for this reason, several institutions are migrating from the classic e-learning platforms to the tools offered by CC, providing a more unified user experience [14], offering quality education even in remote or distant areas that have inadequate and inefficient infrastructure [22].

After the identification of technologies as CC, the Industry 4.0 Node used a three-phase methodology to generate a catalog of competencies that contemplated each of them, the institutions of the Node particularly decide which of these 15 technologies they will implement, in the case of the Tecnológico de Estudios Superiores de Chalco (TESCHA), the possibility of implementing a specialty focused on CC technology was evaluated and that is where the question arises: How can we diagnose the level of competence that teachers have in this technology in the context of Education 4.0? To address this question, the objective was to design a validated instrument to measure CC competencies defined by the Industry 4.0 Node in order to perform a diagnosis in higher education institutions that want to implement them.

The structure of this work includes the topic of education 4.0 and CC, the methodology followed for the design and validation of the instrument, the results obtained after the expert judgment and the pilot test, the link to the questionnaire and finally the conclusions with the projections of possible future work such as the application of the instrument in other higher education institutions are presented.

## 2 Methodology

The type of study was instrumental, according to Montero and León [23], it consists of the development of tests and devices, including their design and adaptation, as well as the study and analysis of their psychometric properties, in this case the CC competencies diagnostic questionnaire. The construction of the instrument was carried out between the months of February-April 2021 and applied in a public institution in the State of Mexico. It was developed in four stages: analysis of the CC competencies of the Industry 4.0 Node, literature review, then content validation by expert judgment, and finally a pilot test was applied.

First, a questionnaire was designed based on the CC competencies defined by the Industry 4.0 Node [3]. The literature was reviewed in search of other instruments related to cloud computing, analyzing five of these. Two of these were focused on cloud computing usage [24, 25], two on cloud computing adoption [22, 26] and one on the level of readiness to migrate to cloud computing [27]. All of these instruments used a Likert scale. In addition each one went through a validation and reliability process among which are, test retest, piloting, Crombach's Alpha. After this, the questionnaire was drafted in collaboration with two experts in Information and Computer Technologies, one from Chile and the other from Mexico. For validation, expert judgment was used, which is defined as an informed opinion of people with experience in the subject, who are recognized by others as qualified to provide information, evidence, judgments and evaluations [28]. Four experts participated and the results were statistically analyzed using Kendall's W coefficient of concordance, which attempts to provide the degree of agreement between various ranks of n objects or individuals [29].

A pilot test was also applied to check the reliability of the instrument [30] using the KR20 - Kuder Richardson. The pilot test involved teachers from TESCHA, a public institution located in the east of the State of Mexico, which is part of the Industry 4.0 Node, the sample was non-probabilistic, by convenience, where teachers of Computer Systems Engineering who meet the characteristics of the target population ($n = 17$), 5 women and 12 men, participated by invitation. Of the total, ($n = 8$) Computer Systems Engineers, ($n = 2$) Masters in Computer Science, ($n = 2$) Chemical Engineers, ($n = 1$) Electronics Engineer, ($n = 1$) Telematics Engineer, ($n = 1$) Master of Science in Energy Systems Engineering, ($n = 1$) Master in Information Technology and ($n = 1$) Bachelor in Computer Science and Systems Development.

## 3 Results and Discussion

Initially, the CC Competencies Diagnosis instrument was composed of 21 items covering 7 competencies (Table 1). After the experts' evaluation, Kendall's W coefficient of concordance was calculated, whose statistic showed a significance of 0.02 and a concordance among experts of 0.548, so it was considered that the items with a high agreement among the judges were maintained. The experts' observations regarding the relevance, coherence, clarity and pertinence of the items were also reviewed in order to make the suggested corrections, which added two items to the instrument, specifically in the competency Apply a language to solve problems for mobile devices.

**Table 1.** Items by competence (first version)

| Competence | Items |
|---|---|
| Uses development tools for web and mobile applications, data and client/server communications | 1–3 |
| Apply the syntax of a language for mobile and web applications | 4–6 |
| Develop embedded systems that enable automatic control and data transfer from a mobile device | 7–9 |
| Apply a troubleshooting language for mobile devices | 10–12 |
| It uses modeling techniques for problem solving | 13–15 |
| It uses security services, access, data, with the purpose of integrating information in the cloud in real time | 16–18 |
| Implements physical and virtual infrastructure for data, web and file transfer servers | 19–21 |

After taking into account the observations of the expert evaluation, the seven competencies were maintained and the result was an instrument with 23 items. After piloting, the K20 - Kuder Richardson calculation resulted in a reliability index of 0.8425, which is considered adequate.

In terms of content, the instrument measures the following seven CC competencies presented in Table 2 (for reasons of space, only the question stem is included). Each item has four response options, only one of which is correct. This questionnaire can be consulted in full at https://doi.org/10.5281/zenodo.4729221.

**Table 2.** Items of the CC competence diagnosis instrument (final version)

| Cloud computing competencies | Items |
|---|---|
| 1- Uses development tools for web and mobile applications, data and client/server communications | R-1 In CSS it is known as the space outside the element that separates it from the others |
| | R-2 It is the most widely used software for client/server communication |
| | R-3 Allows direct management of user data |
| 2- Apply the syntax of a language for mobile and web applications | R-4 Which of the following instructions is correct? |
| | R-5 This is the basic structure of an HTML5 document |
| | R-6 This is the basic structure of a form |
| | R-7 It is the SQL code that connects a web page to a database |

*(continued)*

**Table 2.** (*continued*)

| Cloud computing competencies | Items |
|---|---|
| 3- Develop embedded systems that enable automatic control and data transfer from a mobile device | R-8 Bluetooth permission settings for Android |
| | R-9 Allows you to register a service on the local network |
| | R-10 Allows autocompletion of a database from the file system |
| 4- Apply a troubleshooting language for mobile devices | R-11 It is the basic structure of a Java program |
| | R-12 This is the basic structure of a Kotlin program |
| | R-13 What is the result of the following code? |
| | R14 What is the result of the following code? |
| 5- It uses modeling techniques for problem solving | R15 Which of the following is a modeling language? |
| | R-16 Which of the following models is oriented to model processes of a system? |
| | R-17 With what can an algorithm or process be represented graphically? |
| 6- It uses security services, access, data, with the purpose of integrating information in the cloud in real time | R-18 Which of the following is NOT Cloud Computing? |
| | R-19 What is one of the main security models implemented by Cloud services? |
| | R-20 Cloud resources and workloads are exposed to a wide variety of cybersecurity threats, such as: |
| 7- Implements physical and virtual infrastructure for data, web and file transfer servers | R-21 The most basic category of cloud computing services. IT infrastructure (servers, virtual machines, storage, networks, operating systems) is rented from a cloud service provider and paid for on a per-use basis |
| | R-22 What are the categories (types) of Cloud depending on the role and control exercised by user and provider? |
| | R-23 In cloud environments the update, both software and hardware, is left to the: |

## 4 Conclusions

The objective was achieved; to design a validated instrument to measure CC competencies in teachers of higher education institutions, becoming a tool to answer the question:

How can we diagnose the level of CC competencies that teachers have in the context of Education 4.0?

This instrument was the result of the collaborative work of researchers from four institutions and used as a basis the collaborative work of the Industry 4.0 Node, made up of higher education institutions of the GEM with educational offerings focused on Industry 4.0, which highlights the usefulness and relevance of this type of collaborative networks.

The results show that the instrument to measure CC competencies is pertinent and presented internal consistency when piloted with different teachers specialized in Computer Systems Engineering. On the other hand, the expert judgment methodology was determinant to consolidate and improve the instrument to measure CC competencies, because the participants demonstrated an academic level and experience in the evaluation of instruments.

The instrument designed measures the seven competencies of one of the 15 Industry 4.0 technologies identified by the Industry 4.0 Node. It is relevant to note that there are other instruments that measure the use, adoption and readiness for migration in CC, however the present instrument focuses on measuring competencies in CC. As future work, it is suggested to design instruments that measure the competencies of the other 14 technologies, and to apply this instrument to the other institutions of this collaborative network and to professors of any institution that wants to measure CC competencies.

**Acknowledgments.** The authors would like to acknowledge the experts who collaborated in the design and evaluation of the instrument, as well as the financial support of Writing Lab, TecLabs, Tecnologico de Monterrey, Mexico, in the production of this work y debe decir: The authors would like to acknowledge the experts who collaborated in the design and evaluation of the instrument, as well as the financial support of Writing Lab, Institute for the Future of Education, Tecnologico de Monterrey, Mexico, in the production of this work.

## References

1. World Economic Forum: The future of jobs 2020. Report, World Economic Forum (2020)
2. Carvajal, J.H.: La Cuarta Revolución Industrial o Industria 4.0 y su Impacto en la Educación Superior en Ingeniería en Latinoamérica y el Caribe. In: 5th LACCEI International Multi-Conference for Engineering, Education, and Technology, pp. 19–21. Boca Raton Fl, United States (2017)
3. Gobierno del Estado de México: Fortalecimiento del currículum académico para atender las necesidades de la Industria 4.0. Technical report (2021)
4. Aristin, N.F., Budijanto, B., Taryana, D., Ruja, I.N.: 3D map of dry land use based aerial image as learning media in era of education 4.0. Int. J. Emerg. Technol. Learn. **15**, 171–179 (2020)
5. Hussin, A.A.: Education 4.0 made simple: ideas for teaching. Int. J. Educ. Lit. Stud. **6**, 92–98 (2018)
6. Ishak, R., Mansor, M.: The relationship between knowledge management and organizational learning with academic staff readiness for education 4.0. Eurasian J. Educ. Res. **20**, 169–184 (2020)

7. Kaeophanuek, S., Na-Songkhla, J., Nilsook, P.: A learning process model to enhance digital literacy using critical inquiry through digital storytelling (CIDST). Int. J. Emerg. Technol. Learn. **14**, 22–37 (2019)
8. Bujang, S.D.A., Selamat, A., Krejcar, O., Maresova, P., Nguyen, N.T.: Digital learning demand for future education 4.0—case studies at Malaysia Education Institutions. Informatics. **7**, 1–11 (2020)
9. EY: University of the future. Bringing Education 4.0 to life. EYGM, UK (2018)
10. Rodríguez-García, A.M., Martínez, N.: La competencia digital en la base de Scopus: un estudio de metaanálisis. Rev. Estud. Exp. En Educ. **2**, 15–24 (2018)
11. Ramirez-Montoya, M.S., Loaiza-Aguirre, M.I., Zúñiga-Ojeda, A., Portuguez-Castro, M.: Characterization of the teaching profile within the framework of education 4.0. Future Internet. **13**, 1–17 (2021)
12. Engen, B.K.: Understanding social and cultural aspects of teachers' digital competencies. Comunicar. **27**, 9–19 (2019)
13. Kirkpatrick, D., Barrie, S.: 21st Century Curriculum Project. Project brief, Wester Sydney (2017)
14. Shana, Z., Abu libdeh, E.: Cloud Computing issues for higher education: theory of acceptance model. Int. J. Emerg. Technol. Learn. **12**, 168–184 (2017)
15. Mell, P., Grance, T.: The NIST Definition of Cloud Computing. National Institute of Standards and Technology, Gaithersburg (2011)
16. Karim, F., Goodwin, D.R.: Using cloud computing in e-learning systems. Comput. Sci. **1**, 65–69 (2013)
17. Rojo, E.G.: Cómputo en las nubes, características y beneficios. Cuba y la nube. Universidad & Ciencia. **6**, 15–30 (2017)
18. Gallardo, D.I., Razón, J.P., León, N.: Comparative study between virtualization technologies: cloud computing and host-bases. Pist. Educ. **42**, 39–49 (2020)
19. Báez-Pérez, C.I., Clunie-Beaufond, C.E.: El modelo tecnológico para la implementación de un proceso de educación ubicua en un ambiente de computación en la nube móvil: Rev. UIS Ing. **19**, 77–88 (2020)
20. Bhardwaj, G.L., Garg, A., Gajpal, Y.: E-learning during COVID-19 outbreak: cloud computing adoption in Indian Public Universities. Comput. Mater. Contin. **66**, 2471–2492 (2021)
21. Bora, U.J., Ahmed, M.: E-learning using cloud computing. Int. J. Sci. Mod. Eng. **1**, 9–12 (2013)
22. Hussein, A., Haryani, N., Mat, Z.: Factors influencing cloud computing adoption in higher education institutions of least developed countries: evidence from Republic of Yemen. Appl. Sci. **10**, 1–27 (2020)
23. Montero, I., León, O.: Sistema de clasificación del método en los informes de investigación en Psicología. Int. J. Clin. Health Psychol. **5**, 115–127 (2005)
24. Asadi, Z., Abdekhoda, M., Nadrian, H.: Cloud computing services adoption among higher education faculties: development of a standardized questionnaire. Educ. Inf. Technol. **25**(1), 175–191 (2019). https://doi.org/10.1007/s10639-019-09932-0
25. Qasem, Y.A., Abdullah, R., Yaha, Y., Atana, R.: Continuance use of cloud computing in higher education institutions: a conceptual model. Appl. Sci. **10**(19), 6628 (2020)
26. Amron, M., Ibrahim, R., Bakar, N., Chuprat, S.: The validity and reliability evaluation of instruments for cloud computing acceptance study. In: 2020 6th International Conference on Information Management (ICIM), pp. 269–273 (2020)
27. Restrepo-Palacio, S., Cifuentes, Y.: Design and validation of an instrument for the evaluation of digital competence in Higher Education. Ensaio: Avaliação e Políticas Públicas em Educação **28**, 932–961 (2020)

28. Escobar-Pérez, J., Cuervo-Martínez, Á.: Validez de contenido y juicio de expertos: una aproximación a su utilización. Avances en medición **6**, 27–36 (2008)
29. Siegel, S., Castellan, N.J.: Estadística no paramétrica aplicada a las ciencias de la conducta. Trillas, México (1995)
30. Folgueiras-Bertomeu, P., Ramirez, C.: Elaboración de técnicas de recogida de información en diseños mixtos. Un ejemplo de estudio en apre. REIRE Rev. Innov. Recer. En. Educ. **10**, 64–78 (2017)

# "Speed-Dating" as a Learning Method in Online Synchronous Classes

Donovan Esqueda-Merino(✉), Diego Mondragón, Luis A. Calvillo-Corona, César A. Aldana-Pérez, and Jesús E. Chong-Quero

Escuela de Ingeniería y Ciencias, Tecnológico de Monterrey, Ave. Eugenio Garza Sada 2501, 64849 Monterrey, NL, Mexico
{donovan.esqueda,lcalvillo,caaldanap,jchong}@tec.mx, A01748979@itesm.mx

**Abstract.** Since COVID-19, many educational institutions have focused their attention towards remote digital synchronous learning. While this new kind of learning brings some advantages, it also brings new challenges like keeping the students focused and engaged in the courses being given. Through this paper we introduce a learning strategy based on some of the principles of speed-dating, a tool that has been explored in the entrepreneurship world for networking, in order to maintain the students' focus in the class activities and topics. The proposal was tested in a Process Automation course for Chemical and Biotechnology Engineers, which is usually not one of their preferred ones due to its complexity in relation to other courses. A framework for incorporating the activities in other courses is presented, along with preliminary quantitative and qualitative results to evaluate its efficacy.

**Keywords:** Higher education · Educational innovation · Professional Education · Learning methods · Gamification

## 1 Introduction

Due to the lockdowns implemented as a consequence of the Covid-19 pandemic, the teaching methods have been forced to evolve enormously, not only with the change from a face-to-face environment from the classroom to a virtual environment from home through a screen, but also essentially in the way of teaching. Despite efforts from universities and professors, such as the investment in educational software and the restructuring of the courses, the level of attention of the students is limited in comparison to a traditional lecture. For this reason, educators need to continuously propose ideas that can capture their attention.

From the beginning of the Covid-19 pandemic, students' learning has been affected due to various factors such as a decreased attention span, technology and internet connectivity problems, work overload, and inadequate support from instructors and colleagues [1]. However, the commitment of both students and teachers has remained during the


Published by Springer Nature Switzerland AG 2021
L. M. Camarinha-Matos et al. (Eds.): PRO-VE 2021, IFIP AICT 629, pp. 674–682, 2021.
https://doi.org/10.1007/978-3-030-85969-5_63

pandemic [2], which is the reason behind new learning methods compensating for some of the previously indicated factors. As an example, *Active Learning* is used by interwinding lecture time with questions or activities in which students participate in the acquisition of their own knowledge [3]. Moreover, *Gamification* [4] assists in this objective by attracting the students' attention by means of activities or games, in which badges, awards, achievements and/or markers are used for evaluation [5]. That is why several unusual implementation strategies have been adapted to be used appropriately and obtain the benefit expected of them (*e.g.* the scavengers hunt method). These methods have been effective in different environments, such as business teaching, which is why the present work is interested in the use of *Speed Dating* [6] as a case of Active Learning and Gamification.

With the development of new collaborative tools supported by the Internet and mobile computing, new organizational ways are emerging as a result of the challenges faced by the learning fields. For instance, the web provides a space for communities to practice and share their learnings after a training has been given [7]. In this sense, students working remotely are analogous to collaborative networks in certain aspects: autonomous entities distributed geographically, collaborating towards a common academic goal, with interactions supported by computer networks.

Thus, new perspectives have been established in educational programs to achieve innovative solutions that make the best use of virtual community connections and professional capacities [8, 9]. Lacking a correct implementation has contributed to students struggling in virtual classes to keep their focus, especially when the class is highly demanding, while collaborative work has turned mainly into meetings to define individual task planning for reaching a goal (e.g. a homework assignment). Within this virtual collaborative network context, a question arises: how can we promote real collaboration in an effort to keep students interested in the class?

This paper aims to present structured planning in the implementation of the active learning method based, on the speed dating model, with the purpose of improving the learning and teaching experience with a more strategic and useful approach for professors, in order to better capture the attention of students. The paper is presented as follows: the method is briefly presented in Sect. 2, Sect. 3 provides a case-study with details in the implementation as well as preliminary results based on that case-study, and Sect. 4 opens the discussion on the usefulness of the method.

## 2 Method

The learning method proposed here for online synchronous classes is based on a tool that has been widely used recently in the Entrepreneurship world: *Speed-dating*. In this context, it is used mainly to pitch ideas to investors by assigning them randomly to entrepreneurs for a couple of minutes to get to know each other. During these sessions, different pairs of entrepreneurs-investors alternate, which might lead to further collaborations whenever interest has been raised by any of the parties.

In the context of *online classes*, this method is used as an approach to compensate for the missing interaction between professors and students during traditional in-classroom classes, where the professor can make sure everyone is working on practical exercises.

Instead of that, several activities (hereby named "Speed-Dating Activities" or "SDA") were carried out in each class, where students were separated randomly into small sessions (i.e. Zoom's breakout rooms) so that they could work together. The professor would also switch between sessions to solve any questions related to the activities, whether students proactively called the professor, or the professor randomly visited the teams in the allocated time to validate comprehension.

Moreover, a *gamification* strategy was also combined so students would keep the interest in the activities. For this objective, special *tokens* were proposed so that students could earn depending on their faultlessness and their response time. While the ultimate goal is to have the right answer in order to get more points, a quicker response might foster a more active collaboration in order to get more points.

As expressed by [8], incentives in collaborative networks help to pro-actively engage participants. Thus, these *tokens* are recommended to be exchangeable for something that incentives the students. In this way, during the random sessions, students would motivate and help each other during the SDA with the understanding of the topics that were previously presented in class. Some practical recommendations regarding these tokens are:

- To avoid discouragement, make sure you supply enough tokens for everyone. For example, on every exercise, you could give the maximum number of tokens to the team sending the right answer first. Then give one less token to the next team with the right answer and so on. After all the right answers have been awarded tokens, consider giving some to those teams that had the right procedure but a wrong answer (e.g. due to a wrong sign).
- To reduce the number of people not working, keep teams small and allow students to leave out people who don't work (e.g. those that leave their computer connected even if they are not there or that don't participate).
- To reduce the disadvantage of slow internet connections: promote analytical thinking (so that activities require a good understanding of the topics and some time to develop them), request as evidence low-size files (such as pictures, text or PDF), and avoid that the students know beforehand the upcoming activities (*e.g.* by uploading the slides with the exercise before you present them).

In this way, an active collaboration within a small group of students occurs organically by exploiting the concept of *learnativity* [10], as long as at least two of the students in the team care about doing the activity properly. It is also important to keep teams small so that there is a lesser chance of any student being idle.

## 3 Case Study: Process Automation

The methodology previously described was tested during the August-December 2020 semester at Tecnológico de Monterrey. This course, aimed at undergraduate Chemical and Biotechnical Engineering students, introduces topics related to modeling and control of industrial processes, as well as the design, analysis and use of logic control strategies. A total of 25 students (out of 27 enrolled in the course) accepted to participate in this experimental study by correlating their grades to the SDA points.

As part of the overall learning strategy, students had to develop different activities throughout the semester including:

- 32 SDA, in random teams of maximum 3 students
- 14 exams, individually-graded
- 9 homework assignments, in teams of 3 (formed by the students during the first session)
- 1 individual homework assignment

The final grade was calculated considering 3 periods of evaluation: first and second period would have a 30% impact on the final grade, while the third term would have a 40% weight. In each term, exams would be worth 60% and assignments 40%.

The general instructions for the SDA were as follows: every session 9 teams would be created with Zoom's Breakout Rooms. During the sessions, specific instructions would be given regarding the specific SDA. Each team would work for a period of 10–20 min in order to earn so-called "Automaton Coins" (AC), which were assigned from 9–0 as described in Sect. 2. For most of the exercises, students would require between 10 to 20 min to complete the activity, although they could decide if they would send the answer right away or after the class ended, as long as the professor didn't start reviewing other students' results. This would give them a chance to finish even if they would earn less AC.

The SDA would be a collection of activities including hand-solved practical problems and software-based practices (see Table 1). Exams on their own would be both theoretical and practical, and related to the topics seen in class (with a few of them having similar exercises to the ones developed in the SDA or homework assignments). Exams took random questions from an exam bank, making it a unique experience for each individual. On their side, homework assignments required a certain level of research from the students in a way to reinforce the general learning.

**Table 1.** Activities carried out for the process automation course

| SDA | Homework Assignments |
|---|---|
| Introduction to Process Automation | |
| - Discuss characteristic parameters and variables of a fan<br>- Identify control-oriented variables of a fan and if it has feedback control<br>- Obtain transfer function from differential equations<br>- Solve Laplace transforms in Matlab<br>- Solve differential equations using Laplace Transform with Matlab<br>- ZPK form and pole-zero graph using Matlab of given systems | - Real-life applications of Automatic Process Control<br>- Examples of Open-loop and Closed-loop systems including game from SpaceX<br>- Infographic explaining specific case of partial-fraction expansion |

*(continued)*

**Table 1.** (*continued*)

| SDA | Homework Assignments |
|---|---|
| Dynamic Modeling of Processes | |
| - Reduce Transfer Function (TF) with Matlab<br>- Reduce TF with Block Diagram Algebra<br>- Mason's rule exercise (1 easy/1 medium/1 hard)<br>- Convert block diagram to signal-flow graph<br>- Find open-loop parameters from a first-order TF<br>- Obtain phase lag and lag time from practical example<br>- Get gain values from second-order system with time constraints<br>- Validate approximation of two TFs<br>- Obtain TF and response to step-input in mixed tank heater<br>- Simulate response of non-interacting tanks in Simulink<br>- Find block diagram and TF of interacting tanks | - Control-oriented block diagrams found in research article<br>- Model's parameter identification with Matlab and Simulink<br>- Identify stability conditions of specific exercises |
| Continuously modulated controllers | |
| - Obtain Padés approximation for systems with dead-time<br>- Routh-Hurwitz criterion exercise<br>- Find a range for gain K to validate stability of a system<br>- Obtain frequency of oscillation to make a system marginally stable<br>- Determine PID-controller parameters via oscillation method | - Research PID-related tuning strategies in articles |
| Batch sequences | |
| - Understand logic gates with logic.ly<br>- Research differences between XOR, XNOR, OR, NOR<br>- Validate De Morgan's Theorems with logic.ly<br>- Find minterms and maxterms of a function<br>- Obtain function and diagram from truth table<br>- Simplify function using Karnaugh maps<br>- Obtain a truth table from minterms, draw logic circuits and simplify using only NAND gates | - Design logic system and validate with Simulink<br>- Use TinkerCAD to display numbers in 7-segment display |
| Logic Control Systems | |
| - Simulate pneumatic circuit in FluidSim and record it | - Virtual commissioning with Factory IO and WinSPS |

Through these activities (see Figs. 1 and 2), students used different software packages from their own homes (i.e. Factory IO, Matlab Simulink, FluidSim, TinkerCAD), and they even watched live the remote operation of a laboratory with Programmable Logic Controllers (PLCs). Concepts of Industry 4.0 can be important enablers of collaborative networks [11] and are highly valued by both students and industrial partners [12]. This gives students a sense of a practical approach in those activities as it would happen in a real working environment. Additionally, the overall learning experience was complemented with programming examples, illustrative videos, quizzes, and a conference from an automation expert in the beer industry.

**Fig. 1.** Remote laboratory setup consisting of cylinders being controlled by PLCs. Remote desktop software and a webcam allowed to execute the code in real-time.

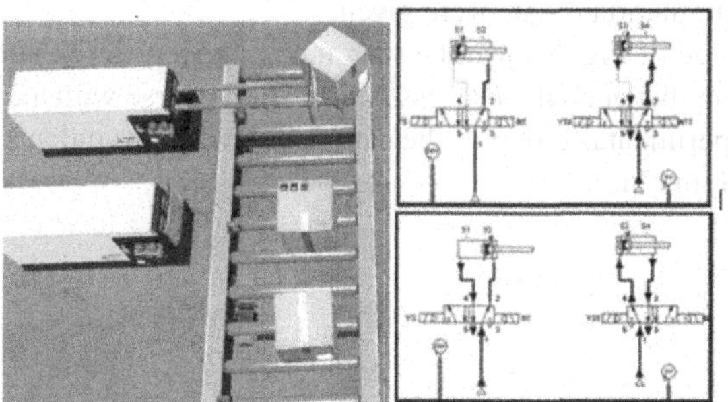

**Fig. 2.** Specialized software complemented the learning experience.

### 3.1 Qualitative Results

In order to have the Voice-of-the-Students represented in decision-making at different levels, the University does an online survey every semester in which professors and certain school managers are evaluated by students in an anonymous manner. While not mandatory, students are very much encouraged to do it. This online survey happens at two moments during the semester: during the first-term evaluations, and about two months later, before the final-term evaluations.

These surveys ask 12 questions related to aspects such as the methodology of the class, commitment of the professor, professor-student interactions, challenge of the course, and it even calculates the Net Promoter Score (NPS) of the professor. Quoting [13], NPS "is a unique metric that quantifies the response to a single direct survey question: How likely are you to recommend this service?" This question measures a customers' satisfaction based on experiences, and provides valuable feedback to improve existing products and services offered by a company.

Professors can check on the results some weeks after the surveys have been collected. In this way, the comments that were related to the methodology were analyzed: during the first-term, several students indicated the class was well-planned with an encouragement to teamwork, yet they considered the time for the SDA was leaving out more detailed explanations of the topics (e.g. "I think the number of activities is excessive, which makes the explanations very quick sometimes").

For the final survey, all comments made in relation to the SDA were positive, and the NPS of the professor increased from 8.35 (calculated with 17 opinions, first-term) to 9.04 (including 26 opinions, end of semester). Students kept on pointing out that the classes were very dynamic and organized, but now they indicated that the constant evaluations made the topics more entertaining and easier to understand.

### 3.2 Quantitative Results

For this part, an analysis between the AC awarded to each student and their overall grade was made. In Fig. 3 (left side) we can see the relationship between these grades in the experimental group. It is important to state that this grade was before any additional points due to accumulation of AC were given.

On the right side of Fig. 3 it can be seen a comparison of the normal distributions of grades happening between the Process Automation course with a control group (CG, in red) and an experimental group of the same class with 14 students, not having SDA implemented (EG, in blue).

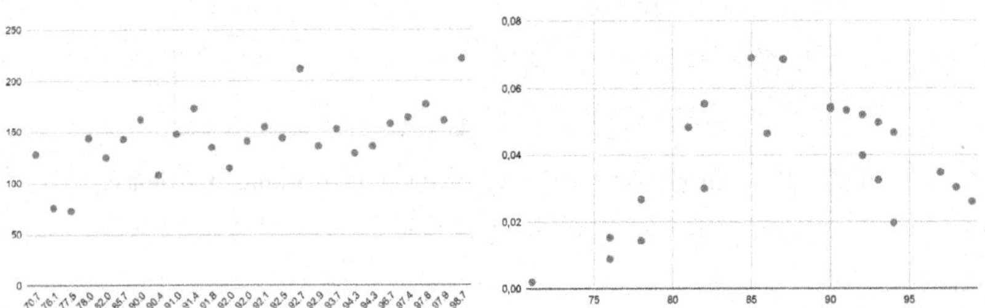


**Fig. 3.** Left) Horizontal axis: final grade of the students in the experimental group on a scale from 0 to 100. Vertical axis: AC points awarded to each student. As 32 activities were proposed, the maximum number of AC a student could get was 288. Right) Gaussian distribution of grades between the CG (red) and the EG (blue). (Color figure online)

From these results, it can be noticed that there seems to be a potential correlation between the final grade and the AC awarded throughout the semesters' activities within the experimental group, even if there are some exceptions (which might be associated with regular teamwork assignments). Moreover, it can be appreciated that some grades shift towards higher values in the experimental group, which could potentially relate to a higher engagement in the class.

## 4 Conclusions and Discussion

As the lockdown context has forced educators to find new ways to foster participation, teamwork and understanding of the topics, in contrast to traditional oral lectures, this methodology presents an approach to promote student's engagement and active participation of collaborative networks of students, inspired by the entrepreneurship activity of Speed-Dating.

While the concept was only applied in a single class and can't be conclusive, both qualitative and quantitative results showed a trend into students having a benefit by this kind of interaction: the grade of the students was higher than a regular group of the same class in the digital format, and also, once they got used to the methodology, they expressed it to be a highly dynamic class in which collaboration was promoted.

The results align to the research question aiming to increase the engagement of the students. The fact that the experiment was done in a complex class to the students just contributed to a rather optimistic outlook on the approach. Particularly, the regular exams and homework assignments allowed us to validate the learning outcome for this class: an understanding of industrial process regulation, as well as the skill to apply basic and advanced control strategies to solve problems in industrial process automation and logic control problems.

The next steps are to test this concept in other engineering classes, define roles for the students during the activities with specific tasks, and finally evaluate the methodology in face-to-face classes to see if it still provides a benefit for them.

**Acknowledgments.** The authors would like to acknowledge the financial support of Writing Lab, Institute for the Future of Education, Tecnologico de Monterrey, Mexico, in the production of this work. Additionally, the authors would like to acknowledge the financial support of NOVUS Grant with PEP No. 19016, *TecLabs, Tecnológico de Monterrey* in the production of this work. Finally, we would also like to thank the students who willingly participated in this study.

## References

1. Husseln, E., Daoud, S., Alrabaiah, H., Badawi, R.: Exploring undergraduate students' attitudes towards emergency online learning during COVID-19: a case from the UAE. Child. Youth Serv. Rev. **119**, 105699 (2020)
2. van Braak, M., van de Pol, J., Poorthuls, A.M.G., Mainhard, T.: A micro-perspective on students' behavioral engagement in the context of teachers' instructional support during seat-work: Sources of variability and the role of teacher adaptive support. Contemp. Educ. Psychol. **64**, 101928 (2021)
3. Felder, R.M., Brent, R.: Active learning: an introduction. ASQ High. Educ. Brief **2**(4), 1–5 (2009)

4. Escamilla, J., et al.: EduTrends gamification. Obs. Educ. Innov. 1–36 (2016)
5. Zepeda, J.S., Abascal, M.D.R., Ornelas, E.: Integración de gamificación y aprendizaje activo en el aula. Ra Ximhai **12**(6), 315–325 (2016)
6. Jowitt, S.M.: Speed dating for entrepreneurship–rapid fire pitching and adaptation of business models. Experiential Entrepreneurship Exercises J. **1**(3), (2015)
7. Gârlaşu, D., Dumitrache, I., Stanescu, A.M.: A new approach for e-learning in collaborative networks. In: Working Conference on Virtual Enterprises, pp. 539–546 (2005)
8. Camarinha-Matos, L.M., Afsarmanesh, H.: Collaborative networks. In: Wang, K., Kovacs, G.L., Wozny, M., Fang, M. (eds.) PROLAMAT 2006. IIFIP, vol. 207, pp. 26–40. Springer, Boston (2006). https://doi.org/10.1007/0-387-34403-9_4
9. Díaz-Gibson, J., Civís-Zaragoza, M., Guàrdia-Olmos, J.: Strengthening education through collaborative networks: leading the cultural change. School Leadersh. Manage. **34**(2), 179–200 (2014)
10. Hodgins, W.: Learnativity: into the future. In: The ASTD e-Learning Handbook, pp. 38–57 (2002)
11. Camarinha-Matos, L.M., Fornasiero, R., Afsarmanesh, H.: Collaborative networks as a core enabler of industry 4.0. In: Camarinha-Matos, L.M., Afsarmanesh, H., Fornasiero, R. (eds.) PRO-VE 2017. IAICT, vol. 506, pp. 3–17. Springer, Cham (2017). https://doi.org/10.1007/978-3-319-65151-4_1
12. Villagomez, L.E., et al.: Laboratory of intelligent operational decisions: a proposal for learning digital and smart manufacturing concepts. In: Proceedings of 2019 IEEE 11th International Conference on Engineering Education ICEED 2019, pp. 153–158 (2019). https://doi.org/10.1109/ICEED47294.2019.8994936
13. Hamilton, D.F., et al.: Assessing treatment outcomes using a single question: the net promoter score. Bone Joint J. **9**(5), 622–628 (2014)

# A Gamified HMI as a Response for Implementing a Smart-Sustainable University Campus

Juana Isabel Méndez[1(✉)], Pedro Ponce[1], Therese Peffer[2], Alan Meier[3], and Arturo Molina[1]

[1] School of Engineering and Sciences, Tecnologico de Monterrey, México City, México
A01165549@itesm.mx, {pedro.ponce,armolina}@tec.mx

[2] Institute for Energy and Environment, University of California, Berkeley, CA 94720, USA
tpeffer@berkeley.edu

[3] Energy and Efficiency Institute, University of California, Davis, CA 95616, USA
akmeier@ucdavis.edu

**Abstract.** Universities need to explore drastic changes regarding their facilities to be more inclusive and sustainable. Those changes must move forward to a Smart university campus. A Smart University Campus involves Smart City's concept because different socio-cultural aspects in the community and services like health care, public safety, mobility, education, transportation, and energy are integrated into the Campus. For instance, 25% of the total electric consumption comes from the cooling in an educational facility. Besides, energy awareness campaigns reach 5% to 15% energy cost savings. Nevertheless, the end-users do not engage in those applications due to multiple platform requirements and the generalization of a conventional user; thus, energy awareness is not reached. Knowing the type of user enhances gamification strategies that engage them in energy reduction activities without being obtrusive. Through collaborative networks, the university members socially interact with others, strengths their relationships, and improve their skills toward saving energy. Hence, this paper proposes a case study located at the Tecnologico de Monterrey, Mexico City Campus and analyzes six different scenarios to understand the energy impacts of using different cooling values on thermostats during classes. Dividing these services into a three-level gamified interface: Smart building, Smart Community, and Smart Campus to promote energy awareness to reduce electrical consumption. Besides, if the reference temperature is set correctly, a terminal comfort is achieved, the students and professors could increment their work performance. This gamified interface runs a feed-forward Artificial Neural Network (ANN) as a decision-making system that supports the proposed structure.

**Keywords:** Smart city · Smart campus · Gamification · Energy awareness · Personality traits


Published by Springer Nature Switzerland AG 2021
L. M. Camarinha-Matos et al. (Eds.): PRO-VE 2021, IFIP AICT 629, pp. 683–691, 2021.
https://doi.org/10.1007/978-3-030-85969-5_64

## 1 Introduction

The electricity end-user sector is often divided into the residential, commercial, and public, transport, industrial, and agricultural sectors. According to the last record in SENER, in 2019, the Mexican electricity consumption were about 284 billion kWh, with 22.7%, 12.3%, 0.4%, 60%, and 4.6% respectively [16]. Therefore, it is a challenge to reduce electrical consumption without being invasive or losing quality of life. Moreover, citizens represent the linkage, the main actor, and the sensor to the city, as they actively interact with it. Consequently, users' interaction plays a primary role in understanding and knowing the city to reduce electrical consumption. However, teaching them how to reduce electrical consumption represents a challenge as sometimes they have other interests rather than reducing their consumption. In that regard, the education offered, for instance, in a university, seems the ideal place, to begin with, the interaction between the user and the city to become energy awareness.

Innovative education considers an interactive, collaborative, and visual model to continually engage students and allow teachers to adapt to new students' skills [7]. Therefore, it requires design, development, implementation, and active use of innovative systems, technologies, teaching, and learning strategies [19]. Besides, smart education is a crucial element in smart city development [9]. In that sense, universities as Tecnologico de Monterrey support smart education through novel learning methods, including open innovation laboratories for knowledge transference [12], for instance, for electrical energy education [15]. 25% of the total electric consumption comes from cooling in an educational facility [7]. Energy awareness campaigns promote electrical energy reduction, and it can reach from 5% to 15% of energy cost savings with scarce to no investment [4, 13, 18]. Therefore, incorporating gamification techniques to target energy reduction as a goal is not as complicated as it may seem. For example, providing an HMI that monitors the cooling setpoint in classrooms can save energy. According to [3], by increasing 1 °C the thermostat during summer periods, 6% of the electricity consumed can be saved. In addition, implementing tailored gamification strategies in Human Machine-Interfaces (HMI) can engage end-users to reduce energy consumption by considering their personality traits [14].

Moreover, collaborative networks consider socio-cultural people, services, facilities, urban planning, or governance systems, for instance, in smart cities [2, 9, 20]. Thus, this paper conceptualizes a Smart Campus as a Smart City. The Tecnologico de Monterrey, Mexico City Campus was employed as a case study.

## 2 Methodology

The smart building model considered six cases for a typical classroom during cooling periods to measure the impact of increasing the cooling setpoint starting from 22 °C and increase a 0.5 °C for each case, ending with 24.5 °C for the sixth case. Each classroom considered a cooling setback of 27 °C, 20 °C for the heating setpoint, and 12.8 °C for the heating setback. This proposal aims to sensibilize the students the importance of well managing the cooling setpoint. Other considerations for the energy model included Mexico City's weather file, the construction materials, the classroom schedule and loads, and the setpoint and setback for cooling and heating. As a result, the energy model gave the total cooling kWh per case. Ladybug Tools for Grasshopper were used for the energy simulation [11]. The ANN model considered for the input values the month, day, hour, and setpoint to predict the kWh usage for that specific conditions. Besides, this proposal considered five personality traits obtained in a worldwide database by [1]. Then, it was related to the eight-core drives proposed by Chou [5] and updated with energy game elements by Ponce et al. [14]. The database was filtered only to consider the Mexican responses. Thus, the ANN model used as input values the gender, age, and personality trait to predict which core drive should consider the HMI proposal. Hence, a two-layer feed-forward ANN decision-making system was modeled using the Neural Network Pattern Recognition from MATLAB. Simulink software was used to implement a dashboard prototype that analyzed the results from the ANN.

## 3 Proposed Framework

Figure 1 displays the proposed framework. This framework proposes three steps per integration: Smart building integration, smart community integration, and smart campus integration. In addition, within each integration, three stages are proposed: knowledge base, decision system, and evaluation stage.

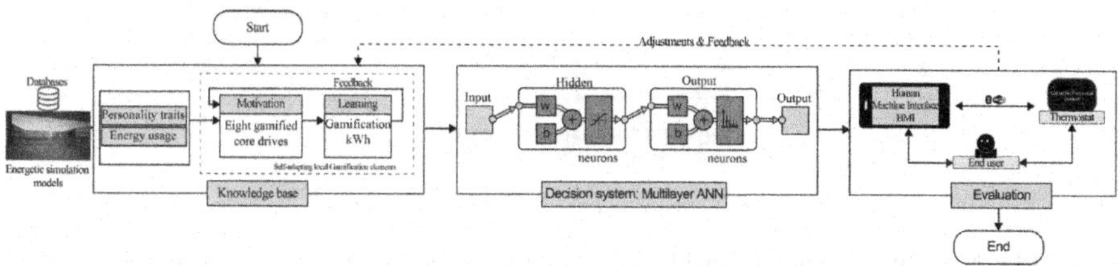


Fig. 1. Proposed framework.

### 3.1 Knowledge Base Stage

Six cases were analyzed using the same classroom in terms of location, orientation, construction material, schedules, loads, heating setpoint/setback, and cooling setback. To recreate the interaction in a building and analyze the different changes based on the setpoint decisions, Fig. 2. depicts the cooling setpoint considered for each case. Besides, the legend shows the total kWh consumption by case and obtained from the energetic model. Table 1 presents the eight-core gamification drives, their associated personality traits, and game elements considered in this paper [5, 14]. The database used to relate the personality traits with the core drives was obtained from [1]. This database had the answers per country, gender, age, and personality traits; thus, the observations were filtered to select Mexico. Openness personalities are open to learning new things. Conscientious personalities are rule followers, competitive, and self-discipline. Extraversion personalities are optimistic, assertive, and appreciate social interactions. Agreeable personalities are sympathetic, tolerant, and cooperative. Neuroticism personalities are impulsive, stressful, and bad-tempered [10, 14].

## 3.2 ANN Decision System Stage

A two-layer feed-forward ANN decision-making system was modeled to predict the kWh consumption depending on the cooling setpoint proposed in Fig. 2. In addition, the gamified core drive was required for the interface design depending on age and gender, and personality traits of the end-user proposed in Table 1. Based on the total kWh consumption by case, the setpoint/setback from the 17105 observations was used to feed the ANN; the input values for the kWh prediction were the month, day, hour, and setpoint; whereas the output value was the kWh consumption by observation. For the case of the type of gamified proposal, 700 observations were used. The input values were the gender, age, and personality traits; the output values were each core drive. For the particular case of Mexico, all the respondents had similarities in the core drives one, three, four, five, and seven. However, core drives three, six, and eight had diverse answers, meaning that some respondents required core drive three, while others core drive six or eight. The ANNs used a two-layer feed-forward network with 100 neurons in its hidden layer and used a hyperbolic tangent sigmoid transfer function. Finally, the ANN was exported into Simulink to design a dashboard prototype.

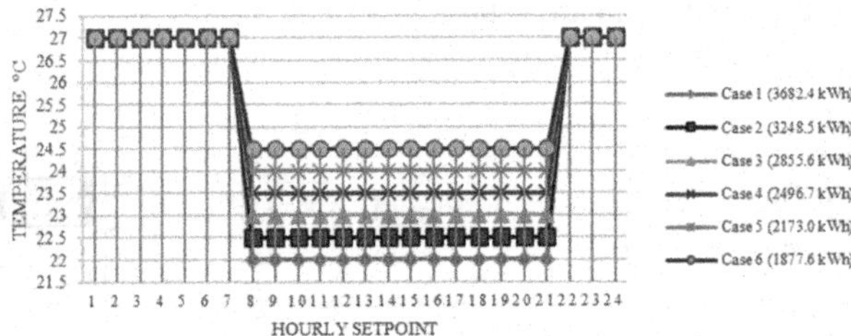


**Fig. 2.** Cooling setpoint considered for each case and its total kWh consumption.

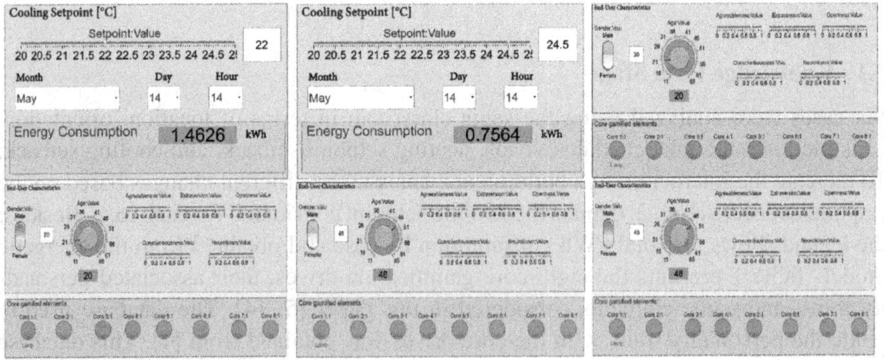


**Fig. 3.** Dashboard prototype.

### 3.3 Evaluation Stage

Figure 3 displays a dashboard prototype programmed using Simulink/MATLAB that the students and professors can access. They can select the cooling setpoint, month, day, and hour to know the energy consumption at this specific time. Besides, depending on the gender, age, and personality traits, the core drive is activated with a green light to determine the gamification elements needed to propose the HMI interface.

**Table 1.** Eight core drives, their associated personality traits, and gamification elements.

| Core drive | Personality trait | Gamification element |
|---|---|---|
| 1. Epic meaning and calling | Extraversion, Agreeableness, Conscientiousness, Openness | Narrative, elitism, beginners lick, higher meaning, co-creator |
| 2. Development and accomplishment | Conscientiousness | Offers, coupons, bill discounts, challenges, levels, badges, points, leaderboard, progress bar |
| 3. Empowerment of creativity and feedback | Extraversion, Neuroticism, Openness | Notifications, messages, tips, real-time control |
| 4. Ownership and possession | Extraversion, Agreeableness, Neuroticism, Openness | Dashboard, statistics, collection set, learning curve, monitoring, degree of control, recruitment |
| 5. Social influence and relatedness | Extraversion, Agreeableness, Conscientiousness, Openness, Neuroticism | Energy community, collaboration, control over peers, social comparison, competition, mentorship |
| 6. Scarcity and patience | Neuroticism | Prize pacing, appointment dynamics |
| 7. Unpredictability and curiosity | Extraversion, Neuroticism, Openness | Mini quests, visual storytelling, rolling rewards, random rewards |
| 8. Loss and avoidance | Neuroticism | Progress loss, evanescence opportunity |

## 4 Results

Figure 4 shows a three-level HMI considering a setpoint of 22 °C during cooling periods. Thus, gamified core drives one, two, four, six, and eight are displayed on an online set of stimuli based on rewards, challenges, and a dashboard to display how much electricity is wasting the building. Figure 4 (a) displays the interface for the classroom considering the professor's perspective interface. Therefore, following the evaluation subsection, this type of user is a 48 years old male with higher agreeableness and openness personality traits and lower extraversion, conscientiousness, and neuroticism personality traits. In addition, this interface requires taking into account core drives one, three, four, five, and seven; thus, it emphasizes the community and coOllaborative networks, displaying messages of the benefits of increasing the thermostat setpoints and gives some tips on improving energy savings.

Figure 4 (b) shows the interfaces from the students' perspective. This student is a 20 years old female with higher agreeableness and extraversion personality traits and lower openness, conscientiousness, and neuroticism personality traits. In addition, this interface requires the six and eight-core drive; thus, the interface displays specific messages that suggest progress loss, evanescence opportunities, and prize pacing as a motivation for this user type to accept and reduce energy consumption. The teacher proposes the setpoint increase, and the student receives the option to accept or decline the proposal. Figure 4 (c) displays the smart community interface as a collaborative network where members can interact with others and visualize which building wins to promote competitions and challenges to motivate each team to reduce energy. Finally, Fig. 4 (d) displays the Smart Campus services and displays the winning community.

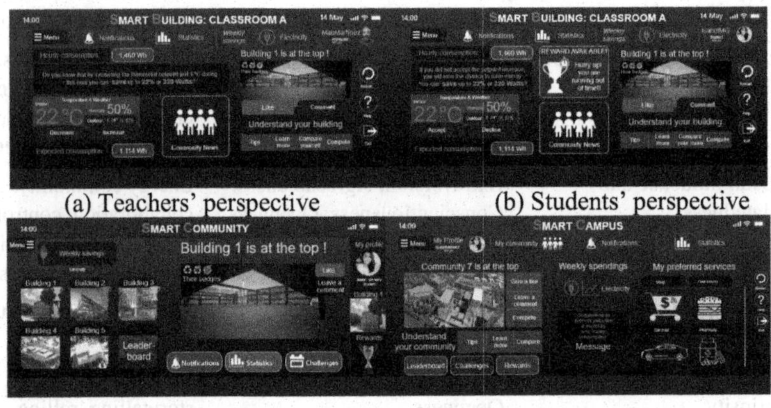


(a) Teachers' perspective (b) Students' perspective

(a) Smart community HMI (b) Smart Campus HMI

**Fig. 4.** Three-level interface proposal for the Smart Campus: (a) Smart Building from the teacher's perspective, (b) student's perspective, (c) Smart Community, and (d) Smart Campus.

## 5 Discussion

The literature shows gamification approaches within a smart city context, including using multiple platforms or applications to promote energy consciousness. However, these approaches do not consider end-users types and often consider typical users or generic users. Thus, users do not engage and use the interfaces because there are complex to use at the same time these multiple applications.

As a university involves different types of collaborative networks, users with different socio-cultural aspects represent a challenge in reducing energy; however, providing a gamification structure could allow all the members to reduce energy reduction strategies. The smart community structure is grouped into faculties by educational level (high school and university), administrative and business areas, cultural buildings, and research facilities. Besides, the management area has the credentials to determine which type of information is displayed to other community members and propose any change and share their tips on saving more energy or improving the quality of life at Campus. An example is sending tips or messages to the end-users and suggesting that increasing the thermostat's setpoint during cooling periods can help the Campus reduce electrical consumption. Besides, all the members can share their tips for saving energy or even build an energy community. Therefore, an achievable goal is to reduce electrical consumption by accepting changes on the setpoint that does not affect the community.

As the Mexican responses coincided with epic meaning and calling, empowerment of creativity and feedback, ownership and possession, social influence and relatedness, unpredictability, and curiosity, any of these drives can be proposed for the HMI. Then, specific types of Mexicans had other personality traits that conveyed the development and accomplishment, scarcity and patience, and loss and avoidance. For instance, the interface can consider using progress loss or appointment dynamics to engage the user in reducing energy consumption. The gamification strategy integrates all the community involved in each building through social sharing activities or group challenges, so the community is motivated to reduce energy consumption. Besides, through the gamified HMIs and big data analytics, energy behavior patterns can be identified, tracked, and forecasted energy behavior patterns to promote energy reductions [8, 17]. However, behavioral adjustment, physiological adaption, and psychological dimensions of thermal adaptation intervene during these group decisions [6].

## 6 Conclusion

The six cases considered the occupied periods in a classroom from 8 am to 9 pm; therefore, students and academics can collaborate in bringing new ideas upon saving electrical energy during cooling periods. A significant determinant to reduce energy consumption during summer periods is the collaboration between students and professors. Collaboration promotes social interaction, strengthens relationships, and improves skills. For instance, during cooling periods, the thermostat setpoints in classrooms ranged from 22 °C to 24.5 °C. There was a 50% of savings from adjusting the thermostat setpoint from 22 °C to 24.5 °C. Therefore, the cooling setpoint in a classroom should be at least 22 °C or above. This paper proposes implementing a gamification structure in three levels through a two-layer feed-forward ANN decision system to promote energy awareness in university students. Thus, the energy model was simulated to propose gamification strategies based on the cooling setpoints. The proposal relies on using a single HMI to access three levels of the smart Campus, access the classroom and building, and the community and the Campus. This proposal aims to profile and know each building's energy patterns and the interaction of the buildings in the community and the whole Campus to deploy an application that improves the quality of life.

**Acknowledgments.** This research project is supported by Tecnologico de Monterrey and CITRIS under the collaboration ITESM-CITRIS Smart thermostat, deep learning, and gamification project (https://citris-uc.org/2019-itesm-seed-funding/).

## References

1. Automoto automoto/big-five-data (2021)
2. Ben Yahia, N., Eljaoued, W., Bellamine Ben Saoud, N., Colomo-Palacios, R.: Towards sustainable collaborative networks for smart cities co-governance. Int. J. Inf. Manage. **56**, 102037 (2021). https://doi.org/10.1016/j.ijinfomgt.2019.11.005
3. Bureau of Energy Efficiency Energy Conservation in Building Space Cooling through recommended optimum temperature setting (2018)
4. Capehart, B.L., Kennedy, W.J., Turner, W.C.: Guide to Energy Management. Fairmont Press, Lilburn (2012)
5. Chou, Y.: Actionable Gamification Beyond Points, Badges, and Leaderboards. CreateSpace Independent Publishing Platform, Scotts Valley (2015)
6. de Dear, R.J., Brager, G.S.: Developing an adaptive model of thermal comfort and preference. ASHRAE Trans. **104**(1), 145–167 (1998)
7. Energy Star 10. Facility Type: K–12 Schools. In: Energy Star (2006). https://www.energystar.gov/sites/default/files/buildings/tools/EPA_BUM_CH10_Schools.pdf
8. Giest, S.: Big data analytics for mitigating carbon emissions in smart cities: opportunities and challenges. Eur. Plan. Stud. **25**, 941–957 (2017). https://doi.org/10.1080/09654313.2017.1294149
9. Glasco, J.: Smart Education for Smart Cities: Visual, Collaborative & Interactive (2019). https://hub.beesmart.city/en/solutions/smart-people/smart-education/viewsonic-smart-education-for-smart-cities. Accessed 28 Nov 2020
10. John, O.P., Srivastava, S.: The big five trait taxonomy: history, measurement, and theoretical perspectives. In: Handbook of personality: Theory and research, 2nd ed. Guilford Press, New York, pp. 102–138 (1999)
11. Ladybug Tools Ladybug Tools. https://www.ladybug.tools/. Accessed 2 May 2021
12. Miranda, J., et al.: Open innovation laboratory for rapid realization of sensing, smart and sustainable products (S3 Products) for higher education. **11**(7), 1215–1221 (2017)
13. Paone, A., Bacher, J.-P.: The impact of building occupant behavior on energy efficiency and methods to influence it: a review of the state of the art. Energies **11**, 953 (2018). https://doi.org/10.3390/en11040953
14. Ponce, P., Meier, A., Mendez, J., Peffer, T., Molina, A., Mata, O.: Tailored gamification and serious game framework based on fuzzy logic for saving energy in smart thermostats. J. Cleaner Prod. 121167 (2020). https://doi.org/10.1016/j.jclepro.2020.121167
15. Ponce, P., Polasko, K., Molina, A.: Open innovation laboratory in electrical energy education based on the knowledge economy. Int. J. Electr. Eng. Educ. 002072091982971 (2019). https://doi.org/10.1177/0020720919829711
16. Secretaría de Energía SENER, Sistema de Información Energética, Electricidad. In: Sistema de Información Energética (2020). https://sie.energia.gob.mx/bdiController.do?action=cuadro&subAction=applyOptions. Accessed 15 Jun 2021
17. Tamym, L., Benyoucef, L., Nait Sidi Moh, A., El Ouadghiri, M.D.: A big data based architecture for collaborative networks: supply chains mixed-network. Comput. Commun. **175**, 102–111 (2021). https://doi.org/10.1016/j.comcom.2021.05.008
18. Turner, W.C., Doty, S.: Energy Management Handbook. Fairmont Press, Lilburn (2013)

19. Uskov, V.L., Howlett, R.J., Jain, L.C.: Smart Education and e-Learning 2020. Springer, Singapore (2020). https://doi.org/10.1007/978-981-15-5584-8
20. Wang, S., Wang, J., Wei, C., Wang, X., Fan, F.: Collaborative innovation efficiency: from within cities to between cities—empirical analysis based on innovative cities in China. Growth Change Grow 12504 (2021). https://doi.org/10.1111/grow.12504

# Education 4.0 Reference Framework for the Design of Teaching-Learning Systems: Two Case Studies Involving Collaborative Networks and Open Innovation

Jhonattan Miranda(✉), Maria Soledad Ramírez-Montoya, and Arturo Molina

School of Engineering and Sciences, Tecnologico de Monterrey, Mexico City, Mexico
{jhonattan.miranda,solramirez,armolina}@tec.mx

**Abstract.** Collaborative networks and open innovation have high potential as co-drivers of value creation for many production and service sectors such as education. In higher education, it is increasingly frequent to observe universities implementing teaching-learning systems with collaborative processes supported by 4.0 technologies. Moreover, various pedagogical procedures, research activities, and co-development projects have complemented these types of collaborative processes, which today are considered desirable to be carried out within Education 4.0. In this paper, the authors propose a reference framework for designing new teaching-learning systems using the concept and vision of Education 4.0. The proposed reference framework considers key enablers of Education 4.0 and three dimensions to analyse and evaluate decisions made: (i) Technological, (ii) Pedagogical, and (iii) Organisational. Finally, two case studies involving collaborative networks and open innovation illustrate how the proposed reference framework is used.

**Keyword:** Collaborative network · Open innovation · Higher education · Educational innovation · Education 4.0

## 1 Introduction

Nowadays, technological advancement due to the capabilities and capacities of 4.0 technologies (connectivity, digitalisation, virtualisation, smartification, datafication, among others) has allowed practically all the productive and service sectors to improve their processes, leverage resources, and even grow and expand to other regions [1]. As a result, 4.0 technologies have played a very relevant role to promote and improve collaboration processes, internally in organisations and externally, in the exponential formation of Collaborative Networks (CNs) [2]. In higher education, implementing strategies based on collaborative processes has been increasingly frequent since these allow improving teaching-learning processes that promote the participation of academicians and students in collaborative environments. Moreover, these strategies put them in real scenarios that


Published by Springer Nature Switzerland AG 2021
L. M. Camarinha-Matos et al. (Eds.): PRO-VE 2021, IFIP AICT 629, pp. 692–701, 2021.
https://doi.org/10.1007/978-3-030-85969-5_65

allow them to work on joint projects to propose solutions to current challenges and problems. Currently, models such as the triple helix (involving the participation of academia, industry, and government) and the quadruple helix that adds the participation of society (e.g., users, consumers, citizens, workers) have been implemented to support these dynamics [3].

In higher education, collaboration is essential to provide adequate active learning environments, activities, and resources for the training and development of the core competencies necessary for the profile of the 21st-century student. In this context, it is necessary to implement new teaching-learning systems that stimulate collaboration and complement their activities using 4.0 technologies, innovative learning processes, and adequate infrastructure. In education, these pedagogical procedures, collaborative activities, and 4.0 technologies are known today as Education 4.0.

Currently, various design approaches focused on innovative educational systems within the Education 4.0 context consider not only the instructional and didactic aspects but also the psychological, motivational, and engagement ones [4]. In addition, approaches for the instructional design of modules meeting the requirements of Education 4.0 exist [5]. Other design approaches take up the specific design of products and tools for learning and infrastructure design for suitable teaching-learning environments. These approaches separately address the product, processes, and infrastructure development in education and are not conceived in an integrated approach. This work proposes an integrated reference framework employing the Education 4.0 vision and concept in the design of teaching-learning systems.

The rest of this paper is structured as follows: Sect. 2 presents the concept of Education 4.0 in higher education and its four key enablers. Section 3 shows the current relevance of collaborative networks applying open innovation strategies. Section 4 presents the proposed reference framework. Section 5 presents two case studies. Finally, the conclusions and future work are presented in Sect. 6.

## 2 Education 4.0 in Higher Education

Education 4.0 is a relatively new concept recently approached by different authors and implemented in various contexts in higher education. This concept arises from the relationship between 4.0 technologies particular to the Fourth Industrial Revolution and the Education sector. Therefore, the use of current and emerging technologies for pedagogical purposes is known today as Education 4.0. However, other authors have been more specific with this concept, referring to Education 4.0 exclusively as developing necessary competencies in engineering education for Industry 4.0 [6]. Recently, the World Economic Forum developed a framework for Education 4.0 based on critical shifts in learning content, development of critical skills and competencies, and experiences that redefine quality learning in the new economy [7]. Recently, the combination of heutagogy, peeragogy, and cybergogy approaches has emerged under Education 4.0 [8].

This work follows the concept of Education 4.0 as described in the following reference:

*"Education 4.0 is the period in which the education sector takes advantage of emerging ICTs to improve pedagogical processes that are complemented by new learning methods and innovative didactic and management tools, as well as the smart and sustainable infrastructure used during current teaching-learning processes for the training and development of key competencies in today's students"* [8].

Therefore, identifying the key enablers to achieve the Education 4.0 vision is necessary to guide educators during the teaching-learning processes. Four categories of key enablers are used during the design and implementation of today's teaching-learning systems: (i) Identifying crucial soft and hard competencies necessary to be developed by today's students; (ii) Incorporating new learning methods in educational programs with different modalities for information transfer and teaching-learning methods; (iii) Implementing current and emerging ICTs considering technology-based solutions and current tools and platforms, and (iv) Employing innovative infrastructure (architecture, facilities, services, and platforms) to improve learning processes at two levels, namely, the classroom/home level and the institutional level. These enablers then allow new teaching-learning systems to emerge under the vision of Education 4.0.

## 3 Collaborative Networks Applying Open Innovation Strategies

Organisations have increasingly adopted collaborative processes from different sectors as part of their continuous improvement, growth, and expansion activities. Nowadays, thanks to technological advancement and the use of 4.0 technologies, the implementation of these activities have grown exponentially. They have led to new tools and best practices. They have also facilitated creating links so key entities and actors can collaborate from different productive-service sectors at local, regional, and international levels [9]. In addition, the global health emergency of 2020–2021 has dramatically increased the implementation of collaborative platforms and accelerated the digital transformation of many organisations and academic institutions [10]. This has opened new opportunities for distance collaboration on synchronous and asynchronous activities. These current dynamics make collaborative-based processes accessible and flexible between different actors [11].

Consequently, encouraged organisations from all sectors (academia, government, industry, and citizens) have generated collaborative and cooperative practices. It is becoming more common to find these actors networked and interdependent. Collaborative networks and open innovation (OI) have served as frameworks to shape these practices. These concepts have shown a high potential to be co-drivers of value creation and sharing resources, knowledge, complementary skills and capacities, and even share responsibilities and risks getting as a consequence not only the creation of disruptive processes, products, and services but also to make the most of resources, to shorten development processes, and to increase social impacts [12].

In this context, CNs are defined as "a network that consists of various entities that are largely autonomous, geographically distributed, and heterogeneous in their operating environment, culture, social capital and goals. They have come together to collaborate to achieve better common or compatible goals; their interactions can be supported by computer networks" [13].

Since CNs induce OI strategies, OI has been used to define the networked nature of innovation processes [9]. Thus, OI strategies combine internal and external ideas, resources and technologies, and create synergies among various multidisciplinary actors [14]. Hence, implementing these strategies plays a primary role in networks ability to facilitate innovation and spur the openness of innovative processes.

Therefore, today, collaborative networks applying open innovation strategies are excellent drivers for collaboration in Education 4.0. Hence, through multidisciplinary collaborative activities, academicians and students can participate in different scenarios internally in their institutions and externally in projects with actors participating in the triple-helix and quadruple-helix models.

Today, in higher education, OI strategies are widely used in different universities because these dynamics allow the structured participation of different actors for education and research, development, technology transfer, and entrepreneurship. Therefore, higher education institutions leverage these dynamics to develop curricular strategies and strategies that link companies and academicians through collaborative projects. These activities have been considered effective in achieving the vision of Education 4.0 because they induce active learning processes and the implementation of current ICTs.

## 4 Education 4.0 Reference Framework for Designing Teaching-Learning Systems

We propose a reference framework for designing new teaching-learning systems based on the concept and vision of Education 4.0. The proposed reference framework relies on the theory of enterprise modelling, using instantiation processes that facilitate enterprise integration [15, 16]. This reference framework aims to guide designers during the design and development of new didactic products, teaching-learning processes, and educational infrastructure through the generation of generic, partial, and particular models. Then, modelling is done through the instantiation of a generic model to partial and particular models. The definition of these models allows designers to systematically perform activities and apply techniques and tools when creating any teaching-learning system. Thus, the generation of these models allows designers to take advantage of previous knowledge and experiences that result in the shortening of the design, development, and implementation processes.

This framework has four stages related to the development life cycle. Hence, didactic products, teaching-learning processes, and educational infrastructure can be created through the following four stages of development: (i) *Ideation*. At this stage, ideas are generated and evaluated, and then they can be created and implemented in new products, programs or facilities. Also, at this stage, activities focus on understanding the educational institution's needs, the social contexts, and the student's profile to migrate these needs into requirements. *(ii) Basic development*: At this stage, designers provide the concepts underlying the proposed solutions. Therefore, all the functions or attributes that the product/process/infrastructure must include are defined. In addition, in this stage, the identified learning goals must be aligned to the proposed concept. (iii) *Advanced development*: The product/process/infrastructure is detailed designed at this stage. At this point, the design process can be complemented using any design methodology for teaching-learning systems to determine the learning content, dynamics, and instructions to be implemented. At this point, designers determine the capacities and capabilities and consider the four key enablers of Education 4.0 as a reference. Then, designers identify: (a) the key competencies to be promoted, (b) the learning methods to be implemented, (c) the ICTs to be applied, and (d) the required infrastructure to carry out the teaching-learning process. Once the proposed solution is obtained, it has to be evaluated and validated; then, the i-scale tool evaluates the innovation, learning outcomes, growth potential, institutional alignment, and financial viability, among others [17]. (iv) *Launching*. At this stage, all the implications to the proposed solution execution process must carry out. Some of the generic activities to be performed are tests of implementation and evaluation, design of experiments, and pilot tests. Finally, the learning assessment must be applied. The evaluation of the students is very relevant at this point since the information obtained serves to discover any weak aspect during the teaching-learning process that can be improved. Therefore, evaluation mechanisms must be applied and aligned with the measurement of learning goals. Figure 1 presents the proposed reference framework for the design of teaching-learning systems in Education 4.0. Then, different activities have been defined to carry out these stages. See Fig. 1.

These activities can be selected according to the following models:

*Generic model*. This model contains generic activities that can be used to design any teaching-learning system in a general way. Consequently, designers can reference generic models and then configure them to obtain partial or particular models.

*Partial model*. During the definition of this model, the designers take advantage of previous knowledge and then apply it within a specific field or discipline. Consequently, the partial activities to be performed and the partial resources to be used must be defined.

*Particular model*. Designers must define the specific topic and themes to be addressed. Also, specific requirements must be considered to define the specific learning methods, tools, ICTs, and infrastructure to be implemented. Therefore, the previously mentioned generic activities receive a deep level of specification. The resulting teaching-learning systems will be highly particularised to a specific social context, field, discipline, and topic.

Also, our proposed reference framework provides a toolbox that allows the designer to reference the type of resources that can be applied. The toolbox is organised per the main enablers considered in the concept and vision of Education 4.0: (i) The main soft and hard competencies to develop; (ii) the learning methods to be considered in new teaching-learning dynamics; (iii) the implementation of current and emerging ICTs for technology-based solutions using existing tools and platforms, and (iv) the use of an innovative infrastructure to improve pedagogical procedures and managerial processes at two levels, the classroom/home level and the institutional level.

Finally, once the product, process or infrastructure has been obtained, it will be necessary to analyse and evaluate it per the following views: (i) Technological, which seeks to validate the use of technologies characteristic of Industry 4.0; (ii) Pedagogical, which seeks to validate the implemented activities that promote the training and development of desirable competencies in Education 4.0; the activities must follow an active teaching-learning methodology of current learning models, and (iii) Organisational, which seeks to verify that the proposed learning dynamics have an organisational structure that is important to identify key participants (internal and external) within teaching-learning processes. In addition, this view verifies that the proposed activities promote collaboration and cooperation initiatives.

Figure 2 presents an example of how each cell of the reference framework includes different activities (analysis, synthesis, and evaluation) to be performed and how these activities are supported by the key enablers of Education 4.0 and analysed and evaluated according to the proposed views (technological, pedagogical, and organisational). See Fig. 2.

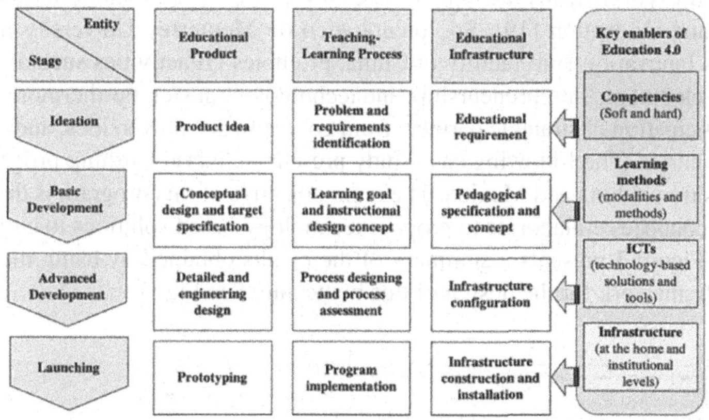


**Fig. 1.** The Education 4.0 reference framework for designing teaching-learning systems

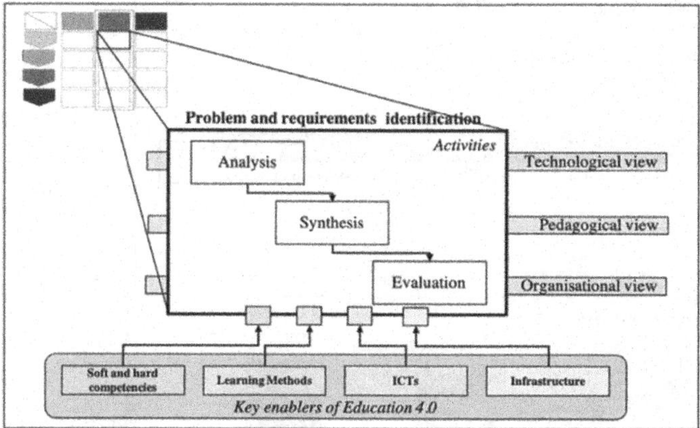


**Fig. 2.** Performed activities at the problem and requirements identification stage (example)

# 5 Design of Teaching-Learning Programs: Two Case Studies Appling Collaborative Networks and Open Innovation

## 5.1 Case Study: The Innovation Challenge Bootcamp as a Driver to Promote Open Innovation

In China, the government, higher education institutions, and organisations are promoting initiatives to improve the quality of engineering education, the internationalisation of higher education through collaborative/joint programs, and the acceleration of China's progress as a manufacturing powerhouse and leader in innovation, technology and science [18]. In this context, there is a lack of alternative credentials in engineering education that address holistically the topics related to developing technology-based products, creativity and innovation [19]. So, Tecnologico de Monterrey University in Mexico, through its Innovation Hub facility in China, promotes OI activities such as co-design and co-development, entrepreneurship, and technology transfer. Furthermore, it considers the participation of strategic partners from governments, universities, and companies in both countries. The following case study presents a hybrid learning program taught to students from China and Mexico. The main objective of this program is that students from both countries collaborate to propose technology-based solutions to current social problems. Figure 3 presents a summary of the results obtained by using the proposed reference framework for the design of this bootcamp. See Fig. 3.

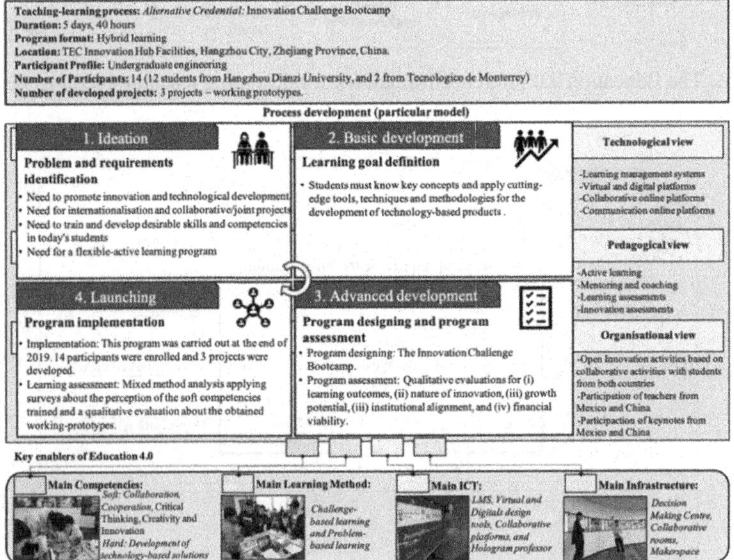


**Fig. 3.** Summarised results of the development process of the Innovation Challenge Bootcamp applying the teaching-learning process of the Education 4.0 reference framework

## 5.2 Case Study: Collaborative Online International Learning

Processes that create new options benefit societal development. Innovation leads to the generation of new services, products and technologies. Analysing the possibilities in different countries will help us propose options in our regions (Latin America). In this case study, the "Collaborative Online International Learning" (COIL) activity provides a collaborative experience among various academic disciplines and countries. The objective of this COIL activity was to develop critical thinking skills, effective communication, innovation and collaborative work. By the end of this experience, the students should have developed their capacity for effective communication through online interactions with people from different cultures and disciplines. This program works with the proposed reference framework to develop competencies using experiential methods, ICT integration, and open infrastructure environments. See Fig. 4.

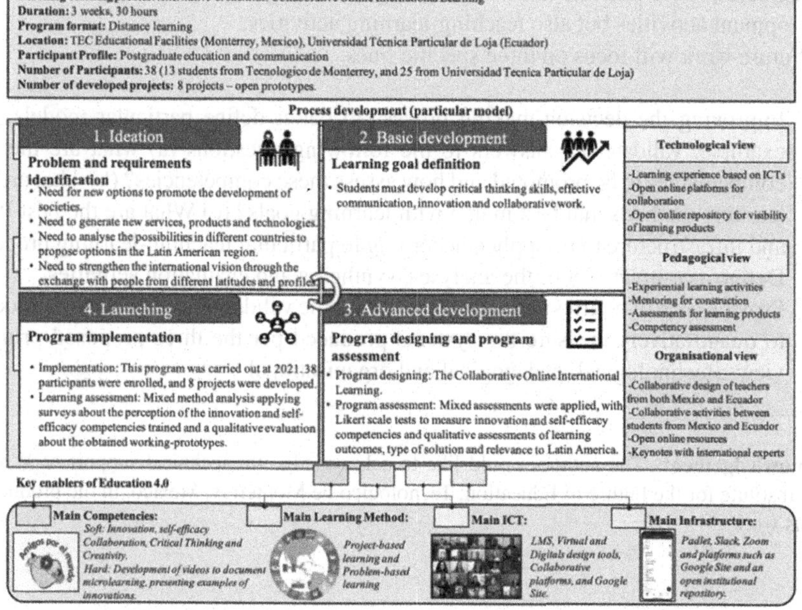


**Fig. 4.** Summarised results of the development process of the collaborative online international learning applying the teaching-learning process of the education 4.0 reference framework

# 6 Conclusions and Future Work

In this work, we propose a reference framework for the design of teaching-learning systems in Education 4.0. Then, the design and development of new educational products, processes and infrastructure are supported. Furthermore, this reference framework allows educational innovators to guide them while creating systems that adopt the concept of Education 4.0. We accomplished this by providing the main components shaping Education 4.0 in a toolbox comprised of its four key enablers. Finally, an evaluation was carried out to validate the technological, pedagogical and organisational components used within the system produced.

We also presented two case studies to illustrate how the proposed framework is used to design teaching-learning processes in academic programs. The presented case studies show three main results: (i) Using the proposed reference framework, new educational systems with their desired components can be obtained in the period of Education 4.0. Hence, this reference framework can be an engine for educational innovation. (ii) Using the proposed reference framework can be a driver to promote collaboration and cooperative activities because the technologies employed and the active learning activities applied induce the forming of collaborative networks and the implementation of open innovation strategies. (iii) The creation of multidisciplinary teams, the participation of international partners during teaching-learning processes, and the shared use of infrastructure were possible thanks to existing CNs that promote not only research and development activities but also teaching-learning activities.

Future work will focus on three specific lines:

(i) Improving the decision-making process to better define particular models. For example, validate the answers to the following questions (a) what are the key competencies to be promoted and how assess these competencies? (b) what are the learning methods that best match with learning goals? (c) What are the best ICTs and infrastructure to be applied according to particular teaching-learning process?
(ii) Define a complete set of the analyses, syntheses and evaluation activities.
(iii) Provide a set of metrics and indicators during the validation and evaluation process to quantitatively measure the systems produced per the three proposed primary views: technological, pedagogical and organisational.

**Acknowledgement.** The authors would like to acknowledge the technical support of Writing Lab, Institute for the Future of Education, Tecnologico de Monterrey, Mexico, in the production of this work.

## References

1. Wan, J., Cai, H., Zhou, K.: Industry 4.0: Enabling Technologies. In: 2015 International Conference on Intelligent Computing and Internet of Things (IC1T), Harbin, China, 2015, pp. 135–140 (2015)
2. Camarinha-Matos, L.M., Fornasiero, R., Afsarmanesh, H.: Collaborative Networks as a Core Enabler of Industry 4.0. In: 18th Working Conference on Virtual Enterprises (PRO-VE), Vicenza, Italy. pp. 3–17 (2017)
3. Roman, M., Varga, H., Cvijanovic, V., Reid, A.: Quadruple Helix Models for Sustainable Regional Innovation Engaging and Facilitating Civil Society Participation. Economies **8**(2), 48 (2020)
4. Mehmet, E.: An IDEA for design pedagogy: devising instructional design in higher education 4.0. Des. Technol. Educ. **26**(1), 118–136 (2021)

5. Ayub, E., Wei, G.W., Luaran, J.E., Keppell, M.J., Leong, L.C., Mohamad, S.N.A.: A design and development research approach to redesigning an online module for education 4.0. In: IEEE Conference on e-Learning, e-Management & e-Services, pp. 1–6 (2019)
6. Das, S., Kleinke, D.K., Pistrui, D.: Reimagining engineering education: does industry 4.0 need education 4.0?. In: ASEE Virtual Annual Conference Experience (2020)
7. World Economic Forum.: Schools of the Future, Defining New Models of Education for the Fourth Industrial Revolution. Geneva: World Economic Forum (2020)
8. Miranda, J., et al.: The core components of education 4.0 in higher education: three case studies in engineering education. Comput. Electr. Eng. **93**, 107278 (2021)
9. Huggins, R., Prokop, D., Thompson, P.: Universities and open innovation: the determinants of network centrality. J. Technol. Transf. **45**(3), 718–757 (2020)
10. Anthony Jr., B., Petersen, S.A.: Examining the digitalisation of virtual enterprises amidst the COVID-19 pandemic: a systematic and meta-analysis. Enter. Inf. Syst. **30**, 1–34 (2020)
11. Borissova, D., Dimitrova, Z., Dimitrov, V.: How to support teams to be remote and productive: group decision-making for distance collaboration software tools. Inf. Secur. **46**(1), 36–52 (2020)
12. Himmelman, A.T.: On coalitions and the transformation of power relations: Collaborative betterment and collaborative empowerment. Am. J. Community Psychol. **29**(2), 277–284 (2001)
13. Camarinha-Matos, L.M., Afsarmanesh, H.: Collaborative networks: a new scientific discipline. J. Intell. Manuf. **16**(4–5), 439–452 (2005)
14. Chesbrough, H.: Open Innovation: The New Imperative for Creating and Profiting from Technology. Harvard Business School Press, Boston (2003)
15. Molina, A., Sánchez, J.M., Kusiak, A. (eds.): Handbook of Life Cycle Engineering: Concepts, Models and Technologies. Springer, US (1999). ISBN 978-0-412-81250-7
16. Molina, A., Ponce, P., Miranda, J., Cortés, D.: Enabling Systems for Intelligent Manufacturing in Industry 4.0: Sensing, Smart and Sustainable Systems for the Design of S3 Products, Processes, Manufacturing Systems, and Enterprises. Springer, Cham (2021). https://doi.org/10.1007/978-3-030-65547-1
17. López-Cruz, C.S., Heredia, Y.: Escala i, Guía de Aplicación. In: Tecnológico de Monterrey, Mexico (2017)
18. Mei, W., Symaco, L.: University-wide entrepreneurship education in China's higher education institutions: issues and challenges. In: Studies in Higher Education, pp. 1–17 (2020)
19. Shen, J., Li, T., Wu, M.: The new engineering education in China. Procedia Comput. Sci. **172**, 886–895 (2020)

# A Framework for Education 4.0 in Digital Education Ecosystems

Claudia-Melania Chituc(✉)

DIPF | Leibniz Institute for Research and Information in Education, Rostocker Straße 6, 60323 Frankfurt am Main, Germany
Chituc@dipf.de

**Abstract.** The digital technologies enable the transformation of the educational institutions, shaping the way teaching and learning knowledge and skills activities are delivered and assessed, and the pursuance of the Digital Education Ecosystems (DEEs). Industry 4.0 requires highly qualified employees, and the concept of Education 4.0 emerged, which focusses on preparing the future workforce for Industry 4.0. Despite the importance of Education 4.0, research and development work in this area is in an incipient phase, and the fields of Education 4.0 and DEEs expand without a clear vision how the necessities of Industry 4.0 will be addressed, and how the DEEs support attaining the goals of Education 4.0. The aim of this article is to present a framework for Education 4.0 developed by performing a literature review, which contains six dimensions: knowledge, skills and qualifications in Education 4.0; teaching; learning; implementation; (e-)assessment; and quality assurance.

**Keywords:** Education 4.0 · Digital technologies · Industry 4.0 · Digital education ecosystem

## 1 Introduction

The digitalization of the education sector is accelerated by the recent advances in the digital tools and technologies, such as: big data analytics, cloud computing, machine learning, Internet of Things (IoT), sensing and actuation technologies, 3D printing, social media. They enable the transformation of the educational institutions, shaping (next to disruptions caused by epidemic occurrences) the educational activities and services, the way teaching and learning knowledge and skills activities are delivered and assessed, and the pursuance of the Digital Education Ecosystems (DEEs). While the concept of DEE is not new in the fields of engineering or social sciences (see: [1, 2]), the interest in digitally enhanced teaching and learning activities is expanding in recent times as numerous benefits are acknowledged.

The DEEs refer in this work to inter-connected heterogeneous and geographically distributed e-learning infrastructure, software tools and devices used in education activities. The IoT and Cyber-Physical Systems (CPSs) (which are pillars of Industry 4.0) enable the realization of the DEEs.


Published by Springer Nature Switzerland AG 2021
L. M. Camarinha-Matos et al. (Eds.): PRO-VE 2021, IFIP AICT 629, pp. 702–709, 2021.
https://doi.org/10.1007/978-3-030-85969-5_66

The Industry 4.0 concept, as noted in [3], emerged from the industrial revolution in Germany, with a solid background (scientific, technical, industrial) constructed on the melding of industrial norms and standards based on a novel DIN (Deutsche Industrie Norm) specification: the Reference Architecture Model (RAMI4.0) [4]. Industry 4.0 requires highly qualified employees [5]. The Education 4.0 concept emerged, which focuses on preparing the future workforce for Industry 4.0.

Despite the importance of Education 4.0, this is a recent field, and research and development work in this area is in an incipient phase [6]. Moreover, the fields of Education 4.0 and DEEs expand without a clear vision how the necessities of Industry 4.0 will be addressed, and how the DEEs support attaining the goals of Education 4.0. Relevant research questions in this area that need to be addressed are: Which are the key dimensions to characterize Education 4.0? How Education 4.0 is currently tackled? Which are enablers for Education 4.0 in the DEEs? Which are challenges for Education 4.0 that need to be further addressed?

Aiming to answer these research questions, this article presents a framework for Education 4.0 in the inter-connected DEEs. The notion of framework is understood here as a structure underlying the concept of Education 4.0. The findings of a literature review performed following PRISMA guidelines [7] represent the basis of the proposed framework, which is structured in six dimensions: knowledge, skills and qualifications; teaching; learning; implementation; (e-)assessment; and quality assurance. This framework reflects the main dimensions and characteristics of Education 4.0, and is useful for educators and educational institutions, enterprises, policy makers in better understanding the emerging fields of Education 4.0, and identifying areas that need to be further addressed by research and development work.

This article is organized as follows. Background information is introduced next. The research approach and related work are presented in Sect. 3. A framework for Education 4.0 is described in Sect. 4. This articles concludes with a section addressing the need for future research and development work.

## 2 Background: The Role of DEEs in Education 4.0

While in the traditional e-learning environments the students and educators connect to an e-learning platform (such as Moodle, moodle.org) to perform basic activities (e.g., execute quizzes, access e-learning material), the DEEs enable the rendering of convoluted e-learning activities (e.g., to support the execution of remote complex group work activities using virtual reality, 3D printing, interactive whiteboards, cloud computing) and real-time analysis of huge volumes of heterogeneous data (e.g., to allow the human or robot teacher to adjust or individualize the teaching activities).

Numerous benefits are associated with the DEEs enabled by the IoT technologies and CPSs, such as: enrich learners' psychological experiences in learning activities, allowing interaction, collaboration and flexibility [8], enhanced learning [9], and help organizations to improve the quality of teaching and learning by allowing a richer learning experience and real-time analysis of learners' performance [10].

Several e-learning management systems exist (e.g., Moodle, Canvas instructure.com/canvas, Blackboard blackboard.com, Army Learning Management System-ALMS atris.mil/ALMS) and standardization initiatives to address interoperability among e-learning infrastructures, such as: Learning Object Metadata promoted by the IEEE Learning Technology Standards Committee (ltsc.ieee.org), which advocates for storing learning objects as well as their descriptions; IMS Question and Test Interoperability (www.imsglobal.org), which specifies an XML format for encoding on-line questions, tests and test banks. As the field of e-learning is expanding without a clear vision on how heterogeneous software systems, "things" and e-learning infrastructures should inter-relate, the attainment of interoperable DEEs[1] is still not achieved, which brings numerous challenges for Education 4.0.

It is important to ensure collaboration and transfer of technology and technology knowledge among the main DEE stakeholders (e.g., students, educators, educational institutions, companies, research centers, government structures) towards ensuring the highly qualified workforce needed in Industry 4.0 (see: [11]). Thus, the DEEs enable Education 4.0, and attaining interoperability in DEEs is crucial for Education 4.0.

## 3 Research Approach and Discussion of Related Work

Aiming to identify the main dimensions to characterize Education 4.0, relevant approaches and challenges, a literature review was conducted following PRISMA guidelines [7]. The digital libraries of IEEE, ACM, Elsevier and Springer were searched as they represent the most important databases in the area of Education 4.0 and Industry 4.0. Queries on Google Scholar were also performed. Keywords identified include: "Education 4.0", "characteristic", "challenge", "Industry 4.0", "work force", "qualification", "skills" "classroom 4.0", "study program", "digital skills", "teaching", "digital learning", "learning factory", "future manufacturing". Queries executed included the Boolean operators OR, AND, NOT, e.g., ("Education 4.0" AND "challenge"); (("Industry 4.0" OR "future manufacturing") AND "work force" AND ("qualification" OR "skills" OR "digital skills")). The search concerned articles published from January 2015 to April 2021. As the list of retrieved articles was vast, inclusion and exclusion criteria were defined. For example, by reading the title and abstract, the clearly out of scope articles were excluded. The articles written in a language other than English and articles to which full access was not possible were also excluded. The relevant articles were read in full, and an analysis of related work was made.

Industry 4.0 determines a shift in the required skills and qualifications of the workforce [12, 13]. The technical and personal skills and qualifications required for Industry 4.0 are analyzed in [14], grouped in "must have", "should have" and "could have". Accordingly, "must have" technical skills include IT knowledge and abilities, data and information processing and analytics, statistical knowledge, organizational and processual understanding, ability to interact with modern interfaces (human-machine/human-robot), "must have" personal skills concern self- and time management, adaptability, ability to change, team work abilities, social and communication skills, "should have" technical skills include knowledge management, interdisciplinary/generic knowledge

[1] Interoperability in the context of DEEs refers here to the ability of inter-connected e-learning ICT infrastructures, software systems and "things" to exchange information and interpret it in the same way.

about technologies and organizations, specialized knowledge of manufacturing activities and processes, awareness of IT security and data protection, and "should have" personal skills include trust in new technologies and mindset for life-long learning [14].

Examining the inter-disciplinary field of Industry 4.0, on one hand, and the traditional engineering study programs, it is very challenging for educators and students (or recent graduates) to meet these demands, e.g., concerning learning, teaching, understanding the informatization, digitalization and networking of the industrial and business ecosystem [3]. Classic lecture-based teaching seems not adequate [15]. Education 4.0 emerged to address these demands and challenges. Although the field of Education 4.0 is in an incipient phase [6], some studies exist that illustrate the implementation of Education 4.0 pilots at educational institutions. The use and importance of "demonstration platforms" for the design, implementation, test, optimization of Industry 4.0-complian solutions by teachers, students in university in a multi-disciplinary fashion is emphasized in [3], where the authors present the "Automated Class Room" demonstrator platform at the University of Applied Sciences in Emden. Upgrades of learning factories (e.g., implementation of CPSs in learning factories, smart factories in Industry 4.0) are referred in the literature as approaches towards preparing highly skilled workforce required in Industry 4.0, e.g., [16–18]. The inclusion of mandatory subjects relevant for Industry 4.0 in education curricula, internships, MOOCs, open day tours, workshops, professional development courses, industry-university collaborations are noted in [14] as approaches to address the "must have" and "should have" skills and qualifications for Industry 4.0. Learning approaches in Education 4.0 noted in [19] include, among others, blended, personalized and experimental learning, and mentoring through peers. The authors also refer to the need for customized learner's evaluation. Gamification is also used in Education 4.0 [20]. The need for adaptive learning powered by artificial intelligence learning portals that allow to adapt the learning process considering the learner's profile is emphasized in [21].

Five clusters of scientific gaps for Education 4.0 are discussed in [6]: to map and assess Education 4.0 challenges and solutions to Industry 4.0, pedagogical alignment, analyze novel teaching methods in Education 4.0, optimize and update Education 4.0 digital platforms. Next to education institutions and companies, the importance of policymakers in Education 4.0 in noted in [19, 22], e.g., for accreditation, global outlook, support in collaborations, implement the Education 4.0 vision.

The finding of the related work represent the basis for the development of the Education 4.0 framework described next.

## 4 Framework for Education 4.0

Figure 1 illustrates the proposed framework for Education 4.0. This framework was constructed considering the main characteristics and challenges of Education 4.0 identified from the literature review conducted, which were grouped in six dimensions: (1) **knowledge, skills** and **qualifications** required by Industry 4.0 that need to be addressed in Education 4.0, (2) **teaching** approaches, concerning methods for teaching technical and personal skills, and pedagogy approaches, (3) **learning** approaches, (4) **implementation** of the Education 4.0 vision, teaching methods, and ensuring an environment where innovation, knowledge and technology transfer are promoted, (5) **(e-)assessment**, which concerns the methods and (technology-based) assessment methods, tools and infrastructures used to evaluate the knowledge and skills, tailored considering the specificities of Education 4.0 and specific teaching and learning methods, (6) **quality assurance**, concerning the methodologies, methods, metrics and tools for evaluating the quality of the teaching, and regulate diploma issuing, accreditation and verification processes. Figure 1 also illustrates examples of approaches used (or which could be relevant) in each dimension. These aspects are also relevant in the construction of the DEEs.

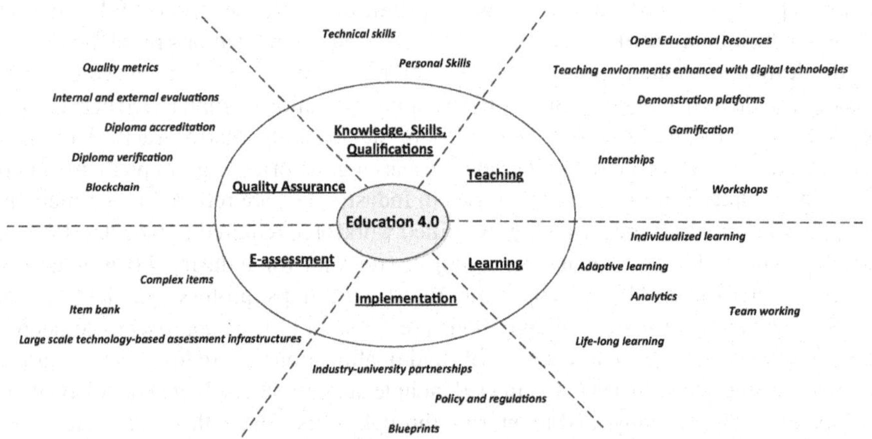


**Fig. 1.** Framework for Education 4.0

Although Education 4.0 is a recent domain, several studies exist in the context of Education 4.0 focusing on the knowledge, skills and qualifications required for Education 4.0 (see: [3, 14]), teaching (see: [3, 20]) and learning (see: [19, 21]) approaches. Several requirements for universities also need to be addressed, such as: advanced infrastructures, skilled staff, increased industrial partnership, revised curricula, effective financial planning [23].

Few studies focus on the actual implementation of Education 4.0 approaches, although the importance of policymakers in this process is acknowledged (e.g. [19, 22]), and on e-assessment approaches. Adequate complex items, item banks, and large scale ICT infrastructures for technology-based assessments are needed. Research in this area has intensified in the past years (e.g., approaches for the development of item banks for complex items are described in: [24, 25]). However, ensuring a kind of "widely-accepted" e-assessment approach (relevant in the context of globalization, students' participation in international educational activities and exchange programs, and life-long learning programs) is very challenging, e.g., this requires the translation of complex items – often accompanied by audio or video files - in different languages, which may change the level of difficulty of the respective item. Technology-based assessments are focusing in recent years on large-scale adaptive testing and multi-testing applications, which require advanced support for item design and editing, assessment assignments, and access to additional test materials. Solutions that reflect the content, interaction patterns, psychometric item and test analysis, quality control software, test delivery software and hardware are needed [26]. However, Education 4.0 does not exclude the use of traditional assessment methods.

Ensuring quality assurance in Education 4.0 is not tackled currently, and this is a crucial topic especially considering the specificities of Education 4.0, mobility in education, and the increasing competition faced nowadays by educational institutions (that are traditionally acknowledged as main providers of educational activities) as more and more companies develop and offer teaching programs. Quality assurance in education is not a new topic (see: [27, 28]). Several quality assurance systems were developed along the years, e.g., by the Educational Testing Service [29], Association for Educational Assessment Europe [30], Cambridge Assessment [31]. However, the primary focus of most such systems, standards, guidelines, or formal reviewing systems is on psychological testing, and they are not fully suitable to assess the quality of educational tests or exams [32], and often they do not address the specificities of technology-based assessments that rely on the concepts of item and item bank. Research and development work needs to address these aspects in the context of Education 4.0. The development of quality assurance metrics, methods, methodologies and software tools for Education 4.0 can build on previous approaches. However, aspects such as ethics and fairness in artificial intelligence-enabled e-assessment approaches need to be carefully tackled, and the policymakers can have an important role in the development of adequate e-assessment and quality assurance methods and methodologies in Education 4.0.

## 5 Conclusions and Future Work

Education 4.0 brings numerous challenging for educational institutions in developing and implementing teaching and learning approaches needed to ensure the technical qualifications and personal skills of young graduates required by Industry 4.0. The DEEs, enhanced with digital technologies, support teaching and learning activities, and the establishment of partnerships or networks among educational institutions and enterprises to tackle these challenges.

The findings of a literature review performed following PRISMA guidelines [7] represent the basis of an Education 4.0 framework (Fig. 1) structured in six dimensions: knowledge, skills and qualifications for Education 4.0; teaching; learning; implementation; (e-)assessment; and quality assurance. While studies exist on identifying the required knowledge and skills, teaching, learning approaches in the context of Industry 4.0, few works focus on e-assessment and quality assurance. Future research and development work in Education 4.0 should focus on these topics. Aspects such as ethics and fairness in artificial intelligence-enabled e-assessment approaches also need to be addressed. The policymakers can have an important role in the development of adequate assessment and quality assurance approaches in Education 4.0, and in defining blueprints for their implementation.

Another important aspects to be tackled is pedagogical knowledge in the context of Education 4.0. Digital technologies enable Education 4.0. However, existing approaches lack pedagogical knowledge and strategy. The educators and educational institutions need to select and implement appropriate techniques to optimally combine adequate educational resources, technology and a pedagogy strategy to address the workforce needs of Industry 4.0. Future research and development work will focus on developing a methodology to support educators in making appropriate decision about e-learning optimally combining these aspects.

## References


1. Ficheman, I.K., de Deus Lopes R.: Digital learning ecosystems: authoring, collaboration, immersion and mobility. In: ACM IDC, pp. 9–12 (2008)
2. Mavrikis, M., Guardia, L., Cukurova, M., Maina, M.: A Digital ecosystem for digital competences: the CRISS project demo. In: Pammer-Schindler, V., Pérez-Sanagustín, M., Drachsler, H., Elferink, R., Scheffel, M. (eds.) EC-TEL 2018. LNCS, vol. 11082, pp. 627–630. Springer, Cham (2018). https://doi.org/10.1007/978-3-319-98572-5_60
3. Wermann, J., Colombo, A.W., Pechmann, A., et al.: Using an interdisciplinary demonstration platform for teaching Industry 4.0. Procedia Manuf. **31**, 302–308 (2019)
4. DIN Deutsches Institut für Normung e.V.: DIN SPEC 91345:2016-04: Referenzarchitekturmodell Industrie 4.0 (RAMI4.0) (2016)
5. Benesova, A., Tupa, J.: Requirements for education and qualification of people in Industry 4.0. Procedia Manuf. **11**, 2195–2202 (2017)
6. da Motta Reis, J., et al.: Education 4.0: gaps research between school formation and technological development. In: Latifi, S. (ed.) 17th International Conference on Information Technology–New Generations (ITNG 2020). AISC, vol. 1134, pp. 415–420. Springer, Cham (2020). https://doi.org/10.1007/978-3-030-43020-7_55
7. Moher, D., et al.: Preferred reporting items for systematic review and meta-analyses: the PRISMA statement. PLOS Med. **6**(7), e1000097 (2009)
8. Chang, F.-C., et al.: Future classroom with the Internet of Things - a service-oriented framework. J. Inf. Hiding Multimedia Signal Process. **6**(5), 869–881 (2015)
9. Bagheri, M., Siavosh, H.M.: The effect of the Internet of Things (IoT) on education business model. In: IEEE SITIS, pp. 435–441 (2016)
10. Boyes, H., Hallaq, B., et al.: The industrial Internet of Things (IIoT): an analysis framework. Comput. Ind. **101**, 1–12 (2018)
11. Tirto, T., Ossik, Y., Omelyanenko, V.: ICT support for Industry 4.0 innovation networks: education and technology transfer issues. In: Ivanov, V., et al. (eds.) DSMIE 2019. LNME, pp. 359–369. Springer, Cham (2020). https://doi.org/10.1007/978-3-030-22365-6_36
12. Siemens, A.G.: Competences for the future of manufacturing. Siemens Ind. J. **2**, 11–25 (2013)
13. Hammer, M., Hippe, M., Schmitz, C., Sellschop, R., Somers, K.: The dirty little secret. Harv. Bus. Rev. (2016). https://hbr.org/2016/05/the-dirty-little-secret-about-digitally-transforming-operations. Accessed 30 Apr 2021
14. Gehrke, L., Kühn, A., Rule, D., Moore, P., Bellmann, C., et al.: A Discussion of Qualifications and Skills in the Factory of the Future: A German and American Perspective. VDI The Association of German Engineers, Düsseldorf, Germany (2015)
15. Karre, H., Hammer, M., Kleindienst, M., et al.: Transition towards an Industry 4.0 state of the LeanLab at Graz University of Technology. Procedia Manuf. **9**, 206–213 (2017)
16. Thiede, S., Juraschek, M., Christoph, H.: Implementing cyber-physical production systems in learning factories. Procedia CIPR **54**, 7–12 (2016)
17. Prinz, C., Morlock, F., Freith, S., et al.: Learning factories modules for smart factories in Industry 4.0. Procedia CIRP **54**, 113–118 (2016)

18. Centea, D., Singh, I., Wanyama, T., Magolon, M., Boer, J., Elbestawi, M.: Using SEPT learning factory for the implementation of Industry 4.0: case of SMEs. Procedia Manuf. **45**, 102–107 (2020)
19. Koul, S., Nayar, B.: The holistic learning educational ecosystem: a classroom 4.0 perspective. High. Educ. Q. **75**, 98–112 (2021)
20. Almeida, F., Simoes, J.: The role of serious games, gamification and Industry 4.0 tools in the Education 4.0 paradigm. Contemp. Educ. Technol. **10**(2), 120–136 (2019)
21. Demartini, B., Benussi, L.: Do web 40 and Industry 4.0 imply Education X.0? IT Prof. **19**, 4–7 (2017)
22. Halili, S.H.: Technological advancements in Education 4.0. Online J. Distance Educ. e-Learning **1**(7), 63–69 (2019)
23. Mian, S.H., Salah, B., Ameen, W., et al.: Adapting universities for sustainability education in Industry 4.0: challenges and opportunities. Sustainability **12**, 6100 (2020)
24. Petersen, M.A., et al.: Development of an item bank for computerized adaptive test (CAT) measurement of pain. Qual. Life Res. **25**(1), 1–11 (2015). https://doi.org/10.1007/s11136-015-1069-5
25. Chituc, C.-M., Herrmann, M., Schiffner, D., Rittberger, M.: Towards the design and deployment of an item bank: an analysis of the requirements elicited. In: Herzog, M.A., Kubincová, Z., Han, P., Temperini, M. (eds.) ICWL 2019. LNCS, vol. 11841, pp. 155–162. Springer, Cham (2019). https://doi.org/10.1007/978-3-030-35758-0_15
26. Luecht, R.M.: Computer-based test delivery models, data, and operational implementation issues. In: Drasgow, F. (ed.) Technology and testing: Improving educational and psychological measurement, pp. 179–205. Routledge, New York (2016)
27. Buros, O.K. (ed.): The 1938 Mental Measurements Yearbook. Rutgers University Press, Oxford (1938)
28. Bartram, D.: Review model for the description and evaluation of psychological tests. European Federation of Psychologists' Associations, Brussels, Belgium (2002)
29. Educational Testing Service: ETS standards for quality and fairness. Educational Testing Service, Princeton (2014)
30. Association of Educational Assessment-Europe: European framework of standards for educational assessment 1.0. Edizione Nova Cultura, Roma (2012). www.aea-europe.net/wpcontent/uploads/2017/07/SW_Framework_of_European_Standards.pdf
31. Cambridge Assessment: Cambridge Approach to Assessment (2017). www.cambridgeassessment.org.uk/Images/cambridge-approach-to-assessment.pdf
32. Veldkamp, B.P., Sluijter, C. (eds.): Theoretical and Practical Advances in Computer-based Educational Measurement. MEMA, Springer, Cham (2019). https://doi.org/10.1007/978-3-030-18480-3

# Collaborative Decision-Making Model of Green Supply Chain: Cloud-Based Metaheuristics

Ehsan Yadegari(✉) and Xavier Delorme

Mines Saint-Etienne, Univ Clermont Auvergne, CNRS, UMR 6158 LIMOS, Institut Henri Fayol, 42023 Saint-Etienne, France
ehsan.yadegari@emse.fr

**Abstract.** The inter-organizational collaborative supply chain (SC) network involves the collaboration of various firms and decision-makers to increase the whole efficiency of an SC network. There is often a conflict between operations and environmental managers in how to design a supply network to simultaneously reduce greenhouse gas emissions and logistics costs. In this paper, a two-dimensional collaborative decision-making (CDM) model for a SC network is developed. The proposed network is assumed to deliver the final product to customers in the forward flow from suppliers through manufacturers and distribution centers (DCs). Simultaneously, collecting recycled products from customers and entering them into a recovery cycle is examined. Mathematical modeling of this problem is going to minimize both the total costs and the environmental negative effects. To effectively manage the conflict, Pareto solutions for the bi-objective model are provided. Moreover, a cloud-based simulated annealing algorithm (CSA) has been applied for the first time in this area. We have compared its performance with the genetic algorithm (GA) and the simulated annealing (SA) algorithm of the literature.

**Keywords:** Collaborative supply chain, green · Cloud-based simulated annealing

## 1 Introduction

Recently, supply-chain network CDM has attracted operations research analysts' attention. A large number of papers have concentrated on problems relevant to this area, like centralized CDM and decentralized CDM.

References on centralized CDM mainly apply operations research tools such as network analysis, dynamic programming, and heuristics to identify the optimal or near-optimal decision items. On the other hand, research on decentralized decision-making has been done to enhance the applicability of CDM solutions [1]. As, this study is in the category of centralized CDM, in this part, we concentrate more on the SC modeling and solution approaches of centralized collaborative SCs, especially Supply chain network design (SCND) problems. Recently, there are some publications in centralized collaborative SCND in which all units of the SC share information regarding demand and rate


Published by Springer Nature Switzerland AG 2021
L. M. Camarinha-Matos et al. (Eds.): PRO-VE 2021, IFIP AICT 629, pp. 710–718, 2021.
https://doi.org/10.1007/978-3-030-85969-5_67

of return [2, 3]. However, these papers only focused on SC costs and there is no focus on environmental costs.

SCND involves strategic decisions that refer to supply chain configuration and as an infrastructure issue in SC management, it has long-lasting effects on other tactical and operational decisions of a company. In general, the network design project faces identifying locations and capacities needed for new facilities and planning to purchase, production, distribution, and maintenance of products.

Pishvaee et al. [4] have classified the integration of SCND into two categories: (1) vertical and (2) horizontal integration. Vertical integration is defined as the integrated decisions at strategic (long-term), tactical (mid-term), and operational (short-term) levels in SCND. Designing the SC network is in the class of a strategic decision that typically involves determining the location of facilities, their capacities, the number of categories in the chain, and how the facilities are related. Therefore, it should be noted that integrating lower-level decisions in network design must be accompanied by maintaining strategic-level decisions.

In this regard, according to the literature review [5, 6], the 2013 to 2021 studies in the SCND area have been investigated in terms of decision problems, and solution approaches. Numerous approaches have been developed regarding the methodologies for representing SCND solutions. The most important ones are Matrix-based, Prufer Numbers, Priority based, and the spanning tree concept. In Table 1 the research background has been classified.

**Table 1.** Literature review on SCND based on decision types and solution methodology.

| Networks | Solution representation | Solution methodology | Decision problem | | |
|---|---|---|---|---|---|
| | | | Location | Distribution organization | Green effect |
| *Forward networks* | | | | | |
| Jayaraman, Gupta [7] | Matrix-based | SA | ✓ | | |
| Pishvaee and Razmi [4] | – | Interactive fuzzy | ✓ | ✓ | ✓ |
| Syarif and Yun [8] | Matrix-based | GA | ✓ | ✓ | |
| Elhedhli and Merrick [9] | – | Lagrangian relaxation | ✓ | ✓ | ✓ |
| *Reverse networks* | | | | | |
| Krikke, van Harten [10] | – | Exact solution | ✓ | ✓ | |
| Min and Ko [11] | Matrix-based | GA | ✓ | | |

(*continued*)

**Table 1.** *(continued)*

| Networks | Solution representation | Solution methodology | Decision problem | | |
|---|---|---|---|---|---|
| | | | Location | Distribution organization | Green effect |
| Aras and Crowther [12] | Matrix-based | Tabu search | ✓ | | ✓ |
| Nezamoddini [13] | Priority-based | GA | ✓ | | |
| *Closed-loop networks* | | | | | |
| Wang and Hsu [14] | Spanning tree | GA | ✓ | ✓ | |
| Devika, Jafarian [15] | Priority-based | Hybrid | ✓ | ✓ | ✓ |
| Yadegari, Zandieh [16] | Spanning tree | Hybrid | ✓ | ✓ | |
| Kaya and Urek [17] | Priority-based | Hybrid heuristics | ✓ | ✓ | |
| Yi, Huang [18] | Other | Genetic algorithm | ✓ | ✓ | |
| This paper | Spanning tree | CSA | ✓ | ✓ | ✓ |

The remainder of the manuscript is dedicated to the mathematical model of the SCND problem with focusing on the conflict between environmental and operational managers. In Sect. 4, the CSA algorithm is applied to the SCND problem for the first time in the literature. Section 5 provides a sample Pareto solution and how sensitivity analysis is applied to smooth the conflict between decision-makers and finally the conclusion is provided in Sect. 6.

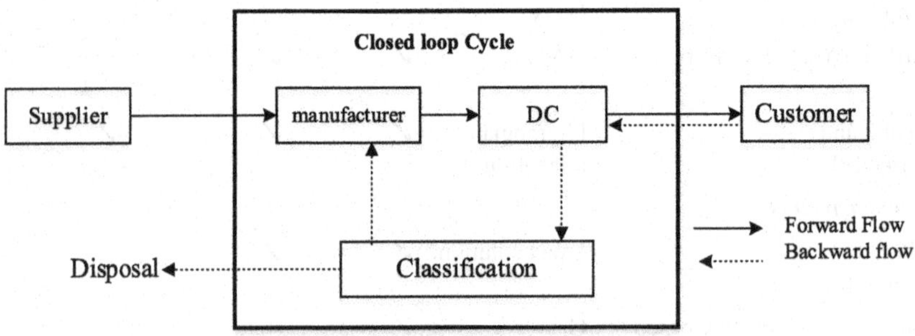


**Fig. 1.** The overall formation of SC network

## 2 Mathematical Model

The proposed CDM model is an extension of the model provided in [14, 16] in which their model only considered one objective function related to the total cost of shpping and developing facilities. However, the provided model in this paper simultaneously considers the cost and environmental effect of the SC. To be concise, in Sect. 2 we only mention the extension of the model so for a better understanding of the model please refer to the mentioned literature.

The following describes the sets, parameters, and variables of the SCND model based on the network configuration provided in Fig. 1.

**Sets:**

| | | | |
|---|---|---|---|
| $I$ | Fixed locations of suppliers | $I = \{1, 2, ..., \|I\|\}$ | $i \in I$ |
| $J$ | Potential locations for developing manufactories | $J = \{1, 2, ..., \|J\|\}$ | $j \in J$ |
| $K$ | Potential locations for developing DCs | $K = \{1, 2, ..., \|K\|\}$ | $k \in K$ |
| $L$ | Fixed locations of customers | $L = \{1, 2, ..., \|L\|\}$ | $l \in L$ |
| $M$ | Potential locations for developing dismantlers | $M = \{1, 2, ..., \|M\|\}$ | $m \in M$ |

**Parameters:**

| | |
|---|---|
| $ERJ_j$ | Emission rate of developing a plant in potential location $j$ |
| $ERK_k$ | Emission rate of developing a DC in potential location $k$ |
| $ERM_m$ | Emission rate of developing a dismantler in potential location $m$ |
| $EIJ_{ij}$ | Emission rate of shipping from supplier $i$ to manufactory j |
| $EJK_{jk}$ | Emission rate of shipping from plant $j$ to DC $k$ |
| $EKL_{kl}$ | Emission rate of shipping from DC $k$ to customer zone $l$ |
| $EKM_{km}$ | Emission rate of shipping from DC $k$ to dismantlers $m$ |
| $EMJ_{mj}$ | Emission rate of shipping from dismantlers $m$ to manufactory $j$ |

**Decision Variables:**

| | |
|---|---|
| $X_{ij}$ | Quantity produced at plant j by raw materials of supplier $i$ |
| $Y_{jk}$ | The amount of product transferred from plant $j$ to DC $k$ |
| $Z_{kl}$ | The amount of product transferred from DC $k$ to customer $l$ |
| $O_{km}$ | The amount of product transferred from DC $k$ to dismantler $m$ |
| $Rd_{mj}$ | The amount of used product transferred from dismantler $m$ to manufactory $j$ |
| $Rz_{lk}$ | The amount of used product received at DC $k$ from customer $l$ |

| | | |
|---|---|---|
| $\alpha_j$ | 1: If a plant is developed in location $j$ | 0: Else |
| $\beta_k$ | 1: If a DC is developed in location $k$ | 0: Else |
| $\delta_m$ | 1: If a dismantler is developed in location $m$ | 0: Else |

According to the aforementioned symbols, the bi-objective mixed-integer linear programming is proposed for the green forward/reverse SCND to minimize costs and emission rate as follows (the first objective and the constraints can be found in [14, 16]):

$$\begin{aligned}\text{Emission Rate}\quad & \sum_{j} ERJ_j\alpha_j + \sum_{k} ERK_k\beta_k + \sum_{m} ERM_m\delta_m \\ & + \sum_{i}\sum_{j} EIJ_{ij}.x_{ij} + \sum_{j}\sum_{k} EJK_{jk}.y_{jk} + \sum_{k}\sum_{i} EKL.z_{kl} \\ & + \sum_{k}\sum_{m} EKM.o_{km} + \sum_{m}\sum_{j} EMJ.Rd_{mj} + \sum_{l}\sum_{k} ELK_{lk}.Rz_{lk}\end{aligned} \tag{1}$$

The objective function in verbal form:

- Minimum cost = Fixed costs of reopening + Shipping costs
- Minimum Emission = Emission of constructing facilities (plants, DCs, and dismantlers) + Shipping emission

The first objective function of the CDM model is to minimize costs, which includes transportation costs within the network and the fixed costs of developing units in potential locations. The second objective function (1) aims to minimize the total emissions of developing units in potential locations and the emission from the transferring of products between different layers of the SC network. The constraints generally contain four types and a verbal description of them is provided as below:

- Facility capacity: the incoming and outgoing products to each facility should be equal to or less than the related capacity.
- Flow constraints: the amount of input to each center must be equal to the amount of output from the same center.
- Demand Constraint: All the demands should be satisfied.
- Logical constraints: non-negativity and binary nature of variables should be considered.

## 3 Solution Approach

Since the closed-loop SCND problem is NP-hard, applying efficient metaheuristics is highly beneficial especially when dealing with large instances. One of the important sections of metaheuristics is a solution encoding method. The spanning-tree encoding method, as an efficient solution encoding method, is generally used in problems where there is no loop. However, the closed-loop SCND problem contains a loop. By dividing it into smaller parts, where there is no loop, this can be resolved. For more information about encoding, decoding, and the repair mechanism of this approach please refer to [14]. The advantage of the spanning tree method comparing to other methods in the literature is its minimum usage of alleles in a chromosome while the disadvantage of this method is the difficulty of coding and decoding since it needs many types of repairing mechanisms.

Following the research activities regarding the development of SA, Lu, Yuan, and Zhang [19] presented a cloud theory-based approach that enabled better neighborhood search and obtaining better solutions. The cloud modeling is a kind of modeling that incorporates qualitative concepts and quantitative representation that utilizes natural language for this purpose (Fig. 2).

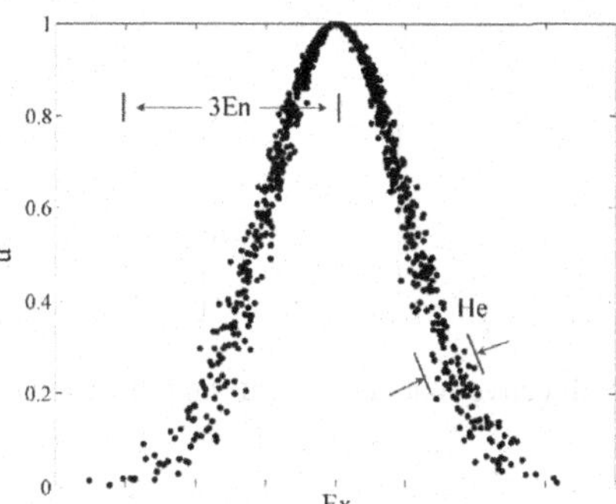


**Fig. 2.** Three digital characteristics of a normal cloud [19].

To obtain almost persistent annealing temperature, the CSA gets advantages of the Metropolis rule and applies the Y status normal cloud generator. By incorporating the cloud theory, the random conversion of annealing temperature can increase the diversity of the searched space and avoid being trapped by a local minimum more efficiently than an original SA algorithm. Furthermore, the permanent tendency of annealing temperature can faster detect better answers and thus improve the efficiency of the SA algorithm. In fact, by revising the temperature change pattern in the SA algorithm, we are likely to see more speed and accuracy in solving the NP-hard problems. In the following section, we will discuss the results of applying CSA on SCND.

## 4 Computational Results

For the integrated problem of forward/reverse SCND, 14 test problem samples are used from small to large sizes based on a steel company in Iran. Some other data are generated based on papers in the literature: Wang and Hsu [14] and Yadegari et al. [16, 20].

In this part, the CSA's performance is compared to the performance of two of the algorithms in the literature that used the spanning tree representation method to solve the NP-hard problem. The first algorithm is GA developed in [14] and the second is the SA developed in [16]. The three mentioned meta-heuristics are compared for efficiency and effectiveness. The results obtained from the implementation of the algorithms for the given problems are pertaining of the best objective function value in the closed-loop SCND.

For coding the algorithms MATLAB 7.11.0 (R2014b) and for comparing the algorithms, Tukey Test and Two-Way ANOVA are applied. The results of implementation of algorithms are analyzed from the following two points of view: 1. The best amount of the objective function and 2. The CPU time.

In Fig. 3 (right side), we examined the output obtained from the variance analysis and 95% confidence interval for the best value of the objective function. According to these two analyses performed on this criterion, the CSA is superior to the GA algorithm, but there is no significant difference between the SA algorithm and GA.

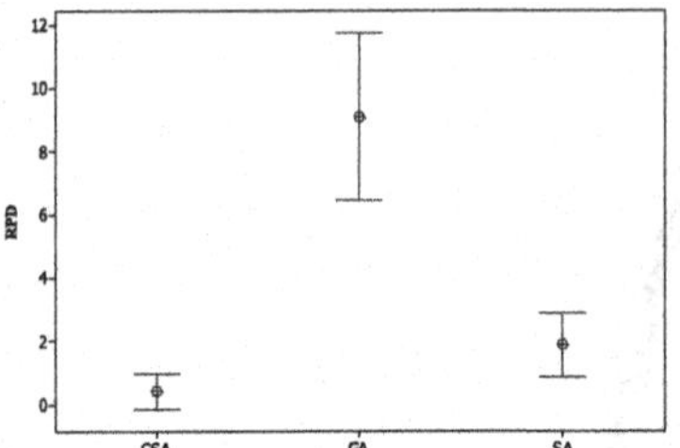

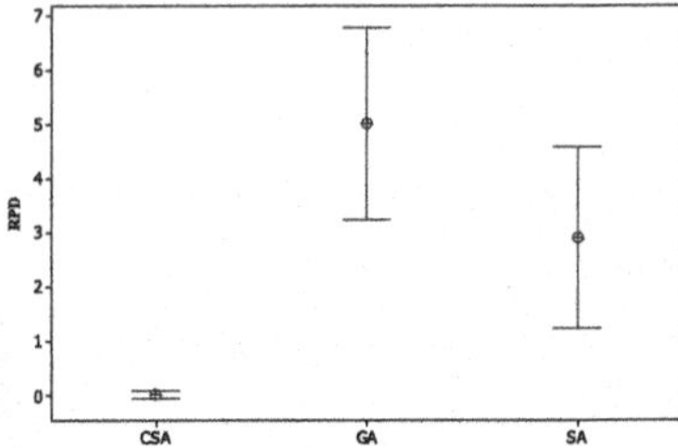


**Fig. 3.** The objective functions (right) and the running time (left)

The results of Tukey's test are illustrated in Fig. 3 (left part) for the algorithms' running time and it shows that the CSA and SA are significantly different from GA in terms of CPU time consumption. It should note that the stopping criteria for each algorithm meet when they show no progress after 20 iterations.

## 5 Managerial Findings of Collaborative Decision Making

In Fig. 4, the trade-off between two objective functions is shown in which the weight of objective function one (total cost) is *w: {0.99, 0.9, 0.8, 0.7, 0.6, 0.5,0.4, 0.3, 0.2, 0.1, and 0.01}*. On the other hand, the weight of the second objective (total environmental negative effect) is *1-w*.

The curve shows us the potentially non-dominated solutions obtained from CSA. As there are usually many conflicts between environmental and operational managers of a collaborative SC contributors, Pareto frontier can help these decision-makers to first avoid non-optimal solutions to their problem as Pareto frontier efficiently eliminate dominated solutions and second, by sensitivity analysis on the weight of each objective, they can find out the cost of environmental decisions on the total SC. For example, in Fig. 4, considering $w = 0.7$ as a point with more emphasis on environmental objective than $w = 0.8$, putting more weight on environmental objective the total cost of the network will increase and this cost growth would be the environmental cost of our decision. Whereas, sometimes, the horizontal collaborative network can bear a little additional cost to gain more competitive advantage through considering environmental issues.

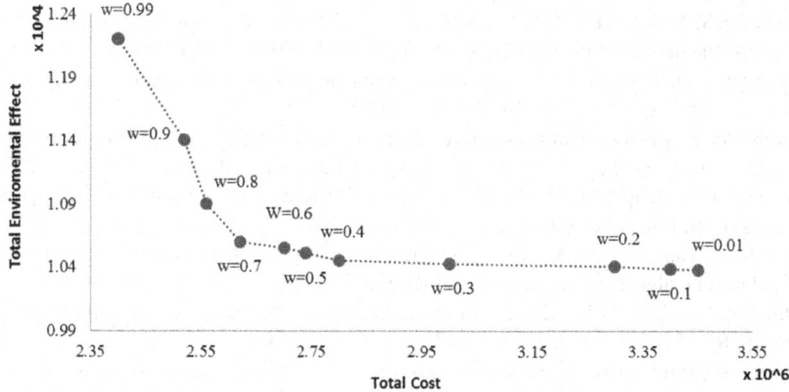


**Fig. 4.** Trade-off between environmental and economics goals

## 6 Conclusion

Recently, horizontal and centralized collaborations have become a very productive strategy in SCs, particularly from a green point of view. The collaborative closed-loop SCND model discussed in this paper was a multi-echelon network, which included suppliers, plants, distribution/collection, dismantler centers, and customer zones. The aim was to minimize the total costs and environmentally negative effects with the collaboration of all parts of the network and enable operations and environmental managers to make a tradeoff analysis between SC costs and the amount of CO2 emission. Considering a variety of characteristics and real-world conditions, a new algorithm in this field was presented using the complex spanning tree representation method to improve the running time and provide more accurate solutions to problems of different sizes. These algorithms were then compared with each other regarding the solutions' quality and the CPU time.

The literature on SCND models considering green principles and the profit is not in its maturity. One of the limitations of this study is that it is usually complicated to determine the exact amount of return product so that one of the future expansion of the paper can be considered as independent possibilistic variables. Moreover, researchers can extend horizontal collaboration with other external sections. Besides, assessment criteria and modeling methodologies should be enhanced for more effective decision-making on green aspects.

## References

1. Long, Q.: A flow-based three-dimensional collaborative decision-making model for supply-chain networks. Knowl.-Based Syst. **97**, 101–110 (2016)
2. Acevedo-Chedid, J., Salas-Navarro, K., Ospina-Mateus, H., Villalobo, A., Sana, S.S.: Production system in a collaborative supply chain considering deterioration. Int. J. Appl. Comput. Math. **7**(3), 1–46 (2021). https://doi.org/10.1007/s40819-021-00965-z
3. Walters, M.: Quantifying the benefits of a collaborative supply chain network using a discrete-time vehicle routing model (2021)

4. Pishvaee, M.S., Razmi, J.: Environmental supply chain network design using multi-objective fuzzy mathematical programming. Appl. Math. Model. **36**(8), 3433–3446 (2012)
5. Van Engeland, J., et al.: Literature review: Strategic network optimization models in waste reverse supply chains. Omega **91**, 102012 (2020)
6. Aloui, A., et al.: Systematic literature review on collaborative sustainable transportation: overview, analysis and perspectives. Transp. Res. Interdiscip. Perspect. **9**, 100291 (2021)
7. Jayaraman, V., Gupta, R., Pirkul, H.: Selecting hierarchical facilities in a service-operations environment. Eur. J. Oper. Res. **147**(3), 613–628 (2003)
8. Syarif, A., Yun, Y., Gen, M.: Study on multi-stage logistic chain network: a spanning tree-based genetic algorithm approach. Comput. Ind. Eng. **43**(1), 299–314 (2002)
9. Elhedhli, S., Merrick, R.: Green supply chain network design to reduce carbon emissions. Transp. Res. Part D Transp. Environ. **17**(5), 370–379 (2012)
10. Krikke, H., van Harten, A., Schuur, P.: Business case Oce: reverse logistic network re-design for copiers. OR-Spektrum **21**(3), 381–409 (1999). https://doi.org/10.1007/s002910050095
11. Min, H., Ko, H.-J.: The dynamic design of a reverse logistics network from the perspective of third-party logistics service providers. Int. J. Prod. Econ. **113**(1), 176–192 (2008)
12. Aras, G., Crowther, D.: Governance and sustainability: an investigation into the relationship between corporate governance and corporate sustainability. Manag. Decis. **46**(3), 433–448 (2008)
13. Nezamoddini, N., Gholami, A., Aqlan, F.: A risk-based optimization framework for integrated supply chains using genetic algorithm and artificial neural networks. Int. J. Prod. Econ. **225**, 107569 (2020)
14. Wang, H.-F., Hsu, H.-W.: A closed-loop logistic model with a spanning-tree based genetic algorithm. Comput. Oper. Res. **37**(2), 376–389 (2010)
15. Devika, K., Jafarian, A., Nourbakhsh, V.: Designing a sustainable closed-loop supply chain network based on triple bottom line approach: a comparison of metaheuristics hybridization techniques. Eur. J. Oper. Res. **235**(3), 594–615 (2014)
16. Yadegari, E., Zandieh, M., Najmi, H.: A hybrid spanning tree-based genetic/simulated annealing algorithm for a closed-loop logistics network design problem. Int. J. Appl. Decis. Sci. **8**(4), 400–426 (2015)
17. Kaya, O., Urek, B.: A mixed integer nonlinear programming model and heuristic solutions for location, inventory and pricing decisions in a closed loop supply chain. Comput. Oper. Res. **65**, 93–103 (2016)
18. Yi, P., et al.: A retailer oriented closed-loop supply chain network design for end of life construction machinery remanufacturing. J. Clean. Prod. **124**, 191–203 (2016)
19. Lv, P., Yuan, L., Zhang, J.: Cloud theory-based simulated annealing algorithm and application. Eng. Appl. Artif. Intell. **22**(4–5), 742–749 (2009)
20. Yadegari, E., Alem-Tabriz, A., Zandieh, M.: A memetic algorithm with a novel neighborhood search and modified solution representation for closed-loop supply chain network design. Comput. Ind. Eng. **128**, 418–436 (2019)

# Collaborative Learning Networks with Industry and Academia

# Education 4.0 and the Smart Manufacturing Paradigm: A Conceptual Gateway for Learning Factories

Leonor Cónego(✉), Rui Pinto, and Gil Gonçalves

Faculty of Engineering of the University of Porto,
Rua Dr. Roberto Frias s/n, 4200-465 Porto, Portugal
{leonorconego,rpinto,gil}@fe.up.pt

**Abstract.** The latest shift in the industry, known as industry 4.0, has introduced new challenges in manufacturing. The main characteristic of this transformation is digital technologies' effect on the way production processes occur. Due to the technological growth, knowledge and skills on manufacturing operations are becoming obsolete. Hence, the need for upskilling and reskilling individuals urges. In collaboration with other key entities, educational institutions are responsible for raising awareness and interest of young students to reach a qualified and equal workforce. Drawing on a thorough literature review focused on key empirical studies on learning factories and fundamental industry 4.0 concepts, trends, teaching approaches, and required skills, the goal of this paper is to provide a gateway to understand effective learning factories' approaches and a holistic understanding of the role of advanced and collaborative learning practices in the so-called education 4.0.

**Keywords:** Industry 4.0 · Education 4.0 · Smart manufacturing · Learning factories

## 1 Introduction

Considering the delivery mechanisms for learning and training in the Industry 4.0 (I4.0) paradigm, it is safe to say that traditional education is no longer fit-for-purpose. Virtual/Augmented Reality, Cyber-Physical Systems (CPS), Co-bots and 3D printing are just a few examples of technologies that are reshaping the way people think, learn, and work [1]. Many of today's students will work in new job types that do not yet exist, with an increased demand for leadership, resourcefulness and creativity. These are crucial skills considering the emerging production processes' demands.

Overall, the current education system follows a standard testing-oriented approach, which fails at measuring qualitative skills that are crucial in the upcoming years. Specifically, in the Smart Manufacturing paradigm, the gap between education and jobs is further widened by limited innovation in learning systems, which should be largely designed to mirror factory-style growth models. Education 4.0 (E4.0) [2–4] is a new learning approach that emerges from this urgent need for education systems to adapt in the I4.0


Published by Springer Nature Switzerland AG 2021
L. M. Camarinha-Matos et al. (Eds.): PRO-VE 2021, IFIP AICT 629, pp. 721–728, 2021.
https://doi.org/10.1007/978-3-030-85969-5_68

context. E4.0 is the desired approach to learning with the emerging Fourth Industrial Revolution, which focuses on the Internet of Things (IoT), Artificial Intelligence (AI), Robotics, among other topics, all of which are already impacting our everyday lives. The main challenge of E4.0 is to prepare students for evolving industries, which means (a) a change on educational approaches must occur and (b) governments, educational institutions and employers should focus on job creation to tackle I4.0 challenges.

This paper provides a Literature Review (LR) regarding theoretical and methodological E4.0 approaches and innovative Learning Factories (LFs). The presented study tries to collect and analyse recent pedagogical strategies in LFs implemented with industrial partnerships, which were best suited to educate future factory engineers while identifying relevant learning skills.

Regarding the structure of the paper, the Introduction is followed by Sect. 2 that provides a detailed description and state-of-art of innovative LFs. Section 3 summarises the body of the review and draws important conclusions about the LFs and E4.0 topics while identifying gaps or inconsistencies in a body of knowledge. Finally, Sect. 4 concludes the paper, stating final remarks about the work presented and provides orientations for future work.

## 2 Innovative Learning Factories

This section consists of reviewing E4.0 approaches and LFs that demonstrate their relevance in supporting I4.0 applied research and education. This review's underlying research question is "*What is the best architecture of LFs to educate the next set of manufacturing engineers?*". The main goals are: 1) getting to know the main adopted teaching approaches when using LFs as a setting to learn; 2) understanding how a LF can establish a partnership and take advantage of it and finally; 3) identifying the most relevant skills to target to shape future engineers.

LFs are mainly present at universities and contribute significantly to the acquisition of a holistic understanding of I4.0 by creating a realistic setting in which academia, industry, and other entities can collaborate and validate the use of novel technologies. The LFs concept has been used worldwide and has proven to be a practical action-oriented approach where participants learn innovative factory procedures and their challenges in a production-technological learning environment [5].

Establishing interactions such as collaborations, partnerships, and integrations between university and I4.0 enterprises contributes to fostering students' employability rate, teacher's continuum learning and, consequently, stimulates regional growth [6]. On the one hand, E4.0 demands students to have skills capable of implementing and maintaining the latest technologies, which entails solving complex problems, being creative, taking quick and intelligent decisions, and analysing information. Often educational institutions lack friendly advanced equipment to provide an appropriate education to students [7]. On the other hand, enterprises need to respond to the globalisation challenges, delivering products and services at lower prices and better quality [6]. Moreover, Rocha Brito and Ciampi [6] stress that regardless of a country's political situation, governments must invest in Science and Technology to pursue socio-economic growth and development, which strongly supports collaborations. According to Karlik *et al.* [7], to be effective, these collaborations should have a considerable length in time, enabling the development of various fields such as science, education and the production industry.

Maia *et al.* [8] describe how two laboratories – one of Digital Manufacturing (DM) and the other of IoT - were developed at the Educational Foundation of Ignatius (FEI) University Center (Brazil) in partnership with two manufacturing companies, aiming to train engineering and computer science students to cope with IoT and I4.0 issues. The IoT laboratory resulted from the collaboration with an international telecommunication company, and its projects were focused on IoT applications, data analytics and hardware prototyping. The learning method used was *Problem-Based Learning*, which provided a challenge for the students to tackle and explore solutions. Additionally, students had a teacher to help find the materials and explain concepts, and tutor from the telecommunication company to help students develop a solution. Students who successfully solved the challenges were invited to work in scientific initiations. Moreover, these students also helped other students solve problems using a *Learning by Teaching* approach. For the implementation of the DM laboratory, two partnerships were established to support it: a DM software provider and an automation company. The first one provided access to 100 DM software licenses. The second one provided its experience in the implementation and offered a digital project of a robotic cell and its physical construction. As a result of the collaboration between these two labs, new problems regarding Machine-to-Machine (M2M) communication emerged, involving societal and business entities in academic research. Besides the evident benefits this active learning environment offered to students, this experience was also significant to enhance each manufacturing companies' particular expertise.

Oberc *et al.* [9] established a LF training on integrating collaborative robots into manual assembly lines through an *Action-Oriented* and *Problem-solving approach* in the LF of the Chair of Production Systems (LPS) at the Ruhr-University in Bochum. This training focused on organizational and personnel topics. Authors defend that this was made possible by the collaboration between academic institutions and industrial companies or academies, which revealed its utility, for example, in the implementation phase. Students could develop code for robots provided by various enterprises. Apart from this, the LPS is involved in research activities related to the Human-Robot Collaboration (HRC) planning and simulation environment, contributing to functional integration of a robot simulation and programming framework in *Ema* [10]. From this perspective, partnerships for research purposes seem to be very feasible and desirable.

Schuh *et al.* [11] work consisted of an empirical *Work-based* approach to understand how learning in production is supported while reducing its complexity at the same time. It took 30 working days to test the integrity of certain assumptions concerning new HRC interfaces for the provision and permanently updated Digital Twin information for work instructions. The survey was conducted by the Laboratory for Machine Tools and Production Engineers at the Demonstration Factory of the Rheinisch-Westfälische Technische Hochschule (RWTH) Aachen Campus. This simple collaboration inside the university allowed the learning content to be immediately linked with the needs and applications of daily work practically and economically. The research was supported by the German Federal Ministry of Education and Research within the collaborative research project *ELIAS* [12]. The authors seek to permanently develop solutions in the future concerning automation for the context-sensitive provision and customized instruction.

The *AutFab*, located at the University of Applied Sciences Darmstadt (h_da) [13], is a fully automated I4.0 LF used for education, research and development purposes. It consists of high bay storage, two assembly and two inspection stations. Students of different courses are educated here, whether by working in labs or directly in the *Autfab*. The *Problem-Based Learning* approach consists of establishing the communication between the software system MATLAB/Simulink and the *AutFab* via OPC and analysing the data they get, or directly in the *Autfab*, focusing on project planning and managing as well as on the presentation and documentation. The constant evaluation of the *AutFab* projects constitute a benefit for students, researchers and different industries involved. On the one hand, students highlight the hands-on relevance for their future work. Usually, students' thesis at h_da are conducted in industry, and often supervisors positively report the students' practical skills. On the other hand, researchers and companies who provide conditions for the undergoing thesis benefit from discoveries and a qualified workforce. This alliance has revealed that *Project-based learning* in the *AutFab* has a crucial effect on students' education. Besides this, *AutFab* usually collaborates with high schools to present them the LF and thus attract new students. Authors mention that working in multidisciplinary teams and contacting suppliers improves students' communication skills and allows teachers to broaden their knowledge continuously.

The *Industry 4.0 Pilot Factory* (I40PF) [14], based in Austria, emphasizes the importance of cooperation with different industries, i.e., machinery and equipment. I40PF provides easy access to I4.0 infrastructures for Small and Medium Enterprises (SMEs), whereas key industrial technology suppliers help build a factory that meets I4.0 requirements. Kemény *et al.* [15] foresee a possible partnership between the I4.0 LF at TU Wien and the premises of MTA SZTAKI in Gyor and Budapest. The authors provide a high-level description of the possibilities of such a partnership by describing the underlying features and types of collaboration to complement capacities. From the authors perspective, cooperation is more advantageous by involving different product life cycles, namely design, procurement, testing prototypes and production. This interconnection between different LFs may create an exciting and productive baseline for research and learning while it provides a meaningful complement to the students' curricula.

Ogorodnyk *et al.* [16] installed a roller skis assembly line in the faculty NTNU in Norway to teach practical skills and theoretical knowledge on waste reduction and push/pull production systems. However, it was built with no technological appliances. Although the authors defend that the activity was able to respond to its main goal, enhancing theoretical and practical knowledge while working on a "real assembly line", students could probably take more advantage of it if some collaboration with a real industry was made, resembling it to an actual production assembly line. Other projects involve *Problem-Based Learning* approach and students at lower levels of studies [17, 18]. However, hitherto, there is no evidence of collaborations such as the ones mentioned previously. Smit *et al.* [19] advocate that Industry-School Partnerships (ISP) foster students' interest in STEM careers, and it is highlighted later in this paper the gender gap persisting in this field. According to PORDATA [20], in Portugal, only 24% of students attending higher education in engineering, manufacturing and construction are female.

And this gap is visible both in education and the workforce [21]. Furthermore, Watters *et al.* [22] stress that despite the challenges and threats (i.e., financial, quality teacher access and ISP model) involved when establishing a partnership, it provides meaningful and authentic learning for students environment. Table 1 sums up the studies mentioned in this review (excluding the ones that did not yet take actual place), identifying the core teaching approaches, type of collaboration, and targets.

**Table 1.** Projects' characteristics

| | | Maia *et al.* [8] | Oberc *et al.* [9] | Schuh *et al.* [11] | Simons *et al.* [13] | Ogorodnyk *et al.* [16] |
|---|---|---|---|---|---|---|
| Approach | Problem-based learning | ✓ | ✓ | | ✓ | |
| | Project-based learning | ✓ | | | ✓ | ✓ |
| | Learning by teaching | ✓ | | | | |
| | Action-oriented | ✓ | ✓ | | ✓ | ✓ |
| | Work-based | | | ✓ | | |
| Collaboration type | Inside institution | ✓ | | ✓ | ✓ | |
| | Outside institution | ✓ | ✓ | | ✓ | |
| Target | University students | ✓ | | | ✓ | |
| | High school students or lower | | | | ✓ | ✓ |
| | Operators | | | ✓ | | |

## 3 Discussion

I4.0 envisions a future where small distributed and digitalized production networks operate autonomously in factories. As a result, they will be able to plan production in response to any change properly. Meanwhile, I4.0 researchers and technology developers still have a long way ahead. LFs contribute significantly to understanding the primary enablers and barriers of the Smart Manufacturing vision since they are commonly used for learning and research purposes. Thus, most of the time, it requires developing and testing models and technologies, new manufacturing processes, interaction, and decision support systems [14]. All of these requirements can be more easily achieved through the establishment of collaboration networks. Collaborative networking between industry and academia allows students to improve their project planning competencies and solve complex problems, which enriches their comprehensive understanding of CPS [8, 9, 11, 13]. In some cases, it also improves students' presentation and documentation skills [13]. Besides that, teachers' knowledge is also enhanced, which can be positively integrated into their courses. Nonetheless, we highlight the importance of long-term collaborations since these are also long-term developments that require extensive investigation. Funded research is also fundamental. More research means more break-throws and advancements, which means better education, a more qualified workforce, and social and economic development. For enterprises, it constitutes an opportunity to develop their knowledge and be able to produce better products.

Concerning teaching approaches, it looks like there has been a steady trend toward Student-Centered learning, such as *Problem* and *Project-Based learning*, aiming to respond to the new challenges. Educational organizations must redefine the required profiles and skills requirements and change their instructional notions based on the idea that I4.0 demands interdisciplinarity [8], communication and analytical skills, and creativity, among others [23]. Tutoring was also something that we retained as a good practice for LF contexts. Students take part in a continuous learning and cooperative process of creating and restructuring knowledge.

Inferring from this review, LFs are mainly implemented at universities to train graduate and undergraduate students. However, one should also consider involving lower levels of studies, motivating young pupils to consider a career in manufacturing and, this way, guarantee a future qualified workforce. A complex modular CPS coupled with a *Problem-Based Learning* approach (prominent in this LR), interdisciplinary teams and tutoring seem to be the key to provide the skills and substantial knowledge of I4.0 concepts to the next set of manufacturing engineers (see Fig. 1). A step forward is to consider a collaboration with a related LF, making its technologies more advanced and accurate to the real smart factory environments. It is expected that it increases the system complexity and thus generates a holistic understanding of I4.0. The latest is halfway there to motivate students to follow a career in engineering.

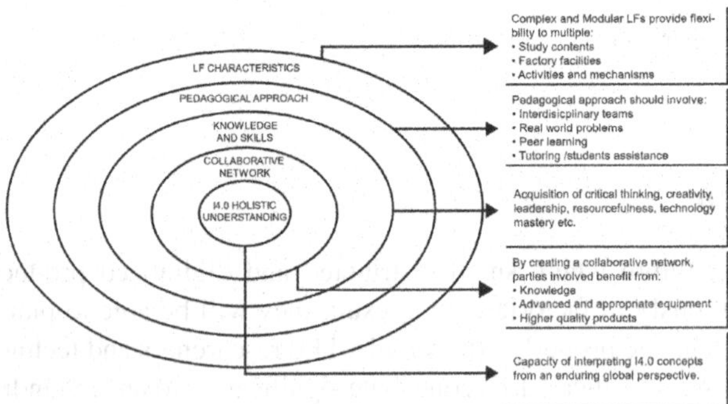


**Fig. 1.** The architecture of an effective LF

## 4 Conclusion

In this paper, we presented a LR regarding theoretical and methodological E4.0 approaches and innovative LFs. We collected and critically analyzed recent pedagogical approaches in LFs implemented with industrial partnerships while identifying relevant learning skills to be tackled in the current I4.0 educational context.

From the review, we conclude that the road map for an I4.0 holistic understanding combines specific LF characteristics, approaches, processes and skills (see Fig. 1). Together, these "blocks" may constitute the key axes to an effective LF architecture, capable of endowing students with the required I4.0 skills and knowledge to succeed. It is expected that by testing such architecture and analysing the most effective ways of connecting the mentioned "blocks", a gateway to further explore and understand learning factories' approaches and the role of advanced and collaborative learning practices, arises.

Regarding future work, we intend to hold an activity in a set of Portuguese schools, in which students are orientated to build a small LF, consisting of a 3D printable production line that uses CPPS related technologies. In this context, we aim to address and validate the collaborative network approach in which the involved schools and targeted related companies can mutually take advantage of it.

**Acknowledgements.** This research is developed within the scope of the European project "ShapiNG" (Shaping the next Generation of Manufacturing Professionals), supported by EIT-Manufacturing.

## References

1. Bongomin, O., Gilibrays Ocen, G., Oyondi Nganyi, E., Musinguzi, A., Omara, T.: Exponential disruptive technologies and the required skills of Industry 4.0. J. Eng. (United Kingdom). 2020, 0–17 (2020). https://doi.org/10.1155/2020/4280156
2. Hussin Aziz, A.: Education 4.0 made simple: ideas for teaching. Int. J. Educ. Lit. Stud. **6**, 92 (2018)
3. Mourtzis, D.: Development of skills and competences in manufacturing towards Education 4.0: a teaching factory approach (2018). https://doi.org/10.2991/iscfec-18.2019.45
4. Mourtzis, D., Vlachou, E., Dimitrakopoulos, G., Zogopoulos, V.: Cyber-physical systems and Education 4.0 -the teaching Factory 4.0 concept. Procedia Manuf. **23**, 129–134 (2018). https://doi.org/10.1016/j.promfg.2018.04.005.
5. Tisch, M., Hertle, C., Cachay, J., Abele, E., Metternich, J., Tenberg, R.: A systematic approach on developing action-oriented, competency-based learning factories. Procedia CIRP **7**, 580–585 (2013). https://doi.org/10.1016/j.procir.2013.06.036
6. Da Rocha Brito, C., Ciampi, M.M.: Research relevance in the world scenario. In: 2015 International Symposium Computers in Education SIIE 2015, pp. 1–4 (2016). https://doi.org/10.1109/SIIE.2015.7451638
7. Karlik, A.E., Platonov, V. V., Iakovleva, E.A., Shirokov, S.N.: Experience of cooperation between St. Petersburg universities and industrial enterprises. In: 2016 IEEE 5th Forum Strategic Partnership Universities and Enterprises of Hi-Tech Branches, Science. Education. Innovations 2016, pp. 9–11 (2017). https://doi.org/10.1109/IVForum.2016.7835838.

8. Maia, R.F., Massote, A.A., Lima, F.: Innovative laboratory model based on partnerships and active learning. In: Proceedings - Frontiers Education Conference FIE. 2017, Octobober 2017. https://doi.org/10.1109/FIE.2017.8190534
9. Oberc, H., Prinz, C., Glogowski, P., Lemmerz, K., Kuhlenkötter, B.: Human robot interaction - learning how to integrate collaborative robots into manual assembly lines. Procedia Manuf. **31**, 26–31 (2019). https://doi.org/10.1016/j.promfg.2019.03.005
10. Fritzsche, L., Jendrusch, R., Leidholdt, W., Bauer, S., Jäckel, T., Pirger, A.: Introducing EMA (editor for manual work activities) – a new tool for enhancing accuracy and efficiency of human simulations in digital production planning. In: Duffy, V.G. (ed.) Digital Human Modeling, pp. 272–281. Springer, Heidelberg (2011)
11. Schuh, G., Gartzen, T., Rodenhauser, T., Marks, A.: Promoting work-based learning through Industry 4.0. Procedia CIRP **32**, 82–87 (2015). https://doi.org/10.1016/j.procir.2015.02.213
12. Research Institute for Industrial Management. https://www.fir.rwth-aachen.de/en/research/research-work-at-fir/detail/elias-01xz13007/
13. Simons, S., Abé, P., Neser, S.: Learning in the AutFab – the fully automated Industrie 4.0 learning factory of the university of applied sciences Darmstadt. Procedia Manuf. **9**, 81–88 (2017). https://doi.org/10.1016/j.promfg.2017.04.023
14. Erol, S., Jäger, A., Hold, P., Ott, K., Sihn, W.: Tangible Industry 4.0: a scenario-based approach to learning for the future of production. Procedia CIRP **54**, 13–18 (2016). https://doi.org/10.1016/j.procir.2016.03.162
15. Kemény, Z., Beregi, R., Nacsa, J., Glawar, R., Sihn, W.: Expanding production perspectives by collaborating learning factories - perceived needs and possibilities. Procedia Manuf. **23**, 111–116 (2018). https://doi.org/10.1016/j.promfg.2018.04.002
16. Ogorodnyk, O., Granheim, M., Holtskog, H., Ogorodnyk, I.: Roller skis assembly line learning factory – development and learning outcomes. Procedia Manuf. **9**, 121–126 (2017). https://doi.org/10.1016/j.promfg.2017.04.045
17. Kaloti-Hallak, F., Armoni, M., Ben-Ari, M.: The effect of robotics activities on learning the engineering design process. Inform. Educ. **18**, 105–129 (2019). https://doi.org/10.15388/infedu.2019.05
18. Peiró-Signes, A., Trull-Dominguez, O., Segarra-Oña, M., Cabrero, J.A.: Bowling game to learn communications between different devices. In: INTED2020 Proceedings, vol. 1, pp. 1490–1495 (2020). https://doi.org/10.21125/inted.2020.0493
19. Smit, R., Robin, N., De Toffol, C., Atanasova, S.: Industry school projects as an aim to foster secondary school.pdf. Int. J. Technol. Des. Educ. **31**, 61–79 (2019). https://doi.org/10.1007/s10798-019-09538-0
20. PORDATA: Alunos do sexo feminino em % dos matriculados no ensino superior: total e por área de educação e formação. https://www.pordata.pt/Portugal/Alunos+do+sexo+feminino+em+percentagem+dos+matriculados+no+ensino+superior+total+e+por+área+de+educação+e+formação+-1051
21. Silva, S.M.: Closing the gender gap in digital technologies (2018)
22. Watters, J., Pillay, H., Flynn, M.: Industry-school partnerships: a strategy to enhance education and training opportunities (2016)
23. Hecklau, F., Galeitzke, M., Flachs, S., Kohl, H.: Holistic approach for human resource management in Industry 4.0. Procedia CIRP **54**, 1–6 (2016). https://doi.org/10.1016/j.procir.2016.05.102.

# Innovative Learning Scheme to Up-skilling and Re-skilling – Designing a Collaborative Training Program Between Industry and Academia Towards Digital Transformation

Ana Correia Simões[1(✉)], Filipe Ferreira[1], António Almeida[1], Ricardo Zimmermann[1], Hélio Castro[1,2], and Américo Azevedo[1]

[1] INESC TEC, Campus da FEUP, R. Dr. Roberto Frias, 4200-465 Porto, Portugal
{ana.c.simoes,filipe.d.ferreira,antonio.h.almeida, ricardo.a.zimmermann,helio.c.castro,americo.azevedo}@inesctec.pt

[2] School of Engineering (ISEP) - Polytechnic of Porto, R. Dr António Bernardino de Almeida, 431, 4249-015 Porto, Portugal

**Abstract.** Small and medium-sized enterprises (SMEs) in Europe are conscious that their competitive position depends on their success to embrace digitalisation challenges. However, some decision-makers in companies discard digital transformation because they do not understand how it can be incorporated into their businesses. Therefore, academia, research centres, and technological clusters are responsible for building the infrastructures and providing the support and the training that will progressively change this mindset. This paper aims to report an experience on designing a training program to train the trainers under the digital transformation topic. To define strategies to understand better the companies (and professionals) needs and motivations and the requisites to deliver the training course, the focus group methodology was applied. In this paper, we present a training program methodology and structure that intend to respond to industrial requests and, in this way to accelerate the digital transformation of companies, especially SMEs.

**Keywords:** Digital transformation · Education 4.0 · Manufacturing · e-learning · Up-skilling · Re-skilling

## 1 Introduction

A non-return trend seems to be the digitalisation of the industry. Addressing the different dimensions underlying digitisation is a challenge for both companies and academia/research centres. Significant challenges are acknowledged: i) Ensure adequate availability of qualified workforce; ii) Achieve a practical awareness and understanding of cost-benefit related to the adoption of digital solutions; iii) Guaranteeing effectiveness in the development of suitable initiatives to transform organisations.


Published by Springer Nature Switzerland AG 2021
L. M. Camarinha-Matos et al. (Eds.): PRO-VE 2021, IFIP AICT 629, pp. 729–737, 2021.
https://doi.org/10.1007/978-3-030-85969-5_69

There are two poles of industrial companies. On one side, we have the big companies, with their intervening power and availability of resources. To increase their competitive position in the market, they launch comprehensive initiatives of test, evaluation and adoption of technologies and operating and organisational practices. On the opposite side, we have small and medium-size enterprises (SME), generally with scarce resources, acting fundamentally on a regional niche basis and without a strategic orientation in business evolution. They end up having a reactive attitude, which is very much sustained by the need for survival in the markets they operate. Consequently, although digitalisation strategies can bring exceptional competitive opportunities to companies, the implementation of this digital transformation in SMEs is not risk-free or straightforward.

Although SMEs in Europe risk their competitiveness if they fail to embrace digitalisation [1, 2], a key obstacle in this process is related to decision makers' lack of awareness concerning digital technologies potential and implications. Some decision-makers renounce digital transformation simply because they do not understand how it can be incorporated into their businesses [3]. In this context, research and technology organisations (RTOs) assume a critical role, as they include in their mission the identification of research and innovation results that can be the object of advanced training actions, providing comprehensive support for organisations to place emerging technologies at the centre of strategic innovation decisions [4]. As the generation of knowledge is built on a rigorous scientific research base and in a dynamic research environment, this allows for mentoring, coaching, technological and business consultancy, supporting the development of technological-based business projects.

However, RTOs, due to their constitution, organisation and structure, are not able to train, on their own, all SMEs and large companies in emerging subjects and technologies related to industry 4.0. In this sense, it is necessary to build a strategy that promotes a more effective way of training professionals with the new competencies required for industry 4.0, taking advantage of new collaborative learning networks between academia and industry supported by the industrial clusters, associations and similar institutions.

European industry sectoral clusters are working to develop transregional cooperation, defining common strategies and roadmaps for joint activities, responding to the needs of companies to better adapt to the trends, challenges and opportunities. Because they know the needs of the industrial sectors and the individual characteristics of the companies, the digital maturity of the sector and the future objectives of remaining competitive in a global domain, they can be actors in the dissemination of knowledge through their network of industrial companies.

These already established networks may form the basis for successful collaborative networks for advanced training, providing the means to scale the upskilling and re-skilling human capital for industry 4.0. At the same time, through these links between RTOs and industrial clusters in the development of advanced training allows an acceleration in the adoption of the industry 4.0 paradigm by manufacturing SMEs through training. Also, it gives a considerable advantage in highly turbulent conditions, such as the current COVID 19 pandemic situation.

Considering the context previously presented, this paper aims to answer to the following research question: How to design a training program to train the trainers under the digital transformation topic? This paper reports an experience on designing a training program, to be implemented in the near future, and that was developed in a collaborative way involving the academia, with the experts in the digital transformation topic, and industrial associations, closer to companies.

## 2 Theoretical Background

Digital transformation has been driving a radical change in work environments. The digitalisation of products, processes and activities requires a whole new set of skills and has led companies to rethink how education and training are performed [24]. Recent studies suggest that work organisation and activities and the respective skills requirements will be significantly different shortly due to the increasing environmental complexity [5, 6].

The development of skills aligned with job requirements is a decisive factor for digital technologies adoption [7, 8]. Many authors have highlighted the lack of qualified personnel and the need for continued training as two of the main barriers to digital transformation [9–11]. Although the development of appropriate skills to face the needs of the dynamic and complex business environments is an important condition for companies' competitiveness [12], the rapid development of new technologies makes skills become obsolete much faster than in the past, generating gaps between companies' needs and workforce availability [13]. Achieving this balance is a crucial aspect of the readiness for the adoption and implementation of new technologies. In this sense, it is imperative to find ways to allow workers to acquire skills that meet the new job requirements and maintain and update these skills over time [13].

As a response to these challenges, two approaches to the development of the workforce have gained ground in the literature in recent years in the context of digitalisation: re-skilling and upskilling. Reskilling is related to the acquisition of entirely new skills sets that will potentially lead to new career positions, while upskilling concerns the learning of new skills that can support the improvement in the current situation. Thus, adopting an education and learning strategy based on re-skilling and/or upskilling workforce helps companies respond more quickly to market changes.

The collaboration between academia and industry is considered an effective way to reduce the existing gaps between workforce capabilities and companies' needs [14]. Previous studies have discussed different approaches on how academia can interact with industry in a mutually beneficial collaboration in terms of research, education, training, students experience, etc. [15, 16]. A demand-driven approach to the development of education and training programs – especially regarding digitalisation – can accelerate the adaptation to new requirements, considering that the traditional pace of education and training programs may not be fast enough to keep up with the changes caused by digital transformation.

Moreover, partnerships between academia and industry tend to be cost-efficient – as the mission to identify and retain skills will be facilitated and more flexible and adaptable [17]. On the other hand, the main obstacles to the success of this type of partnership may be the differing interests of the industry/employee and the students when it comes to career projection and the risk of a short-term view by the industry [14]. In this sense, the collaboration between academia and industry to foster upskilling and re-skilling workforce requires clearly defined roles and mechanisms that allow coherent cooperation between all relevant actors to favour significant gains.

The relevance of active teaching methods has been vastly discussed in the literature over the last years [18]. A more substantial role of the students in their educational process has been highlighted as a central objective in the contemporary environment. This trend promotes the increase of methodologies such as project-based learning, problem-based learning and flipped or inverted classroom [18, 19]. Active learning can be defined as a method that favours students' engagement in the learning process [20]. For instance, in flipped classrooms, students are transformed from passive listeners to active learners [21].

Besides the methods mentioned above, the relevance of the train-the-trainer model has been highlighted in the context of academia and industry collaboration [22]. This model refers to the education or training of potential "instructors" with a set of skills that allow them to train other people. This approach is commonly used with leaders, who will be able to train their teams. Pancucci [22] argues that the skills acquired using the train-the-trainer method, especially in professional learning, enhance the teaching and learning capacity of the community members. In turn, this increased capacity supports other education and training events that emerge from a broader professional development model.

## 3 Material and Methods

This paper aims to describe and explain the design of a training program to train the trainers under the digital transformation topic. Therefore, this paper reports an experience on designing a training program, to be implemented in the near future, and that was developed in a collaborative way involving the academia, with the experts in the topic, and industrial associations, closer to companies.

Aiming to design and propose an innovative "train the trainer" program capable of fostering the digital transition in Europe, structured qualitative research was used in this study. The primary value of this research design is to enable an enriched picture with precise and substantial contributions to developing a training programme for trainers in the topic of digital transformation [23]. In particular, the focus group was applied to accomplish to the research objective. To define strategies to comprehend better the industrial clusters and specific industrial sectors needs and motivations, and consequently, the requisites to deliver a course to train the trainers in the topic of the digital transformation, the focus group methodology can be applied to educational research [24]. Using this method, it was possible to identify the best practices, frameworks and contents to support the training programme, namely the learning and teaching activities [24]. Focus group methodology was conducted involving different groups of participants. Therefore, two focus groups were conducted: i) one internal (academia), with the experts in the digital transformation topic, and ii) one external, with the industrial associations responsible and mentor of this training program. A total of twenty experts in the management, leadership and training areas were involved, ten from academia and ten from sectoral industrial clusters. Focus group methodology resulted very well since the purpose of understanding specific aspects and generating relevant information and context on collective point views. Sharing knowledge and experiences between participants, in an interactive way, in both focus groups resulted in enriched and valuable contributions to design the training program.

The designed training program will be validated in the several modular sessions prepared to be running during June 2021 with a sample of participants from three European sectoral industrial clusters. Based on the results of these sessions, the program will be adjusted to better met the objectives, and other training sessions will be prepared by the sectoral industrial clusters to target the companies. Only after this long process it will be possible to validate and evaluate the success of this initiative.

## 4 Results

Considering the context and ambition previously identified, this paper proposes establishing virtual networks composed of RTOs, industrial clusters and associations, and industry to promote i4.0 training on a large scale. To leverage these European training networks, this paper proposes an innovative training methodology for industrial clusters, based on a "train the trainer" approach, capable of contributing to the training of future trainers from industrial clusters around the fundamentals and concepts, methodologies, technologies and tools inherent to the multidisciplinary challenge of digital transformation that is posed to the organisations. More concretely, after the course, it is expected that clusters become able to:

- Explain to industry companies the relevance, scope, strategies and approaches inherent to the digital transformation initiatives of organisations, and in particular for SMEs;
- Understand the importance of a digital transformation methodology that systematise the effective adoption of digital technologies in manufacturing companies;
- Assess the suitability of a digital transformation strategy applied to a specific organisation;
- Understand how the organisation structure and operating model need to evolve to adopt and take advantage of the digital transformation effectively;
- Identify the key technologies that drive the digital transformation as well as understand the potential and barriers for its adoption;
- Recognise the intrinsic importance of combining different digital technologies towards a customised data-driven digital architecture;
- Understand the importance of the digital transformation to the development and deployment of new digital business models;
- Recognise the importance of digital innovation hubs as a mechanism capable of fostering the digital transformation in the SME ecosystem;
- To draw recommendations for the future delivery of effective services to SMEs, the creation of dedicated exchange opportunities (for cluster members or other organisations) and the definition of individual and joint strategies;
- To draw recommendations for facilitating cluster members better use of advanced technologies, improving productivity, resource efficiency, innovation and creativity.

This training course was developed, implemented and tested with European clusters from textile and advanced production systems sectors within the CLAMTEX European project.

### 4.1 Training Program Methodology

Aiming to achieve the objectives previously identified, an active teaching method was followed, grounded on an interactive teaching-learning methodology, and leveraged by an online platform. Considering the actual pandemic context, it was possible to take the on-site regular classroom-style lecture to a new level by adding interactive and group activities to the online training experience. Here, two types of training sessions were proposed: the theoretical (T) and Practical (P) sessions. In the T sessions, with a shorter duration (30 min), the main objective is to present the fundamental concepts, methods and tools. In the P sessions (longer sessions, 1,5 h), the aim is to stimulate bi-directional communication between the trainer and the trainees by empowering discussion and group interaction, not only to keep high energy and attention levels but also to allow participants to learn from each other's experiences and knowledge. A case-based learning method is used to guarantee high motivation and participation levels, where trainees apply their knowledge to real-world scenarios, promoting higher levels of cognition. Different case studies presenting a real multidisciplinary problem or problems are shared before sessions. Therefore, trainees can read, analyse and prepare their participation in the group exercises that will be promoted and guided by the trainer along with the P session. At the end of these sessions, the trainer compiles the discussion's primary outcomes and exposes/share the main takeaways of the session.

### 4.2 Training Program Structure

A comprehensive digital transformation framework was designed to support the complete digital transformation journeys iteratively based on multidisciplinary scientific and innovation results. The framework allows the analysis of companies' digital maturity, the design of the company's digital vision, the establishment of the roadmap for digital transformation as well as the planning and operationalisation of the digital transformation roadmap.

Furthermore, the framework also supports the implementation of digital transformation, bridging the gap between the companies and technology suppliers, ensuring the strategic alignment of the company's business processes with technologies in a sustained manner, and monitoring the change management process the successful adoption of technology. Therefore, the program is composed of the following modules:

- Module 1 - Basics of digital transformation, explains the emerging technologies and the new management and business models' concepts that emerge with its successful implementation. The digital transformation does not only impact on technology adoption, but also influences the business models and company strategy. It is necessary to explore the concepts that will enable the clusters and their company members to think in a more holistic and business-oriented way. In this module, participants will learn the concepts and challenges of the emerging technologies of digital transformation to create an understanding of the potential and implications of adopting these technologies.
- Module 2 - Maturity assessment and digital strategy design supporting tools for digital transformation. Here, sessions will cover the entire digital transformation life-cycle,

from the digital maturity assessment to the technology strategy and road mapping definition until its implementation, execution and monitoring. The essential tools for the successful planning and execution of each phase of the digital transformation life cycle will be presented.
- Module 3 - Digital strategy implementation and systematisation, to guarantee the successful implementation of the digital transformation in the industry, based on a well-validated methodology and toolkit that has been developed along the time with the consultancy services to industry and clusters. The main objective is to provide clusters with a methodological approach that will support their members to maximise the return of investment in digital technologies.
- Module 4 - Digital innovation hubs as a one-stop-shop capable of providing advanced services to the local industry to foster the digital transformation. This module is based on the five steps for the formation of a Digital Innovation Hub: (1) Assess the readiness of the Region, (2) Analyse the ecosystem and engage stakeholders, (3) Build the service portfolio and the Business Model, (4) Deliver Services, (5) Evaluate DIH's performance and benefits.

The four modules form a comprehensive methodology that allows the cluster managers to support their associates (companies) with digital transformation journeys in a structured, efficient and effective way.

## 5 Conclusions

Several approaches can be found in the literature to accelerate the adoption of digital technologies by manufacturing companies. The companies can only accomplish this journey towards digital transformation with the support of their partners. Two of these privileged partners are i) the academia (or research centres) through the participation in research and innovation collaboration projects and ii) the industrial sectoral clusters. This partnership has also been accomplished during the last years by developing and delivering training courses to professionals in companies to upskill and re-skill their professionals. To target and support more companies interested in embracing the digital transformation challenge, the training program presented in this study was developed to train the trainees. Therefore, with this objective in mind, a collaborative partnership between some industrial sectoral clusters in textile and fashion and a research centre was created to train the people (trainers) of these clusters in the topic of digital transformation. Based on the competencies and knowledge acquired in this training program, these trainers will be better prepared to provide training to professionals in companies in a more effective way. Thus, with this approach, a proximity strategy is addressed. More companies are in conditions to participate in the training programmes that would support them and their companies in the digital transformation challenge and reach the most significant number of SMEs in the shortest amount of time.

To develop an advanced training programme, an active training method was pursued, based on an interactive methodology and supported by an online platform. The training program methodology was mainly oriented to group interaction and sharing experiences among trainers and trainees. Based on multiple case studies and organised in four consistent modules, rich contents ensure SMEs collaborators' awareness and preparedness to perform up-skilling and re-skilling towards industry 4.0 in SMEs.

This study presents the first steps in designing an innovative training program to train trainees under the digital transformation topic. Based on these results, several research topics can be addressed in the future. One of them should be how to evaluate the success of this training program for the trainers. In other words, what KPIs should be defined to assess skills and competencies acquired by the trainees in this training course. Another topic should be how to evaluate the efficacy of this initiative on the professionals and as a consequence in their companies. In this sense, what KPIs should be defined to assess the impact of this initiative in the companies in achieving the goal of digital transformation. Finally, one more topic to be addressed in future research should be the impact of the pandemic situation (and the consecutive lockdown) on the acceleration of the virtual training and, consequently, on the companies' digital transformation.

**Acknowledgements.** This work is financed by National Funds through the Portuguese funding agency, FCT - Fundação para a Ciência e a Tecnologia,. within project UIDB/50014/2020.

## References

1. Li, L., Su, F., Zhang, W., Mao, J.Y.: Digital transformation by SME entrepreneurs: a capability perspective. Inf. Syst. J. **28**, 1129–1157 (2017)
2. Ulas, D.: Digital transformation process and SMEs. Procedia Comput. Sci. **158**, 662–671 (2019)
3. Reis, J., Amorim, M., Melão, N., Matos, P.: Digital transformation: a literature review and guidelines for future research. In: Rocha, Á., Adeli, H., Reis, L.P., Costanzo, S. (eds.) WorldCIST'18 2018. AISC, vol. 745, pp. 411–421. Springer, Cham (2018). https://doi.org/10.1007/978-3-319-77703-0_41
4. Azevedo, A., Almeida, A.H.: Grasp the challenge of digital transition in SMEs—a training course geared towards decision-makers. Educ. Sci. **11**, 151 (2021). https://doi.org/10.3390/educsci11104015
5. Beinicke, A., Kyndt, E.: Evidence-based actions for maximising training effectiveness in corporate E-learning and classroom training. Stud. Continuing Educ. **42**(2), 256–276 (2020). https://doi.org/10.1080/0158037X.2019.1608940
6. Rotatori, D., Lee, E.J., Sleeva, S.: The evolution of the workforce during the fourth industrial revolution. Hum. Resour. Dev. Int. **24**(1), 92–103 (2021). https://doi.org/10.1080/13678868.2020.1767453
7. Horváth, D., Szabó, R.: Driving forces and barriers of Industry 4.0: do multinational and small and medium-sized companies have equal opportunities? Technol. Forecast. Soc. Change 146, 119–132 (2019). https://doi.org/10.1016/j.techfore.2019.05.021
8. Maisiri, W., Van Dyk, L.: Industry 4.0 skills: a perspective of the South African manufacturing industry. SA J. Hum. Resour. Manage. **19**(0), a1416 (2021). https://doi.org/10.4102/sajhrm.v19i0.1416
9. Karadayi-Usta, S.: An interpretive structural analysis for Industry 4.0 adoption challenges. IEEE Trans. Eng. Manage. J. **67**(3), 973–978 (2020). https://doi.org/10.1109/TEM.2018.2890443

10. Stentoft, J., Rajkumar, C.: The relevance of Industry 4.0 and its relationship with moving manufacturing out, back and staying at home. Int. J. Prod. Res. **58**(10), 2953–2973 (2019). https://doi.org/10.1080/00207543.2019.1660823
11. Raj, A., Dwivedi, G., Sharma, A., Jabbour, A.B.L.S., Rajak, S.: Barriers to the adoption of Industry 4.0 technologies in the manufacturing sector: an inter-country comparative perspective. Int. J. Prod. Econ. **224**, 107546 (2020). https://doi.org/10.1016/j.ijpe.2019.107546
12. Doherty, O., Stephens, S.: The skill needs of the manufacturing industry: can higher education keep up? Educ. Train. 63(4), 632–646. https://doi.org/10.1108/ET-05-2020-0134
13. Kim, J., Park, C.-Y.: Education, skill training, and lifelong learning in the era of technological revolution: a review. Asian Pac. Econ. Lit. **34**, 3–19 (2020). https://doi.org/10.1111/apel.12299
14. Taylor, A.: The challenge of partnership in school-to-work transition. J. Vocat. Educ. Train. **58**(3), 319–336 (2006)
15. Prasasd, M., Kumar, B., Swarnamani, A.: OBE based industry academy approach for embedded system design course. J. Eng. Educ. Transform. **30**(3), 150–156 (2017)
16. Morell, L.: Scaffold to build and sustain industry-university partnerships. J. Eng. Educ. Transform. **27**(4), 6–16 (2014)
17. Bridgeford, T., Aman, K.: Academy-Industry Relationships and Partnerships - Perspectives for Technical Communicators. Routledge, New York (2017)
18. Arruabarrena, R., Sánchez, A., Blanco, J.M., Vadillo, J.A., Usandizaga, I.: Integration of good practices of active methodologies with the reuse of student-generated content. Int. J. Educ. Technol. High. Educ. **16**(1), 1–20 (2019). https://doi.org/10.1186/s41239-019-0140-7
19. O'Flaherty, J., Phillips, C.: The use of flipped classrooms in higher education: a scoping review. Internet High. Educ. **25**, 85–95 (2015)
20. Prince, M.: Does active learning work? A review of the research. J. Engr. Educ. **93**(3), 223–231 (2004)
21. Akçayır, G., Akçayır, M.: The flipped classroom: a review of its advantages and challenges. Comput. Educ. **126**, 334–345 (2018)
22. Pancucci, S.: Train the trainer: the bricks in the learning community scaffold of professional development. Int. J. Educ. Pedagogical Sci. **1**(11), 597–604 (2007)
23. Gray, D.E.: Doing Research in the Real World, 2nd edn. Sage Publications (2009)
24. Winlow, H., Simm, D., Marvell, A., Schaaf, R.: Using focus group research to support teaching and learning. J. Geogr. High. Educ. **37**, 292–303 (2013)

# Complementarity of European RIS Territories Towards Manufacturing Educational Products

Panos Stavropoulos(✉), Alexios Papacharalampopoulos, Harry Bikas, Lydia Athanasopoulou, Anna-Maria Korfiati, and Christos K. Michail

Laboratory for Manufacturing Systems and Automation (LMS), Mechanical Engineering and Aeronautics Department, University of Patras, 26504 Patras, Greece

{pstavr,apapacharal,bikas,athanasopoulou,korfiati, michail}@lms.mech.upatras.gr

**Abstract.** Europe is in a position where the complementarity of the workforce in terms of competences and skills is able to produce a high added value for industry. The need for technologies absorption, digitalization and innovation increase dictate a change in the training products, so that every single country is benefited and utilized, simultaneously. Thus, collaborative educational and training programs can be standardized. This is a roadmap towards such a holistic design, taking advantage of the functionalities of RIS hubs that have been established in EU RIS countries. A framework of five phases is presented involving RIS hubs as well as the complementary skills of the stakeholders.

**Keywords:** Complementarity of skills · RIS countries · Technological areas · European innovation · Educational and training programs

## 1 Introduction

The fourth industrial revolution (Industry 4.0), defines the new age of networked and hence digitalized manufacturing, where computers can control automated production lines with the coupling of physical and digital technologies, including technologies such as artificial intelligence, analytics, cognitive control and the internet of things (IoT) [1]. Artificial intelligence will monitor and improve the physical processes of a factory, even solving problems before they occur. A network of hub factories around the world will be controlled and upgraded remotely with little need for local human labor. This will generate abundant opportunities for new products and services, better ways to serve customers, new types of jobs and, hence, a whole new business model. B. Householder, president of Hitachi Vantara claimed that "Automation, artificial intelligence, IoT, machine learning and other advanced technologies can quickly capture and analyze a wealth of data… Our challenge becomes moving to the next phase … to create value from the findings obtained through advanced technologies." [2].


Published by Springer Nature Switzerland AG 2021
L. M. Camarinha-Matos et al. (Eds.): PRO-VE 2021, IFIP AICT 629, pp. 738–745, 2021.
https://doi.org/10.1007/978-3-030-85969-5_70

Recently, the European Commission (EC) has stressed the importance of the real economy and strong industry as the leading head of economic growth and employment. According to its vision, the target for the contribution of industry to GDP by 2020 has been raised to 20%, i.e. reaching a value of €287 billion [3]. Currently, the European manufacturing industry is responsible for 15% of GDP [4].

Additionally, digitalization has diverse and opposing effects on job dynamics, on the development of new products and machines as well as on increased competitiveness. This situation creates new professional needs and these needs lead to the development of new skills, new roles and jobs or lead to the transformation of current jobs. A new type of worker known as a "knowledge worker" ("workers with higher education and characterized by knowledge work that, in turn, requires the generation and application of knowledge" [5]) is evolving, and it is no longer associated with a single work role. Therefore, many skills that aren't essential in manufacturing today will account for 1/3 of the core skills in most jobs in the near future [6].

### 1.1 Demand of Manufacturing Education in Europe

It is difficult to reach the right talent with the adequate skills to fill the role since there are not enough candidates with the right skills and ethics to staff the company and in the future [7]. As the future works will be based on coding skills, it is estimated that by 2020 there will be skills shortage for 800 thousand of skilled IT jobs across the EU [8, 9]. There are about 23 million unemployed people in Europe, with 5 milling of them being young people. Simultaneously, most businesses are having difficulty finding qualified employees to fill open vacancies. It is a fact that, in the manufacturing industry, between 10% and 30% of businesses encounter increased production losses due to a shortage of highly qualified workers. It is anticipated that 80 million jobs were created in 2020, with 16 million of them requiring high-skilled staff [9].

This demand is greater for the less innovative countries (with moderate or modest innovation scores), also known as RIS (Regional innovation scheme) countries [10], such as Bulgaria, Cyprus, Greece, Spain, Lithuania, Portugal etc. that don't have a strong industrial activity and employment in their region. RIS describes the unequal geographic variation of innovation and strategies to boost regional innovation capacity. Academics illustrate the development of new path creation or the various ways of boosting the development of new activities and industries in regions to generate growth using the RIS approach [11]. It is thus important to close the huge gap between supply and demand, in other words, to close the gap between the jobs that are emerging from this radical technological development, need to be filled and talents with the skillset capable to fill industry 4.0 enabling jobs.

Thus, the question is whether there can be a common strategy for training among diversified European countries, so that innovation is accelerated. This study deals with the integration of research innovation and education activities seamlessly within a single initiative that is called Teaching Factory (TF) so as to promote the future perspective of a knowledge based competitive and sustainable manufacturing industry in RIS countries. More specifically, how stakeholders from various countries of different Innovation score can collaborate in order to create manufacturing related educational products based on the concept of TF.

## 2 Educational Areas

To date, a number of educational initiatives are conducted aiming to grow innovation in Regional Innovation Scheme (RIS) countries while increasing the know-how transfer and enhancing the innovation capacity in industrial partners (startups, scale-ups, OEMs) and higher education institutions. Also, collaborations such as EIT-RIS aim at the partnerships of higher education institutions, research organization, industries and others partners in the Knowledge and Innovation Communities (KICs) activities, creating the right foundations. Depending on the regional preference, different specialization among with the Information and Communication Technology (ICT), logistics, industry, energy, environment and sustainability, etc. can be selected by the firm's field [10]. All over industrial applications, integration of ICT technologies seems to be the most relevant strategy. For instance, Greece develops a resistance spot welding testbed targeting on the Cognitive Automation of the process. Another RIS country, Czech Republic, completes a robotic assembly line, a 5-axis milling workstation and a milling robot testbed for research, demonstration and learning of those processes (details are given in the Appendix).

Additionally, Research and Innovation Strategies for Smart Specialization (RIS3), referring to the national/regional economic transformation, are based on five key aspects [12]: i) policy support and investments, ii) enhance national/regional strengths, iii) trigger private sector investments, iv) boost stakeholders, v) evidence-based systems. The vital goals of RIS3 consist from the smart, sustainable and inclusive growth applying on the research, technological development & innovation (RTDI) and ICT [13]. RIS3 also promote the growth of jobs and industries across RIS countries.

RIS and RIS3 are providing the appropriate emergent skills gaps on numerous education areas on the added-value manufacturing. The education area may be tentatively classified in (a) Innovation strategy, (b) Digitalization of manufacturing systems and processes, (c) Emergent technologies in manufacturing, (d) Advanced monitoring and control systems, (e) Cognitive Automation, (f) Digital Twins, (g) Advanced ICTs, (h) Intellectual Property Rights and Security Issues (targeting CEO/executives), (i) Sustainable manufacturing, (h) Digital skills (CAx).

## 3 Framework for Orchestrating Educational Design

An educational framework design has to take into account all the factors affecting its operation and the sustainability. Therefore, the Knowledge Triangle Integration (Education, Innovation, Business Creation) has to be taken into account, and the well-established concept of RIS Hubs [14] can be used to this end, gathering all the basic information needed for this work, such as regional capabilities and needs, technologies offered, as well as partnerships.

Additionally, the concepts of evaluation, certification and communication are vital to the sustainability of such programs and frameworks, guaranteeing their usability and the smooth operation. Additionally, the link to non-RIS countries is also vital, rendering the exchange of technical and monetary flows possible, through networking and establishing information flows and the corresponding value chains.

The following schematic (Fig. 1) is indicative of the flow of information needed to design such frameworks. It is separated in five phases; design, preparation, pilots, evaluation, operation and communication, rendering its implementation a feasible target. The Teaching Factory (TF) paradigm [15] is located at the core, **integrating personalized experiential learning** and reducing the needs for evaluation extra steps.

The Teaching Factory paradigm can be used as a medium of experiential education. When implemented at a network level (involving and connecting multiple industrial and academic actors), the TF paradigm can bring together diverse competences, backgrounds and know-how, enabling the effective exchange of knowledge between them. The network facilitates the launch of collaborative manufacturing training projects with mutual interest. Participating organizations can effectively exchange information, including teaching material, virtual access to state-of-art infrastructure (including Learning Factories (LF) [16]), real industrial challenges and novel solutions. These organizations are classified into two boards. On one hand, the academic board focuses on providing novel concepts, approaches, and remotely-accessed test-beds to address both industrial needs and innovative educational schemes. On the other hand, the industrial board has the chance to express their needs in terms of training and upskilling personnel as well as provide a number of industrial challenges to be elaborated by the developed network. Evidently, stakeholders in both boards can originate from different countries, creating thus an adequately diversified skills spectrum in order for the training to be holistic.

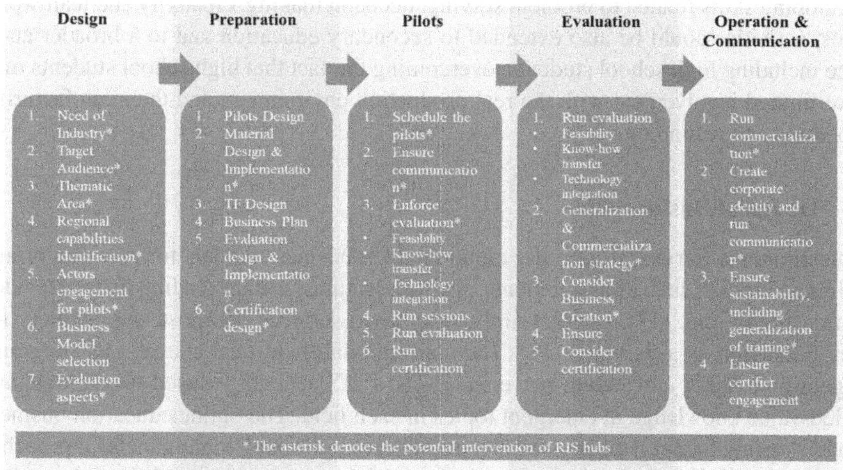


**Fig. 1.** Phases of implementing a complete manufacturing educational program based on collaboration between RIS countries.

As such, a TF can operate in multiple knowledge transfer modes. **"Industry-to-academia"** aims at transferring the real manufacturing environment to the classroom through the adoption of an industrial project involving one factory in a simultaneous interaction with one or several classrooms. This interaction can involve discussions, presentations, live videos from the production, and other knowledge delivery mechanisms. A characteristic example would be solving an industrial challenge, where different entities could focus on different aspects of it (such as mechanical design, mechatronics, electronics, software, HMI, and business-related aspects). Similarly, benefits arise when industrial actors from different industrial sectors openly present their challenges and innovative solutions, best practices or success stories, fostering innovation in other industries (**"industry to industry"**). Finally, **"academia-to-industry"** aims at transferring knowledge from academia to industry. Test-beds and demonstrators for new technological concepts are installed into academic facilities (Learning Factories) in order to be validated by students and researchers or used for professionals training and upskilling.

As an example, the aim of ManuLearn project has been to "to enhance the innovation capacity of the participating EIT RIS countries by improving their educational framework and by boosting their digital capabilities in order to face the future manufacturing challenges". Therefore, different stakeholders from industry and academia can work together to manually develop their skills through co created solutions to real manufacturing problems combining the concepts of Teaching and Learning factories.

Additionally, the main goal of the ShapiNG I project has been to motivate and raise the interest of young Europeans, with particular emphasis on high school students (ages 15–18) and with a special focus on females, for activities in the field of manufacturing, within Portugal, Spain, Greece, and Slovakia. In particular, the aim of the "3D Printing for Pupils" TF has been to engage pupils with a simple Additive Manufacturing concept while helping them gain practical skills and knowledge about designing spare parts and developing skills related to problem solving, decision making, creativity and teamwork. Thus, activities could be also extended to secondary education and to a broader audience including high school students, overcoming the fact that high school students may have limited involvement with the real production environment and the manufacturing processes and technologies.

### 3.1 Design of Business Plan

Education-as-a-Service (EaaS) use cloud-enabled business models for teaching or/and training purposes such as assignments, support, lectures, further reading material, video demonstration etc. [17]. Internet and cloud-based services comprise the enablers for the "Education-as-a-Service" [18]. The conventional/traditional educational programs targeting on static curriculum per course. The EaaS scheme focused on the dynamic added-value knowledge in emergent topics in each field. The online education business models mainly focus on the profitability of the services through four financial approaches [19, 20], i) the charge of certifications/badges, ii) the charge of extended services (documents, demo, etc.), iii) the link of students to potential employers, iv) and last the advertisements. To date, educational business models profiting from the above services are referring to Massive Open Online Courses (MOOCs) and it's free for access [21]. For instance, three major academic-oriented educational platforms are Coursera [22], edX [23] and Khan Academy [24] which close collaborate with top universities and institutes. The number of registrations on these platforms are increasing, however the completion is relative low and the drop-out rate reaches 85–95% [25]. The hot-topic of Artificial Intelligence (AI) occurred only a 17.5% completion rate. Another way of educational scheme is the "blended course scheme" which assist the conventional curriculum with virtual courses with the appropriate credits. Now, both Coursera and edX are offering more advanced course in post-graduate level, which does not require any application form, but typically cost approximately from 1,000 to 5,000 $ [25].

In manufacturing engineering, no specialized holistic approach of educational and training platform exists on the market. Hence, a business plan on highly added-value manufacturing (AVM) is proposed for the developing of a unique educational platform based on emergent technologies, tools and techniques, both theoretical and practical with the use of testbeds [26]. Manufacturing engineering-oriented educational platform is targeting on executives and professional engineers for up/re-skill in RIS/RIS3 countries.

The business model referring on the conceptual framework, while the business plan to the documenting strategy of the project's targets [27]. At the starting point of the training material design, a business model CANVAS is needed to establish all the key components including cost-related factors. Afterwards, a SWOT-PESTEL analysis is to be performed to determine the key factors of the business plan. At the end of the design, a VRIO analysis has to be performed to uncover any competitive advantages of the platform. The EaaS scheme is used to enhance the accessibility of the courses through cloud-based services.

## 4 Conclusions and Future Outlook

It is evident that RIS countries' complementarity can be utilized towards forming proper educational frameworks as well as education material, aiming simultaneously towards (i) technology integration in manufacturing enterprises, (ii) training engineers and operators on these technologies and (iii) educating students and pupils on manufacturing cutting-edge technologies. To this end, the orchestration of such activities should be performed by one framework, taking into account the role of RIS Hubs. The variability in the background of the involved stakeholders seems to be sufficiently large in order to meet the needs of continuously evolving European Industry, addressing the need for further innovation absorption and digitalization.

The details of the preparation lie on the fact that everything should be based on regional needs and capabilities, thus forming even temporary local networks between actors from such regions. Then, evaluation, communication as well as commercialization strategies need to be involved.

For the future activities, the technical areas need to be harmonized, in a formal and structured way, as well as the skills and competencies need to be addressed explicitly through this framework. The way to achieve these is making sure everyone is confident in themselves being engaged with proper evaluation methods. Also, the evaluation of the framework in terms of applicability ought to be formulated and evaluated; this will have to be performed in a twofold way; firstly, with respect to upskilling (knowledge) workers and secondly concerning technology absorption and innovation enhancement as foreseen [28].

**Acknowledgements.** The formation of the current framework has been funded by EIT Manufacturing project "EIT Manufacturing RIS Hubs".

## Appendix

Material from the projects below has been taken, as they complete each other with respect to the goals of the current work.

**Table 1.** Concepts adopted from various educational projects.

| Projects | Carrier | Concepts | Running period |
|---|---|---|---|
| TF KnowNet | EIT Manufacturing | Learning-Transfer Evaluation Model | Jan. 2020 – Dec. 2020 |
| Manulearn | EIT Manufacturing | Academia – Industry TF | As above |
| M-NEST-RIS | EIT Manufacturing | Evaluation, Cognitive Control LF | As above |
| Shaping I | EIT Manufacturing | Industry – Pupils TF | As above |
| InMas | EIT Manufacturing | Workshops to pupils | As above |
| M-NEST-II | EIT Manufacturing | Business Model | Jan. 2021 – Dec. 2021 |

## References


1. Industrie 4.0 site (2021). https://www.plattform-i40.de/PI40/Navigation/EN/Industrie40/WhatIsIndustrie40/what-is-industrie40.html
2. Deloitte: The Fourth Industrial Revolution is here: are you ready? (2018). https://www2.deloitte.com/cn/en/pages/consumer-industrial-products/articles/industry-4-0-technology-manufacturing-revolution.html
3. Alessandrini, M., Celotti, P., Gramillano, A., Lilla, M.: The future of industry in Europe. European Committee of the Regions, Brussels (2017)
4. World bank data. https://data.worldbank.org/indicator/NV.IND.MANF.ZS?locations=EU
5. Razzaq, S., et al.: Knowledge management, organizational commitment and knowledge-worker performance. Business process management journal (2019)
6. Aulbur, W., Arvind, C.J., Bigghe, R.: Whitepaper: Skill Development for Industry 4.0. BRICS Skill Development Group: Roland Berger (2016)
7. Deloitte Insights: Deloitte skills gap and future of work in manufacturing study (2018)
8. The Guardian: Rise of The Machines: Why Coding is the Skill you Have to Learn. https://www.theguardian.com/new-faces-of-tech/2018/oct/25/riseof-the-machines-why-coding-is-the-skill-you-have-to-learn (2018)
9. Bert Maes: The future of European Education and training System. https://bertmaes.wordpress.com/report-skills-shortage/. Accessed 20 June 2021
10. European Institute of Innovation & Technology (EIT): EIT Regional Innovation Scheme. https://eit.europa.eu/our-activities/eit-regional-innovation-scheme-ris (2019). Accessed 10 Apr 2021
11. Hervas-Oliver, J.L., Gonzalez-Alcaidem G., Rojas-Alvarado, R., Monto-Mompo, S.: Emerging regional innovation policies for industry 4.0: analyzing the digital innovation hub program in European regions. Competitiveness Review: An International Business Journal (2020)

12. Foray, D., Goddard, J., Beldarrain, X.G., Landabaso, M., McCann, P., Morgan, K., Nauwelaers, C., Ortega-Argilés, R.: Guide to research and innovation strategies for smart specialisations (2012)
13. Lopes, J., Ferreira, J.J., Farinha, L.: Innovation strategies for smart specialisation (RIS3): Past, present and future research. Growth and Change (2019)
14. EIT Manufacturing RIS Hubs site. https://eitmanufacturing.eu/eit-manufacturing-ris-hubs/. Accessed 27 Apr 2021
15. Chryssolouris, G., Mavrikios, D., Rentzos, L.: The teaching factory: a manufacturing education paradigm. Procedia CIRP **57**, 44–48 (2016)
16. Abele, E., Metternich, J., Tisch, M., Chryssolouris, et al: Learning factories for research, education, and training. Procedia CIRP **32**, 1–6 (2015)
17. Prifti, L., Knigge, M., Löffler, A., Hecht, S., Krcmar, H.: Emerging business models in education provisioning: a case study on providing learning support as education-as-a-service. Int. J. Eng. Ped. (2017)
18. Deepa, N., Sathiyaseelan, R.: The cloud and the changing shape of education - EAAS (education as a service). Int. J. Comput. Appl. **42**, 4–8 (2012)
19. Okoli, C., Wang, N.: Business Models for Online Education and Open Educational Resources. SSRN Working Paper Series (2016)
20. Burd, E.L., Smith, S.P., Reisman, S.: Exploring business models for MOOCs in higher education. Innov. High Educ. **40**, 37–49 (2015)
21. Long, Y.: Explore the business model of MOOCs. In: Nah, F.-H., Tan, C.-H. (eds.) HCIBGO 2017. LNCS, vol. 10293, pp. 181–193. Springer, Cham (2017). https://doi.org/10.1007/978-3-319-58481-2_15
22. Coursera. https://www.coursera.org/. Accessed 4 Apr 2021
23. edX. https://www.edx.org/. Accessed 4 Apr 2021
24. Khan Academy. https://www.khanacademy.org/. Accessed 4 Apr 2021
25. Leighton, M.: edX MicroMasters vs Coursera MasterTracks comparison and FAQ (2021). https://www.businessinsider.com/edx-micromaster-vs-coursera-mastertrack-online-masters-programs. Accessed 13 Apr 2021
26. Teece, D.J.: Business Models, Business Strategy and Innovation. Long Range Planning (2010)
27. Kalman, Y.M.: A race to the bottom: MOOCs and higher education business models. Open Learning: The Journal of Open, Distance and e-Learning (2014)
28. Thalheimer, W.: The learning-transfer evaluation model: Sending messages to enable learning effectiveness (2018). https://www.worklearning.com/wp-content/uploads/2018/02/Thalheimer-The-Learning-Transfer-Evaluation-Model-Report-for-LTEM-v11.pdf. Accessed 15 Apr 2021

# Industrial Workshop

# Exploring the Best Practices for Co-innovation in Industry and Academy Collaboration – Four Practical Case Examples

Katri Valkokari(✉), Pasi Valkokari, Tuija Rantala, and Jutta Nyblom

VTT, Technical Research Centre of Finland, 1306, FI-33101 Tampere, Finland
{Katri.Valkokari,Pasi.Valkokari,Tuija.Rantala,Jutta.Nyblom}@vtt.fi

**Abstract.** Managing the continuation of an innovation funnel from scientific knowledge to commercialisation in a collaborative setting is a challenging task. The purpose of this paper is to explore the best practices for governing the collaborative industry–academy innovation process. As an outcome, the paper presents best practices as well as the weaknesses and strengths of three mechanisms of collaborative innovation. The mechanisms are: (1) having a strong vision and enabling technologies, (2) orchestration by a globally operating core company and (3) regional clusters facilitated by public actors.

**Keywords:** Practices · Industry–academy collaboration · Co-innovation

## 1 Introduction

In a modern innovation, hackathons, innovation laboratories, innovation spaces, living labs, maker spaces and fab labs have been mentioned as necessities for successful innovation. In other words, innovation is based on collaboration between a variety of actors [1]; [2] – including practitioners from industry and researchers representing an academy. The fluent management of the innovation funnel, from research ideas and knowledge towards commercialisation in a collaborative business setting, is a challenging task. The concrete ways by which industrial actors are seeking improvements and renewal or benchmarking are often limited by organisations in their industry sector [3]. Recently, B2B research is increasingly focusing on the broader collaborative settings of actors connected through the various technological systems and platforms [4].

In this study, we follow the research stream of collaborative networks [5] and aim to look beyond traditional organisational boundaries. Although the discussion on collaborative and open innovation has been active in recent years and, for instance, Davey et al., [6] presented a wide study of practical case examples of industry–academy collaboration, longitudinal studies are still scarce. Therefore, instead of zooming out, we seek mechanisms for successful collaborative practices between industry and academia. The purpose of this paper is to explore the best practices for industry–academy innovation


Published by Springer Nature Switzerland AG 2021
L. M. Camarinha-Matos et al. (Eds.): PRO-VE 2021, IFIP AICT 629, pp. 749–758, 2021.
https://doi.org/10.1007/978-3-030-85969-5_71

collaboration. This is done by analysing four different ecosystemic innovation cases in the context of manufacturing and construction domains.

The paper builds on a comparison between three mechanisms of co-evolution within the collaborative innovation funnel. All the cases aim to build a novel competitive advantage through systemic changes to current networks as disruption is driven by servitisation, sustainability and digitalisation. This requires collaborative innovation, crossing the borders of industrial sectors.

## 2 The Theoretical Background

Although in textbooks the process of innovation is often simplified into a linear process [7], in practice it is seldom linear, even in the case of intra-firm innovation. In a collaborative setting, such as industry–academy co-innovation, it can really be a multidimensional, complex process. Since Chesbrough introduced the concept of open innovation in 2003 [8], the related literature has tried to understand and model innovation practices that go beyond the boundaries of a single firm [1, 2]. Such innovation ecosystems can be seen as a special type of collaborative network [9]. In this paper our aim is to explore innovation that is crossing industrial boundaries [3].

Both the collaborative innovation ecosystems as a whole and their components constantly evolve. A successful innovation ecosystem is the result of a process of continuous evolution, which is often a long, complex and slow process, and its development may have different stages of maturity [10]. Beneficial collaboration requires that the actors of the ecosystem are willing to share the knowledge that is required for the co-innovation between ecosystem actors and are capable of doing so. Thus, the cross-industry collaborative setting includes additional challenges due to the different backgrounds and cultures of the actors involved [11]. This ecosystem orchestration should be handled in such a way that the created breeding environment and joint co-innovation processes remain attractive to all actors.

There are different mechanisms that enable co-innovation between multiple actors. One mechanism is that an ecosystem can be an artefact when there is an actor that has a strategic intention to design ecosystemic collaboration [12]. Such an actor can be a keystone company [13]; a public or research organisation may have a strategical intention to create an ecosystem. Another mechanism is that the ecosystem can be formed autonomously when a sufficient number of actors have aligned strategic interests. The latter mechanism is often accompanied by hype around a certain topic which encourages several actors to gather together or it can be based on the geographical proximity of the actors that operate within the same cluster [14, 15].

Based on the earlier research and practical work with ecosystems summarised above, in our study we have identified three main mechanisms (see Fig. 1) that follow: (1) driven by a shared vision and enabling technologies, (2) orchestration by a globally operating core company and (3) regional clusters facilitated by public actors. Each of these mechanisms has its strengths and weaknesses as the roles of the involved actors vary. Cities and local development agencies often play a key role in ecosystems, building on regional strengths. Ecosystems associated with companies that are strong industrial drivers are closely integrated into the international business environment and operations. Ecosystems based on the shared vision enable major transitions even though the process of transforming the visions into practical development work may be slow at first. Ecosystems relying on a strong national vision and a development agenda may encounter fragmented decision-making in ministries and challenges related to continuity in commitment to the vision.

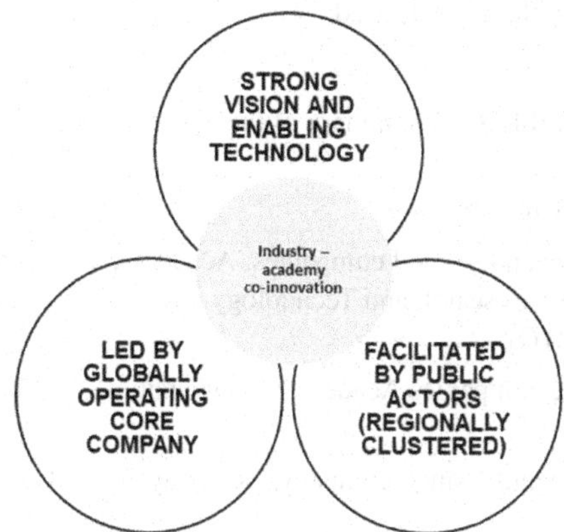


**Fig. 1.** The three mechanisms of innovation ecosystems.

Ensuring sufficient renewal may present a challenge to ecosystems driven by strong industrial leader companies or based on regional clustered actors. In particular, well-established companies may be reluctant to give up their competitive advantages and business operating models.

## 3 Methodology: A Case Study

The goal of the paper is to explore mechanisms enabling industry–academy collaboration within the co-innovation process in a multi-actor setting. We aim to create new understanding of the vital role of shared processes in enhancing co-innovation and how the contributions of the involved industry and academy actors take shape. Accordingly, we formulate the following research question: What are the pros and cons of the different mechanisms of ecosystems that are used in coordinating industry–academy collaborative innovation?

The selection of four case ecosystems was made according to guidelines for case research [16]. In the cases, researchers had access to the industry–academy collaboration in four innovation ecosystem settings, and the selected cases were both comparable and complementary. Table 1 summarises the basic information of these four cases. The level of analysis was industry–academy collaboration within the ecosystems.

The first innovation ecosystem, 'Case A', offers an open innovation marketplace to match make the challenges of the Finnish forest industry and the innovative offerings of the Finnish IT industry with the innovations catalysed by research. The second innovation ecosystem, 'Case B', connects Finnish manufacturing factories, research institutes and SME-sized IoT/IT companies via agile co-creation and experience sharing within real-world production environments. The third innovation ecosystem, 'Case C', is developing a business ecosystem and a platform to promote the development of intelligent data-based services in the context of smart buildings. Finally, the fourth innovation ecosystem, 'Case D', aims to boost the performance of Finnish manufacturing SMEs and accelerate their sustainable digitalisation journey. Currently, it has a regional focus as the involved actors are geographically quite closely situated.

**Table 1.** A summary of the case ecosystems.

| Case | Number of participants | Industry sectors |
|---|---|---|
| Case A | Industry:12 large and 9 small companies, Academy: 2 universities and 1 Research and Technology Organisation (RTO) | Forest, ICT, design |
| Case B | Industry: 8 large companies Academy: 3 universities, 1 RTO | Manufacturing, ICT |
| Case C | Industry: 5 large and 1 small company, Academy: 1 RTO | Construction, services, ICT |
| Case D | Academy and intermediators: 9 research and education organisations and 5 public actors | Smart manufacturing |

The data utilised in this study included, for example, participatory observations on ecosystem activity in numerous meetings and workshops, their results, different kinds of project plans and documents, discussions on on-line tools, interviews and facilitated on-line discussions conducted as part of industry–academy collaboration. In each case, approximately 20 researchers and over 20 practitioners participated in industry–academy collaboration activities. The material covers the time period from the initiation of collaboration to two and half years from then in Case A, three years ahead in Case B, one and half year ahead in Case C and approximately one year ahead in Case D.

## 4 Findings: The Pros and Cons of the Three Mechanisms

The analyses of empirical data from industry–academy collaboration practices were made based on comparison between the three mechanisms of co-evolution (see Fig. 1) within the collaborative innovation funnel. Although the four ecosystems have different modes of operation, similarities were also found. In this section we will first present the operation model of each innovation ecosystem and the key activities in industry–academy collaboration.

The vision-led **Case A** ecosystem operates with three levels of industry–academy collaboration. The long-term vision track is for solving systematic-level industry challenges and affecting systematic change in the related industry. This track includes, for example, vision creation and related insights, and it is led by research. Thus, design thinking and agile methods enable the industry-driven co-creation track to solve use cases and create a joint offering. The forest industry companies have stated that 'we are transforming the way industry works'. Company-driven collaboration is for scaling up and commercialising the ideas for international markets. The broad number of company participants, as well as their different backgrounds, caused some challenges for ecosystem co-operation, and therefore the ecosystem's operation model continuously evolves with the participants (Table 2).

**Table 2.** Case A: Key activities in industry–academy collaboration

| Roles | Company-driven | Vision-led | Public/region-facilitated |
|---|---|---|---|
| Industry | Industrial companies as use case owners as well as IT companies as solvers | The companies are actively involved in vision building | |
| Academy | The identification of new companies and matchmaking | Long-term research work that connects the industrial use cases and the vision for industry renewal | Building linkages to the national agenda through the funding program |

Similarly to Case A, the **Case B** ecosystem is vision-led and operates through sprints and by creating proofs of concept (PoCs) for jointly recognised grand challenges. The participating eight industry actors provide their factories as innovation platforms and are involved in defining the requirements for the different PoCs. Anyhow, the research organisation also has an active role in describing the requirements as well as identifying possible SMEs to provide solutions. Together, the ecosystem steers sprints and PoCs, and SMEs demonstrate their existing solutions. In addition, ecosystem actors (especially the academies) assist SMEs in scaling up within the factories involved at the ecosystem, commercialising the PoC and disseminating the results in, for example, ecosystem workshops, scientific papers and blogs. Anyhow, the SMEs providing the solutions to PoCs are not members of the ecosystem; instead, they have a role as subcontractors (Table 3).

**Table 3.** Case B: The key activities in industry–academy collaboration

| Roles | Company-driven | Vision-led | Public/region-facilitated |
|---|---|---|---|
| Industry | Factories as innovation platforms, benchmarking between them | Leading research work around specific grand challenges; the vision is divided into practical, well-defined PoCs | |
| Academy | Matchmaking and SME engagement | Participating research work around specific grand challenges | Research institutes worked together with a public funding body to boost the launch of the project |

The **Case C** is a company-driven ecosystem in which all the involved companies share the vision of building a platform. The ecosystem has a leader company which has initiated the ecosystem's co-operation and is providing the starting point for the strategic agenda and the ecosystem's paths to international markets. Through hackathons, the ecosystem actors have opened the identified research agenda to SMEs. The aim of the hackathons is to open new business opportunities for these SMEs as subcontractors. The ecosystem has also involved a venture client alliance that has the responsibility of organising the industry hacks. The industry–academy collaboration is based on the cross-functional teams, and this ecosystem also organises the shared problem solving in sprints (Table 4).

**Table 4.** Case C: The key activities in industry–academy collaboration

| Roles | Company-driven | Visio-led | Public/region-facilitated |
|---|---|---|---|
| Industry | Companies initiated the collaboration and actively manage it | Built together by 7 core companies | |
| Academy | Supports the company-initiated co-operation | Participating research work around specific topics | |

The **Case D** ecosystem is based on the national agenda of smart manufacturing. It is strongly led by an academy and, on the other hand, it aims to be a roof ecosystem with several different horizontal and vertical ecosystems and networks. This national initiative improves the Finnish industry's performance and sustainable growth through innovation and knowledge. Currently, it is a quite loosely coupled network of research and education organisations. The engagement of industry actors is based on the involved organisations' independent networks and research projects (Table 5).

**Table 5.** Case D: The key activities in industry–academy collaboration.

| Roles | Company-driven | Vision-led | Public/region-faclitated |
|---|---|---|---|
| Industry | Through involvement, large companies aim to guide research activities | Companies' interests are loosely coupled to the national agenda | |
| Academy | The development of the capabilities of SMEs through research and education | Bridging the national agenda and the research portfolio | The strong national agenda guides the ecosystem's work and linkages to international research networks |

The empirical analyses of four cases showed that each of the three identified mechanisms has its strengths and weaknesses. These pros and cons are summarised in Table 6.

National agendas, as well as local development agencies and cities, often play a key role in ecosystems, building on regional strengths. It can be stated that in Case D, the research organisation has an exceptionally strong role in building the ecosystem. This was partially based on the strategic research agenda of this organisation. Thus, rather broad ecosystems relying on a strong national vision and a development agenda may encounter the fragmented decision-making of different authorities and challenges related to continuity in commitment to the vision.

**Table 6.** A summary of the pros and cons of the three mechanisms.

| Company-driven (Case C) | Vision-driven (Cases A & B) | Regional/public-facilitated (Case D) |
|---|---|---|
| ***Pros*** | | |
| • Direct link to the global business environment, a focus on one's business development (not joint offerings)<br>• Owners' common business ecosystem formation and shared vision<br>• The leader company is boosting the strategic agenda and opening growth/new markets for its subcontractors through its networks | • Actors are equal and have complementary resources<br>• A shared understanding and joint offerings evolve through collaboration<br>• Also gathering opportunities and needs from the perspective of service provider companies<br>• Shaping markets and building growth through complementary resources | • Motivation comes from geographical proximity and well-known partners<br>• Extensive agendas and links to international research<br>• Trust enabled openness and knowledge sharing (on a personal level) |
| ***Cons*** | | |
| • Barriers for new companies to join the ecosystem<br>• Disrupting the traditional operating model and aiming to maintain status quo<br>• Finding a business owner and/or changing interests (business models that benefit all will not be found) | • A variety of actors poses a challenge to staying agile<br>• Scaling solutions for other industries, slowed down by solution ownership<br>• A balance between the parties – the ecosystem's continuity, attractiveness and renewal<br>• Readiness of private investments (including funding the ecosystem orchestration) | • Grows the business beyond regional boundaries<br>• The business phase is far away, there is a focus on technological details, grounding operations in the interests of companies (at strategic level)<br>• The renewal of collaboration and networks |

Ecosystems based on the vision enable major transitions even though the process of transforming the visions into practical development work may be slow at first. Both Case A and B provide empirical evidence that it is important to boost collaboration between the companies who have different competencies and that academies could have an even more active role in matchmaking the companies as well as in challenging their thinking based on research results and novel understanding. Digitalisation has been one of the driving forces for novel collaboration models, but concurrently, it also requires cultural change towards more agile operation models as well as cross-industrial collaboration.

Ecosystems associated with strong industrial driver companies are closely integrated into the international business environment and operations. In Case C, all the six case companies involved share a vision for future business opportunities based around a platform, although they would have different roles and business models. Based on the different roles, the six industry companies also had different ecosystem strategies, which caused some conflicting interest. Therefore, ensuring sufficient renewal may present a challenge to ecosystems driven by strong industrial leader companies. In order to avoid this barrier, the involved research organisation had a role as an ecosystem project coordinator.

Based on the pros and cons analyses of the three mechanisms, we have integrated the best practices for industry–academy collaboration as a process integrating short- and long-term needs and the different interests of the actors involved. This process for industry–academy collaboration (see Fig. 2) aims to optimise the value of research investment with the three interconnected R&D&I tracks.

First, within the research-driven long-term vision track, novel research results support industry's systemic long-term challenge to solve and support companies in directing future strategic competitive-edge building. Then, the industry challenge-driven idea co-creation track supports co-innovation in order to solve common concrete industry problems with relevant research and to create a business impact in the shorter term. Finally, the industry-owned confidential project track boosts the scaling up and out of the results gained through collaboration.

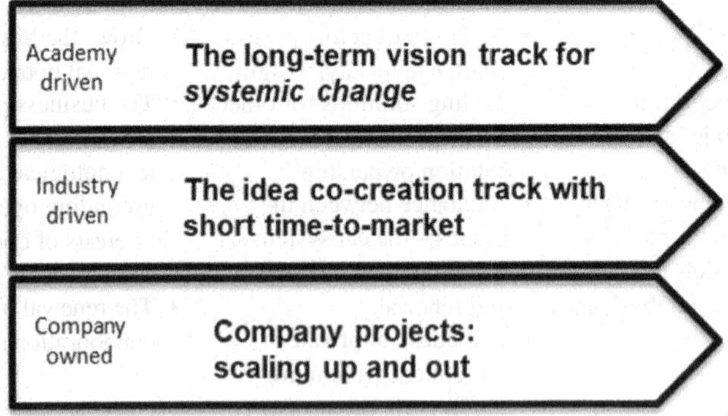


**Fig. 2.** The industry–academy operation mode.

Furthermore, the longitudinal observations of ecosystem cases also indicated that different phases of the ecosystem lifecycle require different operations models. Especially at the beginning, the role of public actors, as well as the role of public funding, was highlighted. When the collaboration proceeds closer to business operations, it is natural that the role of companies is crucial in order to boost the emergence of business ecosystems and networks.

## 5 Conclusions

In order to identify the best practices for industry–academy collaboration, we have analysed four cases. Our empirical cases provide practical implications, although every collaboration within an innovation funnel is heterogeneous with their specialties. Therefore, it is important to understand how a shared aim, structure of collaboration and variety of actors influence best practices. As a starting point, it should be noted that the practices and processes of co-innovation need to be co-created with the involved actors. In other words, they cannot be brought from one collaborative setting to another without mutual understanding about their meaning. Furthermore, the variety of actors is an important factor for the diversity of the ecosystem, which will then bring challenges for coordination. Different interests, as well as different expectations and mind-sets, may even hinder the collaboration. As for the managerial implications of this study, the three mechanisms studied may support the identification of the different perspectives of the involved actors and the concretisation of their roles in co-innovation ecosystems.

Although the literature of collaborative networks provides an excellent baseline for understanding industry–academy collaboration, there is still room for fruitful research. The evaluation of the three mechanisms was done in four innovation ecosystems within their building base; the co-evolution within ecosystems may take years. Therefore, one obvious avenue for further research would be the follow-up of these ecosystems. Then, in order to test the three mechanisms and their impacts on a larger scale, another important dimension for future research would be based on a quantitative approach.

**Acknowledgments.** The authors would like to thank all the parties of the case ecosystems for their support of this study. This study has been done as a part of the funding that the Finnish Government gave to VTT Technical Research Centre of Finland in order to promote the digitalisation and competitiveness of Finnish manufacturing industry in a post-Covid world.

## References

1. Lee, S., Olson, S.M., Trimi, D.L.: Co-Innovation: Convergenomics, collaboration, and co-creation for organizational values. Manag. Decis. **50**(5), 817–831 (2012)
2. Bogers, M., et al.: The open innovation research landscape: established perspectives and emerging themes across different levels of analysis. Ind. Innov. **2716**, 1–33 (2016)
3. Nuutinen, M., Palomäki, K., Valkokari, K.: Understanding industrial service ecosystems as a mechanism for solving systemic challenges, in Forum on Markets and Marketing 2020: Institutions. Aalto University, Service Ecosystems and Emergence (2020)

4. Aarikka-Stenroos, L., Ritala, P.: Network management in the era of ecosystems: systematic review and management framework. Ind. Mark. Manag. **67**, 23–36 (2017)
5. Camarinha-Matos, L.M., Fornasiero, R., Afsarmanesh, H.: Collaborative networks as a core enabler of industry 4.0. In: Camarinha-Matos, L.M., Afsarmanesh, H., Fornasiero, R. (eds.) PRO-VE 2017. IAICT, vol. 506, pp. 3–17. Springer, Cham (2017). https://doi.org/10.1007/978-3-319-65151-4_1
6. Davey, T., Deery, M., Winters, C., Van Der Sijde, P., Kusio, T., Rodriquez, S.: 30 best case studies of good practice in the area of UBC within Europe (2009)
7. Cooper, R., Edgett, S.: Lean, Rapid and Profitable New Product Development. Ancaster, ON: Product Development Institute (2005)
8. Chesbrough, H.: Open Innovation: The New Imperative for Creating and Profiting from Technology. Harvard Business School Press, Boston (2003)
9. Rabelo, R., Bernus, P., Romero, D.: Innovation ecosystems: A collaborative networks perspective, in Risks and Resilience of Collaborative Networks. Springer, (2015).
10. Bittencourt, B.A., Santos, D.A.G., Mignoni, J.: Resource orchestration in innovation ecosystems: a comparative study between innovation ecosystems at different stages of development. Int. Hournal Innov. **9**(1), 108–130 (2021)
11. Valkokari, K., Valkokari, P., Kortelainen, H., Nyblom, J.: Building business impacts of an industry 4.0 ecosystem through collaborative network settings between IT and forest companies. In: Camarinha-Matos, L.M., Afsarmanesh, H., Ortiz, A. (eds.) PRO-VE 2020. IAICT, vol. 598, pp. 463–474. Springer, Cham (2020). https://doi.org/10.1007/978-3-030-62412-5_38
12. Tsujimoto, M., Kajikawa, Y., Tomita, J., Matsumoto, Y.: A review of the ecosystem concept: towards coherent ecosystem design. Technol. Forecast. Soc. Change **136**, 49–58 (2018)
13. Iansiti, M., Levien, R.: Strategy as ecology. Harv. Bus. Rev. **82**(3) (2004)
14. Valkokari, K.: Business, innovation, and knowledge ecosystems: how they differ and how to survive and thrive within them. Technol. Innov. Manag. Rev. **5**(8), 17–24 (2015)
15. Clarysse, B., Wright, M., Bruneel, J., Mahajan, A.: Creating value in ecosystems: crossing the chasm between knowledge and business ecosystems. Res. Policy **43**(7), 1164–1176 (2014)
16. Eisenhardt, K.M.: Building theories from case study research. Acad. Manag. Rev. **14**, 532–550 (1989)

# Simulation Model for a Semi-automated Retail Order Picking System Under Uncertainty

Sawssen Souiden[1,2](✉), Audrey Cerqueus[1], Xavier Delorme[1], and Jean-Lucien Rascle[2]

[1] Mines Saint-Etienne, Univ Clermont Auvergne, CNRS, UMR 6158 LIMOS, Institut Henri Fayol, 42023 Saint-Etienne, France
{audrey.cerqueus,delorme}@emse.fr

[2] Boa Concept SAS, 42000 Saint-Etienne, France
{sawssen.souiden,jean-lucien.rascle}@boaconcept.com

**Abstract.** Due to the growth of e-commerce, retail order picking problems are nowadays one of the most challengeable issues in logistics networks. Conventionally, semi-automated picking systems are implemented, using a conveyor for transportation and operators for preparation. Customer demand being volatile, the sustainability of the system relies on digitalization and reconfigurability, regarding both the physical and information system. From an operational standpoint, the performance is driven by scheduling approaches to manage the bins' flow however the system is prone to uncertainty. We develop a decision tool based on a simulation model to accurately reflect the real-life situation and the human-conveyor interaction. Our aim is to evaluate the practical flow of the system with uncertain preparation times compared to a theoretical schedule obtained by a deterministic optimization approach. Numerical experiments including an industrial case study are presented and discussed.

**Keywords:** Semi-automated retail order picking system · Scheduling · Optimization · Simulation · Uncertainty

## 1 Introduction

Order picking (OP) process is one of the most critical components of supply chain management [1]. It plays a fundamental role in ensuring customer fulfillment and in the smooth running of the logistics warehouses networks. There are several OP methods that could be applied depending on the company requirements. Manual picking methods such as "Picker-to-Part" (also called "Pick-by Order") are commonly used in traditional warehousing systems, when the volume of orders is low and the parts are heavy. In these systems, the order picker travels to storage locations in order to bring together the customer's required products. Despite their simplicity, the travel of pickers is an important unproductive part of the OP process. The "Part-to-Picker" method employs the same physical location as the previous method with the integration of material handling system to bring automatically the products to stationary pickers. Such settings are


Published by Springer Nature Switzerland AG 2021
L. M. Camarinha-Matos et al. (Eds.): PRO-VE 2021, IFIP AICT 629, pp. 759–767, 2021.
https://doi.org/10.1007/978-3-030-85969-5_72

appropriate for high numbers of orders per days and for small and heavy products, as the material handling systems are expensive investment, and have less margin of error. "Zone picking" is a semi-automated process which involves a collaboration between a conveyor system for transportation and order picker for orders preparation. This method is typically used for retail order picking (ROP) where the ordered products are small and the delivery dates are tight, as it is the case in e-commerce. As represented in Fig. 1, the OP process consists in retrieving sequentially different items from one zone into another until the constitution of the whole customer order. This ROP method is efficient since it reflects the therein occurring human-machine interactions and allows pickers to focus only on the picking process. However, it could have some organizational issues such as flow gridlocks, which induce costs and delays. Hence, from an operational perspective, the zoning system's performance relies substantially on scheduling approaches of managing the flow within the conveyor system. As all semi-automated OP systems, it is prone to uncertainty due to the variability of the order pickers preparation times and to the conveyor system's state (failure or obstruction of a cell causing the conveyor to stop fractionally or entirely).

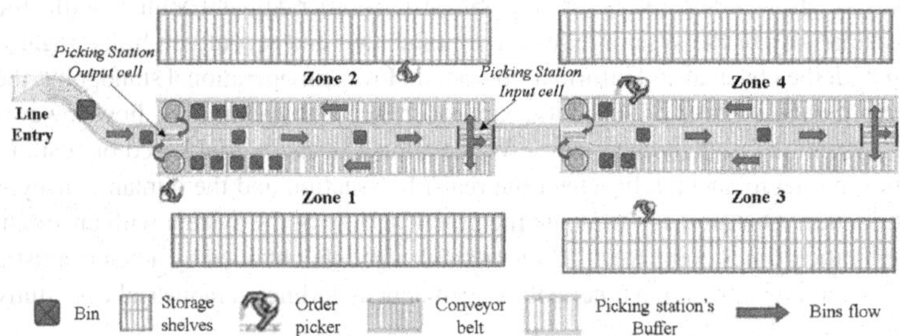


**Fig. 1.** A schematic diagram of a ROP system under zoning configuration

Nowadays, the customer's demand tends to be fickle and unpredictable and we attend to the booming of e-commerce, intensified by the current health situation which has heightened the need for e-commerce as a vital alternative sales solution [2]. Thus, to remain competitive, companies have to implement digitized and reconfigurable supply chains, on both the physical and information system levels. In this context, we need digital decision-making tools that enable real-time retrieval of the system data and interaction with it on an operational scale. Simulation tools and digital twins can be used as such decision tools enabling the ROP system to communicate and share data for optimal workflows. They also take into account uncertain data and business rules and help to evaluate the system's performance and to highlight bottlenecks. In Industry 4.0, certain tendencies begin to emerge, which lead the logistics companies to adopt a servitization approach by offering customized digital tools developed as a service to their customers. This is in order to strengthen the collaboration with their customers.

In this paper, we develop a simulation model for a ROP system under zone picking configuration. The aim is to rely on a digital simulation tool to evaluate the system's practical flow subject to preparation times uncertainty compared to a deterministic schedule that could be obtained through an exact or approximate optimization. The proposed simulation tool enables to exploit data arising from a servitization process. The reminder of the paper is as follows: In the next section, a literature review of related works is presented. Section 3 is dedicated to the ROP simulation model. An industrial study case is discussed in Sect. 4. Finally, some concluding remarks and research perspectives are given in Sect. 5.

## 2 Literature Review

The ROP system we study combines the scheduling aspect along with the consideration of uncertainty. The problem of scheduling for OP systems has been widely studied in the literature under a deterministic manner regarding an exact mathematical modeling. For instance, [3] which minimizes the order picker unproductive times while taking into consideration limited buffer capacity and the possibility of skipping some zones and [4] which minimizes the sum of delivery cost and the makespan for multiple zones and limited vehicle capacity. Likewise, many researchers dealt with the scheduling problem in supply chain system by assuming that the input data are known. However, in real-life, scheduling systems are subject to uncertainty caused by the variability of data due to external constraints or factors inherent to the system [5]. It is therefore crucial to model these uncertainties during the scheduling in order to enhance the schedule quality.

The issue of scheduling under uncertainty has received great attention from the researchers in the past decades and it was handled with different methodologies including stochastic, probabilistic, fuzzy programming and robust optimization methods [6, 7]. Simulation has been successfully adopted in several studies related to scheduling systems, to evaluate the robustness of a schedule and analyze the impact of various uncertain factors [8]. In [9, 10], the authors presented a real-time scheduling methodology based on simulation to optimize job dispatching rules in two different manufacturing systems. They considered different strategies based on various dispatching rules and by comparing those strategies, the efficient one is determined. [11] presents a study for a discrete event simulation with an integrated optimization procedure for a flow-shop layout. A coupling simulation optimization is proposed.

Simulation modeling has also been extensively developed in numerous studies related to logistics and manufacturing systems. However, to the best of our knowledge, simulation approaches for OP systems remain modestly explored in the literature specifically in the context of scheduling. [12] develops queuing simulation models to evaluate the performance of a warehouse that uses sequential zone picking. The proposed queuing network model focuses on several performance measures such as system throughput, order pickers occupancy rate, and the average number of bins in the system based on factors such as the speed and length of the conveyor, the number of picking stations, and the number of picks per station. [13] analyzes the OP system efficiency under congestion situations. The authors drew attention to picker blocking phenomenon and its impact on OP efficiency. The OP system's performance is investigated by implementing a simulation model, which proves that the system efficiency is directly correlated with the number of pickers. The recent work presented in [14] intends to evaluate the performance of bucket brigade OP system in which a simulation study is conducted to analyze the effects of various OP configurations.

There are no works that take into account the uncertainty in the ROP scheduling problem. This paper presents a simulation model for a ROP system modeling the flow with a main focus on the variability of preparation times since in human-machine systems, the human is often the main source of uncertainty.

## 3 Modeling and Simulating the Retail Order Picking System

The aim of this paper is to develop a discrete-event simulation model to evaluate a schedule quality applied in the ROP system under uncertainty. The model was built within Arena simulation software Rockwell Automation to reflect real-life situations and the human-conveyor interaction. This section describes the ROP system components and the fundamental business rules integrated in the simulation model.

We consider that the system does not contain loops, that the zones are visited by the bins in the order of their indices. We suppose that the customer order is known and that the products are partitioned on the zones. Thus, the bins visiting sequences are known in advance.

The ROP conveyor system is modeled in a compartmentalized way, dividing it into cells of unit capacity arranged one after the other. The bins go through the cells with a fixed transportation time. When a bin is on an input cell of a station, it is directed depending on if it needs to go on this station or not. Each picking stations is simulated as a set of two complementary resources: the order picker which process only one bin at a time and an associated buffering resource with a finite capacity.

As illustrated in Fig. 1, when a bin enters a picking station, it is placed in a buffer. The bins are processed in the order of their arrival at the station and are prepared as soon as the order picker is available. Preemption is forbidden.

After the completion of a bin preparation, the order picker tries to evacuate the prepared bins on the conveyor. If the picking station's output cell is empty, the evacuation process is done immediately, otherwise, the bins are maintained in the picking station's buffer and the order picker proceeds with his/her activities. The prepared bins are sent to the conveyor according to the FIFO rule.

Whenever the picking station buffer is saturated, a bin which should access to this station will remain on the input cell. This flow congestion hinders the bin transportation, making it impossible for bins to go from an upstream to a downstream station. Consequently, bins will be accumulated on the conveyor (see Fig. 2).

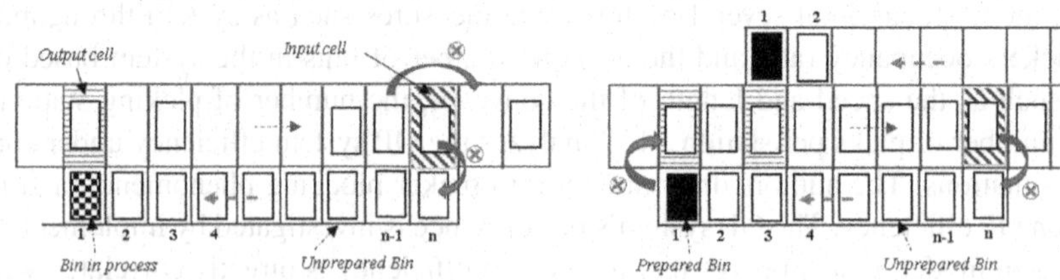


**Fig. 2.** A flow congestion situation

**Fig. 3.** A deadlock situation

If the blocking situation persists and the station's output cell is upstream from its input cell, a deadlock can occur. A deadlock is a definitive blocking of the bins flow on the conveying segment connecting the input and the output cells of a saturated picking station (see Fig. 3). Thus, it requires a human intervention to unlock the flow.

To deal with the deadlock situations, two different business rules have been applied. The first rule aims to prevent the bins stationing in the output cell of the picking station. To do this, a bin is only allowed to access the output cell of a picking station if both the output cell and the one following it are empty. The second rule models the human intervention to handle deadlocks. To solve the deadlock problem, and ensure not falling back into a deadlock situation, only bins coming from the deadlocked station can arrive on the segment connecting the input and output cells. In this degraded mode, the conveyor is stopped right before the output cell and all stations which have their output cell in this segment are not allowed to free bins on the conveyor (see step 1 of Fig. 4). Then the last entered bin is placed on an additional buffer to enable the circulation of the bins (see step 2 of Fig. 4).

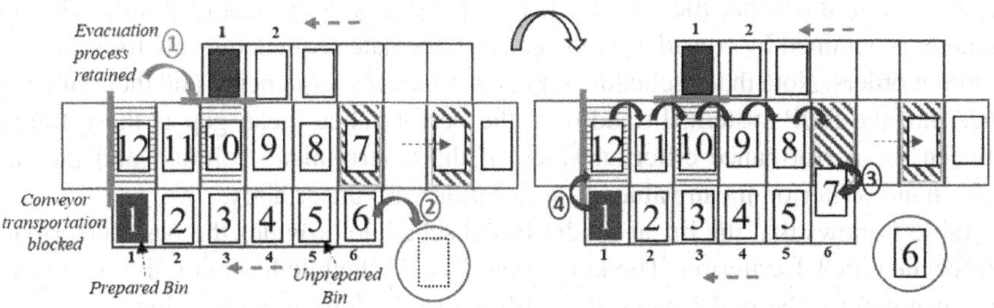


**Fig. 4.** A representation of the picking station's degraded mode in deadlock situation

The bin holding at the station's input cell will then access the picking station's buffer and once the station's output cell is freed up, the order picker evacuates the prepared bin in the order of their preparations (see steps 3 and 4 on Fig. 4). The degraded mode stays on until the station becomes unsaturated. Then, the order picker puts back on the station's buffer the bin that was in the additional buffer and the flow retention is lifted.

To synthesize the key components of our simulation model, the bins are the entities flowing through the ROP system. The resources are: an order picker and a buffer for each picking station, the conveyor cells and an additional buffer of unit capacity for each station which is used only in a deadlock situations.

## 4 Industrial Case Study

The industrial case under study involves a company specialized in the manufacturing and marketing of products and tools for construction and decoration. Their activity volume is about 3500 orders per day.

We aim to study the impact of uncertainty and analyze the performance if the company's ROP system regarding a predictive scheduling. The system's configuration is composed of 4 stations: two pairs of parallel stations, for which the direction is opposite to the conveyor, as represented in Fig. 1. The buffer capacity of each picking station is of 10 bins. There are 50 bins to prepare, which visit on average 65% of the stations with minimum one station to visit and maximum 4. The OP preparation times are centered around the company expected average time of 35s. We consider that preparation times uncertainty follows a truncated normal distribution with a mean of 30s and a standard deviation (SD) of 10.

In this case study, we draw attention to two different performance measurements: the makespan performance measure and the order pickers cumulative presence time (OPCPT) at their stations criterion which measures the order pickers unproductive times. The simulation model is executed for one simulation with 50 replications and the time unit is second.

First, we consider 3 types of predictive schedules obtained from different scheduling methods with the aim is to study the efficiency and the performance of these scheduling solutions while keeping the uncertainty level fixed. The first schedule represents the sequencing approach currently adopted by the company which is based on their know-how. The second schedule is a feasible solution generated by the solving of a deterministic linear model minimizing the OPCPT [3], stopped at a time limit of 3600s. The third schedule is obtained by considering the earliest due date sequencing rule for scheduling customer orders. Note that a schedule represents the bins sequencing and their launching times into the ROP system. In addition, the performance mean gap is the difference between the performance criterion value of the deterministic solution and the same performance criterion mean value of the solution with uncertainty.

Table 1 shows that the linear model-based schedule provides the best performance gap for the OPCPT criterion. The know-how-based schedule has not only the best performance gap for the makespan criterion but also the lowest mean value of makespan comparing to the other schedules. The due date-based schedule is the most unfordable schedule with the bigger performance gap for both makespan and OPCPT performance measurements. This could be explained by the fact that the due date-based scheduling method does not take into account the ROP system workload and only considers an external factor (customers due dates). The simulation model could be a decision tool for the company decision-makers, enabling them to choose the most adequate schedule to apply in the ROP system depending on their interests.

The next experiment focuses on the impact of the variability of the uncertainty level. We considered the know-how-based schedule for which we consider different uncertainty levels by modifying the value of SD.

The experiment shows the linear variation of the makespan performance mean gap with the increase of the level of uncertainty unlike the OPCPT performance mean gap. The reason behind the increasing gaps is that system started to generate blockages. In addition, due to the non-linearity of the number of deadlocks, the number of human interventions would be difficult to predict with increasing of the uncertainty level.

**Table 1.** Difference in performance measurements of the three scheduling approaches under the same uncertainty level.

| | OPCPT for | | | Makespan for | | |
|---|---|---|---|---|---|---|
| Schedule | Know-how-based | Linear model based | Due date based | Know-how-based | Linear model based | Due date based |
| Without uncertainty | 9609 | 8241 | 11865 | 8733 | 8896 | 9701 |
| Simulation Mean value | 10802 | 9004 | 13573 | 9231 | 9788 | 10751 |
| Performance Mean Gap in % | 12.42 | 9.26 | 14.40 | 5.70 | 10.03 | 10.82 |
| Gap Confidence interval in % | [10.94;13.88] | [7.77;10.73] | [12.81;15.97] | [4.30;7.09] | [8.64;11.40] | [9.26;12.40] |

**Table 2.** Impact of the variability of the uncertainty parameter

| | OPCPT Performance Mean Gap in % | OPCPT Confidence Interval in % | Makespan Performance Mean Gap in % | Makespan Confidence Interval in % | Nb of Deadlocks | Nb of deadlocks Confidence interval |
|---|---|---|---|---|---|---|
| SD = 5 | 7.83 | [6.61;9.03] | 5.11 | [3.97;6.24] | 2 | [1;3] |
| SD = 10 | 12.42 | [10.94;13.88] | 5.70 | [4.30;7.09] | 3 | [2;4] |
| SD = 15 | 13.21 | [11.60;14.80] | 6.52 | [5.03;7.99] | 5 | [3;7] |
| SD = 20 | 16.28 | [14.41;18.13] | 7.71 | [6.03;9.37] | 9 | [7;11] |

## 5 Conclusion and Perspectives

This paper develops a simulation model of a zone OP system with the aim to evaluate a predictive picking schedule under uncertainty. The work points out the impact of the variability of the preparation times on the system's performance measurements. By referring to the simulation, industrial decision-makers can anticipate on future deadlocks. They can also compare different scheduling methods and analyze the schedules resilience to uncertainty in order to find the best one that meets their needs.

Further proposed analysis could be by considering other sources of uncertainty like the conveyor's system state (failure of a cell causing the conveyor to stop fractionally or entirely) which will add an extra layer of perturbation. Another complementary work is the coupling and interaction between simulation-based and optimization methods. We think this could be the key to absorb real scheduling uncertainties especially when the problem gets more complex.

## References


1. Wäscher, G.: Order picking: a survey of planning problems and methods. In: Dyckhoff, H., Lackes, R., Reese, J. (eds.) Supply Chain Management and Reverse Logistics, pp. 323–347. Springer, Heidelberg (2004). https://doi.org/10.1007/978-3-540-24815-6_15
2. Guthrie, C., Fosso-Wamba, S., Arnaud, J.B.: Online consumer resilience during a pandemic: An exploratory study of e-commerce behavior before, during and after a COVID-19 lockdown. J. Retailing Consumer Servs. **61**, 102570 (2021). https://doi.org/10.1016/j.jretconser.2021.102570
3. Souiden, S., Cerqueus, A., Delorme, X., Rascle, J.-L.: Retail order picking scheduling with missing operations and limited buffer. IFAC-PapersOnLine. **53**, 10767–10772 (2020). https://doi.org/10.1016/j.ifacol.2020.12.2859
4. Zhang, J., Wang, X., Huang, K.: On-line scheduling of order picking and delivery with multiple zones and limited vehicle capacity. Omega **79**, 104–115 (2018). https://doi.org/10.1016/j.omega.2017.08.004
5. Floudas, C.A., Lin, X.: Continuous-time versus discrete-time approaches for scheduling of chemical processes: a review. Comput. Chem. Eng. **28**, 2109–2129 (2004). https://doi.org/10.1016/j.compchemeng.2004.05.002
6. Sahinidis, N.V.: Optimization under uncertainty: state-of-the-art and opportunities. Comput. Chem. Eng. **28**, 971–983 (2004). https://doi.org/10.1016/j.compchemeng.2003.09.017

7. González-Neira, E.M., Montoya-Torres, J.R., Barrera, D.: Flow-shop scheduling problem under uncertainties: review and trends. Int. J. Ind. Eng. Comput., 399–426 (2017). https://doi.org/10.5267/j.ijiec.2017.2.001
8. Negahban, A., Smith, J.S.: Simulation for manufacturing system design and operation: literature review and analysis. J. Manuf. Syst. **33**, 241–261 (2014). https://doi.org/10.1016/j.jmsy.2013.12.007
9. Jeong, K.-C., Kim, Y.-D.: A real-time scheduling mechanism for a flexible manufacturing system: using simulation and dispatching rules. Int. J. Prod. Res. **36**, 2609–2626 (1998). https://doi.org/10.1080/002075498192733
10. Tavakkoli-Moghaddam, R., Daneshmand-Mehr, M.: A computer simulation model for job shop scheduling problems minimizing makespan. Comput. Ind. Eng. **48**, 811–823 (2005). https://doi.org/10.1016/j.cie.2004.12.010
11. Framinan, J.M., Perez-Gonzalez, P., Escudero, V.F.-V.: The value of real-time data in stochastic flowshop scheduling: a simulation study for makespan. In: 2017 Winter Simulation Conference (WSC), pp. 3299–3310. IEEE, Las Vegas, NV (2017). https://doi.org/10.1109/WSC.2017.8248047
12. de Koster, R.: Performance approximation of pick-to-belt orderpicking systems. Eur. J. Oper. Res. **72**, 558–573 (1994). https://doi.org/10.1016/0377-2217(94)90423-5
13. Klodawski, M., Jachimowski, R., Jacyna-Golda, I., Izdebski, M.: Simulation analysis of order picking efficiency with congestion situations. Int. J. Simul. Modelling **17**, 431–443 (2018). https://doi.org/10.2507/IJSIMM17(3)438
14. Hong, S.: A performance evaluation of bucket brigade order picking systems: analytical and simulation approaches. Comput. Ind. Eng. **135**, 120–131 (2019). https://doi.org/10.1016/j.cie.2019.05.037

# Sustainable Horizontal Collaboration: A Case Study in Moroccan Dry Foods Distribution

Hanan Ouhader(✉) and Malika El Kyal

National School of Applied Sciences, Ibn Zohr University, Agadir, Morocco
ouhader@gmail.com

**Abstract.** The paper develops, for partners, a decision tool to assess the economic and ecological impact of collaborative freight delivery, before accepting to integrate a horizontal cooperative coalition. The proposed mechanism is based on the design of a sustainable collaborative supply chain for specific competing dry food distributors in Morocco. The success of such practice requires addressing different issues, among them: the redesign of the supply chain and the fair cost allocation to participating partners. An extension of the two echelons Location Routing Problem (2E-LRP) was exploited, to investigate how this collaboration can support the participants during a predefined planning horizon. The Shapley value method is used to evaluate the individual opportunities savings. We opt for Multi-objective to detect a good trade-off between the economic objective and the ecological one. Case study confirms the economic and environmental positive impact of the shippers' collaboration with different optimal network configurations.

**Keywords:** Horizontal logistics collaboration · Network design · Two-echelon location routing problem · Multi-objective optimization · Sustainability · Case study

## 1 Background and Motivation of the Research

The multi-stakeholder partnerships and collaboration are crucial in efforts toward sustainable supply chain [1]. Logistic collaboration becomes an interesting topic and it receives considerable attention in recent years. (Cao & Zhang 2011) [2] define supply chain collaboration (SCC) as like «a partnership process where two or more autonomous firms work closely to plan and execute supply chain operations toward common goals and mutual benefits». Different types of classifications for SCC exist. The most expanded referring to its direction. SCC is classified into two categories: vertical and horizontal collaboration. The vertical collaboration concerns two or more organizations (receiver, shipper, carrier), which share their responsibilities, resources, and data information to serve relatively similar end customers [3]. Horizontal collaboration occurs between companies in the same level of supply chain [4]. Vertical cooperation has been the focus of various research efforts over the last decades. Horizontal cooperation (HC) is starting to gain traction as a one of the key policies to assure sustainable supply chain [5, 6]).There are several ways for HC: carriers collaboration and shippers collaboration.


Published by Springer Nature Switzerland AG 2021
L. M. Camarinha-Matos et al. (Eds.): PRO-VE 2021, IFIP AICT 629, pp. 768–777, 2021.
https://doi.org/10.1007/978-3-030-85969-5_73

Over the last years, a good recent reviews on HC appeared in Logistic and Transportation as, [5, 7–10]. These reviews pointed out the scarcity of papers integrated the environmental issue in HC analysis. Compared to carriers' collaboration, there are few works on the problem of shippers' collaboration. From operation research approach, most of papers were based on vehicle routing problem and its variants whereas few papers treated supply chain design directly, where facility location or location routing decisions should be taken in collaboration with other supply chain partners. For interested readers, Prodhon & Prins 2014 [13] published exhaustive literature review of Location Routing problem (LRP).

A few studies have analyzed the benefits of HC by combining location and routing decisions such as [14–17] but they focused on economic indicators. Works as [18–20] quantified the environmental and economic effect of implementing HC but, optimized separately. To minimize costs and carbon emission under a bi-objective approach, (Yong et al. 2018) [21] studied variants of vehicle routing problem (VRP) without integrating facility location (FL) and (Mrabti et al. 2020) [22] suggested a FL model without integrating VRP. Recently, (Aloui et al. 2021) [12] proposed a bi-objective ILRP which combines routing, facility location and inventory decisions to assess the benefits of HC. This study has not been tested in real life-case. It was based on randomly instances and hypothetical data. Furthermore this study did not address the allocation of individual savings between partners.

For that, we note the need to gain a comprehensive perspective of the supply chain design and sustainability in horizontal collaboration between shippers through multi-objective decision-making models. These models permit to decision makers to understand the potentialities of such alliances.

In our previous works [11, 23], we investigated the potential economic and ecological impacts of combining depot location and vehicle routing decisions in urban road freight transportation under HC. We proposed a multi-objective, two echelon location routing problem (2E-LRP) to evaluate, the tradeoff between the objectives. In these works, extended known instances representing the real distribution in urban area were used to test the proposed model.

Due the importance of food wholesale supply chain, we evaluate in the current study, the impact of HC in this supply chain efficiency. We extend the 2E-LRP mathematical model developed in our previous studies to consider multi-period planning framework and we test the applicability of the model on a case of cooperative coalition composed of dry food wholesalers operating in Morocco.

The remainder of the article is structured as follows. In Sect. 2 we introduce the case study, in Sect. 3 we describe our optimization approach, in Sect. 4 we show and discuss the results, and in Sect. 5 we conclude this article and suggest future research directions.

## 2 Case Study Description

We evaluate, in this paper, the effect of implementing HC in distribution for a dry food supply chain in the Moroccan economic region of Souss-Massa. We consider a coalition of three independent dry foods distributors specializing in the wholesale distribution of flour products with more than 20 years of experience in the sector. The companies are designated as (BG, BL and BB) to maintain its anonymity. They service many different types of customers such as bakeries, grocery or retail stores and resellers. All partners compete with each other, but they have to look for new ways to be competitive. Actually, these distributors organize their logistics individually but aim to intensify partnership to reduce cost and emissions by joining their distribution decision. Goods are distributed to customers via transitional depots. Trucks are utilized to transport directly goods to these depots for consolidating flows. Later, goods are delivered to customers using small vehicles. Our study does not suppose inventory planning at depots (cross- docking facilities) (see Fig. 1).

We redesign the distribution network to support horizontal collaboration with the objectives of minimizing, the transportation cost and carbon emissions in a two-echelon distribution system. The current problem combines two decisions: Location –allocation problem and routing problem.

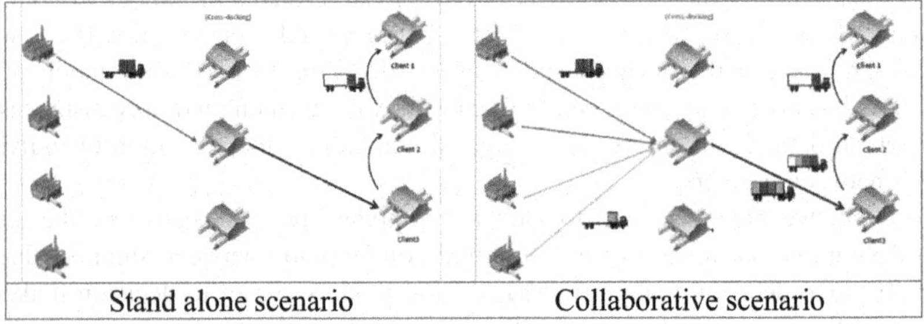


**Fig. 1.** Stand alone scenario Vs Collaborative scenario

## 3 Modeling and Optimization Approach

The problem is modeled as bi-objective 2E-LRP extended from our previous work [11], to consider multi-period planning. The problem consist of selecting a group of depots over the planning horizon, defining customers to visit for each period, allocating customers to chosen depots and assigning the routes serving the customers to each depot. The studied problem is defined on a directed, weighted graph and on a horizon $H$ composed of $P$ periods with shipping date $t \in P$. In order to convert the model to a multi-period model, the index t, which represents each period of the planning horizon, is included in the single period model equations.

We adopt the same assumptions and constraints as presented in [11]. The economic objective function includes the fixed cost of exploiting depots, the handling cost in depots, the fixed costs of trucks and vehicles and the traversal costs of the arcs in the two distribution levels. The environmental objective consists of carbon emissions induced by the trucks and vehicles. These emissions depend on travelled distances, load and capacity of vehicles or trucks, confirmed to European studies such as [24, 25] and [26]. This ecological model is generally easy to apply in optimization problems. Due to space limitation, the rigorous mathematical description of the model is beyond the scope of this article and is detailed in [11].

The 2E-LRP models can be implemented to analyze the two scenarios: Non collaborative scenario (NCS) and the collaborative scenario (CS). Three base cases will be used for analysis: (i) Cost minimization (C_min) where the economic objective is solved (ii) Emissions minimization (Em_min) where environmental objective is solved (iii) Transportation cost minimization versus carbon emissions reduction (C_St_Em) where the bi-objective model is solved.

The model is implemented and solved exactly using commercial solver MATLAB 2014 (which uses a branch-and-bound algorithm) and tested on a 4.2 GHz Core i7 desktop with 16 GB RAM and a 64-bits operating system under Windows 10 environment desktop.

Because of confidentiality, no cost can be shown in this manuscript. Nevertheless, we evaluate the impact of HC based on the percentage of generated savings, comparing collaboration scenario with the stand alone one.

# 4 Results

## 4.1 Data and Information

The studied product is the flour packaged in bags of 25 kg. Partners provided us with a record on four weeks orders placed by the customers. The weekly delivery is once and the average demand per customer is 11 units. Each supplier has its own and unshared customers with other partners. In collaboration, suppliers will share their own depots. Eight potential depot locations and 37 delivery points have been identified (See Table 1). The travel distances and the travel times were calculated using the Google Distance Matrix API which provides travel distance and time for a matrix of origins and destinations. We consider groups of homogeneous vehicles and trucks. Their characteristics are summarized in Table 2. According to the speed limitation and traffic condition, speeds are set as 60 km/h of trucks and as 30 km/h for urban vehicles. All customers must be served between 6 am and 11 pm. Then the urban routes cannot exceed a time length of 5 h. Because of confidentiality, we cannot reveal the sensitive data and information (e.g. demands, geographic localization and costs). Further parameters are available on demand to the corresponding author of this paper.

**Table 1.** Partners' characteristics

| Supplier | Depots | Customers' number | % of the total delivered quantities of the coalition |
|---|---|---|---|
| BG | DC1, DC2 and DC6 | 14 | 40% |
| BL | DC3, DC4 and DC7 | 13 | 41% |
| BB | DC5 and DC8 | 10 | 19% |

**Table 2.** Trucks and vehicles characteristic

| | Urban vehicle | Truck |
|---|---|---|
| Type | RENAULT-Master FORGON TRACTION L2H3 2,8T (Base cases) | Volvo FL514 4 × 2 Platform 14 ton |
| Capacity (Bags) | 55 | 150 |
| $E_{(empty)}$ (g/CO2) | 208 | 650 |
| $E_{(full)}$ (g/CO2) | 234 | 780 |

## 4.2 Single Objective Approach

In this part, we consider a single objective approach to evaluate the potential impacts of cooperatively reducing cost as well as emissions.

**Non Collaborative Scenario (NCS).** First, we evaluate the extreme solutions in the two cases (C_min) and (Em_min). Focusing on the aggregated amounts all over the planning horizon(Four weeks), results are presented in Table 3. The load rates are calculated as (total demand of route)/(capacity of the vehicle/truck) for each vehicle and truck. We calculate the trucks' and vehicles' numbers as the maximum number performed by vehicles or trucks during a period over the horizon planning. Results show that, for the three suppliers, lower environmental impact involves a higher transportation cost. For suppliers BG, BL and BB, carbon emission reduction with 18%, 14% and 38% can be achieved, respectively, at 11%, 9.8% and 6.5% augmentation on the cost of the C_min case. From Table 3, this reduction is related to the decrease of travelled distances after the modification of chosen depots in Em_min case. These DCs are better propagated and closer to customers. These depots have more expensive open or handling costs, which justifies the increase of shipment cost. Compared with C_min case, the vehicle load factor (VLR) decrease in Em_min case as the number of vehicle increases and the number of customers allocated to depots is modified. The average load rates of truck (TLR) do not change because the number of trucks is the same in both cases.

**Collaborative Scenario (CS).** To assess the potential impacts of HC in the studied supply chain, the cooperative scenario is compared to the stand alone scenario. To evaluate the NCS, the sum of transportation cost, emissions and other metrics of individual companies is calculated. The obtained results are presented in the two last columns of Table 3 and in Fig. 2. Results show that the collaborative scenario surpasses the non-collaborative one in all cases. Gaps between the two scenarios are positives, proving the profitability of horizontal collaboration. In C_min case, a profit of 9.40% and emissions reduction of 4.66% are obtained. In Em_min case, a profit of 5.58% and emissions reduction of 23.57% are obtained. As shown in Table 3 and Fig. 2, these positive gaps is related to the diminution of the travelled distances and the vehicles' number after the new assignment of customers to depots and the augmentation of vehicles' load rates. Also the number of selected depots decreases from 5 to 3 after collaboration, leading to the reduction of facility opening costs.

**Table 3.** Summary results for cooperative and non cooperative cases

| | Scenario | (kgCO2) | Travelled distances (Km) | Trucks number | Vehicles number | satellites number : open satellites/ number of assigned customers | TLR % | VLR % |
|---|---|---|---|---|---|---|---|---|
| BG | C_min | 392 | 560 | 3 | 5 | 2:DC2/9;DC1/5 | 65.4 | 87.2 |
| | Em_min | 324 | 452 | 3 | 6 | 2:DC2/10;DC6/4 | 65.4 | 72.6 |
| BL | C_min | 284 | 388 | 3 | 6 | 2:DC4/10;DC3/3 | 66 | 73.4 |
| | Em_min | 244 | 332 | 3 | 6 | 2:DC7/3;DC3/10 | 66 | 73.4 |
| BB | C_min | 96 | 188 | 1 | 3 | 1:DC5/10 | 96 | 71.2 |
| | Em_min | 60 | 92 | 1 | 3 | 1:DC8/10 | 96 | 71.2 |
| Total NCS | C_min | 772 | 1136 | 7 | 14 | 5:DC1/5;DC2/9; DC3/3;DC4/10; DC5/10 | 70 | 77.8 |
| | Em_min | 628 | 876 | 7 | 15 | 5:DC2/10;DC3/10; DC6/4;DC7/3; DC8/10 | 70 | 72.6 |
| CS | C_min | 736 | 960 | 7 | 12 | 3:DC2/10;DC4/11; DC5/16 | 70 | 90.74 |
| | Em_min | 480 | 664 | 7 | 13 | 3:DC2/4;DC3/24; DC8/9 | 70 | 83.76 |

**Cost and Emissions-Sharing Agreement.** Before that the suppliers accept to participate in a HC coalition, an assessment of the individual opportunities savings must be available. Several cost allocation tools were suggested in the literature. (Guajardo 2016) [27] presented a review on cost allocation tools on collaborative transportation. The Shapley value method is quantified as a possible best practice by the industrials participating in European CO3-project ([28] and [29]). As explained by [30], the Shapley value is calculated using the marginal values of the each partner in all possible sub-coalitions and then the it incites partners to be collaborative as it guaranties the stability and fairness among partners. The cost allocated to partner p can be calculated by using (Eq. 1). Given a player i, a coalition N, which consists of sub-coalitions $S \subseteq N$, that each generates a cost c(S), the Shapley value is:

$$\mathbf{C_i^{Shapley}} = \sum\nolimits_{\mathbf{S\subseteq N\backslash i}} \frac{\mathbf{|S|!(n-|S|-1)!}}{\mathbf{n!}} * \left(\mathbf{c}\left(\mathbf{S}\bigcup\mathbf{i}\right) - \mathbf{c(S)}\right) \quad (1)$$

For these reason, we opt for the Shapley value method to allocate the collaborative gains in the current case study. Figure 3 focuses in the individual gains generated after collaboration. Results illustrate the economic and ecologic positive effect of the shippers' collaboration. While the Em_min case induces an average reduction in total cost in the range [4.81%, 8.38%], these values increases to [5.25%, 22.01%], when considering C_min case. For carbon emissions, gains increase from the range [0.64%, 13.53%] in

C_min case to the range [16.97%, 28.52%] in Em_min case. This is due to the fact that minimizing costs requires opening less expensive depots which involve larger distances while minimizing emissions leads to shorter distances due to opening more expensive depots. The small supplier BB was the largest beneficiary of collaboration. This supplier obtained an economic profit of 22% in C_min case and an ecological gain of 13% in Em_min case. The big size suppliers have more customers and demand and then, more cost and emissions were allocated to these suppliers.

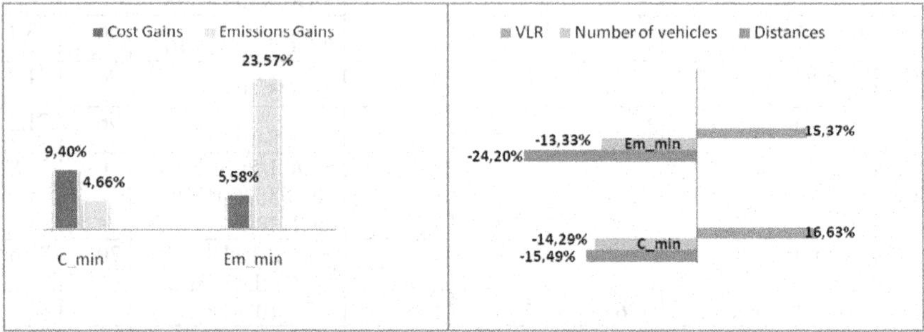


**Fig. 2.** Aggregated gains analysis after collaboration

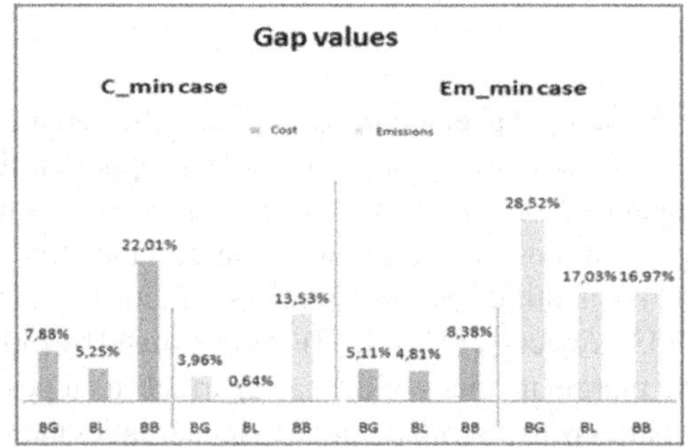


**Fig. 3.** Gains analysis using Shapley value method in the two extreme cases

### 4.3 Trade-off Analysis

The Multi-objective analysis leads to detect a good trade-off between the economic objective and the ecological one. The efficient frontier is the group of non-dominated solutions for the association of different objectives [31]. We generate a set of efficient solutions using the approach adopted by [32] as a simple and easy technique to implement. The approach is based on the weighted sum method where a value of importance ($\alpha$) is assigned to each objective, according to predefined interests of the decision [33]. As described by (Halevy et al. 2006) [32], a normalization of the objectives is required because they have different units of measurement. Normalization utilizes the results of single objective approach. The objectives are aggregated into a single objective function. The function to optimize is as follows:

$$\text{Min Z} = \alpha\left(\frac{\text{C} - \text{Cmin}}{\text{Cmax} - \text{Cmin}}\right) + (\alpha - 1)(\frac{\text{E} - \text{Emin}}{\text{Emax} - \text{Emin}}) \tag{2}$$

***C*** is the function minimizing transportation Cost and ***E*** is the function minimizing transportation Emissions. The value α of ranges between 0 and 1. Values of *Cmin* and *Emax* were obtained by minimizing transportation cost (α = 1). Minimizing transportation emissions allowed us to calculate *Cmax* and *Emin* were (α = 0). The obtained Pareto frontiers is presented in Fig. 4. Varying α 10 times leads to, only 5 different solutions. The case (α = 0,2) is the most favorable scenario for ecological impact. The slopes of Pareto frontiers clearly decrease after this point

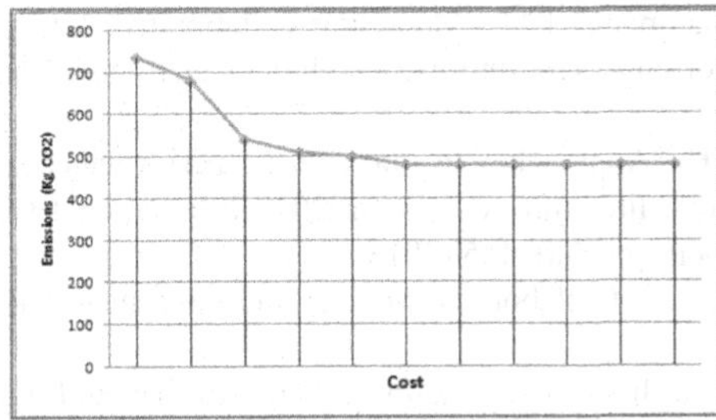


**Fig. 4.** Efficient frontier between the transportation cost and the ecological impact

## 5 Conclusion

Horizontal collaboration is one of the efficient strategies to persevere in the competitive market and to respond to the environmental concerns for wholesale supply chain. Found on multi-objective 2E-LRP, we confirmed the positive impact of horizontal collaboration on costs as well as on carbon emissions. We found that cost's optimization and emissions' optimization are two conflicting objectives. This brings to different optimal configurations of the studied network and leads to the dissimilar selection of depots and allocation of transport flows. Consequently, generated saving changed based on the selected configuration. These savings come from several factors. Collaboration contributed to the decrease of the number of open depots and travelled distances. Before any decision to integrate the coalition, each partner would like to quantify the impact of the collaboration on his own profit and loss. Therefore a fair allocation mechanism should be adopted. The allocation of cost and CO2 emissions is assured using the Shapley value method. The Multi-objective approach contributed to the detection of a good trade-off between the economic objective and the ecological one. Tests revealed that the incorporation of ecological condition into to economic objective influences the generated gains. The partners must decide on the solution based on their preferences and importance of cost and emissions gains. This research can be useful to other supply chain design problems in different areas as e-commerce, drug distribution or retail.

Important extensions to studied problem can be proposed like: The incorporation of additional objectives to optimize as individual preference. Here, each partner can precise, in priori, his preference regarding the reduction of logistical costs versus reduced CO2 emissions. To handle large-scale instances within reasonable computational times, the development of meta-heuristic approaches (such as NSGA-II) would be a meaningful direction.

## References


1. Ayala-orozco, B., et al.: Challenges and strategies in place-based multi-stakeholder collaboration for sustainability: learning from experiences in the global South. Sustainability **10**(9), 3217 (2018)
2. Cao, M., Zhang, Q.: Supply chain collaboration : Impact on collaborative advantage and firm performance. J. Oper. Manag. **29**(3), 163–180 (2011)
3. Okdinawati, L., Simatupang, T.M.: Modelling collaborative transportation management : current state and opportunities for future research. J. Oper. Supply Chain Manag. **8**(2), 96–119 (2015)
4. Taieb, N.H., Affes, H.: Approaches to improve the performance of the collaborative supply chain management: literature review. In: 2013 International Conference on Advanced Logistics and Transport, pp. 440–445 (2013)
5. Gansterer, M., Hartl, R.F.: Collaborative vehicle routing: a survey. Eur. J. Oper. Res. **268**(1), 1–12 (2018)
6. Serrano-Hernández, A., Juan, A.A., Faulin, J., Perez-Bernabeu, E.: Horizontal collaboration in freight transport: concepts, benefits, and environmental challenges. Sort **41**(2), 1–22 (2017)
7. Martin, N., Verdonck, L., Caris, A., Depaire, B.: Horizontal collaboration in logistics: decision framework and typology. Oper. Manag. Res. **11**(1–2), 32–50 (2018). https://doi.org/10.1007/s12063-018-0131-1
8. Cleophas, C., Cottrill, C., Ehmke, J.F., Tierney, K.: Collaborative urban transportation: recent advances in theory and practice. Eur. J. Oper. Res. **273**(3), 801–816 (2018)
9. Pan, S., Trentesaux, D., Ballot, E., Huang, G.Q., Trentesaux, D.: Horizontal collaborative transport : survey of solutions and practical implementation issues. Int. J. Prod. Res. **57**(15–16), 5340–5361 (2019)
10. Aloui, A., Hamani, N., Derrouiche, R., Delahoche, L.: Systematic literature review on collaborative sustainable transportation: overview, analysis and perspectives. Transp. Res. Interdiscip. Perspect. **9**, 100291 (2020)
11. Ouhader, H., El kyal, M.: Combining facility location and routing decisions in sustainable urban freight distribution under horizontal collaboration: How shippers can be benefited? Math. Probl. Eng. **2017**, 1–27 (2017)
12. Aloui, A., Hamani, N., Derrouiche, R., et al.: Assessing the benefits of horizontal collaboration using an integrated planning model for two-echelon energy efficiency-oriented logistics networks design. Int. J. Syst. Sci. Oper. Logist., February 2021
13. Prodhon, C., Prins, C.: A survey of recent research on location-routing problems. Eur. J. Oper. Res. **238**(1), 1–17 (2014)
14. Quintero-Araujo, C.L., Gruler, A., Juan, A.A., Faulin, J.: Using horizontal cooperation concepts in integrated routing and facility-location decisions. Int. Trans. Oper. Res. **26**(2), 551–576 (2017)
15. Wang, Y., et al.: Two-echelon logistics delivery and pickup network optimization based on integrated cooperation and transportation fleet sharing. Expert Syst. Appl. **113**(December), 44–65 (2018)

16. Osicka, O., Guajardo, M., van Oost, T.: Cooperative game-theoretic features of cost sharing in location-routing. Norwegian school of economics (2018)
17. Nataraj, S., Ferone, D., Quintero-araujo, C., Juan, A.A., Festa, P.: Consolidation centers in city logistics: a cooperative approach based on the location routing problem. Int. J. Ind. Eng. Comput. **10**(3), 393–404 (2019)
18. Soysal, M., Bloemhof-, J.M., Haijema, R., Van Der Vorst, J.G.A.J.: Modeling a green inventory routing problem for perishable products with horizontal collaboration. Comput. Oper. Res. **89**, 168–182 (2018)
19. Stellingwerf, H.M., Laporte, G., Cruijssen, F.C.A.M.: Quantifying the environmental and economic benefits of cooperation: a case study in temperature-controlled food logistics. Transp. Res. Part D **65**, 178–193 (2018)
20. Hacardiaux, T., Tancrez, J.-S.: Assessing the environmental benefits of horizontal cooperation using a location-inventory model. CEJOR **28**(4), 1363–1387 (2019). https://doi.org/10.1007/s10100-018-0599-7
21. Wang, Y., Zhang, J., Assogba, K., Liua, Y., Xua, M., Wangd, Y.: Collaboration and transportation resource sharing in multiple centers vehicle routing optimization with delivery and pickup. Knowl.-Based Syst. **160**, 296–310 (2018)
22. Mrabti, N., Hamani, N., Delahoche, L.: The pooling of sustainable freight transport. J. Oper. Res. Soc., 1–16 (2020)
23. Ouhader, H., El kyal, M.: Assessing the economic and environmental benefits of horizontal cooperation in delivery: performance and scenario analysis. Uncertain Supply Chain Manag. **8**, 303–320 (2020)
24. Moutaoukil, A., Derrouich, R.E., Neubert, G., Fayol, I., Fauriel, C.: Modélisation d'une stratégie de mutualisation logistique en intégrant les objectifs de Développement Durable pour des PME agroalimentaires. 13e Congrés Int. G´énie Ind. (CIGI'13), Jun 2013, LA ROCHELLE, Fr. (2013)
25. Pan, S., Ballot, E., Fontane, F.: The reduction of greenhouse gas emissions from freight transport by pooling supply chains. Int. J. Prod. Econ. **143**(1), 86–94 (2013)
26. Moutaoukil, A., Neubert, G., Derrouiche, R., Evs, I.F.-U.M.R.: Urban freight distribution: the impact of delivery time on sustainability. IFAC-PapersOnLine **48**(3), 2455–2460 (2015)
27. Guajardo, M.: A review on cost allocation methods in collaborative transportation. Int. Trans. Oper. Res. **23**, 371–392 (2016)
28. Defryn, C., Sörensen, K., Cornelissens, T.: The selective vehicle routing problem in a collaborative environment. Eur. J. Oper. Res. **250**(2), 400–411 (2016)
29. Cruijssen, F., BV, A.: $CO^3$ position paper: framework for collaboration, CO3 Project (2012)
30. Vanovermeire, C., Sörensen, K., Van Breedam, A., Vannieuwenhuyse, B., Verstrepen, S.: Horizontal logistics collaboration: decreasing costs through flexibility and an adequate cost allocation strategy. Int. J. Logist. Res. Appl. **17**(4), 339–355 (2014)
31. Muñoz-villamizar, A., Quintero-araújo, C.L., Montoya-torres, J.R., Faulin, J.: Short- and mid-term evaluation of the use of electric vehicles in urban freight transport collaborative networks: a case study, vol. 5567 (2018)
32. Halevy, I., Kava, Z., Seeman, T.: Normalization and Other Topics in Multi Objective Optimization, vol. 2, pp. 89–101 (2006)
33. Maghsoudlou, H., Kahag, M.R., Taghi, S., Niaki, A., Pourvaziri, H.: Bi-objective optimization of a three-echelon multi-server supply-chain problem in congested systems: modeling and solution. Comput. Ind. Eng. **99**, 41–62 (2016)

# Extending Value in Legacy Production Systems: Insights from the Liquid Food Processing

Brendan P. Sullivan[1(✉)], Monica Rossi[1(✉)], David Ward[2(✉)], and Carlo Leardi[3(✉)]

[1] Department of Management and Industrial Engineering, Politecnico Di Milano, via Lambruschini 4/B, 20156 Milan, Italy
{brendan.sullivan,monica.rossi}@polimi.it
[2] TMC Italy, Viale dell'Innovazione, 3, 20126 Milan, Italy
david.ward@tmceurope.com
[3] Tetra Pak Packaging Solutions Spa, D&E, Via delfini, 1, 41123 Modena, Italy
Carlo.leardi@tetrapak.com

**Abstract.** Shifts in needs coupled with dynamic markets and technological evolution, requires that products and production infrastructures be capable providing extended value for stakeholders throughout the comprehensive systems life cycle. Product change not only reflects shifts in externalities but also on the legacy manufacturing system that produce it. In such situations where product and production change occur it is critical to actively plan and integrate unique system characteristics that can leverage different change types. This requires consideration of not only the changes needed for the product, but also the relational changes of the manufacturing infrastructure. This research provides a basis to support extended value delivery for legacy systems through a conceptual framework based on literature and a use case that evaluates the types and intensity of specific change states according to existing product and production system specifications. The findings from the food processing industry case suggest that knowledge, enabled via smart collaborative networks, and change histories can be effectively used to increase and extend the value of both products and production systems when subject to dynamic changes.

**Keywords:** Changeability · Ilities · Extended value · Life cycle · Production systems · Systems engineering · Food production · Industrial case · Conceptual framework

## 1 Introduction

New and novel systems continue to be requested including those in manufacturing. However, similar to software development where systems are updated or re-developed through the use of existing system, manufacturing systems are frequently built out of an existing architecture that has in some form been previously deployed [1]. The leveraging of systems to meet new stakeholder needs arises from system complexity and the high development costs associated with creating a completely new solution [1]. By leveraging


Published by Springer Nature Switzerland AG 2021
L. M. Camarinha-Matos et al. (Eds.): PRO-VE 2021, IFIP AICT 629, pp. 778–788, 2021.
https://doi.org/10.1007/978-3-030-85969-5_74

knowledge derived from legacy systems it is possible to evaluate functionalities, reducing costs of change, production down-time, maintenance costs, re-training of employees, un-needed capabilities and undesirable perpetrations [2, 3].

Changeability as a high-level system-ility (flexibility, agility, adaptability, robustness, reconfigurability) is one of the possible solutions that can be applied to extend the value of systems, reducing the time and cost for making changes and improving how system functions are delivered [4–6]. The ability to leverage change for extended value enables legacy systems to be more efficient at adapting to changes that emerge from a variety of sources (shifts in requirements, stakeholder needs, and system functions). To accommodate this, an active and coordinated strategy is required, and while it is not possible to generalize the level of changeability for every system, it is possible to analyze the number of changes the system can easily make (cost vs. time) and the value implications of the suitable changes [7, 8].

The objective of this paper is to provide a literature-based framework, to support the extended value for legacy systems. The paper proposes an approach to support the extension of legacy system value as well as discusses how different types of change can affect the production systems based on an applied use case. The article is structured as follows: Sect. 2 discusses the elements of changeability and implications for legacy production systems. Then, Sect. 3 presents an approach for extending the value of legacy systems in the liquid food processing sector that is implemented through a case study, which is described in Sect. 4. Section 5 concludes the article.

## 2 Changeability and Legacy Production Systems

Changeability represents the modification of systems in anticipation of, or in response to, changes in exogenous variables [9]. In respect to legacy systems this includes extending value throughout a systems life cycle, where the incurrence of change should extend the value of the system in an active manner. This requires distinct contextual and operational knowledge, increasing the complexity of the decision process by requiring an agent to initiate changes that allow for the system to maintain a value throughout its life [10]. In analyzing such systems, it is possible to evaluate change options that reflect on the total number of potential changes the system can make (top-down), or the magnitude of a specific change according to its utility value.

### 2.1 Ilities and Changeability Elements

"Ilities" are grounded in strategic thinking and decision theory and refers to the theoretical and applied notion of change within systems [11]. Changeability represents a high-level system ility that is characterized by the ability of a system to change form, function, or operation, through lower level ilities such as flexibility, agility, adaptability, evolvability, reconfigurability, versatility, and robustness. A change can be understood as any transition of the system from one state to another [12]. Changeability determines what changes, but also how the change occurs and the effect the change has on the system throughout its life cycle [4, 5, 7, 13–17].

Engineering "change" accounts for some of the largest resource intensive processes in engineering design [18] and through the utilization of "ilities" within systems this can be reduced. Regardless of the change, intentional/unintentional stakeholders desire for systems to effectively perform and deliver value (Mekdeci et al., 2012).

While changeability is traditionally viewed as a design decision to enable the change of a system, when applied to the evaluation of legacy systems the real options for modification become the focal point. This transitional view of the concept derives from the fact that even the most experienced engineer/team cannot predict all foreseeable changes. Within production processes where system of systems (SoS) are prevalent this means that even if a system was designed for change there will be elements of the SoS that affect how the change occurs, the agent responsible, and the change effect [19].

## 2.2 Legacy Production Systems

It can be necessary for legacy systems to change according to a variety of affects including changes in product specifications, volumes, materials and stakeholder needs. Such systems previously developed through past efforts, represent deployed and designed systems that operate as/within a SoS architecture requiring consideration of what's being produced, resource availability, stakeholder expectations, utility value and functionality. Systems that were initially developed to provide some form of value to a stakeholder are through dynamic pressures being required to change. Determining how changes can extend value requires consideration of how they fit into the SoS and the long-term change value according to feasible tradeoffs as illustrated in Table 1.

**Table 1.** Techniques to understand and analyze legacy systems.

| Technique | Tools | Legacy type |
|---|---|---|
| Reverse Engineering | CAM software, NC programs, Solid-modeling software, Parametric Diagram | Deployed |
| Change History | Design Structure Matrix, Change Prediction Method, Domain Mapping Matrices | Design, Deployed |
| Documentation | Functional Block Diagram, Use Case Diagrams | Design, Deployed |
| Technical Manual | Requirement Diagram, Functional Block Diagram, Use Case Diagrams | Design, Deployed |
| Generalization | Functional Block Diagram, Internal Block Diagram, Use Case Diagrams | Design, Deployed |
| Interviewing | Sequence Diagram, Use Case Diagrams | Design, Deployed |
| Process Modelling | State Machine diagram, Internal Block Diagram, Analysis Model | Design, Deployed |

## 3 Framework for Extending Legacy System Value

Manufacturing industries, system products and customer services provide value through their ability to fulfil stakeholders' needs and wants. These needs evolve over time and may diverge from an original system's capabilities. Thus, a system's value to its stakeholders diminishes over time. Some reasons for this decrease include growth in stakeholder wants and technological opportunities, which make an existing system seem inadequate. Other reasons are growth in a system's maintenance costs, due to effects such as depreciation and component obsolescence. Still other reasons are changes in the environment, for example new rules and regulations and so forth. As a result, systems have to be periodically upgraded at substantial cost and disruption. Since complete replacement costs are often prohibitive, system adaptability is a valuable characteristic. Current concepts, methods and tools for architecting engineered systems (emanating from engineering disciplines) lack vital business and economic considerations. As a result, most architectures are not easily adaptable to evolving manufacturing needs and product variants [20]. This gap hinders the European industry from delivering updated products/services quickly and cost-effectively, prevents optimal manufacturing performance, and threatens Europe's leading world position. In summary, increasing a system's lifetime value requires improved methods of architecting it.

This framework suggested in this section was developed by leveraging literature and a series of interviews from production and system engineers in the food processing industry to support the management of legacy systems by evaluating the types and intensity of specific change states according to existing product and production system specifications. As illustrated below (Fig. 1) this framework represents a basis to advance and support the evaluation of legacy system changeability for the purpose of extended life cycle value, in response to stakeholder needs and dynamic pressures.

The framework is a question-based framework built around 8 dimensions that characterize changeability in legacy systems, detailed in the following.

1. **System State**: In cases where the system being analyzed has been deployed and are highly embedded into daily routines it is difficult to modify and replace the singular sub-systems or components when new technology or other needs must be brought forth. Additionally, refactoring or modernizing any deployed legacy system requires careful analysis of the extent that any change or failure to that system will have. Similarly legacy systems which were previously designed that have not been deployed require these same incidents to be overcome. While modularity and other lower-level ilities have successfully been used, this requires either a complete analysis of how the system can change, or redesign of the entire system. The redesign of the system design may have the greatest long-term value for the manufacturer of the equipment however can be slow and expensive.
2. **Change Affect**: The inclusion of socio variables has been a regular practice in systems engineering since the 1970's and have been found to be the most critical areas giving rise to system change [17, 21].

   a. Regulatory based externalities refer to norms set by the standardizing organization, governments, governing bodies, and the organization itself. The laws

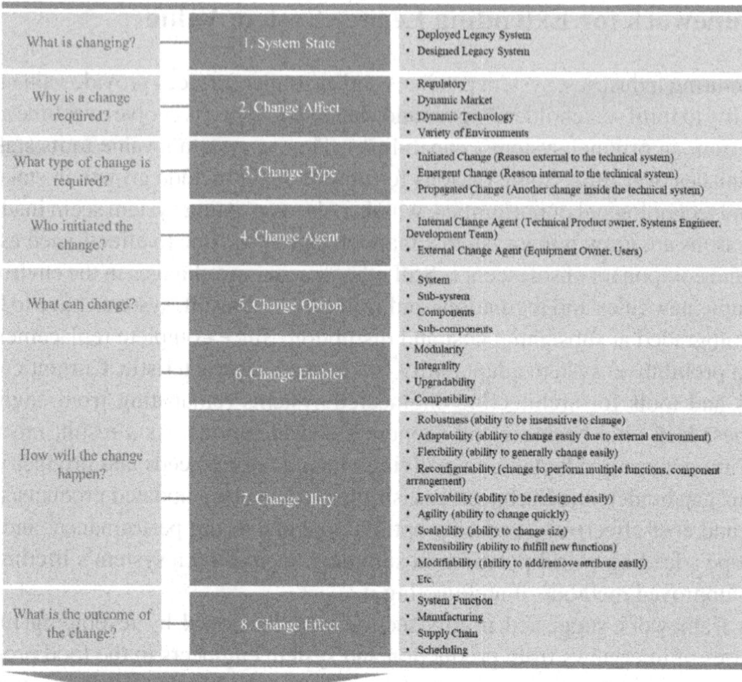


**Fig. 1.** Conceptual framework for the analysis of changeability within legacy systems.

and regulations are models that require companies to analyze the potential impacts of the system (health, safety, compliance). Regulations can include the Stakeholder security interests like Intellectual Property Rights, Information Assurance, Security Laws, Supply Chain Compliance, and Security Standards.

b. Dynamic Market based externalities are an effect of the new markets are emerging rapidly, while existing markets are changing. Staying ahead of competition requires highly responsive abilities that allow for changes to the system throughout the life cycle of the legacy system.
c. Dynamic Technology based externalities are a response to the development of new technologies that are required to produce the specific product, or at behest of the change agent. Technology changes are necessary to keep a system competitive, meet changing market demands, or requirements for customization, what is partially addressed in Schulz [22].
d. Environment based externalities reflect the level of integration, number of subsystems and how they are embedded.

3. **Change Type**: All changes can be seen as both threats and opportunities. On one hand, changes enacted by the agent can increase the amount of rework and can lead to additional changes, thus increasing costs and effort; on the other, they offer the chance to improve the system, increasing the performance, providing useful

functionalities or reducing undesired features [23]. The forces representing what the system must respond is categorized on how each change emerges depending on the agent and the decision taken (impact, observation, decision-making).

a. Initiated Change: Can be planned and unplanned changes that are generated by an outside source and are frequently attributed to a change in requirements.
b. Emergent Change: Are "caused by the state of the design, where problems occurring across the whole design and throughout the product life cycle can lead to changes" [24].
c. Propagated Change: Undesired changes that come due to other changes having been made to the system.

4. **Change Agent**: The forces representing what the system must respond to (change for) are presented and acted upon through a distinct agent. The respective change can be either intentional or implied, but always requires the ability to set the necessary change in motion. As shown in [12] the initiator can either be in or out of the technical system. When classifying the respective change agent it is important to consider what is necessary for the decision maker to initiate this change according to the impact, observation and decision-making [12].
5. **Change Option**: The modelling of features and functions allows for change options to be identified according to the number and magnitude of the changes the system can perform to support value generation. This parameter describes the feasibility of the change, the suitability in respect to value extension and how the change can be facilitated through the subsequent change. The number of potential viable changes the system can afford, magnitude perspective of the change (can be a matrix). Reflecting the most critical changes, and pathway that the system can follow to extend the value of the system.
6. **Change Enabler**: As a system architecture-type ility, enablers allow for a system to change and are related to the change-type ilities [25]. Affecting the inherent complexity of the system, enablers determine the effectiveness of the change.
7. **Change Ility**: The ilities for implementing or enacting the change must be compatible with the functions of the system and needs of the stakeholder. Through the evaluation of suitable changes the architecture of the system can go beyond functionalities (reliability, maintainability, etc.), to include life cycle implications. The application here of lower-level ilities as means for change allow the balancing for the number of changes (volume) and value generation.
8. **Change Effect**: Based on the selected ility the value and utility of the change can be analyzed for the change, the system and the SoS. This can be accomplished through different degrees of abstraction including an impact analysis (new vs old), compliance and regulatory conformance review (when in non-compliance the change is reviewed), and risk analysis (safety, export control).

## 4 Industrial Use Case

Liquid food packaging product lines constitute the assets of a wider eco-system including skill, stakeholders, customers, consumers awareness trends, market needs [26, 27]. The proposed case regards the cap application, one of the relevant sub-systems in a liquid food packaging line and leverages the framework to evaluate and support successful system changeability. Through this, the function of the sub-system (to apply pre-manufactured caps on packages) will be changed to allow for the opening and reclosing function. According to the recent Single-Use Plastics (SUP) EU directive, the caps are expected not to be detached from the package due to growing environmental safe-guard expectations. The architectural and functional impact on the installed packaging lines, alias the legacy systems, is relevant and classified according to the framework (Sect. 3) in Table 2 below.

**Table 2.** Analysis of changeability within industrial use case legacy system.

| Changeability criteria | Legacy system state |
|---|---|
| System State | Designed |
| Change Affect | Regulatory, Dynamic Market |
| Change Type | Initiated Change |
| Change Agent | Internal Change Agent |
| Change Option | Sub-system |
| Change Enabler | Modularity |
| Change Ility | Flexibility and Robustness |
| Change Effect | System Function |

The change enabler, modularity was implemented due to afforded autonomy and ability for non-hierarchical integration [28]. As commonly utilized it satisfies the needs of the change-ilities (flexibility and robustness) allowing for distinct system elements to be developed/changed and supporting the management of the increased technological complexity and interface requirements.

The first implementations relate about legacy systems where the independence assumption was only partly satisfied. The major negative effect was setting-up the interface requirements as a no-one land for fights among conflictual engineering silos. In the case, although limited, the results are being evaluated to determine the utility for each respective change. The time for change implementation was sensibly reduced but the production system life cycle was not guaranteed in long terms due dynamic change affects. This approach identifies and limits the cooperation to the module suppliers, developer and integrator and operational environment. Smart and cooperative networks were not explicitly needed or addressing significant value increase.

Through the consideration of robustness and flexibility it is possible to set higher quality standards, noise-insensitive, growing capacities able to be updated without impacting the overall asset and operational costs. The solutions developed under these concepts are still effectively operating in the market. The efficiency though is limited to the original requirements of the system and are difficult to overcome without incorporating additional change enablers that will further reduce development cost and extend the potential of the respective change options being implemented.

The main misconception of the case related to the limited number of available changes, and the direct level of application. Robustness at the component or sub-system level was often confused with robustness verification at system level with limited opportunities to really implement insensitiveness to noises. Flexibility was partially accomplished, however due to the lack of a consistent architecture and functional description real change options and the subsequent change effects were minimized. Fundamentally a rigorous and wise application of changeability and systems engineering principles is still missing in the liquid food packaging industry and will require the development of additional tools to improve the analysis. However, great benefits came from its introduction. Once again, despite an enlarged stakeholder chain, the collaborative aspect was still reduced and the mutual learning deriving from smart, culturally nonhomogeneous, partnerships improved.

## 4.1 Evolution

The aim was to pass from specific to general changeability through two change-ilities. As discussed throughout this paper, this means that the system is developed to comply with expected future needs. Unlike the conventional design process in which a system is designed for a nominal set of requirements, it is developed to be adapted to different or additional functions beyond their normal operational mode based on forecast information. In the pilot case quantitative estimations were calculated through Monte Carlo applications within the architectural framework through a series of Design Structure Matrices. To quantify the monetary benefit and Expected Net Present Value (ENPV) calculation under uncertainty. The project targets were driven to the following measures Number of Closure Types, Number of Package Types, Damage rate and Noise level as shown in Fig. 2.

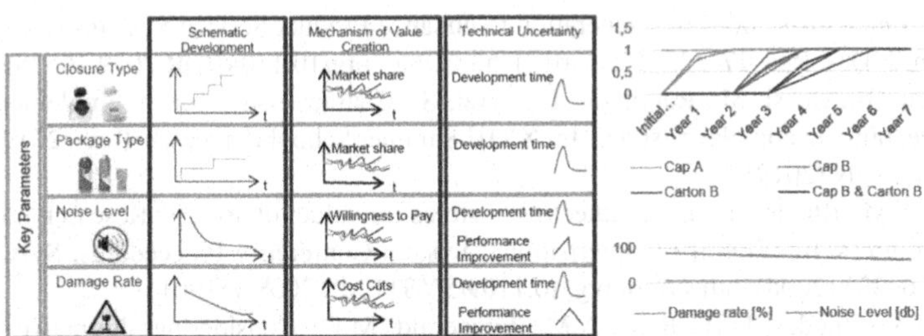


**Fig. 2.** Overview technology forecasting under uncertainty.

The implementation of the framework has the potential to better integrate into the mindset of engineers and increasingly complete systems engineering set of systems engineering methodologies and tools. A wider attention is emerging to the socio-human themes likes as consumers acceptance of environmentally sustainable products that unavoidable shall be different from the ones we are used to. The full changeability concept has so to be acquired and its benefits delivered to the overall chain of stakeholders, starting from us, as consumers, and the finite world we are living. Equally new collaborations, heterogeneous environments, contribute to increase the confidence robustness of the system.

## 5 Concluding Remarks

This research provided evidence that value extension of legacy systems, as shown in the industrial case of liquid food packaging, is challenged by the increasing dynamic markets, technological advancements and regulatory acts. A systemic life-cycle thinking is required. The cooperation of several partners: academic, industrial, SW&HW partners into a smart network is the pre-requisite to framework all the knowledge, empirical, enabling applied methodologies and soft socio-human drivers necessary to understand and successfully drive changeability.

The article is intended as one first step to promote the creation and the characterization of such type of smart and sustainable collaborative networks and will be expanded to a more complex system, to provide more substantive results and better evaluation of the change effect cost and value implications.

## References

1. Ross, A.M., Rhodes, D.H.: The system shell as a construct for mitigating the impact of changing contexts by creating opportunities for value robustness. In: Proceedings of the 1st Annual 2007 IEEE System Conference, pp. 226–232 (2007). https://doi.org/10.1109/SYSTEMS.2007.374677.
2. Sassanelli, C., Rossi, M., Pezzotta, G., Pacheco, DA de J., Terzi, S.: Defining Lean Product Service Systems (PSS) features and research trends through a systematic literature review. Int. J. Prod. Lifecycle Manag. **12**, 37–61 (2019). https://doi.org/10.1504/IJPLM.2019.104371
3. Sassanelli, C., Pezzotta, G., Pirola, F., Rossi, M., Terzi, S.: The PSS Design GuRu Methodology: Guidelines and Rules generation to enhance Product Service Systems (PSS) detailed design. J. Des. Res. **17**, 125–162 (2019). https://doi.org/10.1504/JDR.2019.105756
4. Sullivan, B., Rossi, M., Ramundo, L., Terzi, S.: Characteristics for the implementation of changeability in complex systems. In: XXIII Summer School Francesco Turco 2019, pp. 1–7, Brescia, Italy (2019)
5. Ross, A.M., Rhodes, D.H.: Architecting systems for value robustness: Research motivations and progress. In: 2008 IEEE International System Conference Proceedings, SysCon 2008, pp. 216–223 (2008). https://doi.org/10.1109/SYSTEMS.2008.4519011
6. Ricci, N., Rhodes, D.H., Ross, A.M., Fitzgerald, M.E.: Considering alternative strategies for value sustainment in systems-of-systems. In: SysCon 2013 - 7th Annual IEEE International System Conference Proc., pp. 725–730 (2013). https://doi.org/10.1109/SysCon.2013.6549963
7. Sullivan, B.P., Rossi, M., Terzi, S.: a review of changeability in complex engineering systems. In: IFAC-PapersOnLine, pp. 1567–1572 (2018). https://doi.org/10.1016/j.ifacol.2018.08.273.
8. Rehn, C.F., et al.: Quantification of changeability level for engineering systems. Syst. Eng. **22**, 80–94 (2019). https://doi.org/10.1002/sys.21472
9. Fitzgerald, M.E., Ross, A.M.: Sustaining lifecycle value: Valuable changeability analysis with era simulation. In: SysCon 2012 - 2012 IEEE International System Conference Proceedings, pp. 202–208 (2012). https://doi.org/10.1109/SysCon.2012.6189465

10. Ross, A.M., Rhodes, D.H.: Using natural value-centric time scales for conceptualizing system timelines through epoch-era analysis. In: Incose. 15 (2008). https://doi.org/10.1002/j.2334-5837.2008.tb00871.x
11. Colombo, E.F., Cascini, G., de Weck, O.L.: Classification of change-related ilities based on a literature review of engineering changes. J. Integr. Des. Process Sci. **20**, 1–21 (2016). https://doi.org/10.3233/jid-2016-0019
12. Ross, A.M., Rhodes, D.H., Hastings, D.E.: Defining changeability: reconciling flexibility, adaptability, scalability, modifiability, and robustness for maintaining system lifecycle value. Syst. Eng. **11**, 246–262 (2008). https://doi.org/10.1002/sys
13. McManus, H., Richards, M.G., Ross, A.M., Hastings, D.E.: A framework for incorporating "ilities" in tradespace studies. Am. Inst. Aeronaut. Astronaut. 1–14 (2007). https://doi.org/10.2514/6.2007-6100
14. Altenhofen, J.A., Oyama, K.F., Jacques, D.R.: A methodology to determine the influence of requirements change to support system design. IIE Annu. Conf. Expo **2015**, 2181–2190 (2015)
15. Beesemyer, J.C., Ross, A.M., Rhodes, D.H.: An empirical investigation of system changes to frame links between design decisions and ilities. Procedia Comput. Sci. **8**, 31–38 (2012). https://doi.org/10.1016/j.procs.2012.01.010
16. Colombo, E.F., Cascini, G., De Weck, O.L.: Classification of change-related ilities based on a literature review of engineering changes. J. Integr. Des. Process Sci. **20**, 3–23 (2016). https://doi.org/10.3233/jid-2016-0019
17. Fricke, E., Schulz, A.P.: Design for changeability (DfC): principles to enable changes in systems throughout their entire lifecycle. Syst. Eng. **8**, 342–359 (2005). https://doi.org/10.1002/sys.20039
18. Eckert, C.M., Clarkson, P.J., Zanker, W.: Change and customisation in complex engineering domains. Res. Eng. Des. **15**, 1–21 (2004). https://doi.org/10.1007/s00163-003-0031-7
19. Rhodes, D.H., Ross, A.M.: Five aspects of engineering complex systems: Emerging constructs and methods. In: 2010 IEEE International Systems Conference Proceedings, SysCon 2010, pp. 190–195 (2010). https://doi.org/10.1109/SYSTEMS.2010.5482431
20. Elmaraghy, H.A.: Changing and evolving products and systems – models and enablers. In: Changeable and Reconfigurable Manufacturing Systems, pp. 25–45 (2009)
21. Mehrabi, M.G., Ulsoy, A.G., Koren, Y.: Reconfigurable manufacturing systems: key to future manufacturing. J. Intell. Manuf. **11**, 403–419 (2000). https://doi.org/10.1023/A:1008930403506
22. Schulz, A.P., Fricke, E.: Incorporating flexibility, agility, robustness, and adaptability within the design of integrated systems - key to success? Gatew. to New Millenn. In: 18th Digit. Avion. Syst. Conf. Proc. (Cat. No.99CH37033). 1/17, pp. v, 1–8 (1999). https://doi.org/10.1109/DASC.1999.863677
23. Jarratt, T.A.W., Eckert, C.M., Caldwell, N.H.M., Clarkson, P.J.: Engineering change: an overview and perspective on the literature. Res. Eng. Des. **22**, 103–124 (2011). https://doi.org/10.1007/s00163-010-0097-y
24. Ross, A.M., Rhodes, D.H.: Using attribute classes to uncover latent value during conceptual systems design. In: 2008 IEEE International System Conference Proceedings, SysCon 2008, pp. 7–14 (2008). https://doi.org/10.1109/SYSTEMS.2008.4518981
25. Ross, A.M., Rhodes, D.H.: Towards a prescriptive semantic basis for change-type ilities. Procedia Comput. Sci. **44**, 443–453 (2015). https://doi.org/10.1016/j.procs.2015.03.040
26. Sassanelli, C., Da Costa Fernandes, S., Rozenfeld, H., Mascarenhas, J., Terzi, S.: Enhancing knowledge management in the PSS detailed design: a case study in a food and bakery machinery company. Concurr. Eng. Res. Appl. (2021). https://doi.org/10.1177/1063293X21991806

27. Pinna, C., Galati, F., Rossi, M., Saidy, C., Harik, R., Terzi, S.: Effect of product lifecycle management on new product development performances: evidence from the food industry. Comput. Ind. **100**, 184–195 (2018). https://doi.org/10.1016/j.compind.2018.03.036
28. Boucher, X., et al.: Towards reconfigurable digitalized and servitized manufacturing systems: conceptual framework. In: Ameri, F., Stecke, K.E., von Cieminski, G., Kiritsis, D. (eds.) APMS 2019. IAICT, vol. 566, pp. 214–222. Springer, Cham (2019). https://doi.org/10.1007/978-3-030-30000-5_28

# Advancing Circular Economy: Research Roadmap for Circular Integrated Production Systems

Magdalena Paul[1], Simon Thevenin[2], Julia Schulz[1], Nadjib Brahimi[2,3], Hichem Haddou Benderbal[2](✉), and Alexandre Dolgui[2]

[1] Institute for Machine Tools and Industrial Management, Technical University of Munich, 85748 Garching, Germany
{magdalena.paul,juliaschulz}@iwb.tum.de
[2] IMT Atlantique, LS2N-CNRS Nantes, France
{simon.thevenin,hichem.haddou-ben-derbal, alexandre.dolgui}@imt-atlantique.fr
[3] Rennes School of Business, Rennes, France
nadjib.brahimi@rennes-sb.com

**Abstract.** The coronavirus crisis had a critical impact on supply chains and production worldwide. In particular, closed borders often prevented companies from obtaining the components required for their production. Such disruptions are the results of globalization, with suppliers spreading all over the world. The circular economy is an opportunity to overcome this challenge since components from end-of-life items may substitute supplies from afar. However, many barriers exist in the implementation of circular processes, as manufacturers perceive it as a radical change to their procedures. Therefore, we propose not to use completely new lines for the circular economy, but to use already existing systems. This paper presents the definition of circular integrated production systems (CIPS) and suggests a research roadmap for such to investigate what challenges and potentials arise, and what future research will be needed.

**Keywords:** Disassembly · Remanufacturing · Sustainable production · Integrated production lines · Circular economy

## 1 Introduction

When parts are not available, production is interrupted: the recent coronavirus crisis demonstrates the critical impact of supply chain disruptions, as many companies are unable to source the components required for their productions, often due to closed borders [1, 2]. The circular economy can make a major contribution to address this challenge: Products return to factories at the end of their life cycle instead of ending up in a landfill. In this way, locally available resources are used and companies are less dependent on distant suppliers. In addition, increasing environmental awareness and scarcity of


Published by Springer Nature Switzerland AG 2021
L. M. Camarinha-Matos et al. (Eds.): PRO-VE 2021, IFIP AICT 629, pp. 789–796, 2021.
https://doi.org/10.1007/978-3-030-85969-5_75

available resources are putting pressure on companies to manage available resources in the domestic market. A circular approach can change the company's perspective: Instead of seeing used products as a liability, they can now be a source of parts or materials.

The purpose of this paper is to give a research roadmap for a new production paradigm. So-called circular integrated production systems (CIPS) should help to enable circular economy for more companies. Therefore, this paper compiles the current and previous research results to derive existing research gaps on circular production systems with integrated lines. In addition, specific action areas are defined to describe a roadmap for further research on the outlined topic. After describing the path from conventional production systems to circular integrated production systems (Sect. 2), the manuscript includes a section that divides the aforementioned research roadmap into the design (Sect. 3.1) and operation (Sect. 3.2) of CIPS, leading to a summary overview (Sect. 3.3). Section 4 discusses the results and draws a conclusion.

## 2 The Way from Conventional Production Systems to Circular Integrated Production Systems (CIPS)

The conventional production triangle, which describes the conflict between time, cost, and quality, is gradually being superseded by the holistic approach of sustainable production. Sustainable production combines economic, ecological and social aspects of value-adding activities. Due to regulation and green consumerism, most manufacturing companies are now willing to adopt more sustainable practices such as circular economy. This trend will likely increase in the coming years, since laws and regulations will become stricter pushing the manufacturing industry even more into a sustainable direction. For instance, the European Commission recently adopted the "Right to Repair", obliging the manufacturing industry to provide long-lasting machines and spare parts and to repair electronic equipment. Nevertheless, only a few companies are remanufacturing end-of-life items. Despite the willingness of the industry, several barriers prevent the adoption of circular economy. The barriers can be economical (high costs to build the reverse system, costs to manage the reverse inventory, not realizing the value, etc.), operational (lack of know-how, lack of guideline, coordination issues, etc.), environmental (lack of laws and regulations regarding end-of-life items, lack of government policy to support a return flow, etc.), socio-cultural (acceptance of remanufactured parts from customers, etc.), technological (current information systems mostly do not support circularity, etc.) or strategic (lack of management commitment, lack of performance indicators, etc.) [3].

To mitigate these barriers, the authors suggest a new approach of integrating circular economy into conventional production systems:

> Circular integrated production systems (CIPS) are defined as production systems that can perform both conventional linear processes and circular activities on the same systems.

Disassembly or remanufacturing are examples for circular activities in manufacturing companies. Within CIPS, existing elements, such as assembly lines, transport network, planning and scheduling software, and operation management, of factories mostly remain as they are designed for linear production, and are only adapted to comply with circular flows while minimizing costs of reconfiguration and the environmental impact. CIPS will not only reduce waste and enhance ecological sustainability but will also be a profitable form of processing of used products into existing lines. Returning products e.g. through recycling or remanufacturing can satisfy the rising customer demand for sustainable products. The creation of CIPS opens up local sources of supply for components and can therefore mitigate the risks of production stoppages during global supply chain disruptions.

## 3 Research Roadmap for CIPS

Before CIPS can be implemented in companies, there are still questions to be answered and challenges to be overcome. On the one hand, qualitative research is required to analyze and describe the type of industry that can use the system and methodology to operate the resulting integrated lines. The conditions under which a company can benefit from an integrated circular production system with identical elements being used for linear and circular activities need to be analyzed. This analysis includes the characteristics of the products and those of the factory, along with the internal and external environment. On the other hand, quantitative research must be performed to provide methodologies and software solutions to help manufacturers design a production system integrating an end-of-life item recovery process into an existing production process. More precisely, manufacturers must possess tools for (1) process planning and (2) operating a factory with integrated lines. The integration of circular processes creates challenges for capacity planning since it uses the same resources as the initial production and for requirement planning; for example recovered parts can be used for the initial production. Furthermore, a major challenge in the operation management is to deal with the arising uncertainty regarding the amount, the quality and the condition of revised products or parts.

### 3.1 Designing a Circular Integrated Production System

**Definition of the System Boundaries and External Influences.** Research on sustainability in production systems and supply chain management has been subject of a lot of interest during the last two decades. This research has taken several forms including work related to green logistics [4], design of processes for the treatment of returns through remanufacturing and refurbishing [5] and energy and resource usage along the supply chain [6]. Moreover, recycling and reuse are fundamental processing steps for products and their components, which are incorporated in disassembly. Disassembly is considered an important aspect of end-of-life product treatment [7]. In this context, researchers have either considered that returns are processed in a dedicated plant or within the same assembly plants of new products. The latter are called hybrid systems and have been studied from various perspectives. A classification of these studies can be found in [8]. One of the views considers two completely separate lines, where the disassembly line provides the assembly line with remanufactured parts that can be considered to be as good as new [9].

Further research is required to identify the prerequisites, barriers and enablers for the integration and introduction of circular activities in linear production companies. Such work must systematize the initial situation, analyze the internal and external requirements for implementing CIPS, and define the scope and boundaries. Qualitative research must include the following aspects:

- Analysis of aspects related to industrial circular economy to derive industry sectors that are suitable for integrated production systems
- Analysis of aspects related to in-house logistics, depth of in-house manufacturing as well as the analysis of regulations and legal conditions to identify common areas, as well as advantages and disadvantages of the different systems regarding the industrial circular economy
- Analysis of aspects related to the impact of product design for circular economy to derive suitable product groups
- Analysis of applied loop strategies to identify the nature of the relationship between product, corporate strategy and loop strategy

**System Structure.** To close the cycle successfully, companies must be able to disassemble used parts effectively and efficiently. The costs for disassembly should be lower than the costs for purchasing a new part. Investment of companies in new lines must be kept as low as possible. Therefore, researchers must investigate whether the use of already existing assembly lines is suitable for disassembly. This way, idle times can be exploited and expensive downtimes can be avoided. In addition, the reuse of parts for remanufacturing can help to save energy and thus $CO_2$-emissions by omitting energy-intensive material extraction and manufacturing processes. Moreover, a cheap and readily available solution for disassembly would likely increase the use of remanufacturing, thus reducing the need to produce new products.

Very few studies on the design of disassembly lines from existing assembly lines have been conducted so far. Tiwari et al. [10] argued that disassembly plays an important role in restoring and reusing the parts and components of a product as much as possible. Boothroyd et al. [11] propose a widely used approach to the design of assembly as well as disassembly lines. The objective is to reduce assembly costs and set up principles to improve product sustainability through disassembly. In the same context, Mesa et al. [12] studied open architecture products and presented metrics to assess the complexity of the various modules for assembly and disassembly. Furthermore, a lot of research focuses on disassembly, in which both deterministic and stochastic problems for complete disassembly without any target component are considered [13]. Nevertheless, there is a dearth of research when it comes to CIPSs. Compared to the assembly process, operational and physical properties are more complex in disassembly processes [14]. The most important difference is the production structure. In an assembly system, the parts converge to a single final product, whereas in a disassembly system, the parts diverge to multiple components. The first difference between assembly and disassembly line balancing is the use of various precedence graphs. Disassembly precedence constraints are often modeled using a transformed AND/OR graph [15]. One of the major challenges in disassembly line design is the creation of a line able to cope with the high uncertainties in inputs and outputs, especially regarding the time required for planning or configuration. Hence, these uncertainties can consist of the unknown state of the returned products. The number of returned products may vary as well as their quality and thus the type of operations to perform. While some authors tried to tackle some disassembly problems with these uncertainties (e.g. [16]), there is still unexploited potential: uncertainties have not yet been examined within the scope of integrated linear/circular lines. Mete et al. [17] published the only research paper on the topic of balancing hybrid lines for assembly and disassembly. In this work, a configuration of two parallel lines dedicated to assembly or disassembly is considered. However, the two lines can use shared workstations.

Future research is required to create a methodology that enables companies to define a suitable production system structure according to its conditions. Suitable circular material flow and the corresponding system structure must be elaborated based on qualitative aspects, i.e. the requirements definition and the assessment procedure. Furthermore, quantitative aspects must specify the derived system structure. This includes algorithms to design the circular production line at minimum costs with respect to the given throughput time. In addition, a future research direction is to investigate different possible configurations including the possibility to use the same line for assembly and disassembly or reassembly. The design of a line able to disassemble items in different conditions such as partial disassembly will also be a crucial point.

## 3.2 Operating a Circular Integrated Production System

A production system using the same resources for production and product recovery requires a proper management of resources and inventory. The integration of circular into linear systems creates challenges for operation management. On the one hand, the capacity of the line must be managed differently because the line capacity has to be divided between disassembly and assembly operations. On the other hand, the flow of re-entrant products is subject to various uncertainties in terms of the quantity and quality of items. Therefore, the development of a production planning tool to support the use of integrated assembly/disassembly lines is crucial. The resulting tool must be able to properly account for the capacity of the line, for the level of inventory of the recovered components, and for the high level of uncertainty inherent to the disassembly process.

Since the seminal work of Gupta et al. [18], the disassembly lot-sizing problems have attracted a lot of attention and Slama et al. [19] presented a recent review. Most of the literature on disassembly systems concerns the deterministic incapacitated problem [20, 21], and a small number of studies focus on the stochastic capacitated version [22]. Few works exists on joint planning of reassembly and assembly. For instance, cost-optimized production planning is examined, but without considering set-up times and system dynamics [23]. Further sources for reassembly integration provide approaches for planning and control under consideration of set-up costs [24], in a stochastic environment [25], with the inclusion of set-up times and costs [26], for set-up and production control policies [27] and for batch size and supplier selection [28]. Finally, in practice, the product recovery process is sensitive to various sources of uncertainty, such as uncertain demand from customers, recovery rates, lead times, etc. As in supply planning for assembly systems, these uncertainties create disruptions in the disassembly plan, and lead to unmet customers' demand and difficulties with inventory management [29].

Further research is required to provide tools to help production planners to manage a factory with integrated lines. Firstly, there is currently no methodology to characterize an item and to define the suitable circular activities based on its condition. Such an approach must characterize the product's functional and geometric conditions, examine the capability of the production system with regard to product condition, and compare these characteristics to define the suitable circular activity (repair, refurbish, or disposal). Secondly, there is a need for a planning tool that extends the classical mathematical model for production planning. Such a model must both place orders to suppliers and plan the assembly and disassembly operations under limited capacity. In particular, it must account for component substitution by enabling the possibility of disassembling end-of-life items in order to substitute new components in the event of component shortage. Finally, circular activities are highly uncertain. Not only is the amount of return items unpredictable, but their quality – and thus the circular activity – varies significantly. Therefore, the approach must rely on a robust/stochastic optimization approach to integrate uncertainty in delivery lead times, returned quantity, and component quality in the model.

### 3.3 Summary of the Roadmap

The outlined state of the art as well as the derived need for research is summarized in Fig. 1.

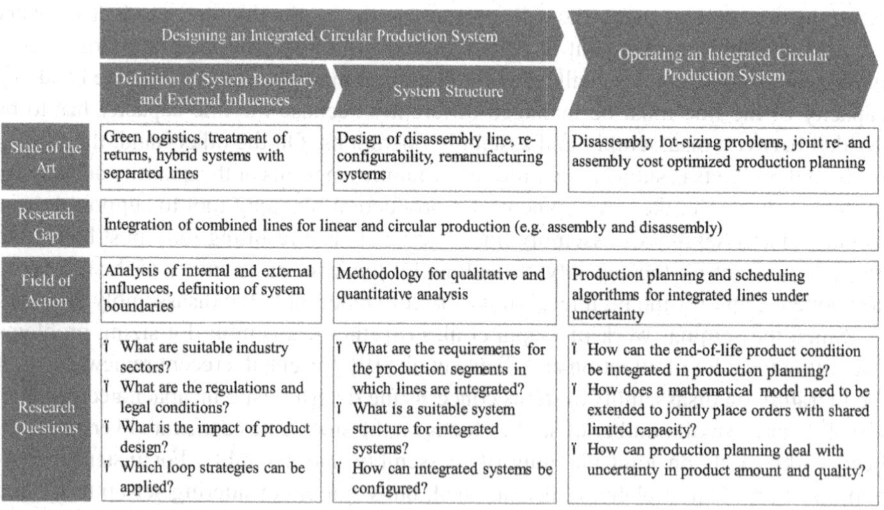


**Fig. 1.** Summarized research roadmap for CIPS

## 4 Conclusion

This paper presents a vision and a road map regarding the integration of reverse flow activities within existing production systems. The innovative ideas behind the project aim to foster the adoption of circular economy by the manufacturing industry through classification of the challenges and requirements of integrated production lines. Integrating lines, especially assembly and disassembly lines, can help manufacturing companies to maintain more products at a higher value-added level. Instead of throwing away and disposing of products at the end of their life, companies can consider how they can preserve products in the best way and which of the circular processes are suitable. The possible circular processes are repairing, reusing, remanufacturing and recycling. Processes that obtain the products at the highest possible value-added level are preferable, and recycling – as material recovery – should only be the last option.

We provide a description of the tools and methods required for decision-makers to design and operate integrated production lines using existing production resources for the entire cycle of manufacturing decisions including process selection, production system design, planning, scheduling, and real-time control.

**Acknowledgement.** This research is supported by the German-French Academy for the Industry of the Future.

## References

1. Ivanov, D.: Predicting the impacts of epidemic outbreaks on global supply chains: a simulation-based analysis on the coronavirus outbreak case. Transp. Res. Part E: Logistics Transp. Rev. **136** (2020). Article ID: 101922
2. Queiroz, M.M., Ivanov, D., Dolgui, A., Wamba, S.F.: Impacts of epidemic outbreaks on supplychains: mapping a research agenda amid the covid-19 pandemic through a structured literature review. Annals of Operations Research (2020)
3. Prajapati, H., Kant, R., Shankar, R.: Prioritizing the solutions of reverse logistics implementation to mitigate its barriers: a hybrid modified SWARA and WASPAS approach. J. Clean. Prod. **240**, 118219 (2019)
4. McKinnon, A., Browne, M., Whiteing, A., Piecyk, M. (eds.): Green logistics: Improving the environmental sustainability of logistics. Kogan Page Publ. (2015)
5. Thierry, M., Salomon, M., Van Nunen, J., Van Wassenhove, L.: Strategic issues in product recovery management. California MGMT Rev. **37**(2), 23 (1995)
6. Lamy, D., Schulz, J., Zaeh, M.: Energy-aware scheduling in reconfigurable multiple path shop floors. Procedia CIRP **93**, 1007–1012 (2020)
7. Pintzos, G., Matsas, M., Papakostas, N., Mourtzis, D.: Disassembly line planning through the generation of end-of-life handling information from design files. Procedia CIRP **57**, 740–745 (2016)
8. Rickert, J., Blömeke, S., Mennenga, M., Cerdas, F., Thiede, S., Herrmann, C.: Refining Circulation Factories: Classification Scheme and Supporting Product and Factory Features for Closed-Loop Production Integration. Springer, Heidelberg (2020)
9. Boutarfa, Y., Senoussi, A., Brahimi, N.: Reverse logistics with disassembly, assembly, repair and substitution. In: IEEE International Conference on Industrial Engineering and Engineering Management (2020)
10. Tiwari, M.K., Sinha, N., Kumar, S., Rai, R., Mukhopadhyay, S.K.: A Petri net based approach to determine the disassembly strategy of a product. Int. J. Prod. Res. 40–45 (2002)
11. Boothroyd, G., Alting, L.: Design for assembly and disassembly. CIRP **41**(2), 625–636 (1992)

12. Mesa, J.A., Esparragoza, I., Maury, H.: Development of a metric to assess the complexity of assembly/disassembly tasks in open architecture products. Int. J. Prod. Res. **56**(24), 7201–7219 (2018)
13. Battaïa, O., Dolgui, A., Heragu, S.S., Meerkov, S.M., Tiwari, M.K.: Design for manufacturing and assembly/disassembly: joint design of products and production systems (2018)
14. Özceylan, E., Kalayci, C.B., Güngör, A., Gupta, S.M.: Disassembly line balancing problem: a review of the state of the art and future directions. Int. J. Prod. Res. **57**(15–16), 4805–4827 (2019)
15. Koc, A., Sabuncuoglu, I., Erel, E.: Two exact formulations for disassembly line balancing problems with task precedence diagram construction using an AND/OR graph. Transactions **41**(10), 866–881 (2009)
16. Bentaha, M.L., Battaïa, O., Dolgui, A.: A sample average approximation method for disassembly line balancing problem under uncertainty. Comput. Oper. Res. **51**, 111–122 (2014)
17. Mete, S., Çil, Z.A., Özceylan, E., Ağpak, K., Battaïa, O.: An optimisation support for the design of hybrid production lines including assembly and disassembly tasks. Int. J. Prod. Res. **56**(24), 7220–7242 (2018)
18. Gupta, S., Taleb, K.: Scheduling disassembly. Int. J. Prod. Res. 32 1857–1886 (1994)
19. Slama, I., Ben-Ammar, O., Masmoudi, F., Dolgui, A.: Disassembly scheduling problem: literature review and future research directions. IFAC-PapersOnLine **52**, 601–606 (2019)
20. Godichaud, M., Amodeo, L.: Eoq inventory models for disassembly systems with disposal and lost sales. Int. J. Prod. Res. **57**, 5685–5704 (2019)
21. Kim, H.W., Park, C., Lee, D.H.: Selective disassembly sequencing with random operation times in parallel disassembly environment. Int. J. Prod. Res. **56**(24), 7243–7257 (2018)
22. Slama, I., Ben-Ammar, O., Thevenin, S., Dolgui, A., Masmoudi, F.: Stochastic program for disassembly lot-sizing under given demand and uncertain component refurbishing lead times. Under review (2021)
23. Macedo, P.B., Alem, D., Santos, M., Junior, M.L., Moreno, A.: Hybrid manufacturing and remanufacturing lot-sizing problem with stochastic demand, return, and setup costs. Int. J. Adv. Manuf. Technol. **82**(5–8), 1241–1257 (2015). https://doi.org/10.1007/s00170-015-7445-z
24. Assid, M., Gharbi, A., Hajji, A.: Production and setup control policy for unreliable hybrid manufacturing-remanufacturing systems. J. Manuf. Syst. **50**, 103–118 (2019)
25. Polotski, V., Kenne, J.-P., Gharbi, A.: Production policy optimization in flexible manufacturing-remanufacturing systems. IFAC-PapersOnLine **49**, 12 (2016)
26. Polotski, V., Kenne, J.-P., Gharbi, A.: Production and setup policy optimization for hybrid manufacturing–remanufacturing systems. Int. J. Prod. Econ. **183**, 539–550 (2017)
27. Polotski, V., Kenne, J.-P., Gharbi, A.: Set-up and production planning in hybrid manufacturing remanufacturing systems with large returns. Int. J. Prod. Res. **55**, 3766–3787 (2017)
28. Zouadi, T., Yalaoui, A., Reghioui, M., El Kadiri, K.: Hybrid manufacturing/remanufacturing lot-sizing problem with returns supplier's selection under, carbon emissions constraint. IFAC-PapersOnLine 49 (2016)
29. Thevenin, S., Adulyasak, Y., Cordeau, J.F.: Material requirements planning under demand uncertainty using stochastic optimization. Prod. Oper. Manage. **30**(2), 475–493 (2021)

# Correction to: Robust Optimization for Collaborative Distribution Network Design Problem

Islem Snoussi, Nadia Hamani, Nassim Mrabti, and Lyes Kermad

**Correction to:**
**Chapter "Robust Optimization for Collaborative Distribution Network Design Problem"**
**in: L. M. Camarinha-Matos et al. (Eds.):**
***Smart and Sustainable Collaborative Networks 4.0*, IFIP AICT 629,**
**https://doi.org/10.1007/978-3-030-85969-5_25**

The original version of this chapter was revised. The chapter was inadvertently published with the incorrect order of authors. This has been corrected.

The updated version of this chapter can be found at
https://doi.org/10.1007/978-3-030-85969-5_25


Published by Springer Nature Switzerland AG 2021
L. M. Camarinha-Matos et al. (Eds.): PRO-VE 2021, IFIP AICT 629, p. C1, 2021.
https://doi.org/10.1007/978-3-030-85969-5_76

# Author Index